Africa 68-69

70

74

76

72

78

Europe 80-81

84

82

94

98

106

108

88

86

110

90

92

100

96

104

102

WORLD
ATLAS

ESSENTIAL

Previously published as *Essential Atlas of the World*

LONDON, NEW YORK, MELBOURNE, MUNICH, DELHI

LONDON, NEW YORK, MELBOURNE, MUNICH, DELHI

FOR THE SEVENTH EDITION

SENIOR CARTOGRAPHIC MANAGER David Roberts
SENIOR CARTOGRAPHIC EDITOR Simon Mumford
CARTOGRAPHY Encompass Graphics Ltd., Brighton, UK
PRODUCTION CONTROLLER Danielle Smith   PRODUCTION EDITOR Joanna Byrne
PUBLISHER Jonathan Metcalf   ART DIRECTOR Philip Ormerod
ASSOCIATE PUBLISHER Liz Wheeler

DORLING KINDERSLEY CARTOGRAPHY
PROJECT CARTOGRAPHY AND DESIGN
Julia Lunn, Julie Turner

CARTOGRAPHERS
James Anderson, Roger Bullen, Martin Darlison,
Simon Mumford, John Plumer, Peter Winfield

DESIGN
Katy Wall

INDEX-GAZETTEER
Natalie Clarkson, Ruth Duxbury, Margaret Hynes, Margaret Stevenson

PRODUCTION
Hilary Stephens, David Proffit

EDITORIAL DIRECTION
Andrew Heritage

ART DIRECTION
Chez Picthall

First American edition 1997. Second Edition 1998. Third Edition 2001.
Fourth Edition 2003. Fifth Edition 2005. Sixth Edition 2008. Seventh Edition 2011.

Previously published as the *Essential Atlas of the World*.

Published in the United States by DK Publishing,
375 Hudson Street, New York, New York 10014
A Penguin Company.

11 12 13 14 15 10 9 8 7 6 5 4 3 2 1

001—180686—Apr/2011

A catalog record for this book is available from the Library of Congress.

ISBN: 978-0-7566-7223-2

Printed and bound by Tien Wah Press, Singapore.

Discover more at **www.dk.com**

Key to map symbols

Physical features

Elevation

6000m/19,686ft
4000m/13,124ft
3000m/9843ft
2000m/6562ft
1000m/3281ft
500m/1640ft
250m/820ft
0
Below sea level

△   Mountain

▽   Depression

⌃   Volcano

)(Pass/tunnel

▨   Sandy desert

Drainage features

——   Major perennial river

——   Minor perennial river

– – –   Seasonal river

——   Canal

| Waterfall

⬭   Perennial lake

⬭   Seasonal lake

▨   Wetland

Ice features

Permanent ice cap/ice shelf

Winter limit of pack ice

Summer limit of pack ice

Borders

Full international border

– – – –   Disputed de facto border

· · · · ·   Territorial claim border

×–×–×–   Cease-fire line

– –   Undefined boundary

——   Internal administrative boundary

Communications

——   Major road

——   Minor road

——   Railroad

✈   International airport

Settlements

▣   Above 500,000

◉   100,000 to 500,000

○   50,000 to 100,000

○   Below 50,000

●   National capital

◉   Internal administrative capital

Miscellaneous features

+   Site of interest

⌐⌐⌐⌐   Ancient wall

Graticule features

——   Line of latitude/longitude/ Equator

– – –   Tropic/Polar circle

25°   Degrees of latitude/ longitude

Names

Physical features

Andes
Sahara | Landscape features
Ardennes

Land's End | Headland

Mont Blanc 4,807m | Elevation/volcano/pass

Blue Nile | River/canal/waterfall

Ross Ice Shelf | Ice feature

PACIFIC OCEAN
Sulu Sea | Sea features
Palk Strait

Chile Rise | Undersea feature

Regions

FRANCE | Country

JERSEY (to UK) | Dependent territory

KANSAS | Administrative region

Dordogne | Cultural region

Settlements

PARIS | Capital city

SAN JUAN | Dependent territory capital city

Chicago
Kettering | Other settlements
Burke

Inset map symbols

Urban area

City

Park

▪   Place of interest

□   Suburb/district

Contents

The World Today

Flags of the World..................................6-7
The Political World..............................8-9
The Physical World............................10-11
Time Zones...12-13
Geology & Structure...........................14-15
World Climate.....................................16-17
Ocean Currents...................................18-19
Life Zones...20-21
Population...22-23
Languages...24-25
Religion...26-27
The Global Economy...........................28-29
Politics and Conflict...........................30-31

The World's Regions

North & Central America

North & Central America....................34-35
Western Canada & Alaska....................36-37
Eastern Canada...................................38-39
USA: The Northeast.............................40-41
USA: The Southeast.............................42-43
   Bermuda
USA: Central States.............................44-45
USA: The West.....................................46-47
   Los Angeles & Hawaii

USA: The Southwest.............................48-49
Mexico..50-51
Central America..................................52-53
The Caribbean....................................54-55
   Jamaica, St. Lucia, & Barbados

South America

South America.....................................56-57
Northern South America......................58-59
Western South America........................60-61
   Galapagos Islands
Brazil..62-63
Southern South America......................64-65
The Atlantic Ocean.............................66-67

Africa

Africa..68-69
Northwest Africa.................................70-71
Northeast Africa..................................72-73
West Africa..74-75
Central Africa......................................76-77
   Sao Tome & Principe
Southern Africa...................................78-79

Europe

Europe..80-81
The North Atlantic..............................82-83
Scandinavia & Finland.........................84-85
The Low Countries..............................86-87
The British Isles..................................88-89
   London

continued....

Europe *continued*

France, Andorra, & Monaco..............90-91
Paris, Andorra, & Monaco
Spain & Portugal.........................92-93
Azores & Gibraltar
Germany & the Alpine States............94-95
Liechtenstein
Italy....................................96-97
San Marino & Vatican City
Central Europe..........................98-99
Southeast Europe......................100-101
Bosnia & Herzegovina
The Mediterranean.....................102-103
Malta & Cyprus
Bulgaria & Greece.....................104-105
The Baltic States & Belarus...........106-107
Ukraine, Moldova,
& Romania.............................108-109
European Russia.......................110-111

North & West Asia

North & West Asia.....................112-113
Russia & Kazakhstan...................114-115
Turkey & the Caucasus.................116-117
The Near East.........................118-119
West Bank
The Middle East.......................120-121
Central Asia..........................122-123

South & East Asia

South & East Asia.....................124-125
Western China & Mongolia..............126-127

Eastern China & Korea.................128-129
Hong Kong (Xianggang)
Japan.................................130-131
Tokyo & Nansei-Shoto
South India & Sri Lanka...............132-133
North India, Pakistan,
& Bangladesh..........................134-135
Mainland Southeast Asia...............136-137
Maritime Southeast Asia...............138-139
Singapore
The Indian Ocean......................140-141

Australasia & Oceania

Australasia & Oceania.................142-143
The Southwest Pacific.................144-145
Western Australia.....................146-147
Eastern Australia.....................148-149
Sydney
New Zealand...........................150-151
The Pacific Ocean.....................152-153
Antarctica................................154
The Arctic Ocean..........................155

Index–Gazetteer

Overseas Territories
& Dependencies........................156-159
Glossary of Geographical
Terms.................................160-161
Continental Factfiles.................162-163
Geographical Comparisons..............164-166
Index-Gazetteer of Places
& Countries...........................167-256

Flags of the World

NORTH & CENTRAL AMERICA

- CANADA PAGES 36-39
- UNITED STATES OF AMERICA PAGES 40-49
- MEXICO PAGES 50-51
- BELIZE PAGES 52-53
- COSTA RICA PAGES 52-53
- EL SALVADOR PAGES 52-53
- GUATEMALA PAGES 52-53
- HONDURAS PAGES 52-53

- GRENADA PAGES 54-55
- HAITI PAGES 54-55
- JAMAICA PAGES 54-55
- ST KITTS & NEVIS PAGES 54-55
- ST LUCIA PAGES 54-55
- ST VINCENT & THE GRENADINES PAGES 54-55
- TRINIDAD & TOBAGO PAGES 54-55

SOUTH AMER

- COLOMBIA PAGES 58-59

- URUGUAY PAGES 64-65
- CHILE PAGES 64-65
- PARAGUAY PAGES 64-65

AFRICA

- ALGERIA PAGES 70-71
- LIBYA PAGES 70-71
- MOROCCO PAGES 70-71
- TUNISIA PAGES 70-71
- BURUNDI PAGES 72-73

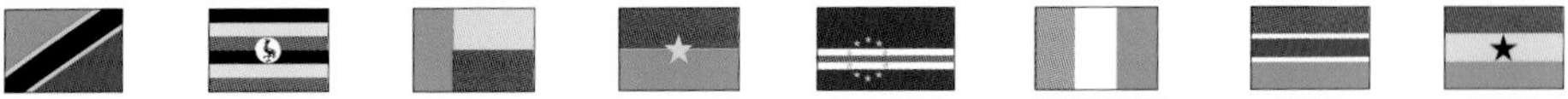

- TANZANIA PAGES 72-73
- UGANDA PAGES 72-73
- BENIN PAGES 74-75
- BURKINA FASO PAGES 74-75
- CAPE VERDE PAGES 74-75
- CÔTE D'IVOIRE (IVORY COAST) PAGES 74-75
- GAMBIA PAGES 74-75
- GHANA PAGES 74-75

- SIERRA LEONE PAGES 74-75
- TOGO PAGES 74-75
- CAMEROON PAGES 76-77
- CENTRAL AFRICAN REPUBLIC PAGES 76-77
- CHAD PAGES 76-77
- CONGO PAGES 76-77
- DEM. REP. CONGO PAGES 76-77
- EQUATORIAL GUINEA PAGES 76-77

- MAURITIUS PAGES 78-79
- MOZAMBIQUE PAGES 78-79
- NAMIBIA PAGES 78-79
- SEYCHELLES PAGES 78-79
- SOUTH AFRICA PAGES 78-79
- SWAZILAND PAGES 78-79
- ZAMBIA PAGES 78-79
- ZIMBABWE PAGES 78-79

- UNITED KINGDOM PAGES 88-89
- FRANCE PAGES 90-91
- MONACO PAGES 90-91
- ANDORRA PAGES 90-91
- PORTUGAL PAGES 92-93
- SPAIN PAGES 92-93
- AUSTRIA PAGES 94-95
- GERMANY PAGES 94-95

- POLAND PAGES 98-99
- SLOVAKIA PAGES 98-99
- ALBANIA PAGES 100-101
- BOSNIA & HERZEGOVINA PAGES 100-101
- CROATIA PAGES 100-101
- KOSOVO PAGES 100-101
- MACEDONIA PAGES 100-101
- MONTENEGRO PAGES 100-101

- MOLDOVA PAGES 108-109
- ROMANIA PAGES 108-109
- UKRAINE PAGES 108-109
- RUSSIAN FEDERATION PAGES 110-115

ASIA

- KAZAKHSTAN PAGES 114-115
- ARMENIA PAGES 116-117
- AZERBAIJAN PAGES 116-117
- GEORGIA PAGES 116-117

- KUWAIT PAGES 120-121
- OMAN PAGES 120-121
- QATAR PAGES 120-121
- SAUDI ARABIA PAGES 120-121
- UNITED ARAB EMIRATES PAGES 120-121
- YEMEN PAGES 120-121
- AFGHANISTAN PAGES 122-123
- KYRGYZSTAN PAGES 122-123

- JAPAN PAGES 130-131
- INDIA PAGES 132-135
- SRI LANKA PAGES 132-133
- MALDIVES PAGES 132-133
- PAKISTAN PAGES 134-135
- BANGLADESH PAGES 134-135
- BHUTAN PAGES 134-135
- NEPAL PAGES 134-135
- CAMBODIA PAGES 136-137

- PHILIPPINES PAGES 138-139
- SINGAPORE PAGES 138-139

AUSTRALASIA & OCEANIA

- FIJI PAGES 144-145
- KIRIBATI PAGES 144-145
- MARSHALL ISLANDS PAGES 144-145
- MICRONESIA PAGES 144-145
- NAURU PAGES 144-145
- PALAU PAGES 144-145

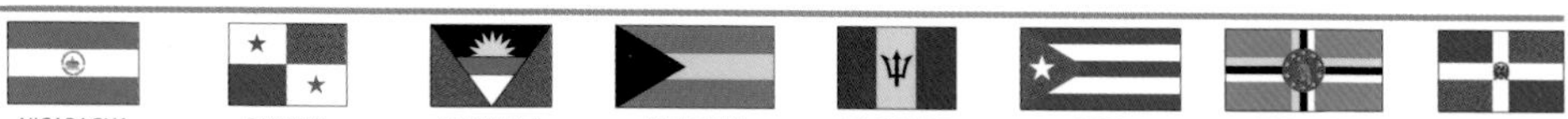

NICARAGUA PAGES 52-53
PANAMA PAGES 52-53
ANTIGUA & BARBUDA PAGES 54-55
BAHAMAS PAGES 54-55
BARBADOS PAGES 54-55
CUBA PAGES 54-55
DOMINICA PAGES 54-55
DOMINICAN REPUBLIC PAGES 54–55

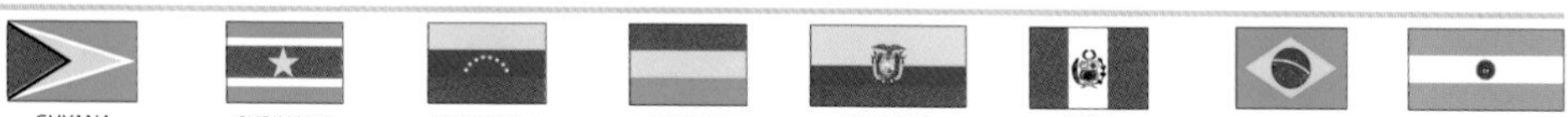

GUYANA PAGES 58-59
SURINAME PAGES 58-59
VENEZUELA PAGES 58-59
BOLIVIA PAGES 60-61
ECUADOR PAGES 60-61
PERU PAGES 60-61
BRAZIL PAGES 62-63
ARGENTINA PAGES 64-65

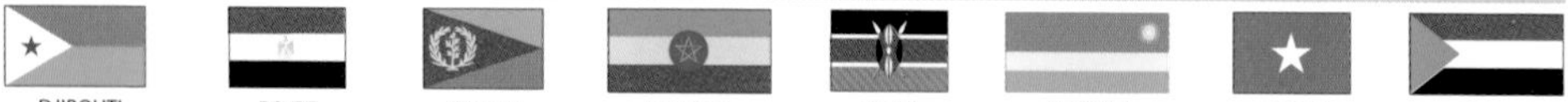

DJIBOUTI PAGES 72-73
EGYPT PAGES 72-73
ERITREA PAGES 72-73
ETHIOPIA PAGES 72-73
KENYA PAGES 72-73
RWANDA PAGES 72-73
SOMALIA PAGES 72-73
SUDAN PAGES 72-73

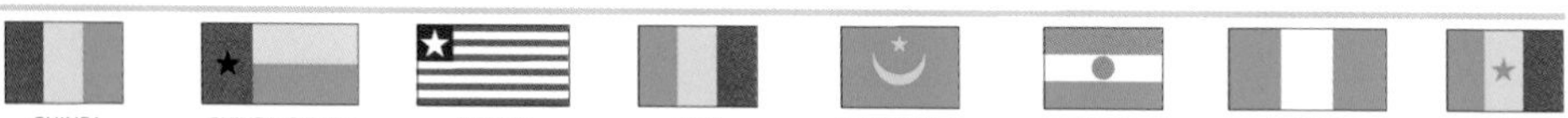

GUINEA PAGES 74-75
GUINEA–BISSAU PAGES 74-75
LIBERIA PAGES 74-75
MALI PAGES 74-75
MAURITANIA PAGES 74-75
NIGER PAGES 74-75
NIGERIA PAGES 74-75
SENEGAL PAGES 74-75

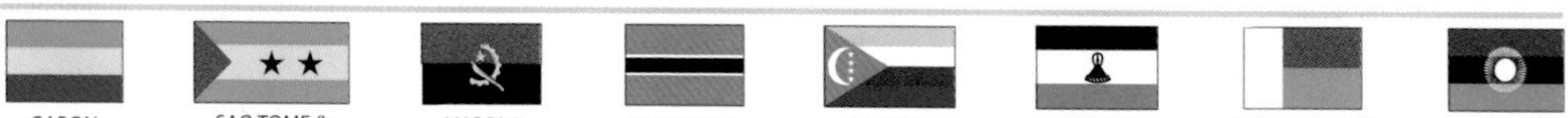

GABON PAGES 76-77
SAO TOME & PRINCIPE PAGES 76-77
ANGOLA PAGES 78-79
BOTSWANA PAGES 78-79
COMOROS PAGES 78-79
LESOTHO PAGES 78-79
MADAGASCAR PAGES 78-79
MALAWI PAGES 78-79

EUROPE

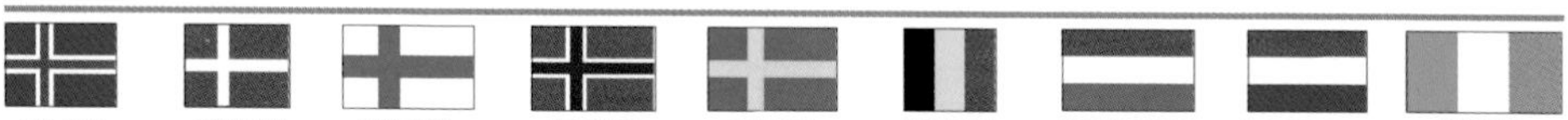

ICELAND PAGES 82-83
DENMARK PAGES 84-85
FINLAND PAGES 84-85
NORWAY PAGES 84-85
SWEDEN PAGES 84-85
BELGIUM PAGES 86-87
LUXEMBOURG PAGES 86-87
NETHERLANDS PAGES 86-87
IRELAND PAGES 88-89

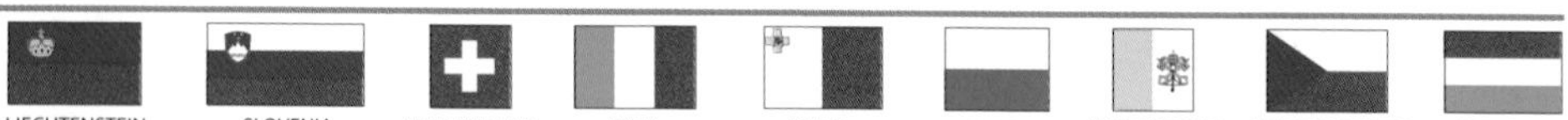

LIECHTENSTEIN PAGES 94-95
SLOVENIA PAGES 94-95
SWITZERLAND PAGES 94-95
ITALY PAGES 96-97
MALTA PAGES 96-97
SAN MARINO PAGES 96-97
VATICAN CITY PAGES 96-97
CZECH REPUBLIC PAGES 98-99
HUNGARY PAGES 98-99

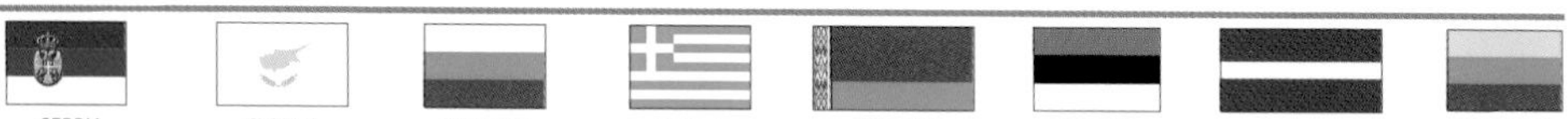

SERBIA PAGES 100-101
CYPRUS PAGES 102-103
BULGARIA PAGES 104-105
GREECE PAGES 104-105
BELARUS PAGES 106-107
ESTONIA PAGES 106-107
LATVIA PAGES 106-107
LITHUANIA PAGES 106-107

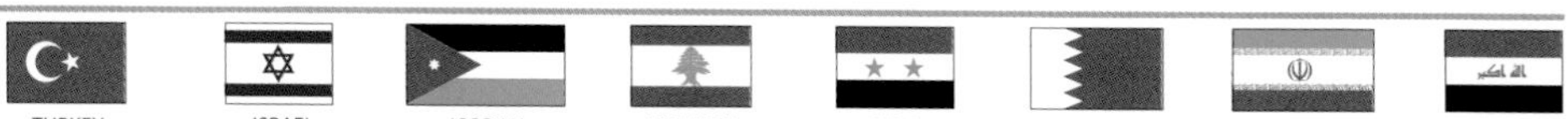

TURKEY PAGES 116-117
ISRAEL PAGES 118-119
JORDAN PAGES 118-119
LEBANON PAGES 118-119
SYRIA PAGES 118-119
BAHRAIN PAGES 120-121
IRAN PAGES 120-121
IRAQ PAGES 120-121

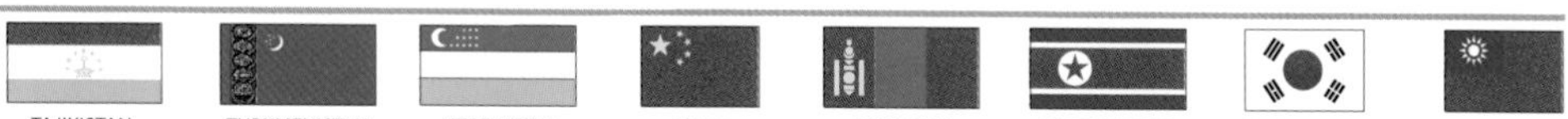

TAJIKISTAN PAGES 122-123
TURKMENISTAN PAGES 122-123
UZBEKISTAN PAGES 122-123
CHINA PAGES 126-129
MONGOLIA PAGES 126-127
NORTH KOREA PAGES 128-129
SOUTH KOREA PAGES 128-129
TAIWAN PAGES 128-129

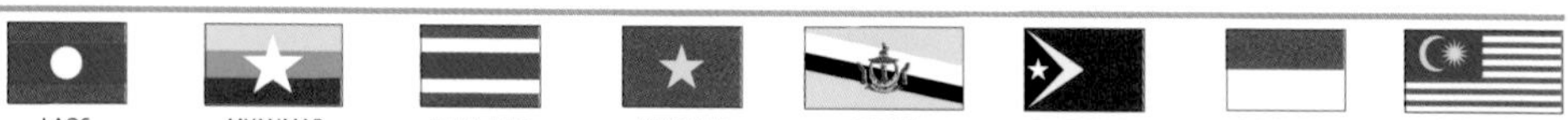

LAOS PAGES 136-137
MYANMAR (BURMA) PAGES 136-137
THAILAND PAGES 136-137
VIETNAM PAGES 136-137
BRUNEI PAGES 138-139
EAST TIMOR PAGES 138-139
INDONESIA PAGES 138-139
MALAYSIA PAGES 138-139

PAPUA NEW GUINEA PAGES 144-145
SAMOA PAGES 144-145
SOLOMON ISLANDS PAGES 144-145
TONGA PAGES 144-145
TUVALU PAGES 144-145
VANUATU PAGES 144-145
AUSTRALIA PAGES 146-149
NEW ZEALAND PAGES 150-151

The Political World

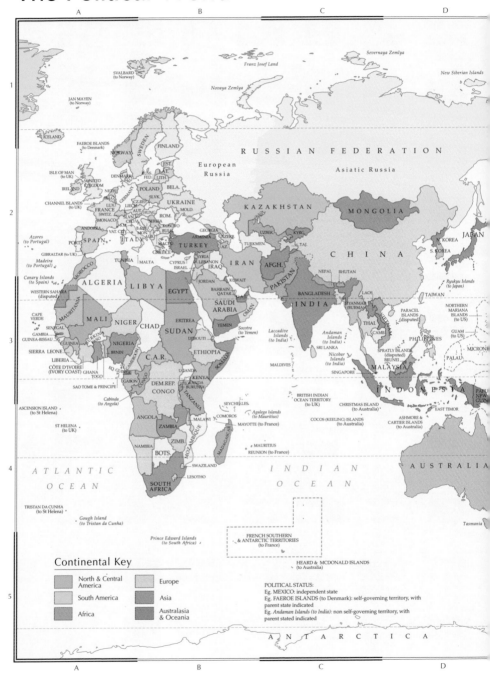

Continental Key

- North & Central America
- South America
- Africa
- Europe
- Asia
- Australasia & Oceania

POLITICAL STATUS:
Eg. MEXICO: independent state
Eg. FAEROE ISLANDS (to Denmark): self-governing territory, with parent state indicated
Eg. *Andaman Islands (to India)*: non self-governing territory, with parent stated indicated

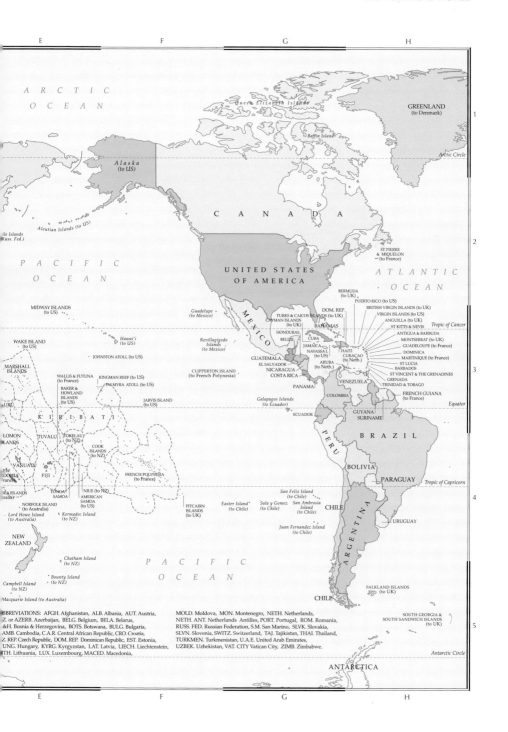

E F G H

A R C T I C
O C E A N

Queen Elizabeth Islands

GREENLAND
(to Denmark)

1

Baffin Island

Arctic Circle

Alaska
(to US)

C A N A D A

2

ile Islands
(Russ. Fed.)

Aleutian Islands (to US)

ST PIERRE
& MIQUELON
(to France)

P A C I F I C
O C E A N

UNITED STATES
OF AMERICA

A T L A N T I C
O C E A N

BERMUDA
(to UK)

PUERTO RICO (to US)

MIDWAY ISLANDS
(to US)

Guadelupe
(to Mexico)

TURKS & CAICOS ISLANDS (to UK)
CAYMAN ISLANDS
(to UK)

BRITISH VIRGIN ISLANDS (to UK)
VIRGIN ISLANDS (to US)
ANGUILLA (to UK)
ST KITTS & NEVIS

Tropic of Cancer

DOM. REP.
BAHAMAS

CUBA

ANTIGUA & BARBUDA
MONTSERRAT (to UK)
GUADELOUPE (to France)
DOMINICA
MARTINIQUE (to France)

WAKE ISLAND
(to US)

Hawai'i
(to US)

Revillagigedo
Islands
(to Mexico)

HONDURAS

BELIZE

JAMAICA
NAVASSA I.
(to US)

HAITI
CURAÇAO
(to Neth.)

JOHNSTON ATOLL (to US)

MARSHALL
ISLANDS

GUATEMALA
EL SALVADOR
NICARAGUA
COSTA RICA

ARUBA
(to Neth.)

ST LUCIA
BARBADOS
ST VINCENT & THE GRENADINES
GRENADA
TRINIDAD & TOBAGO

WALLIS & FUTUNA
(to France)

KINGMAN REEF (to US)

CLIPPERTON ISLAND
(to French Polynesia)

PANAMA

VENEZUELA

FRENCH GUIANA
(to France)

PALMYRA ATOLL (to US)

BAKER &
HOWLAND
ISLANDS
(to US)

COLOMBIA

GUYANA
SURINAME

Equator

URU

K I R I B A T I

JARVIS ISLAND
(to US)

Galapagos Islands
(to Ecuador)

ECUADOR

3

LOMON
LANDS

TUVALU

TOKELAU
(to NZ)

COOK
ISLANDS
(to NZ)

P E R U

B R A Z I L

VANUATU

EW
DONIA
rance)

FIJI

FRENCH POLYNESIA
(to France)

BOLIVIA

PARAGUAY

Tropic of Capricorn

SEA ISLANDS
rralia)

TONGA
SAMOA

NIUE (to NZ)

AMERICAN
SAMOA
(to US)

San Felix Island
(to Chile)

Sala y Gomez
(to Chile)

San Ambrosia
Island
(to Chile)

CHILE

NORFOLK ISLAND
(to Australia)

Kermadec Island
(to NZ)

PITCAIRN
ISLANDS
(to UK)

Easter Island*
(to Chile)

URUGUAY

Lord Howe Island
(to Australia)

A R G E N T I N A

NEW
ZEALAND

Juan Fernandez Island
(to Chile)

4

Chatham Island
(to NZ)

P A C I F I C
O C E A N

Bounty Island
(to NZ)

Campbell Island
(to NZ)

Macquarie Island (to Australia)

FALKLAND ISLANDS
(to UK)

CHILE

ABBREVIATIONS: AFGH. Afghanistan, ALB. Albania, AUT. Austria,
Z. or AZERB. Azerbaijan, BELG. Belgium, BELA. Belarus,
&H. Bosnia & Herzegovina, BOTS. Botswana, BULG. Bulgaria,
AMB. Cambodia, C.A.R. Central African Republic, CRO. Croatia,
Z. REP. Czech Republic, DOM. REP. Dominican Republic, EST. Estonia,
UNG. Hungary, KYRG. Kyrgyzstan, LAT. Latvia, LIECH. Liechtenstein,
TH. Lithuania, LUX. Luxembourg, MACED. Macedonia,

MOLD. Moldova, MON. Montenegro, NETH. Netherlands,
NETH. ANT. Netherlands Antilles, PORT. Portugal, ROM. Romania,
RUSS. FED. Russian Federation, S.M. San Marino, SLVK. Slovakia,
SLVN. Slovenia, SWITZ. Switzerland, TAJ. Tajikistan, THAI. Thailand,
TURKMEN. Turkmenistan, U.A.E. United Arab Emirates,
UZBEK. Uzbekistan, VAT. CITY Vatican City, ZIMB. Zimbabwe.

SOUTH GEORGIA &
SOUTH SANDWICH ISLANDS
(to UK)

Antarctic Circle

ANTARCTICA

5

E F G H

The Physical World

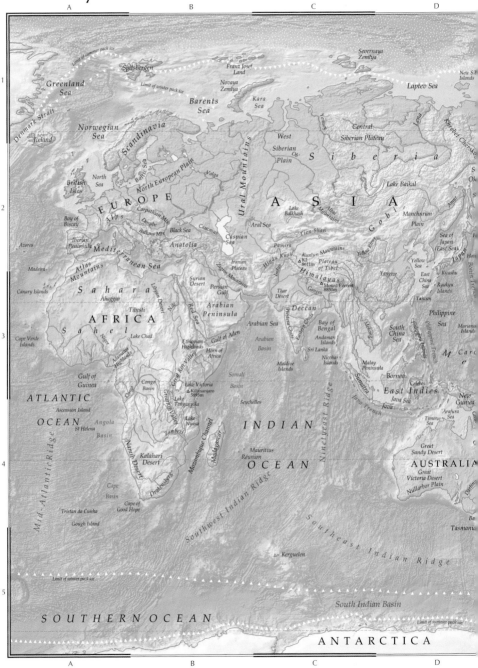

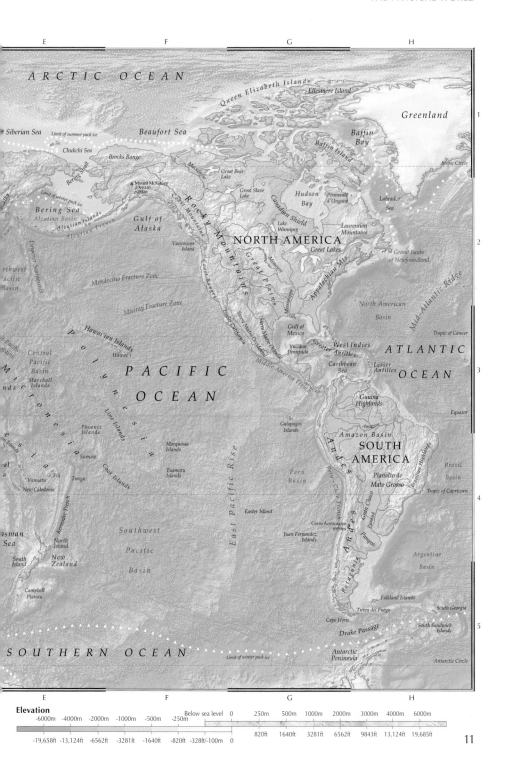

E F G H

ARCTIC OCEAN

Queen Elizabeth Islands
Ellesmere Island

Greenland — 1

Siberian Sea
Limit of summer pack ice
Beaufort Sea

Baffin
Bay

Chukchi Sea

Baffin Island

Arctic Circle

Brooks Range

Mackenzie

Great Bear Lake

Hudson
Bay

Península
d'Ungava

Labrador
Sea

Limit of winter pack ice

△ Mount McKinley
(Denali)
6194m

Great Slave Lake

Canadian Shield

Bering Sea
Aleutian Islands
Aleutian Basin
Aleutian Trench

Gulf of
Alaska

Coast Mountains

Lake
Winnipeg

Laurentian
Mountains

NORTH AMERICA

Great Lakes

Grand Banks
of Newfoundland — 2

Vancouver
Island

Rocky Mountains

Great Plains

Missouri

Appalachian Mts

Emperor Seamounts

Northwest Pacific Basin

Mendocino Fracture Zone

Coast Ranges

Sierra Madre Occidental

Mississippi

North American
Basin

Murray Fracture Zone

Baja California

Sierra Madre Oriental

Gulf of
Mexico

Tropic of Cancer

Hawaiian Islands

Hawai'i

Yucatán
Peninsula

Greater Antilles

West Indies

ATLANTIC

Mid-Atlantic Ridge

Central
Pacific
Basin

PACIFIC

OCEAN

Polynesia

Middle America Trench

Caribbean
Sea

Lesser
Antilles

OCEAN — 3

Micronesia

Marshall
Islands

Line Islands

Phoenix
Islands

Galápagos
Islands

Guiana
Highlands

Equator

Marquesas
Islands

Amazon

Amazon Basin

SOUTH
AMERICA

Samoa

Cook Islands

Tuamotu
Islands

Perú
Basin

Andes

Planalto de
Mato Grosso

Brazil
Basin

Vanuatu *Fiji* *Tonga*

New Caledonia

East Pacific Rise

Easter Island

Perú-Chile Trench

Cerro Aconcagua
6959m

Juan Fernández
Islands

Gran Chaco

Pampas

Brazilian Highlands

Tropic of Capricorn — 4

Tasman
Sea

North
Island

New
Zealand

Southwest

Pacific

Basin

Argentine

Basin

South
Island

Campbell
Plateau

Kermadec Trench

Patagonia

Falkland Islands

South Georgia

Tierra del Fuego

Cape Horn

Drake Passage

South Sandwich
Islands — 5

SOUTHERN OCEAN

Limit of winter pack ice

Antarctic
Peninsula

Antarctic Circle

E F G H

Elevation

| -6000m | -4000m | -2000m | -1000m | -500m | -250m | Below sea level 0 | 250m | 500m | 1000m | 2000m | 3000m | 4000m | 6000m |

| -19,658ft | -13,124ft | -6562ft | -3281ft | -1640ft | -820ft | -328ft/-100m | 0 | 820ft | 1640ft | 3281ft | 6562ft | 9843ft | 13,124ft | 19,685ft |

Time Zones

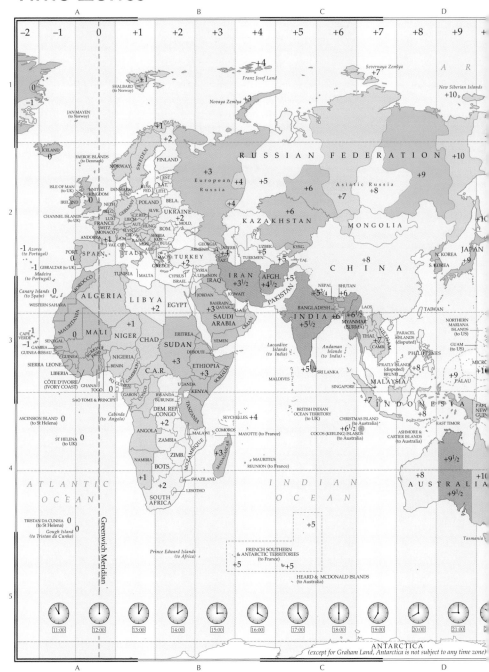

The numbers represented thus; +2/-2, indicate the number of hours each time zone is ahead or behind UCT (Coordinated Universal Time)

The clocks and 24-hour times given at the bottom of the map show time in each time zone when it is 12.00 hours noon UCT

Geology & Structure

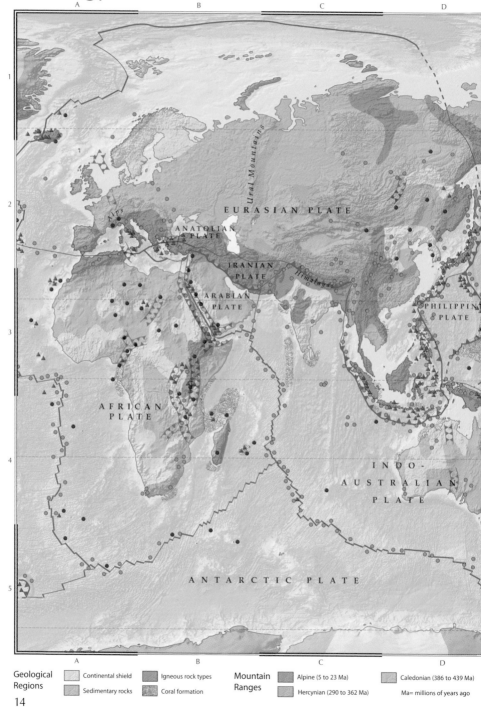

EURASIAN PLATE

Ural Mountains

Alps

ANATOLIAN PLATE

IRANIAN PLATE

ARABIAN PLATE

Himalayas

PHILIPPINE PLATE

AFRICAN PLATE

INDO-AUSTRALIAN PLATE

ANTARCTIC PLATE

Geological Regions		Mountain Ranges	
Continental shield	Igneous rock types	Alpine (5 to 23 Ma)	Caledonian (386 to 439 Ma)
Sedimentary rocks	Coral formation	Hercynian (290 to 362 Ma)	Ma= millions of years ago

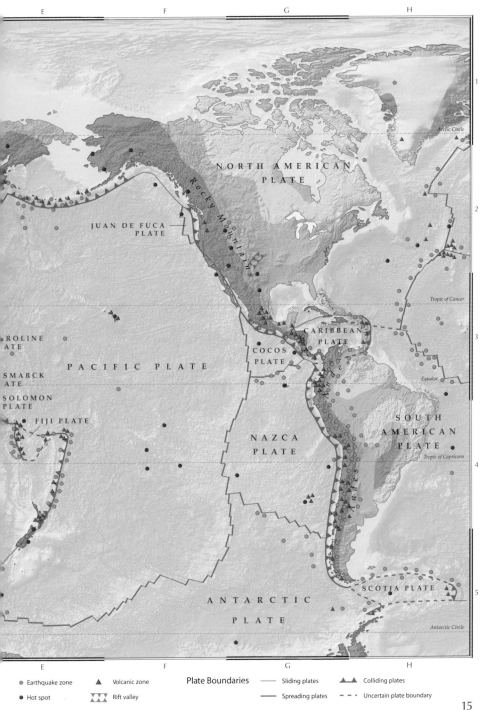

NORTH AMERICAN PLATE

Rocky Mountains

JUAN DE FUCA PLATE

ROLINE ATE

SMARCK ATE

SOLOMON PLATE

FIJI PLATE

PACIFIC PLATE

COCOS PLATE

CARIBBEAN PLATE

Andes

NAZCA PLATE

SOUTH AMERICAN PLATE

Andes

SCOTIA PLATE

ANTARCTIC PLATE

Arctic Circle

Tropic of Cancer

Equator

Tropic of Capricorn

Antarctic Circle

Earthquake zone ●   Volcanic zone ▲   **Plate Boundaries** —— Sliding plates   ▲▲ Colliding plates

Hot spot ●   Rift valley ▼▼▼   —— Spreading plates   – – – Uncertain plate boundary

World Climate

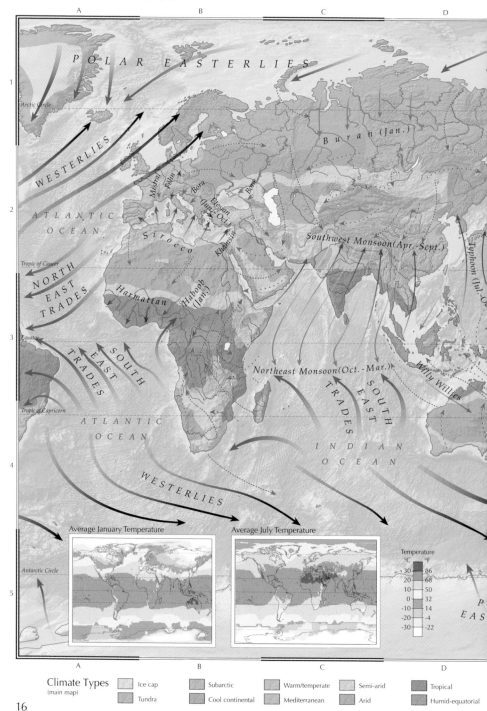

POLAR EASTERLIES

Arctic Circle

WESTERLIES

ATLANTIC
OCEAN

Buran (Jan.)

Mistral
Föhn
Bora
Etesian (June-Oct.)
Bora

Sirocco

Khamsin

Southwest Monsoon(Apr.-Sept.)

Typhoon (Jul.-O

Tropic of Cancer

NORTH
EAST
TRADES

Harmattan

Haboob (Jan.)

Equator

SOUTH
EAST
TRADES

Northeast Monsoon(Oct.-Mar.)

Willy Willies

Tropic of Capricorn

ATLANTIC
OCEAN

SOUTH
EAST
TRADES

INDIAN
OCEAN

WESTERLIES

Average January Temperature

Average July Temperature

Antarctic Circle

Temperature	
°C	°F
30	86
20	68
10	50
0	32
-10	14
-20	-4
-30	-22

P
EAS

Climate Types
(main map)

Ice cap

Tundra

Subarctic

Cool continental

Warm/temperate

Mediterranean

Semi-arid

Arid

Tropical

Humid-equatorial

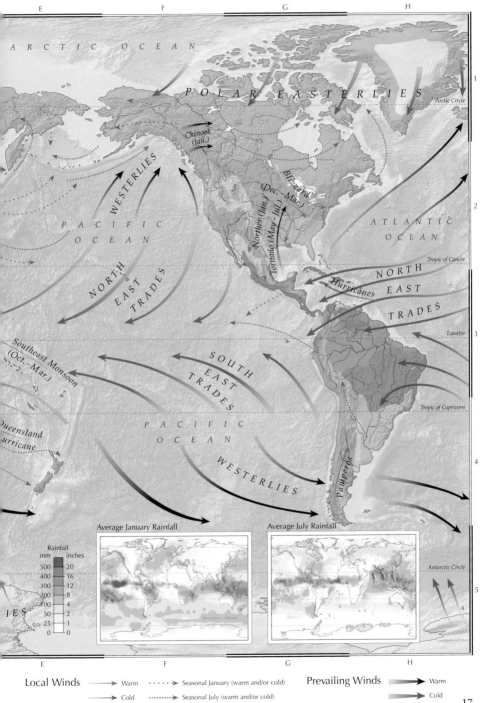

E F G H

ARCTIC OCEAN

POLAR EASTERLIES

1

Arctic Circle

Chinook (Jan.)

WESTERLIES

Blizzard (Dec. - Mar.)

Norther (Jan.)

Tornado (May - Jul.)

PACIFIC OCEAN

ATLANTIC OCEAN

2

Tropic of Cancer

NORTH EAST TRADES

Hurricanes

NORTH EAST TRADES

Equator

3

Southeast Monsoon (Oct. - Mar.)

SOUTH EAST TRADES

Tropic of Capricorn

Queensland Hurricane

PACIFIC OCEAN

WESTERLIES

Pamperos

4

WESTERLIES

Average January Rainfall

Average July Rainfall

Rainfall	
mm	inches
500	20
400	16
300	12
200	8
100	4
50	2
25	1
0	0

Antarctic Circle

5

IES

E F G H

Local Winds
→ Warm
→ Cold
·····▷ Seasonal January (warm and/or cold)
······▷ Seasonal July (warm and/or cold)

Prevailing Winds
➜ Warm
➜ Cold

17

Ocean Currents

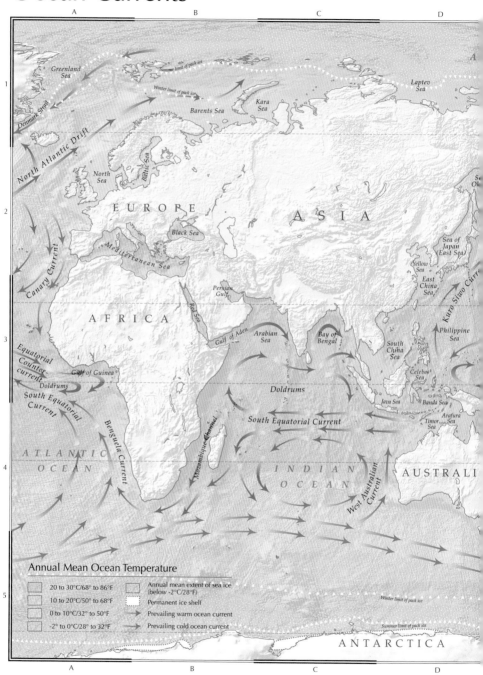

A   B   C   D

Greenland Sea

Summer limit of pack ice

Winter limit of pack ice

Laptev Sea

Denmark Strait

North Atlantic Drift

Barents Sea

Kara Sea

Sea of Okhotsk

North Sea

Baltic Sea

EUROPE

ASIA

Black Sea

Sea of Japan (East Sea)

Canary Current

Mediterranean Sea

Persian Gulf

Yellow Sea

East China Sea

Kuro Siwo Current

AFRICA

Red Sea

Gulf of Aden

Arabian Sea

Bay of Bengal

South China Sea

Philippine Sea

Equatorial Counter current

Gulf of Guinea

Doldrums

Celebes Sea

South Equatorial Current

Benguela Current

Doldrums

Java Sea

Banda Sea

ATLANTIC OCEAN

Mozambique Channel

South Equatorial Current

Timor Sea

Arafura Sea

INDIAN OCEAN

West Australian Current

AUSTRALIA

Annual Mean Ocean Temperature

- 20 to 30°C/68° to 86°F
- 10 to 20°C/50° to 68°F
- 0 to 10°C/32° to 50°F
- -2° to 0°C/28° to 32°F

- Annual mean extent of sea ice (below -2°C/28°F)
- Permanent ice shelf
- → Prevailing warm ocean current
- → Prevailing cold ocean current

Winter limit of pack ice

Summer limit of pack ice

ANTARCTICA

A   B   C   D

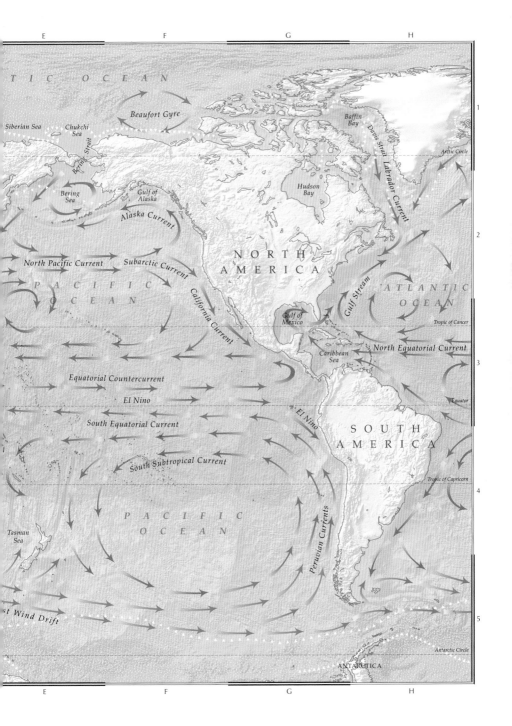

Life Zones

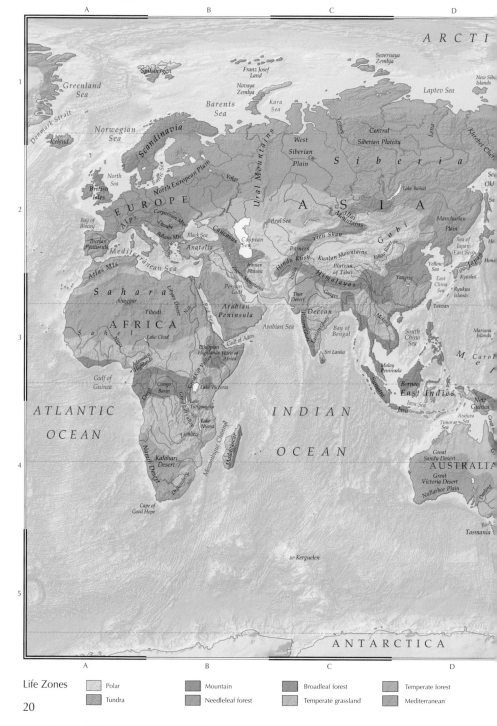

Life Zones

Polar	Mountain	Broadleaf forest	Temperate forest
Tundra	Needleleaf forest	Temperate grassland	Mediterranean

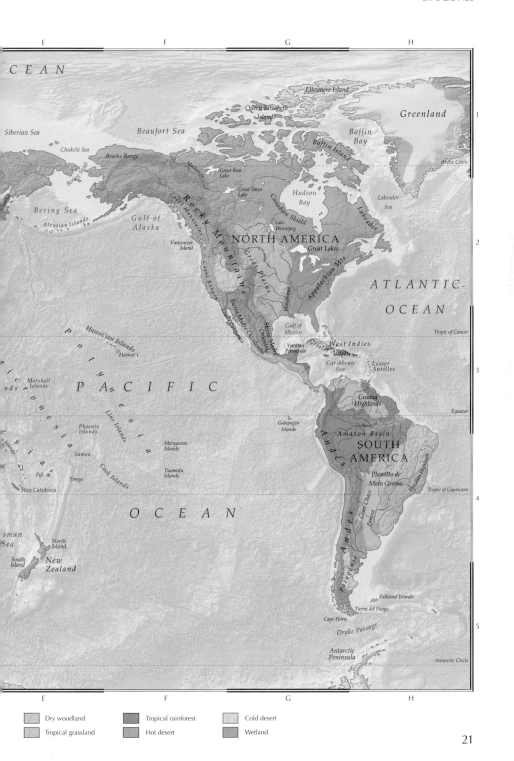

E   F   G   H

OCEAN

Ellesmere Island

Queen Elizabeth
Islands

Greenland

Siberian Sea

Beaufort Sea

Baffin
Bay

Chukchi Sea

Brooks Range

Baffin Island

Arctic Circle

Bering Strait

Mackenzie

Great Bear
Lake

Great Slave
Lake

Hudson
Bay

Labrador
Sea

Bering Sea

Aleutian Islands

Gulf of
Alaska

Rocky Mountains

Coast Mountains

Canadian Shield

Lake
Winnipeg

NORTH AMERICA

Great Lakes

Appalachian Mts

ATLANTIC
OCEAN

Vancouver
Island

Coast Ranges

Great Plains

Sierra Madre Occidental

Mississippi

Hawai'ian Islands

Hawai'i

Polynesia

Baja California

Sierra Madre
Oriental

Gulf of
Mexico

Yucatán
Peninsula

Greater Antilles

West Indies

Caribbean
Sea

Lesser
Antilles

Tropic of Cancer

Micronesia

Marshall
Islands

PACIFIC

Phoenix
Islands

Line Islands

Galapagos
Islands

Guiana
Highlands

Amazon

Equator

Marquesas
Islands

Amazon Basin

SOUTH
AMERICA

Samoa

Fiji

Tonga

Cook Islands

Tuamotu
Islands

New Caledonia

OCEAN

Planalto de
Mato Grosso

Brazilian Highlands

Tropic of Capricorn

Andes

Gran Chaco

Paraná

Tasman
Sea

North
Island

South
Island

New
Zealand

Patagonia

Falkland Islands

Tierra del Fuego

Cape Horn

Drake Passage

Antarctic
Peninsula

Antarctic Circle

E   F   G   H

Dry woodland	Tropical rainforest	Cold desert
Tropical grassland	Hot desert	Wetland

Population

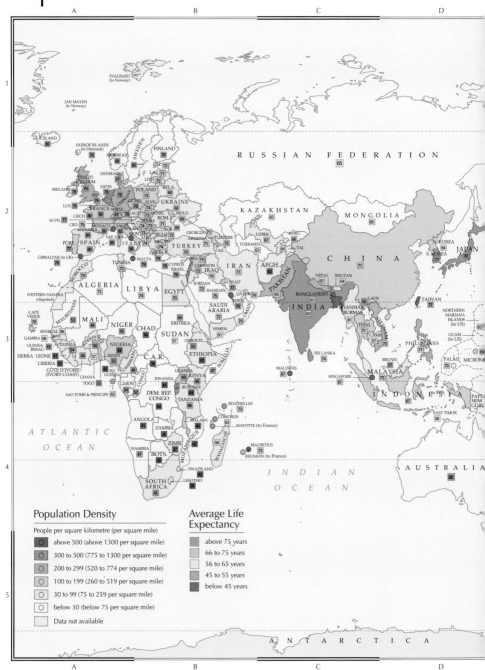

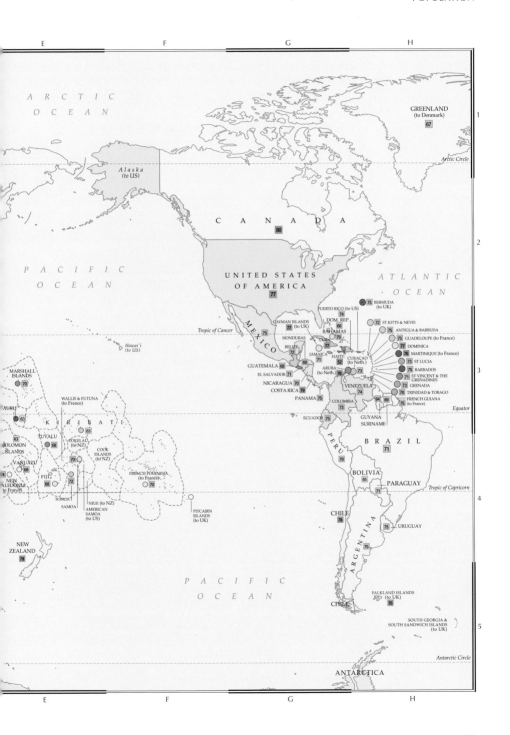

ARCTIC OCEAN

GREENLAND
(to Denmark)
67

Arctic Circle

Alaska
(to US)

C A N A D A
80

PACIFIC
OCEAN

UNITED STATES
OF AMERICA
77

ATLANTIC
OCEAN

BERMUDA
(to UK)
75

PUERTO RICO (to US)
74

ST KITTS & NEVIS
72

CAYMAN ISLANDS
(to UK)
77

DOM. REP.
68

ANTIGUA & BARBUDA
75

Tropic of Cancer

MEXICO

BAHAMAS
68

HONDURAS
70

GUADELOUPE (to France)
75

CUBA
77

DOMINICA
77

BELIZE
72

JAMAICA
71

HAITI
52

MARTINIQUE (to France)
76

Hawai'i
(to US)

CURAÇAO
(to Neth.)

ST LUCIA
73

GUATEMALA
68

68

BARBADOS
75

MARSHALL
ISLANDS
70

EL SALVADOR
71

ARUBA
(to Neth.)
76

73

ST VINCENT & THE
GRENADINES
71

NICARAGUA
70

GRENADA
73

COSTA RICA
79

VENEZUELA
74

TRINIDAD & TOBAGO
70

NAURU
63

WALLIS & FUTUNA
(to France)

PANAMA
75

COLOMBIA
73

FRENCH GUIANA
(to France)
75

GUYANA
64

SURINAME
69

Equator

K I R I B A T I

ECUADOR
75

TUVALU
63

TOKELAU
(to NZ)

63

SOLOMON
ISLANDS
68

BRAZIL
71

COOK
ISLANDS
(to NZ)

PERU
70

VANUATU
70

69

FRENCH POLYNESIA
(to France)

BOLIVIA
65

NEW
CALEDONIA
(to France)
4

FIJI
68

72

70

PARAGUAY
71

Tropic of Capricorn

TONGA
SAMOA

NIUE (to NZ)
AMERICAN
SAMOA
(to US)

PITCAIRN
ISLANDS
(to UK)

CHILE
78

URUGUAY
75

NEW
ZEALAND
79

ARGENTINA
75

PACIFIC
OCEAN

CHILE
78

FALKLAND ISLANDS
(to UK)
78

SOUTH GEORGIA &
SOUTH SANDWICH ISLANDS
(to UK)

Antarctic Circle

ANTARCTICA

Languages

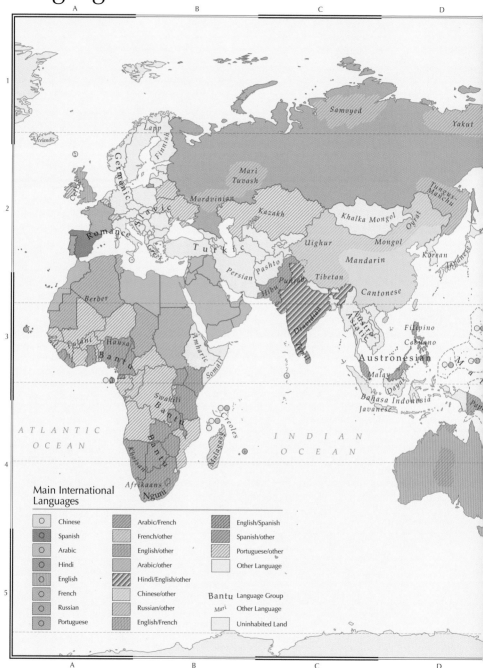

Main International Languages

○ Chinese	Arabic/French	English/Spanish
◉ Spanish	French/other	Spanish/other
○ Arabic	English/other	Portuguese/other
○ Hindi	Arabic/other	Other Language
○ English	Hindi/English/other	
○ French	Chinese/other	**Bantu** Language Group
○ Russian	Russian/other	*Mari* Other Language
○ Portuguese	English/French	Uninhabited Land

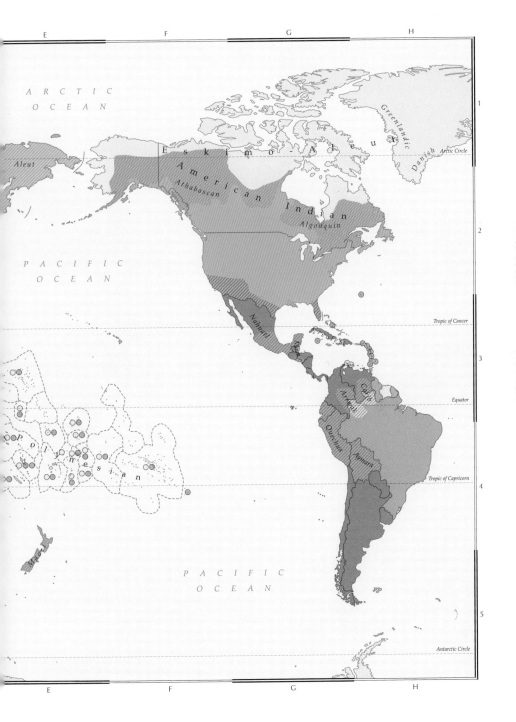

Religion

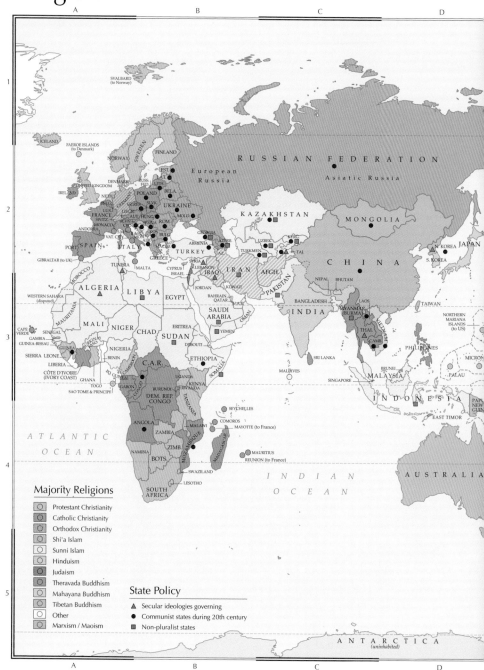

Majority Religions

- Protestant Christianity
- Catholic Christianity
- Orthodox Christianity
- Shi'a Islam
- Sunni Islam
- Hinduism
- Judaism
- Theravada Buddhism
- Mahayana Buddhism
- Tibetan Buddhism
- Other
- Marxism / Maoism

State Policy

- ▲ Secular ideologies governing
- ● Communist states during 20th century
- ■ Non-pluralist states

The Global Economy

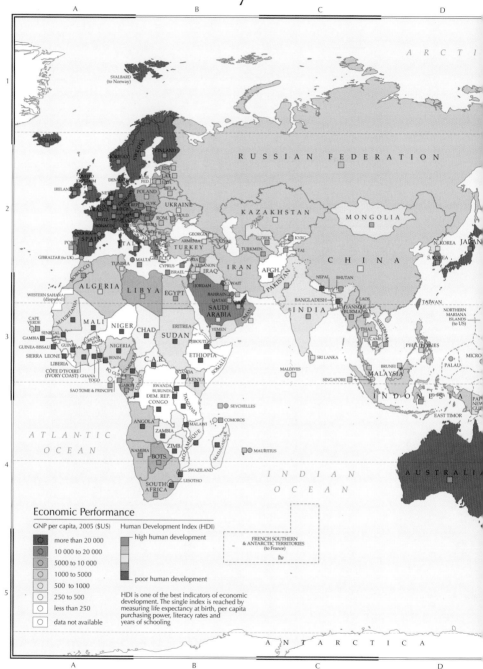

Economic Performance

GNP per capita, 2005 ($US)

- more than 20 000
- 10 000 to 20 000
- 5000 to 10 000
- 1000 to 5000
- 500 to 1000
- 250 to 500
- less than 250
- data not available

Human Development Index (HDI)

- high human development
- poor human development

HDI is one of the best indicators of economic development. The single index is reached by measuring life expectancy at birth, per capita purchasing power, literacy rates and years of schooling

FRENCH SOUTHERN & ANTARCTIC TERRITORIES (to France)

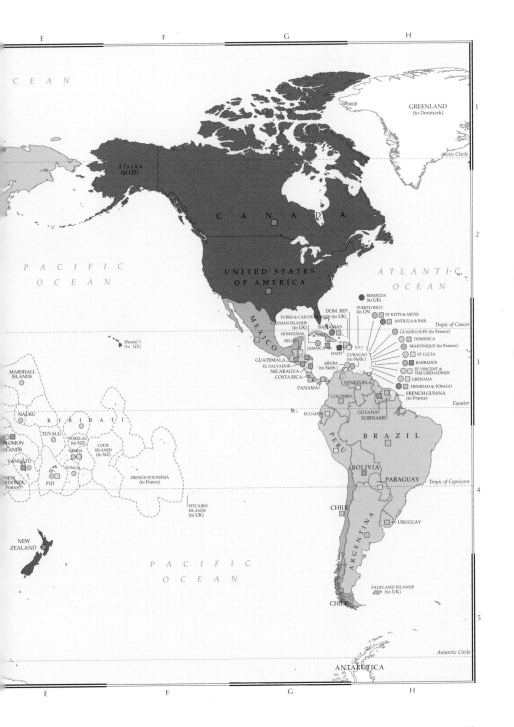

E F G H

C E A N

GREENLAND
(to Denmark)

1

Arctic Circle

Alaska
(to US)

C A N A D A

2

P A C I F I C
O C E A N

UNITED STATES
OF AMERICA

A T L A N T I C
O C E A N

BERMUDA
(to UK)

PUERTO RICO
(to US) ST KITTS & NEVIS
ANTIGUA & BAR.

DOM. REP.
TURKS & CAICOS ISLANDS (to UK)
CAYMAN ISLANDS
(to UK)

Hawai'i
(to US)

MEXICO

Tropic of Cancer

GUADELOUPE (to France)
DOMINICA
MAKTINIQUE (to France)
ST LUCIA
BARBADOS
ST VINCENT &
THE GRENADINES
GRENADA
TRINIDAD & TOBAGO
FRENCH GUIANA
(to France)

HONDURAS
BELIZE

BAHAMAS
CUBA
JAMAICA
HAITI
CURAÇAO
(to Neth.)
ARUBA
(to Neth.)

GUATEMALA
EL SALVADOR
NICARAGUA
COSTA RICA

MARSHALL
ISLANDS

3

VENEZUELA

PANAMA

COLOMBIA

Equator

NAURU

K I R I B A T I

ECUADOR

GUYANA
SURINAME

TUVALU

TOKELAU
(to NZ)

SOLOMON
ISLANDS

SAMOA

COOK
ISLANDS
(to NZ)

P E R U

B R A Z I L

VANUATU

TONGA

BOLIVIA

NEW
CALEDONIA
(to France)

FIJI

FRENCH POLYNESIA
(to France)

PARAGUAY

Tropic of Capricorn

4

PITCAIRN
ISLANDS
(to UK)

CHILE

URUGUAY

A R G E N T I N A

NEW
ZEALAND

P A C I F I C
O C E A N

FALKLAND ISLANDS
(to UK)

CHILE

5

Antarctic Circle

ANTARCTICA

E F G H

Politics and Conflict

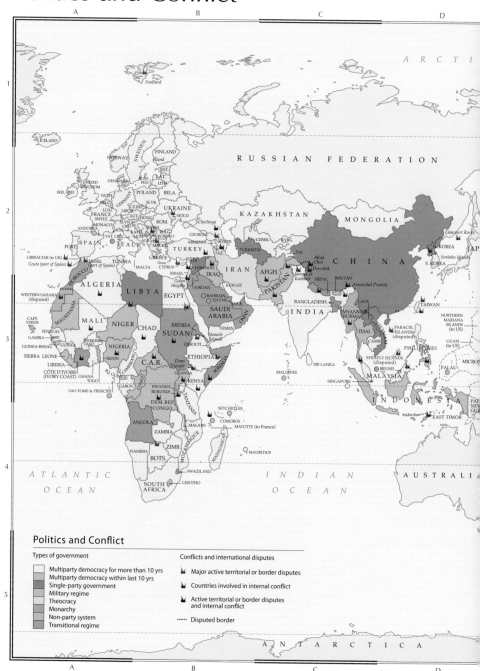

A   B   C   D

ARCTI

Svalbard

ICELAND

NORWAY   SWEDEN   FINLAND
Åland

RUSSIAN FEDERATION

EST.
DENMARK   RUSS.   LAT.
UNITED   FED.   LITH.
KINGDOM
IRELAND   NETH.   POLAND   BELA.
BEL.G.   GERMANY
LUX.   CZ.REP.   SLVK.
FRANCE   LIECH.   UKRAINE
SWITZ.   AUT.   HUNG.
MONACO   SLV.   ROM.   MOLD.   KAZAKHSTAN   MONGOLIA
ANDORRA   CRO.   BOS.   BELG.
VAT. CIT.   MONT.   KOSOVO   GEORGIA
SPAIN   ITALY   ALB.   MACE.   ARMENIA   AZERB.   UZBEK.   KYRG.
   TURKEY   TURKMEN.   TAJ.
GIBRALTAR (to UK)   GREECE   SYRIA   IRAN   AFGH.   CHINA
Ceuta (part of Spain)   Melilla   TUNISIA   MALTA   CYPRUS   LEBANON   IRAQ
   (part of Spain)   ISRAEL   PAKISTAN
MOROCCO   LIBYA   EGYPT   JORDAN   KUWAIT   NEPAL   BHUTAN
ALGERIA   BAHRAIN   QATAR
WESTERN SAHARA   SAUDI   BANGLADESH
(disputed)   ARABIA   OMAN   INDIA   MYANMAR
CAPE   MAURITANIA   MALI   NIGER   CHAD   ERITREA   YEMEN   THAI.   LAOS
VERDE   SENEGAL   BURKINA   SUDAN   DJIBOUTI   CAMB.
GAMBIA   FASO   NIGERIA   ETHIOPIA
GUINEA-BISSAU   GUINEA   BENIN   C.A.R.   SRI LANKA
SIERRA LEONE   CAMEROON   SOMALIA
LIBERIA   UGANDA   MALDIVES
CÔTE D'IVOIRE   GHANA   KENYA   SINGAPORE
(IVORY COAST)   TOGO   GABON   RWANDA   TANZANIA   MALAYSIA
SAO TOME & PRINCIPE   CONGO   BURUNDI   SEYCHELLES   INDONESIA
DEM.REP.   CONGO   COMOROS
ANGOLA   MALAWI   MAYOTTE (to France)   EAST TIMOR
ZAMBIA   MOZAMBIQUE
NAMIBIA   ZIMB.   MADAGASCAR   MAURITIUS
BOTS.   SWAZILAND

ATLANTIC   *INDIAN*   *AUSTRALI*
OCEAN   SOUTH   LESOTHO   *OCEAN*
   AFRICA

N.KOREA   JAP
S.KOREA
Lancang Rocks
Senkaku Islands
Aksai Chin
Jammu &
Kashmir   Arunachal Pradesh
Demchok
TAIWAN
NORTHERN
MARIANA
ISLANDS
(to US)
PARACEL
ISLANDS
(disputed)   GUAM
PHILIPPINES   (to US)
SPRATLY ISLANDS   MICRO
(disputed)   BRUNEI   PALAU
PA
NE
GU
FA

Chechnya
Golan
Heights
Hamish
Islands
Elemi
Triangle

Politics and Conflict

Types of government

	Multiparty democracy for more than 10 yrs
	Multiparty democracy within last 10 yrs
	Single-party government
	Military regime
	Theocracy
	Monarchy
	Non-party system
	Transitional regime

Conflicts and international disputes

Major active territorial or border disputes

Countries involved in internal conflict

Active territorial or border disputes
and internal conflict

······ Disputed border

ANTARCTICA

A   B   C   D

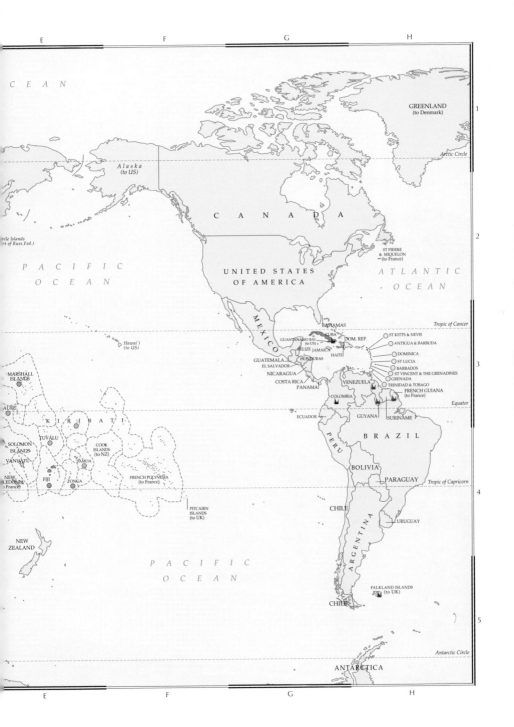

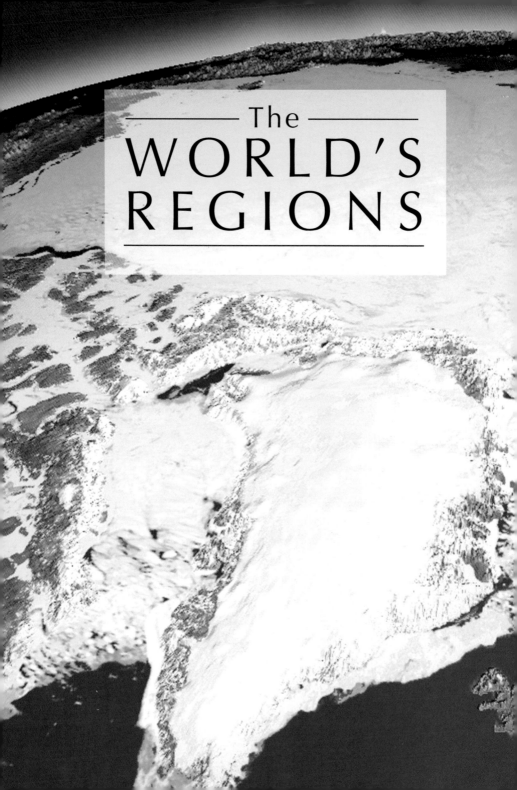

The
WORLD'S
REGIONS

North & Central America

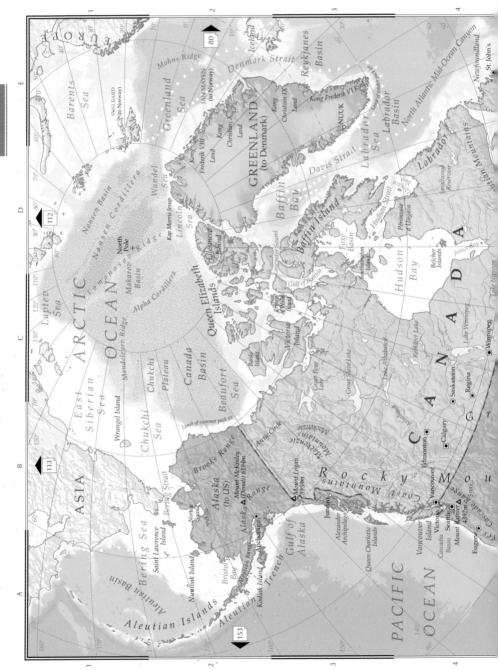

0 km 1000

0 miles 1000

Population   • National capital

o below 50,000   ○ 50,000 to 100,000   ◉ 100,000 to 500,000   ■ above 500,000

Western Canada & Alaska

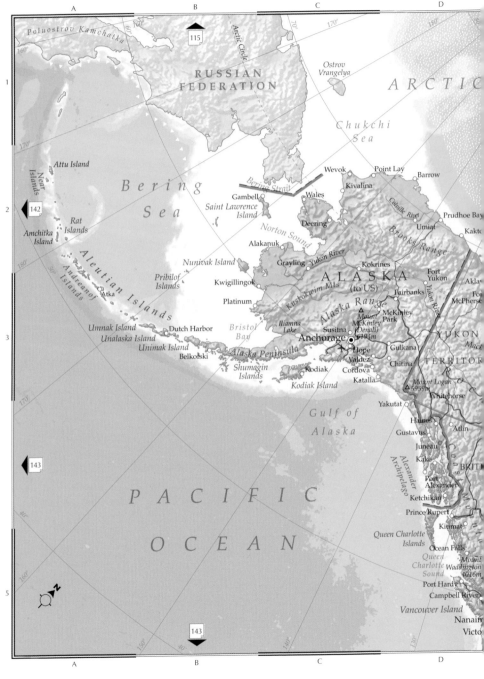

poluostrov Kamchatka

115

Arctic Circle

RUSSIAN
FEDERATION

Ostrov
Vrangelya

ARCTIC

1

Chukchi
Sea

Attu Island

Near
Islands

Bering

Sea

142

Rat
Islands

Amchitka
Island

Saint Lawrence
Island

Gambell

Wevok

Kivalina

Wales

Point Lay

Barrow

2

Deering

Norton Sound

Umiat

Colville River

Prudhoe Bay

Brooks Range

Kakto

Aleutian Islands

Andreanof
Islands

Atka

Nunivak Island

Pribilof
Islands

Kwigillingok

Platinum

Alakanuk

Grayling

Yukon River

Kuskokwim Mts

ALASKA
(to US)

Kokrines

Fort
Yukon

Fairbanks

Akla

Fort
McPherse

Yukon River

Umnak Island

Unalaska Island

Dutch Harbor

Bristol
Bay

Unimak Island

Belkofski

Alaska Peninsula

Iliamna
Lake

Susitna

Anchorage

Alaska Range

Mount
McKinley
(Denali)
6194m

McKinley
Park

YUKON

3

Shumagin
Islands

Kodiak

Kodiak Island

Hope

Valdez

Cordova

Katalla

Gulkana

Chitina

Mack

TERRITOR

Mount Logan
5959m

Whitehorse

Yakutat

Gulf of

Alaska

Haines

Gustavus

Atlin

Juneau

Kake

Alexander
Archipelago

143

PACIFIC

OCEAN

BRIT

Port
Alexander

Ketchikan

Prince Rupert

Kitimat

Queen Charlotte
Islands

Ocean Falls

Queen
Charlotte
Sound

Mount
Waddington
4016m

Port Hardy

Campbell River

Vancouver Island

Nanain

Victo

5

143

0 km   400

0 miles   400

Population

○ below 50,000   ○ 50,000 to 100,000   ◉ 100,000 to 500,000   ■ above 500,000

● Internal administrative capital

OCEAN

Alert

155

Knud Rasmussen Land

GREENLAND
(to Denmark)

Ellesmere Island

Arctic Circle

Axel
Heiberg
Island

Queen Elizabeth Islands

Ellef Ringnes
Island
Isachsen

Amund
Ringnes
Island

*Baffin
Bay*

Prince Patrick
Island

Mould Bay

Davis Strait

Bathurst
Island

Devon Island

Cornwallis
Island

82

Melville
Island

Resolute
(Qausuittuq)

Lancaster Sound

Beaufort

Viscount Melville
Sound

Somerset
Island

Baffin Island

Sea

Banks
Island

Prince of
Wales Island

Byltot
Peninsula

chs Harbour
(Ikaahuk)

Amundsen

Holman

Gulf of Boothia

Igloolik

Cumberland Sound

toyaktuk

Gulf

Victoria
Island

Boothia
Peninsula

Nettilling
Lake

ik

Paulatuk

Cambridge Bay
(Ikaluktutiak)

King William
Island

Kugaaruk
(Pelly Bay)

Melville
Peninsula

*Foxe
Basin*

Amadjuak
Lake

Iqaluit
(Frobisher Bay)

Fort
Good Hope

Kugluktuk
(Coppermine)

Gjoa Haven
(Uqsuqtuuq)

Repulse Bay

Great
Bear
Lake

Echo Bay

Burnside

Southampton
Island

Hudson Strait

Mackenzie

NUNAVUT

Garry Lake

Coral
Harbour

*Péninsule
d'Ungava*

Back

Baker Lake

38

NORTHWEST

Rankin Inlet

Coats
Island

Mansel
Island

QUÉBEC

TERRITORIES

Edzo

Yellowknife

Reliance

Whale Cove

gsten

Fort Simpson

Dubawnt

Arviat

Hudson

Great Slave
Lake

Lutselk'e
(Snowdrift)

Fort Providence

Hay River

Fort Smith

Churchill

Bay

Fort Liard

Lake Athabasca

Belcher
Islands

Fort Nelson

Wollaston Lake

Reindeer Lake

*James
Bay*

LUMBIA

Fort Vermilion

Southern
Indian Lake

Nelson

C   A   N   A   D   A

Fort St. John

Fort
McMurray

Lynn Lake

Thompson

ALBERTA

Grande Prairie

Buffalo
Narrows

SASKATCHEWAN

Flin Flon

ONTARIO

rince George

Athabasca

Saskatchewan

The Pas

Lake
Winnipeg

Edmonton

North Saskatchewan

Saskatchewan

MANITOBA

fount Robson
3954m

Leduc

Prince Albert

Red Deer

Saskatoon

Kamloops

Calgary

Kindersley

Yorkton

Kelowna

Regina

Qu'Appelle

Lake
Manitoba

Winnipeg

Lake of the
Woods

Lake Superior

Medicine Hat

Brandon
Weyburn

Cranbrook

Lethbridge

Melita

Lake
Michigan

couver

Milk River

Estevan

45

U   N   I   T   E   D   S   T   A   T   E   S   O   F   A   M   E   R   I

Elevation

| -6000m | -4000m | -2000m | -1000m | -500m | Below sea level | 0 | 250m | 500m | 1000m | 2000m | 3000m | 4000m | 6000m |
| | | | | | -250m | | | | | | | | |

| -19,658ft | -13,124ft | -6562ft | -3281ft | -1640ft | -820ft | -328ft/-100m | 0 | 820ft | 1640ft | 3281ft | 6562ft | 9843ft | 13,124ft | 19,685ft |

37

Eastern Canada

NORTHWEST TERRITORIES

105° 100° 95° ~90° 85° 80° 75°

60°

NUNAVUT

37

SASKATCHEWAN

Churchill

Southern Indian Lake

Charles Island

Coats Island

Ivujivik

Mansel Island

Péninsul d' Ungav

55°

37

MANITOBA

Nelson

Hayes

Severn

H u d s o n

Ottawa Islands

Inukjuak (Port Harrison)

Rivière Feu

Lac Mintc

B a y

Fort Severn

Belcher Islands

Bien

Cedar Lake

Lake Winnipeg

Lake Winnipegosis

Sandy Lake

Wunisk

Peawanuk

Attawapiskat

J a m e s
B a y

Akimiski Island

QU

Lake Manitoba

C

O N T A R I O

Albany

Attawapiskat

Fort Albany

Eastmain

50°

Lac Seul

Moosonee

Rivière de Rupert

Lae Mistassin

Moose

Armstrong

Kenora

Red River

Dryden

Lake of the Woods

Lake Nipigon

Longlac

Hearst

Harricana

Chibougamau

Fort Frances

Atikokan

Nipigon

Kapuskasing

Cochrane

Amos

Réservoir Gouin

Rainy Lake

Marathon

Tip Top Mountain △640m

Timmins

Rouyn-Noranda

Thunder Bay

Lake Superior

Foleyet

Wawa

Kirkland Lake

Val-d'Or

NORTH DAKOTA

45

45°

MINNESOTA

43°

M I C H I G A N

Sault Ste.Marie

Sudbury

North Bay

SOUTH DAKOTA

Pembroke

Gatineau
Hull

La

U N I T E D   S T A T E S

Manitoulin Island

Georgian Bay

OTTAWA

NEBRASKA

WISCONSIN

Lake Huron

Midland

Peterborough

Kingstc

Lake Michigan

Brampton

Oshawa

Lake Onta

O F   A M E R I C A

IOWA

Kitchener

Toronto

Sarnia

Hamilton

St.Catharines

Windsor

London

Niagara Falls

NEW YORK

Leamington

Lake Erie

ILLINOIS

40

40°

95°

90°

INDIANA

85°

O H I O

80°

PENNSYLVANIA

Mississippi River

0 km 300

0 miles 300

Population

○ below 50,000

○ 50,000 to 100,000

◉ 100,000 to 500,000

■ above 500,000

● National capital

◎ Internal administrative capital

Baffin Island
Resolution Island
Button Islands
Akpatok Island
Strait
Ungava Bay
Inukjuak
Rivière à la Baleine
Nain
Hopedale
Makkovik
Cape Harrison
Caniapiscau
Scheff*erville
NEWFOUNDLAND
Smallwood Reservoir
Lake Melville
Cartwright
Labrador
Labrador Sea
Churchill
Réservoir de Caniapiscau
E C
D
A
& LABRADOR
St.Anthony
Gagnon
Réservoir Manicouagan
Laurentian Mountains
Havre-St-Pierre
Île d'Anticosti
Strait of Belle Isle
Gander
Corner Brook
Grand Falls
Newfoundland
St.John's
Sept-Îles
Baie-Comeau
St.Lawrence
Gaspé
Gulf of St. Lawrence
Cape Race
Chicoutimi
Matane
Peninsula de Gaspé
Îles de la Madeleine
Channel-Port aux Basques
Cabot Strait
ac Jean
Rimouski
Bathurst
PRINCE EDWARD ISLAND
ST PIERRE & MIQUELON (to France)
Jonquière
a Tuque
Rivière-du-Loup
Edmundston
Glace Bay
Charlesbourg
NEW BRUNSWICK
Charlottetown
Sydney
Cape Breton Island
Trois-Rivières
Québec
St-Georges
Moncton
Amherst
New Glasgow
Montréal
Drummondville
Fredericton
Oromocto
Truro
NOVA SCOTIA
MAINE
Saint John
Dartmouth
Sherbrooke
Bay of Fundy
Halifax
Sable Island
Liverpool
NEW HAMPSHIRE
Yarmouth
ATLANTIC
MASSACHUSETTS
Cape Cod
OCEAN
CONNECTICUT
RHODE ISLAND
VERMONT

82
66
66
66

Elevation

-6000m	-4000m	-2000m	-1000m	-500m	-250m	Below sea level 0	250m	500m	1000m	2000m	3000m	4000m	6000m
-19,658ft	-13,124ft	-6562ft	-3281ft	-1640ft	-820ft	-328ft/-100m 0	820ft	1640ft	3281ft	6562ft	9843ft	13,124ft	19,685ft

39

USA: The Northeast

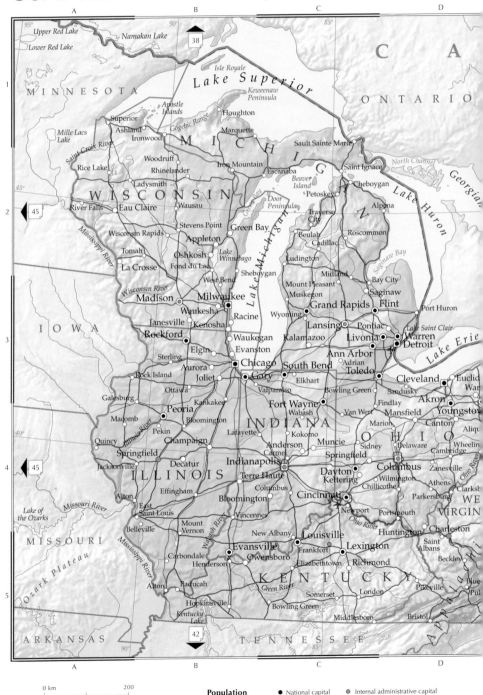

Population

- ○ below 50,000
- ○ 50,000 to 100,000
- ⦿ 100,000 to 500,000
- ▣ above 500,000

● National capital   ○ Internal administrative capital

0 km   200
0 miles   200

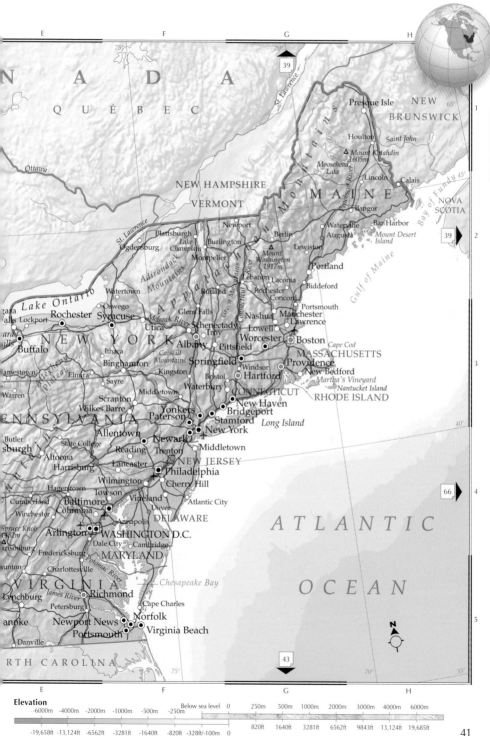

USA: The Southeast

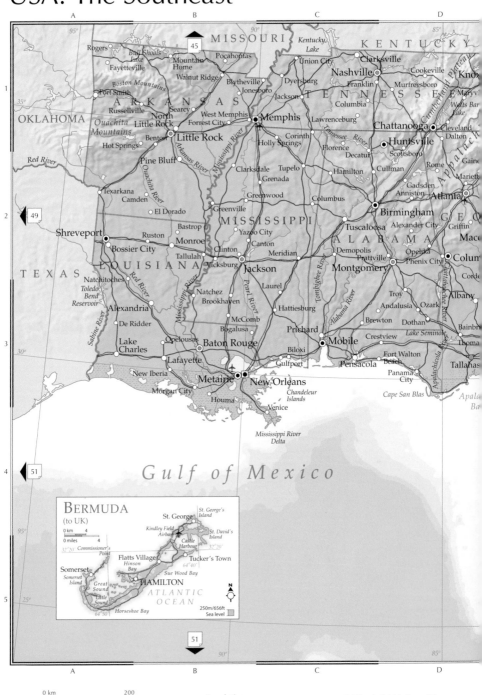

A · B · C · D

MISSOURI

Rogers · Bull Shoals Lake · Pocahontas · Kentucky Lake · KENTUCKY
Fayetteville · Mountain Home · Union City · Clarksville · Cookeville · Knox
Walnut Ridge · Blytheville · Dyersburg · Nashville · Franklin · Murfreesboro · Maryv
Fort Smith · Boston Mountains · Jonesboro · TENNESSEE · Columbia · Watts Bar Lake
Russellville · Searcy · West Memphis · Jackson · Lawrenceburg · Chattanooga · Cleveland
OKLAHOMA · Ouachita Mountains · Little Rock · Forrest City · Memphis · Corinth · Huntsville · Dalton
Hot Springs · Benton · Little Rock · Holly Springs · Florence · Decatur · Scottsboro
Red River · Pine Bluff · Clarksdale · Tupelo · Hamilton · Cullman · Rome · Gadsden · Marietta
Texarkana · Greenwood · Columbus · Anniston · Atlanta
Camden · Greenville · MISSISSIPPI · Birmingham · GEO
El Dorado · Bastrop · Yazoo City · Tuscaloosa · Alexander City · Griffin
Shreveport · Ruston · Monroe · Clinton · Canton · ALABAMA · Macc
Bossier City · Tallulah · Meridian · Demopolis · Opelika · Phenix City · Colun
TEXAS · LOUISIANA · Vicksburg · Jackson · Montgomery · Prattville · Corde
Natchitoches · Toledo Bend Reservoir · Natchez · Laurel · Troy · Albany
Alexandria · Brookhaven · Hattiesburg · Andalusia · Ozark
De Ridder · McComb · Brewton · Dothan · Bainbr
Bogalusa · Prichard · Crestview · Lake Seminole · Thoma
Lake Charles · Opelousas · Baton Rouge · Mobile · Fort Walton Beach · Tallahas
Lafayette · Biloxi · Pensacola · Panama City
New Iberia · Metairie · Gulfport · Cape San Blas · Apala
Morgan City · New Orleans · Chandeleur Islands · Ba
Houma · Venice

Mississippi River Delta

Gulf of Mexico

BERMUDA
(to UK)

0 km 4
0 miles 4

Commissioner's Point · Kindley Field Airbase · St. George · St. George's Island
Flatts Village · Castle Harbour · St. David's Island
Somerset · Hinson Bay · Tucker's Town
Somerset Island · Sue Wood Bay
Great Sound · HAMILTON · ATLANTIC OCEAN
Little Sound · Horseshoe Bay

250m/656ft
Sea level

0 km 200
0 miles 200

Population

○ below 50,000 · ○ 50,000 to 100,000 · ◉ 100,000 to 500,000 · ■ above 500,000 · ● Internal administrative capital

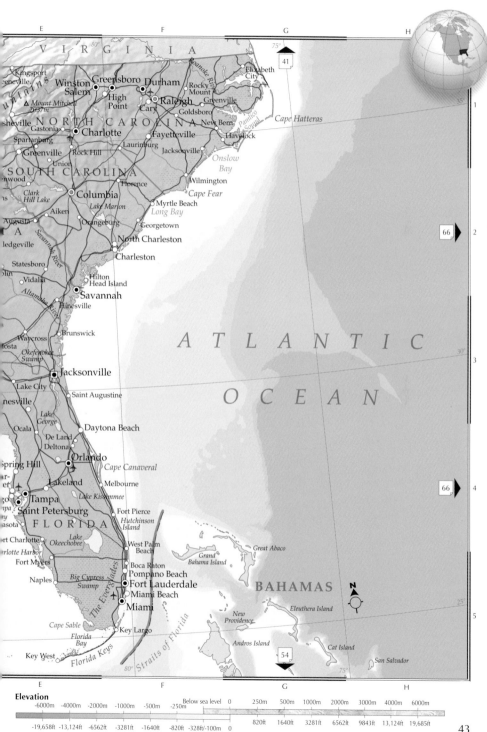

Elevation

						Below sea level								
-6000m	-4000m	-2000m	-1000m	-500m	-250m		0	250m	500m	1000m	2000m	3000m	4000m	6000m
-19,658ft	-13,124ft	-6562ft	-3281ft	-1640ft	-820ft	-328ft/-100m	0	820ft	1640ft	3281ft	6562ft	9843ft	13,124ft	19,685ft

USA: Central States

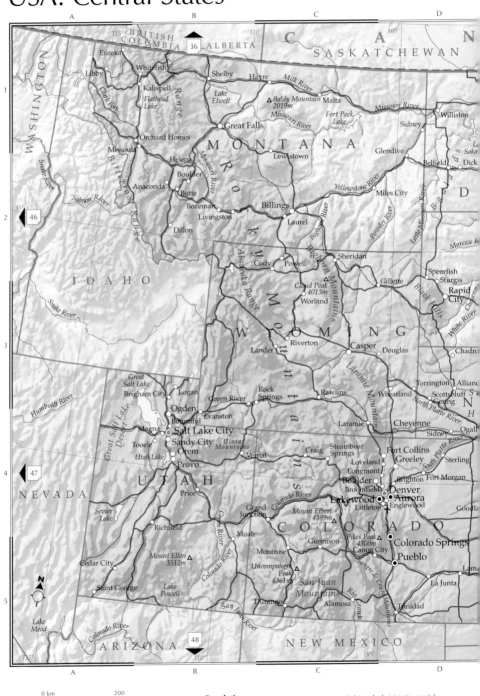

Population

○ below 50,000	● Internal administrative capital
○ 50,000 to 100,000	
● 100,000 to 500,000	
■ above 500,000	

0 km   200

0 miles   200

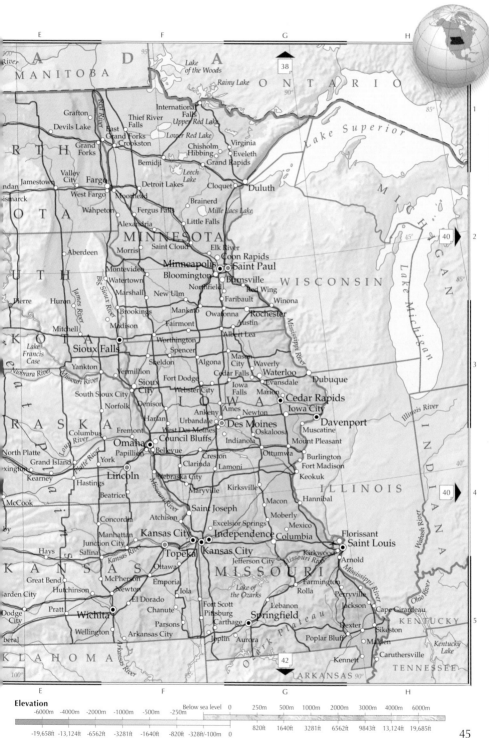

Elevation

-6000m	-4000m	-2000m	-1000m	-500m	-250m	Below sea level 0	250m	500m	1000m	2000m	3000m	4000m	6000m
-19,658ft	-13,124ft	-6562ft	-3281ft	-1640ft	-820ft	-328ft/-100m 0	820ft	1640ft	3281ft	6562ft	9843ft	13,124ft	19,685ft

45

USA: The West

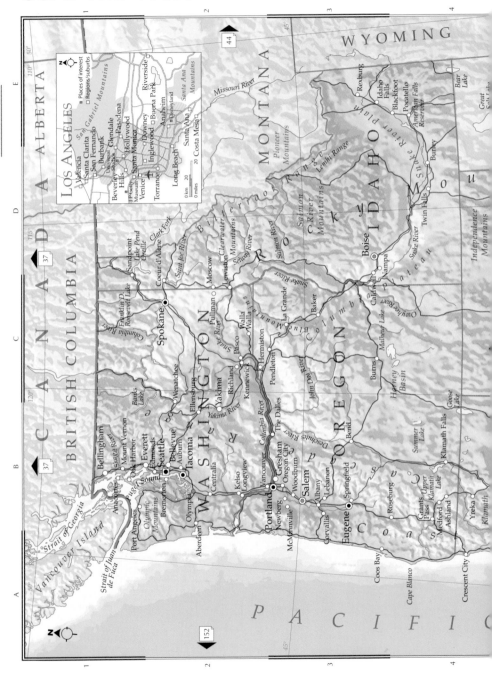

LOS ANGELES

Places of interest
Regions/suburbs

San Gabriel Mountains
Santa Clarita
Valencia
San Fernando
Burbank
Universal Studios
Pasadena
Glendale
Hollywood
Beverly Hills
Santa Monica
Museum
Venice
Inglewood
Downey
Whittier
Disneyland
Buena Park
Anaheim
Santa Ana
Riverside
Santa Ana Mountains
Torrance
Long Beach
Costa Mesa

0 km 20
0 miles 20

CANADA

ALBERTA
BRITISH COLUMBIA

WYOMING

MONTANA

Missouri River
Pioneer Mountains
Lemhi Range
Rexburg
Idaho Falls
Blackfoot
Pocatello
American Falls Reservoir
Burley
Bear Lake
Great Salt Lake

IDAHO

Sandpoint
Lake Pend Oreille
Clark Fork
Coeur d'Alene
Spokane
Moscow
Pullman
Lewiston
Clearwater River
Selway River
Salmon River
Salmon River Mountains
Boise
Nampa
Caldwell
Owyhee River
Snake River
Twin Falls
Independence Mountains

Franklin D. Roosevelt Lake
Columbia River
Banks Lake

WASHINGTON

Bellingham
Mount Vernon
Everett
Edmonds
Oak Harbor
Anacortes
Seattle
Bellevue
Auburn
Tacoma
Bremerton
Olympia
Aberdeen
Port Angeles
Olympic Mountains
Puget Sound
Strait of Juan de Fuca
Vancouver Island
Strait of Georgia

Wenatchee
Ellensburg
Yakima
Yakima River
Richland
Kennewick
Pasco
Walla Walla
Hermiston
Pendleton
La Grande
Baker
Burns
Harney Basin
Malheur Lake

Snake River
Blue Mountains
John Day River
Columbia Plateau

Centralia
Kelso
Longview
Woodburn
Oregon City
Gresham
Portland
Vancouver
Salem
Newberg
McMinnville
Albany
Lebanon
Corvallis
Springfield
Eugene
Bend
Deschutes River
The Dalles
Columbia River

OREGON

Roseburg
Grants Pass
Medford
Ashland
Klamath Falls
Upper Klamath Lake
Summer Lake
Goose Lake
Yreka
Klamath

Coos Bay
Cape Blanco
Crescent City

PACIFIC

0 km 200
0 miles 200

Population

○ below 50,000
○ 50,000 to 100,000
◉ 100,000 to 500,000
◼ above 500,000

◉ Internal administrative capital

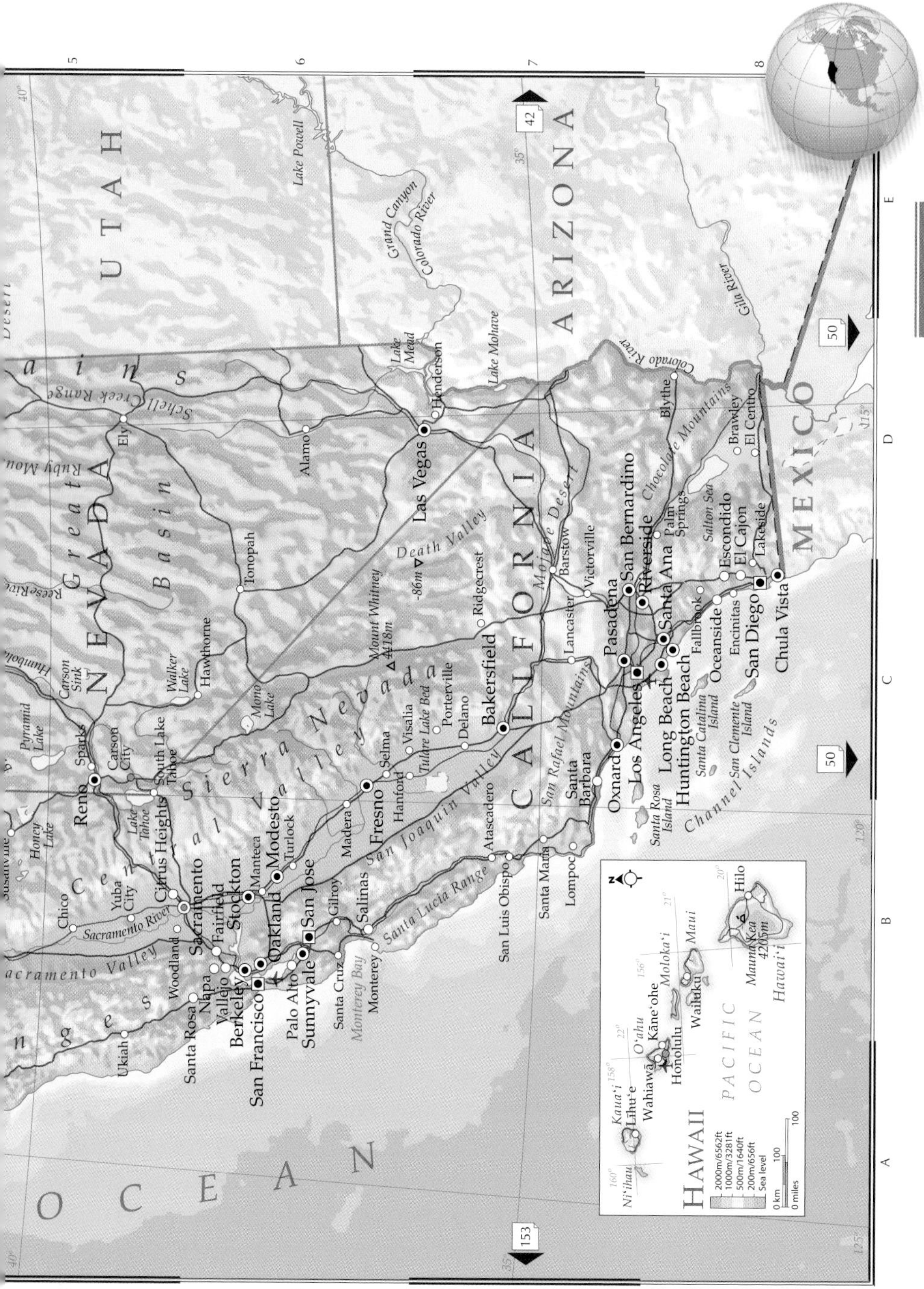
NEVADA
UTAH
ARIZONA
CALIFORNIA
MEXICO
OCEAN
Great Basin
Sierra Nevada
Central Valley
San Joaquin Valley
Sacramento Valley
Death Valley
Mojave Desert
Lake Powell
Grand Canyon
Colorado River
Lake Mead
Lake Mohave
Gila River
Salton Sea
Chocolate Mountains
Mount Whitney 4418m
-86m
Tulare Lake Bed
San Rafael Mountains
Santa Lucia Range
Monterey Bay
Channel Islands
Santa Rosa Island
Santa Catalina Island
San Clemente Island
Pyramid Lake
Honey Lake
Lake Tahoe
Carson Sink
Walker Lake
Mono Lake
Schell Creek Range
Ruby Mou...
Reese River
Humboldt
Sacramento River
Reno
Sparks
Carson City
South Lake Tahoe
Citrus Heights
Sacramento
Stockton
Modesto
Manteca
Turlock
Oakland
Berkeley
San Francisco
San Jose
Sunnyvale
Palo Alto
Santa Cruz
Gilroy
Salinas
Monterey
Fresno
Madera
Hanford
Selma
Visalia
Porterville
Delano
Bakersfield
Ridgecrest
Lancaster
Barstow
Victorville
Los Angeles
Pasadena
Long Beach
Huntington Beach
Santa Ana
Riverside
San Bernardino
Palm Springs
Oxnard
Santa Barbara
Lompoc
Santa Maria
San Luis Obispo
Atascadero
Oceanside
Fallbrook
Encinitas
Escondido
El Cajon
Lakeside
San Diego
Chula Vista
Brawley
El Centro
Blythe
Las Vegas
Henderson
Alamo
Tonopah
Hawthorne
Ely
Chico
Yuba City
Woodland
Fairfield
Vallejo
Napa
Santa Rosa
Ukiah
HAWAII
Ni'ihau
Kaua'i
Līhu'e
O'ahu
Wahiawā
Kāne'ohe
Honolulu
Moloka'i
Maui
Wailuku
Hawai'i
Hilo
Mauna Kea 4205m
PACIFIC OCEAN
2000m/6562ft
1000m/3281ft
500m/1640ft
200m/656ft
Sea level
0 km 100
0 miles 100
42
50
153
A B C D E
5 6 7 8
40° 35° 120° 115° 125°

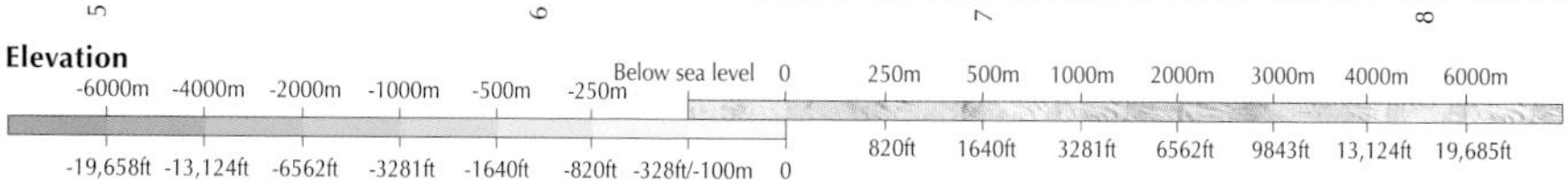
Elevation
-6000m -4000m -2000m -1000m -500m -250m
Below sea level 0
250m 500m 1000m 2000m 3000m 4000m 6000m
-19,658ft -13,124ft -6562ft -3281ft -1640ft -820ft -328ft/-100m 0
820ft 1640ft 3281ft 6562ft 9843ft 13,124ft 19,685ft

USA: The Southwest

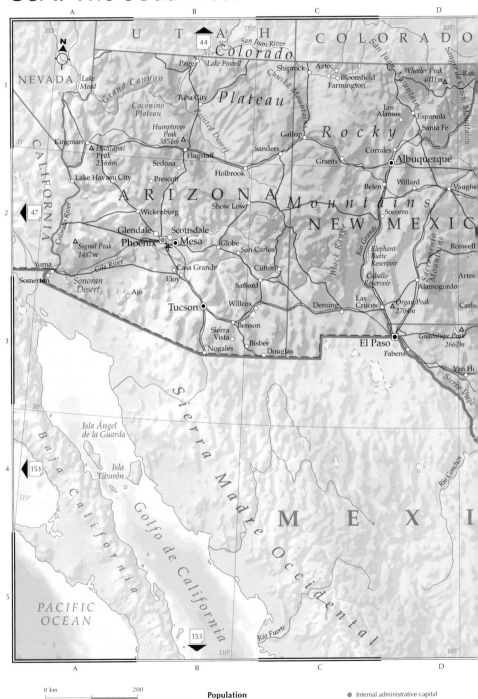

UTAH
COLORADO
115°
110°
105°

N

San Juan River
44
Colorado
Page Lake Powell
Shiprock Aztec
Wheeler Peak
4011m
Rato

NEVADA Lake Mead
Grand Canyon
Bloomfield
Farmington
San Juan Mountains
Sangre de Cristo Mountains

1

Coconino Plateau
Tuba City
Plateau
Chuska Mountains
Los Alamos
Espanola

Humphreys Peak
3851m
Gallup
Rocky
Santa Fe

35°
Kingman
Hualapai Peak
2566m
Flagstaff
Sanders
Corrales
Albuquerque

Sedona
Grants
CALIFORNIA

Lake Havasu City
Prescott
Holbrook
Belen
Willard
Vaughn

ARIZONA
Show Low
Mountains
Socorro

2

47

Wickenburg
NEW MEXICO

Colorado River
Glendale Scottsdale
Rio Grande

Signal Peak
1487m
Phoenix Mesa
Globe
Elephant Butte Reservoir
Roswell

Yuma
Gila River
San Carlos
Black Range
Sacramento Mountains

Somerton
Sonoran Desert
Casa Grande
Clifton
Artes

Eloy
Safford
Caballo Reservoir
Alamogordo

Ajo
Tucson
Willcox
Deming
Las Cruces
Organ Peak
2704m
Carls

3

Sierra Vista
Benson
Guadalupe Peak
2667m

Nogales
Bisbee
Douglas
El Paso
Fabens

Van Ho
Sierra Vieja

30°

Isla Ángel de la Guarda

Baja California

4

153

Isla Tiburón

Sierra Madre Occidental

Rio Conchos

115°

MEXICO

Golfo de California

5

PACIFIC OCEAN

153

Río Fuerte

110°
105°

0 km   200

0 miles   200

Population

○ below 50,000   ○ 50,000 to 100,000   ◉ 100,000 to 500,000   ◼ above 500,000

● Internal administrative capital

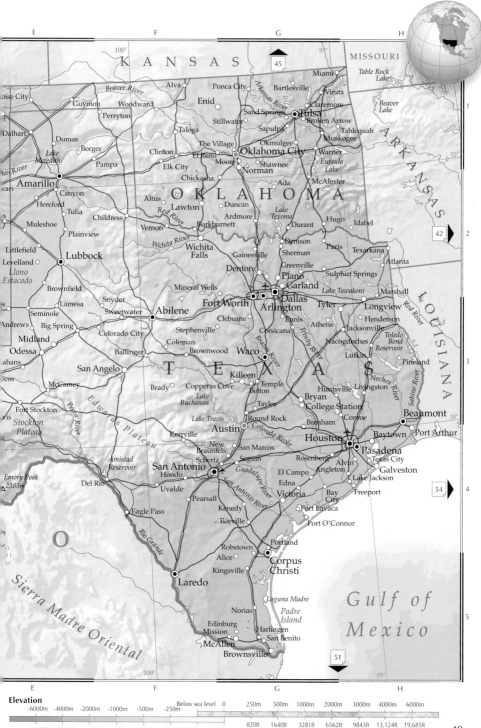

Elevation

-6000m	-4000m	-2000m	-1000m	-500m	-250m	Below sea level 0	250m	500m	1000m	2000m	3000m	4000m	6000m
-19,658ft	-13,124ft	-6562ft	-3281ft	-1640ft	-820ft	-328ft/-100m 0		820ft	1640ft	3281ft	6562ft	9843ft	13,124ft	19,685ft

Mexico

0 km   300

0 miles   300

Population

● National capital

○ below 50,000   ○ 50,000 to 100,000   ◉ 100,000 to 500,000   ■ above 500,000

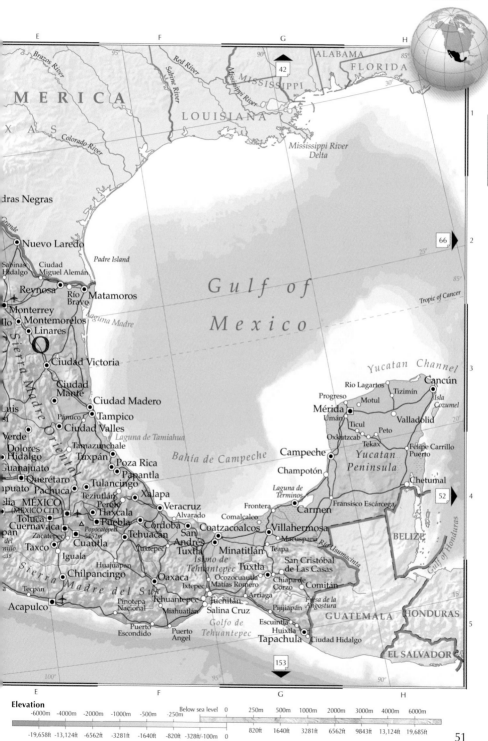

E   F   G   H

ALABAMA

FLORIDA

MERICA

LOUISIANA

Brazos River

Red River

Mississippi River

MISSISSIPPI

42

Colorado River

X A S

Mississippi River Delta

dras Negras

66

Nuevo Laredo

Padre Island

Gulf of

Sabinas Hidalgo

Ciudad Miguel Alemán

Reynosa

Río Bravo

Matamoros

Monterrey

Mexico

Montemorelos

Linares

Laguna Madre

Tropic of Cancer

Sierra Madre Oriental

Ciudad Victoria

Yucatan Channel

Ciudad Mante

Cancún

Río Lagartos

Ciudad Madero

Progreso

Tizimín

Isla Cozumel

Pánuco

Tampico

uis

Mérida

Motul

Umán

Verde

Ciudad Valles

Laguna de Tamiahua

Ticul

Peto

Valladolid

Dolores Hidalgo

Tamazunchale

Tuxpán

Oxkutzcab

Tekax

Felipe Carrillo Puerto

Guanajuato

Poza Rica

Bahía de Campeche

Campeche

Yucatan Peninsula

apuato

Querétaro

Papantla

Champotón

Pachuca

Tulancingo

Laguna de Términos

Chetumal

elia

Teziutlán

Xalapa

52

MEXICO

Perote

Fransisco Escárcega

(MEXICO CITY)

Tlaxcala

Veracruz

Frontera

Toluca

Puebla

Córdoba

Carmen

Cuernavaca

Popocatépetl 5452m

Comalcalco

BELIZE

pan del nillo

Zacatepec

Tehuacán

Coatzacoalcos

Villahermosa

sús

Taxco

Cuautla

Ixtepec

San Andrés

Macuspana

Río Usumacinta

Iguala

Tuxtla

Minatitlán

Teapa

Gulf of Honduras

Chilpancingo

Huajuapan

Istmo de Tehuantepec

San Cristóbal de Las Casas

Tecpán

Oaxaca

Ocozocuautla

Chiapa de Corzo

Comitán

Sierra Madre del Sur

Ixtepec

Tuxtla

Pinotepa Nacional

Tehuantepec

Matías Romero

Arriaga

Presa de la Angostura

Acapulco

Miahuatlán

Salina Cruz

Pijijiapán

GUATEMALA

HONDURAS

Puerto Escondido

Puerto Angel

Golfo de Tehuantepec

Escuintla

Huixtla

Tapachula

Ciudad Hidalgo

EL SALVADOR

153

Elevation

| -6000m | -4000m | -2000m | -1000m | -500m | -250m | Below sea level 0 | 250m | 500m | 1000m | 2000m | 3000m | 4000m | 6000m |

-19,658ft   -13,124ft   -6562ft   -3281ft   -1640ft   -820ft -328ft/-100m   0   820ft   1640ft   3281ft   6562ft   9843ft   13,124ft   19,685ft

Central America

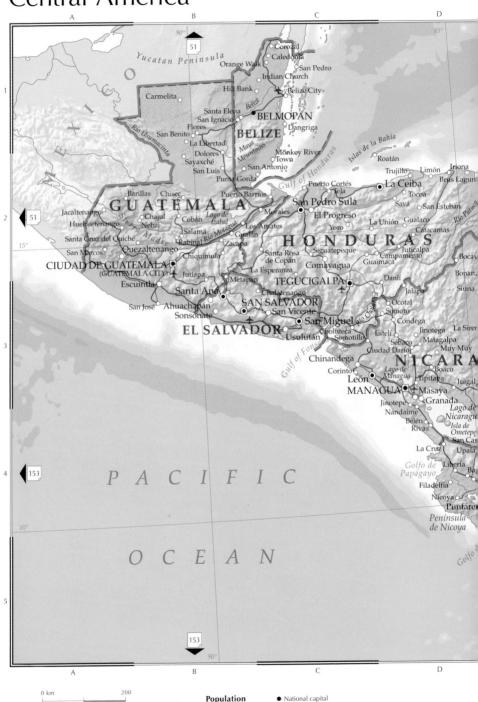

A   B   C   D

90°   85°

1

Yucatan Peninsula

M E X I C O

Corozal
Caledonia
Orange Walk
San Pedro
Indian Church
Hill Bank
Belize City
Carmelita

Santa Elena
San Ignacio
Flores
San Benito
La Libertad
Dolores
Sayaxché
San Luis

BELMOPAN
Dangriga

BELIZE

Río Usumacinta

Belize

Maya Mountains
Monkey River Town
San Antonio
Punta Gorda

Islas de la Bahía

Roatán

Trujillo   Limón   Iriona
Brus Lagun

2

15°

Barillas   Chisec
Jacaltenango
Huehuetenango   Nebaj
Santa Cruz del Quiché
San Marcos   Quezaltenango
CIUDAD DE GUATEMALA
(GUATEMALA CITY)
Escuintla
Santa Ana
San José   Ahuachapán
Sonsonate

GUATEMALA

Chajul   Cobán
Salamá
Rabinal
Chiquimula
Jutiapa
Metapán
Chalatenango
SAN SALVADOR
San Vicente

Lago de Izabal
Los Amates
Gualán
Zacapa
Río Motagua

Puerto Barrios
Morales
San Pedro Sula
El Progreso
Yoro
Santa Rosa de Copán
La Esperanza

Puerto Cortés
Tela
La Ceiba
Savá   San Esteban

HONDURAS

Siguatepeque
Comayagua
TEGUCIGALPA

La Unión   Gualaco
Catacamas
Juticalpa
Campamento
Guaimaca
Danlí

Tocoa

Río Patuca

Bocay
Bonan.
Siuna

Sierra Madre

Gulf of Honduras

EL SALVADOR
San Miguel
Usulután

Choluteca
Somotillo
Chinandega
Corinto
León
MANAGUA

Jalapa
Ocotal
Somoto
Condega
Estelí
Sébaco
Ciudad Darío
Boaco
Lago de Managua
Tipitapa
Masaya
Granada

Jinotega   La Siren
Matagalpa
Muy Muy

NICARA

Juigal

3

Gulf of Fons

Río Coco

Jinotepe
Nandaime
Belén
Rivas
La Cruz
Golfo de Papagayo

Lago de Nicaragu
Isla de Ometepe
San Ca
Upala
Liberia   Ba
Filadelfia
Nicoya
Puntare
Península de Nicoya

4

10°

P A C I F I C

Golfo d

5

O C E A N

90°

A   B   C   D

0 km   200

0 miles   200

Population   ● National capital

○ below 50,000   ○ 50,000 to 100,000   ◉ 100,000 to 500,000   ◼ above 500,000

N

54

Santanilla
(Honduras)

Bajo Nuevo
(to Colombia)

Cayo de Serranilla
(to Colombia)

ia de Caratasca
Puerto Lempira

55

Cayo de Serrana
(to Colombia)

spam

blis
Tuapi
Puerto Cabezas

Cayos Miskitos

C a r i b b e a n

Isla de Providencia
(to Colombia)

Prinzapolka

Barra de Río Grande

S e a

Isla de San Andrés
(to Colombia)

A
ama
Laguna de Perlas

Islas del Maíz

Bluefields

Punta Gorda

San Juan del Norte

58

n Juan
jo
esada

COSTA RICA

Istmo de Panamá

El Porvenir

Gulf of

Heredia
SAN JOSÉ
Cartago

Siquirres
Limón

Portobelo
Colón
Cristóbal
Panama Canal
Lago Gatún
Balboa

Aligandí

Darien

Guabito

Guápiles

rro Chirripó
Grande
pos 3819m
Buenos Aires
Cortés
Palmar Sur
oronado
nsula de Osa

Almirante
Laguna
de Chiriquí
Boquete
La Concepción
David

Golfo de los
Mosquitos

Volcán Barú 3475m
Cordillera Central

Cordillera de San Blas

Lago Bayano

Capira

San Miguelito
PANAMÁ
(PANAMA CITY)
Penonomé
Aguadulce

P A N A M Á

Archipiélago
de las Perlas

Chimán

Isla
del Rey

La Palma

Puerto Obaldía

Serranía del Darién

Yaviza

El Real
Garachiné

COLOMBIA

Santiago
Guarumal

Chitré
Ocú

Las Tablas

Golfo
de Panamá

Jaqué

Golfo
de Chiriquí
Isla de Coiba

Península de
Azuero
Isla
Cébaco

58

Elevation

					Below sea level		250m	500m	1000m	2000m	3000m	4000m	6000m
-6000m	-4000m	-2000m	-1000m	-500m	-250m	0							
-19,658ft	-13,124ft	-6562ft	-3281ft	-1640ft	-820ft	-328ft/-100m	0	820ft	1640ft	3281ft	6562ft	9843ft	13,124ft	19,685ft

The Caribbean

Population

○ below 50,000 ○ 50,000 to 100,000 ◉ 100,000 to 500,000 ▣ above 500,000

● National capital

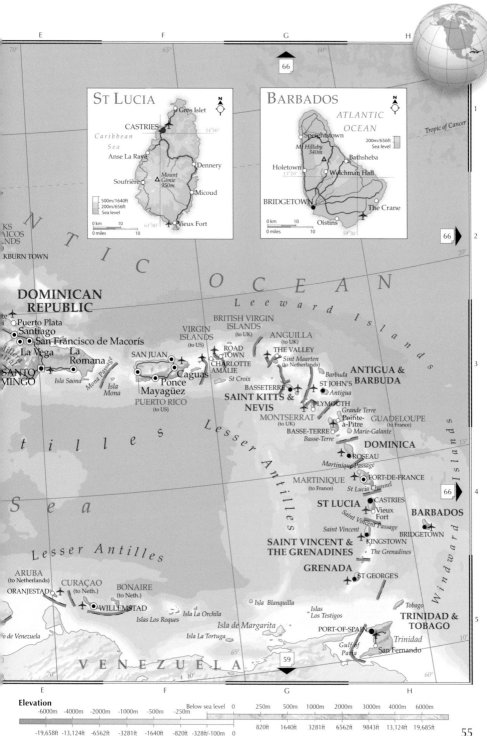

ST LUCIA

N

Gros Islet

CASTRIES

Caribbean Sea

14°00'

Anse La Raye

Dennery

Soufrière

Mount Gimie 950m

Micoud

500m/1640ft
200m/656ft
Sea level

0 km   10
0 miles   10

61°00'

Vieux Fort

BARBADOS

N

ATLANTIC OCEAN

Speightstown

200m/656ft
Sea level

Mt Hillaby 340m

Holetown
13°10'

Bathsheba

Welchman Hall

BRIDGETOWN

The Crane

0 km   10
0 miles   10

Oistins

59°30'

66

66

Tropic of Cancer

20°

KS
AICOS
NDS

KBURN TOWN

DOMINICAN
REPUBLIC

te

Puerto Plata
Santiago
San Francisco de Macorís
La Vega   La
Romana
SANTO
MINGO

Isla Saona

L e e w a r d   I s l a n d s

VIRGIN
ISLANDS
(to US)

BRITISH VIRGIN
ISLANDS
(to UK)

ANGUILLA
(to UK)

THE VALLEY

Sint Maarten
(to Netherlands)

ROAD
TOWN

CHARLOTTE
AMALIE

St Croix

SAN JUAN

Mona Passage

*Isla
Mona*

Caguas
Ponce
Mayagüez

PUERTO RICO
(to US)

BASSETERRE

SAINT KITTS &
NEVIS

Barbuda

ST JOHN'S

Antigua

PLYMOUTH

MONTSERRAT
(to UK)

BASSE-TERRE

Basse-Terre

ANTIGUA &
BARBUDA

Grande Terre

Pointe-
à-Pitre

GUADELOUPE
(to France)

Marie-Galante

DOMINICA

ROSEAU

Martinique Passage

MARTINIQUE
(to France)

FORT-DE-FRANCE

St Lucia Channel

ST LUCIA

CASTRIES
Vieux
Fort

Saint Vincent Passage

Saint Vincent

SAINT VINCENT &
THE GRENADINES

KINGSTOWN

The Grenadines

GRENADA

ST GEORGE'S

BARBADOS

BRIDGETOWN

15°

I s l a n d s

W i n d w a r d

66

66

t   i   l   l   e   s

L e s s e r   A n t i l l e s

S   e   a

L e s s e r   A n t i l l e s

ARUBA
(to Netherlands)

ORANJESTAD

CURAÇAO
(to Neth.)

BONAIRE
(to Neth.)

WILLEMSTAD

Islas Los Roques

Isla La Orchila

Isla Blanquilla

*Islas
Los Testigos*

Isla de Margarita

Tobago

TRINIDAD &
TOBAGO

PORT-OF-SPAIN

Trinidad

San Fernando

*Gulf of
Paria*

10°

o de Venezuela

Isla La Tortuga

V E N E Z U E L A

59

60°

70°

65°

10°

E   F   G   H

Elevation

-6000m	-4000m	-2000m	-1000m	-500m	-250m	Below sea level 0	250m	500m	1000m	2000m	3000m	4000m	6000m
-19,658ft	-13,124ft	-6562ft	-3281ft	-1640ft	-820ft	-328ft/-100m 0	820ft	1640ft	3281ft	6562ft	9843ft	13,124ft	19,685ft

South America

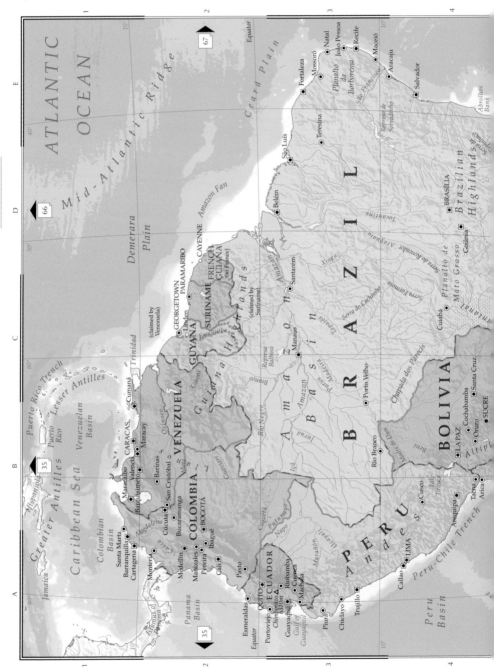

Population   • National capital

o below 50,000   o 50,000 to 100,000   ◉ 100,000 to 500,000   ▪ above 500,000

0 km   500

0 miles   500

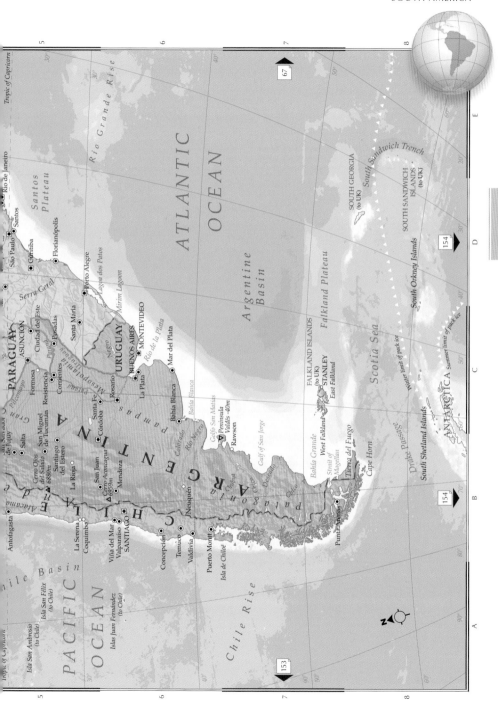

Northern South America

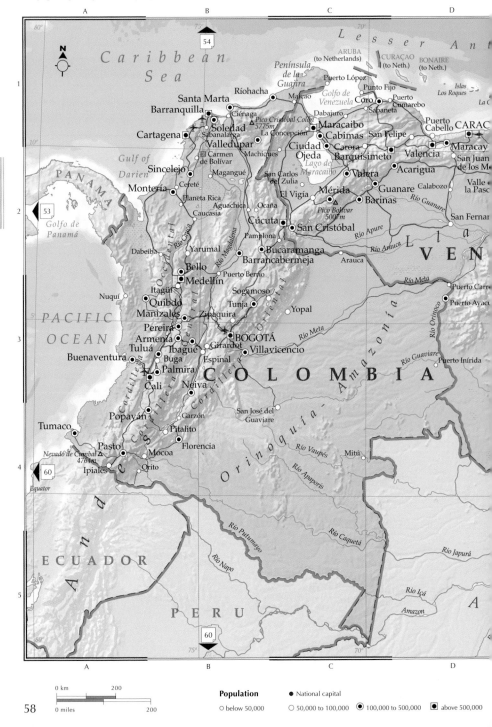

Population   ● National capital

0 km   200
0 miles   200

○ below 50,000   ○ 50,000 to 100,000   ◉ 100,000 to 500,000   ◼ above 500,000

SAINT VINCENT &
THE GRENADINES

BARBADOS

GRENADA

Isla Blanquilla

Isla de
Margarita

La Asunción

Islas Los Testigos

Tobago

Carúpano

TRINIDAD &
TOBAGO

Güiria

Puerto La Cruz

Cariaco

Gulf of
Paria

Trinidad

Barcelona

San Mateo

Maturín

Serpent's Mouth

Anaco

Cantaura

El Tigre

Tucupita

ATLANTIC

OCEAN

67

UELA

Ciudad Guayana

Río Orinoco

Upata

Ciudad
Bolívar

Embalse de Guri

Matthews
Ridge

Charity

El Callao

Spring Garden

GEORGETOWN

El Dorado

Peters Mine

Parika

Aurora

New
Amsterdam

Salto
Ángel

Kamarang

Rockstone

Bartica

Linden

PARAMARIBO

Nieuw Amsterdam

Mount Roraima
2810m

Caroni River

GUYANA

Orealla

Nieuw
Nickerie

Totness

Apoera

Kaaimanston

St-Laurent-du-Maroni

Sinnamary

Kourou

Río Paragua

Río Caura

Río Caroní

Pakaraima Mountains

Kurupukari

Essequibo River

SURINAME

W. J. van
Blommesteinmeer

Maroni River

Montagnes
de la Trinité

CAYENNE

Rio Caura

Rio Caroní

Kamarang

Mount Roraima

Juliana Top
1230m

Grand-
Santi

Montagne
Tortue

Ouanary

St-Georges

uiana

Highlands

(Venezuela claims all
of Guyana west of
Essequibo River)

Lethem

Courantyne River

FRENCH
GUIANA
(to France)

Camopi

Orinoco

Acarai Mountains

Tumuc-Humac Mountains

(claimed by
Suriname)

Rio Negro

(claimed by
Suriname)

62

Equator

B R A Z I L

Amazon

zon

Basin

Amazon

Amazon

Rio Purús

Rio Tapajós

62

Elevation

-6000m -4000m -2000m -1000m -500m -250m   Below sea level 0   250m 500m 1000m 2000m 3000m 6000m

-19,658ft -13,124ft -6562ft -3281ft -1640ft -820ft -328ft/-100m 0   820ft 1640ft 3281ft 6562ft 9843ft 13,124ft 19,685ft

Western South America

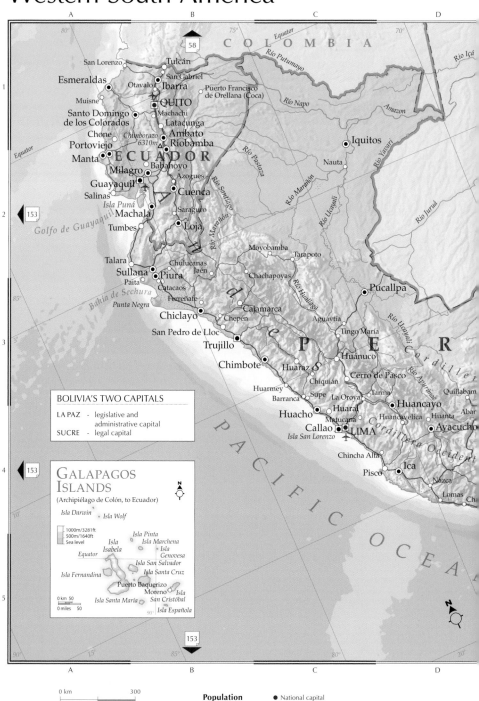

A · B · C · D

58

C O L O M B I A

Equator

Río Putumayo   Río Icá

80°   75°   70°

San Lorenzo   Tulcán
Esmeraldas   San Gabriel
Otavalo   Ibarra   Puerto Francisco
de Orellana (Coca)
Muisne   QUITO
Machachi   Río Napo   Amazon
Santo Domingo   Latacunga
de los Colorados
Chone   Chimborazo   Ambato
6310m   Riobamba   Iquitos
Portoviejo
Manta   E C U A D O R   Nauta
Milagro   Babahoyo   Río Pastaza
Azogues   Río Santiago
Guayaquil   Cuenca   Río Marañón
Salinas
Isla Puná   Saraguro   Río Ucayali   Río Juruá
Machala
Tumbes   Loja   Río Marañón
Golfo de Guayaquil

85°   Moyobamba   Tarapoto

Talara   Chulucanas   Jaén   Chachapoyas   Río Huallaga
Sullana   Piura   Pucallpa
Paita   Catacaos
Punta Negra   Ferreñafe   Cajamarca   Aguaytía   Río Ucayali
Bahía de Sechura
Chiclayo   Chepén   Tingo María   Quillabam
San Pedro de Lloc   P   E   R
Trujillo   Huánuco   Cordille
Chimbote   Huaraz   Cerro de Pasco   Río Apurímac
Chiquián   Abar
Huarmey   La Oroya   Tarma   Huancayo
Barranca   Supe   Quillabam
Huaral   Huancavelica   Huanta
Huacho   Matucana   Ayacucho
Callao   LIMA   Huancayo
Isla San Lorenzo   Cordillera Occidental
Chincha Alta

BOLIVIA'S TWO CAPITALS

LA PAZ - legislative and
            administrative capital
SUCRE - legal capital

Pisco   Ica
Nazca
Lomas
Cha

GALAPAGOS ISLANDS

(Archipiélago de Colón, to Ecuador)

Isla Darwin   Isla Wolf

1000m/3281ft
500m/1640ft
Sea level

Isla Pinta
Isla   Isla Marchena
Isabela   Isla
Equator   Genovesa
Isla San Salvador
Isla Fernandina   Isla Santa Cruz
Puerto Baquerizo
Moreno   Isla
0 km 50   Isla Santa María   San Cristóbal
0 miles 50   Isla Española

P A C I F I C   O C E A N

153

153

153

A · B · C · D

0 km   300

60

0 miles   300

Population ● National capital

○ below 50,000   ○ 50,000 to 100,000   ◉ 100,000 to 500,000   ◼ above 500,000

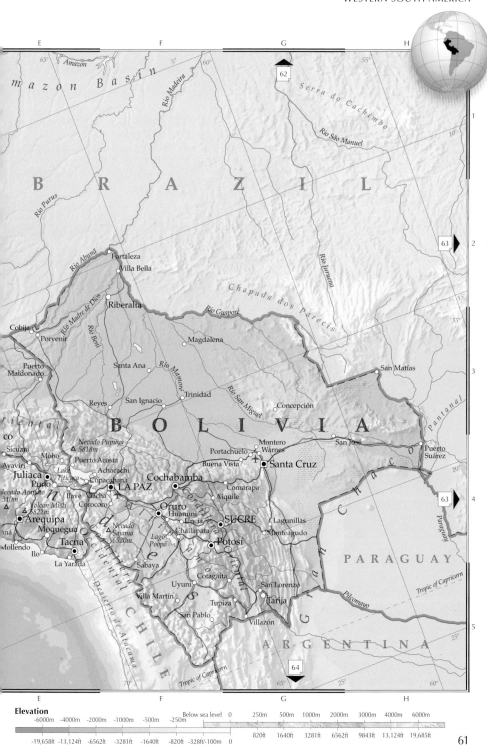

E   F   G   H

65°   Amazon   5°   60°   55°

m a z o n   *B a s i n*

Rio Madeira

Serra do Cachimbo

Rio São Manuel

10°

B R A Z I L

Rio Purus

Rio Abunã   Fortaleza
   Villa Bella

Chapada dos Parecis

Rio Guaporé

Riberalta

Rio Madre de Dios

Rio Juruena

15°

55°

Cobija
Porvenir   Rio Beni

Magdalena

Puerto
Maldonado

Santa Ana   Rio Mamoré

San Matías

Reyes   San Ignacio   Trinidad

Rio San Miguel

Concepción

Pantanal

co
Sicuani   Nevado Pupiya △ 5818m
Moho   Puerto Acosta

B O L I V I A

Montero
Warnes

San José

Puerto
Suárez

20°

Ayaviri
Achacachi   Portachuelo

Ayaviri   Lake   Achacachi   Buena Vista

Juliaca   Titicaca   Copacabana   Cochabamba   ●Santa Cruz

Puno   Ilave   Viacha
evado Ampato   Corocoro   ●LA PAZ

Comarapa
Aiquile

Volcán Misti
5822m

●Arequipa

Oruro
Huanuni   Uncía

SUCRE   Lagunillas

Moquegua   Nevado
Sajama
6520m   Lago
Poopó   Challapata   Monteagudo

Tacna   Potosí

C h a c o

Paraguay

63

P A R A G U A Y

Mollendo   Ilo
La Yarada   Sabaya

Uyuni   Cotagaita

San Lorenzo

Villa Martín

Tupiza   Tarija

San Pablo   Villazón

Pilcomayo   Tropic of Capricorn

25°

A R G E N T I N A

64

Tropic of Capricorn   70°   65°   25°   60°

E   F   G   H

Elevation

| | | | | | Below sea level | 0 | 250m | 500m | 1000m | 2000m | 3000m | 4000m | 6000m |
| -6000m | -4000m | -2000m | -1000m | -500m | -250m | | | | | | | | |

| | | | | | | | 820ft | 1640ft | 3281ft | 6562ft | 9843ft | 13,124ft | 19,685ft |
| -19,658ft | -13,124ft | -6562ft | -3281ft | -1640ft | -820ft | -328ft/-100m | 0 | | | | | | |

Brazil

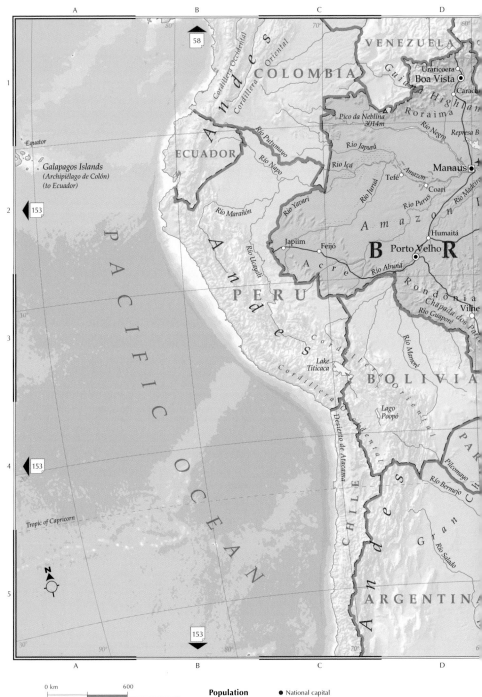

Population ● National capital

○ below 50,000   ○ 50,000 to 100,000   ◉ 100,000 to 500,000   ◼ above 500,000

ATLANTIC OCEAN

66

FRENCH GUIANA
(to France)

Tumuc-Humac Mountains

Amapá

Ilha Caviana de Fora

Macapá

Ilha de Marajó

Baía de Marajó

Belém

Amazon

Santarém

Altamira

Itaituba

São Luís

Parnaíba

Camocim

Baía de São Marcos

Represa de Tucuruí

Bacabal

Piripiri

Fortaleza

Atol das Rocas

San Fernando de Noronha
(to Brazil)

67

Imperatriz

Marabá

Teresina

Mossoró

Cabo de São Roque

Rio Xingu

Maranhão

Ceará

Açu

Natal

Rio Grande do Norte

Marajó

P a r á

Carolina

Floriano

Juazeiro do Norte

João Pessoa

Balsas

Picos

Campina Grande

Serra dos Gradaús

Rio Tocantins

Piauí

Paraíba

Recife

Z I L

Represa de Sobradinho

Juazeiro

Pernambuco

Alagoas

Maceió

Serra Formosa

Palmas do Tocantins

Rio São Francisco

Chapada Diamantina

Aracaju

Estância

Rio Araguaia

Tocantins

Taguatinga

Feira de Santana

Salvador

G r o s s o

Goiás

Bahia

Planalto

Baía de Todos os Santos

Cuiabá

Anápolis

BRASÍLIA

Janaúba

Itabuna

Central

Vitória da Conquista

donópolis

Goiânia

Jataí

Montes Claros

Canavieiras

Mato Grosso do Sul

Araguari

Araçuaí

Minas Gerais

Campo Grande

Uberlândia

Uberaba

Governador Valadares

Espírito Santo

idauana

Ribeirão Preto

Divinópolis

Belo Horizonte

Vitória

dente Prudente

Marília

Juiz de Fora

Campos

São Paulo

Campinas

Londrina

Nova Iguaçu

Rio de Janeiro

Maringá

São Paulo

Santos

Paraná

Represa de Itaipu

Ponta Grossa

Saltos do Rio Iguaçu

Curitiba

Santa Catarina

Joinville

Blumenau

Florianópolis

Passo Fundo

Rio Grande

a Maria

Canoas

Porto Alegre

Lagoa dos Patos

Bagé

Negro

Rio Grande

Mirim Lagoon

UGUAY

ATLANTIC OCEAN

Equator

Tropic of Capricorn

67

67

ATLANTIC OCEAN

Elevation

| -6000m | -4000m | -2000m | -1000m | -500m | -250m | Below sea level | 0 | 250m | 500m | 1000m | 2000m | 3000m | 4000m | 6000m |

| -19,658ft | -13,124ft | -6562ft | -3281ft | -1640ft | -820ft | -328ft/-100m | 0 | 820ft | 1640ft | 3281ft | 6562ft | 9843ft | 13,124ft | 19,685ft |

63

Southern South America

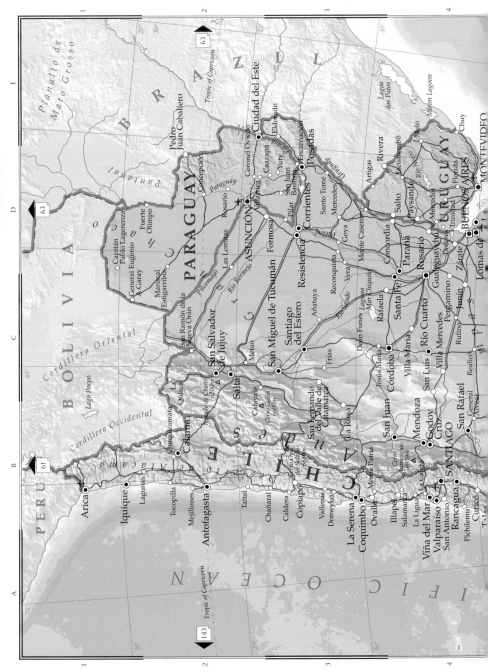

0 km · 200
0 miles · 200

Population   ● National capital

○ below 50,000   ○ 50,000 to 100,000   ◉ 100,000 to 500,000   ◼ above 500,000

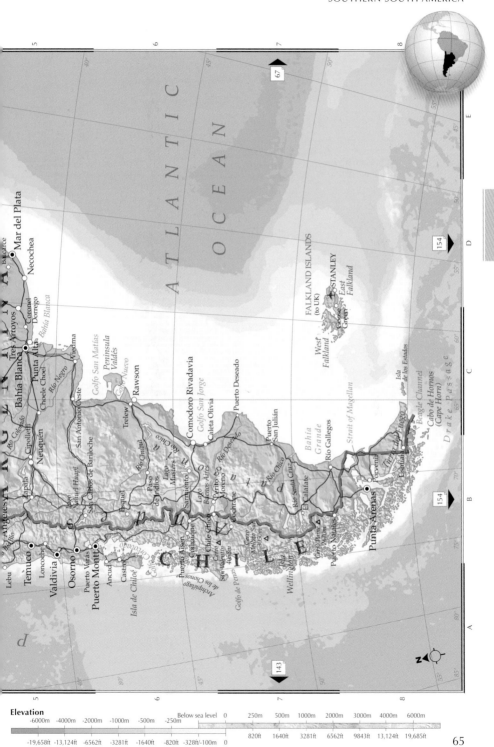

ATLANTIC

OCEAN

Mar del Plata

Necochea

Balcarce

Tres Arroyos
Coronel
Dorrego
Bahía Blanca
Punta Alta
Bahía Blanca
Choele Choel

A R G E N T I N A

Cipolletti
Neuquén

Río Colorado

Río Negro

Viedma

Golfo San Matías

Península
Valdés

Golfo Nuevo

Rawson

San Antonio Oeste

Trelew

Río Chubut

Comodoro Rivadavia
Golfo San Jorge
Caleta Olivia

Puerto Deseado

Puerto
San Julián

Río Deseado

Río Chico

Bahía
Grande

Río Gallegos

Strait of Magellan

FALKLAND ISLANDS
(to UK)

West
Falkland

East
Falkland

STANLEY

Goose
Green

Isla
de los Estados

Cabo de Hornos
(Cape Horn)

Bagle Channel

Drake Passage

Tierra del Fuego

Porvenir

Ushuaia

Puerto Natales

Punta Arenas

El Calafate

Río Santa Cruz

Lago
Buenos Aires

Lago
Musters

Sarmiento

Paso
de Indios

Río Chubut

Río Chico

Cerro
Moreno

Perito
Moreno

Cochrane

Chile Chico

Coihaique

Puerto Aisén

Cerro
San Valentín
4058m

Cerro
Mellizo Sur
3310m

Cerro Fitzroy
3375m

Golfo de Penas

Archipiélago
de los Chonos

Isla de Chiloé

Castro

Ancud

Puerto Varas

Puerto Montt

Osorno

Valdivia

Temuco

Loncoche

Lebu

Río Bío Bío

Los Angeles

Zapala

Sn Carlos de Bariloche

Nahuel Huapi

Esquel

C H I L E

d

Elevation

-6000m	-4000m	-2000m	-1000m	-500m	-250m	Below sea level 0	250m	500m	1000m	2000m	3000m	4000m	6000m
-19,658ft	-13,124ft	-6562ft	-3281ft	-1640ft	-820ft	-328ft/-100m 0	820ft	1640ft	3281ft	6562ft	9843ft	13,124ft	19,685ft

The Atlantic Ocean

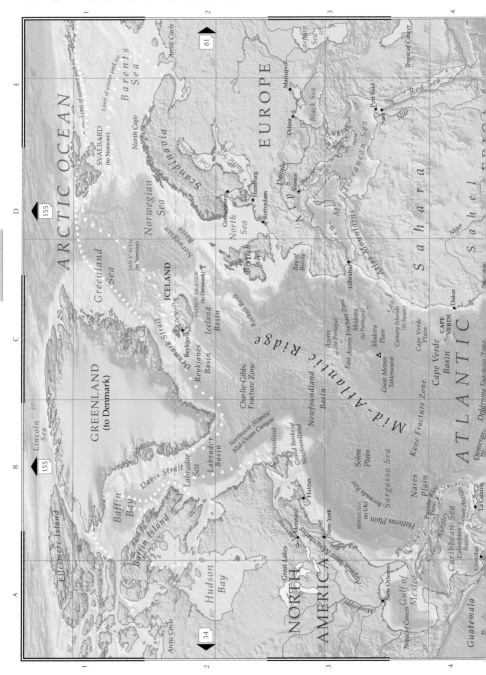

0 km   1000

0 miles   1000

• Major port

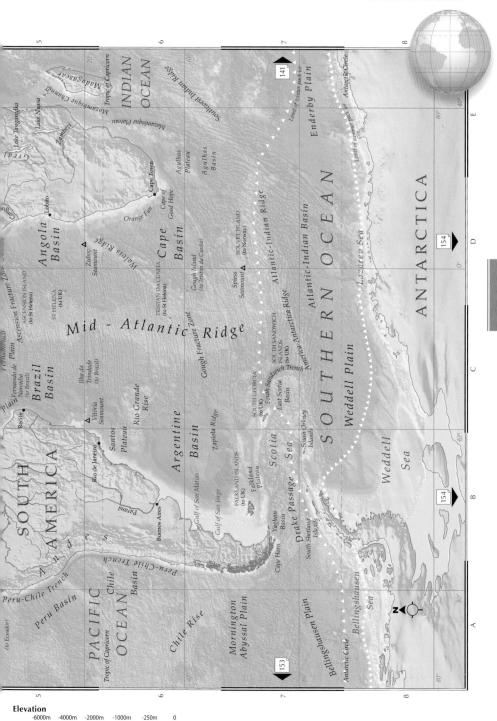

INDIAN OCEAN

Tropic of Capricorn

Madagascar

Mozambique Channel

Lake Nyasa

Lake Tanganyika

Great

Zambezi

Mozambique Plateau

Southwest Indian Ridge

Limit of winter pack ice

141

Enderby Plain

Limit of summer pack ice

Antarctic Circle

Agulhas Plateau

Agulhas Basin

Congo

Luanda

Cape Town

Cape of Good Hope

Angola Basin

Zaire

Orange Fan

Walvis Ridge

Cape Basin

BOUVET ISLAND (to Norway)

Atlantic-Indian Ridge

Atlantic-Indian Basin

ANTARCTICA

154

Ascension Fracture Zone

ASCENSION ISLAND (to St Helena)

ST HELENA (to UK)

Zaboc Seamount

TRISTAN DA CUNHA (to St Helena)

Gough Island (to Tristan da Cunha)

Spiess Seamount

SOUTHERN OCEAN

0°

Lazarev Sea

Pernambuco

Mid - Atlantic Ridge

Ilha da Trindade (to Brazil)

Gough Fracture Zone

SOUTH SANDWICH ISLANDS

America-Antarctica Ridge

Weddell Plain

Plain

Fernando de Noronha (to Brazil)

Brazil Basin

Vitória Seamount

Rio Grande Rise

South Sandwich Trench

SOUTH GEORGIA (to UK)

East Scotia Basin

Recife

Rio de Janeiro

Santos Plateau

Argentine Basin

Zapiola Ridge

Scotia Sea

South Orkney Islands

Weddell Sea

SOUTH AMERICA

Paraná

Buenos Aires

Gulf of San Matías

Gulf of San Jorge

FALKLAND ISLANDS (to UK)

Falkland Plateau

Yaghan Basin

Drake Passage

154

Andes

Cape Horn

South Shetland Islands

Bellingshausen Plain

Peru-Chile Trench

Chile Basin

Mornington Abyssal Plain

Bellingshausen Sea

Antarctic Circle

Peru-Chile Trench

Chile Rise

153

N

PACIFIC OCEAN

Peru Basin

(to Ecuador)

Tropic of Capricorn

Africa

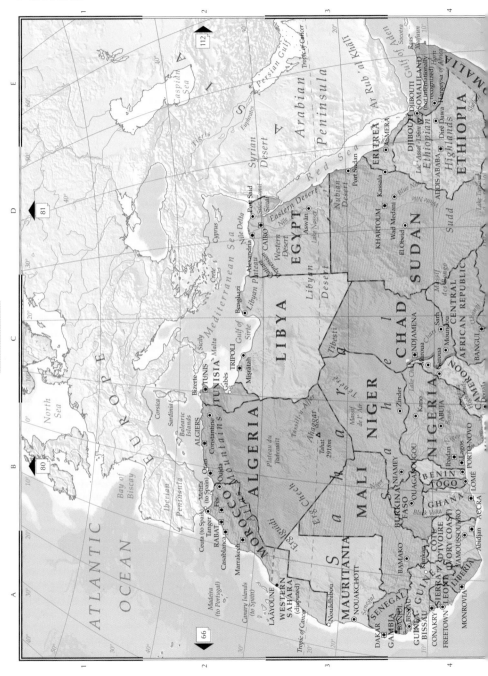

Population • National capital

o below 50,000   o 50,000 to 100,000   ⊙ 100,000 to 500,000   ■ above 500,000

0 km   1000

0 miles   1000

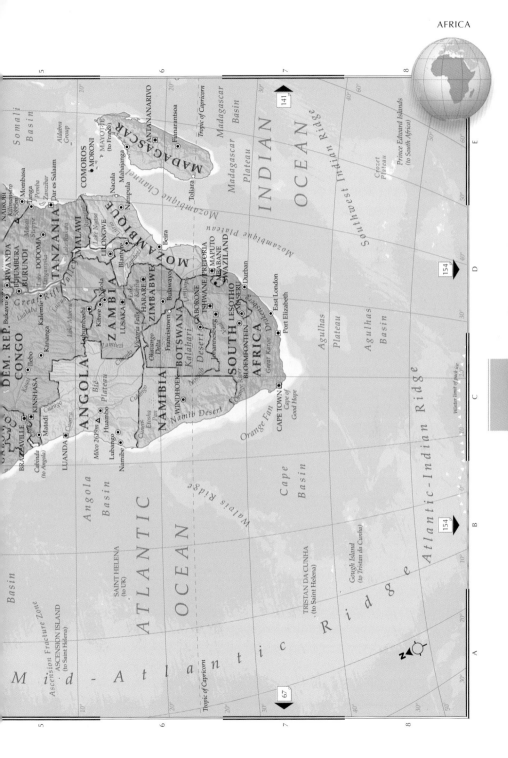

Northwest Africa

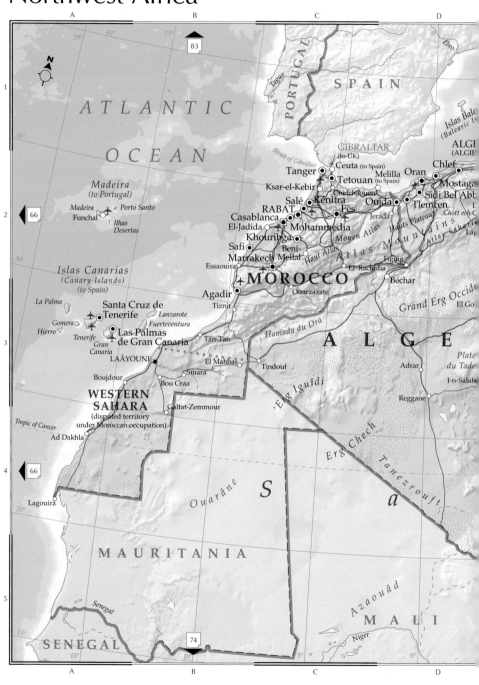

A   B   C   D

83

N

ATLANTIC

OCEAN

PORTUGAL

SPAIN

Tagus

Ebro

Islas Bale
(Balearic Is

GIBRALTAR
(to UK)

Strait of Gibraltar

Ceuta (to Spain)

ALGIE
(ALGE

Tanger

Melilla
(to Spain)

Oran

Chlef

Ksar-el-Kebir

Tetouan

Mostaga

Chefchaouen

Sidi Bel Abl

Salé

Kenitra

Fès

Oujda

Tlemcen

Madeira
(to Portugal)

66

Madeira

Porto Santo

RABAT

Jerada

Chott ech C

Funchal

Ilhas
Desertas

Casablanca

Mohammedia

Moyen Atlas

Hauts Plateaux

Atlas Sahari

El-Jadida

Lag

Khouribga

Safi

Beni-
Mellal

Haut Atlas

Atlas

Mountains

Islas Canarias
(Canary Islands)
(to Spain)

Essaouira

MOROCCO

Figuig

Er-Rachidia

Béchar

La Palma

Agadir

Ouarzazate

Grand Erg Occide

El Go

Gomera

Santa Cruz de
Tenerife

Tiznit

Lanzarote

Fuerteventura

Hamada du Dra

A L G É E

Hierro

Tenerife

Gran
Canaria

Las Palmas
de Gran Canaria

Tan-Tan

Plate
du Tade

LAÂYOUNE

El Mahbas

Tindouf

Adrar

I-n-Salah

Boujdour

Smara

Bou Craa

WESTERN
SAHARA

(disputed territory
under Moroccan occupation)

Galtat-Zemmour

Erg Iguîdi

Reggane

Erg Chech

Tropic of Cancer

Ad Dakhla

Tanezrouft

66

Lagouira

Ouarâne

S

a

MAURITANIA

Azaouâd

M A L I

Senegal

74

Niger

SENEGAL

A   B   C   D

0 km   400

0 miles   400

Population

● National capital

○ below 50,000   ◎ 50,000 to 100,000   ◉ 100,000 to 500,000   ▣ above 500,000

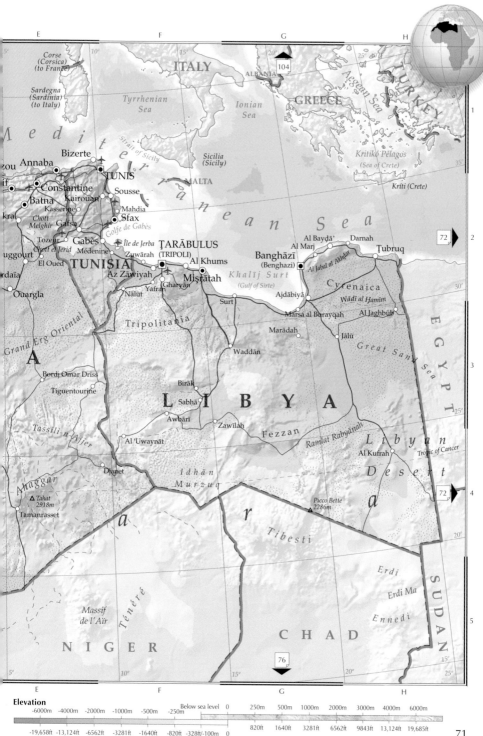

E   10°   F   15°   G   20°   H   25°

ITALY

104

ALBANIA

GREECE

Tyrrhenian Sea

Ionian Sea

Aegean Sea

TURKEY

Corse (Corsica) (to France)

Sardegna (Sardinia) (to Italy)

M e d i t e r

Annaba
Bizerte

zou

if

Constantine

TUNIS

Sousse

Batna
Kairouan

Kasserine

Mahdia

kra

Chott Melghir
Gafsa

Sfax

Strait of Sicily

MALTA

Sicilia (Sicily)

Kritikó Pélagos (Sea of Crete)

35°

Kríti (Crete)

r a

n e a n

S e a

Tozeur
Gabès

Îe de Jerba

ṬARĀBULUS

Al Bayḍā'
Al Marj
Darnah

72

2

uggourt

Chott el Jerid
Médenine

Zuwārah

(TRIPOLI)

Al Khums

Banghāzī
(Benghazi)

Ṭubruq

rdaïa

El Oued

TUNISIA

Az Zāwiyah

Mişrātah

Khalīj Surt (Gulf of Sirte)

Al Jabal al Akhḍar

C y r e n a i c a

30°

Ouargla

Nālūt

Yafran
Gharyān

Surt

Ajdābiyā

Wādī al Ḥamīm

Al Jaghbūb

Marsá al Burayqah

A

T r i p o l i t a n i a

Marādah

Jālū

G r e a t *S a n d* *S e a*

E
G
Y
P
T

3

Bordj Omar Driss

Waddān

Tiguentourine

Birāk

L

I

B

Y

A

25°

Sabhā

Grand Erg Oriental

Awbārī

Zawīlah

F e z z a n

Ramlat Rabyānah

L i b y a n

Al 'Uwaynāt

Tassili n'Ajjer

Al Kufrah

Tropic of Cancer

72

4

Djanet

I d h ā n

M u r z u q

D e s e r t

20°

Ahaggar

△ Tahat
2918m

Tamanrasset

a

r

Picco Bette
△ 2286m

T i b e s t i

Erdi

Erdi Ma

S
U
D
A
N

5

Massif de l'Aïr

Ténéré

Ennedi

N **I** **G** **E** **R**

C **H** **A** **D**

15°

76

5°   E   10°   F   15°   G   20°   H   25°

Elevation

-6000m	-4000m	-2000m	-1000m	-500m	-250m	Below sea level	0	250m	500m	1000m	2000m	3000m	4000m	6000m
-19,658ft	-13,124ft	-6562ft	-3281ft	-1640ft	-820ft	-328ft/-100m	0	820ft	1640ft	3281ft	6562ft	9843ft	13,124ft	19,685ft

71

Northeast Africa

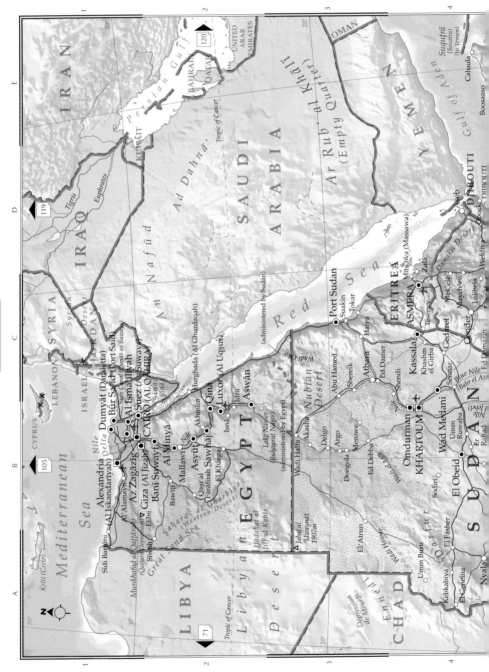

IRAN

UNITED
ARAB
EMIRATES

OMAN

Persian Gulf

120

BAHRAIN
QATAR

KUWAIT

Suqutrā
(Socotra)
(to Yemen)

Caluula

119

Tigris

Euphrates

Tropic of Cancer

Ad Dahnā

A
m

N
a
f
ū
d

SAUDI

ARABIA

Ar Rub' al Khālī
(Empty Quarter)

Y
E
M
E
N

Boosaaso

Gulf of Aden

SYRIA

Syrian   Desert

JORDAN

IRAQ

Aden

DJIBOUTI

DJIBOUTI

Zeila

LEBANON

ISRAEL

CYPRUS

Mediterranean

Sea

Krití (Crete)

Sidi Barrani

Alexandria
(Al Iskandariyah)

Nile   Delta

Dumyāt (Damietta)

Būr Saʿīd (Port Said)

Suez Canal (Qanāt as Suways)

Al Ismāʿīlīyah

Suez (As Suways)

Al Qāhirah)

CAIRO (AL QĀHIRAH)

Sinai
(Sīnā)

Khalīg Suways

Hurghada (Al Ghurdaqah)

Port Sudan

Red   Sea

Suakin

Tokar

Mitsiwa (Massawa)

Zula

Danakil Desert

ERITREA

ASMERA

Weldiya

Adīgrat

Mek'ele

Aksum

Maych'ew

Lālībela

Gonder

Tesseney

Gedaref

El Matamma

(administered by Sudan)

Wadi Oko

Abu Hamed

Nubian

Desert

Haiya

Atbara

Ed Damer

Shendi

Khashm
el Girba

Sennar

Blue Nile

(Bahr al
Azraq)

Kassala

Ed Debba

Wadi Halfa

Akasha

Delgo

Argo

Dongola

Merowe

Omdurman

KHARTOUM

Wad Medani

Umm
Ruwaba

Er Rahad

El Obeid

Sodiri

Blue Nile

Lake Nasser
(Buḩayrat Nāṣir)
(administered by Egypt)

At Alamayn

Az Zagāzig

Giza (Al Jizah)

Bani Suwayf

Al Minyā

Mallawi

Asyūṭ

Sawhāj

Akhmīm

Qinā

Luxor (Al Uqṣur)

Idfū

Isnā

Aswān

Qaṣr al
Farāfirah

Bawiti

El Khārga

Sīwah

Munkhafaḍ al Qaṭṭārah
(Qattara Depression)
-133m

Sahara el Gharbiya
(Western Desert)

Great Sand Sea

Hadabat at
Jilf al Kabīr

Jabal al
Uʿuwaynāt
1907m

L
i
b
y
a
n

D
e
s
e
r
t

El'Atrun

E
G
Y
P
T

S
U
D
A
N

D
a
r
f
u
r

Umm Badr

El Fasher

Kebkabiya

Ed Geneina

Nyala

CHAD

LIBYA

Tropic of Cancer

Depression
de Mourdi

E
n
n
e
d
i

Wadi Howar

N 105

71

N

| 0 km | | 400 |
| 0 miles | | 400 |

Population   ● National capital

○ below 50,000   ◯ 50,000 to 100,000   ◉ 100,000 to 500,000   ■ above 500,000

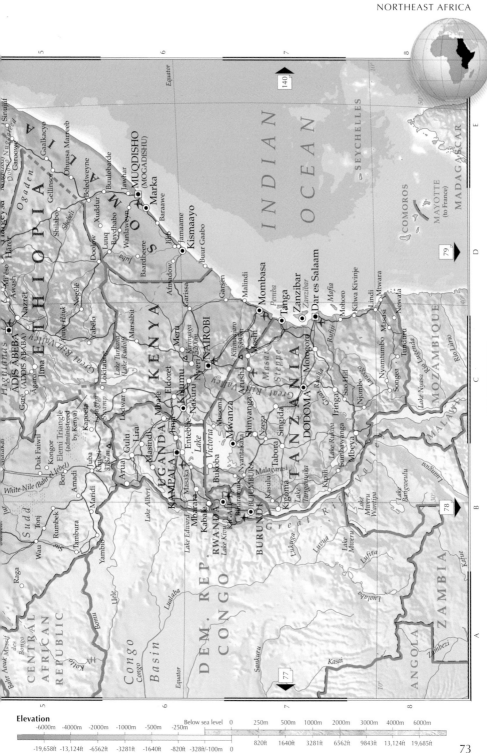

Elevation

-6000m	-4000m	-2000m	-1000m	-500m	-250m	Below sea level	0	250m	500m	1000m	2000m	3000m	4000m	6000m
-19,658ft	-13,124ft	-6562ft	-3281ft	-1640ft	-820ft	-328ft/-100m	0	820ft	1640ft	3281ft	6562ft	9843ft	13,124ft	19,685ft

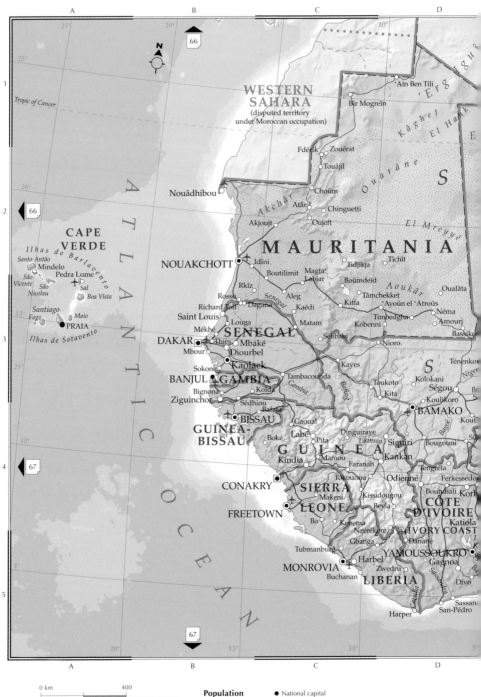

0 km   400

0 miles   400

Population   ● National capital

○ below 50,000   ◯ 50,000 to 100,000   ◉ 100,000 to 500,000   ▣ above 500,000

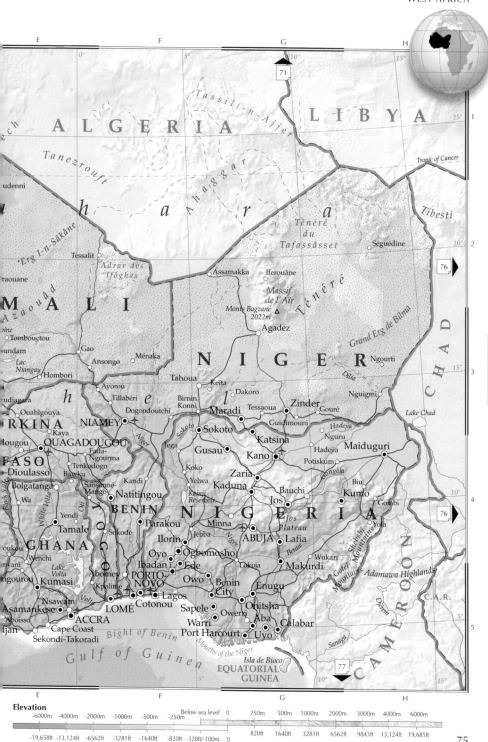

E 0° F 5° G 10° H 15°

71

ALGERIA **LIBYA**
1 25°

Tassili-n-Ajjer

Tanezrouft Tropic of Cancer

Tibesti

'Erg In-Sâkâne Tessalit *Ténéré du Tafassâsset* Séguédine
2 20° 76

Adrar des Ifôghas Assamakka Iferouâne

raouane *Massif de l'Aïr*

Azaouâd Monts Bagzane 2022m △ *Ténéré*

vine Agadez *Grand Erg de Bilma*

Tombouctou Gao **N I G E R** Ngourti

undam Ansongo Ménaka *Dilia*

Lac Niangay Hombori Tahoua Keita Dakoro Nguigmi
3 15°

i Ayorou Birnin Tessaoua Goure Lake Chad

udiagara Tillabéri Konni Zinder

Ouahigouya Dogondoutchi **Maradi** Guidimouni Hadejia

RKINA **NIAMEY** Jega *Sokoto* **Sokoto** Nguru

lougou Kaya Koko **Gusau** **Katsina** **Maiduguri**

QUAGADOUGOU Fada- **Kano** Hadejia

FASO Ngourma Tenkodogo Yelwa *Gongola* Potiskum Biu

-Dioulasso Bawku Sansanné- **Zaria** **Kumo**
4 10° 76

Bolgatanga Mango Kandi **Kaduna** **Bauchi** Gombi

Wa Yendi *Kainji* **Jos**

BENIN **N I G E R I A** *Jos*

Tamale Sokodé Parakou Minna *Plateau* Yola

oukou **Natitingou** Ilorin Jebba **ABUJA** Lafia *Shebshi*

GHANA **Oyo** **Ogbomosho** Lokoja **Makurdi** Wukari *Gotel* *Adamawa Highlands*

Wenchi Lake *Ede* Owo **Enugu** *Mountains*

ngourou Volta **Ibadan** **Benin** C.A.R.

Kumasi Abomey **PORTO-** **City** *Djerem*
5 5°

Nsawam Kpalimé **NOVO** **Owerri** *Dirou*

Asamankese **Lagos** Sapele **Onitsha**

Aboisso **ACCRA** **LOMÉ** Cotonou Warri **Aba** **Calabar**

Ijan Cape Coast *Bight of Benin* **Port Harcourt** **Uyo** *Sanaga*

Sekondi-Takoradi *Mouths of the Niger*

Gulf of Guinea Isla de Bioco 77

EQUATORIAL GUINEA **CAMEROON**

E 0° F 5° G 10° H 15°

Elevation
-6000m -4000m -2000m -1000m -500m -250m Below sea level 0 250m 500m 1000m 2000m 3000m 4000m 6000m

-19,658ft -13,124ft -6562ft -3281ft -1640ft -820ft -328ft/-100m 0 820ft 1640ft 3281ft 6562ft 9843ft 13,124ft 19,685ft

Central Africa

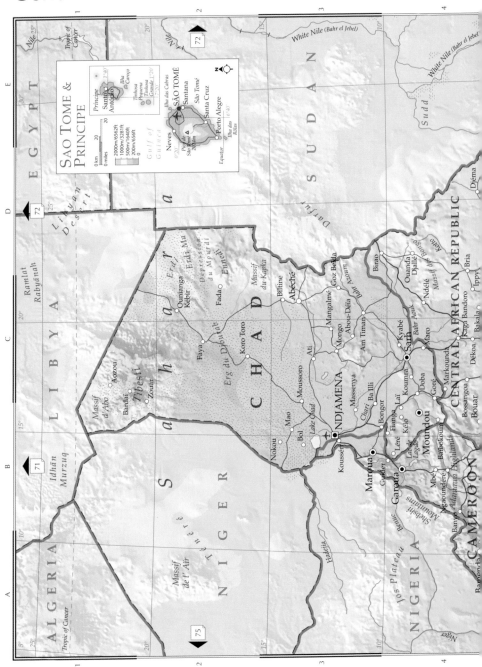

Population   ● National capital

○ below 50,000   ○ 50,000 to 100,000   ◉ 100,000 to 500,000   ■ above 500,000

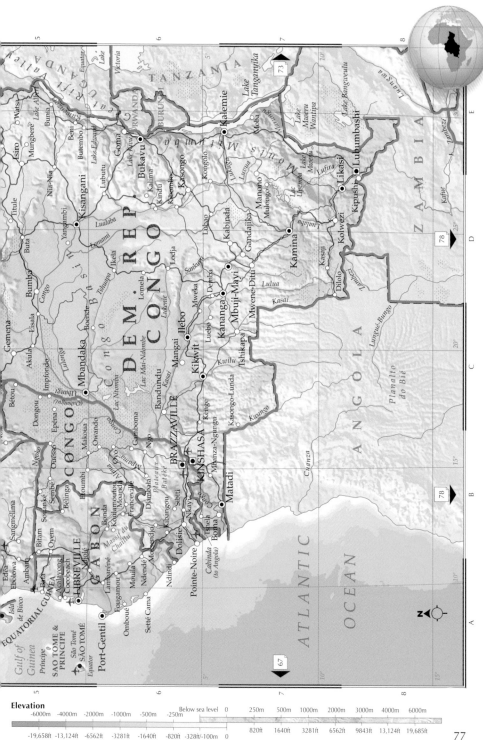

Elevation

-6000m	-4000m	-2000m	-1000m	-500m	-250m	Below sea level	0	250m	500m	1000m	2000m	3000m	4000m	6000m
-19,658ft	-13,124ft	-6562ft	-3281ft	-1640ft	-820ft	-328ft/-100m	0	820ft	1640ft	3281ft	6562ft	9843ft	13,124ft	19,685ft

Southern Africa

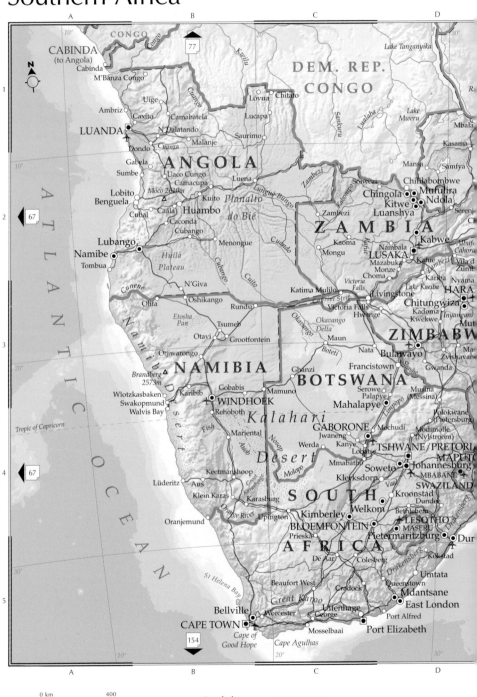

CABINDA
(to Angola)
Cabinda
M'Banza Congo

CONGO

DEM. REP.
CONGO

Lake Tanganyika

Uíge
Lóvua
Chitato
Ambriz
Caxito
Camabatela
Lucapa
N'Dalatando
Saurimo
LUANDA
Malanje
Dondo
Cuanza
Gabela
ANGOLA
Sumbe
Uaco Cungo
Luena
Camacupa
Lobito
Moço 2610m
Kuito
Benguela
Planalto
Cubal
Caála
Huambo
do Bié
Caconda
Cubango
Lubango
Menongue
Namibe
Huíla
Tombua
Plateau
N'Giva
Olifa
Oshikango
Rundu
Etosha
Tsumeb
Pan
Otavi
Grootfontein
Otjiwarongo
NAMIBIA
Brandberg
2573m
Ghanzi
Wlotzkasbaken
Karibib
Gobabis
Mamuno
Swakopmund
WINDHOEK
Walvis Bay
Rehoboth
Kalahari
Fish
Mariental
Lüderitz
Aus
Keetmanshoop
Klein Karas
Karasburg
Oranjemund
Upington
Kimberley
BLOEMFONTEIN
Prieska
De Aar
Colesberg
AFRICA
Beaufort West
Cradock
Great Karoo
Bellville
Worcester
CAPE TOWN
Cape of
Good Hope
Mosselbaai
Cape Agulhas

Mbala
Kasama
Mansa
Samfya
Solwezi
Chililabombwe
Chingola
Mufulira
Kitwe
Ndola
Zambezi
Luanshya
ZAMBIA
Kaoma
Kabwe
Mongu
Nambala
LUSAKA
Mazabuka
Kafue
Monze
Choma
Kariba
Victoria
Livingstone
Falls
Victoria Falls
Hwange
Maun
Nata
Bulawayo
ZIMBABWE
Francistown
Gwanda
BOTSWANA
Serowe
Musina
Palapye
(Messina)
Mahalapye
Polokwane
(Pietersburg)
GABORONE
Mochudi
Modimolle
Jwaneng
(Nylstroom)
Werda
Kanye
TSHWANE / PRETORIA
Lobatse
MAPUTO
Mmabatho
Soweto
MBABANE
Johannesburg
Klerksdorp
SWAZILAND
SOUTH
Vaal
Kroonstad
Dundee
Welkom
Bethlehem
LESOTHO
MASERU
Pietermaritzburg
Durban
Kokstad
Umtata
Queenstown
Mdantsane
East London
Uitenhage
George
Port Alfred
Port Elizabeth

ATLANTIC OCEAN

Tropic of Capricorn

0 km   400
0 miles   400

Population

● National capital

○ below 50,000   ◉ 50,000 to 100,000   ⦿ 100,000 to 500,000   ▣ above 500,000

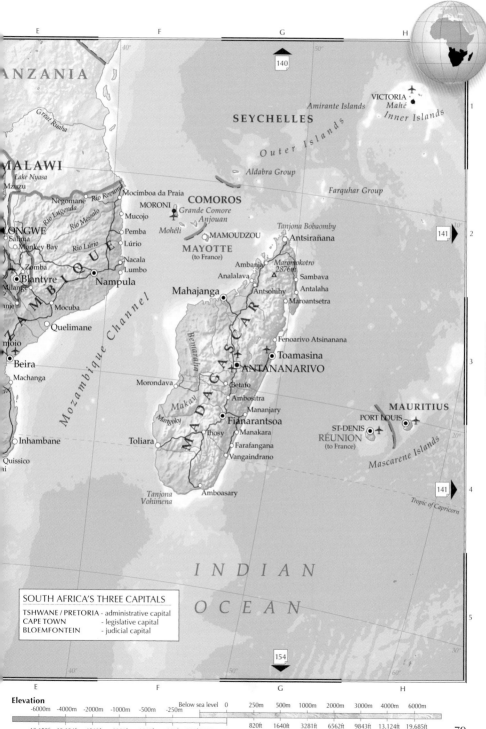

140

ZANZANIA

Great Ruaha

MALAWI
Lake Nyasa
Mzuzu

Negomane Rio Rovuma Mocímboa da Praia
Rio Lugenda
Rio Messalo Mucojo
LONGWE Pemba
Salima Lúrio
Monkey Bay Rio Lúrio Nacala
Zomba Lumbo
Blantyre Nampula
Milange
nje Mocuba
Quelimane

Beira
Machanga

Inhambane
Quissico
ai

VICTORIA
Mahé
SEYCHELLES
Amirante Islands
Inner Islands
Outer Islands

Aldabra Group
Farquhar Group

COMOROS
MORONI Grande Comore
Anjouan
Mohéli
MAMOUDZOU
MAYOTTE
(to France)

Tanjona Bobaomby
Antsirañana

Ambanja Maromokotro
2876m
Analalava Sambava
Antsohihy Antalaha
Mahajanga Maroantsetra

Fenoarivo Atsinanana
Toamasina
ANTANANARIVO

Morondava Betafo
Ambositra
Mananjary MAURITIUS
Fianarantsoa PORT LOUIS
Mangoky Ihosy Manakara ST-DENIS
Toliara Farafangana RÉUNION
Vangaindrano (to France)
Mascarene Islands

Tanjona Amboasary
Vohimena
Tropic of Capricorn

MADAGASCAR
Bemaraha
Makay

Mozambique Channel

INDIAN

OCEAN

SOUTH AFRICA'S THREE CAPITALS
TSHWANE / PRETORIA - administrative capital
CAPE TOWN   - legislative capital
BLOEMFONTEIN   - judicial capital

154

Elevation

-6000m	-4000m	-2000m	-1000m	-500m	-250m	Below sea level 0	250m	500m	1000m	2000m	3000m	4000m	6000m
-19,658ft	-13,124ft	-6562ft	-3281ft	-1640ft	-820ft	-328ft/-100m 0	820ft	1640ft	3281ft	6562ft	9843ft	13,124ft	19,685ft

Europe

A   B   C   D

155

30° 20° 70° 10° 0°

Limit of winter pack ice

REYKJAVÍK
ICELAND
Vatnajökull
Arctic Circle

Charlie-Gibbs Fracture Zone

Reykjanes Ridge

Norwegian Basin

Iceland Basin

Norwegian Sea

FAEROE ISLANDS
(to Denmark)

Faeroe-Iceland Ridge

Trondheim

Hatton Ridge

Faeroe-Shetland Trough

66

Mid - Atlantic Ridge

Rockall Bank

Shetland Islands

Bergen

Stavanger

OSLO

Porcupine Plain

Rockall Trough

Outer Hebrides

Orkney Islands

British Isles

Ireland

Glasgow
Edinburgh

North Sea

Gothenburg
Aalborg
Jönkö

A T L A N T I C

Belfast

IRELAND
DUBLIN

ISLE OF MAN
(to UK)

UNITED KINGDOM

Jylland

Odense

DENMARK COPENH

Liverpool
Manchester

O C E A N

Celtic Sea

Britain

Birmingham

Hamburg

Celtic Shelf

Cardiff

LONDON

NETHERLANDS

THE HAGUE
AMSTERDAM

Elbe

Azores-Biscay Rise

English Channel

BELGIUM

Rotterdam

Hannover

N

Charcot Seamounts

CHANNEL IS.
(to UK)

le Havre

BRUSSELS

BERLIN

Liège

Bonn

Biscay Plain

Rennes

LUXEMBOURG

GERMANY

Wro

Iberian Plain

PARIS

LUXEMBOURG

Frankfurt
am Main

FR

Nantes

Orléans

Strasbourg

Stuttgart

CZE
REPU

A Coruña

Bay of Biscay

FRANCE

Munich

BRA

Galicia Bank

Bordeaux

Zürich

BERN
SWITZERLAND

VIENN
Salzburg

CZECH

66

Cordillera Cantábrica

Bilbao

Lyon

Innsbruck

AUSTRI

Porto

Massif Central

Mont Blanc
4807m

Milan

LJUBLJA

SLOVEN

Horseshoe Seamounts

Toulouse

Turin

Venice

Trieste

PORTUGAL

Iberian

Duero

Zaragoza

ANDORRA

Nice

Bologna

SAN
MARINO

Tagus Plain

LISBON

Tagus

MADRID

Ebro

Marseille

MONACO

Pisa

Madeira
(to Portugal)

SPAIN

Peninsula

Barcelona

Corsica

VATICAN CITY

ROME

Valencia

Guadalquivir

Seville

Strait of Gibraltar

Palma

Sardinia

Naples

Bari

Málaga

Balearic Islands

Algerian Basin

Cagliari

Tyrrhenian Sea

GIBRALTAR
(to UK)

Ceuta
(to Spain)

M e d i t e r r a

Cosenza

Canary Islands
(to Spain)

Melilla
(to Spain)

Palermo

Mount Etna
3340m

Catani

Sicily

A t l a s M o u n t a i n s

MALTA
VALLETTA

68

A F R I C A

10° 30° 0° 10°

A   B   C   D

0 km   500

0 miles   500

Population   ● National capital

o below 50,000   o 50,000 to 100,000   ◉ 100,000 to 500,000   ◼ above 500,000

E   F   G   H

Barents Sea

North Cape

Ostrov Kolguyev

Arctic Circle

Ob'

Irtysh

20° 30° 40° 50° 70° 80° 70° 80°

80°

1

Murmansk

Kola Peninsula

White Sea

Archangel

Ural Mountains

Northern Dvina

F I N L A N D

R U S S I A N

Lake Onega

Perm'

112

2

Tampere

Lake Ladoga

F E D E R A T I O N

70°

50°

Turku HELSINKI

Saint Petersburg

Vologda

Ufa

KHOLM TALLINN

Kazan'

ESTONIA

Yaroslavl'

Caspian Plain

Nizhniy Novgorod

Ul'yanovsk

Orenburg

Syr Darya

LATVIA

MOSCOW

Samara

Ural

RIGA

Volga Uplands

Volga

Aral Sea

3

ITHUANIA Kaunas

Vitsyebsk

Central Russian Upland

KALININGRAD (to Russ Fed.)

VILNIUS

MINSK

Ural

ARSAW Brest

Babruysk

Homyel'

Voronezh

Amu Darya

BELARUS

Pripet Marshes

Dón

AND

Bug

Dnieper Lowlands

KIEV

Kharkiv

Volgograd

60°

L'viv

Dnieper

Dnipropetrovs'k

Astrakhan

Volga Delta

A

ików

UKRAINE

Donets'k

-28m

40°

KIA Chernivtsi

Dniester

Rostov-na-Donu

112

4

EST

MOLDOVA

Caspian Sea

ARY Cluj-Napoca

CHIŞINĂU

Stavropol'

ROMANIA

Odesa

Sea of Azov

Caucasus

LGRADE Braşov

Simferopol

Crimea

El'brus 5642m

S

BUCHAREST

Constanţa

Black Sea

I

IA

Danube

A

OVO BULGARIA

Varna

Balkan Mountains

KRISTINA SOFIA

Burgas

OKOPJE

TURKEY

5

ACED

A

NIA

Aegean Sea

Anatolia

A

GREECE

ATHENS

Piraeus

Zagros Mountains

30°

Irákleio

Cyprus

118

Tigris

Euphrates

50°

Crete

30°

40°

E   F   G   H

The North Atlantic

A   B   C   D

37

Arctic Circle

Gulf of Boothia

90°

Đevon
Island

Ellesmere Island

80°

Nares Strait

1

N U N A V U T

90°

Qaanaaq

Knud Rasmusse

Hudson

Bay

Innaanganeq

Southampton
Island

Savissivik

Foxe

Basin

Qimusseriarsuaq

Baffin

38

C A N A D A

Kullorsuaq

80°

Bay

Baffin Island

Upernavik

Péninsule
d'Ungava

Hudson Strait

2

QUÉBEC

Limit of summer pack ice

Uummannaq

Qeqertarsuaq

Arnaud

Cumberland Sound

Davis Strait

Qeqertarsuaq

Qeqertarsuup Tunua

Qasigianguit

70°

Ungava
Bay

Frobisher Bay

Sisimiut

Kong Frederik IX
Land

G R E E N L A N D

(to Denmark)

3

George

Maniitsoq

NUUK

Kong Christian IX Land

Gunnbjør

Mont Forel
3360m

39

Paamiut

Ammassalik

Den m

NEWFOUNDLAND & LABRADOR

Ivittuut

Labrador

Kong Frederik VI Kyst

4

Sea

Qaqortoq

Nanortalik

Limit of winter pack ice

Reykjanes Basin

Nunap Isua
(Kap Farvel)

A T L A N T I C

5

30°

O C E A N

40°

30°

66

A   B   C   D

0 km   400

0 miles   400

Population   ● National capital

○ below 50,000   ○ 50,000 to 100,000   ◉ 100,000 to 500,000   ◼ above 500,000

ARCTIC OCEAN

Lincoln Sea

Kap Morris Jesup

Wandel Sea

Independence Fjord

Nord

SVALBARD
(to Norway)

Kvitøya

Nordaustlandet

Zemlya
Frantsa-Iosifa

Novaya
Zemlya

Kong Frederik VIII Land

Kong Karls Land

Spitsbergen

LONGYEARBYEN
Barentsburg

Barentsøya

Edgeøya

Storfjorden

Barents
Sea

155

110

Greenland
Sea

Limit of winter pack ice

Kong Christian X Land

Limit of summer pack ice

Petermann Bjerg
2940m

Daneborg

Bjørnøya
(to Norway)

Nordkapp
(North Cape)

Mohns Ridge

Kong Oscar Fjord

Kangertittivaq
Kangikajik

Ittoqqortoormiit

JAN MAYEN
(to Norway)

Norwegian
Sea

Vestfjorden

FINLAND

Arctic Circle

84

Norwegian Basin

Strait

ICELAND

Ólungarvík
Siglufjördhur
Bördhur
Húsavík
Akureyri
Stykkishólmur
REYKJAVÍK
Selfoss
Vatnajökull
Þorlákshöfn
Hvannadalshnúkur
2119m
Surtsey
Vestmannaeyjar

Raufarhöfn

Seydhisfjördhur
Neskaupstadhur
Djúpivogur

SWEDEN

NORWAY

Gulf
of
Bothnia

FAEROE ISLANDS
(to Denmark)

TÓRSHAVN

N

Shetland
Islands

85

Elevation

					Below sea level	0		250m	500m	1000m	2000m	3000m	4000m	6000m

-6000m -4000m -2000m -1000m -500m -250m

-19,658ft -13,124ft -6562ft -3281ft -1640ft -820ft -328ft/-100m 0

820ft 1640ft 3281ft 6562ft 9843ft 13,124ft 19,685ft

Scandinavia & Finland

Population

● National capital

○ below 50,000　○ 50,000 to 100,000　◉ 100,000 to 500,000　■ above 500,000

0 km　　200

0 miles　　　200

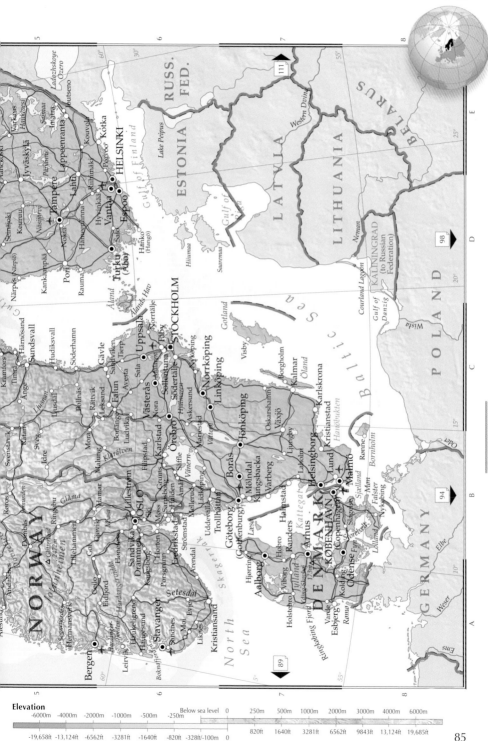

Elevation

-6000m	-4000m	-2000m	-1000m	-500m	Below sea level	0	250m	500m	1000m	2000m	3000m	4000m	6000m
					-250m								
-19,658ft	-13,124ft	-6562ft	-3281ft	-1640ft	-820ft -328ft/-100m	0	820ft	1640ft	3281ft	6562ft	9843ft	13,124ft	19,685ft

85

The Low Countries

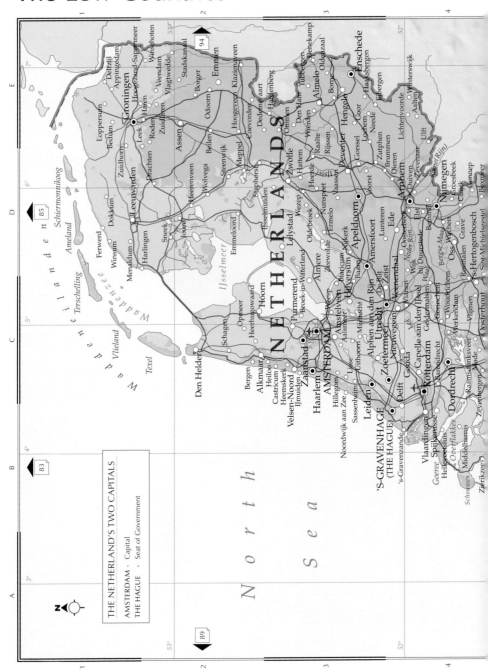

0 km   50

0 miles   50

Population   ● National capital

○ below 50,000   ◎ 50,000 to 100,000   ◉ 100,000 to 500,000   ▣ above 500,000

GERMANY

LUXEMBOURG

LUXEMBOURG

BELGIUM

FRANCE

Lorraine

Rhine (Rhein)

Mosel

Mosselle

Grevenmacher

Weiswampach

Our

Ardenne

Meuse

Sambre

Oise

Somme

Flanders

Fagne

Botrange
694m

Hautes Fagnes

Maastricht

Liège

Namur

Charleroi

Antwerpen (Antwerp)

Schaerbeek

BRUSSEL/BRUXELLES (BRUSSELS)

Gent (Ghent)

Brugge (Bruges)

Oostende (Ostend)

Middelkerke

Zeebrugge

Blankenberge

Knokke-Heist

Koksijde

Veurne

Torhout

Roeselare

Ieper

Poperinge

Diksmuide

Kortrijk

Mouscron

Tournai

Péruwelz

Leuze-en-Hainaut

Ath

Enghien

Mons

Jemappes

Binche

Anderlues

Thuin

Walcourt

Couvin

Chimay

Philippeville

Dinant

Rochefort

Ciney

Marche-en-Famenne

Bastogne

Neufchâteau

Recogne

Arlon

Étalle

Virton

Aubange

Esch-sur-Alzette

Differdange

Pétange

Rodange

Dudelange

Alzette

Sûre

Ettelbrück

Diekirch

Hosingen

Clervaux

Vianden

Houffalize

Malmédy

Eupen

Verviers

Vaals

Kerkrade

Heerlen

Simpelveld

Sittard

Geleen

Genk

Hasselt

Vesdre

Ourthe

Semois

Lesse

Houyet

Andenne

Huy

Waremme

Seraing

Herve

Visé

Eijsden

Meerssen

Riemst

Tongeren

Bilzen

Diepenbeek

Maaseik

Bree

Peer

Lommel

Mol

Balen

Geel

Herentals

Turnhout

Hoogstraten

Brecht

Kapellen

Schoten

Kalmthout

Beveren

Sint-Niklaas

Temse

Dendermonde

Aalst

Ninove

Geraardsbergen

Halle

Braine-le-Comte

La Louvière

Châtelet

Gerpinnes

Gembloux

Wavre

Louvain-la-Neuve

Ottignies

Tervuren

Leuven

Tienen

Landen

Diest

Aarschot

Herk-de-Stad

Zonhoven

Beringen

Tessenderlo

Westerlo

Heist-op-den-Berg

Lier

Mechelen

Vilvoorde

Zaventem

Eghezée

Gerpinnes

Ciney

Couvin

Elevation

Below sea level						0	250m	500m	1000m	2000m	3000m	4000m	6000m
-6000m	-4000m	-2000m	-1000m	-500m	-250m								

| -19,658ft | -13,124ft | -6562ft | -3281ft | -1640ft | -820ft | -328ft/-100m | 0 | 820ft | 1640ft | 3281ft | 6562ft | 9843ft | 13,124ft | 19,685ft |

The British Isles

Population

○ below 50,000
○ 50,000 to 100,000
◉ 100,000 to 500,000
■ above 500,000

● National capital
◎ Internal administrative capital

0 km 100
0 miles 100

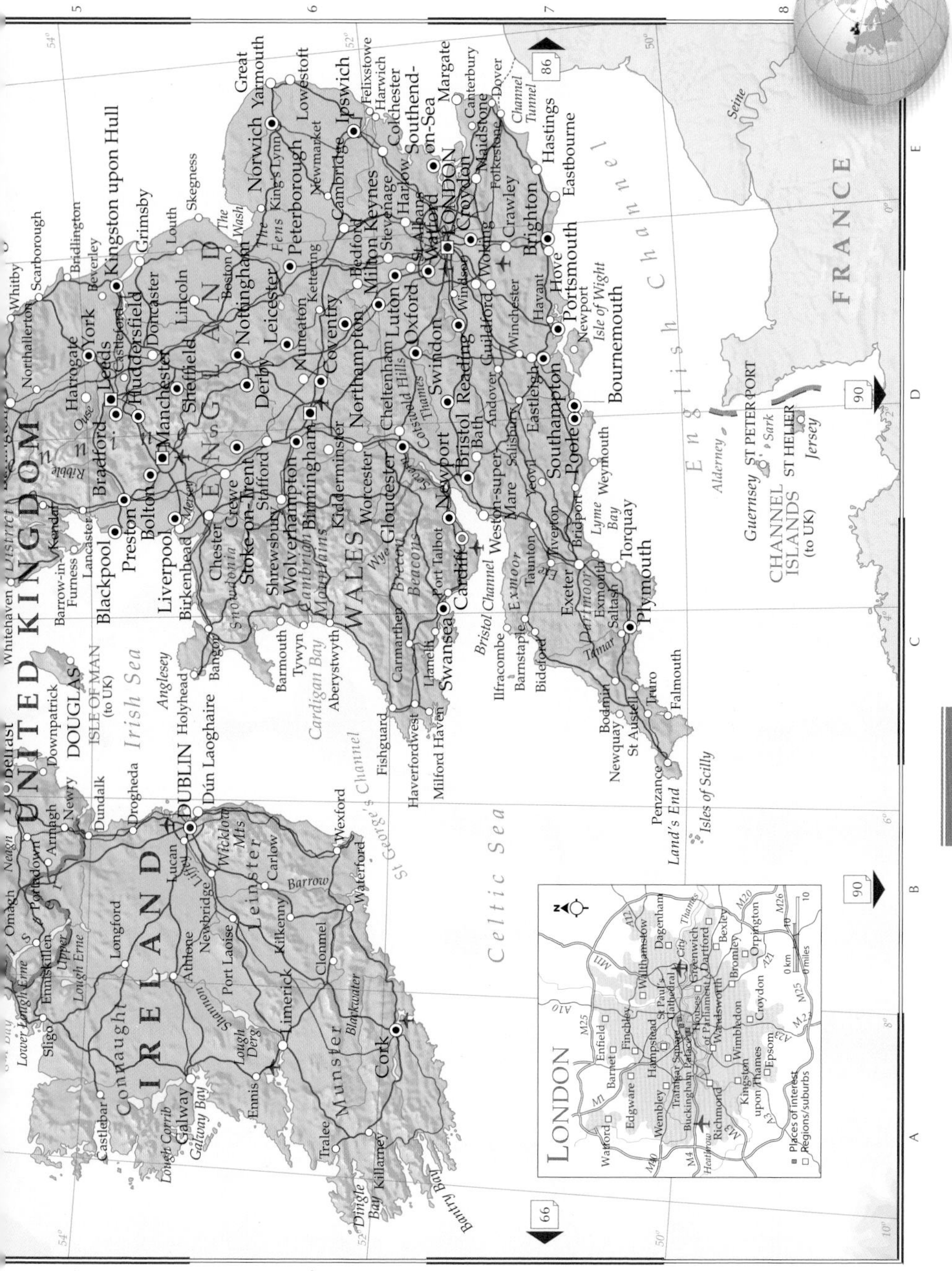

Elevation

Below sea level							0	250m	500m	1000m	2000m	3000m	4000m	6000m
-6000m	-4000m	-2000m	-1000m	-500m	-250m									
-19,658ft	-13,124ft	-6562ft	-3281ft	-1640ft	-820ft	-328ft/-100m	0	820ft	1640ft	3281ft	6562ft	9843ft	13,124ft	19,685ft

France, Andorra & Monaco

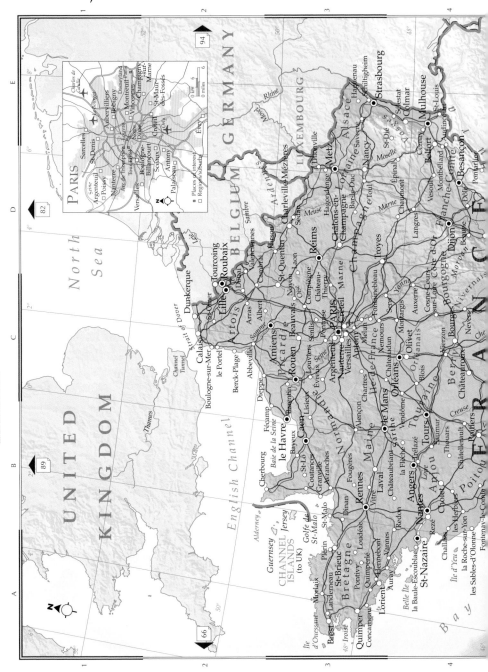

Population

● National capital

○ below 50,000   ○ 50,000 to 100,000   ◉ 100,000 to 500,000   ■ above 500,000

0 km   100

0 miles   100

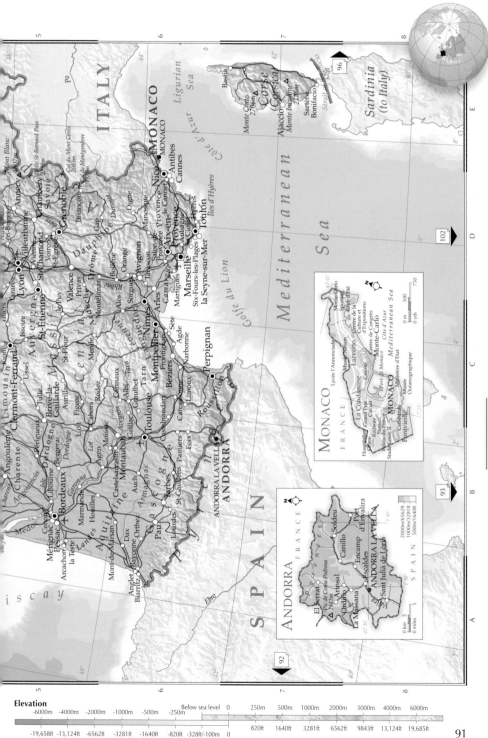

Elevation

					Below sea level	0		250m	500m	1000m	2000m	3000m	4000m	6000m
-6000m	-4000m	-2000m	-1000m	-500m	-250m									
-19,658ft	-13,124ft	-6562ft	-3281ft	-1640ft	-820ft	-328ft/-100m	0		820ft	1640ft	3281ft	6562ft	9843ft	13,124ft	19,685ft

91

Spain & Portugal

0 km 100
0 miles 100

Population ● National capital

○ below 50,000 ○ 50,000 to 100,000 ◉ 100,000 to 500,000 ◼ above 500,000

E · F · G · H

FRANCE

Golfe du Lion

90

96

Bermeo
Zarautz
Eibar
Donostia-San Sebastián
Irun
Tolosa
Bergara
ís Vasco
ria-Gasteiz
Pamplona
(Iruña)
Miranda
de Ebro
Estella
Jaca
Monte Perdido
3348m
La Seo d'Urgel
ANDORRA
groño
Navarra
Calahorra
Huesca
Berga
Ripoll
Figueres
Girona
(Gerona)
Arnedo
Ejea de
los Caballeros
Barbastro
Monzón
Cataluña
Vic
Palafrugell
Palamós
La Rioja
Tudela
Tarazona
Soria
stema Ibérico
Zaragoza
Lleida
(Lérida)
Balaguer
Cervera
Tárrega
Sabadell
Terrassa
Blanes
Arenys de Mar
Mataró
Costa Brava
rgo
sma
Fraga
Vilafranca del Penedès
Valls
Barcelona
L'Hospitalet de Llobregat
Calatayud
Aragón
Reus
Sitges
El Vendrell
Medinaceli
Daroca
Alcañiz
Tarragona
I · N
Tortosa
Teruel
Amposta
Sant Carles de la Ràpita
uadalajara
alá de Henares
ón de Ardoz
Vinaròs
Cuenca
Javalambre
2020m △
País Valenciano
Ciutadella
Menorca
(Minorca)
Mahón
Tarancón
Onda
Castellón de la Plana
Burriana
Vall d'Uxó
Sagunto
(Sagunt)
Pollença
Sa Pobla
stilla-La Mancha
Mota del Cuervo
Campo de Criptana
Socuéllamos
La Roda
Burjassot
Torrent
Valencia
Catarroja
Sueca
Golfo de
Valencia
Palma
Lluchmajor
Manacor
Felanitx
Mallorca
(Majorca)
Júcar
Algemesí
Xàtiva
Cullera
Gandía
Oliva
Dénia
Illa de
Cabrera
Tomelloso
anares
Solana
eñas
Albacete
Almansa
Onteniente
Alcoy
Ibiza
Islas Baleares
(Balearic Islands)
Villanueva de los Infantes
Hellín
Villena
Jumilla
Elda
Benidorm
Villajoyosa (La Vila Joíosa)
Eivissa (Ibiza)
Formentera
Beas de Segura
Moratalla
Segura
Monóvar
Elche
(Elx)
San Juan de Alicante
Alicante (Alacant)
illacarrillo
a
Cazorla
Mula
Cieza
Callosa de Segura
Orihuela
Murcia
Huéscar
Totana
Murcia
Baza
Lorca
La Unión
Cartagena
Aguilas
Guadix
hacén
m
ada
Berja
Mojácar
Mediterranean Sea
Almería
Adra

GIBRALTAR (to UK)

N

SPAIN
5°21'
Gibraltar
Airport
North Mole
Gibraltar
Harbour
Gibraltar Bay
Bay of Gibraltar
The Rock
Catalan Bay
Catalan
Bay
Rosia
Summit
△
Sandy
Bay
Rosia
Bay
Buena Vista
Little
Bay
Europa Point
200m/656ft
Sea level
0 km   1
0 mile   1
Strait of Gibraltar

97

71

ALGERIA

Elevation

-6000m	-4000m	-2000m	-1000m	-500m	-250m	Below sea level 0	250m	500m	1000m	2000m	3000m	4000m	6000m
-19,658ft	-13,124ft	-6562ft	-3281ft	-1640ft	-820ft	-328ft/-100m 0	820ft	1640ft	3281ft	6562ft	9843ft	13,124ft	19,685ft

Germany & the Alpine States

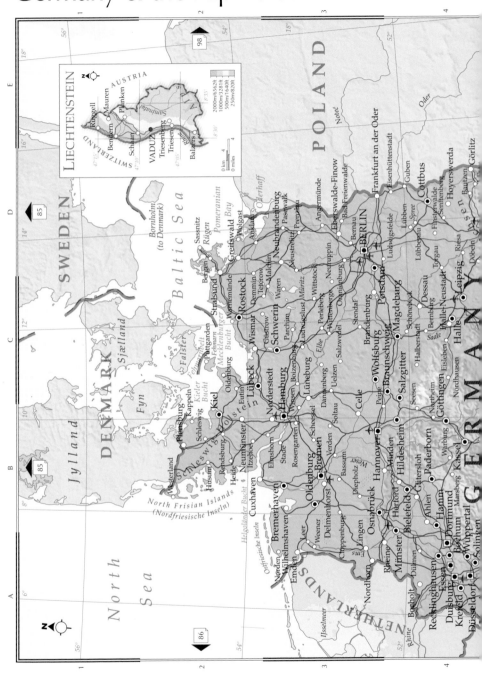

Population
○ below 50,000   ○ 50,000 to 100,000   ◉ 100,000 to 500,000   ■ above 500,000
● National capital

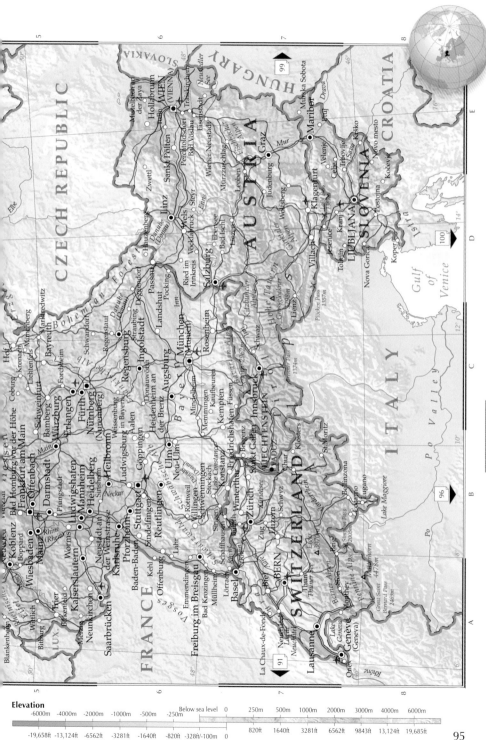

Elevation

					Below sea level	0	250m	500m	1000m	2000m	3000m	4000m	6000m
-6000m	-4000m	-2000m	-1000m	-500m	-250m								
-19,658ft	-13,124ft	-6562ft	-3281ft	-1640ft	-820ft	-328ft/-100m	0	820ft	1640ft	3281ft	6562ft	9843ft	13,124ft	19,685ft

95

Italy

Population • National capital

○ below 50,000   ○ 50,000 to 100,000   ◉ 100,000 to 500,000   ◼ above 500,000

0 km   100

0 miles   100

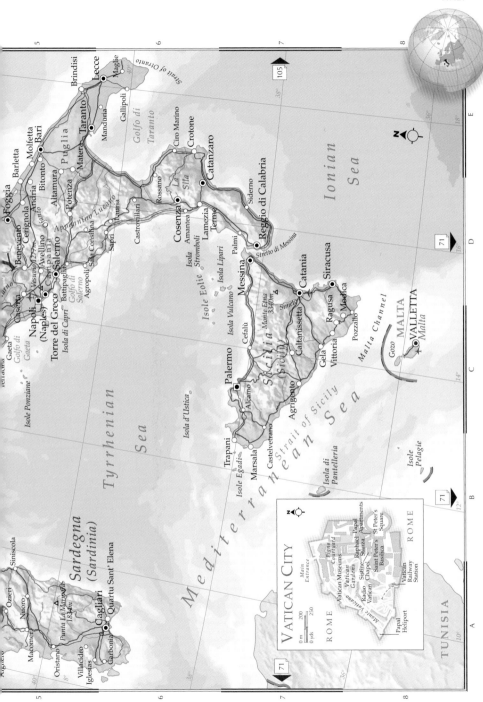

71

71

71

VATICAN CITY

Main
Entrance

Pigna
Courtyard

Papal
Apartments

St Peter's
Square

Raphael
Stanza

Vatican
Museums

Vatican
Gardens

Sistine
Chapel

Saint Peter's
Basilica

Radio
Vatican

Vatican
Railway
Station

Monte Vaticano

Papal
Heliport

ROME

ROME

0 m 200
0 yds 250

Elevation

-6000m	-4000m	-2000m	-1000m	-500m	Below sea level	0	250m	500m	1000m	2000m	3000m	4000m	6000m
-19,658ft	-13,124ft	-6562ft	-3281ft	-1640ft	-820ft	-328ft/-100m	0	820ft	1640ft	3281ft	6562ft	9843ft	13,124ft	19,685ft

97

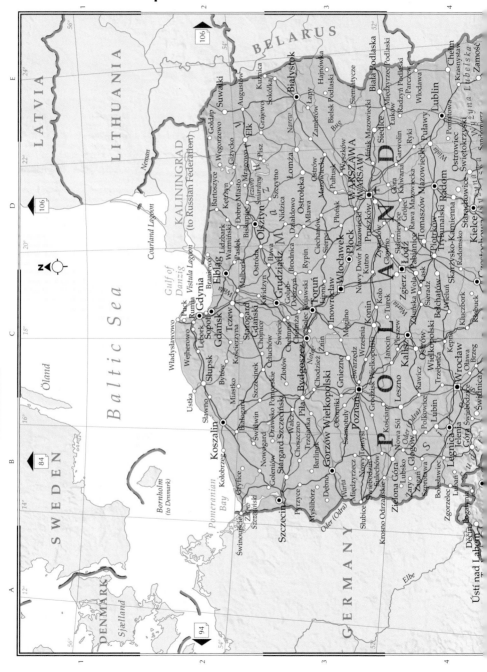

0 km 100

0 miles 100

Population ● National capital

○ below 50,000 ◯ 50,000 to 100,000 ◉ 100,000 to 500,000 ■ above 500,000

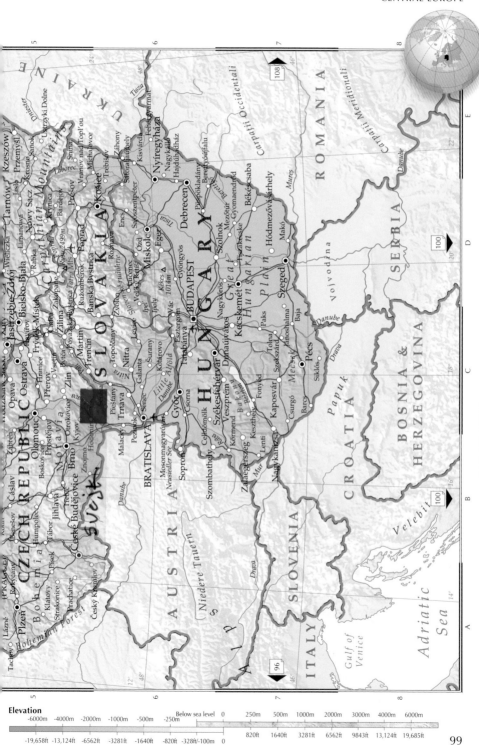

Elevation

-6000m	-4000m	-2000m	-1000m	-500m	-250m	Below sea level 0	250m	500m	1000m	2000m	3000m	4000m	6000m

| -19,658ft | -13,124ft | -6562ft | -3281ft | -1640ft | -820ft | -328ft/-100m 0 | 820ft | 1640ft | 3281ft | 6562ft | 9843ft | 13,124ft | 19,685ft |

Southeast Europe

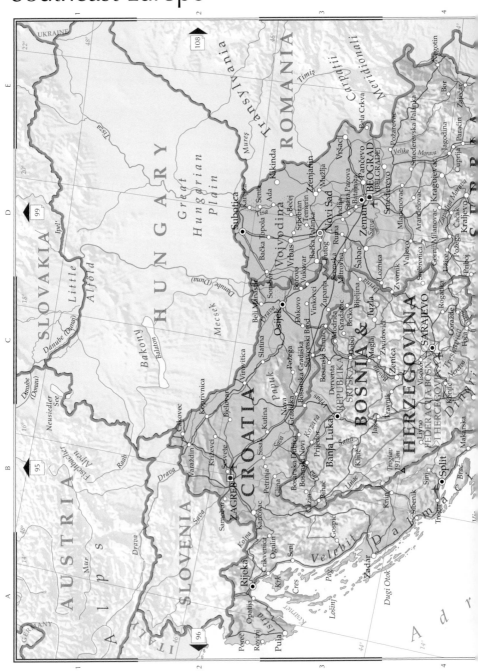

0 km   100

0 miles   100

Population

○ below 50,000   ○ 50,000 to 100,000   ◎ 100,000 to 500,000   ◼ above 500,000

● National capital   ◎ Internal administrative capital

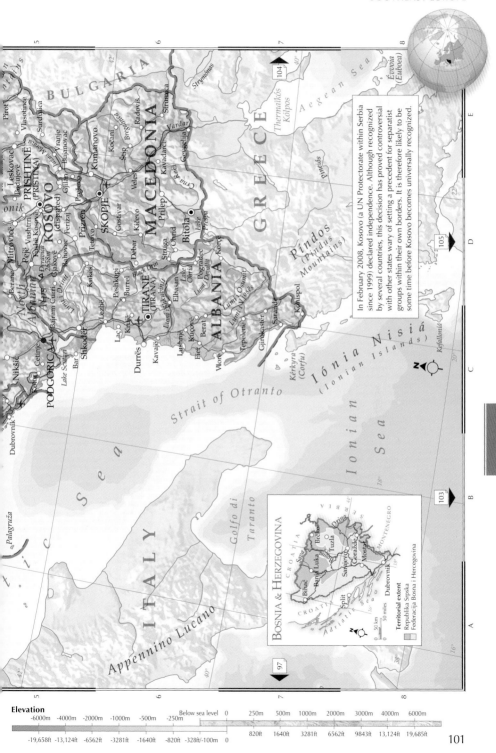

In February 2008, Kosovo (a UN Protectorate within Serbia since 1999) declared independence. Although recognized by several countries, this decision has proved controversial with other states wary of setting a precedent for separatist groups within their own borders. It is therefore likely to be some time before Kosovo becomes universally recognized.

BULGARIA

MACEDONIA

GREECE

KOSOVO

ALBANIA

ITALY

Aegean Sea

Pindos (Pindus Mountains)

Iónia Nisiá (Ionian Islands)

Ionian Sea

Strait of Otranto

Adriatic Sea

Golfo di Taranto

Appennino Lucano

PRISHTINË (PRISTINA) (Disputed)

SKOPJE

TIRANË (TIRANA)

PODGORICA

BOSNIA & HERZEGOVINA

Territorial extent
Republika Srpska
Federacija Bosna I Hercegovina

0   50 km
0   50 miles

Elevation

-6000m	-4000m	-2000m	-1000m	-500m	-250m	Below sea level 0	250m	500m	1000m	2000m	3000m	4000m	6000m
-19,658ft	-13,124ft	-6562ft	-3281ft	-1640ft	-820ft	-328ft/-100m	0	820ft	1640ft	3281ft	6562ft	9843ft	13,124ft	19,685ft

The Mediterranean

MALTA

Nadur
Victoria
Gozo Mgarr
Comino
(Kemmuna)

Mellieħa
St Julian's
Sliema
Mosta
VALLETTA
Ħamrun
Paola

250m/820ft
100m/328ft
Sea Level

0 km   10
0 miles   10

Malta
Rabat
Birżebbuġa

Mediterranean Sea

CYPRUS

TURKISH REPUBLIC OF
NORTHERN CYPRUS
(recognized only
by Turkey)

Lapta
(Lápithos)
Girne
(Kerýneia)
Yenierenköy
(Agialoúsa)

Güzelyurt Körfezi
(Kólpos Mórfou)
Değirmenlik
(Kythrea)
Gazimağusa Körfezi
(Kólpos Ammóchostos)

Pólis
NICOSIA
Dílcelia
Gazimağusa
(Ammóchostos,
Famagusta)

Tróodos

Pápos
Sovereign
Base Area
(to UK)
Lárnaka
Sovereign
Base Area
(to UK)

Akrotírion
Lemesós
(Limassol)

1000m/3281ft
500m/1640ft
250m/820ft
Sea Level

0 km   25
0 miles   25

Mediterranean Sea

S a h a r

0 km   400
0 miles   400

Population   ● National capital

o below 50,000   o 50,000 to 100,000   ◉ 100,000 to 500,000   ▣ above 500,000

SLOVAKIA
WIEN
(ENNA)
Danube
HUNGARY
BUDAPEST
Satu Mare
Tisza
Great
Hungarian
Plain
Targu Mures
BLJANA
ZAGREB
CROATIA
Novi Sad
Sava
BOSNIA
& HERZ.
BEOGRAD
(BELGRADE)
SARAJEVO
SERBIA
PODGORICA
MON
TIRANÉ
(TIRANA)
Bari
oli (Naples)
Vesuvio 1277m
Lecce
Golfo di
Taranto
osenza
Kérkyra
(Corfu)
Catanzaro
Ionian
Kefallonia
Sea
Monte Etna
3340m
Catania
Siracusa
Zákynthos
ALLETTA
TA
Kýthira

Carpathian Mountains
UKRAINE
108
MOLD
CHISINĂU
ROMANIA
Carpatii Meridionali
BUCUREŞTI
(BUCHAREST)
Danube
Constanţa
Bălti
Kakhovs'ka
Vodoskhovyshche
Odesa
Dnieper
Berdyans'k
Sea of Azov
Kryms'kyy
Pivostrov
Kerch
RUSS.
FED.
Sevastopol'
Novorossiysk

Galaţi

BULGARIA
Varna
PRISHTINÉ
(PRISTINA)
Balkan Mountains
KOSOVO
(Mispuced)
SOFIYA
(SOFIA)
Burgas
SKOPJE
MACED.
Rhodope
Mountains
Edirne
Thessaloníki
(Salonica)
PINdus
Límnos
Lárisa
GREECE
Aegean
ATHINA
(ATHENS)
Chíos
Mirtóo
Pélagos
Irakleio
Kríti
(Crete)
Sámos
Dodécanuse
Ródos
(Rhodes)
Kárpathos
Kritikó Pélagos
(Sea of Crete)

Black Sea

İstanbul
Boğazı
(Bosporus)
İstanbul
Marmara
Denizi
Bursa
Zonguldak
Küre Dağları
Samsun
Ordu
Kızıl Irmak
ANKARA
TURKEY
Balıkesir
İzmir
Tuz
Gölü
Kayseri
Antalya
Toros Dağları
Antalya
Körfezi
Adana
Gaziantep
İskenderun Körfezi
NICOSIA
CYPRUS
Lemesós
(Limassol)
Lárnaka
Halab
(Aleppo)
SYRIA
LEBANON
BEYROUTH
(BEIRUT)
DIMASHQ
(DAMASCUS)

Ced’s
Kefbar
117

119

Mişrātah
Surt
Khalīj Surt
(Gulf of Sirte)
Banghāzī
(Benghazi)
Ajdābiyā
Darnah
Ţubruq
Libyan
Plateau
Great Sand Sea
LIBYA
Libyan
Desert
Waddān

Alexandria
(Al Iskandariyah)
Nile
Delta
Būr Sa'īd
(Port Said)
CAIRO
(AL QÁHIRAH)
Giza
(Al Jīzah)
Mtukhfad al Qaţţārah
(Qattari Depression)
Niles
Qanāt as Suways
(Suez Canal)
Suez
(As Suways)
Sahara al Sharqiya
Eastern Desert
EGYPT
72

Hefa
(Haifa)
ISRAEL
Tel Aviv-Yafo
JERUSALEM
Gaza
Al 'Aqabah
Elat
Sinai
(Sīnā)
Gulf of Suez
Red
Sea
Dead Sea
AMMAN
JORDAN
Al 'Aqabah
SAUDI
ARABIA

Elevation

-6000m	-4000m	-2000m	-1000m	-500m	Below sea level -250m	0	250m	500m	1000m	2000m	3000m	4000m	6000m
-19,658ft	-13,124ft	-6562ft	-3281ft	-1640ft	-820ft -328ft/-100m	0	820ft	1640ft	3281ft	6562ft	9843ft	13,124ft	19,685ft

Bulgaria & Greece

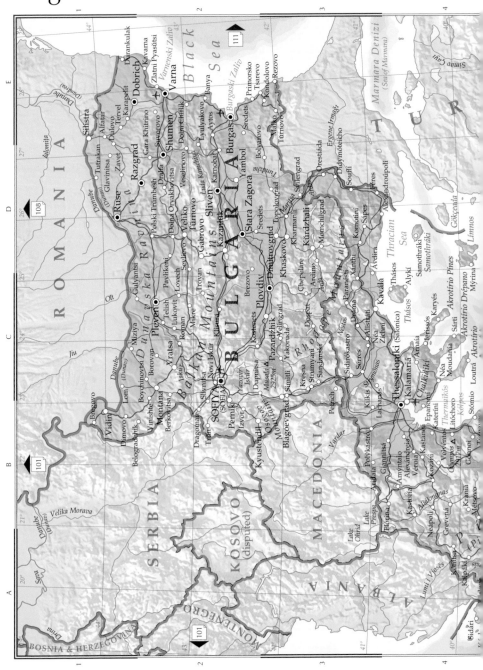

Population

- ● National capital
- ○ below 50,000
- ◎ 50,000 to 100,000
- ◉ 100,000 to 500,000
- ▣ above 500,000

0 km 100

0 miles 100

Ródos
(Rhodes)
Lindos
Ródos
(Rhodes)
Kattaviá
Kárpathos
Kárpathos

Mytilíni
Lésvos
(Lesbos)
Plomári
Büyükmenderes Nehri
Gediz Nehri

Chálki
Tílos
Nísiros
Kos
Agía
Marína
Léros
Arkoí
Kálymnos
Agathonísi
Pátmos
Lipsó
Sými
Dodekánisa (Dodecanese)

Sámos
Sámos
Ikaría
Psará
Chíos
Chíos
Antípsara

Sými
Kásos

Thérma
Amorgós
Astypálaia
Katápola
Akrotírio Floúda
Amorgós

72

Kými
Skýros
Marmári
Kárystos
Ándros
Tínos
Tínos
Mýkonos
Náxos
Náxos
Íos
Thíra
Santoríni
Aníti
Akrotírio Floúda

Neápoli
Ágios Nikólaos
Sitía
Dikti
Zarós
Mýrtos
Ierápetra

Skáthos
Skópelos
Strofyliá
Vória
Évvoia
(Euboea)
Istiaía
Marathónas
Kéa
Tziá
Ioúlis
Kýthnos
Sýros
Ermoúpoli
Páros
Paroikía
Náxos
Kykládes (Cyclades)
Chóra
Kástro

Lamía
Domokós
Sofrpi
Agriniano
Méos
Livanátes
Chalkída
Alivéri
Thíva
Megara
Keratéa
Lávrio
Póros
Emmóni
Ýdra

Kritikó Pélagos
(Sea of Crete)

Kríti (Crete)
Pános
Iráklio
Iráklio
Spíli
Týmpaki
Girados

Panormós

Chaniá
Lefká Óri
Réthymno

Kíssamos
Kándanos
Chóra Sfakíon

ATHÍNA
(ATHENS)
Kálamos
Peiraiás
(Piraeus)
Máhdra
Aígina
Ýdra
Palaiá Epídavros
Ýdra
Emmóni

Korinthiakós Kólpos
Kórinthos
Kiáto
Néa
Naúplio
Árgos
Tripolí
Leonídio
Geráki
Gýtheio

Mediterranean Sea

Aígio Achaía
Pátra
Lampeia
Alféios
Kyparissía
Zachárō
Pýrgos
Kalamáta
Koróni
Messíni
Pýlos
Kýthira
Neápoli
Karavás
Kýthira
Antikýthira
Potamós
Daimoniá
Areópoli
Gerolimḗnas
Lakonikós Kólpos

Mírtoo Pélagos

GREECE
Pelopónnisos
Ionian Sea

Ántanas
Árta Rentína
Karpenísi
Préveza
Lefkáda
Lefkáda
Vasilikí
Neochóri
Thérmo
Pórós
Lechainá
Gastoúni
Kerí

Ámphochia
Nafpaktos
Agrínio
Antírrio
Kató Achaía

Kefalloniá
Argostóli
Zákynthos
Ióni a Nisiá
(Ionian Islands)
Kythira
Antípaxoi

97

z
N

Elevation

Below sea level						Above sea level						
-6000m	-4000m	-2000m	-1000m	-500m	-250m	0	250m	500m	1000m	2000m	3000m	4000m	6000m
-19,658ft	-13,124ft	-6562ft	-3281ft	-1640ft	-820ft -328ft/-100m	0	820ft	1640ft	3281ft	6562ft	9843ft	13,124ft	19,685ft

The Baltic States & Belarus

Population

- ● National capital
- ○ below 50,000
- ⊙ 50,000 to 100,000
- ◉ 100,000 to 500,000
- ◼ above 500,000

0 km 100

0 miles 100

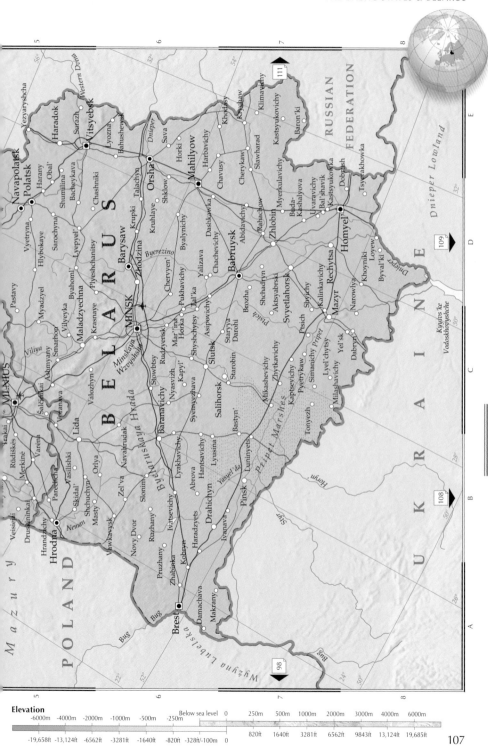

THE BALTIC STATES & BELARUS

RUSSIAN FEDERATION

Dnieper Lowland

Dnieper

BELARUS

MINSK

Navapolatsk
Polatsk
Vitsyebsk
Haradok
Suražh
Lyozna
Bahusheysk
Khodasy
Klimavichy
Krhchaw
Baron'ki
Kastsyukovichy
Slawharad
Tsvyetakhowka
Dobrush
Kastsyukowka
Homyel
Khoyniki
Loyew
Byval'ki
Narowlya
Mazyr
Rechytsa
Kalinkavichy
Spyichy
Svyetlahorsk
Zhlobin
Babruysk
Rahachow
Byda-Kashalyova
Uvaravichy
Bal'shavik
Myerkulavichy
Chavusy
Cherykaw
Mahilyow
Orsha
Sklow
Horki
Harbavichy
Talachyn
Sava
Dnieper
Shumilina
Obal'
Harany
Bachéykava
Chashniki
Lyepyel'
Vyetryna
Hlybokaye
Sarochyna
Byahoml'
Flyeshchanitsy
Barysaw
Zhodzina
Byerezino
Cherven'
Pukhavichy
Byalynichy
Dashkawka
Chachevichy
Yalizava
Abidavichy
Shchadryn
Aktsyabrski
Brozha
Pisich
Zhyrkavichy
Lyel'chytsy
Milashavichy
Dabryn
Yel'sk
Narowlya
Kyدز'ke
Vodoskhovyshche
Pastavy
Myadzyel
Smarhon
Vilyeyka
Krasnaye
Maladzyechna
Minskaye Wzvyshsha
Smarhon
Adamyany
Valozhyn
Stowbtsy
Rudzyensk
Mar'ina Horka
Shyshchytsy
Asipovichy
Starobin
Staryya Darohi
Slutsk
Salihorsk
Svyenzyzhava
Kapyl'
Nyasvizh
Baranavichy
Lyakhavichy
Hantsavichy
Lyusina
Drahichyn
Byelarusskaya Hrada
Navahrudak
Zel'va
Orlya
Slonim
Ivatsevichy
Ruzhany
Pruzhany
Kobryn
Zhabinka
Damachava
Makrany
Brest
Bug
Yasyel'da
Pinsk
Iranava
Luninyets
Lyusina
Bastyn'
Lyusina
Mikashevichy
Simanichy
Tonyezh
Pripet Marshes
Pripet
Stvr
Kaptsevichy
Pyetrykaw
Svyetlahorsk
Horyn'

MLAWUS

Trakai
Vilnius
Salcininkai
Adutiškis
Merkine
Parecha
Šalcininkai
Orlya
Vasilishki
Shchuchyn
Masty
Vawkavysk
Novy Dvor
Haradzyets
Ivanava

POLAND

Mazury

Radviškes
Druskininkai
Veisiejai
Varena
Hrandzichy
Hrodna
Neman
Skidal'
Lida

Wyżyna Lubelska

RUSSIAN FEDERATION

U K R A I N E

POLAND

111
109
108
98

Elevation

-6000m	-4000m	-2000m	-1000m	-500m	-250m	Below sea level 0	250m	500m	1000m	2000m	3000m	4000m	6000m
-19,658ft	-13,124ft	-6562ft	-3281ft	-1640ft	-820ft	-328ft/-100m	0	820ft	1640ft	3281ft	6562ft	9843ft	13,124ft	19,685ft

107

Ukraine, Moldova & Romania

0 km 100

0 miles 100

Population
- ● National capital
- ○ below 50,000
- ○ 50,000 to 100,000
- ◉ 100,000 to 500,000
- ◼ above 500,000

E   F   G   H

32°   34°   36°   38°   40°

110

Dnieper
(Dnyapro)

Horodnya
Shostka
Shchors
Hlukhiv
Chernihiv   Krolevets'
Konotop
Nizhyn   Bakhmach
Nosivka   Romny   Sumy

Desna

Srednerusskaya
Vozvyshennost'

R U S S I A N

52°

40°

1

s'ke
vyshche
Oster

F E D E R A T I O N

Don

Brovary
Pryluky   Lebedyn
Yahotyn   Pyryatyn
Okhtyrka   Zolochiv
a Tserkva   Hrebinka   Lubny   Myrhorod
odoskhovyshche   Kaniv   Derhachi
huslav   Zolotonosha   Lyubotyn   **Kharkiv**

Psel

50°

110

2

I   *N*   *E*

lorodyshche
yhorodka   Cherkasy   Hlobyne   Merefa
Smila   Kremenchuts'ke   Kup"yans'k
Tal'ne   Shpola   Chyhyryn   Vodoskhovyshche   Poltava
Oleksandrivka   Svitlovods'k   **Kremenchuk**   Izyum   Starobil's'k
Mala Vyska   Znam"yanka   Oleksandriya   Dniprodzerzhyns'ke   Kreminna   Rubizhne
olovanivs'k   **Dniprodzerzhyns'k**   Vodoskhovyshche   Slov"yans'k   **Syeverodonets'k**
aniyka   **Kirovohrad**   Zhovti Vody   Novomoskovs'k   Kramators'k   Lysychans'k
Vil'shanka   P"yatykhatky   **Dnipropetrovs'k**   Pavlohrad   Kostyantynivka   Zolote   **Luhans'k**
Pervomays'k   Dolyns'ka   Synel'nykove   Horlivka   Stakhanov
ve Ozero   Arbuzynka   Bobrynets'   **Kryvyy Rih**   Pokrovs'ke   Yenakiyeve   Krasnodon
Novyy Buh   Inhulets'   **Makiyivka**   **Krasnyy Luch**
Voznesens'k   Ordzhonikidze   **Nikopol'**   **Zaporizhzhya**   Orikhiv   **Donets'k**   Torez
Kam"yanka-Dniprovs'ka   Marhanets'   Volnovakha   Dokuchayevs'k   Amvrosiyivka

Donets

48°

3

l   *a*   *c*

Dnieper
(Dnipro)

Kakhovs'ka   Dniprorudne   Polohy
Vodoskhovyshche   Tokmak   Novoazovs'k
Mykolayiv   Kakhovka   Molochans'k   Don
Zhovtneve   **Melitopol'**   **Mariupol'**   Gulf of Taganrog
S   *e*   *a*   Yeya

46°

4

Ochakiv   **Kherson**   *o*   *w*   *l*   *a*   *n*   *d*
Odesa   Hola Prystan'   Yakymivka   Prymors'k   **Berdyans'k**
lichivs'k   Tsyurupyns'k   Novotroyits'ke
Chaplynka   Kalanchak   Armyans'k   Heniches'k

110

Sea of Azov

R U S S I A N

Krasnoperekops'k
Rozdol'ne   Dzhankoy   Kerch Strait

F E D E R A T I O N

Chornomors'ke   Krasnohvardiys'ke   Zatoka
Nyzhn'ohirs'kyy   Syvash   **Kerch**
Yevpatoriya   *Kryms'kyy*   Lenine   Kuban'
Saky   *Pivostriv*   Feodosiya
Simferopol'
Bakhchysaray   *Kryms'ki Hory*
Sevastopol'   Alushta
Yalta
Alupka

44°

5

B   *l*   *a*   *c*   *k*   *S*   *e*   *a*

116

32°   34°   36°   38°   40°

E   F   G   H

Elevation

| -6000m | -4000m | -2000m | -1000m | -500m | -250m | Below sea level 0 | 250m | 500m | 1000m | 2000m | 3000m | 4000m | 6000m |

-19,658ft   -13,124ft   -6562ft   -3281ft   -1640ft   -820ft   -328ft/-100m   0   820ft   1640ft   3281ft   6562ft   9843ft   13,124ft   19,685ft

European Russia

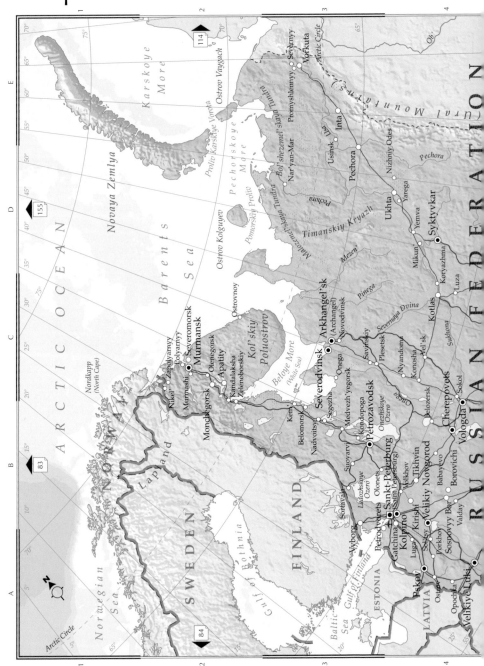

Population

○ below 50,000 ● National capital

○ 50,000 to 100,000 ⊙ 100,000 to 500,000 ◉ above 500,000

0 km   300

0 miles   300

Elevation

					Below sea level	0	250m	500m	1000m	2000m	3000m	4000m	6000m
-6000m	-4000m	-2000m	-1000m	-500m	-250m								
-19,658ft	-13,124ft	-6562ft	-3281ft	-1640ft	-820ft	-328ft/-100m	0	820ft	1640ft	3281ft	6562ft	9843ft	13,124ft	19,685ft

North & West Asia

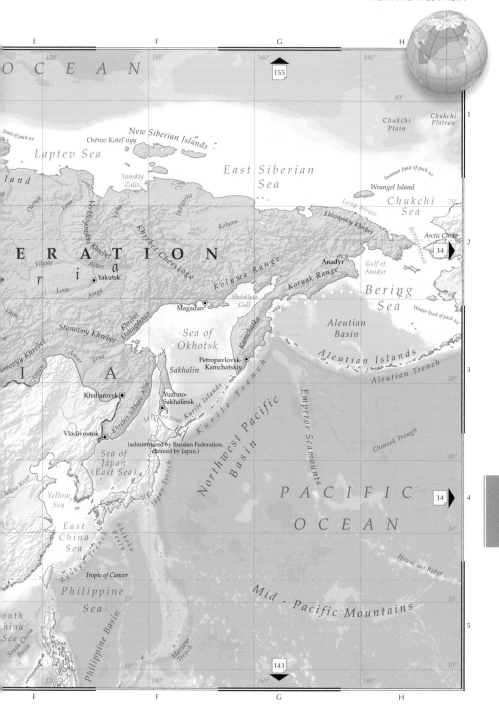

E 120° F 140° G 160° H 180°

155

O C E A N

80°

Chukchi
Plain

Chukchi
Plateau

1

limit of pack ice

New Siberian Islands
Ostrov Kotel'nyy

Laptev Sea

land

*East Siberian
Sea*

Summer limit of pack ice

Wrangel Island

70°

Yanskiy
Zaliv

Long Strait

*Chukchi
Sea*

Okenek

Lena

Jana

Verkhoyanskiy Khrebet

Indigirka

Kolyma

Eklatapskiy Khrebet

Bering Strait

Arctic Circle

E R A T I O N

34

2

Vilyuy

Aldan

a

Anadyr

Gulf of
Anadyr

r   i

Yakutsk

Khrebet Cherskogo

Kolyma Range

Koryak Range

*Bering
Sea*

60°

Lena

Amga

Sheleklion
Gulf

Winter limit of pack ice

Magadan

Stanovoy Khrebet

Khrebet Dzhugdzhur

*Sea of
Okhotsk*

Kamchatka

*Aleutian
Basin*

onovyy Khrebet

Zeya

Petropavlovsk-
Kamchatskiy

Sakhalin

Aleutian Islands

50°

Amur

Argun

Aleutian Trench

I   A

Khabarovsk

Yuzhno-
Sakhalinsk

Kurile Islands

Khrebet Sikhote-Alin

La Perouse Strait

Vladivostok

(administered by Russian Federation,
claimed by Japan.)

*Northwest Pacific
Basin*

Kurile Trench

Emperor Seamounts

Chinook Trough

34

4

Yellow River

*Sea of
Japan
(East Sea)*

Japan Trench

40°

Yellow
Sea

P A C I F I C

outh
hina
Sea

*East
China
Sea*

Shikoku
Basin

O C E A N

30°

South China
Basin

Ryukyu Trench

Tropic of Cancer

*Philippine
Sea*

20°

Hawaiian Ridge

20°

Philippine Basin

Mid - Pacific Mountains

5

Mariana
Trench

143

10°

10°

E 120° F 140° G 160° H 180°

Russia & Kazakhstan

A   B   C   D

NORWAY
SVALBARD
(to Norway)

NETH.
DENMARK
SWEDEN
GERMANY
KALININGRAD
(to Russ. Fed.)
Kaliningrad
POLAND
LITH.
BELARUS
MOLDOVA
UKRAINE
Belgorod
Voronezh

Nordkapp
(North Cape)
FINLAND
Murmansk
Kandalaksha

Zemlya Fr
Iosifa

*Barents
Sea*

ARCT

Novaya Zemlya

Karskoye More

Ostrov Bel
Dik

Sankt-Peterburg
Ladozhskoye
Ozero
Pskov
Petrozavodsk
Severodvinsk
Ostrov
Kolguyev
Velikiy Novgorod
Onezhskoye
Ozero
Arkhangel'sk
Smolensk
Cherepovets
Vel'sk
Nar'yan-Mar
MOSKVA
(MOSCOW)
Tver
Vologda
Bryansk
Tula
Yaroslavl'
Kotlas
Ukhta
Vorkuta
Kineshma
Ryazan
Vladimir
Syktyvkar
Salekhard
Nori
Nizhniy Novgorod
Kirov
Nadym
Igark
Tambov
Solikamsk
Nyagan'
Penza
Kazan
Glazov
Zapadno-
Mikhaylovka
Ul'yanovsk
Izhevsk
Perm'
Serov
Rostov-na-
Donu
Saratov
Tol'yatti
Naberezhnyye
Chelny
Lesnoy
Khanty-Mansiysk
Sibirskaya
Krasnodar
Balakovo
Samara
Ufa
Yekaterinburg
Surgut
Nizhnevartovs
Sochi
Stavropol'
Volgograd
Tyumen'
Tobol'sk
Ravnina
Elbrus
5642m
Ural'sk
Orenburg
Sterlitamak
Chelyabinsk
RUSSIA
Nal'chik
Astrakhan'
Magnitogorsk
Ishim
Chulym
Vladikavkaz
Orsk
Petropavlovsk
Omsk
Seversk
Tomsk
Groznyy
Rudnyy
Kostanay
Makhachkala
Atyrau
(Aktyubinsk)
Kokshetau
Novosibirsk
Krasne
Fort-Shevchenko
Alga
Emba
Atbasar
Shchuchinsk
Kemero
AZERBAIJAN
Aktau
Shalkar
ASTANA
Novokuznetsk
Zhanaozen
Pavlodar
Barnaul
KAZAKHSTAN
Temirtau
Saran'
Karaganda
Semipalatinsk
Ustyurt
Plateau
Aral
Sea
Aral'sk
Ayteke Bi
Zhezkazgan
Melkosopochnik
Shar
Leninogorsk
Dzhusaly
Kyzylorda
Ust'-Kamenogorsk
Zyryanovsk
Kyzyl Kum
Balkhash
Ayagoz
Ozero
Zaysan
Turkestan
Kentau
*Ozero
Balkhash*
Karatau
Taldykorgan
Arys'
Shu
Tekeli
Shymkent
Taraz
Almaty
(Alma-Ata)
CHINA
KYRGYZSTAN
Tien Shan
IRAN
AFGHANISTAN
TURKMENISTAN
UZBEKISTAN
Amu Darya
Syr Darya

A   B   C   D

0 km   600
0 miles   600

Population   ● National capital

○ below 50,000   ○ 50,000 to 100,000   ◉ 100,000 to 500,000   ◼ above 500,000

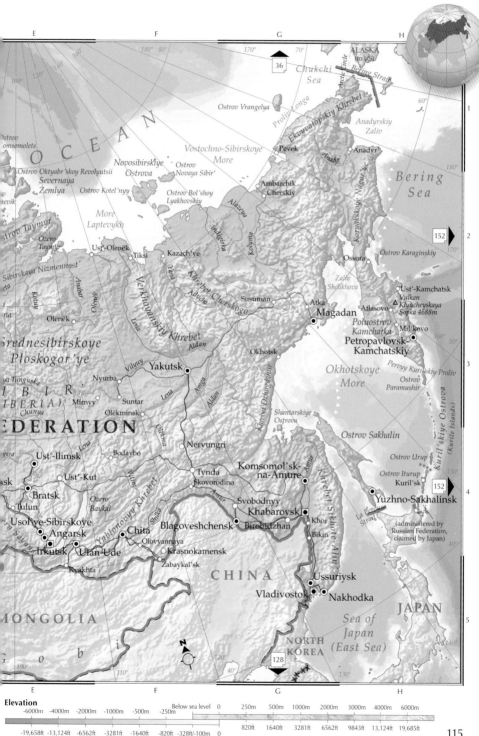

180° 80°   170° 70°   ALASKA
                          (to US)

36   Chukchi   Bering Strait
      Sea

Ostrov Vrangelya   Anadyrskiy
                    Zaliv

Proliv Longa   Ekvyvatapskiy Khrebet

Ostrov
Komsomolets   Vostochno-Sibirskoye   Pevek   Anadyr
               More

Ostrov Oktyabr'skoy Revolyutsii   Novosibirskiye   Ostrov
Ostrova   Novaya Sibir'

Severnaya   Ostrov Kotel'nyy   Ambarchik   B e r i n g
Zemlya   Ostrov Bol'shoy   Cherskiy   S e a
          Lyakhovskiy

More   Alazeya   152

Laptevykh   Zaliv
              Shelikhova   Ust'-Kamchatsk

Ozero   Ust'-Olenëk   Tiksi   Kazach'ye   Ossora   Ostrov Karaginskiy
Taymyr

Sibirskaya Nizmennost'   Susuman   Atka   Atlasovo   Vulkan
                                   Magadan   Klyucheyskaya
Anabar   Sopka 4688m

Olenëk   Verkhoyanskiy Khrebet   Okhotsk   Poluostrov   Mil'kovo
                                              Kamchatka
Srednesibirskoye   Khrebet Cherskogo   Petropavlovsk
Ploskogor'ye   Adycha   Aldan   Kamchatskiy

Nyurba   Yakutsk   Okhotskoye   Pervyy Kuril'skiy Proliv
                     More   Ostrov
Mirnyy   Suntar   Shantarskiye   Paramushir
          Olëkminsk   Ostrova

FEDERATION   Ostrov Sakhalin

Ust'-Ilimsk   Bodaybo   Neryungri   Ostrov Urup

Ust'-Kut   Tynda   Ostrov Iturup   Kuril'sk   152
           Skovorodino
Bratsk   Svobodnyy   Yuzhno-Sakhalinsk
Tulun   Ozero   Khabarovsk
         Baykal
Usol'ye-Sibirskoye   Blagoveshchensk   Birobidzhan   Khor   (administered by
Angarsk   Chita   Bikin   Russian Federation,
                             claimed by Japan)
Irkutsk   Ulan-Ude   Olovyannaya   Krasnokamensk
Kyakhta   Zabaykal'sk   C H I N A   Ussuriysk

MONGOLIA   Vladivostok   Nakhodka   JAPAN

                NORTH   Sea of
                KOREA   Japan
128   (East Sea)

Elevation

					Below sea level	0	250m	500m	1000m	2000m	3000m	4000m	6000m
-6000m	-4000m	-2000m	-1000m	-500m	-250m								
-19,658ft	-13,124ft	-6562ft	-3281ft	-1640ft	-820ft	-328ft/-100m	0	820ft	1640ft	3281ft	6562ft	9843ft	13,124ft	19,685ft

Turkey & the Caucasus

Population

○ below 50,000   ○ 50,000 to 100,000   ◉ 100,000 to 500,000   ◼ above 500,000

● National capital

0 km   200

0 miles   200

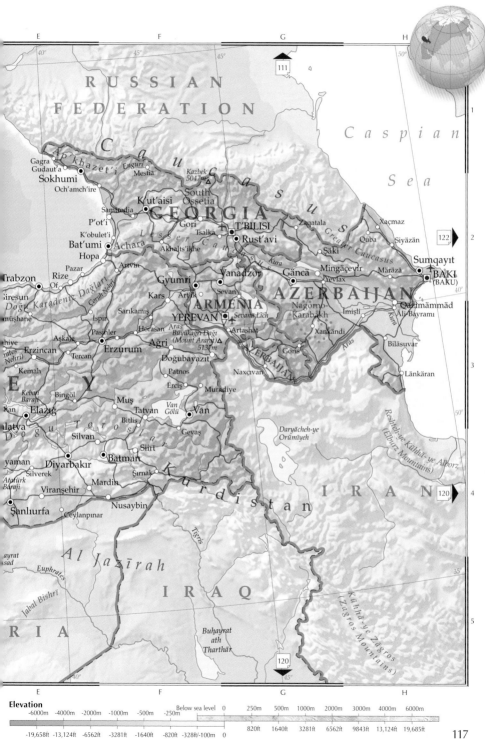

E   F   G   H

40°   45°   45°   50°

RUSSIAN

FEDERATION

Caspian

Sea

C a u c a s u s

Gagra
Gudaut'a
Sokhumi
Och'amch'ire

Mestia

Kazbek
5047m

South
Ossetia

Samtredia

K'ut'aisi

GEORGIA

Gori

Tsalka

T'BILISI

Zaqatala

Xaçmaz

P'ot'i

K'obulet'i

Bat'umi

Achara

Akhalts'ikhe

Rust'avi

Quba

Siyäzän

Hopa

Pazar

Artvin

Vanadzor

Gäncä

Mingäçevir

Säki

Märäzä

Sumqayıt

Trabzon

Rize

Of

Gyumri

Sevan

Kura

Yevlax

BAKI
(BAKU)

Giresun

Kars

Artik

Greater Caucasus

Doğu Karadeniz Dağları

Coruh Nehri

İspir

ARMENIA

YEREVAN

Sevana Lich

Nagorno-
Karabakh

İmişli

Qazımämmäd

müshane

Sarıkamış

Horasan

Artashat

Xankändi

Ali-Bayramı

hiye

Aşkale

Pasinler

Aras

Buyukağrı Dağı
(Mount Ararat)
5137m

Goris

Biläsuvar

Erzincan

Tercan

Erzurum

Ağrı

Doğubayazıt

Naxçıvan

Länkäran

Kemah

Patnos

Keban
Barajı

Bingöl

Erciş

Muradiye

E Y

Kan

Elazığ

Muş

Tatvan

Van
Gölü

Van

latya

Silvan

Bitlis

Gevaş

*Daryācheh-ye
Orūmīyeh*

Siirt

yaman

Diyarbakır

Batman

Silverek

Şırnak

Mardin

Kurdistan

Viranşehir

Nusaybin

I R A N

Şanlıurfa

Ceylanpınar

ayrat
sad

Euphrates

Al Jazīrah

Tigris

I R A Q

Jabal Bishrī

R I A

Buhayrat
ath
Tharthār

*Zagros Mountains
(Kūhhā-ye Zāgros)*

E   F   G   H

Elevation

						Below sea level	0	250m	500m	1000m	2000m	3000m	4000m	6000m
-6000m	-4000m	-2000m	-1000m	-500m	-250m									
-19,658ft	-13,124ft	-6562ft	-3281ft	-1640ft	-820ft	-328ft/-100m	0	820ft	1640ft	3281ft	6562ft	9843ft	13,124ft	19,685ft

The Near East

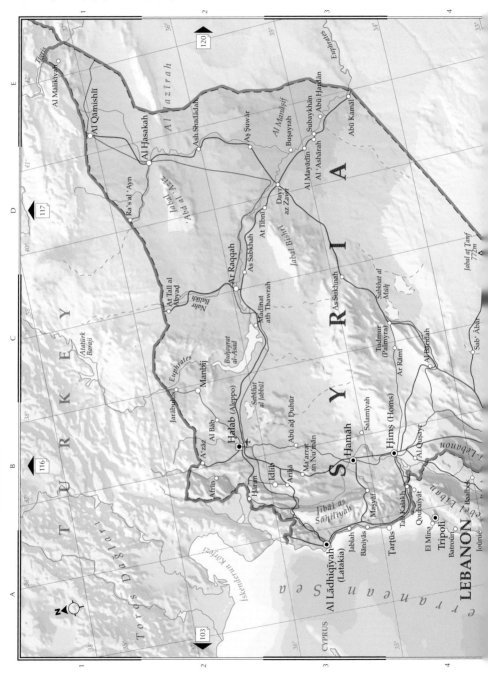

Population

● National capital

○ below 50,000 ○ 50,000 to 100,000 ◉ 100,000 to 500,000 ■ above 500,000

0 km 100

0 miles 100

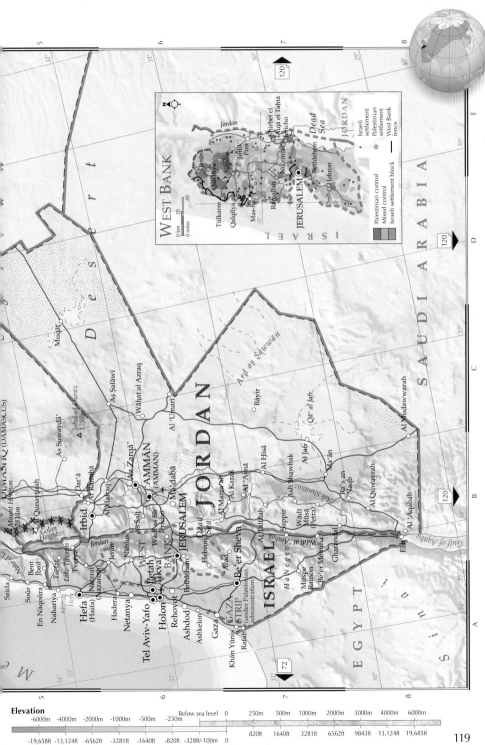

WEST BANK

Jordan

Jenín
Qabátiya
Níablus
Jiftlik
Khirbet el Aujá et Tahtá
Jericho
Dead Sea
JORDAN
Tulkarm
Qalqílya
Mas-ha
Ramalláh
Kúlema
Bethlehem
JERUSALEM
Hebron

ISRAEL

0 km   20
0 miles   20

Israeli settlement
Palestinian settlement
West Bank fence

Palestinian control
Mixed control
Israeli settlement block

120

72

120

120

120

JORDAN

SAUDI ARABIA

Muqát

D e s e r t

Ard aş Shuwān

As Şafāwī
Wāhat Azraq
Jabal ad Durūz
1798m
Al 'Uharí
Báyir
Qár al Jafr
Al Mudawwarah

DIMASHQ (DAMASCUS)

As Suwaydā'
Dar'ā
Ar Ramthā
Az Zarqā'
AMMĀN (AMMAN)
Mádabá
Al 'Uharí
Al Hisá
Al Jafr
Al Quwayrah
Al 'Aqabah
Elat

Mount Hermon
2814m
Qunaytirah
Irbid
Al Mafraq
As Salt
Wadí as Sír
Jericho
Al Mazra'ah
Al Karak
At 'Ayná
Ash Shawbak
Wadí Mūsá (Petra)
Ra's an Naqb

Golan Heights
Jordan
Jenín
Náblus
JERUSALEM
Dead Sea
Hebron
Bethlehem
Be'er Sheva
Afal
Al Qatrāna
Al Hisá
Sappir
Gharandal

Saïda
Soûr
Bent Jbaïl
Naqoûra
Tiberias
Lake Tiberias
Tiverya
Nazerat (Nazareth)
WEST BANK
Tel Aviv-Yafo
Holon
Rehovot
Ashdod
Ashkelon
Gaza
Khān Yūnis
Rafah
GAZA STRIP
(under Palestinian administration)
ISRAEL
Ha Negev
Mitspe Ramon
Be'er Menuha

En Naqoûra
Nahariya
Hefa (Haifa)
Hadera
Netanya
Petah Tikva

EGYPT

Sinai

Gulf of Aqaba

M e d i t e r r a n e a n   S e a

Elevation

-6000m	-4000m	-2000m	-1000m	-500m	-250m	Below sea level 0	250m	500m	1000m	2000m	3000m	4000m	6000m

-19,658ft	-13,124ft	-6562ft	-3281ft	-1640ft	-820ft	-328ft/-100m	0	820ft	1640ft	3281ft	6562ft	9843ft	13,124ft	19,685ft

119

The Middle East

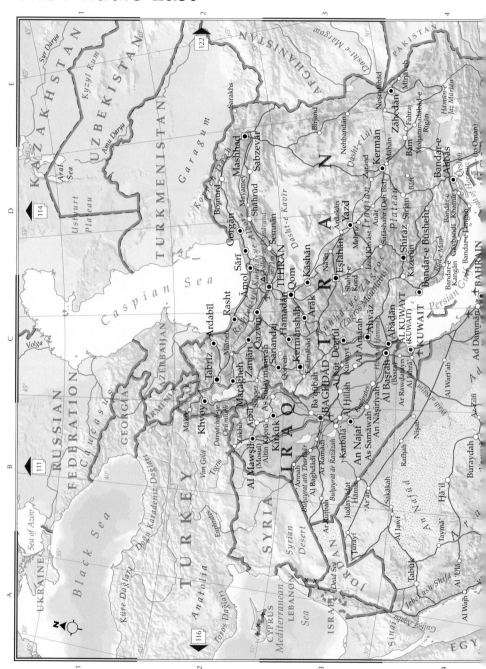

Population

- ● National capital
- ○ below 50,000
- ◎ 50,000 to 100,000
- ◉ 100,000 to 500,000
- ■ above 500,000

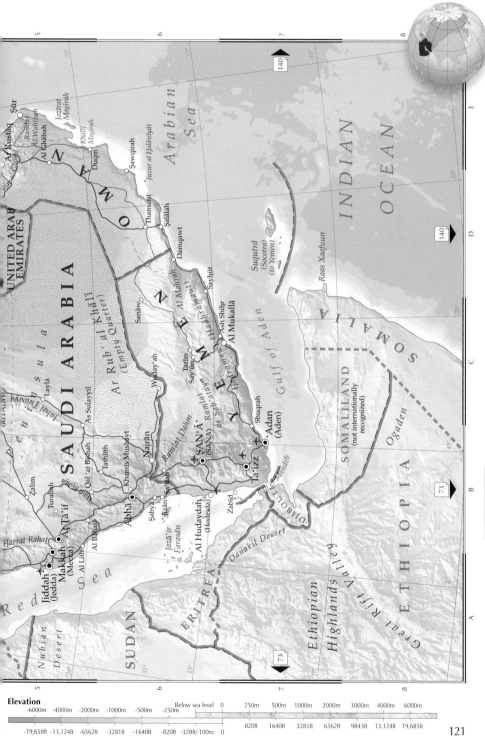

Elevation

-6000m	-4000m	-2000m	-1000m	-500m	-250m	Below sea level 0	250m	500m	1000m	2000m	3000m	4000m	6000m

| -19,658ft | -13,124ft | -6562ft | -3281ft | -1640ft | -820ft | -328ft/-100m | 0 | 820ft | 1640ft | 3281ft | 6562ft | 9843ft | 13,124ft | 19,685ft |

Central Asia

RUSSIAN
FEDERATION

Caspian

Sea

AZERBAIJAN

GEORGIA

50°

45°

55°

60°

114

Ustyurt

Plateau

Aral
Sea

Mo'ynoq

Chimboy

Taxtako'pir

Köneürgenç Nukus
Taxiatosh
Gurbansoltan Eje Gubadag

Daşoguz Urganch

Xiva To'rtko'l

Uchquduq

UZBEI

Zarafs

Garabogaz
Aylagy

Ushaqur Platosy

Türkmenbaşy

Türkmenbaşy
Aylagy
Hazar

Balkanabat

Türkmen
Aylagy

120

Bereket

Derweze

Üngüz Gazojak Lebap

Angyrsyndaky *Garagum*

Amu Darya

Zarafs

G'ijd

Ga

TURKMENISTAN

Köpetdag Serdar
Magtymguly Baharly

Esenguly

Gökdepe
Gora Chapan ▲
2889m

Garagum Gelen

Garagum

Seýdi
Galkynys

Türkmenabat

Sayat

Buxc

Abadan
AŞGABAT

Tejen Mary
Kaka Bayramaly
Murgap

Sarahs

Garagum
Garabil
Belentligi

U

And

Reshteh-ye Kuhhā-ye Alborz

35°

40°

Kuhhā-ye Zāgros

I R A N

Iranian

Plateau

30°

50°

55°

60°

0°

120

120

Balā Morghāb Meyr

Serhetabat
Towraghoudī

Selseleh-ye Safīd Kūh

Ghūrīān Herāt

AFGHA

Shīndand

Farāh Rūd

Farāh Delārām

Dasht-e Khāsh

Hāmūn-e
Şāberī

Lashkar Gāh
Chakhānsūr
Zaranj

Deh Shū

Dasht-e Mārgow

Kūchnay
Darweys

Daryā-ye Helmand

Ge

Rīg

Chāgai Hills

0 km   200

0 miles   200

Population ● National capital

○ below 50,000 ○ 50,000 to 100,000 ◉ 100,000 to 500,000 ◼ above 500,000

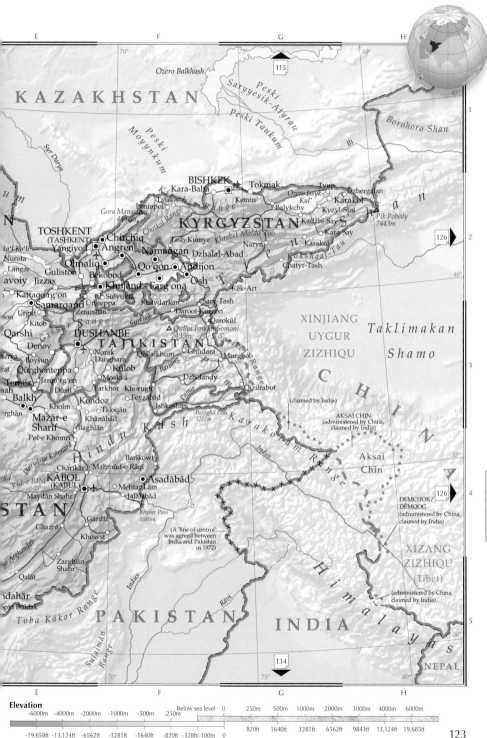

KAZAKHSTAN

Ozero Balkhash

Peski Saryyesik-Atyrau

Peski Taukum

Ili

Borohoro Shan

Peski Moyynkum

Syr Darya

BISHKEK
Kara-Balta • Tokmak
Lalas Kemin *Ozero Issyk Kul'* Dzhergalan
Leninpol Balykchy Kyzyl-Suu Karakol
Gora Manas Kemin *Kul'* Kyzyl-Suu
4488m

KYRGYZSTAN
Kadzhi-Say Karakol
Pik Pobedy
7443m

TOSHKENT
(TASHKENT) • Chirchiq
Yangiyo'l Angren Tash-Kumyr *Khrebet Moldo-Too* Naryn *Kara-Say*
ko'l Ko'li Namangan Naryn Karakol
Nurota *Chatkal Range* Dzhalal-Abad *Kokshaal-Tau*
Langar Guliston Olmaliq Qo'qon Andijon Chatyr-Tash
avoiy Jizzax Bekobod Farg'ona Osh
Kattaqo'rg'on Khujand Sary-Tash
Urteppa Sulyukta Kek-Art
Samarqand Urteppa Khaydarkan
son Zeravshan Daroot-Korgon
Urgut *Range* Qarokül
Qarshi Kitob *Gissar* *Surkhob* *Qullai Ismoili Somoni*
Denov DUSHANBE *7495m*

TAJIKISTAN

XINJIANG
UYGUR
ZIZHIQU

Taklimakan

Shamo

Boysun Norak
terʻya Danghara Qalaikhum Ghúdara
rat Qürghonteppa Kúlob Murghob
Termiz Jargoʻrgʻon Moskva *Bartang*
ah Dusti Farkhor Khorugh Dzhelandy
Balkh Kondoz Feyzábád Qizilrabot
rghān Kholm Tálogán Ishkoshim *Pamir*
Mazār-e Khānābād *Baroghil Pass*
Sharíf Baghlān *3777m*
Pol-e Khomri

CHINA

(claimed by India)

AKSAI CHIN
(administered by China,
claimed by India)

Hindu Kush
Barikowt
Karakoram Range

Aksai
Chin

Daryā-ye Kahmard
Charikar Mahmūd-e Rāqi
KĀBOL Mehtar Lām
(KABUL) Asadābād
Rūh-e Bābā Maydān Shahr Jalālābād
Khyber Pass
1080m

DEMCHOK/
DEMQOG
(administered by China,
claimed by India)

STAN
Ghaznī Gardíz
Khowst
(A 'line of control'
was agreed between
India and Pakistan
in 1972)

XIZANG
ZIZHIQU
(Tibet)

(administered by China,
claimed by India)

Zarghûn
Shahr Qalāt
ye Arghandāb *Indus*

Rāgi

adahār
opin Baldak
Toba Kākar Range

PAKISTAN

INDIA

Himalayas

Suliman Range

NEPAL

Elevation

-6000m	-4000m	-2000m	-1000m	-500m	-250m	Below sea level 0	250m	500m	1000m	2000m	3000m	4000m	6000m
-19,658ft	-13,124ft	-6562ft	-3281ft	-1640ft	-820ft -328ft/-100m	0	820ft	1640ft	3281ft	6562ft	9843ft	13,124ft	19,685ft

South & East Asia

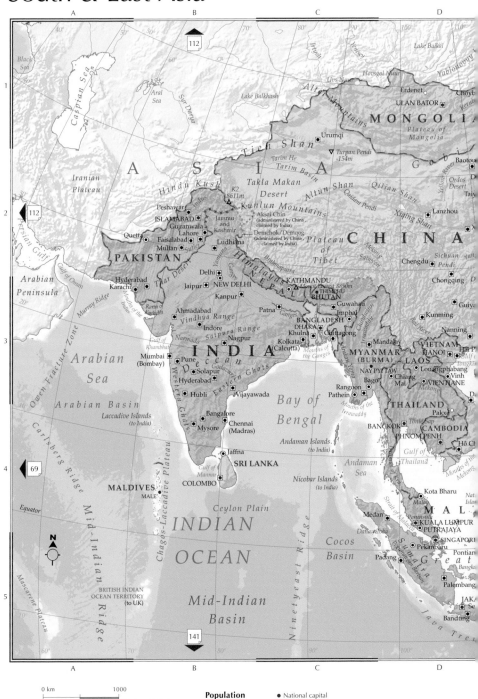

A   B   C   D

112

Black Sea

Caspian Sea

Aral Sea

Sır Darya

Lake Balkhash

40°

50°

60°

70°

80°

90°

100°

110°

Lake Baikal

Hovsgol Nuur

Erdenet

Choyr

ULAN BATOR

MONGOLIA

Plateau of Mongolia

Baotou

Urumqi

Altai Mountains

Irtysh

Yenisey

Uvs Nuur

Yablonovy

112

A S I A

Iranian Plateau

Hindu Kush

Tien Shan

Tarim He

Tarim Basin

Turpan Pendi -154m

G o b i

Takla Makan Desert

Altun Shan

Qilian Shan

Ordos Desert

Tai

Kunlun Mountains

Qaidam Pendi

Xiqing Shan

Lanzhou

Yellow River

K2 8611m

Peshawar

Aksai Chin (administered by China, claimed by India)

Chengdu

Sichuan Pendi

ISLAMABAD

Jammu and Kashmir

Demchok/Demqog (administered by China, claimed by India)

Plateau of Tibet

C H I N A

Persian Gulf

Gulf of Oman

Quetta

Gujranwala
Lahore

Faisalabad

Multan

Sutlej

Indus

Ludhiana

Himalayas

Brahmaputra

Mekong

Salween

Chongqing

PAKISTAN

Thar Desert

Delhi

Ganges

KATHMANDU

Mount Everest 8850m

Guwahati

Guiya

Arabian Peninsula

Mouths of the Indus

Hyderabad

Karachi

Rann of Kachchh

Jaipur

NEW DELHI

NEPAL

THIMPHU

BHUTAN

Imphal

Kunming

20°

Ahmadabad

Vindhya Range

Kanpur

Patna

Ganges

BANGLADESH

DHAKA

Chittagong

Nanning

Gulf of Khambhat

Narmada

Saipura Range

Indore

Nagpur

Khulna

Kolkata (Calcutta)

Mandalay

VIETNAM

Har!

Arabian Sea

Mumbai (Bombay)

Pune

Solapur

Godavari

I N D I A

D e c c a n

Mouths of the Ganges

MYANMAR (BURMA)

HANOI

LAOS

tongkin

Owen Fracture Zone

Hyderabad

Eastern Ghats

Yangtze

NAY PYI TAW

Louangphabang

Vinh

Western Ghats

Rangoon

Bago

Chiang Mai

VIENTIANE

Arabian Basin

Hubli

Vijayawada

Bay of Bengal

Pathein

Mouths of the Irrawaddy

THAILAND

D

Laccadive Islands (to India)

Bangalore

Mysore

Chennai (Madras)

BANGKOK

Tonle Sap

CAMBODIA

Pakxe

Carlsberg Ridge

Andaman Islands (to India)

PHNOM PENH

Gulf of

Hô Ch

Jaffna

SRI LANKA

Andaman Sea

Gulf of Thailand

Mouths of the Mekong

MALDIVES

Gulf of Mannar

COLOMBO

Nicobar Islands (to India)

Kota Bharu

Nat

Equator

MALE

Ceylon Plain

Medan

Malay Peninsula

Strait of Malacca

M A L

KUALA LUMPUR

PUTRAJAYA

Chagos-Laccadive Plateau

Mid-Indian Ridge

INDIAN

Cocos Basin

Dumai

SINGAPORE

Pekanbaru

Pontian

Sumatra

Sunda

G r e a t

OCEAN

Padang

Bangka

Mascarene Plateau

N

BRITISH INDIAN OCEAN TERRITORY (to UK)

Mid-Indian Basin

Ninetyeast Ridge

Palembang

JAK

Se

Java

Bandung

Java Tren

141

A   B   C   D

69

Population   • National capital

0 km 1000	
0 miles 1000	

o below 50,000   o 50,000 to 100,000   ◉ 100,000 to 500,000   ■ above 500,000

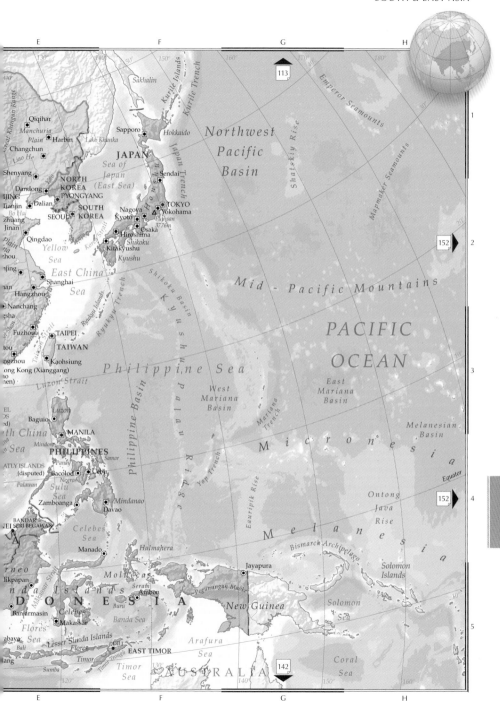

Western China & Mongolia

A   B   C   D

114

RUSSIAN FE

Yenisey

50°

*Kulunda
Steppe*

*Höösgöl
Nuur*

KAZAKHSTAN

Kazakhskiy

Uvs Nuur

Ulaangom

Mö

*Ozero
Zaysan*

Ölgiy

*Hyargas
Nuur*

Melkosopochnik

*Ozero
Balkhash*

Altay

Har-Us Nuur

Har Nuur

Tsetserl

123

45°

Hovd

MON

*Ulungur
Hu*

Altay

Bayanhongor

70°

Karamay

*Gurbantünggüt
Shamo*

△ *Aj Bogd Uul
3802m*

Borohoro Shan

Kuytun

Shamo

Fukang

Jimsar

Atas Bogd
△ 2695m

Yining

Shihezi

Ürümqi

Qitai

Turpan

Hami

G

KYRGYZSTAN

Ozero Issyk-Kul'

Tien Shan

Bosten Hu

*Turpan
Pendi*

Xingxingxia

Dalian

*Tomür Feng
7443m*

Korla

Kuruktag

GH

Kashi

Tarim He

Tarim Basin

Lop Nur

GANSU

Yengisar

XINJIANG UYGUR

Qilian Shan

Shache

ZIZHIQU

Ruoqiang

TAJIKISTAN

Yecheng

Pishan

Taklimakan

Altun Shan

Danghe Nanshan

Qinghai

Moyu

Shamo

Qaidam Pendi

K2
△ 8611m

Hotan

Qira

Kunlun Shan

Golmud

Dulan

Karakoram Range

AKSAI
CHIN

AKSAICHIN
(administered by
China, claimed
by India)

Burhan Budai Shan

134

JAMMU
AND
KASHMIR

Indus

Qingzang Gaoyuan

Yongtian He

QINGHAI

C

H

Bayan Har Sh

DEMCHOK/DÊMQOG
(administered by China,
claimed by India)

Rutog

(Plateau of Tibet)

Yushu

30°

Gar Xincun

Zanda

XIZANG

Tanggula Shan

Mekong

Amdo

Qamdo

Salween

Jinsha Jiang

ZIZHIQU

Gozhê

Siling Co

*Tangra
Yumco*

*Gyaring
Co*

Nam Co

Nagqu

(Tibet)

Ngangzê
Co

Damxung

Nyainqentanglha Shan

Lhaze

Xigazê

Maizhokunggar

Lhasa

ARUNACHAL
PRADESH
(claimed by China)

INDIA

Yamuna

Ganges

△ *Mount Everest
8850m*

Gyangzê

Gonggar

H i m a l a y a s

NEPAL

BHUTAN

INDIA

MYANMAR
(BURMA)

135

25°

A   B   C   D

| 0 km | | 400 |
| 0 miles | | 400 |

Population

○ below 50,000
◎ 50,000 to 100,000
● National capital
○ Internal administrative capital
◉ 100,000 to 500,000
■ above 500,000

RUSS. FED.

E F G H

55° 110° 115° 120° 125° 130° 50° 135°

o Baykal

R A T I O N

Shilka

Ergun Jagdaqi

Hulun Buir
(Hailar)

Onon

Ergun (Ergun He)

HEILONGJIANG

Amur (Heilong Jiang)

45°

Manzhouli

Sühbaatar

Hulun
Nur

Lake
Khanka

135°

Darhan

Onon Gol

Choybalsan

enet

ULAANBAATAR
(ULAN BATOR)

Menengiyn
Tal

JILIN

128

2

Dzuunmod

Ondörhaan

Hulingol

Kerulen

Baruun-Urt

40°

L I A

Tongliao

Xilinhot

Saynshand

Erenhot

Liao He

LIAONING

Chifeng
(Ulanhad)

NORTH
KOREA

Korea
Bay

Sea of
Japan
(East Sea)

Dalandzadgad

Nuruu

Ulan Qab (Jining)

BEIJING

Liaodong Wan

35°

SOUTH
KOREA

130°

Hohhot

Huang He
(Yellow River)

Baotou

TIANJIN

Bo Hai

JAPAN

Wuhai
(Haibowan)

Mu Us
Shadi

Great Wall of China

HEBEI

Korea
Bay

amo

NINGXIA

SHANXI

SHANDONG

Yellow
Sea

N A

GANSU

SHAANXI

Han Shui

HENAN

Huang He (Yellow River)

JIANGSU

ANHUI

SHANGHAI SHI

East

30° 4

129

HUAN

Chang Jiang (Yangtze)

HUBEI

ZHEJIANG

China

CHONGQING

JIANGXI

Sea

Nansei-shotō
(to Japan)

YUNNAN

HUNAN

FUJIAN

25°

GUIZHOU

TAIWAN

Tropic of Cancer

105° 110° 115° 120°

129

E F G H

Elevation

| Below sea level | 0 | 250m | 500m | 1000m | 2000m | 3000m | 4000m | 6000m |

-6000m -4000m -2000m -1000m -500m -250m

820ft 1640ft 3281ft 6562ft 9843ft 13,124ft 19,685ft

-19,658ft -13,124ft -6562ft -3281ft -1640ft -820ft -328ft/-100m 0

Eastern China & Korea

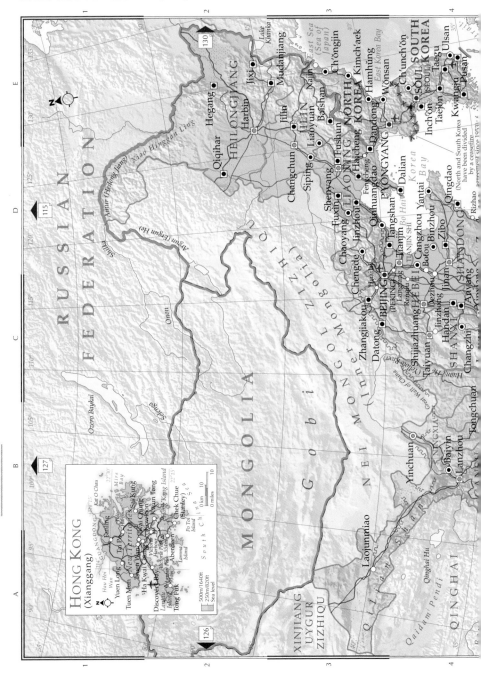

SEOUL SOUTH KOREA (SEOUL) KOREA

(North and South Korea
have been divided
by a ceasefire
agreement since 1953)

Chongjin
Najin
Kimch'aek
Hamhung
Wonsan
Ch'unch'on
Inch'on
Taejon
Kwangju
Taegu
Pusan
Ulsan

PYONGYANG
NORTH KOREA
Sinuiju
Dandong
Haicheng
Fengcheng

HEILONGJIANG
Harbin
Hegang
Jixi
Mudanjiang
Qiqihar
Jiamusi

Changchun
JILIN
Jilin
Liaoyuan
Baishan
Fushun
Siping
Shenyang
LIAONING
Fuxin
Chaoyang
Jinzhou
Qinhuangdao
Benxi

Dalian
Yantai
Qingdao
Rizhao
SHANDONG

Beizhen
Tangshan
TIANJIN SHI
Tianjin
Cangzhou
Botou
Binzhou
Zibo
Jinan
Dezhou
Anyang

Chengde
Huailai
Zhangjiakou
Datong
BEIJING (PEKING)
HEBEI
Baoding
Langfang
Shijiazhuang
Taiyuan
SHANXI
Handan
Changzhi

Yinchuan
Baiyin
Lanzhou
NINGXIA
GANSU

Laojunmiao
Qinghai Hu
QINGHAI
Qaidam Pendi

XINJIANG
UYGUR
ZIZHIQU

RUSSIAN FEDERATION

MONGOLIA

NEI MONGGOL (Inner Mongolia)
BO HAI ZIZHIQU

Gobi

Ozero Baykal
Selenga
Onon
Shilka
Amur (Heilong Jiang)
Argun (Ergun He)
Xiao Hinggan Ling

East Sea
(Sea of Japan)
Lake Khanka
East Korea Bay
Korea Bay
Bo Hai
Korea Strait
Yellow Sea

Great Wall of China
Huang He (Yellow River)

Qilian Shan
Qin Ling

HONG KONG (Xianggang)

Mirs Bay
Kat O Chau
GUANGDONG
Sha Tau Kok
Sheung Shui
Fanling
Sai Kung
Tai Po
Kwun Tong
Kowloon
Tsuen Wan
Victoria Harbour
Chek Chue (Stanley)
Po Toi Island
South China Sea
Hau Hoi Wan
Tuen Mun
Yuen Long
Ha Kwai Chung
Discovery Bay
Lantau Island
Aberdeen
Tong Fuk
Lamma Island

500m/1640ft
250m/820ft
Sea level

0 km 10
0 miles 10

0 km 400
0 miles 400

Population

● National capital
◉ Internal administrative capital
○ below 50,000
◎ 50,000 to 100,000
◉ 100,000 to 500,000
■ above 500,000

East China Sea

Okinawa (part of Japan)

Nansen-shoto (part of Japan)

Tropic of Cancer

PACIFIC OCEAN

TAIWAN

Chilung
TAIPEI
Taichung
Chiai
Tainan
Kaohsiung

(China and Taiwan claim all of each other's territory)

Taiwan Strait

Luzon Strait

PHILIPPINES

152

139

136

South China Sea

PARACEL ISLANDS
(disputed by China, Taiwan and Vietnam)
Amphitrite Group
Crescent Group
Triton Island

SPRATLY ISLANDS
(disputed by China, Malaysia, Philippines, Taiwan and Vietnam)
Flat Island
Nanshan Island
Thitu Island
Loaita Island
Namyit Island
Len Dao
Spratly Island

VIETNAM

CAMBODIA

THAILAND

LAOS

Gulf of Tongking

Gulf of Thailand

MYANMAR (BURMA)

Shanghai
Suzhou
Wuxi
Jiaxing
Ningbo
Hangzhou
Jinhua
Wenzhou
ZHEJIANG
Shangrao
Fuzhou
Nanping
Yong'an
Quanzhou
Xiamen
FUJIAN
Zhangzhou
Shantou
Hong Kong
Dongguan
Macao (Xianggang)
(Aomen)

Bengbu
ANHUI
Anqing
Huangshi
Jingdezhen

Xinyang
HUBEI
Yichang
Wuhan

Yueyang
Changsha
Xiangtan
Hengyang
HUNAN
Yongzhou

Nanchang
JIANGXI
Ji'an
Ganzhou
Longyan

Lichuan
Chongqing
CHONGQING SHI

Zunyi
GUIZHOU
Guiyang
Anshun

Guilin
GUANGXI ZHUANGZU
Liuzhou
Guangzhou
GUANGDONG
Zhaoqing
Jiangmen
Maoming
Zhanjiang
Haikou
Beihai
Qinzhou
Nanning
Yulin
Gejiu

Hechi
Hongzhou

Miaoyang
Sichuan Pendi
Chengdu
Leshan
Zigong
Neijiang
Yibin

Dazhou
Dadu He

Kunming
YUNNAN
Dali
Baoshan

Xichang

Jinsha Jiang

Min Jiang
Tuo Jiang

Yangtze

Hainan Dao
HAINAN
Sanya
Xuwen
Dongfang
Danzhou

Wuliang Shan

Mekong
Salween
Jinghong

Red River

Hengduan Shan

XIZANG ZIZHIQU (TIBET)

INDIA

CHINA

SICHUAN

Elevation
-6000m -4000m -2000m -1000m -500m Below sea level 0 250m 500m 1000m 2000m 3000m 4000m 6000m
-250m
-19,658ft -13,124ft -6562ft -3281ft -1640ft -820ft -328ft/-100m 0 820ft 1640ft 3281ft 6562ft 9843ft 13,124ft 19,685ft

129

Japan

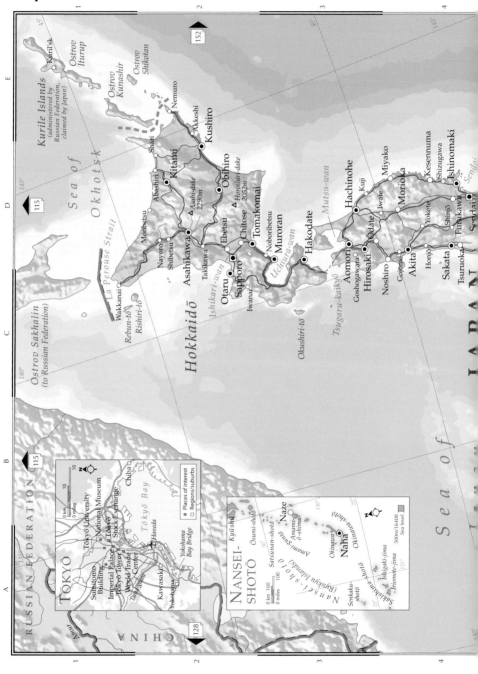

Kurile Islands
(administered by
Russian Federation,
claimed by Japan)

Kuril'sk
Ostrov
Iturup

Ostrov
Shikotan

Ostrov
Kunashir

Nemuro

Akkeshi

Kushiro

Shari

Kitami

Abashiri

Monbetsu

Asahi-dake
2290m

Horoshiri-dake
2052m

Obihiro

Tomakomai

Chitose

Ebetsu

Nayoro

Shibetsu

Asahikawa

Takikawa

Otaru

Sapporo

Noboribetsu

Muroran

Hakodate

Iwanai

Okushiri-tō

Hokkaidō

Ishikari-wan

Uchiura-wan

Tsugaru-kaikyō

Aomori

Goshogawara

Hirosaki

Noshiro

Gojome

Akita

Honjō

Sakata

Tsuruoka

Odate

Kuji

Iwate

Yokote

Shinjō

Funakawa

Hachinohe

Morioka

Miyako

Sendai

Kesennuma

Shizugawa

Ishinomaki

Sendai

Mutsu-wan

Sea of
Okhotsk

La Perouse Strait

Wakkanai

Rebun-tō

Rishiri-tō

Ostrov Sakhalin
(to Russian Federation)

RUSSIAN FEDERATION

Amur

CHINA

Sea of

TŌKYŌ inset

Chiba

Tōkyō Bay

Tokyo University

National Museum

Tokyo
Stock Exchange

Sumitomo
Building

Imperial Palace

Tokyo Tower

World Trade
Center

Tokyo Station

Haneda

Yokohama
Bay Bridge

Kawasaki

Yokohama

TŌKYŌ

■ Places of interest
□ Regions/suburbs

NANSEI-SHOTŌ inset

Ōsumi-shotō

Satsunan-shotō

Kyūshū

Naze

Amami-guntō

Amami-
ō-shima

Okinawa

Naha

Okinawa-shotō

Ishigaki-jima

Iriomote-jima

Sakishima-shotō

Senkaku-
shotō

Nansei-shotō
(Ryūkyū Islands)

NANSEI-
SHOTŌ

500m/1640ft

Sea level

0 km 200

0 miles 200

Population ● National capital

○ below 50,000 ○ 50,000 to 100,000 ◉ 100,000 to 500,000 ■ above 500,000

Honshū

Hitachi
Utsunomiya
Mito
Ōyama
Choshi
Chiba
Kawagoe
Yokohama
Kawasaki
TOKYO
Kōfu
Maebashi
Nagano
Toyama
Matsumoto
Joetsu
Itoigawa
Takaoka
Kanazawa
Komatsu
Fukui
Tsuruga
Nakatsugawa
Gifu
Ōgaki
Nagoya
Kyōto
Ōsaka
Kōbe
Himeji
Okayama
Kurashiki
Tottori
Yonago
Matsue
Gōtsu
Hamada
Masuda
Hiroshima
Iwakuni
Hōfu
Ube
Yamaguchi
Shimonoseki
Kitakyūshū
Fukuoka
Saga
Sasebo
Nagasaki
Kumamoto
Ōmuta
Kurume
Ōita
Nobeoka
Miyazaki
Miyakonojō
Sendai
Kagoshima

TOKYO
Kawasaki
Yokohama
Ōyama
Hamamatsu
Shizuoka
Toyota
Okazaki
Tsu
Ise
Owase
Shingū
Wakayama
Tanabe
Gobō

Fuji-san
3776m

Bōsō-hantō
Sagami-nada
Kashima-nada
Kazusa-uri
Sagami-wan
O-shima
Nii-jima
Kōzu-shima
Miyake-jima
Mikura-jima
Hachijō-jima

Izu-shotō

Izu-hantō

Ise-wan

Kii-suidō

Shikoku
Tokushima
Kōchi
Mihama
Matsuyama
Nakamura
Sukumo

Tosa-wan

Kyūshū
Yatsushiro
Amakusa-nada
Koshikijima-rettō
Sendai
Kagoshima
Kagoshima-wan
Tanega-shima
Yaku-shima
Shibushi-wan
Ōsumi-shotō

Bungo-suidō
Iyo-nada
Suō-nada
Kure
Mihara
Matsuyama

Shinano-gawa
Toyama-wan
Wakasa-wan
Noto-hantō

Oki-shotō
Dōgo
Dōzen

Liancourt Rocks
(under South
Korean control)

SOUTH
KOREA

Korea Strait

Tsushima

Iki
Kō-saki
Gotō-rettō

PACIFIC

OCEAN

East

China Sea

152
152
152
152
128

Elevation

					Below sea level	0							
-6000m	-4000m	-2000m	-1000m	-500m	-250m		250m	500m	1000m	2000m	3000m	4000m	6000m
-19,658ft	-13,124ft	-6562ft	-3281ft	-1640ft	-820ft	-328ft/-100m	0	820ft	1640ft	3281ft	6562ft	9843ft	13,124ft	19,685ft

131

Southern India & Sri Lanka

Kalyān
Mumbai (Bombay)
134
Pune
Ahmadnagar
Bārāmati
Nizāmābād
Nānded
Karimnagar
Jagdalp

INDIA

Vizianagaram
Solāpur
Sāngli
Secunderābād
Visākhapa
Kolhāpur
Gulbarga
Hyderābād
Rājahmu
Kāki
Belgaum
Rāichūr
Krishna
Vijayawāda
Machilīpatr
Panaji
Gadag
Kurnool
Andhra
Chirāla
Hubli
Nandyal
Pradesh
Ongole
Tungabhadra
Reservoir
Tādpatri
Kāvali
Dāvangere
Anantapur
Nellore
Shimoga
Cuddapah
Udupi
Bhadrāvati
Tumkūr
Chennai
Mangalore
Bangalore
Vellore
(Madras)
Kāsaragod
Mandya
Kānchīpuram
Kannur/Cannanore
Krishnagiri
Tiruppattūr
Amīndīvi
Islands
Mysore
Salem
Pondicherry
Kozhikode/Calicut
Erode
Neyveli
Kavaratti
Island
Coimbatore
Thrissur/Trichūr
Tiruchchirāppalli
Kalpeni
Island
Ernākulam
Dindigul
Madurai
Kochi/Cochin
Jaffna
Alappuzha/Alleppey
Rājapālaiyam
Mannar
Kollam/Quilon
Vavuniya
Trincomalee
Minicoy Island
Thiruvananthapuram/
Trivandrum
Tuticorin
Puttalam
Anuradhapura
Nāgercoil
Gulf of
Mannar
Batticalo
Negombo
Matale
Kandy
COLOMBO
Sri Jayewardenap
Kalutara
Ratnapura
K
Galle
Matara

Arabian
Sea

121

Lakshadweep
(Laccadive Islands)
(to India)

Nine Degree
Channel

Eight Degree Channel

Ihavandhippolhu
Atoll

MALDIVES

Faadhippolhu
Atoll

Horsburgh
Atoll

73

Ari Atoll

Male'Atoll
MALE'

Felidhu Atoll

Mulakatholhu

Kolhumadulu

Hadhdhunmathi Atoll

SRI LANI

North Huvadhu Atoll

Equator

South Huvadhu
Atoll

INDIAN

Gan
140

Addu Atoll

0 km   300
0 miles   300

Population   ● National capital

○ below 50,000   ○ 50,000 to 100,000   ◉ 100,000 to 500,000   ◼ above 500,000

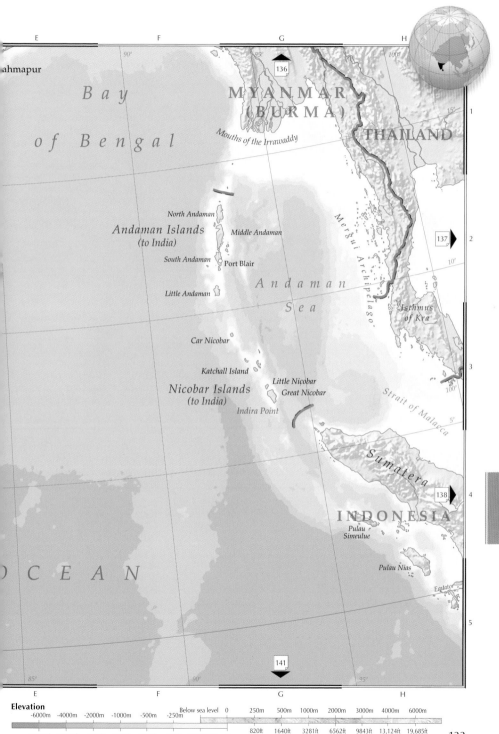

ahmapur

B a y

of B e n g a l

M Y A N M A R
(B U R M A)

THAILAND

Mouths of the Irrawaddy

North Andaman

Andaman Islands
(to India)

Middle Andaman

South Andaman   Port Blair

A n d a m a n

S e a

Little Andaman

M e r g u i   A r c h i p e l a g o

*Isthmus
of Kra*

Car Nicobar

Katchall Island

Nicobar Islands
(to India)

Little Nicobar
Great Nicobar

Indira Point

Strait of Malacca

S u m a t e r a

I N D O N E S I A

Pulau
Simeulue

O C E A N

Pulau Nias

Equator

Elevation

-6000m	-4000m	-2000m	-1000m	-500m	Below sea level	0	250m	500m	1000m	2000m	3000m	4000m	6000m
-19,658ft	-13,124ft	-6562ft	-3281ft	-1640ft	-820ft -328ft/-100m	0	820ft	1640ft	3281ft	6562ft	9843ft	13,124ft	19,685ft

Northern India, Pakistan & Bangladesh

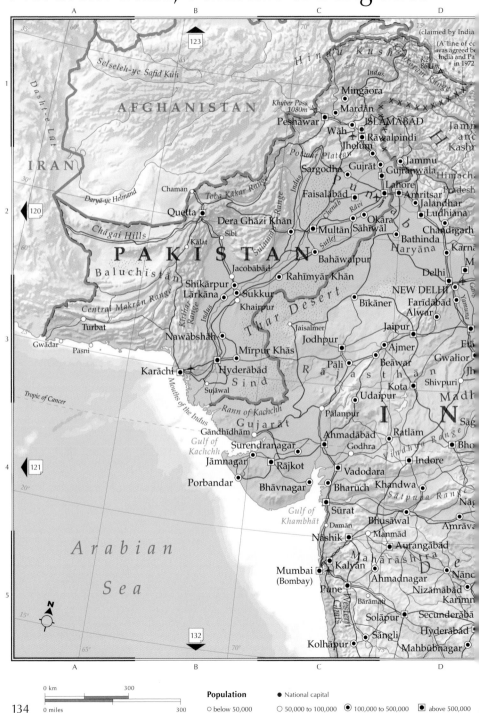

A   B   C   D

123

(claimed by India
(A line of co
was agreed be
India and Pa
K2 in 1972
8611m

Hindu Kush

Selseleh-ye Safid Kūh

Indus

AFGHANISTAN

Khyber Pass
1080m

Mingāora

Mardān

Peshāwar

ISLĀMĀBĀD

Wāh

Rāwalpindi

Jhelum

IRAN

Jammu
and
Kashm

Potwar Plateau

Jammu

Sargodha

Gujrāt

Gujrānwāla

*Himach.
Pradesh*

Daryā-ye Helmand

Chaman

Toba Kākar Range

Faisalābād

Lahore

Amritsar

Jalandhar

Ludhiāna

120

Quetta

Dera Ghāzī Khān

Okāra

Chandīgarh

Chāgai Hills

Kālat

Sibi

Multān

Sāhīwāl

Bathinda

Haryāna

Karna

PAKISTAN

Bahāwalpur

Delhi

M

Baluchistān

Jacobābād

Rahīmyār Khān

NEW DELHI

Gan

Central Makrān Range

Kirthar Range

Shikārpur

Lārkāna

Sukkur

Bīkāner

Farīdābād

Alwar

Yamuna

Khairpur

Thar Desert

Turbat

Jaisalmer

Jaipur

Gwādar

Pasni

Nawābshāh

Jodhpur

Ajmer

Eta

Mīrpur Khās

Pāli

Beāwar

Gwalior

Jh

Karāchi

Hyderābād

Sind

Rajasthān

Kota

Shivpuri

Sujāwal

Udaipur

Mad

Rann of Kachchh

Pālanpur

IN

Gujarāt

Gāndhīdhām

*Gulf of
Kachchh*

Surendranagar

Ahmadābād

Ratlām

Sāg

Godhra

Vindhya Range

Bho

121

Jāmnagar

Rājkot

Vadodara

Indore

Porbandar

Bhāvnagar

Bhārūch

Khandwa

Satpura Range

Nāg

*Gulf of
Khambhāt*

Sūrat

Damān

Bhusāwal

Amrāva

Nāshik

Manmād

Aurangābād

Arabian

Mahārāshtra

Mumbai
(Bombay)

Kalyān

De

Nānc

Ahmadnagar

Sea

Pune

Nizāmābād

Karīmn

Bārāmati

N

Solāpur

Secunderāba

132

Sāngli

Hyderābād

Kolhāpur

Mahbūbnagar

A   B   C   D

0 km   300

Population

● National capital

134

0 miles   300

○ below 50,000   ○ 50,000 to 100,000   ◉ 100,000 to 500,000   ◼ above 500,000

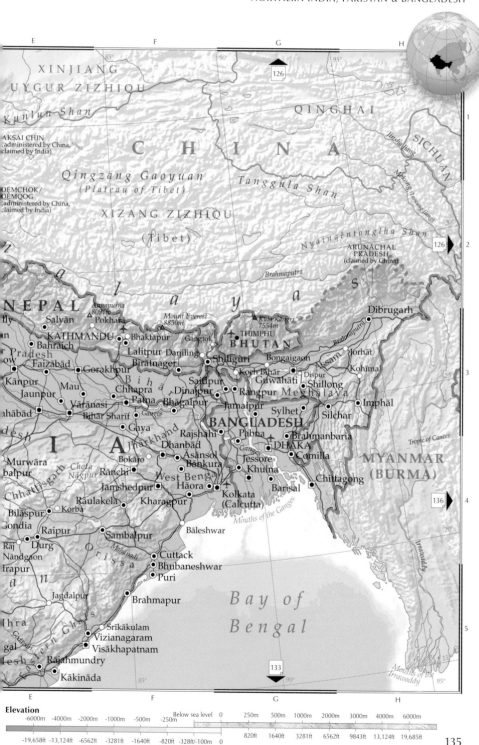

E   F   G   H

126

85°   90°   95°

35°

XINJIANG

UYGUR ZIZHIQU

Kunlun Shan

QINGHAI

Jinshajiang

SICHUAN

AKSAI CHIN
(administered by China,
claimed by India)

C H I N A

Qingzang Gaoyuan
(Plateau of Tibet)

Tanggula Shan

Mekong (Lancang Jiang)

DEMCHOK/
DEMQOG
(administered by China,
claimed by India)

XIZANG ZIZHIQU

(Tibet)

Nyainqêntanglha Shan

30°

126

Brahmaputra

**ARUNACHAL
PRADESH**
(claimed by China)

Dibrugarh

Annapurna
8091m △
△ Mount Everest
8850m
▲ Kula Kangri
7554m

NEPAL

Salyān ● Pokhara

●Bahraich   ●KATHMANDU   ●Bhaktapur

Darjiling   **THIMPHU**

BHUTAN

Assam

Brahmaputra

Jorhat

●Faizābād   ●Gorakhpur   Lalitpur

Biratnagar   Shiliguri   Bongaigaon   Kohima

Koch Bihar   Guwahati   Dispur●   Shillong

25°

Pradesh

Kānpur   Mau   Chhapra   Saidpur

Jaunpur   ●Yārānasi   ●Patna   Dinajpur   Rangpur   **Meghalaya**   Imphāl

Bhagalpur   Jamalpur   Sylhet   Silchar

ahābād   ●Bihar Sharif   *Ganges*

Gaya   Rajshahi   Pabna   **DHAKA**   Brahmanbaria

Jharkhand

Dhanbād   Āsansol   *Ganges*   Comilla

Murwāra   Bokāro   Jessore

balpur   *Chota*   Rānchī   **West Bengal**   Khulna

Nāgpur   Bānkura   Chittagong

**MYANMAR
(BURMA)**

Jamshedpur   Hāora   Barisal

Rāulakela   Kharagpur   Kolkata
(Calcutta)

136

Bilāspur●   ●Korba

Mouths of the Ganges

Gondia

Raipur   Sambalpur   Bāleshwar

20°

Rāj●   Durg

Nāndgaon

Irapur   Cuttack   *Mahanadi*

Orissa   Bhubaneshwar

Jagdalpur   Puri

**Bay of
Bengal**

Brahmapur

Eastern Ghats

Srīkākulam

Vizianagaram

Visākhapatnam

15°

Rajahmundry   *Mouths of the
Irrawaddy*

Kākināda

85°   90°   95°

133

E   F   G   H

Elevation

| -6000m | -4000m | -2000m | -1000m | -500m | -250m | Below sea level | 0 | 250m | 500m | 1000m | 2000m | 3000m | 4000m | 6000m |

| -19,658ft | -13,124ft | -6562ft | -3281ft | -1640ft | -820ft | -328ft/-100m | 0 | 820ft | 1640ft | 3281ft | 6562ft | 9843ft | 13,124ft | 19,685ft |

Mainland Southeast Asia

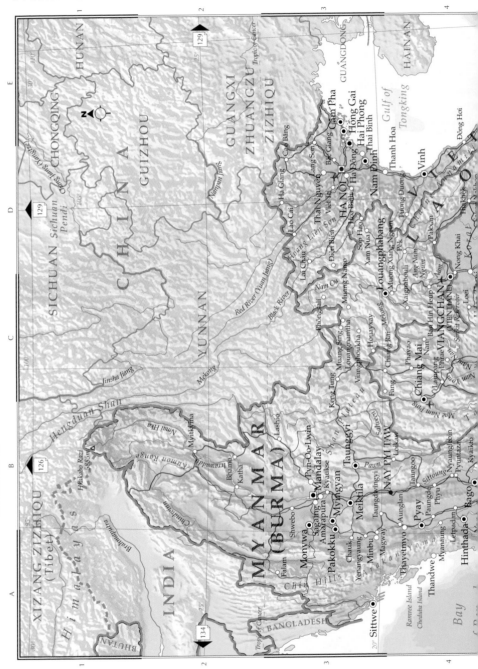

Population

○ below 50,000
○ 50,000 to 100,000
◉ 100,000 to 500,000
◼ above 500,000

● National capital

0 km 200

0 miles 200

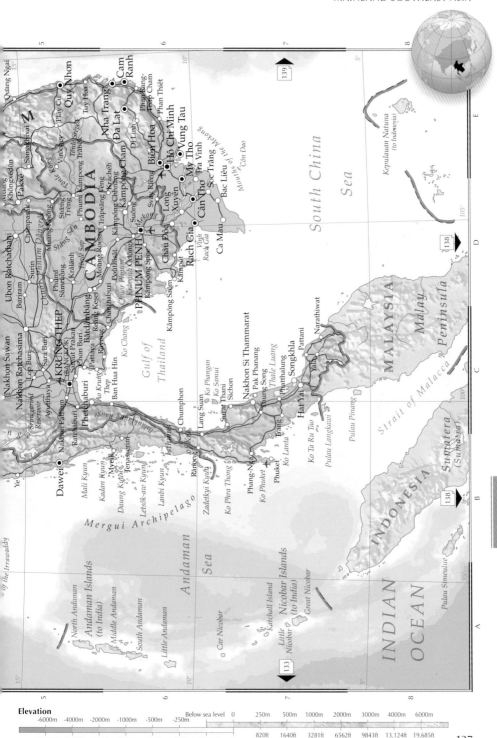

Elevation

-6000m	-4000m	-2000m	-1000m	-500m	-250m	Below sea level	0	250m	500m	1000m	2000m	3000m	4000m	6000m
-19,658ft	-13,124ft	-6562ft	-3281ft	-1640ft	-820ft	-328ft/-100m	0	820ft	1640ft	3281ft	6562ft	9843ft	13,124ft	19,685ft

Maritime Southeast Asia

MYANMAR
(BURMA)

137

Gulf of
Tongking

Hainan Dao
(to China)

SINGAPORE

0 km 10
0 miles 10

MALAYSIA

Johore Strait

Causeway

Lim Chu
Kang
Choa Chu
Kang

Hougang
Bukit Panjang New Town
Bukit Timah 176m
Queenstown

Pulau
Ubin
Pulau
Tekong

Changi

Bedok
City New Town

Jurong
Industrial
Estate
Selat Pandan

Telok Blangah
Sentosa

Pulau Sudong

Pulau Pawai

Strait of Singapore

N

Urban areas
Open areas
Nature reserves

PARACEL ISLANDS
(disputed by China, Taiwan
and Vietnam)

South Chin

Sea

THAILAND

LAOS

VIETNAM

Mekong

CAMBODIA

SPRATLY ISLANDS
(disputed by China, Malaysia,
Philippines, Taiwan and Vietnam)

133

Andaman
Sea

Nicobar Islands
(to India)

Isthmus of Kra

Gulf of
Thailand

Mouths of
the Mekong

Banda Aceh   Sigli

Meulaboh

Pulau Simeulue

Langsa

Medan
Tebingtinggi
Pematangsiantar

Danau
Toba

Kepulauan
Banyak
Sibolga

Pulau Nias

Strait of Malacca

George
Town
Pulau
Pinang

Butterworth

Taiping
Ipoh

Klang

Kota Bharu

Kuala Terengganu
Dungun

Cukai

Kuantan

KUALA LUMPUR
PUTRAJAYA

MALAYSIA

Kepulauan
Natuna

Gunung Kinal
Kota Kinabalu
BANDAR SERI
BEGAWAN
BRUNEI
Miri

Balabac

Bintulu

Baligian
Tembo

Equator

Pulau Siberut

Padang

Kepulauan
Mentawai

Kepulauan
Lingga

Melaka
Muar
Batu Pahat

Keluang
Johor Bahru
SINGAPORE

Pekanbaru

Solok   Rengat

Kualatungkal

Singkawang

Pontianak

Selat Serasan

Sidas

Kuching
Sri Aman

Sibu   Batang Rajang
Sarawak

Sungai Kayi

Borneo

Samarinda
Balikpapan

Banda

Batang Hari

Jambi

Bangka

Selat Karimata

Pegunungan Mullgr

Kalimantan

Sampit

Muller

Sungai Mahak

Sungai Barito

Amuntai
Kandang

133

Sungaipenuh

Pangkalpinang

Palembang

Bengkulu

Lahat

Pulau
Belitung

I   N   D

Banjarmasin

Pulau
Laut

Maka

Sumatera
(Sumatra)

Bandar Lampung

Kotabumi

Cirebon

Tegal

Java   Sea

JAKARTA

Serang

Pekalongan

Semarang
Kudus

INDIAN

Selat Sunda

Bogor
Sukabumi
Bandung

Pulau
Madura
Surabaya
Probolinggo

OCEAN

Tasikmalaya

Jember Mata

Jawa
(Java)

Cilacap
Magelang
Yogyakarta
Surakarta

Malang
Kediri
Madiun

Bali

Denpasar
Pulau
Lombok

MALAYSIA'S TWO CAPITALS

KUALA LUMPUR   - Capital
PUTRAJAYA   - Administrative capital

141

0 km   200
0 miles   200

Population   ● National capital

○ below 50,000   ○ 50,000 to 100,000   ◉ 100,000 to 500,000   ■ above 500,000

E   F   G   H

120°   *Luzon Strait*

131

130°   140°

Babuyan Channel   °Babuyan Island

NORTHERN
MARIANA
ISLANDS
(to US)

Tuguegarao
Ilagan

Luzon

Dagupan
Cabanatuan

P h i l i p p i n e

GUAM
(to US)

Lucena   **PHILIPPINES**

S e a

Naga
Legazpi City

Mindoro   *Sibuyan*

Calbayog

Roxas City   *Samar*

*Panay
Island*   Cadiz   Tacloban

Iloilo   *Leyte*

Bacolod   Cebu
City

Yap

144

MICRONESIA

Negros   *Bohol Sea*   Butuan

Iligan   Cagayan de Oro
Bislig

Zamboanga

*Moro
Gulf*   *Mindanao*
Davao

Basilan

P   A   C   I   F   I   C

Babeldaob

Lebak   *Davao Gulf*
General
Santos

Sulu Archipelago

PALAU

*Kepulauan
Talaud*

O   C   E   A   N

Equator

C e l e b e s   S e a

Manado   Bitung

Pulau Morotai

*Pulau
Halmahera*

Gorontalo

*Gulf of
Tomini*

Pulau Waigeo

*Halmahera
Sea*   Sorong

*Pulau
Biak*

*Pulau
Yapen*

Manokwari

144

Jayapura

*Kepulauan
Banggai*

*Jazirah
Doberai*

*Teluk
Cenderawasih*

Sungai Mamberamo

PAPUA

*Sulawesi
(Celebes)*   *Kepulauan
Sula*

Ceram Sea   Wahai

*Pulau
Misool*

Teluk Berau

Puncak Jaya
5030m   *Pegunungan*
Maoke

I   N   D   O   N   E   S   I   A

*Danau
Towuti*   Waflia

Tifu   Ambon

*Pulau
Seram*

Papua
(Irian Jaya)

NEW
GUINEA

Pare

Kendari

*Pulau
Buru*

Kolaka   *Pulau
Buton*
Watampone

Makassar

*Kepulauan
Kai*

*Kepulauan
Aru*

New Guinea

Bulukumba

B a n d a   S e a

T e n g g a r a

*Kepulauan
Tanimbar*

Sungai Digul

Flores

*Pulau
Wetar*

Kepulauan Alor

DILI

Kepulauan Leti

Pulau Yamdena

Sumba

Savu Sea

EAST TIMOR

Timor

Nikiniki
Kupang

Torres Strait

A r a f u r a

S e a

10°

Timor Sea

148

130°   140°

A U S T R A L I A

E   F   G   H

Elevation

-6000m   -4000m   -2000m   -1000m   -500m   -250m   Below sea level   0   250m   500m   1000m   2000m   3000m   4000m   6000m

820ft   1640ft   3281ft   6562ft   9843ft   13,124ft   19,685ft

-19,658ft   -13,124ft   -6562ft   -3281ft   -1640ft   -820ft   -328ft/-100m   0

The Indian Ocean

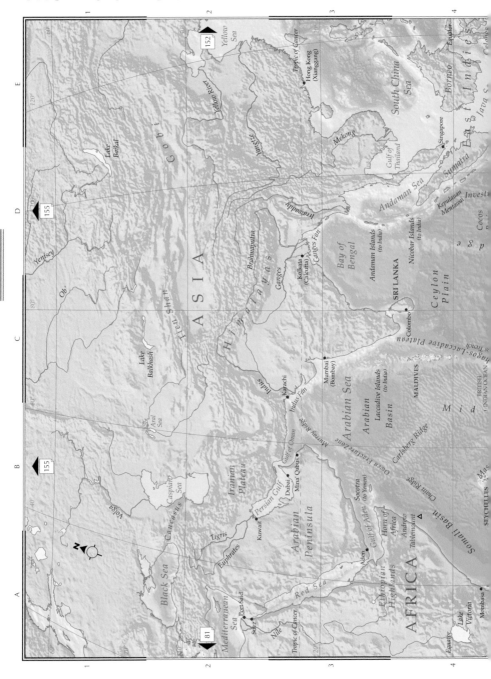

0 km   1500

0 miles   1500

• Major port

Elevation

-6000m	-4000m	-2000m	-1000m	-250m	0
-19,658ft	-13,124ft	-6562ft	-3281ft	-820ft	0

Australasia & Oceania

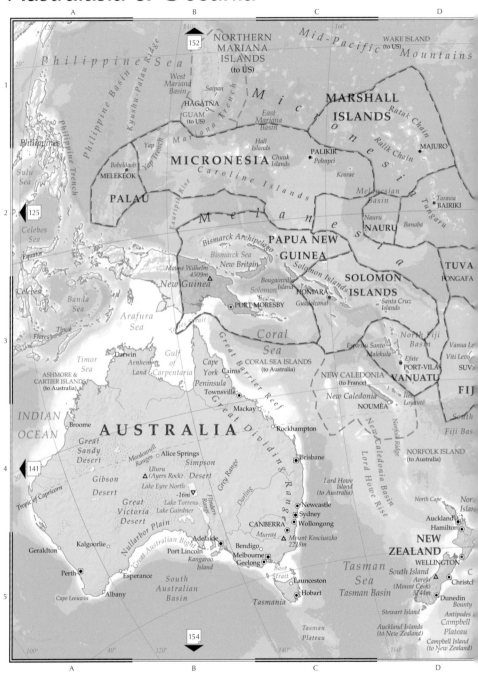

A   B   C   D

152

NORTHERN
MARIANA
ISLANDS
(to US)

Mid-Pacific Mountains

WAKE ISLAND
(to US)

Philippine Sea

West
Mariana
Basin

Saipan

M
i
c

MARSHALL
ISLANDS

Ratak Chain

Philippine Basin

Kyushu-Palau Ridge

HAGÅTNA

GUAM
(to US)

East
Mariana
Basin

r
o
n

Mariana Trench

Yap

Hall
Islands

Chuuk
Islands

PALIKIR

Pohnpei

Ralik Chain

MAJURO

Philippines

Philippine Trench

Babeldaob

Yap Trench

MELEKEOK

MICRONESIA

Caroline Islands

Kosrae

e
s
i

*Melanesian
Basin*

Tarawa
BAIRIKI

Sulu
Sea

PALAU

Eauripik Rise

M
e
l
a
n
e

Nauru

NAURU

Banaba

Tungaru

125

Celebes
Sea

Equator

Celebes

Banda
Sea

Bismarck Archipelago

Bismarck Sea

New Britain

Mount Wilhelm
4509m △

New Guinea

PAPUA NEW
GUINEA

Bougainville

Solomon
Islands

*Solomon
Sea*

HONIARA

Guadalcanal

s

SOLOMON
ISLANDS

Santa Cruz
Islands

a

TUVA
FONGAFA

*Arafura
Sea*

PORT MORESBY

Timor

Flores

Timor

*North Fiji
Basin*

Vanua Le

Darwin

Arnhem
Land

Gulf
of
Carpentaria

Cape
York
Cairns

CORAL SEA ISLANDS
(to Australia)

Espíritu Santo

Malekula

Efate

NEW CALEDONIA
(to France)

PORT-VILA

Viti Levu

SUV

VANUATU

FIJ

ASHMORE &
CARTIER ISLANDS
(to Australia)

*Timor
Sea*

Peninsula
Townsville

*Coral
Sea*

Great Barrier Reef

New Caledonia

NOUMÉA

*Îles
Loyauté*

South
Fiji Bas

Mackay

INDIAN
OCEAN

Broome

AUSTRALIA

Great Dividing Range

Rockhampton

New Caledonia Ridge

Norfolk Ridge

NORFOLK ISLAND
(to Australia)

Great
Sandy
Desert

Macdonnell
Ranges

Alice Springs

Simpson

Brisbane

Lord Howe Basin

141

Gibson
Desert

Uluru
(Ayers Rock) △

Desert

Grey Range

Lord Howe
Island
(to Australia)

Lord Howe Rise

North Cape

Nor
Islan

Tropic of Capricorn

Great
Victoria
Desert

Lake Eyre North ▽

-16m▽

Lake Torrens

Lake Gairdner

Darling

Flinders Range

Newcastle

Sydney

Wollongong

Auckland

Hamilton

Geraldton

Kalgoorlie

Nullarbor Plain

Great Australian Bight

Adelaide

Port Lincoln

Kangaroo
Island

CANBERRA

Murray

Bendigo

Melbourne

Geelong

Mount Kosciuszko
2228m △

NEW
ZEALAND

WELLINGTON

Perth

Esperance

South
Australian
Basin

*Bass
Strait*

Launceston

Hobart

*Tasman
Sea*

South Island

Aoraki
(Mount Cook)
3744m △

C

Christch

Cape Leeuwin

Albany

Tasmania

Tasman Basin

Dunedin

Bounty

Stewart Island

Antipodes i

Campbell
Plateau

154

Tasman
Plateau

Auckland Islands
(to New Zealand)

Campbell Island
(to New Zealand)

A   B   C   D

0 km   1000
0 miles   1000

Population   ● National capital

○ below 50,000   ○ 50,000 to 100,000   ◉ 100,000 to 500,000   ■ above 500,000

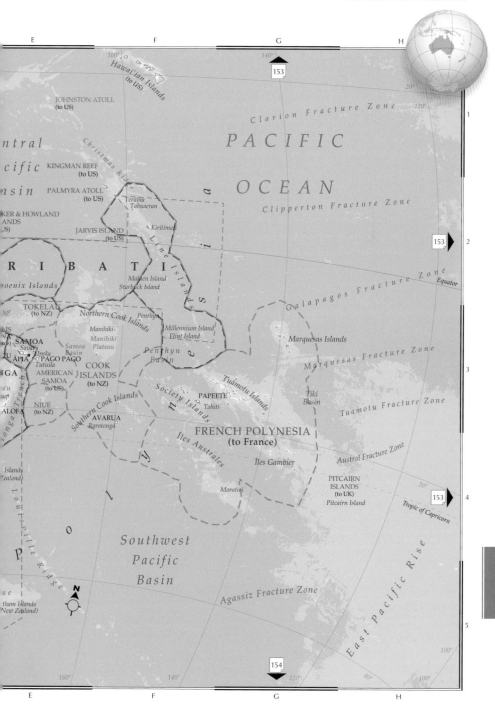

E   F   G   H

160°   Hawai'ian Islands (to US)   140°

153

JOHNSTON ATOLL
(to US)

20°

Clarion Fracture Zone   120°

1

ntral

PACIFIC

cific   KINGMAN REEF
(to US)

Christmas Ridge

sin   PALMYRA ATOLL
(to US)

OCEAN

Teraina
Tabuaeran

Clipperton Fracture Zone

KER & HOWLAND
ANDS
US)

JARVIS ISLAND
(to US)

Kiritimati

153

2

R I B A T I

Line Islands

Malden Island
Starbuck Island

Galapagos Fracture Zone

Equator

oenix Islands

TOKELAU
(to NZ)

Northern Cook Islands

Penrhyn

Manihiki-
Manihiki
Plateau

Millennium Island
Flint Island

Marquesas Islands

NS
A

SAMOA
Savaii

Samoa
Basin

Penrhyn
Basin

Marquesas Fracture Zone

Ipolu

APIA   PAGO PAGO
Tutuila

COOK
ISLANDS
(to NZ)

3

GA

AMERICAN
SAMOA
(to US)

Tuamotu Islands

Tiki
Basin

u
up

PAPEETE
Tahiti

Society Islands

Tuamotu Fracture Zone

ALOFA

NIUE
(to NZ)

Southern Cook Islands

AVARUA
Rarotonga

Îles Australes

FRENCH POLYNESIA
(to France)

Austral Fracture Zone

Islands
ealand)

Îles Gambier

PITCAIRN
ISLANDS
(to UK)
Pitcairn Island

20°

153

4

Marotiri

Tropic of Capricorn

Southwest
Pacific
Basin

East Pacific Rise

Lo

Ridge

0

P

se

tham Islands
New Zealand)

N

Agassiz Fracture Zone

40°

100°

5

100°

160°   140°   120°

154

E   F   G   H

The Southwest Pacific

A · · · · · · · · · · · · · B · · · · · · · · · · · · · C · · · · · · · · · · · · · D

140°   150°   160°   170°

Saipan
Tinian NORTHERN
Rota   MARIANA
        ISLANDS   152
GUAM HAGÁTÑA (to US)
(to US)

MARSHALL
ISLANDS

Enewetak Bikini Atoll Rongelap
Atoll   Atoll

10°   Ailuk A

Yap   Ujelang Atoll   Wotje
Babeldaob   Kwajalein Male
MICRONESIA   Atoll   Atoll
                            Namu Atoll
Babeldaob   Ailinglaplap Atoll· M
MELEKEOK   Chuuk   PALIKIR· Pohnpei Jaluit Atoll
              Islands   Mili ·
        C a r o l i n e   I s l a n d s
PALAU   Kosrae   Ebon Atoll

139   BAIRI

Equator   Aber

Nauru
                                        NAURU   Banaba

Admiralty   St.Matthias Group   Ne
Islands
Bismarck Archipelago
New Guinea Bismarck Sea New Ireland
          Madang PAPUA NEW GUINEA
INDONESIA Central Range Bougainville
          ▲Mount Wilhelm Island
          4509m Lae New
                  Britain Choiseul
          Solomon Sea Santa Isabel SOLOMON
Arafura   Gulf of   New Georgia Malaita
Sea   Papua   Islands
10° PORT MORESBY ●   HONIARA ● + ISLANDS
     Torres Strait   D'Entrecasteaux Guadalcanal
                         Islands   San Cristobal Santa Cruz
                         Louisiade   Islands
                         Archipelago Rennell

Arnhem   Groote   C o r a l S e a   Banks Islands
Land   Eylandt   Maéwo
          Gulf of   Espíritu Santo Pentecost
146   Carpentaria Cape   Ambrym
Barkly   Tableland   York   CORAL SEA ISLANDS Malekula Epi
          Peninsula   (to Australia)   Efate
                                                     PORT-VILA
20° NORTHERN   NEW   Erromango
                                        CALEDONIA VANUATU
     TERRITORY   (to France) Tanna
                                                    Aneityum
Tropic of Capricorn QUEENSLAND   New   Lifou
                                        Caledonia Maré
Macdonnell   NOUMÉA

Ranges   A U S T R A L I A
                        149
140°   150°   160°   170°

A · · · · · · · · · · · · · B · · · · · · · · · · · · · C · · · · · · · · · · · · · D

0 km   750

0 miles   750

Population ● National capital

○ below 50,000   ○ 50,000 to 100,000   ◉ 100,000 to 500,000   ◼ above 500,000

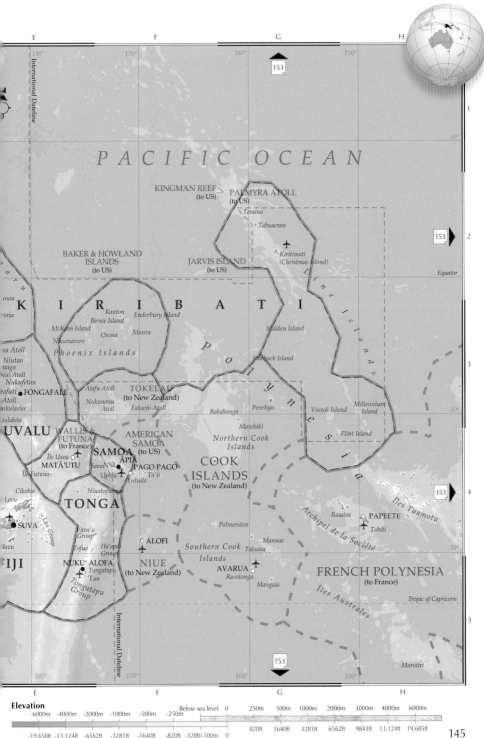

PACIFIC OCEAN

KINGMAN REEF
(to US)

PALMYRA ATOLL
(to US)

Teraina

Tabuaeran

153

BAKER & HOWLAND
ISLANDS
(to US)

JARVIS ISLAND
(to US)

Kiritimati
(Christmas Island)

Equator

K I R I B A T I

Kanton

Birnie Island

Enderbury Island

McKean Island

Nikumaroro

Orona

Manra

Malden Island

Phoenix Islands

Starbuck Island

Niutao

Nui Atoll

Nukufetau

FONGAFALE

Atafu Atoll

TOKELAU
(to New Zealand)

Nukunonu
Atoll

Fakaofo Atoll

Rakahanga

Penrhyn

Vostok Island

Millennium
Island

UVALU

WALLIS &
FUTUNA
(to France)

AMERICAN
SAMOA
(to US)

Northern Cook
Islands

Manihiki

Flint Island

Ile Uvea

SAMOA

MATĀ'UTU

Savai'i

APIA

'Upolu

PAGO PAGO

Ta'ū

COOK

Ile Futuna

Tutuila

ISLANDS
(to New Zealand)

Cikobia

Niuatoputapu

Raiatea

Iles Tuamotu

153

Levu

TONGA

PAPEETE

SUVA

Vava'u
Group

Palmerston

Manuae

Tahiti

Tofua

Ha'apai
Group

Takutea

ALOFI

Southern Cook

Archipel de la Société

IJI

NUKU'ALOFA

'Eua

Tongatapu

NIUE
(to New Zealand)

Islands

AVARUA

FRENCH POLYNESIA
(to France)

Tongatapu
Group

Rarotonga

Mangaia

Iles Australes

Tropic of Capricorn

153

Marotiri

Elevation

| -6000m | -4000m | -2000m | -1000m | -500m | -250m | Below sea level 0 | 250m | 500m | 1000m | 2000m | 3000m | 4000m | 6000m |
| -19,658ft | -13,124ft | -6562ft | -3281ft | -1640ft | -820ft | -328ft/-100m | 0 | 820ft | 1640ft | 3281ft | 6562ft | 9843ft | 13,124ft | 19,685ft |

145

Western Australia

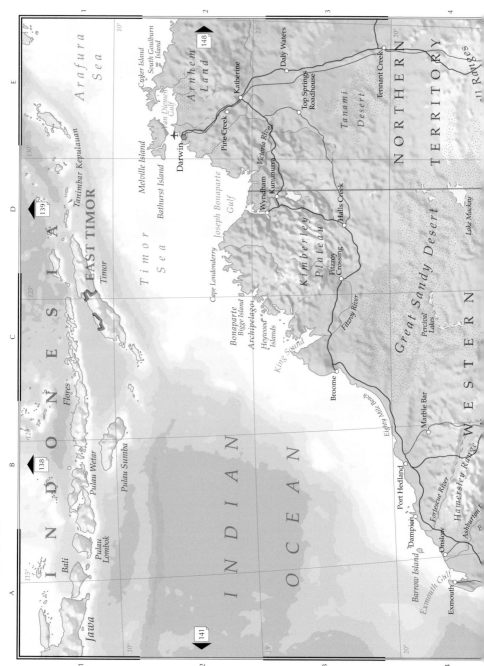

0 km 300

0 miles 300

Population

○ below 50,000 ○ 50,000 to 100,000 ◉ 100,000 to 500,000 ■ above 500,000

● Internal administrative capital

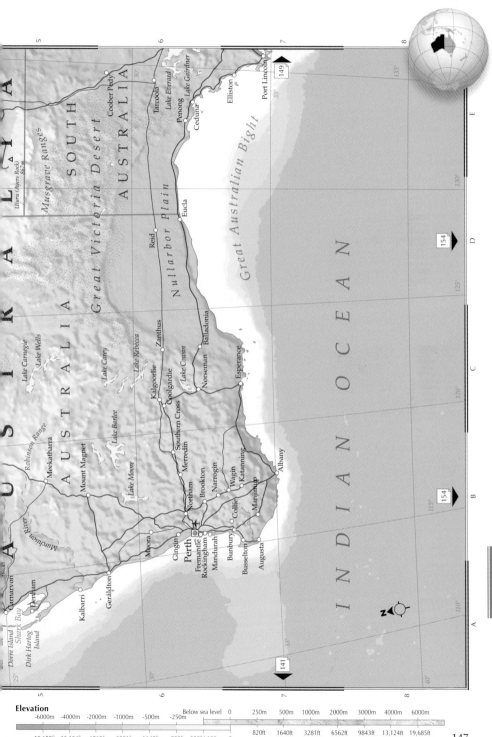

149

154

154

141

Elevation

					Below sea level	0	250m	500m	1000m	2000m	3000m	4000m	6000m
-6000m	-4000m	-2000m	-1000m	-500m	-250m								
-19,658ft	-13,124ft	-6562ft	-3281ft	-1640ft	-820ft -328ft/-100m	0	820ft	1640ft	3281ft	6562ft	9843ft	13,124ft	19,685ft

Eastern Australia

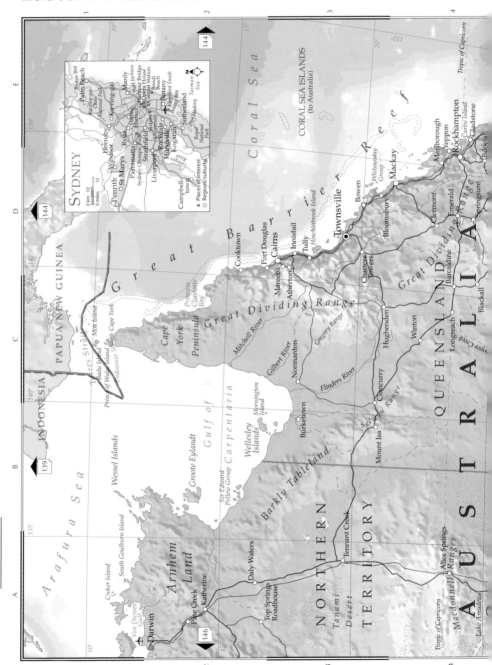

SYDNEY

Frenchs Bay
Palm Beach
Ku\-ring\-gai
Pacific Ocean
National Park
Manly
Botany
Kingsford Smith
Hornsby
Ryde
Central Station
Opera House
Bondi Beach
Windsor
Parramatta
Sydney Olympic Park
Darling Harbour
University
Sutherland
Botany Bay
St Marys
Liverpool
Strathfield
Sydney
Port Hacking
Tasman Sea
Penrith
Hurstville
Rockdale
Kogarah
Royal National Park
Campbell\-town

Cronulla River

- ■ Places of interest
- ☐ Regions/suburbs

0 km 10
0 miles 10

Coral Sea

CORAL SEA ISLANDS
(to Australia)

Great Barrier Reef

PAPUA NEW GUINEA

INDONESIA

Torres Strait

Arafura Sea

Cape York Peninsula

Great Dividing Range

QUEENSLAND

NORTHERN TERRITORY

A U S T R A L I A

Gulf of Carpentaria

Barkly Tableland

Tanami Desert

Macdonnell Ranges

Arnhem Land

Van Diemen Gulf

Darwin
Pine Creek
Katherine
Top Springs Roadhouse
Daly Waters
Tennant Creek
Alice Springs
Lake Amadeus

Croker Island
South Goulburn Island
Wessel Islands
Groote Eylandt
Sir Edward Pellew Group
Mornington Island
Wellesley Islands
Burketown
Normanton
Flinders River
Gilbert River
Mitchell River
Gregory Range
Selwyn Range
Mount Isa
Cloncurry
Hughenden
Winton
Longreach
Barcaldine
Blackall
Cooper Creek

Princess Charlotte Bay
Cooktown
Port Douglas
Cairns
Innisfail
Tully
Hinchinbrook Island
Mareeba
Atherton
Townsville
Bowen
Bloomsbury
Mackay
Whitsunday Group
Proserpine
Clermont
Emerald
Springsure
Marlborough
Yeppoon
Rockhampton
Gladstone
Curtis Island
Biloela

Charters Towers

Tropic of Capricorn

Badu Island
Moa Island
Cape York
Prince of Wales Island
Endeavour Strait

0 km 300
0 miles 300

Population

- ● National capital
- ◉ Internal administrative capital
- ○ below 50,000
- ○ 50,000 to 100,000
- ◉ 100,000 to 500,000
- ■ above 500,000

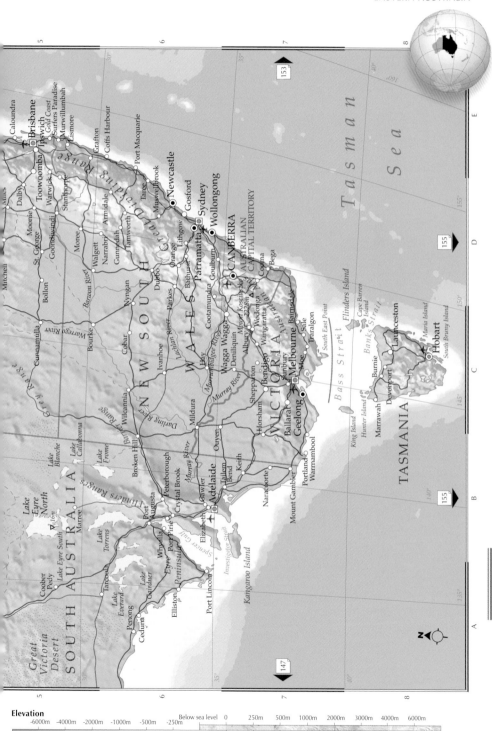

Elevation

| -6000m | -4000m | -2000m | -1000m | -500m | -250m | Below sea level 0 | 250m | 500m | 1000m | 2000m | 3000m | 4000m | 6000m |

| -19,658ft | -13,124ft | -6562ft | -3281ft | -1640ft | -820ft | -328ft/-100m | 0 | 820ft | 1640ft | 3281ft | 6562ft | 9843ft | 13,124ft | 19,685ft |

New Zealand

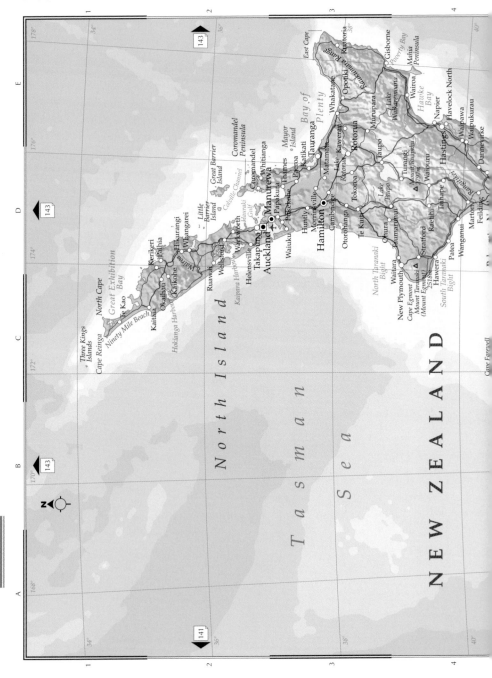

Population	• National capital		
○ below 50,000	○ 50,000 to 100,000	◉ 100,000 to 500,000	▣ above 500,000

0 km   100
0 miles   100

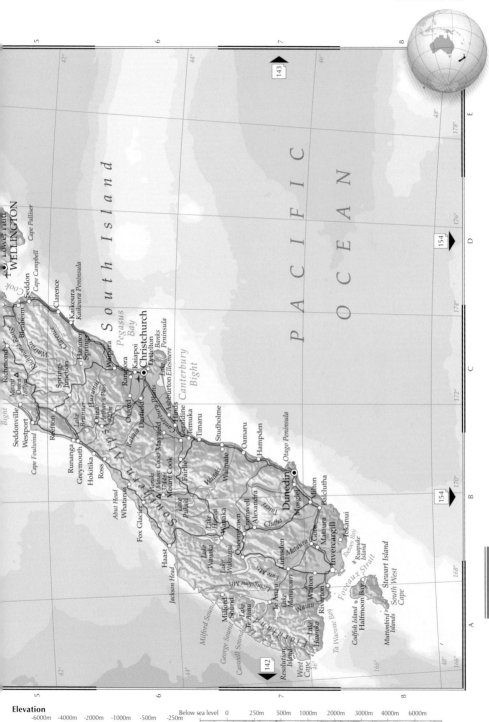

South Island

PACIFIC OCEAN

Cook

WELLINGTON
Lower Hutt
Cape Palliser
Cape Campbell
Seddon
Blenheim
Cape Campbell
Clarence
Kaikoura
Kaikoura Peninsula
Hanmer
Springs
Springs
Junction
Waiau
Rangiora
Kaiapoi
Christchurch
Lyttelton
Banks
Peninsula
Lake
Ellesmere
Pegasus
Bay
Canterbury
Bight

Richmond
Mount
Owen
1875m
Nelson Range
Murchison
Waimea
Tasman
Lake
Rotoiti
Maruia
Hope
Lewis
Pass

Bight
Seddonville
Westport
Cape Foulwind
Reefton
Runanga
Greymouth
Hokitika
Ross
Abut Head
Whataroa
Fox Glacier
Haast
Jackson Head
West
Cape

Lake
Brunner
Otira
Otira
Arthur's
Pass
920m
Oxford
Darfield
Rakaia
Mayfield
Canterbury Plains
Ashburton
Hinds
Geraldine
Temuka
Timaru
Studholme
Oamaru
Hampden
Otago Peninsula

Aoraki
(Mount Cook)
3744m
Mount Cook
Fairlie
Waitaki
Waimate

SOUTHERN ALPS

Lake
Pukaki
Lake
Tekapo

Lake
Hawea
Lake
Wanaka
Lake
Wakatipu

Cromwell
Alexandra
Queenstown

Teviot
Cluthia
Dunedin
Mosgiel
Milton
Balclutha

Lumsden
Mataura
Gore
Mataura
Tokanui
Clinton
Toetoes Bay
Ruapuke
Island

Invercargill
Winton
Riverton
Waiau
Foveaux Strait
Stewart Island
South West
Cape
South Cape

Eyre Mts
Livingstone Mts
Te Anau
Lake
Manapouri
Lake
Manapouri

Codfish
Island
Halfmoon Bay
Mutton bird
Islands

Milford Sound
George Sound
Caswell Sound
Resolution
Island
Milford
Sound
Lake
Te Anau
Lake
Te Anau
Lake
Hauroko
Te Waewae Bay

FIORDLAND

142
143
154
154

Elevation

-6000m	-4000m	-2000m	-1000m	-500m	-250m	Below sea level 0	250m	500m	1000m	2000m	3000m	4000m	6000m
-19,658ft	-13,124ft	-6562ft	-3281ft	-1640ft	-820ft	-328ft/-100m 0	820ft	1640ft	3281ft	6562ft	9843ft	13,124ft	19,685ft

The Pacific Ocean

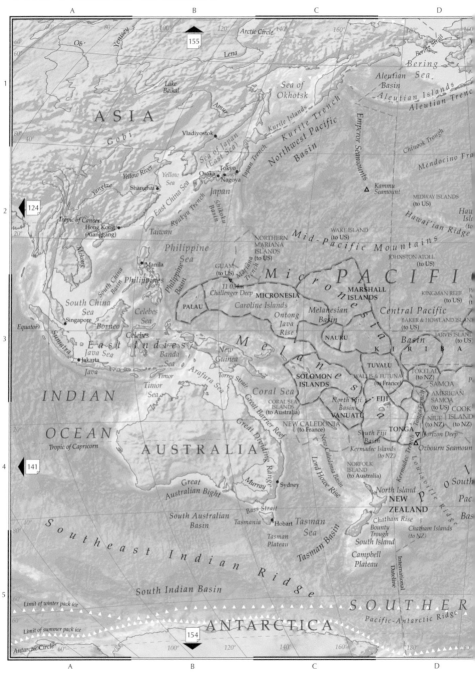

0 km   2000

0 miles   2000

● Major port

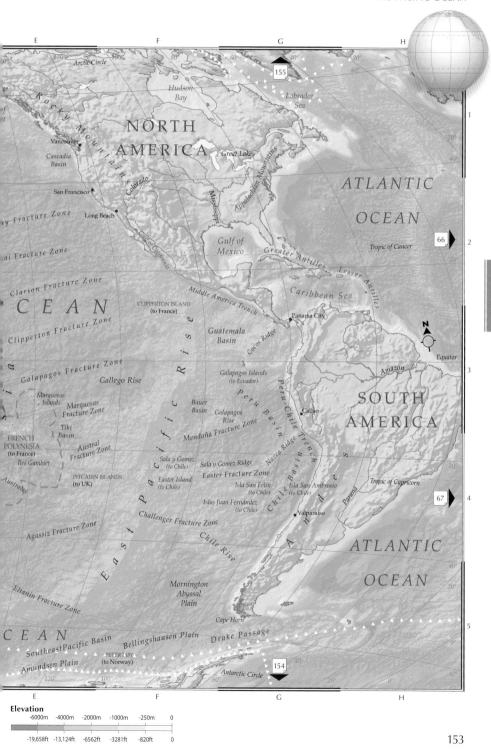

E   F   G   H

155

Arctic Circle

Hudson
Bay

Labrador
Sea

**NORTH
AMERICA**

Great Lakes

Vancouver

Cascadia
Basin

Rocky Mountains

San Francisco

Long Beach

Colorado

Mississippi

Appalachian Mountains

ay Fracture Zone

ai Fracture Zone

Gulf of
California

Gulf of
Mexico

Greater Antilles

ATLANTIC

OCEAN

Tropic of Cancer

66

Clarion Fracture Zone

C E A N

Clipperton Fracture Zone

CLIPPERTON ISLAND
(to France)

Middle America Trench

Guatemala
Basin

Cocos Ridge

Lesser Antilles

Caribbean Sea

Panama City

N

Equator

Galapagos Fracture Zone

Gallego Rise

East Pacific Rise

Galapagos Islands
(to Ecuador)

Bauer
Basin

Galapagos
Rise

Peru Basin

Amazon

**SOUTH
AMERICA**

Callao

sia

Marquesas
Islands

*Marquesas
Fracture Zone*

Tiki
Basin

*Austral
Fracture Zone*

Mendaña Fracture Zone

Nazca Ridge

FRENCH
POLYNESIA
(to France)

Iles Gambier

Sala y Gomez
(to Chile)

Sala y Gomez Ridge

Peru–Chile Trench

Andes

Tropic of Capricorn

Australes

PITCAIRN ISLANDS
(to UK)

Easter Island
(to Chile)

Easter Fracture Zone

Isla San Félix
(to Chile)

Isla San Ambrosio
(to Chile)

Chile Basin

67

Islas Juan Fernández
(to Chile)

Parana

Challenger Fracture Zone

Valparaíso

Agassiz Fracture Zone

Chile Rise

ATLANTIC

OCEAN

Eltanin Fracture Zone

Mornington
Abyssal
Plain

Cape Horn

C E A N

Southeast Pacific Basin

Bellingshausen Plain

Drake Passage

PETER I ØY
(to Norway)

Amundsen Plain

Antarctic Circle

154

E   F   G   H

Elevation

-6000m	-4000m	-2000m	-1000m	-250m	0
-19,658ft	-13,124ft	-6562ft	-3281ft	-820ft	0

Antarctica

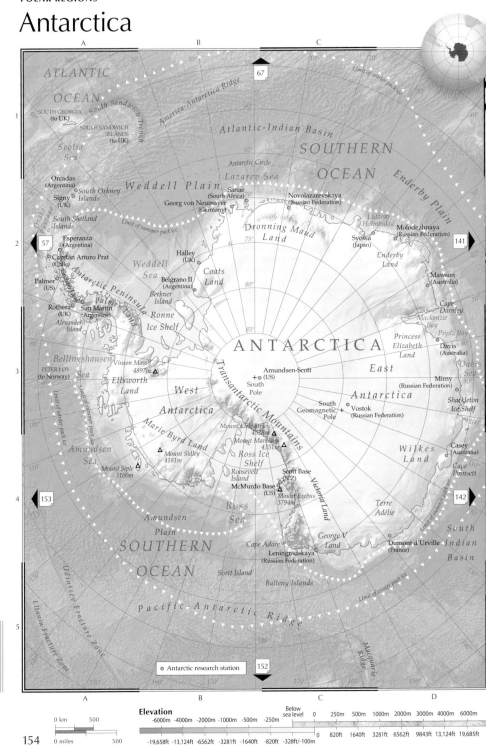

Elevation

						Below sea level	0	250m	500m	1000m	2000m	3000m	4000m	6000m
-6000m	-4000m	-2000m	-1000m	-500m	-250m									
-19,658ft	-13,124ft	-6562ft	-3281ft	-1640ft	-820ft	-328ft/-100m	0	820ft	1640ft	3281ft	6562ft	9843ft	13,124ft	19,685ft

0 km 500
0 miles 500

Arctic Ocean

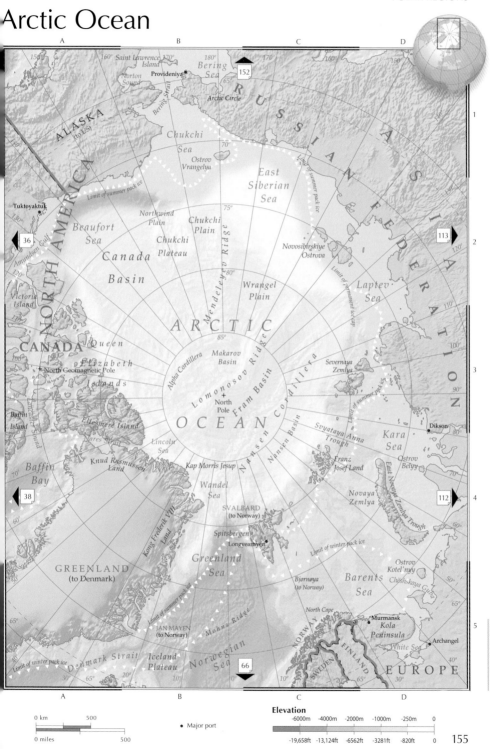

A   B   C   D

150°   160°   Saint Lawrence   170°   180°   170°   160°   150°
Island
Norton   Providenîya   Bering   **152**
Sound   Sea   65°
Arctic Circle

ALASKA   RUSSIAN   FEDERATION
(to US)

Chukchi
Sea   70°
Ostrov
Vrangelya

East
Siberian
Sea

Tuktoyaktuk   Northwind   Chukchi   75°   **113**
Plain   Plain   120°
36   Beaufort   Chukchi   Novosibirskiye
Sea   Plateau   Ostrova
Canada
Basin   80°   Wrangel   Laptev
Plain   Sea
Victoria
Island   A R C T I C   110°
85°
CANADA   Queen   Makarov   Severnaya   100°
Alpha Cordillera   Basin   Zemlya
Elizabeth
North Geomagnetic Pole   Lomonosov Ridge   90°
Islands   North   Fram Basin
Pole   Kara   Dikson
Baffin   O C E A N   Nansen Basin   Sea   80°
Island   Ellesmere Island   Lincoln   Svyataya Anna   Ostrov
Nares Strait   Sea   Trough   Belyy
Knud Rasmussen   Kap Morris Jesup   Franz   70°
Baffin   Land   Wandel   Josef Land   **112**
Bay   Sea   Novaya
38   SVALBARD   Zemlya   60°
(to Norway)
Spitsbergen   Ostrov
Longyearbyen   Kotel'nyy
GREENLAND   Greenland   Barents   Chesh-skaya Guba
(to Denmark)   Sea   Bjørnøya   Sea   65°
(to Norway)
North Cape   White Sea
65°   JAN MAYEN   Mohns Ridge   Murmansk   Kola
(to Norway)   NORWAY   Peninsula   Archangel
Denmark Strait   Iceland   Norwegian   FINLAND   40°
Plateau   Sea   **66**   SWEDEN   E U R O P E
30°   65°   20°   10°   0°   10°   20°   30°

A   B   C   D

0 km   500   • Major port

0 miles   500

Elevation
-6000m   -4000m   -2000m   -1000m   -250m   0

-19,658ft   -13,124ft   -6562ft   -3281ft   -820ft   0

Overseas territories & dependencies

Despite the rapid process of global decolonization since the Second World War, around 8 million people in more than 50 territories around the world continue to live under the protection of France, Australia, the Netherlands, Denmark, Norway, New Zealand, the UK, or the USA. These remnants of former colonial empires may have persisted for economic, strategic or political reasons and are administered in a variety of ways.

AUSTRALIA

Australia's overseas territories have not been an issue since Papua New Guinea became independent in 1975. Consequently there is no overriding policy toward them. Norfolk Island is inhabited by descendants of the H.M.S Bounty mutineers and more recent Australian migrants.

Ashmore & Cartier Islands
Indian Ocean
Status: External territory
Claimed: 1931
Capital: Not applicable
Population: None
Area: 2 sq miles
(5.2 sq km)

Christmas Island
Indian Ocean
Status: External territory
Claimed: 1958
Capital: The Settlement
Population: 1403
Area: 52 sq miles
(135 sq km)

Cocos Islands
Indian Ocean
Status: External territory
Claimed: 1955
Capital: No official capital
Population: 596
Area: 5.5 sq miles
(14 sq km)

Coral Sea Islands
South Pacific
Status: External territory
Claimed: 1969
Capital: None
Population: 8 (meteorologists)
Area: Less than 1.2 sq miles
(3 sq km)

Heard & McDonald Is.
Indian Ocean
Status: External territory
Claimed: 1947
Capital: Not applicable
Population: None
Area: 161 sq miles
(417 sq km)

Norfolk Island
South Pacific
Status: External territory
Claimed: 1774
Capital: Kingston
Population: 2141
Area: 13 sq miles
(34 sq km)

DENMARK

The Faeroe Islands have been under Danish administration since Queen Margreth I of Denmark inherited Norway in 1380. The Home Rule Act of 1948 gave the Faeroese control over all their internal affairs. Greenland first came under Danish rule in 1380. Today, Denmark is responsible for the island's foreign affairs and defense.

Faeroe Islands
North Atlantic
Status: External territory
Claimed: 1380
Capital: Tórshavn
Population: 48,917
Area: 540 sq miles
(1399 sq km)

Greenland
North Atlantic
Status: External territory
Claimed: 1380
Capital: Nuuk
Population: 56,452
Area: 840,000 sq miles
(2,175,516 sq km)

FRANCE

France has developed economic ties with its *Territoires d'Outre-Mer*, thereby stressing interdependence over independence. Overseas *départements*, officially part of France, have their own governments. Territorial *collectivités* and overseas *territoires* have varying degrees of autonomy.

Clipperton Island
East Pacific
Status: Dependency of French Polynesia
Claimed: 1935
Capital: Not applicable
Population: None
Area: 2.7 sq miles
(7 sq km)

French Guiana
South America
Status: Overseas department
Claimed: 1817
Capital: Cayenne
Population: 229,000
Area: 32,253 sq miles
(83,534 sq km)

French Polynesia
South Pacific
Status: Overseas territory
Claimed: 1843
Capital: Papeete
Population: 264,000
Area: 1608 sq miles
(4165 sq km)

Guadeloupe
West Indies
Status: Overseas department
Claimed: 1635
Capital: Basse-Terre
Population: 405,500
Area: 687 sq miles
(1780 sq km)

Martinique
West Indies
Status: Overseas
department
Claimed: 1635
Capital: Fort-de-France
Population: 397,000
Area: 425 sq miles
(1100 sq km)

Mayotte
Indian Ocean
Status: Territorial
collectivity
Claimed: 1843
Capital: Mamoudzou
Population: 194,000
Area: 144 sq miles
(374 sq km)

New Caledonia
South Pacific
Status: Overseas territory
Claimed: 1853
Capital: Nouméa
Population: 249,000
Area: 7374 sq miles
(19,100 sq km)

Réunion
Indian Ocean
Status: Overseas
department
Claimed: 1638
Capital: Saint-Denis
Population: 827,000
Area: 970 sq miles
(2500 sq km)

St. Pierre
& Miquelon
North America
Status: Territorial collectivity
Claimed: 1604
Capital: Saint-Pierre
Population: 7063
Area: 93 sq miles
(242 sq km)

Wallis & Futuna
South Pacific
Status: Overseas territory
Claimed: 1842
Capital: Matá'Utu
Population: 15,289
Area: 106 sq miles
(274 sq km)

NETHERLANDS

The country's remaining overseas
territories were formerly part of the
Dutch West Indies. The Netherlands
Antilles dissolved in 2010 leaving
the constituent islands with varying
degrees of autonomy, but the
Netherlands remains responsible for
their security.

Aruba
West Indies
Status: Autonomous
part of the Netherlands
Claimed: 1643
Capital: Oranjestad
Population: 103,065
Area: 75 sq miles (194 sq km)

Bonaire
West Indies
Status: Special municipality of
the Netherlands
Claimed: 1816
Capital: Kralendijk
Population: 14,006
Area: 113 sq miles
(294 sq km)

Curaçao
West Indies
Status: Autonomous
part of the Netherlands
Claimed: 1816
Capital: Willemstad
Population: 141,766
Area: 171 sq miles
(444 sq km)

Sint Maarten
West Indies
Status: Autonomous
part of the Netherlands
Claimed: 1816
Capital: Philipsburg
Population: 40,917
Area: 13 sq miles (34 sq km)

NEW ZEALAND

New Zealand's government
has no desire to retain any overseas
territories. However, the economic
weakness of its dependent territory
Tokelau and its freely associated
states, Niue and the Cook Islands,
has forced New Zealand to
remain responsible for their
foreign policy and defense.

Cook Islands
South Pacific
Status: Associated territory
Claimed: 1901
Capital: Avarua
Population: 19,596
Area: 91 sq miles
(235 sq km)

Niue
South Pacific
Status: Associated territory
Claimed: 1901
Capital: Alofi
Population: 1398
Area: 102 sq miles
(264 sq km)

Tokelau
South Pacific
Status: Dependent territory
Claimed: 1926
Capital: Not applicable
Population: 1416
Area: 4 sq miles (10 sq km)

NORWAY

In 1920, 41 nations signed the
Spits-bergen Treaty recognizing
Norwegian sovereignty over
Svalbard. There is a NATO base
on Jan Mayen. Bouvet Island is
a nature reserve.

Bouvet Island
South Atlantic
Status: Dependency
Claimed: 1928
Capital: Not applicable
Population: None
Area: 22 sq miles (58 sq km)

Jan Mayen
North Atlantic
Status: Dependency
Claimed: 1929
Capital: Not applicable
Population: None
Area: 147 sq miles
(381 sq km)

Continued on page158

Overseas territories & dependencies

Peter I. Island
Southern Ocean
Status: Dependency
Claimed: 1931
Capital: Not applicable
Population: None
Area: 69 sq miles (180 sq km)

Svalbard
Arctic Ocean
Status: Dependency
Claimed: 1920
Capital: Longyearbyen
Population: 2572
Area: 24,289 sq miles
(62,906 sq km)

UNITED KINGDOM

The UK still has the largest number
of overseas territories. These are
locally-governed by a mixture
of elected representatives and
appointed officials, and they
all enjoy a large measure of internal
self-government, but certain powers,
such as foreign affairs and defense,
are reserved for Governors
of the British Crown.

Anguilla
West Indies
Status: Dependent
territory
Claimed: 1650
Capital: The Valley
Population: 13,600
Area: 37 sq miles
(96 sq km)

Ascension Island
South Atlantic
Status: Dependency
of St. Helena
Claimed: 1673
Capital: Georgetown
Population: 940
Area: 34 sq miles
(88 sq km)

Bermuda
North Atlantic
Status: Crown colony
Claimed: 1612
Capital: Hamilton
Population: 67,837
Area: 20 sq miles (53 sq km)

**British Indian
Ocean Territory**
Status: Dependent
territory
Claimed: 1814
Capital: Diego Garcia
Population: 4000
Area: 23 sq miles
(60 sq km)

British Virgin Islands
West Indies
Status: Dependent territory
Claimed: 1672
Capital: Road Town
Population: 27,000
Area: 59 sq miles
(153 sq km)

Cayman Islands
West Indies
Status: Dependent territory
Claimed: 1670
Capital: George Town
Population: 60,456
Area: 100 sq miles (259 sq km)

Falkland Islands
South Atlantic
Status: Dependent territory
Claimed: 1832
Capital: Stanley
Population: 3140
Area: 4699 sq miles
(12,173 sq km)

Gibraltar
Southwest Europe
Status: Crown colony
Claimed: 1713
Capital: Gibraltar
Population: 29,286
Area: 2.5 sq miles (6.5 sq km)

Guernsey
Channel Islands
Status: Crown dependency
Claimed: 1066
Capital: St. Peter Port
Population: 65,573
Area: 25 sq miles (65 sq km)

Isle of Man
British Isles
Status: Crown dependency
Claimed: 1765
Capital: Douglas
Population: 80,085
Area: 221 sq miles (572 sq km)

Jersey
Channel Islands
Status: Crown dependency
Claimed: 1066
Capital: St. Helier
Population: 91,626
Area: 45 sq miles (116 sq km)

Montserrat
West Indies
Status: Dependent territory
Claimed: 1632
Capital: Plymouth
(currently uninhabitable)
Population: 4655
Area: 40 sq miles (102 sq km)

Pitcairn Islands
South Pacific
Status: Dependent territory
Claimed: 1887
Capital: Adamstown
Population: 50
Area: 18 sq miles (47 sq km)

St. Helena
South Atlantic
Status: Dependent territory
Claimed: 1673
Capital: Jamestown
Population: 4255
Area: 47 sq miles (122 sq km)

**South Georgia & The
South Sandwich Islands**
South Atlantic
Status: Dependent territory
Claimed: 1775
Capital: Not applicable
Population: No permanent
residents
Area: 1387 sq miles
(3592 sq km)

Tristan da Cunha
South Atlantic
Status: Dependency
of St. Helena
Claimed: 1612
Capital: Edinburgh
Population: 276
Area: 38 sq miles (98 sq km)

Turks & Caicos Islands
West Indies
Status: Dependent territory
Claimed: 1766
Capital: Cockburn Town
Population: 36,605
Area: 166 sq miles
(430 sq km)

UNITED STATES OF AMERICA

America's overseas territories
have been seen as strategically
useful, if expensive, links with its
"backyards." The US has, in most
cases, given the local population a
say in deciding their own status.
A US Commonwealth territory, such
as Puerto Rico, has a greater level
of independence than that of a US
unincorporated or external territory.

American Samoa
South Pacific
Status: Unincorporated
territory
Claimed: 1900
Capital: Pago Pago
Population: 65,628
Area: 75 sq miles (195 sq km)

Baker & Howland Islands
South Pacific
Status: Unincorporated
territory
Claimed: 1856
Capital: Not applicable
Population: None
Area: 0.5 sq miles (1.4 sq km)

Guam
West Pacific
Status: Unincorporated
territory
Claimed: 1898
Capital: Hagåtña
Population: 178,000
Area: 212 sq miles
(549 sq km)

Jarvis Island
South Pacific
Status: Unincorporated territory
Claimed: 1856
Capital: Not applicable
Population: None
Area: 1.7 sq miles (4.5 sq km)

Johnston Atoll
Central Pacific
Status: Unincorporated
territory
Claimed: 1858
Capital: Not applicable
Population: Not applicable
Area: 1 sq mile (2.8 sq km)

Kingman Reef
Central Pacific
Status: Administered territory
Claimed: 1856
Capital: Not applicable
Population: None
Area: 0.4 sq mile
(1 sq km)

Midway Islands
Central Pacific
Status: Administered
territory
Claimed: 1867
Capital: Not applicable
Population: None
Area: 2 sq miles
(5.2 sq km)

Navassa Island
West Indies
Status: Unincorporated
territory
Claimed: 1856
Capital: Not applicable
Population: None
Area: 2 sq miles (5.2 sq km)

Northern Mariana Islands
West Pacific
Status: Commonwealth
territory
Claimed: 1947
Capital: Saipan
Population: 86,616
Area: 177 sq miles (457 sq km)

Palmyra Atoll
Central Pacific
Status: Unincorporated
territory
Claimed: 1898
Capital: Not applicable
Population: None
Area: 5 sq miles (12 sq km)

Puerto Rico
West Indies
Status: Commonwealth
territory
Claimed: 1898
Capital: San Juan
Population: 4.0 million
Area: 3515 sq miles
(9104 sq km)

Virgin Islands
West Indies
Status: Unincorporated
territory
Claimed: 1917
Capital: Charlotte Amalie
Population: 108,448
Area: 137 sq miles
(355 sq km)

Wake Island
Central Pacific
Status: Unincorporated
territory
Claimed: 1898
Capital: Not applicable
Population: 200
Area: 2.5 sq miles
(6.5 sq km)

Glossary of geographical terms

The following glossary lists all geographical terms occuring on the maps and in the main-entry names in the Index–Gazetteer. These terms may precede, follow or be run together with the proper elements of the name; where they precede it the term is reversed for indexing purposes – thus Poluostov Yamal is indexed as Yamal, Poluostrov.

A

À Danish, Norwegian, River
Alpen German, Alps
Altiplanicie Spanish, Plateau
Älv(en) Swedish, River
Anse French, Bay
Archipiélago Spanish, Archipelago
Arcipelago Italian, Archipelago
Arquipélago Portuguese, Archipelago
Aukštuma Lithuanian, Upland

B

Bahía Spanish, Bay
Baía Portuguese, Bay
Baḥr Arabic, River
Baie French, Bay
Bandao Chinese, Peninsula
Banjaran Malay, Mountain range
Batang Malay, Stream
-berg Afrikaans, Norwegian, Mountain
Birket Arabic, Lake
Boğazı Turkish, Strait
Bucht German, Bay
Bugten Danish, Bay
Buḥayrat Arabic, Lake, reservoir
Buḥeiret Arabic, Lake
Bukit Malay, Mountain
-bukta Norwegian, Bay
bukten Swedish, Bay
Burnu Turkish, Cape, point
Buuraha Somali, Mountains

C

Cabo Portuguese, Cape
Cap French, Cape
Cascada Portuguese, Waterfall
Cerro Spanish, Mountain
Chaîne French, Mountain range
Chau Cantonese, Island
Cháy Turkish, Stream
Chhâk Cambodian, Bay
Chhu Tibetan, River
-chôsuji Korean, Reservoir

Chott Arabic, Salt lake, depression
Ch'ün-tao Chinese, Island group
Cordillera Spanish, Mountain range
Costa Spanish, Coast
Côte French, Coast
Cuchilla Spanish, Mountains

D

Dağı Azerbaijani, Turkish, Mountain
Dağları Azerbaijani, Turkish, Mountains
-dake Japanese, Peak
Danau Indonesian, Lake
Dao Vietnamese, Island
Daryá Persian, River
Daryácheh Persian, Lake
Dasht Persian, Plain, desert
Dawḥat Arabic, Bay
Dere Turkish, Stream
Dili Azerbaijani, Spit
-do Korean, Island
Dooxo Somali, Valley
Düzü Azerbaijani, Steppe

E

Embalse Spanish, Reservoir
Erg Arabic, Dunes
Estany Catalan, Lake
Estrecho Spanish, Strait
-ey Icelandic, Island
Ezero Bulgarian, Macedonian, Lake

F

Fjord Danish, Fjord
-fjorden Norwegian, Fjord
-fjørdhur Faeroese, Fjord
Fleuve French, River
Fliegu Maltese, Channel
-fljót Icelandic, River

G

-gang Korean, River
Ganga Nepali, Sinhala, River
Gaoyuan Chinese, Plateau
-gawa Japanese, River

Gebel Arabic, Mountain
-gebirge German, Mountains
Ghubbat Arabic, Bay
Gjiri Albanian, Bay
Gol Mongolian, River
Golfe French, Gulf
Golfo Italian, Spanish, Gulf
Gora Russian, Serbian, Mountain
Gory Russian, Mountains
Guba Russian, Bay
Gunung Malay, Mountain

H

Ḥadd Arabic, Spit
-haehyôp Korean, Strait
Haff German, Lagoon
Hai Chinese, Sea, bay
Ḥammádat Arabic, Plateau
Hámún Persian, Lake
Hawr Arabic, Lake
Háyk' Amharic, Lake
He Chinese, River
Helodrano Malagasy, Bay
-hegység Hungarian, Mountain range
Hka Burmese, River
-ho Korean, Lake
Hô Korean, Reservoir
/olot Hebrew, Dunes
Hora Belorussian, Mountain
Hrada Belorussian, Mountains, ridge
Hsi Chinese, River
Hu Chinese, Lake

I

Île(s) French, Island(s)
Ilha(s) Portuguese, Island(s)
Ilhéu(s) Portuguese, Islet(s)
Irmak Turkish, River
Isla(s) Spanish, Island(s)
Isola (Isole) Italian, Island(s)

J

Jabal Arabic, Mountain
Jál Arabic, Ridge
-järvi Finnish, Lake
Jazírat Arabic, Island
Jazíreh Persian, Island

Jebel Arabic, Mountain
Jezero Serbian/Croatian, Lake
Jiang Chinese, River
-joki Finnish, River
-jökull Icelandic, Glacier
Juzur Arabic, Islands

K

Kaikyó Japanese, Strait
-kaise Lappish, Mountain
Kali Nepali, River
Kalnas Lithuanian, Mountain
Kalns Latvian, Mountain
Kang Chinese, Harbor
Kangri Tibetan, Mountain(s)
Kaôh Cambodian, Island
Kapp Norwegian, Cape
Kavir Persian, Desert
K'edi Georgian, Mountain range
Kediet Arabic, Mountain
Kepulauan Indonesian, Malay, Island group
Khalîg, Khalíj Arabic, Gulf
Khawr Arabic, Inlet
Khola Nepali, River
Khrebet Russian, Mountain range
Ko Thai, Island
Kolpos Greek, Bay
-kopf German, Peak
Körfäzi Azerbaijani, Bay
Körfezi Turkish, Bay
Kõrgustik Estonian, Upland
Koshi Nepali, River
Kowtal Persian, Pass
Kúh(há) Persian, Mountain(s)
-kundo Korean, Island group
-kysten Norwegian, Coast
Kyun Burmese, Island

L

Laaq Somali, Watercourse
Lac French, Lake
Lacul Romanian, Lake
Lago Italian, Portuguese, Spanish, Lake

Laguna *Spanish*,
Lagoon, Lake
Laht *Estonian*, Bay
Laut *Indonesian*, Sea
Lembalemba *Malagasy*,
Plateau
Lerr *Armenian*,
Mountain
Lerrnashght'a *Armenian*,
Mountain range
Les *Czech*, Forest
Lich *Armenian*, Lake
Liqeni *Albanian*, Lake
Lumi *Albanian*, River
Lyman *Ukrainian*,
Estuary

M

Mae Nam *Thai*, River
-mägi *Estonian*, Hill
Maja *Albanian*, Mountain
-man *Korean*, Bay
Marios *Lithuanian*, Lake
-meer *Dutch*, Lake
Melkosopochnik
Russian, Plain
-meri *Estonian*, Sea
Mifraz *Hebrew*, Bay
Monkhafad *Arabic*,
Depression
Mont(s) *French*,
Mountain(s)
Monte *Italian*,
Portuguese, Mountain
More *Russian*, Sea
Mörön *Mongolian*, River

N

Nagor'ye *Russian*,
Upland
Na¡al *Hebrew*, River
Nahr *Arabic*, River
Nam *Laotian*, River
Nehri *Turkish*, River
Nevado *Spanish*,
Mountain (snow-
capped)
Nisoi *Greek*, Islands
Nizmennost' *Russian*,
Lowland, plain
Nosy *Malagasy*, Island
Nur *Mongolian*, Lake
Nuruu *Mongolian*,
Mountains
Nuur *Mongolian*, Lake
Nyzovyna *Ukrainian*,
Lowland, plain

O

Ostrov(a) *Russian*,
Island(s)
Oued *Arabic*,
Watercourse
-oy *Faeroese*, Island
-øy(a) *Norwegian*,
Island
Oya *Sinhala*, River
Ozero *Russian*,
Ukrainian, Lake

P

Passo *Italian*, Pass
Pegunungan
Indonesian, Malay,
Mountain range
Pelagos *Greek*, Sea
Penisola *Italian*,
Peninsula
Peski *Russian*, Sands
Phanom *Thai*, Mountain
Phou *Laotian*,
Mountain
Pic *Catalan*, Peak
Pico *Portuguese*,
Spanish, Peak
Pik *Russian*, Peak
Planalto *Portuguese*,
Plateau
Planina, Planini
Bulgarian, Macedonian,
Serbian, Croatian,
Mountain range
Ploskogor'ye *Russian*,
Upland
Poluostrov *Russian*,
Peninsula
Potamos *Greek*, River
Proliv *Russian*, Strait
Pulau *Indonesian*,
Malay, Island
Pulu *Malay*, Island
Punta *Portuguese*,
Spanish, Point

Q

Qá' *Arabic*, Depression
Qolleh *Persian*,
Mountain

R

Raas *Somali*, Cape
-rags *Latvian*, Cape
Ramlat *Arabic*, Sands
Ra's *Arabic*, Cape,
point, headland
Ravnina *Bulgarian*,
Russian, Plain
Récif *French*, Reef
Represa (Rep.) *Spanish*,
Portuguese, Reservoir
-rettó *Japanese*, Island
chain
Riacho *Spanish*,
Stream
Riban' *Malagasy*,
Mountains
Rio *Portuguese*, River
Río *Spanish*, River
Riu *Catalan*, River
Rivier *Dutch*, River
Rivière *French*, River
Rowd *Pashtu*, River
Rúd *Persian*, River
Rudohorie *Slovak*,
Mountains
Ruisseau *French*,
Stream

S

Sabkhat *Arabic*, Salt
marsh
Ṣaḥrá' *Arabic*, Desert
Samudra *Sinhala*,
Reservoir
-san *Japanese, Korean*,
Mountain
-sanchi *Japanese*,
Mountains
-sanmaek *Korean*,
Mountains
Sarír *Arabic*, Desert
Sebkha, Sebkhet *Arabic*,
Salt marsh, depression
See *German*, Lake
Selat *Indonesian*, Strait
-selkä *Finnish*, Ridge
Selseleh *Persian*,
Mountain range
Serra *Portuguese*,
Mountain
Serranía *Spanish*,
Mountain
Sha'íb *Arabic*,
Watercourse
Shamo *Chinese*,
Desert
Shan *Chinese*,
Mountain(s)
Shan-mo *Chinese*,
Mountain range
Shaṭṭ *Arabic*,
Distributary
-shima *Japanese*, Island
Shui-tao *Chinese*,
Channel
Sierra *Spanish*,
Mountains
Sòn *Vietnamese*,
Mountain
Sông *Vietnamese*, River
-spitze *German*, Peak
Štít *Slovak*, Peak
Stoeng *Cambodian*,
River
Stretto *Italian*, Strait
Su Anbarı *Azerbaijani*,
Reservoir
Sungai *Indonesian*,
Malay, River
Suu *Turkish*, River

T

Tal *Mongolian*, Plain
Tandavan' *Malagasy*,
Mountain range
Tangorombohitr'
Malagasy, Mountain
massif
Tao *Chinese*, Island
Tassili *Berber*, Plateau,
mountain
Tau *Russian*,
Mountain(s)
Taungdan *Burmese*,
Mountain range

Teluk *Indonesian*,
Malay, Bay
Terara *Amharic*,
Mountain
Tog *Somali*, Valley
Tônlé *Cambodian*,
Lake
Top *Dutch*, Peak
-tunturi *Finnish*,
Mountain
Tur'at *Arabic*,
Channel

V

Väin *Estonian*, Strait
-vatn *Icelandic*, Lake
-vesi *Finnish*, Lake
Vinh *Vietnamese*, Bay
Vodokhranilishche
(Vdkhr.) *Russian*,
Reservoir
Vodoskhovyshche
(Vdskh.) *Ukrainian*,
Reservoir
Volcán *Spanish*,
Volcano
Vozvyshennost'
Russian, Upland,
plateau
Vrh *Macedonian*,
Peak
Vysochyna *Ukrainian*,
Upland
Vysočina *Czech*,
Upland

W

Waadi *Somali*,
Watercourse
Wádí *Arabic*,
Watercourse
Wáḥat, Wâhat *Arabic*,
Oasis
Wald *German*, Forest
Wan *Chinese*, Bay
Wyżyna *Polish*,
Upland

X

Xé *Laotian*, River

Y

Yarımadası *Azerbaijani*,
Peninsula
Yazovir *Bulgarian*,
Reservoir
Yoma *Burmese*,
Mountains
Yü *Chinese*, Island

Z

Zaliv *Bulgarian*,
Russian, Bay
Zatoka *Ukrainian*, Bay
Zemlya *Russian*, Land

Continental factfile

North & Central America

Total area:
9,400,000 sq miles
(24,346,000 sq km)

Total number of countries: 23

Total population:
512 million

Largest city with population: Mexico City, Mexico 22.8 million

Country with highest population density: Barbados 1692 people per sq mile (653 people per sq km)

Largest country:
Canada 3,854,085 sq miles
(9,984,670 sq km)

Smallest country:
St. Kitts & Nevis 101 sq miles
(261 sq km)

Largest lake: Lake Superior, Canada/ USA 32,151 sq miles (83,270 sq km)

Longest river: Mississippi-Missouri, USA 3710 miles (5969 km)

Highest point: Mt. McKinley (Denali), Alaska, USA 20,322 ft (6194 m)

lowest point: Death Valley, California, USA 282 ft (86 m) below sea level

South America

Total area:
6,880,000 sq miles
(17,819,000 sq km)

Total number of countries: 12

Total population:
375 million

Largest city with population: São Paulo, Brazil 20.2 million

Country with highest population density: Ecuador 127 people per sq mile (49 people per sq km)

Largest country:
Brazil 3,286,470 sq miles
(8,511,965 sq km)

Smallest country:
Suriname 63,039 sq miles
(163,270 sq km)

Largest lake: Lake Titicaca, Bolivia/Peru 3220 sq miles (8340 sq km)

Longest river: Amazon, Brazil 4049 miles (6516 km)

Highest point: Cerro Aconcagua, Argentina 22,831 ft (6959 m)

Lowest point: Peninsula Valdés, Argentina 131 ft (40 m) below sea level

Africa

Total area:
11,677,250 sq miles
(30,244,050 sq km)

Total number of countries: 53

Total population:
910 million

Largest city with population: Cairo, Egypt 15.6 million

Country with highest population density: Mauritius 1811 people per sq mile (699 people per sq km)

Largest country:
Sudan 967,493 sq miles
(2,505,810 sq km)

Smallest country:
Seychelles 176 sq miles
(455 sq km)

Largest lake: Lake Victoria, Uganda, Kenya, Tanzania 26,828 sq miles (69,484 sq km)

Longest river: Nile, Uganda/Sudan/Egypt 4160 miles (6695 km)

Highest point: Kilimanjaro, Tanzania 19,340 ft (5895 m)

Lowest point: Lac', Assal, Djibouti 512 ft (156 m) below sea level

Europe

Total area:
4,809,200 sq miles
(12,456,000 sq km)

Total number of countries: 46

Total population:
697 million

Largest city with population: Moscow, Euro Russia 13.8 million

Country with highest population density: Monaco 43,561 people per sq mile (16,754 people per sq km)

Largest country: European Russia 1,527,341 sq miles (3,955,818 sq km)

Smallest country:
Vatican City, Italy 0.17 sq miles
(0.44 sq km)

Largest lake: Ladoga, European Russia 7100 sq miles (18,390 sq km)

Longest river: Volga, European Russia 2290 miles (3688 km)

Highest point: El'brus, Caucasus Mts, European Russia 18,510 ft (5642 m)

Lowest point: Volga Delta, Caspian Sea, European Russia 92 ft (28 m) below sea level

North & West Asia

 Total area:
9,585,500 sq miles
(24,826,600 sq km)

 Total number of
countries: 24

 Total population:
398 million

 Largest city with
population: Tehran, Iran
11.9 million

 Country with highest
population density: Bahrain
2596 people per sq mile
(1004 people per sq km)

 Largest country: Asiatic
Russia 5,065,471 sq miles
(13,119,582 sq km)

 Smallest country:
Bahrain 239 sq miles
(620 sq km)

 Largest lake:
Caspian Sea 142,243 sq miles
(371,000 sq km)

 Longest river: Ob'-Irtysh,
Asiatic Russia 3461 miles
(5570 km)

 Highest point: Pik Pobedy,
Kyrgyzstan/China 24,408 ft
(7439 m)

 Lowest point: Dead Sea,
Israel/Jordan 1286 ft
(392 m) below sea level

South & East Asia

 Total area:
7,936,200 sq miles
(20,554,700 sq km)

 Total number of
countries: 24

 Total population:
3979 million

 Largest city with
population: Tokyo,
Japan 34.2 million

 Country with highest
population density: Singapore
18,644 people per sq mile
(7213 people per sq km)

 Largest country:
China 3,705,386 sq miles
(9,596,960 sq km)

 Smallest country:
Maldives 116 sq miles
(300 sq km)

 Largest lake: Tonle Sap,
Cambodia 1000 sq miles
(2850 sq km)

 Longest river: Chang Jiang
(Yangtze) 3965 miles
(6380 km)

 Highest point:
Mount Everest, Nepal
29,035 ft (8850 m)

 Lowest point: Turpan Hami,
(Turfan basin), China 505 ft
(154 m) below sea level

Australasia & Oceania

 Total area:
3,376,700 sq miles
(8,745,750 sq km)

 Total number of
countries: 14

 Total population:
32 million

 Largest city with
population: Sydney,
Australia 4.4 million

 Country with highest
population density: Nauru
1670 people per sq mile
(644 people per sq km)

 Largest country:
Australia 2,967,893 sq miles
(7,686,850 sq km)

 Smallest country:
Nauru 8 sq miles
(21 sq km)

 Largest lake: Lake Eyre,
Australia 3700 sq miles
(9583 sq km)

 Longest river: Murray-
Darling, Australia
2330 miles (3750 km)

 Highest point: Mt. Wilhelm,
Papua New Guinea 14,795 ft
(4509 m)

 Lowest point: Lake Eyre,
Australia 52 ft
(16 m) below sea level

Antarctica

 Total area: 5,450,500 sq miles (14,000,000 sq km)
of which approx. 324,300 sq miles
(840,000 sq km) is ice-free.

 Total number of countries: The Antarctic Treaty has
30 participating nations and 14 with observer status.
Claims by Australia, France, New Zealand, Norway,
Argentina, Chile, and the UK are not recognized by
other member states.

 Total Population: No indigenous population.
74 research stations, (42 are staffed all year-round).
Population varies between about 1000 (winter)
and 4000 (summer).

 Total volume of ice:
7,200,000 cu miles (30,000,000 cu km):
contains 90% of Earth's fresh water

 Sea ice: 1,158,300 sq miles (3,000,000
sq km) in February. 7,722,000 sq miles
(20,000,000 sq km) in October

 Lowest temperature: Vostok station
-89.5°C (-129°F)

 Highest point: Vinson Massif
16,072 ft (4897 m)

 Lowest Point: Coastline 0ft/m

Geographical comparisons

Largest countries

Russ. Fed.	6,592,735 sq miles	(17,075,200 sq km)
Canada	3,854,085 sq miles	(9,984,670 sq km)
USA	3,717,792 sq miles	(9,629,091 sq km)
China	3,705,386 sq miles	(9,596,960 sq km)
Brazil	3,286,470 sq miles	(8,511,965 sq km)
Australia	2,967,893 sq miles	(7,686,850 sq km)
India	1,269,339 sq miles	(3,287,590 sq km)
Argentina	1,068,296 sq miles	(2,766,890 sq km)
Kazakhstan	1,049,150 sq miles	(2,717,300 sq km)
Sudan	967,493 sq miles	(2,505,810 sq km)

Smallest countries

Vatican City	0.17 sq miles	(0.44 sq km)
Monaco	0.75 sq miles	(1.95 sq km)
Nauru	8 sq miles	(21 sq km)
Tuvalu	10 sq miles	(26 sq km)
San Marino	24 sq miles	(61 sq km)
Liechtenstein	62 sq miles	(160 sq km)
Marshall Islands	70 sq miles	(181 sq km)
St. Kitts & Nevis	101 sq miles	(261 sq km)
Maldives	116 sq miles	(300 sq km)
Malta	122 sq miles	(316 sq km)

Largest islands

Greenland	849,400 sq miles	(2,200,000 sq km)
New Guinea	312,000 sq miles	(808,000 sq km)
Borneo	292,222 sq miles	(757,050 sq km)
Madagascar	229,300 sq miles	(594,000 sq km)
Sumatra	202,300 sq miles	(524,000 sq km)
Baffin Island	183,800 sq miles	(476,000 sq km)
Honshu	88,800 sq miles	(230,000 sq km)
Britain	88,700 sq miles	(229,800 sq km)
Victoria Island	81,900 sq miles	(212,000 sq km)
Ellesmere Island	75,700 sq miles	(196,000 sq km)

Richest countries   (GNI per capita, in US$)

Luxembourg	65,630
Norway	59,590
Switzerland	54,930
Liechtenstein	50,000
Denmark	47,390
Iceland	46,320
USA	43,740
Sweden	41,060
Ireland	40,150
Japan	38,980

Poorest countries   (GNI per capita, in US$)

Burundi	100
Somalia	120
Congo, Dem. Rep	120
Liberia.	130
Malawi	160
Ethiopia	160
Guinea-Bissau	180
Sierra Leone	220
Eritrea	220
Afghanistan	222

Most populous countries

China	1,331,400,000
India	1,135,600,000
USA	303,900,000
Indonesia	228,100,000
Brazil	191,300,000
Pakistan	164,600,000
Bangladesh	147,100,000
Russian Federation	141,900,000
Nigeria	137,200,000
Japan	128,300,000

Least populous countries

Vatican City	821
Tuvalu	11,992
Nauru	13,528
Palau	20,842
San Marino	29,615
Monaco	32,671
Liechtenstein	34,247
St. Kitts & Nevis	39,349
Marshall Islands	61,815
Antigua & Barbuda	69,481

Most densely populated countries

Monaco	43,561 people per sq mile	(16,754 per sq km)
Singapore	18,644 people per sq mile	(7213 per sq km)
Vatican City	4829 people per sq mile	(1866 per sq km)
Malta	3241 people per sq mile	(1256 per sq km)
Maldives	3181 people per sq mile	(1230 per sq km)
Bangladesh	2845 people per sq mile	(1098 per sq km)
Bahrain	2596 people per sq mile	(1004 per sq km)
Taiwan	1835 people per sq mile	(709 per sq km)
Mauritius	1811 people per sq mile	(699 per sq km)
Barbados	1692 people per sq mile	(653 per sq km)

Most sparsely populated countries

Mongolia.........4 people per sq mile......... (2 per sq km)
Namibia...........7 people per sq mile......... (3 per sq km)
Australia..........7 people per sq mile......... (3 per sq km)
Iceland ....8 people per sq mile......... (3 per sq km)
Suriname.........8 people per sq mile......... (3 per sq km)
Botswana.........8 people per sq mile......... (3 per sq km)
Mauritania ......8 people per sq mile......... (3 per sq km)
Libya ....9 people per sq mile......... (4 per sq km)
Canada ....9 people per sq mile......... (4 per sq km)
Guyana ....10 people per sq mile......... (4 per sq km)

Most widely spoken languages

1. Chinese (Mandarin)	6. Arabic
2. English	7. Bengali
3. Hindi	8. Portuguese
4. Spanish	9. Malay-Indonesian
5. Russian	10. French

Largest conurbations

Tokyo......................................34,200,000
Mexico City 22,800,000
Seoul 22,300,000
New York 21,900,000
São Paulo.................................20,200,000
Mumbai 19,850,000
Delhi..19,700,000
Shanghai..................................18,150,000
Los Angeles 18,000,000
Osaka 16,800,000
Jakarta.....................................16,550,000
Kolkata.....................................15,650,000
Cairo..15,600,000
Manila......................................14,950,000
Karachi.....................................14,300,000
Moscow....................................13,750,000
Buenos Aires 13,450,000
Dacca.......................................13,250,000
Rio de Janeiro...........................12,150,000
Beijing 12,100,000
London 12,000,000
Tehran......................................11,850,000
Istanbul 11,500,000
Lagos 11,100,000
Shenzhen 10,700,000

Longest rivers

Nile (NE Africa) ....4160 miles ...... (6695 km)
Amazon (South America) ....4049 miles ...... (6516 km)
Yangtze (China)..........................3915 miles ...... (6299 km)
Mississippi/Missouri (US) ....3710 miles........ (5969 km)
Ob'-Irtysh (Russ. Fed.) ....3461 miles ...... (5570 km)
Yellow River (China) ....3395 miles ...... (5464 km)
Congo (Central Africa) ....2900 miles ...... (4667 km)
Mekong (Southeast Asia) ....2749 miles...... (4425 km)
Lena (Russian Federation).......2734 miles...... (4400 km)
Mackenzie (Canada) ....2640 miles....... (4250 km)
Yenisey (Russ. Federation) ......2541 miles...... (4090 km)

Highest mountains   (Height above sea level)

Everest...................................... 29,035 ft....... (8850 m)
K2 .... 28,253 ft....... (8611 m)
Kanchenjunga I....................... 28,210 ft....... (8598 m)
Makalu I .... 27,767 ft....... (8463 m)
Cho Oyu .... 26,907 ft....... (8201 m)
Dhaulagiri I.............................. 26,796 ft....... (8167 m)
Manaslu I .... 26,783 ft....... (8163 m)
Nanga Parbat I......................... 26,661 ft....... (8126 m)
Annapurna I .... 26,547 ft....... (8091 m)
Gasherbrum I.......................... 26,471 ft....... (8068 m)

Largest bodies of inland water   (Area & depth)

Caspian Sea
    143,243 sq miles (371,000 sq km)....... 3215 ft (980 m)
Lake Superior
    32,151 sq miles (83,270 sq km)....... 1289 ft (393 m)
Lake Victoria
    26,560 sq miles (68,880 sq km).........328 ft (100 m)
Lake Huron
    23,436 sq miles (60,700 sq km).........751 ft (229 m)
Lake Michigan
    22,402 sq miles (58,020 sq km).........922 ft (281 m)
Lake Tanganyika
    12,703 sq miles (32,900 sq km).... 4700 ft (1435 m)
Great Bear Lake
    12,274 sq miles (31,790 sq km)...... 1047 ft (319 m)
Lake Baikal
    11,776 sq miles (30,500 sq km).... 5712 ft (1741 m)
Great Slave Lake
    10,981 sq miles (28,440 sq km).........459 ft (140 m)
Lake Erie
    9915 sq miles (25,680 sq km)...........197 ft (60 m)

......continued on page 166

Geographical comparisons continued

Deepest ocean features

Challenger Deep, Mariana Trench (Pacific)
36,201 ft .... (11,034 m)
Vityaz III Depth, Tonga Trench (Pacific)
35,704 ft .... (10,882 m)
Vityaz Depth, Kurile-Kamchatka Trench (Pacific)
34,588 ft .... (10,542 m)
Cape Johnson Deep, Philippine Trench (Pacific)
34,441 ft .... (10,497 m)
Kermadec Trench (Pacific)
32,964 ft .... (10,047 m)
Ramapo Deep, Japan Trench (Pacific)
32,758 ft .... (9984 m)
Milwaukee Deep, Puerto Rico Trench (Atlantic)
30,185 ft .... (9200 m)
Argo Deep, Torres Trench (Pacific)
30,070 ft .... (9165 m)
Meteor Depth, South Sandwich Trench (Atlantic)
30,000 ft .... (9144 m)
Planet Deep, New Britain Trench (Pacific)
29,988 ft .... (9140 m)

Greatest waterfalls (Mean flow of water)

Boyoma (Congo) ....600,400 cu. ft/sec (17,000 cu.m/sec)
Khône (Laos/Cambodia) ... 410,000 cu. ft/sec (11,600 cu.m/sec)
Niagara (USA/Canada) .... 195,000 cu. ft/sec (5500 cu.m/sec)
Grande (Uruguay) .... 160,000 cu. ft/sec (4500 cu.m/sec)
Paulo Afonso (Brazil) .... 100,000 cu. ft/sec(2800 cu.m/sec)
Urubupunga (Brazil) ....97,000 cu. ft/sec (2750 cu.m/sec)
Iguaçu (Argentina/Brazil)..........62,000 cu. ft/sec (1700 cu.m/sec)
Maribondo (Brazil)................53,000 cu. ft/sec (1500 cu.m/sec)
Victoria (Zimbabwe)................39,000 cu. ft/sec (1100 cu.m/sec)
Kabalega (Uganda)..................42,000 cu. ft/sec (1200 cu.m/sec)
Churchill (Canada)..................35,000 cu. ft/sec (1000 cu.m/sec)
Cauvery (India) ....33,000 cu. ft/sec (900 cu.m/sec)

Highest waterfalls

Angel (Venezuela) ....3212 ft............... (979 m)
Tugela (South Africa) ....3110 ft............... (948 m)
Utigard (Norway)..............................2625 ft............... (800 m)
Mongefossen (Norway) ....2539 ft............... (774 m)
Mtarazi (Zimbabwe) ....2500 ft............... (762 m)
Yosemite (USA) ....2425 ft............... (739 m)
Ostre Mardola Foss (Norway) .....2156 ft .... (657 m)
Tyssestrengane (Norway)............2119 ft............... (646 m)
*Cuquenan (Venezuela)................2001 ft............... (610 m)
Sutherland (New Zealand)...........1903 ft .... (580 m)
*Kjellfossen (Norway) ....1841 ft ....(561 m)

indicates that the total height is a single leap

Largest deserts

Sahara ....3,450,000 sq miles (9,065,000 sq km)
Gobi .... 500,000 sq miles (1,295,000 sq km)
Ar Rub al Khali ...... 289,600 sq miles (750,000 sq km)
Great Victorian ..... 249,800 sq miles (647,000 sq km)
Sonoran .... 120,000 sq miles (311,000 sq km)
Kalahari .... 120,000 sq miles (310,800 sq km)
Garagum .... 115,800 sq miles (300,000 sq km)
Takla Makan .... 100,400 sq miles (260,000 sq km)
Namib....................52,100 sq miles (135,000 sq km)
Thar.......................33,670 sq miles (130,000 sq km)

NB – Most of Antarctica is a polar desert, with only 2 inches (50 mm) of precipitation annually

Hottest inhabited places

Djibouti (Djibouti) .... 86.0°F .... (30.0°C)
Timbouctou (Mali)..................... 84.7°F .... (29.3°C)
Tirunelveli (India) .... 84.7°F .... (29.3°C)
Tuticorin (India).......................... 84.7°F .... (29.3°C)
Nellore (India)............................ 84.5°F .... (29.2°C)
Santa Marta (Colombia) .... 84.5°F .... (29.2°C)
Aden (Yemen) .... 84.0°F .... (29.0°C)
Madurai (India)........................... 84.0°F .... (29.0°C)
Niamey (Niger)............................ 84.0°F .... (29.0°C)

Driest inhabited places

Aswân (Egypt) ....0.02 in ......(0.5 mm)
Luxor (Egypt)..............................0.03 in ......(0.7 mm)
Arica (Chile) ....0.04 in ......(1.1 mm)
Ica (Peru)....................................0.10 in ......(2.3 mm)
Antofagasta (Chile)....................0.20 in ......(4.9 mm)
El Minya (Egypt) ....0.20 in ......(5.1 mm)
Asyût (Egypt) ....0.20 in ......(5.2 mm)
Callao (Peru)...............................0.50 in ......(12.0 mm)
Trujillo (Peru)..............................0.55 in ......(14.0 mm)
El Faiyûm (Egypt) ....0.80 in .....(19.0 mm)

Wettest inhabited places

Buenaventura (Colombia) .... 265 in .... (6743 mm)
Monrovia (Liberia) .... 202 in .... (5131 mm)
Pago Pago (American Samoa) .... 196 in .... (4990 mm)
Moulmein (Myanmar) .... 191 in .... (4852 mm)
Lae (Papua New Guinea) .... 183 in .... (4645 mm)
Baguio (Luzon I., Philippines)..... 180 in .... (4573 mm)
Sylhet (Bangladesh)..................... 176 in .... (4457 mm)
Padang (Sumatra, Indonesia)...... 166 in .... (4225 mm)
Bogor (Java, Indonesia)................166 in......(4225 mm)
Conakry (Guinea).........................171 in......(4341 mm)

GLOSSARY OF ABBREVIATIONS

This Glossary provides a comprehensive guide to the abbreviations used in this Atlas, and in the Index.

A
abbrev. abbreviated
Afr. Afrikaans
Alb. Albanian
Amh. Amharic
anc. ancient
Ar. Arabic
Arm. Armenian
Az. Azerbaijani

B
Basq. Basque
Bel. Belorussian
Ben. Bengali
Bibl. Biblical
Bret. Breton
Bul. Bulgarian
Bur. Burmese

C
Cam. Cambodian
Cant. Cantonese
Cast. Castilian
Cat. Catalan
Chin. Chinese
Cro. Croat
Cz. Czech

D
Dan. Danish
Dut. Dutch

E
Eng. English
Est. Estonian
est. estimated

F
Faer. Faeroese
Fij. Fijian
Fin. Finnish
Flem. Flemish
Fr. French
Fris. Frisian

G
Geor. Georgian
Ger. German
Gk. Greek
Guj. Gujarati

H
Haw. Hawaiian
Heb. Hebrew
Hind. Hindi
hist. historical
Hung. Hungarian

I
Icel. Icelandic
Ind. Indonesian
In. Inuit
Ir. Irish
It. Italian

J
Jap. Japanese

K
Kaz. Kazakh
Kir. Kirghiz
Kor. Korean
Kurd. Kurdish

L
Lao. Laotian
Lapp. Lappish
Lat. Latin
Latv. Latvian

Lith. Lithanian
Lus. Lusatian

M
Mac. Macedonian
Mal. Malay
Malg. Malagasy
Malt. Maltese
Mon. Montenegro
Mong. Mongolian

N
Nepali. Nepali
Nor. Norwegian

O
off. officially

P
Pash. Pashtu
Per. Persian
Pol. Polish
Port. Portuguese
prev. previously

R
Rmsch. Romansch
Roman. Romanian
Rus. Russian

S
SCr. Serbo - Croatian
Serb. Serbian
Slvk. Slovak
Slvn. Slovene
Som. Somali
Sp. Spanish
Swa. Swahili
Swe. Swedish

T
Taj. Tajik
Th. Thai
Tib. Tibetan
Turk. Turkish
Turkm. Turkmenistan

U
Uigh. Uighur
Ukr. Ukrainian
Uzb. Uzbek

V
var. variant
Vtn. Vietnamese

W
Wel. Welsh

X
Xh. Xhosa

Key to country factboxes within the Index:

Formation
Date of independence

Population
Total population / population density - based on total land area .

Calorie consumption
Average number of calories consumed daily per person.

A

Aa *see* Gauja
Aachen *94 A4 Dut.* Aken, *Fr.* Aix-la-Chapelle; *anc.* Aquae Grani, Aquisgranum. Nordrhein-Westfalen, W Germany
Aiún *see* Laâyoune
Aalborg *85 B7 var.* Ålborg, Ålborg-Nørresundby; *anc.* Alburgum. Nordjylland, N Denmark
Aalen *95 B6* Baden-Württemberg, S Germany
Aalsmeer *86 C3* Noord-Holland, C Netherlands
Aalst *87 B6* Oost-Vlaanderen, C Belgium
Aalten *86 E4* Gelderland, E Netherlands
Aalter *87 B5* Oost-Vlaanderen, NW Belgium
Aanaarjävri *see* Inarijärvi
Äänekoski *85 D5* Länsi-Suomi, W Finland
Aar *see* Aare
Aare *95 A7 var.* Aar. *river* W Switzerland
Aarhus *see* Århus
Aarlen *see* Arlon
Aat *see* Ath
Aba *77 E5* Orientale, NE Dem. Rep. Congo
Aba *75 G5* Abia, S Nigeria
Abā as Su'ūd *see* Najrān
Abaco Island *see* Great Abaco, N Bahamas
Ābādān *120 C4* Khūzestān, SW Iran
Abadan *122 C3 prev.* Bezmeïn, Büzmeyin, *Rus.* Byuzmeyin. Ahal Welaýaty, C Turkmenistan
Abai *see* Blue Nile
Abakan *114 D4* Respublika Khakasiya, S Russian Federation
Abancay *60 D4* Apurímac, SE Peru
Abariringa *see* Kanton
Abashiri *130 D2 var.* Abasiri. Hokkaidō, NE Japan
Abasiri *see* Abashiri
Äbay Wenz *see* Blue Nile
Abaya Häyk' *see* Ābaya Häyk'
Abbatis Villa *see* Abbeville
Abbazia *see* Opatija
Abbeville *90 C2 anc.* Abbatis Villa. Somme, N France
'Abd al 'Azīz, Jabal *118 D2 mountain range* NE Syria
Abéché *76 C3 var.* Abécher, Abeshr. Ouaddaï, SE Chad
Abécher *see* Abéché
Abela *see* Ávila
Abellinum *see* Avellino
Abemama *144 D2 var.* Apamama; *prev.* Roger Simpson Island. *atoll* Tungaru, W Kiribati
Abengourou *75 E5* E Côte d'Ivoire
Aberbrothock *see* Arbroath
Abercorn *see* Mbala
Aberdeen *88 D3 anc.* Devana. NE Scotland, United Kingdom
Aberdeen *45 E2* South Dakota, N USA
Aberdeen *46 B2* Washington, NW USA
Abergwaun *see* Fishguard
Abertawe *see* Swansea
Aberystwyth *89 C6* W Wales, United Kingdom
Abeshr *see* Abéché
Abhā *121 B6* 'Asīr, SW Saudi Arabia
Abidavichy *107 D7 Rus.* Obidovichi. Mahilyowskaya Voblasts', E Belarus
Abidjan *75 E5* S Côte d'Ivoire
Abilene *49 F3* Texas, SW USA
Abingdon *see* Pinta, Isla
Abkhazia *see* Ap'khazet'i
Åbo *see* Turku
Aboisso *75 E5* SE Côte d'Ivoire
Abo, Massif d' *76 B1 mountain range* NW Chad
Abomey *75 F5* S Benin
Abou-Déïa *76 C3* Salamat, SE Chad
Aboudouhour *see* Abū aḍ Ḍuhūr
Abou Kémal *see* Abū Kamāl
Abrantes *92 B3 var.* Abrántes. Santarém, C Portugal
Abrashlare *see* Brezovo
Abrolhos Bank *56 E4 undersea bank* W Atlantic Ocean
Abrova *107 B6 Rus.* Obrovo. Brestskaya Voblasts', SW Belarus
Abrud *108 B4 Ger.* Gross-Schlatten, *Hung.* Abrudbánya. Alba, SW Romania

Abrudbánya *see* Abrud
Abruzzese, Appennino *96 C4 mountain range* C Italy
Absaroka Range *44 B2 mountain range* Montana/Wyoming, NW USA
Abū aḍ Ḍuhūr *118 B3 Fr.* Aboudouhour. Idlib, NW Syria
Abu Dhabi *see* Abū Ẓabī
Abu Hamed *72 C3* River Nile, N Sudan
Abū Ḥardān *118 E3 var.* Hajîne. Dayr az Zawr, E Syria
Abuja *75 G4 country capital* (Nigeria) (Nigeria) Federal Capital District, C Nigeria
Abū Kamāl *118 E3 Fr.* Abou Kémal. Dayr az Zawr, E Syria
Abula *see* Ávila
Abunã, Rio *62 C2 var.* Río Abuná. *river* Bolivia/Brazil
Abut Head *151 B6 headland* South Island, New Zealand
Abū Ẓabī *121 C5 var.* Abū Ẓabī, *Eng.* Abu Dhabi. *country capital* (United Arab Emirates) (United Arab Emirates) Abū Ẓaby, C United Arab Emirates
Abū Ẓaby *see* Abū Ẓabī
Abyad, Al Baḥr al *see* White Nile
Abyla *see* Ávila
Abyssinia *see* Ethiopia
Acalayong *77 A5* SW Equatorial Guinea
Acaponeta *50 D4* Nayarit, C Mexico
Acapulco *51 E5 var.* Acapulco de Juárez, Guerrero, S Mexico
Acapulco de Juárez *see* Acapulco
Acarai Mountains *59 F4 Sp.* Serra Acaraí. *mountain range* Brazil/Guyana
Acaraí, Serra *see* Acarai Mountains
Acarigua *58 D2* Portuguesa, N Venezuela
Accra *75 E5 country capital* (Ghana) (Ghana)SE Ghana
Achacachi *61 E4* La Paz, W Bolivia
Achara *117 F2 var.* Ajaria. *autonomous republic* SW Georgia
Acklins Island *54 C2 island* SE Bahamas
Aconcagua, Cerro *64 B4 mountain* W Argentina
Açores/Açores, Arquipélago dos/ Açores, Ilhas dos *see* Azores
A Coruña *92 B1 Cast.* La Coruña, *Eng.* Corunna; *anc.* Caronium. Galicia, NW Spain
Acre *62 C2 off.* Estado do Acre. *region* W Brazil
Acre *62 C2 off.* Estado do Acre. *state* W Brazil
Açu *63 G2 var.* Assu. Rio Grande do Norte, E Brazil
Acunum Acusio *see* Montélimar
Ada *100 D3* Vojvodina, N Serbia
Ada *49 G2* Oklahoma, C USA
Ada Bazar *see* Adapazari
Adalia *see* Antalya
Adalia, Gulf of *see* Antalya Körfezi
Adama *see* Nazrēt
'Adan *121 B7 Eng.* Aden. SW Yemen
Adana *116 D4 var.* Seyhan. Adana, S Turkey
Adâncata *see* Horlivka
Adapazari *116 B2 prev.* Ada Bazar. Sakarya, NW Turkey
Adare, Cape *154 B4 cape* Antarctica
Ad Dahna *120 C4 desert* E Saudi Arabia
Ad Dakhla *70 A4 var.* Dakhla. SW Western Sahara
Ad Dalanj *see* Dilling
Ad Damar *see* Ed Damer
Ad Damazin *see* Ed Damazin
Ad Dāmir *see* Ed Damer
Ad Dammām *120 C4 var.* Dammām. Ash Sharqiyah, NE Saudi Arabia
Ad Dāmūr *see* Damoūr
Ad Dawḥah *120 C4 Eng.* Doha. *country capital* (Qatar) (Qatar) C Qatar
Ad Diffah *see* Libyan Plateau
Addis Ababa *see* Ādīs Ābeba
Addoo Atoll *see* Addu Atoll
Addu Atoll *132 A5 var.* Addu Atoll, Seenu Atoll. *atoll* S Maldives
Adelaide *149 B6 state capital* South Australia
Adelsberg *see* Postojna
Aden *see* 'Adan
Aden, Gulf of *121 C7 gulf* SW Arabian Sea
Adige *96 C2 Ger.* Etsch. *river* N Italy

Adirondack Mountains *41 F2 mountain range* New York, NE USA
Ådis Åbeba *73 C5 Eng.* Addis Ababa. *country capital* (Ethiopia) (Ethiopia) Ådis Åbeba, C Ethiopia
Adıyaman *117 E4* Adıyaman, SE Turkey
Adjud *108 C4* Vrancea, E Romania
Admiralty Islands *144 B3 island group* N Papua New Guinea
Adra *93 E5* Andalucía, S Spain
Adrar *70 D3* C Algeria
Adrian *40 C3* Michigan, N USA
Adrianople/Adrianopolis *see* Edirne
Adriatico, Mare *see* Adriatic Sea
Adriatic Sea *103 E2 Alb.* Deti Adriatik, *It.* Mare Adriatico, *SCr.* Jadransko More, *Slvn.* Jadransko Morje. *sea* N Mediterranean Sea
Adriatik, Deti *see* Adriatic Sea
Adycha *115 F2 river* NE Russian Federation
Aegean Sea *105 C5 Gk.* Aigaíon Pelagos, Aigaío Pélagos, *Turk.* Ege Denizi. *sea* NE Mediterranean Sea
Aegviidu *106 D2 Ger.* Charlottenhof. Harjumaa, NW Estonia
Aegyptus *see* Egypt
Aelana *see* Al 'Aqabah
Aelok *see* Ailuk Atoll
Aelönlaplap *see* Ailinglaplap Atoll
Aemona *see* Ljubljana
Aeolian Islands *97 C6 var.* Isole Lipari, *Eng.* Aeolian Islands, Lipari Islands. *island group* S Italy
Aeolian Islands *see* Eolie, Isole
Æsernia *see* Isernia
Afar Depression *see* Danakil Desert
Afars et des Issas, Territoire Français des *see* Djibouti
Afghānestān, Dowlat-e Eslāmī-ye *see* Afghanistan
Afghanistan *122 C4 off.* Islamic Republic of Afghanistan, *Per.* Dowlat-e Eslāmī-ye Afghānestān; *prev.* Republic of Afghanistan. *country* C Asia

AFGHANISTAN
Central Asia

Official name The Islamic Republic of Afghanistan
Formation 1919 / 1919
Capital Kabul
Population 32.3 million / 128 people per sq mile (50 people per sq km) / 24%
Total area 250,000 sq. miles (647,500 sq. km)
Languages Pashtu*, Tajik, Dari*, Farsi, Uzbek, Turkmen
Religions Sunni Muslim 84%, Shi'a Muslim 15%, Other 1%
Ethnic mix Pashtun 38%, Tajik 25%, Hazara 19%, Uzbek and Turkmen 16%, Other 3%
Government Presidential system
Currency Afghani = 100 puls
Literacy rate 28%
Calorie consumption 1539 calories

Afmadow *73 D6* Jubbada Hoose, S Somalia
Africa *68 continent*
Africa, Horn of *68 E4 physical region* Ethiopia/Somalia
Africana Seamount *141 A6 seamount* SW Indian Ocean
'Afrin *118 B2* Ḥalab, N Syria
Afyon *116 B3 prev.* Afyonkarahisar. Afyon, W Turkey
Agadès *see* Agadez
Agadez *75 G3 prev.* Agadès. Agadez, C Niger
Agadir *70 B3* SW Morocco
Agana/Agaña *see* Hagåtña
Āgaro *73 C5* Oromīya, C Ethiopia
Agassiz Fracture Zone *143 G5 fracture zone* S Pacific Ocean
Agatha *see* Agde
Agathónisi *105 D6 island* Dodekánisa, Greece, Aegean Sea
Agde *91 D6 anc.* Agatha. Hérault, S France
Agedabia *see* Ajdābiyā
Agen *91 B5 anc.* Aginnum. Lot-et-Garonne, SW France
Agendicum *see* Sens
Aghri Dagh *see* Büyükağrı Dağı

Agiá *104 B4 var.* Ayiá. Thessalía, C Greece
Agialoúsa *see* Yenierenköy
Agía Marína *105 E6* Léros, Dodekánisa, Greece, Aegean Sea
Aginnum *see* Agen
Ágios Efstrátios *104 D4 var.* Áyios Evstrátios, Hagios Evstrátios. *island* E Greece
Ágios Nikólaos *105 D8 var.* Áyios Nikólaos. Kríti, Greece, E Mediterranean Sea
Āgra *134 D3* Uttar Pradesh, N India
Agra and Oudh, United Provinces of *see* Uttar Pradesh
Agram *see* Zagreb
Ağrı *117 F3 var.* Karaköse; *prev.* Karakılısse. Ağrı, NE Turkey
Agri Dagi *see* Büyükağrı Dağı
Agrigento *97 C7 Gk.* Akragas; *prev.* Girgenti. Sicilia, Italy, C Mediterranean Sea
Agrínio *105 C5* Évvoia, C Greece
Agropoli *97 D5* Campania, S Italy
Aguachica *58 B2* Cesar, N Colombia
Aguadulce *53 F5* Coclé, S Panama
Agua Prieta *50 B1* Sonora, NW Mexico
Aguascalientes *50 D4* Aguascalientes, C Mexico
Aguaytía *60 C3* Ucayali, C Peru
Aguilas *93 E4* Murcia, SE Spain
Aguililla *50 D4* Michoacán, SW Mexico
Agulhas Basin *69 D8 undersea basin* SW Indian Ocean
Agulhas Plateau *67 D6 undersea plateau* SW Indian Ocean
Ahaggar *75 F2 high plateau region* SE Algeria
Ahlen *94 B4* Nordrhein-Westfalen, W Germany
Ahmadābād *134 C4 var.* Ahmedabad. Gujarāt, W India
Ahmadnagar *134 C5 var.* Ahmednagar. Mahārāshtra, W India
Ahmedabad *see* Ahmadābād
Ahmednagar *see* Ahmadnagar
Ahuachapán *52 B3* Ahuachapán, W El Salvador
Ahvāz *120 C3 var.* Ahwāz; *prev.* Nāsiri. Khūzestān, SW Iran
Ahvenanmaa *see* Åland
Ahwāz *see* Ahvāz
Aigaíon Pelagos/Aigaío Pélagos *see* Aegean Sea
Aígina *105 C6 var.* Aíyina, Egina. Aígina, C Greece
Aígio *105 B5 var.* Egio; *prev.* Aíyion. Dytikí Ellás, S Greece
Aiken *43 E2* South Carolina, SE USA
Ailinglaplap Atoll *144 D2 var.* Aelönlaplap. *atoll* Ralik Chain, S Marshall Islands
Ailuk Atoll *144 D1 var.* Aelok. *atoll* Ratak Chain, NE Marshall Islands
Ainaži *106 D3 Est.* Heinaste, *Ger.* Hainasch. Limbaži, N Latvia
'Aïn Ben Tili *74 D1* Tiris Zemmour, N Mauritania
Aintab *see* Gaziantep
Aïoun el Atrous/Aïoun el Atroûss *see* 'Ayoûn el 'Atroûs
Aiquile *61 F4* Cochabamba, C Bolivia
Air *see* Aïr, Massif de l'
Air du Azbine *see* Aïr, Massif de l'
Aïr, Massif de l' *75 G2 var.* Aïr, Aïr du Azbine, Asben. *mountain range* NC Niger
Aiud *108 B4 Ger.* Strassburg, *Hung.* Nagyenyed; *prev.* Engeten. Alba, SW Romania
Aix *see* Aix-en-Provence
Aix-en-Provence *91 D6 var.* Aix; *anc.* Aquae Sextiae. Bouches-du-Rhône, SE France
Aix-la-Chapelle *see* Aachen
Aíyina *see* Aígina
Aíyion *see* Aígio
Aizkraukle *106 C4* Aizkraukle, S Latvia
Ajaccio *91 E7* Corse, France, C Mediterranean Sea
Ajaria *see* Achara
Ajastan *see* Armenia
Aj Bogd Uul *126 D2 mountain* SW Mongolia
Ajdabiya *see* Ajdābiyā. Ajdābiyah. NE Libya
Ajdābiyah *see* Ajdābiyā

Ajjinena *see* El Geneina
Ajmer *134 D3 var.* Ajmere. Rājasthān, N India
Ajo *48 A3* Arizona, SW USA
Akaba *see* Al 'Aqabah
Akamagaseki *see* Shimonoseki
Akasha *72 B3* Northern, N Sudan
Akchâr *74 C2 desert* W Mauritania
Aken *see* Aachen
Akermanceaster *see* Bath
Akhalts'ikhe *117 F2* SW Georgia
Akhisar *116 A3* Manisa, W Turkey
Akhmîm *72 B2 var.* Akhmîm; *anc.* Panopolis. C Egypt
Akhtubinsk *111 C7* Astrakhanskaya Oblast', SW Russian Federation
Akhtyrka *see* Okhtyrka
Akimiski Island *38 C3 island* Nunavut, C Canada
Akinovka *109 F4* Zaporiz'ka Oblast', S Ukraine
Akita *130 D4* Akita, Honshū, C Japan
Akjoujt *74 C2 prev.* Fort-Repoux. Inchiri, W Mauritania
Akkeshi *130 E2* Hokkaidō, NE Japan
Aklavik *36 D3* Northwest Territories, NW Canada
Akmola *see* Astana
Akmolinsk *see* Astana
Aknavásár *see* Târgu Ocna
Akpatok Island *39 E1 island* Nunavut, E Canada
Akragas *see* Agrigento
Akron *40 D4* Ohio, N USA
Akrotiri *see* Akrotírion
Akrotírion *102 C5 var.* Akrotiri. *UK air base* S Cyprus
Aksai Chin *124 B2 Chin.* Aksayqin. *disputed region* China/India
Aksaray *116 C4* Aksaray, C Turkey
Aksayqin *see* Aksai Chin
Akşehir *116 B4* Konya, W Turkey
Aktash *see* Oqtosh
Aktau *114 A4 Kaz.* Aqtaū; *prev.* Shevchenko. Mangistau, W Kazakhstan
Aktjubinsk/Aktyubinsk *see* Aktobe
Aktobe *114 B4 Kaz.* Aqtöbe; *prev.* Aktjubinsk, Aktyubinsk. Aktyubinsk, NW Kazakhstan
Aktsyabrski *107 C7 Rus.* Oktyabr'skiy; *prev.* Karpilovka. Homyel'skaya Voblasts', SE Belarus
Aktyubinsk *see* Aktobe
Akula *77 C5* Equateur, NW Dem. Rep. Congo
Akureyri *83 E4* Norðurland Eystra, N Iceland
Akyab *see* Sittwe
Alabama *42 C2 off.* State of Alabama, *also known as* Camellia State, Heart of Dixie, The Cotton State, Yellowhammer State. *state* S USA
Alabama River *42 C3 river* Alabama, S USA
Alaca *116 C3* Çorum, N Turkey
Alacant *see* Alicante
Alagoas *63 G2 off.* Estado de Alagoas. *region* E Brazil
Alagoas *63 G2 off.* Estado de Alagoas. *state* E Brazil
Alais *see* Alès
Alajuela *53 E4* Alajuela, C Costa Rica
Alakanuk *36 C2* Alaska, USA
Al 'Alamayn *72 B1 var.* El 'Alamein. N Egypt
Al 'Amārah *120 C3 var.* Amara. Maysān, E Iraq
Alamo *47 D6* Nevada, W USA
Alamogordo *48 D3* New Mexico, SW USA
Alamosa *44 C5* Colorado, C USA
Åland Islands *85 C6 var.* Åland Islands, *Fin.* Ahvenanmaa. *island group* SW Finland
Åland Islands *see* Åland
Åland Sea *85 C6 var.* Åland Sea. *strait* Baltic Sea/Gulf of Bothnia
Åland Sea *see* Ålands Hav
Alanya *116 C4* Antalya, S Turkey
Al 'Aqabah *119 B8 var.* Akaba, Aqaba, 'Aqaba; *anc.* Aelana, Elath. Al 'Aqabah, SW Jordan
Al 'Arabīyah as Su'ūdīyah *see* Saudi Arabia
Alasca, Golfo de *see* Alaska, Gulf of
Alaşehir *116 A4* Manisa, W Turkey

Al 'Ashārah *118 E3 var.* Ashara. Dayr az Zawr, E Syria
Alaska *36 C3 off.* State of Alaska, *also known as* Land of the Midnight Sun, The Last Frontier, Seward's Folly; *prev.* Russian America. *state* NW USA
Alaska, Gulf of *36 C4 var.* Golfo de Alasca. *gulf* Canada/USA
Alaska Peninsula *36 C3 peninsula* Alaska, USA
Alaska Range *34 B2 mountain range* Alaska, USA
Al-Asnam *see* Chlef
Alattio *see* Alta
Al Awaynāt *see* Al 'Uwaynāt
Alaykel'/Alay-Kuu *see* Kёk-Art
Al 'Aynā *119 B7* Al Karak, W Jordan
Alazeya *115 G2 river* NE Russian Federation
Al Bāb *118 B2* Ḥalab, N Syria
Albacete *93 E3* Castilla-La Mancha, C Spain
Al Baghdādī *120 B3 var.* Khān al Baghdādī. Al Anbār, SW Iraq
Al Bāha *see* Al Bāḥah
Al Bāḥah *121 B5 var.* Al Bāha. Al Bāḥah, SW Saudi Arabia
Al Baḥrayn *see* Bahrain
Alba Iulia *108 B4 Ger.* Weissenburg, *Hung.* Gyulafehérvár; *prev.* Bălgrad, Karlsburg, Károly-Fehérvár. Alba, W Romania
Albania *101 C7 off.* Republic of Albania, *Alb.* Republika e Shqipërisë, Shqipëria; *prev.* People's Socialist Republic of Albania. *country* SE Europe

ALBANIA
Southeast Europe

Official name Republic of Albania
Formation 1912 / 1921
Capital Tirana
Population 3.2 million / 302 people per sq mile (117 people per sq km) / 44%
Total area 11,100 sq. miles (28,748 sq. km)
Languages Albanian*, Greek
Religions Sunni Muslim 70%, Orthodox Christian 20%, Roman Catholic 10%
Ethnic mix Albanian 93%, Greek 5%, Other 2%
Government Parliamentary system
Currency Lek = 100 qindarka (qintars)
Literacy rate 99%
Calorie consumption 2848 calories

Albania *see* Aubagne
Albany *147 B7* Western Australia
Albany *42 D3* Georgia, SE USA
Albany *41 F3 state capital* New York, NE USA
Albany *46 B3* Oregon, NW USA
Albany *38 C3 river* Ontario, S Canada
Alba Regia *see* Székesfehérvár
Al Bāridah *118 C4 var.* Bāridah. Ḥimṣ, C Syria
Albany *134 B3 Ter.* Albert Nyanza, Lac Mobutu Sese Seko. *lake* Uganda/ Dem. Rep. Congo
Albert Lea *45 F3* Minnesota, N USA
Albert Nyanza *see* Albert, Lake
Albertville *see* Kalemie
Albi *91 C6 anc.* Albiga. Tarn, S France
Albiga *see* Albi
Ålborg *see* Aalborg
Ålborg-Nørresundby *see* Aalborg
Albuquerque *48 D2* New Mexico, SW USA
Alburgum *see* Aalborg
Albury *149 C7* New South Wales, SE Australia
Alcácer do Sal *92 B4* Setúbal, W Portugal

Alcalá de Henares 93 E3 Ar. Alkal'a; anc.
  Complutum. Madrid, C Spain
Alcamo 97 C7 Sicilia, Italy,
  C Mediterranean Sea
Alcañiz 93 F2 Aragón, NE Spain
Alcántara, Embalse de 92 C3 reservoir
  W Spain
Alcaudete 92 D4 Andalucía, S Spain
Alcázar see Ksar-el-Kebir
Alcazarquivir see Ksar-el-Kebir
Alcoi see Alcoy
Alcoy 93 F4 Cat. Alcoi. País Valenciano,
  E Spain
Aldabra Group 79 G2 island group
  SW Seychelles
Aldan 115 F3 river NE Russian
  Federation
al Dar al Baida see Rabat
Alderney 90 A2 island Channel
  Islands
Aleg 74 C3 Brakna, SW Mauritania
Aleksandriya see Oleksandriya
Aleksandropol' see Gyumri
Aleksandrovka see Oleksandrivka
Aleksandrovsk see Zaporizhzhya
Aleksin 111 B5 Tul'skaya Oblast',
  W Russian Federation
Aleksinac 100 E4 Serbia, SE Serbia
Alençon 90 B3 Orne, N France
Alenquer 63 E2 Pará, NE Brazil
Alep/Aleppo see Ḥalab
Alert 37 F1 Ellesmere Island, Nunavut,
  N Canada
Alès 91 C6 prev. Alais. Gard,
  S France
Aleşd 108 B3 Hung. Élesd. Bihor,
  SW Romania
Alessandria 96 B2 Fr. Alexandrie.
  Piemonte, N Italy
Ålesund 85 A5 Møre og Romsdal,
  S Norway
Aleutian Basin 113 G3 undersea basin
  Bering Sea
Aleutian Islands 36 A3 island group
  Alaska, USA
Aleutian Range 34 A2 mountain range
  Alaska, USA
Aleutian Trench 113 H3 trench
  S Bering Sea
Alexander Archipelago 36 D4 island
  group Alaska, USA
Alexander City 42 D2 Alabama, S USA
Alexander Island 154 A3 island
  Antarctica
Alexander Range see Kirghiz Range
Alexandra 151 B7 Otago, South Island,
  New Zealand
Alexándreia 104 B4 var. Aléxandria.
  Kentrikí Makedonía, N Greece
Alexandretta see İskenderun
Alexandretta, Gulf of see İskenderun
  Körfezi
Alexandria 72 B1 Ar. Al Iskandariyah.
  N Egypt
Alexandria 108 C5 Teleorman,
  S Romania
Alexandria 42 B3 Louisiana, S USA
Alexandria 45 F2 Minnesota, N USA
Aléxandria see Alexándreia
Alexandrie see Alessandria
Alexandroúpoli 104 B4 var. Alexándria
  Alexandroúpolis, Turk. Dedeagaç,
  Dedeagach. Anatolikí Makedonía kai
  Thráki, NE Greece
Alexandroúpolis see Alexandroúpoli
Al Fāshir see El Fasher
Alfatar 104 E1 Silistra, NE Bulgaria
Alfeiós 105 B6 prev. Alfiós; anc.
  Alpheius, Alpheus. river S Greece
Alfiós see Alfeiós
Alföld see Great Hungarian Plain
Al-Furāt see Euphrates
Alga 114 B4 Kaz. Algha. Aktyubinsk,
  NW Kazakhstan
Algarve 92 B4 cultural region
  S Portugal
Algeciras 92 C5 Andalucía,
  SW Spain
Algemesí 93 F3 País Valenciano,
  E Spain
Al-Genain see El Geneina
Alger 71 E1 var. Algiers, El Djazaïr,
  Al Jazair. country capital (Algeria)
  (Algeria) N Algeria
Algeria 70 C3 off. Democratic and
  Popular Republic of Algeria. country
  N Africa

ALGERIA
  North Africa

Official name People's Democratic
  Republic of Algeria
Formation 1962 / 1962
Capital Algiers
Population 33.9 million / 37 people
  per sq mile (14 people per sq km) / 59%
Total area 919,590 sq. miles
  (2,381,740 sq. km)
Languages Arabic*, Tamazight (Kabyle,
  Shawia, Tamashek), French
Religions Sunni Muslim 99%,
  Christian and Jewish 1%
Ethnic mix Arab 75%, Berber 24%,
  European and Jewish 1%
Government Presidential system
Currency Algerian dinar = 100 centimes
Literacy rate 70%
Calorie consumption 3022 calories

Algeria, Democratic and Popular
  Republic of see Algeria
Algerian Basin 80 C5 var. Balearic Plain.
  undersea basin W Mediterranean Sea
Algha see Alga
Al Ghābah 121 E5 var. Ghaba. C Oman
Alghero 97 A5 Sardegna, Italy,
  C Mediterranean Sea
Al Ghurdaqah see Hurghada
Algiers see Alger
Al Golea see El Goléa
Algona 45 F3 Iowa, C USA
Al Hajar al Gharbi 121 D5 mountain
  range N Oman
Al Hamad see Syrian Desert
Al Ḥasakah 118 D2 var. Al Hasijah, El
  Haseke, Fr. Hassetché. Al Ḥasakah,
  NE Syria
Al Hasijah see Al Ḥasakah
Al Ḥillah 120 B3 var. Hilla. Bābil, C Iraq
Al Ḥisā 119 B7 Aṭ Ṭafīlah, W Jordan
Al Ḥudaydah 121 B6 Eng. Hodeida.
  W Yemen
Al Hufūf 120 C4 var. Hofuf. Ash
  Sharqīyah, NE Saudi Arabia
Aliákmon see Aliákmonas
Aliákmonas 104 B4 prev. Aliákmon; anc.
  Haliacmon. river N Greece
Aliartos 105 C5 Stereá Ellás, C Greece
Alicante 93 F4 Cat. Alacant, Lat.
  Lucentum. País Valenciano, SE Spain
Alice 49 G5 Texas, SW USA
Alice Springs 148 A4 Northern
  Territory, C Australia
Alifu Atoll see Ari Atoll
Aligandí 53 G4 Kuna Yala, NE Panama
Aliki see Alykí
Alima 77 B6 river C Congo
Al Imārāt al 'Arabīyahal Muttaḥidah
  see United Arab Emirates
Alindao 76 C4 Basse-Kotto, S Central
  African Republic
Aliquippa 40 D4 Pennsylvania, NE USA
Al Iskandariyah see Alexandria
Al Ismā'īlīya 72 B1 var. Ismailia,
  Ismâ'ilīya. N Egypt
Alistráti 104 C3 Kentrikí Makedonía,
  NE Greece
Alivéri 105 C5 var. Alivérion. Évvoia,
  C Greece
Alivérion see Alivéri
Al Jabal al Akḥdar 71 G2 mountain
  range NE Libya
Al Jafr 119 B7 Ma'ān, S Jordan
Al Jaghbūb 71 H3 NE Libya
Al Jahrā' 120 C4 var. Al Jahrah, Jahra.
  C Kuwait
Al Jahrah see Al Jahrā'
Al Jamāhīrīyah al 'Arabīyah al Lībīyah
  ash Sha'bīyah al Ishtirākīy see Libya
Al Jawf 120 B4 off. Jauf. Al Jawf,
  NW Saudi Arabia
Al Jawlan see Golan Heights
Al Jazair see Alger
Al Jazirah 118 E2 physical region
  Iraq/Syria
Al Jīzah see Gîza
Al Junaynah see El Geneina
Alkal'a see Alcalá de Henares
Al Karak 119 B7 var. El Kerak, Karak,
  Kerak; anc. Kir Moab, Kir of Moab. Al
  Karak, W Jordan
Al-Kasr al-Kebir see Ksar-el-Kebir
Al Khalīl see Hebron

Al Khārijah 72 B2 var. El Khârga.
  C Egypt
Al Khums 71 F2 var. Homs, Khoms,
  Khums. NW Libya
Alkmaar 86 C2 Noord-Holland,
  NW Netherlands
Al Kufrah 71 H4 SE Libya
Al Kūt 120 C3 var. Kūt al 'Amārah, Kut
  al Imara. Wāsiṭ, E Iraq
Al-Kuwait see Al Kuwayt
Al Kuwayt 120 C4 var. Al-Kuwait, Eng.
  Kuwait, Kuwait City; prev. Qurein.
  country capital (Kuwait) (Kuwait)
  E Kuwait
Al Lādhiqīyah 118 A3 Eng. Latakia, Fr.
  Lattaquié; anc. Laodicea, Laodicea ad
  Mare. Al Lādhiqīyah, W Syria
Allahābād 135 E3 Uttar Pradesh, N India
Allanmyo see Aunglan
Allegheny Plateau 41 E3 mountain
  range New York/Pennsylvania, NE USA
Allenstein see Olsztyn
Allentown 41 F4 Pennsylvania, NE USA
Alleppey 132 C3 var. Alappuzha. Kerala,
  SW India
Alliance 44 D3 Nebraska, C USA
Al Līth 121 B5 Makkah, SW Saudi Arabia
Al Lubnān see Lebanon
Alma-Ata see Almaty
Almada 92 B4 Setúbal, W Portugal
Al Madīnah 121 A5 Eng. Medina. Al
  Madīnah, W Saudi Arabia
Al Mafraq see Mafraq
Al Mafraq 119 B6 var. Mafraq. Al
  Mafraq, N Jordan
Al Mahdīyah see Mahdia
Al Mahrah 121 C6 mountain range
  E Yemen
Al Majma'ah 120 B4 Ar Riyāḍ, C Saudi
  Arabia
Al Mālikīyah 118 E1 var. Malkiye. Al
  Ḥasakah, N Syria
Almalyk see Olmaliq
Al Mamlakah see Morocco
Al Mamlaka al Urdunīya al
  Hashemīyah see Jordan
Al Manāmah 120 C4 Eng. Manama.
  country capital (Bahrain) (Bahrain)
  N Bahrain
Al Manāṣif 118 E3 mountain range
  E Syria
Almansa 93 F4 Castilla-La Mancha,
  C Spain
Al-Mariyya see Almería
Al Marj 71 G2 var. Barka, It. Barce.
  NE Libya
Almaty 114 C5 var. Alma-Ata. Almaty,
  SE Kazakhstan
Al Mawṣil 120 B2 Eng. Mosul. Nīnawá,
  N Iraq
Al Mayādīn 118 D3 var. Mayadin, Fr.
  Meyadine. Dayr az Zawr, E Syria
Al Mazra' see Al Mazra'ah
Al Mazra'ah 119 B6 var. Al Mazra',
  Mazra'a. Al Karak, W Jordan
Almelo 86 E3 Overijssel, E Netherlands
Almendra, Embalse de 92 C2 reservoir
  Castilla-León, W Spain
Almendralejo 92 C4 Extremadura,
  W Spain
Almere 86 C3 var. Almere-stad.
  Flevoland, C Netherlands
Almere-stad see Almere
Almería 93 E5 Ar. Al-Mariyya; anc. Unci,
  Lat. Portus Magnus. Andalucía, S Spain
Al Mīnā' see El Mina
Al Minyā 72 B2 var. El Minya, Minya.
  C Egypt
Almirante 53 E4 Bocas del Toro,
  NW Panama
Al Mudawwarah 119 B8 Ma'ān,
  SW Jordan
Al Mukallā 121 C6 var. Mukalla.
  SE Yemen
Al Obayyid see El Obeid
Alofi 145 F4 dependent territory capital
  (Niue) W Niue
Aloha State see Hawai'i
Aloja 106 D3 Limbaži, N Latvia
Alónnisos 105 C5 island Vóreies
  Sporádes, Greece, Aegean Sea
Alor, Kepulauan 139 E5 island group
  E Indonesia
Al Oued see El Oued
Alpen see Alps

Alpena 40 D2 Michigan, N USA
Alpes see Alps
Alpha Cordillera 155 B3 var. Alpha
  Ridge. seamount range Arctic Ocean
Alpha Ridge see Alpha Cordillera
Alpheius see Alfeiós
Alphen aan den Rijn see Alphen aan den
  Rijn
Alphen aan den Rijn 86 C3 var. Alphen.
  Zuid-Holland, C Netherlands
Alpheus see Alfeiós
Alpi see Alps
Alpine 49 E4 Texas, SW USA
Alps 102 C1 Fr. Alpes, Ger. Alpen, It.
  Alpi. mountain range C Europe
Al Qadārif see Gedaref
Al Qāhirah see Cairo
Al Qāmishlī 118 E1 var. Kamishli,
  Qamishly. Al Ḥasakah, NE Syria
Al Qaṣrayn see Kasserine
Al Qayrawān see Kairouan
Al-Qsar al-Kbir see Ksar-el-Kebir
Al Qubayyāt see Qoubaïyât
Al Quds/Al Quds ash Sharif see
  Jerusalem
Alqueva, Barragem do 92 C4 reservoir
  Portugal/Spain
Al Qunayṭirah 119 B5 var. El Kuneitra,
  El Quneitra, Kuneitra, Qunaytra. Al
  Qunayṭirah, SW Syria
Al Quṣayr 118 B4 var. El Quseir, Quṣayr,
  Fr. Kousseir. Ḥimṣ, W Syria
Al Quwayrah 119 B8 var. El Quweira. Al
  'Aqabah, SW Jordan
Alsace 90 E3 Ger. Elsass; anc. Alsatia.
  cultural region NE France
Alsatia see Alsace
Alsdorf 94 A4 Nordrhein-Westfalen,
  W Germany
Alte see Olt
Alta 84 D2 Fin. Alattio. Finnmark,
  N Norway
Altai Mountains 126 C2 var. Altai, Chin.
  Altay Shan, Rus. Altay. mountain range
  Asia/Europe
Altamaha River 43 E3 river Georgia,
  SE USA
Altamira 63 E2 Pará, NE Brazil
Altamura 97 E5 anc. Lupatia. Puglia,
  SE Italy
Altar, Desierto de 50 A1 var. Sonoran
  Desert. desert Mexico/USA
Altar, Desierto de see Sonoran Desert
Altay 126 C2 Xinjiang Uygur Zizhiqu,
  NW China
Altay 126 C2 prev. Yösönbulag. Govĭ-
  Altay, W Mongolia
Altay Mountains see Altai Mountains
Altay Shan see Altai Mountains
Altenburg see Bucureşti, Romania
Altın Köprü 120 B3 var. Altun Kupri. At
  Ta'mīn, N Iraq
Altiplano 61 F4 physical region W South
  America
Altkanischa see Kanjiža
Alton 40 B5 Illinois, N USA
Alton 40 B4 Pennsylvania, NE USA
Altoona 41 E4 Pennsylvania,
  NE USA
Alto Paraná see Paraná
Altpassaue see Stara Pazova
Alt-Schwanenburg see Gulbene
Altsohl see Zvolen
Altun Kupri see Altin Köprü
Alupka 109 F5 Respublika Krym,
  S Ukraine
Al Urdunn see Jordan
Alushta 109 F5 Respublika Krym,
  S Ukraine
Al 'Uwaynāt 71 F4 var. Al Awaynāt.
  SW Libya
Alva 49 F1 Oklahoma, C USA
Alvarado 51 F4 Veracruz-Llave,
  E Mexico
Alvin 49 H4 Texas, SW USA

Al Wajh *120 A4* Tabūk, NW Saudi Arabia
Alwar *134 D3* Rājasthān, N India
Al Wari'ah *120 C4* Ash Sharqīyah, N Saudi Arabia
Al Yaman *see* Yemen
Alyki *104 C4 var.* Aliki. Thásos, N Greece
Alytus *107 B5 Pol.* Olita. Alytus, S Lithuania
Alzette *87 D8 river* S Luxembourg
Amadeus, Lake *147 D5 seasonal lake* Northern Territory, C Australia
Amadi *73 B5* Western Equatoria, SW Sudan
Amadjuak Lake *37 G3 lake* Baffin Island, Nunavut, N Canada
Amakusa-nada *131 A7 gulf* SW Japan
Åmål *85 B6* Västra Götaland, S Sweden
Amami-gunto *130 A3 island group* SW Japan
Amami-o-shim *130 A3 island* S Japan
Amantea *97 D6* Calabria, SW Italy
Amapá *63 E1 off.* Estado de Amapá; *prev.* Território de Amapá. *state* NE Brazil
Amapá *63 E1 off.* Estado de Amapá; *prev.* Território de Amapá. *region* NE Brazil
Amapá, Estado de *see* Amapá
Amapá, Território de *see* Amapá
Amara *see* Al 'Amārah
Amarapura *136 B3* Mandalay, C Burma (Myanmar)
Amarillo *49 E2* Texas, SW USA
Amay *87 C6* Liège, E Belgium
Amazon *63 E1 Sp.* Amazonas. *river* Brazil/Peru
Amazonas *see* Amazon
Amazon Basin *62 D2 basin* N South America
Amazon, Mouths of the *63 F1 delta* NE Brazil
Ambam *77 B5* Sud, S Cameroon
Ambanja *79 G2* Antsiraňana, N Madagascar
Ambarchik *115 G2* Respublika Sakha (Yakutiya), NE Russian Federation
Ambato *60 B1* Tungurahua, C Ecuador
Ambérieu-en-Bugey *91 D5* Ain, E France
Ambianum *see* Amiens
Amboasary *79 F4* Toliara, S Madagascar
Amboina *see* Ambon
Ambon *139 F4 prev.* Amboina, Amboyna. Pulau Ambon, E Indonesia
Ambositra *79 G3* Fianarantsoa, SE Madagascar
Amboyna *see* Ambon
Ambracia *see* Árta
Ambre, Cap d' *see* Bobaomby, Tanjona
Ambrim *see* Ambrym
Ambriz *78 A1* Bengo, NW Angola
Ambrym *144 D4 var.* Ambrim. *island* C Vanuatu
Amchitka Island *36 A2 island* Aleutian Islands, Alaska, USA
Amdo *126 C5* Xizang Zizhiqu, W China
Ameland *86 D1* Fris. It Amelân. *island* Waddeneilanden, N Netherlands
Amelân, It *see* Ameland
America *see* United States of America
America-Antarctica Ridge *67 C7 undersea ridge* S Atlantic Ocean
America in Miniature *see* Maryland
American Falls Reservoir *46 E4 reservoir* Idaho, NW USA
American Samoa *145 E4 US unincorporated territory* W Polynesia
Amersfoort *86 D3* Utrecht, C Netherlands
Ames *45 F3* Iowa, C USA
Amfilochía *105 A5 var.* Amfilokhía. Dytikí Ellás, C Greece
Amfilokhía *see* Amfilochía
Amga *115 F3 river* NE Russian Federation
Amherst *39 F4* Nova Scotia, SE Canada
Amherst *see* Kyaikkami
Amida *see* Diyarbakır
Amiens *90 C3 anc.* Ambianum, Samarobriva. Somme, N France
Amindaion/Amindeo *see* Amýntaio
Amíndivi Islands *132 A2 island group* Lakshadweep, India, N Indian Ocean
Amirante Islands *79 G1 var.* Amirantes Group. *island group* C Seychelles

Amirantes Group *see* Amirante Islands
Amistad, Presa de la *see* Amistad Reservoir
Amistad Reservoir *49 F4 var.* Presa de la Amistad. *reservoir* Mexico/USA
Amisus *see* Samsun
Ammaia *see* Portalegre
'Ammān *119 B6 var.* Amman; *anc.* Philadelphia, *Bibl.* Rabbah Ammon, Rabbath Ammon. *country capital* (Jordan) (Jordan) 'Ammān, NW Jordan
Ammassalik *82 D4 var.* Angmagssalik. Tunu, S Greenland
Ammóchostos *see* Gazimağusa
Ammóchostos, Kólpos *see* Gazimağusa Körfezi
Amnok-kang *see* Yalu
Amoea *see* Portalegre
Amoentai *see* Amuntai
Åmol *120 D2 var.* Amul. Māzandarān, N Iran
Amorgós *105 D6* Amorgós, Kykládes, Greece, Aegean Sea
Amorgós *105 D6 island* Kykládes, Greece, Aegean Sea
Amos *38 D4* Québec, SE Canada
Amourj *74 D3* Hodh ech Chargui, SE Mauritania
Amoy *see* Xiamen
Ampato, Nevado *61 E4 mountain* S Peru
Amposta *93 F2* Cataluña, NE Spain
Amraoti *see* Amrāvati
Amrāvati *134 D4 prev.* Amraoti. Mahārāshtra, C India
Amritsar *134 D2* Punjab, N India
Amstelveen *86 C3* Noord-Holland, C Netherlands
Amsterdam *86 C3 country capital* (Netherlands) (Netherlands) Noord-Holland, C Netherlands
Amsterdam Island *141 C6 island* NE French Southern and Antarctic Territories
Am Timan *76 C3* Salamat, SE Chad
Amu Darya *122 D2 Rus.* Amudar'ya, *Taj.* Dar"yoi Amu, *Turkm.* Amyderya, *Uzb.* Amudaryo; *anc.* Oxus. *river* C Asia
Amu-Dar'ya *see* Amyderýa
Amudar"ya/Amudaryo/Amu, Dar"yoi *see* Amu Darya
Amul *see* Åmol
Amund Ringnes Island *37 F2 Island* Nunavut, N Canada
Amundsen Basin *see* Fram Basin
Amundsen Plain *154 A4 abyssal plain* S Pacific Ocean
Amundsen-Scott *154 B3 US research station* Antarctica
Amundsen Sea *154 A4 sea* S Pacific Ocean
Amuntai *138 D4 prev.* Amoentai. Borneo, C Indonesia
Amur *115 G4 Chin.* Heilong Jiang. *river* China/Russian Federation
Amvrosiyevka *see* Amvrosiyivka
Amvrosiyivka *109 H3 Rus.* Amvrosiyevka. Donets'ka Oblast', SE Ukraine
Amyderýa *123 E3 Rus.* Amu-Dar'ya. Lebap Welaýaty, NE Turkmenistan
Amyderya *see* Amu Darya
Amýntaio *104 B4 var.* Amindeo; *prev.* Amíndaion. Dytikí Makedonía, N Greece
Anabar *115 E2 river* NE Russian Federation
An Abhainn Mhór *see* Blackwater
Anaco *59 E2* Anzoátegui, NE Venezuela
Anaconda *44 B2* Montana, NW USA
Anacortes *46 B1* Washington, NW USA
Anadolu Dağları *see* Doğu Karadeniz Dağları
Anadyr' *115 H1* Chukotskiy Avtonomnyy Okrug, NE Russian Federation
Anadyr' *115 G1 river* NE Russian Federation
Anadyr, Gulf of *115 H1 Eng.* Gulf of Anadyr. *gulf* NE Russian Federation
Anadyr, Gulf of *see* Anadyrskiy Zaliv
Anáfi *105 D7 anc.* Anaphe. Kykládes, Greece, Aegean Sea
'Ānah *see* 'Annah
Anaheim *46 E2* California, W USA
Anaiza *see* 'Unayzah

Analalava *79 G2* Mahajanga, NW Madagascar
Anamur *116 C5* İçel, S Turkey
Anantapur *132 C2* Andhra Pradesh, S India
Anaphe *see* Anáfi
Anápolis *63 F3* Goiás, C Brazil
Anār *120 D3* Kermān, C Iran
Anatolia *116 C4 plateau* C Turkey
Anatom *see* Aneityum
Añatuya *64 C3* Santiago del Estero, N Argentina
An Bhearú *see* Barrow
Anchorage *36 C3* Alaska, USA
Ancona *96 C3* Marche, C Italy
Ancud *65 B6 prev.* San Carlos de Ancud. Los Lagos, S Chile
Ancyra *see* Ankara
Åndalsnes *85 A5* Møre og Romsdal, S Norway
Andalucía *92 D4 cultural region* S Spain
Andalusia *42 C3* Alabama, S USA
Andaman Islands *124 B4 island group* India, NE Indian Ocean
Andaman Sea *124 C4 sea* NE Indian Ocean
Andenne *87 C6* Namur, SE Belgium
Anderlues *87 B7* Hainaut, S Belgium
Anderson *40 C4* Indiana, N USA
Andes *64 B3 mountain range* W South America
Andhra Pradesh *135 E5 cultural region* E India
Andijon *123 F2 Rus.* Andizhan. Andijon Viloyati, E Uzbekistan
Andikíthira *see* Antikýthira
Andipaxi *see* Antipaxoi
Andípsara *see* Antípsara
Ándissa *see* Ántissa
Andizhan *see* Andijon
Andkhvoy *122 D3* Fāryāb, N Afghanistan
Andorra *91 A7 off.* Principality of Andorra, *Cat.* Valls d'Andorra, *Fr.* Vallée d'Andorre. *country* SW Europe

Andorra *see* Andorra la Vella
Andorra la Vella *91 A8 var.* Andorra, *Fr.* Andorre la Vielle, *Sp.* Andorra la Vieja. *country capital* (Andorra) (Andorra) C Andorra
Andorra la Vieja *see* Andorra la Vella
Andorra, Principality of *see* Andorra
Andorra, Valls d'Andorra, Vallée d' *see* Andorra
Andorre la Vielle *see* Andorra la Vella
Andover *89 D7* S England, United Kingdom
Andøya *84 C2 island* C Norway
Andreanof Islands *36 A3 island group* Aleutian Islands, Alaska, USA
Andrews *49 E3* Texas, SW USA
Andrew Tablemount *140 A4 var.* Gora Andryu. *seamount* W Indian Ocean
Andria *97 D5* Puglia, SE Italy
An Droichead Nua *see* Newbridge
Andropov *see* Rybinsk
Ándros *105 D6* Ándros, Kykládes, Greece, Aegean Sea
Ándros *105 C6 island* Kykládes, Greece, Aegean Sea
Andros Island *54 B2 island* NW Bahamas
Andros Town *54 C1* Andros Island, NW Bahamas
Andryu, Gora *see* Andrew Tablemount
Aneityum *144 D5 var.* Anatom; *prev.* Kéamu. *island* S Vanuatu

Ånewetak *see* Enewetak Atoll
Angara *115 E4 river* C Russian Federation
Angarsk *115 E4* Irkutskaya Oblast', S Russian Federation
Ånge *85 C5* Västernorrland, C Sweden
Ángel de la Guarda, Isla *50 B2 island* NW Mexico
Angeles *139 E1 off.* Angeles City. Luzon, N Philippines
Angeles City *see* Angeles
Angel Falls *59 F3 Eng.* Angel Falls. *waterfall* E Venezuela
Angel Falls *see* Ángel, Salto
Angerburg *see* Węgorzewo
Ängermanälven *84 C4 river* N Sweden
Angermünde *94 D3* Brandenburg, NE Germany
Angers *90 B4 anc.* Juliomagus. Maine-et-Loire, NW France
Anglesey *89 C5 island* NW Wales, United Kingdom
Anglet *91 A6* Pyrénées-Atlantiques, SW France
Angleton *49 H4* Texas, SW USA
Anglia *see* England
Anglo-Egyptian Sudan *see* Sudan
Angmagssalik *see* Ammassalik
Ang Nam Ngum *136 C4 lake* C Laos
Angola *78 B2 off.* Republic of Angola; *prev.* People's Republic of Angola, Portuguese West Africa. *country* SW Africa

ANGOLA
Southern Africa

Official name Republic of Angola
Formation 1975 / 1975
Capital Luanda
Population 16.9 million / 35 people per sq mile (14 people per sq km) / 36%
Total area 481,351 sq. miles (1,246,700 sq. km)
Languages Portuguese*, Umbundu, Kimbundu, Kikongo
Religions Roman Catholic 50%, Other 30%, Protestant 20%
Ethnic mix Ovimbundu 37%, Other 25%, Kimbundu 25%, Bakongo 13%
Government Presidential system
Currency Readjusted kwanza = 100 lwei
Literacy rate 67%
Calorie consumption 2083 calories

Angola Basin *69 B5 undersea basin* E Atlantic Ocean
Angola, People's Republic of *see* Angola
Angola, Republic of *see* Angola
Angora *see* Ankara
Angostura *see* Ciudad Bolívar
Angostura, Presa de la *51 G5 reservoir* SE Mexico
Angoulême *91 B5 anc.* Iculisma. Charente, W France
Angoumois *91 B5 cultural region* W France
Angra Pequena *see* Lüderitz
Angren *123 F2* Toshkent Viloyati, E Uzbekistan
Anguilla *55 G3 UK dependent territory* E West Indies
Anguilla Cays *54 B2 islets* SW Bahamas
Anhui *128 C5 var.* Anhui Sheng, Anhwei, Wan. *province* E China
AnhuiSheng/Anhwei Wan *see* Anhui
Anicium *see* le Puy
Anina *108 A4 Ger.* Steierdorf, *Hung.* Stájerlakanina; *prev.* Ștaierdorf-Anina, Steierdorf-Anina, Steyerlak-Anina. Caraș-Severin, SW Romania
Anjou *90 B4 cultural region* NW France
Anjouan *79 F2 var.* Ndzouani, Nzwani. *island* SE Comoros
Ankara *116 C3 prev.* Angora; *anc.* Ancyra. *country capital* (Turkey) (Turkey) Ankara, C Turkey
Ankeny *45 F3* Iowa, C USA
Anklam *94 D2* Mecklenburg-Vorpommern, NE Germany
An Mhuir Cheilteach *see* Celtic Sea
An Nafud *120 B4 desert* NW Saudi Arabia
'Annah *120 B3 var.* 'Ānah. Al Anbār, NW Iraq

An Najaf 120 B3 var. Najaf. An Najaf, S Iraq
Annamitique, Chaîne 136 D4 mountain range C Laos
Annapolis 41 F4 state capital Maryland, NE USA
Annapurna 135 E3 mountain C Nepal
An Nāqūrah see En Nâqoûra
Ann Arbor 40 C3 Michigan, N USA
An Nāşirīyah 120 C3 var. Nasiriya. Dhi Qār, SE Iraq
Anneciacum see Annecy
Annecy 91 D5 anc. Anneciacum. Haute-Savoie, E France
An Nîl al Abyad see White Nile
An Nîl al Azraq see Blue Nile
Anniston 42 D2 Alabama, S USA
Annotto Bay 54 B4 C Jamaica
An Ómaigh see Omagh
Anqing 128 D5 Anhui, E China
Anse La Raye 55 F1 NW Saint Lucia
Anshun 128 B6 Guizhou, S China
Ansongo 75 E3 Gao, E Mali
An Srath Bán see Strabane
Antakya 116 D4 anc. Antioch, Antiochia. Hatay, S Turkey
Antalaha 79 G2 Antsiranana, NE Madagascar
Antalya 116 B4 prev. Adalia; anc. Attaleia, Bibl. Attalia. Antalya, SW Turkey
Antalya, Gulf of 116 B4 var. Gulf of Adalia, Eng. Gulf of Antalya. gulf SW Turkey
Antalya, Gulf of see Antalya Körfezi
Antananarivo 79 G3 prev. Tananarive. country capital (Madagascar) (Madagascar) Antananarivo, C Madagascar
Antarctica 154 B3 continent
Antarctic Peninsula 154 A2 peninsula Antarctica
Antep see Gaziantep
Antequera 92 D5 anc. Anticaria, Antiquaria. Andalucía, S Spain
Antequera see Oaxaca
Antibes 91 D6 anc. Antipolis. Alpes-Maritimes, SE France
Anticaria see Antequera
Anticosti, Île d' 39 F3 Eng. Anticosti Island. island Québec, E Canada
Anticosti Island see Anticosti, Île d'
Antigua 55 G3 island S Antigua and Barbuda, Leeward Islands
Antigua and Barbuda 55 G3 country E West Indies

ANTIGUA & BARBUDA
West Indies

Official name Antigua and Barbuda
Formation 1981 / 1981
Capital St. John's
Population 69,481 / 409 people per sq mile (158 people per sq km) / 38%
Total area 170 sq. miles (442 sq. km)
Languages English*, English patois
Religions Anglican 45%, Other Protestant 42%, Roman Catholic 10%, Other 2%, Rastafarian 1%
Ethnic mix Black African 95%, Other 5%
Government Parliamentary system
Currency Eastern Caribbean dollar = 100 cents
Literacy rate 86%
Calorie consumption 2349 calories

Antikythira 105 B7 var. Andikíthira. island S Greece
Anti-Lebanon 118 B4 var. Jebel esh Sharqi, Ar. Al Jabal ash Sharqī, Fr. Anti-Liban. mountain range Lebanon/Syria
Anti-Liban see Anti-Lebanon
Antioch see Antakya
Antiochia see Antakya
Antípaxoi 105 A5 var. Andipaxi. island Iónia Nisiá, Greece, C Mediterranean Sea
Antipodes Islands 142 D5 island group S New Zealand
Antipolis see Antibes
Antípsara 105 D5 var. Andípsara. island E Greece
Antiquaria see Antequera
Ántissa 105 C5 var. Ándissa. Lésvos, E Greece
An tIúr see Newry

Antivari see Bar
Antofagasta 64 B2 Antofagasta, N Chile
Antony 90 E2 Hauts-de-Seine, N France
An tSionainn see Shannon
Antsirañana 79 G2 province N Madagascar
Antsohihy 79 G2 Mahajanga, NW Madagascar
An-tung see Dandong
Antwerpen 87 C5 Eng. Antwerp, Fr. Anvers. Antwerpen, N Belgium
Anuradhapura 132 D3 North Central Province, C Sri Lanka
Anvers see Antwerpen
Anyang 128 C4 Henan, C China
A'nyêmaqên Shan 126 D4 mountain range C China
Anykščiai 106 C4 Utena, E Lithuania
Anzio 97 C5 Lazio, C Italy
Ao Krung Thep 137 C5 var. Krung Thep Mahanakhon, Eng. Bangkok. country capital (Thailand) (Thailand) Bangkok, C Thailand
Aomen see Macao
Aomori 130 D3 Aomori, Honshū, C Japan
Aóos see Vjosës, Lumi i
Aoraki 151 B6 prev. Aorangi, Mount Cook. mountain South Island, New Zealand
Aorangi see Aoraki
Aosta 96 A1 anc. Augusta Praetoria. Valle d'Aosta, NW Italy
Aoukâr 74 D3 var. Aouker. plateau C Mauritania
Aouk, Bahr 76 C4 river Central African Republic/Chad
Aouker see Aoukâr
Aozou 76 C1 Borkou-Ennedi-Tibesti, N Chad
Apalachee Bay 42 D3 bay Florida, SE USA
Apalachicola River 42 D3 river Florida, SE USA
Apamama see Abemama
Apaporis, Río 58 C4 river Brazil/ Colombia
Apatity 110 C2 Murmanskaya Oblast', NW Russian Federation
Ape 106 D3 Alūksne, NE Latvia
Apeldoorn 86 D3 Gelderland, E Netherlands
Apennines 96 E2 Eng. Apennines. mountain range Italy/San Marino
Apennines see Appennino
Ãpia 145 F4 country capital (Samoa) (Samoa) Upolu, SE Samoa
Ap'khazet'i 117 E1 var. Abkhazia. autonomous republic NW Georgia
Apoera 59 G3 Sipaliwini, NW Suriname
Apostle Islands 40 B1 island group Wisconsin, N USA
Appalachian Mountains 35 D5 mountain range E USA
Appingedam 86 E1 Groningen, NE Netherlands
Appleton 40 B2 Wisconsin, N USA
Apulia see Puglia
Apure, Río 58 C2 river W Venezuela
Apurímac, Río 60 D3 river S Peru
Apuseni, Munții 108 A4 mountain range W Romania
Aqaba/'Aqaba see Al 'Aqabah
Aqaba, Gulf of 120 A4 var. Gulf of Elat, Ar. Khalij al 'Aqabah; anc. Sinus Aelaniticus. gulf NE Red Sea
'Aqabah, Khalīj al see Aqaba, Gulf of
Āqchah 123 E3 var. Āqcheh. Jowzjān, N Afghanistan
Āqcheh see Āqchah
Aqmola see Astana
Aqtöbe see Aktobe
Aquae Augustae see Dax
Aquae Calidae see Bath
Aquae Flaviae see Chaves
Aquae Grani see Aachen
Aquae Sextiae see Aix-en-Provence
Aquae Solis see Bath
Aquae Tarbelicae see Dax
Aquidauana 63 E4 Mato Grosso do Sul, S Brazil
Aquila/Aquila degli Abruzzi see L'Aquila
Aquisgranum see Aachen
Aquitaine 91 B6 cultural region SW France

'Arabah, Wadi al 119 B7 Heb. Ha'Arava. dry watercourse Israel/Jordan
Arabian Basin 124 A4 undersea basin N Arabian Sea
Arabian Desert see Sahara el Sharqīya
Arabian Peninsula 121 B5 peninsula SW Asia
Arabian Sea 124 A3 sea NW Indian Ocean
Arabicus, Sinus see Red Sea
'Arabī, Khalīj al see Gulf, The
'Arabīyah as Su'ūdīyah, Al Mamlakah al see Saudi Arabia
'Arabīyah Jumhūrīyah, Mişr al see Egypt
Arab Republic of Egypt see Egypt
Aracaju 63 G3 state capital Sergipe, E Brazil
Araçuaí 63 F3 Minas Gerais, SE Brazil
Arad 119 B7 Southern, S Israel
Arad 108 A4 Arad, W Romania
Arafura Sea 142 A3 Ind. Laut Arafuru. sea W Pacific Ocean
Arafuru, Laut see Arafura Sea
Aragón 93 E2 autonomous community E Spain
Araguaia, Río 63 E3 var. Araguaya. river C Brazil
Araguari 63 F3 Minas Gerais, SE Brazil
Araguaya see Araguaia, Río
Ara Jovis see Aranjuez
Arāk 120 C3 prev. Sultānābād. Markazī, W Iran
Arakan Yoma 136 A3 mountain range W Burma (Myanmar)
Araks/Arak's see Aras
Aral Sea 122 C1 Kaz. Aral Tengizi, Rus. Aral'skoye More, Uzb. Orol Dengizi. inland sea Kazakhstan/Uzbekistan
Aral'sk 114 B4 Kaz. Aral. Kzylorda, SW Kazakhstan
Aral'skoye More/Aral Tengizi see Aral Sea
Aranda de Duero 92 D2 Castilla-León, N Spain
Arandelovac 100 D4 prev. Arandjelovac. Serbia, C Serbia
Arandjelovac see Arandelovac
Aranjuez 92 D3 anc. Ara Jovis. Madrid, C Spain
Araouane 75 E2 Tombouctou, N Mali
'Ar'ar 120 B3 Al Ḩudūd ash Shamālīyah, NW Saudi Arabia
Mount Ararat 117 F3 var. Aghri Dagh, Agri Dagi, Koh I Noh, Masis, Eng. Great Ararat, Mount Ararat. mountain E Turkey
Ararat, Mount see Büyükağrı Dağı
Aras 117 G3 Arm. Arak's, Az. Araz Nehri, Per. Rūd-e Aras, Rus. Araks; prev. Araxes. river SW Asia
Aras, Rūd-e see Aras
Arauca 58 C2 Arauca, NE Colombia
Arauca, Río 58 C2 river Colombia/ Venezuela
Arausio see Orange
Araxes see Aras
Arbela see Arbil
Arbil 120 B2 var. Erbil, Irbil, Kurd. Hawlêr; anc. Arbela. Arbil, N Iraq
Arbroath 88 D3 anc. Aberbrothock. E Scotland, United Kingdom
Arbuzinka see Arbuzynka
Arbuzynka 109 E3 Rus. Arbuzinka. Mykolayivs'ka Oblast', S Ukraine
Arcachon 91 B5 Gironde, SW France
Arcae Remorum see Châlons-en-Champagne
Arcata 46 A4 California, W USA
Archangel Bay see Chëshskaya Guba
Archidona 92 D5 Andalucía, S Spain
Arco 96 C2 Trentino-Alto Adige, N Italy
Arctic Mid Oceanic Ridge see Nansen Cordillera
Arctic Ocean 155 B3 ocean
Arda 104 C3 var. Ardha, Bul. Ardas. river Bulgaria/Greece
Ardabil 120 C2 var. Ardebil. Ardabīl, NW Iran
Ardakān 120 D3 Yazd, C Iran
Ardas 104 D3 var. Ardhas, Bul. Arda. river Bulgaria/Greece
Ard aş Şawwān 119 C7 var. Ardh es Suwwān. plain S Jordan
Ardeal see Transylvania

Ardebil see Ardabil
Ardèche 91 C5 cultural region E France
Ardennes 87 C8 physical region Belgium/ France
Ardhas see Arda/Ardas
Ardh es Suwwān see Ard aş Şawwān
Ardino 104 D3 Kŭrdzhali, S Bulgaria
Ard Mhacha see Armagh
Ardmore 49 G2 Oklahoma, C USA
Arel see Arlon
Arelas/Arelate see Arles
Arendal 85 A6 Aust-Agder, S Norway
Arensburg see Kuressaare
Arenys de Mar 93 G2 Cataluña, NE Spain
Areópoli 105 B7 prev. Areópolis. Pelopónnisos, S Greece
Areópolis see Areópoli
Arequipa 61 E4 Arequipa, SE Peru
Arezzo 96 C3 anc. Arretium. Toscana, C Italy
Argalastí 105 C5 Thessalía, C Greece
Argenteuil 90 D1 Val-d'Oise, N France
Argentina 65 B5 off. Argentine Republic. country S South America

ARGENTINA
South America

Official name The Argentine Republic
Formation 1816 / 1816
Capital Buenos Aires
Population 39.5 million / 37 people per sq mile (14 people per sq km) / 90%
Total area 1,068,296 sq. miles (2,766,890 sq. km)
Languages Spanish*, Italian, Amerindian languages
Religions Roman Catholic 90%, Other 6%, Protestant 2%, Jewish 2%
Ethnic mix Indo-European 83%, Mestizo 14%, Jewish 2%, Amerindian 1%
Government Presidential system
Currency new Argentine peso = 100 centavos
Literacy rate 97%
Calorie consumption 2992 calories

Argentina Basin see Argentine Basin
Argentine Basin 57 C7 var. Argentina Basin. undersea basin SW Atlantic Ocean
Argentine Republic see Argentina
Argentine Rise see Falkland Plateau
Argentoratum see Strasbourg
Darya-ye Arghandab 123 E5 river SE Afghanistan
Argirocastro see Gjirokastër
Argo 72 B3 Northern, N Sudan
Argo Fracture Zone 141 C5 tectonic feature C Indian Ocean
Árgos 105 B6 Pelopónnisos, S Greece
Argostóli 105 A5 var. Argostólion. Kefalloniá, Iónia Nisiá, Greece, C Mediterranean Sea
Argostólion see Argostóli
Argun 125 E1 Chin. Ergun He, Rus. river China/Russian Federation
Argyrokastron see Gjirokastër
Århus 85 B7 var. Aarhus. Århus, C Denmark
Aria see Herāt
Ari Atoll 132 A4 var. Alifu Atoll. atoll C Maldives
Arica 64 B1 hist. San Marcos de Arica. Tarapacá, N Chile
Aridaía 104 B3 var. Aridaia, Aridhaía. Dytikí Makedonía, N Greece
Aridea see Aridaía
Aridhaía see Aridaía
Arīḩā 118 B3 Al Karak, W Jordan
Arīḩā see Jericho
Ariminum see Rimini
Arinsal 91 H7 NW Andorra Europe
Arizona 48 A2 off. State of Arizona, also known as Copper State, Grand Canyon State. state SW USA
Arkansas 42 A1 off. State of Arkansas, also known as The Land of Opportunity. state S USA
Arkansas City 45 F5 Kansas, C USA
Arkansas River 49 G1 river C USA
Arkhangel'sk 114 B2 Eng. Archangel. Arkhangel'skaya Oblast', NW Russian Federation
Arkoí 105 E6 island Dodekánisa, Greece, Aegean Sea

Arles *91 D6 var.* Arles-sur-Rhône; *anc.*
Arelas, Arelate. Bouches-du-Rhône,
SE France
Arles-sur-Rhône *see* Arles
Arlington *49 G2* Texas, SW USA
Arlington *41 E4* Virginia, NE USA
Arlon *87 D8 Dut.* Aarlen, *Ger.* Arel, *Lat.*
Orolaunum. Luxembourg, SE Belgium
Armagh *89 B5 Ir.* Ard Mhacha.
S Northern Ireland, United Kingdom
Armagnac *91 B6 cultural region* S France
Armenia *58 B3* Quindío, W Colombia
Armenia *117 F3 off.* Republic of
Armenia, *var.* Ajastan, *Arm.* Hayastani
Hanrapetut'yun; *prev.* Armenian Soviet
Socialist Republic. *country* SW Asia

ARMENIA
Southwest Asia

Official name	Republic of Armenia
Formation	1991 / 1991
Capital	Yerevan
Population	3 million / 261 people
per sq mile (101 people per sq km) / 64%	
Total area	11,506 sq. miles (29,800 sq. km)
Languages	Armenian*, Azeri, Russian
Religions	Armenian Apostolic Church
(Orthodox) 88%, Other 6%,	
Armenian Catholic Church 6%	
Ethnic mix	Armenian 98%, Other 1%,
Yezidi 1%	
Government	Parliamentary system
Currency	Dram = 100 luma
Literacy rate	99%
Calorie consumption	2268 calories

Armenian Soviet Socialist Republic
see Armenia
Armenia, Republic of *see* Armenia
Armidale *149 D6* New South Wales,
SE Australia
Armstrong *38 B3* Ontario, S Canada
Armyans'k *109 F4 Rus.* Armyansk.
Respublika Krym, S Ukraine
Arnaía *104 C4 Cont.* Arnea. Kentrikí
Makedonía, N Greece
Arnaud *82 A3 river* Québec, E Canada
Arnea *see* Arnaía
Arnedo *93 E2* La Rioja, N Spain
Arnhem *86 D4* Gelderland,
SE Netherlands
Arnhem Land *148 A2 physical region*
Northern Territory, N Australia
Arno *96 B3 river* C Italy
Arnold *45 G4* Missouri, C USA
Arnswalde *see* Choszczno
Aroe Islands *see* Aru, Kepulauan
Arorae *145 E3 atoll* Tungaru, W Kiribati
Arrabona *see* Győr
Ar Rahad *see* Er Rahad
Ar Ramādī *120 B3 var.* Ramadi,
Rumadiya. Al Anbar, SW Iraq
Ar Rāmī *118 C4* Ḩimṣ, C Syria
Ar Ramtha *119 B5 var.* Ramtha. Irbid,
N Jordan
Arran, Isle of *88 C4 island* SW Scotland,
United Kingdom
Ar Raqqah *118 C2 var.* Rakka; *anc.*
Nicephorium. Ar Raqqah, N Syria
Arras *90 C2 anc.* Nemetocenna. Pas-de-
Calais, N France
Ar Rawḍatayn *120 C4 var.* Raudhatain.
N Kuwait
Arretium *see* Arezzo
Arriaca *see* Guadalajara
Arriaga *51 G5* Chiapas, SE Mexico
Ar Riyāḍ *121 C5 Eng.* Riyadh. *country
capital* (Saudi Arabia) (Saudi Arabia)
Ar Riyāḍ, C Saudi Arabia
Ar Rub 'al Khali *121 C6 Eng.* Empty
Quarter, Great Sandy Desert. *desert*
SW Asia
Ar Rustāq *121 E5 var.* Rostak, Rustaq.
N Oman
Ar Rutbah *120 B3 var.* Rutba. Al Anbar,
SW Iraq
Árta *105 A5 anc.* Ambracia. Ípeiros,
W Greece
Artashat *117 F3* S Armenia
Artemisa *54 B2* La Habana, W Cuba
Artesia *48 D3* New Mexico, SW USA
Arthur's Pass *151 C6 pass* South Island,
New Zealand
Artigas *64 D3 prev.* San Eugenio,
San Eugenio del Cuareim. Artigas,
N Uruguay

Art'ik *117 F2* W Armenia
Artois *90 C2 cultural region* N France
Artsiz *see* Artsyz
Artsyz *108 D4 Rus.* Artsiz. Odes'ka
Oblast', SW Ukraine
Artvin *117 F2* Artvin, NE Turkey
Arua *73 B6* NW Uganda
Aruba *58 C1 var.* Oruba. *Dutch
autonomous region* S West Indies
Aru Islands *see* Aru, Kepulauan
Aru, Kepulauan *139 G4 Eng.* Aru
Islands; *prev.* Aroe Islands. *island
group* E Indonesia
Arunāchal Pradesh *135 G3 prev.* North
East Frontier Agency, North East
Frontier Agency of Assam. *cultural
region* NE India
Arusha *73 C7* Arusha, N Tanzania
Arviat *37 G4 prev.* Eskimo Point.
Nunavut, C Canada
Arvidsjaur *84 C4* Norrbotten, N Sweden
Arys' *114 B5 Kaz.* Arys. Yuzhnyy
Kazakhstan, S Kazakhstan
Arys *see* Arys'
Asadābād *123 F4 var.* Asadābād; *prev.*
Chaghasarāy. Konar, E Afghanistan
Asadābād *see* Asadābād
Asahi-dake *130 D2 mountain* Hokkaidō,
N Japan
Asahikawa *130 D2* Hokkaidō, N Japan
Asamankese *75 E5* SE Ghana
Āsansol *135 F4* West Bengal, NE India
Asben *see* Aïr, Massif de l'
Ascension Fracture Zone *69 A5 tectonic
Feature* C Atlantic Ocean
Ascension Island *67 C5 dependency of*
St.Helena C Atlantic Ocean
Ascoli Piceno *96 C4 anc.* Asculum
Picenum. Marche, C Italy
Asculum Picenum *see* Ascoli Piceno
'Aseb *72 D4 var.* Assab, *Amh.* Āseb.
SE Eritrea
Assen *86 E2* Drenthe, NE Netherlands
Asgabat *122 C3 prev.* Ashgabat,
Ashkhabad, Poltoratsk. *country capital*
(Turkmenistan) (Turkmenistan) Ahal
Welaýaty, C Turkmenistan
Ashara *see* Al 'Ashārah
Ashburton *151 C6* Canterbury, South
Island, New Zealand
Ashburton River *146 A4 river* Western
Australia
Ashdod *119 A6 anc.* Azotos, *Lat.* Azotus.
Central, W Israel
Asheville *43 E1* North Carolina, SE USA
Ashgabat *see* Aşgabat
Ashkelon *119 A6 prev.* Ashqelon.
Southern, C Israel
Ashkhabad *see* Aşgabat
Ashland *46 B4* Oregon, NW USA
Ashland *40 B1* Wisconsin, N USA
Ashmore and Cartier Islands *142 A3
Australian external territory* E Indian
Ocean
Ashmyany *107 C5 Rus.* Oshmyany.
Hrodzyenskaya Voblasts', W Belarus
Ashqelon *see* Ashkelon
Ash Shaddādah *118 D2 var.* Ash
Shaddādah, Jisr ash Shadadi, Shaddādī,
Shedadi, Tell Shedadi. Al Ḩasakah,
NE Syria
Ash Shaddādah *see* Ash Shaddādah
Ash Sharah *119 B7 var.* Esh Sharā.
mountain range W Jordan
Ash Shāriqah *120 D4 Eng.* Sharjah. Ash
Shāriqah, NE United Arab Emirates
Ash Shawbak *119 B7* Ma'ān, W Jordan
Ash Shiḩr *121 C6* SE Yemen
Asia *112 continent*
Asinara *96 A4 island* W Italy
Asipovichy *107 D6 Rus.* Osipovichi.
Mahilyowskaya Voblasts', C Belarus
Aşkale *117 E3* Erzurum, NE Turkey
Askersund *85 C6* Örebro, C Sweden
Asmara *see* Asmera
Asmera *72 C4 var.* Asmara. *country
capital* (Eritrea) (Eritrea) C Eritrea
Aspadana *see* Eşfahān
Asphaltites, Lacus *see* Dead Sea
Aspinwall *see* Colón
Assab *see* 'Aseb
Ash Shaddādah *118 D2 var.* Sabkha. Ar
Raqqah, NE Syria
Assad, Lake *118 C2 Eng.* Lake Assad.
lake N Syria
Assad, Lake *see* Asad, Buḩayrat al
Aş Şafāwī *119 C6* Al Mafraq, N Jordan

Aş Şaḩrā' ash Sharqīyah *see* Sahara el
Sharqīya
As Salamīyah *see* Salamīyah
'Assal, Lac *68 E4 lake* C Djibouti
As Salṭ *119 B6 var.* Salt. Al Balqā',
NW Jordan
Assamaka *see* Assamakka
Assamakka *75 F2 var.* Assamaka.
Agadez, NW Niger
As Samāwah *120 B3 var.* Samawa. Al
Muthanná, S Iraq
Assenede *87 B5* Oost-Vlaanderen,
NW Belgium
Assiout *see* Asyūṭ
Assiut *see* Asyūṭ
Assling *see* Jesenice
Assouan *see* Aswān
Assu *see* Açu
Assuan *see* Aswān
As Sukhnah *118 C3 var.* Sukhne, *Fr.*
Soukhné. Ḩimṣ, C Syria
As Sulaymānīyah *120 C3 var.*
Sulaimaniya, *Kurd.* Slēmāni. As
Sulaymānīyah, NE Iraq
As Sulayyil *121 B5* Ar Riyāḍ, S Saudi
Arabia
Aş Şuwār *118 D2 var.* Ṣuwār. Dayr az
Zawr, E Syria
As Suwaydā' *119 B5 var.* El Suweida,
Es Suweida, Suweida, *Fr.* Soueida. As
Suwaydā', SW Syria
As Suways *see* Suez
Asta Colonia *see* Asti
Astacus *see* İzmit
Astana *114 C4 prev.* Akmola,
Akmolinsk, Tselinograd, Aqmola.
country capital (Kazakhstan)
(Kazakhstan) Akmola, N Kazakhstan
Asta Pompeia *see* Asti
Astarabad *see* Gorgān
Asterābād *see* Gorgān
Asti *96 A2 anc.* Asta Colonia, Asta
Pompeia, Hasta Colonia, Hasta
Pompeia. Piemonte, NW Italy
Astigi *see* Ecija
Astipálaia *see* Astypálaia
Astorga *92 C1 anc.* Asturica Augusta.
Castilla-León, N Spain
Astrabad *see* Gorgān
Astrakhan' *111 C7* Astrakhanskaya
Oblast', SW Russian Federation
Asturias *92 C1 autonomous community*
NW Spain
Asturias *see* Oviedo
Asturica Augusta *see* Astorga
Astypálaia *105 D7 var.* Astipálaia, *It.*
Stampalia. *island* Kykládes, Greece,
Aegean Sea
Asunción *64 D2 country capital*
(Paraguay) (Paraguay) Central,
S Paraguay
Aswān *72 B2 var.* Assouan, Assuan,
Aswân; *anc.* Syene. SE Egypt
Aswân *see* Aswān
Asyūṭ *72 B2 var.* Assiout, Assiut, Asyût;
Siut; *anc.* Lycopolis. C Egypt
Asyût *see* Asyūṭ
Atacama Desert *see* Atacama
Atacama Desert *62 B2 Eng.* Atacama
Desert. *desert* N Chile
Atacama Desert *see* Atacama, Desierto de
Atafu Atoll *145 E3 island* NW Tokelau
Atamyrat *122 D3 prev.* Kerki. Lebap
Welaýaty, E Turkmenistan
Aṭār *74 C2* Adrar, W Mauritania
Atas Bogd *126 D3 mountain*
SW Mongolia
Atascadero *47 B7* California, W USA
Atatürk Baraji *117 E4 reservoir*
S Turkey
Atbara *72 C3 var.* 'Aṭbarah. River Nile,
NE Sudan
'Aṭbārah/'Aṭbarah, Nahr *see* Atbara
Atbasar *114 C4* Akmola, N Kazakhstan
Atchison *45 F4* Kansas, C USA
Aternum *see* Pescara
Ath *87 B6 var.* Aat. Hainaut, SW Belgium
Athabasca *37 E5* Alberta, SW Canada
Athabasca *37 E5 var.* Athabaska. *river*
Alberta, SW Canada
Athabasca, Lake *37 F4 lake* Alberta/
Saskatchewan, SW Canada
Athabaska *see* Athabasca
Athenae *see* Athína
Athenae *see* Athína
Athens *43 E2* Georgia, SE USA
Athens *40 D4* Ohio, N USA
Athens *49 G3* Texas, SW USA
Athens *see* Athína

Atherton *148 D3* Queensland,
NE Australia
Athína *105 C6 Eng.* Athens, *prev.*
Athínai; *anc.* Athenae. *country capital*
(Greece) (Greece) Attikí, C Greece
Athínai *see* Athína
Athlone *89 B5 Ir.* Baile Átha Luain.
C Ireland
Ath Thawrah *see* Madīnat ath Thawrah
Ati *76 C3* Batha, C Chad
Atikokan *38 B4* Ontario, S Canada
Atka *35 G3* Magadanskaya Oblast',
E Russian Federation
Atka *36 A3* Atka Island, Alaska, USA
Atlanta *42 D2 state capital* Georgia,
SE USA
Atlanta *49 H2* Texas, SW USA
Atlantic City *41 F4* New Jersey,
NE USA
Atlantic-Indian Basin *67 D7 undersea
basin* SW Indian Ocean
Atlantic-Indian Ridge *69 B8 undersea
ridge* SW Indian Ocean
Atlantic Ocean *66 B4 ocean*
Atlas Mountains *70 C2 mountain range*
NW Africa
Atlasovo *115 H3* Kamchatskaya Oblast',
E Russian Federation
Atlas, Tell *102 C3 Eng.* Tell Atlas.
mountain range N Algeria
Atlas, Tell *see* Atlas Tellien
Atlin *36 D4* British Columbia, W Canada
Aṭ Ṭafīlah *119 B7 var.* Et Tafila, Tafila,
Ṭafīla. Aṭ Ṭafīlah, W Jordan
Aṭ Ṭafīlah *see* Aṭ Ṭafīlah
Aṭ Ṭā'if *121 B5* Makkah, W Saudi Arabia
Attaleia/Attalia *see* Antalya
At Tall al Abyaḍ *118 C2 var.* Tall al
Abyaḍ, Tell Abyad, *Fr.* Tell Abiad. Ar
Raqqah, N Syria
At Ṭanf *118 D4* Ḩimṣ, S Syria
Attapu *see* Samakhixai
Attawapiskat *38 C3* Ontario, C Canada
Attawapiskat *38 C3 river* Ontario,
S Canada
At Tibni *118 D2 var.* Tibni. Dayr az
Zawr, NE Syria
Attopeu *see* Samakhixai
Attu Island *36 A2 island* Aleutian
Islands, Alaska, USA
Atyrau *114 B4 prev.* Gur'yev. Atyrau,
W Kazakhstan
Aubagne *91 D6 anc.* Albania. Bouches-
du-Rhône, SE France
Aubange *87 D8* Luxembourg,
SE Belgium
Aubervilliers *90 E1* Seine-St-Denis,
Île-de-France, N France France Europe
Auburn *46 B2* Washington, NW USA
Auch *91 B6 Lat.* Augusta Auscorum,
Elimberrum. Gers, S France
Auckland *150 D2* Auckland, North
Island, New Zealand
Auckland Islands *142 C5 island group*
S New Zealand
Audern *see* Audru
Audincourt *90 E4* Doubs, E France
Audru *106 D2 Ger.* Audern. Pärnumaa,
SW Estonia
Augathella *149 D5* Queensland,
E Australia
Augsbourg *see* Augsburg
Augsburg *95 C6 Fr.* Augsbourg; *anc.*
Augusta Vindelicorum. Bayern,
S Germany
Augusta *147 A7* Western Australia
Augusta *97 D7* Sicilia, Italy
Augusta *41 G3 state capital* Maine,
NE USA
Augusta *see* London
Augusta Auscorum *see* Auch
Augusta Emerita *see* Mérida
Augusta Praetoria *see* Aosta
Augusta Trajana *see* Stara Zagora
Augusta Treverorum *see* Trier
Augusta Vangionum *see* Worms
Augusta Vindelicorum *see* Augsburg
Augustobona Tricassium *see* Troyes
Augustodurum *see* Bayeux
Augustoritum Lemovicensium *see*
Limoges
Augustów *98 E2 Rus.* Avgustov.
Podlaskie, NE Poland
Aulie Ata/Auliye-Ata *see* Taraz
Aunglan *136 B4 var.* Allanmyo, Myaydo.
Magway, C Burma (Myanmar)
Auob *78 B4 var.* Oup. *river* Namibia/
South Africa

Aurangābād *134 D5* Mahārāshtra, C India
Auray *90 A3* Morbihan, NW France
Aurelia Aquensis *see* Baden-Baden
Aurelianum *see* Orléans
Aurès, Massif de l' *102 C4 mountain range* NE Algeria
Aurillac *91 C5* Cantal, C France
Aurium *see* Ourense
Aurora *59 F2* NW Guyana
Aurora *44 D4* Colorado, C USA
Aurora *40 B3* Illinois, N USA
Aurora *45 G5* Missouri, C USA
Aurora *see* Maéwo, Vanuatu
Ausa *see* Vic
Aussig *see* Ústí nad Labem
Austin *45 G3* Minnesota, N USA
Austin *49 G3 state capital* Texas, SW USA
Australes, Archipel des *see* Australes, Îles
Australes et Antarctiques Françaises, Terres *see* French Southern and Antarctic Territories
Australes, Îles *143 F4 var.* Archipel des Australes, Îles Tubuai, Tubuai Islands, *Eng.* Austral Islands. *island group* SW French Polynesia
Austral Fracture Zone *143 H4 tectonic feature* S Pacific Ocean
Australia *142 A4 off.* Commonwealth of Australia. *country*

AUSTRALIA
Australasia & Oceania

Official name Commonwealth of Australia
Formation 1901 / 1901
Capital Canberra
Population 20.9 million / 7 people per sq mile (3 people per sq km) / 92%
Total area 2,967,893 sq. miles (7,686,850 sq. km)
Languages English*, Italian, Cantonese, Greek, Arabic, Vietnamese, Aboriginal languages
Religions Roman Catholic 26%, Anglican 24%, Other 23%, Nonreligious 13%, United Church 8%, Other Protestant 6%
Ethnic mix European 92%, Asian 5%, Aboriginal 2%, Other 1%
Government Parliamentary system
Currency Australian dollar = 100 cents
Literacy rate 99%
Calorie consumption 3054 calories

Australia, Commonwealth of *see* Australia
Australian Alps *149 C7 mountain range* SE Australia
Australian Capital Territory *149 D7 prev.* Federal Capital Territory. *territory* SE Australia
Australie, Bassin Nord de l' *see* North Australian Basin
Austral Islands *see* Australes, Îles
Austrava *see* Ostrov
Austria *95 D7 off.* Republic of Austria, *Ger.* Österreich. *country* C Europe

AUSTRIA
Central Europe

Official name Republic of Austria
Formation 1918 / 1919
Capital Vienna
Population 8.2 million / 257 people per sq mile (99 people per sq km) / 66%
Total area 32,378 sq. miles (83,858 sq. km)
Languages German*, Croatian, Slovenian, Hungarian (Magyar)
Religions Roman Catholic 78%, Nonreligious 9%, Other (including Jewish and Muslim) 8%, Protestant 5%
Ethnic mix Austrian 93%, Croat, Slovene, and Hungarian 6%, Other 1%
Government Parliamentary system
Currency Euro = 100 cents
Literacy rate 99%
Calorie consumption 3673 calories

Austria, Republic of *see* Austria
Autesiodorum *see* Auxerre
Autissiodorum *see* Auxerre
Autricum *see* Chartres
Auvergne *91 C5 cultural region* C France
Auxerre *90 C4 anc.* Autesiodorum, Autissiodorum. Yonne, C France
Avaricum *see* Bourges
Avarua *145 G5 dependent territory capital* (Cook Islands) Rarotonga, S Cook Islands
Avasfelsőfalu *see* Negreşti-Oaş
Ávdira *104 C3* Anatolikí Makedonía kai Thráki, NE Greece
Aveiro *92 B2 anc.* Talabriga. Aveiro, W Portugal
Avela *see* Ávila
Avellino *97 D5 anc.* Abellinum. Campania, S Italy
Avenio *see* Avignon
Avesta *85 C6* Dalarna, C Sweden
Aveyron *91 C6 river* S France
Avezzano *96 C4* Abruzzo, C Italy
Avgustov *see* Augustów
Aviemore *88 C3* N Scotland, United Kingdom
Avignon *91 D6 anc.* Avenio. Vaucluse, SE France
Ávila *92 D3 var.* Avila; *anc.* Abela, Abula, Abyla, Avela. Castilla-León, C Spain
Avilés *92 C1* Asturias, NW Spain
Avranches *90 B3* Manche, N France
Avveel *see* Ivalo, Finland
Avvil *see* Ivalo
Awaji-shima *131 C6 island* SW Japan
Āwash *73 D5* Āfar, NE Ethiopia
Awbārī *71 F3* SW Libya
Ax *see* Dax
Axel *87 B5* Zeeland, SW Netherlands
Axel Heiberg Island *37 E1 var.* Axel Heiburg. *island* Nunavut, N Canada
Axel Heiburg *see* Axel Heiberg Island
Axiós *see* Vardar
Ayacucho *60 D4* Ayacucho, S Peru
Ayagoz *114 C5 var.* Ayaguz, *Kaz.* Ayakoz. *river* E Kazakhstan
Ayamonte *92 C4* Andalucía, S Spain
Ayaviri *61 E4* Puno, S Peru
Aydarko'l Ko'li *123 E2 Rus.* Ozero Aydarkul'; *lake* C Uzbekistan
Aydarkul', Ozero *see* Aydarko'l Ko'li
Aydın *116 A4 var.* Aidin; *anc.* Tralles Aydin. Aydın, SW Turkey
Ayers Rock *see* Uluru
Ayeyarwady *see* Irrawaddy
Ayiá *see* Agiá
Áyios Evstrátios *see* Ágios Efstrátios
Áyios Nikólaos *see* Ágios Nikólaos
Ayorou *75 E3* Tillabéri, W Niger
'Ayoûn el 'Atroûs *74 D3 var.* Aïoun el Atrous, Aïoun el Atroûss. Hodh el Gharbi, SE Mauritania
Ayr *88 C4* W Scotland, United Kingdom
Ayteke Bi *114 B4 Kaz.* Zhangaqazaly; *prev.* Novokazalinsk. Kzylorda, SW Kazakhstan
Aytos *104 E2* Burgas, E Bulgaria
Ayutthaya *137 C5 var.* Phra Nakhon Si Ayutthaya. Phra Nakhon Si Ayutthaya, C Thailand
Ayvalık *116 A3* Balıkesir, W Turkey
Azahar, Costa del *93 F3 coastal region* E Spain
Azaouâd *75 E3 desert* C Mali
Azärbaycan/Azärbaycan Respublikasī *see* Azerbaijan
A'zāz *118 B2* Ḩalab, NW Syria
Azerbaijan *117 G2 off.* Azerbaijani Republic, *Az.* Azärbaycan, Azärbaycan Respublikasī; *prev.* Azerbaijan SSR. *country* SE Asia

AZERBAIJAN
Southwest Asia

Official name Republic of Azerbaijan
Formation 1991 / 1991
Capital Baku
Population 8.5 million / 254 people per sq mile (98 people per sq km) / 50%
Total area 33,436 sq. miles (86,600 sq. km)
Languages Azeri*, Russian
Religions Shi'a Muslim 68%, Sunni Muslim 26%, Russian Orthodox 3%, Armenian Apostolic Church (Orthodox) 2%, Other 1%
Ethnic mix Azeri 91%, Other 3%, Lazs 2%, Armenian 2%, Russian 2%
Government Presidential system

AZERBAIJAN
(continued)

Currency New manat = 100 gopik
Literacy rate 99%
Calorie consumption 2575 calories

Azerbaijani Republic *see* Azerbaijan
Azerbaijan SSR *see* Azerbaijan
Azimabad *see* Patna
Azizie *see* Telish
Azogues *60 B2* Cañar, S Ecuador
Azores *92 A4 var.* Açores, Ilhas dos Açores, *Port.* Arquipélago dos Açores. *island group* Portugal, NE Atlantic Ocean
Azores-Biscay Rise *80 A3 undersea rise* E Atlantic Ocean
Azotos/Azotus *see* Ashdod
Azoum, Bahr *76 C3 seasonal river* SE Chad
Azov, Sea of *103 H1 Rus.* Azovskoye More, *Ukr.* Azovs'ke More. *sea* NE Black Sea
Azovs'ke More/Azovskoye More *see* Azov, Sea of
Azraq, Wāḩat al *119 C6 oasis* N Jordan
Aztec *48 C1* New Mexico, SW USA
Azuaga *92 C4* Extremadura, W Spain
Azuero, Península de *53 F5 peninsula* S Panama
Azul *65 D5* Buenos Aires, E Argentina
Azur, Côte d' *91 E6 coastal region* SE France
'Azza *see* Gaza
Az Zaqāzīq *72 B1 var.* Zagazig *var.* Az Zaqāzīq. N Egypt
Az Zaqāzīq *see* Az Zaqāzīq
Az Zarqā' *119 B6 var.* Zarqa. Az Zarqā', NW Jordan
Az Zāwiyah *71 F2 var.* Zawia. NW Libya
Az Zilfī *120 B4* Ar Riyāḍ, N Saudi Arabia

B

Baalbek *118 B4 var.* Ba'labakk; *anc.* Heliopolis. E Lebanon
Baardheere *73 D6 var.* Bardere, *It.* Bardera. Gedo, SW Somalia
Baarle-Hertog *87 C5* Antwerpen, N Belgium
Baarn *86 C3* Utrecht, C Netherlands
Babadag *108 D5* Tulcea, SE Romania
Babahoyo *60 B2 prev.* Bodegas. Los Ríos, C Ecuador
Bābā, Kūh-e *123 E4 mountain range* C Afghanistan
Babayevo *110 B4* Vologodskaya Oblast', NW Russian Federation
Babeldaob *144 A1 var.* Babeldaop, Babelthuap. *island* N Palau
Babeldaop *see* Babeldaob
Bab el Mandeb *121 B7 strait* Gulf of Aden/Red Sea
Babelthuap *see* Babeldaob
Babian Jiang *see* Black River
Babruysk *107 D7 Rus.* Bobruysk. Mahilyowskaya Voblasts', E Belarus
Babuyan Channel *139 E1 channel* N Philippines
Babuyan Islands *139 E1 island group* N Philippines
Bacabal *63 F2* Maranhão, E Brazil
Bacău *108 C4 Hung.* Bákó. Bacău, NE Romania
Bắc Bộ, Vịnh *see* Tongking, Gulf of
Bắc Giang *136 D3* Ha Bắc, N Vietnam
Bacheykava *107 D5 Rus.* Bocheykovo. Vitsyebskaya Voblasts', N Belarus
Bắc Liêu *137 D6 var.* Vinh Loi. Minh Hai, S Vietnam
Bacolod *125 E4 off.* Bacolod City. Negros, C Philippines
Bacolod City *see* Bacolod
Bácsszenttamás *see* Srbobran
Bácstopolya *see* Bačka Topola
Bactra *see* Balkh
Badajoz *92 C4 anc.* Pax Augusta. Extremadura, W Spain
Baden-Baden *95 B6 anc.* Aurelia Aquensis. Baden-Württemberg, SW Germany
Bad Freienwalde *94 D3* Brandenburg, NE Germany
Badger State *see* Wisconsin
Bad Hersfeld *94 B4* Hessen, C Germany
Bad Homburg *see* Bad Homburg vor der Höhe
Bad Homburg vor der Höhe *95 B5 var.* Bad Homburg. Hessen, W Germany
Bad Ischl *95 D7* Oberösterreich, N Austria
Bad Krozingen *95 A6* Baden-Württemberg, SW Germany
Badlands *44 D2 physical region* North Dakota/South Dakota, N USA
Badu Island *148 C1 island* Queensland, NE Australia
Bad Vöslau *95 E6* Niederösterreich, NE Austria
Baeterrae/Baeterrae Septimanorum *see* Béziers
Baetic Cordillera/Baetic Mountains *see* Béticos, Sistemas
Bafatá *74 C4* C Guinea-Bissau
Baffin Bay *37 G2 bay* Canada/Greenland
Baffin Island *37 G2 island* Nunavut, NE Canada
Bafing *74 C3 river* W Africa
Bafoussam *76 A4* Ouest, W Cameroon
Bafra *116 D2* Samsun, N Turkey
Bāft *120 D4* Kermān, S Iran
Bagaces *52 D4* Guanacaste, NW Costa Rica
Bagdad *see* Baghdād
Bagé *63 E5* Rio Grande do Sul, S Brazil
Baghdād *120 B3 var.* Bagdad, *Eng.* Baghdad. *country capital* (Iraq) Baghdād, C Iraq
Baghdad *see* Baghdād
Baghlān *123 E3* Baghlān, NE Afghanistan
Bago *136 B4 var.* Pegu. Bago, SW Burma (Myanmar)
Bagoé *74 D4 river* Côte d'Ivoire/Mali
Bagrationovsk *106 A4 Ger.* Preussisch Eylau. Kaliningradskaya Oblast', W Russian Federation
Bagrax Hu *see* Bosten Hu
Baguio *139 E1 off.* Baguio City. Luzon, N Philippines
Baguio City *see* Baguio
Bagzane, Monts *75 F3 mountain* N Niger
Bahama Islands *see* Bahamas
Bahamas *54 C2 off.* Commonwealth of the Bahamas. *country* N West Indies

BAHAMAS
West Indies

Official name Commonwealth of the Bahamas
Formation 1973 / 1973
Capital Nassau
Population 305,655 / 79 people per sq mile (31 people per sq km) / 90%
Total area 5382 sq. miles (13,940 sq. km)
Languages English*, English Creole, French Creole
Religions Baptist 32%, Anglican 20%, Roman Catholic 19%, Other 17%, Methodist 6%, Church of God 6%
Ethnic mix Black African 85%, Other 15%
Government Parliamentary system
Currency Bahamian dollar = 100 cents
Literacy rate 96%
Calorie consumption 2755 calories

Bahamas *35 D6 var.* Bahama Islands. *island group* N West Indies
Bahamas, Commonwealth of the *see* Bahamas
Baharly *122 C3 var.* Bäherden, *prev.* Bakherden; *prev.* Bakharden. Ahal Welaýaty, C Turkmenistan
Bahāwalpur *134 C2* Punjab, E Pakistan
Bäherden *see* Baharly
Bahia *63 F3 off.* Estado da Bahia. *state* E Brazil
Bahia, Estado da *see* Bahia. *region* E Brazil
Bahía Blanca *65 C5* Buenos Aires, E Argentina
Bahia, Estado da *see* Bahia
Bahir Dar *72 C4 var.* Bahr Dar, Bahrdar Giyorgis. Āmara, N Ethiopia

Bahraich *135 E3* Uttar Pradesh, N India
Bahrain *120 C4 off.* State of Bahrain,
Dawlat al Bahrayn, *Ar.* Al Bahrayn,
prev. Bahrein; *anc.* Tylos, Tyros.
country SW Asia

BAHRAIN
Southwest Asia

Official name Kingdom of Bahrain
Formation 1971 / 1971
Capital Manama
Population 708,573 / 2596 people per
sq mile (1004 people per sq km) / 90%
Total area 239 sq. miles (620 sq. km)
Languages Arabic
Religions Muslim (mainly Shi'a) 99%,
Other 1%
Ethnic mix Bahraini 70%, Iranian, Indian,
and Pakistani 24%, Other Arab 4%,
European 2%
Government Mixed monarchical–
parliamentary system
Currency Bahraini dinar = 1000 fils
Literacy rate 87%
Calorie consumption Not available

Bahrain, State of *see* Bahrain
Bahrayn, Dawlat al *see* Bahrain
Bahr Dar/Bahrdar Giyorgis *see*
Bahir Dar
Bahrein *see* Bahrain
Bahr el, Azraq *see* Blue Nile
Bahr Tabariya, Sea of *see* Tiberias, Lake
Bahushewsk *107 E6 Rus.* Bogushëvsk.
Vitsyebskaya Voblasts', NE Belarus
Baia Mare *108 B3 Ger.* Frauenbach,
Hung. Nagybánya; *prev.* Neustadt.
Maramureş, NW Romania
Baia Sprie *108 B3 Ger.* Mittelstadt,
Hung. Felsőbánya. Maramureş,
NW Romania
Baïbokoum *76 B4* Logone-Oriental,
SW Chad
Baidoa *see* Baydhabo
Baie-Comeau *39 E3* Québec, SE Canada
Baikal, Lake *115 E4 Eng.* Lake Baikal.
lake S Russian Federation
Baikal, Lake *see* Baykal, Ozero
Baile Átha Cliath *see* Dublin
Baile Átha Luain *see* Athlone
Bailén *92 D4* Andalucía, S Spain
Baile na Mainistreach *see* Newtownabbey
Băileşti *108 B5* Dolj, SW Romania
Ba Illi *76 B3* Chari-Baguirmi, SW Chad
Bainbridge *42 D3* Georgia, SE USA
Bā'ir *see* Bāyir
Baireuth *see* Bayreuth
Bairiki *144 D2 country capital* (Kiribati)
(Kiribati) Tarawa, NW Kiribati
Bairnsdale *149 C7* Victoria, SE Australia
Baishan *129 E3 prev.* Hunjiang. Jilin,
NE China
Baiyin *128 B4* Gansu, C China
Baja *99 C7* Bács-Kiskun, S Hungary
Baja California Norte *50 B2 state*
NW Mexico
Bajo Boquete *see* Boquete
Bajram Curri *101 D5* Kukës, N Albania
Bakala *76 C4* Ouaka, C Central African
Republic
Bakan *see* Shimonoseki
Baker *46 C3* Oregon, NW USA
Baker and Howland Islands *145 E2 US*
unincorporated territory W Polynesia
Baker Lake *37 F3* Nunavut, N Canada
Bakersfield *47 C7* California, W USA
Bakharden *see* Baharly
Bakhchisaray *see* Bakhchysaray
Bakhchysaray *109 F5 Rus.* Bakhchisaray.
Respublika Krym, S Ukraine
Bakherden *see* Baharly
Bakhmach *109 F1* Chernihivs'ka Oblast',
N Ukraine
Bākhtarān *see* Kermānshāh
Baki *117 H2 Eng.* Baku. *country capital*
(Azerbaijan) (Azerbaijan) E Azerbaijan
Bákó *see* Bacău
Bakony *99 C7 Eng.* Bakony Mountains,
Ger. Bakonywald. *mountain range*
W Hungary
Bakony Mountains/Bakonywald *see*
Bakony
Baku *see* Bakı
Bakwanga *see* Mbuji-Mayi
Balabac Island *129 C8 island*
W Philippines

Balabac, Selat *see* Balabac Strait
Balabac Strait *138 D2 var.* Selat Balabac.
strait Malaysia/Philippines
Ba'labakk *see* Baalbek
Balaguer *93 F2* Cataluña, NE Spain
Balakovo *111 C6* Saratovskaya Oblast',
W Russian Federation
Bāla Morghāb *122 D4* Laghmān,
NW Afghanistan
Balashov *111 B6* Saratovskaya Oblast',
W Russian Federation
Balasore *see* Bāleshwar
Balaton, Lake *99 C7 var.* Lake Balaton,
Ger. Plattensee. *lake* W Hungary
Balaton, Lake *see* Balaton
Balbina, Represa *62 D1 reservoir*
NW Brazil
Balboa *53 G4* Panamá, C Panama
Balcarce *65 D5* Buenos Aires,
E Argentina
Balclutha *151 B7* Otago, South Island,
New Zealand
Baldy Mountain *44 C1 mountain*
Montana, NW USA
Bâle *see* Basel
Balearic Plain *see* Algerian Basin
Baleares Major *see* Mallorca
Balearic Islands *93 G3 Eng.* Balearic
Islands. *island group* Spain,
W Mediterranean Sea
Balearic Islands *see* Baleares, Islas
Balearis Minor *see* Menorca
Baleine, Rivière à la *39 E2 river* Québec,
E Canada
Balen *87 C5* Antwerpen, N Belgium
Bāleshwar *135 F4 prev.* Balasore. Orissa,
E India
Bâlgrad *see* Alba Iulia
Bali *138 D5 island* C Indonesia
Balıkesir *116 A3* Balıkesir, W Turkey
Balikh, Nahr *118 C2 river* N Syria
Balikpapan *138 D4* Borneo, C Indonesia
Balkanabat *122 B2 Rus.* Nebitdag.
Balkan Welaýaty, W Turkmenistan
Balkan Mountains *104 C2 Bul./*
SCr. Stara Planina. *mountain range*
Bulgaria/Serbia
Balkh *123 E3 anc.* Bactra. Balkh,
N Afghanistan
Balkhash *114 C5 Kaz.* Balqash.
Karaganda, SE Kazakhstan
Balkhash, Lake *see* Balkhash, Ozero
Balkhash, Lake *114 C5 Eng.* Lake
Balkhash, *Kaz.* Balqash. *lake*
SE Kazakhstan
Balkhash, Lake *see* Balkhash, Ozero
Balladonia *147 C6* Western Australia
Ballarat *149 C7* Victoria,
SE Australia
Balleny Islands *154 B5 island group*
Antarctica
Ballinger *49 F3* Texas, SW USA
Balochistān *see* Baluchistān
Balqash *see* Balkhash/Balkhash, Ozero
Bals *108 B5* Olt, S Romania
Balsas *63 F2* Maranhão, E Brazil
Balsas, Río *51 E4 var.* Río Mexcala. *river*
S Mexico
Bal'shavik *107 D7 Rus.* Bol'shevik.
Homyel'skaya Voblasts', SE Belarus
Balta *108 D3 Rus.* Odes'ka Oblast',
SW Ukraine
Bălţi *108 D3 Rus.* Bel'tsy. N Moldova
Baltic Port *see* Paldiski
Baltic Sea *85 C7 Ger.* Ostee, *Rus.*
Baltiskoye More. *sea* N Europe
Baltimore *41 F4* Maryland, NE USA
Baltischport/Baltiski *see* Paldiski
Baltiskoye More *see* Baltic Sea
Baltkrievija *see* Belarus
Baluchistān *134 B3 var.* Balochistān,
Beluchistan. *province* SW Pakistan
Balvi *106 D4* Balvi, NE Latvia
Balykchy *123 G2 Kir.* Ysyk-Köl; *prev.*
Issyk-Kul', Rybach'ye. Issyk-Kul'skaya
Oblast', NE Kyrgyzstan
Balzers *94 E2* S Liechtenstein
Bam *120 E4* Kermān, SE Iran
Bamako *74 D4 country capital* (Mali)
(Mali) Capital District, SW Mali
Bambari *76 C4* Ouaka, C Central African
Republic
Bamberg *95 C5* Bayern, SE Germany
Bamenda *76 A4* Nord-Ouest,
W Cameroon
Banaba *144 D2 var.* Ocean Island. *island*
Tungaru, W Kiribati
Banaras *see* Vārānasi

Bandaaceh *138 A3 var.* Banda Atjeh;
prev. Koetaradja, Kutaradja, Kutaraja.
Sumatera, W Indonesia
Banda Atjeh *see* Bandaaceh
Banda, Laut *see* Banda Sea
Bandama *74 D5 var.* Bandama Fleuve.
river S Côte d'Ivoire
Bandama Fleuve *see* Bandama
Bandar 'Abbās *see* Bandar-e 'Abbās
Bandarbeyla *73 E5 var.* Bender Beila,
Bender Beyla. Bari, NE Somalia
Bandar-e 'Abbās *120 D4 var.* Bandar
'Abbās; *prev.* Gombroon. Hormozgān,
S Iran
Bandar-e Būshehr *120 C4 var.* Būshehr,
Eng. Bushire. Būshehr, S Iran
Bandar-e Kangān *120 D4 var.* Kangān.
Būshehr, S Iran
Bandar-e Khamīr *120 D4* Hormozgān,
S Iran
Bandar-e Langeh *see* Bandar-e
Lengeh
Bandar-e Lengeh *120 D4 var.*
Bandar-e Langeh, Lingeh. Hormozgān,
S Iran
Bandar Kassim *see* Boosaaso
Bandar Lampung *138 C4 var.*
Bandarlampung, Tanjungkarang-
Telukbetung; *prev.* Tandjoengkarang,
Tanjungkarang, Teloekbetoeng,
Telukbetung. Sumatera,
W Indonesia
Bandarlampung *see* Bandar Lampung
Bandar Maharani *see* Muar
Bandar Masulipatnam *see*
Machilipatnam
Bandar Penggaram *see* Batu Pahat
Bandar Seri Begawan *138 D3 prev.*
Brunei Town. *country capital* (Brunei)
(Brunei) N Brunei
Banda Sea *139 F5 var.* Laut Banda. *sea*
E Indonesia
Bandiagara *75 E3* Mopti, C Mali
Bandırma *116 A3 var.* Penderma.
Balıkesir, NW Turkey
Bandjarmasin *see* Banjarmasin
Bandoeng *see* Bandung
Bandundu *77 C6 prev.* Banningville.
Bandundu, W Dem. Rep. Congo
Bandung *138 C5 prev.* Bandoeng. Jawa,
C Indonesia
Bangalore *132 C2 var.* Bengalooru. *state*
capital Karnātaka, S India
Bangassou *76 D4* Mbomou, SE Central
African Republic
Banggai, Kepulauan *139 E4 island*
group C Indonesia
Banghāzī *71 G2 Eng.* Bengazi, Benghazi,
It. Bengasi. NE Libya
Bangka, Pulau *138 C4 island*
W Indonesia
Bangkok *see* Ao Krung Thep
Bangkok, Bight of *see* Krung Thep, Ao
Bangladesh *135 G3 off.* People's
Republic of Bangladesh; *prev.* East
Pakistan. *country* S Asia

BANGLADESH
South Asia

Official name People's Republic
of Bangladesh
Formation 1971 / 1971
Capital Dhaka
Population 147 million / 2845 people
per sq mile (1098 people per sq km) / 25%
Total area 55,598 sq. miles
(144,000 sq. km)
Languages Bengali*, Urdu, Chakma,
Marma (Magh), Garo, Khasi, Santhali,
Tripuri, Mro
Religions Muslim (mainly Sunni) 87%,
Hindu 12%, Other 1%
Ethnic mix Bengali 98%, Other 2%
Government Transitional regime
Currency Taka = 100 poisha
Literacy rate 41%
Calorie consumption 2205 calories

Bangladesh, People's Republic of *see*
Bangladesh
Bangor *89 C6* NW Wales, United
Kingdom
Bangor *89 B5 Ir.* Beannchar. E Northern
Ireland, United Kingdom
Bangor *41 G2* Maine, NE USA
Bang Pla Soi *see* Chon Buri

Bangui *77 B5 country capital* (Central
African Republic) (Central African
Republic) Ombella-Mpoko, SW Central
African Republic
Bangweulu, Lake *73 B8 var.* Lake
Bengweulu. *lake* N Zambia
Ban Hat Yai *see* Hat Yai
Ban Hin Heup *136 C4* Viangchan,
C Laos
Ban Houayxay/Ban Houei Sai *see*
Houayxay
Ban Hua Hin *137 C6 var.* Hua Hin.
Prachuap Khiri Khan, SW Thailand
Bani *74 D3 river* S Mali
Bani *see* Bāniyās
Banias *see* Bāniyās
Banijska Palanka *see* Glina
Bani Suwayf *72 B2 var.* Beni Suef.
N Egypt
Bāniyās *118 B3 var.* Banias, Baniyas,
Paneas. Ţarţūs, W Syria
Banjak, Kepulauan *see* Banyak,
Kepulauan
Banja Luka *100 B3* Republika Srpska,
NW Bosnia and Herzegovina
Banjarmasin *138 D4 prev.*
Bandjarmasin. Borneo, C Indonesia
Banjul *74 B3 prev.* Bathurst. *country*
capital (Gambia) (Gambia) W Gambia
Banks, Îles *see* Banks Islands
Banks Island *37 E2 island* Northwest
Territories, NW Canada
Banks Islands *144 D4 Fr.* Îles Banks.
island group N Vanuatu
Banks Lake *46 B1 reservoir* Washington,
NW USA
Banks Peninsula *151 C6 peninsula*
South Island, New Zealand
Banks Strait *149 C8 strait* SW Tasman
Sea
Bankura *135 F4* West Bengal, NE India
Ban Mak Khaeng *see* Udon Thani
Banmo *see* Bhamo
Banningville *see* Bandundu
Ban Pak Phanang *see* Pak Phanang
Ban Sichon *see* Sichon
Banská Bystrica *99 C6 Ger.*
Neusohl, *Hung.* Besztercebánya.
Banskobystrický Kraj, C Slovakia
Bantry Bay *89 A7 Ir.* Bá Bheanntraí. *bay*
SW Ireland
Banya *104 E2* Burgas, E Bulgaria
Banyak, Kepulauan *138 A3 prev.*
Kepulauan Banjak. *island group*
NW Indonesia
Banyo *76 B4* Adamaoua, NW Cameroon
Banyoles *93 G2 var.* Bañolas. Cataluña,
NE Spain
Banzare Seamounts *141 C7 seamount*
range S Indian Ocean
Banzart *see* Bizerte
Baoji *128 B4 var.* Pao-chi, Paoki.
Shaanxi, C China
Baoro *76 B4* Nana-Mambéré, W Central
African Republic
Baoshan *128 A3 var.* Pao-shan. Yunnan,
SW China
Baotou *127 F3 var.* Pao-t'ou, Paotow.
Nei Mongol Zizhiqu, N China
Ba'qūbah *120 B3 var.* Qubba. Diyālá,
C Iraq
Baquerizo Moreno *see* Puerto Baquerizo
Moreno
Bar *101 C5 It.* Antivari. S Montenegro
Baraawe *73 D6 It.* Brava. Shabeellaha
Hoose, S Somalia
Bārāmati *134 C5* Mahārāshtra, W India
Baranavichy *107 B6 Pol.* Baranowicze,
Rus. Baranovichi. Brestskaya Voblasts',
SW Belarus
Baranovichi/Baranowicze *see*
Baranavichy
Barbados *55 G1 country* SE West Indies

BARBADOS
West Indies

Official name Barbados
Formation 1966 / 1966
Capital Bridgetown
Population 280,946 / 1692 people
per sq mile (653 people per sq km) / 52%
Total area 166 sq. miles (430 sq. km)
Languages English*, Bajan
(Barbadian English)
Religions Anglican 40%, Other 24%,
Nonreligious 17%, Pentecostal 8%,

BARBADOS
(continued)

Methodist 7%, Roman Catholic 4%
Ethnic mix Black African 92%, White 3%,
Other 3%, Mixed race 2%
Government Parliamentary system
Currency Barbados dollar = 100 cents
Literacy rate 99%
Calorie consumption 3091 calories

Barbastro 93 F2 Aragón, NE Spain
Barbate de Franco 92 C5 Andalucía,
S Spain
Barbuda 55 G3 *island* N Antigua and
Barbuda
Barcaldine 148 C4 Queensland,
E Australia
Barcarozsnyó *see* Râşnov
Barcău *see* Berettyó
Barce *see* Al Marj
Barcelona 93 G2 *anc.* Barcino,
Barcinona. Cataluña, E Spain
Barcelona 59 E2 Anzoátegui,
NE Venezuela
Barcino/Barcinona *see* Barcelona
Barcoo *see* Cooper Creek
Barcs 99 C7 Somogy, SW Hungary
Bardaï 76 C1 Borkou-Ennedi-Tibesti,
N Chad
Bardejov 99 D5 *Ger.* Bartfeld, *Hung.*
Bártfa. Presovský Kraj, E Slovakia
Bardera/Bardere *see* Baardheere
Barduli *see* Barletta
Bareilly 135 E3 *var.* Bareli. Uttar
Pradesh, N India
Bareli *see* Bareilly
Barendrecht 86 C4 Zuid-Holland,
SW Netherlands
Barentin 90 C3 Seine-Maritime,
N France
Barentsburg 83 G2 Spitsbergen,
W Svalbard
Barentsevo More/Barents Havet *see*
Barents Sea
Barentsøya 83 G2 *island* E Svalbard
Barents Sea 110 C2 *Nor.* Barents Havet,
Rus. Barentsevo More. *sea* Arctic
Ocean
Bar Harbor 41 H2 Mount Desert Island,
Maine, NE USA
Bari 97 E5 *var.* Bari delle Puglie; *anc.*
Barium. Puglia, SE Italy
Baridah *see* Al Bāridah
Bari delle Puglie *see* Bari
Barikowt 123 F4 *var.* Barikot. Konar,
NE Afghanistan
Barikot *see* Barikowt
Barillas 52 A2 *var.* Santa Cruz Barillas.
Huehuetenango, NW Guatemala
Barinas 58 C2 Barinas, W Venezuela
Barisal 139 G4 Barisal, S Bangladesh
Barisan, Pegunungan 138 B4 *mountain
range* Sumatera, W Indonesia
Barito, Sungai 138 D4 *river* Borneo,
C Indonesia
Barium *see* Bari
Barka *see* Al Marj
Barkly Tableland 148 B3 *plateau*
Northern Territory/Queensland,
N Australia
Bârlad 108 D4 *prev.* Bîrlad. Vaslui,
E Romania
Barlavento, Ilhas de 74 A2 *var.*
Windward Islands. *island group*
N Cape Verde
Bar-le-Duc 90 D3 *var.* Bar-sur-Ornain.
Meuse, NE France
Barlee, Lake 147 B6 *lake* Western
Australia
Barlee Range 146 A4 *mountain range*
Western Australia
Barletta 97 D5 *anc.* Barduli. Puglia,
SE Italy
Barlinek 98 B3 *Ger.* Berlinchen.
Zachodnio-pomorskie,
NW Poland
Barmen-Elberfeld *see* Wuppertal
Barmouth 89 C6 NW Wales, United
Kingdom
Barnaul 114 D4 Altayskiy Kray,
C Russian Federation
Barnet 89 A7 United Kingdom
Barnstaple 89 C7 SW England, United
Kingdom
Baroda *see* Vadodara

Baroghil Pass 123 F3 *var.* Kowtal-e
Barowghil. *pass* Afghanistan/Pakistan
Baron'ki 107 E7 *Rus.* Boron'ki.
Mahilyowskaya Voblasts', E Belarus
Barowghil, Kowtal-e *see* Baroghil Pass
Barquisimeto 58 C2 Lara,
NW Venezuela
Barra 88 B3 *island* NW Scotland, United
Kingdom
Barra de Río Grande 53 E3 Región
Autónoma Atlántico Sur, E Nicaragua
Barranca 60 C3 Lima, W Peru
Barrancabermeja 58 B2 Santander,
N Colombia
Barranquilla 58 B1 Atlántico,
N Colombia
Barreiro 92 B4 Setúbal, W Portugal
Barrier Range 149 C6 *hill range* New
South Wales, SE Australia
Barrow 36 D2 Alaska, USA
Barrow 89 B6 *Ir.* An Bhearú. *river*
SE Ireland
Barrow-in-Furness 89 C5 NW England,
United Kingdom
Barrow Island 149 A4 *island* Western
Australia
Barstow 47 C7 California, W USA
Bar-sur-Ornain *see* Bar-le-Duc
Bartang 123 F3 *river* SE Tajikistan
Bartenstein *see* Bartoszyce
Bártfa/Bartfeld *see* Bardejov
Bartica 59 F3 N Guyana
Bartın 116 C2 Bartın, NW Turkey
Bartlesville 49 G1 Oklahoma, C USA
Bartoszyce 98 D2 *Ger.* Bartenstein.
Warmińsko-mazurskie, NE Poland
Baruun-Urt 127 F2 Sühbaatar,
E Mongolia
Barú, Volcán 53 E5 *var.* Volcán de
Chiriquí. *volcano* W Panama
Barwon River 149 D5 *river* New South
Wales, SE Australia
Barysaw 107 D6 *Rus.* Borisov. Minskaya
Voblasts', NE Belarus
Basarabeasca 108 D4 *Rus.* Bessarabka.
SE Moldova
Basel 95 A7 *Eng.* Basle, *Fr.* Bâle. Basel-
Stadt, NW Switzerland
Basilan 139 E3 *island* Sulu Archipelago,
SW Philippines
Basle *see* Basel
Basra *see* Al Başrah
Bassano del Grappa 96 C2 Veneto,
NE Italy
Bassein *see* Pathein
Basse-Terre 55 G4 *country capital* (Saint
Kitts and Nevis) (Saint Kitts and Nevis)
Saint Kitts, Saint Kitts and Nevis
Basse-Terre 55 G3 *dependent territory
capital* (Guadeloupe) Basse Terre,
SW Guadeloupe
Basse Terre 55 G4 *island* W Guadeloupe
Bassikounou 74 D3 Hodh ech Chargui,
SE Mauritania
Bass, Îlots de *see* Marotiri
Bass Strait 149 C7 *strait* SE Australia
Bassum 94 B3 Niedersachsen,
NW Germany
Bastia 91 E7 Corse, France,
C Mediterranean Sea
Bastogne 87 D7 Luxembourg,
SE Belgium
Bastrop 42 B2 Louisiana, S USA
Bastyn' 107 B7 *Rus.* Bostyn'. Brestskaya
Voblasts', SW Belarus
Basuo *see* Dongfang
Basutoland *see* Lesotho
Bata 77 A5 NW Equatorial Guinea
Batae Coritanorum *see* Leicester
Batajnica 100 D3 Vojvodina, N Serbia
Batangas 139 E2 *off.* Batangas City.
Luzon, N Philippines
Batangas City *see* Batangas
Batavia *see* Jakarta
Bătdâmbâng 137 C5 *prev.* Battambang.
Bătdâmbâng, NW Cambodia
Batéké, Plateaux 77 B6 *plateau* S Congo
Bath 89 D7 *hist.* Akermanceaster;
anc. Aquae Calidae, Aquae Solis.
SW England, United Kingdom
Bathinda 134 D2 Punjab, NW India
Bathsheba 55 G1 E Barbados
Bathurst 149 D6 New South Wales,
SE Australia
Bathurst 39 F4 New Brunswick,
SE Canada
Bathurst *see* Banjul

Bathurst Island 146 D2 *island* Northern
Territory, N Australia
Bathurst Island 37 F2 *island* Parry
Islands, Nunavut, N Canada
Wadi al Batin 120 C4 *dry watercourse*
SW Asia
Batman 117 E4 *var.* Iluh. Batman,
SE Turkey
Batna 71 E2 NE Algeria
Baton Rouge 42 B3 *state capital*
Louisiana, S USA
Batroûn 118 A4 *var.* Al Batrūn.
N Lebanon
Battambang *see* Bătdâmbâng
Batticaloa 132 D3 Eastern Province,
E Sri Lanka
Battipaglia 97 D5 Campania, S Italy
Battle Born State *see* Nevada
Bat'umi 117 F2 W Georgia
Batu Pahat 138 B3 *prev.* Bandar
Penggaram. Johor, Peninsular Malaysia
Bauchi 75 G4 Bauchi, NE Nigeria
Bauer Basin 153 F3 *undersea basin*
E Pacific Ocean
Bauska 106 C3 *Ger.* Bauske. Bauska,
S Latvia
Bauske *see* Bauska
Bautzen 94 D4 *Lus.* Budyšin. Sachsen,
E Germany
Bauzanum *see* Bolzano
Bavaria *see* Bayern
Bavarian Alps 95 C7 *Ger.* Bayrische
Alpen. *mountain range* Austria/
Germany
Bavière *see* Bayern
Bavispe, Río 50 C2 *river* NW Mexico
Bawiti 72 B2 *var.* Bawiti. N Egypt
Bawiti *see* Bawiti
Bawku 75 E4 N Ghana
Bayamo 54 C3 Granma, E Cuba
Bayan Har Shan 126 D4 *var.* Bayan
Khar. *mountain range* C China
Bayanhongor 126 D2 Bayanhongor,
C Mongolia
Bayan Khar *see* Bayan Har Shan
Bayano, Lago 53 G4 *lake* E Panama
Bay City 43 C5 Michigan, N USA
Bay City 49 G4 Texas, SW USA
Baydhabo 73 D6 *var.* Baydhowa, Isha
Baydhabo, *It.* Baidoa. Bay, SW Somalia
Baydhowa *see* Baydhabo
Bayern 95 C6 *Eng.* Bavaria, *Fr.* Bavière.
state SE Germany
Bayeux 90 B3 *anc.* Augustodurum.
Calvados, N France
Bāyir 119 C7 *var.* Bā'ir. Ma'ān, S Jordan
Bay Islands 52 C1 *Eng.* Bay Islands.
island group N Honduras
Bay Islands *see* Bahía, E Honduras
Baymak 111 D6 Respublika
Bashkortostan, W Russian Federation
Bayonne 91 A6 *anc.* Lapurdum.
Pyrénées-Atlantiques, SW France
Bayou State *see* Mississippi
Bayram-Ali *see* Bayramaly
Bayramaly 122 D3 *var.* Bayram-Ali;
prev. Bayram-Ali. Mary Welaýaty,
S Turkmenistan
Bayreuth 95 C5 *var.* Baireuth. Bayern,
SE Germany
Bayrische Alpen *see* Bavarian Alps
Bayrūt *see* Beyrouth
Bay State *see* Massachusetts
Baysun *see* Boysun
Bayt Laḥm *see* Bethlehem
Baytown 49 H4 Texas, SE USA
Baza 93 E4 Andalucía, S Spain
Bazargic *see* Dobrich
Bazin *see* Pezinok
Beagle Channel 65 C8 *channel*
Argentina/Chile
Béal Feirste *see* Belfast
Beannchar *see* Bangor, Northern
Ireland, UK
Bear Island *see* Bjørnøya
Bear Lake 46 E4 *lake* Idaho/Utah,
NW USA
Beas de Segura 93 E4 Andalucía, S Spain
Beata, Isla 55 E3 *island* SW Dominican
Republic
Beatrice 45 F4 Nebraska, C USA
Beaufort Sea 36 D2 *sea* Arctic Ocean
Beaufort West *see* Beaufort-Wes
Beaufort-Wes 78 C5 *Afr.* Beaufort-Wes.
Western Cape, SW South Africa
Beaumont 49 H3 Texas, SW USA
Beaune 90 D4 Côte d'Or, C France

Beauvais 90 C3 *anc.* Bellovacum,
Caesaromagus. Oise, N France
Beaver Island 40 C2 *island* Michigan,
N USA
Beaver Lake 49 H1 *reservoir* Arkansas,
C USA
Beaver River 49 F1 *river* Oklahoma,
C USA
Beaver State *see* Oregon
Beáwar 134 C3 Rājasthān, N India
Bečej 100 D3 *Ger.* Altbetsche, *Hung.*
Óbecse, Rácz-Becse; *prev.* Magyar-
Becse, Stari Bečej. Vojvodina, N Serbia
Béchar 70 D2 *prev.* Colomb-Béchar.
W Algeria
Beckley 40 D5 West Virginia, NE USA
Bécs *see* Wien
Bedford 89 D6 E England, United
Kingdom
Bedum 86 E1 Groningen,
NE Netherlands
Beehive State *see* Utah
Be'er Menuha 119 B7 *prev.* Be'er
Menuḥa. Southern, S Israel
Be'ér Menuḥa *see* Be'er Menuha
Beernem 87 A5 West-Vlaanderen,
NW Belgium
Beersheba *see* Be'er Sheva
Be'er Sheva 119 A7 *var.* Beersheba,
Ar. Bir es Saba; *prev.* Be'ér Sheva'.
Southern, S Israel
Be'ér Sheva' *see* Be'er Sheva
Beesel 87 D5 Limburg, SE Netherlands
Beeville 49 G4 Texas, SW USA
Bega 149 D7 New South Wales,
SE Australia
Begoml' *see* Byahoml'
Begovat *see* Bekobod
Behagle *see* Laï
Behar *see* Bihār
Beibu Wan *see* Tongking, Gulf of
Beida *see* Al Bayḍā'
Beihai 128 B6 Guangxi Zhuangzu
Zizhiqu, S China
Beijing 128 C3 *var.* Pei-ching, *Eng.*
Peking; *prev.* Pei-p'ing. *country
capital* (China) (China) Beijing Shi,
E China
Beilen 86 E2 Drenthe, NE Netherlands
Beira 79 E3 Sofala, C Mozambique
Beirut *see* Beyrouth
Beit Lekhem *see* Bethlehem
Beiuş 108 B3 *Hung.* Belényes. Bihor,
NW Romania
Beja 92 B4 *anc.* Pax Julia. Beja,
SE Portugal
Béjar 92 C3 Castilla-León, N Spain
Bejraburi *see* Phetchaburi
Bekabad *see* Bekobod
Békás *see* Bicaz
Bek-Budi *see* Qarshi
Békéscsaba 99 D7 *Rom.* Bichiş-Ciaba.
Békés, SE Hungary
Bekobod 123 E2 *Rus.* Bekabad;
prev. Begovat. Toshkent Viloyati,
E Uzbekistan
Bela Crkva 100 E3 *Ger.* Weisskirchen,
Hung. Fehértemplom. Vojvodina,
W Serbia
Belarus 107 B6 *off.* Republic of Belarus,
var. Belorussia, *Latv.* Baltkrievija; *prev.*
Belorussian SSR, *Rus.* Belorusskaya
SSR. *country* E Europe

BELARUS
Eastern Europe

Official name Republic of Belarus
Formation 1991 / 1991
Capital Minsk
Population 9.6 million / 120 people
per sq mile (46 people per sq km) / 71%
Total area 80,154 sq. miles
(207,600 sq. km)
Languages Belorussian*, Russian*
Religions Orthodox Christian 80%,
Other 32%, Roman Catholic 8%
Ethnic mix Belorussian 81%, Russian 11%,
Polish 4%, Other 2%, Ukrainian 2%
Government Presidential system
Currency Belorussian rouble = 100 kopeks
Literacy rate 99%
Calorie consumption 3000 calories

Belarus, Republic of *see* Belarus
Belau *see* Palau
Belaya Tserkov' *see* Bila Tserkva

Bełchatów 98 C4 var. Belchatow.
Łódzski, C Poland
Belchatow see Bełchatów
Belcher, Îles see Belcher Islands
Belcher Islands 38 C2 Fr. Îles Belcher.
island group Nunavut, SE Canada
Beledweyne 73 D5 var. Belet Huen, It.
Belet Uen. Hiiraan, C Somalia
Belém 63 F1 var. Pará.
Pará, N Brazil
Belén 52 D4 Rivas, SW Nicaragua
Belen 48 D2 New Mexico, SW USA
Belényes see Beiuş
Belet Huen/Belet Uen see Beledweyne
Belfast 89 B5 Ir. Béal Feirste. national
capital E Northern Ireland, United
Kingdom
Belfield 44 D2 North Dakota, N USA
Belfort 90 E4 Territoire-de-Belfort,
E France
Belgard see Białogard
Belgaum 132 B1 Karnātaka, W India
Belgian Congo see Congo (Democratic
Republic of)
België/Belgique see Belgium
Belgium 87 B6 off. Kingdom of Belgium,
Dut. België, Fr. Belgique. country
NW Europe

BELGIUM
Northwest Europe

Official name Kingdom of Belgium
Formation 1830 / 1919
Capital Brussels
Population 10.5 million / 829 people
per sq mile (320 people per sq km) / 97%
Total area 11,780 sq. miles (30,510 sq. km)
Languages Dutch*, French*, German*
Religions Roman Catholic 88%,
Other 10%, Muslim 2%
Ethnic mix Fleming 58%, Walloon 33%,
Other 6%, Italian 2%, Moroccan 1%
Government Parliamentary system
Currency Euro = 100 cents
Literacy rate 99%
Calorie consumption 3584 calories

Belgium, Kingdom of see Belgium
Belgorod 111 A6 Belgorodskaya Oblast',
W Russian Federation
Belgrano II 154 A2 Argentinian research
station Antarctica
Belice see Belize/Belize City
Beligrad see Berat
Beli Manastir 100 C3 Hung.
Pélmonostor; prev. Monostor. Osijek-
Baranja, NE Croatia
Belinga 77 B5 Ogooué-Ivindo,
NE Gabon
Belitung, Pulau 138 C4 island
W Indonesia
Belize 52 B1 Sp. Belice; prev. British
Honduras, Colony of Belize. country
Central America

BELIZE
Central America

Official name Belize
Formation 1981 / 1981
Capital Belmopan
Population 294,385 / 33 people
per sq mile (13 people per sq km) / 48%
Total area 8867 sq. miles (22,966 sq. km)
Languages English*, English Creole,
Spanish, Mayan, Garifuna (Carib)
Religions Roman Catholic 62%,
Other 13%, Anglican 12%,
Methodist 6%, Mennonite 4%,
Seventh-day Adventist 3%
Ethnic mix Mestizo 49%, Creole 25%,
Maya 11%, Other 6%, Garifuna 6%,
Asian Indian 3%
Government Parliamentary system
Currency Belizean dollar = 100 cents
Literacy rate 75%
Calorie consumption 2869 calories

Belize 52 B1 river Belize/Guatemala
Belize see Belize City
Belize City 52 C1 var. Belize, Sp. Belice.
Belize, NE Belize
Belize, Colony of see Belize
Beljak see Villach
Belkofski 36 B3 Alaska, USA
Belle Île 90 A4 island NW France

Belle Isle, Strait of 39 G3 strait
Newfoundland and Labrador, E Canada
Bellenz see Bellinzona
Belleville 40 B4 Illinois, N USA
Bellevue 45 F4 Iowa, C USA
Bellevue 46 B2 Washington, NW USA
Bellingham 46 B1 Washington,
NW USA
Belling Hausen Mulde see Southeast
Pacific Basin
Bellingshausen Abyssal Plain see
Bellingshausen Plain
Bellingshausen Plain 153 F5 var.
Bellingshausen Abyssal Plain. abyssal
plain SE Pacific Ocean
Bellingshausen Sea 154 A3 sea
Antarctica
Bellinzona 95 B8 Ger. Bellenz. Ticino,
S Switzerland
Bello 58 B2 Antioquia, W Colombia
Bello Horizonte see Belo Horizonte
Bellovacum see Beauvais
Bellville 78 B5 Western Cape, SW South
Africa
Belmopan 52 C1 country capital (Belize)
(Belize) Cayo, C Belize
Belogradchik 104 B1 Vidin,
NW Bulgaria
Belo Horizonte 63 F4 prev. Bello
Horizonte. state capital Minas Gerais,
SE Brazil
Belomorsk 110 B3 Respublika Kareliya,
NW Russian Federation
Beloretsk 111 D6 Respublika
Bashkortostan, W Russian Federation
Belorussia/Belorussian SSR see Belarus
Belorusskaya Gryada see Byelaruskaya
Hrada
Belorusskaya SSR see Belarus
Beloshchel'ye see Nar'yan-Mar
Belostok see Białystok
Belovár see Bjelovar
Belozërsk 110 B4 Vologodskaya Oblast',
NW Russian Federation
Belton 49 G3 Texas, SW USA
Bel'tsy see Bălţi
Beluchistan see Baluchistān
Belukha, Gora 114 D5 mountain
Kazakhstan/Russian Federation
Belynichi see Byalynichy
Belyy, Ostrov 114 D2 island N Russian
Federation
Bemaraha 79 F3 var. Plateau du
Bemaraha. mountain range
W Madagascar
Bemaraha, Plateau du see Bemaraha
Bemidji 45 F1 Minnesota, N USA
Bemmel 86 D4 Gelderland,
SE Netherlands
Benaco see Garda, Lago di
Benares see Vārānasi
Benavente 92 D2 Castilla-León, N Spain
Bend 46 B3 Oregon, NW USA
Bender see Tighina
Bender Beila/Bender Beyla see
Bandarbeyla
Bender Cassim/Bender Qaasim see
Boosaaso
Bendern 94 E1 NW Liechtenstein Europe
Bendery see Tighina
Bendigo 149 C7 Victoria, SE Australia
Beneschau see Benešov
Beneški Zaliv see Venice, Gulf of
Benešov 99 B5 Ger. Beneschau.
Středočeský Kraj, W Czech Republic
Benevento 97 D5 anc. Beneventum,
Malventum. Campania, S Italy
Beneventum see Benevento
Bengal, Bay of 124 C4 bay N Indian
Ocean
Bengalooru see Bangalore
Bengasi see Banghāzī
Bengazi see Banghāzī
Bengbu 128 D5 var. Peng-pu. Anhui,
E China
Benghazi see Banghāzī
Bengkulu 138 B4 prev. Bengkoeloe,
Benkoelen, Benkulen. Sumatera,
W Indonesia
Benguela 78 A2 var. Benguella.
Benguela, W Angola
Benguella see Benguela
Bengweulu, Lake see Bangweulu, Lake
Ben Hope 88 B2 mountain N Scotland,
United Kingdom
Beni 77 E5 Nord-Kivu, NE Dem. Rep.
Congo

Benidorm 93 F4 País Valenciano,
SE Spain
Beni-Mellal 70 C2 C Morocco
Benin 75 F4 off. Republic of Benin; prev.
Dahomey. country W Africa

BENIN
West Africa

Official name Republic of Benin
Formation 1960 / 1960
Capital Porto-Novo
Population 9 million / 211 people
per sq mile (81 people per sq km) / 45%
Total area 43,483 sq. miles (112,620 sq. km)
Languages French*, Fon, Bariba, Yoruba,
Adja, Houeda, Somba
Religions Voodoo 50%, Muslim 30%,
Christian 20%
Ethnic mix Fon 41%, Other 21%, Adja 16%,
Yoruba 12%, Bariba 10%
Government Presidential system
Currency CFA franc = 100 centimes
Literacy rate 35%
Calorie consumption 2548 calories

Benin, Bight of 75 F5 gulf W Africa
Benin City 75 F5 Edo, SW Nigeria
Benin, Republic of see Benin
Beni, Río 61 E3 river N Bolivia
Beni Suef see Banī Suwayf
Ben Nevis 88 C3 mountain N Scotland,
United Kingdom
Bénoué see Benue
Benson 48 B3 Arizona, SW USA
Bent Jbaïl 119 A5 var. Bint Jubayl.
S Lebanon
Benton 42 B1 Arkansas, C USA
Benue 76 B4 Fr. Bénoué. river
Cameroon/Nigeria
Beograd 100 D3 Eng. Belgrade. Serbia,
N Serbia
Berane 101 D5 prev. Ivangrad.
E Montenegro
Berat 101 C6 var. Berati, SCr. Beligrad.
Berat, C Albania
Berătău see Berettyó
Berati see Berat
Berau, Teluk 139 G4 var. MacCluer Gulf.
bay Papua, E Indonesia
Berbera 72 D4 Sahil, NW Somalia
Berbérati 77 B5 Mambéré-Kadéï,
SW Central African Republic
Berck-Plage 90 C2 Pas-de-Calais,
N France
Berdichev see Berdychiv
Berdyans'k 109 G4 Rus. Berdyansk;
prev. Osipenko. Zaporiz'ka Oblast',
SE Ukraine
Berdychiv 108 D2 Rus. Berdichev.
Zhytomyrs'ka Oblast', N Ukraine
Beregovo/Beregszász see Berehove
Berehove 108 B3 Cz. Berehovo,
Hung. Beregszász, Rus. Beregovo.
Zakarpats'ka Oblast', W Ukraine
Berehovo see Berehove
Bereket 122 B2 prev. Rus. Gazandzhyk,
Kazandzhik, Turkm. Gazanjyk. Balkan
Welaýaty, W Turkmenistan
Beretău see Berettyó
Berettyó 99 D7 Rom. Barcău; prev.
Berătău, Beretău. river Hungary/
Romania
Berettyóújfalu 99 D6 Hajdú-Bihar,
E Hungary
Berezhany 108 C2 Pol. Brzeżany.
Ternopil's'ka Oblast', W Ukraine
Berezina see Byerezino
Berezniki 111 D5 Permskaya Oblast',
NW Russian Federation
Berga 93 G2 Cataluña, NE Spain
Bergamo 96 B2 anc. Bergomum.
Lombardia, N Italy
Bergara 93 E1 País Vasco, N Spain
Bergen 94 D2 Mecklenburg-
Vorpommern, NE Germany
Bergen 86 C2 Noord-Holland,
NW Netherlands
Bergen 85 A5 Hordaland, S Norway
Bergen see Mons
Bergerac 91 B5 Dordogne, SW France
Bergeyk 87 C5 Noord-Brabant,
S Netherlands
Bergomum see Bergamo
Bergse Maas 86 D4 river S Netherlands
Beringen 87 C5 Limburg, NE Belgium
Beringov Proliv see Bering Strait

Bering Sea 36 A2 sea N Pacific Ocean
Bering Strait 36 C2 Rus. Beringov Proliv,
strait Bering Sea/Chukchi Sea
Berja 93 E5 Andalucía, S Spain
Berkeley 47 B6 California, W USA
Berkner Island 154 A2 island Antarctica
Berkovitsa 104 C2 Montana,
NW Bulgaria
Berlin 94 D3 country capital (Germany)
(Germany) Berlin, NE Germany
Berlin 41 G2 New Hampshire, NE USA
Berlinchen see Barlinek
Bermejo, Río 64 C2 river N Argentina
Bermeo 93 E1 País Vasco, N Spain
Bermuda 35 D6 var. Bermuda Islands,
Bermudas; prev. Somers Islands. UK
crown colony NW Atlantic Ocean
Bermuda Islands see Bermuda
Bermuda Rise 35 E6 undersea rise
C Sargasso Sea
Bermudas see Bermuda
Bern 95 A7 Fr. Berne. country capital
(Switzerland) (Switzerland) Bern,
W Switzerland
Bernau 94 D3 Brandenburg,
NE Germany
Bernburg 94 C4 Sachsen-Anhalt,
C Germany
Berne see Bern
Berner Alpen 95 A7 var. Berner
Oberland, Eng. Bernese Oberland.
mountain range SW Switzerland
Berner Oberland/Bernese Oberland see
Berner Alpen
Bernier Island 147 A5 island Western
Australia
Beroea see Ḥalab
Berry 90 C4 cultural region C France
Berry Islands 54 C1 island group
N Bahamas
Bertoua 77 B5 Est, E Cameroon
Beru 145 E2 var. Peru. atoll Tungaru,
W Kiribati
Berwick-upon-Tweed 88 D4 N England
United Kingdom
Berytus see Beyrouth
Besançon 90 D4 anc. Besontium,
Vesontio. Doubs, E France
Beskra see Biskra
Besontium see Besançon
Bessarabka see Basarabeasca
Beszterce see Bistriţa
Besztercebánya see Banská Bystrica
Betafo 79 G3 Antananarivo,
C Madagascar
Betanzos 92 B1 Galicia, NW Spain
Bethlehem 78 D4 Free State, C South
Africa
Bethlehem 119 B6 var. Beit Lehem,
Ar. Bayt Laḥm, Heb. Bet Leḥem.
C West Bank
Béticos, Sistemas 92 D4 var. Sistema
Penibético, Eng. Baetic Cordillera,
Baetic Mountains. mountain range
S Spain
Bet Leḥem see Bethlehem
Bétou 77 C5 Likouala, N Congo
Bette, Picco 71 A4 var. Bette, Picco
Bette. mountain S Libya
Bette, Picco see Bette, Picco
Beulah 40 C2 Michigan, N USA
Beuthen see Bytom
Beveren 87 B5 Oost-Vlaanderen,
N Belgium
Beverley 89 D5 E England, United
Kingdom
Bexley 89 B8 Bexley, SE England, United
Kingdom
Beyla 74 D4 SE Guinea
Beyrouth 118 A4 var. Bayrūt, Eng.
Beirut; anc. Berytus. country capital
(Lebanon) (Lebanon) W Lebanon
Beyşehir 116 B4 Konya, SW Turkey
Beyşehir Gölü 116 B4 lake C Turkey
Béziers 91 C6 anc. Baeterrae, Baeterrae
Septimanorum, Julia Beterrae. Hérault
S France
Bezwada see Vijayawāda
Bhādrāvati 132 C2 Karnātaka, SW India
Bhāgalpur 135 F3 Bihār, NE India
Bhaktapur 135 F3 Central, C Nepal
Bhamo 136 B2 var. Banmo. Kachin
State, N Burma (Myanmar)
Bhārat see India
Bharūch 134 C4 Gujarāt, W India
Bhaunagar see Bhāvnagar

hāvnagar 134 C4 prev. Bhaunagar.
  Gujarāt, W India
heanntraí, Bá see Bantry Bay
hopāl 134 D4 state capital Madhya
  Pradesh, C India
hubaneshwar 135 F5 prev.
  Bhubaneswar, Bhuvaneshwar. state
  capital Orissa, E India
hubaneswar see Bhubaneshwar
huket see Phuket
husaval see Bhusāwal
husāwal 134 D4 prev. Bhusaval.
  Mahārāshtra, C India
hutan 135 G3 off. Kingdom of Bhutan,
  var. Druk-yul. country S Asia

BHUTAN
South Asia

Official name Kingdom of Bhutan
Formation 1656 / 1865
Capital Thimphu
Population 2.3 million / 127 people
  per sq mile (49 people per sq km) / 9%
Total area 18,147 sq. miles (47,000 sq. km)
Languages Dzongkha*, Nepali, Assamese
Religions Mahayana Buddhist 70%,
  Hindu 24%, Other 6%
Ethnic mix Bhute 50%, Other 25%,
  Nepalese 25%
Government Mixed monarchical–
  parliamentary system
Currency Ngultrum = 100 chetrum
Literacy rate 47%
Calorie consumption Not available

hutan, Kingdom of see Bhutan
huvaneshwar see Bhubaneshwar
iak, Pulau 139 G4 island E Indonesia
iała Podlaska 98 E3 Lubelskie,
  E Poland
iałogard 98 B2 Ger. Belgard.
  Zachodnio-pomorskie, NW Poland
iałystok 98 E3 Rus. Belostok, Bielostok.
  Podlaskie, NE Poland
ianco, Monte see Blanc, Mont
iarritz 91 A6 Pyrénées-Atlantiques,
  SW France
icaz 108 C3 Hung. Békás. Neamţ,
  NE Romania
ichiş-Ciaba see Békéscsaba
iddeford 41 G2 Maine, NE USA
ideford 89 C7 SW England, United
  Kingdom
iel 95 A7 Fr. Bienne. Bern,
  W Switzerland
ielefeld 94 B4 Nordrhein-Westfalen,
  NW Germany
ielitz/Bielitz-Biala see Bielsko-Biała
ielostok see Białystok
ielsko-Biała 99 C5 Ger. Bielitz, Bielitz-
  Biala. Śląskie, S Poland
ielsk Podlaski 98 E3 Białystok,
  E Poland
ien Bien see Điên Biên
iên Đông see South China Sea
iên Hoa 137 E6 Đông Nai, S Vietnam
ienne see Biel
ienville, Lac 38 D2 lake Québec,
  C Canada
ié Plateau 78 B2 var. Bié Plateau.
  plateau C Angola
ié Plateau see Bié, Planalto do
ig Cypress Swamp 43 E5 wetland
  Florida, SE USA
igge Island 146 C2 island Western
  Australia
ighorn Mountains 44 C2 mountain
  range Wyoming, C USA
ighorn River 44 C2 river Montana/
  Wyoming, NW USA
ignona 74 B3 SW Senegal
igorra see Tarbes
igosovo see Bihosava
ig Sioux River 45 E2 river Iowa/South
  Dakota, N USA
ig Spring 49 E3 Texas, SW USA
ihać 100 B3 Federacija Bosna I
  Hercegovina, NW Bosnia and
  Herzegovina
ihār 135 F3 prev. Behar. cultural
  region N India
ihār see Bihār Sharif
iharamulo 73 B7 Kagera,
  NW Tanzania
ihār Sharif 135 F3 var. Bihār. Bihār,
  N India

Bihosava 107 D5 Rus. Bigosovo.
  Vitsyebskaya Voblasts', NW Belarus
Bijeljina 100 C3 Republika Srpska,
  NE Bosnia and Herzegovina
Bijelo Polje 101 D5 E Montenegro
Bīkāner 134 C3 Rājasthān, NW India
Bikin 115 G4 Khabarovskiy Kray,
  SE Russian Federation
Bikini Atoll 144 C1 var. Pikinni. atoll
  Ralik Chain, NW Marshall Islands
Bīkkū Bīttī see Bette, Picco
Bilāspur 135 E4 Chhattisgarh, C India
Bilāsuvar 117 H3 Rus. Bilyasuvar; prev.
  Pushkino. SE Azerbaijan
Bila Tserkva 109 E2 Rus. Belaya
  Tserkov'. Kyyivs'ka Oblast', N Ukraine
Bilauktaung Range 137 C6 var.
  Thanintari Taungdan. mountain range
  Burma (Myanmar)/Thailand
Bilbao 93 E1 Basq. Bilbo. País Vasco,
  N Spain
Bilbo see Bilbao
Bilecik 116 B3 Bilecik, NW Turkey
Billings 44 C2 Montana, NW USA
Bilma, Grand Erg de 75 H3 desert
  NE Niger
Biloela 148 D4 Queensland, E Australia
Biloxi 42 C3 Mississippi, S USA
Biltine 76 C3 Biltine, E Chad
Bilwi see Puerto Cabezas
Bilyasuvar see Bilāsuvar
Bilzen 87 D6 Limburg, NE Belgium
Bimini Islands 54 C1 island group
  W Bahamas
Binche 87 B7 Hainaut, S Belgium
Bindloe Island see Marchena, Isla
Bin Ghalfān, Jazāʾir see Ḥālāniyāt,
  Juzur al
Binghamton 41 F3 New York, NE USA
Bingöl 117 E3 Bingöl, E Turkey
Bint Jubayl see Bent Jbaïl
Bintulu 138 D3 Sarawak, East Malaysia
Binzhou 128 D4 Shandong, E China
Bío Bío, Río 65 B5 river C Chile
Bioco, Isla de 77 A5 var. Bioko, Eng.
  Fernando Po, Sp. Fernando Póo;
  prev. Macías Nguema Biyogo. island
  NW Equatorial Guinea
Bioko see Bioco, Isla de
Birāk 71 F3 var. Brak. C Libya
Birao 76 D3 Vakaga, NE Central African
  Republic
Birātnagar 135 F3 Eastern, SE Nepal
Bir es Saba see Be'er Sheva
Bīrjand 120 E3 Khorāsān-e Janūbī,
  E Iran
Birkenfeld 95 A5 Rheinland-Pfalz,
  SW Germany
Birkenhead 89 C5 NW England, United
  Kingdom
Bîrlad see Bârlad
Birmingham 89 C6 C England, United
  Kingdom
Birmingham 42 C2 Alabama, S USA
Bir Moghreïn see Bir Mogreïn
Bir Mogreïn 74 C1 var. Bir Moghreïn;
  prev. Fort-Trinquet. Tiris Zemmour,
  N Mauritania
Birnie Island 145 E3 atoll Phoenix
  Islands, C Kiribati
Birnin Konni 75 F3 var. Birni-Nkonni.
  Tahoua, SW Niger
Birni-Nkonni see Birnin Konni
Birobidzhan 115 G4 Yevreyskaya
  Avtonomnaya Oblast', SE Russian
  Federation
Birsen see Biržai
Birsk 111 D5 Respublika Bashkortostan,
  W Russian Federation
Biržai 106 C4 Ger. Birsen. Panevėžys,
  NE Lithuania
Birżebbuġa 102 B5 SE Malta
Bisanthe see Tekirdağ
Bisbee 48 B3 Arizona, SW USA
Biscaia, Baía de see Biscay, Bay of
Biscay, Bay of 80 B4 Sp. Golfo de
  Vizcaya, Port. Baía de Biscaia. bay
  SW Europe
Biscay Plain 80 B3 abyssal plain SE Bay
  of Biscay
Bischofsburg see Biskupiec
Bishah, Wadi 121 B5 dry watercourse
  C Saudi Arabia
Bishkek 123 G2 var. Pishpek; prev.
  Frunze. country capital (Kyrgyzstan)
  (Kyrgyzstan) Chuyskaya Oblast',
  N Kyrgyzstan

Bishop's Lynn see King's Lynn
Bishrī, Jabal 118 D3 mountain range
  E Syria
Biskara see Biskra
Biskra 71 E2 var. Beskra, Biskara.
  NE Algeria
Biskupiec 98 D2 Ger. Bischofsburg.
  Warmińsko-Mazurskie, NE Poland
Bislig 139 F2 Mindanao, S Philippines
Bismarck 45 E2 state capital North
  Dakota, N USA
Bismarck Archipelago 144 B3 island
  group NE Papua New Guinea
Bismarck Sea 144 B3 sea W Pacific
  Ocean
Bisnulok see Phitsanulok
Bissau 74 B4 country capital
  (Guinea-Bissau) (Guinea-Bissau)
  W Guinea-Bissau
Bistriţa 108 B3 Ger. Bistritz, Hung.
  Besztercze; prev. Nösen. Bistriţa-
  Năsăud, N Romania
Bistritz see Bistriţa
Bitam 77 B5 Woleu-Ntem, N Gabon
Bitburg 95 A5 Rheinland-Pfalz,
  SW Germany
Bitlis 117 F3 Bitlis, SE Turkey
Bitoeng see Bitung
Bitola 101 D6 Turk. Monastir; prev.
  Bitolj. S FYR Macedonia
Bitolj see Bitola
Bitonto 97 D5 anc. Butuntum. Puglia,
  SE Italy
Bitterroot Range 46 D2 mountain range
  Idaho/Montana, NW USA
Bitung 139 F3 prev. Bitoeng. Sulawesi,
  C Indonesia
Biu 75 H4 Borno, E Nigeria
Biwa-ko 131 C6 lake Honshū, SW Japan
Bizerta see Bizerte
Bizerte 71 E1 Ar. Banzart, Eng. Bizerta.
  N Tunisia
Bjelovar 100 B2 Hung. Belovár.
  Bjelovar-Bilogora, N Croatia
Bjeshkët e Namuna see North Albanian
  Alps
Björneborg see Pori
Bjørnøya 83 F3 Eng. Bear Island. island
  N Norway
Blackall 148 C4 Queensland, E Australia
Black Drin 101 D6 Alb. Lumi i Drinit të
  Zi, SCr. Crni Drim. river Albania/FYR
  Macedonia
Blackfoot 46 E4 Idaho, NW USA
Black Forest 95 B6 Eng. Black Forest.
  mountain range SW Germany
Black Forest see Schwarzwald
Black Hills 44 D3 mountain range South
  Dakota/Wyoming, N USA
Blackpool 89 C5 NW England, United
  Kingdom
Black Range 48 C2 mountain range New
  Mexico, SW USA
Black River 54 A5 W Jamaica
Black River 136 C3 Chin. Babian Jiang,
  Lixian Jiang, Fr. Rivière Noire, Vtn.
  Sông Đa. river China/Vietnam
Black Rock Desert 47 C5 desert Nevada,
  W USA
Black Sand Desert see Garagum
Black Sea 116 B1 var. Euxine Sea, Bul.
  Cherno More, Rom. Marea Neagră,
  Chernoye More, Turk. Karadeniz, Ukr.
  Chorne More. sea Asia/Europe
Black Sea Lowland 109 E4 Ukr.
  Prychornomors'ka Nyzovyna.
  depression SE Europe
Blackwater 89 A6 Ir. An Abhainn Mhór.
  river S Ireland
Blackwater see Nebraska
Blagoevgrad 104 C3 prev. Gorna
  Dzhumaya. Blagoevgrad, W Bulgaria
Blagoveshchensk 115 G4 Amurskaya
  Oblast', SE Russian Federation
Blake Plateau 35 D6 var. Blake Terrace.
  undersea plateau W Atlantic Ocean
Blake Terrace see Blake Plateau
Blanca, Bahía 65 C5 bay E Argentina
Blanca, Costa 93 F4 physical region
  SE Spain
Blanche, Lake 149 B5 lake South
  Australia
Blanc, Mont 91 D5 It. Monte Bianco.
  mountain France/Italy

Blanco, Cape 46 A4 headland Oregon,
  NW USA
Blanes 93 G2 Cataluña, NE Spain
Blankenberge 87 A5 West-Vlaanderen,
  NW Belgium
Blankenheim 95 A5 Nordrhein-
  Westfalen, W Germany
Blanquilla, Isla 59 E1 var. La Blanquila.
  island N Venezuela
Blanquilla, La see Blanquilla, Isla
Blantyre 79 E2 var. Blantyre-Limbe.
  Southern, S Malawi
Blantyre-Limbe see Blantyre
Blaricum 86 C3 Noord-Holland,
  C Netherlands
Blatnitsa see Durankulak
Blenheim 151 C5 Marlborough, South
  Island, New Zealand
Blesae see Blois
Blida 70 D2 var. El Boulaida, El
  Boulaïda. N Algeria
Bloemfontein 78 C4 var. Mangaung.
  country capital (South Africa-judicial
  capital) (South Africa-judicial capital)
  Free State, C South Africa
Blois 90 C4 anc. Blesae. Loir-et-Cher,
  C France
Bloomfield 48 C1 New Mexico, SW USA
Bloomington 40 B4 Illinois, N USA
Bloomington 40 C4 Indiana, N USA
Bloomington 45 F2 Minnesota, N USA
Bloomsbury 148 D3 Queensland,
  NE Australia
Bluefield 40 D5 West Virginia, NE USA
Bluefields 53 E3 Región Autónoma
  Atlántico Sur, SE Nicaragua
Bluegrass State see Kentucky
Blue Hen State see Delaware
Blue Law State see Connecticut
Blue Mountain Peak 54 B5 mountain
  E Jamaica
Blue Mountains 46 C3 mountain range
  Oregon/Washington, NW USA
Blue Nile 72 C4 var. Abai, Bahr el,
  Azraq, Amh. Ābay Wenz, Ar. An Nīl al
  Azraq. river Ethiopia/Sudan
Blumenau 63 E5 Santa Catarina, S Brazil
Blythe 47 D8 California, W USA
Blytheville 42 C1 Arkansas, C USA
Bo 74 C4 S Sierra Leone
Boaco 52 D3 Boaco, S Nicaragua
Boa Vista 62 D1 state capital Roraima,
  NW Brazil
Boa Vista 74 A3 island Ilhas de
  Barlavento, E Cape Verde
Bobaomby, Tanjona 79 G2 Fr. Cap
  d'Ambre. headland N Madagascar
Bobigny 90 E1 Seine-St-Denis, N France
Bobo-Dioulasso 74 D4 SW Burkina Faso
Bobrinets see Bobrynets'
Bobruysk see Babruysk
Bobrynets' 109 E3 Rus. Bobrinets.
  Kirovohrads'ka Oblast', C Ukraine
Boca Raton 43 F5 Florida, SE USA
Bocay 52 D2 Jinotega, N Nicaragua
Bocheykovo see Bacheykava
Bocholt 94 A4 Nordrhein-Westfalen,
  W Germany
Bochum 94 A4 Nordrhein-Westfalen,
  W Germany
Bocşa 108 A4 Ger. Bokschen, Hung.
  Boksánbánya. Caraş-Severin,
  SW Romania
Bodaybo 115 F4 Irkutskaya Oblast',
  E Russian Federation
Bodegas see Babahoyo
Boden 84 D4 Norrbotten, N Sweden
Bodensee see Constance, Lake,
  C Europe
Bodmin 89 C7 SW England, United
  Kingdom
Bodø 84 C3 Nordland, C Norway
Bodrum 116 A4 Muğla, SW Turkey
Boeloekoemba see Bulukumba
Boende 77 C5 Equateur, C Dem. Rep.
  Congo
Boeroe see Buru, Pulau
Boetoeng see Buton, Pulau
Bogale 136 B4 Ayeyarwady, SW Burma
  (Myanmar)
Bogalusa 42 B3 Louisiana, S USA
Bogatynia 98 B4 Ger. Reichenau.
  Dolnośląskie, SW Poland
Bogazliyan 116 D3 Yozgat, C Turkey
Bogendorf see Łuków
Bogor 138 C5 Dut. Buitenzorg. Jawa,
  C Indonesia

Bogotá 58 B3 prev. Santa Fe, Santa Fe de Bogotá. country capital (Colombia) (Colombia) Cundinamarca, C Colombia
Bogushëvsk see Bahushewsk
Boguslav see Bohuslav
Bo Hai 128 D4 var. Gulf of Chihli. gulf NE China
Bohemia 99 A5 Cz. Čechy, Ger. Böhmen. W Czech Republic
Bohemian Forest 95 C5 Cz. Ceský Les, Šumava, Ger. Böhmerwald. mountain range C Europe
Böhmen see Bohemia
Böhmerwald see Bohemian Forest
Böhmisch-Krumau see Český Krumlov
Bohol Sea 139 E2 var. Mindanao Sea. sea S Philippines
Bohuslav 109 E2 Rus. Boguslav. Kyyivs'ka Oblast', N Ukraine
Boise 46 D3 var. Boise City. state capital Idaho, NW USA
Boise City 49 E1 Oklahoma, C USA
Boise City see Boise
Bois, Lac des see Woods, Lake of the
Bois-le-Duc see 's-Hertogenbosch
Boizenburg 94 C3 Mecklenburg-Vorpommern, N Germany
Bojador see Boujdour
Bojnûrd 120 D2 var. Bujnurd. Khorāsān-e Shemālī, N Iran
Bokāro 135 F4 Jhārkhand, N India
Boké 74 C4 W Guinea
Bokhara see Buxoro
Boknafjorden 85 A6 fjord S Norway
Boksánbánya/Bokschen see Bocşa
Bol 76 B3 Lac, W Chad
Bolgatanga 75 E4 N Ghana
Bolgrad see Bolhrad
Bolhrad 108 D4 Rus. Bolgrad. Odes'ka Oblast', SW Ukraine
Bolívar, Pico 58 C2 mountain W Venezuela
Bolivia 61 F3 off. Republic of Bolivia. country W South America

BOLIVIA
South America

Official name Republic of Bolivia
Formation 1825 / 1938
Capital La Paz (administrative); Sucre (judicial)
Population 9.5 million / 23 people per sq mile (9 people per sq km) / 64%
Total area 424,162 sq. miles (1,098,580 sq. km)
Languages Aymara*, Quechua*, Spanish*
Religions Roman Catholic 93%, Other 7%
Ethnic mix Quechua 37%, Aymara 32%, Mixed race 13%, European 10%, Other 8%
Government Presidential system
Currency Boliviano = 100 centavos
Literacy rate 87%
Calorie consumption 2235 calories

Bolivia, Republic of see Bolivia
Bollène 91 D6 Vaucluse, SE France
Bollnäs 85 C5 Gävleborg, C Sweden
Bollon 149 D5 Queensland, C Australia
Bologna 96 C3 Emilia-Romagna, N Italy
Bol'shevik see Bal'shavik
Bol'shevik, Ostrov 115 E2 island Severnaya Zemlya, N Russian Federation
Bol'shezemel'skaya Tundra 110 E3 physical region NW Russian Federation
Bol'shoy Lyakhovskiy, Ostrov 115 F2 island NE Russian Federation
Bolton 89 D5 prev. Bolton-le-Moors. NW England, United Kingdom
Bolton-le-Moors see Bolton
Bolu 116 B3 Bolu, NW Turkey
Bolungarvík 83 E4 Vestfirðir, NW Iceland
Bolyarovo 104 D3 prev. Pashkeni. Yambol, E Bulgaria
Bolzano 96 C1 Ger. Bozen; anc. Bauzanum. Trentino-Alto Adige, N Italy
Boma 76 B6 Bas-Congo, W Dem. Rep. Congo
Bombay see Mumbai
Bomu 76 D4 var. M'Bomou, Mbomu, M'Bomu. river Central African Republic/Dem. Rep. Congo

Bonaire 55 F5 Dutch autonomous region S Caribbean Sea
Bonanza 52 D2 Región Autónoma Atlántico Norte, NE Nicaragua
Bonaparte Archipelago 146 C2 island group Western Australia
Bon, Cap 102 D3 headland N Tunisia
Bonda 77 B6 Ogooué-Lolo, C Gabon
Bondoukou 75 E4 E Côte d'Ivoire
Bône see Annaba, Algeria
Bone see Watampone, Indonesia
Bone, Teluk 139 E4 bay Sulawesi, C Indonesia
Bongaigaon 135 G3 Assam, NE India
Bongo, Massif des 76 D4 var. Chaîne des Mongos. mountain range NE Central African Republic
Bongor 76 B3 Mayo-Kébbi, SW Chad
Bonifacio 91 E7 Corse, France, C Mediterranean Sea
Bonifacio, Bocche de/Bonifacio, Bouches de see Bonifacio, Strait of
Bonifacio, Strait of 96 A4 Fr. Bouches de Bonifacio, It. Bocche di Bonifacio. strait C Mediterranean Sea
Bonn 95 A5 Nordrhein-Westfalen, W Germany
Bononia see Vidin, Bulgaria
Bononia see Boulogne-sur-Mer, France
Boosaaso 72 E4 var. Bandar Kassim, Bender Qaasim, Bosaso, It. Bender Cassim. Bari, N Somalia
Boothia Felix see Boothia Peninsula
Boothia, Gulf of 37 F2 gulf Nunavut, NE Canada
Boothia Peninsula 37 F2 prev. Boothia Felix. peninsula Nunavut, NE Canada
Boppard 95 A5 Rheinland-Pfalz, W Germany
Boquete 53 E5 var. Bajo Boquete. Chiriquí, W Panama
Boquillas 50 D2 var. Boquillas del Carmen. Coahuila, NE Mexico
Boquillas del Carmen see Boquillas
Bor 100 E4 Serbia, E Serbia
Bor 73 B5 Jonglei, S Sudan
Borås 85 B7 Västra Götaland, S Sweden
Borbetomagus see Worms
Borborema, Planalto da 56 E3 plateau NE Brazil
Bordeaux 91 B5 anc. Burdigala. Gironde, SW France
Bordj Omar Driss 71 E3 E Algeria
Borgå see Porvoo
Børgefjell 84 C4 mountain range C Norway
Borger 86 E2 Drenthe, NE Netherlands
Borger 49 E1 Texas, SW USA
Borgholm 85 C7 Kalmar, S Sweden
Borgo Maggiore 96 E1 NW San Marino
Borislav see Boryslav
Borisoglebsk 111 B6 Voronezhskaya Oblast', W Russian Federation
Borisov see Barysaw
Borlänge 85 C6 Dalarna, C Sweden
Borne 86 E3 Overijssel, E Netherlands
Borneo 138 C4 island Brunei/Indonesia/Malaysia
Bornholm 85 B8 island E Denmark
Borohoro Shan 126 B2 mountain range NW China
Borongo see Black Volta
Boron'ki see Baron'ki
Borosjenő see Ineu
Borovan 104 C2 Vratsa, NW Bulgaria
Borovichi 110 B4 Novgorodskaya Oblast', W Russian Federation
Borovo 100 C3 Vukovar-Srijem, NE Croatia
Borşa 108 C3 Hung. Borsa. Maramureş, N Romania
Boryslav 108 B2 Pol. Borysław, Rus. Borislav. L'viv's'ka Oblast', NW Ukraine
Borysław see Boryslav
Bosanska Dubica 100 B3 var. Kozarska Dubica. Republika Srpska, NW Bosnia and Herzegovina
Bosanska Gradiška 100 B3 var. Gradiška. Republika Srpska, N Bosnia and Herzegovina
Bosanski Novi 100 B3 var. Novi Grad. Republika Srpska, NW Bosnia and Herzegovina
Bosanski Šamac 100 C3 var. Šamac. Republika Srpska, N Bosnia and Herzegovina
Bosaso see Boosaaso

Bösing see Pezinok
Boskovice 99 B5 Ger. Boskowitz. Jihomoravský Kraj, SE Czech Republic
Boskowitz see Boskovice
Bosna 100 C4 river N Bosnia and Herzegovina
Bosnia and Herzegovina 100 B3 off. Republic of Bosnia and Herzegovina. country SE Europe

BOSNIA & HERZEGOVINA
Southeast Europe

Official name Bosnia and Herzegovina
Formation 1992 / 1992
Capital Sarajevo
Population 3.9 million / 198 people per sq mile (76 people per sq km) / 45%
Total area 19,741 sq. miles (51,129 sq. km)
Languages Bosnian*, Croatian*, Serbian*
Religions Muslim (mainly Sunni) 40%, Orthodox Christian 31%, Roman Catholic 15%, Other 10%, Protestant 4%
Ethnic mix Bosniak 44%, Serb 31%, Croat 17%, Other 8%
Government Parliamentary system
Currency Marka = 100 pfeninga
Literacy rate 97%
Calorie consumption 2894 calories

Bosnia and Herzegovina, Republic of see Bosnia and Herzegovina
Boso-hanto 131 D6 peninsula Honshū, S Japan
Bosphorus/Bosporus see İstanbul Boğazı
Bosporus 116 B2 var. Bosporus Thracius, Eng. Bosphorus, Bosporus, Turk. Karadeniz Boğazı. strait NW Turkey
Bosporus Cimmerius see Kerch Strait
Bosporus Thracius see İstanbul Boğazı
Bossangoa 76 C4 Ouham, C Central African Republic
Bossembélé 76 C4 Ombella-Mpoko, C Central African Republic
Bossier City 42 A2 Louisiana, S USA
Bosten Hu 126 C3 var. Bagrax Hu. lake NW China
Boston 89 E6 prev. St.Botolph's Town. E England, United Kingdom
Boston 41 G3 state capital Massachusetts, NE USA
Boston Mountains 42 B1 mountain range Arkansas, C USA
Bostyn' see Bastyn'
Botany 148 E2 New South Wales, E Australia
Botany Bay 148 E2 inlet New South Wales, SE Australia
Boteti 78 C3 var. Botletle. river N Botswana
Bothnia, Gulf of 85 D5 Fin. Pohjanlahti, Swe. Bottniska Viken. gulf N Baltic Sea
Botletle see Boteti
Botoşani 108 C3 Hung. Botosány. NE Romania
Botosány see Botoşani
Botou 128 C2 prev. Bozhen. Hebei, E China
Botrange 87 D6 mountain E Belgium
Botswana 78 C3 off. Republic of Botswana. country S Africa

BOTSWANA
Southern Africa

Official name Republic of Botswana
Formation 1966 / 1966
Capital Gaborone
Population 1.8 million / 8 people per sq mile (3 people per sq km) / 52%
Total area 231,803 sq. miles (600,370 sq. km)
Languages English*, Setswana, Shona, San, Khoikhoi, isiNdebele
Religions Traditional beliefs 50%, Christian (mainly Protestant) 30%, Other (including Muslim) 20%
Ethnic mix Tswana 98%, Other 2%
Government Presidential system
Currency Pula = 100 thebe
Literacy rate 81%
Calorie consumption 2151 calories

Botswana, Republic of see Botswana
Bottniska Viken see Bothnia, Gulf of

Bouar 76 B4 Nana-Mambéré, W Central African Republic
Bou Craa 70 B3 var. Bu Craa. NW Western Sahara
Bougainville Island 142 B3 island NE Papua New Guinea
Bougaroun, Cap 102 C3 headland NE Algeria
Bougouni 74 D4 Sikasso, SW Mali
Boujdour 70 A3 var. Bojador. W Western Sahara
Boulder 44 C4 Colorado, C USA
Boulder 44 B2 Montana, NW USA
Boulogne see Boulogne-sur-Mer
Boulogne-Billancourt 90 D1 Île-de-France, N France
Boulogne-sur-Mer 90 C2 var. Boulogne; anc. Bononia, Gesoriacum, Gessoriacum. Pas-de-Calais, N France
Boûmdeïd 74 C3 var. Boumdeit. Assaba, S Mauritania
Boumdeit see Boûmdeïd
Boundiali 74 D4 N Côte d'Ivoire
Bountiful 44 B4 Utah, W USA
Bounty Basin see Bounty Trough
Bounty Islands 142 D5 island group S New Zealand
Bounty Trough 152 C5 var. Bounty Basin. trough S Pacific Ocean
Bourbonnais 90 C4 cultural region C France
Bourbon Vendée see La Roche-sur-Yon
Bourg see Bourg-en-Bresse
Bourgas see Burgas
Bourge-en-Bresse see Bourg-en-Bresse
Bourg-en-Bresse 91 D5 var. Bourg, Bourge-en-Bresse. Ain, E France
Bourges 90 C4 anc. Avaricum. Cher, C France
Bourgogne 90 C4 Eng. Burgundy. cultural region E France
Bourke 149 C5 New South Wales, SE Australia
Bournemouth 89 D7 S England, United Kingdom
Boutilimit 74 C3 Trarza, SW Mauritania
Bouvet Island 67 D7 Norwegian dependency S Atlantic Ocean
Bowen 148 D3 Queensland, NE Australia
Bowling Green 40 B5 Kentucky, S USA
Bowling Green 40 D3 Ohio, N USA
Boxmeer 86 D4 Noord-Brabant, SE Netherlands
Boyarka 109 E2 Kyyivs'ka Oblast', N Ukraine
Boysun 123 E3 Rus. Baysun. Surkhondaryo Viloyati, S Uzbekistan
Bozeman 44 B2 Montana, NW USA
Bozen see Bolzano
Bozhen see Botou
Bozüyük 116 B3 Bilecik, NW Turkey
Brač 100 B4 var. Brach, It. Brazza; anc. Brattia. island S Croatia
Bracara Augusta see Braga
Brach see Brač
Bradford 89 D5 N England, United Kingdom
Brady 49 F3 Texas, SW USA
Braga 92 B2 anc. Bracara Augusta. Braga, NW Portugal
Braga see Braga
Bragança 92 C2 Eng. Braganza; anc. Juliobriga. Bragança, NE Portugal
Braganza see Bragança
Brahestad see Raahe
Brahmanbaria 135 G4 Chittagong, E Bangladesh
Brahmapur 135 F5 Orissa, E India
Brahmaputra 135 H3 var. Padma, Tsangpo, Ben. Jamuna, Chin. Yarlung Zangbo Jiang, Ind. Bramaputra, Dihang, Siang. river S Asia
Bräila 108 D4 Brăila, SE Romania
Braine-le-Comte 87 B6 Hainaut, SW Belgium
Brainerd 45 F2 Minnesota, N USA
Brak see Birāk
Bramaputra see Brahmaputra
Brampton 38 D5 Ontario, S Canada
Branco, Rio 58 C3 river N Brazil
Brandberg 78 A3 mountain NW Namibia
Brandenburg 94 C3 var. Brandenburg an der Havel. Brandenburg, NE Germany
Brandenburg an der Havel see Brandenburg
Brandon 37 F5 Manitoba, S Canada

Braniewo 98 D2 Ger. Braunsberg.
Warmińsko-mazurskie, N Poland
Brasil see Brazil
Brasília 63 F3 country capital (Brazil)
(Brazil) Distrito Federal, C Brazil
Brasil, Republica Federativa do see
Brazil
Braşov 108 C4 Ger. Kronstadt, Hung.
Brassó; prev. Oraşul Stalin. Braşov,
C Romania
Brassó see Braşov
Bratislava 99 C6 Ger. Pressburg, Hung.
Pozsony. country capital (Slovakia)
(Slovakia) Bratislavský Kraj, W Slovakia
Bratsk 115 E4 Irkutskaya Oblast',
C Russian Federation
Brattia see Brač
Braunsberg see Braniewo
Braunschweig 94 C4 Eng./Fr.
Brunswick. Niedersachsen, N Germany
Brava see Baraawe
Brava, Costa 93 H2 coastal region
NE Spain
Bravo del Norte, Río/Bravo, Río see
Grande, Rio
Bravo, Río 50 C1 river Mexico/USA
North America
Brawley 47 D8 California, W USA
Brazil 62 C2 off. Federative Republic of
Brazil, Port. República Federativa do
Brasil, Sp. Brasil; prev. United States of
Brazil. country South America
Brazil Basin 67 C5 var. Brazilian Basin,
Brazil'skaya Kotlovina. undersea basin
W Atlantic Ocean

BRAZIL
South America

Official name Federative Republic
of Brazil
Formation 1822 / 1828
Capital Brasília
Population 191 million / 59 people
per sq mile (23 people per sq km) / 84%
Total area 3,286,470 sq. miles
(8,511,965 sq. km)
Languages Portuguese*, German,
Italian, Spanish, Polish, Japanese,
Amerindian languages
Religions Roman Catholic 74%,
Protestant 15%, Atheist 7%, Other 4%,
Black 6%, Other 2%
Government Presidential system
Currency Real = 100 centavos
Literacy rate 89%
Calorie consumption 3049 calories

Brazil, Federative Republic of see Brazil
Brazilian Basin see Brazil Basin
Brazilian Highlands 63 F3 var. Brazilian
Highlands. mountain range E Brazil
Brazilian Highlands see Central, Planalto
Brazil'skaya Kotlovina see Brazil Basin
Brazil, United States of see Brazil
Brazos River 49 G3 river Texas, SW USA
Brazza see Brač
Brazzaville 77 B6 country capital
(Congo) (Congo) Capital District,
S Congo
Brčko 100 C3 Republika Srpska,
NE Bosnia and Herzegovina
Brecht 87 C5 Antwerpen, N Belgium
Brecon Beacons 89 C6 mountain range
S Wales, United Kingdom
Breda 86 C4 Noord-Brabant,
S Netherlands
Bree 87 D5 Limburg, NE Belgium
Bregalnica 101 E6 river E FYR
Macedonia
Bregenz 57 B7 anc. Brigantium.
Vorarlberg, W Austria
Bregovo 104 E1 Vidin, NW Bulgaria
Bremen 94 B3 Fr. Brême. Bremen,
NW Germany
Bremerhaven 94 B3 Bremen,
NW Germany
Bremerton 46 B2 Washington, NW USA
Brenham 49 G3 Texas, SW USA
Brenner, Col du/Brennero, Passo del
see Brenner Pass
Brenner Pass 96 C1 var. Brenner Sattel,
Fr. Col du Brenner, Ger. Brennerpass,
It. Passo del Brennero. pass Austria/
Italy
Brennerpass see Brenner Pass

Brenner Sattel see Brenner Pass
Brescia 96 B2 anc. Brixia. Lombardia,
N Italy
Breslau see Wrocław
Bressanone 96 C1 Ger. Brixen.
Trentino-Alto Adige, N Italy
Brest 107 A6 Pol. Brześć nad Bugiem,
Rus. Brest-Litovsk; prev. Brześć
Litewski. Brestskaya Voblasts',
SW Belarus
Brest 90 A3 Finistère, NW France
Brest-Litovsk see Brest
Bretagne 90 A3 Eng. Brittany, Lat.
Britannia Minor. cultural region
NW France
Brewster, Kap see Kangikajik
Brewton 42 C3 Alabama, S USA
Brezhnev see Naberezhnyye Chelny
Brezovo 104 D2 prev. Abrashlare.
Plovdiv, C Bulgaria
Bria 76 D4 Haute-Kotto, C Central
African Republic
Briançon 91 D5 anc. Brigantio. Hautes-
Alpes, SE France
Bricgstow see Bristol
Bridgeport 41 F3 Connecticut, NE USA
Bridgetown 55 G2 country capital
(Barbados) (Barbados) SW Barbados
Bridlington 89 D5 E England, United
Kingdom
Bridport 89 D7 S England, United
Kingdom
Brieg see Brzeg
Brig 95 A7 Fr. Brigue, It. Briga. Valais,
SW Switzerland
Briga see Brig
Brigantio see Briançon
Brigantium see Bregenz
Brigham City 44 B3 Utah, W USA
Brighton 89 E7 SE England, United
Kingdom
Brighton 44 D4 Colorado, C USA
Brigue see Brig
Brindisi 97 E5 anc. Brundisium,
Brundusium. Puglia, SE Italy
Briovera see St-Lô
Brisbane 149 E5 state capital
Queensland, E Australia
Bristol 89 D7 anc. Bricgstow.
SW England, United Kingdom
Bristol 41 F3 Connecticut, NE USA
Bristol 40 D5 Tennessee, S USA
Bristol Bay 36 B3 bay Alaska, USA
Bristol Channel 89 C7 inlet England/
Wales, United Kingdom
Britain 80 C3 var. Great Britain. island
United Kingdom
Britannia Minor see Bretagne
British Columbia 36 D4 Fr. Colombie-
Britannique. province SW Canada
British Guiana see Guyana
British Honduras see Belize
British Indian Ocean Territory 141 B5
UK dependent territory C Indian Ocean
British Isles 80 B3 island group NW Europe
British North Borneo see Sabah
British Solomon Islands Protectorate
see Solomon Islands
British Virgin Islands 55 F3 var.
Virgin Islands. UK dependent territory
E West Indies
Brittany see Bretagne
Briva Curretia see Brive-la-Gaillarde
Briva Isarae see Pontoise
Brive see Brive-la-Gaillarde
Brive-la-Gaillarde 91 C5 prev. Brive;
anc. Briva Curretia. Corrèze, C France
Brixen see Bressanone
Brixia see Brescia
Brno 99 B5 Ger. Brünn. Jihomoravský
Kraj, SE Czech Republic
Broceni 106 B3 Saldus, SW Latvia
Brod/Bród see Slavonski Brod
Brodeur Peninsula 37 F2 peninsula
Baffin Island, Nunavut, NE Canada
Brod na Savi see Slavonski Brod
Brodnica 98 C3 Ger. Buddenbrock.
Kujawski-pomorskie, C Poland
Broek-in-Waterland 86 C3 Noord-
Holland, C Netherlands
Broken Arrow 49 G1 Oklahoma, C USA
Broken Bay 148 E1 bay New South
Wales, SE Australia
Broken Hill 149 B6 New South Wales,
SE Australia
Broken Ridge 141 D6 undersea plateau
S Indian Ocean

Bromberg see Bydgoszcz
Bromley 89 B8 United Kingdom
Brookhaven 42 B3 Mississippi, S USA
Brookings 45 F3 South Dakota, N USA
Brooks Range 36 D2 mountain range
Alaska, USA
Brookton 147 B6 Western Australia
Broome 146 B3 Western Australia
Broomfield 44 D4 Colorado, C USA
Broucsella see Brussel/Bruxelles
Brovary 109 E2 Kyyivs'ka Oblast',
N Ukraine
Brownfield 49 E2 Texas, SW USA
Brownsville 49 G5 Texas, SW USA
Brownwood 49 F3 Texas, SW USA
Brozha 107 D7 Mahilyowskaya Voblasts',
E Belarus
Bruges see Brugge
Brugge 87 A5 Fr. Bruges. West-
Vlaanderen, NW Belgium
Brummen 86 D3 Gelderland,
E Netherlands
Brundisium/Brundusium see Brindisi
Brunei 138 D3 off. Brunei Darussalam,
Mal. Negara Brunei Darussalam.
country SE Asia

BRUNEI
Southeast Asia

Official name Brunei Darussalam
Formation 1984 / 1984
Capital Bandar Seri Begawan
Population 381,371 / 184 people
per sq mile (71 people per sq km) / 77%
Total area 2228 sq. miles (5770 sq. km)
Languages Malay*, English, Chinese
Religions Muslim (mainly Sunni) 66%,
Buddhist 14%, Other 10%, Christian 10%
Ethnic mix Malay 67%, Chinese 16%,
Other 11%, Indigenous 6%
Government Monarchy
Currency Brunei dollar = 100 cents
Literacy rate 93%
Calorie consumption 2855 calories

Brunei Darussalam see Brunei
Brunei Town see Bandar Seri Begawan
Brünn see Brno
Brunner, Lake 151 C5 lake South Island,
New Zealand
Brunswick 43 E3 Georgia, SE USA
Brunswick see Braunschweig
Brusa see Bursa
Brus Laguna 52 D2 Gracias a Dios,
E Honduras
Brussa see Bursa
Brussel 87 C6 var. Brussels, Fr. Bruxelles,
Ger. Brüssel; anc. Broucsella. country
capital (Belgium) (Belgium) Brussels,
C Belgium
Brüssel/Brussels see Brussel/Bruxelles
Brüx see Most
Bruxelles see Brussel
Bryan 49 G3 Texas, SW USA
Bryansk 111 A5 Bryanskaya Oblast',
W Russian Federation
Brzeg 98 C4 Ger. Brieg; anc. Civitas Altae
Ripae. Opolskie, S Poland
Brześć Litewski/Brześć nad Bugiem
see Brest
Brzeżany see Berezhany
Bucaramanga 58 B2 Santander,
N Colombia
Buchanan 74 C5 prev. Grand Bassa.
SW Liberia
Buchanan, Lake 49 F3 reservoir Texas,
SW USA
Bucharest see București
Buckeye State see Ohio
Bu Craa see Bou Craa
București 108 C5 Eng. Bucharest, Ger.
Bukarest, prev. Altenburg; anc. Cetatea
Dâmboviței. country capital (Romania)
(Romania) București, S Romania
Buda-Kashalyova 107 D7 Rus.
Koshelëvo. Homyel'skaya Voblasts',
SE Belarus
Buda-Koshelëvo see Buda-Kashalyova
Budapest 99 C6 off. Budapest Főváros,
SCr. Budimpešta. country capital
(Hungary) (Hungary) Pest, N Hungary
Budapest Főváros see Budapest
Budaun 133 D3 Uttar Pradesh, N India
Buddenbrock see Brodnica
Budimpešta see Budapest
Budweis see České Budějovice

Bromberg see Bydgoszcz

Budyšin see Bautzen
Buena Park 46 E2 California, W USA
North America
Buenaventura 58 A3 Valle del Cauca,
W Colombia
Buena Vista 61 G4 Santa Cruz, C Bolivia
Buena Vista 93 H5 S Gibraltar Europe
Buena Vista 93 H5 S Gibraltar Europe
Buenavista 93 H5 Baja California Sur,
NW Mexico
Buenavista 93 H5 Sonora, NW Mexico
Buena Vista 93 H5 Cerro Largo,
Uruguay
Buena Vista 93 H5 Colorado, C USA
Buena Vista 93 H5 Georgia, SE USA
Buena Vista 93 H5 Virginia, NE USA
Buenos Aires 64 D4 hist. Santa Maria del
Buen Aire. country capital (Argentina)
(Argentina) Buenos Aires, E Argentina
Buenos Aires 53 E5 Puntarenas,
SE Costa Rica
Buenos Aires, Lago 65 B6 var. Lago
General Carrera. lake Argentina/Chile
Buffalo 41 E3 New York, NE USA
Buffalo Narrows 37 F4 Saskatchewan,
C Canada
Buff Bay 54 B5 E Jamaica
Buftea 108 C5 Ilfov, S Romania
Bug 81 E3 Bel. Zakhodni Buh, Eng.
Western Bug, Rus. Zapadnyy Bug, Ukr.
Zakhidnyy Buh. river E Europe
Buga 58 B3 Valle del Cauca, W Colombia
Bughotu see Santa Isabel
Buguruslan 111 D6 Orenburgskaya
Oblast', W Russian Federation
Buitenzorg see Bogor
Bujalance 92 D4 Andalucía, S Spain
Bujanovac 101 E5 SE Serbia
Bujnurd see Bojnūrd
Bujumbura 73 B7 prev. Usumbura.
country capital (Burundi) (Burundi)
W Burundi
Bukarest see București
Bukavu 77 E6 prev. Costermansville.
Sud-Kivu, E Dem. Rep. Congo
Bukhàra see Buxoro
Bukoba 73 B6 Kagera, NW Tanzania
Bülach 95 B7 Zürich, NW Switzerland
Bulawayo 78 D3 Matabeleland North,
SW Zimbabwe
Bulgan 127 E2 Bulgan, N Mongolia
Bulgaria 104 C2 off. Republic of Bulgaria,
Bul. Bŭlgariya; prev. People's Republic
of Bulgaria. country SE Europe

BULGARIA
Southeast Europe

Official name Republic of Bulgaria
Formation 1908 / 1947
Capital Sofia
Population 7.6 million / 178 people
per sq mile (69 people per sq km) / 70%
Total area 42,822 sq. miles (110,910 sq. km)
Languages Bulgarian*, Turkish, Romani
Religions Orthodox Christian 83%,
Muslim 12%, Other 4%, Roman
Catholic 1%
Ethnic mix Bulgarian 84%, Turkish 9%,
Roma 5%, Other 2%
Government Parliamentary system
Currency Lev = 100 stotinki
Literacy rate 98%
Calorie consumption 2848 calories

Bulgaria, People's Republic of see
Bulgaria
Bulgaria, Republic of see Bulgaria
Bŭlgariya see Bulgaria
Bullion State see Missouri
Bull Shoals Lake 42 B1 reservoir
Arkansas/Missouri, C USA
Bulukumba 139 E4 prev. Boeloekoemba.
Sulawesi, C Indonesia
Bumba 77 D5 Equateur, N Dem. Rep.
Congo
Bunbury 147 A7 Western Australia
Bundaberg 148 E4 Queensland,
E Australia
Bungo-suido 131 B7 strait SW Japan
Bunia 77 E5 Orientale, NE Dem. Rep.
Congo
Bünyan 116 D3 Kayseri, C Turkey
Buraida see Buraydah
Buraydah 120 B4 var. Buraida. Al
Qaşim, N Saudi Arabia
Burdigala see Bordeaux

Burdur *116 B4 var.* Buldur. Burdur, SW Turkey
Burdur Gölü *116 B4 salt lake* SW Turkey
Burë *72 C4* Åmara, N Ethiopia
Burgas *104 E2 var.* Bourgas. Burgas, E Bulgaria
Burgaski Zaliv *104 E2 gulf* E Bulgaria
Burgos *92 D2* Castilla-León, N Spain
Burgundy *see* Bourgogne
Burhan Budai Shan *126 D4 mountain range* C China
Buriram *137 D5 var.* Buri Ram, Puriramya. Buri Ram, E Thailand
Buri Ram *see* Buriram
Burjassot *93 F3* País Valenciano, E Spain
Burkburnett *49 F2* Texas, SW USA
Burketown *148 B3* Queensland, NE Australia
Burkina *see* Burkina Faso
Burkina Faso *75 E4 off.* Burkina Faso; *prev.* Upper Volta. *country* W Africa

BURKINA FASO
West Africa

Official name Burkina Faso
Formation 1960 / 1960
Capital Ouagadougou
Population 14 million / 132 people per sq mile (51 people per sq km) / 18%
Total area 105,869 sq. miles (274,200 sq. km)
Languages French*, Mossi, Fulani, Tuareg, Dyula, Songhai
Religions Muslim 55%, Traditional beliefs 35%, Roman Catholic 9%, Other Christian 1%
Ethnic mix Mossi 48%, Other 21%, Peul 10%, Lobi 7%, Bobo 7%, Mandé 7%
Government Presidential system
Currency CFA franc = 100 centimes
Literacy rate 22%
Calorie consumption 2462 calories

Burley *46 D4* Idaho, NW USA
Burlington *45 G4* Iowa, C USA
Burlington *41 F2* Vermont, NE USA
Burma *136 A3 off.* Union of Myanmar. *country* SE Asia. *See also* Myanmar
Burnie *149 C8* Tasmania, SE Australia
Burns *46 C3* Oregon, NW USA
Burnside *37 F3 river* Nunavut, NW Canada
Burnsville *45 F2* Minnesota, N USA
Burrel *101 D6 var.* Burreli. Dibër, C Albania
Burreli *see* Burrel
Burriana *93 F3* País Valenciano, E Spain
Bursa *116 B3 var.* Brussa, *prev.* Brusa; *anc.* Prusa. Bursa, NW Turkey
Bûr Sa'îd *72 B1 var.* Port Said. N Egypt
Burtnieks *106 C3 var.* Burtnieks Ezers. *lake* N Latvia
Burtnieks Ezers *see* Burtnieks
Burundi *73 B7 off.* Republic of Burundi; *prev.* Kingdom of Burundi, Urundi. *country* C Africa

BURUNDI
Central Africa

Official name Republic of Burundi
Formation 1962 / 1962
Capital Bujumbura
Population 8.1 million / 818 people per sq mile (316 people per sq km) / 10%
Total area 10,745 sq. miles (27,830 sq. km)
Languages Kirundi*, French*, Kiswahili
Religions Christian (mainly Roman Catholic) 60%, Traditional beliefs 39%, Muslim 1%
Ethnic mix Hutu 85%, Tutsi 14%, Twa 1%
Government Presidential system
Currency Burundian franc = 100 centimes
Literacy rate 59%
Calorie consumption 1649 calories

Burundi, Kingdom of *see* Burundi
Burundi, Republic of *see* Burundi
Buru, Pulau *139 F4 prev.* Boeroe. *island* E Indonesia
Busan *see* Pusan
Buşayrah *118 D3* Dayr az Zawr, E Syria
Büsheher/Bushehr *see* Bandar-e Büsheher
Busra *see* Al Başrah, Iraq
Busselton *147 A7* Western Australia
Bussora *see* Al Başrah

Buta *77 D5* Orientale, N Dem. Rep. Congo
Butembo *77 E5* Nord-Kivu, NE Dem. Rep. Congo
Butler *41 E4* Pennsylvania, NE USA
Buton, Pulau *139 E4 var.* Pulau Butung; *prev.* Boetoeng. *island* C Indonesia
Bütow *see* Bytów
Butte *44 B2* Montana, NW USA
Butterworth *138 A3* Pinang, Peninsular Malaysia
Button Islands *39 E1 island group* Nunavut, NE Canada
Butuan *139 F2 off.* Butuan City. Mindanao, S Philippines
Butuan City *see* Butuan
Butung, Pulau *see* Buton, Pulau
Butuntum *see* Bitonto
Buulobarde *73 D5 var.* Buulo Berde. Hiiraan, C Somalia
Buulo Berde *see* Buulobarde
Buur Gaabo *73 D6* Jubbada Hoose, S Somalia
Buxoro *122 D2 var.* Bokhara, *Rus.* Bukhara. Buxoro Viloyati, C Uzbekistan
Buynaksk *111 B8* Respublika Dagestan, SW Russian Federation
Büyükmenderes Nehri *116 A4 river* SW Turkey
Buzău *108 C4* Buzău, SE Romania
Büzmeyin *see* Abadan
Buzuluk *111 D6* Orenburgskaya Oblast', W Russian Federation
Byahoml' *107 D5 Rus.* Begoml'. Vitsyebskaya Voblasts', N Belarus
Byalynichy *107 D6 Rus.* Belynichi. Mahilyowskaya Voblasts', E Belarus
Byan Tumen *see* Choybalsan
Bydgoszcz *98 C3 Ger.* Bromberg. Kujawski-pomorskie, C Poland
Byelaruskaya Hrada *107 B6 Rus.* Belorusskaya Gryada. *ridge* N Belarus
Byerezino *107 D6 Rus.* Berezina. *river* C Belarus
Byron Island *see* Nikunau
Bystrovka *see* Kemin
Bytča *99 C5* Žilinský Kraj, N Slovakia
Bytom *99 C5 Ger.* Beuthen. Śląskie, S Poland
Bytów *98 C2 Ger.* Bütow. Pomorskie, N Poland
Byuzmeyin *see* Abadan
Byval'ki *107 D8* Homyel'skaya Voblasts', SE Belarus
Byzantium *see* İstanbul

C

Caála *78 B2 var.* Kaala, Robert Williams, *Port.* Vila Robert Williams. Huambo, C Angola
Caazapá *64 D3* Caazapá, S Paraguay
Caballo Reservoir *48 C3 reservoir* New Mexico, SW USA
Cabañaquinta *92 D1* Asturias, N Spain
Cabanatuan *139 E1 off.* Cabanatuan City. Luzon, N Philippines
Cabanatuan City *see* Cabanatuan
Cabillonum *see* Chalon-sur-Saône
Cabimas *58 C1* Zulia, NW Venezuela
Cabinda *78 A1 var.* Kabinda. Cabinda, NW Angola
Cabinda *78 A1 var.* Kabinda. *province* NW Angola
Lake Cabora Bassa *78 D2 var.* Lake Cabora Bassa. *reservoir* NW Mozambique
Cabora Bassa, Lake *see* Cabora Bassa, Albufeira de
Caborca *50 B1* Sonora, NW Mexico
Cabot Strait *39 G4 strait* E Canada
Cabo Verde, Ilhas do *see* Cape Verde
Cabras, Ilha das *76 E2 island* S Sao Tome and Principe, Africa, E Atlantic Ocean
Cabrera *93 G3 river* NW Spain
Cáceres *92 C3 Ar.* Qazris. Extremadura, W Spain
Cachimbo, Serra do *63 E2 mountain range* C Brazil
Caconda *78 B2* Huíla, C Angola
Čadca *99 C5 Hung.* Csaca. Žilinský Kraj, N Slovakia
Cadillac *40 C2* Michigan, N USA

Cadiz *139 E2 off.* Cadiz City. Negros, C Philippines
Cádiz *92 C5 anc.* Gades, Gadier, Gadir, Gadire. Andalucía, SW Spain
Cadiz City *see* Cadiz
Gulf of Cadiz *92 B5 Eng.* Gulf of Cadiz. *gulf* Portugal/Spain
Cadiz, Gulf of *see* Cádiz, Golfo de
Cadurcum *see* Cahors
Caen *90 B3* Calvados, N France
Caene/Caenepolis *see* Qinā
Caerdydd *see* Cardiff
Caer Glou *see* Gloucester
Caer Gybi *see* Holyhead
Caerleon *see* Chester
Caer Luel *see* Carlisle
Caesaraugusta *see* Zaragoza
Caesarea Mazaca *see* Kayseri
Caesarobriga *see* Talavera de la Reina
Caesarodunum *see* Tours
Caesaromagus *see* Beauvais
Caesena *see* Cesena
Cafayate *64 C2* Salta, N Argentina
Cagayan de Oro *139 E2 off.* Cagayan de Oro City. Mindanao, S Philippines
Cagayan de Oro City *see* Cagayan de Oro
Cagliari *97 A6 anc.* Caralis. Sardegna, Italy, C Mediterranean Sea
Caguas *55 F3* E Puerto Rico
Cahors *91 C5 anc.* Cadurcum. Lot, S France
Cahul *108 D4 Rus.* Kagul. S Moldova
Caicos Passage *54 D2 strait* Bahamas/Turks and Caicos Islands
Caiffa *see* Hefa
Cailungo *96 E1* N San Marino
Caiphas *see* Hefa
Cairns *148 D3* Queensland, NE Australia
Cairo *72 B2 var.* El Qâhira, *Ar.* Al Qâhirah. *country capital* (Egypt) (Egypt) N Egypt
Caisleán an Bharraigh *see* Castlebar
Cajamarca *60 B3 prev.* Caxamarca. Cajamarca, NW Peru
Čakovec *100 B2 Ger.* Csakathurn, *Hung.* Csáktornya; *prev. Ger.* Tschakathurn. Medimurje, N Croatia
Calabar *75 G5* Cross River, S Nigeria
Calabozo *58 D2* Guárico, C Venezuela
Calafat *108 B5* Dolj, SW Romania
Calafate *see* El Calafate
Calahorra *93 E2* La Rioja, N Spain
Calais *90 C2* Pas-de-Calais, N France
Calais *41 H2* Maine, NE USA
Calais, Pas de *see* Dover, Strait of
Calama *64 B2* Antofagasta, N Chile
Călăras *see* Călărași
Călărași *108 D3 var.* Călăras, Rus. Kalarash. C Moldova
Călărași *108 C5* Călărași, SE Romania
Calatayud *93 E2* Aragón, NE Spain
Calbayog *139 E2 off.* Calbayog City. Samar, C Philippines
Calbayog City *see* Calbayog
Calcutta *135 G4* West Bengal, N India
Caldas da Rainha *92 B3* Leiria, W Portugal
Caldera *64 B3* Atacama, N Chile
Caldwell *46 C3* Idaho, NW USA
Caledonia *52 C1* Corozal, N Belize
Caleta Olivia *65 B6* Santa Cruz, SE Argentina
Calgary *37 E5* Alberta, SW Canada
Cali *58 B3* Valle del Cauca, W Colombia
Calicut *132 C2 var.* Kozhikode. Kerala, SW India
California *47 B7 off.* State of California, *also known as* El Dorado, The Golden State. *state* W USA
Gulf of California *50 B2 Eng.* Gulf of California; *prev.* Sea of Cortez. *gulf* W Mexico
California, Gulf of *see* California, Golfo de
Călimănești *108 B4* Vâlcea, SW Romania
Calisia *see* Kalisz
Callabonna, Lake *149 B5 lake* South Australia
Callao *60 C4* Callao, W Peru
Callatis *see* Mangalia
Callosa de Segura *93 F4* País Valenciano, E Spain
Calmar *see* Kalmar

Caloundra *149 E5* Queensland, E Australia
Caltanissetta *97 C7* Sicilia, Italy, C Mediterranean Sea
Caluula *72 E4* Bari, NE Somalia
Camabatela *78 B1* Cuanza Norte, NW Angola
Camacupa *78 B2 var.* General Machado, *Port.* Vila General Machado. Bié, C Angola
Camagüey *54 C2 prev.* Puerto Príncipe. Camagüey, C Cuba
Camagüey, Archipiélago de *54 C2 island group* C Cuba
Camana *61 E4 var.* Camaná. Arequipa, SW Peru
Camargue *91 D6 physical region* SE France
Ca Mau *137 D6 var.* Quan Long. Minh Hai, S Vietnam
Cambay, Gulf of *see* Khambhāt, Gulf of
Camberia *see* Chambéry
Cambodia *137 D5 off.* Kingdom of Cambodia, *var.* Democratic Kampuchea, Roat Kampuchea, Cam. Kampuchea; *prev.* People's Democratic Republic of Kampuchea. *country* SE Asia

CAMBODIA
Southeast Asia

Official name Kingdom of Cambodia
Formation 1953 / 1953
Capital Phnom Penh
Population 14.6 million / 214 people per sq mile (83 people per sq km) / 19%
Total area 69,900 sq. miles (181,040 sq. km)
Languages Khmer*, French, Chinese, Vietnamese, Cham
Religions Buddhist 93%, Muslim 6%, Christian 1%
Ethnic mix Khmer 90%, Other 5%, Vietnamese 4%, Chinese 1%
Government Parliamentary system
Currency Riel = 100 sen
Literacy rate 74%
Calorie consumption 2046 calories

Cambodia, Kingdom of *see* Cambodia
Cambrai *90 C2 Flem.* Kambryk, *prev.* Cambray; *anc.* Cameracum. Nord, N France
Cambray *see* Cambrai
Cambrian Mountains *89 C6 mountain range* C Wales, United Kingdom
Cambridge *54 A4* W Jamaica
Cambridge *150 D3* Waikato, North Island, New Zealand
Cambridge *89 E6 Lat.* Cantabrigia. E England, United Kingdom
Cambridge *41 F4* Maryland, NE USA
Cambridge *40 D4* Ohio, NE USA
Cambridge Bay *37 F3 var.* Ikaluktutiak. Victoria Island, Nunavut, NW Canada
Camden *42 B2* Arkansas, C USA
Camellia State *see* Alabama
Cameracum *see* Cambrai
Cameroon *76 A4 off.* Republic of Cameroon, *Fr.* Cameroun. *country* W Africa

CAMEROON
Central Africa

Official name Republic of Cameroon
Formation 1960 / 1961
Capital Yaoundé
Population 16.3 million / 94 people per sq mile (36 people per sq km) / 52%
Total area 183,567 sq. miles (475,440 sq. km)
Languages English*, French*, Bamileke, Fang, Fulani
Religions Roman Catholic 35%, Traditional beliefs 25%, Muslim 22%, Protestant 18%
Ethnic mix Cameroon highlanders 31%, Other 21%, Equatorial Bantu 19%, Kirdi 11%, Fulani 10%, Northwestern Bantu 8%
Government Presidential system
Currency CFA franc = 100 centimes
Literacy rate 68%
Calorie consumption 2273 calories

Cameroon, Republic of *see* Cameroon
Cameroun *see* Cameroon
Camocim 63 F2 Ceará, E Brazil
Camopi 59 H3 E French Guiana
Campamento 52 C2 Olancho,
  C Honduras
Campania 97 D5 Eng. Champagne.
  region S Italy
Campbell, Cape 151 D5 *headland* South
  Island, New Zealand
Campbell Island 142 D5 *island* S New
  Zealand
Campbell Plateau 142 D5 *undersea
  plateau* SW Pacific Ocean
Campbell River 36 D5 Vancouver
  Island, British Columbia, SW Canada
Campeche 51 G4 Campeche, SE Mexico
Bay of Campeche 51 F4 *Eng.* Bay of
  Campeche. *bay* E Mexico
Campeche, Bay of *see* Campeche,
  Bahía de
Câm Pha 136 E3 Quang Ninh,
  N Vietnam
Câmpina 108 C4 *prev.* Cîmpina.
  Prahova, SE Romania
Campina Grande 63 G2 Paraíba, E Brazil
Campinas 63 F4 São Paulo, S Brazil
Campobasso 97 D5 Molise, C Italy
Campo Criptana *see* Campo de Criptana
Campo de Criptana 93 E3 *var.* Campo
  Criptana. Castilla-La Mancha, C Spain
Campo dos Goitacazes *see* Campos
Campo Grande 63 E4 *state capital* Mato
  Grosso do Sul, SW Brazil
Campos 63 F4 *var.* Campo dos
  Goitacazes. Rio de Janeiro, SE Brazil
Câmpulung 108 B4 *prev.* Câmpulung-
  Muşcel, Cîmpulung. Argeş, S Romania
Câmpulung-Muşcel *see* Câmpulung
Campus Stellae *see* Santiago
Cam Ranh 137 E6 Khanh Hoa,
  S Vietnam
Canada 34 B4 *country* N North America

CANADA
North America

Official name Canada
Formation 1867 / 1949
Capital Ottawa
Population 32.9 million / 9 people
  per sq mile (4 people per sq km) / 81%
Total area 3,854,085 sq. miles
  (9,984,670 sq. km)
Languages English*, French*, Chinese,
  Italian, German, Ukrainian, Portuguese,
  Inuktitut, Cree
Religions Roman Catholic 44%,
  Protestant 29%, Other and
  nonreligious 27%
Government Parliamentary system
Currency Canadian dollar = 100 cents
Literacy rate 99%
Calorie consumption 3589 calories

Canada Basin 34 C2 *undersea basin*
  Arctic Ocean
Canadian River 49 E2 *river* SW USA
Çanakkale 116 A3 *var.* Dardanelli; *prev.*
  Chanak, Kale Sultanie. Çanakkale,
  W Turkey
Cananea 50 B1 Sonora,
  NW Mexico
Canarreos, Archipiélago de los 54 B2
  island group W Cuba
Canary Islands 70 A2 *Eng.* Canary
  Islands. *island group* Spain,
  NE Atlantic Ocean
Canary Islands *see* Canarias, Islas
Cañas 52 D4 Guanacaste, NW Costa Rica
Canaveral, Cape 43 E4 *headland* Florida,
  SE USA
Canavieiras 63 G3 Bahia, E Brazil
Canberra 142 C4 *country capital*
  (Australia) (Australia) Australian
  Capital Territory, SE Australia
Cancún 51 H3 Quintana Roo, SE Mexico
Candia *see* Irákleio
Canea *see* Chaniá
Cangzhou 128 D4 Hebei, E China
Caniapiscau 39 E2 *river* Québec,
  E Canada
Caniapiscau, Réservoir de 38 D3
  reservoir Québec, C Canada
Canik Dağları 116 D2 *mountain range*
  N Turkey
Canillo 91 A7 Canillo, C Andorra Europe

Çankırı 116 C3 *var.* Chankiri; *anc.*
  Gangra, Germanicopolis. Çankırı,
  N Turkey
Cannanore 132 B2 *var.* Kannur. Kerala,
  SW India
Cannes 91 D6 Alpes-Maritimes,
  SE France
Canoas 63 E5 Rio Grande do Sul, S Brazil
Canon City 44 C5 Colorado, C USA
Cantabria 92 D1 *autonomous
  community* N Spain
Cantábrica, Cordillera 92 C1 *mountain
  range* N Spain
Cantabrigia *see* Cambridge
Cantaura 59 E2 Anzoátegui,
  NE Venezuela
Canterbury 89 E7 *hist.* Cantwaraburh;
  anc. Durovernum, *Lat.* Cantuaria.
  SE England, United Kingdom
Canterbury Bight 151 C6 *bight* South
  Island, New Zealand
Canterbury Plains 151 C6 *plain* South
  Island, New Zealand
Cân Thơ 137 E6 Cân Thơ, S Vietnam
Canton 42 B3 Mississippi, S USA
Canton 40 D4 Ohio, N USA
Canton *see* Guangzhou
Canton Island *see* Kanton
Cantuaria/Cantwaraburh *see*
  Canterbury
Canyon 49 E2 Texas, SW USA
Cao Băng 136 D3 *var.* Caobang. Cao
  Băng, N Vietnam
Caobang *see* Cao Băng
Cap-Breton, Île du *see* Cape Breton
  Island
Cape Barren Island 149 C8 *island*
  Furneaux Group, Tasmania,
  SE Australia
Cape Basin 69 B7 *undersea basin*
  S Atlantic Ocean
Cape Breton Island 39 G4 *Fr.* Île du
  Cap-Breton. *island* Nova Scotia,
  SE Canada
Cape Charles 41 F5 Virginia, NE USA
Cape Coast 75 E5 *prev.* Cape Coast
  Castle. S Ghana
Cape Coast Castle *see* Cape Coast
Cape Girardeau 45 H5 Missouri, C USA
Capelle aan den IJssel 86 C4 Zuid-
  Holland, SW Netherlands
Cape Palmas *see* Harper
Cape Saint Jacques *see* Vung Tau
Cape Town 78 B5 *var.* Ekapa, *Afr.*
  Kaapstad, Kapstad. *country capital*
  (South Africa-legislative capital) (South
  Africa-legislative capital) Western Cape,
  SW South Africa
Cape Verde 74 A2 *off.* Republic of Cape
  Verde, *Port.* Cabo Verde, Ilhas do Cabo
  Verde. *country* E Atlantic Ocean

CAPE VERDE
Atlantic Ocean

Official name Republic of Cape Verde
Formation 1975 / 1975
Capital Praia
Population 423,613 / 272 people
  per sq mile (105 people per sq km) / 57%
Total area 1557 sq. miles (4033 sq. km)
Languages Portuguese*,
  Portuguese Creole**Religions** Roman
  Catholic 97%, Other 2%, Protestant
  (Church of the Nazarene) 1%
Ethnic mix Mestiço 60%, African 30%,
  Other 10%
Government Mixed presidential–
  parliamentary system
Currency Cape Verde escudo
  = 100 centavos
Literacy rate 76%
Calorie consumption 3243 calories

Cape Verde Basin 66 C4 *undersea basin*
  E Atlantic Ocean
Cape Verde Plain 66 C4 *abyssal plain*
  E Atlantic Ocean
Cape Verde, Republic of *see* Cape
  Verde
Cape York Peninsula 148 C2 *peninsula*
  Queensland, N Australia
Cap-Haïtien 54 D3 *var.* Le Cap. N Haiti
Capira 53 G5 Panamá, C Panama
Capitán Arturo Prat 154 A2 *Chilean
  research station* South Shetland Islands,
  Antarctica

Capitán Pablo Lagerenza 64 D1 *var.*
  Mayor Pablo Lagerenza. Chaco,
  N Paraguay
Capodistria *see* Koper
Capri 97 C5 *island* S Italy
Caprivi Concession *see* Caprivi Strip
Caprivi Strip 78 C3 *Ger.* Caprivizipfel;
  prev. Caprivi Concession. *cultural
  region* NE Namibia
Caprivizipfel *see* Caprivi Strip
Cap Saint-Jacques *see* Vung Tau
Caquetá, Río 58 C5 *var.* Rio Japurá,
  Yapurá. *river* Brazil/Colombia
Caquetá, Rio *see* Japurá, Rio
CAR *see* Central African Republic
Caracal 108 B5 Olt, S Romania
Caracaraí 62 D1 Rondônia, W Brazil
Caracas 58 D1 *country capital*
  (Venezuela) (Venezuela) Distrito
  Federal, N Venezuela
Caralis *see* Cagliari
Caratasca, Laguna de 53 E2 *lagoon*
  NE Honduras
Carballiño *see* O Carballiño
Carbondale 40 B5 Illinois, N USA
Carbonia 97 A6 *var.* Carbonia Centro.
  Sardegna, Italy, C Mediterranean Sea
Carbonia Centro *see* Carbonia
Carcaso *see* Carcassonne
Carcassonne 91 C6 *anc.* Carcaso. Aude,
  S France
Cardamomes, Chaine des *see* Krâvanh,
  Chuŏr Phnum
Cardamom Mountains *see* Krâvanh,
  Chuŏr Phnum
Cárdenas 54 B2 Matanzas, W Cuba
Cardiff 89 C7 *Wel.* Caerdydd. *national
  capital* S Wales, United Kingdom
Cardigan Bay 89 C6 *bay* W Wales,
  United Kingdom
Carei 108 B3 *Ger.* Gross-Karol, Karol,
  Hung. Nagykároly; *prev.* Careii-Mari.
  Satu Mare, NW Romania
Careii-Mari *see* Carei
Carey, Lake 147 B6 *lake* Western
  Australia
Cariaco 59 E1 Sucre, NE Venezuela
Caribbean Sea 54 C4 *sea* W Atlantic
  Ocean
Caribrod *see* Dimitrovgrad
Carlisle 88 C4 *anc.* Caer Luel,
  Luguvallium, Luguvallum.
  NW England, United Kingdom
Carlow 89 B6 *Ir.* Ceatharlach. SE Ireland
Carlsbad 48 D3 New Mexico, SW USA
Carlsbad *see* Karlovy Vary
Carlsberg Ridge 140 B4 *undersea ridge*
  S Arabian Sea
Carlsruhe *see* Karlsruhe
Carmana/Carmania *see* Kermān
Carmarthen 89 C6 SW Wales, United
  Kingdom
Carmaux 91 C6 Tarn, S France
Carmel 40 C4 Indiana, N USA
Carmelita 52 B1 Petén, N Guatemala
Carmen 51 G4 *var.* Ciudad del Carmen.
  Campeche, SE Mexico
Carmona 92 C4 Andalucía, S Spain
Carmona *see* Uíge
Carnaro *see* Kvarner
Carnarvon 147 A5 Western Australia
Carnegie, Lake 147 B5 *salt lake* Western
  Australia
Car Nicobar 133 F3 *island* Nicobar
  Islands, India, NE Indian Ocean
Caroaço, Ilha 76 E1 *island* N Sao Tome
  and Principe, Africa, E Atlantic Ocean
Carolina 63 F2 Maranhão, E Brazil
Caroline Island *see* Millennium Island
Caroline Islands 144 B2 *island group*
  C Micronesia
Carolopois *see* Châlons-en-Champagne
Caroní, Río 59 E3 *river* E Venezuela
Caronium *see* A Coruña
Carora 58 C1 Lara, N Venezuela
Carpathian Mountains 81 F4 *var.*
  Carpathians, Cz./Pol. Karpaty, Ger.
  Karpaten. *mountain range* E Europe
Carpathians *see* Carpathian Mountains
Carpathos/Carpathus *see* Kárpathos
Carpaţii Sudici *see* Carpaţii Meridionali
Carpentaria, Gulf of 148 B2 *gulf*
  N Australia
Carpi 96 C2 Emilia-Romagna, N Italy
Carrara 96 B3 Toscana, C Italy
Carson City 47 C5 *state capital* Nevada,
  W USA

Carson Sink 47 C5 *salt flat* Nevada,
  W USA
Carstensz, Puntjak *see* Jaya, Puncak
Cartagena 58 B1 *var.* Cartagena de los
  Indes. Bolívar, NW Colombia
Cartagena 93 F4 *anc.* Carthago Nova.
  Murcia, SE Spain
Cartagena de los Indes *see* Cartagena
Cartago 53 E4 Cartago, C Costa Rica
Carthage 45 F5 Missouri, C USA
Carthago Nova *see* Cartagena
Cartwright 39 F2 Newfoundland and
  Labrador, E Canada
Carúpano 59 E1 Sucre, NE Venezuela
Carusbur *see* Cherbourg
Caruthersville 45 H5 Missouri, C USA
Cary 43 F1 North Carolina, SE USA
Casablanca 70 C2 *Ar.* Dar-el-Beida.
  NW Morocco
Casa Grande 48 B2 Arizona, SW USA
Cascade Range 46 B3 *mountain range*
  Oregon/Washington, NW USA
Cascadia Basin 34 A4 *undersea basin*
  NE Pacific Ocean
Cascais 92 B4 Lisboa, C Portugal
Caserta 97 D5 Campania, S Italy
Casey 154 D4 *Australian research station*
  Antarctica
Casiquiare, Río *see* Tschaslau. Střední
  Čechy, C Czech Republic
Casper 44 C3 Wyoming, C USA
Caspian Depression 111 B7 *Kaz.* Kaspiy
  Mangy Oypaty, *Rus.* Prikaspiyskaya
  Nizmennost'. *depression* Kazakhstan/
  Russian Federation
Caspian Sea 114 A4 *Az.* Xäzär Dänizi,
  Kaz. Kaspiy Tengizi, *Per.* Bahr-e
  Khazar, Darýa-ye Khazar, *Rus.*
  Kaspiyskoye More. *inland sea* Asia/
  Europe
Cassai *see* Kasai
Cassel *see* Kassel
Castamoni *see* Kastamonu
Casteggio 96 B2 Lombardia, N Italy
Castelló de la Plana *see* Castellón de
  la Plana
Castellón *see* Castellón de la Plana
Castellón de la Plana 93 F3 *var.*
  Castellón, *Cat.* Castelló de la Plana.
  País Valenciano, E Spain
Castelnaudary 91 C6 Aude, S France
Castelo Branco 92 C3 Castelo Branco,
  C Portugal
Castelsarrasin 91 B6 Tarn-et-Garonne,
  S France
Castelvetrano 97 C7 Sicilia, Italy,
  C Mediterranean Sea
Castilla-La Mancha 93 E3 *autonomous
  community* NE Spain
Castilla-León 92 C2 *var.* Castilla
  y León. *autonomous community*
  NW Spain
Castilla y Leon *see* Castilla-León
Castlebar 89 A5 *Ir.* Caisleán an
  Bharraigh. W Ireland
Castleford 89 D5 N England, United
  Kingdom
Castle Harbour 42 B5 *inlet* Bermuda,
  NW Atlantic Ocean
Castra Regina *see* Regensburg
Castricum 86 C3 Noord-Holland,
  W Netherlands
Castries 55 F1 *country capital* (Saint
  Lucia) (Saint Lucia) N Saint Lucia
Castro 65 B6 Los Lagos, W Chile
Castrovillari 97 D6 Calabria, SW Italy
Castuera 92 D4 Extremadura, W Spain
Caswell Sound 151 A7 *sound* South
  Island, New Zealand
Catacamas 52 D2 Olancho, C Honduras
Catacaos 60 B3 Piura, NW Peru
Catalan Bay 93 H4 *bay* E Gibraltar,
  Mediterranean Sea
Cataluña 93 G2 N Spain
Catamarca *see* San Fernando del Valle
  de Catamarca
Catania 97 D7 Sicilia, Italy,
  C Mediterranean Sea
Catanzaro 97 D6 Calabria, SW Italy
Catarroja 93 F3 País Valenciano, E Spain
Cat Island 54 C1 *island* C Bahamas
Catskill Mountains 41 F3 *mountain
  range* New York, NE USA
Cattaro *see* Kotor
Cauca, Río 58 B2 *river* N Colombia
Caucasia 58 B2 Antioquia,
  NW Colombia

Caucasus *81 G4 Rus.* Kavkaz. *mountain range* Georgia/Russian Federation
Caura, Río *59 E3 river* C Venezuela
Cavaia *see* Kavajë
Cavalla *74 D5 var.* Cavally, Cavally Fleuve. *river* Côte d'Ivoire/Liberia
Cavally/Cavally Fleuve *see* Cavalla
Caviana de Fora, Ilha *63 E1 var.* Ilha Caviana. *island* N Brazil
Caviana, Ilha *see* Caviana de Fora, Ilha
Cawnpore *see* Kānpur
Caxamarca *see* Cajamarca
Caxito *78 B1* Bengo, NW Angola
Cayenne *59 H3 dependent territory/ arrondissement capital* (French Guiana) NE French Guiana
Cayes *54 D3 var.* Les Cayes. SW Haiti
Cayman Brac *54 B3 island* E Cayman Islands
Cayman Islands *54 B3 UK dependent territory* W West Indies
Cayo *see* San Ignacio
Cay Sal *54 B2 islet* SW Bahamas
Cazin *100 B3* Federacija Bosna I Hercegovina, NW Bosnia and Herzegovina
Cazorla *93 E4* Andalucía, S Spain
Ceadâr-Lunga *see* Ciadir-Lunga
Ceará *63 F2 off.* Estado do Ceará. *region* C Brazil
Ceará *63 F2 off.* Estado do Ceará. *state* C Brazil
Ceará *see* Fortaleza
Ceara Abyssal Plain *see* Ceará Plain
Ceará, Estado do *see* Ceará
Ceará Plain *56 E3 var.* Ceara Abyssal Plain. *abyssal plain* W Atlantic Ocean
Ceatharlach *see* Carlow
Cébaco, Isla *53 F5 island* SW Panama
Cebu *139 E2 off.* Cebu City. Cebu, C Philippines
Cebu City *see* Cebu
Čechy *see* Bohemia
Cecina *96 B3* Toscana, C Italy
Cedar City *44 A5* Utah, W USA
Cedar Falls *45 G3* Iowa, C USA
Cedar Lake *38 A2 lake* Manitoba, C Canada
Cedar Rapids *45 G3* Iowa, C USA
Cedros, Isla *50 A2 island* W Mexico
Ceduna *149 A6* South Australia
Cefalù *97 C7 anc.* Cephaloedium. Sicilia, Italy, C Mediterranean Sea
Celebes *139 E4 Eng.* Celebes. *island* C Indonesia
Celebes *see* Sulawesi
Celebes Sea *139 E3 Ind.* Laut Sulawesi. *sea* Indonesia/Philippines
Celje *95 E7 Ger.* Cilli. C Slovenia
Celldömölk *99 C6* Vas, W Hungary
Celle *94 B3 var.* Zelle. Niedersachsen, N Germany
Celovec *see* Klagenfurt
Celtic Sea *89 B7 Ir.* An Mhuir Cheilteach. *sea* SW British Isles
Celtic Shelf *84 B3 continental shelf* E Atlantic Ocean
Cenderawasih, Teluk *139 G4 var.* Teluk Irian, Teluk Sarera. *bay* W Pacific Ocean
Cenon *91 B5* Gironde, SW France
Centennial State *see* Colorado
Centrafricaine, République *see* Central African Republic
Central African Republic *76 C4 var.* République Centrafricaine, *prev.* CAR; *prev.* Ubangi-Shari, Oubangui-Chari, Territoire de l'Oubangui-Chari. *country* C Africa

CENTRAL AFRICAN REPUBLIC
Central Africa

Official name Central African Republic
Formation 1960 / 1960
Capital Bangui
Population 4.2 million / 17 people per sq mile (7 people per sq km) / 43%
Total area 240,534 sq. miles (622,984 sq. km)
Languages French*, Sango, Banda, Gbaya
Religions Traditional beliefs 60%, Christian (mainly Roman Catholic) 35%, Muslim 5%
Ethnic mix Baya 34%, Banda 27%, Mandjia 21%, Sara 10%, Other 8%
Government Presidential system

CENTRAL AFRICAN REPUBLIC
(continued)

Currency CFA franc = 100 centimes
Literacy rate 49%
Calorie consumption 1980 calories

Central, Cordillera *58 B3 mountain range* W Colombia
Cordillera Central *55 E3 mountain range* C Dominican Republic
Cordillera Central *53 F5 mountain range* C Panama
Central, Cordillera *139 E1 mountain range* Luzon, N Philippines
Central Group *see* Inner Islands
Centralia *46 B2 mountain*, NW USA
Central Indian Ridge *see* Mid-Indian Ridge
Central Makran Range *134 A3 mountain range* W Pakistan
Central Pacific Basin *142 D1 undersea basin* C Pacific Ocean
Central Provinces and Berar *see* Madhya Pradesh
Central Range *144 B3 mountain range* NW Papua New Guinea
Central Russian Upland *109 G1 Eng.* Central Russian Upland. *mountain range* W Russian Federation
Central Russian Upland *see* Srednerusskaya Vozvyshennost'
Central Siberian Plateau *114 D3 var.* Central Siberian Uplands, *Eng.* Central Siberian Plateau. *mountain range* N Russian Federation
Central Siberian Plateau/Central Siberian Uplands *see* Srednesibirskoye Ploskogor'ye
Central, Sistema *92 D3 mountain range* C Spain
Central Valley *47 B6 valley* California, W USA
Centum Cellae *see* Civitavecchia
Ceos *see* Tziá
Cephaloedium *see* Cefalù
Ceram *see* Seram, Pulau
Ceram Sea *139 F4 Ind.* Laut Seram. *sea* E Indonesia
Cerasus *see* Giresun
Cereté *58 B2* Córdoba, NW Colombia
Cergy-Pontoise *see* Pontoise
Cerignola *97 D5* Puglia, SE Italy
Çerkeş *116 C2* Çankin, N Turkey
Cernăuţi *see* Chernivtsi
Cernay *90 E4* Haut-Rhin, NE France
Cerro de Pasco *60 C3* Pasco, C Peru
Cervera *93 F2* Cataluña, NE Spain
Cervino, Monte *see* Matterhorn
Cesena *96 C3 anc.* Caesena. Emilia-Romagna, N Italy
Cēsis *106 D3 Ger.* Wenden. Cēsis, C Latvia
Česká Republika *see* Czech Republic
České Budějovice *99 B5 Ger.* Budweis. Jihočeský Kraj, S Czech Republic
Český Krumlov *99 A5 var.* Böhmisch-Krumau, *Ger.* Krummau. Jihočeský Kraj, S Czech Republic
Český Les *see* Böhmian Forest
Cetatea Damboviţei *see* Bucureşti
Cetinje *101 C5 It.* Cettigne. S Montenegro
Cette *see* Sète
Cettigne *see* Cetinje
Ceuta *70 C2 enclave* Spain, N Africa
Cévennes *91 C6 mountain range* S France
Ceyhan *116 D4* Adana, S Turkey
Ceylanpınar *117 E4* Şanlıurfa, SE Turkey
Ceylon *see* Sri Lanka
Ceylon Plain *124 B4 abyssal plain* N Indian Ocean
Ceyre to the Caribs *see* Marie-Galante
Chachapoyas *60 B2* Amazonas, NW Peru
Chachevichy *107 D6 Rus.* Chechevichi. Mahilyowskaya Voblasts', E Belarus
Chaco *see* Gran Chaco
Chad *76 C3 off.* Republic of Chad, *Fr.* Tchad. *country* C Africa

CHAD
Central Africa

Official name Republic of Chad
Formation 1960 / 1960
Capital N'Djamena

CHAD
(continued)

Population 10.3 million / 21 people per sq mile (8 people per sq km) / 25%
Total area 495,752 sq. miles (1,284,000 sq. km)
Languages Arabic*, French*, Sara, Maba
Religions Muslim 55%, Traditional beliefs 35%, Christian 10%
Ethnic mix Other 30%, Sara 28%, Mayo-Kebbi 12%, Arab 12%, Ouaddaï 9%, Kanem-Bornou 9%
Government Presidential system
Currency CFA franc = 100 centimes
Literacy rate 26%
Calorie consumption 2114 calories

Chad, Lake *76 B3 Fr.* Lac Tchad. *lake* C Africa
Chad, Republic of *see* Chad
Chadron *44 D3* Nebraska, C USA
Chadyr-Lunga *see* Ciadir-Lunga
Chagai Hills *134 A2 var.* Chāh Gay. *mountain range* Afghanistan/Pakistan
Chaghasarāy *see* Asadābād
Chagos-Laccadive Plateau *124 B4 undersea plateau* N Indian Ocean
Chagos Trench *141 C5 trench* N Indian Ocean
Chāh Gay *see* Chāgai Hills
Chaillu, Massif du *77 B6 mountain range* C Gabon
Chain Ridge *140 B4 undersea ridge* W Indian Ocean
Chajul *52 B2* Quiché, W Guatemala
Chakhānsūr *122 D5* Nīmrūz, SW Afghanistan
Chala *60 D4* Arequipa, SW Peru
Chalatenango *52 C3* Chalatenango, N El Salvador
Chalcidice *see* Chalkidikí
Chalcis *see* Chalkída
Chalki *105 E7 island* Dodekánisa, Greece, Aegean Sea
Chalkída *105 C5 var.* Halkída, *prev.* Khalkís; *anc.* Chalcis. Evvoia, E Greece
Chalkidikí *104 C4 var.* Khalkidhikí; *anc.* Chalcidice. *peninsula* NE Greece
Challans *90 B4* Vendée, NW France
Challapata *61 F4* Oruro, SW Bolivia
Challenger Deep *152 B3 trench* W Pacific Ocean
Challenger Deep *see* Mariana Trench
Challenger Fracture Zone *153 F4 tectonic feature* SE Pacific Ocean
Châlons-en-Champagne *90 D3 prev.* Châlons-sur-Marne, *hist.* Arcae Remorum; *anc.* Carolopois. Marne, NE France
Châlons-sur-Marne *see* Châlons-en-Champagne
Chalon-sur-Saône *90 D4 anc.* Cabillonum. Saône-et-Loire, C France
Cha Mai *see* Thung Song
Chaman *134 B2* Baluchistān, SW Pakistan
Chambéry *91 D5 anc.* Cambaria. Savoie, E France
Champagne *90 D3 cultural region* N France
Champagne *see* Campania
Champaign *40 B4* Illinois, N USA
Champasak *137 D5* Champasak, S Laos
Champlain, Lake *41 F2 lake* Canada/USA
Champotón *51 G4* Campeche, SE Mexico
Chanak *see* Çanakkale
Chañaral *64 B3* Atacama, N Chile
Chan-chiang/Chanchiang *see* Zhanjiang
Chandeleur Islands *42 C3 island group* Louisiana, S USA
Chandigarh *134 D2 state capital* Punjab, N India
Chandrapur *135 E5* Mahārāshtra, C India
Changan *see* Xi'an, Shaanxi, C China
Changane *79 E3 river* S Mozambique
Changchun *128 D3 var.* Ch'angch'un, Ch'ang-ch'un; *prev.* Hsinking. *province capital* Jilin, NE China
Ch'angch'un/Ch'ang-ch'un *see* Changchun
Changkiakow *see* Zhangjiakou
Chang, Ko *137 C6 island* S Thailand

Changsha *128 C5 var.* Ch'angsha, Ch'ang-sha. *province capital* Hunan, S China
Ch'angsha/Ch'ang-sha *see* Changsha
Changzhi *128 C4* Shanxi, C China
Chaniá *105 C7 var.* Hania, Khaniá, *Eng.* Canea; *anc.* Cydonia. Kríti, Greece, E Mediterranean Sea
Chañi, Nevado de *64 B2 mountain* NW Argentina
Chankiri *see* Çankırı
Channel Islands *89 C8 Fr.* Iles Normandes. *island group* S English Channel
Channel Islands *47 B8 island group* California, W USA
Channel-Port aux Basques *39 G4* Newfoundland and Labrador, SE Canada
Channel, The *see* English Channel
Channel Tunnel *90 C2 tunnel* France/United Kingdom
Chantabun/Chantaburi *see* Chanthaburi
Chantada *92 C1* Galicia, NW Spain
Chanthaburi *137 C6 var.* Chantabun, Chantaburi. Chantaburi, S Thailand
Chanute *45 F5* Kansas, C USA
Chaouèn *see* Chefchaouen
Chaoyang *128 D3* Liaoning, NE China
Chapala, Lago de *50 D4 lake* C Mexico
Chapan, Gora *122 B3 mountain* C Turkmenistan
Chapayevsk *111 C6* Samarskaya Oblast', W Russian Federation
Chaplynka *109 F4* Khersons'ka Oblast', S Ukraine
Chapra *see* Chhapra
Charcot Seamounts *80 B3 seamount range* E Atlantic Ocean
Chardzhev *see* Türkmenabat
Chardzhou/Chardzhui *see* Türkmenabat
Charente *91 B5 cultural region* W France
Charente *91 B5 river* W France
Chari *76 B3 var.* Shari. *river* Central African Republic/Chad
Chārīkār *123 E4* Parvān, NE Afghanistan
Charity *59 F2* NW Guyana
Chärjew *see* Türkmenabat
Charkhlik/Charkhliq *see* Ruoqiang
Charleroi *87 C7* Hainaut, S Belgium
Charlesbourg *39 E4* Québec, SE Canada
Charles de Gaulle *90 E1* (Paris) Seine-et-Marne, N France
Charles Island *38 D1 island* Nunavut, NE Canada
Charles Island *see* Santa María, Isla
Charleston *43 F2* South Carolina, SE USA
Charleston *40 D5 state capital* West Virginia, NE USA
Charleville *149 D5* Queensland, E Australia
Charleville-Mézières *90 D3* Ardennes, N France
Charlie-Gibbs Fracture Zone *66 C2 tectonic feature* N Atlantic Ocean
Charlotte *43 E1* North Carolina, SE USA
Charlotte Amalie *55 F3 prev.* Saint Thomas. *dependent territory capital* (Virgin Islands (US)) Saint Thomas, N Virgin Islands (US)
Charlotte Harbor *43 E5 inlet* Florida, SE USA
Charlottenhof *see* Aegviidu
Charlottesville *41 E5* Virginia, NE USA
Charlottetown *39 F4 province capital* Prince Edward Island, Prince Edward Island, SE Canada
Charlotte Town *see* Roseau, Dominica
Charsk *see* Shar
Charters Towers *148 D3* Queensland, NE Australia
Chartres *90 C3 anc.* Autricum, Civitas Carnutum. Eure-et-Loir, C France
Chashniki *107 D5* Vitsyebskaya Voblasts', N Belarus
Châteaubriant *90 B3* Loire-Atlantique, NW France
Châteaudun *90 C3* Eure-et-Loir, C France
Châteauroux *90 C4 prev.* Indreville. Indre, C France
Château-Thierry *90 C3* Aisne, N France
Châtelet *87 C7* Hainaut, S Belgium
Châtellerault *90 B4 var.* Châtelherault. Vienne, W France

Chatham Island *see* San Cristóbal, Isla
Chatham Island Rise *see* Chatham Rise
Chatham Islands 143 E5 *island group* New Zealand, SW Pacific Ocean
Chatham Rise 142 D5 *var.* Chatham Island Rise. *undersea rise* S Pacific Ocean
Chatkal Range 123 F2 *Rus.* Chatkal'skiy Khrebet. *mountain range* Kyrgyzstan/ Uzbekistan
Chatkal'skiy Khrebet *see* Chatkal Range
Chättagām *see* Chittagong
Chattahoochee River 42 D3 *river* SE USA
Chattanooga 42 D1 Tennessee, S USA
Chatyr-Tash 123 G2 Narynskaya Oblast', C Kyrgyzstan
Châu Độc 137 D6 *var.* Chauphu, Chau Phu. An Giang, S Vietnam
Chauk 136 A3 Magway, W Burma (Myanmar)
Chaumont 90 D4 *prev.* Chaumont-en-Bassigny. Haute-Marne, N France
Chaumont-en-Bassigny *see* Chaumont
Chau Phu *see* Châu Độc
Chausy *see* Chavusy
Chaves 92 C2 *anc.* Aquae Flaviae. Vila Real, N Portugal
Chávez, Isla *see* Santa Cruz, Isla
Chavusy 107 E6 *Rus.* Chausy. Mahilyowskaya Voblasts', E Belarus
Chaykovskiy 111 D5 Permskaya Oblast', NW Russian Federation
Cheb 99 A5 *Ger.* Eger. Karlovarský Kraj, W Czech Republic
Cheboksary 111 C5 Chuvashskaya Respublika, W Russian Federation
Cheboygan 40 C2 Michigan, N USA
Chechaouèn *see* Chefchaouen
Chech, Erg 74 D1 *desert* Algeria/Mali
Chechevichi *see* Chachevichy
Che-chiang *see* Zhejiang
Cheduba Island 136 A4 *island* W Burma (Myanmar)
Chefchaouen 70 C2 *var.* Chaouèn, Chechaouèn, Sp. Xauen. N Morocco
Chefoo *see* Yantai
Cheju-do 129 E4 *Jap.* Saishū; *prev.* Quelpart. *island* S South Korea
Cheju Strait 129 E4 *Eng.* Cheju Strait. *strait* S South Korea
Cheju Strait *see* Cheju-haehyŏp
Chekiang *see* Zhejiang
Cheleken *see* Hazar
Chelkar *see* Shalkar
Chelm 98 E4 *Rus.* Kholm. Lubelskie, SE Poland
Chelmno 98 C3 *Ger.* Culm, Kulm. Kujawski-pomorskie, C Poland
Chelmza 98 C3 *Ger.* Culmsee, Kulmsee. Kujawski-pomorskie, C Poland
Cheltenham 89 D6 C England, United Kingdom
Chelyabinsk 114 C3 Chelyabinskaya Oblast', C Russian Federation
Chemnitz 94 D4 *prev.* Karl-Marx-Stadt. Sachsen, E Germany
Chemulpo *see* Inch'ŏn
Chenāb 134 C2 *river* India/Pakistan
Chengchiatun *see* Liaoyuan
Ch'eng-chou/Chengchow *see* Zhengzhou
Chengde 128 D3 *var.* Jehol. Hebei, E China
Chengdu 128 B5 *var.* Chengtu, Ch'eng-tu. *province capital* Sichuan, C China
Chenghsien *see* Zhengzhou
Chengtu/Ch'eng-tu *see* Chengdu
Chennai 132 D2 *prev.* Madras. *state capital* Tamil Nādu, S India
Chenstokhov *see* Częstochowa
Chen Xian/Chenxian/Chen Xiang *see* Chenzhou
Chenzhou 128 C6 *var.* Chenxian, Chen Xian, Chen Xiang. Hunan, S China
Chepelare 104 C3 Smolyan, S Bulgaria
Chepén 60 B3 La Libertad, C Peru
Cher 102 C4 *river* C France
Cherbourg 90 B3 *anc.* Carusbur. Manche, N France
Cherepovets 114 B4 Vologodskaya Oblast', NW Russian Federation
Chergui, Chott ech 70 D2 *salt lake* NW Algeria
Cherikov *see* Cherykaw
Cherkassy *see* Cherkasy

Cherkasy 109 E2 *Rus.* Cherkassy. Cherkas'ka Oblast', C Ukraine
Cherkessk 111 B7 Karachayevo-Cherkesskaya Respublika, SW Russian Federation
Chernigov *see* Chernihiv
Chernihiv 109 E1 *Rus.* Chernigov. Chernihivs'ka Oblast', NE Ukraine
Chernivtsi 108 C3 *Ger.* Czernowitz, *Rom.* Cernăuţi, *Rus.* Chernovtsy. Chernivets'ka Oblast', W Ukraine
Cherno More *see* Black Sea
Chernomorskoye *see* Chornomors'ke
Chernovtsy *see* Chernivtsi
Chernoye More *see* Black Sea
Chernyakhovsk 106 A4 *Ger.* Insterburg. Kaliningradskaya Oblast', W Russian Federation
Cherry Hill 41 F4 New Jersey, NE USA
Cherski Range *see* Cherskogo, Khrebet
Cherskiy 115 G2 Respublika Sakha (Yakutiya), NE Russian Federation
Cherskogo, Khrebet 115 F2 *var.* Cherski Range. *mountain range* NE Russian Federation
Cherso *see* Cres
Cherven' *see* Chervyen'
Chervonograd *see* Chervonohrad
Chervonohrad 108 C2 *Rus.* Chervonograd. L'vivs'ka Oblast', NW Ukraine
Chervyen' 107 D6 *Rus.* Cherven'. Minskaya Voblasts', C Belarus
Cherykaw 107 E7 *Rus.* Cherikov. Mahilyowskaya Voblasts', E Belarus
Chesapeake Bay 41 F5 *inlet* NE USA
Chesha Bay *see* Chëshskaya Guba
Chëshskaya Guba 155 D5 *var.* Archangel Bay, Chesha Bay, Dvina Bay. *bay* NW Russian Federation
Chester 89 C6 *Wel.* Caerleon, *hist.* Legaceaster, *Lat.* Deva, Devana Castra. C England, United Kingdom
Chetumal 51 H4 *var.* Payo Obispo. Quintana Roo, SE Mexico
Cheviot Hills 88 D4 *hill range* England/ Scotland, United Kingdom
Cheyenne 44 D4 *state capital* Wyoming, C USA
Cheyenne River 44 D3 *river* South Dakota/Wyoming, N USA
Chezdi-Oşorheiu *see* Târgu Secuiesc
Chhapra 135 F3 *prev.* Chapra. Bihār, N India
Chhattīsgarh 135 E4 *cultural region* E India
Chiai 128 D6 *var.* Chia-i, Chiayi, Kiayi, Jiayi, *Jap.* Kagi. C Taiwan
Chia-i *see* Chiai
Chiang-hsi *see* Jiangxi
Chiang Mai 136 B4 *var.* Chiangmai, Chiengmai, Kiangmai. Chiang Mai, NW Thailand
Chiangmai *see* Chiang Mai
Chiang Rai 136 C3 *var.* Chianpai, Chienrai, Muang Chiang Rai. Chiang Rai, NW Thailand
Chiang-su *see* Jiangsu
Chianning/Chian-ning *see* Nanjing
Chianpai *see* Chiang Rai
Chianti 96 C3 *cultural region* C Italy
Chiapa *see* Chiapa de Corzo
Chiapa de Corzo 51 G5 *var.* Chiapa. Chiapas, SE Mexico
Chiayi *see* Chiai
Chiba 130 B1 *var.* Tiba. Chiba, Honshū, S Japan
Chibougamau 38 D3 Québec, SE Canada
Chicago 40 B3 Illinois, N USA
Ch'i-ch'i-ha-erh *see* Qiqihar
Chickasha 49 G2 Oklahoma, C USA
Chiclayo 60 B3 Lambayeque, NW Peru
Chico 47 B5 California, W USA
Chico, Río 60 C7 *river* S Argentina
Chico, Río 65 B6 *river* S Argentina
Chicoutimi 39 E4 Québec, SE Canada
Chiengmai *see* Chiang Mai
Chienrai *see* Chiang Rai
Chiesanuova 96 D2 SW San Marino
Chieti 96 D4 *var.* Teate. Abruzzo, C Italy
Chifeng 127 G2 *var.* Ulanhad. Nei Mongol Zizhiqu, N China
Chigirin *see* Chyhyryn
Chih-fu *see* Yantai
Chihli *see* Hebei
Chihli, Gulf of *see* Bo Hai
Chihuahua 50 C2 Chihuahua, NW Mexico

Childress 49 F2 Texas, SW USA
Chile 64 B3 *off.* Republic of Chile. *country* SW South America

Chile Basin 57 A5 *undersea basin* E Pacific Ocean
Chile Chico 65 B6 Aisén, W Chile
Chile, Republic of *see* Chile
Chile Rise 57 A7 *undersea rise* SE Pacific Ocean
Chilia-Nouă *see* Kiliya
Chililabombwe 78 D2 Copperbelt, C Zambia
Chi-lin *see* Jilin
Chillán 65 B5 Bío Bío, C Chile
Chillicothe 40 D4 Ohio, N USA
Chill Mhantáin, Sléibhte *see* Wicklow Mountains
Chiloé, Isla de 65 A6 *var.* Isla Grande de Chiloé. *island* W Chile
Chilpancingo 51 E5 *var.* Chilpancingo de los Bravos. Guerrero, S Mexico
Chilpancingo de los Bravos *see* Chilpancingo
Chilung 128 D6 *var.* Keelung, *Jap.* Kirun, Kirun'; *prev. Sp.* Santissima Trinidad. N Taiwan
Chimán 53 G5 Panamá, E Panama
Chimbay *see* Chimboy
Chimborazo 60 A1 *volcano* C Ecuador
Chimbote 60 C3 Ancash, W Peru
Chimboy 122 D1 *Rus.* Chimbay. Qoraqalpog'iston Respublikasi, NW Uzbekistan
Chimkent *see* Shymkent
Chimoio 79 E3 Manica, C Mozambique
China 124 C2 *off.* People's Republic of China, *Chin.* Chung-hua Jen-min Kung-ho-kuo, Zhonghua Renmin Gongheguo; *prev.* Chinese Empire. *country* E Asia

Chi-nan/Chinan *see* Jinan
Chinandega 52 C3 Chinandega, NW Nicaragua
China, People's Republic of *see* China
China, Republic of *see* Taiwan
Chincha Alta 60 D4 Ica, SW Peru
Chin-chiang *see* Quanzhou
Chin-chou/Chinchow *see* Jinzhou
Chindwin *see* Chindwin

Chindwinn 136 B2 *var.* Chindwin. *river* N Burma (Myanmar)
Chinese Empire *see* China
Chinghai *see* Qinghai
Ch'ing Hai *see* Qinghai Hu, China
Chingola 78 D2 Copperbelt, C Zambia
Ching-Tao/Ch'ing-tao *see* Qingdao
Chinguetti 74 C2 *var.* Chinguetti. Adrar, C Mauritania
Chin Hills 136 A3 *mountain range* W Burma (Myanmar)
Chinhsien *see* Jinzhou
Chinnereth *see* Tiberias, Lake
Chinook Trough 113 H4 *trough* N Pacific Ocean
Chioggia 96 C2 *anc.* Fossa Claudia. Veneto, NE Italy
Chíos 105 D5 *var.* Hios, Khíos, *It.* Scio, *Turk.* Sakiz-Adasi. Chíos, E Greece
Chíos 105 D5 *var.* Khíos. *island* E Greece
Chipata 78 D2 *prev.* Fort Jameson. Eastern, E Zambia
Chiquián 60 C3 Ancash, W Peru
Chiquimula 52 B2 Chiquimula, SE Guatemala
Chírala 132 D1 Andhra Pradesh, E India
Chirchik *see* Chirchiq
Chirchiq 123 E2 *Rus.* Chirchik. Toshkent Viloyati, E Uzbekistan
Chiriquí Gulf 53 E5 *Eng.* Chiriquí Gulf. *gulf* SW Panama
Chiriquí, Laguna de 53 E5 *lagoon* NW Panama
Chiriquí, Volcán de *see* Barú, Volcán
Chirripó, Cerro *see* Chirripó Grande, Cerro
Chirripó Grande, Cerro 52 D4 *var.* Cerro Chirripó. *mountain* SE Costa Rica
Chisec 52 B2 Alta Verapaz, C Guatemala
Chisholm 45 F1 Minnesota, N USA
Chisimaio/Chisimayu *see* Kismaayo
Chişinău 108 D4 *Rus.* Kishinev. *country capital* (Moldova) (Moldova) C Moldova
Chita 115 F4 Chitinskaya Oblast', S Russian Federation
Chitangwiza *see* Chitungwiza
Chitato 78 C1 Lunda Norte, NE Angola
Chitina 36 D3 Alaska, USA
Chitose 130 D2 *var.* Titose. Hokkaidō, NE Japan
Chitré 53 F5 Herrera, S Panama
Chittagong 135 G4 *Ben.* Châttagām. Chittagong, SE Bangladesh
Chitungwiza 78 D3 *prev.* Chitangwiza. Mashonaland East, NE Zimbabwe
Chkalov *see* Orenburg
Chlef 70 D2 *var.* Ech Cheliff, Ech Chleff; *prev.* Al-Asnam, El Asnam, Orléansville. NW Algeria
Chocolate Mountains 47 D8 *mountain range* California, W USA
Chodorów *see* Khodoriv
Chodzież 98 C3 Wielkopolskie, C Poland
Choele Choel 65 C5 Río Negro, C Argentina
Choiseul 144 C3 *var.* Lauru. *island* NW Solomon Islands
Chojnice 98 C2 *Ger.* Konitz. Pomorskie, N Poland
Ch'ok'ē 72 C4 *var.* Choke Mountains. *mountain range* NW Ethiopia
Choke Mountains *see* Ch'ok'ē
Cholet 90 B4 Maine-et-Loire, NW France
Choluteca 52 C3 Choluteca, S Honduras
Choluteca, Río 52 C3 *river* SW Honduras
Choma 78 D2 Southern, S Zambia
Chomutov 98 A4 *Ger.* Komotau. Ústecký Kraj, NW Czech Republic
Chona 113 E2 *river* C Russian Federation
Chon Buri 137 C5 *prev.* Bang Pla Soi. Chon Buri, S Thailand
Chone 60 A1 Manabí, W Ecuador
Ch'ŏngjin 128 B3 *var.* Ch'ung-ching, Ch'ung-ch'ing, Chungking, Pahsien, Tchongking, Yuzhou. Chongqing Shi, C China
Chongqing *see* Connaught
Chonos, Archipiélago de los 65 A6 *island group* S Chile
Chóra Sfakíon 105 C8 *var.* Sfákia. Kríti, Greece, E Mediterranean Sea
Chorne More *see* Black Sea

Chornomors'ke 109 E4 Rus.
Chernomorskoye. Respublika Krym,
S Ukraine
Chorokh/Chorokhi see Çoruh Nehri
Chortkiv 108 C2 Rus. Chortkov.
Ternopil's'ka Oblast', W Ukraine
Chortkov see Chortkiv
Chorzów 99 C5 Ger. Königshütte; prev.
Królewska Huta. Śląskie, S Poland
Chōsebuz see Cottbus
Chōsen-kaikyō see Korea Strait
Chōshi 131 D5 var. Tyōsi. Chiba,
Honshū, S Japan
Chosŏn-minjujuŭi-inmin-kanghwaguk
see North Korea
Choszczno 98 B3 Ger. Arnswalde.
Zachodnio-pomorskie, NW Poland
Chota Nagpur 135 E6 plateau N India
Choûm 74 C2 Adrar, C Mauritania
Choybalsan 127 F2 prev. Byan Tumen.
Dornod, E Mongolia
Christchurch 151 C6 Canterbury, South
Island, New Zealand
Christiana 54 B5 C Jamaica
Christiania see Oslo
Christiansand see Kristiansand
Christianshåb see Qasigiannguit
Christiansund see Kristiansund
Christmas Island 141 D5 Australian
external territory E Indian Ocean
Christmas Island see Kiritimati
Christmas Ridge 143 E1 undersea ridge
C Pacific Ocean
Chuan see Sichuan
Ch'uan-chou see Quanzhou
Chubek see Moskva
Chubut, Río 65 B6 river SE Argentina
Ch'u-chiang see Shaoguan
Chudskoye Ozero see Peipus, Lake
Chugoku-sanchi 131 B6 mountain range
Honshū, SW Japan
Chui see Chuy
Chukai see Cukai
Chukchi Plain 155 B2 abyssal plain
Arctic Ocean
Chukchi Plateau 34 C2 undersea plateau
Arctic Ocean
Chukchi Sea 34 B2 Rus. Chukotskoye
More. see Arctic Ocean
Chukotskoye More see Chukchi Sea
Chula Vista 47 C8 California, W USA
Chulucanas 60 B2 Piura, NW Peru
Chulym 114 D4 river C Russian
Federation
Chumphon 137 C6 var. Jumporn.
Chumphon, SW Thailand
Ch'unch'ŏn 129 E4 Jap. Shunsen.
N South Korea
Ch'ung-ch'ing/Ch'ung-ching see
Chongqing
Chung-hua Jen-min Kung-ho-kuo
see China
Chungking see Chongqing
Chunya 115 E3 river C Russian
Federation
Chuquicamata 64 B2 Antofagasta,
N Chile
Chuquisaca see Sucre
Chur 95 B7 Fr. Coire, It. Coira, Rmsch.
Cuera, Quera; anc. Curia Rhaetorum.
Graubünden, E Switzerland
Churchill 37 G4 Manitoba,
C Canada
Churchill 38 B2 river Manitoba/
Saskatchewan, C Canada
Churchill 39 F2 river Newfoundland and
Labrador, E Canada
Chuska Mountains 48 C1 mountain
range Arizona/New Mexico, SW USA
Chusovoy 111 D5 Permskaya Oblast',
NW Russian Federation
Chust see Khust
Chuuk Islands 144 B2 var. Hogoley
Islands; prev. Truk Islands. island
group Caroline Islands, C Micronesia
Chuy 64 E4 var. Chuí. Rocha, E Uruguay
Chyhyryn 109 E2 Rus. Chigirin.
Cherkas'ka Oblast', N Ukraine
Ciadir-Lunga 108 D4 var. Ceadâr-
Lunga, Rus. Chadyr-Lunga. S Moldova
Cide 116 C2 Kastamonu, N Turkey
Ciechanów 98 D3 prev. Zichenau.
Mazowieckie, C Poland
Ciego de Ávila 54 C2 Ciego de Ávila,
C Cuba
Ciénaga 58 B1 Magdalena, N Colombia
Cienfuegos 54 B2 Cienfuegos, C Cuba

Cieza 93 E4 Murcia, SE Spain
Cihanbeyli 116 C3 Konya, C Turkey
Cikobia 145 E4 prev. Thikombia.
island N Fiji
Cilacap 138 C5 prev. Tjilatjap. Jawa,
C Indonesia
Cill Airne see Killarney
Cill Chainnigh see Kilkenny
Cilli see Celje
Cill Mhantáin see Wicklow
Cîmpina see Câmpina
Cîmpulung see Câmpulung
Cina Selatan, Laut see South China Sea
Cincinnati 40 C4 Ohio, N USA
Ciney 87 C7 Namur, SE Belgium
Cinto, Monte 91 E7 mountain Corse,
France, C Mediterranean Sea
Cintra see Sintra
Cipolletti 65 B5 Río Negro, C Argentina
Cirebon 138 C4 prev. Tjirebon. Jawa,
S Indonesia
Cirkvenica see Crikvenica
Ciro Marino 97 E6 Calabria, S Italy
Cirquenizza see Crikvenica
Cisnădie 108 B4 Ger. Heltau, Hung.
Nagydisznód. Sibiu, SW Romania
Citharista see la Ciotat
Citlaltépetl see Orizaba, Volcán Pico de
Citrus Heights 47 B5 California, W USA
Ciudad Acuña see Villa Acuña
Ciudad Bolívar 59 E2 prev. Angostura.
Bolívar, E Venezuela
Ciudad Camargo 50 D2 Chihuahua,
N Mexico
Ciudad Cortés see Cortés
Ciudad Darío 52 D3 var. Dario.
Matagalpa, W Nicaragua
Ciudad de Dolores Hidalgo see Dolores
Hidalgo
Ciudad de Guatemala 52 B2 Eng.
Guatemala City; prev. Santiago
de los Caballeros. country capital
(Guatemala) (Guatemala) Guatemala,
C Guatemala
Ciudad del Carmen see Carmen
Ciudad del Este 64 E2 prev. Ciudad
Presidente Stroessner, Presidente
Stroessner, Puerto Presidente
Stroessner. Alto Paraná, SE Paraguay
Ciudad Delicias see Delicias
Ciudad de México see México
Ciudad de Panamá see Panamá
Ciudad Guayana 59 E2 prev. San Tomé
de Guayana, Santo Tomé de Guayana.
Bolívar, NE Venezuela
Ciudad Guzmán 50 D4 Jalisco,
SW Mexico
Ciudad Hidalgo 51 G5 Chiapas,
SE Mexico
Ciudad Juárez 50 C1 Chihuahua,
N Mexico
Ciudad Lerdo 50 D3 Durango, C Mexico
Ciudad Madero 51 E3 var. Villa Cecilia.
Tamaulipas, C Mexico
Ciudad Mante 51 E3 Tamaulipas,
C Mexico
Ciudad Miguel Alemán 51 E2
Tamaulipas, C Mexico
Ciudad Obregón 50 B2 Sonora,
NW Mexico
Ciudad Ojeda 58 C1 Zulia,
NW Venezuela
Ciudad Porfirio Díaz see Piedras Negras
Ciudad Presidente Stroessner see
Ciudad del Este
Ciudad Quesada see Quesada
Ciudad Real 92 D3 Castilla-La Mancha,
C Spain
Ciudad-Rodrigo 92 C3 Castilla-León,
N Spain
Ciudad Trujillo see Santo Domingo
Ciudad Valles 51 E3 San Luis Potosí,
C Mexico
Ciudad Victoria 51 E3 Tamaulipas,
C Mexico
Ciutadella 93 H3 var. Ciutadella
de Menorca. Menorca, Spain,
W Mediterranean Sea
Ciutadella Ciutadella de Menorca see
Ciutadella
Civitanova Marche 96 D3 Marche,
C Italy
Civitas Altae Ripae see Brzeg
Civitas Carnutum see Chartres
Civitas Eburovicum see Évreux
Civitavecchia 96 C4 anc. Centum Cellae,
Trajani Portus. Lazio, C Italy

Claremore 49 G1 Oklahoma, C USA
Clarence 151 C5 Canterbury, South
Island, New Zealand
Clarence 151 C5 river South Island,
New Zealand
Clarence Town 54 D2 Long Island,
C Bahamas
Clarinda 45 F4 Iowa, C USA
Clarion Fracture Zone 153 E2 tectonic
feature NE Pacific Ocean
Clarión, Isla 50 A5 island W Mexico
Clark Fork 44 A1 river Idaho/Montana,
NW USA
Clark Hill Lake 43 E2 var. J.Storm
Thurmond Reservoir. reservoir
Georgia/South Carolina, SE USA
Clarksburg 40 D4 West Virginia,
NE USA
Clarksdale 42 B2 Mississippi, S USA
Clarksville 42 C1 Tennessee, S USA
Clausentum see Southampton
Clayton 49 E1 New Mexico, SW USA
Clearwater 43 E4 Florida, SE USA
Clearwater Mountains 46 D2 mountain
range Idaho, NW USA
Cleburne 49 G3 Texas, SW USA
Clermont 148 D4 Queensland,
E Australia
Clermont-Ferrand 91 C5 Puy-de-Dôme,
C France
Cleveland 40 D3 Ohio, N USA
Cleveland 42 D1 Tennessee, S USA
Clifton 48 C2 Arizona, SW USA
Clinton 42 B2 Mississippi, S USA
Clinton 49 F1 Oklahoma, C USA
Clipperton Fracture Zone 153 E3
tectonic feature E Pacific Ocean
Clipperton Island 35 A7 French
dependency of French Polynesia
E Pacific Ocean
Cloncurry 148 B3 Queensland,
C Australia
Clonmel 89 B6 Ir. Cluain Meala.
S Ireland
Cloppenburg 94 B3 Niedersachsen,
NW Germany
Cloquet 45 G2 Minnesota, N USA
Cloud Peak 44 C3 mountain Wyoming,
C USA
Clovis 49 E2 New Mexico, SW USA
Cluain Meala see Clonmel
Cluj see Cluj-Napoca
Cluj-Napoca 108 B3 Ger. Klausenburg,
Hung. Kolozsvár; prev. Cluj. Cluj,
NW Romania
Clutha 151 B7 river South Island, New
Zealand
Clyde 88 C4 river W Scotland, United
Kingdom
Coari 62 D2 Amazonas, N Brazil
Coast Mountains 36 D4 Fr. Chaîne
Côtière. mountain range Canada/USA
Coast Ranges 46 A4 mountain range
W USA
Coats Island 37 G3 island Nunavut,
NE Canada
Coats Land 154 B2 physical region
Antarctica
Coatzacoalcos 51 G4 var. Quetzalcoalco;
prev. Puerto México. Veracruz-Llave,
E Mexico
Cobán 52 B2 Alta Verapaz, C Guatemala
Cobar 149 C6 New South Wales,
SE Australia
Cobija 61 E3 Pando, NW Bolivia
Coblence/Coblenz see Koblenz
Coburg 95 C5 Bayern, SE Germany
Cocanada see Kakinada
Cochabamba 61 F4 hist. Oropeza.
Cochabamba, C Bolivia
Cochin 132 C3 var. Kochchi, Kochi.
Kerala, SW India
Cochrane 38 C4 Ontario, S Canada
Cochrane 65 B7 Aisén, S Chile
Cocibolca see Nicaragua, Lago de
Cockade State see Maryland
Cockburn Town 51 E2 San Salvador,
E Bahamas
Cockpit Country, The 54 A4 physical
region W Jamaica
Cocobeach 77 A5 Estuaire, NW Gabon
Coconino Plateau 48 B1 plain Arizona,
SW USA
Coco, Río 53 E2 var. Río Wanki,
Segoviao Wangkí. river Honduras/
Nicaragua

Cocos Basin 124 C5 undersea basin
E Indian Ocean
Cocos Island Ridge see Cocos Ridge
Cocos Islands 141 D5 island group
E Indian Ocean
Cocos Ridge 35 C8 var. Cocos Island
Ridge. undersea ridge E Pacific Ocean
Cod, Cape 41 G3 headland
Massachusetts, NE USA
Codfish Island 151 A8 island SW New
Zealand
Codlea 108 C4 Ger. Zeiden, Hung.
Feketehalom. Braşov, C Romania
Cody 44 C2 Wyoming, C USA
Coeur d'Alene 46 C2 Idaho, NW USA
Coevorden 86 E2 Drenthe,
NE Netherlands
Coffs Harbour 149 E6 New South
Wales, SE Australia
Cognac 91 B5 anc. Compniacum.
Charente, W France
Cohalm see Rupea
Coiba, Isla de 53 F5 island SW Panama
Coihaique 65 B6 var. Coyhaique. Aisén,
S Chile
Coimbatore 132 C3 Tamil Nādu, S India
Coimbra 92 B3 anc. Conímbria,
Conímbriga. Coimbra, W Portugal
Coín 92 D5 Andalucía, S Spain
Coira/Coire see Chur
Coirib, Loch see Corrib, Lough
Colby 45 E4 Kansas, C USA
Colchester 89 E6 Connecticut, NE USA
Coleman 49 F3 Texas, SW USA
Coleraine 88 B4 Ir. Cúil Raithin.
N Northern Ireland, United Kingdom
Colesberg 78 C5 Northern Cape,
C South Africa
Colima 50 D4 Colima, S Mexico
Coll 88 B3 island W Scotland, United
Kingdom
College Station 49 G3 Texas, SW USA
Collie 147 A7 Western Australia
Collipo see Leiria
Colmar 90 E4 Ger. Kolmar. Haut-Rhin,
NE France
Cöln see Köln
Cologne see Köln
Colomb-Béchar see Béchar
Colombia 58 B3 off. Republic of
Colombia. country N South America

COLOMBIA
South America

Official name Republic of Colombia
Formation 1819 / 1903
Capital Bogotá
Population 47 million / 117 people
per sq mile (45 people per sq km) / 77%
Total area 439,733 sq. miles
(1,138,910 sq. km)
Languages Spanish*, Wayuu, Páez, and
other Amerindian languages
Religions Roman Catholic 95%, Other 5%
Ethnic mix Mestizo 58%, White 20%,
European–African 14%, African 4%,
African–Amerindian 3%, Amerindian 1%
Government Presidential system
Currency Colombian peso = 100 centavos
Literacy rate 93%
Calorie consumption 2585 calories

Colombian Basin 56 A1 undersea basin
SW Caribbean Sea
Colombia, Republic of see Colombia
Colombie-Britannique see British
Columbia
Colombo 132 C4 country capital (Sri
Lanka) (Sri Lanka) Western Province,
W Sri Lanka
Colón 53 G4 prev. Aspinwall. Colón,
C Panama
Colonia Agrippina see Köln
Colón Ridge 35 B8 undersea ridge
E Pacific Ocean
Colorado 44 C4 off. State of Colorado,
also known as Centennial State, Silver
State. state C USA
Colorado City 49 F3 Texas, SW USA
Colorado Plateau 48 B1 plateau W USA
Colorado, Río 65 C5 river E Argentina
Colorado, Río see Colorado River
Colorado River 33 B5 var. Río Colorado.
river Mexico/USA
Colorado River 49 G4 river Texas,
SW USA

Colorado Springs *44 D5* Colorado, C USA
Columbia *41 E4* Maryland, NE USA
Columbia *45 G4* Missouri, C USA
Columbia *43 E2 state capital* South Carolina, SE USA
Columbia *42 C1* Tennessee, S USA
Columbia River *46 B3 river* Canada/ USA
Columbia Plateau *46 C3 plateau* Idaho/ Oregon, NW USA
Columbus *42 D2* Georgia, SE USA
Columbus *40 C4* Indiana, N USA
Columbus *42 C2* Mississippi, S USA
Columbus *45 F4* Nebraska, C USA
Columbus *40 D4 state capital* Ohio, N USA
Colville Channel *150 D2 channel* North Island, New Zealand
Colville River *36 D2 river* Alaska, USA
Comacchio *96 C3 var.* Commachio; *anc.* Comactium. Emilia-Romagna, N Italy
Comactium *see* Comacchio
Comalcalco *51 G4* Tabasco, SE Mexico
Coma Pedrosa, Pic de *91 A7 mountain* NW Andorra
Comarapa *61 F4* Santa Cruz, C Bolivia
Comayagua *52 C2* Comayagua, W Honduras
Comer See *see* Como, Lago di
Comilla *135 G4 Ben.* Kumillā. Chittagong, E Bangladesh
Comino *102 A5 Malt.* Kemmuna. *island* C Malta
Comitán *51 G5 var.* Comitán de Domínguez. Chiapas, SE Mexico
Comitán de Domínguez *see* Comitán
Commachio *see* Comacchio
Commissioner's Point *42 A5 headland* W Bermuda
Communism Peak *123 F3 prev.* Qullai Kommunizm. *mountain* E Tajikistan
Como *96 B2 anc.* Comum. Lombardia, N Italy
Comodoro Rivadavia *65 B6* Chubut, SE Argentina
Como, Lake *96 B2 var.* Lario, Eng. Lake Como, *Ger.* Comer See. *lake* N Italy
Como, Lake *see* Como, Lake
Comores, République Fédérale Islamique des *see* Comoros
Comoros *79 F2 off.* Federal Islamic Republic of the Comoros, *Fr.* République Fédérale Islamique des Comores. *country* W Indian Ocean

COMOROS
Indian Ocean

Official name Union of the Comoros
Formation 1975 / 1975
Capital Moroni
Population 711,417 / 826 people per sq mile (319 people per sq km) / 36%
Total area 838 sq. miles (2,170 sq. km)
Languages Arabic*, Comoran*, French*
Religions Muslim (mainly Sunni) 98%, Other 1%, Roman Catholic 1%
Ethnic mix Comoran 97%, Other 3%
Government Presidential system
Currency Comoros franc = 100 centimes
Literacy rate 56%
Calorie consumption 1754 calories

Comoros, Federal Islamic Republic of the *see* Comoros
Compiègne *90 C3* Oise, N France
Complutum *see* Alcalá de Henares
Compniacum *see* Cognac
Compostela *see* Santiago
Comrat *108 D4 Rus.* Komrat. S Moldova
Comum *see* Como
Conakry *74 C4 country capital* (Guinea) (Guinea) SW Guinea
Conca *see* Cuenca
Concarneau *90 A3* Finistère, NW France
Concepción *61 G3* Santa Cruz, E Bolivia
Concepción *65 B5* Bío Bío, C Chile
Concepción *64 D2 var.* Villa Concepción. Concepción, C Paraguay
Concepción *see* La Concepción
Concepción de la Vega *see* La Vega
Conchos, Río *48 D4 river* NW Mexico
Conchos, Río *50 D2 river* C Mexico

Concord *41 G3 state capital* New Hampshire, NE USA
Concordia *64 D4* Entre Ríos, E Argentina
Concordia *45 E4* Kansas, C USA
Côn Đao *137 E7 var.* Con Son. *island* S Vietnam
Condate *see* Rennes, Ille-et-Vilaine, France
Condate *see* St-Claude, Jura, France
Condega *52 D3* Estelí, NW Nicaragua
Condivincum *see* Nantes
Confluentes *see* Koblenz
Cộng Hoa Xa Hội Chu Nghia Việt Nam *see* Vietnam
Congo *77 D5 off.* Republic of the Congo, *Fr.* Moyen-Congo; *prev.* Middle Congo. *country* C Africa

CONGO
Central Africa

Official name Republic of the Congo
Formation 1960 / 1960
Capital Brazzaville
Population 4.2 million / 32 people per sq mile (12 people per sq km) / 54%
Total area 132,046 sq. miles (342,000 sq. km)
Languages French*, Kongo, Teke, Lingala
Religions Traditional beliefs 50%, Roman Catholic 25%, Protestant 23%, Muslim 2%
Ethnic mix Bakongo 51%, Teke 17%, Other 16%, Mbochi 11%, Mbédé 5%
Government Presidential system
Currency CFA franc = 100 centimes
Literacy rate 83%
Calorie consumption 2162 calories

Congo *77 C6 off.* Democratic Republic of Congo; *prev.* Zaire, Belgian Congo, Congo (Kinshasa). *country* C Africa

CONGO, DEM. REP.
Central Africa

Official name Democratic Republic of the Congo
Formation 1960 / 1960
Capital Kinshasa
Population 61.2 million / 70 people per sq mile (27 people per sq km) / 33%
Total area 905,563 sq. miles (2,345,410 sq. km)
Languages French*, Kiswahili, Tshiluba, Kikongo, Lingala
Religions Roman Catholic 50%, Protestant 20%, Traditional beliefs and other 10%, Muslim 10%, Kimbanguist 10%
Ethnic mix Other 55%, Mongo, Luba, Kongo, and Mangbetu-Azande 45%
Government Presidential system
Currency Congolese franc = 100 centimes
Literacy rate 67%
Calorie consumption 1599 calories

Congo *77 C6 var.* Kongo, Fr. Zaire. *river* C Africa
Congo Basin *77 C6 drainage basin* W Dem. Rep. Congo
Congo/Congo (Kinshasa) *see* Congo (Democratic Republic of)
Coni *see* Cuneo
Conimbria/Conimbriga *see* Coimbra
Conjeeveram *see* Kānchipuram
Connacht *see* Connaught
Connaught *89 A5 var.* Connacht, Ir. Chonnacht, Cúige. *province* W Ireland
Connecticut *41 F3 off.* State of Connecticut, *also known as* Blue Law State, Constitution State, Land of Steady Habits, Nutmeg State. *state* NE USA
Connecticut *41 G3 river* Canada/USA
Conroe *49 G3* Texas, SW USA
Consentia *see* Cosenza
Consolación del Sur *54 A2* Pinar del Río, W Cuba
Con Son *see* Côn Đao
Constance *see* Konstanz
Constance, Lake *95 B7 Ger.* Bodensee. *lake* C Europe
Constanța *108 D5 var.* Küstendje, *Eng.* Constanza, *Ger.* Konstanza, *Turk.* Küstence. Constanța, SE Romania
Constantia *see* Coutances
Constantia *see* Konstanz

Constantine *71 E2 var.* Qacentina, Ar. Qoussantina. NE Algeria
Constantinople *see* İstanbul
Constantiola *see* Oltenița
Constanz *see* Konstanz
Constanza *see* Constanța
Constitution State *see* Connecticut
Coo *see* Kos
Coober Pedy *149 A5* South Australia
Cookeville *42 D1* Tennessee, S USA
Cook Islands *145 F4 territory in free association with New Zealand* S Pacific Ocean
Cook, Mount *see* Aoraki
Cook Strait *151 D5 var.* Raukawa. *strait* New Zealand
Cooktown *148 D2* Queensland, NE Australia
Coolgardie *147 B6* Western Australia
Cooma *149 D7* New South Wales, SE Australia
Coomassie *see* Kumasi
Coon Rapids *45 F2* Minnesota, N USA
Cooper Creek *148 C4 var.* Barcoo, Cooper's Creek. *seasonal river* Queensland/South Australia
Cooper's Creek *see* Cooper Creek
Coos Bay *46 A3* Oregon, NW USA
Cootamundra *149 D6* New South Wales, SE Australia
Copacabana *61 E4* La Paz, W Bolivia
Copenhagen *see* København
Copiapó *64 B3* Atacama, N Chile
Copperas Cove *49 G3* Texas, SW USA
Coppermine *see* Kugluktuk
Copper State *see* Arizona
Coquilhatville *see* Mbandaka
Coquimbo *64 B3* Coquimbo, N Chile
Corabia *108 B5* Olt, S Romania
Coral Harbour *37 G3* Southampton Island, Nunavut, NE Canada
Coral Sea *142 B3 sea* SW Pacific Ocean
Coral Sea Islands *144 B4 Australian external territory* SW Pacific Ocean
Corantijn Rivier *see* Courantyne River
Corcovado, Golfo *65 B6 gulf* S Chile
Corcyra Nigra *see* Korčula
Cordele *42 D3* Georgia, SE USA
Córdoba *64 C3* Córdoba, C Argentina
Córdoba *51 F4* Veracruz-Llave, E Mexico
Córdoba *92 D4 var.* Cordoba, *Eng.* Cordova; *anc.* Corduba. Andalucía, SW Spain
Cordova *36 C3* Alaska, USA
Cordova/Cordoba *see* Córdoba
Corduba *see* Córdoba
Corentyne River *see* Courantyne River
Corfu *104 A4 var.* Kérkira, *Eng.* Corfu. *island* Ionía Nisiá, Greece, C Mediterranean Sea
Corfu *see* Kérkyra
Coria *92 C3* Extremadura, W Spain
Corinth *42 C1* Mississippi, S USA
Corinth *see* Kórinthos
Corinth, Gulf of *105 B5 Eng.* Gulf of Corinth; *anc.* Corinthiacus Sinus. *gulf* C Greece
Corinth, Gulf of/Corinthiacus Sinus *see* Korinthiakós Kólpos
Corinthus *see* Kórinthos
Corinto *52 C3* Chinandega, NW Nicaragua
Cork *89 A6 Ir.* Corcaigh. S Ireland
Çorlu *116 A2* Tekirdağ, NW Turkey
Corner Brook *39 G3* Newfoundland, Newfoundland and Labrador, E Canada
Cornhusker State *see* Nebraska
Corn Islands *53 E3 var.* Corn Islands. *island group* SE Nicaragua
Corn Islands *see* Maíz, Islas del
Cornwallis Island *37 F2 Island* Nunavut, N Canada
Coro *58 C1 prev.* Santa Ana de Coro. Falcón, NW Venezuela
Corocoro *61 F4* La Paz, W Bolivia
Coromandel *150 D2* Waikato, North Island, New Zealand
Coromandel Coast *132 D2 coast* E India
Coromandel Peninsula *150 D2 peninsula* North Island, New Zealand
Coronado, Bahía de *52 D5 bay* S Costa Rica
Coronel Dorrego *65 C5* Buenos Aires, E Argentina
Coronel Oviedo *64 D2* Caaguazú, SE Paraguay

Corozal *52 C1* Corozal, N Belize
Corpus Christi *49 G4* Texas, SW USA
Corrales *48 D2* New Mexico, SW USA
Corrib, Lough *89 A5 Ir.* Loch Coirib. *lake* W Ireland
Corrientes *64 D3* Corrientes, NE Argentina
Corriza *see* Korçë
Corsica *91 E7 Eng.* Corsica. *island* France, C Mediterranean Sea
Corsica *see* Corse
Corsicana *49 G3* Texas, SW USA
Cortegana *92 C4* Andalucía, S Spain
Cortés *53 E5 var.* Ciudad Cortés. Puntarenas, SE Costa Rica
Cortez, Sea of *see* California, Golfo de
Cortina d'Ampezzo *96 C3 var.* Veneto, NE Italy
Coruche *92 B3* Santarém, C Portugal
Çoruh Nehri *117 E3 Geor.* Chorokh, *Rus.* Chorokhi. *river* Georgia/Turkey
Çorum *116 D3 var.* Chorum. Çorum, N Turkey
Corunna *see* A Coruña
Corvallis *46 B3* Oregon, NW USA
Corvo *92 A5 var.* Ilha do Corvo. *island* Azores, Portugal, NE Atlantic Ocean
Corvo, Ilha do *see* Corvo
Cos *see* Kos
Cosenza *97 D6 anc.* Consentia. Calabria, SW Italy
Cosne-Cours-sur-Loire *90 C4* Nièvre, Bourgogne, C France Europe
Costa Mesa *47 C7* California, W USA
North America
Costa Rica *53 E4 off.* Republic of Costa Rica. *country* Central America

COSTA RICA
Central America

Official name Republic of Costa Rica
Formation 1838 / 1838
Capital San José
Population 4.5 million / 228 people per sq mile (88 people per sq km) / 61%
Total area 19,730 sq. miles (51,100 sq. km)
Languages Spanish*, English Creole, Bribri, Cabecar
Religions Roman Catholic 76%, Other (including Protestant) 24%
Ethnic mix Mestizo and European 96%, Black 2%, Chinese 1%, Amerindian 1%
Government Presidential system
Currency Costa Rican colón = 100 céntimos
Literacy rate 95%
Calorie consumption 2876 calories

Costa Rica, Republic of *see* Costa Rica
Costermansville *see* Bukavu
Cotagaita *61 F5* Potosí, S Bolivia
Côte d'Ivoire *74 D4 off.* Republic of Côte d'Ivoire, *Fr.* Côte d'Ivoire, République de la Côte d'Ivoire, *Eng.* Ivory Coast. *country* W Africa

CÔTE D'IVOIRE (IVORY COAST)
West Africa

Official name Republic of Côte d'Ivoire
Formation 1960 / 1960
Capital Yamoussoukro
Population 16.8 million / 153 people per sq mile (59 people per sq km) / 45%
Total area 124,502 sq. miles (322,460 sq. km)
Languages Akan, French*, Krou, Voltaïque
Religions Muslim 38%, Traditional beliefs 25%, Roman Catholic 25%, Other 6%, Protestant 6%
Ethnic mix Akan 42%, Voltaïque 18%, Mandé du Nord 17%, Krou 11%, Mandé du Sud 10%, Other 2%
Government Presidential system
Currency CFA franc = 100 centimes
Literacy rate 49%
Calorie consumption 2631 calories

Côte d'Ivoire, République de la *see* Côte d'Ivoire
Côte d'Or *90 D4 cultural region* C France
Côte Française des Somalis *see* Djibouti
Côtière, Chaîne *see* Coast Mountains
Cotonou *75 F5 var.* Kotonu. S Benin
Cotrone *see* Crotone

Cotswold Hills 89 *D6 var.* Cotswolds.
hill range S England, United Kingdom
Cotswolds *see* Cotswold Hills
Cottbus 94 *D4 Lus.* Chośebuz; *prev.*
Kottbus. Brandenburg, E Germany
Cotton State, The *see* Alabama
Cotyora *see* Ordu
Couentrey *see* Coventry
Council Bluffs 45 *F4* Iowa, C USA
Courantyne River 59 *G4 var.* Corantijn
Rivier, Corentyne River. *river* Guyana/
Suriname
Courland Lagoon 106 *A4 Ger.* Kurisches
Haff, *Rus.* Kurskiy Zaliv. *lagoon*
Lithuania/Russian Federation
Courtrai *see* Kortrijk
Coutances 90 *B3 anc.* Constantia.
Manche, N France
Couvin 87 *C7* Namur, S Belgium
Coventry 89 *D6 anc.* Couentrey.
C England, United Kingdom
Covilhã 92 *C3* Castelo Branco, E Portugal
Cowan, Lake 147 *B6 lake* Western
Australia
Coxen Hole *see* Roatán
Coxin Hole *see* Roatán
Coyhaique *see* Coihaique
Coyote State, The *see* South Dakota
Cozhĕ 126 *C5* Xizang Zizhiqu, W China
Cozumel, Isla 51 *H3 island* SE Mexico
Cracovia/Cracow *see* Kraków
Cradock 78 *C5* Eastern Cape, S South
Africa
Craig 44 *C4* Colorado, C USA
Craiova 108 *B5* Dolj, SW Romania
Cranbrook 37 *E5* British Columbia,
SW Canada
Crane *see* The Crane
Cranz *see* Zelenogradsk
Crawley 89 *E7* SE England, United
Kingdom
Cremona 96 *B2* Lombardia, N Italy
Creole State *see* Louisiana
Cres 100 *A3 It.* Cherso; *anc.* Crexa.
island W Croatia
Crescent City 46 *A4* California, W USA
Crescent Group 128 *C7 island group*
C Paracel Islands
Creston 45 *F4* Iowa, C USA
Crestview 42 *D3* Florida, SE USA
Crete 105 *C7 Eng.* Crete. *island* Greece,
Aegean Sea
Créteil 90 *E2* Val-de-Marne, N France
Sea of Crete 105 *D7 var.* Kretikon
Delagos, *Eng.* Sea of Crete; *anc.* Mare
Creticum. *sea* Greece, Aegean Sea
Crete, Sea of/Creticum, Mare *see* Kritikó
Pélagos
Creuse 90 *B4 river* C France
Crewe 89 *D6* C England, United
Kingdom
Crexa *see* Cres
Crikvenica 100 *A3 It.* Cirquenizza; *prev.*
Cirkvenica, Crjkvenica. Primorje-
Gorski Kotar, NW Croatia
Crimea 81 *F4 peninsula* SE Ukraine
Europe
Cristóbal 53 *G4* Colón, C Panama
Cristóbal Colón, Pico 58 *B1 mountain*
N Colombia
Cristur/Cristuru Săcuiesc *see* Cristuru
Secuiesc
Cristuru Secuiesc 108 *C4 prev.* Cristur,
Cristuru Săcuiesc, Sitaş Cristuru.
Kreutz, *Hung.* Székelykeresztúr, Szitás-
Keresztúr. Harghita, C Romania
Crjkvenica *see* Crikvenica
Crna Gora *see* Montenegro
Crna Reka 101 *D6 river* S FYR
Macedonia
Crni Drim *see* Black Drin
Croatia 100 *B3 off.* Republic of Croatia,
Ger. Kroatien, *SCr.* Hrvatska. *country*
SE Europe

CROATIA
Southeast Europe

Official name Republic of Croatia
Formation 1991 / 1991
Capital Zagreb
Population 4.6 million / 211 people
per sq mile (81 people per sq km) / 59%
Total area 21,831 sq. miles (56,542 sq. km)
Languages Croatian*
Religions Roman Catholic 88%, Other 7%,
Orthodox Christian 4%, Muslim 1%

CROATIA
(continued)

Ethnic mix Croat 90%, Other 5%, Serb 5%
Government Parliamentary system
Currency Kuna = 100 lipa
Literacy rate 98%
Calorie consumption 2799 calories

Croatia, Republic of *see* Croatia
Crocodile *see* Limpopo
Croia *see* Krujë
Croker Island 146 *E2 island* Northern
Territory, N Australia
Cromwell 151 *B7* Otago, South Island,
New Zealand
Crooked Island 54 *D2 island* SE Bahamas
Crooked Island Passage 54 *D2 channel*
SE Bahamas
Crookston 45 *F1* Minnesota, N USA
Crossen *see* Krosno Odrzańskie
Croton/Crotona *see* Crotone
Crotone 97 *E6 var.* Cotrone; *anc.* Croton,
Crotona. Calabria, SW Italy
Croydon 89 *A8* SE England, United
Kingdom
Crozet Basin 141 *B6 undersea basin*
S Indian Ocean
Crozet Islands 141 *B7 island group*
French Southern and Antarctic
Territories
Crozet Plateau 141 *B7 var.* Crozet
Plateaus. *undersea plateau* SW Indian
Ocean
Crozet Plateaus *see* Crozet Plateau
Crystal Brook 149 *B6* South Australia
Csaca *see* Čadca
Csakathurn/Csáktornya *see* Čakovec
Csíkszereda *see* Miercurea-Ciuc
Csorna 99 *C6* Győr-Moson-Sopron,
NW Hungary
Csurgó 99 *C7* Somogy, SW Hungary
Cuando 78 *C2 var.* Kwando. *river*
S Africa
Cuango 78 *B1 var.* Kwango. *river*
Angola/Dem. Rep. Congo
Cuango *see* Kwango
Cuanza 78 *B1 var.* Kwanza. *river*
C Angola
Cuauhtémoc 50 *C2* Chihuahua,
N Mexico
Cuautla 51 *E4* Morelos, S Mexico
Cuba 54 *B2 off.* Republic of Cuba.
country W West Indies

CUBA
West Indies

Official name Republic of Cuba
Formation 1902 / 1902
Capital Havana
Population 11.3 million / 264 people
per sq mile (102 people per sq km) / 76%
Total area 42,803 sq. miles (110,860 sq. km)
Languages Spanish
Religions Nonreligious 49%, Roman
Catholic 40%, Atheist 6%, Other 4%,
Protestant 1%
Ethnic mix White 66%, European–African
22%, Black 12%
Government One-party state
Currency Cuban peso = 100 centavos
Literacy rate 99%
Calorie consumption 3152 calories

Cubal 78 *B2* Benguela, W Angola
Cubango 78 *B2 var.* Kuvango, *Port.* Vila
Artur de Paiva, Vila da Ponte. Huíla,
SW Angola
Cubango 78 *B2 var.* Kavango, Kuvango,
Kubango, Okavango, Okavanggo.
river S Africa
Cuba, Republic of *see* Cuba
Cúcuta 58 *C2 var.* San José de Cúcuta.
Norte de Santander, N Colombia
Cuddapah 132 *C2* Andhra Pradesh,
S India
Cuenca 60 *B2* Azuay, S Ecuador
Cuenca 93 *E3 anc.* Conca. Castilla-La
Mancha, C Spain
Cuera *see* Chur
Cuernavaca 51 *E4* Morelos, S Mexico
Cuiabá 63 *E3 prev.* Cuyabá. *state capital*
Mato Grosso, SW Brazil
Cúige *see* Connaught

Cúige Laighean *see* Leinster
Cúige Mumhan *see* Munster
Cuijck 86 *D4* Noord-Brabant,
SE Netherlands
Cúil Raithin *see* Coleraine
Cuito 78 *B2 var.* Kwito. *river* SE Angola
Cukai 138 *B3 var.* Chukai, Kemaman.
Terengganu, Peninsular Malaysia
Cularo *see* Grenoble
Culiacán 50 *C3 var.* Culiacán Rosales,
Culiacán-Rosales. Sinaloa, C Mexico
Culiacán-Rosales/Culiacán Rosales
see Culiacán
Cullera 93 *F3* País Valenciano, E Spain
Cullman 42 *C2* Alabama, S USA
Culm *see* Chełmno
Culmsee *see* Chełmża
Cumaná 59 *E1* Sucre, NE Venezuela
Cumbal, Nevado de 58 *A4 elevation*
S Colombia
Cumberland 41 *E4* Maryland, NE USA
Cumberland Plateau 42 *D1 plateau*
E USA
Cumberland Sound 37 *H3 inlet* Baffin
Island, Nunavut, NE Canada
Cumpas 50 *B2* Sonora, NW Mexico
Cuneo 96 *A2 Fr.* Coni. Piemonte,
NW Italy
Cunnamulla 149 *C5* Queensland,
E Australia
Ćuprija 100 *E4* Serbia, E Serbia
Curaçao 55 *E5 Dutch autonomous region*
S Caribbean Sea
Curia Rhaetorum *see* Chur
Curicó 64 *B4* Maule, C Chile
Curieta *see* Krk
Curitiba 63 *E4 prev.* Curytiba. *state*
capital Paraná, S Brazil
Curtbunar *see* Tervel
Curtea de Argeş 108 *C4 var.* Curtea-de-
Arges. Argeş, S Romania
Curtea-de-Arges *see* Curtea de Argeş
Curtici 108 *A4 Ger.* Kurtitsch, *Hung.*
Kürtös. Arad, W Romania
Curtis Island 148 *E4 island* Queensland,
SE Australia
Curytiba *see* Curitiba
Curzola *see* Korčula
Cusco 61 *E4 var.* Cuzco. Cusco, C Peru
Cusset 91 *C5* Allier, C France
Cutch, Gulf of *see* Kachchh, Gulf of
Cuttack 135 *F4* Orissa, E India
Cuvier Plateau 141 *E6 undersea plateau*
E Indian Ocean
Cuxhaven 94 *B2* Niedersachsen,
NW Germany
Cuyabá *see* Cuiabá
Cuyuni, Río *see* Cuyuni River
Cuyuni River 59 *F3 var.* Río Cuyuni.
river Guyana/Venezuela
Cuzco *see* Cusco
Cyclades 105 *D6 var.* Kikládhes, *Eng.*
Cyclades. *island group* SE Greece
Cyclades *see* Kykládes
Cydonia *see* Chaniá
Cymru *see* Wales
Cyprus 102 *C4 off.* Republic of
Cyprus, *Gk.* Kypros, *Turk.* Kıbrıs,
Kıbrıs Cumhuriyeti. *country*
E Mediterranean Sea

CYPRUS
Southeast Europe

Official name Republic of Cyprus
Formation 1960 / 1960
Capital Nicosia
Population 788,457 / 221 people
per sq mile (85 people per sq km) / 69%
Total area 3571 sq. miles (9250 sq. km)
Languages Greek*, Turkish*
Religions Orthodox Christian 78%,
Muslim 18%, Other 4%
Ethnic mix Greek 81%, Turkish 11%,
Other 8%
Government Presidential system
Currency Euro (Turkish Cypriot area: new
cents (euro); 100 kurus (Turkish lira)
Literacy rate 97%
Calorie consumption 3255 calories

Cyprus, Republic of *see* Cyprus
Cythnos *see* Kýthnos
Czech Republic 99 *A5 Cz.* Česká
Republika. *country* C Europe

CZECH REPUBLIC
Central Europe

Official name Czech Republic
Formation 1993 / 1993
Capital Prague
Population 10.2 million / 335 people
per sq mile (129 people per sq km) / 74%
Total area 30,450 sq. miles (78,866 sq. km)
Languages Czech*, Slovak,
Hungarian (Magyar)
Religions Roman Catholic 39%,
Atheist 38%, Other 18%, Protestant 3%,
Hussite 2%
Ethnic mix Czech 90%, Other 4%,
Moravian 4%, Slovak 2%
Government Parliamentary system
Currency Czech koruna = 100 haleru
Literacy rate 99%
Calorie consumption 3171 calories

Czenstochau *see* Częstochowa
Czernowitz *see* Chernivtsi
Częstochowa 98 *C4 Ger.* Czenstochau,
Tschenstochau, *Rus.* Chenstokhov.
Śląskie, S Poland
Człuchów 98 *C3. Ger.* Schlochau.
Pomorskie, NW Poland

Dabajuro 58 *C1* Falcón, NW Venezuela
Dabeiba 58 *B2* Antioquia, NW Colombia
Dąbrowa Tarnowska 99 *D5*
Małopolskie, S Poland
Dabryn' 107 *C8 Rus.* Dobryn'.
Homyel'skaya Voblasts', SE Belarus
Dacca *see* Dhaka
Daegu *see* Taegu
Dagana 74 *B3* N Senegal
Dagda 106 *D4* Krāslava, SE Latvia
Dagden *see* Hiiumaa
Dagenham 89 *B8* United Kingdom
Dağlıq Quarabağ *see* Nagorno-Karabakh
Dagö *see* Hiiumaa
Dagupan 139 *E1 off.* Dagupan City.
Luzon, N Philippines
Dagupan City *see* Dagupan
Dahm, Ramlat 121 *B6 desert* NW Yemen
Dahomey *see* Benin
Daihoku *see* T'aipei
Daimiel 92 *D3* Castilla-La Mancha,
C Spain
Daimoniá 105 *B7* Pelopónnisos, S Greece
Dainan *see* T'ainan
Daingin, Bá an *see* Dingle Bay
Dairen *see* Dalian
Dakar 74 *B3 country capital* (Senegal)
(Senegal) W Senegal
Dakhla *see* Ad Dakhla
Dakoro 75 *G3* Maradi, S Niger
Đakovica *see* Gjakovë
Đakovo 100 *D3 var.* Djakovo, *Hung.*
Diakovár. Osijek-Baranja, E Croatia
Dakshin *see* Deccan
Dalain Hob 126 *D3 var.* Ejin Qi. Nei
Mongol Zizhiqu, N China
Dalai Nor *see* Hulun Nur
Dalaman 116 *A4* Muğla, SW Turkey
Dalandzadgad 127 *E3* Ömnögovĭ,
S Mongolia
Đa Lat 137 *E6* Lâm Đông, S Vietnam
Dalby 149 *D5* Queensland, E Australia
Dale City 41 *F4* Virginia, NE USA
Dalhart 49 *E1* Texas, SW USA
Dali 128 *A4 var.* Xiaguan. Yunnan,
SW China
Dalian 128 *D4 var.* Dairen, Dalien, Jay
Dairen, Lüda, Ta-lien, *Rus.* Dalny.
Liaoning, NE China
Dalien *see* Dalian
Dallas 49 *G2* Texas, SW USA
Dalmacija 100 *B4 Eng.* Dalmatia, *Ger.*
Dalmatien, *It.* Dalmazia. *cultural region*
S Croatia
Dalmatia/Dalmatien/Dalmazia *see*
Dalmacija
Dalny *see* Dalian
Dalton 42 *D1* Georgia, SE USA
Dálvvadis *see* Jokkmokk
Daly Waters 148 *A2* Northern Territory,
N Australia
Damachava 107 *A6 var.* Damachova,
Pol. Domaczewo, *Rus.* Domachëvo.
Brestskaya Voblasts', SW Belarus

Damachova *see* Damachava
Damān *134 C4* Damān and Diu, W India
Damara *76 C4* Ombella-Mpoko,
S Central African Republic
Damas *see* Dimashq
Damasco *see* Dimashq
Damascus *see* Dimashq
Qolleh-ye Damavand *120 D3 mountain*
N Iran
Damietta *see* Dumyāt
Dammām *see* Ad Dammān
Damoûr *119 A5 var.* Ad Dāmūr.
W Lebanon
Dampier *146 A4* Western Australia
Dampier, Selat *139 F4 strait* Papua,
E Indonesia
Damqawt *121 D6 var.* Damqut.
E Yemen
Damqut *see* Damqawt
Damxung *126 C5 var.* Gongtang. Xizang
Zizhiqu, W China
Danakil Desert *72 D4 var.* Afar
Depression, Danakil Plain. *desert*
E Africa
Danakil Plain *see* Danakil Desert
Danané *74 D5* W Côte d'Ivoire
Đà Nâng *137 E5 prev.* Tourane. Quang
Nam-Đa Nâng, C Vietnam
Danborg *see* Daneborg
Dandong *128 D3 var.* Tan-tung; *prev.*
An-tung. Liaoning, NE China
Daneborg *83 E3 var.* Danborg. Tunu,
N Greenland
Dänew *see* Galkynyş
Dangara *see* Danghara
Dangerous Archipelago *see* Tuamotu,
Îles
Danghara *123 E3 Rus.* Dangara.
SW Tajikistan
Danghe Nanshan *126 D3 mountain*
range W China
**Dang Raek, Phanom/Dangrek, Chaine
des** *see* Dângrêk, Chuôr Phnum
Chuor Phnum Dangrek *137 D5 var.*
Phanom Dang Raek, Phanom Dong
Rak, *Fr.* Chaîne des Dangrek. *mountain
range* Cambodia/Thailand
Dangriga *52 C1 prev.* Stann Creek.
Stann Creek, E Belize
Danish West Indies *see* Virgin Islands
(US)
Danli *52 D2* El Paraíso, S Honduras
Danmark *see* Denmark
Danmarksstraedet *see* Denmark Strait
Dannenberg *94 C3* Niedersachsen,
N Germany
Dannevirke *150 D4* Manawatu-
Wanganui, North Island, New Zealand
Dantzig *see* Gdańsk
Danube *81 E4 Bul.* Dunav, *Cz.* Dunaj,
Ger. Donau, *Hung.* Duna, *Rom.*
Dunărea. *river* C Europe
Danubian Plain *104 C2 Eng.* Danubian
Plain. *lowlands* N Bulgaria
Danubian Plain *see* Dunavska Ravnina
Danum *see* Doncaster
Danville *41 E5* Virginia, NE USA
Danxian/Dan Xian *see* Danzhou
Danzhou *128 C7 prev.* Danxian, Dan
Xian, Nada. Hainan, S China
Danzig *see* Gdańsk
Danziger Bucht *see* Danzig, Gulf of
Danzig, Gulf of *98 C2 var.* Gulf of
Gdańsk, *Ger.* Danziger Bucht, *Pol.*
Zatoka Gdańska, *Rus.* Gdan'skaya
Bukhta. *gulf* N Poland
Daqm *see* Duqm
Dar'ā *119 B5 var.* Der'a, *Fr.* Déraa.
Dar'ā, SW Syria
Darabani *108 C3* Botoşani,
NW Romania
Daraut-Kurgan *see* Daroot-Korgon
Dardanelles *116 A2 Eng.* Dardanelles.
strait NW Turkey
Dardanelles *see* Çanakkale Boğazı
Dardaneli *see* Çanakkale
Dar-el-Beida *see* Casablanca
Dar es Salaam *73 C7* Dar es Salaam,
E Tanzania
Darfield *151 C6* Canterbury, South
Island, New Zealand
Darfur *72 A4 var.* Darfur Massif.
cultural region W Sudan
Darfur Massif *see* Darfur
Darhan *127 E2* Darhan Uul, N Mongolia
Darién, Golfo del *see* Darien, Gulf of
Darien, Gulf of *58 A2 Sp.* Golfo del
Darién. *gulf* S Caribbean Sea

Darien, Isthmus of *see* Panama, Istmo de
Darién, Serranía del *53 H5 mountain
range* Colombia/Panama
Dario *see* Ciudad Darío
Dariorigum *see* Vannes
Darjeeling *see* Dārjiling
Dārjiling *135 F3 prev.* Darjeeling. West
Bengal, NE India
Darling River *149 C6 river* New South
Wales, SE Australia
Darlington *89 D5* N England, United
Kingdom
Darmstadt *95 B5* Hessen, SW Germany
Darnah *71 G2 var.* Dérna. NE Libya
Darnley, Cape *154 D2 cape* Antarctica
Daroca *93 E2* Aragón, NE Spain
Daroot-Korgon *123 F3 var.*
Daraut-Kurgan. Oshskaya Oblast',
SW Kyrgyzstan
Dartford *89 B8* SE England, United
Kingdom
Dartmoor *89 C7 moorland* SW England,
United Kingdom
Dartmouth *39 F4* Nova Scotia, SE Canada
Darvaza *see* Derweze, Turkmenistan
Darwin *146 D2 prev.* Palmerston, Port
Darwin. *territory capital* Northern
Territory, N Australia
Darwin, Isla *60 A4 island* Galápagos,
Galapagos Islands, W Ecuador
Dashhowuz *see* Daşoguz
Dashkawka *107 D6 Rus.* Dashkovka.
Mahilyowskaya Voblasts', E Belarus
Dashkovka *see* Dashkawka
Daşoguz *122 C2 Rus.* Dashkhovuz,
Turkm. Dashhowuz; *prev.* Tashauz.
Daşoguz Welaýaty, N Turkmenistan
Đa, Sông *see* Black River
Datong *128 C3 var.* Tatung, Ta-t'ung.
Shanxi, C China
Daugava *see* Western Dvina
Daugavpils *106 D4 Ger.* Dünaburg; *prev.*
Rus. Dvinsk. Daugvapils, SE Latvia
Daung Kyun *137 B6 island* S Burma
(Myanmar)
Dauphiné *91 D5 cultural region* E France
Dāvangere *132 C2* Karnātaka, W India
Davao *139 F3 off.* Davao City.
Mindanao, S Philippines
Davao City *see* Davao
Davao Gulf *139 F3 gulf* Mindanao,
S Philippines
Davenport *45 G3* Iowa, C USA
David *53 E5* Chiriquí, W Panama
Davie Ridge *141 A5 undersea ridge*
W Indian Ocean
Davis *154 D3 Australian research station*
Antarctica
Davis Sea *154 D3 sea* Antarctica
Davis Strait *82 B3 strait* Baffin Bay/
Labrador Sea
Dawei *137 B5 var.* Tavoy, Htawei.
Tanintharyi, S Burma (Myanmar)
Dawlat Qatar *see* Qatar
Dax *91 B6 var.* Ax; *anc.* Aquae Augustae,
Aquae Tarbellicae. Landes, SW France
Dayr az Zawr *118 D3 var.* Deir ez Zor.
Dayr az Zawr, E Syria
Dayton *40 C4* Ohio, N USA
Daytona Beach *43 E4* Florida, SE USA
De Aar *78 C5* Northern Cape, C South
Africa
Dead Sea *119 B6 var.* Bahret Lut, Lacus
Asphaltites, *Ar.* Al Baḥr al Mayyit,
Baḥrat Lūt, *Heb.* Yam HaMelaḥ. *salt
lake* Israel/Jordan
Deán Funes *64 C3* Córdoba, C Argentina
Death Valley *47 C7 valley* California,
W USA
Deatnu *see* Tana
Debar *101 D6 Ger.* Dibra, *Turk.* Debre.
W FYR Macedonia
De Behagle *see* Laï
Dęblin *99 D5* Podkarpackie, SE Poland
De Bildt *see* De Bilt
De Bilt *86 C3 var.* De Bildt. Utrecht,
C Netherlands
Dębno *98 B3* Zachodnio-pomorskie,
NW Poland
Debrecen *99 D6 Ger.* Debreczin, *Rom.*
Debreţin; *prev.* Debreczen. Hajdú-
Bihar, E Hungary
Debreczen/Debreczin *see* Debrecen
Debreţin *see* Debrecen
Decatur *42 C1* Alabama, S USA

Decatur *40 B4* Illinois, N USA
Deccan *134 D5 Hind.* Dakshin. *plateau*
C India
Děčín *98 B4 Ger.* Tetschen. Ústecký Kraj,
NW Czech Republic
Dedeagaç/Dedeagach *see* Alexandroúpoli
Dedemsvaart *86 E3* Overijssel,
E Netherlands
Dee *88 C3 river* NE Scotland, United
Kingdom
Deering *36 C2* Alaska, USA
Deés *see* Dej
Deggendorf *95 D6* Bayern, SE Germany
Değirmenlik *102 C5 Gk.* Kythréa.
N Cyprus
Deh Bīd *see* Şafāshahr
Dehli *see* Delhi
Deh Shū *122 D5 var.* Deshu. Helmand,
S Afghanistan
Deinze *87 B5* Oost-Vlaanderen,
NW Belgium
Deir ez Zor *see* Dayr az Zawr
Deirgeirt, Loch *see* Derg, Lough
Dej *108 B3 Hung.* Dés; *prev.* Deés. Cluj,
NW Romania
De Jouwer *see* Joure
Dekéleia *see* Dhekélia
Dékoa *76 C4* Kémo, C Central African
Republic
De Land *43 E4* Florida, SE USA
Delano *47 C7* California, W USA
Delārām *122 D5* Nīmrūz,
SW Afghanistan
Delaware *40 D4* Ohio, N USA
Delaware *41 F4 off.* State of Delaware,
also known as Blue Hen State, Diamond
State, First State. *state* NE USA
Delft *86 B4* Zuid-Holland,
W Netherlands
Delfzijl *86 E1* Groningen,
NE Netherlands
Delgo *72 B3* Northern, N Sudan
Delhi *134 D3 var.* Dehli, *Hind.* Dilli, *hist.*
Shahjahanabad. *union territory capital*
Delhi, N India
Delicias *50 D2 var.* Ciudad Delicias.
Chihuahua, N Mexico
Déli-Kárpátok *see* Carpaţii Meridionali
Delmenhorst *94 B3* Niedersachsen,
NW Germany
Del Rio *49 F4* Texas, SW USA
Deltona *43 E4* Florida, SE USA
Demba *77 D6* Kasai-Occidental, C Dem.
Rep. Congo
Dembia *76 D4* Mbomou, SE Central
African Republic
Demchok *126 A5 var.* Dêmqog. *disputed
region* China/India
Demerara Plain *56 C2 abyssal plain*
W Atlantic Ocean
Deming *48 C3* New Mexico, SW USA
Demmin *94 C2* Mecklenburg-
Vorpommern, NE Germany
Demopolis *42 C2* Alabama, S USA
Dêmqog *126 A5 var.* Demchok. China/
India
Denali *see* McKinley, Mount
Denau *see* Denov
Dender *87 B6 Fr.* Dendre. *river*
W Belgium
Dendre *see* Dender
Denekamp *86 E3* Overijssel,
E Netherlands
Den Haag *see* 's-Gravenhage
Denham *147 A5* Western Australia
Den Ham *86 E3* Overijssel, E Netherlands
Den Helder *86 C2* Noord-Holland,
NW Netherlands
Dénia *93 F4* País Valenciano, E Spain
Deniliquin *149 C7* New South Wales,
SE Australia
Denison *45 F3* Iowa, C USA
Denison *49 G2* Texas, SW USA
Denizli *116 B4* Denizli, SW Turkey
Denmark *85 A7 off.* Kingdom of
Denmark, *Dan.* Danmark; *anc.* Hafnia.
country N Europe

DENMARK
Northern Europe

Official name Kingdom of Denmark
Formation 950 / 1944
Capital Copenhagen
Population 5.5 million / 336 people
per sq mile (130 people per sq km) / 85%
Total area 16,639 sq. miles (43,094 sq. km)

DENMARK
(continued)

Languages Danish
Religions Evangelical Lutheran 89%,
Other 10%, Roman Catholic 1%
Ethnic mix Danish 96%, Other
(including Scandinavian and Turkish) 3%,
Faeroese and Inuit 1%
Government Parliamentary system
Currency Danish krone = 100 øre
Literacy rate 99%
Calorie consumption 3439 calories

Denmark, Kingdom of *see* Denmark
Denmark Strait *82 D4 var.*
Danmarksstraedet. *strait* Greenland/
Iceland
Dennery *55 F1* E Saint Lucia
Denov *123 E3 Rus.* Denau.
Surkhondaryo Viloyati, S Uzbekistan
Denpasar *138 D5 prev.* Paloe. Bali,
C Indonesia
Denton *49 G2* Texas, SW USA
D'Entrecasteaux Islands *144 B3 island
group* SE Papua New Guinea
Denver *44 D4 state capital* Colorado,
C USA
Der'a/Derá/Déraa *see* Dar'ā
Dera Ghāzi Khān *134 C2 var.* Dera
Ghāzikhān. Punjab, C Pakistan
Dera Ghāzikhān *see* Dera Ghāzi Khān
Đeravica *101 D5 mountain* S Serbia
Derbent *111 B8* Respublika Dagestan,
SW Russian Federation
Derby *89 D6* C England, United
Kingdom
Dereli *see* Gönnoi
Dergachi *see* Derhachi
Derg, Lough *89 A6 Ir.* Loch Deirgeirt.
lake W Ireland
Derhachi *109 G2 Rus.* Dergachi.
Kharkivs'ka Oblast', E Ukraine
De Ridder *42 A3* Louisiana, S USA
Dérna *see* Darnah
Derry *see* Londonderry
Dertosa *see* Tortosa
Derventa *100 B3* Republika Srpska,
N Bosnia and Herzegovina
Derweze *122 C2 Rus.* Darvaza. Ahal
Welaýaty, C Turkmenistan
Dés *see* Dej
Deschutes River *46 B3 river* Oregon,
NW USA
Desë *72 C4 var.* Desse, It. Dessie. Āmara,
N Ethiopia
Deseado, Río *65 B7 river* S Argentina
Desertas, Ilhas *70 A2 island group*
Madeira, Portugal, NE Atlantic Ocean
Deshu *see* Deh Shū
Des Moines *45 F3 state capital* Iowa,
C USA
Desna *109 E2 river* Russian Federation/
Ukraine
Dessau *94 C4* Sachsen-Anhalt,
E Germany
Desse *see* Desë
Dessie *see* Desë
Destêrro *see* Florianópolis
Detroit *40 D3* Michigan, N USA
Detroit Lakes *45 F2* Minnesota, N USA
Deurne *87 D5* Noord-Brabant,
SE Netherlands
Deutschendorf *see* Poprad
Deutsch-Eylau *see* Iława
Deutsch Krone *see* Wałcz
**Deutschland/Deutschland,
Bundesrepublik** *see* Germany
Deutsch-Südwestafrika *see* Namibia
Deva *108 B4 Ger.* Diemrich, *Hung.* Déva.
Hunedoara, W Romania
Déva *see* Deva
Deva *see* Chester
Devana Castra *see* Chester
Devdelija *see* Gevgelija
Deventer *86 D3* Overijssel, E Netherlands
Devils Lake *45 E1* North Dakota, N USA
Devoll *see* Devollit, Lumi i
Devollit, Lumi i *101 D6 var.* Devoll.
river SE Albania
Devon Island *37 F2 prev.* North Devon
Island. *island* Parry Islands, Nunavut,
NE Canada
Devonport *149 C8* Tasmania,
SE Australia

Devrek *116 C2* Zonguldak, N Turkey
Dexter *45 H5* Missouri, C USA
Deynau *see* Galkynyş
Dezfūl *120 C3 var.* Dizful. Khūzestān,
  SW Iran
Dezhou *128 D4* Shandong, E China
Dhaka *135 G4 prev.* Dacca. *country
  capital* (Bangladesh) (Bangladesh)
  Dhaka, C Bangladesh
Dhanbād *135 F4* Jhārkhand, NE India
Dhekélia *102 C5 Eng.* Dhekelia, *Gk.*
  Dekéleia. *UK air base* SE Cyprus
  see Dhekélia
Dhidhimótikhon *see* Didymóteicho
Dhíkti Ori *see* Dikti
Dhodhekánisos *see* Dodekánisa
Dhomokós *see* Domokós
Dhráma *see* Dráma
Dhrepanon, Akrotírio *see* Drépano,
  Akrotírio
Dhún na nGall, Bá *see* Donegal Bay
Dhuusa Marreeb *73 E5 var.* Dusa
  Marreb, *It.* Dusa Mareb. Galguduud,
  C Somalia
Diakovár *see* Ðakovo
Diamantina, Chapada *63 F3 mountain
  range* E Brazil
Diamantina Fracture Zone *141 E6
  tectonic feature* E Indian Ocean
Diamond State *see* Delaware
Diarbekr *see* Diyarbakır
Dibio *see* Dijon
Dibra *see* Debar
Dibrugarh *135 H3* Assam, NE India
Dickinson *44 D2* North Dakota, N USA
Dicle *see* Tigris
Didimótiho *see* Didymóteicho
Didymóteicho *104 D3 var.*
  Dhidhimótikhon, Didimotiho.
  Anatolikí Makedonía kai Thráki,
  NE Greece
Diedenhofen *see* Thionville
Diekirch *87 D7* Diekirch, C Luxembourg
Diemrich *see* Deva
Ðiên Biên *136 D3 var.* Bien Bien, Dien
  Bien Phu. Lai Châu, N Vietnam
Dien Bien Phu *see* Ðiên Biên
Diepenbeek *87 D6* Limburg, NE Belgium
Diepholz *94 B3* Niedersachsen,
  NW Germany
Dieppe *90 C2* Seine-Maritime, N France
Dieren *86 D4* Gelderland, E Netherlands
Differdange *87 D8* Luxembourg,
  SW Luxembourg
Digne *91 D6 var.* Digne-les-Bains.
  Alpes-de-Haute-Provence, SE France
Digne-les-Bains *see* Digne
Digoel *see* Digul, Sungai
Digoin *90 C4* Saône-et-Loire, C France
Digul, Sungai *139 H5 prev.* Digoel. *river*
  Papua, E Indonesia
Dihang *see* Brahmaputra
Dijlah *see* Tigris
Dijon *90 D4 anc.* Dibio. Côte d'Or,
  C France
Dikhil *72 D4* SW Djibouti
Dikson *114 D2* Taymyrskiy (Dolgano-
  Nenetskiy) Avtonomnyy Okrug,
  N Russian Federation
Dikti *105 D8 var.* Dhíkti Ori.
  mountain range Kríti, Greece,
  E Mediterranean Sea
Dili *139 F5 var.* Dilli, Dilly. *country
  capital* (East Timor) (East Timor)
  N East Timor
Dilia *75 G3 var.* Dillia. *river* SE Niger
Di Linh *137 E6* Lâm Ðông, S Vietnam
Dilli *see* Dili, East Timor
Dilli *see* Delhi, India
Dillia *see* Dilia
Dilling *72 B4 var.* Ad Dalanj. Southern
  Kordofan, C Sudan
Dillon *44 B2* Montana, NW USA
Dilly *see* Dili
Dilolo *77 D7* Katanga, S Dem. Rep. Congo
Dimashq *119 B5 var.* Ash Shām, Esh
  Sham, *Eng.* Damascus, *Fr.* Damas,
  It. Damasco. *country capital* (Syria)
  Dimashq, SW Syria
Dimitrovgrad *104 D3* Khaskovo,
  S Bulgaria
Dimitrovgrad *111 C6 prev.* Caribrod.
  Serbia, SE Serbia
Dimitrovo *see* Pernik
Dimovo *104 B1* Vidin, NW Bulgaria
Dinajpur *135 F3* Rajshahi,
  NW Bangladesh

Dinan *90 B3* Côtes d'Armor, NW France
Dinant *87 C7* Namur, S Belgium
Dinar *116 B4* Afyon, SW Turkey
Dinara *see* Dinaric Alps
Dinaric Alps *100 C4 var.* Dinara.
  mountain range Bosnia and
  Herzegovina/Croatia
Dindigul *132 C3* Tamil Nādu, SE India
Dingle Bay *89 A6 Ir.* Bá an Daingin. *bay*
  SW Ireland
Dinguiraye *74 C4* N Guinea
Diourbel *74 B3* W Senegal
Dirē Dawa *73 D5* Dirē Dawa, E Ethiopia
Dirē Dawa *73 D5* Dirē Dawa, E Ethiopia
Dirk Hartog Island *147 A5 island*
  Western Australia
Dirschau *see* Tczew
Disappointment, Lake *146 C4 salt lake*
  Western Australia
Discovery Bay *54 B4* Middlesex,
  Jamaica, Greater Antilles, C Jamaica
Disko Bugt *see* Qeqertarsuup Tunua
Dispur *135 G3 state capital* Assam,
  NE India
Divinópolis *63 F4* Minas Gerais, SE Brazil
Divo *74 D5* S Côte d'Ivoire
Divodurum Mediomatricum *see* Metz
Diyarbakır *117 E4 var.* Diarbekr; *anc.*
  Amida. Diyarbakır, SE Turkey
Dizful *see* Dezfūl
Djailolo *see* Halmahera, Pulau
Djajapura *see* Jayapura
Djakarta *see* Jakarta
Djakovo *see* Ðakovo
Djambala *77 B6* Plateaux, C Congo
Djambi *see* Jambi
Djambi *see* Hari, Batang
Djanet *71 E4 prev.* Fort Charlet.
  SE Algeria
Djéblé *see* Jablah
Djelfa *70 D2 var.* El Djelfa. N Algeria
Djéma *76 D4* Haut-Mbomou, E Central
  African Republic
Djember *see* Jember
Djérablous *see* Jarābulus
Djerba *71 F2 var.* Djerba, Jazīrat Jarbah.
  island E Tunisia
Djerba *see* Jerba, Île de
Djérem *76 B4 river* C Cameroon
Djevdjelija *see* Gevgelija
Djibouti *72 D4 var.* Jibuti. *country
  capital* (Djibouti) (Djibouti) E Djibouti
Djibouti *72 D4 off.* Republic of Djibouti,
  var. Jibuti; *prev.* French Somaliland,
  French Territory of the Afars and
  Issas, *Fr.* Côte Française des Somalis,
  Territoire Français des Afars et des
  Issas. *country* E Africa

DJIBOUTI
East Africa

Official name Republic of Djibouti
Formation 1977 / 1977
Capital Djibouti
Population 496,374 / 555 people
  per sq mile (21 people per sq km) / 84%
Total area 8494 sq. miles (22,000 sq. km)
Languages Arabic*, French*, Somali, Afar
Religions Muslim (mainly Sunni) 94%,
  Christian 6%
Ethnic mix Issa 60%, Afar 35%, Other 5%
Government Presidential system
Currency Djibouti franc = 100 centimes
Literacy rate 66%
Calorie consumption 2220 calories

Djibouti, Republic of *see* Djibouti
Djokjakarta *see* Yogyakarta
Djourab, Erg du *76 C2 desert* N Chad
Djúpivogur *83 E5* Austurland,
  SE Iceland
Dmitriyevsk *see* Makiyivka
Dnepr *see* Dnieper
Dneprodzerzhinsk *see* Romaniv
**Dneprodzerzhinskoye
  Vodokhranilishche** *see*
  Dniprodzerzhyns'ke Vodoskhovyshche
Dnepropetrovsk *see* Dnipropetrovs'k
Dneprorudnoye *see* Dniprorudne
Dnestr *see* Dniester
Dnieper *81 F4 Bel.* Dnyapro, *Rus.* Dnepr,
  Ukr. Dnipro. *river* E Europe
Dnieper Lowland *109 E2 Bel.*
  Prydnyaprowskaya Nizina, *Ukr.*
  Prydniprovs'ka Nyzovyna. *lowlands*
  Belarus/Ukraine

Dniester *81 E4 Rom.* Nistru, *Rus.*
  Dnestr, *Ukr.* Dnister; *anc.* Tyras. *river*
  Moldova/Ukraine
Dnipro *see* Dnieper
Dniprodzerzhyns'k *see* Romaniv
Dniprodzerzhyns'ke Vodoskhovyshche
  109 F3. Rus. Dneprodzerzhinskoye
  Vodokhranilishche. *reservoir*
  C Ukraine
Dnipropetrovs'k *109 F3 Rus.*
  Dnepropetrovsk; *prev.* Yekaterinoslav.
  Dnipropetrovs'ka Oblast', E Ukraine
Dniprorudne *109 F3 Rus.*
  Dneprorudnoye. Zaporiz'ka Oblast',
  SE Ukraine
Dnister *see* Dniester
Dnyapro *see* Dnieper
Doba *76 C4* Logone-Oriental, S Chad
Döbeln *94 D4* Sachsen, E Germany
Doberai Peninsula *139 G4 Dut.*
  Vogelkop. *peninsula* Papua,
  E Indonesia
Doboj *100 C3* Republiks Srpska,
  N Bosnia and Herzegovina
Dobre Miasto *98 D2 Ger.* Guttstadt.
  Warmińsko-mazurskie, NE Poland
Dobrich *104 E1 Rom.* Bazargic; *prev.*
  Tolbukhin. Dobrich, NE Bulgaria
Dobrush *107 D7* Homyel'skaya
  Voblasts', SE Belarus
Dobryn' *see* Dabryn'
Dodecanese *105 D6 var.* Nóties
  Sporádes, *Eng.* Dodecanese; *prev.*
  Dhodhekánisos, Dodekanisos. *island
  group* SE Greece
Dodecanese *see* Dodekánisa
Dodekanisos *see* Dodekánisa
Dodge City *45 E5* Kansas, C USA
Dodoma *69 D5 country capital*
  (Tanzania) (Tanzania) Dodoma,
  C Tanzania
Dogana *96 E1* NE San Marino Europe
Dogo *131 B6 island* Oki-shotō, SW Japan
Dogondoutchi *75 F3* Dosso, SW Niger
Dogrular *see* Pravda
Doğubayazıt *117 F3* Ağrı, E Turkey
Doğu Karadeniz Dağları *117 E3 var.*
  Anadolu Dağları. *mountain range*
  NE Turkey
Doha *see* Ad Dawḥah
Doire *see* Londonderry
Dokkum *86 D1* Friesland, N Netherlands
Dokuchayevs'k *109 G3 var.*
  Dokuchayevsk. Donets'ka Oblast',
  SE Ukraine
Dokuchayevsk *see* Dokuchayevs'k
Doldrums Fracture Zone *66 C4 fracture
  zone* W Atlantic Ocean
Dôle *90 D4* Jura, E France
Dolina *see* Dolyna
Dolinskaya *see* Dolyns'ka
Dolisie *77 B6 prev.* Loubomo. Niari,
  S Congo
Dolomites *96 C1 var.* Dolomiti, *Eng.*
  Dolomites. *mountain range* NE Italy
Dolomites/Dolomiti *see* Dolomitiche,
  Alpi
Dolores *64 D4* Buenos Aires, E Argentina
Dolores *52 B1* Petén, N Guatemala
Dolores *64 D4* Soriano, SW Uruguay
Dolores Hidalgo *51 E4 var.* Ciudad
  de Dolores Hidalgo. Guanajuato,
  C Mexico
Dolyna *108 B2 Rus.* Dolina. Ivano-
  Frankivs'ka Oblast', W Ukraine
Dolyns'ka *109 F3 Rus.* Dolinskaya.
  Kirovohrads'ka Oblast', S Ukraine
Domachëvo/Domachevo *see* Damachava
Dombås *85 B5* Oppland, S Norway
Domel Island *see* Letsôk-aw Kyun
Domesnes, Cape *see* Kolkasrags
Domeyko *64 B3* Atacama, N Chile
Dominica *55 H4 off.* Commonwealth of
  Dominica. *country* E West Indies

DOMINICA
West Indies

Official name Commonwealth
  of Dominica
Formation 1978 / 1978
Capital Roseau
Population 72,386 / 250 people
  per sq mile (97 people per sq km) / 72%
Total area 291 sq. miles (754 sq. km)
Languages English*, French Creole
Religions Roman Catholic 77%, Dominica

DOMINICA
(continued)

Protestant 15%, Other 8%
Ethnic mix Black 87%, Mixed race 9%,
  Carib 3%, Other 1%
Government Parliamentary system
Currency Eastern Caribbean dollar
  = 100 cents
Literacy rate 88%
Calorie consumption 2763 calories

Dominica Channel *see* Martinique
  Passage
Dominica, Commonwealth of *see*
  Dominica
Dominican Republic *55 E2 country*
  C West Indies

DOMINICAN REPUBLIC
West Indies

Official name Dominican Republic
Formation 1865 / 1865
Capital Santo Domingo
Population 9.1 million / 487 people
  per sq mile (188 people per sq km) / 60%
Total area 18,679 sq. miles (48,380 sq. km)
Languages Spanish*, French Creole
Religions Roman Catholic 92%,
  Other and nonreligious 8%
Ethnic mix Mixed race 75%, White 15%,
  Black 10%
Government Presidential system
Currency Dominican Republic peso
  = 100 centavos
Literacy rate 87%
Calorie consumption 2347 calories

Domokós *105 B5 var.* Dhomokós. Stereá
  Ellás, C Greece
Don *111 B6 var.* Duna, Tanais. *river*
  SW Russian Federation
Donau *see* Danube
Donauwörth *95 C6* Bayern, S Germany
Don Benito *92 C3* Extremadura,
  W Spain
Doncaster *89 D5 anc.* Danum.
  N England, United Kingdom
Dondo *78 B1* Cuanza Norte, NW Angola
Donegal *89 B5 Ir.* Dún na nGall.
  Donegal, NW Ireland
Donegal Bay *89 A5 Ir.* Bá Dhún na nGall.
  bay NW Ireland
Donets *109 G2 river* Russian Federation/
  Ukraine
Donets'k *109 G3 Rus.* Donetsk; *prev.*
  Stalino. Donets'ka Oblast', E Ukraine
Dongfang *128 B7 var.* Basuo. Hainan,
  S China
Dongguan *128 C6* Guangdong, S China
Ðông Ha *136 E4* Quang Tri, C Vietnam
Dong Hai *see* East China Sea
Ðông Hoi *136 D4* Quang Binh,
  C Vietnam
Dongliao *see* Liaoyuan
Dongola *72 B3 var.* Donqola, Dunqulah.
  Northern, N Sudan
Dongou *77 C5* Likouala, NE Congo
Dong Rak, Phanom *see* Dângrêk, Chuŏr
  Phnum
Dongting Hu *128 C5 var.* Tung-t'ing
  Hu. *lake* S China
Donostia-San Sebastián *93 E1* País
  Vasco, N Spain
Donqola *see* Dongola
Doolow *73 D5* Sumalē, E Ethiopia
Doornik *see* Tournai
Door Peninsula *40 C2 peninsula*
  Wisconsin, N USA
Dooxo Nugaaleed *73 E5 var.* Nogal
  Valley. *valley* E Somalia
Dordogne *91 B5 cultural region*
  SW France
Dordogne *91 B5 river* W France
Dordrecht *86 C4 var.* Dordt, Dort.
  Zuid-Holland, SW Netherlands
Dordt *see* Dordrecht
Dorohoi *108 C3* Botoşani, NE Romania
Dorotea *84 C4* Västerbotten, N Sweden
Dorpat *see* Tartu
Dorre Island *147 A5 island* Western
  Australia
Dort *see* Dordrecht
Dortmund *94 A4* Nordrhein-Westfalen,
  W Germany

Dos Hermanas 92 C4 Andalucía, S Spain
Dospad Dagh see Rhodope Mountains
Dospat 104 C3 Smolyan, S Bulgaria
Dothan 42 D3 Alabama, S USA
Dotnuva 106 B4 Kaunas, C Lithuania
Douai 90 C2 prev. Douay; anc. Duacum. Nord, N France
Douala 77 A5 var. Duala. Littoral, W Cameroon
Douay see Douai
Douglas 89 C5 dependent territory capital (Isle of Man) E Isle of Man
Douglas 48 C3 Arizona, SW USA
Douglas 44 D3 Wyoming, C USA
Douma see Dūmā
Douro see Duero
Douvres see Dover
Dover 89 E7 Fr. Douvres, Lat. Dubris Portus. SE England, United Kingdom
Dover 41 F4 state capital Delaware, NE USA
Dover, Strait of 90 C2 var. Straits of Dover, Fr. Pas de Calais. strait England, United Kingdom/France
Dover, Straits of see Dover, Strait of
Dovrefjell 85 B5 plateau S Norway
Downpatrick 89 B5 Ir. Dún Pádraig. SE Northern Ireland, United Kingdom
Dozen 131 B6 island Oki-shotō, SW Japan
Drâa, Hamada du see Dra, Hamada du
Dra, Hamada du 70 C3 var. Hamada du Drâa, Haut Plateau du Dra. plateau W Algeria
Dra, Haut Plateau du see Dra, Hamada du
Drahichyn 107 B6 Pol. Drohiczyn Poleski, Rus. Drogichin. Brestskaya Voblasts', SW Belarus
Drakensberg 78 D5 mountain range Lesotho/South Africa
Drake Passage 57 B8 passage Atlantic Ocean/Pacific Ocean
Dralfa 104 D2 Türgovishte, N Bulgaria
Dráma 104 C3 var. Dhráma. Anatolikí Makedonía kai Thráki, NE Greece
Dramburg see Drawsko Pomorskie
Drammen 85 B6 Buskerud, S Norway
Drau see Drava
Drava 100 C3 var. Drau, Drave, Hung. Dráva. river C Europe
Dráva/Drave see Drau/Drava
Drawsko Pomorskie 98 B3 Ger. Dramburg. Zachodnio-pomorskie, NW Poland
Drépano, Akrotírio 104 C4 var. Akrotírio Dhrepanon. headland N Greece
Drepanum see Trapani
Dresden 94 D4 Sachsen, E Germany
Drin see Drinit, Lumi i
Drina 100 C3 river Bosnia and Herzegovina/Serbia
Drinit, Lumi i 101 D5 var. Drin. river NW Albania
Drinit të Zi, Lumi i see Black Drin
Drissa see Drysa
Drobeta-Turnu Severin 108 B5 prev. Turnu Severin. Mehedinți, SW Romania
Drogheda 89 B5 Ir. Droichead Átha. NE Ireland
Drogichin see Drahichyn
Drogobych see Drohobych
Drohiczyn Poleski see Drahichyn
Drohobych 108 B2 Pol. Drohobycz, Rus. Drogobych. L'vivs'ka Oblast', NW Ukraine
Drohobycz see Drohobych
Droichead Átha see Drogheda
Drôme 91 D5 cultural region E France
Dronning Maud Land 154 B2 physical region Antarctica
Drontheim see Trondheim
Drug see Durg
Druk-yul see Bhutan
Drummondville 39 E4 Québec, SE Canada
Druskieniki see Druskininkai
Druskininkai 107 B5 Pol. Druskienniki. Alytus, S Lithuania
Dryden 38 B3 Ontario, C Canada

Drysa 107 D5 Rus. Drissa. river N Belarus
Duacum see Douai
Duala see Douala
Dubai see Dubayy
Dubāsari 108 D3 Rus. Dubossary. NE Moldova
Dubawnt 37 F4 river Nunavut, NW Canada
Dubayy 120 D4 Eng. Dubai. Dubayy, NE United Arab Emirates
Dubbo 149 D6 New South Wales, SE Australia
Dublin 89 B5 Ir. Baile Átha Cliath; anc. Eblana. country capital (Ireland) (Ireland) Dublin, E Ireland
Dublin 43 E2 Georgia, SE USA
Dubno 108 C2 Rivnens'ka Oblast', NW Ukraine
Dubossary see Dubāsari
Dubris Portus see Dover
Dubrovnik 101 B5 It. Ragusa. Dubrovnik-Neretva, SE Croatia
Dubuque 45 G3 Iowa, C USA
Dudelange 87 D8 var. Forge du Sud, Ger. Dudelingen. Luxembourg, S Luxembourg
Dudelingen see Dudelange
Duero 92 D2 Port. Douro. river Portugal/Spain
Duesseldorf see Düsseldorf
Duffel 87 C5 Antwerpen, C Belgium
Dugi Otok 100 A4 var. Isola Grossa, It. Isola Lunga. island W Croatia
Duinekerke see Dunkerque
Duisburg 94 A4 prev. Duisburg-Hamborn. Nordrhein-Westfalen, W Germany
Duisburg-Hamborn see Duisburg
Duiven 86 D4 Gelderland, E Netherlands
Duk Faiwil 73 B5 Jonglei, SE Sudan
Dulan 126 D4 var. Qagan Us. Qinghai, C China
Dulce, Golfo 53 E5 gulf S Costa Rica
Dulce, Golfo see Izabal, Lago de
Dülmen 94 A4 Nordrhein-Westfalen, W Germany
Dulovo 104 E1 Silistra, NE Bulgaria
Duluth 45 G2 Minnesota, N USA
Dūmā 119 B5 Fr. Douma. Dimashq, SW Syria
Dumas 49 E1 Texas, SW USA
Dumfries 88 C4 S Scotland, United Kingdom
Dumont d'Urville 154 C4 French research station Antarctica
Dumyât 72 B1 var. Dumyāt, Eng. Damietta. N Egypt
Duna see Danube, C Europe
Dúna see Western Dvina
Duna see Don, Russian Federation
Dünaburg see Daugavpils
Dunaj see Wien, C Europe
Dunaj see Danube, C Europe
Dunapentele see Dunaújváros
Dunărea see Danube
Dunaújváros 99 C7 prev. Dunapentele, Sztálinváros. Fejér, C Hungary
Dunav see Danube
Duncan 49 G2 Oklahoma, C USA
Dundalk 89 B5 Ir. Dún Dealgan. Louth, NE Ireland
Dún Dealgan see Dundalk
Dundee 78 D4 KwaZulu/Natal, E South Africa
Dundee 88 C4 E Scotland, United Kingdom
Dunedin 151 B7 Otago, South Island, New Zealand
Dunfermline 88 C4 C Scotland, United Kingdom
Dungu 77 E5 Orientale, NE Dem. Rep. Congo
Dungun 138 B3 var. Kuala Dungun. Terengganu, Peninsular Malaysia
Dunholme see Durham
Dunkerque 90 C2 Eng. Dunkirk, Flem. Duinekerke; prev. Dunquerque. Nord, N France
Dunkirk see Dunkerque
Dún Laoghaire 89 B6 Eng. Dunleary; prev. Kingstown. E Ireland
Dunleary see Dún Laoghaire
Dún Pádraig see Downpatrick
Dunquerque see Dunkerque
Dunqulah see Dongola

Dupnitsa 104 C2 prev. Marek, Stanke Dimitrov. Kyustendil, W Bulgaria
Duqm 121 E5 var. Daqm. E Oman
Durance 91 D6 river SE France
Durango 50 D3 var. Victoria de Durango. Durango, W Mexico
Durango 44 C5 Colorado, C USA
Durankulak 104 E1 Rom. Răcari; prev. Blatnitsa, Duranulac. Dobrich, NE Bulgaria
Durant 49 G2 Oklahoma, C USA
Duranulac see Durankulak
Durazzo see Durrës
Durban 78 D4 var. Port Natal. KwaZulu/Natal, E South Africa
Durbe 106 B3 Ger. Durben. Liepāja, W Latvia
Durben see Durbe
Durg 135 E4 prev. Drug. Chhattisgarh, C India
Durham 89 D5 hist. Dunholme. N England, United Kingdom
Durham 43 F1 North Carolina, SE USA
Durocortorum see Reims
Durostorum see Silistra
Durrës 101 C6 var. Durrësi, Dursi, It. Durazzo, SCr. Drač, Turk. Draç. Durrës, W Albania
Durrësi see Durrës
Dursi see Durrës
Durüz, Jabal ad 119 C5 mountain SW Syria
D'Urville Island 150 C4 island C New Zealand
Dusa Mareb/Dusa Marreb see Dhuusa Marreeb
Dushanbe 123 E3 var. Dyushambe; prev. Stalinabad, Taj. Stalinobod. country capital (Tajikistan) (Tajikistan) W Tajikistan
Düsseldorf 94 A4 var. Duesseldorf. Nordrhein-Westfalen, W Germany
Düsti 123 E3 Rus. Dusti. SW Tajikistan
Dutch East Indies see Indonesia
Dutch Guiana see Suriname
Dutch Harbor 36 B3 Unalaska Island, Alaska, USA
Dutch New Guinea see Papua
Dutch West Indies see Netherlands Antilles
Duzdab see Zāhedān
Dvina Bay see Chëshskaya Guba
Dvinsk see Daugavpils
Dyanev see Galkynyş
Dyersburg 42 C1 Tennessee, S USA
Dyushambe see Dushanbe
Dza Chu see Mekong
Dzaudzhikau see Vladikavkaz
Dzerzhinsk 111 C5 Nizhegorodskaya Oblast', W Russian Federation
Dzerzhinskiy see Nar'yan-Mar
Dzhalal-Abad 123 F2 Kir. Jalal-Abad. Dzhalal-Abadskaya Oblast', W Kyrgyzstan
Dzhambul see Taraz
Dzhankoy 109 F4 Respublika Krym, S Ukraine
Dzharkurgan see Jarqo'rg'on
Dzhelandy 123 F3 SE Tajikistan
Dzhergalan 123 G2 Kir. Jyrgalan. Issyk-Kul'skaya Oblast', NE Kyrgyzstan
Dzhezkazgan see Zhezkazgan
Dzhizak see Jizzax
Dzhugdzhur, Khrebet 115 G3 mountain range E Russian Federation
Dzhusaly 114 B4 Kaz. Zhosaly. Kzylorda, SW Kazakhstan
Działdowo 98 D3 Warmińsko-Mazurskie, C Poland
Dzuunmod 127 E2 Töv, C Mongolia
Dzvina see Western Dvina

Eagle Pass 49 F4 Texas, SW USA
East Açores Fracture Zone see East Azores Fracture Zone
East Antarctica 154 C3 var. Greater Antarctica. physical region Antarctica
East Australian Basin see Tasman Basin
East Azores Fracture Zone 80 B4 var. East Açores Fracture Zone. tectonic feature E Atlantic Ocean

Eastbourne 89 E7 SE England, United Kingdom
East Cape 150 E3 headland North Island, New Zealand
East China Sea 125 E2 Chin. Dong Hai. sea W Pacific Ocean
Easter Fracture Zone 153 G4 tectonic feature E Pacific Ocean
Easter Island 153 F4 var. Rapa Nui, Easter Island. island E Pacific Ocean
Easter Island see Pascua, Isla de
Eastern Desert 68 D3 var. Aş Şaḩrā' ash Sharqiyah, Eng. Arabian Desert, Eastern Desert. desert E Egypt
Eastern Desert see Sahara el Sharqiya
Eastern Ghats 124 B3 mountain range SE India
Eastern Sayans 115 E4 Mong. Dzüün Soyonï Nuruu, Rus. Vostochnyy Sayan. mountain range Mongolia/Russian Federation
Eastern Sierra Madre see Madre Oriental, Sierra
East Falkland 65 D8 var. Isla Soledad. island E Falkland Islands
East Frisian Islands 94 A3 Eng. East Frisian Islands. island group NW Germany
East Frisian Islands see Ostfriesische Inseln
East Grand Forks 45 E1 Minnesota, N USA
East Indiaman Ridge 141 D6 undersea ridge E Indian Ocean
East Indies 152 A3 island group SE Asia
East Kilbride 88 C4 S Scotland, United Kingdom
East Korea Bay 129 E3 bay E North Korea
Eastleigh 89 D7 S England, United Kingdom
East London 78 D5 Afr. Oos-Londen; prev. Emonti, Port Rex. Eastern Cape, S South Africa
Eastmain 38 D3 river Québec, C Canada
East Mariana Basin 142 B1 undersea basin W Pacific Ocean
East Novaya Zemlya Trough 112 C1 var. Novaya Zemlya Trough. trough W Kara Sea
East Pacific Rise 153 F4 undersea rise E Pacific Ocean
East Saint Louis 40 B4 Illinois, N USA
East Scotia Basin 67 C7 undersea basin SE Scotia Sea
East Sea 130 A4 var. Sea of Japan, Rus. Yapanskoye More. Sea NW Pacific Ocean
East Siberian Sea 115 F1 Eng. East Siberian Sea. sea Arctic Ocean
East Siberian Sea see Vostochno-Sibirskoye More
East Timor 139 F5 var. Loro Sae; prev. Portuguese Timor, Timor Timur. country S Indonesia

EAST TIMOR
Southeast Asia
Official name Democratic Republic of Timor-Leste
Formation 2002 / 2002
Capital Dili
Population 1.1 million / 192 people per sq mile (74 people per sq km) / 8%
Total area 5756 sq. miles (14,874 sq. km)
Languages Tetum (Portuguese/Austronesian)*, Bahasa Indonesia, and Portuguese*
Religions Roman Catholic 95%, Other (including Muslim and Protestant) 5%
Government Parliamentary system
Currency US dollar = 100 cents
Literacy rate 59%
Calorie consumption 2806 calories

Eau Claire 40 A2 Wisconsin, N USA
Eau Claire, Lac à l' see St. Clair, Lake
Eauripik Rise 142 B2 undersea rise W Pacific Ocean
Ebensee 95 D6 Oberösterreich, N Austria
Eberswalde-Finow 94 D3 Brandenburg, E Germany
Ebetsu 130 D2 var. Ebetu. Hokkaidō, NE Japan

Ebetu see Ebetsu
Eblana see Dublin
Ebolowa 77 A5 Sud, S Cameroon
Ebon Atoll 144 D2 var. Epoon. atoll
Ralik Chain, S Marshall Islands
Ebora see Évora
Eboracum see York
Ebro 93 E2 river NE Spain
Eburacum see York
Ebusus see Eivissa
Ebusus see Eivissa
Ebusus see Eivissa
Ecbatana see Hamadān
Ech Cheliff/Ech Chlef see Chlef
Echo Bay 37 E3 Northwest Territories,
NW Canada
Echt 87 D5 Limburg, SE Netherlands
Ecija 92 D4 anc. Astigi. Andalucía,
SW Spain
Eckengraf see Viesīte
Ecuador 60 B1 off. Republic of Ecuador.
country NW South America

ECUADOR
South America

Official name Republic of Ecuador
Formation 1830 / 1942
Capital Quito
Population 13.6 million / 127 people
per sq mile (49 people per sq km) / 62%
Total area 109,483 sq. miles
(283,560 sq. km)
Languages Spanish*, Quechua,
other Amerindian languages
Religions Roman Catholic 93%,
Protestant, Jewish, and other 7%
Ethnic mix Mestizo 55%, Amerindian 25%,
White 10%, Black 10%
Government Presidential system
Currency US dollar = 100 cents
Literacy rate 91%
Calorie consumption 2754 calories

Ecuador, Republic of see Ecuador
Ed Da'ein 72 A4 Southern Darfur,
W Sudan
Ed Damazin 72 C4 var. Ad Damazin.
Blue Nile, E Sudan
Ed Damer 72 C3 var. Ad Dāmir, Ad
Damar. River Nile, NE Sudan
Ed Debba 72 B3 Northern, N Sudan
Ede 86 D4 Gelderland, C Netherlands
Ede 75 F5 Osun, SW Nigeria
Edéa 77 A5 Littoral, SW Cameroon
Edessa see Şanlıurfa
Edfu see Idfū
Edgeøya 83 G2 island S Svalbard
Edgware 89 A7 Harrow, SE England,
United Kingdom
Edinburg 49 G5 Texas, SW USA
Edinburgh 88 C4 national capital
S Scotland, United Kingdom
Edingen see Enghien
Edirne 116 A2 Eng. Adrianople; anc.
Adrianopolis, Hadrianopolis. Edirne,
NW Turkey
Edmonds 46 B2 Washington, NW USA
Edmonton 37 E5 province capital
Alberta, SW Canada
Edmundston 39 F4 New Brunswick,
SE Canada
Edna 49 G4 Texas, SW USA
Edolo 96 B1 Lombardia, N Italy
Edremit 116 A3 Balıkesir, NW Turkey
Edward, Lake 77 E5 var. Albert Edward
Nyanza, Edward Nyanza, Lac Idi
Amin, Lake Rutanzige. lake Uganda/
Dem. Rep. Congo
Edward Nyanza see Edward, Lake
Edwards Plateau 49 F3 plain Texas,
SW USA
Edzo 53 E4 prev. Rae-Edzo. Northwest
Territories, NW Canada
Eeklo 87 B5 var. Eekloo. Oost-
Vlaanderen, NW Belgium
Eekloo see Eeklo
Eems see Ems
Eersel 87 C5 Noord-Brabant,
S Netherlands
Eesti Vabariik see Estonia
Efate 144 D4 var. Efate, Fr. Vaté; prev.
Sandwich Island. island C Vanuatu
Efate see Efate
Effingham 40 B4 Illinois, N USA
Eforie Sud 108 D5 Constanţa, E Romania
Egadi Is. 97 B7 island group S Italy

Ege Denizi see Aegean Sea
Eger 99 D6 Ger. Erlau. Heves,
NE Hungary
Eger see Cheb, Czech Republic
Egeria Fracture Zone 141 C5 tectonic
feature W Indian Ocean
Éghezèe 87 C6 Namur, C Belgium
Egina see Aígina
Egio see Aígio
Egmont see Taranaki, Mount
Egmont, Cape 150 C4 headland North
Island, New Zealand
Egoli see Johannesburg
Egypt 72 B2 off. Arab Republic of Egypt,
Ar. Jumhūrīyah Miṣr al 'Arabīyah, prev.
United Arab Republic; anc. Aegyptus.
country NE Africa

EGYPT
North Africa

Official name Arab Republic of Egypt
Formation 1936 / 1982
Capital Cairo
Population 76.9 million / 200 people
per sq mile (77 people per sq km) / 42%
Total area 386,660 sq. miles
(1,001,450 sq. km)
Languages Arabic*, French,
English, Berber
Religions Muslim (mainly Sunni) 94%,
Coptic Christian and other 6%
Ethnic mix Egyptian 99%, Nubian,
Armenian, Greek, and Berber 1%
Government Presidential system
Currency Egyptian pound = 100 piastres
Literacy rate 71%
Calorie consumption 3338 calories

Eibar 93 E1 País Vasco, N Spain
Eibergen 86 E3 Gelderland,
E Netherlands
Eidfjord 85 A5 Hordaland, S Norway
Eier-Berg see Suur Munamägi
Eifel 95 A5 plateau W Germany
Eiger 95 B7 mountain C Switzerland
Eigg 88 B3 island W Scotland, United
Kingdom
Eight Degree Channel 132 B3 channel
India/Maldives
Eighty Mile Beach 146 B4 beach
Western Australia
Eijsden 87 D6 Limburg, SE Netherlands
Eilat see Elat
Eindhoven 87 D5 Noord-Brabant,
S Netherlands
Eipel see Ipel'
Éire see Ireland
Éireann, Muir see Irish Sea
Eisenhüttenstadt 94 D4 Brandenburg,
E Germany
Eisenmark see Hunedoara
Eisenstadt 95 E6 Burgenland, E Austria
Eisleben 94 C4 Sachsen-Anhalt,
C Germany
Eivissa 93 G3 var. Iviza, Cast.
Ibiza; anc. Ebusus. Ibiza, Spain,
W Mediterranean Sea
Eivissa 93 G3 var. Iviza, Cast.
Ibiza; anc. Ebusus. Ibiza, Spain,
W Mediterranean Sea
Eivissa 93 G3 var. Iviza, Cast.
Ibiza; anc. Ebusus. Ibiza, Spain,
W Mediterranean Sea
Ejea de los Caballeros 93 E2 Aragón,
NE Spain
Ejin Qi see Dalain Hob
Ekapa see Cape Town
Ekaterinodar see Krasnodar
Ekvvyatapskiy Khrebet 115 G1
mountain range NE Russian Federation
El 'Alamein see Al 'Alamayn
El Asnam see Chlef
Elat 119 B8 var. Eilat, Elath. Southern,
S Israel
Elat, Gulf of see Aqaba, Gulf of
Elath see Elat, Israel
Elath see Al 'Aqabah, Jordan
El'Atrun 72 B3 Northern Darfur,
NW Sudan
Elâziğ 117 E3 var. Elâzig, Elâziz. Elâziğ,
E Turkey
Elba 96 B4 island Archipelago Toscano,
C Italy
Elbasani see Elbasan

Elbe 80 D3 Cz. Labe. river Czech
Republic/Germany
Elbert, Mount 44 C4 mountain
Colorado, C USA
Elbing see Elbląg
Elbląg 98 C2 var. Elblag, Ger. Elbing.
Warmińsko-Mazurskie, NE Poland
El Boulaida/El Boulaïda see Blida
El'brus 111 A8 var. Gora El'brus.
mountain SW Russian Federation
El'brus, Gora see El'brus
El Burgo de Osma 93 E2 Castilla-León,
C Spain
Elburz Mountains 120 C2 Eng. Elburz
Mountains. mountain range N Iran
Elburz Mountains see Alborz, Reshteh-ye
Kūhhā-ye
El Cajon 47 C8 California, W USA
El Calafate 65 B7 var. Calafate. Santa
Cruz, S Argentina
El Callao 59 E2 Bolívar, E Venezuela
El Campo 49 G4 Texas, SW USA
El Carmen de Bolívar 58 B2 Bolívar,
NW Colombia
El Cayo see San Ignacio
El Centro 47 D8 California, W USA
Elche 93 F4 Cat. Elx; anc. Ilici, Lat. Illicis.
País Valenciano, E Spain
Elda 93 F4 País Valenciano, E Spain
El Djazaïr see Alger
El Djelfa see Djelfa
Eldorado 64 E3 Misiones, NE Argentina
El Dorado 50 C3 Sinaloa, C Mexico
El Dorado 42 B2 Arkansas, C USA
El Dorado 45 F5 Kansas, C USA
El Dorado 59 E2 Bolívar, E Venezuela
El Dorado see California
Eldoret 73 C6 Rift Valley, W Kenya
Elektrostal' 111 B5 Moskovskaya
Oblast', W Russian Federation
Elemi Triangle 73 B5 disputed region
Kenya/Sudan
Elephant Butte Reservoir 48 C2
reservoir New Mexico, SW USA
Élesd see Aleşd
Eleuthera Island 54 C1 island
N Bahamas
El Fasher 72 A4 var. Al Fāshir. Northern
Darfur, W Sudan
El Ferrol/El Ferrol del Caudillo see
Ferrol
El Gedaref see Gedaref
El Geneina 72 A4 var. Ajjinena, Al-
Genain, Al Junaynah. Western Darfur,
W Sudan
Elgin 88 C3 NE Scotland, United
Kingdom
Elgin 40 B3 Illinois, N USA
El Gîza see Gîza
El Goléa 70 D3 var. Al Golea. C Algeria
El Hank 74 D1 cliff N Mauritania
El Haseke see Al Ḩasakah
Elimberrum see Auch
Eliocroca see Lorca
Élisabethville see Lubumbashi
Elista 111 B7 Respublika Kalmykiya,
SW Russian Federation
Elizabeth 149 B6 South Australia
Elizabeth City 43 G1 North Carolina,
SE USA
Elizabethtown 40 C5 Kentucky, S USA
El-Jadida 70 C2 prev. Mazagan.
W Morocco
Elk 98 E2 Ger. Lyck. Warmińsko-
mazurskie, NE Poland
Elk City 49 F1 Oklahoma, C USA
El Khalil see Hebron
El Khârga see Al Khārijah
Elkhart 40 C3 Indiana, N USA
El Khartum see Khartoum
Elk River 45 F2 Minnesota, N USA
El Kuneitra see Al Qunayţirah
Ellás see Greece
Ellef Ringnes Island 37 E1 island
Nunavut, N Canada
Ellen, Mount 44 B5 mountain Utah,
W USA
Ellensburg 46 B2 Washington, NW USA
Ellesmere Island 37 F1 island Queen
Elizabeth Islands, Nunavut, N Canada
Ellesmere, Lake 151 C6 lake South
Island, New Zealand
Ellice Islands see Tuvalu
Elliston 149 A6 South Australia
Ellsworth Land 154 A3 physical region
Antarctica

El Mahbas 70 B3 var. Mahbés.
SW Western Sahara
El Mina 118 B4 var. Al Mīnâ'.
N Lebanon
El Minya see Al Minyā
Elmira 41 E3 New York, NE USA
El Mreyyé 74 D2 desert E Mauritania
Elmshorn 94 B3 Schleswig-Holstein,
N Germany
El Muglad 72 B4 Western Kordofan,
C Sudan
El Obeid 72 B4 var. Al Obayyid, Al
Ubayyiḑ. Northern Kordofan, C Sudan
El Ouâdi see El Oued
El Oued 71 E2 var. Al Oued, El Ouâdi, El
Wad. NE Algeria
Eloy 48 B2 Arizona, SW USA
El Paso 48 D3 Texas, SW USA
El Porvenir 53 G4 Kuna Yala, N Panama
El Progreso 52 C2 Yoro, NW Honduras
El Puerto de Santa María 92 C5
Andalucía, S Spain
El Qâhira see Cairo
El Quneitra see Al Qunayţirah
El Quseir see Quşayr
El Quweira see Al Quwayrah
El Rama 53 E3 Región Autónoma
Atlántico Sur, SE Nicaragua
El Real 53 H5 var. El Real de Santa María.
Darién, SE Panama
El Real de Santa María see El Real
El Reno 49 F1 Oklahoma, C USA
El Salvador 52 B3 off. Republica de El
Salvador. country Central America

EL SALVADOR
Central America

Official name Republic of El Salvador
Formation 1841 / 1841
Capital San Salvador
Population 7.1 million / 888 people
per sq mile (343 people per sq km) / 60%
Total area 8124 sq. miles (21,040 sq. km)
Languages Spanish
Religions Roman Catholic 80%,
Evangelical 18%, other 2%
Ethnic mix Mestizo 94%,
Amerindian 5%, White 1%
Government Presidential system
Currency Salvadorean colón & US dollar =
100 centavos (colón); 100 cents (US dollar)
Literacy rate 80%
Calorie consumption 2584 calories

El Salvador, Republica de see El Salvador
Elsass see Alsace
El Sáuz 50 C2 Chihuahua, N Mexico
El Serrat 91 A7 N Andorra Europe
Elst 86 D4 Gelderland, E Netherlands
El Sueco 50 C2 Chihuahua, N Mexico
El Suweida see As Suwaydā'
El Suweis see Suez
Eltanin Fracture Zone 153 E5 tectonic
feature SE Pacific Ocean
El Tigre 59 E2 Anzoátegui, NE Venezuela
Elvas 92 C4 Portalegre, C Portugal
El Vendrell 93 G2 Cataluña, NE Spain
El Vigía 58 C2 Mérida, NW Venezuela
El Wad see El Oued
Elwell, Lake 44 B1 reservoir Montana,
NW USA
Elx see Elche
Ely 47 D5 Nevada, W USA
El Yopal see Yopal
Emajõgi 106 D3 Ger. Embach. river
SE Estonia
Emāmrūd see Shāhrūd
Emāmshahr see Shāhrūd
Emba 114 B4 Kaz. Embi. Aktyubinsk,
W Kazakhstan
Embach see Emajõgi
Embi see Emba
Emden 94 A3 Niedersachsen,
NW Germany
Emerald 148 D4 Queensland, E Australia
Emerald Isle see Montserrat
Emesa see Ḩimş
Emmaste 106 C2 Hiiumaa, W Estonia
Emmeloord 86 D2 Flevoland,
N Netherlands
Emmen 86 E2 Drenthe, NE Netherlands
Emmendingen 95 A6 Baden-
Württemberg, SW Germany
Emona see Ljubljana
Emonti see East London

Emory Peak *49 E4 mountain* Texas, SW USA
Empalme *50 B2* Sonora, NW Mexico
Emperor Seamounts *113 G3 seamount range* NW Pacific Ocean
Empire State of the South *see* Georgia
Emporia *45 F5* Kansas, C USA
Empty Quarter *see* Ar Rub 'al Khālī
Ems *94 A3 Dut.* Eems. *river* NW Germany
Enareträsk *see* Inarijärvi
Encamp *91 A8* Encamp, C Andorra Europe
Encarnación *64 D3* Itapúa, S Paraguay
Encinitas *47 C8* California, W USA
Encs *99 D6* Borsod-Abaúj-Zemplén, NE Hungary
Endeavour Strait *148 C1 strait* Queensland, NE Australia
Enderbury Island *145 F3 atoll* Phoenix Islands, C Kiribati
Enderby Land *154 C2 physical region* Antarctica
Enderby Plain *154 D2 abyssal plain* S Indian Ocean
Endersdorf *see* Jędrzejów
Enewetak Atoll *144 C1 var.* Ānewetak, Eniwetok. *atoll* Ralik Chain, W Marshall Islands
Enfield *89 A7* United Kingdom
Engeten *see* Aiud
Enghien *87 B6 Dut.* Edingen. Hainaut, SW Belgium
England *89 D5 Lat.* Anglia. *cultural region* England, United Kingdom
Englewood *44 D4* Colorado, C USA
English Channel *89 D8 var.* The Channel, *Fr.* la Manche. *channel* NW Europe
Engure *106 C3* Tukums, W Latvia
Engures Ezers *106 B3 lake* NW Latvia
Enguri *117 F1 Rus.* Inguri. *river* NW Georgia
Enid *49 F1* Oklahoma, C USA
Enikale Strait *see* Kerch Strait
Eniwetok *see* Enewetak Atoll
En Nâqoûra *119 A5 var.* An Nāqūrah. SW Lebanon
En Nazira *see* Natzrat
Ennedi *76 D2 plateau* E Chad
Ennis *89 A6 Ir.* Inis. Clare, W Ireland
Ennis *49 G3* Texas, SW USA
Enniskillen *89 B5 var.* Inniskilling, *Ir.* Inis Ceithleann. SW Northern Ireland, United Kingdom
Enns *95 D6 river* C Austria
Enschede *86 E3* Overijssel, E Netherlands
Ensenada *50 A1* Baja California Norte, NW Mexico
Entebbe *73 B6* S Uganda
Entroncamento *92 B3* Santarém, C Portugal
Enugu *75 G5* Enugu, S Nigeria
Epanomí *104 B4* Kentrikí Makedonía, N Greece
Epéna *77 B5* Likouala, NE Congo
Eperies/Eperjes *see* Prešov
Epi *144 D4 var.* Épi. *island* C Vanuatu
Épi *see* Epi
Epinal *90 D4* Vosges, NE France
Epiphania *see* Hamāh
Epitoli *see* Tshwane
Epoon *see* Ebon Atoll
Epsom *89 A8* United Kingdom
Equality State *see* Wyoming
Equatorial Guinea *77 A5 off.* Equatorial Guinea, Republic of. *country* C Africa
Equatorial Guinea, Republic of *see* Equatorial Guinea

EQUATORIAL GUINEA
Central Africa

Official name Republic of Equatorial Guinea
Formation 1968 / 1968
Capital Malabo
Population 551,201 / 51 people per sq mile (20 people per sq km) / 49%
Total area 10,830 sq. miles (28,051 sq. km)
Languages French*, Spanish*, Fang, Bubi
Religions Roman Catholic 90%, Other 10%
Ethnic mix Fang 85%, Other 11%, Bubi 4%
Government Presidential system
Currency CFA franc = 100 centimes
Literacy rate 87%
Calorie consumption Not available

Erautini *see* Johannesburg
Erbil *see* Arbil
Erciş *117 F3* Van, E Turkey
Erdély *see* Transylvania
Erdélyi-Havasok *see* Carpaţii Meridionalii
Erdenet *127 E2* Orhon, N Mongolia
Erdi *76 C2 plateau* NE Chad
Erdi Ma *76 D2 desert* NE Chad
Erebus, Mount *154 B4 volcano* Ross Island, Antarctica
Ereğli *116 C4* Konya, S Turkey
Erenhot *127 F2 var.* Erlian. Nei Mongol Zizhiqu, NE China
Erfurt *94 C4* Thüringen, C Germany
Ergene Çayı *see* Ergene Irmaği
Ergene Irmaği *116 A2 var.* Ergene Çayı. *river* NW Turkey
Ergun *127 F1 var.* Labudalin; *prev.* Ergun Youqi. Nei Mongol Zizhiqu, N China
Ergun He *see* Ergun
Ergun Youqi *see* Ergun
Erie *40 D3* Pennsylvania, NE USA
Érié, Lac *see* Erie, Lake
Erie, Lake *40 D3 Fr.* Lac Érié. *lake* Canada/USA
Eritrea *72 C4 off.* State of Eritrea, Ērtra. *country* E Africa

ERITREA
East Africa

Official name State of Eritrea
Formation 1993 / 2002
Capital Asmara
Population 4.7 million / 104 people per sq mile (40 people per sq km) / 20%
Total area 46,842 sq. miles (121,320 sq. km)
Languages Tigrinya*, English*, Tigre, Afar, Arabic*, Bileri, Kunama, Nara, Saho, Hadareb
Religions Christian 45%, Muslim 45%, Other 10%
Ethnic mix Tigray 50%, Tigray and Kunama 40%, Afar 4%, Other 3%, Saho 3%
Government Transitional regime
Currency Nakfa = 100 cents
Literacy rate 57%
Calorie consumption 1513 calories

Eritrea, State of *see* Eritrea
Erivan *see* Yerevan
Erlangen *95 C5* Bayern, S Germany
Erlau *see* Eger
Erlian *see* Erenhot
Ermelo *86 E3* Gelderland, C Netherlands
Ermióni *105 C6* Pelopónnisos, S Greece
Ermoúpoli *105 D6 var.* Hermoupolis; *prev.* Ermoúpolis. Sýyros, Kykládes, Greece, Aegean Sea
Ermoúpolis *see* Ermoúpoli
Ernäkulam *132 C3* Kerala, SW India
Erode *132 C2* Tamil Nādu, SE India
Erquelinnes *87 B7* Hainaut, S Belgium
Er-Rachidia *70 C2 var.* Ksar al Soule. E Morocco
Er Rahad *72 B4 var.* Ar Rahad. Northern Kordofan, C Sudan
Erromango *144 D4 island* S Vanuatu
Ertis *see* Irtysh, C Asia
Ērtra *see* Eritrea
Erzerum *see* Erzurum
Erzincan *117 E3 var.* Erzinjan. Erzincan, E Turkey
Erzinjan *see* Erzincan
Erzurum *117 E3 prev.* Erzerum. Erzurum, NE Turkey
Esbjerg *85 A7* Ribe, W Denmark
Esbo *see* Espoo
Escaldes *91 A8* Escaldes Engordany, C Andorra Europe
Escaut *see* Scheldt
Esch-sur-Alzette *87 D8* Luxembourg, S Luxembourg
Esclaves, Grand Lac des *see* Great Slave Lake
Escondido *47 C8* California, W USA
Escuinapa *50 D3 var.* Escuinapa de Hidalgo. Sinaloa, C Mexico
Escuinapa de Hidalgo *see* Escuinapa
Escuintla *52 B2* Escuintla, S Guatemala
Escuintla *51 G5* Chiapas, SE Mexico
Esenguly *122 B3 Rus.* Gasan-Kuli. Balkan Welaýaty, W Turkmenistan
Eşfahān *120 C3 Eng.* Isfahan; *anc.* Aspadana. Eşfahān, C Iran
Esh Sharā *see* Ash Sharāh

Esil *see* Ishim, Kazakhstan/Russian Federation
Eskimo Point *see* Arviat
Eskişehir *116 B3 var.* Eskishehr. Eskişehir, W Turkey
Eskishehr *see* Eskişehir
Eslāmābād *120 C3 var.* Eslāmābād-e Gharb; *prev.* Harunabad, Shāhābād. Kermānshāhān, W Iran
Eslāmābād-e Gharb *see* Eslāmābād
Esmeraldas *60 A1* Esmeraldas, N Ecuador
Esna *see* Isnā
España *see* Spain
Espanola *48 D1* New Mexico, SW USA
Esperance *147 B7* Western Australia
Esperanza *50 B2* Sonora, NW Mexico
Esperanza *154 A2 Argentinian research station* Antarctica
Espinal *58 B3* Tolima, C Colombia
Espinhaço, Serra do *56 D4 mountain range* SE Brazil
Espírito Santo *63 F4 off.* Estado do Espírito Santo. *state* E Brazil
Espírito Santo *63 F4 off.* Estado do Espírito Santo. *region* E Brazil
Espírito Santo, Estado do *see* Espírito Santo
Espíritu Santo *144 C4 var.* Santo. *island* W Vanuatu
Espoo *85 D6 Swe.* Esbo. Etelä-Suomi, S Finland
Esquel *65 B6* Chubut, SW Argentina
Essaouira *70 B2 prev.* Mogador. W Morocco
Esseg *see* Osijek
Essen *87 C5* Antwerpen, N Belgium
Essen *94 A4 var.* Essen an der Ruhr. Nordrhein-Westfalen, W Germany
Essen an der Ruhr *see* Essen
Essequibo River *59 F3 river* C Guyana
Es Suweida *see* As Suwaydā'
Estacado, Llano *49 E2 plain* New Mexico/Texas, SW USA
Estados, Isla de los *65 C8 prev. Eng.* Staten Island. *island* S Argentina
Estância *63 G3* Sergipe, E Brazil
Estelí *52 D3* Estelí, NW Nicaragua
Estella *93 E1 Bas.* Lizarra. Navarra, N Spain
Estepona *92 D5* Andalucía, S Spain
Estevan *37 F5* Saskatchewan, S Canada
Estland *see* Estonia
Estonia *106 D2 off.* Republic of Estonia, *Est.* Eesti Vabariik, *Ger.* Estland, *Latv.* Igaunija; *prev.* Estonian SSR, *Rus.* Estonskaya SSR. *country* NE Europe

ESTONIA
Northeast Europe

Official name Republic of Estonia
Formation 1991 / 1991
Capital Tallinn
Population 1.3 million / 75 people per sq mile (29 people per sq km) / 70%
Total area 17,462 sq. miles (45,226 sq. km)
Languages Estonian*, Russian
Religions Evangelical Lutheran 56%, Orthodox Christian 25%, Other 19%
Ethnic mix Estonian 68%, Russian 26%, Other 4%, Ukrainian 2%
Government Parliamentary system
Currency Euro = 100 cents
Literacy rate 99%
Calorie consumption 3002 calories

Estonian SSR *see* Estonia
Estonia, Republic of *see* Estonia
Estonskaya SSR *see* Estonia
Estrela, Serra da *92 C3 mountain range* C Portugal
Estremadura *see* Extremadura
Estremoz *92 C4* Évora, S Portugal
Esztergom *99 C6 Ger.* Gran; *anc.* Strigonium. Komárom-Esztergom, N Hungary
Étaile *87 D8* Luxembourg, SE Belgium
Etāwah *134 D3* Uttar Pradesh, N India
Ethiopia *73 C5 off.* Federal Democratic Republic of Ethiopia; *prev.* Abyssinia, People's Democratic Republic of Ethiopia. *country* E Africa

ETHIOPIA
East Africa

Official name Federal Democratic Republic of Ethiopia
Formation 1896 / 2002
Capital Addis Ababa
Population 81.2 million / 189 people per sq mile (73 people per sq km) / 16%
Total area 435,184 sq. miles (1,127,127 sq. km)
Languages Amharic*, Tigrinya, Galla, Sidamo, Somali, English, Arabic
Religions Orthodox Christian 40%, Muslim 40%, Traditional beliefs 15%, Other 5%
Ethnic mix Oromo 32%, Amhara 30%, Other 22%, Tigrean 6%, Somali 6%, Guragie 4%
Government Parliamentary system
Currency Ethiopian birr = 100 cents
Literacy rate 42%
Calorie consumption 1857 calories

Ethiopia, Federal Democratic Republic of *see* Ethiopia
Ethiopian Highlands *73 C5 var.* Ethiopian Plateau. *plateau* N Ethiopia
Ethiopian Plateau *see* Ethiopian Highlands
Ethiopia, People's Democratic Republic of *see* Ethiopia
Mount Etna *97 C7 Eng.* Mount Etna. *volcano* Sicilia, Italy, C Mediterranean Sea
Etna, Mount *see* Etna, Monte
Etosha Pan *78 B3 salt lake* N Namibia
Etoumbi *77 B5* Cuvette Ouest, NW Congo
Etsch *see* Adige
Et Tafila *see* Aţ Ţafilah
Ettelbrück *87 D8* Diekirch, C Luxembourg
'Eua *145 E5 prev.* Middleburg Island. *island* Tongatapu Group, SE Tonga
Euboea *105 C5 Lat.* Euboea. *island* C Greece
Euboea *see* Évvoia
Eucla *147 D6* Western Australia
Euclid *40 D3* Ohio, N USA
Eufaula Lake *49 G1 var.* Eufaula Reservoir. *reservoir* Oklahoma, C USA
Eufaula Reservoir *see* Eufaula Lake
Eugene *46 B3* Oregon, NW USA
Eumolpias *see* Plovdiv
Eupen *87 D6* Liège, E Belgium
Euphrates *128 B4 Ar.* Al-Furât, *Turk.* Firat Nehri. *river* SW Asia
Eureka *47 A5* California, W USA
Eureka *44 A1* Nevada, NW USA
Europa Point *93 H5 headland* S Gibraltar
Europe *80 continent*
Eutin *94 C2* Schleswig-Holstein, N Germany
Euxine Sea *see* Black Sea
Evansdale *45 G3* Iowa, C USA
Evanston *40 B3* Illinois, N USA
Evanston *44 B4* Wyoming, C USA
Evansville *40 B5* Indiana, N USA
Eveleth *45 G1* Minnesota, N USA
Everard, Lake *149 A6 salt lake* South Australia
Everest, Mount *126 B5 Chin.* Qomolangma Feng, *Nep.* Sagarmāthā. *mountain* China/Nepal
Everett *46 B2* Washington, NW USA
Everglades, The *43 F5 wetland* Florida, SE USA
Evje *85 A6* Aust-Agder, S Norway
Evmolpia *see* Plovdiv
Évora *92 B4 anc.* Ebora, *Lat.* Liberalitas Julia. Évora, C Portugal
Évreux *90 C3 anc.* Civitas Eburovicum. Eure, N France
Évros *see* Maritsa
Évry *90 E2* Essonne, N France
Ewarton *54 B5* C Jamaica
Excelsior Springs *45 F4* Missouri, C USA
Exe *89 C7 river* SW England, United Kingdom
Exeter *89 C7 anc.* Isca Damnoniorum. SW England, United Kingdom
Exmoor *89 C7 moorland* SW England, United Kingdom

Exmouth *146 A4* Western Australia
Exmouth *89 C7* SW England, United Kingdom
Exmouth Gulf *146 A4* *gulf* Western Australia
Exmouth Plateau *141 E5* *undersea plateau* E Indian Ocean
Extremadura *92 C3* *var.* Estremadura.
autonomous community W Spain
Exuma Cays *54 C1* *islets* C Bahamas
Exuma Sound *54 C1* *sound* C Bahamas
Eyre Mountains *151 A7* *mountain range* South Island, New Zealand
Eyre North, Lake *149 A5* *salt lake* South Australia
Eyre Peninsula *149 A6* *peninsula* South Australia
Eyre South, Lake *149 A5* *salt lake* South Australia
Ezo *see* Hokkaidō

F

Faadhippolhu Atoll *132 B4* *var.*
Fadiffolu, Lhaviyani Atoll. *atoll*
N Maldives
Fabens *48 D3* Texas, SW USA
Fada *76 C2* Borkou-Ennedi-Tibesti, E Chad
Fada-Ngourma *75 E4* E Burkina Faso
Fadiffolu *see* Faadhippolhu Atoll
Faenza *96 C3* *anc.* Faventia. Emilia-Romagna, N Italy
Faeroe-Iceland Ridge *80 C1* *undersea ridge* NW Norwegian Sea
Faeroe Islands *83 E5* *Dan.* Færøerne, *Faer.* Føroyar. *Danish external territory* N Atlantic Ocean
Færøerne *see* Faeroe Islands
Faeroe-Shetland Trough *80 C2* *trough* NE Atlantic Ocean
Faetano *96 E2* E San Marino
Făgăraş *108 C4* *Ger.* Fogarasch, *Hung.* Fogaras. Braşov, C Romania
Fagibina, Lake *see* Faguibine, Lac
Fagne *87 C7* *hill range* S Belgium
Faguibine, Lac *75 E3* *var.* Lake Fagibina. *lake* NW Mali
Fahlun *see* Falun
Fahraj *120 E4* Kermān, SE Iran
Faial *92 A5* *var.* Ilha do Faial. *island* Azores, Portugal, NE Atlantic Ocean
Faial, Ilha do *see* Faial
Faifo *see* Hôi An
Fairbanks *36 D3* Alaska, USA
Fairfield *47 B6* California, W USA
Fair Isle *88 D2* *island* NE Scotland, United Kingdom
Fairlie *151 B6* Canterbury, South Island, New Zealand
Fairmont *45 F3* Minnesota, N USA
Faisalābād *134 C2* *prev.* Lyallpur. Punjab, NE Pakistan
Faizābād *135 E3* Uttar Pradesh, N India
Faizabad/Faizābād *see* Feyzābād
Fakaofo Atoll *145 F3* *island* SE Tokelau
Falam *136 A3* Chin State, W Burma (Myanmar)
Falconara Marittima *96 C3* Marche, C Italy
Falkenau an der Eger *see* Sokolov
Falkland Islands *65 D7* *var.* Falklands, Islas Malvinas. *UK dependent territory* SW Atlantic Ocean
Falkland Plateau *57 D7* *var.* Argentine Rise. *undersea feature* SW Atlantic Ocean
Falklands *see* Falkland Islands
Falknov nad Ohří *see* Sokolov
Fallbrook *47 C8* California, W USA
Falmouth *54 A4* W Jamaica
Falmouth *89 C7* SW England, United Kingdom
Falster *85 B8* *island* SE Denmark
Fălticeni *108 C3* *Hung.* Falticsén. Suceava, NE Romania
Falticsén *see* Fălticeni
Falun *85 C6* *var.* Fahlun. Kopparberg, C Sweden
Famagusta *see* Gazimağusa
Famagusta Bay *see* Gazimağusa Bay, *Gk.* Kólpos Ammóchostos. *bay* E Cyprus
Famagusta Bay *see* Gazimağusa Körfezi

Famenne *87 C7* *physical region* SE Belgium
Fang *136 C3* Chiang Mai, NW Thailand
Fanning Island *see* Tabuaeran
Fanø *96 C3* *island* W Denmark
Farafangana *79 G4* Fianarantsoa, SE Madagascar
Farāh *122 D4* *var.* Farah, Fararud.
Farāh, W Afghanistan
Farah Rud *122 D4* *river* W Afghanistan
Faranah *74 C4* Haute-Guinée, S Guinea
Fararud *see* Farāh
Farasan, Jaza'ir *121 A6* *island group* SW Saudi Arabia
Farewell, Cape *150 C4* *headland* South Island, New Zealand
Farewell, Cape *see* Nunap Isua
Fargo *45 F2* North Dakota, N USA
Farg'ona *123 F2* *Rus.* Fergana; *prev.* Novyy Margilan. Farg'ona Viloyati, E Uzbekistan
Faribault *45 F2* Minnesota, N USA
Farīdābād *134 D3* Haryāna, N India
Farkhor *123 E3* *Rus.* Parkhar. SW Tajikistan
Farmington *45 G5* Missouri, C USA
Farmington *48 C1* New Mexico, SW USA
Faro *92 B5* Faro, S Portugal
Farquhar Group *79 G2* *island group* S Seychelles
Fars, Khalīj-e *see* Gulf, The
Farvel, Kap *see* Nunap Isua
Fastiv *109 E2* *Rus.* Fastov. Kyyivs'ka Oblast', NW Ukraine
Fastov *see* Fastiv
Fauske *84 C3* Nordland, C Norway
Faventia *see* Faenza
Faxa Bay *see* Faxaflói
Faxaflói *82 D5* *Eng.* Faxa Bay. *bay* W Iceland
Faya *76 C2* *prev.* Faya-Largeau, Largeau. Borkou-Ennedi-Tibesti, N Chad
Faya-Largeau *see* Faya
Fayetteville *42 A1* Arkansas, C USA
Fayetteville *43 F1* North Carolina, SE USA
Fdérick *see* Fdérik
Fdérik *74 C2* *var.* Fdérick, *Fr.* Fort Gouraud. Tiris Zemmour, NW Mauritania
Fear, Cape *43 F2* *headland* Bald Head Island, North Carolina, SE USA
Fécamp *90 B3* Seine-Maritime, N France
Fédala *see* Mohammedia
Federal Capital Territory *see* Australian Capital Territory
Fehérgyarmat *99 E6* Szabolcs-Szatmár-Bereg, E Hungary
Fehértemplom *see* Bela Crkva
Fehmarn *94 C2* *island* N Germany
Fehmarn Belt *94 C2* *Dan.* Femern Bælt, *Ger.* Fehmarnbelt. *strait* Denmark/Germany
Fehmarnbelt *see* Fehmarn Belt/Femer Bælt
Feijó *62 C2* Acre, W Brazil
Feilding *150 D4* Manawatu-Wanganui, North Island, New Zealand
Feira *see* Feira de Santana
Feira de Santana *63 G3* *var.* Feira. Bahia, E Brazil
Feketehalom *see* Codlea
Felanitx *93 G3* Mallorca, Spain, W Mediterranean Sea
Felicitas Julia *see* Lisboa
Felidhu Atoll *132 B4* *atoll* C Maldives
Felipe Carrillo Puerto *51 H4* Quintana Roo, SE Mexico
Felixstowe *89 E6* E England, United Kingdom
Fellin *see* Viljandi
Felsőbánya *see* Baia Sprie
Felsőmuzslya *see* Mužlja
Femunden *85 B5* *lake* S Norway
Fénérive *see* Fenoarivo Atsinanana
Fengcheng *128 D3* *var.* Feng-cheng, Fenghwangcheng. Liaoning, NE China
Feng-cheng *see* Fengcheng
Fenghwangcheng *see* Fengcheng
Fengtien *see* Liaoning, China
Fengtien *see* Shenyang, China
Fenoarivo Atsinanana *79 G3* *Fr.* Fénérive. Toamasina, E Madagascar
Fens, The *89 E6* *wetland* E England, United Kingdom
Feodosiya *109 F5* *var.* Kefe, *It.* Kaffa; *anc.* Theodosia. Respublika Krym, S Ukraine

Ferdinand *see* Montana, Bulgaria
Ferdinandsberg *see* Oţelu Roşu
Féres *104 D3* Anatolikí Makedonía kai Thráki, NE Greece
Fergana *see* Farg'ona
Fergus Falls *45 F2* Minnesota, N USA
Ferizaj *101 D5* *Serb.* Uroševac. C Kosovo
Ferkessédougou *74 D4* N Côte d'Ivoire
Fermo *96 C4* *anc.* Firmum Picenum. Marche, C Italy
Fernandina, Isla *60 A5* *var.* Narborough Island. *island* Galápagos Islands, Ecuador, E Pacific Ocean
Fernando de Noronha *63 H2* *island* E Brazil
Fernando Po/Fernando Póo *see* Bioco, Isla de
Ferrara *96 C2* *anc.* Forum Alieni. Emilia-Romagna, N Italy
Ferreñafe *60 B3* Lambayeque, W Peru
Ferro *see* Hierro
Ferrol *92 B1* *var.* El Ferrol; *prev.* El Ferrol del Caudillo. Galicia, NW Spain
Fertő *see* Neusiedler See
Ferwerd *86 D1* *Fris.* Ferwert. Friesland, N Netherlands
Ferwert *see* Ferwerd
Fès *70 C2* *Eng.* Fez. N Morocco
Fetești *108 D5* Ialomiţa, SE Romania
Fethiye *116 B4* Muğla, SW Turkey
Fetlar *88 D1* *island* NE Scotland, United Kingdom
Feyzābād *123 F3* *var.* Faizabad, Faizābād, Feyzābād, Fyzabad. Badakhshān, NE Afghanistan
Feyẕābād *see* Feyzābād
Fez *see* Fès
Fianarantsoa *79 F3* Fianarantsoa, C Madagascar
Fianga *76 B4* Mayo-Kébbi, SW Chad
Fier *101 C6* *var.* Fieri. Fier, SW Albania
Fieri *see* Fier
Figeac *91 C5* Lot, S France
Figig *see* Figuig
Figueira da Foz *92 B3* Coimbra, W Portugal
Figueres *93 G2* Cataluña, E Spain
Figuig *70 D2* *var.* Figig. E Morocco
Fiji *145 E5* *off.* Sovereign Democratic Republic of Fiji, *Fij.* Viti. *country* SW Pacific Ocean

---

FIJI
Australasia & Oceania

Official name Republic of the Fiji Islands
Formation 1970 / 1970
Capital Suva
Population 918,675 / 130 people
per sq mile (50 people per sq km) / 52%
Total area 7054 sq. miles (18,270 sq. km)
Languages Fijian, English*, Hindi, Urdu, Tamil, Telugu
Religions Hindu 38%, Methodist 37%,
Roman Catholic 9%, Other 8%,
Muslim 8%
Ethnic mix Melanesian 51%, Indian 44%, Other 5%
Government Democratic National regime
Currency Fiji dollar = 100 cents
Literacy rate 93%
Calorie consumption 2894 calories

Fiji, Sovereign Democratic Republic of *see* Fiji
Filadelfia *52 D4* Guanacaste, W Costa Rica
Filiaşi *108 B5* Dolj, SW Romania
Filipstad *85 B6* Värmland, C Sweden
Finale Ligure *96 A3* Liguria, NW Italy
Finchley *89 A7* United Kingdom
Findlay *40 C4* Ohio, N USA
Finike *116 B4* Antalya, SW Turkey
Finland *84 D4* *off.* Republic of Finland, *Fin.* Suomen Tasavalta, Suomi. *country* N Europe

---

FINLAND
Northern Europe

Official name Republic of Finland
Formation 1917 / 1947
Capital Helsinki
Population 5.3 million / 45 people
per sq mile (17 people per sq km) / 61%
Total area 130,127 sq. miles (337,030 sq. km)

FINLAND
(continued)

Languages Finnish*, Swedish*, Sámi
Religions Evangelical Lutheran 89%,
Other 9%, Orthodox Christian 1%,
Roman Catholic 1%
Ethnic mix Finnish 93%,
Other (including Sámi) 7%
Government Parliamentary system
Currency Euro = 100 cents
Literacy rate 99%
Calorie consumption 3100 calories

Finland, Gulf of *85 D6* *Est.* Soome Laht, *Fin.* Suomenlahti, *Ger.* Finnischer Meerbusen, *Rus.* Finskiy Zaliv, *Swe.* Finska Viken. *gulf* E Baltic Sea
Finland, Republic of *see* Finland
Finnischer Meerbusen *see* Finland, Gulf of
Finnmarksvidda *84 D2* *physical region* N Norway
Finska Viken/Finskiy Zaliv *see* Finland, Gulf of
Finsterwalde *94 D4* Brandenburg, E Germany
Fiordland *151 A7* *physical region* South Island, New Zealand
Fiorina *96 E1* NE San Marino
Firat Nehri *see* Euphrates
Firenze *96 C3* *Eng.* Florence; *anc.* Florentia. Toscana, C Italy
Firmum Picenum *see* Fermo
First State *see* Delaware
Fischbacher Alpen *95 E7* *mountain range* E Austria
Fischhausen *see* Primorsk
Fish *78 B4* *var.* Vis. *river* S Namibia
Fishguard *89 C6* *Wel.* Abergwaun. SW Wales, United Kingdom
Fisterra, Cabo *92 B1* *headland* NW Spain
Fitzroy Crossing *146 C3* Western Australia
Fitzroy River *146 C3* *river* Western Australia
Fiume *see* Rijeka
Flagstaff *48 B2* Arizona, SW USA
Flanders *87 A6* *Dut.* Vlaanderen, *Fr.* Flandre. *cultural region* Belgium/France
Flandre *see* Flanders
Flathead Lake *44 B1* *lake* Montana, NW USA
Flat Island *128 C8* *island* NE Spratly Islands
Flatts Village *42 B5* *var.* The Flatts Village. C Bermuda
Flensburg *94 B2* Schleswig-Holstein, N Germany
Flessingue *see* Vlissingen
Flickertail State *see* North Dakota
Flinders Island *149 C8* *island* Furneaux Group, Tasmania, SE Australia
Flinders Ranges *149 B6* *mountain range* South Australia
Flinders River *148 C3* *river* Queensland, NE Australia
Flin Flon *37 F5* Manitoba, C Canada
Flint *40 C3* Michigan, N USA
Flint Island *145 G4* *island* Line Islands, E Kiribati
Floreana, Isla *see* Santa María, Isla
Florence *42 C1* Alabama, S USA
Florence *43 F2* South Carolina, SE USA
Florence *see* Firenze
Florencia *58 B4* Caquetá, S Colombia
Florentia *see* Firenze
Flores *52 B1* Petén, N Guatemala
Flores *139 E5* *island* Nusa Tenggara, C Indonesia
Flores *92 A5* *island* Azores, Portugal, NE Atlantic Ocean
Flores, Laut *see* Flores Sea
Flores Sea *138 D5* *Ind.* Laut Flores. *sea* C Indonesia
Floriano *63 F2* Piauí, E Brazil
Florianópolis *63 F5* *prev.* Destêrro. *state capital* Santa Catarina, S Brazil
Florida *64 D4* Florida, S Uruguay
Florida *43 E4* *off.* State of Florida, *also known as* Peninsular State, Sunshine State. *state* SE USA
Florida Bay *43 E5* *bay* Florida, SE USA
Florida Keys *43 E5* *island group* Florida, SE USA

Florida, Straits of *54 B1 strait* Atlantic Ocean/Gulf of Mexico
Flórina *104 B4 var.* Phlórina. Dytikí Makedonía, N Greece
Florissant *45 G4* Missouri, C USA
Floúda, Akrotírio *105 D7 headland* Astypálaia, Kykládes, Greece, Aegean Sea
Flushing *see* Vlissingen
Flylân *see* Vlieland
Foča *100 C4 var.* Srbinje. SE Bosnia and Herzegovina
Focşani *108 C4* Vrancea, E Romania
Fogaras/Fogarasch *see* Făgăraş
Foggia *97 D5* Puglia, SE Italy
Fogo *74 A3 island* Ilhas de Sotavento, SW Cape Verde
Foix *91 B6* Ariège, S France
Folégandros *105 C7 island* Kykládes, Greece, Aegean Sea
Foleyet *38 C4* Ontario, S Canada
Foligno *96 C4* Umbria, C Italy
Folkestone *89 E7* SE England, United Kingdom
Fond du Lac *40 B2* Wisconsin, N USA
Fongafale *145 E3 var.* Funafuti. *country capital* (Tuvalu) (Tuvalu) Funafuti Atoll, SE Tuvalu
Fonseca, Golfo de *see* Fonseca, Gulf of
Fonseca, Gulf of *52 C3 Sp.* Golfo de Fonseca. *gulf* C Central America
Fontainebleau *90 C3* Seine-et-Marne, N France
Fontenay-le-Comte *90 B4* Vendée, NW France
Fontvieille *91 B8* SW Monaco Europe
Fonyód *99 C7* Somogy, W Hungary
Foochow *see* Fuzhou
Foochow *see* Fuzhou
Forchheim *95 C5* Bayern, SE Germany
Forel, Mont *82 D4 mountain* SE Greenland
Forfar *88 C3* E Scotland, United Kingdom
Forge du Sud *see* Dudelange
Forlì *96 C3 anc.* Forum Livii. Emilia-Romagna, N Italy
Formentera *93 G4 anc.* Ophiusa, *Lat.* Frumentum. *island* Islas Baleares, Spain, W Mediterranean Sea
Formosa *64 D2* Formosa, NE Argentina
Formosa/Formo'sa *see* Taiwan
Formosa, Serra *63 E3 mountain range* C Brazil
Formosa Strait *see* Taiwan Strait
Føroyar *see* Faeroe Islands
Forrest City *42 B1* Arkansas, C USA
Fort Albany *38 C3* Ontario, C Canada
Fortaleza *61 F2* Pando, N Bolivia
Fortaleza *63 G2 prev.* Ceará. *state capital* Ceará, NE Brazil
Fort-Archambault *see* Sarh
Fort-Bayard *see* Zhanjiang
Fort-Cappolani *see* Tidjikja
Fort Charlet *see* Djanet
Fort-Chimo *see* Kuujjuaq
Fort Collins *44 D4* Colorado, C USA
Fort-Crampel *see* Kaga Bandoro
Fort Davis *49 E3* Texas, SW USA
Fort-de-France *55 H4 prev.* Fort-Royal. *dependent territory capital* (Martinique) W Martinique
Fort Dodge *45 F3* Iowa, C USA
Fortescue River *146 A4 river* Western Australia
Fort-Foureau *see* Kousséri
Fort Frances *38 B4* Ontario, S Canada
Fort Good Hope *37 E3 var.* Rádeyilikóe. Northwest Territories, NW Canada
Fort Gouraud *see* Fdérik
Forth *88 C4 river* C Scotland, United Kingdom
Forth, Firth of *88 C4 estuary* E Scotland, United Kingdom
Fortín General Eugenio Garay *see* General Eugenio A. Garay
Fort Jameson *see* Chipata
Fort-Lamy *see* Ndjamena
Fort Lauderdale *43 F5* Florida, SE USA
Fort Liard *37 E4 var.* Liard. Northwest Territories, W Canada
Fort Madison *45 G4* Iowa, C USA
Fort McMurray *37 E4* Alberta, C Canada
Fort McPherson *36 D3 var.* McPherson. Northwest Territories, NW Canada
Fort Morgan *44 D4* Colorado, C USA
Fort Myers *43 E5* Florida, SE USA

Fort Nelson *37 E4* British Columbia, W Canada
Fort Peck Lake *44 C1 reservoir* Montana, NW USA
Fort Pierce *43 F4* Florida, SE USA
Fort Providence *37 E4 var.* Providence. Northwest Territories, W Canada
Fort-Repoux *see* Akjoujt
Fort Rosebery *see* Mansa
Fort Rousset *see* Owando
Fort-Royal *see* Fort-de-France
Fort St. John *37 E4* British Columbia, W Canada
Fort Scott *45 F5* Kansas, C USA
Fort Severn *38 C2* Ontario, C Canada
Fort-Shevchenko *114 A4* Mangistau, W Kazakhstan
Fort-Sibut *see* Sibut
Fort Simpson *37 E4 var.* Simpson. Northwest Territories, W Canada
Fort Smith *42 B1* Arkansas, C USA
Fort Stockton *49 E3* Texas, SW USA
Fort-Trinquet *see* Bir Mogrein
Fort Vermilion *37 E4* Alberta, W Canada
Fort Victoria *see* Masvingo
Fort Walton Beach *42 C3* Florida, SE USA
Fort Wayne *40 C4* Indiana, N USA
Fort William *88 C3* N Scotland, United Kingdom
Fort Worth *49 G2* Texas, SW USA
Fort Yukon *36 D3* Alaska, USA
Forum Alieni *see* Ferrara
Forum Livii *see* Forlì
Fossa Claudia *see* Chioggia
Fougamou *77 A6* Ngounié, C Gabon
Fougères *90 B3* Ille-et-Vilaine, NW France
Fou-hsin *see* Fuxin
Foulwind, Cape *151 B5 headland* South Island, New Zealand
Foumban *76 A4* Ouest, NW Cameroon
Fou-shan *see* Fushun
Foveaux Strait *151 A8 strait* S New Zealand
Foxe Basin *37 G3 sea* Nunavut, N Canada
Fox Glacier *151 B6* West Coast, South Island, New Zealand
Fraga *93 F2* Aragón, NE Spain
Fram Basin *155 C3 var.* Amundsen Basin. *undersea basin* Arctic Ocean
France *90 B4 off.* French Republic, *It./Sp.* Francia; *prev.* Gaul, Gaule, *Lat.* Gallia. *country* W Europe

---
FRANCE
Western Europe

Official name French Republic
Formation 987 / 1919
Capital Paris
Population 60.9 million / 287 people per sq mile (111 people per sq km) / 76%
Total area 211,208 sq. miles (547,030 sq. km)
Languages French*, Provençal, German, Breton, Catalan, Basque
Religions Roman Catholic 88%, Muslim 8%, Protestant 2%, Buddhist 1%, Jewish 1%
Ethnic mix French 90%, North African (mainly Algerian) 6%, German (Alsace) 2%, Breton 1%, Other (including Corsicans) 1%
Government Mixed presidential–parliamentary system
Currency Euro = 100 cents
Literacy rate 99%
Calorie consumption 3654 calories

Franceville *77 B6 var.* Massoukou, Masuku. Haut-Ogooué, E Gabon
Francfort *see* Frankfurt am Main
Franche-Comté *90 D4 cultural region* E France
Francia *see* France
Francis Case, Lake *45 E3 reservoir* South Dakota, N USA
Francisco Escárcega *51 G4* Campeche, SE Mexico
Francistown *78 D3* North East, NE Botswana
Franconian Jura *see* Fränkische Alb

Frankenalb *see* Fränkische Alb
Frankenstein/Frankenstein in Schlesien *see* Ząbkowice Śląskie
Frankfort *40 C5 state capital* Kentucky, S USA
Frankfort on the Main *see* Frankfurt am Main
Frankfurt *see* Frankfurt am Main, Germany
Frankfurt *see* Słubice, Poland
Frankfurt am Main *95 B5 var.* Frankfurt, *Fr.* Francfort; *prev. Eng.* Frankfort on the Main. Hessen, SW Germany
Frankfurt an der Oder *94 D3* Brandenburg, E Germany
Fränkische Alb *95 C6 var.* Frankenalb, *Eng.* Franconian Jura. *mountain range* S Germany
Franklin *42 C1* Tennessee, S USA
Franklin D. Roosevelt Lake *46 C1 reservoir* Washington, NW USA
Franz Josef Land *114 D1 Eng.* Franz Josef Land. *island group* N Russian Federation
Franz Josef Land *see* Frantsa-Iosifa, Zemlya
Fraserburgh *88 D3* NE Scotland, United Kingdom
Fraser Island *148 E4 var.* Great Sandy Island. *island* Queensland, E Australia
Frauenbach *see* Baia Mare
Frauenburg *see* Saldus, Latvia
Fredericksburg *41 E5* Virginia, NE USA
Fredericton *39 F4 province capital* New Brunswick, SE Canada
Frederikshåb *see* Paamiut
Frederikshald *see* Halden
Fredrikstad *85 B6* Østfold, S Norway
Freeport *54 C1* Grand Bahama Island, N Bahamas
Freeport *49 H4* Texas, SW USA
Free State *see* Maryland
Freetown *74 C4 country capital* (Sierra Leone) (Sierra Leone) W Sierra Leone
Freiburg *see* Freiburg im Breisgau, Germany
Freiburg *see* Fribourg, Switzerland
Freiburg im Breisgau *95 A6 var.* Freiburg, *Fr.* Fribourg-en-Brisgau. Baden-Württemberg, SW Germany
Freiburg in Schlesien *see* Świebodzice
Fremantle *147 A6* Western Australia
Fremont *45 F4* Nebraska, C USA
French Guiana *59 H3 var.* Guiana, Guyane. *French overseas department* N South America
French Guinea *see* Guinea
French Polynesia *143 F4 French overseas territory* S Pacific Ocean
French Republic *see* France
French Somaliland *see* Djibouti
French Southern and Antarctic Territories *141 B7 Fr.* Terres Australes et Antarctiques Françaises. *French overseas territory* S Indian Ocean
French Sudan *see* Mali
French Territory of the Afars and Issas *see* Djibouti
French Togoland *see* Togo
Fresnillo *50 D3 var.* Fresnillo de González Echeverría. Zacatecas, C Mexico
Fresnillo de González Echeverría *see* Fresnillo
Fresno *47 C6* California, W USA
Frías *64 C3* Catamarca, N Argentina
Fribourg-en-Brisgau *see* Freiburg im Breisgau
Friedek-Mistek *see* Frýdek-Místek
Friedrichshafen *95 B7* Baden-Württemberg, S Germany
Friendly Islands *see* Tonga
Frisches Haff *see* Vistula Lagoon
Frobisher Bay *33 B3 inlet* Baffin Island, Nunavut, NE Canada
Frobisher Bay *see* Iqaluit
Frohavet *84 B4 sound* C Norway
Frome, Lake *149 B6 salt lake* South Australia
Frontera *51 G4* Tabasco, SE Mexico
Frontignan *91 C6* Hérault, S France
Frostviken *see* Kvarnbergsvattnet
Frøya *84 A4 island* W Norway
Frumentum *see* Formentera
Frunze *see* Bishkek

Frýdek-Místek *99 C5 Ger.* Friedek-Mistek. Moravskoslezský Kraj, E Czech Republic
Fu-chien *see* Fujian
Fu-chou *see* Fuzhou
Fu-chou *see* Fuzhou
Fuengirola *92 D5* Andalucía, S Spain
Fuerte Olimpo *64 D2 var.* Olimpo. Alto Paraguay, NE Paraguay
Fuerte, Río *48 C5 river* C Mexico
Fuerteventura *70 B3 island* Islas Canarias, Spain, NE Atlantic Ocean
Fuhkien *see* Fujian
Fu-hsin *see* Fuxin
Fuji *131 D6 var.* Huzi. Shizuoka, Honshū, S Japan
Fujian *128 D6 var.* Fu-chien, Fuhkien, Fukien, Min, Fujian Sheng. *province* SE China
Fujian Sheng *see* Fujian
Mount Fuji *131 D6 var.* Fujiyama, *Eng.* Mount Fuji. *mountain* Honshū, SE Japan
Fuji, Mount/Fujiyama *see* Fuji-san
Fukang *126 C2* Xinjiang Uygur Zizhiqu, W China
Fukien *see* Fujian
Fukui *131 C6 var.* Hukui. Fukui, Honshū, SW Japan
Fukuoka *131 A7 var.* Hukuoka, *hist.* Najima. Fukuoka, Kyūshū, SW Japan
Fukushima *130 D4 var.* Hukusima. Fukushima, Honshū, C Japan
Fulda *95 B5* Hessen, C Germany
Funafuti *see* Fongafale
Funafuti Atoll *145 E3 atoll* C Tuvalu
Funchal *70 A2* Madeira, Portugal, NE Atlantic Ocean
Fundy, Bay of *39 F5 bay* Canada/USA
Fünen *see* Fyn
Fünfkirchen *see* Pécs
Furnes *see* Veurne
Fürth *95 C5* Bayern, S Germany
Furukawa *130 D4 var.* Hurukawa, Ōsaki. Miyagi, Honshū, C Japan
Fusan *see* Pusan
Fushë Kosovë *101 D5 Serb.* Kosovo Polje. C Kosovo
Fushun *128 D3 var.* Fou-shan, Fu-shun. Liaoning, NE China
Fu-shun *see* Fushun
Fusin *see* Fuxin
Füssen *95 C7* Bayern, S Germany
Futog *100 D3* Vojvodina, NW Serbia
Futuna, Île *145 E4 island* S Wallis and Futuna
Fuxin *128 D3 var.* Fou-hsin, Fu-hsin, Fusin. Liaoning, NE China
Fuzhou *128 D5 var.* Foochow, Fu-chou. *province capital* Fujian, SE China
Fuzhou *128 D6 var.* Foochow, Fu-chou. *province capital* Fujian, SE China
Fyn *85 B8 Ger.* Fünen. *island* C Denmark
FYR Macedonia/FYROM *see* Macedonia, FYR
Fyzabad *see* Feyzābād

G

Gaafu Alifu Atoll *see* North Huvadhu Atoll
Gaalkacyo *73 E5 var.* Galka'yo, *It.* Galcaio. Mudug, C Somalia
Gabela *78 B2* Cuanza Sul, W Angola
Gaberones *see* Gaborone
Gabès *71 E2 var.* Qābis. E Tunisia
Gabès, Golfe de *71 F2 Ar.* Khalīj Qābis. *gulf* E Tunisia
Gabon *77 B6 off.* Gabonese Republic. *country* C Africa

GABON
Central Africa

Official name Gabonese Republic
Formation 1960 / 1960
Capital Libreville
Population 1.4 million / 14 people per sq mile (5 people per sq km) / 84%
Total area 103,346 sq. miles (267,667 sq. km)
Languages Fang, French*, Punu, Sira, Nzebi, Mpongwe
Religions Christian (mainly Roman Catholic) 55%, Traditional beliefs 40%, Other 4%, Muslim 1%

GABON
(continued)

Ethnic mix Fang 26%, Shira-punu 24%,
Other 16%, Foreign residents 15%,
Nzabi-duma 11%, Mbédé-Teke 8%
Government Presidential system
Currency CFA franc = 100 centimes
Literacy rate 71%
Calorie consumption 2637 calories

Gabonese Republic *see* Gabon
Gaborone 78 *C4 prev.* Gaberones.
  country capital (Botswana) (Botswana)
  South East, SE Botswana
Gabrovo 104 *D2* Gabrovo, N Bulgaria
Gadag 132 *C1* Karnātaka, W India
Gades/Gadier/Gadir/Gadire *see* Cádiz
Gadsden 42 *D2* Alabama, S USA
Gaeta 97 *C5* Lazio, C Italy
Gaeta, Gulf of 97 *C5 var.* Gulf of Gaeta.
  gulf C Italy
Gaeta, Gulf of *see* Gaeta, Golfo di
Gäfle *see* Gävle
Gafsa 71 *E2 var.* Qafşah. W Tunisia
Gagnoa 74 *D5* C Côte d'Ivoire
Gagra 117 *E1* NW Georgia
Gaillac 91 *C6 var.* Gaillac-sur-Tarn.
  Tarn, S France
Gaillac-sur-Tarn *see* Gaillac
Gaillimh *see* Galway
Gaillimhe, Cuan na *see* Galway Bay
Gainesville 43 *E3* Florida, SE USA
Gainesville 42 *D2* Georgia, SE USA
Gainesville 49 *G2* Texas, SW USA
Lake Gairdner 149 *A6 salt lake* South
  Australia
Gaizina Kalns *see* Gaiziņkalns
Gaiziņkalns 106 *C3 var.* Gaizina Kalns.
  mountain E Latvia
Galán, Cerro 64 *B3 mountain*
  NW Argentina
Galanta 99 *C6 Hung.* Galánta. Trnavský
  Kraj, W Slovakia
Galapagos Fracture Zone 153 *E3*
  tectonic feature E Pacific Ocean
Galapagos Islands 153 *F3 var.* Islas de
  los Galápagos, *Eng.* Galapagos Islands,
  Tortoise Islands. *island group* Ecuador,
  E Pacific Ocean
Galapagos Islands *see* Colón,
  Archipiélago de
Galápagos, Islas de los *see* Colón,
  Archipiélago de
Galapagos Rise 153 *F3 undersea rise*
  E Pacific Ocean
Galashiels 88 *C4* SE Scotland, United
  Kingdom
Galați 108 *D4 Ger.* Galatz. Galați,
  E Romania
Galatz *see* Galați
Galcaio *see* Gaalkacyo
Galesburg 40 *B3* Illinois, N USA
Galicia 92 *B1 anc.* Gallaecia.
  autonomous community NW Spain
Galicia Bank 80 *B4 undersea bank*
  E Atlantic Ocean
Galilee, Sea of *see* Tiberias, Lake
Galka'yo *see* Gaalkacyo
Galkynyş 122 *D3 prev. Rus.* Deynau,
  Dyanev, *Turkm.* Dänew. Lebap
  Welaýaty, NE Turkmenistan
Gallaecia *see* Galicia
Galle 132 *D4 prev.* Point de Galle.
  Southern Province, SW Sri Lanka
Gallego Rise 153 *F3 undersea rise*
  E Pacific Ocean
Gallegos *see* Río Gallegos
Gallia *see* France
Gallipoli 97 *E6* Puglia, SE Italy
Gällivare 84 *C3 Lapp.* Váhtjer.
  Norrbotten, N Sweden
Gallup 48 *C1* New Mexico, SW USA
Galtat-Zemmour 70 *B3* C Western
  Sahara
Galveston 49 *H4* Texas, SW USA
Galway 89 *A5 Ir.* Gaillimh. W Ireland
Galway Bay 89 *A6 Ir.* Cuan na Gaillimhe.
  bay W Ireland
Gámas *see* Kaamanen
Gambell 36 *C2* Saint Lawrence Island,
  Alaska, USA
Gambia 74 *B3 off.* Republic of The
  Gambia, The Gambia. *country*
  W Africa

GAMBIA
West Africa

Official name Republic of the Gambia
Formation 1965 / 1965
Capital Banjul
Population 1.6 million / 414 people
  per sq mile (160 people per sq km) / 26%
Total area 4363 sq. miles (11,300 sq. km)
Languages English*, Mandinka, Fulani,
  Wolof, Jola, Soninke
Religions Sunni Muslim 90%,
  Christian 9%, Traditional beliefs 1%
Ethnic mix Mandinka 40%, Fulani 19%,
  Wolof 15%, Jola 11%, Serahuli 9%,
  Other 6%
Government Presidential system
Currency Dalasi = 100 butut
Literacy rate 38%
Calorie consumption 2273 calories

Gambia 74 *C3 Fr.* Gambie. *river* W Africa
Gambia, Republic of The *see* Gambia
Gambia, The *see* Gambia
Gambie *see* Gambia
Gambier, Îles 143 *G4 island group*
  E French Polynesia
Gamboma 77 *B6* Plateaux, E Congo
Gamlakarleby *see* Kokkola
Gan 132 *B5* Addu Atoll, C Maldives
Gan *see* Gansu, China
Gan *see* Jiangxi, China
Ganaane *see* Juba
Gäncä 117 *G2 Rus.* Gyandzha; *prev.*
  Kirovabad, Yelisavetpol. W Azerbaijan
Gand *see* Gent
Gandajika 77 *D7* Kasai-Oriental, S Dem.
  Rep. Congo
Gander 39 *G3* Newfoundland and
  Labrador, SE Canada
Gāndhīdhām 134 *C4* Gujarāt, W India
Gandía 93 *F3* País Valenciano, E Spain
Ganges 135 *F3 Ben.* Padma. *river*
  Bangladesh/India
Ganges Cone *see* Ganges Fan
Ganges Fan 140 *D3 var.* Ganges Cone.
  undersea fan N Bay of Bengal
Ganges, Mouths of the 135 *G4 delta*
  Bangladesh/India
Gangra *see* Çankırı
Gangtok 135 *F3 state capital* Sikkim,
  N India
Gansos, Lago dos *see* Goose Lake
Gansu 128 *B4 var.* Gan, Gansu Sheng,
  Kansu. *province* N China
Gansu Sheng *see* Gansu
Gantsevichi *see* Hantsavichy
Ganzhou 128 *D6* Jiangxi, S China
Gao 75 *E3* Gao, E Mali
Gaocheng *see* Litang
Gaoual 74 *C4* N Guinea
Gaoxiong *see* Kaohsiung
Gap 91 *D5 anc.* Vapincum. Hautes-
  Alpes, SE France
Gaplaňgyr Platosy 122 *C2 Rus.* Plato
  Kaplangky. *ridge* Turkmenistan/
  Uzbekistan
Gar *see* Gar Xincun
Garabil Belentligi 122 *D3 Rus.*
  Vozvyshennost' Karabil'. *mountain
  range* S Turkmenistan
Garabogaz Aylagy 122 *B2 Rus.*
  Zaliv Kara-Bogaz-Gol. *bay*
  NW Turkmenistan
Garachiné 53 *G5* Darién, SE Panama
Garagum 122 *var.* Garagumy, Qara
  Qum, *Eng.* Black Sand Desert, Kara
  Kum; *prev.* Peski Karakumy. *desert*
  C Turkmenistan
Garagum Canal 122 *D3 var.* Kara
  Kum Canal, *Rus.* Karagumskiy
  Kanal, Karakumskiy Kanal. *canal*
  C Turkmenistan
Garagumy *see* Garagum
Gara Khitrino 104 *D2* Shumen,
  NE Bulgaria
Gárassavon *see* Kaaresuvanto
Garda, Lake 96 *C2 var.* Benaco, *Eng.*
  Lake Garda, *Ger.* Gardasee. *lake*
  NE Italy
Garda, Lake *see* Garda, Lago di
Gardasee *see* Garda, Lago di
Garden City 45 *E5* Kansas, C USA
Garden State, The *see* New Jersey
Gardner Island *see* Nikumaroro
Garegeasnjárga *see* Karigasniemi

Gargždai 106 *B3* Klaipėda,
  W Lithuania
Garissa 73 *D6* Coast, E Kenya
Garland 49 *G2* Texas, SW USA
Garoe *see* Garoowe
Garonne 91 *B5 anc.* Garumna. *river*
  S France
Garoowe 73 *E5 var.* Garoe. Nugaal,
  N Somalia
Garoua 76 *B4 var.* Garua. Nord,
  N Cameroon
Garry Lake 37 *F3 lake* Nunavut,
  N Canada
Garsen 73 *D6* Coast, S Kenya
Garua *see* Garoua
Garumna *see* Garonne
Garwolin 98 *D4* Mazowieckie, E Poland
Gar Xincun 126 *A4 prev.* Gar. Xizang
  Zizhiqu, W China
Gary 40 *B3* Indiana, N USA
Garzón 58 *B4* Huila, S Colombia
Gasan-Kuli *see* Esenguly
Gascogne 91 *B6 Eng.* Gascony. *cultural
  region* S France
Gascony *see* Gascogne
Gascoyne River 147 *A5 river* Western
  Australia
Gaspé 39 *F3* Québec, SE Canada
Gaspé, Péninsule de 39 *E4 var.*
  Péninsule de la Gaspésie. *peninsula*
  Québec, SE Canada
Gaspésie, Péninsule de la *see* Gaspé,
  Péninsule de
Gastonia 43 *E1* North Carolina, SE USA
Gastoúni 105 *B6* Dytikí Ellás, S Greece
Gatchina 110 *B4* Leningradskaya Oblast',
  NW Russian Federation
Gatineau 38 *D4* Québec, SE Canada
Gatooma *see* Kadoma
Gatún, Lake 53 *F4 reservoir* C Panama
Gauhāti *see* Guwāhāti
Gauja 106 *D3 Ger.* Aa. *river* Estonia/
  Latvia
Gaul/Gaule *see* France
Gauteng *see* Johannesburg, South Africa
Gävbandī 120 *D4* Hormozgān, S Iran
Gávdos 105 *C8 island* SE Greece
Gavere 87 *B6* Oost-Vlaanderen,
  NW Belgium
Gävle 85 *C6 var.* Gäfle; *prev.* Gefle.
  Gävleborg, C Sweden
Gawler 149 *B6* South Australia
Gaya 135 *F3* Bihār, N India
Gaya *see* Kyjov
Gayndah 149 *E5* Queensland, E Australia
Gaysin *see* Haysyn
Gaza 119 *A6 Ar.* Ghazzah, *Heb.* 'Azza.
  NE Gaza Strip
Gaz-Achak *see* Gazojak
Gazandzhyk/Gazanjyk *see* Bereket
Gaza Strip 119 *A7 Ar.* Qita Ghazzah.
  disputed region SW Asia
Gaziantep 116 *D4 var.* Gazi Antep; *prev.*
  Aintab, Antep. Gaziantep, S Turkey
Gazi Antep *see* Gaziantep
Gazimağusa 102 *D5 var.* Famagusta, *Gk.*
  Ammóchostos. E Cyprus
Gazli 122 *D2* Buxoro Viloyati,
  C Uzbekistan
Gazojak 122 *D2 Rus.* Gaz-Achak. Lebap
  Welaýaty, NE Turkmenistan
Gbanga 74 *D5 var.* Gbarnga. N Liberia
Gbarnga *see* Gbanga
Gdańsk 98 *C2 Fr.* Dantzig, *Ger.* Danzig.
  Pomorskie, N Poland
Gdan'skaya Bukhta/Gdańsk, Gulf of *see*
  Danzig, Gulf of
Gdańska, Zakota *see* Danzig, Gulf of
Gdingen *see* Gdynia
Gdynia 98 *C2 Ger.* Gdingen. Pomorskie,
  N Poland
Gedaref 72 *C4 var.* Al Qadārif, El
  Gedaref. Gedaref, E Sudan
Gediz 116 *B3* Kütahya, W Turkey
Gediz Nehri 116 *A3 river* W Turkey
Geel 87 *C5 var.* Gheel. Antwerpen,
  N Belgium
Geelong 149 *C7* Victoria, SE Australia
Ge'e'mu *see* Golmud
Gefle *see* Gävle
Geilo 85 *A5* Buskerud, S Norway
Gejiu 128 *B6 var.* Kochiu. Yunnan,
  S China
Gëkdepe *see* Gökdepe
Gela 97 *C7 prev.* Terranova di Sicilia.
  Sicilia, Italy, C Mediterranean Sea

Geldermalsen 86 *C4* Gelderland,
  C Netherlands
Geleen 87 *D6* Limburg, SE Netherlands
Gelib *see* Jilib
Gellinsor 73 *E5* Mudug, C Somalia
Gembloux 87 *C6* Namur, C Belgium
Gemena 77 *C5* Equateur, NW Dem.
  Rep. Congo
Gem of the Mountains *see* Idaho
Gemona del Friuli 96 *D2* Friuli-Venezia
  Giulia, NE Italy
Gem State *see* Idaho
Genalē Wenz *see* Juba
Genck *see* Genk
General Alvear 64 *B4* Mendoza,
  W Argentina
General Carrera, Lago *see* Buenos
  Aires, Lago
General Eugenio A. Garay 64 *C1*
  var. Fortín General Eugenio Garay;
  prev. Yrendagüé. Nueva Asunción,
  NW Paraguay
General José F.Uriburu *see* Zárate
General Machado *see* Camacupa
General Santos 139 *F3 off.* General
  Santos City. Mindanao, S Philippines
General Santos City *see* General Santos
Gênes *see* Genova
Geneva *see* Genève
Geneva, Lake 95 *A7 Fr.* Lac de Genève,
  Lac Léman, *le* Léman, *Ger.* Genfer See.
  lake France/Switzerland
Genève 95 *A7 Eng.* Geneva, *Ger.* Genf, *It.*
  Ginevra. Genève, SW Switzerland
Genève, Lac de *see* Geneva, Lake
Genf *see* Genève
Genfer See *see* Geneva, Lake
Genichesk *see* Heniches'k
Genk 87 *D6 var.* Genck. Limburg,
  NE Belgium
Gennep 86 *D4* Limburg, SE Netherlands
Genoa *see* Genova
Genoa, Gulf of 96 *A3 Eng.* Gulf of
  Genoa. *gulf* NW Italy
Genoa, Gulf of *see* Genova, Golfo di
Genova 102 *D1 Eng.* Genoa; *anc.* Genua,
  Fr. Gênes. Liguria, NW Italy
Genovesa, Isla 60 *B5 var.* Tower Island.
  island Galapagos Islands, Ecuador,
  E Pacific Ocean
Gent 87 *B5 Eng.* Ghent, *Fr.* Gand. Oost-
  Vlaanderen, NW Belgium
Genua *see* Genova
Geok-Tepe *see* Gökdepe
George 78 *C5* Western Cape, S South
  Africa
George 82 *A4 river* Newfoundland and
  Labrador/Québec, E Canada
George, Lake 43 *E3 lake* Florida, SE USA
Georgenburg *see* Jurbarkas
Georges Bank 35 *D5 undersea bank*
  W Atlantic Ocean
George Sound 151 *A7 sound* South
  Island, New Zealand
Georges River 148 *D2 river* New South
  Wales, E Australia
Georgetown 59 *F2 country capital*
  (Guyana) (Guyana) N Guyana
George Town 54 *C2* Great Exuma Island,
  C Bahamas
George Town 54 *B3 var.* Georgetown.
  dependent territory capital (Cayman
  Islands) Grand Cayman, SW Cayman
  Islands
George Town 138 *B3 var.* Penang,
  Pinang. Pinang, Peninsular Malaysia
Georgetown 43 *F2* South Carolina,
  SE USA
Georgetown *see* George Town
George V Land 154 *C4 physical region*
  Antarctica
Georgia 117 *F2 off.* Republic of Georgia,
  Geor. Sak'art'velo, *Rus.* Gruzinskaya
  SSR, Gruziya. *country* SW Asia

GEORGIA
Southwest Asia

Official name Georgia
Formation 1991 / 1991
Capital Tbilisi
Population 4.4 million / 164 people
  per sq mile (63 people per sq km) / 52%
Total area 26,911 sq. miles (69,700 sq. km)
Languages Georgian*, Russian, Azeri,
  Armenian, Mingrelian, Ossetian,
  Abkhazian* (*in Abkhazia*)

GEORGIA
(continued)

Religions Georgian Orthodox 65%,
Muslim 11%, Russian Orthodox 10%,
Armenian Apostolic Church
(Orthodox) 8%, Other 6%
Ethnic mix Georgian 84%, Armenian 6%,
Azeri 6%, Russian 2%, Other 1%,
Ossetian 1%
Government Presidential system
Currency Lari = 100 tetri
Literacy rate 99%
Calorie consumption 2354 calories

Georgia *42 D2 off.* State of Georgia, *also
known as* Empire State of the South,
Peach State. *state* SE USA
Georgian Bay *40 D2 lake bay* Ontario,
S Canada
Georgia, Republic of *see* Georgia
Georgia, Strait of *46 A1 strait* British
Columbia, W Canada
Georgi Dimitrov *see* Kostenets
Georgiu-Dezh *see* Liski
Georg von Neumayer *154 A2 German
research station* Antarctica
Gera *94 C4* Thüringen, E Germany
Geráki *105 B6* Pelopónnisos, S Greece
Geraldine *151 B6* Canterbury, South
Island, New Zealand
Geraldton *147 A6* Western Australia
Geral, Serra *57 D5 mountain range*
S Brazil
Gerede *116 C2* Bolu, N Turkey
Gereshk *122 D5* Helmand,
SW Afghanistan
Gering *44 D3* Nebraska, C USA
German East Africa *see* Tanzania
Germanicopolis *see* Çankırı
Germanicum, Mare/German Ocean
see North Sea
German Southwest Africa *see* Namibia
Germany *94 B4 off.* Federal Republic
of Germany, Bundesrepublik
Deutschland, *Ger.* Deutschland.
country N Europe

GERMANY
Northern Europe

Official name Federal Republic
of Germany
Formation 1871 / 1990
Capital Berlin
Population 82.7 million / 613 people
per sq mile (237 people per sq km) / 88%
Total area 137,846 sq. miles
(357,021 sq. km)
Languages German*, Turkish
Religions Protestant 34%, Roman
Catholic 33%, Other 30%, Muslim 3%
Ethnic mix German 92%, Other
European 3%, Other 3%, Turkish 2%
Government Parliamentary system
Currency Euro = 100 cents
Literacy rate 99%
Calorie consumption 3496 calories

Germany, Federal Republic of *see*
Germany
Geroliménas *105 B7* Pelopónnisos,
S Greece
Gerona *see* Girona
Gerpinnes *87 C7* Hainaut, S Belgium
Gerunda *see* Girona
Gerze *116 D2* Sinop, N Turkey
Gesoriacum *see* Boulogne-sur-Mer
Gessoriacum *see* Boulogne-sur-Mer
Getafe *92 D3* Madrid, C Spain
Gevaş *117 F3* Van, SE Turkey
Gevgeli *see* Gevgelija
Gevgelija *101 E6 var.* Đevđelija,
Djevdjelija, *Turk.* Gevgeli.
SE Macedonia
Ghaba *see* Al Ghābah
Ghana *75 E5 off.* Republic of Ghana.
country W Africa

GHANA
West Africa

Official name Republic of Ghana
Formation 1957 / 1957
Capital Accra
Population 23 million / 259 people
per sq mile (100 people per sq km) / 46%

GHANA
(continued)

Total area 92,100 sq. miles (238,540 sq. km)
Languages English*, Twi, Fanti, Ewe, Ga,
Adangbe, Gurma, Dagomba (Dagbani)
Religions Christian 69%, Muslim 16%,
Traditional beliefs 9%, Other 6%
Ethnic mix Akan 49%, Mole-Dagbani 17%,
Ewe 13%, Other 9%, Ga and
Ga-Adangbe 8%, Guan 4%
Government Presidential system
Currency Cedi = 100 pesewas
Literacy rate 58%
Calorie consumption 2667 calories

Ghanzi *78 C3 var.* Khanzi. Ghanzi,
W Botswana
Gharandal *119 B7* Al'Aqabah,
SW Jordan
Gharbt, Jabal al *see* Liban, Jebel
Ghardaïa *70 D2* N Algeria
Gharvān *see* Gharyān
Gharyān *71 F2 var.* Gharvān. NW Libya
Ghawdex *see* Gozo
Ghaznī *123 E4 var.* Ghazni. Ghazni,
E Afghanistan
Ghazzah *see* Gaza
Gheel *see* Geel
Ghent *see* Gent
Gheorghieni *108 C4 prev.* Gheorghieni,
Sîn-Miclâuş, *Ger.* Niklasmarkt, *Hung.*
Gyergyószentmiklós. Harghita,
C Romania
Gheorghieni *see* Gheorghieni
Ghūdara *123 F3 var.* Gudara, *Rus.*
Kudara. SE Tajikistan
Ghurdaqah *see* Hurghada
Ghūrīān *122 D4* Herāt, W Afghanistan
Giamame *see* Jamaame
Giannitsá *104 B4 var.* Yiannitsá.
Kentrikí Makedonía, N Greece
Gibraltar *93 G4* UK dependent territory
SW Europe
Gibraltar, Bay of *93 G5 bay* Gibraltar/
Spain Europe Mediterranean Sea
Atlantic Ocean
**Gibraltar, Détroit de/Gibraltar,
Estrecho de** *see* Gibraltar, Strait of
Gibraltar, Strait of *92 C5 Fr.* Détroit de
Gibraltar, *Sp.* Estrecho de Gibraltar.
strait Atlantic Ocean/Mediterranean Sea
Gibson Desert *147 B5 desert* Western
Australia
Giedraičiai *107 C5* Utena, E Lithuania
Giessen *95 B5* Hessen, W Germany
Gifu *131 C6 var.* Gihu. Gifu, Honshū,
SW Japan
Giganta, Sierra de la *50 B3 mountain
range* NW Mexico
Gihu *see* Gifu
G'ijduvon *122 D2 Rus.* Gizhduvon.
Buxoro Viloyati, C Uzbekistan
Gijón *92 D1 var.* Xixón. Asturias,
NW Spain
Gila River *48 A2 river* Arizona, SW USA
Gilbert Islands *see* Tungaru
Gilbert River *148 C3 river* Queensland,
NE Australia
Gilf Kebir Plateau *see* Haḍabat al Jilf
al Kabīr
Gillette *44 D3* Wyoming, C USA
Gilolo *see* Halmahera, Pulau
Gilroy *47 B6* California, W USA
Gimie, Mount *55 F1 mountain* C Saint
Lucia
Gimma *see* Jīma
Ginevra *see* Genève
Gingin *147 A6* Western Australia
Giohar *see* Jawhar
Gipeswic *see* Ipswich
Girardot *58 B3* Cundinamarca,
C Colombia
Giresun *117 E2 var.* Kerasunt; *anc.*
Cerasus, Pharnacia. Giresun, NE Turkey
Girgenti *see* Agrigento
Girin *see* Jilin
Girne *102 C5 Gk.* Kerýneia, Kyrenia.
N Cyprus
Giron *see* Kiruna
Girona *93 G2 var.* Gerona; *anc.* Gerunda.
Cataluña, NE Spain
Gisborne *150 E3* Gisborne, North Island,
New Zealand
Gissar Range *123 E3 Rus.* Gissarskiy
Khrebet. *mountain range* Tajikistan/
Uzbekistan

Gissarskiy Khrebet *see* Gissar Range
Githio *see* Gýtheio
Giulianova *96 D4* Abruzzi, C Italy
Giumri *see* Gyumri
Giurgiu *108 C5* Giurgiu, S Romania
Giza *72 B1 var.* Al Jīzah, El Gīza, Gizeh.
N Egypt
Gizhduvon *see* G'ijduvon
Giżycko *98 D2 Ger.* Lötzen. Warmińsko-
Mazurskie, NE Poland
Gjakovë *101 D5 Serb.* Đakovica.
W Kosovo
Gjilan *101 D5 Serb.* Gnjilane. E Kosovo
Gjinokastër *see* Gjirokastër
Gjirokastër *101 C7 var.* Gjirokastra;
prev. Gjinokastër, *Gk.* Argyrokastron,
It. Argirocastro. Gjirokastër, S Albania
Gjirokastra *see* Gjirokastër
Gjoa Haven *37 F3 var.* Uqsuqtuuq. King
William Island, Nunavut, NW Canada
Gjøvik *85 B5* Oppland, S Norway
Glace Bay *39 G4* Cape Breton Island,
Nova Scotia, SE Canada
Gladstone *148 E4* Queensland,
E Australia
Gláma *85 B5 var.* Glommen. *river*
S Norway
Glasgow *88 C4* S Scotland, United
Kingdom
Glavn'a Morava *see* Velika Morava
Glazov *111 D5* Udmurtskaya Respublika,
NW Russian Federation
Gleiwitz *see* Gliwice
Glendale *48 B2* Arizona, SW USA
Glendive *44 D2* Montana, NW USA
Glens Falls *41 F3* New York, NE USA
Glevum *see* Gloucester
Glina *100 B3 var.* Banijska Palanka.
Sisak-Moslavina, NE Croatia
Glittertind *85 A5 mountain* S Norway
Gliwice *99 C5 Ger.* Gleiwitz. Śląskie,
S Poland
Globe *48 B2* Arizona, SW USA
Globino *see* Hlobyne
Głogau *see* Głogów
Głogów *98 B4 Ger.* Glogau, Glogow.
Dolnośląskie, SW Poland
Glogow *see* Głogów
Glomma *see* Gláma
Glommen *see* Gláma
Gloucester *89 D6 hist.* Caer Glou, *Lat.*
Glevum. C England, United Kingdom
Głowno *98 D4* Łódź, C Poland
Glubokoye *see* Hlybokaye
Glukhov *see* Hlukhiv
Gnesen *see* Gniezno
Gniezno *98 C3 Ger.* Gnesen.
Weilkopolskie, C Poland
Gnjilane *see* Gjilan
Gobabis *78 B3* Omaheke, E Namibia
Gobi *126 D3 desert* China/Mongolia
Gobō *131 C6* Wakayama, Honshū,
SW Japan
Godavari *124 B3 var.* Godavari. *river*
C India
Godavari *see* Godāvari
Godhavn *see* Qeqertarsuaq
Godhra *134 C4* Gujarāt, W India
Göding *see* Hodonín
Godoy Cruz *64 B4* Mendoza,
W Argentina
Godthaab/Godthåb *see* Nuuk
Godwin Austen, Mount *see* K2
Goede Hoop, Kaap de *see* Good Hope,
Cape of
Goeie Hoop, Kaap die *see* Good Hope,
Cape of
Goeree *86 B4 island* SW Netherlands
Goes *87 B5* Zeeland, SW Netherlands
Goettingen *see* Göttingen
Gogebic Range *40 B1 hill range*
Michigan/Wisconsin, N USA
Goiânia *63 E3 prev.* Goyania. *state
capital* Goiás, C Brazil
Goiás *63 E3 off.* Estado de Goiás; *prev.*
Goiaz, Goyaz. *region* C Brazil
Goiás *63 E3 off.* Estado de Goiás; *prev.*
Goiaz, Goyaz. *state* C Brazil
Goiás, Estado de *see* Goiás
Goiaz *see* Goiás
Goidhoo Atoll *see* Horsburgh Atoll
Gojōme *130 D4* Akita, Honshū,
NW Japan
Gökçeada *104 D4 var.* Imroz Adasī, *Gk.*
Imbros. *island* NW Turkey
Gökdepe *122 C3 Rus.* Gëkdepe, Geok-
Tepe. Ahal Welaýaty, C Turkmenistan

Göksun *116 D4* Kahramanmaraş,
C Turkey
Gol *85 A5* Buskerud, S Norway
Golan Heights *119 B5 Ar.* Al Jawlān,
Heb. HaGolan. *mountain range*
SW Syria
Golaya Pristan *see* Hola Prystan'
Gołdap *98 E2 Ger.* Goldap. Warmińsko-
Mazurskie, NE Poland
Gold Coast *149 E5 cultural region*
Queensland, E Australia
Golden Bay *150 C4 bay* South Island,
New Zealand
Golden State, The *see* California
Goldingen *see* Kuldīga
Goldsboro *43 F1* North Carolina,
SE USA
Goleniów *98 B3 Ger.* Gollnow.
Zachodnio-pomorskie, NW Poland
Gollnow *see* Goleniów
Golmo *see* Golmud
Golmud *126 D4 var.* Ge'e'mu, Golmo,
Chin. Ko-erh-mu. Qinghai, C China
Golovanevsk *see* Holovanivs'k
Golub-Dobrzyń *98 C3* Kujawski-
pomorskie, C Poland
Goma *77 E6* Nord-Kivu, NE Dem.
Rep. Congo
Gombi *75 H4* Adamawa, E Nigeria
Gombroon *see* Bandar-e 'Abbās
Gomel' *see* Homyel'
Gómera *70 A3 island* Islas Canarias,
Spain, NE Atlantic Ocean
Gómez Palacio *50 D3* Durango,
C Mexico
Gonaïves *54 D3 var.* Les Gonaïves.
N Haiti
Gonâve, Île de la *54 D3 island* C Haiti
Gonder *see* Gondar
Gonder *72 C4 var.* Gondar. Āmara,
NW Ethiopia
Gondia *135 E4* Mahārāshtra, C India
Gonggar *126 C5 var.* Gyixong. Xizang
Zizhiqu, W China
Gongola *75 G4 river* E Nigeria
Gongtang *see* Damxung
Gonni/Gónnos *see* Gónnoi
Gónnoi *104 B4 var.* Gonni, Gónnos;
prev. Dereli. Thessalía, C Greece
Good Hope, Cape of *78 B5 Afr.* Kaap de
Goede Hoop, Kaap die Goeie Hoop.
headland SW South Africa
Goodland *44 D4* Kansas, C USA
Goondiwindi *149 D5* Queensland,
E Australia
Goor *86 E3* Overijssel, E Netherlands
Goose Green *65 D7 var.* Prado del
Ganso. East Falkland, Falkland Islands
Goose Lake *46 B4 var.* Lago dos Gansos.
lake California/Oregon, W USA
Gopher State *see* Minnesota
Göppingen *95 B6* Baden-Württemberg,
SW Germany
Góra Kalwaria *114 D4* Mazowieckie,
C Poland
Gorakhpur *135 E3* Uttar Pradesh,
N India
Gorany *see* Harany
Goražde *100 C4* Federacija Bosna
I Hercegovina, SE Bosnia and
Herzegovina
Gorbovichi *see* Harbavichy
Goré *76 C4* Logone-Oriental, S Chad
Gorë *73 C5* Oromīya, C Ethiopia
Gore *151 B7* Southland, South Island,
New Zealand
Gorgān *120 D2 var.* Astarabad,
Astrabad, Gurgan, *prev.* Asterābād;
anc. Hyrcania. Golestán, N Iran
Gorinchem *86 C4 var.* Gorkum.
Holland, C Netherlands
Goris *117 G3* SE Armenia
Gorki *see* Horki
Gor'kiy *see* Nizhniy Novgorod
Gorkum *see* Gorinchem
Görlitz *94 D4* Sachsen, E Germany
Gorlovka *see* Horlivka
Gorna Dzhumaya *see* Blagoevgrad
Gorna Oryahovitsa *see* Gorna
Oryahovitsa
Gornji Milanovac *100 C4* Serbia,
C Serbia
Gorodets *see* Haradzyets
Gorodishche *see* Horodyshche
Gorodnya *see* Horodnya
Gorodok *see* Haradok

Gorodok/Gorodok Yagellonski *see*
    Horodok
Gorontalo 139 E4 Sulawesi, C Indonesia
Gorontalo, Teluk *see* Tomini, Gulf of
Gorssel 86 D3 Gelderland, E Netherlands
Goryn *see* Horyn'
Gorzów Wielkopolski 98 B3 Ger.
    Landsberg, Landsberg an der Warthe.
    Lubuskie, W Poland
Gosford 149 D6 New South Wales,
    SE Australia
Goshogawara 130 D3 var. Gosyogawara.
    Aomori, Honshū, C Japan
Gospić 100 A3 Lika-Senj, C Croatia
Gostivar 101 D6 W FYR Macedonia
Gosyogawara *see* Goshogawara
Göteborg 85 B7 Eng. Gothenburg.
    Västra Götaland, S Sweden
Gotel Mountains 75 G5 mountain range
    E Nigeria
Gotha 94 C4 Thüringen, C Germany
Gothenburg *see* Göteborg
Gotland 85 C7 island SE Sweden
Goto-retto 131 A7 island group
    SW Japan
Gotska Sandön 106 B1 island SE Sweden
Götsu 131 B6 var. Gôtu. Shimane,
    Honshū, SW Japan
Göttingen 94 B4 var. Goettingen.
    Niedersachsen, C Germany
Gottschee *see* Kočevje
Gottwaldov *see* Zlín
Gôtu *see* Götsu
Gouda 86 C4 Zuid-Holland,
    C Netherlands
Gough Fracture Zone 67 C6 tectonic
    feature S Atlantic Ocean
Gough Island 69 B8 island Tristan da
    Cunha, S Atlantic Ocean
Gouin, Réservoir 38 D4 reservoir
    Québec, SE Canada
Goulburn 149 D6 New South Wales,
    SE Australia
Goundam 75 E3 Tombouctou, NW Mali
Gouré 75 G3 Zinder, SE Niger
Goverla, Gora *see* Hoverla, Hora
Governador Valadares 63 F4 Minas
    Gerais, SE Brazil
Govi Altayn Nuruu 127 E3 mountain
    range S Mongolia
Goya 64 D3 Corrientes, NE Argentina
Goyania *see* Goiânia
Goyaz *see* Goiás
Goz Beïda 76 C3 Ouaddaï, SE Chad
Gozo 97 C8 var. Ghawdex. island
    N Malta
Graciosa 92 A5 var. Ilha Graciosa. island
    Azores, Portugal, NE Atlantic Ocean
Graciosa, Ilha *see* Graciosa
Gradačac 100 C3 Federacija Bosna
    I Hercegovina, N Bosnia and
    Herzegovina
Gradaús, Serra dos 63 E3 mountain
    range C Brazil
Gradiška *see* Bosanska Gradiška
Grafton 149 E5 New South Wales,
    SE Australia
Grafton 45 E1 North Dakota, N USA
Graham Land 154 A2 physical region
    Antarctica
Grajewo 98 E3 Podlaskie, NE Poland
Grampian Mountains 88 C3 mountain
    range C Scotland, United Kingdom
Gran *see* Esztergom, Hungary
Granada 52 D3 Granada, SW Nicaragua
Granada 92 D5 Andalucía, S Spain
Gran Canaria 70 A3 var. Grand Canary.
    island Islas Canarias, Spain, NE Atlantic
    Ocean
Gran Chaco 64 D2 var. Chaco. lowland
    plain South America
Grand Bahama Island 54 B1 island
    N Bahamas
Grand Banks of Newfoundland 34 E4
    undersea basin NW Atlantic Ocean
Grand Bassa *see* Buchanan
Grand Canary *see* Gran Canaria
Grand Canyon 48 A1 canyon Arizona,
    SW USA
Grand Canyon State *see* Arizona
Grand Cayman 54 B3 island
    SW Cayman Islands
Grand Duchy of Luxembourg *see*
    Luxembourg
Grande, Bahía 65 B7 bay S Argentina
Grande-Comor *see* Ngazidja
Grande de Chiloé, Isla *see* Chiloé, Isla de

Grande Prairie 37 E4 Alberta, W Canada
Grand Erg Occidental 70 D3 desert
    W Algeria
Grand Erg Oriental 71 E3 desert
    Algeria/Tunisia
Río Grande 51 E2 var. Río Bravo, Sp. Río
    Bravo del Norte, Bravo del Norte. river
    Mexico/USA
Grande Terre 55 G3 island E West Indies
Grand Falls 39 G3 Newfoundland,
    Newfoundland and Labrador,
    SE Canada
Grand Forks 45 E1 North Dakota,
    N USA
Grandichi *see* Hrandzichy
Grand Island 45 E4 Nebraska, C USA
Grand Junction 44 C4 Colorado, C USA
Grand Paradis *see* Gran Paradiso
Grand Rapids 40 C3 Michigan, N USA
Grand Rapids 45 F1 Minnesota, N USA
Grand-Saint-Bernard, Col du *see* Great
    Saint Bernard Pass
Grand-Santi 59 G3 W French Guiana
Granite State *see* New Hampshire
Gran Lago *see* Nicaragua, Lago de
Gran Malvina *see* West Falkland
Gran Paradiso 96 A2 Fr. Grand Paradis.
    mountain NW Italy
Gran San Bernardo, Passo di *see* Great
    Saint Bernard Pass
Gran Santiago *see* Santiago
Grants 48 C2 New Mexico, SW USA
Grants Pass 46 B4 Oregon, NW USA
Granville 90 B3 Manche, N France
Gratianopolis *see* Grenoble
Gratz *see* Graz
Graudenz *see* Grudziądz
Graulhet 91 C6 Tarn, S France
Grave 86 D4 Noord-Brabant,
    SE Netherlands
Grayling 36 C2 Alaska, USA
Graz 95 E7 prev. Gratz. Steiermark,
    SE Austria
Great Abaco 54 C1 var. Abaco Island.
    island N Bahamas
Great Alfold *see* Great Hungarian Plain
Great Ararat *see* Büyükağrı Dağı
Great Australian Bight 147 D7 bight
    S Australia
Great Barrier Island 150 D2 island
    N New Zealand
Great Barrier Reef 148 D2 reef
    Queensland, NE Australia
Great Basin 47 C5 basin W USA
Great Bear Lake 37 E3 Fr. Grand Lac
    de l'Ours. lake Northwest Territories,
    NW Canada
Great Belt 85 B8 var. Store Bælt, Eng.
    Great Belt, Storebelt. channel Baltic
    Sea/Kattegat
Great Belt *see* Storebælt
Great Bend 45 E5 Kansas, C USA
Great Britain *see* Britain
Great Dividing Range 148 D4 mountain
    range NE Australia
Greater Antilles 54 D3 island group
    West Indies
Greater Caucasus 117 G2 mountain
    range Azerbaijan/Georgia/Russian
    Federation Asia/Europe
Greater Sunda Islands 124 D5 var.
    Sunda Islands. island group Indonesia
Great Exhibition Bay 150 C1 inlet North
    Island, New Zealand
Great Exuma Island 54 C2 island
    C Bahamas
Great Falls 44 B1 Montana, NW USA
Great Grimsby *see* Grimsby
Great Hungarian Plain 99 C7 var. Great
    Alfold, Plain of Hungary, Hung. Alföld.
    plain SE Europe
Great Inagua 54 D2 var. Inagua Islands.
    island S Bahamas
Great Indian Desert *see* Thar Desert
Great Khingan Range 127 G1 Eng.
    Great Khingan Range. mountain range
    NE China
Great Khingan Range *see* Da Hinggan
    Ling
Great Lake *see* Tônlé Sap
Great Lakes 35 C5 lakes Ontario,
    Canada/USA
Great Lakes State *see* Michigan
Great Meteor Seamount *see* Great
    Meteor Tablemount
Great Meteor Tablemount 66 B3 var.
    Great Meteor Seamount. seamount
    E Atlantic Ocean

Great Nicobar 133 G3 island Nicobar
    Islands, India, NE Indian Ocean
Great Plain of China 125 E2 plain
    E China
Great Plains 45 E3 var. High Plains.
    plains Canada/USA
Great Rift Valley 73 C5 var. Rift Valley.
    depression Asia/Africa
Great Ruaha 73 C7 river S Tanzania
Great Saint Bernard Pass 96 A4 Fr.
    Col du Grand-Saint-Bernard, It. Passo
    del Gran San Bernardo. pass Italy/
    Switzerland
Great Salt Desert *see* Kavīr, Dasht-e
Great Salt Lake 44 A3 salt lake Utah,
    W USA
Great Salt Lake Desert 44 A4 plain
    Utah, W USA
Great Sand Sea 71 H3 desert Egypt/Libya
Great Sandy Desert 146 C4 desert
    Western Australia
Great Sandy Desert *see* Ar Rub 'al Khālī
Great Sandy Island *see* Fraser Island
Great Slave Lake 37 E4 Fr. Grand
    Lac des Esclaves. lake Northwest
    Territories, NW Canada
Great Socialist People's Libyan Arab
    Jamahiriya *see* Libya
Great Sound 42 A5 sound Bermuda,
    NW Atlantic Ocean
Great Victoria Desert 147 C5 desert
    South Australia/Western Australia
Great Wall of China 128 C4 ancient
    monument N China Asia
Great Yarmouth 89 E6 var. Yarmouth.
    E England, United Kingdom
Grebenka *see* Hrebinka
Gredos, Sierra de 92 D3 mountain
    range W Spain
Greece 105 A5 off. Hellenic Republic, Gk.
    Ellás; anc. Hellas. country SE Europe

GREECE
Southeast Europe

Official name Hellenic Republic
Formation 1829 / 1947
Capital Athens
Population 11.2 million / 222 people
    per sq mile (86 people per sq km) / 61%
Total area 50,942 sq. miles (131,940 sq. km)
Languages Greek*, Turkish, Macedonian,
    Albanian
Religions Orthodox Christian 98%,
    Other 1%, Muslim 1%
Ethnic mix Greek 98%, Other 2%
Government Parliamentary system
Currency Euro = 100 cents
Literacy rate 96%
Calorie consumption 3721 calories

Greeley 44 D4 Colorado, C USA
Green Bay 40 B2 Wisconsin, N USA
Green Bay 40 B2 lake bay Michigan/
    Wisconsin, N USA
Greeneville 43 E1 Tennessee, S USA
Greenland 83 D3 Dan. Grønland, Inuit
    Kalaallit Nunaat. Danish external
    territory NE North America
Greenland Sea 83 F2 sea Arctic Ocean
Green Mountains 41 G2 mountain
    range Vermont, NE USA
Green Mountain State *see* Vermont
Greenock 88 C4 W Scotland, United
    Kingdom
Green River 44 B3 Wyoming, C USA
Green River 40 C5 river Kentucky,
    C USA
Green River 44 B4 river Utah, W USA
Greensboro 43 F1 North Carolina,
    SE USA
Greenville 42 B2 Mississippi, S USA
Greenville 43 F1 North Carolina, SE USA
Greenville 43 E1 North Carolina, SE USA
Greenville 49 G2 Texas, SW USA
Greenwich 89 B8 United Kingdom
Greenwood 42 B2 Mississippi, S USA
Greenwood 43 E2 South Carolina,
    SE USA
Gregory Range 148 C3 mountain range
    Queensland, E Australia
Greifenberg/Greifenberg in Pommern
    see Gryfice
Greifswald 94 D2 Mecklenburg-
    Vorpommern, NE Germany
Grenada 42 C2 Mississippi, S USA

Grenada 55 G5 country SE West Indies

GRENADA
West Indies

Official name Grenada
Formation 1974 / 1974
Capital St. George's
Population 89,971 / 687 people
    per sq mile (265 people per sq km) / 41%
Total area 131 sq. miles (340 sq. km)
Languages English*, English Creole
Religions Roman Catholic 68%,
    Anglican 17%, Other 15%
Ethnic mix Black African 82%, Mulatto
    (mixed race) 13%, East Indian 3%,
    Other 2%
Government Parliamentary system
Currency Eastern Caribbean dollar
    = 100 cents
Literacy rate 96%
Calorie consumption 2932 calories

Grenadines, The 55 H4 island group
    Grenada/St Vincent and the
    Grenadines
Grenoble 91 D5 anc. Cularo,
    Gratianopolis. Isère, E France
Gresham 46 B3 Oregon, NW USA
Grevená 104 B4 Dytiki Makedonía,
    N Greece
Grevenmacher 87 E8 Grevenmacher,
    E Luxembourg
Greymouth 151 B5 West Coast, South
    Island, New Zealand
Grey Range 149 C5 mountain range New
    South Wales/Queensland, E Australia
Greytown *see* San Juan del Norte
Griffin 42 D2 Georgia, SE USA
Grimari 76 C4 Ouaka, C Central African
    Republic
Grimsby 89 E5 prev. Great Grimsby.
    E England, United Kingdom
Grobin *see* Grobina
Grobiņa 106 B3 Ger. Grobin. Liepāja,
    W Latvia
Gródek Jagielloński *see* Horodok
Grodno *see* Hrodna
Grodzisk Wielkopolski 98 B3
    Wielkopolskie, C Poland
Groesbeek 86 D4 Gelderland,
    SE Netherlands
Grójec 98 D4 Mazowieckie, C Poland
Groningen 86 E1 Groningen,
    NE Netherlands
Gronland *see* Greenland
Groote Eylandt 148 B2 island Northern
    Territory, N Australia
Grootfontein 78 B3 Otjozondjupa,
    N Namibia
Groot Karasberge 78 B4 mountain
    range S Namibia
Gros Islet 55 F1 N Saint Lucia
Grossa, Isola *see* Dugi Otok
Grossbetschkerek *see* Zrenjanin
Grosse Morava *see* Velika Morava
Grosser Sund *see* Suur Väin
Grosseto 96 B4 Toscana, C Italy
Grossglockner 95 C7 mountain
    W Austria
Grosskanizsa *see* Nagykanizsa
Gross-Karol *see* Carei
Grosskikinda *see* Kikinda
Grossmichel *see* Michalovce
Gross-Schlatten *see* Abrud
Grosswardein *see* Oradea
Groznyy 111 B8 Chechenskaya
    Respublika, SW Russian Federation
Grudovo *see* Sredets
Grudziądz 98 C3 Ger. Graudenz.
    Kujawsko-pomorskie, C Poland
Grums 85 B6 Värmland, C Sweden
Grünberg/Grünberg in Schlesien *see*
    Zielona Góra
Grüneberg *see* Zielona Góra
Gruzinskaya SSR/Gruziya *see* Georgia
Gryazi 117 B6 Lipetskaya Oblast',
    W Russian Federation
Gryfice 98 B2 Ger. Greifenberg,
    Greifenberg in Pommern. Zachodnio-
    pomorskie, NW Poland
Guabito 53 E4 Bocas del Toro,
    NW Panama
Guadalajara 50 D4 Jalisco, C Mexico
Guadalajara 93 E3 Ar. Wad Al-Hajarah;
    anc. Arriaca. Castilla-La Mancha,
    C Spain

Guadalcanal *144 C3 island* C Solomon
Islands
Guadalquivir *92 D4 river* W Spain
Guadalupe *50 D3* Zacatecas, C Mexico
Guadalupe Peak *48 D3 mountain* Texas,
SW USA
Guadalupe River *49 G4 river* SW USA
Guadarrama, Sierra de *93 E2 mountain
range* C Spain
Guadeloupe *55 H3 French overseas
department* E West Indies
Guadiana *92 C4 river* Portugal/Spain
Guadix *93 E4* Andalucía, S Spain
Guaimaca *52 C2* Francisco Morazán,
C Honduras
Guajira, Península de la *58 B1
peninsula* N Colombia
Gualaco *52 D2* Olancho, C Honduras
Gualán *52 B2* Zacapa, C Guatemala
Guanabacoa *54 B2* La Habana, W Cuba
Guanajuato *51 E4* Guanajuato, C Mexico
Guanare *58 C2* Portuguesa, N Venezuela
Guanare, Río *58 D2 river* W Venezuela
Guangdong *128 C6 var.* Guangdong
Sheng, Kuang-tung, Kwangtung, Yue.
province S China
Guangdong Sheng *see* Guangdong
Guangju *see* Kwangju
Guangxi *see* Guangxi Zhuangzu Zizhiqu
Guangxi Zhuangzu Zizhiqu *128
C6 var.* Guangxi, Gui, Kuang-hsi,
Kwangsi, *Eng.* Kwangsi Chuang
Autonomous Region. *autonomous
region* S China
Guangyuan *128 B5 var.* Kuang-yuan,
Kwangyuan. Sichuan, C China
Guangzhou *128 C6 var.* Kuang-chou,
Kwangchow, *Eng.* Canton. *province
capital* Guangdong, S China
Guantánamo *54 D3* Guantánamo,
SE Cuba
Guantánamo, Bahía de *54 D3 Eng.*
Guantanamo Bay. *US military base*
SE Cuba
Guantanamo Bay *see* Guantánamo,
Bahía de
Guaporé, Río *62 D3 var.* Río Iténez.
river Bolivia/Brazil
Guarda *92 C3* Guarda, N Portugal
Guarumal *53 F5* Veraguas, S Panama
Guasave *50 C3* Sinaloa, C Mexico
Guatemala *52 A2 off.* Republic of
Guatemala. *country* Central America

GUATEMALA
Central America

Official name Republic of Guatemala
Formation 1838 / 1838
Capital Guatemala City
Population 13.2 million / 315 people
per sq mile (122 people per sq km) / 47%
Total area 42,042 sq. miles
(108,890 sq. km)
Languages Spanish*, Quiché, Mam,
Cakchiquel, Kekchí
Religions Roman Catholic 65%,
Protestant 33%, Other and
nonreligious 2%
Ethnic mix Amerindian 60%,
Mestizo 30%, Other 10%
Government Presidential system
Currency Quetzal = 100 centavos
Literacy rate 69%
Calorie consumption 2219 calories

Guatemala Basin *35 B7 undersea basin*
E Pacific Ocean
Guatemala City *see* Ciudad de Guatemala
Guatemala, Republic of *see* Guatemala
Guaviare *56 B2 off.* Comisaría Guaviare.
province S Colombia
Guaviare, Comisaría *see* Guaviare
Guaviare, Río *58 C3 river* E Colombia
Guayanas, Macizo de las *see* Guiana
Highlands
Guayaquil *60 A2 var.* Santiago de
Guayaquil. Guayas, SW Ecuador
Guayaquil, Gulf of *60 A2 var.* Gulf of
Guayaquil. *gulf* SW Ecuador

Guayaquil, Gulf of *see* Guayaquil,
Golfo de
Guaymas *50 B2* Sonora, NW Mexico
Gubadag *122 C2 Turkm.* Tel'man;
prev. Tel'mansk. Daşoguz Welaýaty,
N Turkmenistan
Guben *94 D4 var.* Wilhelm-Pieck-Stadt.
Brandenburg, E Germany
Gudara *see* Ghüdara
Gudaut'a *117 E1* NW Georgia
Guéret *90 C4* Creuse, C France
Guernsey *89 D8 island* Channel Islands,
NW Europe
Guerrero Negro *50 A2* Baja California
Sur, NW Mexico
Gui *see* Guangxi Zhuangzu Zizhiqu
Guiana *see* French Guiana
Guiana Highlands *62 D1 var.* Macizo de
las Guayanas. *mountain range* N South
America
Guiba *see* Juba
Guidder *see* Guider
Guider *76 B4 var.* Guidder. Nord,
N Cameroon
Guidimouni *75 G3* Zinder, S Niger
Guildford *89 D7* SE England, United
Kingdom
Guilin *128 C6 var.* Kuei-lin, Kweilin.
Guangxi Zhuangzu Zizhiqu, S China
Guimarães *92 B2 var.* Guimarães. Braga,
N Portugal
Guimarães *see* Guimarães
Guinea *74 C4 off.* Republic of Guinea,
var. Guinée; *prev.* French Guinea,
People's Revolutionary Republic of
Guinea. *country* W Africa

GUINEA
West Africa

Official name Republic of Guinea
Formation 1958 / 1958
Capital Conakry
Population 9.8 million / 103 people
per sq mile (40 people per sq km) / 36%
Total area 94,925 sq. miles
(245,857 sq. km)
Languages French*, Pulaar, Malinke,
Soussou
Religions Muslim 65%, Traditional
beliefs 33%, Christian 2%
Ethnic mix Peul 39%, Malinké 23%,
Other 16%, Soussou 11%, Kissi 6%,
Kpellé 5%
Government Presidential system
Currency Guinea franc = 100 centimes
Literacy rate 30%
Calorie consumption 2409 calories

Guinea Basin *69 A5 undersea basin*
E Atlantic Ocean
Guinea-Bissau *74 B4 off.* Republic of
Guinea-Bissau, *Fr.* Guinée-Bissau, *Port.*
Guiné-Bissau; *prev.* Portuguese Guinea.
country W Africa

GUINEA-BISSAU
West Africa

Official name Republic of Guinea-Bissau
Formation 1974 / 1974
Capital Bissau
Population 1.7 million / 157 people
per sq mile (60 people per sq km) / 35%
Total area 13,946 sq. miles (36,120 sq. km)
Languages Portuguese*, Portuguese
Creole, Balante, Fulani, Malinke
Religions Traditional beliefs 52%,
Muslim 40%, Christian 8%
Ethnic mix Balante 30%, Fulani 20%,
Other 17%, Mandyako 14%,
Mandinka 12%, Papel 7%
Government Presidential system
Currency CFA franc = 100 centimes
Literacy rate 40%
Calorie consumption 2024 calories

Guinea-Bissau, Republic of *see*
Guinea-Bissau
Guinea, Gulf of *68 B4 Fr.* Golfe de
Guinée. *gulf* E Atlantic Ocean
Guinea, People's Revolutionary
Republic of *see* Guinea
Guinea, Republic of *see* Guinea
Guiné-Bissau *see* Guinea-Bissau
Guinée *see* Guinea
Guinée-Bissau *see* Guinea-Bissau

Guinée, Golfe de *see* Guinea, Gulf of
Güiria *59 E1* Sucre, NE Venezuela
Guiyang *128 B6 var.* Kuei-Yang,
Kuei-yang, Kueyang, Kweiyang; *prev.*
Kweichu. *province capital* Guizhou,
S China
Guizhou *128 B6* Guangdong, SE China
Gujarāt *134 C4 var.* Gujerat. *cultural
region* W India
Gujerat *see* Gujarāt
Gujrānwāla *134 D2* Punjab, NE Pakistan
Gujrāt *134 D2* Punjab, E Pakistan
Gulbarga *132 C1* Karnātaka, C India
Gulbene *106 D3* Est. Alt-Schwanenburg.
Gulbene, NE Latvia
Gulf of Liaotung *see* Liaodong Wan
Gulfport *42 C3* Mississippi, S USA
Gulf, The *see* Persian Gulf
Gulistan *see* Guliston
Guliston *123 E2* Rus. Gulistan. Sirdaryo
Viloyati, E Uzbekistan
Gulja *see* Yining
Gulkana *36 D3* Alaska, USA
Gulu *73 B6* N Uganda
Gulyantsi *104 C1* Pleven, N Bulgaria
Guma *see* Pishan
Gumbinnen *see* Gusev
Gumpolds *see* Humpolec
Gümülcine/Gümüljina *see* Komotiní
Gümüşane *see* Gümüşhane
Gümüşhane *117 E3 var.* Gümüşane,
Gumushkhane. Gümüşhane,
NE Turkey
Gumushkhane *see* Gümüşhane
Güney Doğu Toroslar *117 E4 mountain
range* SE Turkey
Gunnbjørn Fjeld *82 D4 var.*
Gunnbjörns Bjerge. *mountain*
C Greenland
Gunnbjörns Bjerge *see* Gunnbjørn
Fjeld
Gunnedah *149 D6* New South Wales,
SE Australia
Gunnison *44 C5* Colorado, C USA
Gurbansoltan Eje *122 C2 prev.* Ýylanly,
Rus. Il'yaly. Daşoguz Welaýaty,
N Turkmenistan
Gurbantünggüt Shamo *126 B2 desert*
W China
Gurgan *see* Gorgān
Guri, Embalse de *59 E2 reservoir*
E Venezuela
Gurkfeld *see* Krško
Gurktaler Alpen *95 D7 mountain range*
S Austria
Gürün *116 D3* Sivas, C Turkey
Gur'yev/Gur'yevskaya Oblast' *see*
Atyrau
Gusau *75 G4* Zamfara, NW Nigeria
Gusev *106 B4 Ger.* Gumbinnen.
Kaliningradskaya Oblast', W Russian
Federation
Gustavus *36 D4* Alaska, USA
Güstrow *94 C3* Mecklenburg-
Vorpommern, NE Germany
Gütersloh *94 B4* Nordrhein-Westfalen,
W Germany
Gutta *see* Kolárovo
Guttstadt *see* Dobre Miasto
Guwāhāti *135 G3 prev.* Gauhāti. Assam,
NE India
Guyana *59 F3 off.* Co-operative Republic
of Guyana; *prev.* British Guiana.
country N South America

GUYANA
South America

Official name The Co-operative Republic
of Guyana
Formation 1966 / 1966
Capital Georgetown
Population 769,095 / 10 people
per sq mile (4 people per sq km) / 28%
Total area 83,000 sq. miles
(214,970 sq. km)
Languages English*, English Creole, Hindi,
Tamil, Amerindian languages
Religions Christian 57%, Hindu 33%,
Muslim 9%, Other 1%
Ethnic mix East Indian 43%, Black
African 30%, Mixed race 17%,
Amerindian 9%, Other 1%
Government Presidential system
Currency Guyanese dollar = 100 cents
Literacy rate 97%
Calorie consumption 2692 calories

Guyana, Co-operative Republic of
see Guyana
Guyane *see* French Guiana
Guymon *49 E1* Oklahoma, C USA
Güzelyurt *102 C5 Gk.* Kólpos Mórfu,
Morphou. W Cyprus
Gvardeysk *106 A4 Ger.* Tapaiu.
Kaliningradskaya Oblast', W Russian
Federation
Gwādar *134 A3 var.* Gwadur.
Baluchistān, SW Pakistan
Gwadur *see* Gwādar
Gwalior *134 D3* Madhya Pradesh,
C India
Gwanda *78 D3* Matabeleland South,
SW Zimbabwe
Gwy *see* Wye
Gyandzha *see* Gäncä
Gyangzê *126 C5* Xizang Zizhiqu,
W China
Gyaring Co *126 C5 lake* W China
Gyêgu *see* Yushu
Gyergyószentmiklós *see* Gheorgheni
Gyixong *see* Gonggar
Gympie *149 E5* Queensland, E Australia
Gyomaendrőd *99 D7* Békés, SE Hungary
Gyöngyös *99 D6* Heves, NE Hungary
Győr *99 C6 Ger.* Raab, *Lat.* Arrabona.
Győr-Moson-Sopron, NW Hungary
Gytheio *105 B6 var.* Githio; *prev.*
Ýíthion. Pelopónnisos, S Greece
Gyulafehérvár *see* Alba Iulia
Gyumri *117 F2 var.* Giumri, *Rus.*
Kumayri; *prev.* Aleksandropol',
Leninakan. W Armenia
Gyzylarbat *see* Serdar

H

Haabai *see* Ha'apai Group
Haacht *87 C6* Vlaams Brabant, C Belgium
Haaksbergen *86 E3* Overijssel,
E Netherlands
Ha'apai Group *145 F4 var.* Haabai.
island group C Tonga
Haapsalu *106 D2 Ger.* Hapsal.
Läänemaa, W Estonia
Ha'Arava *see* 'Arabah, Wādī al
Haarlem *86 C3 prev.* Harlem. Noord-
Holland, W Netherlands
Haast *151 B6* West Coast, South Island,
New Zealand
Hachijo-jima *131 D6 island* Izu-shotō,
SE Japan
Hachinohe *130 D3* Aomori, Honshū,
C Japan
Hadama *see* Nazrēt
Hadejia *75 G4* Jigawa, N Nigeria
Hadejia *75 G3 river* N Nigeria
Hadera *119 A6 var.* Khadera; *prev.*
Ḥadera. Haifa, C Israel
Ḥadera *see* Hadera
Hadhdhunmathi Atoll *132 A5 atoll*
S Maldives
Ha Đông *136 D3 var.* Hadong. Ha Tây,
N Vietnam
Hadong *see* Ha Đông
Hadramaut *121 C6 Eng.* Hadramaut.
mountain range S Yemen
Hadramaut *see* Ḥaḍramawt
Hadrianopolis *see* Edirne
Haerbin/Haerhpin/Ha-erh-pin *see*
Harbin
Hafnia *see* Denmark
Hafnia *see* København
Hafren *see* Severn
Hafun, Ras *see* Xaafuun, Raas
Hagåtña *144 B1 , var.* Agaña. *dependent
territory capital* (Guam) NW Guam
Hagerstown *41 F4* Maryland, NE USA
Ha Giang *136 D3* Ha Giang, N Vietnam
Hagios Evstrátios *see* Ágios Efstrátios
HaGolan *see* Golan Heights
Hagondange *90 D3* Moselle, NE France
Haguenau *90 E3* Bas-Rhin, NE France
Haibowan *see* Wuhai
Haicheng *128 D3* Liaoning, NE China
Haidarabad *see* Hyderābād
Haifa *see* Hefa
Haifa, Bay of *see* Mifrats Hefa
Haifong *see* Hai Phong
Haikou *128 C7 var.* Hai-k'ou, Hoihow,
Fr. Hoï-Hao. *province capital* Hainan,
S China

Hai-k'ou *see* Haikou
Ḩāʾil *120 B4* Ḩāʾil, NW Saudi Arabia
Hailuoto *84 D4* Swe. Karlö. *island*
W Finland
Hainan *128 B7* var. Hainan Sheng,
Qiong. *province* S China
Hainan Dao *128 C7* *island* S China
Hainan Sheng *see* Hainan
Hainasch *see* Ainaži
Haines *36 D4* Alaska, USA
Hainichen *94 D4* Sachsen, E Germany
Hai Phong *136 D3* var. Haifong,
Haiphong. N Vietnam
Haiphong *see* Hai Phong
Haiti *54 D3* off. Republic of Haiti.
country C West Indies

HAITI
West Indies

Official name Republic of Haiti
Formation 1804 / 1844
Capital Port-au-Prince
Population 8.8 million / 827 people
per sq mile (319 people per sq km) / 38%
Total area 10,714 sq. miles (27,750 sq. km)
Languages French*, French Creole*
Religions Roman Catholic 80%,
Protestant 16%, Other (including
Voodoo) 3%, Nonreligious 1%
Ethnic mix Black African 95%,
Mulatto (mixed race) and European 5%
Government Presidential system
Currency Gourde = 100 centimes
Literacy rate 52%
Calorie consumption 2086 calories

Haiti, Republic of *see* Haiti
Haiya *72 C3* Red Sea, NE Sudan
Hajdúhadház *99 D6* Hajdú-Bihar,
E Hungary
Hajine *see* Abū Ḩardān
Hajnówka *98 E3* Ger. Hermhausen.
Podlaskie, NE Poland
Hakodate *130 D3* Hokkaidō, NE Japan
Hal *see* Halle
Ḩalab *142 B2* Eng. Aleppo, Fr. Alep; anc.
Beroea. Ḩalab, NW Syria
Ḩalāniyāt, Juzur al *121 D6* var. Jazā'ir
Bin Ghalfān, Eng. Kuria Muria Islands.
island group S Oman
Halberstadt *94 C4* Sachsen-Anhalt,
C Germany
Halden *85 B6* prev. Fredrikshald.
Østfold, S Norway
Halfmoon Bay *151 A8* var. Oban.
Stewart Island, Southland, New Zealand
Haliacmon *see* Aliákmonas
Halifax *39 F4* province capital Nova
Scotia, SE Canada
Halkida *see* Chalkída
Halle *87 B6* Fr. Hal. Vlaams Brabant,
C Belgium
Halle *94 C4* var. Halle an der Saale.
Sachsen-Anhalt, C Germany
Halle an der Saale *see* Halle
Halle-Neustadt *94 C4* Sachsen-Anhalt,
C Germany
Halley *154 B2* UK research station
Antarctica
Hall Islands *142 B2* island group
C Micronesia
Halls Creek *146 C3* Western Australia
Halmahera, Laut *see* Halmahera Sea
Halmahera, Pulau *139 F3* prev. Djailolo,
Gilolo, Jailolo. island E Indonesia
Halmahera Sea *139 F4* Ind. Laut
Halmahera. sea E Indonesia
Halmstad *85 B7* Halland, S Sweden
Hälsingborg *see* Helsingborg
Hamada *131 B6* Shimane, Honshū,
SW Japan
Hamadān *120 C3* anc. Ecbatana.
Hamadān, W Iran
Ḩamāh *118 B3* var. Hama; anc. Epiphania,
Bibl. Hamath. Ḩamāh, W Syria
Hamamatsu *131 D6* var. Hamamatu.
Shizuoka, Honshū, S Japan
Hamamatu *see* Hamamatsu
Hamar *85 B5* prev. Storhammer.
Hedmark, S Norway
Hamath *see* Ḩamāh
Hamburg *94 B3* Hamburg, N Germany
Hamd, Wadi al *120 A4* dry watercourse
W Saudi Arabia
Hämeenlinna *85 D5* Swe. Tavastehus.
Etelä-Suomi, S Finland

HaMela h, Yam *see* Dead Sea
Hamersley Range *146 A4* mountain
range Western Australia
Hamhŭng *129 E3* C North Korea
Hami *126 C3* var. Ha-mi, Uigh. Kumul,
Qomul. Xinjiang Uygur Zizhiqu,
NW China
Ha-mi *see* Hami
Hamilton *42 A5* dependent territory
capital (Bermuda) C Bermuda
Hamilton *38 D5* Ontario, S Canada
Hamilton *150 D3* Waikato, North Island,
New Zealand
Hamilton *88 C4* S Scotland, United
Kingdom
Hamilton *42 C2* Alabama, S USA
Hamim, Wadi al *71 G2* river NE Libya
Hamīs Musaīt *see* Khamīs Mushayt
Hamm *94 B4* var. Hamm in Westfalen.
Nordrhein-Westfalen, W Germany
Ḩammāmāt, Khalīj al *see* Hammamet,
Golfe de
Hammamet, Golfe de *102 D3* Ar. Khalīj
al Ḩammāmāt. gulf NE Tunisia
Hammar, Hawr al *120 C3* lake SE Iraq
Hamm in Westfalen *see* Hamm
Hampden *151 B7* Otago, South Island,
New Zealand
Hampstead *89 A7* Maryland, USA
Hamrun *102 B5* C Malta
Hāmūn, Daryācheh-ye *see* Şāberī,
Hāmūn-e/Sīstān, Daryācheh-ye
Hamwih *see* Southampton
Hâncești *see* Hîncești
Hancewicze *see* Hantsavichy
Handan *128 C4* var. Han-tan. Hebei,
E China
Haneda *130 A2* (Tōkyō) Tōkyō, Honshū,
S Japan
Hanford *47 C6* California, W USA
Hangayn Nuruu *126 D2* mountain
range C Mongolia
Hang-chou/Hangchow *see* Hangzhou
Hangö *see* Hanko
Hangzhou *128 D5* var. Hang-chou,
Hangchow. province capital Zhejiang,
SE China
Hania *see* Chaniá
Hanka, Lake *see* Khanka, Lake
Hanko *85 D6* Swe. Hangö. Etelä-Suomi,
SW Finland
Han-kou/Han-k'ou/Hankow *see* Wuhan
Hanmer Springs *151 C5* Canterbury,
South Island, New Zealand
Hannibal *45 G4* Missouri, C USA
Hannover *94 B3* Eng. Hanover.
Niedersachsen, NW Germany
Hanöbukten *85 B7* bay S Sweden
Ha Nôi *136 D3* Eng. Hanoi, Fr. Hanoï.
country capital (Vietnam) (Vietnam)
N Vietnam
Hanover *see* Hannover
Han Shui *127 E4* river C China
Han-tan *see* Handan
Hantsavichy *107 B6* Pol. Hancewicze,
Rus. Gantsevichi. Brestskaya Voblasts',
SW Belarus
Hanyang *see* Wuhan
Hanzhong *128 B5* Shaanxi, C China
Hāora *135 F4* prev. Howrah. West
Bengal, NE India
Haparanda *84 D4* Norrbotten, N Sweden
Hapsal *see* Haapsalu
Haradok *107 E5* Rus. Gorodok.
Vitsyebskaya Voblasts', N Belarus
Haradzyets *107 B6* Rus. Gorodets.
Brestskaya Voblasts', SW Belarus
Haramachi *130 D4* Fukushima, Honshū,
E Japan
Harany *107 D5* Rus. Gorany.
Vitsyebskaya Voblasts', N Belarus
Harare *78 D3* prev. Salisbury. country
capital (Zimbabwe) (Zimbabwe)
Mashonaland East, NE Zimbabwe
Harbavichy *107 E6* Rus. Gorbovichi.
Mahilyowskaya Voblasts', E Belarus
Harbel *74 C5* W Liberia
Harbin *128 E2* var. Haerbin, Ha-
erh-pin, Kharbin; prev. Haerhpin,
Pingkiang, Pinkiang. province capital
Heilongjiang, NE China
Hardangerfjorden *85 A6* fjord S Norway
Hardangervidda *85 A6* plateau S Norway
Harderwijk *86 D3* Gelderland,
C Netherlands
Harelbeke *87 A6* var. Harlebeke. West-
Vlaanderen, W Belgium

Harem *see* Ḩārim
Haren *86 E2* Groningen, NE Netherlands
Härer *73 D5* E Ethiopia
Hargeisa *see* Hargeysa
Hargeysa *73 D5* var. Hargeisa. Woqooyi
Galbeed, NW Somalia
Hariana *see* Haryāna
Hari, Batang *138 B4* prev. Djambi. river
Sumatera, W Indonesia
Ḩārim *118 B2* var. Harem. Idlib, W Syria
Harima-nada *131 B6* sea S Japan
Harirud *123 E4* var. Tedzhen, Turkm.
Tejen. river Afghanistan/Iran
Harlan *45 F3* Iowa, C USA
Harlebeke *see* Harelbeke
Harlem *see* Haarlem
Harlingen *86 D2* Fris. Harns. Friesland,
N Netherlands
Harlingen *49 G5* Texas, SW USA
Harlow *89 E6* E England, United
Kingdom
Harney Basin *46 B4* basin Oregon,
NW USA
Härnösand *83 C5* var. Hernösand.
Västernorrland, C Sweden
Harns *see* Harlingen
Harper *74 D5* var. Cape Palmas.
NE Liberia
Harricana *38 D3* river Québec,
SE Canada
Harris *88 B3* physical region
NW Scotland, United Kingdom
Harrisburg *41 E4* state capital
Pennsylvania, NE USA
Harrison, Cape *39 F2* headland
Newfoundland and Labrador, E Canada
Harris Ridge *see* Lomonosov Ridge
Harrogate *89 D5* N England, United
Kingdom
Hârșova *108 D5* prev. Hîrșova.
Constanța, SE Romania
Harstad *84 C2* Troms, N Norway
Hartford *41 G3* state capital Connecticut,
NE USA
Hartlepool *89 D5* N England, United
Kingdom
Harunabad *see* Eslāmābād
Har Us Gol *126 C2* lake Hovd,
W Mongolia
Har Us Nuur *126 C2* lake NW Mongolia
Harwich *89 E6* E England, United
Kingdom
Haryāna *134 D2* var. Hariana. cultural
region N India
Hashemite Kingdom of Jordan *see*
Jordan
Hasselt *87 C6* Limburg, NE Belgium
Hassetché *see* Al Ḩasakah
Hasta Colonia/Hasta Pompeia *see* Asti
Hastings *150 E4* Hawke's Bay, North
Island, New Zealand
Hastings *89 E7* SE England, United
Kingdom
Hastings *45 E4* Nebraska, C USA
Ḩaţeg *108 B4* Ger. Wallenthal, Hung.
Hátszeg; prev. Hatzeg, Hötzing.
Hunedoara, SW Romania
Hátszeg *see* Ḩaţeg
Hattem *86 D3* Gelderland, E Netherlands
Hatteras, Cape *43 G1* headland North
Carolina, SE USA
Hatteras Plain *35 D6* abyssal plain
W Atlantic Ocean
Hattiesburg *42 C3* Mississippi, S USA
Hatton Bank *see* Hatton Ridge
Hatton Ridge *80 B2* var. Hatton Bank.
undersea ridge N Atlantic Ocean
Hat Yai *137 C7* var. Ban Hat Yai.
Songkhla, SW Thailand
Hatzeg *see* Ḩaţeg
Hatzfeld *see* Jimbolia
Haugesund *85 A6* Rogaland, S Norway
Haukeligrend *85 A6* Telemark,
S Norway
Haukivesi *85 E5* lake SE Finland
Hauraki Gulf *150 D2* gulf North Island,
N New Zealand
Hauroko, Lake *151 A7* lake South
Island, New Zealand
Hautes Fagnes *87 D6* Ger. Hohes Venn.
mountain range E Belgium
Hauts Plateaux *70 D2* plateau Algeria/
Morocco
Hauzenberg *95 D6* Bayern, SE Germany
Havana *35 D6* Illinois, N USA
Havana *see* La Habana

Havant *89 D7* S England, United
Kingdom
Havelock *43 F1* North Carolina, SE USA
Havelock North *150 E4* Hawke's Bay,
North Island, New Zealand
Haverfordwest *89 C6* SW Wales, United
Kingdom
Havířov *99 C5* Moravskoslezský Kraj,
E Czech Republic
Havre *44 C1* Montana, NW USA
Havre *see* le Havre
Havre-St-Pierre *39 F3* Québec,
E Canada
Hawai'i *47 A8* off. State of Hawai'i,
also known as Aloha State, Paradise
of the Pacific, var. Hawaii. state USA,
C Pacific Ocean
Hawai'i *47 B8* var. Hawaii. island
Hawaiian Islands, USA, C Pacific Ocean
Hawaiian Islands *152 D2* prev.
Sandwich Islands. island group
Hawaii, USA
Hawaiian Ridge *152 H4* undersea ridge
N Pacific Ocean
Hawea, Lake *151 B6* lake South Island,
New Zealand
Hawera *150 D4* Taranaki, North Island,
New Zealand
Hawick *88 C4* SE Scotland, United
Kingdom
Hawke Bay *150 E4* bay North Island,
New Zealand
Hawkeye State *see* Iowa
Hawler *see* Arbil
Hawthorne *47 C6* Nevada, W USA
Hay *149 C6* New South Wales,
SE Australia
HaYarden *see* Jordan
Hayastani Hanrapetut'yun *see* Armenia
Hayes *45 F1* river Manitoba, C Canada
Hay River *37 E4* Northwest Territories,
W Canada
Hays *45 E5* Kansas, C USA
Haysyn *108 D3* Rus. Gaysin. Vinnyts'ka
Oblast', C Ukraine
Hazar *122 B2* prev. Rus. Cheleken.
Balkan Welaýaty, W Turkmenistan
Heard and McDonald Islands *141 B7*
Australian external territory S Indian
Ocean
Hearst *38 C4* Ontario, S Canada
Heart of Dixie *see* Alabama
Heathrow *89 A8* (London) SE England,
United Kingdom
Hebei *128 C4* var. Hebei Sheng, Hopeh,
Hopei, Ji; prev. Chihli. province
E China
Hebei Sheng *see* Hebei
Hebron *119 A6* var. Al Khalīl, El Khalīl,
Heb. Hevron; anc. Kiriath-Arba.
S West Bank
Heemskerk *86 C3* Noord-Holland,
W Netherlands
Heerde *86 D3* Gelderland, E Netherlands
Heerenveen *86 D2* Fris. It Hearrenfean.
Friesland, N Netherlands
Heerhugowaard *86 C2* Noord-Holland,
NW Netherlands
Heerlen *87 D6* Limburg, SE Netherlands
Heerwegen *see* Polkowice
Hefa *119 A5* var. Haifa, hist. Caiffa,
Caiphas; anc. Sycaminum. Haifa, N Israel
Hefa, Mifraz *see* Mifrats Hefa
Hefei *128 D5* var. Hefeng, hist. Luchow.
province capital Anhui, E China
Hegang *129 E2* Heilongjiang, NE China
Hei *see* Heilongjiang
Heide *94 B2* Schleswig-Holstein,
N Germany
Heidelberg *95 B5* Baden-Württemberg,
SW Germany
Heidenheim *see* Heidenheim an der
Brenz
Heidenheim an der Brenz *95 B6* var.
Heidenheim. Baden-Württemberg,
S Germany
Hei-ho *see* Nagqu
Heilbronn *95 B6* Baden-Württemberg,
SW Germany
Heiligenbeil *see* Mamonovo
Heilongjiang *128 D2* var. Hei,
Heilongjiang Sheng, Hei-lung-chiang,
Heilungkiang. province NE China
Heilong Jiang *see* Amur
Heilongjiang Sheng *see* Heilongjiang
Heiloo *86 C3* Noord-Holland,
NW Netherlands

Heilsberg *see* Lidzbark Warmiński
Hei-lung-chiang/Heilungkiang *see*
   Heilongjiang
Heimdal *85 B5* Sør-Trøndelag, S Norway
Heinaste *see* Ainaži
Hekimhan *116 D3* Malatya, C Turkey
Helena *44 B2 state capital* Montana,
   NW USA
Helensville *150 D2* Auckland, North
   Island, New Zealand
Helgoland Bay *see* Helgoländer Bucht
Helgoländer Bucht *94 A2 var.*
   Helgoland Bay, Heligoland Bight. *bay*
   NW Germany
Heligoland Bight *see* Helgoländer Bucht
Heliopolis *see* Baalbek
Hellas *see* Greece
Hellenic Republic *see* Greece
Hellevoetsluis *86 B4* Zuid-Holland,
   SW Netherlands
Hellín *93 E4* Castilla-La Mancha, C Spain
Darya-ye Helmand *122 D5 var.* Rūd-e
   Hīrmand. *river* Afghanistan/Iran
Helmantica *see* Salamanca
Helmond *87 D5* Noord-Brabant,
   S Netherlands
Helsingborg *85 B7 prev.* Hälsingborg.
   Skåne, S Sweden
Helsingfors *see* Helsinki
Helsinki *85 D6 Swe.* Helsingfors.
   country capital (Finland) (Finland)
   Etelä-Suomi, S Finland
Heltau *see* Cisnădie
Helvetia *see* Switzerland
Henan *128 C5 var.* Henan Sheng,
   Honan, Yu. *province* C China
Henderson *40 B5* Kentucky, S USA
Henderson *47 D7* Nevada, W USA
Henderson *49 H3* Texas, SW USA
Hendū Kosh *see* Hindu Kush
Hengchow *see* Hengyang
Hengduan Shan *128 A5 mountain range*
   SW China
Hengelo *86 E3* Overijssel, E Netherlands
Hengnan *see* Hengyang
Hengyang *128 C6 var.* Hengnan, Heng-
   yang; *prev.* Hengchow. Hunan, S China
Heng-yang *see* Hengyang
Heniches'k *109 F4 Rus.* Genichesk.
   Khersons'ka Oblast', S Ukraine
Hennebont *90 A3* Morbihan, NW France
Henrique de Carvalho *see* Saurimo
Henzada *see* Hinthada
Herakleion *see* Irákleio
Herāt *122 D4 var.* Herat; *anc.* Aria.
   Herāt, W Afghanistan
Heredia *53 E4* Heredia, C Costa Rica
Hereford *49 E2* Texas, SW USA
Herford *94 B4* Nordrhein-Westfalen,
   NW Germany
Héristal *see* Herstal
Herk-de-Stad *87 C6* Limburg,
   NE Belgium
Herlen Gol/Herlen He *see* Kerulen
Hermannstadt *see* Sibiu
Hermansverk *85 A5* Sogn Og Fjordane,
   S Norway
Hermhausen *see* Hajnówka
Hermiston *46 C2* Oregon, NW USA
Hermon, Mount *119 B5 Ar.* Jabal ash
   Shaykh. *mountain* S Syria
Hermosillo *50 B2* Sonora, NW Mexico
Hermoupolis *see* Ermoúpoli
Hernösand *see* Härnösand
Herrera del Duque *92 D3* Extremadura,
   W Spain
Herselt *87 C5* Antwerpen, C Belgium
Herstal *87 D6 Fr.* Héristal. Liège,
   E Belgium
Herzogenbusch *see* 's-Hertogenbosch
Hesse *see* Hessen
Hessen *95 B5 Eng./Fr.* Hesse. *state*
   C Germany
Hevron *see* Hebron
Heydebrech *see* Kędzierzyn-Kozle
Heydekrug *see* Šilutė
Heywood Islands *146 C3 island group*
   Western Australia
Hibbing *45 F1* Minnesota, N USA
Hibernia *see* Ireland
Hidalgo del Parral *50 C2 var.* Parral.
   Chihuahua, N Mexico
Hida-sanmyaku *131 C5 mountain range*
   Honshū, S Japan
Hierosolyma *see* Jerusalem
Hierro *70 A3 var.* Ferro. *island* Islas
   Canarias, Spain, NE Atlantic Ocean

High Atlas *70 C2 Eng.* High Atlas.
   mountain range C Morocco
High Atlas *see* Haut Atlas
High Plains *see* Great Plains
High Point *43 E1* North Carolina,
   SE USA
Hiiumaa *106 C2 Ger.* Dagden, *Swe.*
   Dagö. *island* W Estonia
Hikurangi *150 D2* Northland, North
   Island, New Zealand
Hildesheim *94 B4* Niedersachsen,
   N Germany
Hilla *see* Al Ḥillah
Hillaby, Mount *55 G1 mountain*
   N Barbados
Hill Bank *52 C1* Orange Walk, N Belize
Hillegom *86 C3* Zuid-Holland,
   W Netherlands
Hilo *47 B8* Hawaii, USA, C Pacific Ocean
Hilton Head Island *43 E2* South
   Carolina, SE USA
Hilversum *86 C3* Noord-Holland,
   C Netherlands
Himalaya/Himalaya Shan *see* Himalayas
Himalayas *135 E2 var.* Himalaya, *Chin.*
   Himalaya Shan. *mountain range* S Asia
Himeji *131 C6 var.* Himezi. Hyōgo,
   Honshū, SW Japan
Himezi *see* Himeji
Ḥimş *118 B4 var.* Homs; *anc.* Emesa.
   Ḥimş, C Syria
Hînceşti *108 D4 var.* Hânceşti; *prev.*
   Kotovsk. C Moldova
Hinchinbrook Island *148 D3 island*
   Queensland, NE Australia
Hinds *151 C6* Canterbury, South Island,
   New Zealand
Hindu Kush *123 F4 Per.* Hendū Kosh.
   mountain range Afghanistan/Pakistan
Hinesville *43 E3* Georgia, SE USA
Hinnøya *84 C3 Lapp.* Iinnasuolu. *island*
   C Norway
Hinson Bay *42 A5 bay* W Bermuda,
   W Atlantic Ocean
Hinthada *136 B4 var.* Henzada.
   Ayeyarwady, SW Burma (Myanmar)
Híos *see* Chíos
Hirfanlı Baraji *116 C3 reservoir*
   C Turkey
Hîrmand, Rūd-e *see* Helmand, Darya-ye
Hirosaki *130 D3* Aomori, Honshū,
   C Japan
Hiroshima *131 B6 var.* Hirosima.
   Hiroshima, Honshū, SW Japan
**Hirschberg/Hirschberg im
   Riesengebirge/Hirschberg in
   Schlesien** *see* Jelenia Góra
Hirson *90 D3* Aisne, N France
Hîrşova *see* Hârşova
Hispalis *see* Sevilla
Hispana/Hispania *see* Spain
Hispaniola *56 B1 island* Dominion
   Republic/Haiti
Hitachi *131 D5 var.* Hitati. Ibaraki,
   Honshū, S Japan
Hitati *see* Hitachi
Hitra *84 A4 prev.* Hitteren. *island*
   S Norway
Hitteren *see* Hitra
Hjälmaren *85 C6 Eng.* Lake Hjalmar.
   lake C Sweden
Hjalmar, Lake *see* Hjälmaren
Hjørring *85 B7* Nordjylland, N Denmark
Hkakabo Razi *136 B1 mountain* Burma
   (Myanmar)/China
Hlobyne *109 F2* Poltav's'ka Oblast',
   NE Ukraine
Hlukhiv *109 F1 Rus.* Glukhov. Sums'ka
   Oblast', NE Ukraine
Hlybokaye *107 D5 Rus.* Glubokoye.
   Vitsyebskaya Voblasts', N Belarus
Hoa Binh *136 D3* Hoa Binh, N Vietnam
Hoang Lien Son *136 D3 mountain range*
   N Vietnam
Hobart *149 C8 prev.* Hobarton, Hobart
   Town. *state capital* Tasmania,
   SE Australia
Hobarton/Hobart Town *see* Hobart
Hobbs *49 E3* New Mexico, SW USA
Hobro *85 A7* Nordjylland, N Denmark
Hô Chi Minh *137 E6 var.* Hô Chi Minh
   City; *prev.* Saigon. S Vietnam
Hô Chi Minh City *see* Hô Chi Minh
Hodeida *see* Al Ḥudaydah
Hódmezővásárhely *99 D7* Csongrád,
   SE Hungary

Hodna, Chott El *102 C4 var.* Chott
   el-Hodna, *Ar.* Shatt al-Hodna. *salt
   lake* N Algeria
Hodna, Chott el-/Hodna, Shatt al- *see*
   Hodna, Chott El
Hodonín *99 C5 Ger.* Göding.
   Jihomoravský Kraj, SE Czech Republic
Hoei *see* Huy
Hoey *see* Huy
Hof *95 C5* Bayern, SE Germany
Hofei *see* Hefei
Hōfu *131 B7* Yamaguchi, Honshū,
   SW Japan
Hofuf *see* Al Hufūf
Hogoley Islands *see* Chuuk Islands
Hohensalza *see* Inowrocław
Hohenstadt *see* Zábřeh
Hohes Venn *see* Hautes Fagnes
Hohe Tauern *95 C7 mountain range*
   W Austria
Hohhot *127 F3 var.* Huhehot,
   Huhohaote, *Mong.* Kukukhoto; *prev.*
   Kweisui, Kwesui. Nei Mongol Zizhiqu,
   N China
Hôi An *137 E5 prev.* Faifo. Quang Nam-
   Đa Nǎng, C Vietnam
Hoï-Hao/Hoihow *see* Haikou
Hokianga Harbour *150 C2 inlet*
   SE Tasman Sea
Hokitika *151 B5* West Coast, South
   Island, New Zealand
Hokkaido *130 C2 prev.* Ezo, Yeso, Yezo.
   island NE Japan
Hola Prystan' *109 E4 Rus.* Golaya
   Pristan. Khersons'ka Oblast', S Ukraine
Holbrook *48 B2* Arizona, SW USA
Holetown *55 G1 prev.* Jamestown.
   W Barbados
Holguín *54 C2* Holguín, SE Cuba
Hollabrunn *95 E6* Niederösterreich,
   NE Austria
Holland *see* Netherlands
Hollandia *see* Jayapura
Holly Springs *42 C1* Mississippi, S USA
Holman *37 E3* Victoria Island, Northwest
   Territories, N Canada
Holmsund *84 D4* Västerbotten, N Sweden
Holon *119 A6 var.* Kholon; *prev.* Ḥolon.
   Tel Aviv, C Israel
Ḥolon *see* Holon
Holovanivs'k *109 E3 Rus.* Golovanevsk.
   Kirovohrads'ka Oblast', C Ukraine
Holstebro *85 A7* Ringkøbing,
   W Denmark
**Holstenborg/Holsteinsborg/
   Holstenborg/Holstensborg** *see*
   Sisimiut
Holyhead *89 C5 Wel.* Caer Gybi.
   NW Wales, United Kingdom
Hombori *75 E3* Mopti, S Mali
Homs *see* Al Khums, Libya
Homs *see* Ḥimş, Syria
Homyel' *107 D7 Rus.* Gomel'.
   Homyel'skaya Voblasts', SE Belarus
Honan *see* Luoyang, China
Honan *see* Henan, China
Hondo *49 F4* Texas, SW USA
Hondo *see* Honshū
Honduras *52 C2 off.* Republic of
   Honduras. *country* Central America

HONDURAS
Central America

Official name Republic of Honduras
Formation 1838 / 1838
Capital Tegucigalpa
Population 7.5 million / 174 people
per sq mile (67 people per sq km) / 46%
Total area 43,278 sq. miles (112,090 sq. km)
Languages Spanish*, Garífuna (Carib),
English Creole
Religions Roman Catholic 97%,
Protestant 3%
Ethnic mix Mestizo 90%, Black
African 5%, Amerindian 4%, White 1%
Government Presidential system
Currency Lempira = 100 centavos
Literacy rate 80%
Calorie consumption 2356 calories

Honduras, Golfo de *see* Honduras,
   Gulf of
Honduras, Gulf of *52 C2 Sp.* Golfo de
   Honduras. *gulf* W Caribbean Sea
Honduras, Republic of *see* Honduras
Hønefoss *85 B6* Buskerud, S Norway

Honey Lake *47 B5 lake* California,
   W USA
Hon Gai *see* Hông Gai
Hongay *see* Hông Gai
Hông Gai *136 E3 var.* Hon Gai, Hongay.
   Quang Ninh, N Vietnam
Hông Hà, Sông *see* Red River
Hong Kong *128 A1 Chin.* Xianggang.
   Hong Kong, S China
Hong Kong Island *128 B2 island*
   S China Asia
Honiara *144 C3 country capital*
   (Solomon Islands) (Solomon Islands)
   Guadalcanal, C Solomon Islands
Honjō *130 D4 var.* Honzyô, Yurihonjô.
   Akita, Honshū, C Japan
Honolulu *47 A8 state capital* O'ahu,
   Hawaii, USA, C Pacific Ocean
Honshu *131 E5 var.* Hondo, Honsyû.
   island SW Japan
Honsyû *see* Honshū
Honte *see* Westerschelde
Honzyô *see* Honjō
Hoogeveen *86 E2* Drenthe,
   NE Netherlands
Hoogezand-Sappemeer *86 E2*
   Groningen, NE Netherlands
Hoorn *86 C2* Noord-Holland,
   NW Netherlands
Hoosier State *see* Indiana
Hopa *117 E2* Artvin, NE Turkey
Hope *36 C3* British Columbia,
   SW Canada
Hopedale *39 F2* Newfoundland and
   Labrador, NE Canada
Hopei/Hopei *see* Hebei
Hopkinsville *40 B5* Kentucky, S USA
Horasan *117 F3* Erzurum, NE Turkey
Horizon Deep *152 D4 trench* W Pacific
   Ocean
Horki *107 E6 Rus.* Gorki.
   Mahilyowskaya Voblasts', E Belarus
Horlivka *109 G3 Rom.* Adâncata, *Rus.*
   Gorlovka. Donets'ka Oblast', E Ukraine
Hormuz, Tangeh-ye *see* Hormuz, Strait of
Hormuz, Strait of *120 D4 var.* Strait of
   Ormuz, *Per.* Tangeh-ye Hormoz. *strait*
   Iran/Oman
Cape Horn *65 C8 Eng.* Cape Horn.
   headland S Chile
Horn, Cape *see* Hornos, Cabo de
Hornsby *148 E1* New South Wales,
   SE Australia
Horodnya *109 E1 Rus.* Gorodnya.
   Cherníhiv's'ka Oblast', NE Ukraine
Horodok *108 B2 Pol.* Gródek
   Jagielloński, *Rus.* Gorodok, Gorodok
   Yagellonski. L'vivs'ka Oblast',
   NW Ukraine
Horodyshche *109 E2 Rus.* Gorodishche.
   Cherkas'ka Oblast', C Ukraine
Horoshiri-dake *130 D2 var.* Horosiri
   Dake. *mountain* Hokkaidô, N Japan
Horosiri Dake *see* Horoshiri-dake
Horsburgh Atoll *132 A4 var.* Goidhoo
   Atoll. *atoll* N Maldives
Horseshoe Bay *42 A5 bay* W Bermuda,
   W Atlantic Ocean
Horseshoe Seamounts *80 A4 seamount
   range* E Atlantic Ocean
Horsham *149 B7* Victoria, SE Australia
Horst *87 D5* Limburg, SE Netherlands
Horten *85 B6* Vestfold, S Norway
Horyn' *107 B7 Rus.* Goryn. *river*
   NW Ukraine
Hosingen *87 D7* Diekirch,
   NE Luxembourg
Hospitalet *see* L'Hospitalet de Llobregat
Hotan *126 B4 var.* Khotan, *Chin.*
   Ho-t'ien. Xinjiang Uygur Zizhiqu,
   NW China
Ho-t'ien *see* Hotan
Hoting *84 C4* Jämtland, C Sweden
Hot Springs *42 B1* Arkansas, C USA
Hôtzing *see* Hațeg
Houayxay *136 C3 var.* Ban Houayxay.
   Bokèo, N Laos
Houghton *40 B1* Michigan, N USA
Houilles *91 B5* Yvelines, Île-de-France,
   N France Europe
Houlton *41 H1* Maine, NE USA
Houma *42 B3* Louisiana, S USA
Houma *see* Tianjin
Houma *23 H4* Texas, SW USA
Hovd *126 C2 var.* Khovd, Kobdo; *prev.*
   Jirgalanta. Hovd, W Mongolia
Hove *89 E7* SE England, United Kingdom

Hoverla, Hora *108 C3 Rus.* Gora
  Goverla. *mountain* W Ukraine
Hovsgol, Lake *see* Hövsgöl Nuur
Hövsgöl Nuur *126 D1 var.* Lake
  Hovsgol. *lake* N Mongolia
Howa, Ouadi *see* Howar, Wâdi
Howar, Wadi *72 A3 var.* Ouadi Howa.
  river Chad/Sudan
Howrah *see* Hāora
Hoy *88 C2 island* N Scotland, United
  Kingdom
Hoyerswerda *94 D4 Lus.* Wojerecy.
  Sachsen, E Germany
Hpa-an *136 B4 var.* Pa-an. Kayin State,
  S Burma (Myanmar)
Hpyu *see* Phyu
Hradec Králové *99 B5 Ger.* Königgrätz.
  Královéhradecký Kraj, N Czech
  Republic
Hrandzichy *107 B5 Rus.* Grandichi.
  Hrodzyenskaya Voblasts', W Belarus
Hranice *99 C5 Ger.* Mährisch-
  Weisskirchen. Olomoucký Kraj,
  E Czech Republic
Hrebinka *109 E2 Rus.* Grebenka.
  Poltavs'ka Oblast', NE Ukraine
Hrodna *107 B5 Pol.* Grodno.
  Hrodzyenskaya Voblasts', W Belarus
Hrvatska *see* Croatia
Hsia-men *see* Xiamen
Hsiang-t'an *see* Xiangtan
Hsi Chiang *see* Xi Jiang
Hsing-K'ai Hu *see* Khanka, Lake
Hsi-ning/Hsining *see* Xining
Hsinking *see* Changchun
Hsin-yang *see* Xinyang
Hsu-chou *see* Xuzhou
Htawei *see* Dawei
Huacho *60 C4* Lima, W Peru
Hua Hin *see* Ban Hua Hin
Huaihua *128 C5* Hunan, S China
Huailai *128 C3 var.* Shacheng. Hebei,
  E China
Huainan *128 D5 var.* Huai-nan,
  Hwainan. Anhui, E China
Huai-nan *see* Huainan
Huajuapan *51 F5 var.* Huajuapan de
  León. Oaxaca, SE Mexico
Huajuapan de León *see* Huajuapan
Hualapai Peak *48 A2 mountain* Arizona,
  SW USA
Huallaga, Río *60 C3 river* N Peru
Huambo *78 B2 Port.* Nova Lisboa.
  Huambo, C Angola
Huancavelica *60 D4* Huancavelica, SW Peru
Huancayo *60 D3* Junín, C Peru
Huang Hai *see* Yellow Sea
Huangshi *128 C5 var.* Huang-shih,
  Hwangshih. Hubei, C China
Huang-shih *see* Huangshi
Huanta *60 D4* Ayacucho, C Peru
Huánuco *60 C3* Huánuco, C Peru
Huanuni *61 F4* Oruro, W Bolivia
Huaral *60 C4* Lima, W Peru
Huarás *see* Huaraz
Huaraz *60 C3 var.* Huarás. Ancash,
  W Peru
Huarmey *60 C3* Ancash, W Peru
Huatabampo *50 C2* Sonora, NW Mexico
Hubli *124 B1* Karnātaka, SW India
Huddersfield *89 D5* N England, United
  Kingdom
Hudiksvall *85 C5* Gävleborg, C Sweden
Hudson Bay *37 G4 bay* NE Canada
Hudson, Détroit d' *see* Hudson Strait
Hudson Strait *37 H3 Fr.* Détroit
  d'Hudson. *strait* Northwest Territories/
  Québec, NE Canada
Hudur *see* Xuddur
Huê *136 E4* Th.a Thièn-Huê, C Vietnam
Huehuetenango *52 A2* Huehuetenango,
  W Guatemala
Huelva *92 C4 anc.* Onuba. Andalucía,
  SW Spain
Huesca *93 F2 anc.* Osca. Aragón,
  NE Spain
Huéscar *93 E4* Andalucía, S Spain
Hughenden *148 C3* Queensland,
  NE Australia
Hugo *49 G2* Oklahoma, C USA
Huhehot/Huhohaote *see* Hohhot
Huíla Plateau *78 B2 plateau* S Angola
Huixtla *51 G5* Chiapas, SE Mexico
Hulingol *127 G2 prev.* Huolin Gol. Nei
  Mongol Zizhiqu, N China
Hull *38 D4* Québec, SE Canada
Hull *see* Kingston upon Hull

Hull Island *see* Orona
Hulst *87 B5* Zeeland, SW Netherlands
Hulun *see* Hulun Buir
Hulun Buir *127 F1 var.* Hailar; *prev.*
  Hulun. Nei Mongol Zizhiqu, N China
Hu-lun Ch'ih *see* Hulun Nur
Hulun Nur *127 F1 var.* Hu-lun Ch'ih;
  prev. Dalai Nor. *lake* NE China
Humaitá *62 D2* Amazonas, N Brazil
Humboldt River *47 C5 river* Nevada,
  W USA
Humphreys Peak *48 B1 mountain*
  Arizona, SW USA
Humpolec *99 B5 Ger.* Gumpolds,
  Humpoletz. Vysočina, C Czech Republic
Humpoletz *see* Humpolec
Hunan *128 C6 var.* Hunan Sheng,
  Xiang. *province* S China
Hunan Sheng *see* Hunan
Hunedoara *108 B4 Ger.* Eisenmarkt,
  Hung. Vajdahunyad. Hunedoara,
  SW Romania
Hünfeld *95 B5* Hessen, C Germany
Hungarian People's Republic *see*
  Hungary
Hungary *99 C6 off.* Republic of Hungary,
  Ger. Ungarn, *Hung.* Magyarország,
  Rom. Ungaria, *SCr.* Madarska, *Ukr.*
  Uhorshchyna; *prev.* Hungarian People's
  Republic. *country* C Europe

HUNGARY
Central Europe

Official name	Republic of Hungary
Formation	1918 / 1947
Capital	Budapest
Population	10 million / 280 people per sq mile (108 people per sq km) / 66%
Total area	35,919 sq. miles (93,030 sq. km)
Languages	Hungarian (Magyar)*
Religions	Roman Catholic 52%, Calvinist 16%, Other 15%, Nonreligious 14%, Lutheran 3%
Ethnic mix	Magyar 94%, Other 5%, Roma 1%
Government	Parliamentary system
Currency	Forint = 100 fillér
Literacy rate	99%
Calorie consumption	3483 calories

Hungary, Plain of *see* Great Hungarian
  Plain
Hungary, Republic of *see* Hungary
Hunjiang *see* Baishan
Hunter Island *149 B8 island* Tasmania,
  SE Australia
Huntington *40 D4* West Virginia, NE USA
Huntington Beach *47 B8* California,
  W USA
Huntly *150 D3* Waikato, North Island,
  New Zealand
Huntsville *42 D1* Alabama, S USA
Huntsville *49 G3* Texas, SW USA
Huolin Gol *see* Hulingol
Hurghada *72 C2 var.* Al Ghurdaqah,
  Ghurdaqah. E Egypt
Huron *45 E3* South Dakota, N USA
Huron, Lake *40 D2 lake* Canada/USA
Hurukawa *see* Furukawa
Hurunui *151 C5 river* South Island,
  New Zealand
Húsavík *83 E4* Nordhurland Eystra,
  NE Iceland
Husté *see* Khust
Husum *94 B2* Schleswig-Holstein,
  N Germany
Huszt *see* Khust
Hutchinson *45 E5* Kansas, C USA
Hutchinson Island *43 F4 island* Florida,
  SE USA
Huy *87 C6 Dut.* Hoei, Hoey. Liège,
  E Belgium
Huzi *see* Fuji
Hvannadalshnúkur *83 E5 volcano*
  S Iceland
Hvar *100 B4 It.* Lesina; *anc.* Pharus.
  island S Croatia
Hwainan *see* Huainan
Hwange *78 D3 prev.* Wankie.
  Matabeleland North, W Zimbabwe
Hwang-Hae *see* Yellow Sea
Hwangshih *see* Huangshi
Hyargas Nuur *126 C2 lake*
  NW Mongolia
Hyderābād *134 D5 var.* Haidarabad.
  state capital Andhra Pradesh, C India

Hyderābād *134 B3 var.* Haidarabad.
  Sind, SE Pakistan
Hyères *91 D6* Var, SE France
Hyères, Îles d' *91 D6 island group*
  S France
Hypanis *see* Kuban'
Hyrcania *see* Gorgān
Hyvinge *see* Hyvinkää
Hyvinkää *85 D5 Swe.* Hyvinge. Etelä-
  Suomi, S Finland

I

Iader *see* Zadar
Ialomiţa *108 C5 river* SE Romania
Iaşi *108 D3 Ger.* Jassy. Iaşi, NE Romania
Ibadan *75 F5* Oyo, SW Nigeria
Ibagué *58 B3* Tolima, C Colombia
Ibar *100 D4 Alb.* Ibër. *river* C Serbia
Ibarra *60 B1 var.* San Miguel de Ibarra.
  Imbabura, N Ecuador
Ibër *see* Ibar
Iberia *see* Spain
Iberian Mountains *see* Ibérico, Sistema
Iberian Peninsula *80 B4 physical region*
  Portugal/Spain
Iberian Plain *80 B4 abyssal plain*
  E Atlantic Ocean
Ibérica, Cordillera *see* Ibérico, Sistema
Ibérico, Sistema *93 E2 var.* Cordillera
  Ibérica, *Eng.* Iberian Mountains.
  mountain range NE Spain
Ibiza *see* Eivissa
Ibiza *see* Eivissa
Ibiza *see* Eivissa
Ibo *see* Sassandra
Ica *60 D4* Ica, SW Peru
Icaria *see* Ikaría
Içá, Rio *62 C2 var.* Río Putumayo. *river*
  NW South America
Içá, Rio *see* Putumayo, Río
İçel *see* Mersin
Iceland *83 E4 off.* Republic of Iceland,
  Dan. Island, *Icel.* Ísland. *country*
  N Atlantic Ocean

ICELAND
Northwest Europe

Official name	Republic of Iceland
Formation	1944 / 1944
Capital	Reykjavík
Population	301,931 / 8 people per sq mile (3 people per sq km) / 93%
Total area	39,768 sq. miles (103,000 sq. km)
Languages	Icelandic*
Religions	Evangelical Lutheran 93%, Nonreligious 6%, Other (mostly Christian) 1%
Ethnic mix	Icelandic 94%, Other 4%, Danish 1%
Government	Parliamentary system
Currency	Icelandic króna = 100 aurar
Literacy rate	99%
Calorie consumption	3249 calories

Iceland Basin *88 B1 undersea basin*
  N Atlantic Ocean
Icelandic Plateau *see* Iceland Plateau
Iceland Plateau *155 B6 var.* Icelandic
  Plateau. *undersea plateau* S Greenland
  Sea
Iceland, Republic of *see* Iceland
Iconium *see* Konya
Iculisma *see* Angoulême
Idabel *49 H2* Oklahoma, C USA
Idaho *46 D3 off.* State of Idaho, *also
  known as* Gem of the Mountains, Gem
  State. *state* NW USA
Idaho Falls *46 E3* Idaho, NW USA
Idensalmi *see* Iisalmi
Idfu *72 B2 var.* Edfu. SE Egypt
Idi Amin, Lac *see* Edward, Lake
Idini *74 B2* Trarza, W Mauritania
Idlib *118 B3* Idlib, NW Syria
Idre *85 B5* Dalarna, C Sweden
Iecava *106 C3* Bauska, S Latvia
Ieper *87 A6 Fr.* Ypres. West-Vlaanderen,
  W Belgium
Ierápetra *105 D8 Kríti*, Kríti,
  E Mediterranean Sea
Ierisós *see* Ierissós
Ierissós *104 C4 var.* Ierisós. Kentrikí
  Makedonía, N Greece
Iferouâne *75 G2* Agadez, N Niger

Ifôghas, Adrar des *75 E2 var.* Adrar des
  Iforas. *mountain range* NE Mali
Iforas, Adrar des *see* Ifôghas, Adrar des
Igarka *114 D3* Krasnoyarskiy Kray,
  N Russian Federation
Igaunija *see* Estonia
Iglau/Iglawa/Iglawa *see* Jihlava
Iglesias *97 A5* Sardegna, Italy,
  C Mediterranean Sea
Igloolik *37 G2* Nunavut, N Canada
Igoumenítsa *104 A4* Ípeiros, W Greece
Iguaçu, Rio *63 E4 Sp.* Río Iguazú. *river*
  Argentina/Brazil
Iguaçu, Salto do *63 E4 Sp.* Cataratas del
  Iguazú; *prev.* Victoria Falls. *waterfall*
  Argentina/Brazil
Iguala *51 E4 var.* Iguala de la
  Independencia. Guerrero, S Mexico
Iguala de la Independencia *see* Iguala
Iguazú, Cataratas del *see* Iguaçu, Salto do
Iguazú, Río *see* Iguaçu, Rio
Iguid, Erg *see* Iguidi, 'Erg
Iguidi, 'Erg *70 C3 var.* Erg Iguid. *desert*
  Algeria/Mauritania
Ihavandhippolhu Atoll *132 A3 var.*
  Ihavandiffulu Atoll. *atoll* N Maldives
Ihavandiffulu Atoll *see* Ihavandhippolhu
  Atoll
Ihosy *79 F4* Fianarantsoa,
  S Madagascar
Iinnasuolu *see* Hinnøya
Iisalmi *84 E4 var.* Idensalmi. Itä-Suomi,
  C Finland
IJmuiden *86 C3* Noord-Holland,
  W Netherlands
IJssel *86 D3 var.* Yssel. *river* Netherlands
IJsselmeer *86 C2 prev.* Zuider Zee. *lake*
  N Netherlands
IJsselmuiden *86 D3* Overijssel,
  E Netherlands
IJzer *87 A6 river* W Belgium
Ikaahuk *see* Sachs Harbour
Ikaluktutiak *see* Cambridge Bay
Ikaría *105 D6 var.* Kariot, Nicaria,
  Nikaria; *anc.* Icaria. *island* Dodekánisa,
  Greece, Aegean Sea
Ikela *77 D6* Equateur, C Dem. Rep. Congo
Iki *131 A7 island* SW Japan
Ilagan *139 E1* Luzon, N Philippines
Ilave *61 E4* Puno, S Peru
Iława *98 D3 Ger.* Deutsch-Eylau.
  Warmińsko-Mazurskie, NE Poland
Ilebo *77 C6 prev.* Port-Francqui. Kasai-
  Occidental, W Dem. Rep. Congo
Île-de-France *90 C3 cultural region*
  N France
Ilerda *see* Lleida
Ilfracombe *89 C7* SW England, United
  Kingdom
Ílhavo *92 B2* Aveiro, N Portugal
Iliamna Lake *36 C3* Alaska, USA
Il'ichevsk *see* Illichivs'k, Ukraine
Ilici *see* Elche
Iligan *139 E2 off.* Iligan City. Mindanao,
  S Philippines
Iligan City *see* Iligan
Ilapel *64 B4* Coquimbo, C Chile
Illichivs'k *109 E4 Rus.* Il'ichevsk.
  Odes'ka Oblast', SW Ukraine
Illicis *see* Elche
Illinois *40 A4 off.* State of Illinois, *also
  known as* Prairie State, Sucker State.
  state C USA
Illinois River *40 B4 river* Illinois, N USA
Illurco *see* Lorca
Illuro *see* Mataró
Ilo *61 E4* Moquegua, SW Peru
Iloilo *139 E2 off.* Iloilo City. Panay
  Island, C Philippines
Iloilo City *see* Iloilo
Ilorin *75 F4* Kwara, W Nigeria
Ilovlya *111 B6* Volgogradskaya Oblast',
  SW Russian Federation
Iluh *see* Batman
Il'yaly *see* Gurbansoltan Eje
Imatra *85 E5* Etelä-Suomi, SE Finland
Imbros *see* Gökçeada
Imishli *see* İmişli
İmişli *117 H3 Rus.* Imishli. C Azerbaijan
Imola *96 C3* Emilia-Romagna, N Italy
Imperatriz *63 F2* Maranhão, NE Brazil
Imperia *96 A3* Liguria, NW Italy
Impfondo *77 C5* Likouala, NE Congo
Imphal *135 H3 state capital* Manipur,
  NE India
Imroz Adası *see* Gökçeada
Inagua Islands *see* Great Inagua

Inagua Islands *see* Little Inagua
Inarijärvi *84 D2 Lapp.* Aanaarjävri, *Swe.*
  Enareträsk. *lake* N Finland
Inău *see* Ineu
Inawashiro-ko *131 D5 var.* Inawasiro
  Ko. *lake* Honshū, C Japan
Inawasiro Ko *see* Inawashiro-ko
Incesu *116 D3* Kayseri, Turkey Asia
Inch'ŏn *129 E4 off.* Inch'ŏn-gwangyŏksi,
  Jap. Jinsen; *prev.* Chemulpo. NW South
  Korea
Inch'ŏn-gwangyŏksi *see* Inch'ŏn
Incudine, Monte *91 E7 mountain* Corse,
  France, C Mediterranean Sea
Indefatigable Island *see* Santa Cruz, Isla
Independence *45 F4* Missouri, C USA
Independence Fjord *83 E1 fjord*
  N Greenland
Independence Island *see* Malden Island
Independence Mountains *46 C4*
  mountain range Nevada, W USA
India *124 B3 off.* Republic of India, *var.*
  Indian Union, Union of India, *Hind.*
  Bhārat. *country* S Asia

INDIA
South Asia

Official name Republic of India
Formation 1947 / 1947
Capital New Delhi
Population 1.14 billion / 989 people
  per sq mile (382 people per sq km) / 29%
Total area 1,269,338 sq. miles
  (3,287,590 sq. km)
Languages Hindi*, English*, Urdu,
  Bengali, Marathi, Telugu, Tamil, Bihari,
  Gujarati, Kanarese
Religions Hindu 81%, Muslim 13%,
  Christian 2%, Sikh 2%, Other 1%,
  Buddhist 1%
Ethnic mix Indo-Aryan 72%,
  Dravidian 25%, Mongoloid and other 3%
Government Parliamentary system
Currency Indian rupee = 100 paise
Literacy rate 61%
Calorie consumption 2459 calories

India *see* Indija
Indiana *40 B4 off.* State of Indiana, *also
  known as* Hoosier State. *state* N USA
Indianapolis *40 C4 state capital* Indiana,
  N USA
Indian Church *52 C1* Orange Walk,
  N Belize
Indian Desert *see* Thar Desert
Indianola *45 F4* Iowa, C USA
Indian Union *see* India
India, Republic of *see* India
Indigirka *115 F2 river* NE Russian
  Federation
Indija *100 D3 Hung.* India; *prev.* Indjija.
  Vojvodina, N Serbia
Indira Point *132 G3 headland* Andaman
  and Nicobar Island, India, NE Indian
  Ocean
Indjija *see* Indija
Indomed Fracture Zone *141 B6 tectonic
  feature* SW Indian Ocean
Indonesia *138 B4 off.* Republic of
  Indonesia, *Ind.* Republik Indonesia;
  prev. Dutch East Indies, Netherlands
  East Indies, United States of Indonesia.
  country SE Asia

INDONESIA
Southeast Asia

Official name Republic of Indonesia
Formation 1949 / 1999
Capital Jakarta
Population 228 million / 329 people
  per sq mile (127 people per sq km) / 47%
Total area 741,096 sq. miles
  (1,919,440 sq. km)
Languages Bahasa Indonesia*, Javanese,
  Sundanese, Madurese, Dutch
Religions Sunni Muslim 87%,
  Protestant 6%, Roman Catholic 3%,
  Hindu 2%, Other 1%, Buddhist 1%
Ethnic mix Javanese 42%, Sundanese 15%,
  Coastal Malays 12%, Madurese 3%,
  Other 28%
Government Presidential system
Currency Rupiah = 100 sen
Literacy rate 90%
Calorie consumption 2904 calories

Indonesian Borneo *see* Kalimantan
Indonesia, Republic of *see* Indonesia
Indonesia, Republik *see* Indonesia
Indonesia, United States of *see*
  Indonesia
Indore *134 D4* Madhya Pradesh, C India
Indreville *see* Châteauroux
Indus *134 C2 Chin.* Yindu Ho; *prev.*
  Yin-tu Ho. *river* S Asia
Indus Cone *see* Indus Fan
Indus Fan *112 C5 var.* Indus Cone.
  undersea fan N Arabian Sea
Indus, Mouths of the *134 B4 delta*
  S Pakistan
İnebolu *116 C2* Kastamonu, N Turkey
Ineu *108 A4 Hung.* Borosjenő; *prev.* Inău.
  Arad, W Romania
Infiernillo, Presa del *51 E4 reservoir*
  S Mexico
Inglewood *46 D2* California, W USA
Ingolstadt *95 C6* Bayern, S Germany
Ingulets *see* Inhulets'
Inguri *see* Enguri
Inhambane *79 E4* Inhambane,
  SE Mozambique
Inhulets' *109 F3 Rus.* Ingulets.
  Dnipropetrovs'ka Oblast', E Ukraine
I-ning *see* Yining
Inis *see* Ennis
Inis Ceithleann *see* Enniskillen
Inn *95 C6 river* C Europe
Innaanganeq *82 C1 var.* Kap York.
  headland NW Greenland
Inner Hebrides *88 B4 island group*
  W Scotland, United Kingdom
Inner Islands *79 H1 var.* Central Group.
  island group NE Seychelles
Innisfail *148 D3* Queensland, NE Australia
Inniskilling *see* Enniskillen
Innsbruck *see* Innsbruck
Innsbruck *95 C7 var.* Innsbruck. Tirol,
  W Austria
Inoucdjouac *see* Inukjuak
Inowrazlaw *see* Inowrocław
Inowrocław *98 C3 Ger.* Hohensalza;
  prev. Inowrazlaw. Kujawski-
  pomorskie, C Poland
I-n-Sakane, 'Erg *75 E2 desert* N Mali
I-n-Salah *70 D3 var.* In Salah. C Algeria
Insterburg *see* Chernyakhovsk
Insula *see* Lille
Inta *110 E3* Respublika Komi,
  NW Russian Federation
Interamna *see* Teramo
Interamna Nahars *see* Terni
International Falls *45 F1* Minnesota,
  N USA
Inukjuak *38 D2 var.* Inoucdjouac; *prev.*
  Port Harrison. Québec, NE Canada
Inuuvik *see* Inuvik
Inuvik *36 D3 var.* Inuuvik. Northwest
  Territories, NW Canada
Invercargill *151 A7* Southland, South
  Island, New Zealand
Inverness *88 C3* N Scotland, United
  Kingdom
Investigator Ridge *141 D5 undersea
  ridge* E Indian Ocean
Investigator Strait *149 B7 strait* South
  Australia
Inyangani *78 D3 mountain* NE Zimbabwe
Ioánnina *104 A4 var.* Janina, Yannina.
  Ípeiros, W Greece
Iola *45 F5* Kansas, C USA
Ionia Basin *see* Ionian Basin
Ionian Basin *80 D5 var.* Ionia
  Basin. *undersea basin* Ionian Sea,
  C Mediterranean Sea
Ionian Sea *103 E3 Gk.* Iónio Pélagos, *It.*
  Mar Ionio. *sea* C Mediterranean Sea
Iónioi Nísoi *105 A5 Eng.* Ionian Islands.
  region W Greece
Ionio, Mar/Iónio Pélagos *see* Ionian Sea
Íos *105 D6 var.* Nio. *island* Kykládes,
  Greece, Aegean Sea
Íos *105 D6 var.* Nio. *island* Kykládes,
  Greece, Aegean Sea
Íos *105 D6 var.* Nio. *island* Kykládes,
  Greece, Aegean Sea
Ioulís *105 C6 prev.* Kéa. Tziá, Kykládes,
  Greece, Aegean Sea
Iowa *45 F3 off.* State of Iowa, *also known
  as* Hawkeye State. *state* C USA
Iowa City *45 G3* Iowa, C USA
Iowa Falls *45 G3* Iowa, C USA
Ipel' *99 C6 var.* Ipoly, *Ger.* Eipel. *river*
  Hungary/Slovakia

Ipiales *58 A4* Nariño, SW Colombia
Ipoh *138 B3* Perak, Peninsular Malaysia
Ipoly *see* Ipel'
Ippy *76 C4* Ouaka, C Central African
  Republic
Ipswich *149 E5* Queensland, E Australia
Ipswich *89 E6 hist.* Gipeswic. E England,
  United Kingdom
Iqaluit *37 H3 prev.* Frobisher Bay.
  province capital Baffin Island, Nunavut,
  NE Canada
Iquique *64 B1* Tarapacá, N Chile
Iquitos *60 C1* Loreto, N Peru
Irákleio *105 D7 var.* Herakleion, *Eng.*
  Candia; *prev.* Iráklion. Kríti, Greece,
  E Mediterranean Sea
Iráklion *see* Irákleio
Iráklion *see* Irákleio
Iran *120 C3 off.* Islamic Republic of Iran;
  prev. Persia. *country* SW Asia

IRAN
Southwest Asia

Official name Islamic Republic of Iran
Formation 1502 / 1990
Capital Tehran
Population 71.2 million / 113 people
  per sq mile (44 people per sq km) / 67%
Total area 636,293 sq. miles
  (1,648,000 sq. km)
Languages Farsi*, Azeri, Luri, Gilaki,
  Kurdish, Mazanderani, Turkmen,
  Arabic, Baluchi
Religions Shi'a Muslim 93%, Sunni
  Muslim 6%, Other 1%
Ethnic mix Persian 50%, Azari 24%,
  Other 10%, Kurdish 8%, Lur and
  Bakhtiari 8%
Government Islamic theocracy
Currency Iranian rial = 100 dinars
Literacy rate 77%
Calorie consumption 3085 calories

Iranian Plateau *120 D3 var.* Plateau of
  Iran. *plateau* N Iran
Iran, Islamic Republic of *see* Iran
Iran, Plateau of *see* Iranian Plateau
Irapuato *51 E4* Guanajuato, C Mexico
Iraq *120 B3 off.* Republic of Iraq, *Ar.*
  'Irāq. *country* SW Asia

IRAQ
Southwest Asia

Official name Republic of Iraq
Formation 1932 / 1990
Capital Baghdad
Population 30.3 million / 179 people
  per sq mile (69 people per sq km) / 67%
Total area 168,753 sq. miles
  (437,072 sq. km)
Languages Arabic*, Kurdish*, Turkic
  languages, Armenian, Assyrian
Religions Shi'a Muslim 60%,
  Sunni Muslim 35%, Other (including
  Christian) 5%
Ethnic mix Arab 80%, Kurdish 15%,
  Turkmen 3%, Other 2%
Government Parliamentary system
Currency New Iraqi dinar = 1000 fils
Literacy rat e 74%
Calorie consumption 2197 calories

'Irāq *see* Iraq
Iraq, Republic of *see* Iraq
Irbid *119 B5* Irbid, N Jordan
Irbil *see* Arbīl
Ireland *80 A3 off.* Republic of Ireland, *Ir.*
  Éire. *country* NW Europe

IRELAND
Northwest Europe

Official name Ireland
Formation 1922 / 1922
Capital Dublin
Population 4.3 million / 162 people
  per sq mile (63 people per sq km) / 60%
Total area 27,135 sq. miles (70,280 sq. km)
Languages English*, Irish Gaelic*
Religions Roman Catholic 88%,
  Other 9%, Anglican 3%
Ethnic mix Irish 99%, Other 1%
Government Parliamentary system
Currency Euro = 100 cents
Literacy rate 99%
Calorie consumption 3656 calories

Ireland *80 C3 Lat.* Hibernia. *island*
  Ireland/United Kingdom
Ireland, Republic of *see* Ireland
Irian *see* New Guinea
Irian Barat *see* Papua
Irian Jaya *see* Papua
Irian, Teluk *see* Cenderawasih, Teluk
Iringa *73 C7* Iringa, C Tanzania
Iriomote-jima *130 A4 island* Sakishima-
  shotō, SW Japan
Iriona *52 D2* Colón, NE Honduras
Irish Sea *89 C7 Ir.* Muir Éireann. *sea*
  C British Isles
Irkutsk *115 E4* Irkutskaya Oblast',
  S Russian Federation
Irminger Basin *see* Reykjanes Basin
Iroise *90 A3 sea* NW France
Iron Mountain *40 B2* Michigan,
  N USA
Ironwood *40 B1* Michigan, N USA
Irrawaddy *136 B4 var.* Ayeyarwady.
  river W Burma (Myanmar)
Irrawaddy, Mouths of the *137 A5 delta*
  SW Burma (Myanmar)
Irtish *see* Irtysh
Irtysh *114 C4 var.* Irtish, *Kaz.* Ertis.
  river C Asia
Irun *93 E1 Cast.* Irún. País Vasco,
  N Spain
Irún *see* Irun
Iruña *see* Pamplona
Isabela, Isla *60 A5 var.* Albemarle Island.
  island Galapagos Islands, Ecuador,
  E Pacific Ocean
Isaccea *108 D4* Tulcea, E Romania
Isachsen *37 F1* Ellef Ringnes Island,
  Nunavut, N Canada
Ísafjördhur *83 E4* Vestfirdhir,
  NW Iceland
Isbarta *see* Isparta
Isca Damnoniorum *see* Exeter
Ise *131 C6* Mie, Honshū, SW Japan
Iseghem *see* Izegem
Isère *91 D5 river* E France
Isernia *97 D5 var.* Æsernia. Molise,
  C Italy
Ise-wan *131 C6 bay* S Japan
Isfahan *see* Eşfahān
Isha Baydhabo *see* Baydhabo
Ishigaki-jima *130 A4 island* Sakishima-
  shotō, SW Japan
Ishikari-wan *130 C2 bay* Hokkaidō,
  NE Japan
Ishim *114 C4* Tyumenskaya Oblast',
  C Russian Federation
Ishim *114 C4 Kaz.* Esil. *river*
  Kazakhstan/Russian Federation
Ishinomaki *130 D4 var.* Isinomaki.
  Miyagi, Honshū, C Japan
Ishkashim *see* Ishkoshim
Ishkoshim *123 F3 Rus.* Ishkashim.
  S Tajikistan
Isinomaki *see* Ishinomaki
Isiro *77 E5* Orientale, NE Dem. Rep.
  Congo
Iskär *see* Iskūr
İskenderun *116 D4 Eng.* Alexandretta.
  Hatay, S Turkey
İskenderun Körfezi *118 A2 Eng.* Gulf of
  Alexandretta. *gulf* S Turkey
Iskur *104 C2 var.* Iskär. *river*
  NW Bulgaria
Yazovir Iskur *104 B2 prev.* Yazovir
  Stalin. *reservoir* W Bulgaria
Isla Cristina *92 C4* Andalucía, S Spain
Isla de León *see* San Fernando
Islāmābād *134 C1 country capital*
  (Pakistan) (Pakistan) Federal Capital
  Territory Islāmābād, NE Pakistan
Island/Ísland *see* Iceland
Islay *88 B4 island* SW Scotland, United
  Kingdom
Isle *91 B5 river* W France
Isle of Man *89 B5 UK crown dependency*
  NW Europe
Isles of Scilly *89 B8 island group*
  SW England, United Kingdom
Ismailia *see* Al Ismā'iliya
Ismâ'iliya *see* Al Ismā'iliya
Ismid *see* İzmit
Isnā *72 B2 var.* Esna. SE Egypt
Isna *see* Isnā
Isola d'Istria *see* Izola
Isparta *116 B4 var.* Isbarta. Isparta,
  SW Turkey
Ispir *117 E3* Erzurum, NE Turkey

Israel 119 A7 off. State of Israel, var.
Medinat Israel, Heb. Yisrael, Yisra'el.
country SW Asia

ISRAEL
Southwest Asia

Official name State of Israel
Formation 1948 / 1994
Capital Jerusalem (not internationally
recognized)
Population 7 million / 892 people
per sq mile (344 people per sq km) / 92%
Total area 8019 sq. miles (20,770 sq. km)
Languages Hebrew*, Arabic*,
Yiddish, German, Russian, Polish,
Romanian, Persian
Religions Jewish 76%, Muslim (mainly
Sunni) 16%, Other 4%, Druze 2%,
Christian 2%
Ethnic mix Jewish 76%, Other
(mostly Arab) 24%
Government Parliamentary system
Currency Shekel = 100 agorot
Literacy rate 97%
Calorie consumption 3666 calories

Israel, State of see Israel
Issa see Vis
Issiq Köl see Issyk-Kul', Ozero
Issoire 91 C5 Puy-de-Dôme, C France
Issyk-Kul' see Balykchy
Issyk-Kul', Ozero 123 G2 var. Issiq Köl,
Kir. Ysyk-Köl. lake E Kyrgyzstan
İstanbul 116 B2 Bul. Tsarigrad, Eng.
Istanbul, prev. Constantinople; anc.
Byzantium. Istanbul, NW Turkey
Istarska Županija see Istra
Istra 100 A3 off. Istarska Županija.
province NW Croatia
Istra 100 A3 Eng. Istria, Ger. Istrien.
cultural region NW Croatia
Istria/Istrien see Istra
Itabuna 63 G3 Bahia, E Brazil
Itagüí 58 B3 Antioquia, W Colombia
Itaipú, Represa de 63 E4 reservoir Brazil/
Paraguay
Itaituba 63 E2 Pará, NE Brazil
**Italia/Italiana, Republica/Italian
Republic, The** see Italy
Italian Somaliland see Somalia
Italy 96 C3 off. The Italian Republic, It.
Italia, Repubblica Italiana. country
S Europe

ITALY
Southern Europe

Official name Italian Republic
Formation 1861 / 1947
Capital Rome
Population 58.2 million / 513 people
per sq mile (198 people per sq km) / 67%
Total area 116,305 sq. miles
(301,230 sq. km)
Languages Italian*, German, French,
Rhaeto-Romanic, Sardinian
Religions Roman Catholic 85%,
Other and nonreligious 13%, Muslim 2%
Ethnic mix Italian 94%, Other 4%,
Sardinian 2%
Government Parliamentary system
Currency Euro = 100 cents
Literacy rate 98%
Calorie consumption 3671 calories

Iténez, Río see Guaporé, Rio
Ithaca 41 E3 New York, NE USA
It Hearrenfean see Heerenveen
Itoigawa 131 C5 Niigata, Honshū,
C Japan
Itseqqortoormiit see Ittoqqortoormiit
Ittoqqortoormiit 83 E3 var.
Itseqqortoormiit, Dan. Scoresbysund,
Eng. Scoresby Sound. Tunu,
C Greenland
Iturup, Ostrov 130 E1 island Kuril'skiye
Ostrova, SE Russian Federation
Itzehoe 94 B2 Schleswig-Holstein,
N Germany
Ivalo 84 D2 Lapp. Avveel, Avvil. Lappi,
N Finland
Ivanava 107 B7 Pol. Janów, Janów
Poleski, Rus. Ivanovo. Brestskaya
Voblasts', SW Belarus
Ivangrad see Berane

Ivanhoe 149 C6 New South Wales,
SE Australia
Ivano-Frankivs'k 108 C2 Ger. Stanislau,
Pol. Stanisławów, Rus. Ivano-
Frankovsk; prev. Stanislav. Ivano-
Frankivs'ka Oblast', W Ukraine
Ivano-Frankovsk see Ivano-Frankivs'k
Ivanovo 111 B5 Ivanovskaya Oblast',
W Russian Federation
Ivanovo see Ivanava
Ivantsevichi/Ivatsevichi see Ivatsevichy
Ivatsevichy 107 B6 Pol. Iwacewicze, Rus.
Ivantsevichi, Ivatsevichi. Brestskaya
Voblasts', SW Belarus
Ivigtut see Ivittuut
Ivittuut 82 B4 var. Ivigtut. Kitaa,
S Greenland
Iviza see Eivissa\Ibiza
Iviza see Eivissa\Ibiza
Iviza see Eivissa\Ibiza
Ivory Coast see Côte d'Ivoire
Ivory Coast, Republic of the see Côte
d'Ivoire
Ivujivik 38 D1 Québec, NE Canada
Iwacewicze see Ivatsevichy
Iwaki 131 D5 Fukushima, Honshū,
N Japan
Iwakuni 131 B7 Yamaguchi, Honshū,
SW Japan
Iwanai 130 C2 Hokkaidō, NE Japan
Iwate 130 D3 Iwate, Honshū, N Japan
Ixtapa 51 E5 Guerrero, S Mexico
Ixtepec 51 F5 Oaxaca, SE Mexico
Iyo-nada 131 B7 sea S Japan
Izabal, Lago de 52 B2 prev. Golfo Dulce.
lake E Guatemala
Izad Khvāst 120 D3 Fārs, C Iran
Izegem 87 A6 prev. Iseghem. West-
Vlaanderen, W Belgium
Izhevsk 111 D5 prev. Ustinov.
Udmurtskaya Respublika, NW Russian
Federation
Izmail see Izmayil
Izmayil 108 D4 Rus. Izmail. Odes'ka
Oblast', SW Ukraine
İzmir 116 A3 prev. Smyrna. İzmir,
W Turkey
İzmit 116 B2 var. Ismid; anc. Astacus.
Kocaeli, NW Turkey
Iznik Gölü 116 B3 lake NW Turkey
Izu-hanto 131 D6 peninsula Honshū,
S Japan
Izu Shichito see Izu-shotō
Izu-shoto 131 D6 var. Izu Shichito.
island group S Japan
Izvor 104 B2 Pernik, W Bulgaria
Izyaslav 108 C2 Khmel'nyts'ka Oblast',
W Ukraine
Izyum 109 G2 Kharkivs'ka Oblast',
E Ukraine

J

Jabal ash Shifa 120 A4 desert NW Saudi
Arabia
Jabalpur 135 E4 prev. Jubbulpore.
Madhya Pradesh, C India
Jabbūl, Sabkhat al 118 B2 sabkha
NW Syria
Jablah 118 A3 var. Jeble, Fr. Djéblé. Al
Lādhiqīyah, W Syria
Jaca 93 F1 Aragón, NE Spain
Jacaltenango 52 A2 Huehuetenango,
W Guatemala
Jackson 42 B2 state capital Mississippi,
S USA
Jackson 45 H5 Missouri, C USA
Jackson 42 C1 Tennessee, S USA
Jackson Head 151 A6 headland South
Island, New Zealand
Jacksonville 43 E3 Florida, SE USA
Jacksonville 40 B4 Illinois, N USA
Jacksonville 43 F1 North Carolina,
SE USA
Jacksonville 49 G3 Texas, SW USA
Jacmel 54 D3 var. Jaquemel. S Haiti
Jacob see Nkayi
Jacobābād 134 B3 Sind, SE Pakistan
Jadotville see Likasi
Jadransko More/Jadransko Morje see
Adriatic Sea
Jaén 60 B2 Cajamarca, N Peru
Jaén 92 D4 Andalucía, SW Spain
Jaffna 132 D3 Northern Province,
N Sri Lanka
Jagannath see Puri

Jagdalpur 135 E5 Chhattīsgarh, C India
Jagdaqi 127 G1 Nei Mongol Zizhiqu,
N China
Jagodina 100 D4 prev. Svetozarevo.
Serbia, C Serbia
Jahra see Al Jahrā'
Jailolo see Halmahera, Pulau
Jaipur 134 D3 prev. Jeypore. state capital
Rājasthān, N India
Jaisalmer 134 C3 Rājasthān, NW India
Jajce 100 B3 Federacija Bosna
I Hercegovina, W Bosnia and
Herzegovina
Jakarta 138 C5 prev. Djakarta, Dut.
Batavia. country capital (Indonesia)
(Indonesia) Jawa, C Indonesia
Jakobstad 84 D4 Fin. Pietarsaari. Länsi-
Suomi, W Finland
Jakobstadt see Jēkabpils
Jalālābād 123 F4 var. Jalalabad,
Jelalabad. Nangarhār, E Afghanistan
Jalal-Abad see Dzhalal-Abad, Dzhalal-
Abadskaya Oblast', Kyrgyzstan
Jalandhar 134 D2 prev. Jullundur.
Punjab, N India
Jalapa 52 D3 Nueva Segovia,
NW Nicaragua
Jalpa 50 D4 Zacatecas, C Mexico
Jālū 71 G3 var. Jālā. NE Libya
Jaluit Atoll 144 D2 var. Jālwōj. atoll
Ralik Chain, S Marshall Islands
Jālwōj see Jaluit Atoll
Jamaame 73 D6 It. Giamame; prev.
Margherita. Jubbada Hoose, S Somalia
Jamaica 54 A4 country W West Indies

JAMAICA
West Indies

Official name Jamaica
Formation 1962 / 1962
Capital Kingston
Population 2.7 million / 646 people
per sq mile (249 people per sq km) / 52%
Total area 4243 sq. miles (10,990 sq. km)
Languages English*, English Creole
Religions Other and nonreligious 45%,
Other Protestant 20%, Church
of God 18%, Baptist 10%, Anglican 7%
Ethnic mix Black African 92%,
Mulatto (mixed race) 6%, East Indian 1%,
European and Chinese 1%
Government Parliamentary system
Currency Jamaican dollar = 100 cents
Literacy rate 80%
Calorie consumption 2685 calories

Jamaica 56 A1 island W West Indies
Jamaica Channel 54 D3 channel Haiti/
Jamaica
Jamālpur 135 F3 Bihār, NE India
Jambi 138 B4 var. Telanaipura; prev.
Djambi. Sumatera, W Indonesia
Jamdena see Yamdena, Pulau
James Bay 38 C3 bay Ontario/Québec,
E Canada
James River 45 E2 river North Dakota/
South Dakota, N USA
James River 41 E5 river Virginia,
NE USA
Jamestown 41 E3 New York, NE USA
Jamestown 45 E2 North Dakota,
N USA
Jamestown see Holetown
Jammu 134 D2 prev. Jummoo. state
capital Jammu and Kashmir,
NW India
Jammu and Kashmīr 134 D1 disputed
region India/Pakistan
Jāmnagar 134 C4 prev. Navanagar.
Gujarāt, W India
Jamshedpur 135 F4 Jhārkhand, NE India
Jamuna see Brahmaputra
Janaúba 63 F3 Minas Gerais, SE Brazil
Janesville 40 B3 Wisconsin, N USA
Janina see Ioánnina
Janischken see Joniškis
Jankovac see Jánoshalma
Jan Mayen 83 F4 Norwegian dependency
N Atlantic Ocean
Jánoshalma 99 C7 SCr. Jankovac. Bács-
Kiskun, S Hungary
Jánossomorja 99 C6 Győr-Moson-
Sopron, NW Hungary
Janów see Ivanava, Belarus
Janow/Janów see Jonava, Lithuania
Janów Poleski see Ivanava

JAPAN
East Asia

Official name Japan
Formation 1590 / 1972
Capital Tokyo
Population 128 million / 883 people
per sq mile (341 people per sq km) / 66%
Total area 145,882 sq. miles
(377,835 sq. km)
Languages Japanese*, Korean, Chinese
Religions Shinto and Buddhist 76%,
Buddhist 16%, Other (including
Christian) 8%
Ethnic mix Japanese 99%, Other
(mainly Korean) 1%
Government Parliamentary system
Currency Yen = 100 sen
Literacy rate 99%
Calorie consumption 2761 calories

Japan 130 C4 var. Nippon, Jap. Nihon.
country E Asia
Japan, Sea of 130 A4 var. East Sea, Rus.
Yaponskoye More. sea NW Pacific
Ocean
Japan Trench 125 F1 trench NW Pacific
Ocean
Japen see Yapen, Pulau
Japiim 62 C2 var. Máncio Lima. Acre,
W Brazil
Japurá, Rio 62 C2 var. Río Caquetá,
Yapurá. river Brazil/Colombia
Japurá, Rio see Caquetá, Río
Jaqué 53 G5 Darién, SE Panama
Jaquemel see Jacmel
Jarablos see Jarābulus
Jarābulus 118 C2 var. Jarablos, Jerablus,
Fr. Djérablous. Ḥalab, N Syria
Jarbah, Jazīrat see Jerba, Île de
**Jardines de la Reina, Archipiélago de
los** 54 B2 island group C Cuba
Jarid, Shaṭṭ al see Jerid, Chott el
Jarocin 98 C4 Wielkopolskie, C Poland
Jarosław see Jaroslaw
Jarosław 99 E5 Ger. Jaroslau, Rus.
Yaroslav. Podkarpackie, SE Poland
Jarqo'rg'on 123 E3 Rus. Dzharkurgan.
Surkhondaryo Viloyati, S Uzbekistan
Jarvis Island 145 G2 US unincorporated
territory C Pacific Ocean
Jaslo 99 D5 Podkarpackie, SE Poland
Jastrzębie-Zdrój 99 C5 Śląskie, S Poland
Jataí 63 E3 Goiás, C Brazil
Jativa see Xàtiva
Jauf see Al Jawf
Jaunpiebalga 106 D3 Gulbene, NE Latvia
Jaunpur 135 E3 Uttar Pradesh, N India
Java 152 A3 South Dakota, N USA
Javalambre 93 E3 mountain S Spain
Java Sea 138 D4 Ind. Laut Jawa. sea
W Indonesia
Java Trench 124 D5 var. Sunda Trench.
trench E Indian Ocean
Jawa, Laut see Java Sea
Jawhar 73 D6 var. Jowhar, It. Giohar.
Shabeellaha Dhexe, S Somalia
Jaworów see Yavoriv
Jaya, Puncak 139 G4 prev. Puntjak
Carstensz, Puntjak Sukarno. mountain
Papua, E Indonesia
Jayapura 139 H4 var. Djajapura,
Dut. Hollandia; prev. Kotabaru,
Sukarnapura. Papua, E Indonesia
Jay Dairen see Dalian
Jayhawker State see Kansas
Jaz Murian, Hamun-e 120 E4 lake
SE Iran
Jebba 75 F4 Kwara, W Nigeria
Jebel, Bahr el see White Nile
Jeble see Jablah
Jedda see Jiddah
Jędrzejów 98 D4 Ger. Endersdorf.
Świętokrzyskie, C Poland
Jefferson City 45 G5 state capital
Missouri, C USA
Jega 75 F4 Kebbi, NW Nigeria
Jehol see Chengde
Jēkabpils 106 D4 Ger. Jakobstadt.
Jēkabpils, S Latvia
Jelalabad see Jalālābād
Jelenia Góra 98 B4 Ger. Hirschberg,
Hirschberg im Riesengebirge,
Hirschberg in Riesengebirge, Hirschberg
in Schlesien. Dolnośląskie, SW Poland
Jelgava 106 C3 Ger. Mitau. Jelgava,
C Latvia

Jemappes 87 B6 Hainaut, S Belgium
Jember 138 D5 prev. Djember.
C Indonesia
Jena 94 C4 Thüringen, C Germany
Jenin 119 A6 N West Bank
Jerablus see Jarābulus
Jerada 70 D2 NE Morocco
Jérémie 54 D3 SW Haiti
Jerez see Jeréz de la Frontera, Spain
Jeréz de la Frontera 92 C5 var. Jerez;
prev. Xeres. Andalucía, SW Spain
Jeréz de los Caballeros 92 C4
Extremadura, W Spain
Jericho 119 B6 Ar. Arīḥā, Heb. Yeriḥo.
E West Bank
Jerid, Chott el 71 E2 var. Shaṭṭ al Jarid.
salt lake SW Tunisia
Jersey 89 D8 uk crown dependency
Channel Islands, NW Europe
Jerusalem 103 H4 Ar. Al Quds, Al Quds
ash Sharīf, Heb. Yerushalayim; anc.
Hierosolyma. country capital (Israel)
(Israel) Jerusalem, NE Israel
Jesenice 95 D7 Ger. Assling. NW Slovenia
Jesselton see Kota Kinabalu
Jessore 135 G4 Khulna, W Bangladesh
Jesús María 64 C3 Córdoba, C Argentina
Jeypore see Jaipur, Rājasthān, India
Jhānsi 134 D3 Uttar Pradesh, N India
Jhārkhand 135 F4 cultural region
NE India
Jhelum 134 C2 Punjab, NE Pakistan
Ji see Hebei, China
Ji see Jilin, China
Jiangmen 128 C6 Guangdong, S China
Jiangsu 128 D4 var. Chiang-su, Jiangsu
Sheng, Kiangsu, Su. province E China
Jiangsu see Nanjing
Jiangsu Sheng see Jiangsu
Jiangxi 128 C6 var. Chiang-hsi, Gan,
Jiangxi Sheng, Kiangsi. province
S China
Jiangxi Sheng see Jiangxi
Jiaxing 128 D5 Zhejiang, SE China
Jiayi see Chiai
Jibuti see Djibouti
Jiddah 121 A5 Eng. Jedda. (Saudi
Arabia) Makkah, W Saudi Arabia
Jih-k'a-tse see Xigazê
Jihlava 99 B5 Ger. Iglau, Pol. Igława.
Vysocina, S Czech Republic
Jilib 73 D6 It. Gelib. Jubbada Dhexe,
S Somalia
Jilin 128 E3 var. Chi-lin, Girin, Kirin;
prev. Yungki, Yunki. Jilin, NE China
Jilin 128 E3 var. Chi-lin, Girin, Ji, Jilin
Sheng, Kirin. province NE China
Jilin Sheng see Jilin
Jima 73 C5 var. Jimma, It. Gimma.
Oromīya, C Ethiopia
Jimbolia 108 A4 Ger. Hatzfeld, Hung.
Zsombolya. Timiș, W Romania
Jiménez 50 D2 Chihuahua, N Mexico
Jimma see Jima
Jimsar 126 C3 Xinjiang Uygur Zizhiqu,
NW China
Jin see Shanxi
Jin see Tianjin Shi
Jinan 128 C4 var. Chinan, Chi-nan,
Tsinan. province capital Shandong,
E China
Jingdezhen 128 C5 Jiangxi, S China
Jinghong 128 A6 var. Yunjinghong.
Yunnan, SW China
Jinhua 128 D5 Zhejiang, SE China
Jining 127 F3 Shandong, E China
Jinja 73 C6 S Uganda
Jinotega 52 D3 Jinotega, NW Nicaragua
Jinotepe 52 D3 Carazo, SW Nicaragua
Jinsen see Inch'ŏn
Jinsha Jiang 124 A5 Eng. Yangtze. river
SW China
Jinzhong 128 C4 var. Yuci. Shanxi,
C China
Jinzhou 128 D3 var. Chin-chou,
Chinchow; prev. Chinhsien. Liaoning,
NE China
Jirgalanta see Hovd
Jisr ash Shadadi see Ash Shadādah
Jiu 108 B5 Ger. Schyl, Schyl, Hung. Zsil,
Zsily. river S Romania
Jiujiang 128 C5 Jiangxi, S China
Jixi 129 E2 Heilongjiang, NE China
Jīzān 121 B6 var. Qīzān. Jīzān, SW Saudi
Arabia
Jizzax 123 E2 Rus. Dzhizak. Jizzax
Viloyati, C Uzbekistan

João Belo see Xai-Xai
João Pessoa 63 G2 prev. Paraíba. state
capital Paraíba, E Brazil
Joazeiro see Juazeiro
Job'urg see Johannesburg
Jo-ch'iang see Ruoqiang
Jodhpur 134 C3 Rājasthān, NW India
Joensuu 85 E5 Itä-Suomi, SE Finland
Jōetsu 131 C5 var. Zyôetu. Niigata,
Honshū, C Japan
Jogjakarta see Yogyakarta
Johannesburg 78 D4 var. Egoli,
Erautini, Gauteng, abbrev. Job'urg.
Gauteng, NE South Africa
Johannisburg see Pisz
John Day River 46 C3 river Oregon,
NW USA
John o'Groats 88 C2 N Scotland, United
Kingdom
Johnston Atoll 143 E1 US unincorporated
territory ◊ Pacific Ocean
Johor Baharu see Johor Bahru
Johor Bahru 138 B3 var. Johor Baharu,
Johore Bahru. Johor, Peninsular
Malaysia
Johore Bahru see Johor Bahru
Johore Strait 138 A1 strait Johor,
Peninsular Malaysia, Malaysia/Singapore
Asia Andaman Sea/South China Sea
Joinvile see Joinville
Joinville 63 E4 var. Joinvile. Santa
Catarina, S Brazil
Jokkmokk 84 C3 Lapp. Dálvvadis.
Norrbotten, N Sweden
Jokyakarta see Yogyakarta
Joliet 40 B3 Illinois, N USA
Jonava 106 B4 Ger. Janow, Pol. Janów.
Kaunas, C Lithuania
Jonesboro 42 B1 Arkansas, C USA
Joniškis 106 C3 Ger. Janischken. Šiauliai,
N Lithuania
Jönköping 85 B7 Jönköping, S Sweden
Jonquière 39 E4 Québec, SE Canada
Joplin 45 F5 Missouri, C USA
Jordan 119 B6 off. Hashemite Kingdom
of Jordan, Ar. Al Mamlaka al Urdunīya
al Hashemīyah, Al Urdunn; prev.
Transjordan. country SW Asia

JORDAN
Southwest Asia

Official name Hashemite Kingdom
of Jordan
Formation 1946 / 1967
Capital Amman
Population 6 million / 175 people
per sq mile (67 people per sq km) / 79%
Total area 35,637 sq. miles (92,300 sq. km)
Languages Arabic*
Religions Muslim (mainly Sunni) 92%,
Other (mostly Christian) 8%
Ethnic mix Arab 98%, Circassian 1%,
Armenian 1%
Government Monarchy
Currency Jordanian dinar = 1000 fils
Literacy rate 90%
Calorie consumption 2673 calories

Jordan 119 B5 Ar. Urdunn, Heb.
HaYarden. river SW Asia
Jorhāt 135 H3 Assam, NE India
Jos 75 G4 Plateau, C Nigeria
Joseph Bonaparte Gulf 146 D2 gulf
N Australia
Jos Plateau 75 G4 plateau C Nigeria
Jotunheimen 85 A5 mountain range
S Norway
Joûnié 118 A4 var. Junīyah. W Lebanon
Joure 86 D2 Fris. De Jouwer. Friesland,
N Netherlands
Joutseno 85 E5 Etelä-Suomi, SE Finland
Jowhar see Jawhar
J.Storm Thurmond Reservoir see Clark
Hill Lake
Juan Aldama 50 D3 Zacatecas, C Mexico
Juan de Fuca, Strait of 46 A1 strait
Canada/USA
Juan Fernández Islands 57 A6 Eng.
Juan Fernandez Islands. island group
W Chile
Juan Fernandez Islands see Juan
Fernández, Islas
Juazeiro 63 G2 prev. Joazeiro. Bahia,
E Brazil
Juazeiro do Norte 63 G2 Ceará, E Brazil

Juba 73 B5 var. Jūbā. Bahr el Gabel,
S Sudan
Juba 73 D6 Amh. Genalē Wenz, It. Guiba,
Som. Ganaane, Webi Jubba. river
Ethiopia/Somalia
Jubba, Webi see Juba
Jubbulpore see Jabalpur
Júcar 93 E3 var. Jucar. river C Spain
Juchitán 51 F5 var. Juchitán de Zaragosa.
Oaxaca, SE Mexico
Juchitán de Zaragosa see Juchitán
Judayyidat Hāmir 120 B3 Al Anbār,
S Iraq
Judenburg 95 D7 Steiermark, C Austria
Jugoslavija see Serbia
Juigalpa 52 D3 Chontales, S Nicaragua
Juiz de Fora 63 F4 Minas Gerais,
SE Brazil
Jujuy see San Salvador de Jujuy
Jūlā see Jālū, Libya
Julia Beterrae see Béziers
Juliaca 61 E4 Puno, SE Peru
Juliana Top 59 G3 mountain C Suriname
Julianehåb see Qaqortoq
Julio Briga see Bragança
Julióbriga see Logroño
Juliomagus see Angers
Jullundur see Jalandhar
Jumilla 93 E4 Murcia, SE Spain
Jummoo see Jammu
Jumna see Yamuna
Jumporn see Chumphon
Junction City 45 F4 Kansas, C USA
Juneau 36 D4 state capital Alaska, USA
Junín 64 C4 Buenos Aires, E Argentina
Juniyah see Joûnié
Junkseylon see Phuket
Jur 73 B5 river C Sudan
Jura 90 D4 cultural region E France
Jura 95 A7 var. Jura Mountains.
mountain range France/Switzerland
Jura 88 B4 island SW Scotland, United
Kingdom
Jura Mountains see Jura
Jurbarkas 106 B4 Ger. Georgenburg,
Jurburg. Tauragė, W Lithuania
Jurburg see Jurbarkas
Jūrmala 106 C3 Rīga, C Latvia
Juruá, Rio 62 C2 var. Río Yuruá. river
Brazil/Peru
Juruena, Rio 62 D3 river
W Brazil
Jutiapa 52 B2 Jutiapa, S Guatemala
Juticalpa 52 D2 Olancho, C Honduras
Jutland 85 A7 Eng. Jutland. peninsula
W Denmark
Jutland see Jylland
Juvavum see Salzburg
Južna Morava 101 E5 Ger. Südliche
Morava. river SE Serbia
Jwaneng 78 C4 Southern, S Botswana
Jyrgalan see Dzhergalan
Jyväskylä 85 D5 Länsi-Suomi, C Finland

K

K2 126 A4 Chin. Qogir Feng, Eng. Mount
Godwin Austen. mountain China/
Pakistan
Kaafu Atoll see Male' Atoll
Kaaimanston 59 G3 Sipaliwini,
N Suriname
Kaakhka see Kaka
Kaala see Caála
Kaamanen 84 D2 Lapp. Gámas. Lappi,
N Finland
Kaapstad see Cape Town
Kaaresuvanto 84 C3 Lapp. Gárassavon.
Lappi, N Finland
Kabale 73 B6 SW Uganda
Kabinda 77 D7 Kasai-Oriental, SE Dem.
Rep. Congo
Kabinda see Cabinda
Kābol 123 E4 var. Kabul, Pash.
Kābul. country capital (Afghanistan)
(Afghanistan) Kābul, E Afghanistan
Kabompo 78 C2 river W Zambia
Kabul 123 E4 var. Darya-ye Kābul. river
Afghanistan/Pakistan
Kābul see Kābol
Kābul, Darya-ye see Kabul
Kabwe 78 D2 Central, C Zambia
Kachchh, Gulf of 134 B4 var. Gulf of
Cutch, Gulf of Kutch. gulf W India
Kachchh, Rann of 134 B4 var. Rann
of Kachh, Rann of Kutch. salt marsh
India/Pakistan

Kachh, Rann of see Kachchh, Rann of
Kadan Kyun 137 B5 prev. King Island.
island Mergui Archipelago, S Burma
(Myanmar)
Kadavu 145 E4 prev. Kandavu. island
S Fiji
Kadoma 78 D3 prev. Gatooma.
Mashonaland West, C Zimbabwe
Kadugli 72 B4 Southern Kordofan,
S Sudan
Kaduna 75 G4 Kaduna, C Nigeria
Kadzhi-Say 123 G2 Kir. Kajisay. Issyk-
Kul'skaya Oblast', NE Kyrgyzstan
Kaédi 74 C3 Gorgol, S Mauritania
Kaffa see Feodosiya
Kafue 78 D2 Lusaka, SE Zambia
Kafue 72 C2 river C Zambia
Kaga Bandoro 76 C4 prev. Fort-
Crampel. Nana-Grébizi, C Central
African Republic
Kagan see Kogon
Kághet 74 D1 var. Karet. physical region
N Mauritania
Kagi see Chiai
Kagoshima 131 B8 var. Kagosima.
Kagoshima, Kyūshū, SW Japan
Kagoshima-wan 131 A8 bay SW Japan
Kagosima see Kagoshima
Kagul see Cahul
Darya-ye Kahmard 123 E4 prev. Darya-
i-surkhab. river NE Afghanistan
Kahramanmaraş 116 D4 var.
Kahraman Maraş, Maraş, Marash.
Kahramanmaraş, S Turkey
Kaiapoi 151 C6 Canterbury, South
Island, New Zealand
Kaifeng 128 C4 Henan, C China
Kai, Kepulauan 139 F4 prev. Kei Islands.
island group Maluku, SE Indonesia
Kaikohe 150 C2 Northland, North
Island, New Zealand
Kaikoura 151 C5 Canterbury, South
Island, New Zealand
Kaikoura Peninsula 151 C5 peninsula
South Island, New Zealand
Kainji Lake see Kainji Reservoir
Kainji Reservoir 75 F4 var. Kainji Lake.
reservoir W Nigeria
Kaipara Harbour 150 C2 harbour North
Island, New Zealand
Kairouan 71 E2 var. Al Qayrawān.
E Tunisia
Kaisaria see Kayseri
Kaiserslautern 95 A5 Rheinland-Pfalz,
SW Germany
Kaišiadorys 107 B5 Kaunas,
S Lithuania
Kaitaia 150 C2 Northland, North Island,
New Zealand
Kajaani 84 E4 Swe. Kajana. Oulu,
C Finland
Kajan see Kayan, Sungai
Kajana see Kajaani
Kajisay see Kadzhi-Say
Kaka 122 C2 Rus. Kaakhka. Ahal
Welaýaty, S Turkmenistan
Kake 36 D4 Kupreanof Island, Alaska,
USA
Kakhovka 109 F4 Khersons'ka Oblast',
S Ukraine
Kakhovs'ke Vodoskhovyshche 109 F4
Rus. Kakhovskoye Vodokhranilishche.
reservoir SE Ukraine
Kakhovskoye Vodokhranilishche see
Kakhovs'ke Vodoskhovyshche
Kākināda 132 D1 prev. Cocanada.
Andhra Pradesh, E India
Kakshaal-Too, Khrebet see
Kokshaal-Tau
Kaktovik 36 D2 Alaska, USA
Kalaallit Nunaat see Greenland
Kalahari Desert 78 B4 desert Southern
Africa
Kalaikhum see Qal'aikhum
Kalámai see Kalámata
Kalamariá 104 B4 Kentrikí Makedonía,
N Greece
Kalamás 104 A4 var. Thiamis; prev.
Thýamis. river W Greece
Kalámata 105 B6 prev. Kalámai.
Pelopónnisos, S Greece
Kalamazoo 40 C3 Michigan, N USA
Kálamos 105 C5 Attikí, C Greece
Kalampáka 104 B4 var. Kalambaka.
Thessalía, C Greece

Kalanchak *109 F4* Khersons'ka Oblast', S Ukraine
Kalarash *see* Călăraşi
Kalasin *136 D4 var.* Muang Kalasin. Kalasin, E Thailand
Kālat *134 B2 var.* Kelat, Khelat. Baluchistān, SW Pakistan
Kalāt *see* Qalāt
Kalbarri *147 A5* Western Australia
Kalecik *116 C3* Ankara, N Turkey
Kalemie *77 E6 prev.* Albertville. Katanga, SE Dem. Rep.
Kale Sultanie *see* Çanakkale
Kalgan *see* Zhangjiakou
Kalgoorlie *147 B6* Western Australia
Kalima *77 D6* Maniema, E Dem. Rep. Congo
Kalimantan *138 D4 Eng.* Indonesian Borneo. *geopolitical region* Borneo, C Indonesia
Kalinin *see* Tver'
Kaliningrad *106 A4* Kaliningradskaya Oblast', W Russian Federation
Kaliningrad *see* Kaliningradskaya Oblast'
Kaliningradskaya Oblast' *106 B4 var.* Kaliningrad. *province and enclave* W Russian Federation
Kalinkavichy *107 C7 Rus.* Kalinkovichi. Homyel'skaya Voblasts', SE Belarus
Kalinkovichi *see* Kalinkavichy
Kalisch/Kalish *see* Kalisz
Kalispell *44 B1* Montana, NW USA
Kalisz *98 C4 Ger.* Kalisch, *Rus.* Kalish; *anc.* Calisia. Wielkopolskie, C Poland
Kalix *84 D4* Norrbotten, N Sweden
Kalixälven *84 D3 river* N Sweden
Kallaste *106 E3* Ger. Krasnogor. Tartumaa, SE Estonia
Kallavesi *85 E5 lake* SE Finland
Kalloni *105 D5* Lésvos, E Greece
Kalmar *85 C7 var.* Calmar. Kalmar, S Sweden
Kalmthout *87 C5* Antwerpen, N Belgium
Kalpáki *104 A4* Ípeiros, W Greece
Kalpeni Island *132 B3 island* Lakshadweep, N Indian Ocean
Kaltdorf *see* Pruszków
Kaluga *111 B5* Kaluzhskaya Oblast', W Russian Federation
Kalush *108 C2 Pol.* Kałusz. Ivano-Frankivs'ka Oblast', W Ukraine
Kałusz *see* Kalush
Kalutara *132 D4* Western Province, SW Sri Lanka
Kalvarija *107 B5 Pol.* Kalwaria. Marijampolė, S Lithuania
Kalwaria *see* Kalvarija
Kalyān *134 C5* Mahārāshtra, W India
Kálymnos *105 D6 var.* Kálimnos. *island* Dodekánisa, Greece, Aegean Sea
Kama *110 D4 river* NW Russian Federation
Kamarang *59 F3* W Guyana
Kambryk *see* Cambrai
Kamchatka *115 G3 Eng.* Kamchatka. *peninsula* E Russian Federation
Kamchatka *see* Kamchatka, Poluostrov
Kamenets-Podol'skiy *see* Kam"yanets'-Podil's'kyy
Kamenka Dneprovskaya *see* Kam"yanka-Dniprovs'ka
Kamenskoye *see* Romaniv
Kamensk-Shakhtinskiy *111 B6* Rostovskaya Oblast', SW Russian Federation
Kamina *77 D7* Katanga, S Dem. Rep. Congo
Kamishli *see* Al Qāmishlī
Kamloops *37 E5* British Columbia, SW Canada
Kammu Seamount *152 C2 guyot* N Pacific Ocean
Kampala *73 B6 country capital* (Uganda) (Uganda) S Uganda
Kâmpóng Cham *137 D6 prev.* Kompong Cham. Kâmpóng Cham, C Cambodia
Kâmpóng Chhnăng *137 D6 prev.* Kompong. Kâmpóng Chhnăng, C Cambodia
Kâmpóng Saôm *137 D6 prev.* Kompong Som, Sihanoukville. Kâmpóng Saôm, SW Cambodia
Kâmpóng Spoe *137 D6 prev.* Kompong Speu. Kâmpóng Spoe, S Cambodia
Kâmpôt *137 D6* Kâmpôt, SW Cambodia
Kampuchea *see* Cambodia
Kampuchea, Democratic *see* Cambodia

Kampuchea, People's Democratic Republic of *see* Cambodia
Kam"yanets'-Podil's'kyy *108 C3 Rus.* Kamenets-Podol'skiy. Khmel'nyts'ka Oblast', W Ukraine
Kam"yanka-Dniprovs'ka *109 F3 Rus.* Kamenka Dneprovskaya. Zaporiz'ka Oblast', SE Ukraine
Kamyshin *111 B6* Volgogradskaya Oblast', SW Russian Federation
Kanaky *see* New Caledonia
Kananga *77 D6 prev.* Luluabourg. Kasai-Occidental, S Dem. Rep. Congo
Kanara *see* Karnātaka
Kanash *111 C5* Chuvashskaya Respublika, W Russian Federation
Kanazawa *131 C5* Ishikawa, Honshū, SW Japan
Kanbe *136 B4* Yangon, SW Burma (Myanmar)
Kānchipuram *132 C2 prev.* Conjeeveram. Tamil Nādu, SE India
Kandahār *123 E5 Per.* Qandahār. Kandahār, S Afghanistan
Kandalaksa *see* Kandalaksha
Kandalaksha *110 B2 var.* Kandalaksa, *Fin.* Kantalahti. Murmanskaya Oblast', NW Russian Federation
Kandangan *138 D4* Borneo, C Indonesia
Kandau *see* Kandava
Kandava *106 C3 Ger.* Kandau. Tukums, W Latvia
Kanduvu *see* Kadavu
Kandi *75 F4* N Benin
Kandy *132 D3* Central Province, C Sri Lanka
Kane Fracture Zone *66 B4 fracture zone* NW Atlantic Ocean
Kāne'ohe *47 A8 var.* Kaneohe. O'ahu, Hawaii, USA, C Pacific Ocean
Kanestron, Akrotírio *see* Palioúri, Akrotírio
Kanëv *see* Kaniv
Kanevskoye Vodokhranilishche *see* Kanivs'ke Vodokhovyshche
Kangän *see* Bandar-e Kangān
Kangaroo Island *149 A7 island* South Australia
Kangertittivaq *83 E4 Dan.* Scoresby Sund. *fjord* E Greenland
Kangikajik *83 E4 var.* Kap Brewster. *headland* E Greenland
Kaniv *109 E2 Rus.* Kanëv. Cherkas'ka Oblast', C Ukraine
Kanivs'ke Vodoskhovyshche *109 E2 Rus.* Kanevskoye Vodokhranilishche. *reservoir* C Ukraine
Kanjiža *100 D2 Ger.* Altkanischa, *Hung.* Magyarkanizsa, Ókanizsa; *prev.* Stara Kanjiža. Vojvodina, N Serbia
Kankaanpää *85 D5* Länsi-Suomi, SW Finland
Kankakee *40 B3* Illinois, N USA
Kankan *74 D4* E Guinea
Kano *75 G4* Kano, N Nigeria
Kānpur *135 E3 Eng.* Cawnpore. Uttar Pradesh, N India
Kansas *45 F5 off.* State of Kansas, *also known as* Jayhawker State, Sunflower State. *state* C USA
Kansas City *45 F4* Kansas, C USA
Kansas City *45 F4* Missouri, C USA
Kansas River *45 F5 river* Kansas, C USA
Kansk *115 E4* Krasnoyarskiy Kray, S Russian Federation
Kansu *see* Gansu
Kantalahti *see* Kandalaksha
Kántanos *105 C7* Kríti, Greece, E Mediterranean Sea
Kantemirovka *111 B6* Voronezhskaya Oblast', W Russian Federation
Kantipur *see* Kathmandu
Kanton *145 F3 var.* Abariringa, Canton Island; *prev.* Mary Island. *atoll* Phoenix Islands, C Kiribati
Kanye *78 C4* Southern, SE Botswana
Kaohsiung *128 D6 var.* Gaoxiong, *Jap.* Takao, Takow. S Taiwan
Kaolack *74 B3 var.* Kaolak. W Senegal
Kaolak *see* Kaolack
Kaolan *see* Lanzhou
Kaoma *78 C2* Western, W Zambia
Kapelle *87 B5* Zeeland, SW Netherlands
Kapellen *87 C5* Antwerpen, N Belgium
Kapka, Massif du *76 C2 mountain range* E Chad
Kaplangky, Plato *see* Gaplaňgyr Platosy
Kapoeas *see* Kapuas, Sungai

Kapoeta *73 C5* Eastern Equatoria, SE Sudan
Kaposvár *99 C7* Somogy, SW Hungary
Kappeln *94 B2* Schleswig-Holstein, N Germany
Kapronczsa *see* Koprivnica
Kapstad *see* Cape Town
Kapsukas *see* Marijampolė
Kaptsevichy *107 C7 Rus.* Koptsevichi. Homyel'skaya Voblasts', SE Belarus
Kapuas, Sungai *138 C4 prev.* Kapoeas. *river* Borneo, C Indonesia
Kapuskasing *38 C4* Ontario, S Canada
Kapyl' *107 C6 Rus.* Kopyl'. Minskaya Voblasts', C Belarus
Kara-Balta *123 F2* Chuyskaya Oblast', N Kyrgyzstan
Karabil', Vozvyshennost' *see* Garabil Belentligi
Kara-Bogaz-Gol, Zaliv *see* Garabogaz Aylagy
Karabük *116 C2* Karabük, NW Turkey
Karāchi *134 B3* Sind, SE Pakistan
Karácsonkő *see* Piatra-Neamţ
Karadeniz *see* Black Sea
Karadeniz Boğazı *see* İstanbul Boğazı
Karaferiye *see* Véroia
Karaganda *114 C4 Kaz.* Qaraghandy. Karaganda, C Kazakhstan
Karaginskiy, Ostrov *115 H2 island* E Russian Federation
Karagumskiy Kanal *see* Garagum Kanaly
Karak *see* Al Karak
Karakax *see* Moyu
Karakılısse *see* Ağrı
Karakol *123 G2 prev.* Przheval'sk. Issyk-Kul'skaya Oblast', NE Kyrgyzstan
Karakol *123 G2 var.* Karakolka. Issyk-Kul'skaya Oblast', NE Kyrgyzstan
Karakolka *see* Karakol
Karakoram Range *134 D1 mountain range* C Asia
Karaköse *see* Ağrı
Karakul' *see* Qarokŭl, Tajikistan
Kara Kum *see* Garagum
Kara Kum Canal/Karakumskiy Kanal *see* Garagum Kanaly
Karakumy, Peski *see* Garagum
Karamai *see* Karamay
Karaman *116 C4* Karaman, S Turkey
Karamay *126 B2 var.* Karamai, Kelamayi; *prev. Chin.* K'o-la-ma-i. Xinjiang Uygur Zizhiqu, NW China
Karama Bight *151 B5 gulf* South Island, New Zealand
Karapelit *104 E1 Rom.* Stejarul. Dobrich, NE Bulgaria
Kara-Say *123 G2* Issyk-Kul'skaya Oblast', NE Kyrgyzstan
Karasburg *78 B4* Karas, S Namibia
Kara Sea *114 D2 Eng.* Kara Sea. *sea* Arctic Ocean
Kara Sea *see* Karskoye More
Kara Strait *110 E2 Eng.* Kara Strait. *strait* N Russian Federation
Kara Strait *see* Karskiye Vorota, Proliv
Karatau *114 C5 Kaz.* Qarataū. Zhambyl, S Kazakhstan
Karavás *105 B7* Kýthira, S Greece
Karbalā' *120 B3 var.* Kerbala, Kerbela. Karbalā', S Iraq
Kardeljevo *see* Ploče
Kardhítsa *see* Kardítsa
Karditsa *105 B5 var.* Kardhítsa. Thessalía, C Greece
Kärdla *106 C2 Ger.* Kertel. Hiiumaa, W Estonia
Karet *see* Kâghet
Kargı *116 C2* Çorum, N Turkey
Kargilik *see* Yecheng
Kariba *78 D2* Mashonaland West, N Zimbabwe
Kariba, Lake *78 D3 reservoir* Zambia/Zimbabwe
Karibib *78 B3* Erongo, C Namibia
Karies *see* Karyés
Karigasniemi *84 D2 Lapp.* Garegasnjárga. Lappi, N Finland
Karimata, Selat *138 C4 strait* W Indonesia
Karīmnagar *134 D5* Andhra Pradesh, C India
Karin *72 D4* Sahil, N Somalia
Kariot *see* Ikaría
Káristos *see* Kárystos
Karkinits'ka Zatoka *109 E4 Rus.* Karkinitskiy Zaliv. *gulf* S Ukraine

Karkinitskiy Zaliv *see* Karkinits'ka Zotoka
Karkük *see* Kirkūk
Karleby *see* Kokkola
Karl-Marx-Stadt *see* Chemnitz
Karlö *see* Hailuoto
Karlovac *100 B3 Ger.* Karlstadt, *Hung.* Károlyváros. Karlovac, C Croatia
Karlovy Vary *99 A5 Ger.* Karlsbad; *prev. Eng.* Carlsbad. Karlovarský Kraj, W Czech Republic
Karlsbad *see* Karlovy Vary
Karlsburg *see* Alba Iulia
Karlskrona *85 C7* Blekinge, S Sweden
Karlsruhe *95 B6 var.* Carlsruhe. Baden-Württemberg, SW Germany
Karlstad *85 B6* Värmland, C Sweden
Karlstadt *see* Karlovac
Karnāl *134 D2* Haryāna, N India
Karnātaka *132 C1 var.* Kanara; *prev.* Maisur, Mysore. *cultural region* W India
Karnobat *104 D2* Burgas, E Bulgaria
Karnul *see* Kurnool
Karol *see* Carei
Károly-Fehérvár *see* Alba Iulia
Károlyváros *see* Karlovac
Karpaten *see* Carpathian Mountains
Kárpathos *105 E7* Kárpathos, SE Greece
Kárpathos *105 E7 It.* Scarpanto; *anc.* Carpathos, Carpathus. *island* SE Greece
Karpaty *see* Carpathian Mountains
Karpenísi *105 B5 prev.* Karpenísion. Stereá Ellás, C Greece
Karpenísion *see* Karpenísi
Karpilovka *see* Aktsyabrski
Kars *117 F3 var.* Qars. Kars, NE Turkey
Karsau *see* Kārsava
Kārsava *106 D4 Ger.* Karsau; *prev. Rus.* Korsovka. Ludza, E Latvia
Karshi *see* Qarshi, Uzbekistan
Karyés *104 C4 var.* Karies. Ágion Óros, N Greece
Kárystos *105 C6 var.* Káristos. Évvoia, C Greece
Kasai *77 C6 var.* Cassai, Kassai. *river* Angola/Dem. Rep. Congo
Kasaji *77 D7* Katanga, S Dem. Rep. Congo
Kasama *78 D1* Northern, N Zambia
Kasan *see* Koson
Käsaragod *132 B2* Kerala, SW India
Kaschau *see* Košice
Kāshān *120 C3* Eşfahān, C Iran
Kashgar *see* Kashi
Kashi *126 A3 Chin.* Kaxgar, K'o-shih, *Uigh.* Kashgar. Xinjiang Uygur Zizhiqu, NW China
Kāshī *see* Vārānasi
Kasongo *77 D6* Maniema, E Dem. Rep. Congo
Kasongo-Lunda *77 C7* Bandundu, SW Dem. Rep. Congo
Kásos *105 D7 island* S Greece
Kaspiy Mangy Oypaty *see* Caspian Depression
Kaspiysk *111 B8* Respublika Dagestan, SW Russian Federation
Kaspiyskoye More/Kaspiy Tengizi *see* Caspian Sea
Kassa *see* Košice
Kassai *see* Kasai
Kassala *72 C4* Kassala, E Sudan
Kassel *94 B4 prev.* Cassel. Hessen, C Germany
Kasserine *71 E2 var.* Al Qaşrayn, N Tunisia
Kastamonu *116 C2 var.* Castamoni, Kastamuni. Kastamonu, N Turkey
Kastamuni *see* Kastamonu
Kastaneá *104 B4* Kentrikí Makedonía, N Greece
Kastélli *see* Kissamos
Kastoría *104 B4* Dytikí Makedonía, N Greece
Kástro *105 C6* Sífnos, Kykládes, Greece, Aegean Sea
Kastsyukovichy *107 E7 Rus.* Kostyukovichi. Mahilyowskaya Voblasts', E Belarus
Kastsyukowka *107 D7 Rus.* Kostyukovka. Homyel'skaya Voblasts', SE Belarus
Kasulu *73 B7* Kigoma, W Tanzania
Kasumiga-ura *131 D5 lake* Honshū, S Japan
Katahdin, Mount *41 G1 mountain* Maine, NE USA

Katalla 36 C3 Alaska, USA
Katana see Qaṭanā
Katanning 147 B7 Western Australia
Katawaz see Zarghūn Shahr
Katchall Island 133 F3 island Nicobar Islands, India, NE Indian Ocean
Katerini 104 B4 Kentrikí Makedonía, N Greece
Katha 136 B2 Sagaing, N Burma (Myanmar)
Katherine 148 A2 Northern Territory, N Australia
Kathmandu 124 C3 prev. Kantipur. country capital (Nepal) (Nepal) Central, C Nepal
Katikati 150 D3 Bay of Plenty, North Island, New Zealand
Katima Mulilo 78 C3 Caprivi, NE Namibia
Katiola 74 D4 C Côte d'Ivoire
Káto Achaía 105 B5 var. Kato Ahaia, Káto Akhaía. Dytikí Ellás, S Greece
Kato Ahaia/Káto Akhaía see Káto Achaía
Katoúna 105 A5 Dytikí Ellás, C Greece
Katowice 99 C5 Ger. Kattowitz. Śląskie, S Poland
Katsina 75 G3 Katsina, N Nigeria
Kattakurgan see Kattaqo'rg'on
Kattaqo'rg'on 123 E2 Rus. Kattakurgan. Samarqand Viloyati, C Uzbekistan
Kattavía 105 E7 Ródos, Dodekánisa, Greece, Aegean Sea
Kattegat 85 B7 Dan. Kattegatt. strait N Europe
Kattegatt see Kattegat
Kattowitz see Katowice
Kaua'i 47 A7 var. Kauai. island Hawaiian Islands, Hawai'i, USA, C Pacific Ocean
Kauai see Kaua'i
Kauen see Kaunas
Kaufbeuren 95 C6 Bayern, S Germany
Kaunas 106 B4 Ger. Kauen, Pol. Kowno; prev. Rus. Kovno. Kaunas, C Lithuania
Kavadar see Kavadarci
Kavadarci 101 E6 Turk. Kavadar. C Macedonia
Kavaja see Kavajë
Kavajë 101 C6 It. Cavaia, Kavaja. Tiranë, W Albania
Kavakli see Topolovgrad
Kavála 104 C3 prev. Kaválla. Anatolikí Makedonía kai Thráki, NE Greece
Kávali 132 D2 Andhra Pradesh, E India
Kaválla see Kavála
Kavango see Cubango/Okavango
Kavaratti Island 132 A3 island Lakshadweep, Lakshadweep, SW India Asia N Indian Ocean
Kavarna 104 E2 Dobrich, NE Bulgaria
Kavengo see Cubango/Okavango
Kavir, Dasht-e 120 D3 var. Great Salt Desert. salt pan N Iran
Kavkaz see Caucasus
Kawagoe 131 D5 Saitama, Honshū, S Japan
Kawasaki 130 A2 Kanagawa, Honshū, S Japan
Kawerau 150 E3 Bay of Plenty, North Island, New Zealand
Kaxgar see Kashi
Kaya 75 E3 C Burkina Faso
Kayan 136 B4 Yangon, SW Burma (Myanmar)
Kayan, Sungai 138 D3 prev. Kajan. river Borneo, C Indonesia
Kayes 74 C3 Kayes, W Mali
Kayseri 116 D3 var. Kaisaria; anc. Caesarea Mazaca, Mazaca. Kayseri, C Turkey
Kazach'ye 115 F2 Respublika Sakha (Yakutiya), NE Russian Federation
Kazakhskaya SSR/Kazakh Soviet Socialist Republic see Kazakhstan
Kazakhstan 114 B4 off. Republic of Kazakhstan, var. Kazak, Kaz. Qazaqstan, Qazaqstan Respublikasy; prev. Kazakh Soviet Socialist Republic, Rus. Kazakhskaya SSR. country C Asia

KAZAKHSTAN
Central Asia

Official name Republic of Kazakhstan
Formation 1991 / 1991
Capital Astana

KAZAKHSTAN
(continued)

Population 14.8 million / 14 people per sq mile (5 people per sq km) / 56%
Total area 1,049,150 sq. miles (2,717,300 sq. km)
Languages Kazakh*, Russian, Ukrainian, German, Uzbek, Tatar, Uighur
Religions Muslim (mainly Sunni) 47%, Orthodox Christian 44%, Other 9%
Ethnic mix Kazakh 57%, Russian 27%, Other 8%, Uzbek 3%, Ukrainian 3%, German 2%
Government Presidential system
Currency Tenge = 100 tiyn
Literacy rate 99%
Calorie consumption 2677 calories

Kazakhstan, Republic of see Kazakhstan
Kazakh Uplands 114 C4 Eng. Kazakh Uplands, Kirghiz Steppe, Kaz. Saryarqa. uplands C Kazakhstan
Kazakh Uplands see Kazakhskiy Melkosopochnik
Kazakstan see Kazakhstan
Kazan' 111 C5 Respublika Tatarstan, W Russian Federation
Kazandzhik see Bereket
Kazanlik see Kazanlŭk
Kazanlŭk 104 D2 prev. Kazanlik. Stara Zagora, C Bulgaria
Kazatin see Kozyatyn
Kazbegi see Kazbek
Kazbek 117 F1 var. Kazbegi, Geor. Mqinvartsveri. mountain N Georgia
Kāzerūn 120 D4 Fārs, S Iran
Kazi Magomed see Qazimämmäd
Kazvin see Qazvin
Kéa see Tziá
Kéa see Ioulís
Kea, Mauna 47 B8 mountain Hawai'i, USA
Kéamu see Aneityum
Kearney 45 E4 Nebraska, C USA
Keban Baraji 117 E3 reservoir C Turkey
Kebkabiya 72 A4 Northern Darfur, W Sudan
Kebnekaise 84 C3 mountain N Sweden
Kecskemét 99 D7 Bács-Kiskun, C Hungary
Kediri 138 D5 Jawa, C Indonesia
Kędzierzyn-Kozle 99 C5 Ger. Heydebrech. Opolskie, S Poland
Keelung see Chilung
Keetmanshoop 78 B4 Karas, S Namibia
Kefallinía see Kefallonía
Kefallonía 105 A5 var. Kefallinía. island Iónia Nisiá, Greece, C Mediterranean Sea
Kefe see Feodosiya
Kegel see Keila
Kehl 95 A6 Baden-Württemberg, SW Germany
Kei Islands see Kai, Kepulauan
Keijō see Sŏul
Keila 106 D2 Ger. Kegel. Harjumaa, NW Estonia
Keita 75 F3 Tahoua, C Niger
Keith 149 B7 South Australia
Kēk-Art 123 G2 prev. Alaykel', Alay-Kuu. Oshskaya Oblast', SW Kyrgyzstan
Kékes 99 C6 mountain N Hungary
Kelamayi see Karamay
Kelang see Klang
Kelat see Kālat
Kelifskiy Uzboy see Kelif Uzboýy
Kelif Uzboýy 122 D3 var. Kelif Uzboy. salt marsh E Turkmenistan
Kelkit Çayı 117 E3 river N Turkey
Kelmė 106 B4 Šiauliai, C Lithuania
Kélo 76 B4 Tandjilé, SW Chad
Kelowna 37 E5 British Columbia, SW Canada
Kelso 46 B2 Washington, NW USA
Keltsy see Kielce
Keluang 138 B3 var. Kluang. Johor, Peninsular Malaysia
Kem' 110 B3 Respublika Kareliya, NW Russian Federation
Kemah 117 E3 Erzincan, E Turkey
Kemaman see Cukai
Kemerovo 114 D4 prev. Shcheglovsk. Kemerovskaya Oblast', C Russian Federation

Kemi 84 D4 Lappi, NW Finland
Kemijärvi 84 D3 Swe. Kemiträsk. Lappi, N Finland
Kemijoki 84 D3 river NW Finland
Kemin 123 G2 prev. Bystrovka. Chuyskaya Oblast', N Kyrgyzstan
Kemins Island see Nikumaroro
Kemiträsk see Kemijärvi
Kemmuna see Comino
Kempele 84 D4 Oulu, C Finland
Kempten 95 B7 Bayern, S Germany
Kendal 89 D5 NW England, United Kingdom
Kendari 139 E4 Sulawesi, C Indonesia
Kenedy 49 G4 Texas, SW USA
Kenema 74 C4 SE Sierra Leone
Këneurgench see Köneürgenç
Kenge 77 C6 Bandundu, SW Dem. Rep. Congo
Keng Tung 136 C3 var. Kentung. Shan State, E Burma (Myanmar)
Kénitra 70 C2 prev. Port-Lyautey. NW Morocco
Kennett 45 H5 Missouri, C USA
Kennewick 46 C2 Washington, NW USA
Kenora 38 A3 Ontario, S Canada
Kenosha 40 B3 Wisconsin, N USA
Kentau 114 B5 Yuzhnyy Kazakhstan, S Kazakhstan
Kentucky 40 C5 off. Commonwealth of Kentucky, also known as Bluegrass State. state C USA
Kentucky Lake 40 B5 reservoir Kentucky/Tennessee, S USA
Kentung see Keng Tung
Kenya 73 C6 off. Republic of Kenya. country E Africa

KENYA
East Africa

Official name Republic of Kenya
Formation 1963 / 1963
Capital Nairobi
Population 36 million / 164 people per sq mile (63 people per sq km) / 40%
Total area 224,961 sq. miles (582,650 sq. km)
Languages Kiswahili*, English*, Kikuyu, Luo, Kalenjin, Kamba
Religions Christian 60%, Traditional beliefs 25%, Other 9%, Muslim 6%
Ethnic mix Other 31%, Kikuyu 20%, Luhya 14%, Luo 13%, Kalenjin 11%, Kamba 11%
Government Mixed Presidential–Parliamentary system
Currency Kenya shilling = 100 cents
Literacy rate 74%
Calorie consumption 2090 calories

Kenya, Mount see Kirinyaga
Kenya, Republic of see Kenya
Keokuk 45 G4 Iowa, C USA
Kéos see Tziá
Kepno 98 C4 Wielkopolskie, C Poland
Keppel Island see Niuatoputapu
Kerak see Al Karak
Kerala 132 C2 cultural region S India
Kerasunt see Giresun
Keratéa 105 C6 var. Keratea. Attikí, C Greece
Keratea see Keratéa
Kerbala/Kerbela see Karbalā'
Kerch 109 G5 Rus. Kerch'. Respublika Krym, SE Ukraine
Kerch' see Kerch
Kerchens'ka Protska/Kerchenskiy Proliv see Kerch Strait
Kerch Strait 109 G4 var. Bosporus Cimmerius, Enikale Strait, Rus. Kerchenskiy Proliv, Ukr. Kerchens'ka Protska. strait Black Sea/Sea of Azov
Keremitlik see Lyulyakovo
Kerguelen 141 C7 island C French Southern and Antarctic Territories
Kerguelen Plateau 141 C7 undersea plateau S Indian Ocean
Kéri 105 A6 Zákynthos, Iónia Nisiá, Greece, C Mediterranean Sea
Kerikeri 150 D2 Northland, North Island, New Zealand
Kerkenah, Îles de 102 D4 var. Kerkenna Islands, Ar. Juzur Qarqannah. island group E Tunisia

Kerkenna Islands see Kerkenah, Îles de
Kerki see Atamyrat
Kérkira see Kérkyra
Kerkrade 87 D6 Limburg, SE Netherlands
Kerkuk see Kirkūk
Kérkyra 104 A4 var. Kérkira, Eng. Corfu. Kérkyra, Iónia Nisiá, Greece, C Mediterranean Sea
Kermadec Islands 152 C4 island group New Zealand, SW Pacific Ocean
Kermadec Trench 143 E4 trench SW Pacific Ocean
Kermān 120 D3 var. Kirman; anc. Carmana. Kermān, C Iran
Kermānshāh 120 C3 var. Qahremānshahr; prev. Bākhtarān. Kermānshāhān, W Iran
Kerrville 49 F4 Texas, SW USA
Kertel see Kärdla
Kerulen 127 E2 Chin. Herlen He, Mong. Herlen Gol. river China/Mongolia
Kerÿneia see Girne
Kesennuma 130 D4 Miyagi, Honshū, C Japan
Keszthely 99 C7 Zala, SW Hungary
Ketchikan 36 D4 Revillagigedo Island, Alaska, USA
Kętrzyn 98 D2 Ger. Rastenburg. Warmińsko-Mazurskie, NE Poland
Kettering 89 D6 C England, United Kingdom
Kettering 40 C4 Ohio, N USA
Keupriya see Primorsko
Keurau 85 D5 Länsi-Suomi, C Finland
Keweenaw Peninsula 40 B1 peninsula Michigan, N USA
Key Largo 43 F5 Key Largo, Florida, SE USA
Keystone State see Pennsylvania
Key West 43 E5 Florida Keys, Florida, SE USA
Kezdivásárhely see Târgu Secuiesc
Khabarovsk 115 G4 Khabarovskiy Kray, SE Russian Federation
Khachmas see Xaçmaz
Khadera see Hadera
Khairpur 134 B3 Sind, SE Pakistan
Khalij as Suways 72 B2 var. Suez, Gulf of. gulf NE Egypt
Khalkidhikí see Chalkidikí
Khalkís see Chalkída
Gulf of Khambhat 134 C4 Eng. Gulf of Cambay. gulf W India
Khamis Mushayt 121 B6 var. Hamis Musait. 'Asīr, SW Saudi Arabia
Khānābād 123 E3 Kunduz, NE Afghanistan
Khān al Baghdādī see Al Baghdādī
Khandwa 134 D4 Madhya Pradesh, C India
Khanh Hung see Soc Trăng
Khaniá see Chaniá
Khanka, Lake 129 E2 var. Hsing-K'ai Hu, Lake Hanka, Chin. Xingkai Hu, Rus. Ozero Khanka. lake China/Russian Federation
Khanka, Ozero see Khanka, Lake
Khankendi see Xankändi
Khanthabouli 136 D4 prev. Savannakhét. Savannakhét, S Laos
Khanty-Mansiysk 114 C3 prev. Ostyako-Voguls'k. Khanty-Mansiyskiy Avtonomnyy Okrug-Yugra, C Russian Federation
Khān Yūnis 119 A7 var. Khān Yūnus. S Gaza Strip
Khān Yūnus see Khān Yūnis
Khanzi see Ghanzi
Kharagpur 135 F4 West Bengal, NE India
Kharbin see Harbin
Kharkiv 109 G2 Rus. Khar'kov. Kharkiv'ska Oblast', NE Ukraine
Khar'kov see Kharkiv
Kharmanli 104 D3 Khaskovo, S Bulgaria
Khartoum 72 B4 var. El Khartûm. country capital (Sudan) (Sudan) Khartoum, C Sudan
Khartum see Khartoum
Khasavyurt 111 B8 Respublika Dagestan, SW Russian Federation
Khash, Dasht-e 122 D5 Eng. Khash Desert. desert SW Afghanistan
Khash Desert see Khash, Dasht-e
Khashim Al Qirba/Khashm al Qirbah see Khashm el Girba

Khashm el Girba 72 C4 var. Khashim Al Qirba, Khashm al Qirbah. Kassala, E Sudan
Khaskovo 104 D3 Khaskovo, S Bulgaria
Khaybar, Kowtal-e see Khyber Pass
Khaydarkan 123 F2 var. Khaydarken. Batkenskaya Oblast', SW Kyrgyzstan
Khaydarken see Khaydarkan
Khazar, Baḥr-e/Khazar, Daryā-ye see Caspian Sea
Khelat see Kālat
Kherson 109 E4 Khersons'ka Oblast', S Ukraine
Kheta 115 E2 river N Russian Federation
Khíos see Chíos
Khirbet el 'Aujā et Taḥtā 119 E7 E West Bank Asia
Khiva/Khiwa see Xiva
Khmel'nitskiy see Khmel 'nyts'kyy
Khmel'nyts'kyy 108 C2 Rus. Khmel'nitskiy; prev. Proskurov. Khmel'nyts'ka Oblast', W Ukraine
Khodasy 107 E6 Rus. Khodosy. Mahilyowskaya Voblasts', E Belarus
Khodoriv 108 C2 Pol. Chodorów, Rus. Khodorov. L'vivs'ka Oblast', NW Ukraine
Khodorov see Khodoriv
Khodosy see Khodasy
Khodzhent see Khujand
Khoi see Khvoy
Khojend see Khujand
Khokand see Qo'qon
Kholm 123 E3 var. Tashqurghan, Pash. Khulm. Balkh, N Afghanistan
Kholm see Chełm
Kholon see Holon
Khoms see Al Khums
Khong Sedone see Muang Khôngxédôn
Khon Kaen 136 D4 var. Muang Khon Kaen. Khon Kaen, E Thailand
Khor 115 G4 Khabarovskiy Kray, SE Russian Federation
Khorat see Nakhon Ratchasima
Khorog see Khorugh
Khorugh 123 F3 Rus. Khorog. S Tajikistan
Khotan see Hotan
Khouribga 70 B2 C Morocco
Khovd see Hovd
Khowst 123 F4 Khowst, E Afghanistan
Khoy see Khvoy
Khoyniki 107 D8 Homyel'skaya Voblasts', SE Belarus
Khudzhand see Khujand
Khujand 123 E2 var. Khodzhent, Khojend, Rus. Khudzhand; prev. Leninabad, Taj. Leninobod. N Tajikistan
Khulm see Kholm
Khulna 135 G4 Khulna, SW Bangladesh
Khums see Al Khums
Khust 108 B3 var. Husté, Cz. Chust, Hung. Huszt. Zakarpats'ka Oblast', W Ukraine
Khvoy 120 C2 var. Khoi, Khoy. Āzarbāyjān-e Bākhtarī, NW Iran
Khyber Pass 134 C1 var. Kowtal-e Khaybar. pass Afghanistan/Pakistan
Kiangmai see Chiang Mai
Kiang-ning see Nanjing
Kiangsi see Jiangxi
Kiangsu see Jiangsu
Kiáto 105 B6 prev. Kiáton. Pelopónnisos, S Greece
Kiáton see Kiáto
Kiayi see Chiai
Kibangou 77 B6 Niari, SW Congo
Kibombo 77 D6 Maniema, E Dem. Rep. Congo
Kıbrıs/Kıbrıs Cumhuriyeti see Cyprus
Kičevo 101 D6 SW FYR Macedonia
Kidderminster 89 D6 C England, United Kingdom
Kiel 94 B2 Schleswig-Holstein, N Germany
Kielce 98 D4 Rus. Keltsy. Świętokrzyskie, C Poland
Kieler Bucht 94 B2 bay N Germany
Kiev see Kyyiv
Kiev Reservoir 109 E1 Eng. Kiev Reservoir, Rus. Kiyevskoye Vodokhranilishche. reservoir N Ukraine
Kiev Reservoir see Kyyivs'ke Vodokhovyshche
Kiffa 74 C3 Assaba, S Mauritania

Kigali 73 B6 country capital (Rwanda) (Rwanda) C Rwanda
Kigoma 73 B7 Kigoma, W Tanzania
Kihnu 106 C2 var. Kihnu Saar, Ger. Kühnö. island SW Estonia
Kihnu Saar see Kihnu
Kii-suido 131 C7 strait S Japan
Kikinda 100 D3 Ger. Grosskikinda, Hung. Nagykikinda; prev. Velika Kikinda. Vojvodina, N Serbia
Kikládhes see Kykládes
Kikwit 77 C6 Bandundu, W Dem. Rep. Congo
Kilien Mountains see Qilian Shan
Kilimane see Quelimane
Kilimanjaro 69 E5 region E Tanzania
Kilimanjaro 73 C7 var. Uhuru Peak. volcano NE Tanzania
Kilingi-Nômme 106 D3 Ger. Kurkund. Pärnumaa, SW Estonia
Kilis 116 D4 Kilis, S Turkey
Kiliya 108 D4 Rom. Chilia-Nouă. Odes'ka Oblast', SW Ukraine
Kilkenny 89 B6 Ir. Cill Chainnigh. Kilkenny, S Ireland
Kilkis 104 B3 Kentrikí Makedonía, N Greece
Killarney 89 A6 Ir. Cill Airne. Kerry, SW Ireland
Killeen 49 G3 Texas, SW USA
Kilmain see Quelimane
Kilmarnock 88 C4 W Scotland, United Kingdom
Kilwa see Kilwa Kivinje
Kilwa Kivinje 73 C7 var. Kilwa. Lindi, SE Tanzania
Kimberley 78 C4 Northern Cape, C South Africa
Kimberley Plateau 146 C3 plateau Western Australia
Kimch'aek 129 E3 prev. Sŏngjin. E North Korea
Kími see Kými
Kinabalu, Gunung 138 D3 mountain East Malaysia
Kindersley 37 F5 Saskatchewan, S Canada
Kindia 74 C4 Guinée-Maritime, SW Guinea
Kindley Field 42 A4 air base E Bermuda
Kindu 77 D6 prev. Kindu-Port-Empain. Maniema, C Dem. Rep. Congo
Kindu-Port-Empain see Kindu
Kineshma 111 C5 Ivanovskaya Oblast', W Russian Federation
King Charles Islands see Kong Karls Land
King Christian IX Land see Kong Christian IX Land
King Frederik VI Coast see Kong Frederik VI Kyst
King Frederik VIII Land see Kong Frederik VIII Land
King Island 149 B8 island Tasmania, SE Australia
King Island see Kadan Kyun
Kingissepp see Kuressaare
Kingman 48 A1 Arizona, SW USA
Kingman Reef 145 E2 US territory C Pacific Ocean
Kingsford Smith 148 E2 (Sydney) New South Wales, SE Australia
King's Lynn 89 E6 var. Bishop's Lynn, Kings Lynn, Lynn, Lynn Regis. E England, United Kingdom
Kings Lynn see King's Lynn
King Sound 146 B3 sound Western Australia
Kingsport 43 E1 Tennessee, S USA
Kingston 54 B5 country capital (Jamaica) (Jamaica) E Jamaica
Kingston 38 D5 Ontario, SE Canada
Kingston 41 F3 New York, NE USA
Kingston upon Hull 89 D5 var. Hull. E England, United Kingdom
Kingston upon Thames 89 A8 SE England, United Kingdom
Kingstown 55 H4 country capital (Saint Vincent and the Grenadines) (Saint Vincent and the Grenadines) Saint Vincent, Saint Vincent and the Grenadines
Kingstown see Dún Laoghaire
Kingsville 49 G5 Texas, SW USA
King William Island 37 F3 island Nunavut, N Canada
Kinneret, Yam see Tiberias, Lake

Kinrooi 87 D5 Limburg, NE Belgium
Kinshasa 77 B6 prev. Léopoldville. country capital (Dem. Rep. Congo) Kinshasa, W Dem. Rep. Congo
Kintyre 88 B4 peninsula W Scotland, United Kingdom
Kinyeti 73 B5 mountain S Sudan
Kiparissía see Kyparissía
Kipili 73 B7 Rukwa, W Tanzania
Kipushi 77 D8 Katanga, SE Dem. Rep. Congo
Kirdzhali see Kürdzhali
Kirghizia see Kyrgyzstan
Kirghiz Range 123 F2 Rus. Kirgizskiy Khrebet; prev. Alexander Range. mountain range Kazakhstan/Kyrgyzstan
Kirghiz SSR see Kyrgyzstan
Kirgizskaya SSR see Kyrgyzstan
Kirgizskiy Khrebet see Kirghiz Range
Kiriath-Arba see Hebron
Kiribati 145 F2 off. Republic of Kiribati. country C Pacific Ocean

KIRIBATI
Australasia & Oceania

Official name Republic of Kiribati
Formation 1979 / 1979
Capital Bairiki (Tarawa Atoll)
Population 107,817 / 393 people per sq mile (152 people per sq km) / 49%
Total area 277 sq. miles (717 sq. km)
Languages English*, Kiribati
Religions Roman Catholic 53%, Kiribati Protestant Church 39%, Other 8%
Ethnic mix Micronesian 99%, Other 1%
Government Nonparty system
Currency Australian dollar = 100 cents
Literacy rate 99%
Calorie consumption 2859 calories

Kiribati, Republic of see Kiribati
Kırıkhan 116 D4 Hatay, S Turkey
Kırıkkale 116 C3 province C Turkey
Kirin see Jilin
Kirinyaga 73 C6 prev. Mount Kenya. volcano C Kenya
Kirishi 110 B4 var. Kirisi. Leningradskaya Oblast', NW Russian Federation
Kirisi see Kirishi
Kiritimati 145 G2 prev. Christmas Island. atoll Line Islands, E Kiribati
Kirkenes 84 E2 Fin. Kirkkoniemi. Finnmark, N Norway
Kirk-Kilissa see Kırklareli
Kirkkoniemi see Kirkenes
Kirkland Lake 38 D4 Ontario, S Canada
Kırklareli 116 A2 prev. Kirk-Kilissa. Kırklareli, NW Turkey
Kirkpatrick, Mount 154 B3 mountain Antarctica
Kirksville 45 G4 Missouri, C USA
Kirkūk 120 B3 var. Karkūk, Kerkuk. Al Ta'mīn, N Iraq
Kirkwall 88 C2 NE Scotland, United Kingdom
Kirkwood 45 G4 Missouri, C USA
Kirov 111 C5 prev. Vyatka. Kirovskaya Oblast', NW Russian Federation
Kirovabad see Gäncä
Kirovakan see Vanadzor
Kirovo-Chepetsk 111 D5 Kirovskaya Oblast', NW Russian Federation
Kirovohrad 109 E3 Rus. Kirovograd; prev. Kirovo, Yelizavetgrad, Zinov'yevsk. Kirovohrads'ka Oblast', C Ukraine
Kirovo/Kirovograd see Kirovohrad
Kirthar Range 134 B3 mountain range S Pakistan
Kiruna 84 C3 Lapp. Giron. Norrbotten, N Sweden
Kirun/Kirun' see Chilung
Kisalföld see Little Alföld
Kisangani 77 D5 prev. Stanleyville. Orientale, NE Dem. Rep. Congo
Kishinev see Chişinău
Kislovodsk 111 B7 Stavropol'skiy Kray, SW Russian Federation
Kismaayo 73 D6 var. Chisimayu, Chismayu, It. Chisimaio. Jubbada Hoose, S Somalia
Kismayu see Kismaayo

Kíssamos 105 C7 prev. Kastélli. Kríti, Greece, E Mediterranean Sea
Kissidougou 74 C4 Guinée-Forestière, S Guinea
Kissimmee, Lake 43 E4 lake Florida, SE USA
Kistna see Krishna
Kisumu 73 C6 prev. Port Florence. Nyanza, W Kenya
Kisvárda 99 E6 Ger. Kleinwardein. Szabolcs-Szatmár-Bereg, E Hungary
Kita 74 D3 Kayes, W Mali
Kitab see Kitob
Kitakyūshū 131 A7 var. Kitakyûsyû. Fukuoka, Kyūshū, SW Japan
Kitakyûsyû see Kitakyūshū
Kitami 130 D2 Hokkaidō, NE Japan
Kitchener 38 C5 Ontario, S Canada
Kíthnos see Kýthnos
Kitimat 36 D4 British Columbia, SW Canada
Kitinen 84 D3 river N Finland
Kitob 123 E3 Rus. Kitab. Qashqadaryo Viloyati, S Uzbekistan
Kitwe 78 D2 var. Kitwe-Nkana. Copperbelt, C Zambia
Kitwe-Nkana see Kitwe
Kitzbüheler Alpen 95 C7 mountain range W Austria
Kivalina 36 C2 Alaska, USA
Kivalo 84 D3 ridge C Finland
Kivertsi 108 C1 Pol. Kiwerce, Rus. Kivertsy. Volyns'ka Oblast', NW Ukraine
Kivertsy see Kivertsi
Kivu, Lac see Kivu, Lake
Kivu, Lake 77 E6 Fr. Lac Kivu. lake Rwanda/Dem. Rep. Congo
Kiwerce see Kivertsi
Kiyev see Kyyiv
Kiyevskoye Vodokhranilishche see Kyyivs'ke Vodokhovyshche
Kızıl Irmak 116 C3 river C Turkey
Kizil Kum see Kyzyl Kum
Kizyl-Arvat see Serdar
Kjølen see Kölen
Kladno 99 A5 Středočeský, NW Czech Republic
Klagenfurt 95 D7 Slvn. Celovec. Kärnten, S Austria
Klaipėda 106 B3 Ger. Memel. Klaipėda, NW Lithuania
Klamath Falls 46 B4 Oregon, NW USA
Klamath Mountains 46 A4 mountain range California/Oregon, W USA
Klang 138 B3 var. Kelang; prev. Port Swettenham. Selangor, Peninsular Malaysia
Klarälven 85 A5 river Norway/Sweden
Klatovy 99 A5 Ger. Klattau. Plzeňský Kraj, W Czech Republic
Klattau see Klatovy
Klausenburg see Cluj-Napoca
Klazienaveen 86 E2 Drenthe, NE Netherlands
Kleines Ungarisches Tiefland see Little Alföld
Klein Karas 78 B4 Karas, S Namibia
Kleinwardein see Kisvárda
Kleisoúra 105 A5 Ípeiros, W Greece
Klerksdorp 78 D4 North-West, N South Africa
Klimavichy 107 E7 Rus. Klimovichi. Mahilyowskaya Voblasts', E Belarus
Klimovichi see Klimavichy
Klintsy 111 A5 Bryanskaya Oblast', W Russian Federation
Klisura 104 C2 Plovdiv, C Bulgaria
Ključ 100 B3 Federacija Bosna I Hercegovina, NW Bosnia and Herzegovina
Kłobuck 98 C4 Śląskie, S Poland
Klosters 95 B7 Graubünden, SE Switzerland
Kluang see Keluang
Kluczbork 98 C4 Ger. Kreuzburg, Kreuzburg in Oberschlesien. Opolskie, S Poland
Klyuchevskaya Sopka, Vulkan 115 H3 volcano E Russian Federation
Knin 100 B4 Šibenik-Knin, S Croatia
Knjaževac 100 E4 Serbia, E Serbia
Knokke-Heist 87 A5 West-Vlaanderen, NW Belgium
Knoxville 42 D1 Tennessee, S USA
Knud Rasmussen Land 82 D1 physical region N Greenland
Kobdo see Hovd

Köbe *131 C6* Hyōgo, Honshū, SW Japan
København *85 B7* Eng. Copenhagen; *anc.* Hafnia. *country capital* (Denmark)
(Denmark) Sjælland, København, E Denmark
Kobenni *74 D3* Hodh el Gharbi, S Mauritania
Koblenz *95 A5 prev.* Coblenz, Fr. Coblence; *anc.* Confluentes. Rheinland-Pfalz, W Germany
Kobrin *see* Kobryn
Kobryn *107 A6 Rus.* Kobrin. Brestskaya Voblasts', SW Belarus
K'obulet'i *117 F2* W Georgia
Kočani *101 E6* NE FYR Macedonia
Kočevje *95 D8 Ger.* Gottschee. S Slovenia
Koch Bihār *135 G3* West Bengal, NE India
Kochchi Cochin/Kochi
Kōchi *131 B7 var.* Kôti. Kōchi, Shikoku, SW Japan
Kochiu *see* Gejiu
Kodiak *36 C3* Kodiak Island, Alaska, USA
Kodiak Island *36 C3 island* Alaska, USA
Koedoes *see* Kudus
Koeln *see* Köln
Koepang *see* Kupang
Ko-erh-mu *see* Golmud
Koetai *see* Mahakam, Sungai
Koetaradja *see* Bandaaceh
Kōfu *131 D5 var.* Kôhu. Yamanashi, Honshū, S Japan
Kogarah *148 E2* New South Wales, E Australia
Kogon *122 D2 Rus.* Kagan. Buxoro Viloyati, C Uzbekistan
Kôhalom *see* Rupea
Kohīma *135 H3 state capital* Nāgāland, E India
Koh I Noh *see* Büyükağrı Dağı
Kohtla-Järve *106 E2* Ida-Virumaa, NE Estonia
Kôhu *see* Kōfu
Kokand *see* Qo'qon
Kokchetav *see* Kokshetau
Kokkola *84 D4 Swe.* Karleby; *prev.* Swe. Gamlakarleby. Länsi-Suomi, W Finland
Koko *75 F4* Kebbi, W Nigeria
Kokomo *40 C4* Indiana, N USA
Koko Nor *see* Qinghai, China
Koko Nor *see* Qinghai Hu, China
Kokrines *36 C2* Alaska, USA
Kokshaal-Tau *123 G2 Rus.* Khrebet Kakshaal-Too. *mountain range* China/Kyrgyzstan
Kokshetau *114 C4 Kaz.* Kökshetaü; *prev.* Kokchetav. Kokshetau, N Kazakhstan
Kökshetaü *see* Kokshetau
Koksijde *87 A5* West-Vlaanderen, W Belgium
Koksoak *38 D2 river* Québec, E Canada
Kokstad *78 D5* KwaZulu/Natal, E South Africa
Kolaka *139 E4* Sulawesi, C Indonesia
K'o-la-ma-i *see* Karamay
Kola Peninsula *112 C2 Eng.* Kola Peninsula. *peninsula* NW Russian Federation
Kola Peninsula *see* Kol'skiy Poluostrov
Kolari *84 D3* Lappi, NW Finland
Kolárovo *99 C6 Ger.* Gutta; *prev.* Guta, Hung. Gúta. Nitriansky Kraj, SW Slovakia
Kolberg *see* Kołobrzeg
Kolda *74 C3* S Senegal
Kolding *85 A7* Vejle, C Denmark
Kolen *81 E1 Nor.* Kjølen. *mountain range* Norway/Sweden
Kolguyev, Ostrov *110 C2 island* NW Russian Federation
Kolhāpur *132 B1* Mahārāshtra, SW India
Kolhumadulu *132 A5 var.* Thaa Atoll. *atoll* S Maldives
Kolín *99 B5 Ger.* Kolin. Střední Čechy, C Czech Republic
Kolka *106 C2* Talsi, NW Latvia
Kolkasrags *106 C2 prev. Eng.* Cape Domesnes. *headland* NW Latvia
Kolmar *see* Colmar
Köln *94 A4 var.* Koeln, *Eng./Fr.* Cologne, *prev.* Cöln; *anc.* Colonia Agrippina, Oppidum Ubiorum. Nordrhein-Westfalen, W Germany
Koło *98 C3* Wielkopolskie, C Poland

Kołobrzeg *98 B2 Ger.* Kolberg. Zachodnio-pomorskie, NW Poland
Kolokani *74 D3* Koulikoro, W Mali
Kolomea *see* Kolomyya
Kolomna *111 B5* Moskovskaya Oblast', W Russian Federation
Kolomyya *108 C3 Ger.* Kolomea. Ivano-Frankivs'ka Oblast', W Ukraine
Kolosjoki *see* Nikel'
Kolozsvár *see* Cluj-Napoca
Kolpa *100 A2 Ger.* Kulpa, *SCr.* Kupa. *river* Croatia/Slovenia
Kolpino *110 B4* Leningradskaya Oblast', NW Russian Federation
Kólpos Mórfu *see* Güzelyurt
Kolwezi *77 D7* Katanga, S Dem. Rep. Congo
Kolyma *115 G2 river* NE Russian Federation
Komatsu *131 C5 var.* Komatu. Ishikawa, Honshū, SW Japan
Komatu *see* Komatsu
Kommunizm, Qullai *see* Ismoili Somoní, Qullai
Komoé *75 E4 var.* Komoé Fleuve. *river* E Côte d'Ivoire
Komoé Fleuve *see* Komoé
Komotau *see* Chomutov
Komotiní *104 D3 var.* Gümüljina, *Turk.* Gümülcine. Anatolikí Makedonía kai Thráki, NE Greece
Kompong *see* Kâmpóng Chhnāng
Kompong Cham *see* Kâmpóng Cham
Kompong Som *see* Kâmpóng Saôm
Kompong Speu *see* Kâmpóng Spoe
Komrat *see* Comrat
Komsomolets, Ostrov *115 E1 island* Severnaya Zemlya, N Russian Federation
Komsomol'sk-na-Amure *115 G4* Khabarovskiy Kray, SE Russian Federation
Kondolovo *104 E3* Burgas, E Bulgaria
Kondopoga *110 B3* Respublika Kareliya, NW Russian Federation
Kondoz *123 E3 Pash.* Kunduz. *province* NE Afghanistan
Köneürgenç *122 C2 var.* Köneürgench, *Rus.* Këneurgench; *prev.* Kunya-Urgench. Dasoguz Welaýaty, N Turkmenistan
Kong Christian IX Land *82 D4 Eng.* King Christian IX Land. *physical region* SE Greenland
Kong Frederik IX Land *82 C3 physical region* SW Greenland
Kong Frederik VIII Land *83 E2 Eng.* King Frederik VIII Land. *physical region* NE Greenland
Kong Frederik VI Kyst *82 C4 Eng.* Frederik VI Coast. *physical region* SE Greenland
Kong Karls Land *83 G2 Eng.* King Charles Islands. *island group* SE Svalbard
Kongo *see* Congo (river)
Kongolo *77 D6* Katanga, E Dem. Rep. Congo
Kongor *73 B5* Jonglei, SE Sudan
Kong Oscar Fjord *83 E3 fjord* E Greenland
Kongsberg *85 B6* Buskerud, S Norway
Kông, Tônle *137 E5 var.* Xê Kong. *river* Cambodia/Laos
Kong, Xê *see* Kông, Tônle
Königgrätz *see* Hradec Králové
Königshütte *see* Chorzów
Konin *98 C3 Ger.* Kuhnau. Weilkopolskie, C Poland
Koninkrijk der Nederlanden *see* Netherlands
Konispol *101 C7 var.* Konispoli. Vlorë, S Albania
Konispoli *see* Konispol
Kónitsa *104 A4* Ípeiros, W Greece
Konitz *see* Chojnice
Konjic *100 C4* Federacija Bosna I Hercegovina, S Bosnia and Herzegovina
Konosha *110 C4* Arkhangel'skaya Oblast', NW Russian Federation
Konotop *109 F1* Sums'ka Oblast', NE Ukraine
Konstantinovka *see* Kostyantynivka
Konstanz *95 B7 var.* Constanz, *Eng.* Constance, *hist.* Kostnitz; *anc.* Constantia. Baden-Württemberg, S Germany

Konstanza *see* Constanţa
Konya *116 C4 var.* Konieh, *prev.* Konia; *anc.* Iconium. Konya, C Turkey
Kopaonik *101 D5 mountain range* S Serbia
Kopar *see* Koper
Koper *95 D8 It.* Capodistria; *prev.* Kopar. SW Slovenia
Köpetdag Gershi *122 C3 mountain range* Iran/Turkmenistan
Köpetdag Gershi/Kopetdag, Khrebet *see* Koppeh Dāgh
Koppeh Dagh *120 D2 Rus.* Khrebet Kopetdag, *Turkn.* Köpetdag Gershi. *mountain range* Iran/Turkmenistan
Kopreinitz *see* Koprivnica
Koprivnica *100 B2 Ger.* Kopreinitz, *Hung.* Kaproncza. Koprivnica-Križevci, N Croatia
Köprülü *see* Veles
Koptsevichi *see* Kaptsevichy
Kopyl' *see* Kapyl'
Korat *see* Nakhon Ratchasima
Korat Plateau *136 D4 plateau* E Thailand
Korba *135 E4* Chhattisgarh, C India
Korçë *see* Korçë
Korçë *101 D6 var.* Korça, *Gk.* Korytsa, *It.* Corriza; *prev.* Korça, Korçë, SE Albania
Korčula *100 B4 It.* Curzola; *anc.* Corcyra Nigra. *island* S Croatia
Korea Bay *127 G3 bay* China/North Korea
Korea, Democratic People's Republic of *see* North Korea
Korea, Republic of *see* South Korea
Korea Strait *131 A7 Jap.* Chōsen-kaikyō, *Kor.* Taehan-haehyōp. *channel* Japan/South Korea
Korhogo *74 D4* N Côte d'Ivoire
Kórinthos *105 B6 Eng.* Corinth *anc.* Corinthus. Pelopónnisos, S Greece
Koritsa *see* Korçë
Kōriyama *131 D5* Fukushima, Honshū, C Japan
Korla *126 C3 Chin.* K'u-erh-lo. Xinjiang Uygur Zizhiqu, NW China
Körmend *99 B7* Vas, W Hungary
Koróni *105 B6* Pelopónnisos, S Greece
Koror *144 A2* (Palau) Oreor, N Palau
Körös *see* Križevci
Korosten' *108 D1* Zhytomyrs'ka Oblast', NW Ukraine
Koro Toro *76 C2* Borkou-Ennedi-Tibesti, N Chad
Korsovka *see* Kārsava
Kortrijk *87 A6 Fr.* Courtrai. West-Vlaanderen, W Belgium
Koryak Range *115 H2 var.* Koryakskiy Khrebet, *Eng.* Koryak Range. *mountain range* NE Russian Federation
Koryak Range *see* Koryakskoye Nagor'ye
Koryakskiy Khrebet *see* Koryakskoye Nagor'ye
Koryazhma *110 C4* Arkhangel'skaya Oblast', NW Russian Federation
Korytsa *see* Korçë
Kos *105 E6* Kos, Dodekánisa, Greece, Aegean Sea
Kos *105 E6 It.* Coo; *anc.* Cos. *island* Dodekánisa, Greece, Aegean Sea
Ko-saki *131 A7 headland* Nagasaki, Tsushima, SW Japan
Kościan *98 B4 Ger.* Kosten.
Kościerzyna *98 C2* Pomorskie, NW Poland
Kosciusko, Mount *see* Kosciuszko, Mount
Kosciuszko, Mount *149 C7 prev.* Mount Kosciusko. *mountain* New South Wales, SE Australia
K'o-shih *see* Kashi
Koshikijima-retto *131 A8 var.* Kosikizima Rettô. *island group* SW Japan
Košice *99 D6 Ger.* Kaschau, *Hung.* Kassa. Košický Kraj, E Slovakia
Kosikizima Rettô *see* Koshikijima-retto
Köslin *see* Koszalin
Koson *123 E3 Rus.* Kasan. Qashqadaryo Viloyati, S Uzbekistan
Kosova *see* Kosovo
Kosovo *101 D5 prev.* Autonomous Province of Kosovo and Metohija. *country* SE Europe

Kosovo (not yet fully recognized) *Southeast Europe*
Official name Republic of Kosovo
Formation 2008 / 2008
Capital Pristina
Population 2.1 million / 499 people per sq mile (193 people per sq km) / 40%
Total area 4212 sq miles (10,908 sq km)
Languages Albanian*, Serbian*, Bosniak, Gorani, Roma, Turkish
Religions Muslim 92%, Roman Catholic 4%, Orthodox Christian 4%
Ethnic mix Albanian 92%, Serb 4%, Bosniak and Gorani 2%, Turkish 1%, Roma 1%
Government Parliamentary system
Currency Euro = 100 cents
Literacy rate 92%
Calorie consumption Not available

Kosovo and Metohija, Autonomous Province of *see* Kosovo
Kosovo Polje *see* Fushë Kosovë
Kosovska Mitrovica *see* Mitrovicë
Kosrae *144 C2 prev.* Kusaie. *island* Caroline Islands, E Micronesia
Kossou, Lac de *74 D5 lake* C Ivory Coast
Kostanay *114 C4 var.* Kustanay, *Kaz.* Qostanay. Kostanay, N Kazakhstan
Kosten *see* Kościan
Kostenets *104 C2 prev.* Georgi Dimitrov. Sofiya, W Bulgaria
Kostnitz *see* Konstanz
Kostroma *110 B4* Kostromskaya Oblast', NW Russian Federation
Kostyantynivka *109 G3 Rus.* Konstantinovka. Donets'ka Oblast', SE Ukraine
Kostyukovichi *see* Kastsyukovichy
Koszalin *98 B2 Ger.* Köslin. Zachodnio-pomorskie, NW Poland
Kota *134 D3 prev.* Kotah. Rājasthān, N India
Kota Baharu *see* Kota Bharu
Kota Baru *see* Kota Bharu
Kota Bharu *138 B3 var.* Kota Baharu, Kota Bahru. Kelantan, Peninsular Malaysia
Kotabumi *138 B4 prev.* Kotaboemi. Sumatera, W Indonesia
Kotah *see* Kota
Kota Kinabalu *138 D3 prev.* Jesselton. Sabah, East Malaysia
Kotel'nyy, Ostrov *115 E2 island* Novosibirskiye Ostrova, N Russian Federation
Kotka *85 E5* Etelä-Suomi, S Finland
Kotlas *110 C4* Arkhangel'skaya Oblast', NW Russian Federation
Kotonu *see* Cotonou
Kotor *101 C5 It.* Cattaro. SW Montenegro
Kotovs'k *108 D3 Rus.* Kotovsk. Odes'ka Oblast', SW Ukraine
Kottbus *see* Cottbus
Kotto *76 D4 river* Central African Republic/Dem. Rep. Congo
Kotuy *115 E2 river* N Russian Federation
Koudougou *75 E4* C Burkina Faso
Koulamoutou *77 B6* Ogooué-Lolo, C Gabon
Koulikoro *74 D3* Koulikoro, SW Mali
Koumra *76 C4* Moyen-Chari, S Chad
Kourou *59 H3* N French Guiana
Kousséir *see* Al Quşayr
Kousséri *76 B3 prev.* Fort-Foureau. Extrême-Nord, NE Cameroon
Koutiala *74 D4* Sikasso, S Mali
Kouvola *85 E5* Etelä-Suomi, S Finland
Kovačica *100 D3* Vojvodina, N Serbia
Kovel' *108 C1 Pol.* Kowel. Volyns'ka Oblast', NW Ukraine
Kovno *see* Kaunas
Kowel *see* Kovel'
Kowloon *128 A2* Hong Kong, S China
Kowno *see* Kaunas
Kozáni *104 B4* Dytikí Makedonía, N Greece
Kozara *100 B3 mountain range* NW Bosnia and Herzegovina

Kozarska Dubica see Bosanska Dubica
Kozu-shima 131 D6 island E Japan
Kozyatyn 108 D2 Rus. Kazatin.
  Vinnyts'ka Oblast', C Ukraine
Kpalimé 75 E5 var. Palimé. SW Togo
Kráchéh 137 D6 prev. Kratie. Kráchéh,
  E Cambodia
Kragujevac 100 D4 Serbia, C Serbia
Krainburg see Kranj
Kra, Isthmus of 137 B6 isthmus
  Malaysia/Thailand
Krakau see Kraków
Kraków 99 D5 Eng. Cracow, Ger.
  Krakau; anc. Cracovia. Małopolskie,
  S Poland
Králánh 137 D5 Siĕmréab,
  NW Cambodia
Kraljevo 100 D4 prev. Rankovićevo.
  Serbia, C Serbia
Kramators'k 109 G3 Rus. Kramatorsk.
  Donets'ka Oblast', SE Ukraine
Kramatorsk see Kramators'k
Kramfors 85 C5 Västernorrland,
  C Sweden
Kranéa see Kraniá
Kraniá 104 B4 var. Kranéa. Dytikí
  Makedonía, N Greece
Kranj 95 D7 Ger. Krainburg.
  NW Slovenia
Kranz see Zelenogradsk
Kräslava 106 D4 Kräslava, SE Latvia
Krasnaye 107 C5 Rus. Krasnoye.
  Minskaya Voblasts', C Belarus
Krasnoarmeysk 111 C6 Saratovskaya
  Oblast', W Russian Federation
Krasnodar 111 A7 prev. Ekaterinodar,
  Yekaterinodar. Krasnodarskiy Kray,
  SW Russian Federation
Krasnodon 109 H3 Luhans'ka Oblast',
  E Ukraine
Krasnogor see Kallaste
Krasnovardeyskoye see
  Krasnohvardiys'ke
Krasnohvardiys'ke 109 F4 Rus.
  Krasnogvardeyskoye. Respublika
  Krym, S Ukraine
Krasnokamensk 115 F4 Chitinskaya
  Oblast', S Russian Federation
Krasnokamsk 111 D5 Permskaya
  Oblast', W Russian Federation
Krasnoperekops'k 109 F4 Rus.
  Krasnoperekopsk. Respublika Krym,
  S Ukraine
Krasnoperekopsk see Krasnoperekops'k
Krasnostav see Krasnystaw
Krasnovodsk see Türkmenbaşy
Krasnovodskiy Zaliv see Türkmenbasy
  Aylagy
Krasnowodsk Aylagy see Türkmenbasy
  Aylagy
Krasnoyarsk 114 D4 Krasnoyarskiy
  Kray, S Russian Federation
Krasnoye see Krasnaye
Krasnystaw 98 E4 Rus. Krasnostav.
  Lubelskie, SE Poland
Krasnyy Kut 111 C6 Saratovskaya
  Oblast', W Russian Federation
Krasnyy Luch 109 H3 prev.
  Krindachevka. Luhans'ka Oblast',
  E Ukraine
Kratie see Kráchéh
Krăvanh, Chuŏr Phnum 137 C6 Eng.
  Cardamom Mountains, Fr. Chaîne
  des Cardamomes. mountain range
  W Cambodia
Krefeld 94 A4 Nordrhein-Westfalen,
  W Germany
Kreisstadt see Krosno Odrzańskie
Kremenchug see Kremenchuk
Kremenchugskoye Vodokhranilishche/
  Kremenchuk Reservoir see
  Kremenchuts'ke Vodoskhovyshche
Kremenchuk 109 F2 Rus. Kremenchug.
  Poltavs'ka Oblast', NE Ukraine
Kremenchuk Reservoir 109 F2
  Eng. Kremenchuk Reservoir, Rus.
  Kremenchugskoye Vodokhranilishche.
  reservoir C Ukraine
Kremenets' 108 C2 Pol. Krzemieniec,
  Rus. Kremenets. Ternopil's'ka Oblast',
  W Ukraine
Kremennaya see Kreminna
Kreminna 109 G2 Rus. Kremennaya.
  Luhans'ka Oblast', E Ukraine
Kresena see Kresna
Kresna 104 C3 var. Kresena.
  Blagoevgrad, SW Bulgaria

Kretikon Delagos see Kritikó Pélagos
Kretinga 106 B3 Ger. Krottingen.
  Klaipėda, NW Lithuania
Kreutz see Cristuru Secuiesc
Kreuz see Križevci, Croatia
Kreuz see Risti, Estonia
Kreuzburg/Kreuzburg in
  Oberschlesien see Kluczbork
Krichëv see Krychaw
Krievija see Russian Federation
Krindachevka see Krasnyy Luch
Krishna 132 C1 prev. Kistna. river
  C India
Krishnagiri 132 C2 Tamil Nādu,
  SE India
Kristiania see Oslo
Kristiansand 85 A6 var. Christiansand.
  Vest-Agder, S Norway
Kristianstad 85 B7 Skåne, S Sweden
Kristiansund 84 A4 var. Christiansund.
  Møre og Romsdal, S Norway
Krivoy Rog see Kryvyy Rih
Križevci 100 D2 Ger. Kreuz, Hung.
  Kőrös. Varaždin, NE Croatia
Krk 100 A3 It. Veglia; anc. Curieta.
  island NW Croatia
Kroatien see Croatia
Krolevets' 109 F1 Rus. Krolevets.
  Sums'ka Oblast', NE Ukraine
Krolevets see Krolevets'
Królewska Huta see Chorzów
Kronach 95 C5 Bayern, E Germany
Kronstadt see Braşov
Kroonstad 78 D4 Free State, C South
  Africa
Kropotkin 111 A7 Krasnodarskiy Kray,
  SW Russian Federation
Krosno 99 D5 Ger. Krossen.
  Podkarpackie, SE Poland
Krosno Odrzańskie 98 B3 Ger. Crossen,
  Kreisstadt. Lubuskie, W Poland
Krossen see Krosno
Krottingen see Kretinga
Krško 95 E8 Ger. Gurkfeld; prev. Videm-
  Krško. E Slovenia
Krugloye see Kruhlaye
Kruhlaye 107 D6 Rus. Krugloye.
  Mahilyowskaya Voblasts', E Belarus
Kruja see Krujë
Krujë 100 C4 var. Kruja, It. Croia.
  Durrës, C Albania
Krummau see Český Krumlov
Krung Thep, Ao 137 C5 var. Bight of
  Bangkok. bay S Thailand
Krung Thep Mahanakhon see Ao
  Krung Thep
Krupki 107 D6 Minskaya Voblasts',
  C Belarus
Krušné Hory see Erzgebirge
Krychaw 107 E7 Rus. Krichëv.
  Mahilyowskaya Voblasts', E Belarus
Kryms'ki Hory 109 F5 mountain range
  S Ukraine
Kryms'kyy Pivostriv 109 F5 peninsula
  S Ukraine
Krynica 99 D5 Ger. Tannenhof.
  Małopolskie, S Poland
Kryve Ozero 109 E3 Odes'ka Oblast',
  SW Ukraine
Kryvyy Rih 109 F3 Rus. Krivoy Rog.
  Dnipropetrovs'ka Oblast', SE Ukraine
Krzemieniec see Kremenets'
Ksar al Kabir see Ksar-el-Kebir
Ksar al Soule see Er-Rachidia
Ksar-el-Kebir 70 C2 var. Alcázar,
  Ksar al Kabir, Ksar-el-Kébir, Ar.
  Al-Kasr al-Kebir, Al-Qsar al-Kbir, Sp.
  Alcazarquivir. NW Morocco
Kuala Dungun see Dungun
Kuala Lumpur 138 B3 country capital
  (Malaysia) (Malaysia) Kuala Lumpur,
  Peninsular Malaysia
Kuala Terengganu 138 B3 var. Kuala
  Trengganu. Terengganu, Peninsular
  Malaysia
Kualatungkal 138 B4 Sumatera,
  W Indonesia
Kuang-chou see Guangzhou
Kuang-hsi see Guangxi Zhuangzu Zizhiqu
Kuang-tung see Guangdong
Kuang-yuan see Guangyuan
Kuantan 138 B3 Pahang, Peninsular
  Malaysia
Kuba see Quba
Kuban' 109 G5 var. Hypanis. river
  SW Russian Federation

Kubango see Cubango/Okavango
Kuching 138 C3 prev. Sarawak. Sarawak,
  East Malaysia
Küchnay Darweyshān 122 D5 Helmand,
  S Afghanistan
Kuçova see Kuçovë
Kuçovë 101 C6 var. Kuçova; prev. Qyteti
  Stalin. Berat, C Albania
Kudara see Ghūdara
Kudus 138 C5 prev. Koedoes. Jawa,
  C Indonesia
Kuei-lin see Guilin
Kuei-Yang/Kuei-yang see Guiyang
K'u-erh-lo see Korla
Kueyang see Guiyang
Kugaaruk 37 G3 prev. Pelly Bay.
  Nunavut, N Canada
Kugluktuk 53 E3 var. Qurlurtuuq; prev.
  Coppermine. Nunavut, NW Canada
Kuhmo 84 E4 Oulu, E Finland
Kuhnau see Konin
Kühnö see Kihnu
Kuibyshev see Kuybyshevskoye
  Vodokhranilishche
Kuito 78 B2 Port. Silva Porto. Bié,
  C Angola
Kuji 130 D3 var. Kuzi. Iwate, Honshū,
  C Japan
Kukës 101 D5 var. Kukёsi. Kukës,
  NE Albania
Kukёsi see Kukës
Kukong see Shaoguan
Kukukhoto see Hohhot
Kula Kangri 135 G3 var. Kulhakangri.
  mountain Bhutan/China
Kuldīga 106 B3 Ger. Goldingen. Kuldiga,
  W Latvia
Kuldja see Yining
Kulhakangri see Kula Kangri
Kullorsuaq 82 D2 var. Kuvdlorssuak.
  Kitaa, C Greenland
Kulm see Chełmno
Kulmsee see Chełmża
Külob 123 F3 Rus. Kulyab.
  SW Tajikistan
Kulpa see Kolpa
Kulu 116 C3 Konya, W Turkey
Kulunda Steppe 114 C4 Kaz. Qulyndy
  Zhazyghy, Rus. Kulundinskaya
  Ravnina. grassland Kazakhstan/
  Russian Federation
Kulundinskaya Ravnina see Kulunda
  Steppe
Kulyab see Külob
Kum see Qom
Kuma 111 B7 river SW Russian
  Federation
Kumamoto 131 A7 Kumamoto, Kyūshū,
  SW Japan
Kumanova see Kumanovo
Kumanovo 101 E5 Turk. Kumanova.
  N Macedonia
Kumasi 75 E5 prev. Coomassie. C Ghana
Kumayri see Gyumri
Kumba 77 A5 Sud-Ouest, W Cameroon
Kumertau 111 D6 Respublika
  Bashkortostan, W Russian Federation
Kumillä see Comilla
Kumo 75 G4 Gombe, E Nigeria
Kumon Range 136 B2 mountain range
  N Burma (Myanmar)
Kumul see Hami
Kunashiri see Kunashir, Ostrov
Kunashir, Ostrov 130 E1 var. Kunashiri.
  island Kuril'skiye Ostrova, SE Russian
  Federation
Kunda 106 E2 Lääne-Virumaa, NE Estonia
Kunduz see Kondoz
Kunene 69 C6 var. Kunene. river
  Angola/Namibia
Kunene see Cunene
Kungsbacka 85 B7 Halland, S Sweden
Kungur 111 D5 Permskaya Oblast',
  NW Russian Federation
Kunlun Mountains see Kunlun Shan
Kunlun Shan 126 B4 Eng. Kunlun
  Mountains. mountain range NW China
Kunming 128 B6 var. K'un-ming; prev.
  Yunnan. province capital Yunnan,
  SW China
K'un-ming see Kunming
Kununurra 146 D3 Western Australia
Kunya-Urgench see Köneürgenç
Kuopio 85 E5 Itä-Suomi, C Finland
Kupa see Kolpa
Kupang 139 E5 prev. Koepang. Timor,
  C Indonesia

Kup"yans'k 109 G2 Rus. Kupyansk.
  Kharkivs'ka Oblast', E Ukraine
Kupyansk see Kup"yans'k
Kür see Kura
Kura 117 H3 Az. Kür, Geor. Mtkvari,
  Turk. Kura Nehri. river SW Asia
Kura Nehri see Kura
Kurashiki 131 B6 var. Kurasiki.
  Okayama, Honshū, SW Japan
Kurasiki see Kurashiki
Kurdistan 117 F4 cultural region SW Asia
Kürdzhali 104 D3 var. Kirdzhali.
  Kürdzhali, S Bulgaria
Kure 131 B7 Hiroshima, Honshū,
  SW Japan
Küre Dağları 116 C2 mountain range
  N Turkey
Kuressaare 106 C2 Ger. Arensburg; prev.
  Kingissepp. Saaremaa, W Estonia
Kureyka 112 D2 river N Russian
  Federation
Kurgan-Tyube see Qürghonteppa
Kurieshes Haff see Courland Lagoon
Kuria Muria Islands see Ḥalāniyāt,
  Juzur al
Kurile Islands 115 H4 Eng. Kurile
  Islands. island group SE Russian
  Federation
Kurile Islands see Kuril'skiye Ostrova
Kurile-Kamchatka Depression see
  Kurile Trench
Kurile Trench 113 F3 var. Kurile-
  Kamchatka Depression. trench
  NW Pacific Ocean
Kuril'sk 130 E1 Jap. Shana. Kuril'skiye
  Ostrova, Sakhalinskaya Oblats',
  SE Russian Federation
Ku-ring-gai 148 E1 New South Wales,
  E Australia
Kurische Haff see Courland Lagoon
Kurkund see Kilingi-Nõmme
Kurnool 132 C1 var. Karnul. Andhra
  Pradesh, S India
Kursk 111 A6 Kurskaya Oblast',
  W Russian Federation
Kurskiy Zaliv see Courland Lagoon
Kuršumlija 101 D5 Serbia, S Serbia
Kurtbunar see Tervel
Kurtitsch/Kürtös see Curtici
Kuruktag 126 C3 mountain range
  NW China
Kurume 131 A7 Fukuoka, Kyūshū,
  SW Japan
Kurupukari 59 F3 C Guyana
Kusaie see Kosrae
Kushiro 130 D2 var. Kusiro. Hokkaidō,
  NE Japan
Kushka see Serhetabat
Kusiro see Kushiro
Kuskokwim Mountains 36 C3
  mountain range Alaska, USA
Kustanay see Kostanay
Küstence/Küstendje see Constanța
Kütahya 116 B3 prev. Kutaia. Kütahya,
  W Turkey
Kutai see Mahakam, Sungai
K'ut'aisi 117 F2 W Georgia
Kūt al 'Amārah see Al Kūt
Kut al Imara see Al Kūt
Kutaradja/Kutaraja see Bandaaceh
Kutch, Gulf of see Kachchh, Gulf of
Kutch, Rann of see Kachchh, Rann of
Kutina 100 B3 Sisak-Moslavina, NE Croatia
Kutno 98 C3 Łódzkie, C Poland
Kuujjuaq 39 E2 prev. Fort-Chimo.
  Québec, E Canada
Kuusamo 84 E3 Oulu, E Finland
Kuvango see Cubango
Kuvdlorssuak see Kullorsuaq
Kuwait 120 C4 off. State of Kuwait, var.
  Dawlat al Kuwait, Koweit, Kuwt.
  country SW Asia

KUWAIT
Southwest Asia

Official name State of Kuwait
Formation 1961 / 1961
Capital Kuwait City
Population 2.8 million / 407 people
per sq mile (157 people per sq km) / 96%
Total area 6880 sq. miles (17,820 sq. km)
Languages Arabic*, English
Religions Sunni Muslim 45%, Shi'a
Muslim 40%, Christian, Hindu,
& other 15%
Ethnic mix Kuwaiti 45%, Other Arab 35%,
South Asian 9%, Other 7%, Iranian 4%

KUWAIT
(continued)

Government Monarchy
Currency Kuwaiti dinar = 1000 fils
Literacy rate 93%
Calorie consumption 3010 calories

Kuwait *see* Al Kuwayt
Kuwait City *see* Al Kuwayt
Kuwait, Dawlat al *see* Kuwait
Kuwait, State of *see* Kuwait
Kuwajleen *see* Kwajalein Atoll
Kuwayt 120 C3 Maysän, E Iraq
Kuweit *see* Kuwait
Kuybyshev *see* Samara
Kuybyshev Reservoir 111 C5 *var.*
  Kuibyshev, Eng. Kuybyshev
  Reservoir. *reservoir* W Russian
  Federation
Kuybyshev Reservoir *see*
  Kuybyshevskoye
  Vodokhranilishche
Kuytun 126 B2 Xinjiang Uygur Zizhiqu,
  NW China
Kuzi *see* Kuji
Kuznetsk 111 B6 Penzenskaya Oblast',
  W Russian Federation
Kuźnica 98 E2 Białystok, NE Poland
  Europe
Kvaløya 84 C2 *island* N Norway
Kvarnbergsvattnet 84 B4 *var.*
  Frostviken. *lake* N Sweden
Kvarner 100 A3 *var.* Carnaro, *It.*
  Quarnero. *gulf* W Croatia
Kvitøya 83 G1 *island* NE Svalbard
Kwajalein Atoll 144 C1 *var.*
  Kuwajleen. *atoll* Ralik Chain,
  C Marshall Islands
Kwando *see* Cuando
Kwangchow *see* Guangzhou
Kwangchu *see* Kwangju
Kwangju 129 E4 *off.* Kwangju-
  gwangyŏksi, *var.* Guangju, Kwangchu,
  Jap. Kōshū. SW South Korea
Kwangju-gwangyŏksi *see* Kwangju
Kwango 77 C7 Port. Cuango. *river*
  Angola/Dem. Rep. Congo
Kwango *see* Cuango
Kwangsi/Kwangsi Chuang
  Autonomous Region *see* Guangxi
  Zhuangzu Zizhiqu
Kwangtung *see* Guangdong
Kwangyuan *see* Guangyuan
Kwanza *see* Cuanza
Kweichu *see* Guiyang
Kweilin *see* Guilin
Kweisui *see* Hohhot
Kweiyang *see* Guiyang
Kwekwe 78 D3 *prev.* Que Que. Midlands,
  C Zimbabwe
Kwesui *see* Hohhot
Kwidzyń 98 C2 Ger. Marienwerder.
  Pomorskie, N Poland
Kwigillingok 36 C3 Alaska, USA
Kwilu 77 C6 *river* W Dem. Rep.
  Congo
Kwito *see* Cuito
Kyabé 76 C4 Moyen-Chari, S Chad
Kyaikkami 137 B5 *prev.* Amherst. Mon
  State, S Burma (Myanmar)
Kyaiklat 136 B4 Ayeyarwady, SW Burma
  (Myanmar)
Kyaikto 136 B4 Mon State, S Burma
  (Myanmar)
Kyakhta 115 E5 Respublika Buryatiya,
  S Russian Federation
Kyaukse 136 B3 Mandalay, C Burma
  (Myanmar)
Kyjov 99 C5 Ger. Gaya. Jihomoravský
  Kraj, SE Czech Republic
Kými 105 C5 *var.* Kími. Évvoia,
  C Greece
Kyōngsŏng *see* Sŏul
Kyōto 131 C6 Kyōto, Honshū, SW Japan
Kyparissía 105 B6 *var.* Kiparissía.
  Pelopónnisos, S Greece
Kypros *see* Cyprus
Kyrá Panagía 105 C5 *island* Vóreies
  Sporádes, Greece, Aegean Sea
Kyrenia *see* Girne
Kyrgyz Republic *see* Kyrgyzstan
Kyrgyzstan 123 F2 *off.* Kyrgyz Republic,
  var. Kirghizia; *prev.* Kirgizskaya SSR,
  Kirghiz SSR, Republic of Kyrgyzstan.
  country C Asia

KYRGYZSTAN
Central Asia

Official name Kyrgyz Republic
Formation 1991 / 1991
Capital Bishkek
Population 5.4 million / 70 people
  per sq mile (27 people per sq km) / 34%
Total area 76,641 sq. miles (198,500 sq. km)
Languages Kyrgyz*, Russian*, Uzbek,
  Tatar, Ukrainian
Religions Muslim (mainly Sunni) 70%,
  Orthodox Christian 30%
Ethnic mix Kyrgyz 65%, Uzbek 14%,
  Russian 13%, Other 6%,
  Dungan 1%, Ukrainian 1%
Government Presidential system
Currency Som = 100 tyiyn
Literacy rate 99%
Calorie consumption 2999 calories

Kyrgyzstan, Republic of *see* Kyrgyzstan
Kythira 105 C7 *var.* Kíthira, *It.* Cerigo,
  Lat. Cythera. *island* S Greece
Kýthnos 105 C6 Knýthnos, Kykládes,
  Greece, Aegean Sea
Kythnos 105 C6 *var.* Kithnos, Thermiá,
  It. Termia; *anc.* Cythnos. *island*
  Kykládes, Greece, Aegean Sea
Kythréa *see* Değirmenlik
Kyushu 131 B7 *var.* Kyūshū. *island*
  SW Japan
Kyushu-Palau Ridge 125 F3 *var.*
  Kyusyu-Palau Ridge. *undersea ridge*
  W Pacific Ocean
Kyustendil 104 B2 *anc.* Pautalia.
  Kyustendil, W Bulgaria
Kyūsyū *see* Kyūshū
Kyusyu-Palau Ridge *see* Kyushu-Palau
  Ridge
Kyyiv 109 E2 Eng. Kiev, *Rus.* Kiyev.
  country capital (Ukraine) (Ukraine)
  Kyyivs'ka Oblast', N Ukraine
Kyzyl 114 D4 Respublika Tyva, C Russian
  Federation
Kyzyl Kum 122 D2 *var.* Kizil Kum,
  Qizil Qum, *Uzb.* Qizilqum. *desert*
  Kazakhstan/Uzbekistan
Kyzylrabot *see* Qizilrabot
Kyzyl-Suu 123 G2 *prev.* Pokrovka.
  Issyk-Kul'skaya Oblast', NE Kyrgyzstan
Kzylorda 114 B5 *var.* Kzyl-Orda, Qizil
  Orda, Qyzylorda; *prev.* Perovsk.
  Kzylorda, S Kazakhstan
Kzyl-Orda *see* Kzylorda

L

Laaland *see* Lolland
La Algaba 92 C4 Andalucía, S Spain
Laarne 87 B5 Oost-Vlaanderen,
  NW Belgium
La Asunción 59 E1 Nueva Esparta,
  NE Venezuela
Laatokka *see* Ladozhskoye, Ozero
Laâyoune 70 B3 *var.* Aaiún. *country
  capital* (Western Sahara) (Western
  Sahara) NW Western Sahara
La Banda Oriental *see* Uruguay
la Baule-Escoublac 90 A4 Loire-
  Atlantique, NW France
Labé 74 C4 NW Guinea
Labe *see* Elbe
Laborca *see* Laborec
Laborec 99 E5 Hung. Laborca. *river*
  E Slovakia
Labrador 39 F2 *cultural region*
  Newfoundland and Labrador,
  SW Canada
Labrador Basin 34 E3 *var.* Labrador Sea
  Basin. *undersea basin* NW Atlantic
  Ocean
Labrador Sea 82 A4 *sea* NW Atlantic
  Ocean
Labrador Sea Basin *see* Labrador Basin
Labudalin *see* Ergun
Labutta 137 A5 Ayeyarwady, SW Burma
  (Myanmar)
Laç 101 C6 *var.* Laci. Lezhë, C Albania
La Calera 64 B4 Valparaíso, C Chile
La Carolina 92 D4 Andalucía, S Spain
Laccadive Islands 132 A3 Eng. Laccadive
  Islands. *island group* India, N Indian
  Ocean
Laccadive Islands/Laccadive Minicoy
  and Amindivi Islands, the *see*
  Lakshadweep

La Ceiba 52 D2 Atlántida, N Honduras
Lachanás 104 B3 Kentrikí Makedonía,
  N Greece
La Chaux-de-Fonds 95 A7 Neuchâtel,
  W Switzerland
Lachlan River 149 C6 *river* New South
  Wales, SE Australia
Laci *see* Laç
la Ciotat 91 D6 *anc.* Citharista. Bouches-
  du-Rhône, SE France
Lacobriga *see* Lagos
La Concepción 53 E5 *var.* Concepción.
  Chiriquí, W Panama
La Concepción 58 C1 Zulia,
  NW Venezuela
La Condamine 91 C8 W Monaco
Laconia 41 G2 New Hampshire, NE USA
La Crosse 40 A2 Wisconsin, N USA
La Cruz 52 D4 Guanacaste, NW Costa
  Rica
Lake Ladoga 110 B3 Eng. Lake Ladoga,
  Fin. Laatokka. *lake* NW Russian
  Federation
Ladoga, Lake *see* Ladozhskoye, Ozero
Ladysmith 40 B2 Wisconsin, N USA
Lae 144 B3 Morobe, W Papua New
  Guinea
La Esperanza 52 C2 Intibucá,
  SW Honduras
Lafayette 40 C4 Indiana, N USA
Lafayette 42 B3 Louisiana, S USA
La Fé 54 A2 Pinar del Río, W Cuba
Lafia 75 G4 Nassarawa, C Nigeria
la Flèche 90 B4 Sarthe, NW France
Lagdo, Lac de 76 B4 *lake* N Cameroon
Laghouat 70 D2 N Algeria
Lagos 75 F5 Lagos, SW Nigeria
Lagos 92 B5 *anc.* Lacobriga. Faro,
  S Portugal
Lagos de Moreno 51 E4 Jalisco,
  SW Mexico
Lagouira 70 A4 SW Western Sahara
La Grande 46 C3 Oregon, NW USA
La Guaira 66 B4 Distrito Federal,
  N Venezuela
Lagunas 64 B1 Tarapacá, N Chile
Lagunillas 61 G4 Santa Cruz, SE Bolivia
La Habana 54 B2 *var.* Havana. *country
  capital* (Cuba) (Cuba) Ciudad de La
  Habana, W Cuba
Lahat 138 B4 Sumatera, W Indonesia
La Haye *see* 's-Gravenhage
Laholm 85 B7 Halland, S Sweden
Lahore 134 D2 Punjab, NE Pakistan
Lahr 95 A6 Baden-Württemberg,
  S Germany
Lahti 85 D5 Swe. Lahtis. Etelä-Suomi,
  S Finland
Lahtis *see* Lahti
Laï 76 B4 *prev.* Behagle, De Behagle.
  Tandjilé, S Chad
Laibach *see* Ljubljana
Lai Châu 136 D3 Lai Châu, N Vietnam
Laila *see* Laylā
La Junta 44 D5 Colorado, C USA
Lake Charles 42 A3 Louisiana, S USA
Lake City 43 E3 Florida, SE USA
Lake District 89 C5 *physical region*
  NW England, United Kingdom
Lake Havasu City 48 A2 Arizona,
  SW USA
Lake Jackson 49 H4 Texas, SW USA
Lakeland 43 E4 Florida, SE USA
Lakeside 47 C8 California, W USA
Lake State *see* Michigan
Lakewood 44 D4 Colorado, C USA
Lakhnau *see* Lucknow
Lakonikós Kólpos 105 B7 *gulf* S Greece
Lakselv 84 D2 Lapp. Leavdnja.
  Finnmark, N Norway
La Laon *see* Laon
Lalibela 72 C4 Amara, Ethiopia
La Libertad 52 B1 Petén, N Guatemala
La Ligua 64 B4 Valparaíso, C Chile
Lalin 92 C1 Galicia, NW Spain
Lalitpur 135 F3 Central, C Nepal
La Louvière 87 B6 Hainaut, S Belgium
la Maddalena 96 A4 Sardegna, Italy,
  C Mediterranean Sea
la Manche *see* English Channel
Lamar 44 D5 Colorado, C USA
La Marmora, Punta 97 A5 *mountain*
  Sardegna, Italy, C Mediterranean Sea
La Massana 91 A5 La Massana,
  W Andorra Europe
Lambaréné 77 A6 Moyen-Ogooué,
  W Gabon

Lamego 92 C2 Viseu, N Portugal
Lamesa 49 E3 Texas, SW USA
Lamezia Terme 97 D6 Calabria, SE Italy
Lamía 105 B5 Stereá Ellás, C Greece
Lamoni 45 F4 Iowa, C USA
Lampang 136 C4 *var.* Muang Lampang.
  Lampang, NW Thailand
Lámpeia 105 B6 Dytikí Ellás, S Greece
Lanbi Kyun 137 B6 *var.* Sullivan Island.
  island Mergui Archipelago, S Burma
  (Myanmar)
Lancang Jiang *see* Mekong
Lancaster 89 D5 NW England, United
  Kingdom
Lancaster 47 C7 California, W USA
Lancaster 41 F4 Pennsylvania, NE USA
Lancaster Sound 37 F2 *sound* Nunavut,
  N Canada
Lan-chou/Lan-chow/Lanchow *see*
  Lanzhou
Landao *see* Lantau Island
Landen 87 C6 Vlaams Brabant, C Belgium
Lander 44 C3 Wyoming, C USA
Landerneau 90 A3 Finistère, NW France
Landes 91 B5 *cultural region* SW France
Land of Enchantment *see* New Mexico
The Land of Opportunity *see* Arkansas
Land of Steady Habits *see* Connecticut
Land of the Midnight Sun *see* Alaska
Landsberg *see* Gorzów Wielkopolski,
  Lubuskie, Poland
Landsberg an der Warthe *see* Gorzów
  Wielkopolski
Land's End 89 B8 *headland* SW England,
  United Kingdom
Landshut 95 C6 Bayern, SE Germany
Langar 123 E2 *Rus.* Lyangar. Navoiy
  Viloyati, C Uzbekistan
Langfang 128 D4 Hebei, E China
Langkawi, Pulau 137 B7 *island*
  Peninsular Malaysia
Langres 91 D4 Haute-Marne, N France
Langsa 138 A3 Sumatera, W Indonesia
Lang Shan 127 E3 *mountain range*
  N China
Lang Son 136 D3 *var.* Langson. Lang
  Son, N Vietnam
Langson *see* Lang Son
Lang Suan 137 B6 Chumphon,
  SW Thailand
Languedoc 91 C6 *cultural region* S France
Länkäran 117 H3 *Rus.* Lenkoran'.
  S Azerbaijan
Lansing 40 C3 *state capital* Michigan,
  N USA
Lanta, Ko 137 B7 *island* S Thailand
Lantau Island 128 A2 Cant. Tai Yue
  Shan, *Chin.* Landao. *island* Hong
  Kong, S China
Lan-ts'ang Chiang *see* Mekong
Lantung, Gulf of *see* Liaodong Wan
Lanzarote 70 B3 *island* Islas Canarias,
  Spain, NE Atlantic Ocean
Lanzhou 128 B4 *var.* Lan-chou,
  Lanchow, Lan-chow; *prev.* Kaolan.
  province capital Gansu, C China
Lao Cai 136 D3 Lao Cai, N Vietnam
Laodicea/Laodicea ad Mare *see* Al
  Lädhiqiyah
Laoet *see* Laut, Pulau
Laojunmiao 128 A3 *prev.* Yumen.
  Gansu, N China
Laon 90 D3 *var.* la Laon; *anc.* Laudunum.
  Aisne, N France
Lao People's Democratic Republic
  see Laos
La Orchila, Isla 58 D1 *island*
  N Venezuela
La Oroya 60 C3 Junín, C Peru
Laos 136 D4 *off.* Lao People's Democratic
  Republic. *country* SE Asia

LAOS
Southeast Asia

Official name Lao People's Democratic
  Republic
Formation 1953 / 1953
Capital Vientiane
Population 6.2 million / 70 people
  per sq mile (27 people per sq km) / 21%
Total area 91,428 sq. miles
  (236,800 sq. km)
Languages Lao*, Mon-Khmer, Yao,
  Vietnamese, Chinese, French
Religions Buddhist 85%,
  Other (including animist) 15%

LAOS
(continued)

Ethnic mix Lao Loum 66%, Lao
Theung 30%, Other 2%, Lao Soung 2%
Government One-party state
Currency New kip = 100 at
Literacy rate 69%
Calorie consumption 2312 calories

La Palma 53 G5 Darién, SE Panama
La Palma 70 A3 island Islas Canarias,
Spain, NE Atlantic Ocean
La Paz 61 F4 var. La Paz de Ayacucho.
country capital (Bolivia-legislative
and administrative capital) (Bolivia-
legislative and administrative capital) La
Paz, W Bolivia
La Paz 50 B3 Baja California Sur,
NW Mexico
La Paz, Bahía de 50 B3 bay NW Mexico
La Paz de Ayacucho see La Paz
La Perouse Strait 130 D1 Jap. Sōya-
kaikyō, Rus. Proliv Laperuza. strait
Japan/Russian Federation
Laperuza, Proliv see La Perouse Strait
Lápithos see Lapta
Lapland 84 D3 Fin. Lappi, Swe.
Lappland. cultural region N Europe
La Plata 64 D4 Buenos Aires, E Argentina
La Plata see Sucre
Lappeenranta 85 E5 Swe. Villmanstrand.
Etelä-Suomi, SE Finland
Lappi/Lappland see Lapland
Lappo see Lapua
Lapta 102 C5 Gk. Lápithos. NW Cyprus
Laptev Sea 115 E2 Eng. Laptev Sea. sea
Arctic Ocean
Laptev Sea see Laptevykh, More
Lapua 85 D5 Swe. Lappo. Länsi-Suomi,
W Finland
Lapurdum see Bayonne
Łapy 98 E3 Podlaskie, NE Poland
La Quiaca 64 C2 Jujuy, N Argentina
L'Aquila 96 C4 var. Aquila, Aquila degli
Abruzzi. Abruzzo, C Italy
Laracha 92 B1 Galicia, NW Spain
Laramie 44 C4 Wyoming, C USA
Laramie Mountains 44 C3 mountain
range Wyoming, C USA
Laredo 93 E1 Cantabria, N Spain
Laredo 49 F5 Texas, SW USA
La Réunion see Réunion
Largeau see Faya
Largo 43 E4 Florida, SE USA
Largo, Cayo 54 B2 island W Cuba
Lario see Como, Lago di
La Rioja 64 C3 La Rioja, NW Argentina
La Rioja 93 E2 autonomous community
N Spain
Lárisa 104 B4 var. Larissa. Thessalía,
C Greece
Larissa see Lárisa
Lárkāna 134 B3 var. Larkhana. Sind,
SE Pakistan
Larkhana see Lārkāna
Larnaca see Lárnaka
Lárnaka 102 C5 var. Larnaca, Larnax.
SE Cyprus
Larnax see Lárnaka
la Rochelle 90 B4 anc. Rupella.
Charente-Maritime, W France
la Roche-sur-Yon 90 B4 prev. Bourbon
Vendée, Napoléon-Vendée. Vendée,
NW France
La Roda 93 E3 Castilla-La Mancha, C Spain
La Romana 55 E3 E Dominican Republic
Larvotto 91 C8 N Monaco Europe
La-sa see Lhasa
Las Cabezas de San Juan 92 C5
Andalucía, S Spain
Las Cruces 48 D3 New Mexico, SW USA
La See d'Urgell 93 G1 var. La Seu
d'Urgell, Seo de Urgel. Cataluña,
NE Spain
La Serena 64 B3 Coquimbo, C Chile
La Seu d'Urgell see La See d'Urgell
la Seyne-sur-Mer 91 D6 Var, SE France
Lashio 136 B3 Shan State, E Burma
(Myanmar)
Lashkar Gāh 122 D4 var. Lash-Kar-Gar'.
Helmand, S Afghanistan
Lash-Kar-Gar' see Lashkar Gāh
La Sila 97 D6 mountain range SW Italy
La Sirena 52 D3 Región Autónoma
Atlántico Sur, E Nicaragua

Łask 98 C4 Lódzkie, C Poland
Las Lomitas 64 D2 Formosa,
N Argentina
La Solana 93 E4 Castilla-La Mancha,
C Spain
Las Palmas 70 A3 var. Las Palmas de
Gran Canaria. Gran Canaria, Islas
Canarias, Spain, NE Atlantic Ocean
Las Palmas de Gran Canaria see Las
Palmas
La Spezia 96 B3 Liguria, NW Italy
Lassa see Lhasa
Las Tablas 53 F5 Los Santos, S Panama
Last Frontier, The see Alaska
Las Tunas 54 C2 var. Victoria de las
Tunas. Las Tunas, E Cuba
La Suisse see Switzerland
Las Vegas 47 D7 Nevada, W USA
Latacunga 60 B1 Cotopaxi, C Ecuador
la Teste 91 B5 Gironde, SW France
Latina 97 C5 prev. Littoria. Lazio, C Italy
La Tortuga, Isla 59 E1 var. Isla Tortuga.
island N Venezuela
La Tuque 39 E4 Québec, SE Canada
Latvia 106 C3 off. Republic of Latvia,
Ger. Lettland, Latv. Latvija, Latvijas
Republika; prev. Latvian SSR, Rus.
Latviyskaya SSR. country NE Europe

LATVIA
Northeast Europe

Official name Republic of Latvia
Formation 1991 / 1991
Capital Riga
Population 2.3 million / 92 people
per sq mile (36 people per sq km) / 66%
Total area 24,938 sq. miles (64,589 sq. km)
Languages Latvian*, Russian
Religions Lutheran 55%, Roman
Catholic 24%, Other 12%, Orthodox
Christian 9%
Ethnic mix Latvian 59%, Russian 29%,
Belarussian 4%, Polish 3%, Ukrainian 3%,
Other 2%
Government Parliamentary system
Currency Lats = 100 santimi
Literacy rate 99%
Calorie consumption 2938 calories

Latvian SSR/Latvija/Latvijas
Republika/Latviyskaya SSR see Latvia
Latvia, Republic of see Latvia
Laudunum see Laon
Laudus see St-Lô
Lauenburg/Lauenburg in Pommern
see Lębork
Lau Group 145 E4 island group E Fiji
Lauis see Lugano
Launceston 149 C8 Tasmania,
SE Australia
La Unión 52 C2 Olancho, C Honduras
La Unión 93 F4 Murcia, SE Spain
Laurel 42 C3 Mississippi, S USA
Laurel 44 C2 Montana, NW USA
Laurentian Highlands see Laurentian
Mountains
Laurentian Mountains 39 E3 var.
Laurentian Highlands, Fr. Les
Laurentides. plateau Newfoundland
and Labrador/Québec, Canada
Laurentides, Les see Laurentian
Mountains
Lauria 97 D6 Basilicata, S Italy
Laurinburg 43 F1 North Carolina,
SE USA
Lauru see Choiseul
Lausanne 95 A7 It. Losanna. Vaud,
SW Switzerland
Laut, Pulau 138 D4 prev. Laoet. island
Borneo, C Indonesia
Laval 39 E4 Québec, SE Canada
Laval 90 B3 Mayenne, NW France
La Vall d'Uixó 93 F3 var. Vall D'Uxó.
País Valenciano, E Spain
La Vega 55 E3 var. Concepción de la
Vega. C Dominican Republic
La Vila Joïosa see Villajoyosa
Lávrio 105 C6 prev. Lávrion. Attikí,
C Greece
Lávrion see Lávrio
Lawrence 41 G3 Massachusetts, NE USA
Lawrenceburg 42 C1 Tennessee, S USA
Lawton 49 F2 Oklahoma, C USA
La Yarada 61 E4 Tacna, SW Peru
Laylā 121 C5 var. Laila. Ar Riyāḍ,
C Saudi Arabia

Lazarev Sea 154 B1 sea Antarctica
Lázaro Cárdenas 51 E5 Michoacán,
SW Mexico
Leal see Lihula
Leamhcán see Lucan
Leamington 38 C5 Ontario, S Canada
Leavdnja see Lakselv
Lebak 139 E3 Mindanao, S Philippines
Lebanese Republic see Lebanon
Lebanon 45 G5 Missouri, C USA
Lebanon 41 G2 New Hampshire,
NE USA
Lebanon 46 B3 Oregon, NW USA
Lebanon 118 A4 off. Lebanese Republic,
Ar. Al Lubnān, Fr. Liban. country
SW Asia

LEBANON
Southwest Asia

Official name The Lebanese Republic
Formation 1941 / 1941
Capital Beirut
Population 3.7 million / 937 people
per sq mile (362 people per sq km) / 88%
Total area 4015 sq. miles (10,400 sq. km)
Languages Arabic*, French,
Armenian, Assyrian
Religions Muslim 70%, Christian 30%
Ethnic mix Arab 94%, Armenian 4%,
Other 2%
Government Parliamentary system
Currency Lebanese pound = 100 piastres
Literacy rate 86%
Calorie consumption 3196 calories

Lebanon, Mount see Liban, Jebel
Lebap 122 D2 Lebapskiy Velayat,
NE Turkmenistan
Lebedin see Lebedyn
Lebedyn 109 F2 Rus. Lebedín. Sums'ka
Oblast', NE Ukraine
Lębork 98 C2 var. Lębórk, Ger.
Lauenburg, Lauenburg in Pommern.
Pomorskie, N Poland
Lebrija 92 C5 Andalucía, S Spain
Lebu 65 A5 Bío Bío, C Chile
le Cannet 91 D6 Alpes-Maritimes,
SE France
Le Cap see Cap-Haïtien
Lecce 97 E6 Puglia, SE Italy
Lechainá 105 B6 var. Lehaina, Lekhainá.
Dytikí Ellás, S Greece
Ledo Salinarius see Lons-le-Saunier
Leduc 37 E5 Alberta, SW Canada
Leech Lake 45 F2 lake Minnesota, N USA
Leeds 89 D5 N England, United Kingdom
Leek 86 E2 Groningen, NE Netherlands
Leer 94 A3 Niedersachsen, NW Germany
Leeuwarden 86 D1 Fris. Ljouwert.
Friesland, N Netherlands
Leeuwin, Cape 142 A5 headland
Western Australia
Leeward Islands 55 G3 island group
E West Indies
Leeward Islands see Sotavento, Ilhas de
Lefkáda 105 A5 prev. Levkás.
Lefkáda, Iónia Nisiá, Greece,
C Mediterranean Sea
Lefkáda 105 A5 It. Santa Maura, prev.
Levkás; anc. Leucas. island Iónia Nisiá,
Greece, C Mediterranean Sea
Lefká Óri 105 C7 mountain range Kríti,
Greece, E Mediterranean Sea
Lefkímmi 105 A5 var. Levkímmi.
Kérkyra, Iónia Nisiá, Greece,
C Mediterranean Sea
Lefkosía/Lefkoşa see Nicosia
Legaceaster see Chester
Legaspi see Legazpi City
Leghorn see Livorno
Legnica 98 B4 Ger. Liegnitz.
Dolnośląskie, SW Poland
le Havre 90 B3 Eng. Havre; prev. le
Havre-de-Grâce. Seine-Maritime,
N France
le Havre-de-Grâce see le Havre
Lehena see Lechainá
Leicester 89 D6 Lat. Batae Coritanorum.
C England, United Kingdom
Leiden 86 B3 prev. Leyden; anc.
Lugdunum Batavorum. Zuid-Holland,
W Netherlands
Leie 90 D2 Fr. Lys. river Belgium/France
Leinster 89 B6 cultural region E Ireland
Leipsic see Leipzig

Leipsoí 105 E6 island Dodekánisa,
Greece, Aegean Sea
Leipzig 94 C4 Pol. Lipsk, hist. Leipsic;
anc. Lipsia. Sachsen, E Germany
Leiria 92 B3 anc. Collipo. Leiria,
C Portugal
Leirvik 85 A6 Hordaland, S Norway
Lek 86 C4 river SW Netherlands
Lekhainá see Lechainá
Lekhchevo 104 C2 Montana,
NW Bulgaria
Leksand 85 C5 Dalarna, C Sweden
Lel'chitsy see Lyel'chytsy
le Léman see Geneva, Lake
Léman, Lac see Geneva, Lake
le Mans 90 B3 Sarthe, NW France
Lemberg see L'viv
Lemesós 102 C5 var. Limassol.
SW Cyprus
Lemhi Range 46 D3 mountain range
Idaho, C USA North America
Lemnos see Límnos
Lemovices see Limoges
Lena 115 F3 river NE Russian Federation
Lena Tablemount 141 B7 seamount
S Indian Ocean
Len Dao 128 C8 island S Spratly Islands
Lengshuitan see Yongzhou
Leninabad see Khujand
Leninakan see Gyumri
Lenine 109 G5 Rus. Lenino. Respublika
Krym, S Ukraine
Leningor see Ridder
Leningrad see Sankt-Peterburg
Leningradskaya 154 B4 Russian research
station Antarctica
Lenino see Lenine, Ukraine
Leninobod see Khujand
Leninpol' 123 F2 Talasskaya Oblast',
NW Kyrgyzstan
Lenin-Turkmenski see Türkmenabat
Lenkoran' see Lǝnkǝran
Lenti 99 B7 Zala, SW Hungary
Lentia see Linz
Leoben 95 E7 Steiermark, C Austria
León 51 E4 var. León de los Aldamas.
Guanajuato, C Mexico
León 52 C3 León, NW Nicaragua
León 92 D1 Castilla-León, NW Spain
León de los Aldamas see León
Leonídi see Leonídio
Leonídio 105 B6 var. Leonídi.
Peloponnisos, S Greece
Léopold II, Lac see Mai-Ndombe, Lac
Léopoldville see Kinshasa
Lepe 92 C4 Andalucía, S Spain
Lepel' see Lyepyel'
le Portel 90 C2 Pas-de-Calais, N France
Le Puglie see Puglia
le Puy 91 C5 prev. le Puy-en-Velay, hist.
Anicium, Podium Anicensis. Haute-
Loire, C France
le Puy-en-Velay see le Puy
Léré 76 B4 Mayo-Kébbi, SW Chad
Lérida see Lleida
Lerma 92 D2 Castilla-León, N Spain
Leros 105 D6 island Dodekánisa, Greece,
Aegean Sea
Lerrnayin Gharabakh see
Nagorno-Karabakh
Lerwick 88 D1 NE Scotland, United
Kingdom
Lesbos 113 A4 anc. Lesbos. island
E Greece
Lesbos see Lésvos
Les Cayes see Cayes
Les Gonaïves see Gonaïves
les Herbiers 90 B4 Vendée, NW France
Lesh/Leshi see Lezhë
Lesina see Hvar
Leskovac 101 E5 Serbia, SE Serbia
Lesnoy 114 C3 Sverdlovskaya Oblast',
C Russian Federation
Lesotho 78 D4 off. Kingdom of Lesotho;
prev. Basutoland. country S Africa

LESOTHO
Southern Africa

Official name Kingdom of Lesotho
Formation 1966 / 1966
Capital Maseru
Population 1.8 million / 154 people
per sq mile (59 people per sq km) / 18%
Total area 11,720 sq. miles (30,355 sq. km)

LESOTHO
(continued)

Languages English*, Sesotho*, isiZulu
Religions Christian 90%, Traditional
 beliefs 10%
Ethnic mix Sotho 97%, European
 and Asian 3%
Government Parliamentary system
Currency Loti = 100 lisente
Literacy rate 82%
Calorie consumption 2638 calories

Lesotho, Kingdom of see Lesotho
les Sables-d'Olonne *90 B4* Vendée,
 NW France
Lesser Antarctica see West Antarctica
Lesser Antilles *55 G4* island group
 E West Indies
Lesser Caucasus *117 F2* Rus. Malyy
 Kavkaz. mountain range SW Asia
Lesser Khingan Range see Xiao Hinggan
 Ling
Lesser Sunda Islands *139 E5* Eng.
 Lesser Sunda Islands. island group
 C Indonesia
Lesser Sunda Islands see Nusa Tenggara
Leszno *98 B4* Ger. Lissa. Wielkopolskie,
 C Poland
Lethbridge *37 E5* Alberta, SW Canada
Lethem *59 F3* S Guyana
Leti, Kepulauan *139 F5* island group
 E Indonesia
Letpadan *136 B4* Bago, SW Burma
 (Myanmar)
Letsôk-aw Kyun *137 B6* var. Letsutan
 Island; prev. Domel Island. island
 Mergui Archipelago, S Burma
 (Myanmar)
Letsutan Island see Letsôk-aw Kyun
Lettland see Latvia
Lëtzebuerg see Luxembourg
Leucas see Lefkáda
Leuven *87 C6* Fr. Louvain, Ger. Löwen.
 Vlaams Brabant, C Belgium
Leuze see Leuze-en-Hainaut
Leuze-en-Hainaut *87 B6* var. Leuze.
 Hainaut, SW Belgium
Léva see Levice
Levanger *84 B4* Nord-Trøndelag,
 C Norway
Levelland *49 E2* Texas, SW USA
Leverkusen *94 A4* Nordrhein-Westfalen,
 W Germany
Levice *99 C6* Ger. Lewentz, Hung. Léva,
 Lewenz. Nitriansky Kraj, SW Slovakia
Levin *150 D4* Manawatu-Wanganui,
 North Island, New Zealand
Levkás see Lefkáda
Levkímmi see Lefkímmi
Lewentz/Lewenz see Levice
Lewis, Isle of *88 B2* island NW Scotland,
 United Kingdom
Lewis Range *44 B1* mountain range
 Montana, NW USA
Lewiston *46 C2* Idaho, NW USA
Lewiston *41 G2* Maine, NE USA
Lewistown *44 C1* Montana, NW USA
Lexington *40 C5* Kentucky, S USA
Lexington *45 E4* Nebraska, C USA
Leyden see Leiden
Leyte *139 F2* island C Philippines
Leżajsk *99 E5* Podkarpackie,
 SE Poland
Lezha see Lezhë
Lezhë *101 C6* var. Lezha; prev. Lesh,
 Leshi. Lezhë, NW Albania
Lhasa *126 C5* var. La-sa, Lassa. Xizang
 Zizhiqu, W China
Lhaviyani Atoll see Faadhippolhu Atoll
Lhazê *126 C5* var. Quxar. Xizang
 Zizhiqu, China E Asia
L'Hospitalet de Llobregat *93 G2* var.
 Hospitalet. Cataluña, NE Spain
Liancourt Rocks *131 A5* island group
 Japan/South Korea
Lianyungang *128 D4* var. Xinpu.
 Jiangsu, E China
Liao see Liaoning
Liaodong Wan *127 G3* Eng. Gulf of
 Lantung, Gulf of Liaotung. gulf
 NE China
Liao He *125 E1* river NE China
Liaoning *128 D3* var. Liao, Liaoning
 Sheng, Shengking, hist. Fengtien,
 Shenking. province NE China
Liaoning Sheng see Liaoning
Liaoyuan *129 E3* var. Dongliao,
 Shuang-liao, Jap. Chengchiatun. Jilin,
 NE China
Liard see Fort Liard
Liban see Lebanon
Liban, Jebel *118 B4* Ar. Jabal al Gharbt,
 Jabal Lubnân, Eng. Mount Lebanon.
 mountain range C Lebanon
Libau see Liepâja
Libby *44 A1* Montana, NW USA
Liberal *45 E5* Kansas, C USA
Liberalitas Julia see Évora
Liberec *98 B4* Ger. Reichenberg.
 Liberecký Kraj, N Czech Republic
Liberia *52 D4* Guanacaste, NW Costa
 Rica
Liberia *74 C5* off. Republic of Liberia.
 country W Africa

LIBERIA
West Africa

Official name Republic of Liberia
Formation 1847 / 1847
Capital Monrovia
Population 3.5 million / 94 people
 per sq mile (36 people per sq km) / 47%
Total area 43,000 sq. miles (111,370 sq. km)
Languages English*, Kpelle, Vai, Bassa, Kru,
 Grebo, Kissi, Gola, Loma
Religions Christian 68%, Traditional
 beliefs 18%, Muslim 14%
Ethnic mix Indigenous tribes (16 main
 groups) 95%, Americo-Liberians 5%
Government Presidential system
Currency Liberian dollar = 100 cents
Literacy rate 58%
Calorie consumption 1900 calories

Liberia, Republic of see Liberia
Libian Desert see Libyan Desert
Libîyah, Aş Şahrâ' al see Libyan Desert
Libourne *91 B5* Gironde,
 SW France
Libreville *77 A5* country capital (Gabon)
 (Gabon) Estuaire, NW Gabon
Libya *71 F3* off. Great Socialist People's
 Libyan Arab Jamahiriya, Ar. Al
 Jamâhîrîyah al 'Arabîyah al Lîbîyah ash
 Sha'bîyah al Ishtirâkîy; prev. Libyan
 Arab Republic. country N Africa

LIBYA
North Africa

Official name The Great Socialist
 People's Libyan Arab Jamahiriyah
Formation 1951 / 1951
Capital Tripoli
Population 6.1 million / 9 people
 per sq mile (3 people per sq km) / 87%
Total area 679,358 sq. miles
 (1,759,540 sq. km)
Languages Arabic*, Tuareg
Religions Muslim (mainly Sunni) 97%,
 Other 3%
Ethnic mix Arab and Berber 95%,
 Other 5%
Government One-party state
Currency Libyan dinar = 1000 dirhams
Literacy rate 82%
Calorie consumption 3320 calories

Libyan Arab Republic see Libya
Libyan Desert *71 H4* var. Libian
 Desert, Ar. Aş Şahrâ' al Lîbîyah. desert
 N Africa
Libyan Plateau *103 F4* var. Ad Diffah.
 plateau Egypt/Libya
Lichtenfels *95 C5* Bayern, SE Germany
Lichtenvoorde *86 E4* Gelderland,
 E Netherlands
Lichuan *128 C5* Hubei, C China
Lida *107 B5* Hrodzyenskaya Voblasts',
 W Belarus
Lidhorikión see Lidoríki
Lidköping *85 B6* Västra Götaland,
 S Sweden
Lidokhorikion see Lidoríki
Lidoríki *105 B5* prev. Lidhorikión,
 Lidokhorikion. Stereá Ellád, S
 C Greece
Lidzbark Warmiński *98 D2* Ger.
 Heilsberg. Olsztyn, NE Poland
Liechtenstein *94 D1* off. Principality of
 Liechtenstein. country C Europe

LIECHTENSTEIN
Central Europe

Official name Principality of
 Liechtenstein
Formation 1719 / 1719
Capital Vaduz
Population 34,247 / 552 people
 per sq mile (214 people per sq km) / 22%
Total area 62 sq. miles (160 sq. km)
Languages German*, Alemannish
 dialect, Italian
Religions Roman Catholic 81%,
 Other 12%, Protestant 7%
Ethnic mix Liechtensteiner 66%,
 Other 12%, Swiss 10%, Austrian 6%,
 German 3%, Italian 3%
Government Parliamentary system
Currency Swiss franc = 100 rappen/
 centimes
Literacy rate 99%
Calorie consumption Not available

Liechtenstein, Principality of see
 Liechtenstein
Liège *81 D6* Dut. Luik, Ger. Lüttich.
 Liège, E Belgium
Liegnitz see Legnica
Lienz *95 D7* Tirol, W Austria
Liepâja *106 B3* Ger. Libau. Liepâja,
 W Latvia
Lietuva see Lithuania
Lievenhof see Līvāni
Liezen *95 D7* Steiermark, C Austria
Liffey *89 B6* river Ireland
Lifou *144 D5* island Îles Loyauté, E New
 Caledonia
Liger see Loire
Ligure, Appennino *96 A2* Eng. Ligurian
 Mountains. mountain range NW Italy
Ligure, Mar see Ligurian Sea
Ligurian Mountains see Ligure,
 Appennino
Ligurian Sea *96 A3* Fr. Mer
 Ligurienne, It. Mar Ligure. sea
 N Mediterranean Sea
Ligurienne, Mer see Ligurian Sea
Lihu'e *47 A7* var. Lihue. Kaua'i,
 Hawaii, USA
Lihue see Lihu'e
Lihula *106 D2* Ger. Leal. Läänemaa,
 W Estonia
Liivi Laht see Riga, Gulf of
Likasi *77 D7* prev. Jadotville. Shaba,
 SE Dem. Rep. Congo
Liknes *85 A6* Vest-Agder, S Norway
Lille *90 C2* var. l'Isle, Dut. Rijssel, Flem.
 Ryssel; prev. Lisle; anc. Insula. Nord,
 N France
Lillehammer *85 B5* Oppland, S Norway
Lillestrøm *85 B6* Akershus, S Norway
Lilongwe *79 E2* country capital (Malawi)
 (Malawi) Central , W Malawi
Lilybaeum see Marsala
Lima *60 C4* country capital (Peru) (Peru)
 Lima, W Peru
Limanowa *99 D5* Małopolskie, S Poland
Limassol see Lemesós
Limerick *89 A6* Ir. Luimneach. Limerick,
 SW Ireland
Limín Vathéos see Sámos
Límnos *103 F3* anc. Lemnos. island
 E Greece
Limoges *91 C5* anc. Augustoritum
 Lemovicensium, Lemovices. Haute-
 Vienne, C France
Limón *53 E4* var. Puerto Limón. Limón,
 E Costa Rica
Limón *52 D2* Colón, NE Honduras
Limonum see Poitiers
Limousin *91 C5* cultural region C France
Limoux *91 C6* Aude, S France
Limpopo *78 D3* var. Crocodile. river
 S Africa
Linares *64 A5* Maule, C Chile
Linares *51 E3* Nuevo León, NE Mexico
Linares *93 E4* Andalucía, S Spain
Lincoln *89 D5* anc. Lindum, Lindum
 Colonia. E England, United Kingdom
Lincoln *41 H2* Maine, NE USA
Lincoln *45 F4* state capital Nebraska,
 C USA
Lincoln Sea *34 D2* sea Arctic Ocean
Linden *59 F3* E Guyana
Líndhos see Líndos
Lindi *73 D8* Lindi, SE Tanzania
Líndos *105 E7* var. Líndhos. Ródos,
 Dodekánisa, Greece, Aegean Sea
Lindum/Lindum Colonia see Lincoln
Line Islands *145 G3* island group
 E Kiribati
Lingeh see Bandar-e Lengeh
Lingen *94 A3* var. Lingen an der Ems.
 Niedersachsen, NW Germany
Lingen an der Ems see Lingen
Lingga, Kepulauan *138 B4* island group
 W Indonesia
Linköping *85 C6* Östergötland, S Sweden
Linz *95 D6* anc. Lentia. Oberösterreich,
 N Austria
Lion, Gulf of *91 C7* Eng. Gulf of Lion,
 Gulf of Lions; anc. Sinus Gallicus. gulf
 S France
Lion, Gulf of/Lions, Gulf of see Lion,
 Golfe du
Liozno see Lyozna
Lipari *76 D6* island Isole Eolie, S Italy
Lipari Islands/Lipari, Isole see Eolie,
 Isole
Lipetsk *111 B5* Lipetskaya Oblast',
 W Russian Federation
Lipno *98 C3* Kujawsko-pomorskie,
 C Poland
Lipova *108 A4* Hung. Lippa. Arad,
 W Romania
Lipovets see Lypovets'
Lippa see Lipova
Lipsia/Lipsk see Leipzig
Lira *73 B6* N Uganda
Lisala *77 C5* Equateur, N Dem. Rep.
 Congo
Lisboa *92 B4* Eng. Lisbon; anc.
 Felicitas Julia, Olisipo. country
 capital (Portugal) (Portugal) Lisboa,
 W Portugal
Lisbon see Lisboa
Lisichansk see Lysychans'k
Lisieux *90 B3* anc. Noviomagus.
 Calvados, N France
Liski *111 B6* prev. Georgiu-Dezh.
 Voronezhskaya Oblast', W Russian
 Federation
Lisle/l'Isle see Lille
Lismore *149 E5* New South Wales,
 SE Australia
Lissa see Vis, Croatia
Lissa see Leszno, Poland
Lisse *86 C3* Zuid-Holland,
 W Netherlands
Litang *128 A5* var. Gaocheng. Sichuan,
 C China
Litani, Nahr el *119 B5* var. Nahr al
 Litant. river C Lebanon
Litant, Nahr al see Litani, Nahr el
Litauen see Lithuania
Lithgow *149 D6* New South Wales,
 SE Australia
Lithuania *106 B4* off. Republic of
 Lithuania, Ger. Litauen, Lith. Lietuva,
 Pol. Litwa, Rus. Litva; prev. Lithuanian
 SSR, Rus. Litovskaya SSR. country
 NE Europe

LITHUANIA
Northeast Europe

Official name Republic of Lithuania
Formation 1991 / 1991
Capital Vilnius
Population 3.4 million / 135 people
 per sq mile (52 people per sq km) / 67%
Total area 25,174 sq. miles (65,200 sq. km)
Languages Lithuanian*, Russian
Religions Roman Catholic 83%,
 Other 12%, Protestant 5%
Ethnic mix Lithuanian 83%, Polish 7%,
 Russian 6%, Other 3%, Belorussian 1%
Government Parliamentary system
Currency Litas = 100 centu
Literacy rate 99%
Calorie consumption 3324 calories

Lithuanian SSR see Lithuania
Lithuania, Republic of see Lithuania
Litóchoro *104 B4* var. Litochoron,
 Litókhoron. Kentrikí Makedonía,
 N Greece
Litóchoron see Litóchoro
Litohoro/Litókhoron see Litóchoro
Litovskaya SSR see Lithuania
Little Alföld *99 C6* Ger. Kleines
 Ungarisches Tiefland, Hung. Kisalföld,
 Slvk. Podunajská Rovina. plain
 Hungary/Slovakia

Little Andaman 133 F2 island Andaman Islands, India, NE Indian Ocean
Little Barrier Island 150 D2 island N New Zealand
Little Bay 93 H5 bay Alboran Sea, Mediterranean Sea
Little Cayman 54 B3 island E Cayman Islands
Little Falls 45 F2 Minnesota, N USA
Littlefield 49 E2 Texas, SW USA
Little Inagua 54 D2 var. Inagua Islands. island S Bahamas
Little Minch, The 88 B3 strait NW Scotland, United Kingdom
Little Missouri River 44 D2 river NW USA Islands, India, NE Indian Ocean
Little Nicobar 133 G3 island Nicobar Islands, India, NE Indian Ocean
Little Rhody see Rhode Island
Little Rock 42 B1 state capital Arkansas, C USA
Little Saint Bernard Pass 91 D5 Fr. Col du Petit St-Bernard, It. Colle del Piccolo San Bernardo. pass France/Italy
Little Sound 42 A5 bay Bermuda, NW Atlantic Ocean
Littleton 44 D4 Colorado, C USA
Littoria see Latina
Litva/Litwa see Lithuania
Liu-chou/Liuchow see Liuzhou
Liuzhou 128 C6 var. Liu-chou, Liuchow. Guangxi Zhuangzu Zizhiqu, S China
Livanátai see Livanátes
Livanátes 105 B5 prev. Livanátai. Stereá Ellás, C Greece
Liváni 106 D4 Ger. Lievenhof. Preiļi, SE Latvia
Liverpool 39 F5 Nova Scotia, SE Canada
Liverpool 52 C5 NW England, United Kingdom
Livingston 44 B2 Montana, NW USA
Livingston 49 H3 Texas, SW USA
Livingstone 49 H3 var. Maramba. Southern, S Zambia
Livingstone 78 C3 var. Maramba. Southern, S Zambia
Livingstone Mountains 151 A7 mountain range South Island, New Zealand
Livno 100 B4 Federicija Bosna I Hercegovina, SW Bosnia and Herzegovina
Livojoki 84 D4 river C Finland
Livonia 40 D3 Michigan, N USA
Livorno 96 B3 Eng. Leghorn. Toscana, C Italy
Lixian Jiang see Black River
Lixoúri 105 A5 prev. Lixoúrion. Kefallinía, Iónia Nisiá, Greece, C Mediterranean Sea
Lixoúrion see Lixoúri
Lizarra see Estella
Ljouwert see Leeuwarden
Ljubelj see Loibl Pass
Ljubljana 95 C7 Ger. Laibach, It. Lubiana; anc. Aemona, Emona. country capital (Slovenia) (Slovenia) C Slovenia
Ljungby 85 B7 Kronoberg, S Sweden
Ljusdal 85 C5 Gävleborg, C Sweden
Ljusnan 85 C5 river C Sweden
Llanelli 89 C6 prev. Llanelly. SW Wales, United Kingdom
Llanelly see Llanelli
Llanes 92 D1 Asturias, N Spain
Llanos 58 D2 physical region Colombia/Venezuela
Lleida 93 F2 Cast. Lérida; anc. Ilerda. Cataluña, NE Spain
Llucmajor 93 G3 Mallorca, Spain, W Mediterranean Sea
Loaíta Island 128 C8 island W Spratly Islands
Loanda see Luanda
Lobatse 78 C4 var. Lobatsi. Kgatleng, SE Botswana
Lobatsi see Lobatse
Löbau 94 D4 Sachsen, E Germany
Lobito 78 B2 Benguela, W Angola
Lob Nor see Lop Nur
Lobositz see Lovosice
Loburi see Lop Buri
Locarno 95 B8 Ger. Luggarus. Ticino, S Switzerland
Lochem 86 E3 Gelderland, E Netherlands
Lockport 41 E3 New York, NE USA
Lodja 77 D6 Kasai-Oriental, C Dem. Rep. Congo

Lodwar 73 C6 Rift Valley, NW Kenya
Łódź 98 D4 Rus. Lodz. Łódź, C Poland
Loei 136 C4 var. Loey, Muang Loei. Loei, C Thailand
Loey see Loei
Lofoten 84 B3 var. Lofoten Islands. island group C Norway
Lofoten Islands see Lofoten
Logan 44 B3 Utah, W USA
Logan, Mount 36 D3 mountain Yukon Territory, W Canada
Logroño 93 E1 anc. Vareia, Lat. Juliobriga. La Rioja, N Spain
Loibl Pass 95 D7 Ger. Loiblpass, Slvn. Ljubelj. pass Austria/Slovenia
Loiblpass see Loibl Pass
Loikaw 136 B4 Kayah State, C Burma (Myanmar)
Loire 90 B4 var. Liger. river C France
Loja 60 B2 Loja, S Ecuador
Lokitaung 73 C5 Rift Valley, NW Kenya
Lokoja 75 G4 Kogi, C Nigeria
Loksa 106 E2 Ger. Loxa. Harjumaa, NW Estonia
Lolland 85 B8 prev. Laaland. island S Denmark
Lom 104 C1 prev. Lom-Palanka. Montana, NW Bulgaria
Lomami 77 D6 river C Dem. Rep. Congo
Lomas 60 D4 Arequipa, SW Peru
Lomas de Zamora 64 D4 Buenos Aires, E Argentina
Lombardia 96 B2 Eng. Lombardy. region N Italy
Lombardy see Lombardia
Lombok, Pulau 138 D5 island Nusa Tenggara, C Indonesia
Lomé 75 F5 country capital (Togo) (Togo) S Togo
Lomela 77 D6 Kasai-Oriental, C Dem. Rep. Congo
Lommel 87 C5 Limburg, N Belgium
Lomond, Loch 88 B4 lake C Scotland, United Kingdom
Lomonosov Ridge 155 B3 var. Harris Ridge, Rus. Khrebet Homonsova. undersea feature Arctic Ocean
Lomonsova, Khrebet see Lomonosov Ridge
Lom-Palanka see Lom
Lompoc 47 B7 California, W USA
Lom Sak 136 C4 var. Muang Lom Sak. Phetchabun, C Thailand
Łomża 98 E3 Rus. Lomzha. Podlaskie, NE Poland
Lomzha see Łomża
Loncoche 65 B5 Araucanía, C Chile
Londinium see London
London 89 A7 anc. Augusta, Lat. Londinium. country capital (United Kingdom) (United Kingdom) SE England, United Kingdom
London 38 C5 Ontario, S Canada
London 40 C5 Kentucky, S USA
Londonderry 88 B4 var. Derry, Ir. Doire. NW Northern Ireland, United Kingdom
Londonderry, Cape 146 C2 cape Western Australia
Londrina 63 E4 Paraná, S Brazil
Lone Star State see Texas
Long Bay 43 F2 bay W Jamaica
Long Beach 47 C7 California, W USA
Longford 89 B5 Ir. An Longfort. Longford, C Ireland
Long Island 54 D2 island C Bahamas
Long Island 41 G4 island New York, NE USA
Longlac 38 C3 Ontario, S Canada
Longmont 44 C4 Colorado, C USA
Longreach 148 C4 Queensland, E Australia
Long Strait 115 G1 Eng. Long Strait. strait NE Russian Federation
Long Strait see Longa, Proliv
Longview 49 H3 Texas, SW USA
Longview 46 B2 Washington, NW USA
Long Xuyên 137 D6 var. Longxuyen. An Giang, S Vietnam
Longxuyen see Long Xuyên
Longyan 128 D6 Fujian, SE China
Longyearbyen 83 G2 dependent territory capital (Svalbard) Spitsbergen, W Svalbard
Lons-le-Saunier 90 D4 anc. Ledo Salinarius. Jura, E France
Lop Buri 137 C5 var. Loburi. Lop Buri, C Thailand

Lop Nor see Lop Nur
Lop Nur 126 C3 var. Lob Nor, Lop Nor, Lo-pu Po. seasonal lake NW China
Loppersum 86 E1 Groningen, NE Netherlands
Lo-pu Po see Lop Nur
Lorca 93 E4 Ar. Lurka; anc. Eliocroca, Lat. Illurco. Murcia, S Spain
Lord Howe Island 142 C4 island E Australia
Lord Howe Rise 142 C4 undersea rise SW Pacific Ocean
Loreto 50 B3 Baja California Sur, NW Mexico
Lorient 90 A3 prev. l'Orient. Morbihan, NW France
l'Orient see Lorient
Lorn, Firth of 88 B4 inlet W Scotland, United Kingdom
Loro Sae see East Timor
Lörrach 95 A7 Baden-Württemberg, S Germany
Lorraine 90 D3 cultural region NE France
Los Alamos 48 C1 New Mexico, SW USA
Los Amates 52 B2 Izabal, E Guatemala
Los Ángeles 65 B5 Bío Bío, C Chile
Los Angeles 47 C7 California, W USA
Losanna see Lausanne
Lošinj 100 A3 Ger. Lussin, It. Lussino. island W Croatia
Loslau see Wodzisław Śląski
Los Mochis 50 C3 Sinaloa, C Mexico
Losonc/Losontz see Lučenec
Los Roques, Islas 58 D1 island group N Venezuela
Lot 91 B5 cultural region S France
Lot 91 B5 river S France
Lotagipi Swamp 73 C5 wetland Kenya/Sudan
Lötzen see Giżycko
Loualaba see Lualaba
Louangnamtha 136 C3 var. Luong Nam Tha. Louang Namtha, N Laos
Louangphabang 124 D3 var. Louangphrabang, Luang Prabang. Louangphabang, N Laos
Louangphrabang see Louangphabang
Loubomo see Dolisie
Loudéac 90 A3 Côtes d'Armor, NW France
Loudi 128 C5 Hunan, S China
Louga 74 B3 NW Senegal
Louisiade Archipelago 144 B4 island group SE Papua New Guinea
Louisiana 42 A2 off. State of Louisiana, also known as Creole State, Pelican State. state S USA
Louisville 40 C5 Kentucky, S USA
Louisville Ridge 143 E4 undersea ridge S Pacific Ocean
Loup River 45 E4 river Nebraska, C USA
Lourdes 91 B6 Hautes-Pyrénées, S France
Lourenço Marques see Maputo
Louth 89 E5 E England, United Kingdom
Loutrá 104 C4 Kentrikí Makedonía, N Greece
Louvain see Leuven
Louvain-la-Neuve 87 C6 Walloon Brabant, C Belgium
Louviers 90 C3 Eure, N France
Lovech 104 C2 Lovech, N Bulgaria
Loveland 44 D4 Colorado, C USA
Lovosice 98 A4 Ger. Lobositz. Ústecký Kraj, NW Czech Republic
Lóvua 78 C1 Moxico, E Angola
Lowell 41 G3 Massachusetts, NE USA
Löwen see Leuven
Lower California see Baja California
Lower California Ridge see Baja California
Lower Hutt 151 D5 Wellington, North Island, New Zealand
Lower Lough Erne 89 A5 lake SW Northern Ireland, United Kingdom
Lower Red Lake 45 F1 Minnesota, N USA
Lower Rhine see Neder Rijn
Lower Tunguska 115 E3 Eng. Lower Tunguska. river N Russian Federation
Lower Tunguska see Nizhnyaya Tunguska
Lowestoft 89 E6 E England, United Kingdom
Loxa see Loksa
Lo-yang see Luoyang
Loyauté, Îles 144 D5 island group S New Caledonia

Loyev see Loyew
Loyew 107 D8 Rus. Loyev. Homyel'skaya Voblasts', SE Belarus
Loznica 100 C3 Serbia, W Serbia
Lu see Shandong, China
Lualaba 77 D6 Fr. Loualaba. river SE Dem. Rep. Congo
Luanda 78 A1 var. Loanda, Port. São Paulo de Loanda. country capital (Angola) Luanda, NW Angola
Luang Prabang see Louangphabang
Luang, Thale 137 C7 lagoon S Thailand
Luangua, Rio see Luangwa
Luangwa 73 B8 var. Aruângua, Rio Luangua. river Mozambique/Zambia
Luanshya 78 D2 Copperbelt, C Zambia
Luarca 92 C1 Asturias, N Spain
Lubaczów 99 E5 var. Lúbaczów. Podkarpackie, SE Poland
Lubang Islands 139 E1 island group N Philippines
Lubao 77 D6 Kasai-Oriental, C Dem. Rep. Congo
Lübben 94 D4 Brandenburg, E Germany
Lübbenau 94 D4 Brandenburg, E Germany
Lubbock 49 E2 Texas, SW USA
Lübeck 94 C2 Schleswig-Holstein, N Germany
Lubelska, Wyżyna 98 E4 plateau SE Poland
Lüben see Lubin
Lubiana see Ljubljana
Lubin 98 B4 Ger. Lüben. Dolnośląskie, SW Poland
Lublin 98 E4 Rus. Lyublin. Lubelskie, E Poland
Lubliniec 98 C4 Śląskie, S Poland
Lubnán, Jabal see Liban, Jebel
Lubny 109 F2 Poltavs'ka Oblast', NE Ukraine
Lubsko 94 B4 Ger. Sommerfeld. Lubuskie, W Poland
Lubumbashi 77 E8 prev. Élisabethville. Shaba, SE Dem. Rep. Congo
Lubutu 77 D6 Maniema, E Dem. Rep. Congo
Luca see Lucca
Lucan 89 B5 Ir. Leamhcán. Dublin, E Ireland
Lucania, Mount 36 C3 mountain Yukon Territory, W Canada
Lucania, Appennino 97 D5 Eng. Lucanian Mountains. mountain range S Italy
Lucanian Mountains see Lucano, Appennino
Lucapa 78 C1 var. Lukapa. Lunda Norte, NE Angola
Lucca 96 B3 anc. Luca. Toscana, C Italy
Lucea 54 A4 W Jamaica
Lucena 139 E1 off. Lucena City. Luzon, N Philippines
Lucena 92 D4 Andalucía, S Spain
Lucena City see Lucena
Lučenec 99 D6 Ger. Losontz, Hung. Losonc. Banskobystrický Kraj, C Slovakia
Lucentum see Alicante
Lucerna/Lucerne see Luzern
Luchow see Hefei
Łuck see Luts'k
Lucknow 135 E3 var. Lakhnau. state capital Uttar Pradesh, N India
Lüda see Dalian
Luda Kamchiya 104 D2 river E Bulgaria
Ludasch see Luduş
Ludus 108 B4 Ger. Ludasch, Hung. Marosludas. Mureş, C Romania
Ludvika 85 C6 Dalarna, C Sweden
Ludwigsburg 95 B6 Baden-Württemberg, SW Germany
Ludwigsfelde 94 D3 Brandenburg, NE Germany
Ludwigshafen 95 B5 var. Ludwigshafen am Rhein. Rheinland-Pfalz, SW Germany
Ludwigshafen am Rhein see Ludwigshafen

Ludwigslust 94 C3 Mecklenburg-Vorpommern, N Germany
Ludza 106 D4 Ger. Ludsan. Ludza, E Latvia
Luebo 77 C6 Kasai-Occidental, SW Dem. Rep. Congo
Luena 78 C2 var. Lwena, Port. Luso. Moxico, E Angola
Lufira 77 E7 river SE Dem. Rep. Congo
Lufkin 49 H3 Texas, SW USA
Luga 110 A4 Leningradskaya Oblast', NW Russian Federation
Lugano 95 B8 Ger. Lauis. Ticino, S Switzerland
Lugansk see Luhans'k
Lugdunum see Lyon
Lugdunum Batavorum see Leiden
Lugenda, Rio 79 E2 river N Mozambique
Luggarus see Locarno
Lugh Ganana see Luuq
Lugo 92 C1 anc. Lugus Augusti. Galicia, NW Spain
Lugoj 108 A4 Ger. Lugosch, Hung. Lugos. Timiş, W Romania
Lugos/Lugosch see Lugoj
Lugus Augusti see Lugo
Luguvallium/Luguvalium see Carlisle
Luhans'k 109 H3 Rus. Lugansk; prev. Voroshilovgrad. Luhans'ka Oblast', E Ukraine
Luimneach see Limerick
Lukapa see Lucapa
Lukenie 77 C6 river C Dem. Rep. Congo
Lukovit 104 C2 Lovech, N Bulgaria
Łuków 98 E4 Ger. Bogendorf. Lubelskie, E Poland
Lukuga 77 D7 river SE Dem. Rep. Congo
Luleå 84 D4 Norrbotten, N Sweden
Luleälven 84 C3 river N Sweden
Lulonga 77 C5 river NW Dem. Rep. Congo
Lulua 77 D7 river S Dem. Rep. Congo
Luluabourg see Kananga
Lumber State see Maine
Lumbo 79 F2 Nampula, NE Mozambique
Lumsden 151 A7 Southland, South Island, New Zealand
Lund 85 B7 Skåne, S Sweden
Lüneburg 94 C3 Niedersachsen, N Germany
Lunga, Isola see Dugi Otok
Lungkiang see Qiqihar
Lungué-Bungo 78 C2 var. Lungwebungu. river Angola/Zambia
Lungwebungu see Lungué-Bungo
Luninets see Luninyets
Luniniec see Luninyets
Luninyets 107 B7 Pol. Luniniec, Rus. Luninets. Brestskaya Voblasts', SW Belarus
Lunteren 86 D4 Gelderland, C Netherlands
Luong Nam Tha see Louangnamtha
Luoyang 128 C4 var. Honan, Lo-yang. Henan, C China
Lupatia see Altamura
Lúrio 79 F2 Nampula, NE Mozambique
Lúrio, Rio 79 E2 river NE Mozambique
Lurka see Lorca
Lusaka 78 D2 country capital (Zambia) (Zambia) Lusaka, SE Zambia
Lushnja see Lushnjë
Lushnjë 101 C6 var. Lushnja. Fier, C Albania
Luso see Luena
Lussin/Lussino see Lošinj
Lüt, Baḥrat/Lut, Bahret see Dead Sea
Lut, Dasht-e 120 D3 var. Kavir-e Lūt. desert E Iran
Lutetia/Lutetia Parisiorum see Paris
Lüt, Kavir-e see Lut, Dasht-e
Luton 89 D6 E England, United Kingdom
Łutselk'e 37 F4 prev. Snowdrift. Northwest Territories, W Canada
Luts'k 108 C2 Pol. Łuck, Rus. Lutsk. Volyns'ka Oblast', NW Ukraine
Lutsk see Luts'k
Lüttich see Liège
Lutzow-Holm Bay 154 C2 var. Lutzow-Holm Bay. bay Antarctica
Lutzow-Holm Bay see Lützow Holmbukta
Luuq 73 D6 It. Lugh Ganana. Gedo, SW Somalia
Luvua 77 D7 river SE Dem. Rep. Congo
Luwego 73 C8 river S Tanzania
Luxembourg 87 D8 country capital (Luxembourg) (Luxembourg) Luxembourg, S Luxembourg

Luxembourg 87 D8 off. Grand Duchy of Luxembourg, var. Lëtzebuerg, Luxemburg. country NW Europe

LUXEMBOURG
Northwest Europe

Official name Grand Duchy of Luxembourg
Formation 1867 / 1867
Capital Luxembourg-Ville
Population 480,222 / 481 people per sq mile (186 people per sq km) / 92%
Total area 998 sq. miles (2586 sq. km)
Languages French*, German*, Luxembourgish*
Religions Roman Catholic 97%, Protestant, Orthodox Christian, and Jewish 3%
Ethnic mix Luxembourger 62%, Foreign residents 38%
Government Parliamentary system
Currency Euro = 100 cents
Literacy rate 99%
Calorie consumption 3701 calories

Luxemburg see Luxembourg
Luxor 72 B2 Ar. Al Uqşur. E Egypt
Luza 110 C4 Kirovskaya Oblast', NW Russian Federation
Luz, Costa de la 92 C5 coastal region SW Spain
Luzern 95 B7 Fr. Lucerne, It. Lucerna. Luzern, C Switzerland
Luzon 139 E1 island N Philippines
Luzon Strait 125 E3 strait Philippines/Taiwan
L'viv 108 B2 Ger. Lemberg, Pol. Lwów, Rus. L'vov. L'vivs'ka Oblast', W Ukraine
L'vov see L'viv
Lwena see Luena
Lwów see L'viv
Lyakhavichy 107 B6 Rus. Lyakhovichi. Brestskaya Voblasts', SW Belarus
Lyakhovichi see Lyakhavichy
Lyallpur see Faisalābād
Lyangar see Langar
Lyck see Ełk
Lycksele 84 C4 Västerbotten, N Sweden
Lycopolis see Asyūţ
Lyel'chytsy 107 C7 Rus. Lel'chitsy. Homyel'skaya Voblasts', SE Belarus
Lyepyel' 107 D5 Rus. Lepel'. Vitsyebskaya Voblasts', N Belarus
Lyme Bay 89 C7 bay S England, United Kingdom
Lynchburg 41 E5 Virginia, NE USA
Lynn see King's Lynn
Lynn Lake 37 F4 Manitoba, C Canada
Lynn Regis see King's Lynn
Lyon 91 D5 Eng. Lyons; anc. Lugdunum. Rhône, E France
Lyons see Lyon
Lyozna 107 E6 Rus. Liozno. Vitsyebskaya Voblasts', NE Belarus
Lypovets' 108 D2 Rus. Lipovets. Vinnyts'ka Oblast', C Ukraine
Lys see Leie
Lysychans'k 109 H3 Rus. Lisichansk. Luhans'ka Oblast', E Ukraine
Lyttelton 151 C6 South Island, New Zealand
Lyublin see Lublin
Lyubotin see Lyubotyn
Lyubotyn 109 G2 Rus. Lyubotin. Kharkivs'ka Oblast', E Ukraine
Lyulyakovo 104 E2 prev. Keremitlik. Burgas, E Bulgaria
Lyusina 107 B6 Rus. Lyusino. Brestskaya Voblasts', SW Belarus
Lyusino see Lyusina

M

Maale see Male'
Ma'ān 119 B7 Ma'än, SW Jordan
Maardu 106 D2 Ger. Maart. Harjumaa, NW Estonia
Ma'aret-en-Nu'man see Ma'arrat an Nu'mān
Ma'arrat an Nu'mān 118 B3 var. Ma'aret-en-Nu'man, Fr. Maarret enn Naamâne. Idlib, NW Syria
Maarret enn Naamâne see Ma'arrat an Nu'mân

Maart see Maardu
Maas see Meuse
Maaseik 87 D5 prev. Maeseyck. Limburg, NE Belgium
Maastricht 87 D6 var. Maestricht; anc. Traiectum ad Mosam, Traiectum Tungorum. Limburg, SE Netherlands
Macao 129 C6 Chin. Aomen, Port. Macau. Guangdong, SE China
Macapá 63 E1 state capital Amapá, N Brazil
Macarscra see Makarska
Macassar see Makassar
Macāu see Makó, Hungary
Macau see Macao
MacCluer Gulf see Berau, Teluk
Macdonnell Ranges 146 D4 mountain range Northern Territory, C Australia
Macedonia see Macedonia, FYR
Macedonia, FYR 101 D6 off. the Former Yugoslav Republic of Macedonia, var. Macedonia, Mac. Makedonija, abbrev. FYR Macedonia, FYROM. country SE Europe

MACEDONIA
Southeast Europe

Official name Republic of Macedonia
Formation 1991 / 1991
Capital Skopje
Population 2 million / 201 people per sq mile (78 people per sq km) / 60%
Total area 9781 sq. miles (25,333 sq. km)
Languages Macedonian*, Albanian*, Turkish, Romani, Serbian
Religions Orthodox Christian 59%, Muslim 26%, Other 10%, Roman Catholic 4%, Protestant 1%
Ethnic mix Macedonian 64%, Albanian 25%, Turkish 4%, Roma 3%, Other 2%, Serb 2%
Government Mixed presidential–parliamentary system
Currency Macedonian denar = 100 deni
Literacy rate 96%
Calorie consumption 2655 calories

Macedonia, the Former Yugoslav Republic of see Macedonia, FYR
Maceió 63 G3 state capital Alagoas, E Brazil
Machachi 60 B1 Pichincha, C Ecuador
Machala 60 B2 El Oro, SW Ecuador
Machanga 79 E3 Sofala, E Mozambique
Machilipatnam 132 D1 var. Bandar Masulipatnam. Andhra Pradesh, E India
Machiques 58 C2 Zulia, NW Venezuela
Macías Nguema Biyogo see Bioco, Isla de
Măcin 108 D5 Tulcea, SE Romania
Mackay 148 D4 Queensland, NE Australia
Mackay, Lake 146 C4 salt lake Northern Territory/Western Australia
Mackenzie 37 E3 river Northwest Territories, NW Canada
Mackenzie Bay 154 D3 bay Antarctica
Mackenzie Mountains 36 D3 mountain range Northwest Territories, NW Canada
Macleod, Lake 146 A4 lake Western Australia
Macomb 40 A4 Illinois, N USA
Macomer 97 A5 Sardegna, Italy, C Mediterranean Sea
Mâcon 91 D5 anc. Matisco, Matisco Ædourum. Saône-et-Loire, C France
Macon 42 D2 Georgia, SE USA
Macon 45 G4 Missouri, C USA
Macquarie Ridge 154 C5 undersea ridge SW Pacific Ocean
Macuspana 51 G4 Tabasco, SE Mexico
Ma'dabā 119 B6 var. Mādabā, Madeba; anc. Medeba. Ma'dabā, NW Jordan
Mādabā see Ma'dabā
Madagascar 79 F3 off. Democratic Republic of Madagascar, Malg. Madagasikara; prev. Malagasy Republic. country W Indian Ocean

MADAGASCAR
Indian Ocean

Official name Republic of Madagascar
Formation 1960 / 1960
Capital Antananarivo

MADAGASCAR
(continued)

Population 19.6 million / 87 people per sq mile (34 people per sq km) / 27%
Total area 226,656 sq. miles (587,040 sq. km)
Languages French*, Malagasy*, English*
Religions Traditional beliefs 52%, Christian (mainly Roman Catholic) 41%, Muslim 7%
Ethnic mix Other Malay 46%, Merina 26%, Betsimisaraka 15%, Betsileo 12%, Other 1%
Government Presidential system
Currency Ariary = 5 iraimbilanja
Literacy rate 71%
Calorie consumption 2005 calories

Madagascar 79 F3 island W Indian Ocean
Madagascar Basin 69 E7 undersea basin W Indian Ocean
Madagascar, Democratic Republic of see Madagascar
Madagascar Plateau 69 E7 var. Madagascar Ridge, Madagascar Rise, Rus. Madagaskarskiy Khrebet. undersea plateau W Indian Ocean
Madagascar Rise/Madagascar Ridge see Madagascar Plateau
Madagasikara see Madagascar
Madagaskarskiy Khrebet see Madagascar Plateau
Madang 144 B3 Madang, N Papua New Guinea
Madaniyin see Médenine
Madarska see Hungary
Made 86 C4 Noord-Brabant, S Netherlands
Madeba see Ma'dabā
Madeira 70 A2 var. Ilha da Madeira. island Madeira, Portugal, NE Atlantic Ocean
Madeira, Ilha de see Madeira
Madeira Plain 66 C3 abyssal plain E Atlantic Ocean
Madeira, Rio 62 D2 var. Río Madera. river Bolivia/Brazil
Madeleine, Îles de la 39 F4 Eng. Magdalen Islands. island group Québec, E Canada
Madera 47 B6 California, W USA
Madera, Río see Madeira, Rio
Madhya Pradesh 135 E4 prev. Central Provinces and Berar. cultural region C India
Madinat ath Thawrah 118 C2 var. Ath Thawrah. Ar Raqqah, N Syria
Madioen see Madiun
Madison 45 F3 South Dakota, N USA
Madison 40 B3 state capital Wisconsin, N USA
Madiun 138 D5 prev. Madioen. Jawa, C Indonesia
Madoera see Madura, Pulau
Madona 106 D4 Ger. Modohn. Madona, E Latvia
Madras see Chennai
Madras see Tamil Nādu
Madre de Dios, Río 61 E3 river Bolivia/Peru
Madre del Sur, Sierra 51 E5 mountain range S Mexico
Madre, Laguna 51 F3 lagoon NE Mexico
Madre, Laguna 49 G5 lagoon Texas, SW USA
Madre Occidental, Sierra 50 C3 var. Western Sierra Madre. mountain range C Mexico
Madre Oriental, Sierra 51 E3 var. Eastern Sierra Madre. mountain range C Mexico
Madre, Sierra 52 B2 var. Sierra de Soconusco. mountain range Guatemala/Mexico
Madrid 92 D3 country capital (Spain) (Spain) Madrid, C Spain
Madura see Madurai
Madurai 132 C3 prev. Madura, Mathurai. Tamil Nādu, S India
Madura, Pulau 138 D5 prev. Madoera. island C Indonesia
Maebashi 131 D5 var. Maebasi, Mayebashi. Gunma, Honshū, S Japan
Maebasi see Maebashi

Mae Nam Khong *see* Mekong
Mae Nam Nan 136 C4 *river* NW Thailand
Mae Nam Yom 136 C4 *river* W Thailand
Maeseyck *see* Maaseik
Maestricht *see* Maastricht
Maéwo 144 D4 *prev.* Aurora. *island* C Vanuatu
Mafia 73 D7 *island* E Tanzania
Mafraq/Muḥāfaẓat al Mafraq *see* Al Mafraq
Magadan 115 G3 Magadanskaya Oblast', E Russian Federation
Magallanes *see* Punta Arenas
Magallanes, Estrecho de *see* Magellan, Strait of
Magangué 58 B2 Bolívar, N Colombia
Magdalena 61 F3 Beni, N Bolivia
Magdalena 50 B1 Sonora, NW Mexico
Isla Magdalena 50 B3 *island* NW Mexico
Magdalena, Río 58 B2 *river* C Colombia
Magdalen Islands *see* Madeleine, Îles de la
Magdeburg 94 C4 Sachsen-Anhalt, C Germany
Magelang 138 C5 Jawa, C Indonesia
Magellan, Strait of 65 B8 *Sp.* Estrecho de Magallanes. *strait* Argentina/Chile
Mageroy *see* Magerøya
Mageroya 84 D1 *var.* Magerøy, *Lapp.* Máhkarávju. *island* N Norway
Maggiore, Lago *see* Maggiore, Lake
Maggiore, Lake 96 B1 *It.* Lago Maggiore. *lake* Italy/Switzerland
Maglaj 100 C3 Federacija Bosna I Hercegovina, N Bosnia and Herzegovina
Maglie 97 E6 Puglia, SE Italy
Magna 44 B4 Utah, W USA
Magnesia *see* Manisa
Magnitogorsk 114 B4 Chelyabinskaya Oblast', C Russian Federation
Magnolia State *see* Mississippi
Magta' Lahjar 74 C3 *var.* Magta Lahjar, Magta' Lahjar, Magtá Lahjar. Brakna, SW Mauritania
Magway 136 A3 *var.* Magwe. Magway, W Burma (Myanmar)
Magyar-Becse *see* Bečej
Magyarkanizsa *see* Kanjiža
Magyarország *see* Hungary
Mahajanga 79 F2 *var.* Majunga. Mahajanga, NW Madagascar
Mahakam, Sungai 138 D4 *var.* Koetai, Kutai. *river* Borneo, C Indonesia
Mahalapye 78 D3 *var.* Mahalatswe. Central, SE Botswana
Mahalatswe *see* Mahalapye
Māhān 120 D3 Kermān, E Iran
Mahanádi 135 F4 *river* E India
Mahārāshtra 134 D5 *cultural region* W India
Mahbés *see* El Mahbas
Mahbūbnagar 134 D5 Andhra Pradesh, C India
Mahdia 71 F2 *var.* Al Mahdīyah, Mehdia. NE Tunisia
Mahé 79 H1 *island* Inner Islands, NE Seychelles
Mahia Peninsula 150 E4 *peninsula* North Island, New Zealand
Mahilyow 107 D6 *Rus.* Mogilëv. Mahilyowskaya Voblasts', E Belarus
Máhkarávju *see* Mageroya
Mahmūd-e 'Erāqī *see* Maḥmūd-e Rāqī
Maḥmūd-e Rāqī 123 E4 *var.* Maḥmūd-e 'Erāqī. Kāpīsā, NE Afghanistan
Mahón 93 H3 *Cat.* Maó, *Eng.* Port Mahon; *anc.* Portus Magonis. Menorca, Spain, W Mediterranean Sea
Mähren *see* Moravia
Mährisch-Weisskirchen *see* Hranice
Maicao 58 C1 La Guajira, N Colombia
Mai Ceu/Mai Chio *see* Maych'ew
Maidstone 89 E7 SE England, United Kingdom
Maiduguri 75 H4 Borno, NE Nigeria
Mailand *see* Milano
Maimāna *see* Meymaneh
Main 95 B5 *river* C Germany
Mai-Ndombe, Lac 77 C6 *prev.* Lac Léopold II. *lake* W Dem. Rep. Congo
Maine 41 G2 *off.* State of Maine, *also known as* Lumber State, Pine Tree State. *state* NE USA
Maine 90 B3 *cultural region* NW France
Maine, Gulf of 41 H2 *gulf* NE USA

Mainland 88 C2 *island* N Scotland, United Kingdom
Mainland 88 D1 *island* NE Scotland, United Kingdom
Mainz 95 B5 *Fr.* Mayence. Rheinland-Pfalz, SW Germany
Maio 74 A3 *var.* Mayo. *island* Ilhas de Sotavento, SE Cape Verde
Maisur *see* Karnātaka, India
Maisur *see* Mysore, India
Maizhokunggar 126 C5 Xizang Zizhiqu, W China
Majorca 93 G3 *Eng.* Majorca; *anc.* Baleares Major. *island* Islas Baleares, Spain, W Mediterranean Sea
Majorca *see* Mallorca
Mājro *see* Majuro Atoll
Majunga *see* Mahajanga
Majuro Atoll 144 D2 *var.* Mājro. *atoll* Ratak Chain, SE Marshall Islands
Makale *see* Mek'elē
Makarov Basin 155 B3 *undersea basin* Arctic Ocean
Makarska 100 B4 *It.* Macarsca. Split-Dalmacija, SE Croatia
Makasar *see* Makassar
Makasar, Selat *see* Makassar Straits
Makassar 139 E4 *var.* Macassar, Makasar; *prev.* Ujungpandang. Sulawesi, C Indonesia
Makassar Straits 138 D4 *Ind.* Makasar Selat. *strait* C Indonesia
Makay 79 F3 *var.* Massif du Makay. *mountain range* SW Madagascar
Makay, Massif du *see* Makay
Makedonija *see* Macedonia, FYR
Makeni 74 C4 C Sierra Leone
Makeyevka *see* Makiyivka
Makhachkala 114 A4 *prev.* Petrovsk-Port. Respublika Dagestan, SW Russian Federation
Makin 144 D2 *prev.* Pitt Island. *atoll* Tungaru, W Kiribati
Makira *see* San Cristobal
Makiyivka 109 G3 *Rus.* Makeyevka; *prev.* Dmitriyevsk. Donets'ka Oblast', E Ukraine
Makkah 121 A5 *Eng.* Mecca. Makkah, W Saudi Arabia
Makkovik 39 F2 Newfoundland and Labrador, NE Canada
Makó 99 D7 *Rom.* Macău. Csongrád, SE Hungary
Makoua 77 B5 Cuvette, C Congo
Makran Coast 120 E4 *coastal region* SE Iran
Makrany 107 A6 *Rus.* Mokrany. Brestskaya Voblasts', SW Belarus
Mākū 120 B2 Āzarbāyjān-e Gharbī, NW Iran
Makurdi 75 G4 Benue, C Nigeria
Mala *see* Malaita, Solomon Islands
Malabār Coast 132 B3 *coast* SW India
Malabo 71 A5 *prev.* Santa Isabel. *country capital* (Equatorial Guinea) (Equatorial Guinea) Isla de Bioco, NW Equatorial Guinea
Malaca *see* Málaga
Malacca, Strait of 138 B3 *Ind.* Selat Malaka. *strait* Indonesia/Malaysia
Malacka *see* Malacky
Malacky 99 C6 Hung. Malacka. Bratislavský Kraj, W Slovakia
Maladzyechna 107 C5 Pol. Molodeczno, Rus. Molodechno. Minskaya Voblasts', C Belarus
Málaga 92 D5 *anc.* Malaca. Andalucía, S Spain
Malagarasi River 73 B7 *river* W Tanzania Africa
Malagasy Republic *see* Madagascar
Malaita 144 C3 *var.* Mala. *island* N Solomon Islands
Malakal 73 B5 Upper Nile, S Sudan
Malakula *see* Malekula
Malang 138 D5 Jawa, C Indonesia
Malange *see* Malanje
Malanje 78 B1 *var.* Malange. Malanje, NW Angola
Mälaren 85 C6 *lake* C Sweden
Malatya 117 E4 *anc.* Melitene. Malatya, SE Turkey
Mala Vyska 109 E3 *Rus.* Malaya Viska. Kirovohrads'ka Oblast', S Ukraine
Malawi 79 E1 *off.* Republic of Malaŵi; *prev.* Nyasaland, Nyasaland Protectorate. *country* S Africa

MALAWI
Southern Africa

Official name Republic of Malawi
Formation 1964 / 1964
Capital Lilongwe
Population 13.5 million / 372 people per sq mile (143 people per sq km) / 17%
Total area 45,745 sq. miles (118,480 sq. km)
Languages English*, Chewa, Lomwe, Yao, Ngoni
Religions Protestant 55%, Roman Catholic 20%, Muslim 20%, Traditional beliefs 5%
Ethnic mix Bantu 99%, Other 1%
Government Presidential system
Currency Malawi kwacha = 100 tambala
Literacy rate 64%
Calorie consumption 2155 calories

Malawi, Lake *see* Nyasa, Lake
Malaŵi, Republic of *see* Malawi
Malaya Viska *see* Mala Vyska
Malay Peninsula 124 D4 *peninsula* Malaysia/Thailand
Malaysia 138 B3 *off.* Malaysia, *var.* Federation of Malaysia; *prev.* the separate territories of Federation of Malaya, Sarawak and Sabah (North Borneo) and Singapore. *country* SE Asia

MALAYSIA
Southeast Asia

Official name Malaysia
Formation 1963 / 1965
Capital Kuala Lumpur; Putrajaya (administrative)
Population 26.2 million / 207 people per sq mile (80 people per sq km) / 64%
Total area 127,316 sq. miles (329,750 sq. km)
Languages Bahasa Malaysia*, Malay, Chinese, Tamil, English
Religions Muslim (mainly Sunni) 53%, Buddhist 19%, Chinese faiths 12%, Other 7%, Christian 7%, Traditional beliefs 2%
Ethnic mix Malay 50%, Chinese 25%, Indigenous tribes 11%, Other 7%, Indian 7%
Government Parliamentary system
Currency Ringgit = 100 sen
Literacy rate 89%
Calorie consumption 2881 calories

Malaysia, Federation of *see* Malaysia
Malbork 98 C2 *Ger.* Marienburg, Marienburg in Westpreussen. Pomorskie, N Poland
Malchin 94 C3 Mecklenburg-Vorpommern, N Germany
Malden 45 H5 Missouri, C USA
Malden Island 145 G3 *prev.* Independence Island. *atoll* E Kiribati
Maldives 132 A4 *off.* Maldivian Divehi, Republic of Maldives. *country* N Indian Ocean

MALDIVES
Indian Ocean

Official name Republic of Maldives
Formation 1965 / 1965
Capital Male'
Population 369,031 / 3181 people per sq mile (1230 people per sq km) / 29%
Total area 116 sq. miles (300 sq. km)
Languages Dhivehi (Maldivian)*, Sinhala, Tamil, Arabic
Religions Sunni Muslim 100%
Ethnic mix Arab-Sinhalese-Malay 100%
Government Presidential system
Currency Rufiyaa = 100 laari
Literacy rate 96%
Calorie consumption 2548 calories

Maldives, Republic of *see* Maldives
Maldivian Divehi *see* Maldives
Male' 132 B4 *Div.* Maale. *country capital* (Maldives) (Maldives) Male' Atoll, C Maldives
Male' Atoll 132 B4 *var.* Kaafu Atoll. *atoll* C Maldives
Malekula 144 C4 *var.* Malakula; *prev.* Mallicolo. *island* W Vanuatu

Malesína 105 C5 Stereá Ellás, E Greece
Malheur Lake 46 C3 *lake* Oregon, NW USA
Mali 75 E3 *off.* Republic of Mali, *Fr.* République du Mali; *prev.* French Sudan, Sudanese Republic. *country* W Africa

MALI
West Africa

Official name Republic of Mali
Formation 1960 / 1960
Capital Bamako
Population 14.3 million / 30 people per sq mile (12 people per sq km) / 33%
Total area 478,764 sq. miles (1,240,000 sq. km)
Languages French*, Bambara, Fulani, Senufo, Soninke
Religions Muslim (mainly Sunni) 80%, Traditional beliefs 18%, Christian 1%, Other 1%
Ethnic mix Bambara 32%, Other 26%, Fulani 14%, Senufo 12%, Soninka 9%, Tuareg 7%
Government Presidential system
Currency CFA franc = 100 centimes
Literacy rate 19%
Calorie consumption 2174 calories

Malik, Wadi al *see* Milk, Wadi el
Mali Kyun 137 B5 *var.* Tavoy Island. *island* Mergui Archipelago, S Burma (Myanmar)
Malin *see* Malyn
Malindi 73 D7 Coast, SE Kenya
Malines *see* Mechelen
Mali, Republic of *see* Mali
Mali, République du *see* Mali
Malkiye *see* Al Mālikīyah
Malko Túrnovo 104 E3 Burgas, E Bulgaria
Mallaig 88 B3 N Scotland, United Kingdom
Mallawī 72 B2 *var.* Mallawi. C Egypt
Mallawi *see* Mallawī
Mallicolo *see* Malekula
Malmberget 84 C3 *Lapp.* Malmivaara. Norrbotten, N Sweden
Malmédy 87 D6 Liège, E Belgium
Malmivaara *see* Malmberget
Malmö 85 B7 Skåne, S Sweden
Maloelap *see* Maloelap Atoll
Maloelap Atoll 144 D1 *var.* Maḷoeḷap. *atoll* E Marshall Islands
Małopolska, Wyżyna 98 D4 *plateau* S Poland
Malozemel'skaya Tundra 110 D3 *physical region* NW Russian Federation
Malta 106 D4 Rēzekne, SE Latvia
Malta 44 C1 Montana, NW USA
Malta 97 C8 *off.* Republic of Malta. *country* C Mediterranean Sea

MALTA
Southern Europe

Official name Republic of Malta
Formation 1964 / 1964
Capital Valletta
Population 401,880 / 3241 people per sq mile (1256 people per sq km) / 92%
Total area 122 sq. miles (316 sq. km)
Languages Maltese*, English*
Religions Roman Catholic 98%, Other and nonreligious 2%
Ethnic mix Maltese 96%, Other 4%
Government Parliamentary system
Currency Euro = 100 cents
Literacy rate 88%
Calorie consumption 3587 calories

Malta 97 C8 *island* Malta, C Mediterranean Sea
Malta, Canale di *see* Malta Channel
Malta Channel 97 C8 *It.* Canale di Malta. *strait* Italy/Malta
Malta, Republic of *see* Malta
Maluku, Laut *see* Molucca Sea
Malung 85 B6 Dalarna, C Sweden
Malventum *see* Benevento
Malvinas, Islas *see* Falkland Islands
Malyn 108 D2 *Rus.* Malin. Zhytomyrs'ka Oblast', N Ukraine
Malyy Kavkaz *see* Lesser Caucasus

Mamberamo, Sungai *139 H4 river* Papua, E Indonesia
Mambij *see* Manbij
Mamonovo *106 A4 Ger.* Heiligenbeil. Kaliningradskaya Oblast', W Russian Federation
Mamoré, Rio *61 F3 river* Bolivia/Brazil
Mamou *74 C4* W Guinea
Mamoudzou *79 F2 dependent territory capital* (Mayotte) C Mayotte
Mamuno *78 C3* Ghanzi, W Botswana
Manacor *93 G3* Mallorca, Spain, W Mediterranean Sea
Manado *139 F3 prev.* Menado. Sulawesi, C Indonesia
Managua *52 D3 country capital* (Nicaragua) (Nicaragua) Managua, W Nicaragua
Managua, Lake *52 C3 var.* Xolotlán. *lake* W Nicaragua
Manakara *79 G4* Fianarantsoa, SE Madagascar
Manama *see* Al Manāmah
Mananjary *79 G3* Fianarantsoa, SE Madagascar
Manáos *see* Manaus
Manapouri, Lake *151 A7 lake* South Island, New Zealand
Manar *see* Mannar
Manas, Gora *123 E2 mountain* Kyrgyzstan/Uzbekistan
Manaus *62 D2 prev.* Manáos. *state capital* Amazonas, NW Brazil
Manavgat *116 B4* Antalya, SW Turkey
Manbij *118 C2 var.* Mambij, Fr. Membidj. Ḥalab, N Syria
Manchester *89 D5 Lat.* Mancunium. NW England, United Kingdom
Manchester *41 G3* New Hampshire, NE USA
Man-chou-li *see* Manzhouli
Manchurian Plain *125 E1 plain* NE China
Mâncio Lima *see* Japiim
Mancunium *see* Manchester
Mand *see* Mand, Rūd-e
Mandalay *136 B3* Mandalay, C Burma (Myanmar)
Mandan *45 E2* North Dakota, N USA
Mandeville *54 B5* C Jamaica
Mándra *105 C6* Attikí, C Greece
Rud-e Mand *120 D4 var.* Mand. *river* S Iran
Mandurah *147 A6* Western Australia
Manduria *97 E5* Puglia, SE Italy
Mandya *132 C2* Karnātaka, C India
Manfredonia *97 D5* Puglia, SE Italy
Mangai *77 C6* Bandundu, W Dem. Rep. Congo
Mangaia *145 G5 island group* S Cook Islands
Mangalia *108 D5 anc.* Callatis. Constanţa, SE Romania
Mangalmé *76 C3* Guéra, SE Chad
Mangalore *132 B2* Karnātaka, W India
Mangaung *see* Bloemfontein
Mango *see* Sansanné-Mango, Togo
Mangoky *79 F3 river* W Madagascar
Manhattan *45 F4* Kansas, C USA
Manicouagan, Réservoir *38 D3 lake* Québec, E Canada
Manihiki *145 G4 atoll* N Cook Islands
Manihiki Plateau *143 E3 undersea plateau* C Pacific Ocean
Maniitsoq *82 C3 var.* Manîtsoq, *Dan.* Sukkertoppen. Kitaa, S Greenland
Manila *139 E1 off.* City of Manila. *country capital* (Philippines) (Philippines) Luzon, N Philippines
Manila, City of *see* Manila
Manisa *116 A3 var.* Manissa, *prev.* Saruhan; *anc.* Magnesia. Manisa, W Turkey
Manissa *see* Manisa
Manitoba *37 F5 province* S Canada
Manitoba, Lake *37 F5 lake* Manitoba, S Canada
Manitoulin Island *38 C4 island* Ontario, S Canada
Manîtsoq *see* Maniitsoq
Manizales *58 B3* Caldas, W Colombia
Manjimup *147 A7* Western Australia
Mankato *45 F3* Minnesota, N USA
Manlleu *93 G2* Cataluña, NE Spain
Manly *148 E1* Iowa, C USA
Manmād *134 C5* Mahārāshtra, W India
Mannar *132 C3 var.* Manar. Northern Province, NW Sri Lanka

Mannar, Gulf of *132 C3 gulf* India/ Sri Lanka
Mannheim *95 B5* Baden-Württemberg, SW Germany
Manono *77 E7* Shaba, SE Dem. Rep. Congo
Manosque *91 D6* Alpes-de-Haute-Provence, SE France
Manra *145 F3 prev.* Sydney Island. *atoll* Phoenix Islands, C Kiribati
Mansa *78 D2 prev.* Fort Rosebery. Luapula, N Zambia
Mansel Island *37 G3 island* Nunavut, NE Canada
Mansfield *40 D4* Ohio, N USA
Manta *60 A2* Manabí, W Ecuador
Manteca *47 B6* California, W USA
Mantoue *see* Mantova
Mantova *96 B2 Eng.* Mantua, *Fr.* Mantoue. Lombardia, NW Italy
Mantua *see* Mantova
Manuae *145 G4 island* S Cook Islands
Manukau *see* Manurewa
Manurewa *150 D3 var.* Manukau. Auckland, North Island, New Zealand
Manzanares *93 E3* Castilla-La Mancha, C Spain
Manzanillo *54 C3* Granma, E Cuba
Manzanillo *50 D4* Colima, SW Mexico
Manzhouli *127 F1 var.* Man-chou-li. Nei Mongol Zizhiqu, N China
Mao *76 B3* Kanem, W Chad
Maó *see* Mahón
Maoke, Pegunungan *139 H4 Dut.* Sneeuw-gebergte, *Eng.* Snow Mountains. *mountain range* Papua, E Indonesia
Maoming *128 C6* Guangdong, S China
Mapmaker Seamounts *125 H2 seamount range* N Pacific Ocean
Maputo *78 D4 prev.* Lourenço Marques. *country capital* (Mozambique) (Mozambique) Maputo, S Mozambique
Marabá *63 F2* Pará, NE Brazil
Maracaibo *58 C1* Zulia, NW Venezuela
Maracaibo, Gulf of *see* Venezuela, Golfo de
Maracaibo, Lake *58 C2 var.* Lake Maracaibo. *inlet* NW Venezuela
Maracaibo, Lake *see* Maracaibo, Lago de
Maracay *58 D2* Aragua, N Venezuela
Marada *see* Marādah
Marādah *71 G3 var.* Marada. N Libya
Maradi *75 G3* Maradi, S Niger
Maragha *see* Marāgheh
Marāgheh *120 C2 var.* Maragha. Āzarbāyjān-e Khāvarī, NW Iran
Marajó, Baía de *61 F1 bay* N Brazil
Marajó, Ilha de *63 E1 island* N Brazil
Marakesh *see* Marrakech
Maramba *see* Livingstone
Maramba *see* Livingstone
Maranhão *63 F2 off.* Estado do Maranhão. *region* E Brazil
Maranhão *63 F2 off.* Estado do Maranhão. *state* E Brazil
Maranhão, Estado do *see* Maranhão
Marañón, Río *60 B2 river* N Peru
Marathon *38 C4* Ontario, S Canada
Marathón *see* Marathónas
Marathónas *105 C5 prev.* Marathón. Attikí, C Greece
Mārāzā *117 H2 Rus.* Maraza. E Azerbaijan
Maraza *see* Mārāzā
Marbella *93 D5* Andalucía, S Spain
Marble Bar *146 B4* Western Australia
Marburg *see* Marburg an der Lahn, Germany
Marburg *see* Maribor, Slovenia
Marburg an der Lahn *94 B4 hist.* Marburg. Hessen, W Germany
March *see* Morava
Marche *96 C3 Eng.* Marches. C Italy
Marche *91 C5 cultural region* C France
Marche-en-Famenne *87 C7* Luxembourg, SE Belgium
Marchena, Isla *60 B5 var.* Bindloe Island. *island* Galapagos Islands, Ecuador, E Pacific Ocean
Marches *see* Marche
Mar Chiquita, Laguna *64 C3 lake* C Argentina
Marcounda *see* Markounda
Mardān *134 C1* North-West Frontier Province, N Pakistan

Mar del Plata *65 D5* Buenos Aires, E Argentina
Mardin *117 E4* Mardin, SE Turkey
Maré *144 D5 island* Îles Loyauté, E New Caledonia
Marea Neagrǎ *see* Black Sea
Mareeba *148 D3* Queensland, NE Australia
Marek *see* Dupnitsa
Margarets *see* Marhanets'
Margarita, Isla de *59 E1 island* N Venezuela
Margate *89 E7 prev.* Mergate. SE England, United Kingdom
Margherita *see* Jamaame
Margherita, Lake *73 C5 Eng.* Lake Margherita, *It.* Abbaia. *lake* SW Ethiopia
Margherita, Lake *see* Ābaya Hāyk'
Marghita *108 B3 Hung.* Margitta. Bihor, NW Romania
Margitta *see* Marghita
Marhanets' *109 F3 Rus.* Marganets. Dnipropetrovs'ka Oblast', E Ukraine
María Cleofas, Isla *50 C4 island* C Mexico
Maria Island *149 C8 island* Tasmania, SE Australia
María Madre, Isla *50 C4 island* C Mexico
María Magdalena, Isla *50 C4 island* C Mexico
Mariana Trench *125 G4 var.* Challenger Deep. *trench* W Pacific Ocean
Mariánské Lázně *99 A5 Ger.* Marienbad. Karlovarský Kraj, W Czech Republic
Marías, Islas *50 C4 island group* C Mexico
Maria-Theresiopel *see* Subotica
Maribor *95 E7 Ger.* Marburg. NE Slovenia
Marica *see* Maritsa
Maridi *73 B5* Western Equatoria, SW Sudan
Marie Byrd Land *154 A3 physical region* Antarctica
Marie-Galante *55 G4 var.* Ceyre to the Caribs. *island* SE Guadeloupe
Marienbad *see* Mariánské Lázně
Marienburg *see* Alūksne, Latvia
Marienburg *see* Malbork, Poland
Marienburg in Westpreussen *see* Malbork
Marienhausen *see* Viļaka
Mariental *78 B4* Hardap, SW Namibia
Marienwerder *see* Kwidzyń
Mariestad *85 B6* Västra Götaland, S Sweden
Marietta *42 D2* Georgia, SE USA
Marijampolė *106 B4 prev.* Kapsukas. Marijampolė, S Lithuania
Marília *63 E4* São Paulo, S Brazil
Marín *92 B1* Galicia, NW Spain
Mar'ina Gorka *see* Mar"ina Horka
Mar"ina Horka *107 C6 Rus.* Mar'ina Gorka. Minskaya Voblasts', C Belarus
Maringá *63 E4* Paraná, S Brazil
Marion *45 G3* Iowa, C USA
Marion *40 D4* Ohio, N USA
Marion, Lake *43 E2 reservoir* South Carolina, SE USA
Mariscal Estigarribia *64 D2* Boquerón, NW Paraguay
Maritsa *104 D3 var.* Marica, *Gk.* Évros, *Turk.* Meriç; *anc.* Hebrus. *river* SW Europe
Maritzburg *see* Pietermaritzburg
Mariupol' *109 G4 prev.* Zhdanov. Donets'ka Oblast', SE Ukraine
Marka *73 D6 var.* Merca. Shabeellaha Hoose, S Somalia
Markham, Mount *154 B4 mountain* Antarctica
Markounda *76 C4 var.* Marcounda. Ouham, NW Central African Republic
Marktredwitz *95 C5* Bayern, E Germany
Marlborough *148 D4* Queensland, E Australia
Marmanda *see* Marmande
Marmande *91 B5 anc.* Marmanda. Lot-et-Garonne, SW France
Marmara, Sea of *see* Marmara Denizi
Marmaris *116 A4* Muğla, SW Turkey
Marne *90 D3 cultural region* N France
Marne *90 D3 river* N France
Maro *76 C4* Moyen-Chari, S Chad
Maroantsetra *79 G2* Toamasina, NE Madagascar

Maromokotro *79 G2 mountain* N Madagascar
Maroni *59 G3 Dut.* Marowijne. *river* French Guiana/Suriname
Marosheviz *see* Toplița
Marosludas *see* Luduş
Marosvásárhely *see* Târgu Mureş
Marotiri *143 F4 anc.* Îlots de Bass, Morotiri. *island group* Îles Australes, SW French Polynesia
Maroua *76 B3* Extrême-Nord, N Cameroon
Marowijne *see* Maroni
Marquesas Fracture Zone *153 E3 fracture zone* E Pacific Ocean
Marquette *40 B1* Michigan, N USA
Marrakech *70 C2 var.* Marakesh, *Eng.* Marrakesh; *prev.* Morocco. W Morocco
Marrakesh *see* Marrakech
Marrawah *149 C8* Tasmania, SE Australia
Marree *149 B5* South Australia
Marsá al Burayqah *71 G3 var.* Al Burayqah. N Libya
Marsabit *73 C6* Eastern, N Kenya
Marsala *97 B7 anc.* Lilybaeum. Sicilia, Italy, C Mediterranean Sea
Marsberg *94 B4* Nordrhein-Westfalen, W Germany
Marseille *91 D6 Eng.* Marseilles; *anc.* Massilia. Bouches-du-Rhône, SE France
Marseilles *see* Marseille
Marshall *45 F2* Minnesota, N USA
Marshall *49 H2* Texas, SW USA
Marshall Islands *144 C1 off.* Republic of the Marshall Islands. *country* W Pacific Ocean

Marshall Islands, Republic of the *see* Marshall Islands
Marshall Seamounts *125 H3 seamount range* SW Pacific Ocean
Marsh Harbour *54 C1* Great Abaco, W Bahamas
Martaban *136 B4 var.* Moktama. Mon State, S Burma (Myanmar)
Martha's Vineyard *41 G3 island* Massachusetts, NE USA
Martigues *91 D6* Bouches-du-Rhône, SE France
Martin *99 C5 Ger.* Sankt Martin, *Hung.* Turócszentmárton; *prev.* Turčiansky Svätý Martin, *Ger.* Žilinský Kraj, N Slovakia
Martinique *55 F4 French overseas department* E West Indies
Martinique Channel *see* Martinique Passage
Martinique Passage *55 G4 var.* Dominica Channel, Martinique Channel. *channel* Dominica/ Martinique
Marton *150 D4* Manawatu-Wanganui, North Island, New Zealand
Martos *92 D4* Andalucía, S Spain
Marungu *77 E7 mountain range* SE Dem. Rep. Congo
Mary *122 D3 prev.* Merv. *Mary* Welayaty, S Turkmenistan
Maryborough *149 D4* Queensland, E Australia
Maryborough *see* Port Laoise
Maryland *41 E5 off.* State of Maryland, *also known as* America in Miniature, Cockade State, Free State, Old Line State. *state* NE USA
Maryland, State of *see* Maryland

Maryville *45 F4* Missouri, C USA
Maryville *42 D1* Tennessee, S USA
Masai Steppe *73 C7* grassland
 NW Tanzania
Masaka *73 B6* SW Uganda
Masallı *117 H3* Rus. Masally.
 S Azerbaijan
Masally see Masallı
Masasi *73 C8* Mtwara, SE Tanzania
Masawa/Massawa see Mits'iwa
Masaya *52 D3* Masaya, W Nicaragua
Mascarene Basin *141 B5* undersea basin
 W Indian Ocean
Mascarene Islands *79 H4* island group
 W Indian Ocean
Mascarene Plain *141 B5* abyssal plain
 W Indian Ocean
Mascarene Plateau *141 B5* undersea
 plateau W Indian Ocean
Maseru *78 D4* country capital (Lesotho)
 (Lesotho) W Lesotho
Mas-ha *119 D7* W West Bank Asia
Mashhad *120 E2* var. Meshed.
 Khorāsān-Razavī, NE Iran
Masindi *73 B6* W Uganda
Masira see Maṣīrah, Jazīrat
Masira, Gulf of *121 E5* var. Gulf of
 Masira. bay E Oman
Masira, Gulf of see Maṣīrah, Khalīj
Maṣīrah, Jazīrat *121 E5* var. Masira.
 island E Oman
Masis see Büyükağrı Dağı
Maskat see Masqaṭ
Mason City *45 F3* Iowa, C USA
Masqaṭ *121 E5* var. Maskat, Eng. Muscat.
 country capital (Oman) (Oman)
 NE Oman
Massa *96 B3* Toscana, C Italy
Massachusetts *41 G3* off.
 Commonwealth of Massachusetts, also
 known as Bay State, Old Bay State, Old
 Colony State. state NE USA
Massenya *76 B3* Chari-Baguirmi,
 SW Chad
Massif Central *91 C5* plateau C France
Massilia see Marseille
Massoukou see Franceville
Mastanli see Momchilgrad
Masterton *151 D5* Wellington, North
 Island, New Zealand
Masty *107 B5* Rus. Mosty.
 Hrodzyenskaya Voblasts', W Belarus
Masuda *131 B6* Shimane, Honshū,
 SW Japan
Masuku see Franceville
Masvingo *78 D3* prev. Fort Victoria,
 Nyanda, Victoria. Masvingo,
 SE Zimbabwe
Maşyāf *118 B3* Fr. Misiaf. Ḥamāh,
 C Syria
Matadi *77 B6* Bas-Congo, W Dem.
 Rep. Congo
Matagalpa *52 D3* Matagalpa,
 C Nicaragua
Matale *132 D3* Central Province,
 C Sri Lanka
Matam *74 C3* NE Senegal
Matamata *150 D3* Waikato, North
 Island, New Zealand
Matamoros *50 D3* Coahuila, NE Mexico
Matamoros *51 E2* Tamaulipas,
 C Mexico
Matane *39 E4* Québec, SE Canada
Matanzas *54 B2* Matanzas, NW Cuba
Matara *132 D4* Southern Province,
 S Sri Lanka
Mataram *138 D5* Pulau Lombok,
 C Indonesia
Mataró *93 G2* anc. Illuro. Cataluña,
 E Spain
Mataura *151 B7* Southland, South Island,
 New Zealand
Mataura *151 B7* river South Island,
 New Zealand
Mata Uta see Matā'utu
Matā'utu *145 E4* var. Mata Uta.
 dependent territory capital (Wallis and
 Futuna) Île Uvea, Wallis and Futuna
Matera *97 E5* Basilicata, S Italy
Mathurai see Madurai
Matianus see Orūmīyeh, Daryācheh-ye
Matías Romero *51 F5* Oaxaca,
 SE Mexico
Matisco/Matisco Ædourum see Mâcon
Mato Grosso *63 E3* Estado de Mato
 Grosso; prev. Matto Grosso. state
 W Brazil

Mato Grosso *63 E3* off. Estado de Mato
 Grosso; prev. Matto Grosso. region
 W Brazil
Mato Grosso do Sul *63 E4* off. Estado de
 Mato Grosso do Sul. state S Brazil
Mato Grosso do Sul *63 E4* off. Estado de
 Mato Grosso do Sul. region S Brazil
Mato Grosso, Estado de see Mato
 Grosso do Sul
Mato Grosso, Estado de see Mato Grosso
Mato Grosso, Planalto de *56 C4* plateau
 C Brazil
Matosinhos *92 B2* prev. Matozinhos.
 Porto, NW Portugal
Matozinhos see Matosinhos
Matsue *131 B6* var. Matsuye, Matue.
 Shimane, Honshū, SW Japan
Matsumoto *131 C5* var. Matumoto.
 Nagano, Honshū, S Japan
Matsuyama *131 B7* var. Matuyama.
 Ehime, Shikoku, SW Japan
Matsuye see Matsue
Matterhorn *95 A8* It. Monte Cervino.
 mountain Italy/Switzerland
Matthews Ridge *59 F2* N Guyana
Matthew Town *54 D2* Great Inagua,
 S Bahamas
Matto Grosso see Mato Grosso
Matucana *60 C4* Lima, W Peru
Matue see Matsue
Matumoto see Matsumoto
Maturín *59 E2* Monagas, NE Venezuela
Matuyama see Matsuyama
Mau *135 E3* var. Maunāth Bhanjan.
 Uttar Pradesh, N India
Maui *47 B8* island Hawai'i, USA,
 C Pacific Ocean
Maun *78 C3* North-West, C Botswana
Maunāth Bhanjan see Mau
Mauren *94 E1* NE Liechtenstein Europe
Maurice see Mauritius
Mauritania *74 C2* off. Islamic Republic of
 Mauritania, Ar. Mūrītāniyah. country
 W Africa

MAURITANIA
West Africa

Official name Islamic Republic
 of Mauritania
Formation 1960 / 1960
Capital Nouakchott
Population 3.2 million / 8 people
 per sq mile (3 people per sq km) / 63%
Total area 397,953 sq. miles
 (1,030,700 sq. km)
Languages Hassaniyah Arabic*,
 Wolof, French
Religions Sunni Muslim 100%
Ethnic mix Maure 81%, Wolof 7%,
 Tukolor 5%, Other 4%, Soninka 3%
Government Presidential system
Currency Ouguiya = 5 khoums
Literacy rate 51%
Calorie consumption 2772 calories

Mauritania, Islamic Republic of see
 Mauritania
Mauritius *79 H3* off. Republic of
 Mauritius, Fr. Maurice. country
 W Indian Ocean

MAURITIUS
Indian Ocean

Official name Republic of Mauritius
Formation 1968 / 1968
Capital Port Louis
Population 1.3 million / 1811 people
 per sq mile (699 people per sq km) / 44%
Total area 718 sq. miles (1860 sq. km)
Languages English*, French Creole, Hindi,
 Urdu, Tamil, Chinese, French
Religions Hindu 52%, Roman
 Catholic 26%, Muslim 17%, Other 3%,
 Protestant 2%
Ethnic mix Indo-Mauritian 68%,
 Creole 27%, Sino-Mauritian 3%,
 Franco-Mauritian 2%
Government Parliamentary system
Currency Mauritian rupee = 100 cents
Literacy rate 84%
Calorie consumption 2955 calories

Mauritius *141 B5* island W Indian Ocean
Mauritius, Republic of see Mauritius
Mawlamyaing see Mawlamyine

Mawlamyine *136 B4* var. Mawlamyaing,
 Moulmein. Mon State, S Burma
 (Myanmar)
Mawson *154 D2* Australian research
 station Antarctica
Mayadin see Al Mayādīn
Mayaguana *54 D2* island SE Bahamas
Mayaguana Passage *54 D2* passage
 SE Bahamas
Mayagüez *55 F3* W Puerto Rico
Mayamey *120 D2* Semnān, N Iran
Maya Mountains *52 B2* Sp. Montañas
 Mayas. mountain range Belize/
 Guatemala
Mayas, Montañas see Maya Mountains
Maych'ew *72 C4* var. Mai Chio, It. Mai
 Ceu. Tigray, N Ethiopia
Maydān Shahr see Meydān Shahr
Mayebashi see Maebashi
Mayence see Mainz
Mayfield *151 B6* Canterbury, South
 Island, New Zealand
Maykop *111 A7* Respublika Adygeya,
 SW Russian Federation
Maymana see Meymaneh
Maymyo see Pyin-Oo-Lwin
Mayo see Maio
Mayor Island *150 D3* island NE New
 Zealand
Mayor Pablo Lagerenza see Capitán
 Pablo Lagerenza
Mayotte *79 F2* French territorial
 collectivity E Africa
May Pen *54 B5* C Jamaica
Mayyit, Al Baḥr al see Dead Sea
Mazabuka *78 D2* Southern, S Zambia
Mazaca see Kayseri
Mazagan see El-Jadida
Mazār-e Sharif *123 E3* var. Mazàr-i
 Sharif. Balkh, N Afghanistan
Mazār-i Sharif see Mazār-e Sharif
Mazatlán *50 C3* Sinaloa, C Mexico
Mažeikiai *106 B3* Telšiai, NW Lithuania
Mazirbe *106 C2* Talsi, NW Latvia
Mazra'a see Al Mazra'ah
Mazury *98 D3* physical region NE Poland
Mazyr *107 C7* Rus. Mozyr'.
 Homyel'skaya Voblasts', SE Belarus
Mbabane *78 D4* country capital
 (Swaziland) (Swaziland) NW Swaziland
Mbacké see Mbaké
Mbaïki *77 C5* var. M'Baiki. Lobaye,
 SW Central African Republic
M'Baiki see Mbaïki
Mbaké *74 B3* var. Mbacké. W Senegal
Mbala *78 D1* prev. Abercorn. Northern,
 NE Zambia
Mbale *73 C6* E Uganda
Mbandaka *77 C5* prev. Coquilhatville.
 Equateur, NW Dem. Rep. Congo
M'Banza Congo *78 B1* var. Mbanza
 Congo; prev. São Salvador, São
 Salvador do Congo. Dem. Rep. Congo,
 NW Angola
Mbanza-Ngungu *77 B6* Bas-Congo,
 W Dem. Rep. Congo
Mbarara *73 B6* SW Uganda
Mbé *76 B4* Nord, N Cameroon
Mbeya *73 C7* Mbeya, SW Tanzania
Mbomou/M'Bomu/Mbomu see Bomu
Mbour *74 B3* W Senegal
Mbuji-Mayi *77 D7* prev. Bakwanga.
 Kasai-Oriental, S Dem. Rep. Congo
McAlester *49 G2* Oklahoma, C USA
McAllen *49 G5* Texas, SW USA
McCamey *49 E3* Texas, SW USA
McClintock Channel *37 F2* channel
 Nunavut, N Canada
McComb *42 B3* Mississippi, S USA
McCook *45 E4* Nebraska, C USA
McKean Island *145 E3* island Phoenix
 Islands, C Kiribati
Mount McKinley *36 C3* var. Denali.
 mountain Alaska, USA
McKinley Park *36 C3* Alaska, USA
McMinnville *46 B3* Oregon, NW USA
McMurdo *154 B4* US research station
 Antarctica
McPherson *45 E5* Kansas, C USA
McPherson see Fort McPherson
Mdantsane *78 D5* Eastern Cape,
 SE South Africa
Mead, Lake *47 D6* reservoir Arizona/
 Nevada, W USA
Mecca see Makkah
Mechelen *87 C5* Eng. Mechlin, Fr.
 Malines. Antwerpen, C Belgium

Mechlin see Mechelen
Mecklenburger Bucht *94 C2* bay
 N Germany
Mecsek *99 C7* mountain range
 SW Hungary
Medan *138 B3* Sumatera, E Indonesia
Medeba see Ma'dabā
Medellín *58 B3* Antioquia,
 NW Colombia
Médenine *71 F2* var. Madanīyīn.
 SE Tunisia
Medeshamstede see Peterborough
Medford *46 B4* Oregon, NW USA
Medgidia *108 D5* Constanţa, SE Romania
Medgyes see Mediaş
Mediaş *108 B4* Ger. Mediasch, Hung.
 Medgyes. Sibiu, C Romania
Mediasch see Mediaş
Medicine Hat *37 F5* Alberta, SW Canada
Medina see Al Madīnah
Medinaceli *93 E2* Castilla-León, N Spain
Medina del Campo *92 D2* Castilla-León,
 N Spain
Medinat Israel see Israel
Mediolanum see Saintes, France
Mediolanum see Milano, Italy
Mediomatrica see Metz
Mediterranean Sea *102 D3* Fr. Mer
 Méditerranée. sea Africa/Asia/Europe
Méditerranée, Mer see Mediterranean
 Sea
Médoc *91 B5* cultural region SW France
Medvezh'yegorsk *110 B3* Respublika
 Kareliya, NW Russian Federation
Meekatharra *147 B5* Western Australia
Meemu Atoll see Mulakatholhu
Meerssen *87 D6* var. Mersen. Limburg,
 SE Netherlands
Meerut *134 D2* Uttar Pradesh, N India
Mégáli Préspa, Límni see Prespa, Lake
Meghālaya *113 G3* cultural region
 NE India
Mehdia see Mahdia
Meheso see M'ēso
Me Hka see Nmai Hka
Mehriz *120 D3* Yazd, C Iran
Mehtar Lām *123 F4* var. Mehtarlām,
 Meterlam, Methariam, Metharlam.
 Laghmān, E Afghanistan
Mehtarlām see Mehtar Lām
Meiktila *136 B3* Mandalay, C Burma
 (Myanmar)
Méjico see Mexico
Mejillones *64 B2* Antofagasta, N Chile
Mek'elē *72 C4* var. Makale. Tigray,
 N Ethiopia
Mékhé *74 B3* NW Senegal
Mekong *124 D3* var. Lan-ts'ang Chiang,
 Cam. Mékôngk, Chin. Lancang Jiang,
 Lao. Mènam Khong, Th. Mae Nam
 Khong, Tib. Dza Chu, Vtn. Sông Tiên
 Giang. river SE Asia
Mékôngk see Mekong
Mekong, Mouths of the *137 E6* delta
 S Vietnam
Melaka *138 B3* var. Malacca. Melaka,
 Peninsular Malaysia
Melaka, Selat see Malacca, Strait of
Melanesia *144 D3* island group W Pacific
 Ocean
Melanesian Basin *142 C2* undersea
 basin W Pacific Ocean
Melbourne *149 C7* state capital Victoria,
 SE Australia
Melbourne *43 E4* Florida, SE USA
Meleda see Mljet
Melghir, Chott *71 E2* var. Chott Melrhir.
 salt lake E Algeria
Melilla *80 B5* anc. Rusaddir, Russadir.
 Melilla, Spain, N Africa
Melilla *70 D2* enclave Spain, N Africa
Melita *37 F5* Manitoba, S Canada
Melita see Mljet
Melitene see Malatya
Melitopol' *109 F4* Zaporiz'ka Oblast',
 SE Ukraine
Melle *87 B5* Oost-Vlaanderen,
 NW Belgium
Mellerud *85 B6* Västra Götaland,
 S Sweden
Mellieha *102 B5* E Malta
Mellizo Sur, Cerro *65 A7* mountain
 S Chile
Melo *64 E4* Cerro Largo, NE Uruguay
Melodunum see Melun
Melrhir, Chott see Melghir, Chott
Melsungen *94 B4* Hessen, C Germany

Melun 90 C3 anc. Melodunum. Seine-et-Marne, N France
Melville Bay/Melville Bugt see Qimusseriarsuaq
Melville Island 146 D2 island Northern Territory, N Australia
Melville Island 37 E2 island Parry Islands, Northwest Territories, NW Canada
Melville, Lake 39 F2 lake Newfoundland and Labrador, E Canada
Melville Peninsula 37 G3 peninsula Nunavut, NE Canada
Melville Sound see Viscount Melville Sound
Membidj see Manbij
Memel see Neman, NE Europe
Memel see Klaipeda, Lithuania
Memmingen 95 B6 Bayern, S Germany
Memphis 42 C1 Tennessee, S USA
Menaam see Menaldum
Menado see Manado
Ménaka 75 F3 Goa, E Mali
Menaldum 86 D1 Fris. Menaam. Friesland, N Netherlands
Mènam Khong see Mekong
Mendaña Fracture Zone 153 F4 fracture zone E Pacific Ocean
Mende 91 C5 anc. Mimatum. Lozère, S France
Mendeleyev Ridge 155 B2 undersea ridge Arctic Ocean
Mendocino Fracture Zone 152 D2 fracture zone NE Pacific Ocean
Mendoza 64 B4 Mendoza, W Argentina
Menemen 116 A3 İzmir, W Turkey
Menengiyn Tal 127 F2 plain E Mongolia
Menongue 78 B2 var. Vila Serpa Pinto, Port. Serpa Pinto. Cuando Cubango, C Angola
Mentawai, Kepulauan 138 A4 island group W Indonesia
Meppel 86 D2 Drenthe, NE Netherlands
Meran see Merano
Merano 96 C1 Ger. Meran. Trentino-Alto Adige, N Italy
Merca see Marka
Mercedes 64 D3 Corrientes, NE Argentina
Mercedes 64 D4 Soriano, SW Uruguay
Meredith, Lake 49 E1 reservoir Texas, SW USA
Merefa 109 G2 Kharkivs'ka Oblast', E Ukraine
Mergate see Margate
Mergui see Myeik
Mergui Archipelago 137 B6 island group S Burma (Myanmar)
Mérida 51 H3 Yucatán, SW Mexico
Mérida 92 C4 anc. Augusta Emerita. Extremadura, W Spain
Mérida 58 C2 Mérida, W Venezuela
Meridian 42 C2 Mississippi, S USA
Mérignac 91 B5 Gironde, SW France
Merin, Laguna see Mirim Lagoon
Merowe 72 B3 Northern, N Sudan
Merredin 147 B6 Western Australia
Mersen see Meerssen
Mersey 89 C5 river NW England, United Kingdom
Mersin 116 C4 var. İçel. İçel, S Turkey
Mērsrags 106 C3 Talsi, NW Latvia
Meru 73 C6 Eastern, C Kenya
Merv see Mary
Merzifon 116 D2 Amasya, N Turkey
Merzig 95 A5 Saarland, SW Germany
Mesa 48 B2 Arizona, SW USA
Meseritz see Międzyrzecz
Meshed see Mashhad
Mesopotamia 57 C5 var. Mesopotamia Argentina. physical region NE Argentina
Mesopotamia Argentina see Mesopotamia
Messalo, Rio 79 E2 var. Mualo. river NE Mozambique
Messana/Messene see Messina
Messina 97 D7 var. Messana, Messene; anc. Zancle. Sicilia, Italy, C Mediterranean Sea
Messina see Musina
Messina, Strait of 97 D7 Eng. Strait of Messina. strait SW Italy
Messina, Strait of see Messina, Stretto di
Messini 105 B6 Pelopónnisos, S Greece
Mesta see Néstos
Mestghanem see Mostaganem

Mestia 117 F1 var. Mestiya. N Georgia
Mestiya see Mestia
Mestre 96 C2 Veneto, NE Italy
Metairie 42 B3 Louisiana, S USA
Metán 64 C2 Salta, N Argentina
Metapán 52 B2 Santa Ana, NW El Salvador
Meta, Río 58 D3 river Colombia/Venezuela
Meterlam see Mehtar Läm
Methariam/Metharlam see Mehtar Läm
Metis see Metz
Metković 100 B4 Dubrovnik-Neretva, SE Croatia
Métsovo 104 B4 prev. Métsovon. Ípeiros, C Greece
Métsovon see Métsovo
Metz 90 D3 anc. Divodurum Mediomatricum, Mediomatrica, Metis. Moselle, NE France
Meulaboh 138 A3 Sumatera, W Indonesia
Meuse 87 C6 Dut. Maas. river W Europe
Mexcala, Río see Balsas, Río
Mexicali 50 A1 Baja California Norte, NW Mexico
Mexicanos, Estados Unidos see Mexico
México 51 E4 var. Ciudad de México, Eng. Mexico City. country capital (Mexico) (Mexico) México, C Mexico
Mexico 45 G4 Missouri, C USA
Mexico 50 C3 off. United Mexican States, var. Méjico, México, Sp. Estados Unidos Mexicanos. country N Central America

MEXICO
North America

Official name United Mexican States
Formation 1836 / 1848
Capital Mexico City
Population 110 million / 149 people per sq mile (57 people per sq km) / 76%
Total area 761,602 sq. miles (1,972,550 sq. km)
Languages Spanish*, Nahuatl, Mayan, Zapotec, Mixtec, Otomi, Totonac, Tzotzil, Tzeltal
Religions Roman Catholic 88%, Other 7%, Protestant 5%
Ethnic mix Mestizo 60%, Amerindian 30%, European 9%, Other 1%
Government Presidential system
Currency Mexican peso = 100 centavos
Literacy rate 91%
Calorie consumption 3145 calories

México see Mexico
Mexico City see México
México, Golfo de see Mexico, Gulf of
Mexico, Gulf of 51 F2 Sp. Golfo de México. gulf W Atlantic Ocean
Meyadine see Al Mayādīn
Meydān Shahr 123 E4 var. Maydān Shahr. Vardak, E Afghanistan
Meymaneh 122 D3 var. Maimāna, Maymana. Fāryāb, NW Afghanistan
Mezen' 110 D3 river NW Russian Federation
Mezőtúr 99 D7 Jász-Nagykun-Szolnok, E Hungary
Mgarr 102 A5 Gozo, N Malta
Miadziol Nowy see Myadzyel
Miahuatlán 51 F5 var. Miahuatlán de Porfirio Díaz. Oaxaca, SE Mexico
Miahuatlán de Porfirio Díaz see Miahuatlán
Miami 43 F5 Florida, SE USA
Miami 49 G1 Oklahoma, C USA
Miami Beach 43 F5 Florida, SE USA
Miāneh 120 C2 var. Miyāneh. Āžarbāyjān-e Sharqī, NW Iran
Mianyang 128 B5 Sichuan, C China
Miastko 98 C2 Ger. Rummelsburg in Pommern. Pomorskie, N Poland
Mi Chai see Nong Khai
Michalovce 99 E5 Ger. Grossmichel, Hung. Nagymihály. Košický Kraj, E Slovakia
Michigan 40 C1 off. State of Michigan, also known as Great Lakes State, Lake State, Wolverine State. state N USA
Michigan, Lake 40 C2 lake N USA
Michurin see Tsarevo
Michurinsk 111 B5 Tambovskaya Oblast', W Russian Federation

Micoud 55 F2 SE Saint Lucia
Micronesia 144 B1 off. Federated States of Micronesia. country W Pacific Ocean

MICRONESIA
Australasia & Oceania

Official name Federated States of Micronesia
Formation 1986 / 1986
Capital Palikir (Pohnpei Island)
Population 107,862 / 398 people per sq mile (154 people per sq km) / 30%
Total area 271 sq. miles (702 sq. km)
Languages English*, Trukese, Pohnpeian, Mortlockese, Kosraean
Religions Roman Catholic 50%, Protestant 48%, Other 2%
Ethnic mix Chuukese 49%, Pohnpeian 24%, Other 14%, Kosraean 6%, Yapese 5%, Asian 2%
Government Nonparty system
Currency US dollar = 100 cents
Literacy rate 81%
Calorie consumption Not available

Micronesia 144 C1 island group W Pacific Ocean
Micronesia, Federated States of see Micronesia
Mid-Atlantic Cordillera see Mid-Atlantic Ridge
Mid-Atlantic Ridge 66 C3 var. Mid-Atlantic Cordillera, Mid-Atlantic Rise, Mid-Atlantic Swell. undersea ridge Atlantic Ocean
Mid-Atlantic Rise/Mid-Atlantic Swell see Mid-Atlantic Ridge
Middelburg 87 B5 Zeeland, SW Netherlands
Middelharnis 86 B4 Zuid-Holland, SW Netherlands
Middelkerke 87 A5 West-Vlaanderen, W Belgium
Middle America Trench 35 B7 trench E Pacific Ocean
Middle Andaman 133 F2 island Andaman Islands, India, NE Indian Ocean
Middle Atlas 70 C2 Eng. Middle Atlas. mountain range N Morocco
Middle Atlas see Moyen Atlas
Middleburg Island see 'Eua
Middle Congo see Congo (Republic of)
Middlesboro 40 C5 Kentucky, S USA
Middlesbrough 89 D5 N England, United Kingdom
Middletown 41 F4 New Jersey, NE USA
Middletown 41 F3 New York, NE USA
Mid-Indian Basin 141 C5 undersea basin N Indian Ocean
Mid-Indian Ridge 141 C5 var. Central Indian Ridge. undersea ridge C Indian Ocean
Midland 38 D5 Ontario, S Canada
Midland 40 C3 Michigan, N USA
Midland 49 E3 Texas, SW USA
Mid-Pacific Mountains 152 C2 var. Mid-Pacific Seamounts. seamount range NW Pacific Ocean
Mid-Pacific Seamounts see Mid-Pacific Mountains
Midway Islands 152 D2 US territory C Pacific Ocean
Miechów 99 D5 Małopolskie, S Poland
Międzyrzec Podlaski 98 E3 Lubelskie, E Poland
Międzyrzecz 98 B3 Ger. Meseritz. Lubuskie, W Poland
Mielec 99 D5 Podkarpackie, SE Poland
Miercurea-Ciuc 108 C4 var. Szeklerburg, Hung. Csíkszereda. Harghita, C Romania
Mieres del Camín see Mieres del Camino
Mieres del Camino 92 D1 var. Mieres del Camín. Asturias, NW Spain
Mì'èso 73 D5 var. Meheso, Miesso. Oromīya, C Ethiopia
Miesso see Mì'èso
Mifrats Hefa 119 A5 Eng. Bay of Haifa; prev. MifrazHefa. bay N Israel
MifrazHefa see Mifrats Hefa
Miguel Asua see Miguel Auza
Miguel Auza 50 D3 var. Miguel Auza. Zacatecas, C Mexico

Mikashevichy 107 C7 Pol. Mikaszewicze, Rus. Mikashevichi. Brestskaya Voblasts', SW Belarus
Mikashevichi see Mikashevichy
Mikaszewicze see Mikashevichy
Mikhaylovgrad see Montana
Mikhaylovka 111 B6 Volgogradskaya Oblast', SW Russian Federation
Míkonos see Mýkonos
Mikre 104 C2 Lovech, N Bulgaria
Mikun' 110 D4 Respublika Komi, NW Russian Federation
Mikuni-sanmyaku 131 D5 mountain range Honshū, N Japan Asia
Mikura-jima 131 D6 island E Japan
Milagro 60 B2 Guayas, SW Ecuador
Milan see Milano
Milange 79 E2 Zambézia, NE Mozambique
Milano 96 B2 Eng. Milan, Ger. Mailand; anc. Mediolanum. Lombardia, N Italy
Milas 116 A4 Muğla, SW Turkey
Milashavichy 107 C7 Rus. Milashevichi. Homyel'skaya Voblasts', SE Belarus
Milashevichi see Milashavichy
Mildura 149 C6 Victoria, SE Australia
Mile see Mili Atoll
Miles 149 D5 Queensland, E Australia
Miles City 44 C2 Montana, NW USA
Milford see Milford Haven
Milford Haven 89 C6 prev. Milford. SW Wales, United Kingdom
Milford Sound 151 A6 Southland, South Island, New Zealand
Milford Sound 151 A6 inlet South Island, New Zealand
Milḩ, Baḩr al see Razāzah, Buḩayrat ar
Mili Atoll 144 D2 var. Mile. atoll Ratak Chain, SE Marshall Islands
Mil'kovo 113 H3 Kamchatskaya Oblast', E Russian Federation
Milk River 37 E5 Alberta, SW Canada
Milk River 44 C1 river Montana, NW USA
Milk, Wadi el 88 B4 var. Wadi al Malik. river C Sudan
Milledgeville 43 E2 Georgia, SE USA
Mille Lacs Lake 45 F2 lake Minnesota, N USA
Millennium Island 143 F3 prev. Caroline Island, Thornton Island. atoll Line Islands, E Kiribati
Millerovo 111 B6 Rostovskaya Oblast', SW Russian Federation
Mílos 105 C6 island Kykládes, Greece, Aegean Sea
Mílos 105 C7 island Kykládes, Greece, Aegean Sea
Mílos 105 C7 island Kykládes, Greece, Aegean Sea
Milton 151 B7 Otago, South Island, New Zealand
Milton Keynes 89 D6 SE England, United Kingdom
Milwaukee 40 B3 Wisconsin, N USA
Mimatum see Mende
Min see Fujian
Minā' Qābūs 140 B3 NE Oman
Minas Gerais 63 F3 off. Estado de Minas Gerais. state E Brazil
Minas Gerais 63 F3 off. Estado de Minas Gerais. region E Brazil
Minas Gerais, Estado de see Minas Gerais
Minatitlán 51 F4 Veracruz-Llave, E Mexico
Minbu 136 A3 Magway, W Burma (Myanmar)
Minch, The 88 B3 var. North Minch. strait NW Scotland, United Kingdom
Mindanao 139 F3 island S Philippines
Mindanao Sea see Bohol Sea
Mindelheim 95 C6 Bayern, S Germany
Mindello see Mindelo
Mindelo 74 A2 var. Mindello; prev. Porto Grande. São Vicente, N Cape Verde
Minden 94 B4 anc. Minthun. Nordrhein-Westfalen, NW Germany
Mindoro 139 E2 island N Philippines
Mindoro Strait 139 E2 strait W Philippines
Mineral Wells 49 F2 Texas, SW USA
Mingäçevir 117 G2 Rus. Mingechaur, Mingechevir. C Azerbaijan
Mingechaur/Mingechevir see Mingäçevir
Mingora see Saidu Sharif
Minho 92 B2 former province N Portugal
Minho 92 B2 Sp. Miño. river Portugal/Spain

Minho, Rio see Miño
Minicoy Island 132 B3 island SW India
Minius see Miño
Minna 75 G4 Niger, C Nigeria
Minneapolis 45 F2 Minnesota, N USA
Minnesota 45 F2 off. State of Minnesota, also known as Gopher State, New England of the West, North Star State. state N USA
Miño 92 B2 var. Mino, Minius, Port. Rio Minho. river Portugal/Spain
Miño see Minho, Rio
Minorca 93 H3 Eng. Minorca; anc. Balearis Minor. island Islas Baleares, Spain, W Mediterranean Sea
Minorca see Menorca
Minot 45 E1 North Dakota, N USA
Minsk 107 C6 country capital (Belarus) (Belarus) Minskaya Voblasts', C Belarus
Minskaya Wzvyshsha 107 C6 mountain range C Belarus
Mińsk Mazowiecki 98 D3 var. Nowo-Minsk. Mazowieckie, C Poland
Minthun see Minden
Minto, Lac 38 D2 lake Québec, C Canada
Minya see Al Minyā
Miraflores 50 C3 Baja California Sur, NW Mexico
Miranda de Ebro 93 E1 La Rioja, N Spain
Mirgorod see Myrhorod
Miri 138 D3 Sarawak, East Malaysia
Mirim Lagoon 63 G5 var. Lake Mirim, Sp. Laguna Merín. lagoon Brazil/Uruguay
Mirim, Lake see Mirim Lagoon
Mírina see Mýrina
Mirjāveh 120 E4 Sīstān va Balūchestān, SE Iran
Mirny 154 C3 Russian research station Antarctica
Mirnyy 115 F3 Respublika Sakha (Yakutiya), NE Russian Federation
Mīrpur Khās 134 B3 Sind, SE Pakistan
Mirtoan Sea 105 C6 Eng. Mirtoan Sea; anc. Myrtoum Mare. sea S Greece
Mirtoan Sea see Mirtóo Pélagos
Misiaf see Maṣyāf
Miskito Coast see La Mosquitia
Miskitos, Cayos 53 E2 island group NE Nicaragua
Miskolc 99 D6 Borsod-Abaúj-Zemplén, NE Hungary
Misool, Pulau 139 F4 island Maluku, E Indonesia
Miṣrātah 71 F2 var. Misurata. NW Libya
Mission 49 G5 Texas, SW USA
Mississippi 42 B2 off. State of Mississippi, also known as Bayou State, Magnolia State. state C USA
Mississippi Delta 42 B4 delta Louisiana, S USA
Mississippi River 35 C6 river C USA
Missoula 44 B1 Montana, NW USA
Missouri 45 F5 off. State of Missouri, also known as Bullion State, Show Me State. state C USA
Missouri River 45 E3 river C USA
Mistassini, Lac 38 D3 lake Québec, SE Canada
Mistelbach an der Zaya 95 E6 Niederösterreich, NE Austria
Misti, Volcán 61 E4 volcano S Peru
Misurata see Miṣrātah
Mitau see Jelgava
Mitchell 149 D5 Queensland, E Australia
Mitchell 45 E3 South Dakota, N USA
Mitchell, Mount 43 E1 mountain North Carolina, SE USA
Mitchell River 148 C2 river Queensland, NE Australia
Mi Tho see Mỹ Tho
Mitilíni see Mytilíni
Mito 131 D5 Ibaraki, Honshū, S Japan
Mitrovica/Mitrovicë see Kosovska Mitrovica, Serbia
Mitrovica/Mitrowitz see Sremska Mitrovica, Serbia
Mitrovicë 101 D5 Serb. Mitrovica, Kosovska Mitrovica, Titova Mitrovica. N Kosovo
Mits'iwa 72 C4 var. Masawa, Massawa. E Eritrea
Mitspe Ramon 119 A7 prev. Mizpe Ramon. Southern, S Israel
Mittelstadt see Baia Sprie
Mitú 58 C4 Vaupés, SE Colombia

Mitumba, Chaîne des/Mitumba Range see Mitumba, Monts
Mitumba Range 77 E7 var. Chaîne des Mitumba, Mitumba Range. mountain range E Dem. Rep. Congo
Miueru Wantipa, Lake 77 E7 lake N Zambia
Miyake-jima 131 D6 island Sakishima-shotō, SW Japan
Miyakonojō 131 B8 var. Miyakonzyô. Miyazaki, Kyūshū, SW Japan
Miyakonzyô see Miyakonojō
Miyāneh see Mīāneh
Miyazaki 131 B8 Miyazaki, Kyūshū, SW Japan
Mizil 108 C5 Prahova, SE Romania
Miziya 104 C1 Vratsa, NW Bulgaria
Mizpe Ramon see Mitspe Ramon
Mjøsa 85 B6 var. Mjøsen. lake S Norway
Mjøsen see Mjøsa
Mladenovac 100 D4 Serbia, C Serbia
Mława 98 D3 Mazowieckie, C Poland
Mljet 101 B5 It. Meleda; anc. Melita. island S Croatia
Mmabatho 78 C4 North-West, N South Africa
Moab 44 B5 Utah, W USA
Moa Island 148 C1 island Queensland, NE Australia
Moanda 77 B6 var. Mouanda. Haut-Ogooué, SE Gabon
Moba 77 E7 Katanga, E Dem. Rep. Congo
Mobay see Montego Bay
Mobaye 77 C5 Basse-Kotto, S Central African Republic
Moberly 45 G4 Missouri, C USA
Mobile 42 C3 Alabama, S USA
Mobutu Sese Seko, Lac see Albert, Lake
Moçâmedes see Namibe
Mochudi 78 C4 Kgatleng, SE Botswana
Mocímboa da Praia 79 F2 var. Vila de Mocímboa da Praia. Cabo Delgado, N Mozambique
Môco 78 B2 var. Morro de Môco. mountain W Angola
Mocoa 58 A4 Putumayo, SW Colombia
Môco, Morro de see Môco
Mocuba 79 E3 Zambézia, NE Mozambique
Modena 96 B3 anc. Mutina. Emilia-Romagna, N Italy
Modesto 47 B6 California, W USA
Modica 97 C7 anc. Motyca. Sicilia, Italy, C Mediterranean Sea
Modimolle 78 D4 prev. Nylstroom. Limpopo, NE South Africa
Modohn see Madona
Modriča 100 C3 Republika Srpska, N Bosnia and Herzegovina
Moe 149 C7 Victoria, SE Australia
Møen see Møn, Denmark
Moero, Lac see Mweru, Lake
Moeskroen see Mouscron
Mogadiscio/Mogadishu see Muqdisho
Mogador see Essaouira
Mogilëv see Mahilyow
Mogilev-Podol'skiy see Mohyliv-Podil's'kyy
Mogilno 98 C3 Kujawsko-pomorskie, C Poland
Moḩammadābād-e Rīgān 120 E4 Kermān, SE Iran
Mohammedia 70 C2 prev. Fédala. NW Morocco
Mohave, Lake 47 D7 reservoir Arizona/Nevada, W USA
Mohawk River 41 F3 river New York, NE USA
Mohéli see Mwali
Mohns Ridge 83 F3 undersea ridge Greenland Sea/Norwegian Sea
Moho 61 E4 Puno, SE Peru
Mohoro 73 C7 Pwani, E Tanzania
Mohyliv-Podil's'kyy 108 D3 Rus. Mogilev-Podol'skiy. Vinnyts'ka Oblast', C Ukraine
Moi 85 A6 Rogaland, S Norway
Moili see Mwali
Mo i Rana 84 C3 Nordland, C Norway
Mõisaküla 106 D3 Ger. Moiseküll. Viljandimaa, S Estonia
Moiseküll see Mõisaküla
Moissac 91 B6 Tarn-et-Garonne, S France
Mojácar 93 E5 Andalucía, S Spain

Mojave Desert 47 D7 plain California, W USA
Mokrany see Makrany
Moktama see Martaban
Mol 87 C5 prev. Moll. Antwerpen, N Belgium
Moldavia see Moldova
Moldavian SSR/Moldavskaya SSR see Moldova
Molde 85 A5 Møre og Romsdal, S Norway
Moldotau, Khrebet see Moldo-Too, Khrebet
Moldo-Too, Khrebet 123 G2 prev. Khrebet Moldotau. mountain range C Kyrgyzstan
Moldova 108 D3 off. Republic of Moldova, var. Moldavia; prev. Moldavian SSR, Rus. Moldavskaya SSR. country SE Europe

Moldova Nouă 108 A4 Ger. Neumoldowa, Hung. Ujmoldova. Caraş-Severin, SW Romania
Moldova, Republic of see Moldova
Moldoveanul see Vârful Moldoveanu
Molfetta 97 E5 Puglia, SE Italy
Moll see Mol
Mollendo 61 E4 Arequipa, SW Peru
Mölndal 85 B7 Västra Götaland, S Sweden
Molochans'k 109 G4 Rus. Molochansk. Zaporiz'ka Oblast', SE Ukraine
Molodechno/Molodeczno see Maladzyechna
Molodezhnaya 154 C2 Russian research station Antarctica
Moloka'i 47 B8 var. Molokai. island Hawaiian Islands, Hawai'i, USA
Molokai Fracture Zone 153 E2 tectonic feature NE Pacific Ocean
Molopo 78 C4 seasonal river Botswana/South Africa
Mólos 105 B5 Stereá Ellás, C Greece
Molotov see Severodvinsk, Arkhangel'skaya Oblast', Russian Federation
Molotov see Perm', Permskaya Oblast', Russian Federation
Moluccas 139 F4 Dut. Molukken, Eng. Moluccas; prev. Spice Islands. island group E Indonesia
Moluccas see Maluku
Molucca Sea 139 F4 Ind. Laut Maluku. sea E Indonesia
Molukken see Maluku
Mombasa 73 D7 Coast, SE Kenya
Mombetsu see Monbetsu
Momchilgrad 104 D3 prev. Mastanli. Kürdzhali, S Bulgaria
Møn 85 B8 prev. Møen. island SE Denmark
Mona, Canal de la see Mona Passage
Monaco 91 C7 var. Monaco-Ville; anc. Monoecus. country capital (Monaco) (Monaco) S Monaco
Monaco 91 E6 off. Principality of Monaco. country W Europe

Monaco see München
Monaco, Port de 91 C8 bay S Monaco W Mediterranean Sea
Monaco, Principality of see Monaco
Monaco-Ville see Monaco
Monahans 49 E3 Texas, SW USA
Mona, Isla 55 E3 island W Puerto Rico
Mona Passage 55 E3 Sp. Canal de la Mona. channel Dominican Republic/Puerto Rico
Monastir see Bitola
Monbetsu 130 D2 var. Mombetsu, Monbetu. Hokkaidō, NE Japan
Monbetu see Monbetsu
Moncalieri 96 A2 Piemonte, NW Italy
Monchegorsk 110 C2 Murmanskaya Oblast', NW Russian Federation
Monclova 50 D2 Coahuila, NE Mexico
Moncton 39 F4 New Brunswick, SE Canada
Mondovì 96 A2 Piemonte, NW Italy
Monfalcone 96 D2 Friuli-Venezia Giulia, NE Italy
Monforte de Lemos 92 C1 Galicia, NW Spain
Mongo 76 C3 Guéra, C Chad
Mongolia 126 C2 Mong. Mongol Uls. country E Asia

Mongolia, Plateau of 124 D1 plateau E Mongolia
Mongol Uls see Mongolia
Mongora see Saidu Sharif
Mongos, Chaîne des see Bongo, Massif des
Mongu 78 C2 Western, W Zambia
Monkchester see Newcastle upon Tyne
Monkey Bay 79 E2 Southern, SE Malawi
Monkey River see Monkey River Town
Monkey River Town 52 C2 var. Monkey River. Toledo, SE Belize
Monoecus see Monaco
Mono Lake 47 C6 lake California, W USA
Monostor see Beli Manastir
Monovar 93 F4 Cat. Monover. País Valenciano, E Spain
Monover see Monovar
Monroe 42 B2 Louisiana, S USA
Monrovia 74 C5 country capital (Liberia) W Liberia
Mons 87 B6 Dut. Bergen. Hainaut, S Belgium
Monselice 96 C2 Veneto, NE Italy
Montana 104 C2 prev. Ferdinand, Mikhaylovgrad. Montana, NW Bulgaria
Montana 44 B1 off. State of Montana, also known as Mountain State, Treasure State. state NW USA

Montargis *90 C4* Loiret, C France
Montauban *91 B6* Tarn-et-Garonne,
S France
Montbéliard *90 D4* Doubs, E France
Mont Cenis, Col du *91 D5* *pass* E France
Mont-de-Marsan *91 B6* Landes,
SW France
Monteagudo *61 G4* Chuquisaca,
S Bolivia
Montecarlo *91 C8* Misiones,
NE Argentina
Monte Caseros *64 D3* Corrientes,
NE Argentina
Monte Cristi *54 D3* *var.* San Fernando
de Monte Cristi. NW Dominican
Republic
Monte Croce Carnico, Passo di *see*
Plöcken Pass
Montegiardino *96 E2* SE San Marino
Montego Bay *54 A4* *var.* Mobay.
W Jamaica
Montélimar *91 D5* *anc.* Acunum Acusio,
Montilium Adhemari. Drôme, E France
Montemorelos *51 E3* Nuevo León,
NE Mexico
Montenegro *101 C5* Serb. Crna Gora.
country SW Europe

MONTENEGRO
Southeast Europe

Official name Republic of Montenegro
Formation 2006 / 2006
Capital Podgorica
Population 684,736 / 128 people
per sq mile (50 people per sq km) / 62%
Total area 5332 sq. miles (13,812 sq. km)
Languages Montenegrin*, Serbian,
Albanian, Bosniak, Croatian
Religions Orthodox Christian 74%,
Muslim 18%, Other 4%Roman Catholic 4%
Ethnic mix Montenegrin 43%, Serb 32%,
Other 12%, Bosniak 8%, Albanian 5%
Government Parliamentary system
Currency Euro = 100 cents
Literacy rate 98%
Calorie consumption Not available

Monte Patria *64 B3* Coquimbo, N Chile
Monterey *47 B6* California, W USA
Monterey *see* Monterrey
Monterey Bay *47 A6* *bay* California,
W USA
Montería *58 B2* Córdoba, NW Colombia
Montero *61 G4* Santa Cruz, C Bolivia
Monterrey *51 E3* *var.* Monterey. Nuevo
León, NE Mexico
Montes Claros *63 F3* Minas Gerais,
SE Brazil
Montevideo *64 D4* *country capital*
(Uruguay) (Uruguay) Montevideo,
S Uruguay
Montevideo *45 F2* Minnesota, N USA
Montgenèvre, Col de *91 D5* *pass*
France/Italy
Montgomery *42 D2* *state capital*
Alabama, S USA
Montgomery *see* Sāhīwāl
Monthey *95 A7* Valais, SW Switzerland
Montilium Adhemari. *see* Montélimar
Montluçon *90 C4* Allier, C France
Montoro *92 D4* Andalucía, S Spain
Montpelier *41 G2* *state capital* Vermont,
NE USA
Montpellier *91 C6* Hérault, S France
Montréal *39 E4* Eng. Montreal. Québec,
SE Canada
Montrose *88 D3* E Scotland, United
Kingdom
Montrose *44 C5* Colorado, C USA
Montserrat *55 G3* *var.* Emerald Isle. UK
dependent territory E West Indies
Monywa *136 B3* Sagaing, C Burma
(Myanmar)
Monza *96 B2* Lombardia, N Italy
Monze *78 D2* Southern, S Zambia
Monzón *93 F2* Aragón, NE Spain
Moonie *149 D5* Queensland, E Australia
Moon-Sund *see* Väinameri
Moora *147 A6* Western Australia
Moore *49 G1* Oklahoma, C USA
Moore, Lake *147 B6* *lake* Western
Australia
Moorhead *45 F2* Minnesota, N USA
Moose *38 C3* river Ontario, S Canada
Moosehead Lake *41 G1* *lake* Maine,
NE USA

Moosonee *38 C3* Ontario, SE Canada
Mopti *75 E3* Mopti, C Mali
Moquegua *61 E4* Moquegua, SE Peru
Mora *85 C5* Dalarna, C Sweden
Morales *52 C2* Izabal, E Guatemala
Morant Bay *54 B5* E Jamaica
Moratalla *93 E4* Murcia, SE Spain
Morava *99 C5* *var.* March. *river*
C Europe
Morava *see* Moravia, Czech Republic
Morava *see* Velika Morava, Serbia
Moravia *99 B5* Cz. Morava, Ger. Mähren.
cultural region E Czech Republic
Moray Firth *88 C3* *inlet* N Scotland,
United Kingdom
Morea *see* Pelopónnisos
Moreau River *44 D2* river South Dakota,
N USA
Moree *149 D5* New South Wales,
SE Australia
Morelia *51 E4* Michoacán, S Mexico
Morena, Sierra *92 C4* *mountain range*
S Spain
Moreni *108 C5* Dâmboviţa, S Romania
Morgan City *42 B3* Louisiana, S USA
Darya-ye Morghab *122 D3* Rus.
Murgab, Murghab, Turkm. Murgap,
Murgap Deryasy. *river* Afghanistan/
Turkmenistan
Darya-ye Morghab *122 D3* Rus.
Murgab, Murghab, Turkm. Murgap,
Murgap Deryasy. *river* Afghanistan/
Turkmenistan
Morghāb, Daryā-ye *see* Murgap
Morioka *130 D4* Iwate, Honshū,
C Japan
Morlaix *90 A3* Finistère, NW France
Mormon State *see* Utah
Mornington Abyssal Plain *67 A7*
abyssal plain SE Pacific Ocean
Mornington Island *148 B2* island
Wellesley Islands, Queensland,
N Australia
Morocco *70 B3* off. Kingdom of
Morocco, Ar. Al Mamlakah. *country*
N Africa

MOROCCO
North Africa

Official name Kingdom of Morocco
Formation 1956 / 1969
Capital Rabat
Population 32.4 million / 188 people
per sq mile (73 people per sq km) / 58%
Total area 172,316 sq. miles
(446,300 sq. km)
Languages Arabic*, Tamazight (Berber),
French, Spanish
Religions Muslim (mainly Sunni) 99%,
Other (mostly Christian) 1%
Ethnic mix Arab 70%, Berber 29%,
European 1%
Government Mixed monarchical–
parliamentary system
Currency Moroccan dirham =
100 centimes
Literacy rate 52%
Calorie consumption 3052 calories

Morocco *see* Marrakech
Morocco, Kingdom of *see* Morocco
Morogoro *73 C7* Morogoro,
E Tanzania
Moro Gulf *139 E3* gulf S Philippines
Morón *54 C2* Ciego de Ávila, C Cuba
Mörön *126 D2* Hövsgöl, N Mongolia
Morondava *79 F3* Toliara,
W Madagascar
Moroni *79 F2* country capital (Comoros)
(Comoros) Grande Comore,
NW Comoros
Morotai, Pulau *139 F3* island Maluku,
E Indonesia
Morotiri *see* Marotiri
Morphou *see* Güzelyurt
Morrinsville *150 D3* Waikato, North
Island, New Zealand
Morris *45 F2* Minnesota, N USA
Morris Jesup, Kap *83 E1* headland
N Greenland
Morvan *90 D4* physical region C France
Moscow *46 C2* Idaho, NW USA
Moscow *see* Moskva
Mosel *95 A5* Fr. Moselle. *river*
W Europe
Mosel *see* Moselle

Moselle *87 E8* Ger. Mosel. *river*
W Europe
Moselle *see* Mosel
Mosgiel *151 B7* Otago, South Island,
New Zealand
Moshi *73 C7* Kilimanjaro, NE Tanzania
Mosjøen *84 B4* Nordland, C Norway
Moskovskiy *see* INDEX
Moskva *111 B5* Eng. Moscow. *country
capital* (Russian Federation) (Russian
Federation) Gorod Moskva, W Russian
Federation
Moskva *123 E3* Rus. Moskovskiy; prev.
Chubek. SW Tajikistan
Moson and Magyaróvár *see*
Mosonmagyaróvár
Mosonmagyaróvár *99 C6* Ger.
Wieselburg-Ungarisch-Altenburg;
prev. Moson and Magyaróvár, Ger.
Wieselburg and Ungarisch-Altenburg.
Győr-Moson-Sopron, NW Hungary
Mosquito Coast *53 E3* var. Miskito
Coast, Eng. Mosquito Coast. *coastal
region* E Nicaragua
Mosquito Coast *see* La Mosquitia
Mosquito Gulf *53 F4* Eng. Mosquito
Gulf. *gulf* N Panama
Mosquito Gulf *see* Mosquitos, Golfo
de los
Moss *85 B6* Østfold, S Norway
Mossâmedes *see* Namibe
Mosselbaai *78 C5* var. Mosselbai, Eng.
Mossel Bay. Western Cape, SW South
Africa
Mosselbai/Mossel Bay *see* Mosselbaai
Mossendjo *77 B6* Niari, SW Congo
Mossoró *63 G2* Rio Grande do Norte,
NE Brazil
Most *98 A4* Ger. Brüx. Ústecký Kraj,
NW Czech Republic
Mosta *102 B5* var. Musta. C Malta
Mostaganem *70 D2* var. Mestghanem.
NW Algeria
Mostar *100 C4* Federacija Bosna I
Hercegovina, S Bosnia and Herzegovina
Mosty *see* Masty
Mosul *see* Al Mawşil
Mota del Cuervo *93 E3* Castilla-La
Mancha, C Spain
Motagua, Río *52 B2* river Guatemala/
Honduras
Mother of Presidents/Mother of States
see Virginia
Motril *92 D5* Andalucía, S Spain
Motru *108 B4* Gorj, SW Romania
Motueka *151 C5* Tasman, South Island,
New Zealand
Motul *51 H3* var. Motul de Felipe Carrillo
Puerto. Yucatán, SE Mexico
Motul de Felipe Carrillo Puerto *see*
Motul
Motyca *see* Modica
Mouanda *see* Moanda
Mouhoun *see* Black Volta
Mouila *77 A6* Ngounié, C Gabon
Moukden *see* Shenyang
Mould Bay *37 E2* Prince Patrick Island,
Northwest Territories, N Canada
Moulins *90 C4* Allier, C France
Moulmein *see* Mawlamyine
Moundou *76 B4* Logone-Occidental,
SW Chad
Moüng Roessei *137 D5* Bătdâmbâng,
W Cambodia
Moun Hou *see* Black Volta
Mountain Home *42 B1* Arkansas, C USA
Mountain State *see* Montana
Mountain State *see* West Virginia
Mount Cook *151 B6* Canterbury, South
Island, New Zealand
Mount Desert Island *41 H2* island
Maine, NE USA
Mount Gambier *149 B7* South Australia
Mount Isa *148 B3* Queensland,
C Australia
Mount Magnet *147 B5* Western Australia
Mount Pleasant *45 G4* Iowa, C USA
Mount Pleasant *40 C3* Michigan, N USA
Mount Pleasant *40 D3* Pennsylvania,
NE USA
Mount Vernon *40 B5* Illinois, N USA
Mount Vernon *46 B1* Washington,
NW USA
Mourdi, Dépression du *76 C2* desert
lowland Chad/Sudan
Mouscron *87 A6* Dut. Moeskroen.
Hainaut, W Belgium
Mouse River *see* Souris River
Moussoro *76 B3* Kanem, W Chad

Moselle *87 E8* Ger. Mosel. *river*
Moyen-Congo *see* Congo (Republic of)
Mo'ynoq *122 C1* Rus. Muynak.
Qoraqalpog'iston Respublikasi,
NW Uzbekistan
Moyobamba *60 B2* San Martín, NW Peru
Moyu *126 B3* var. Karakax. Xinjiang
Uygur Zizhiqu, NW China
Moyynkum, Peski *123 F1* Kaz.
Moyynqum. desert S Kazakhstan
Moyynqum *see* Moyynkum, Peski
Mozambika, Lakandranon' i *see*
Mozambique Channel
Mozambique *79 E3* off. Republic of
Mozambique; prev. People's Republic of
Mozambique, Portuguese East Africa.
country S Africa

MOZAMBIQUE
Southern Africa

Official name Republic of Mozambique
Formation 1975 / 1975
Capital Maputo
Population 20.5 million / 68 people
per sq mile (26 people per sq km) / 37%
Total area 309,494 sq. miles
(801,590 sq. km)
Languages Portuguese*, Makua,
Xitsonga, Sena, Lomwe
Religions Traditional beliefs 56%,
Christian 30%, Muslim 14%
Ethnic mix Makua Lomwe 47%,
Tsonga 23%, Malawi 12%, Shona 11%,
Yao 4%, Other 3%
Government Presidential system
Currency New metical = 100 centavos
Literacy rate 46%
Calorie consumption 2079 calories

Mozambique Basin *see* Natal Basin
Mozambique, Canal de *see* Mozambique
Channel
Mozambique Channel *79 E3* Fr. Canal
de Mozambique, Mal. Lakandranon' i
Mozambika. strait W Indian Ocean
Mozambique, People's Republic of *see*
Mozambique
Mozambique Plateau *69 D7* var.
Mozambique Rise. undersea plateau
SW Indian Ocean
Mozambique, Republic of *see*
Mozambique
Mozambique Rise *see* Mozambique
Plateau
Mozyr' *see* Mazyr
Mpama *77 B6* river C Congo
Mpika *78 D2* Northern, NE Zambia
Mqinvartsveri *see* Kazbek
Mragowo *98 D2* Ger. Sensburg.
Warmińsko-Mazurskie, NE Poland
Mtkvari *see* Kura
Mtwara *73 D8* Mtwara, SE Tanzania
Mualo *see* Messalo, Rio
Muang Chiang Rai *see* Chiang Rai
Muang Kalasin *see* Kalasin
Muang Khammouan *see* Thakhèk
Muang Không *137 D5* Champasak,
S Laos
Muang Khôngxédôn *137 D5* var. Khong
Sedone. Salavan, S Laos
Muang Khon Kaen *see* Khon Kaen
Muang Lampang *see* Lampang
Muang Loei *see* Loei
Muang Lom Sak *see* Lom Sak
Muang Nakhon Sawan *see* Nakhon Sawan
Muang Namo *136 C3* Oudômxai, N Laos
Muang Nan *see* Nan
Muang Phalan *136 D4* var. Muang
Phalane. Savannakhét, S Laos
Muang Phalane *see* Muang Phalan
Muang Phayao *see* Phayao
Muang Phitsanulok *see* Phitsanulok
Muang Phrae *see* Phrae
Muang Roi Et *see* Roi Et
Muang Sakon Nakhon *see* Sakon
Nakhon
Muang Samut Prakan *see* Samut Prakan
Muang Xaignabouri *136 C3* Louang Namtha,
N Laos
Muang Ubon *see* Ubon Ratchathani
Muang Xaignabouri *see* Xaignabouli
Muar *138 B3* var. Bandar Maharani.
Johor, Peninsular Malaysia
Mucojo *79 F2* Cabo Delgado,
N Mozambique
Mudanjiang *129 E3* var. Mu-tan-chiang.
Heilongjiang, NE China

Mudon *137 B5* Mon State, S Burma
(Myanmar)
Muenchen *see* München
Muenster *see* Münster
Mufulira *78 D2* Copperbelt, C Zambia
Mughla *see* Muğla
Muğla *116 A4 var.* Mughla. Muğla,
SW Turkey
Mûh, Sabkhat al *118 C3 lake* C Syria
Muhu Väin *see* Väinameri
Muisne *60 A1* Esmeraldas, NW Ecuador
Mukacheve *108 B3 Hung.* Munkács,
Rus. Mukachevo. Zakarpats'ka Oblast',
W Ukraine
Mukachevo *see* Mukacheve
Mukalla *see* Al Mukallā
Mukden *see* Shenyang
Mula *93 E4* Murcia, SE Spain
Mulakatholhu *132 B4 var.* Meemu Atoll,
Mulaku Atoll. *atoll* C Maldives
Mulaku Atoll *see* Mulakatholhu
Muleshoe *49 E2* Texas, SW USA
Mulhacén *93 E5 var.* Cerro de Mulhacén.
mountain S Spain
Mulhacén, Cerro de *see* Mulhacén
Mülhausen *see* Mulhouse
Mülheim *95 A6 var.* Mulheim an der Ruhr.
Nordrhein-Westfalen, W Germany
Mulheim an der Ruhr *see* Mülheim
Mulhouse *90 E4 Ger.* Mülhausen. Haut-
Rhin, NE France
Müller-gerbergte *see* Muller,
Pegunungan
Muller, Pegunungan *138 D4 Dut.*
Müller-gerbergte. *mountain range*
Borneo, C Indonesia
Mull, Isle of *88 B4 island* W Scotland,
United Kingdom
Mulongo *77 D7* Katanga, SE Dem.
Rep. Congo
Multän *134 C2* Punjab, E Pakistan
Mumbai *134 C5 prev.* Bombay. *state
capital* Mahārāshtra, W India
Munamägi *see* Suur Munamägi
Münchberg *95 C5* Bayern, E Germany
München *95 C6 var.* Muenchen,
Eng. Munich, *It.* Monaco. Bayern,
SE Germany
Muncie *40 C4* Indiana, N USA
Mungbere *77 E5* Orientale, NE Dem.
Rep. Congo
Mu Nggava *see* Rennell
Munich *see* München
Munkács *see* Mukacheve
Münster *94 A4 var.* Muenster, Münster
in Westfalen. Nordrhein-Westfalen,
W Germany
Munster *89 A6 Ir.* Cúige Mumhan.
cultural region S Ireland
Münster in Westfalen *see* Münster
Muong Xiang Ngeun *136 C4 var.* Xieng
Ngeun. Louangphabang, N Laos
Muonio *84 D3* Lappi, N Finland
Muonioälv/Muoniojoki *see* Muonionjoki
Muonionjoki *84 D3 var.* Muoniojoki,
Swe. Muonioälv. *river* Finland/Sweden
Muqät *119 C5* Al Mafraq, E Jordan
Muqdisho *73 D6 Eng.* Mogadishu, *It.*
Mogadiscio. *country capital* (Somalia)
(Somalia) Banaadir, S Somalia
Mur *95 E7 SCr.* Mura. *river* C Europe
Mura *see* Mur
Muradiye *117 F3* Van, E Turkey
Murapara *see* Murupara
Murata *96 E2* S San Marino
Murchison River *147 A5 river* Western
Australia
Murcia *93 E4* Murcia, SE Spain
Murcia *93 E4 autonomous community*
SE Spain
Mureş *108 A4 river* Hungary/Romania
Murfreesboro *42 D1* Tennessee, S USA
Murgab *see* Morghāb, Daryā-ye/Murgap/
Murghob
Murgab *see* Morghāb, Daryā-ye/Murgap/
Murghob
Murgab *see* Murghob
Murgap *122 D3* Mary Welaýaty,
S Turkmenistan
Murgap *122 D3 var.* Deryasy Murgap,
Murghab, *Pash.* Daryā-ye Morghāb,
Rus. Murgab. *river* Afghanistan/
Turkmenistan
Murgap *see* Morghāb, Daryā-ye
Murgap *see* Morghāb, Daryā-ye

Murgap Deryasy *see* Morghāb, Daryā-ye
Murgap Deryasy *see* Morghāb, Daryā-ye
Murghab *see* Morghāb, Daryā-ye
Murghab *see* Morghāb, Daryā-ye
Murghob *123 F3 Rus.* Murgab.
SE Tajikistan
Murgon *149 E5* Queensland, E Australia
Mūritāniyah *see* Mauritania
Müritz *94 C3 var.* Müritzee. *lake*
NE Germany
Müritzee *see* Müritz
Murmansk *110 C2* Murmanskaya
Oblast', NW Russian Federation
Murmashi *110 C2* Murmanskaya
Oblast', NW Russian Federation
Murom *111 B5* Vladimirskaya Oblast',
W Russian Federation
Muroran *130 D3* Hokkaidō, NE Japan
Muros *92 B1* Galicia, NW Spain
Murray Fracture Zone *153 E2 fracture
zone* NE Pacific Ocean
Murray Range *see* Murray Ridge
Murray Ridge *121 C5 var.* Murray
Range. *undersea ridge* N Arabian Sea
Murray River *149 B6 river* SE Australia
Murrumbidgee River *149 C6 river* New
South Wales, SE Australia
Murska Sobota *95 E7 Ger.* Olsnitz.
NE Slovenia
Murupara *150 E3 var.* Murapara. Bay of
Plenty, North Island, New Zealand
Murviedro *see* Sagunto
Murwāra *135 E4* Madhya Pradesh,
N India
Murwillumbah *149 E5* New South
Wales, SE Australia
Murzuq, Edeyin *see* Murzuq, Idhān
Murzuq, Idhan *71 F4 var.* Edeyin
Murzuq. *desert* SW Libya
Mürzzuschlag *95 E7* Steiermark,
E Austria
Muş *117 F3 var.* Mush. Muş, E Turkey
Musa, Gebel *72 C2 var.* Gebel Mûsa.
mountain NE Egypt
Mûsa, Gebel *see* Mûsa, Jabal
Musala *104 B3 mountain* W Bulgaria
Muscat *see* Masqaṭ
Muscat and Oman *see* Oman
Muscatine *45 G3* Iowa, C USA
Musgrave Ranges *147 D5 mountain
range* South Australia
Musina *78 D3 prev.* Messina. Limpopo,
NE South Africa
Muskegon *40 C3* Michigan, N USA
Muskogean *see* Tallahassee
Muskogee *49 G1* Oklahoma, C USA
Musoma *73 B6* Mara, N Tanzania
Musta *see* Mosta
Mustafa-Pasha *see* Svilengrad
Musters, Lago *65 B6 lake* S Argentina
Muswellbrook *149 D6* New South
Wales, SE Australia
Mut *116 C4* İçel, S Turkey
Mu-tan-chiang *see* Mudanjiang
Mutare *78 D3 var.* Mutari; *prev.* Umtali.
Manicaland, E Zimbabwe
Mutari *see* Mutare
Mutina *see* Modena
Mutsu-wan *130 D3 bay* N Japan
Muttonbird Islands *151 A8 island group*
SW New Zealand
Mu Us Shadi *127 E3 var.* Ordos Desert;
prev. Mu Us Shamo. *desert* N China
Mu Us Shamo *see* Mu Us Shadi
Muy Muy *52 D3* Matagalpa, C Nicaragua
Muynak *see* Mo'ynoq
Mužlja *100 D3 Hung.* Felsőmuzslya; *prev.*
Gornja Mužlja. Vojvodina, N Serbia
Mwali *79 F2 var.* Moili, *Fr.* Mohéli.
island S Comoros
Mwanza *73 B6* Mwanza,
NW Tanzania
Mweka *77 C6* Kasai-Occidental, C Dem.
Rep. Congo
Mwene-Ditu *77 D7* Kasai-Oriental,
S Dem. Rep. Congo
Mweru, Lake *77 D7 var.* Lac Moero. *lake*
Dem. Rep. Congo/Zambia
Myadel' *see* Myadzyel
Myadzyel *107 C5 Pol.* Miadzioł Nowy,
Rus. Myadel'. Minskaya Voblasts',
N Belarus
Myanaung *136 B4* Ayeyarwady,
SW Burma (Myanmar)
Myanmar *136 A3 off.* Union of Myanmar,
Myanmar. *country* SE Asia. *See also*
Burma

MYANMAR (BURMA)
Southeast Asia

Official name Union of Myanmar
Formation 1948 / 1948
Capital Nay Pyi Taw
Population 51.5 million / 203 people
per sq mile (78 people per sq km) / 30%
Total area 261,969 sq. miles
(678,500 sq. km)
Languages Burmese*, Shan, Karen,
Rakhine, Chin, Yangbye, Kachin, Mon
Religions Buddhist 87%, Christian 6%,
Muslim 4%, Other 2%, Hindu 1%
Ethnic mix Burman (Bamah) 68%,
Other 13%, Shan 9%, Karen 6%,
Rakhine 4%
Government Military-based regime
Currency Kyat = 100 pyas
Literacy rate 90%
Calorie consumption 2937 calories

Myaungmya *136 A4* Ayeyarwady,
SW Burma (Myanmar)
Myaydo *see* Aunglan
Myeik *137 B6 var.* Mergui. Tanintharyi,
S Burma (Myanmar)
Myerkulavichy *107 D7 Rus.*
Merkulovichi. Homyel'skaya Voblasts',
SE Belarus
Myingyan *136 B3* Mandalay, C Burma
(Myanmar)
Myitkyina *136 B2* Kachin State, N Burma
(Myanmar)
Mykolayiv *109 E4 Rus.* Nikolayev.
Mykolayivs'ka Oblast', S Ukraine
Mykonos *105 D6 var.* Míkonos. *island*
Kykládes, Greece, Aegean Sea
Myrhorod *109 F2 Rus.* Mirgorod.
Poltavs'ka Oblast', NE Ukraine
Mýrina *104 D4 var.* Mírina. Límnos,
SE Greece
Myrtle Beach *43 F2* South Carolina,
SE USA
Mýrtos *105 D8* Kríti, Greece,
E Mediterranean Sea
Myrtoum Mare *see* Mirtóo Pélagos
Myślibórz *98 B3* Zachodnio-pomorskie,
NW Poland
Mysore *132 C2 var.* Maisur. Karnātaka,
W India
Mysore *see* Karnātaka
My Tho *137 E6 var.* Mi Tho. Tiền Giang,
S Vietnam
Mytilene *see* Mytilíni
Mytilíni *105 D5 var.* Mitilíni; *anc.*
Mytilene. Lésvos, E Greece
Mzuzu *79 E2* Northern, N Malawi

N

Naberezhnyye Chelny *111 D5 prev.*
Brezhnev. Respublika Tatarstan,
W Russian Federation
Nablus *119 A6 var.* Nābulus, *Heb.*
Shekhem; *anc.* Neapolis, *Bibl.* Shechem.
N West Bank
Nābulus *see* Nablus
Nacala *79 F2* Nampula, NE Mozambique
Na-Ch'ii *see* Nagqu
Nada *see* Danzhou
Nadi *145 E4 prev.* Nandi. Viti Levu, W Fiji
Nadur *102 A5* Gozo, N Malta
Nadvirna *108 C3 Pol.* Nadwórna, *Rus.*
Nadvornaya. Ivano-Frankivs'ka
Oblast', W Ukraine
Nadvoitsy *110 B3* Respublika Kareliya,
NW Russian Federation
Nadvornaya/Nadwórna *see* Nadvirna
Nadym *114 C3* Yamalo-Nenetskiy
Avtonomnyy Okrug, N Russian
Federation
Náfpaktos *105 B5 var.* Návpaktos.
Dytikí Ellás, C Greece
Náfplio *105 B6 prev.* Návplion.
Pelopónnisos, S Greece
Naga *139 E1 off.* Naga City; *prev.* Nueva
Caceres. Luzon, N Philippines
Naga City *see* Naga
Nagano *131 C5* Nagano, Honshū, S Japan
Nagaoka *131 D5* Niigata, Honshū, S Japan
Nagara Pathom *see* Nakhon Pathom
Nagara Sridharmaraj *see* Nakhon Si
Thammarat
Nagara Svarga *see* Nakhon Sawan
Nagasaki *131 A7* Nagasaki, Kyūshū,
SW Japan

Nagato *131 A7* Yamaguchi, Honshū,
SW Japan
Nägercoil *132 C3* Tamil Nādu, SE India
Nagorno-Karabakh *117 G3 var.*
Nagorno- Karabakhskaya
Avtonomnaya Oblast, *Arm.* Lerrnayin
Gharabakh, *Az.* Dağliq Quarabağ,
Rus. Nagornyy Karabakh. *former
autonomous region* SW Azerbaijan
**Nagorno- Karabakhskaya
Avtonomnaya Oblast** *see*
Nagorno-Karabakh
Nagornyy Karabakh *see*
Nagorno-Karabakh
Nagoya *131 C6* Aichi, Honshū, SW Japan
Nägpur *134 D4* Mahārāshtra, C India
Nagqu *126 C5 Chin.* Na-Ch'ii; *prev.* Hei-
ho. Xizang Zizhiqu, W China
Nagybánya *see* Baia Mare
Nagybecskerek *see* Zrenjanin
Nagydisznód *see* Cisnădie
Nagyenyed *see* Aiud
Nagykálló *99 E6* Szabolcs-Szatmár-
Bereg, E Hungary
Nagykanizsa *99 C7 Ger.* Grosskanizsa.
Zala, SW Hungary
Nagykároly *see* Carei
Nagykikinda *see* Kikinda
Nagykőrös *99 D7* Pest, C Hungary
Nagymihály *see* Michalovce
Nagyszalonta *see* Salonta
Nagyszeben *see* Sibiu
Nagyszentmiklós *see* Sânnicolau Mare
Nagyszöllős *see* Vynohradiv
Nagyszombat *see* Trnava
Nagytapolcsány *see* Topoľčany
Nagyvárad *see* Oradea
Naha *130 A3* Okinawa, Okinawa,
SW Japan
Nahariya *119 A5 prev.* Nahariyya.
Northern, N Israel
Nahariyya *see* Nahariya
Nahuel Huapí, Lago *65 B5 lake*
W Argentina
Nain *39 F2* Newfoundland and Labrador,
NE Canada
Nā'īn *120 D3* Eşfahān, C Iran
Nairobi *69 E5 country capital* (Kenya)
(Kenya) Nairobi Area, S Kenya
Nairobi *73 C6* Nairobi Area, S Kenya
Naissus *see* Niš
Najaf *see* An Najaf
Najima *see* Fukuoka
Najin *129 E3* NE North Korea
Najrān *121 B6 var.* Abā as Su'ūd. Najrān,
S Saudi Arabia
Nakambé *see* White Volta
Nakamura *131 B7 var.* Shimanto. Kōchi,
Shikoku, SW Japan
Nakatsugawa *131 C6 var.* Nakatugawa.
Gifu, Honshū, SW Japan
Nakatugawa *see* Nakatsugawa
Nakhichevan' *see* Naxçivan
Nakhodka *115 G5* Primorskiy Kray,
SE Russian Federation
Nakhon Pathom *137 C5 var.* Nagara
Pathom, Nakon Pathom. Nakhon
Pathom, W Thailand
Nakhon Ratchasima *137 C5 var.*
Khorat, Korat. Nakhon Ratchasima,
E Thailand
Nakhon Sawan *137 C5 var.* Muang
Nakhon Sawan, Nagara Svarga.
Nakhon Sawan, W Thailand
Nakhon Si Thammarat *137 C7 var.*
Nagara Sridharmaraj, Nakhon
Sithammarat. Nakhon Si Thammarat,
SW Thailand
Nakhon Sithamnaraj *see* Nakhon Si
Thammarat
Nakorn Pathom *see* Nakhon Pathom
Nakuru *73 C6* Rift Valley, SW Kenya
Nal'chik *111 B8* Kabardino-Balkarskaya
Respublika, SW Russian Federation
Nālūt *71 F2* NW Libya
Namakan Lake *40 A1* lake Canada/USA
Namangan *123 F2* Namangan Viloyati,
E Uzbekistan
Nambala *78 D2* Central, C Zambia
Nam Co *126 C5* lake W China
Nam Đinh *136 D3* Nam Ha,
N Vietnam
Namib Desert *78 B3 desert* W Namibia
Namibe *78 A2 Port.* Moçâmedes,
Mossâmedes. Namibe, SW Angola

Namibia *78 B3 off.* Republic of Namibia, *var.* South West Africa, *Afr.* Suidwes-Afrika, *Ger.* Deutsch-Südwestafrika; *prev.* German Southwest Africa, South-West Africa. *country* S Africa

NAMIBIA
Southern Africa

Official name Republic of Namibia
Formation 1990 / 1994
Capital Windhoek
Population 2.1 million / 7 people per sq mile (3 people per sq km) / 33%
Total area 318,694 sq. miles (825,418 sq. km)
Languages English*, Ovambo, Kavango, Bergdama, German, Afrikaans
Religions Christian 90%, Traditional beliefs 10%
Ethnic mix Ovambo 50%, Other tribes 24%, Kavango 9%, Damara 8%, Herero 8%, Other 1%
Government Presidential system
Currency Namibian dollar = 100 cents
Literacy rate 85%
Calorie consumption 2278 calories

Namibia, Republic of *see* Namibia
Namnetes *see* Nantes
Namo *see* Namu Atoll
Nam Ou *136 C3 river* N Laos
Nampa *46 D3* Idaho, NW USA
Nampula *79 E2* Nampula, NE Mozambique
Namsos *84 B4* Nord-Trøndelag, C Norway
Nam Tha *136 C4 river* N Laos
Namu Atoll *144 D2 var.* Namo. *atoll* Ralik Chain, C Marshall Islands
Namur *87 C6 Dut.* Namen. Namur, SE Belgium
Namyit Island *128 C8 island* S Spratly Islands
Nan *136 C4 var.* Muang Nan. Nan, NW Thailand
Nanaimo *36 D5* Vancouver Island, British Columbia, SW Canada
Nanchang *128 C5 var.* Nan-ch'ang, Nanch'ang-hsien. *province capital* Jiangxi, S China
Nan-ch'ang *see* Nanchang
Nanch'ang-hsien *see* Nanchang
Nancy *90 D3* Meurthe-et-Moselle, NE France
Nandaime *52 D3* Granada, SW Nicaragua
Nänded *134 D5* Mahārāshtra, C India
Nandi *see* Nadi
Nándorhgy *see* Oţelu Roşu
Nandyäl *132 C1* Andhra Pradesh, E India
Nan Hai *see* South China Sea
Naniwa *see* Ōsaka
Nanjing *128 D5 var.* Nan-ching, Nanking; *prev.* Chianning, Chian-ning, Kiang-ning, Jiangsu. *province capital* Jiangsu, E China
Nanking *see* Nanjing
Nanning *128 B6 var.* Nan-ning; *prev.* Yung-ning. Guangxi Zhuangzu Zizhiqu, S China
Nan-ning *see* Nanning
Nanortalik *82 C5* Kitaa, S Greenland
Nanpan Jiang *136 D2 river* C China
Nanping *128 D6 var.* Nan-p'ing; *prev.* Yenping. Fujian, SE China
Nan-p'ing *see* Nanping
Nansei Syotō Trench *see* Ryukyu Trench
Nansen Basin *155 C4 undersea basin* Arctic Ocean
Nansen Cordillera *155 B3 var.* Arctic Mid Oceanic Ridge, Nansen Ridge. *seamount range* Arctic Ocean
Nansen Ridge *see* Nansen Cordillera
Nansha Qundao *see* Spratly Islands
Nanterre *90 D1* Hauts-de-Seine, N France
Nantes *90 B4 Bret.* Naoned; *anc.* Condivincum, Namnetes. Loire-Atlantique, NW France
Nantucket Island *41 G3 island* Massachusetts, NE USA
Nanumaga *145 E3 var.* Nanumanga. *atoll* NW Tuvalu

Nanyang *128 C5 var.* Nan-yang. Henan, C China
Nan-yang *see* Nanyang
Naoned *see* Nantes
Napa *47 B6* California, W USA
Napier *150 E4* Hawke's Bay, North Island, New Zealand
Naples *43 E5* Florida, SE USA
Naples *see* Napoli
Napo *56 A3 province* NE Ecuador
Napoléon-Vendée *see* la Roche-sur-Yon
Napoli *97 C5 Eng.* Naples, *Ger.* Neapel; *anc.* Neapolis. Campania, S Italy
Napo, Río *60 C1 river* Ecuador/Peru
Naracoorte *149 B7* South Australia
Naradhivas *see* Narathiwat
Narathiwat *137 C7 var.* Naradhivas. Narathiwat, SW Thailand
Narbada *see* Narmada
Narbo Martius *see* Narbonne
Narbonne *91 C6 anc.* Narbo Martius. Aude, S France
Narborough Island *see* Fernandina, Isla
Nares Abyssal Plain *see* Nares Plain
Nares Plain *35 E6 var.* Nares Abyssal Plain. *abyssal plain* NW Atlantic Ocean
Nares Stræde *see* Nares Strait
Nares Strait *82 D1 Dan.* Nares Stræde. *strait* Canada/Greenland
Narew *98 E3 river* E Poland
Narmada *124 B3 var.* Narbada. *river* C India
Narova *see* Narva
Narovlya *107 C8 Rus.* Narovlya.
Homyel'skaya Voblasts', SE Belarus
Närpes *85 D5 Fin.* Närpiö. Länsi-Suomi, W Finland
Närpiö *see* Närpes
Narrabri *149 D6* New South Wales, SE Australia
Narrogin *147 B6* Western Australia
Narva *106 E2* Ida-Virumaa, NE Estonia
Narva *106 E2 prev.* Narova. *river* Estonia/Russian Federation
Narva Bay *106 E2 Est.* Narva Laht, *Ger.* Narwa-Bucht, *Rus.* Narvskiy Zaliv. *bay* Estonia/Russian Federation
Narva Laht *see* Narva Bay
Narva Reservoir *106 E2 Est.* Narva Veehoidla, *Rus.* Narvskoye Vodokhranilishche. *reservoir* Estonia/Russian Federation
Narva Veehoidla *see* Narva Reservoir
Narvik *84 C3* Nordland, C Norway
Narvskiy Zaliv *see* Narva Bay
Narvskoye Vodokhranilishche *see* Narva Reservoir
Narwa-Bucht *see* Narva Bay
Nar'yan-Mar *110 D3 prev.* Beloshchel'ye, Dzerzhinskiy. Nenetskiy Avtonomnyy Okrug, NW Russian Federation
Naryn *123 G2* Narynskaya Oblast', C Kyrgyzstan
Nassau *54 C1 country capital* (Bahamas) (Bahamas) New Providence, N Bahamas
Năsăud *108 B3 Ger.* Nussdorf, *Hung.* Naszód. Bistriţa-Năsăud, N Romania
Nase *see* Naze
Näshik *134 C5 prev.* Nāsik. Mahārāshtra, W India
Nashua *41 G3* New Hampshire, NE USA
Nashville *42 C1 state capital* Tennessee, S USA
Näsijärvi *85 D5 lake* SW Finland
Näsik *see* Nāshik
Nasir, Buhayrat/Nāşir,Buḥeiret *see* Nasser, Lake
Nāsiri *see* Ahvāz
Nasiriya *see* An Nāşirīyah
Nasser, Lake *72 B3 var.* Buhayrat Nasir, Buḥayrat Nāşir, Buḥeiret Nâşir. *lake* Egypt/Sudan
Naszód *see* Năsăud
Nata *78 C4* Central, NE Botswana
Natal *63 G2 state capital* Rio Grande do Norte, E Brazil
Natal Basin *141 A6 var.* Mozambique Basin. *undersea basin* W Indian Ocean
Natanya *see* Netanya
Natchez *42 B3* Mississippi, S USA
Natchitoches *42 A2* Louisiana, S USA
Nathanya *see* Netanya
Natitingou *75 F4* NW Benin
Natsrat *see* Natzrat
Natuna Islands *see* Natuna, Kepulauan

Natuna, Kepulauan *124 D4 var.* Natuna Islands. *island group* W Indonesia
Naturaliste Plateau *141 E6 undersea plateau* E Indian Ocean
Natzrat *119 A5 var.* Natsrat, *Ar.* En Nazira, *Eng.* Nazareth; *prev.* Naẓerat. Northern, N Israel
Naugard *see* Nowogard
Naujamiestis *106 C4* Panevėžys, C Lithuania
Nauru *144 D2 off.* Republic of Nauru; *prev.* Pleasant Island. *country* W Pacific Ocean

NAURU
Australasia & Oceania

Official name Republic of Nauru
Formation 1968 / 1968
Capital None
Population 13,528 / 1670 people per sq mile (644 people per sq km) /
Total area 8.1 sq. miles (21 sq. km)
Languages Nauruan*, Kiribati, Chinese, Tuvaluan, English
Religions Nauruan Congregational Church 60%, Roman Catholic 35%, Other 5%
Ethnic mix Nauruan 62%, Other Pacific islanders 27%, Asian 8%, European 3%
Government Nonparty system
Currency Australian dollar = 100 cents
Literacy rate 95%
Calorie consumption Not available

Nauru, Republic of *see* Nauru
Nauta *60 C2* Loreto, N Peru
Navahrudak *107 C6 Pol.* Nowogródek, *Rus.* Novogrudok. Hrodzyenskaya Voblasts', W Belarus
Navanagar *see* Jāmnagar
Navapolatsk *107 D5 Rus.* Novopolotsk. Vitsyebskaya Voblasts', N Belarus
Navarra *93 E2 Eng./Fr.* Navarre. *autonomous community* N Spain
Navarre *see* Navarra
Navassa Island *54 C3 US unincorporated territory* C West Indies
Navoi *see* Navoiy
Navoiy *123 E2 Rus.* Navoi. Navoiy Viloyati, C Uzbekistan
Navojoa *50 C2* Sonora, NW Mexico
Navolat *see* Navolato
Navolato *50 C3 var.* Navolat. Sinaloa, C Mexico
Návpaktos *see* Náfpaktos
Návplion *see* Náfplio
Nawabashah *see* Nawābshāh
Nawābshāh *134 B3 var.* Nawabashah. Sind, S Pakistan
Naxçıvan *117 G3 Rus.* Nakhichevan'. SW Azerbaijan
Náxos *105 D6 var.* Naxos. Náxos, Kykládes, Greece, Aegean Sea
Náxos *105 D6 island* Kykládes, Greece, Aegean Sea
Nayoro *130 D2* Hokkaidō, NE Japan
Nay Pyi Taw *136 B4 country capital* (Myanmar (Burma)) Mandalay, C Burma (Myanmar)
Nazareth *see* Natzrat
Nazca *60 D4* Ica, S Peru
Nazca Ridge *57 A5 undersea ridge* E Pacific Ocean
Naze *130 B3 var.* Nase. Kagoshima, Amami-ōshima, SW Japan
Naẓerat *see* Natzrat
Nazilli *116 A4* Aydın, SW Turkey
Nazrēt *73 C5 var.* Adama, Hadama. Oromiya, C Ethiopia
N'Dalatando *78 B1 Port.* Salazar, Vila Salazar. Cuanza Norte, NW Angola
Ndélé *76 C4* Bamingui-Bangoran, N Central African Republic
Ndendé *77 B6* Ngounié, S Gabon
Ndindi *77 A6* Nyanga, S Gabon
Ndjamena *76 B3 var.* N'Djamena; *prev.* Fort-Lamy. *country capital* (Chad) Chari-Baguirmi, W Chad
N'Djamena *see* Ndjamena
Ndjolé *77 A5* Moyen-Ogooué, W Gabon
Ndola *78 D2* Copperbelt, C Zambia
Ndzouani *see* Anjouan
Neagh, Lough *89 B5 lake* E Northern Ireland, United Kingdom
Néa Moudhaniá *104 C4 var.* Néa Moudhaniá. Kentrikí Makedonía, N Greece

Néa Moudhaniá *see* Néa Moudanía
Neapel *see* Napoli
Neápoli *104 B4 prev.* Neápolis. Dytikí Makedonía, N Greece
Neápoli *105 D8* Kríti, Greece, E Mediterranean Sea
Neápoli *105 C7* Pelopónnisos, S Greece
Neápolis *see* Napoli, Italy
Neapolis *see* Nablus, West Bank
Near Islands *36 A2 island group* Aleutian Islands, Alaska, USA
Néa Zíchni *104 C3 var.* Néa Zíkhni; *prev.* Néa Zíkhna. Kentrikí Makedonía, NE Greece
Néa Zíkhna/Néa Zíkhni *see* Néa Zíchni
Nebaj *52 B2* Quiché, W Guatemala
Nebitdag *see* Balkanabat
Neblina, Pico da *62 C1 mountain* NW Brazil
Nebraska *44 D4 off.* State of Nebraska, *also known as* Blackwater State, Cornhusker State, Tree Planters State. *state* C USA
Nebraska City *45 F4* Nebraska, C USA
Neches River *49 H3 river* Texas, SW USA
Neckar *95 B6 river* SW Germany
Necochea *65 D5* Buenos Aires, E Argentina
Nederland *see* Netherlands
Neder Rijn *86 D4 Eng.* Lower Rhine. *river* C Netherlands
Nederweert *87 D5* Limburg, SE Netherlands
Neede *86 E3* Gelderland, E Netherlands
Neerpelt *87 D5* Limburg, NE Belgium
Neftekamsk *111 D5* Respublika Bashkortostan, W Russian Federation
Neftezavodsk *see* Seýdi
Negara Brunei Darussalam *see* Brunei
Negêlê *73 D5 var.* Negelli, *It.* Neghelli. Oromiya, C Ethiopia
Negelli *see* Negêlê
Negev *119 A7 Eng.* Negev. *desert* S Israel
Negev *see* HaNegev
Neghelli *see* Negêlê
Negomane *79 E2 var.* Negomano. Cabo Delgado, N Mozambique
Negomano *see* Negomane
Negombo *132 C3* Western Province, SW Sri Lanka
Negotin *100 E4* Serbia, E Serbia
Negra, Punto *60 A3 headland* NW Peru
Negreşti *see* Negreşti-Oaş
Negreşti-Oaş *108 B3 Hung.* Avasfelsőfalu; *prev.* Negreşti. Satu Mare, NE Romania
Negro, Río *65 C5 river* E Argentina
Negro, Río *62 D1 river* N South America
Negro, Río *64 D4 river* Brazil/Uruguay
Negro, Río *63 G2 river* E Brazil
Negros *139 E2 island* C Philippines
Nehbandān *120 E3* Khorāsān, E Iran
Neijiang *128 B5* Sichuan, C China
Neiva *58 B3* Huila, S Colombia
Nellore *132 D2* Andhra Pradesh, E India
Nelson *151 C5* Nelson, South Island, New Zealand
Nelson *37 G4 river* Manitoba, C Canada
Néma *74 D3* Hodh ech Chargui, SE Mauritania
Neman *106 B4 Bel.* Nyoman, *Ger.* Memel, *Lith.* Nemunas, *Pol.* Niemen. *river* NE Europe
Nemausus *see* Nîmes
Neméa *105 B6* Pelopónnisos, S Greece
Nemetocenna *see* Arras
Nemours *90 C3* Seine-et-Marne, N France
Nemunas *see* Neman
Nemuro *130 E2* Hokkaidō, NE Japan
Neochóri *105 B5* Dytikí Ellás, C Greece
Nepal *135 E3 off.* Nepal. *country* S Asia

NEPAL
South Asia

Official name Nepal
Formation 1769 / 1769
Capital Kathmandu
Population 26.3 million / 534 people per sq mile (206 people per sq km) / 15%
Total area 54,363 sq. miles (140,800 sq. km)

NEPAL
(converted)

Languages Nepali*, Maithili, Bhojpuri
Religions Hindu 90%, Buddhist 5%,
Muslim 3%, Other (including Christian) 2%
Ethnic mix Other 52%, Chhetri 16%,
Hill Brahman 13%, Tharu 7%, Magar 7%,
Tamang 5%
Government Parliamentary system
Currency Nepalese rupee = 100 paisa
Literacy rate 49%
Calorie consumption 2453 calories

Nepal *see* Nepal
Nereta 106 C4 Aizkraukle, S Latvia
Neretva 100 C4 *river* Bosnia and
Herzegovina/Croatia
Neris 107 C5 *Bel.* Viliya, *Pol.* Wilia; *prev.*
Pol. Wilja. *river* Belarus/Lithuania
Neris *see* Viliya
Nerva 92 C4 Andalucía, S Spain
Neryungri 115 F4 Respublika Sakha
(Yakutiya), NE Russian Federation
Neskaupstadhur 83 E5 Austurland,
E Iceland
Ness, Loch 88 C3 *lake* N Scotland,
United Kingdom
Nesterov *see* Zhovkva
Néstos 104 C3 *Bul.* Mesta, *Turk.* Kara Su.
river Bulgaria/Greece
Nesvizh *see* Nyasvizh
Netanya 119 A6 *var.* Natanya, Nathanya.
Central, C Israel
Netherlands 86 C3 *off.* Kingdom
of the Netherlands, *var.* Holland,
Dut. Koninkrijk der Nederlanden,
Nederland. *country* NW Europe

NETHERLANDS
Northwest Europe

Official name Kingdom of the
Netherlands
Formation 1648 / 1839
Capital Amsterdam; The Hague
(administrative)
Population 16.4 million / 1252 people
per sq mile (483 people per sq km) / 66%
Total area 16,033 sq. miles (41,526 sq. km)
Languages Dutch*, Frisian
Religions Roman Catholic 36%,
Other 34%, Protestant 27%, Muslim 3%
Ethnic mix Dutch 82%, Other 12%,
Surinamese 2%, Turkish 2%, Moroccan 2%
Government Parliamentary system
Currency Euro = 100 cents
Literacy rate 99%
Calorie consumption 3362 calories

Netherlands East Indies *see* Indonesia
Netherlands Guiana *see* Suriname
Netherlands, Kingdom of the *see*
Netherlands
Netherlands New Guinea *see* Papua
Nettilling Lake 37 G3 *lake* Baffin Island,
Nunavut, N Canada
Netze *see* Noteć
Neu Amerika *see* Puławy
Neubrandenburg 94 D3 Mecklenburg-
Vorpommern, NE Germany
Neuchâtel 95 A7 *Ger.* Neuenburg.
Neuchâtel, W Switzerland
Neuchâtel, Lac de 95 A7 *Ger.*
Neuenburger See. *lake* W Switzerland
Neuenburg *see* Neuchâtel
Neuenburger See *see* Neuchâtel, Lac de
Neufchâteau 87 D8 Luxembourg,
SE Belgium
Neugradisk *see* Nova Gradiška
Neuhof *see* Zgierz
Neukuhren *see* Pionerskiy
Neumarkt *see* Târgu Secuiesc, Covasna,
Romania
Neumarkt *see* Târgu Mureş
Neumoldowa *see* Moldova Nouă
Neumünster 94 B2 Schleswig-Holstein,
N Germany
Neunkirchen 95 A5 Saarland,
SW Germany
Neuquén 65 B5 Neuquén, SE Argentina
Neuruppin 94 C3 Brandenburg,
NE Germany
Neusalz an der Oder *see* Nowa Sól
Neu Sandec *see* Nowy Sącz
Neusatz *see* Novi Sad
Neusiedler See 95 E6 *Hung.* Fertő.
Austria/Hungary

Neusohl *see* Banská Bystrica
Neustadt *see* Baia Mare, Maramureş,
Romania
Neustadt an der Haardt *see* Neustadt an
der Weinstrasse
Neustadt an der Weinstrasse 95
B5 *prev.* Neustadt an der Haardt,
hist. Niewenstat; *anc.* Nova Civitas.
Rheinland-Pfalz, SW Germany
Neustadtl *see* Novo mesto
Neustettin *see* Szczecinek
Neustrelitz 94 D3 Mecklenburg-
Vorpommern, NE Germany
Neutra *see* Nitra
Neu-Ulm 95 B6 Bayern, S Germany
Neuwied 95 A5 Rheinland-Pfalz,
W Germany
Neuzen *see* Terneuzen
Nevada 47 C5 *off.* State of Nevada, *also
known as* Battle Born State, Sagebrush
State, Silver State. *state* W USA
Nevada Sierra 92 D5 *mountain range*
S Spain
Nevada, Sierra 47 C6 *mountain range*
W USA
Nevers 90 C4 *anc.* Noviodunum. Nièvre,
C France
Neves 76 E2 São Tomé, S Sao Tome and
Principe, Africa
Nevinnomyssk 111 B7 Stavropol'skiy
Kray, SW Russian Federation
Nevşehir 116 C3 *var.* Nevshehr.
Nevşehir, C Turkey
Newala 73 C8 Mtwara, SE Tanzania
New Albany 40 C5 Indiana, N USA
New Amsterdam 59 G3 E Guyana
Newark 41 F4 New Jersey, NE USA
New Bedford 41 G3 Massachusetts,
NE USA
Newberg 46 B3 Oregon, NW USA
New Bern 43 F1 North Carolina,
SE USA
New Braunfels 49 G4 Texas, SW USA
Newbridge 89 B6 *Ir.* An Droichead Nua.
Kildare, C Ireland
New Britain 144 B3 *island* E Papua
New Guinea
New Brunswick 39 E4 *Fr.* Nouveau-
Brunswick. *province* SE Canada
New Caledonia 144 D4 *var.* Kanaky, *Fr.*
Nouvelle-Calédonie. *French overseas
territory* SW Pacific Ocean
New Caledonia 144 C5 *island* SW Pacific
Ocean
New Caledonia Basin 142 C4 *undersea
basin* W Pacific Ocean
Newcastle 149 D6 New South Wales,
SE Australia
Newcastle *see* Newcastle upon Tyne
Newcastle upon Tyne 88 D4 *var.*
Newcastle, *hist.* Monkchester, *Lat.* Pons
Aelii. NE England, United Kingdom
New Delhi 134 D3 *country capital*
(India) (India) Delhi, N India
New England of the West *see*
Minnesota
Newfoundland 39 G3 *Fr.* Terre-Neuve.
island Newfoundland and Labrador,
SE Canada
Newfoundland and Labrador 39 F2 *Fr.*
Terre Neuve. *province* E Canada
Newfoundland Basin 66 B3 *undersea
feature* NW Atlantic Ocean
New Georgia Islands 144 C3 *island
group* NW Solomon Islands
New Glasgow 39 F4 Nova Scotia,
SE Canada
New Goa *see* Panaji
New Guinea 144 A3 *Dut.* Nieuw Guinea,
Ind. Irian. *island* Indonesia/Papua
New Guinea
New Hampshire 41 F2 *off.* State of New
Hampshire, *also known as* Granite
State. *state* NE USA
New Haven 41 G3 Connecticut,
NE USA
New Hebrides *see* Vanuatu
New Iberia 42 B3 Louisiana, S USA
New Ireland 144 C3 *island* NE Papua
New Guinea
New Jersey 41 F4 *off.* State of New
Jersey, *also known as* The Garden State.
state NE USA
Newman 146 B4 Western Australia
Newmarket 89 E6 E England, United
Kingdom

New Mexico 48 C2 *off.* State of New
Mexico, *also known as* Land of
Enchantment, Sunshine State. *state*
SW USA
New Orleans 42 B3 Louisiana, S USA
New Plymouth 150 C4 Taranaki, North
Island, New Zealand
Newport 89 D7 S England, United
Kingdom
Newport 89 C7 SE Wales, United
Kingdom
Newport 40 C4 Kentucky, S USA
Newport 41 G2 Vermont, NE USA
Newport News 41 F5 Virginia, NE USA
New Providence 54 C1 *island*
N Bahamas
Newquay 89 C7 SW England, United
Kingdom
Newry 89 B5 *Ir.* An tIúr. SE Northern
Ireland, United Kingdom
New Sarum *see* Salisbury
New Siberian Islands 115 F1 *Eng.*
New Siberian Islands. *island group*
N Russian Federation
New Siberian Islands *see* Novosibirskiye
Ostrova
New South Wales 149 C6 *state*
SE Australia
Newton 45 G3 Iowa, C USA
Newton 45 F5 Kansas, C USA
Newtownabbey 89 B5 *Ir.* Baile na
Mainistreach. E Northern Ireland,
United Kingdom
New Ulm 45 F2 Minnesota, N USA
New York 41 F4 New York, NE USA
New York 41 F3 *state* NE USA
New Zealand 150 A4 *country* SW Pacific
Ocean

NEW ZEALAND
Australasia & Oceania

Official name New Zealand
Formation 1947 / 1947
Capital Wellington
Population 4.1 million / 40 people
per sq mile (15 people per sq km) / 86%
Total area 103,737 sq. miles
(268,680 sq. km)
Languages English*, Maori*
Religions Anglican 24%, Other 22%,
Presbyterian 18%, Nonreligious 16%,
Roman Catholic 15%, Methodist 5%
Ethnic mix European 75%, Maori 15%,
Other 7%, Samoan 3%
Government Parliamentary system
Currency New Zealand dollar = 100 cents
Literacy rate 99%
Calorie consumption 3219 calories

Neyveli 132 C2 Tamil Nādu, SE India
Nezhin *see* Nizhyn
Ngangze Co 126 B5 *lake* W China
Ngaoundéré 76 B4 *var.* N'Gaoundéré.
Adamaoua, N Cameroon
N'Gaoundéré *see* Ngaoundéré
Ngazidja 79 F2 *Fr.* Grande-Comore.
island NW Comoros
N'Giva 78 B3 *var.* Ondjiva, *Port.* Vila
Pereira de Eça. Cunene, S Angola
Ngo 77 B6 Plateaux, SE Congo
Ngoko 75 B5 *river* Cameroon/Congo
Ngourti 75 H3 Diffa, E Niger
Nguigmi 75 H3 *var.* N'Guigmi. Diffa,
SE Niger
N'Guigmi *see* Nguigmi
N'Gunza *see* Sumbe
Nguru 75 G3 Yobe, NE Nigeria
Nha Trang 137 E6 Khanh Hoa,
S Vietnam
Niagara Falls 38 D5 Ontario, S Canada
Niagara Falls 41 E3 New York, NE USA
Niagara Falls 40 D3 *waterfall* Canada/
USA
Niamey 75 F3 *country capital* (Niger)
(Niger) Niamey, SW Niger
Niangay, Lac 75 E3 *lake* E Mali
Nia-Nia 77 E5 Orientale, N Dem.
Rep. Congo
Nias, Pulau 138 A3 *island* W Indonesia
Nicaea *see* Nice
Nicaragua 52 D3 *off.* Republic of
Nicaragua. *country* Central America

NICARAGUA
Central America

Official name Republic of Nicaragua
Formation 1838 / 1838

NICARAGUA
(continued)

Capital Managua
Population 5.7 million / 124 people
per sq mile (48 people per sq km) / 58%
Total area 49,998 sq. miles (129,494 sq. km)
Languages Spanish*, English
Creole, Miskito
Religions Roman Catholic 80%,
Protestant Evangelical 17%, Other 3%
Ethnic mix Mestizo 69%, White 14%,
Black 8%, Amerindian 5%, Zambo 4%
Government Presidential system
Currency Córdoba oro = 100 centavos
Literacy rate 77%
Calorie consumption 2298 calories

Lake Nicaragua 52 D4 *var.* Cocibolca,
Gran Lago, *Eng.* Lake Nicaragua. *lake*
S Nicaragua
Nicaragua, Lake *see* Nicaragua, Lago de
Nicaragua, Republic of *see* Nicaragua
Nicaria *see* Ikaría
Nice 91 D6 *It.* Nizza; *anc.* Nicaea. Alpes-
Maritimes, SE France
Nicephorium *see* Ar Raqqah
Nicholas II Land *see* Severnaya Zemlya
Nicholls Town 54 C1 Andros Island,
NW Bahamas
Nicobar Islands 124 B4 *island group*
India, E Indian Ocean
Nicosia 102 C5 *Gk.* Lefkosía, *Turk.*
Lefkoşa. *country capital* (Cyprus)
(Cyprus) C Cyprus
Nicoya 52 D4 Guanacaste, W Costa Rica
Nicoya, Golfo de 52 D5 *gulf* W Costa Rica
Nicoya, Península de 52 D4 *peninsula*
NW Costa Rica
Nida 106 A3 *Ger.* Nidden. Klaipėda,
SW Lithuania
Nidaros *see* Trondheim
Nidden *see* Nida
Nidzica 98 D3 *Ger.* Niedenburg.
Warmińsko-Mazurskie, NE Poland
Niedenburg *see* Nidzica
Niedere Tauern 99 A6 *mountain range*
C Austria
Niemen *see* Neman
Nieśwież *see* Nyasvizh
Nieuw Amsterdam 59 G3 Commewijne,
NE Suriname
Nieuw-Bergen 86 D4 Limburg,
SE Netherlands
Nieuwegein 86 C4 Utrecht,
C Netherlands
Nieuw Guinea *see* New Guinea
Nieuw Nickerie 59 G3 Nickerie,
NW Suriname
Niewenstat *see* Neustadt an der
Weinstrasse
Niğde 116 C4 Niğde, C Turkey
Niger 75 F3 *off.* Republic of Niger.
country W Africa

NIGER
West Africa

Official name Republic of Niger
Formation 1960 / 1960
Capital Niamey
Population 14.9 million / 30 people
per sq mile (12 people per sq km) / 23%
Total area 489,188 sq. miles
(1,267,000 sq. km)
Languages French*, Hausa, Djerma,
Fulani, Tuareg, Teda
Religions Muslim 85%, Traditional
beliefs 14%, Other (including Christian) 1%
Ethnic mix Hausa 54%, Djerma and
Songhai 21%, Peul 9%, Tuareg 9%,
Other 6%
Government Presidential system
Currency CFA franc = 100 centimes
Literacy rate 29%
Calorie consumption 2130 calories

Niger 75 F4 *river* W Africa
Nigeria 75 F4 *off.* Federal Republic of
Nigeria. *country* W Africa

NIGERIA
West Africa

Official name Federal Republic of Nigeria
Formation 1960 / 1961
Capital Abuja

NIGERIA
(continued)

Population 137 million / 390 people
per sq mile (151 people per sq km) / 47%
Total area 356,667 sq. miles
(923,768 sq. km)
Languages English*, Hausa, Yoruba, Ibo
Religions Muslim 50%, Christian 40%,
Traditional beliefs 10%
Ethnic mix Other 29%, Hausa 21%,
Yoruba 21%, Ibo 18%, Fulani 11%
Government Presidential system
Currency Naira = 100 kobo
Literacy rate 67%
Calorie consumption 2726 calories

Nigeria, Federal Republic of *see* Nigeria
Niger, Mouths of the 75 F5 *delta*
S Nigeria
Niger, Republic of *see* Niger
Nihon *see* Japan
Niigata 131 D5 Niigata, Honshū, C Japan
Niihama 131 B7 Ehime, Shikoku,
SW Japan
Ni'ihau 47 A7 *var.* Niihau. *island*
Hawai'i, USA, C Pacific Ocean
Nii-jima 131 D6 *island* E Japan
Nijkerk 86 D3 Gelderland, C Netherlands
Nijlen 87 C5 Antwerpen, N Belgium
Nijmegen 86 D4 Ger. Nimwegen; *anc.*
Noviomagus. Gelderland, SE Netherlands
Nikaria *see* Ikaría
Nikel' 110 C2 Finn. Kolosjoki.
Murmanskaya Oblast', NW Russian
Federation
Nikiniki 139 E5 Timor, S Indonesia
Niklasmarkt *see* Gheorgheni
Nikolainkaupunki *see* Vaasa
Nikolayev *see* Mykolayiv
Nikol'sk *see* Ussuriysk
Nikol'sk-Ussuriyskiy *see* Ussuriysk
Nikopol' 109 F3 Dnipropetrovs'ka
Oblast', SE Ukraine
Nikšić 101 C5 C Montenegro
Nikumaroro 145 E3 ; *prev.* Gardner
Island. *atoll* Phoenix Islands, C Kiribati
Nikunau 145 E3 *var.* Nukunau; *prev.*
Byron Island. *atoll* Tungaru, W Kiribati
Nile 75 F2 *former province* NW Uganda
Nile 68 D3 Ar. Nahr an Nīl. *river* N Africa
Nile Delta 72 B1 *delta* N Egypt
Nīl, Nahr an *see* Nile
Nimes 91 C6 *anc.* Nemausus, Nismes.
Gard, S France
Nimwegen *see* Nijmegen
Nine Degree Channel 132 B3 *channel*
India/Maldives
Ninetyeast Ridge 141 D5 *undersea
feature* N Indian Ocean
Ninety Mile Beach 150 C1 *beach* North
Island, New Zealand
Ningbo 128 D5 *var.* Ning-po, Yin-hsien;
prev. Ninghsien. Zhejiang, SE China
Ning-hsia *see* Ningxia
Ninghsien *see* Ningbo
Ning-po *see* Ningbo
Ningsia/Ningsia Hui/Ningsia Hui
Autonomous Region *see* Ningxia
Ningxia 128 B4 *off.* Ningxia Huizu
Zizhiqu, *var.* Ning-hsia, Ningsia, *Eng.*
Ningsia Hui, Ningsia Hui Autonomous
Region. *autonomous region* N China
Ningxia Huizu Zizhiqu *see* Ningxia
Nio *see* Íos
Nio *see* Íos
Nio *see* Íos
Niobrara River 45 E3 *river* Nebraska/
Wyoming, C USA
Nioro 74 D3 *var.* Nioro du Sahel. Kayes,
W Mali
Nioro du Sahel *see* Nioro
Niort 90 B4 Deux-Sèvres, W France
Nipigon 38 B4 Ontario, S Canada
Nipigon, Lake 38 B3 *lake* Ontario,
S Canada
Nippon *see* Japan
Niš 101 E5 *Eng.* Nish, *Ger.* Nisch; *anc.*
Naissus. Serbia, SE Serbia
Nisab 120 B4 Al Ḩudūd ash Shamālīyah,
N Saudi Arabia
Nisch/Nish *see* Niš
Nisibin *see* Nusaybin
Nisiros *see* Nísyros
Nisko 98 E4 Podkrapackie, SE Poland
Nismes *see* Nimes

Nistru *see* Dniester
Nísyros 105 E7 *var.* Nisiros. *island*
Dodekánisa, Greece, Aegean Sea
Nitra 99 C6 *Ger.* Neutra, *Hung.* Nyitra.
Nitriansky Kraj, SW Slovakia
Nitra 99 C6 *Ger.* Neutra, *Hung.* Nyitra.
river W Slovakia
Niuatobutabu *see* Niuatoputapu
Niuatoputapu 145 E4 *var.*
Niuatobutabu; *prev.* Keppel Island.
island N Tonga
Niue 145 F4 *self-governing territory in
free association with New Zealand*
S Pacific Ocean
Niulakita 145 E3 *var.* Nurakita. *atoll*
S Tuvalu
Niutao 145 E3 *atoll* NW Tuvalu
Nivernais 90 C4 *cultural region* C France
Nizāmābād 134 D5 Andhra Pradesh,
C India
Nizhnegorskiy *see* Nyzhn'ohirs'kyy
Nizhnekamsk 111 C5 Respublika
Tatarstan, W Russian Federation
Nizhnevartovsk 114 D3 Khanty-
Mansiyskiy Avtonomnyy Okrug-Yugra,
C Russian Federation
Nizhniy Novgorod 111 C5 *prev.* Gor'kiy.
Nizhegorodskaya Oblast', W Russian
Federation
Nizhniy Odes 110 D4 Respublika Komi,
NW Russian Federation
Nizhyn 109 E1 *Rus.* Nezhin.
Chernihivs'ka Oblast', NE Ukraine
Nizza *see* Nice
Njombe 73 C8 Iringa, S Tanzania
Nkayi 77 B6 *prev.* Jacob. Bouenza,
S Congo
Nkongsamba 76 A4 *var.* N'Kongsamba.
Littoral, W Cameroon
N'Kongsamba *see* Nkongsamba
Nmai Hka 136 B2 *var.* Me Hka. *river*
N Burma (Myanmar)
Nobeoka 131 B7 Miyazaki, Kyūshū,
SW Japan
Noboribetsu 130 D3 *var.* Noboribetu.
Hokkaidō, NE Japan
Noboribetu *see* Noboribetsu
Nogales 50 B1 Sonora, NW Mexico
Nogales 48 B3 Arizona, SW USA
Nogal Valley *see* Dooxo Nugaaleed
Noire, Rivi`ere *see* Black River
Nokia 85 D5 Länsi-Suomi, W Finland
Nokou 76 B3 Kanem, W Chad
Nola 77 B5 Sangha-Mbaéré, SW Central
African Republic
Nolinsk 111 C5 Kirovskaya Oblast',
NW Russian Federation
Nongkaya *see* Nong Khai
Nong Khai 136 C4 *var.* Mi Chai,
Nongkaya. Nong Khai, E Thailand
Nonouti 144 D2 *prev.* Sydenham Island.
atoll Tungaru, W Kiribati
Noord-Beveland 84 B4 *var.* North
Beveland. *island* SW Netherlands
Noordwijk aan Zee 86 C3 Zuid-Holland,
W Netherlands
Noordzee *see* North Sea
Nora 85 C6 Örebro, C Sweden
Norak 123 E3 *Rus.* Nurek. W Tajikistan
Nord 83 F1 Avannaarsua, N Greenland
Nordaustlandet 83 G1 *island*
NE Svalbard
Norden 94 A3 Niedersachsen,
NW Germany
Norderstedt 94 B3 Schleswig-Holstein,
N Germany
Nordfriesische Inseln *see* North Frisian
Islands
Nordhausen 94 C4 Thüringen,
C Germany
Nordhorn 94 A3 Niedersachsen,
NW Germany
Nord, Mer du *see* North Sea
Nord-Ouest, Territoires du *see*
Northwest Territories
Nordsee/Nordsjøen/Nordsøen *see*
North Sea
Norfolk 45 E3 Nebraska, C USA
Norfolk 41 F5 Virginia, NE USA
Norfolk Island 142 D4 *Australian
external territory* SW Pacific Ocean
Norfolk Ridge 142 D4 *undersea feature*
W Pacific Ocean
Norge *see* Norway
Norias 49 G5 Texas, SW USA
Noril'sk 114 D3 Taymyrskiy (Dolgano-
Nenetskiy) Avtonomnyy Okrug,
N Russian Federation

Norman 49 G1 Oklahoma, C USA
Normandes, Îles *see* Channel Islands
Normandie 90 B3 *Eng.* Normandy.
cultural region N France
Normandy *see* Normandie
Normanton 148 C3 Queensland,
NE Australia
Norrköping 85 C6 Östergötland,
S Sweden
Norrtälje 85 C6 Stockholm, C Sweden
Norseman 147 B6 Western Australia
Norske Havet *see* Norwegian Sea
North Albanian Alps 101 C5 *Alb.*
Bjeshkët e Namuna, *SCr.* Prokletije.
mountain range SE Europe
Northallerton 89 D5 N England, United
Kingdom
Northam 147 A6 Western Australia
North America 34 *continent*
Northampton 89 D6 C England, United
Kingdom
North Andaman 133 F2 *island*
Andaman Islands, India, NE Indian
Ocean
North Australian Basin 141 E5 *Fr.*
Bassin Nord de l' Australie. *undersea
feature* E Indian Ocean
North Bay 38 D4 Ontario, S Canada
North Beveland *see* Noord-Beveland
North Borneo *see* Sabah
North Cape 150 C1 *headland* North
Island, New Zealand
North Cape 84 D1 *Eng.* North Cape.
headland N Norway
North Cape *see* Nordkapp
North Carolina 43 E1 *off.* State of North
Carolina, *also known as* Old North
State, Tar Heel State, Turpentine State.
state SE USA
North Channel 40 D2 *lake channel*
Canada/USA
North Charleston 43 F2 South Carolina,
SE USA
North Dakota 44 D2 *off.* State of North
Dakota, *also known as* Flickertail
State, Peace Garden State, Sioux State.
state N USA
North Devon Island *see* Devon Island
North East Frontier Agency/North
East Frontier Agency of Assam *see*
Arunāchal Pradesh
Northeast Providence Channel 54 C1
channel N Bahamas
Northeim 94 B4 Niedersachsen,
C Germany
Northern Cook Islands 145 F4 *island
group* N Cook Islands
Northern Dvina 110 C4 *var.* Northern
Dvina. *river* N Russian Federation
Northern Dvina *see* Severnaya Dvina
Northern Ireland 88 B4 *var.* The Six
Counties. *cultural region* Northern
Ireland, United Kingdom
Northern Mariana Islands 142 B1 US
commonwealth territory W Pacific Ocean
Northern Rhodesia *see* Zambia
Northern Sporades 105 C5 *var.* Vóreioi
Sporádes, Vórioi Sporádhes, *Eng.*
Northern Sporades. *island group*
E Greece
Northern Sporades *see* Vóreies Sporádes
Northern Territory 144 A5 *territory*
N Australia
North European Plain 81 E3 *plain*
N Europe
Northfield 45 F2 Minnesota, N USA
North Fiji Basin 142 D3 *undersea
feature* N Coral Sea
North Frisian Islands 94 B2 *var.*
Nordfriesische Inseln. *island group*
N Germany
North Huvadhu Atoll 132 B5 *var.* Gaafu
Alifu Atoll. *atoll* S Maldives
North Island 150 B2 *island* N New
Zealand
North Korea 129 E3 *off.* Democratic
People's Republic of Korea, *Kor.*
Chosŏn-minjujuŭi-inmin-kanghwaguk.
country E Asia

NORTH KOREA
East Asia

Official name Democratic People's
Republic of Korea
Formation 1948 / 1953
Capital Pyongyang

NORTH KOREA
(continued)

Population 22.7 million / 488 people
per sq mile (189 people per sq km) / 61%
Total area 46,540 sq. miles
(120,540 sq. km)
Languages Korean*
Religions Atheist 100%
Ethnic mix Korean 100%
Government One-party state
Currency North Korean won = 100 chon
Literacy rate 98%
Calorie consumption 2142 calories

North Little Rock 42 B1 Arkansas, C USA
North Minch *see* Minch, The
North Mole 93 G4 *harbour wall*
NW Gibraltar Europe
North Platte 45 E4 Nebraska, C USA
North Platte River 44 D4 *river* C USA
North Pole 155 B3 *pole* Arctic Ocean
North Saskatchewan 37 F5 *river*
Alberta/Saskatchewan, S Canada
North Sea 80 D3 *Dan.* Nordsøen, *Dut.*
Noordzee, *Fr.* Mer du Nord, *Ger.*
Nordsee, *Nor.* Nordsjøen; *prev.* German
Ocean, *Lat.* Mare Germanicum. *sea*
NW Europe
North Siberian Lowland 115 E2 *var.*
North Siberian Plain, *Eng.* North
Siberian Lowland. *lowlands* N Russian
Federation
North Siberian Lowland/North
Siberian Plain *see* Severo-Sibirskaya
Nizmennost'
North Star State *see* Minnesota
North Taranaki Bight 150 C3 *gulf* North
Island, New Zealand
North Uist 88 B3 *island* NW Scotland,
United Kingdom
Northwest Atlantic Mid-Ocean Canyon
34 E4 *undersea feature* N Atlantic Ocean
North West Highlands 88 C3 *mountain
range* N Scotland, United Kingdom
Northwest Pacific Basin 113 G4
undersea feature NW Pacific Ocean
Northwest Territories 37 E3 *Fr.*
Territoires du Nord-Ouest. *territory*
NW Canada
Northwind Plain 155 B2 *undersea
feature* Arctic Ocean
Norton Sound 36 C2 *inlet* Alaska, USA
Norway 85 A5 *off.* Kingdom of Norway,
Nor. Norge. *country* N Europe

NORWAY
Northern Europe

Official name Kingdom of Norway
Formation 1905 / 1905
Capital Oslo
Population 4.7 million / 40 people
per sq mile (15 people per sq km) / 80%
Total area 125,181 sq. miles (324,220 sq. km)
Languages Norwegian* (Bokmål
"book language" and Nynorsk
"new Norsk"), Sámi
Religions Evangelical Lutheran 89%,
Other and nonreligious 10%,
Roman Catholic 1%
Ethnic mix Norwegian 93%, Other 6%,
Sámi 1%
Government Parliamentary system
Currency Norwegian krone = 100 øre
Literacy rate 99%
Calorie consumption 3484 calories

Norway, Kingdom of *see* Norway
Norwegian Basin 83 F4 *undersea feature*
NW Norwegian Sea
Norwegian Sea 83 F4 *var.* Norske Havet.
sea NE Atlantic Ocean
Norwich 89 E6 E England, United
Kingdom
Nösen *see* Bistrița
Noshiro 130 D4 *var.* Nosiro; *prev.*
Noshirominato. Akita, Honshū,
C Japan
Noshirominato/Nosiro *see* Noshiro
Nosivka 109 E1 *Rus.* Nosovka.
Chernihivs'ka Oblast', NE Ukraine
Nosovka *see* Nosivka
Noșratābād 120 E3 Sīstān va
Balūchestān, E Iran
Nossob 78 C4 *river* E Namibia
Noteć 98 C3 *Ger.* Netze. *river* NW Poland

Nóties Sporádes see Dodekánisa
Nottingham 89 D6 C England, United Kingdom
Nouâdhibou 74 B2 prev. Port-Étienne. Dakhlet Nouâdhibou, W Mauritania
Nouakchott 74 B2 country capital (Mauritania) (Mauritania) Nouakchott District, SW Mauritania
Nouméa 144 C5 dependent territory capital (New Caledonia) Province Sud, S New Caledonia
Nouveau-Brunswick see New Brunswick
Nouvelle-Calédonie see New Caledonia
Nouvelle Écosse see Nova Scotia
Nova Civitas see Neustadt an der Weinstrasse
Nova Gorica 95 D8 W Slovenia
Nova Gradiška 100 C3 Ger. Neugradisk, Hung. Újgradiska. Brod-Posavina, NE Croatia
Nova Iguaçu 63 F4 Rio de Janeiro, SE Brazil
Nova Lisboa see Huambo
Novara 96 B2 anc. Novaria. Piemonte, NW Italy
Novaria see Novara
Nova Scotia 39 F4 Fr. Nouvelle Écosse. province SE Canada
Nova Scotia 35 E5 physical region SE Canada
Novaya Sibir', Ostrov 115 F1 island Novosibirskiye Ostrova, NE Russian Federation
Novaya Zemlya 110 D1 island group N Russian Federation
Novaya Zemlya Trough see East Novaya Zemlya Trough
Novgorod see Velikiy Novgorod
Novi Grad see Bosanski Novi
Novi Iskŭr 104 C2 Sofiya-Grad, N Bulgaria
Noviodunum see Nevers, Nièvre, France
Noviomagus see Lisieux, Calvados, France
Noviomagus see Nijmegen, Netherlands
Novi Pazar 101 D5 Turk. Yenipazar. Serbia, S Serbia
Novi Sad 100 D3 Ger. Neusatz, Hung. Újvidék. Vojvodina, N Serbia
Novoazovs'k 109 G4 Rus. Novoazovsk. Donets'ka Oblast', E Ukraine
Novocheboksarsk 111 C5 Chuvashskaya Respublika, W Russian Federation
Novocherkassk 111 B7 Rostovskaya Oblast', SW Russian Federation
Novodvinsk 110 C3 Arkhangel'skaya Oblast', NW Russian Federation
Novograd-Volynskiy see Novohrad-Volyns'kyy
Novogrudok see Navahrudak
Novohrad-Volyns'kyy 108 D2 Rus. Novograd-Volynskiy. Zhytomyrs'ka Oblast', N Ukraine
Novokazalinsk see Ayteke Bi
Novokuznetsk 114 D4 prev. Stalinsk. Kemerovskaya Oblast', S Russian Federation
Novolazarevskaya 154 C2 Russian research station Antarctica
Novo mesto 95 E8 Ger. Rudolfswert; prev. Ger. Neustadtl. SE Slovenia
Novomoskovsk 111 B5 Tul'skaya Oblast', W Russian Federation
Novomoskovs'k 109 F3 Rus. Novomoskovsk. Dnipropetrovs'ka Oblast', E Ukraine
Novopolotsk see Navapolatsk
Novoradomsk see Radomsko
Novo Redondo see Sumbe
Novorossiysk 111 A7 Krasnodarskiy Kray, SW Russian Federation
Novoshakhtinsk 111 B6 Rostovskaya Oblast', SW Russian Federation
Novosibirsk 114 D4 Novosibirskaya Oblast', C Russian Federation
Novotroitsk 111 D6 Orenburgskaya Oblast', W Russian Federation
Novotroitskoye see Novotroyits'ke, Ukraine
Novotroyits'ke 109 F4 Rus. Novotroitskoye. Khersons'ka Oblast', S Ukraine
Novo-Urgench see Urganch
Novovolyns'k 108 C1 Rus. Novovolynsk. Volyns'ka Oblast', NW Ukraine
Novy Dvor 107 B6 Rus. Novyy Dvor. Hrodzyenskaya Voblasts', W Belarus
Novyy Bug see Novyy Buh

Novyy Buh 109 E3 Rus. Novyy Bug. Mykolayivs'ka Oblast', S Ukraine
Novyy Dvor see Novy Dvor
Novyy Margilan see Farg'ona
Novyy Uzen' see Zhanaozen
Nowa Sól 98 B4 var. Nowasól, Ger. Neusalz an der Oder. Lubuskie, W Poland
Nowasól see Nowa Sól
Nowogard 98 B2 var. Nowógard, Ger. Naugard. Zachodnio-pomorskie, NW Poland
Nowogródek see Navahrudak
Nowo-Minsk see Mińsk Mazowiecki
Nowy Dwór Mazowiecki 98 D3 Mazowieckie, C Poland
Nowy Sącz 99 D5 Ger. Neu Sandec. Małopolskie, S Poland
Nowy Tomyśl 98 B3 var. Nowy Tomyśl. Wielkopolskie, C Poland
Nowy Tomyśl see Nowy Tomyśl
Noyon 90 C3 Oise, N France
Nsanje 79 E3 Southern, S Malawi
Nsawam 75 E5 SE Ghana
Ntomba, Lac 77 C6 var. Lac Tumba. lake NW Dem. Rep. Congo
Nubian Desert 72 B3 desert NE Sudan
Nu Chiang see Salween
Nu'eima 119 E7 E West Bank Asia
Nueva Caceres see Naga
Nueva Gerona 54 B2 Isla de la Juventud, S Cuba
Nueva Rosita 50 D2 Coahuila, NE Mexico
Nuevitas 54 C2 Camagüey, E Cuba
Nuevo, Bajo 53 G1 island NW Colombia South America
Nuevo Casas Grandes 50 C1 Chihuahua, N Mexico
Nuevo, Golfo 65 C6 gulf S Argentina
Nuevo Laredo 51 E2 Tamaulipas, NE Mexico
Nui Atoll 145 E3 atoll W Tuvalu
Nu Jiang see Salween
Nûk see Nuuk
Nukha see Şäki
Nuku'alofa 145 E5 country capital (Tonga) (Tonga) Tongatapu, S Tonga
Nukufetau Atoll 145 E3 atoll C Tuvalu
Nukulaelae Atoll 145 E3 var. Nukulailai. atoll E Tuvalu
Nukulailai see Nukulaelae Atoll
Nukunau see Nikunau
Nukunonu Atoll 145 E3 island C Tokelau
Nukus 122 C2 Qoraqalpog'iston Respublikasi, W Uzbekistan
Nullarbor Plain 147 C6 plateau South Australia/Western Australia
Nunap Isua 82 C5 var. Uummannarsuaq, Dan. Kap Farvel, Eng. Cape Farewell. cape S Greenland
Nunavut 37 F3 territory N Canada
Nuneaton 89 D6 C England, United Kingdom
Nunivak Island 36 B2 island Alaska, USA
Nunspeet 86 D3 Gelderland, E Netherlands
Nuoro 97 A5 Sardegna, Italy, C Mediterranean Sea
Nuquí 58 A3 Chocó, W Colombia
Nurakita see Niulakita
Nurata see Nurota
Nurek see Norak
Nuremberg see Nürnberg
Nurmes 84 E4 Itä-Suomi, E Finland
Nürnberg 95 C5 Eng. Nuremberg. Bayern, S Germany
Nurota 123 E2 Rus. Nurata. Navoiy Viloyati, C Uzbekistan
Nusaybin 117 F4 var. Nisibin. Manisa, SE Turkey
Nussdorf see Näsaud
Nutmeg State see Connecticut
Nuuk 82 C4 var. Nûk, Dan. Godthaab, Godthåb. dependent territory capital (Greenland) Kitaa, SW Greenland
Nyagan' 114 C3 Khanty-Mansiyskiy Avtonomnyy Okrug-Yugra, N Russian Federation
Nyainqentanglha Shan 126 C5 mountain range W China
Nyala 72 A4 Southern Darfur, W Sudan
Nyamapanda 78 D3 Mashonaland East, NE Zimbabwe

Nyamtumbo 73 C8 Ruvuma, S Tanzania
Nyanda see Masvingo
Nyandoma 110 C4 Arkhangel'skaya Oblast', NW Russian Federation
Nyantakara 73 B7 Kagera, NW Tanzania
Nyasa, Lake 79 E2 var. Lake Malawi; prev. Lago Nyassa. lake E Africa
Nyasaland/Nyasaland Protectorate see Malawi
Nyassa, Lago see Nyasa, Lake
Nyasvizh 107 C6 Pol. Nieśwież, Rus. Nesvizh. Minskaya Voblasts', C Belarus
Nyaunglebin 136 B4 Bago, SW Burma (Myanmar)
Nyeri 73 C6 Central, C Kenya
Nyíregyháza 99 D6 Szabolcs-Szatmár-Bereg, NE Hungary
Nyitra see Nitra
Nykøbing 85 B8 Storstrøm, SE Denmark
Nyköping 85 C6 Södermanland, S Sweden
Nylstroom see Modimolle
Nyngan 149 D6 New South Wales, SE Australia
Nyoman see Neman
Nyurba 115 F3 Respublika Sakha (Yakutiya), NE Russian Federation
Nyzhn'ohirs'kyy 109 F4 Rus. Nizhnegorskiy. Respublika Krym, S Ukraine
NZ see New Zealand
Nzega 73 C7 Tabora, C Tanzania
Nzérékoré 74 D4 SE Guinea
Nzwani see Anjouan

O

Oa'hu 47 A7 var. Oahu. island Hawai'ian Islands, Hawai'i, USA
Oak Harbor 46 B1 Washington, NW USA
Oakland 47 B6 California, W USA
Oamaru 151 B7 Otago, South Island, New Zealand
Oaxaca 51 F5 var. Oaxaca de Juárez; prev. Antequera. Oaxaca, SE Mexico
Oaxaca de Juárez see Oaxaca
Ob' 112 C2 river C Russian Federation
Obal' 107 D5 Rus. Obol'. Vitsyebskaya Voblasts', N Belarus
Oban 88 C4 W Scotland, United Kingdom
Oban see Halfmoon Bay
Obando see Puerto Inírida
Obdorsk see Salekhard
Óbecse see Bečej
Obeliai 106 C4 Panevėžys, NE Lithuania
Oberhollabrunn see Tulln
Ob', Gulf of 114 D3 Eng. Gulf of Ob. gulf N Russian Federation
Ob', Gulf of see Obskaya Guba
Obidovichi see Abidavichy
Óbihiro 130 D2 Hokkaidō, NE Japan
Obo 76 D4 Haut-Mbomou, E Central African Republic
Obock 72 D4 E Djibouti
Obol' see Obal'
Oborniki 98 C3 Wielkopolskie, W Poland
Obrovo see Abrova
Ob' Tablemount 141 B7 undersea feature S Indian Ocean
Ocala 23 E4 Florida, SE USA
Ocaña 58 B2 Norte de Santander, N Colombia
Ocaña 92 D3 Castilla-La Mancha, C Spain
O Carballiño 92 C1 Cast. Carballiño. Galicia, NW Spain
Occidental, Cordillera 58 B2 mountain range W South America
Occidental, Cordillera 61 E4 mountain range Bolivia/Chile
Ocean Falls 36 D5 British Columbia, SW Canada
Ocean Island see Banaba
Oceanside 47 C8 California, W USA
Ocean State see Rhode Island
Ochakiv 109 E4 Rus. Ochakov. Mykolayivs'ka Oblast', S Ukraine
Ochakov see Ochakiv
Ochamchira see Och'amch'ire
Och'amch'ire 117 E2 Rus. Ochamchira. W Georgia
Ocho Rios 54 B5 C Jamaica
Ochrida see Ohrid
Ochrida, Lake see Ohrid, Lake

Ocotal 52 D3 Nueva Segovia, NW Nicaragua
Ocozocuautla 51 G5 Chiapas, SE Mexico
October Revolution Island 115 E2 Eng. October Revolution Island. island Severnaya Zemlya, N Russian Federation
October Revolution Island see Oktyabr'skoy Revolyutsii, Ostrov
Ocú 53 F5 Herrera, S Panama
Ódate 130 D3 Akita, Honshū, C Japan
Oddur see Xuddur
Ödemiş 116 A4 İzmir, SW Turkey
Ödenburg see Sopron
Odenpäh see Otepää
Odense 85 B7 Fyn, C Denmark
Oder 98 B3 Cz./Pol. Odra. river C Europe
Oderhaff see Szczeciński, Zalew
Odesa 109 E4 Rus. Odessa. Odes'ka Oblast', SW Ukraine
Odessa 49 E3 Texas, SW USA
Odessa see Odesa
Odessus see Varna
Odienné 74 D4 NW Côte d'Ivoire
Ódóngk 137 D6 Kâmpóng Spœ, S Cambodia
Odoorn 86 E2 Drenthe, NE Netherlands
Odra see Oder
Oesel see Saaremaa
Of 117 E2 Trabzon, NE Turkey
Ofanto 97 D5 river S Italy
Offenbach 95 B5 var. Offenbach am Main. Hessen, W Germany
Offenbach am Main see Offenbach
Offenburg 95 B6 Baden-Württemberg, SW Germany

Ogaadeen see Ogaden
Ogaden 73 D5 Som. Ogaadeen. plateau Ethiopia/Somalia
Ógaki 131 C6 Gifu, Honshū, SW Japan
Ogallala 44 D4 Nebraska, C USA
Ogbomosho 75 F4 var. Ogmoboso. Oyo, W Nigeria
Ogden 44 B4 Utah, W USA
Ogdensburg 41 F2 New York, NE USA
Ogmoboso see Ogbomosho
Ogulin 100 A3 Karlovac, NW Croatia
Ohio 40 C4 off. State of Ohio, also known as Buckeye State. state N USA
Ohio River 40 C4 river N USA
Ohlau see Oława
Ohri see Ohrid
Ohrid 101 D6 Turk. Ochrida, Ohri. SW FYR Macedonia
Ohrid, Lake 101 D6 var. Lake Ochrida, Alb. Liqeni i Ohrit, Mac. Ohridsko Ezero. lake Albania/FYR Macedonia
Ohridsko Ezero/Ohrit, Liqeni i see Ohrid, Lake
Ohura 150 D3 Manawatu-Wanganui, North Island, New Zealand
Oirschot 87 C5 Noord-Brabant, S Netherlands
Oise 90 C3 river N France
Oistins 55 G2 S Barbados
Óita 131 B7 Óita, Kyūshū, SW Japan
Ojinaga 50 D2 Chihuahua, N Mexico
Ojos del Salado, Cerro 64 B3 mountain W Argentina
Okaihau 150 C2 Northland, North Island, New Zealand
Ókanizsa see Kanjiža
Ókára 134 C2 Punjab, E Pakistan
Okavanggo see Cubango/Okavango
Okavango Delta 78 C3 wetland N Botswana
Okayama 131 B6 Okayama, Honshū, SW Japan
Okazaki 131 C6 Aichi, Honshū, C Japan
Okeechobee, Lake 43 E4 lake Florida, SE USA
Okefenokee Swamp 43 E3 wetland Georgia, SE USA
Okhotsk 115 G3 Khabarovskiy Kray, E Russian Federation
Okhotsk, Sea of 113 F3 sea NW Pacific Ocean
Okhtyrka 109 F2 Rus. Akhtyrka. Sums'ka Oblast', NE Ukraine
Oki-guntó see Oki-shotó
Okinawa 130 A3 SW Japan
Okinawa-shoto 130 A3 island group Nansei-shotō, SW Japan
Oki-shoto 131 B6 var. Oki-guntó. island group SW Japan

Oklahoma *49 F2 off.* State of Oklahoma, *also known as* The Sooner State. *state* C USA

Oklahoma City *49 G1 state capital* Oklahoma, C USA

Okmulgee *49 G1* Oklahoma, C USA

Oko, Wadi *72 C3 river* NE Sudan

Oktyabr'skiy *111 D6* Volgogradskaya Oblast', SW Russian Federation

Oktyabr'skiy *see* Aktsyabrski

Okulovka *110 B4 var.* Okulovka. Novgorodskaya Oblast', W Russian Federation

Okulovka *see* Okulovka

Okushiri-tō *130 C3 var.* Okusiri Tō.

Okusiri Tō *see* Okushiri-tō

Oláh-Toplicza *see* Topliţa

Öland *85 C7 island* S Sweden

Olavarría *65 D5* Buenos Aires, E Argentina

Oława *98 C4 Ger.* Ohlau. Dolnośląskie, SW Poland

Olbia *97 A5 prev.* Terranova Pausania. Sardegna, Italy, C Mediterranean Sea

Old Bay State/Old Colony State *see* Massachusetts

Old Dominion *see* Virginia

Oldebroek *86 D3* Gelderland, E Netherlands

Oldenburg *94 B3* Niedersachsen, NW Germany

Oldenburg *94 C2 var.* Oldenburg in Holstein. Schleswig-Holstein, N Germany

Oldenburg in Holstein *see* Oldenburg

Oldenzaal *86 E3* Overijssel, E Netherlands

Old Harbour *54 B5* C Jamaica

Old Line State *see* Maryland

Old North State *see* North Carolina

Olëkma *115 F4 river* C Russian Federation

Olëkminsk *115 F3* Respublika Sakha (Yakutiya), NE Russian Federation

Oleksandrivka *109 E3 Rus.* Aleksandrovka. Kirovohrads'ka Oblast', C Ukraine

Oleksandriya *109 F3 Rus.* Aleksandriya. Kirovohrads'ka Oblast', C Ukraine

Olenegorsk *110 C2* Murmanskaya Oblast', NW Russian Federation

Olenëk *115 E3* Respublika Sakha (Yakutiya), NE Russian Federation

Olenëk *115 E3 river* NE Russian Federation

Oléron, Île d' *91 A5 island* W France

Olevs'k *108 D1 Rus.* Olevsk. Zhytomyrs'ka Oblast', N Ukraine

Olevsk *see* Olevs'k

Ólgiy *126 C2* Bayan-Ölgiy, W Mongolia

Olhão *92 B5* Faro, S Portugal

Olifa *78 B3* Kunene, NW Namibia

Ólimbos *see* Ólympos

Olimpo *see* Fuerte Olimpo

Olisipo *see* Lisboa

Olita *see* Alytus

Oliva *93 F4* País Valenciano, E Spain

Olivet *90 C4* Loiret, C France

Olmaliq *123 E2 Rus.* Almalyk. Toshkent Viloyati, E Uzbekistan

Olmütz *see* Olomouc

Olomouc *99 C5 Ger.* Olmütz, *Pol.* Ołomuniec. Olomoucký Kraj, E Czech Republic

Ołomuniec *see* Olomouc

Olonets *110 B3* Respublika Kareliya, NW Russian Federation

Olovyannaya *115 F4* Chitinskaya Oblast', S Russian Federation

Olpe *94 B4* Nordrhein-Westfalen, W Germany

Olshanka *see* Vil'shanka

Olsnitz *see* Murska Sobota

Olsztyn *98 D2 Ger.* Allenstein. Warmińsko-Mazurskie, N Poland

Olt *108 B5 var.* Oltul, *Ger.* Alt. *river* S Romania

Olteniţa *108 C5 prev. Eng.* Oltenitsa; *anc.* Constantiola. Călăraşi, SE Romania

Oltenitsa *see* Olteniţa

Oltul *see* Olt

Ol'viopol' *see* Pervomays'k

Olympia *46 B2 state capital* Washington, NW USA

Olympic Mountains *46 A2 mountain range* Washington, NW USA

Olympus, Mount *104 B4 var.* Ólimbos, *Eng.* Mount Olympus. *mountain* N Greece

Omagh *89 B5 Ir.* An Ómaigh. W Northern Ireland, United Kingdom

Omaha *45 F4* Nebraska, C USA

Oman *121 D6 off.* Sultanate of Oman, *Ar.* Salṭanat 'Umān; *prev.* Muscat and Oman. *country* SW Asia

OMAN
Southwest Asia

Official name Sultanate of Oman
Formation 1951 / 1951
Capital Muscat
Population 2.7 million / 33 people per sq mile (13 people per sq km) / 78%
Total area 82,031 sq. miles (212,460 sq. km)
Languages Arabic*, Baluchi, Farsi, Hindi, Punjabi
Religions Ibadi Muslim 75%, Other Muslim and Hindu 25%
Ethnic mix Arab 88%, Baluchi 4%, Persian 3%, Indian and Pakistani 3%, African 2%
Government Monarchy
Currency Omani rial = 1000 baisa
Literacy rate 81%
Calorie consumption Not available

Oman, Gulf of *120 E4 Ar.* Khalīj 'Umān. *gulf* N Arabian Sea

Oman, Sultanate of *see* Oman

Omboué *77 A6* Ogooué-Maritime, W Gabon

Omdurman *72 B4 var.* Umm Durmān. Khartoum, C Sudan

Ometepe, Isla de *52 D4 island* S Nicaragua

Ommen *86 E3* Overijssel, E Netherlands

Omsk *114 C4* Omskaya Oblast', C Russian Federation

Ōmuta *131 A7* Fukuoka, Kyūshū, SW Japan

Onda *93 F3* País Valenciano, E Spain

Ondjiva *see* N'Giva

Öndörhaan *127 E2 var.* Undur Khan; *prev.* Tsetsen Khan. Hentiy, E Mongolia

Onega *110 C3* Arkhangel'skaya Oblast', NW Russian Federation

Onega *110 B4 river* NW Russian Federation

Lake Onega *110 B4 Eng.* Lake Onega. *lake* NW Russian Federation

Onega, Lake *see* Onezhskoye Ozero

Onex *95 A7* Genève, SW Switzerland

Ongole *132 D1* Andhra Pradesh, E India

Onitsha *75 G5* Anambra, S Nigeria

Onon Gol *127 E2 river* N Mongolia

Onslow *146 A4* Western Australia

Onslow Bay *43 F1 bay* North Carolina, E USA

Ontario *38 B3 province* S Canada

Ontario, Lake *41 E3 lake* Canada/USA

Onteniente *see* Ontinyent

Ontinyent *93 F4 var.* Onteniente. País Valenciano, E Spain

Ontong Java Rise *125 H4 undersea feature* W Pacific Ocean

Onuba *see* Huelva

Oodeypore *see* Udaipur

Oos-Londen *see* East London

Oostakker *87 B5* Oost-Vlaanderen, NW Belgium

Oostburg *87 B5* Zeeland, SW Netherlands

Oostende *87 A5 Eng.* Ostend, *Fr.* Ostende. West-Vlaanderen, NW Belgium

Oosterbeek *86 D4* Gelderland, SE Netherlands

Oosterhout *86 C4* Noord-Brabant, S Netherlands

Opatija *100 A2 It.* Abbazia. Primorsko-Gorski Kotar, NW Croatia

Opava *99 C5 Ger.* Troppau. Moravskoslezský Kraj, E Czech Republic

Ópazova *see* Stara Pazova

Opelika *42 D2* Alabama, S USA

Opelousas *42 B3* Louisiana, S USA

Ophiusa *see* Formentera

Opmeer *86 C2* Noord-Holland, NW Netherlands

Opochka *110 A4* Pskovskaya Oblast', W Russian Federation

Opole *98 C4 Ger.* Oppeln. Opolskie, S Poland

Oporto *see* Porto

Opotiki *150 E3* Bay of Plenty, North Island, New Zealand

Oppeln *see* Opole

Oppidum Ubiorum *see* Köln

Oqtosh *123 E2 Rus.* Aktash. Samarqand Viloyati, C Uzbekistan

Oradea *108 B3 prev.* Oradea Mare, *Ger.* Grosswardein, *Hung.* Nagyvárad. Bihor, NW Romania

Oradea Mare *see* Oradea

Orahovac *see* Rahovec

Oral *see* Ural'sk

Oran *70 D2 var.* Ouahran, Wahran. NW Algeria

Orange *149 D6* New South Wales, SE Australia

Orange *91 D6 anc.* Arausio. Vaucluse, SE France

Orangeburg *43 E2* South Carolina, SE USA

Orange Cone *see* Orange Fan

Orange Fan *69 C7 var.* Orange Cone. *undersea feature* SW Indian Ocean

Orange Mouth/Orangemund *see* Oranjemund

Orange River *78 B4 Afr.* Oranjerivier. *river* S Africa

Orange Walk *52 C1* Orange Walk, N Belize

Oranienburg *94 D3* Brandenburg, NE Germany

Oranjemund *78 B4 var.* Orangemund; *prev.* Orange Mouth. Karas, SW Namibia

Oranjerivier *see* Orange River

Oranjestad *55 E5 dependent territory capital* (Aruba) W Aruba

Orany *see* Varėna

Oraşul Stalin *see* Braşov

Oravicabánya *see* Oraviţa

Oraviţa *108 A4 Ger.* Orawitza, *Hung.* Oravicabánya. Caraş-Severin, SW Romania

Orawitza *see* Oraviţa

Orbetello *96 B4* Toscana, C Italy

Orcadas *154 A1 Argentinian research station* South Orkney Islands, Antarctica

Orchard Homes *44 B1* Montana, NW USA

Ordino *91 A8* Ordino, NW Andorra Europe

Ordos Desert *see* Mu Us Shadi

Ordu *116 D2 anc.* Cotyora. Ordu, N Turkey

Ordzhonikidze *109 F3* Dnipropetrovs'ka Oblast', E Ukraine

Ordzhonikidze *see* Vladikavkaz, Russian Federation

Ordzhonikidze *see* Yenakiyeve, Ukraine

Orealla *59 G3* E Guyana

Örebro *85 C6* Örebro, C Sweden

Oregon *46 B3 off.* State of Oregon, *also known as* Beaver State, Sunset State, Valentine State, Webfoot State. *state* NW USA

Oregon City *46 B3* Oregon, NW USA

Oregon, State of *see* Oregon

Orekhov *see* Orikhiv

Orël *111 B5* Orlovskaya Oblast', W Russian Federation

Orem *44 B4* Utah, W USA

Ore Mountains *see* Erzgebirge/Krušné Hory

Orenburg *111 D6 prev.* Chkalov. Orenburgskaya Oblast', W Russian Federation

Orense *see* Ourense

Orestiáda *104 D3 prev.* Orestiás. Anatolikí Makedonía kai Thráki, NE Greece

Orestiás *see* Orestiáda

Organ Peak *48 D3 mountain* New Mexico, SW USA

Orgeyev *see* Orhei

Orhei *108 D3 var.* Orheiu, *Rus.* Orgeyev. N Moldova

Orheiu *see* Orhei

Oriental, Cordillera *60 D3 mountain range* Bolivia/Peru

Oriental, Cordillera *58 B3 mountain range* C Colombia

Orihuela *93 F4* País Valenciano, E Spain

Orikhiv *109 G3 Rus.* Orekhov. Zaporiz'ka Oblast', SE Ukraine

Orinoco, Río *59 E2 river* Colombia/ Venezuela

Orissa *135 F4 cultural region* NE India

Orissaar *see* Orissaare

Orissaare *106 C2 Ger.* Orissaar. Saaremaa, W Estonia

Oristano *97 A5* Sardegna, Italy, C Mediterranean Sea

Orito *58 A4* Putumayo, SW Colombia

Orizaba, Volcán Pico de *35 C7 var.* Citlaltépetl. *mountain* S Mexico

Orkney *see* Orkney Islands

Orkney Islands *88 C2 var.* Orkney, Orkneys. *island group* N Scotland, United Kingdom

Orkneys *see* Orkney Islands

Orlando *43 E4* Florida, SE USA

Orléanais *90 C4 cultural region* C France

Orléans *90 C4 anc.* Aurelianum. Loiret, C France

Orléansville *see* Chlef

Orly *90 E2* (Paris) Essonne, N France

Orlya *107 B6* Hrodzyenskaya Voblasts', W Belarus

Ormsö *see* Vormsi

Ormuz, Strait of *see* Hormuz, Strait of

Örnsköldsvik *85 C5* Västernorrland, C Sweden

Orolaunum *see* Arlon

Orol Dengizi *see* Aral Sea

Oromocto *39 F4* New Brunswick, SE Canada

Orona *145 F3 prev.* Hull Island. *atoll* Phoenix Islands, C Kiribati

Oropeza *see* Cochabamba

Orosirá Rodhópis *see* Rhodope Mountains

Orpington *89 B8* United Kingdom

Orscha *see* Orsha

Orsha *107 E6* Vitsyebskaya Voblasts', NE Belarus

Orsk *114 B4* Orenburgskaya Oblast', W Russian Federation

Orşova *108 A4 Ger.* Orschowa, *Hung.* Orsova. Mehedinţi, SW Romania

Orschowa *see* Orşova

Ortelsburg *see* Szczytno

Orthez *91 B6* Pyrénées-Atlantiques, SW France

Ortona *96 D4* Abruzzo, C Italy

Oruba *see* Aruba

Oruro *61 F4* Oruro, W Bolivia

Oryokko *see* Yalu

Oss *86 D4* Noord-Brabant, S Netherlands

Ōsaka *131 C6 Hist.* Naniwa. Ōsaka, Honshū, SW Japan

Ōsaki *see* Furukawa

Osa, Península de *53 E5 peninsula* S Costa Rica

Osborn Plateau *141 D5 undersea feature* E Indian Ocean

Ösel *see* Saaremaa

Osh *123 F2* Oshskaya Oblast', SW Kyrgyzstan

Oshawa *38 D5* Ontario, SE Canada

Oshikango *78 B3* Ohangwena, N Namibia

O-shima *131 D6 island* S Japan

Oshkosh *40 B2* Wisconsin, N USA

Oshmyany *see* Ashmyany

Osiek *see* Osijek

Osijek *100 C3 prev.* Osijek, Osjek, *Ger.* Esseg, *Hung.* Eszék. Osijek-Baranja, E Croatia

Osipenko *see* Berdyans'k

Osipovichi *see* Asipovichy

Osjek *see* Osijek

Oskaloosa *45 G4* Iowa, C USA

Oskarshamn *85 C7* Kalmar, S Sweden

Öskemen *see* Ust'-Kamenogorsk

Oskil *109 G2 Rus.* Oskil. *river* Russian Federation/Ukraine

Oskil *see* Oskil

Oslo *85 B6 prev.* Christiania, Kristiania. *country capital* (Norway) (Norway) Oslo, S Norway

Osmaniye *116 D4* Osmaniye, S Turkey

Osnabrück *94 A3* Niedersachsen, NW Germany

Osogov Mountains *104 B3 var.* Osogovske Planine, Osogovski Planina, *Mac.* Osogovski Planini. *mountain range* Bulgaria/FYR Macedonia

Osogovske Planine/Osogovski Planina/
Osogovski Planini see Osogov
Mountains
Oșorhei see Târgu Mureş
Osorno 65 B5 Los Lagos, C Chile
Ossa, Serra d' 92 C4 mountain range
SE Portugal
Ossora 115 H2 Koryakskiy Avtonomnyy
Okrug, E Russian Federation
Ostee see Baltic Sea
Ostend/Ostende see Oostende
Oster 109 E1 Chernihivs'ka Oblast',
N Ukraine
Östermyra see Seinäjoki
Osterode/Osterode in Ostpreussen
see Ostróda
Österreich see Austria
Östersund 85 C5 Jämtland, C Sweden
Ostia Aterni see Pescara
Ostiglia 96 C2 Lombardia, N Italy
Ostrava 99 C5 Moravskoslezský Kraj,
E Czech Republic
Ostróda 98 D3 Ger. Osterode, Osterode
in Ostpreussen. Warmińsko-
Mazurskie, NE Poland
Ostrołęka 98 D3 var. Ostrolenka, Rus.
Ostrolenka. Mazowieckie, C Poland
Ostrolenka see Ostrołęka
Ostrov 110 A4 Latv. Austrava.
Pskovskaya Oblast', W Russian
Federation
Ostrovets see Ostrowiec Świętokrzyski
Ostrovnoy 110 C2 Murmanskaya
Oblast', NW Russian Federation
Ostrów see Ostrów Wielkopolski
Ostrowiec see Ostrowiec Świętokrzyski
Ostrowiec Świętokrzyski 98 D4
var. Ostrowiec, Rus. Ostrovets.
Świętokrzyskie, C Poland
Ostrów Mazowiecka 98 D3 var. Ostrów
Mazowiecki. Mazowieckie, NE Poland
Ostrów Mazowiecki see Ostrów
Mazowiecka
Ostrowo see Ostrów Wielkopolski
Ostrów Wielkopolski 98 C4 var.
Ostrów, Ger. Ostrowo. Wielkopolskie,
C Poland
Ostyako-Voguls'k see Khanty-Mansiysk
Osum see Osumit, Lumi i
Osumi-shoto 131 A8 island group
Kagoshima, Nansei-shotō, SW Japan
Asia East China Sea Pacific Ocean
Osumit, Lumi i 101 D7 var. Osum. river
SE Albania
Osuna 92 D4 Andalucía, S Spain
Oswego 41 F2 New York, NE USA
Otago Peninsula 151 B7 peninsula
South Island, New Zealand
Otaki 150 D4 Wellington, North Island,
New Zealand
Otaru 130 C2 Hokkaidō, NE Japan
Otavalo 60 B1 Imbabura, N Ecuador
Otavi 78 B3 Otjozondjupa, N Namibia
Oțelu Roșu 108 B4 Ger. Ferdinandsberg,
Hung. Nándorhgy. Caras-Severin,
SW Romania
Otepää 106 D3 Ger. Odenpäh.
Valgamaa, SE Estonia
Oti 75 E4 river N Togo
Otira 151 C6 West Coast, South Island,
New Zealand
Otjiwarongo 78 B3 Otjozondjupa,
N Namibia
Otorohanga 150 D3 Waikato, North
Island, New Zealand
Otranto, Canale d' see Otranto, Strait of
Otranto, Strait of 101 C6 It. Canale
d'Otranto. strait Albania/Italy
Otrokovice 99 C5 Ger. Otrokowitz.
Zlínský Kraj, E Czech Republic
Otrokowitz see Otrokovice
Ōtsu 131 C6 var. Ōtu. Shiga, Honshū,
SW Japan
Ottawa 38 D3 country capital (Canada)
(Canada) Ontario, SE Canada
Ottawa 40 B3 Illinois, N USA
Ottawa 45 F5 Kansas, C USA
Ottawa 41 E2 Fr. Outaouais. river
Ontario/Québec, SE Canada
Ottawa Islands 38 C1 island group
Nunavut, C Canada
Ottignies 87 C6 Wallon Brabant,
C Belgium
Ottumwa 45 G4 Iowa, C USA
Ōtu see Ōtsu
Ouachita Mountains 42 A1 mountain
range Arkansas/Oklahoma, C USA

Ouachita River 42 B2 river Arkansas/
Louisiana, C USA
Ouagadougou 75 E4 var. Wagadugu.
country capital (Burkina Faso)
C Burkina Faso
Ouahigouya 75 E3 NW Burkina Faso
Ouahran see Oran
Oualâta 74 D3 var. Oualata. Hodh ech
Chargui, SE Mauritania
Ouanary 59 H3 E French Guiana
Ouanda Djallé 76 D4 Vakaga,
NE Central African Republic
Ouarâne 74 D2 desert C Mauritania
Ouargla 71 E2 var. Wargla. NE Algeria
Ouarzazate 70 C3 S Morocco
Oubangui 77 C5 Fr. Oubangui. river
C Africa
Oubangui see Ubangi
Oubangui-Chari see Central African
Republic
Oubangui-Chari, Territoire de l' see
Central African Republic
Oudjda see Oujda
Ouessant, Île d' 90 A3 Eng. Ushant.
island NW France
Ouésso 77 B5 Sangha, NW Congo
Oujda 70 D2 Ar. Oudjda, Ujda.
NE Morocco
Oujeft 74 C2 Adrar, C Mauritania
Oulu 84 D4 Swe. Uleåborg. Oulu,
C Finland
Oulujärvi 84 D4 Swe. Uleträsk. lake
C Finland
Oulujoki 84 D4 Swe. Uleälv. river C Finland
Ounasjoki 84 D3 river N Finland
Ounianga Kébir 76 C2 Borkou-Ennedi-
Tibesti, N Chad
Oup see Auob
Oupeye 87 D6 Liège, E Belgium
Our 87 D6 river NW Europe
Ourense 92 C1 Cast. Orense, Lat.
Aurium. Galicia, NW Spain
Ourique 92 B4 Beja, S Portugal
Ours, Grand Lac de l' see Great Bear Lake
Ourthe 87 D7 river E Belgium
Ouse 89 D5 river N England, United
Kingdom
Outaouais see Ottawa
Outer Hebrides 88 B3 var. Western
Isles. island group NW Scotland,
United Kingdom
Outer Islands 79 G1 island group
SW Seychelles Africa W Indian Ocean
Outes 92 B1 Galicia, NW Spain
Ouvéa 144 D5 island Îles Loyauté,
NE New Caledonia
Ouyen 149 C6 Victoria, SE Australia
Ovalle 64 B3 Coquimbo, N Chile
Ovar 92 B2 Aveiro, N Portugal
Overflakkee 86 B4 island SW Netherlands
Overijse 87 C6 Vlaams Brabant, C Belgium
Oviedo 92 C1 anc. Asturias. Asturias,
NW Spain
Ovilava see Wels
Ovruch 108 D1 Zhytomyrs'ka Oblast',
N Ukraine
Owando 77 B5 prev. Fort Rousset.
Cuvette, C Congo
Owase 131 C6 Mie, Honshū, SW Japan
Owatonna 45 F3 Minnesota, N USA
Owen Fracture Zone 140 B4 tectonic
feature W Arabian Sea
Owen, Mount 151 C5 mountain South
Island, New Zealand
Owensboro 40 B5 Kentucky, S USA
Owen Stanley Range 144 B3 mountain
range S Papua New Guinea
Owerri 75 G5 Imo, S Nigeria
Owo 75 F5 Ondo, SW Nigeria
Owyhee River 46 C4 river Idaho/Oregon,
NW USA
Oxford 151 C6 Canterbury, South Island,
New Zealand
Oxford 89 D6 Lat. Oxonia. S England,
United Kingdom
Oxkutzcab 51 H4 Yucatán, SE Mexico
Oxnard 47 B7 California, W USA
Oxonia see Oxford
Oxus see Amu Darya
Oyama 131 D5 Tochigi, Honshū, S Japan
Oyem 77 B5 Woleu-Ntem, N Gabon
Oyo 77 B6 Cuvette, C Congo
Oyo 75 F4 Oyo, W Nigeria
Ozark 42 D3 Alabama, S USA
Ozark Plateau 45 G5 plain Arkansas/
Missouri, C USA
Ozarks, Lake of the 45 F5 reservoir
Missouri, C USA

Ozbourn Seamount 152 D4 undersea
feature W Pacific Ocean
Ózd 99 D6 Borsod-Abaúj-Zemplén,
NE Hungary
Ozieri 97 A5 Sardegna, Italy,
C Mediterranean Sea

P

Paamiut 82 B4 var. Pâmiut, Dan.
Frederikshåb. S Greenland
Pa-an see Hpa-an
Pabianice 98 C4 Łódzki, Poland
Pabna 135 G4 Rajshahi, W Bangladesh
Pacaraima, Sierra/Pacaraim, Serra see
Pakaraima Mountains
Pachuca 51 E4 var. Pachuca de Soto.
Hidalgo, C Mexico
Pachuca de Soto see Pachuca
Pacific-Antarctic Ridge 154 B5
undersea feature S Pacific Ocean
Pacific Ocean 152 D3 ocean
Padalung see Phatthalung
Padang 138 B4 Sumatera, W Indonesia
Paderborn 94 B4 Nordrhein-Westfalen,
NW Germany
Padma see Brahmaputra
Padma see Ganges
Padova 96 C2 Eng. Padua; anc. Patavium.
Veneto, NE Italy
Padre Island 49 G5 island Texas, SW USA
Padua see Padova
Paducah 40 B5 Kentucky, S USA
Paeroa 150 D3 Waikato, North Island,
New Zealand
Páfos 102 C5 var. Paphos. W Cyprus
Pag 100 A3 It. Pago. island Zadar,
C Croatia
Page 48 B1 Arizona, SW USA
Pago see Pag
Pago Pago 145 F4 dependent territory
capital (American Samoa) Tutuila,
W American Samoa
Pahiatua 150 D4 Manawatu-Wanganui,
North Island, New Zealand
Pahsien see Chongqing
Paide 106 D2 Ger. Weissenstein.
Järvamaa, N Estonia
Paihia 150 D2 Northland, North Island,
New Zealand
Päijänne 85 D5 lake S Finland
Paine, Cerro 65 A7 mountain S Chile
Painted Desert 48 B1 desert Arizona,
SW USA
Paisance see Piacenza
Paisley 88 C4 W Scotland, United Kingdom
País Valenciano 93 F3 var. Valencia,
Cat. València; anc. Valentia.
autonomous community NE Spain
País Vasco 93 E1 cultural region
N Spain
Paita 60 B3 Piura, NW Peru
Pakanbaru see Pekanbaru
Pakaraima Mountains 59 E3 var. Serra
Pacaraim, Sierra Pacaraima. mountain
range N South America
Pakistan 134 A2 off. Islamic Republic
of Pakistan, var. Islami Jamhuriya e
Pakistan. country S Asia

PAKISTAN
South Asia

Official name Islamic Republic
of Pakistan
Formation 1947 / 1971
Capital Islamabad
Population 165 million / 553 people
per sq mile (214 people per sq km) / 34%
Total area 310,401 sq. miles
(803,940 sq. km)
Languages Urdu*, Punjabi, Sindhi, Pashtu,
Baluchi, Brahui
Religions Sunni Muslim 77%, Shi'a
Muslim 20%, Hindu 2%, Christian 1%
Ethnic mix Punjabi 56%, Pashtun
(Pashtun) 15%, Sindhi 14%, Mohajir 7%,
Other 4%, Baluchi 4%
Government Presidential system
Currency Pakistani rupee = 100 paisa
Literacy rate 50%
Calorie consumption 2419 calories

Pakistan, Islamic Republic of see
Pakistan

Pakistan, Islami Jamhuriya e see
Pakistan
Paknam see Samut Prakan
Pakokku 136 A3 Magway, C Burma
(Myanmar)
Pak Phanang 137 C7 var. Ban Pak
Phanang. Nakhon Si Thammarat,
SW Thailand
Pakruojis 106 C4 Šiauliai, N Lithuania
Paks 99 C7 Tolna, S Hungary
Paksé see Pakxé
Pakxé 137 D5 var. Paksé. Champasak,
S Laos
Palafrugell 93 G2 Cataluña, NE Spain
Palagruža 101 B5 It. Pelagosa. island
SW Croatia
Palaiá Epídavros 105 C6 Pelopónnisos,
S Greece
Palaiseau 90 D2 Essonne, N France
Palamós 93 G2 Cataluña, NE Spain
Palamuse 106 E2 Ger. Sankt-
Bartholomäi. Jõgevamaa, E Estonia
Palanka see Bačka Palanka
Pālanpur 134 C4 Gujarāt, W India
Palantia see Palencia
Palapye 78 D3 Central, SE Botswana
Palau 144 A2 var. Belau. country
W Pacific Ocean

PALAU
Australasia & Oceania

Official name Republic of Palau
Formation 1994 / 1994
Capital Melekeok
Population 20,842 / 106 people
per sq mile (41 people per sq km) /
68% Total area 177 sq. miles (458 sq. km)
Languages Palauan*, English*, Japanese,
Angaur, Tobi, Sonsorolese
Religions Christian 66%, Modekngei 34%
Ethnic mix Palauan 74%, Filipino 16%,
Other 6%, Chinese and other Asian 4%
Government Nonparty system
Currency US dollar = 100 cents
Literacy rate 98%
Calorie consumption Not available

Palawan 139 E2 island W Philippines
Palawan Passage 138 D2 passage
W Philippines
Paldiski 106 D2 prev. Baltiski, Eng. Baltic
Port, Ger. Baltischport. Harjumaa,
NW Estonia
Palembang 138 B4 Sumatera, W Indonesia
Palencia 92 D2 anc. Palantia, Palantia.
Castilla-León, NW Spain
Palerme see Palermo
Palermo 97 C7 Fr. Palerme; anc.
Panhormus, Panormus. Sicilia, Italy,
C Mediterranean Sea
Pāli 134 C3 Rājasthān, N India
Palikir 144 C2 country capital
(Micronesia) (Micronesia) Pohnpei,
E Micronesia
Palimé see Kpalimé
Palioúri, Akrotírio 104 C4 var. Akrotírio
Kanestron. headland N Greece
Palk Strait 132 C3 strait India/Sri Lanka
Pallantia see Palencia
Palliser, Cape 151 D5 headland North
Island, New Zealand
Palma 93 G3 var. Palma de Mallorca.
Mallorca, Spain, W Mediterranean Sea
Palma del Río 92 D4 Andalucía, S Spain
Palma de Mallorca see Palma
Palmar Sur 53 E5 Puntarenas, SE Costa
Rica
Palma Soriano 54 C3 Santiago de Cuba,
E Cuba
Palm Beach 148 E1 New South Wales,
E Australia
Palmer 154 A2 US research station
Antarctica
Palmer Land 154 A3 physical region
Antarctica
Palmerston 145 F4 island S Cook Islands
Palmerston see Darwin
Palmerston North 150 D4 Manawatu-
Wanganui, North Island, New Zealand
The Palmetto State see South Carolina
Palmi 97 D7 Calabria, SW Italy
Palmira 58 B3 Valle del Cauca,
W Colombia
Palm Springs 47 D7 California, W USA
Palmyra see Tudmur

Palmyra Atoll 145 G2 US privately owned unincorporated territory C Pacific Ocean
Palo Alto 47 B6 California, W USA
Paloe see Denpasar, Bali, C Indonesia
Paloe see Palu
Palu 139 E4 prev. Paloe. Sulawesi, C Indonesia
Pamiers 91 B6 Ariège, S France
Pamir 123 F3 var. Daryā-ye Pāmīr, Taj. Dar''yoi Pomir. river Afghanistan/Tajikistan
Pāmir, Daryā-ye see Pamir
Pamir/Pāmir, Daryā-ye see Pamirs
Pamirs 123 F3 Pash. Daryā-ye Pāmīr, Rus. Pamir. mountain range C Asia
Pāmiut see Paamiut
Pamlico Sound 43 G1 sound North Carolina, SE USA
Pampa 49 E1 Texas, SW USA
Pampa Aullagas, Lago see Poopó, Lago
Pampas 64 C4 plain C Argentina
Pampeluna see Pamplona
Pamplona 58 C2 Norte de Santander, N Colombia
Pamplona 93 E1 Basq. Iruña, prev. Pampeluna; anc. Pompaelo. Navarra, N Spain
Panaji 132 B1 var. Pangim, Panjim, New Goa. state capital Goa, W India
Panamá 53 G4 var. Ciudad de Panama, Eng. Panama City. country capital (Panama) (Panama) Panamá, C Panama
Panama 53 G5 off. Republic of Panama. country Central America

PANAMA
Central America
Official name Republic of Panama
Formation 1903 / 1903
Capital Panama City
Population 3.3 million / 112 people per sq mile (43 people per sq km) / 57%
Total area 30,193 sq. miles (78,200 sq. km)
Languages English Creole, Spanish*, Amerindian languages, Chibchan languages
Religions Roman Catholic 86%, Other 8%, Protestant 6%
Ethnic mix Mestizo 60%, White 14%, Black 12%, Amerindian 8%, Asian 4%, Other 2%
Government Presidential system
Currency Balboa = 100 centésimos
Literacy rate 92%
Calorie consumption 2272 calories

Panama Basin 35 C8 undersea feature E Pacific Ocean
Panama Canal 53 F4 canal E Panama
Panama City 42 D3 Florida, SE USA
Panama City see Panamá
Gulf of Panama 53 G5 var. Gulf of Panama. gulf S Panama
Panama, Gulf of see Panamá, Golfo de
Isthmus of Panama 53 G4 Eng. Isthmus of Panama; prev. Isthmus of Darien. isthmus E Panama
Panama, Isthmus of see Panama, Istmo de
Panama, Republic of see Panama
Panay Island 139 E2 island C Philippines
Pančevo 100 D3 Ger. Pantschowa, Hung. Pancsova. Vojvodina, N Serbia
Pancsova see Pančevo
Paneas see Bāniyās
Panevėžys 106 C4 Panevėžys, C Lithuania
Pangim see Panaji
Pangkalpinang 138 C4 Pulau Bangka, W Indonesia
Pang-Nga see Phang-Nga
Panhormus see Palermo
Panjim see Panaji
Panopolis see Akhmim
Pánormos 105 C7 Kríti, Greece, E Mediterranean Sea
Panormus see Palermo
Pantanal 63 E3 var. Pantanalmato-Grossense. swamp SW Brazil
Pantanalmato-Grossense see Pantanal
Pantelleria, Isola di 97 B7 island SW Italy

Pantschowa see Pančevo
Pánuco 51 E3 Veracruz-Llave, E Mexico
Pao-chi/Paoki see Baoji
Paola 102 B5 E Malta
Pao-shan see Baoshan
Pao-t'ou/Paotow see Baotou
Papagayo, Golfo de 52 C4 gulf NW Costa Rica
Papakura 150 D3 Auckland, North Island, New Zealand
Papantla 51 F4 var. Papantla de Olarte. Veracruz-Llave, E Mexico
Papantla de Olarte see Papantla
Papeete 145 H4 dependent territory capital (French Polynesia) Tahiti, W French Polynesia
Paphos see Páfos
Papile 106 B3 Šiauliai, NW Lithuania
Papillion 45 F4 Nebraska, C USA
Papua 139 H4 var. Irian Barat, West Irian, West New Guinea, West Papua; prev. Dutch New Guinea, Irian Jaya, Netherlands New Guinea. province E Indonesia
Papua and New Guinea, Territory of see Papua New Guinea
Papua, Gulf of 144 B3 gulf S Papua New Guinea
Papua New Guinea 144 B3 off. Independent State of Papua New Guinea; prev. Territory of Papua and New Guinea. country NW Melanesia

PAPUA NEW GUINEA
Australasia & Oceania
Official name Independent State of Papua New Guinea
Formation 1975 / 1975
Capital Port Moresby
Population 6.1 million / 35 people per sq mile (13 people per sq km) / 13%
Total area 178,703 sq. miles (462,840 sq. km)
Languages English*, Pidgin English, Papuan, Motu, 750 (est.) native languages
Religions Protestant 60%, Roman Catholic 37%, Other 3%
Ethnic mix Melanesian and mixed race 100%
Government Parliamentary system
Currency Kina = 100 toea
Literacy rate 57%
Calorie consumption 2193 calories

Papua New Guinea, Independent State of see Papua New Guinea
Papuk 100 C3 mountain range NE Croatia
Pará 63 E2 off. Estado do Pará. state NE Brazil
Pará 63 E2 off. Estado do Pará. region NE Brazil
Pará see Belém
Paracel Islands 125 E3 disputed territory SE Asia
Paraćin 100 D4 Serbia, C Serbia
Paradise of the Pacific see Hawai'i
Pará, Estado do see Pará
Paragua, Río 59 E3 river SE Venezuela
Paraguay 64 C2 country C South America

PARAGUAY
South America
Official name Republic of Paraguay
Formation 1811 / 1938
Capital Asunción
Population 6.4 million / 42 people per sq mile (16 people per sq km) / 58%
Total area 157,046 sq. miles (406,750 sq. km)
Languages Spanish*, Guaraní, German
Religions Roman Catholic 96%, Protestant (including Mennonite) 4%
Ethnic mix Mestizo 91%, Other 7%, Amerindian 2%
Government Presidential system
Currency Guaraní = 100 céntimos
Literacy rate 93%
Calorie consumption 2565 calories

Paraguay 64 D2 var. Río Paraguay. river C South America

Paraguay, Río see Paraguay
Parahiba/Parahyba see Paraíba
Paraíba 63 G2 off. Estado da Paraíba; prev. Parahiba, Parahyba. region E Brazil
Paraíba 63 G2 off. Estado da Paraíba; prev. Parahiba, Parahyba. state E Brazil
Paraíba see João Pessoa
Paraíba, Estado da see Paraíba
Parakou 75 F4 C Benin
Paramaribo 59 G3 country capital (Suriname) Paramaribo, N Suriname
Paramushir, Ostrov 115 H3 island SE Russian Federation
Paraná 63 E4 Entre Ríos, E Argentina
Paraná 63 E5 off. Estado do Paraná. state S Brazil
Paraná 57 C5 var. Alto Paraná. river C South America
Paraná, Estado do see Paraná
Paranésti 104 C3 var. Paranestio. Anatolikí Makedonía kai Thráki, NE Greece
Paranestio see Paranésti
Paraparaumu 151 D5 Wellington, North Island, New Zealand
Parchim 94 C3 Mecklenburg-Vorpommern, N Germany
Parczew 98 E4 Lubelskie, E Poland
Pardubice 99 B5 Ger. Pardubitz. Pardubický Kraj, C Czech Republic
Pardubitz see Pardubice
Parechcha 107 B5 Pol. Porzecze, Rus. Porech'ye. Hrodzyenskaya Voblasts', W Belarus
Parecis, Chapada dos 63 D3 var. Serra dos Parecis. mountain range W Brazil
Parecis, Serra dos see Parecis, Chapada dos
Parenzo see Poreč
Parepare 139 E4 Sulawesi, C Indonesia
Párga 105 A5 Ípeiros, W Greece
Paria, Golfo de see Paria, Gulf of
Paria, Gulf of 59 E1 var. Golfo de Paria. gulf Trinidad and Tobago/Venezuela
Parika 59 F2 NE Guyana
Paris 90 D1 anc. Lutetia, Lutetia Parisiorum, Parisii. country capital (France) (France) Paris, N France
Parisii see Paris
Parkersburg 40 D4 West Virginia, NE USA
Parkes 149 D6 New South Wales, SE Australia
Parkhar see Farkhor
Parma 96 B2 Emilia-Romagna, N Italy
Parnahyba see Parnaíba
Parnaíba 63 F2 var. Parnahyba. Piauí, E Brazil
Pärnu 106 D2 Ger. Pernau, Latv. Pērnava; prev. Rus. Pernov. Pärnumaa, SW Estonia
Pärnu 106 D2 var. Parnu Jõgi, Ger. Pernau. river SW Estonia
Pärnu-Jaagupi 106 D2 Ger. Sankt-Jakobi. Pärnumaa, SW Estonia
Parnu Jõgi see Pärnu
Pärnu Laht 106 D2 Ger. Pernauer Bucht. bay SW Estonia
Paropamisus Range see Sefid Kūh, Selseleh-ye
Páros 105 D6 island Kykládes, Greece, Aegean Sea
Páros 105 D6 island Kykládes, Greece, Aegean Sea
Páros 105 C6 island Kykládes, Greece, Aegean Sea
Parral 64 B4 Maule, C Chile
Parral see Hidalgo del Parral
Parramatta 148 D1 New South Wales, SE Australia
Parras 50 D3 var. Parras de la Fuente. Coahuila, NE Mexico
Parras de la Fuente see Parras
Parsons 45 F5 Kansas, C USA
Pasadena 47 C7 California, W USA
Pasadena 49 H4 Texas, SW USA
Pașcani 108 C3 Hung. Páskán. Iași, NE Romania
Paseo 46 C2 Washington, NW USA
Pasewalk 94 D3 Mecklenburg-Vorpommern, NE Germany
Pashkeni see Bolyarovo
Pasinler 117 F3 Erzurum, NE Turkey

Páskán see Pașcani
Pasłęk 98 D2 Ger. Preußisch Holland. Warmińsko-Mazurskie, NE Poland
Pasni 134 A3 Baluchistān, SW Pakistan
Paso de Indios 65 B6 Chubut, S Argentina
Passarowitz see Požarevac
Passau 95 D6 Bayern, SE Germany
Passo Fundo 63 E5 Rio Grande do Sul, S Brazil
Pastavy 107 C5 Pol. Postawy, Rus. Postavy. Vitsyebskaya Voblasts', NW Belarus
Pastaza, Río 60 B2 river Ecuador/Peru
Pasto 58 A4 Nariño, SW Colombia
Pasvalys 106 C4 Panevėžys, N Lithuania
Patagonia 57 B7 physical region Argentina/Chile
Patalung see Phatthalung
Patani see Pattani
Patavium see Padova
Patea 150 D4 Taranaki, North Island, New Zealand
Paterson 41 F3 New Jersey, NE USA
Pathein 136 A4 var. Bassein. Ayeyarwady, SW Burma (Myanmar)
Pátmos 105 D6 island Dodekánisa, Greece, Aegean Sea
Patna 135 F3 var. Azimabad. state capital Bihār, N India
Patnos 117 F3 Ağrı, E Turkey
Patos, Lagoa dos 63 E5 lagoon S Brazil
Pátra 105 B5 Eng. Patras; prev. Pátrai. Dytikí Ellás, S Greece
Pátrai/Patras see Pátra
Pattani 137 C7 var. Patani. Pattani, SW Thailand
Pattaya 137 C5 Chon Buri, S Thailand
Patuca, Río 52 D2 river E Honduras
Pau 91 B6 Pyrénées-Atlantiques, SW France
Paulatuk 37 E3 Northwest Territories, NW Canada
Paungde 136 B4 Bago, C Burma (Myanmar)
Pautalia see Kyustendil
Pavia 96 B2 anc. Ticinum. Lombardia, N Italy
Pāvilosta 106 B3 Liepāja, W Latvia
Pavlikeni 104 D2 Veliko Tŭrnovo, N Bulgaria
Pavlodar 114 C4 Pavlodar, NE Kazakhstan
Pavlograd see Pavlohrad
Pavlohrad 109 G3 Rus. Pavlograd. Dnipropetrovs'ka Oblast', E Ukraine
Pawai, Pulau 138 A2 island SW Singapore Asia
Pawn 136 B3 river C Burma (Myanmar)
Pax Augusta see Badajoz
Pax Julia see Beja
Paxoí 105 A5 island Iónia Nisiá, Greece, C Mediterranean Sea
Payo Obispo see Chetumal
Paysandú 64 D4 Paysandú, W Uruguay
Pazar 117 E2 Rize, NE Turkey
Pazardzhik 114 C3 prev. Tatar Pazardzhik. Pazardzhik, SW Bulgaria
Peace Garden State see North Dakota
Peach State see Georgia
Pearl Islands 53 Eng. Pearl Islands. island group SE Panama
Pearl Islands see Perlas, Archipiélago de las
Pearl Lagoon 53 Eng. Pearl Lagoon. lagoon E Nicaragua
Pearl River 42 B3 river Louisiana/Mississippi, S USA
Pearsall 49 F4 Texas, SW USA
Peawanuk 38 C2 river Ontario, S Canada
Peć see Pejë
Pechora 110 D3 Respublika Komi, NW Russian Federation
Pechora 110 D3 river NW Russian Federation
Pechora Sea see Pechorskoye More
Pechorskoye More 110 D2 Eng. Pechora Sea. sea NW Russian Federation
Pecos 49 E3 Texas, SW USA
Pecos River 49 E3 river New Mexico/Texas, SW USA
Pécs 99 C7 Ger. Fünfkirchen, Lat. Sopianae. Baranya, SW Hungary
Pedra Lume 74 A3 Sal, NE Cape Verde
Pedro Cays 54 C3 island group Greater Antilles, S Jamaica North America N Caribbean Sea W Atlantic Ocean

Pedro Juan Caballero 64 D2 Amambay, E Paraguay
Peer 87 D5 Limburg, NE Belgium
Pegasus Bay 151 C6 bay South Island, New Zealand
Pegu see Bago
Pehuajó 64 C4 Buenos Aires, E Argentina
Pei-ching see Beijing/Beijing Shi
Peine 94 B3 Niedersachsen, C Germany
Pei-p'ing see Beijing/Beijing Shi
Peipsi Järv/Peipus-See see Peipus, Lake
Peipus, Lake 106 E3 Est. Peipsi Järv, Ger. Peipus-See, Rus. Chudskoye Ozero. lake Estonia/Russian Federation
Peiraías 105 C6 prev. Piraiévs, Eng. Piraeus. Attikí, C Greece
Pejë 101 D5 Serb. Peć. W Kosovo
Pèk 136 D4 var. Xieng Khouang; prev. Xiangkhoang. Xiangkhoang, N Laos
Pekalongan 138 C4 Jawa, C Indonesia
Pekanbaru 138 B3 var. Pakanbaru. Sumatera, W Indonesia
Pekin 40 B4 Illinois, N USA
Peking see Beijing/Beijing Shi
Pelagie 97 B8 island group SW Italy
Pelagosa see Palagruža
Pelican State see Louisiana
Pelly Bay see Kugaaruk
Pélmonostor see Beli Manastir
Peloponnese 105 B6 var. Morea, Eng. Peloponnese; anc. Peloponnesus. peninsula S Greece
Peloponnese/Peloponnesus see Peloponnese
Pelopónnisos
Pematangsiantar 138 B3 Sumatera, W Indonesia
Pemba 79 F2 prev. Port Amelia, Porto Amélia. Cabo Delgado, NE Mozambique
Pemba 73 D7 island E Tanzania
Pembroke 38 D4 Ontario, SE Canada
Penang see Pinang, Pulau, Peninsular Malaysia
Penang see George Town
Penas, Golfo de 65 A7 gulf S Chile
Penderma see Bandırma
Pendleton 46 C3 Oregon, NW USA
Pend Oreille, Lake 46 D2 lake Idaho, NW USA
Peneius see Pineiós
Peng-pu see Bengbu
Penibético, Sistema see Béticos, Sistemas
Peniche 92 B3 Leiria, W Portugal
Peninsular State see Florida
Pennine, Alpes/Pennine, Alpi see Pennine Alps
Pennine Alps 95 A8 Fr. Alpes Pennines, It. Alpi Pennine, Lat. Alpes Penninae. mountain range Italy/Switzerland
Pennine Chain see Pennines
Pennines 89 D5 var. Pennine Chain. mountain range N England, United Kingdom
Pennines, Alpes see Pennine Alps
Pennsylvania 41 E4 off. Commonwealth of Pennsylvania, also known as Keystone State. state NE USA
Penobscot River 41 G2 river Maine, NE USA
Penong 149 A6 South Australia
Penonomé 53 F5 Coclé, C Panama
Penrhyn 145 G3 atoll N Cook Islands
Penrhyn Basin 143 F3 undersea feature C Pacific Ocean
Penrith 148 D1 New South Wales, SE Australia
Penrith 89 D5 NW England, United Kingdom
Pensacola 42 C3 Florida, SE USA
Pentecost 144 D4 Fr. Pentecôte. island C Vanuatu
Pentecôte see Pentecost
Penza 111 C6 Penzenskaya Oblast', W Russian Federation
Penzance 89 C7 SW England, United Kingdom
Peoria 40 B4 Illinois, N USA
Perchtoldsdorf 95 E6 Niederösterreich, NE Austria
Percival Lakes 146 C4 lakes Western Australia
Perdido, Monte 93 F1 mountain NE Spain
Perece Vela Basin see West Mariana Basin
Pereira 58 B3 Risaralda, W Colombia
Peremyshl see Przemyśl

Pergamino 64 C4 Buenos Aires, E Argentina
Périgueux 91 C5 anc. Vesuna. Dordogne, SW France
Perito Moreno 65 B6 Santa Cruz, S Argentina
Perleberg 94 C3 Brandenburg, N Germany
Perlepe see Prilep
Perm' 114 C3 prev. Molotov. Permskaya Oblast', NW Russian Federation
Pernambuco 63 G2 off. Estado de Pernambuco. state E Brazil
Pernambuco 63 G2 off. Estado de Pernambuco. region E Brazil
Pernambuco see Recife
Pernambuco Abyssal Plain see Pernambuco Plain
Pernambuco, Estado de see Pernambuco
Pernambuco Plain 67 C5 var. Pernambuco Abyssal Plain. undersea feature E Atlantic Ocean
Pernau see Pärnu
Pernauer Bucht see Pärnu Laht
Pērnava see Pärnu
Pernik 104 B2 prev. Dimitrovo. Pernik, W Bulgaria
Pernov see Pärnu
Perote 51 F4 Veracruz-Llave, E Mexico
Pérouse see Perugia
Perovsk see Kzylorda
Perpignan 91 C6 Pyrénées-Orientales, S France
Perryton 49 F1 Texas, SW USA
Perryville 45 H5 Missouri, C USA
Persia see Iran
Persian Gulf 120 C4 var. The Gulf, Ar. Khalīj al 'Arabī, Per. Khalīj-e Fars. gulf SW Asia
Perth 147 A6 state capital Western Australia
Perth 88 C4 C Scotland, United Kingdom
Perth Basin 141 E6 undersea feature SE Indian Ocean
Peru 60 C3 off. Republic of Peru. country W South America

PERU
South America
Official name Republic of Peru
Formation 1824 / 1941
Capital Lima
Population 28.8 million / 58 people per sq mile (22 people per sq km) / 74%
Total area 496,223 sq. miles (1,285,200 sq. km)
Languages Spanish*, Quechua*, Aymara
Religions Roman Catholic 95%, Other 5%
Ethnic mix Amerindian 50%, Mestizo 40%, White 7%, Other 3%
Government Presidential system
Currency New sol = 100 céntimos
Literacy rate 88%
Calorie consumption 2571 calories

Peru see Beru
Peru Basin 67 A5 undersea feature E Pacific Ocean
Peru-Chile Trench 56 A4 undersea feature E Pacific Ocean
Perugia 96 C4 Fr. Pérouse; anc. Perusia. Umbria, C Italy
Perugia, Lake of see Trasimeno, Lago
Peru, Republic of see Peru
Perusia see Perugia
Péruwelz 87 B6 Hainaut, SW Belgium
Pervomay'sk 109 E3 prev. Ol'viopol'. Mykolayivs'ka Oblast', S Ukraine
Pervyy Kuril'skiy Proliv 115 H3 strait E Russian Federation
Pesaro 96 C3 anc. Pisaurum. Marche, C Italy
Pescara 96 D4 anc. Aternum, Ostia Aterni. Abruzzo, C Italy
Peshāwar 134 C1 North-West Frontier Province, N Pakistan
Peshkopi 101 C6 var. Peshkopia, Peshkopija. Dibër, NE Albania
Peshkopia/Peshkopija see Peshkopi
Pessac 91 B5 Gironde, SW France
Petah-Tikva see Petah Tikva
Petah Tikva 119 A6 var. Petach-Tikva, Petah Tiqwa, Petakh Tikva; prev. Petaḥ Tiqwa. Tel Aviv, C Israel
Petaḥ Tiqwa see Petah Tikva

Petakh Tikva/Petah Tiqva see Petah Tikva
Pétange 87 D8 Luxembourg, SW Luxembourg
Petchaburi see Phetchaburi
Peterborough 38 D5 South Australia
Peterborough 38 D5 Ontario, SE Canada
Peterborough 89 E6 prev. Medeshamstede. E England, United Kingdom
Peterhead 88 D3 NE Scotland, United Kingdom
Peter I Øy 154 A3 Norwegian dependency Antarctica
Petermann Bjerg 83 E3 mountain C Greenland
Petersburg 41 E5 Virginia, NE USA
Peters Mine 59 F3 var. Peter's Mine. N Guyana
Petit St-Bernard, Col du see Little Saint Bernard Pass
Peto 51 H4 Yucatán, SE Mexico
Petoskey 40 C2 Michigan, N USA
Petra see Wādī Mūsā
Petrich 104 C3 Blagoevgrad, SW Bulgaria
Petrikau see Piotrków Trybunalski
Petrikov see Pyetrykaw
Petrinja 100 B3 Sisak-Moslavina, C Croatia
Petroaleksandrovsk see To'rtkok'l
Petrodvorets 110 A4 Fin. Pietarhovi. Leningradskaya Oblast', NW Russian Federation
Petrograd see Sankt-Peterburg
Petrokov see Piotrków Trybunalski
Petropavl see Petropavlovsk
Petropavlovsk 114 C4 Kaz. Petropavl. Severnyy Kazakhstan, N Kazakhstan
Petropavlovsk-Kamchatskiy 115 H3 Kamchatskaya Oblast', E Russian Federation
Petroşani 108 B4 var. Petroșeni, Ger. Petroschen, Hung. Petrozsény. Hunedoara, W Romania
Petroschen/Petroşeni see Petroşani
Petroskoi see Petrozavodsk
Petrovgrad see Zrenjanin
Petrovsk-Port see Makhachkala
Petrozavodsk 114 B2 Fin. Petroskoi. Respublika Kareliya, NW Russian Federation
Petrozsény see Petroşani
Pettau see Ptuj
Pevek 115 G1 Chukotskiy Avtonomnyy Okrug, NE Russian Federation
Pezinok 99 C6 Ger. Bösing, Hung. Bazin. Bratislavský Kraj, W Slovakia
Pforzheim 95 B6 Baden-Württemberg, SW Germany
Pfungstadt 95 B5 Hessen, W Germany
Phangan, Ko 137 C6 island SW Thailand
Phang-Nga 137 B7 var. Pang-Nga, Phangnga. Phangnga, SW Thailand
Phangnga see Phang-Nga
Phan Rang/Phanrang see Phan Rang-Thap Cham
Phan Rang-Thap Cham 137 E6 var. Phanrang, Phan Rang, Phan Rang Thap Cham. Ninh Thuận, S Vietnam
Phan Thiết 137 E6 Bình Thuận, S Vietnam
Pharnacia see Giresun
Pharus see Hvar
Phatthalung 137 C7 var. Padalung, Patalung. Phatthalung, SW Thailand
Phayao 136 C4 var. Muang Phayao. Phayao, NW Thailand
Phenix City 42 D2 Alabama, S USA
Phet Buri see Phetchaburi
Phetchaburi 137 C5 var. Bejraburi, Petchaburi, Phet Buri. Phetchaburi, SW Thailand
Philadelphia 41 F4 Pennsylvania, NE USA
Philadelphia see 'Ammān
Philippine Basin 125 F3 undersea feature W Pacific Ocean
Philippine Islands 139 E1 island group W Pacific Ocean
Philippines 139 E1 off. Republic of the Philippines. country SE Asia

PHILIPPINES
Southeast Asia
Official name Republic of the Philippines
Formation 1946 / 1946

PHILIPPINES
(continued)
Capital Manila
Population 85.9 million / 746 people per sq mile (288 people per sq km) / 62%
Total area 115,830 sq. miles (300,000 sq. km)
Languages English*, Filipino*, Tagalog, Cebuano, Ilocano, Hiligaynon, many other local languages
Religions Roman Catholic 83%, Protestant 9%, Muslim 5%, Other (including Buddhist) 3%
Ethnic mix Other 34%, Tagalog 28%, Cebuano 13%, Ilocano 9%, Hiligaynon 8%, Bisaya 8%
Government Presidential system
Currency Philippine peso = 100 centavos
Literacy rate 93%
Calorie consumption 2379 calories

Philippine Sea 125 F3 sea W Pacific Ocean
Philippines, Republic of the see Philippines
Philippine Trench 142 A1 undersea feature W Philippine Sea
Philippopolis see Plovdiv
Phitsanulok 136 C4 var. Bisnulok, Muang Phitsanulok, Pitsanulok. Phitsanulok, C Thailand
Phlórina see Flórina
Phnom Penh see Phnum Penh
Phnum Penh 137 D6 var. Phnom Penh. country capital (Cambodia) (Cambodia) Phnum Penh, S Cambodia
Phoenix 48 B2 state capital Arizona, SW USA
Phoenix Islands 145 E3 island group C Kiribati
Phôngsali 136 C3 var. Phong Saly. Phôngsali, N Laos
Phong Saly see Phôngsali
Phrae 136 C4 var. Muang Phrae, Prae. Phrae, NW Thailand
Phra Nakhon Si Ayutthaya see Ayutthaya
Phra Thong, Ko 137 B6 island SW Thailand
Phuket 137 B7 var. Bhuket, Puket, Mal. Ujung Salang; prev. Junkseylon, Salang. Phuket, SW Thailand
Phuket, Ko 137 B7 island SW Thailand
Phumĭ Kâmpóng Trábêk 137 D5 prev. Phum Kompong Trabek. Kâmpóng Thum, C Cambodia
Phumĭ Sâmraông 137 D5 prev. Phum Samrong. Siêmréab, NW Cambodia
Phum Kompong Trabek see Phumĭ Kâmpóng Trábêk
Phum Samrong see Phumĭ Sâmraông
Phu Vinh see Tra Vinh
Phyu 136 B4 var. Hpyu, Pyu. Bago, C Burma (Myanmar)
Piacenza 96 B2 Fr. Paisance; anc. Placentia. Emilia-Romagna, N Italy
Piatra-Neamţ 108 C4 Hung. Karácsonkő. Neamţ, NE Romania
Piauhy see Piauí
Piauí 63 F2 off. Estado do Piauí; prev. Piauhy. state E Brazil
Piauí 63 F2 off. Estado do Piauí; prev. Piauhy. region E Brazil
Piauí, Estado do see Piauí
Picardie 90 C3 Eng. Picardy. cultural region N France
Picardy see Picardie
Piccolo San Bernardo, Colle di see Little Saint Bernard Pass
Pichilemu 64 B4 Libertador, C Chile
Pico 92 A5 var. Ilha do Pico. island Azores, Portugal, NE Atlantic Ocean
Pico, Ilha do see Pico
Picos 63 F2 Piauí, E Brazil
Picton 151 C5 Marlborough, South Island, New Zealand
Piedmont see Piemonte
Piedras Negras 51 E2 var. Ciudad Porfirio Díaz. Coahuila, NE Mexico
Pielavesi 84 D4 Itä-Suomi, C Finland
Pielinen 84 E4 var. Pielisjärvi. lake E Finland
Pielisjärvi see Pielinen
Piemonte 96 A2 Eng. Piedmont. region NW Italy

Pierre 45 E3 *state capital* South Dakota, N USA
Piešt'any 99 C6 *Ger.* Pistyan, *Hung.* Pöstyén. Tranavský Kraj, W Slovakia
Pietarhovi *see* Petrodvorets
Pietari *see* Sankt-Peterburg
Pietarsaari *see* Jakobstad
Pietermaritzburg 78 C5 *var.* Maritzburg. KwaZulu/Natal, E South Africa
Pietersburg *see* Polokwane
Bay of Pigs 54 B2 *Eng.* Bay of Pigs. *bay* SE Cuba
Pigs, Bay of *see* Cochinos, Bahía de
Pihkva Järv *see* Pskov, Lake
Pijijiapán 51 G5 Chiapas, SE Mexico
Pikes Peak 44 C5 *mountain* Colorado, C USA
Pikeville 40 D5 Kentucky, S USA
Pikinni *see* Bikini Atoll
Piła 98 B3 *Ger.* Schneidemühl. Wielkopolskie, C Poland
Pilar 64 D3 *var.* Villa del Pilar. Neembucú, S Paraguay
Pilcomayo, Rio 57 C5 *river* C South America
Pilos *see* Pýlos
Pilsen *see* Plzeň
Pilzno *see* Plzeň
Pinang *see* George Town
Pinang *see* Pinang, Pulau, Peninsular Malaysia
Pinang, Pulau 138 B3 *var.* Penang, Pinang; *prev.* Prince of Wales Island. *island* Peninsular Malaysia
Pinar del Río 54 A2 Pinar del Río, W Cuba
Píndhos/Píndhos Óros *see* Píndos
Pindus Mountains 104 A4 *var.* Píndhos Óros, *Eng.* Pindus Mountains; *prev.* Píndhos. *mountain range* C Greece
Pindus Mountains *see* Píndos
Pine Bluff 42 B2 Arkansas, C USA
Pine Creek 146 D2 Northern Territory, N Australia
Pinega 110 C3 *river* NW Russian Federation
Pineíos 104 B4 *var.* Piniós; *anc.* Peneius. *river* C Greece
Pineland 49 H3 Texas, SW USA
Pínes, Akrotírio 104 C4 *var.* Akrotírio Pínnes. *headland* N Greece
Pines, The Isle of the *see* Juventud, Isla de la
Pine Tree State *see* Maine
Pingdingshan 128 C4 Henan, C China
Pingkiang *see* Harbin
Ping, Mae Nam 136 B4 *river* W Thailand
Piniós *see* Pineíos
Pinkiang *see* Harbin
Pínnes, Akrotírio *see* Pínes, Akrotírio
Pinos, Isla de *see* Juventud, Isla de la
Pinotepa Nacional 51 F5 *var.* Santiago Pinotepa Nacional. Oaxaca, SE Mexico
Pinsk 107 B7 *Pol.* Pińsk. Brestskaya Voblasts', SW Belarus
Pinta, Isla 60 A5 *var.* Abingdon. *island* Galapagos Islands, Ecuador, E Pacific Ocean
Piombino 96 B3 Toscana, C Italy
Pioneer Mountains 46 D3 *mountain range* Montana, N USA North America
Pionerskiy 106 A4 *Ger.* Neukuhren. Kaliningradskaya Oblast', W Russian Federation
Piotrków Trybunalski 98 D4 *Ger.* Petrikau, *Rus.* Petrokov. Łódzkie, C Poland
Piraeus/Piraiévs *see* Peiraías
Pírgos *see* Pýrgos
Pirineos *see* Pyrenees
Piripiri 63 F2 Piauí, E Brazil
Pirna 94 D4 Sachsen, E Germany
Pirot 101 E5 Serbia, SE Serbia
Piryatin *see* Pyryatyn
Pisa 96 B3 *var.* Pisae. Toscana, C Italy
Pisae *see* Pisa
Pisaurum *see* Pesaro
Pisco 60 D4 Ica, SW Peru
Písek 99 A5 Budějovický Kraj, S Czech Republic
Pishan 126 A3 *var.* Guma. Xinjiang Uygur Zizhiqu, NW China
Pishpek *see* Bishkek
Pistoia 96 B3 *anc.* Pistoria, Pistoriæ. Toscana, C Italy
Pistoria/Pistoriæ *see* Pistoia

Pistyan *see* Piešt'any
Pisz 98 D3 *Ger.* Johannisburg. Warmińsko-Mazurskie, NE Poland
Pita 74 C4 NW Guinea
Pitalito 58 B4 Huila, S Colombia
Pitcairn Island 143 G4 *island* S Pitcairn Islands
Pitcairn Islands 143 G4 *UK dependent territory* C Pacific Ocean
Piteå 84 D4 Norrbotten, N Sweden
Pitești 108 B5 Argeș, S Romania
Pitsanulok *see* Phitsanulok
Pitt Island *see* Makin
Pittsburg 45 F5 Kansas, C USA
Pittsburgh 41 E4 Pennsylvania, NE USA
Pittsfield 41 F3 Massachusetts, NE USA
Piura 60 B2 Piura, NW Peru
Pivdennyy Buh 109 E3 *Rus.* Yuzhnyy Bug. *river* S Ukraine
Placentia *see* Piacenza
Placetas 54 B2 Villa Clara, C Cuba
Plainview 49 E2 Texas, SW USA
Planeta Rica 58 B2 Córdoba, NW Colombia
Planken 94 E1 C Liechtenstein Europe
Plano 49 G2 Texas, SW USA
Plasencia 92 C3 Extremadura, W Spain
Plate, River 64 D4 *var.* River Plate. *estuary* Argentina/Uruguay
Plate, River *see* Plata, Río de la
Platinum 36 C3 Alaska, USA
Plattensee *see* Balaton
Platte River 45 E4 *river* Nebraska, C USA
Plattsburgh 41 F2 New York, NE USA
Plauen 95 C5 *var.* Plauen im Vogtland. Sachsen, E Germany
Plauen im Vogtland *see* Plauen
Pļaviņas 106 D4 *Ger.* Stockmannshof. Aizkraukle, S Latvia
Plây Cu 137 E5 *var.* Pleiku. Gia Lai, C Vietnam
Pleasant Island *see* Nauru
Pleiku *see* Plây Cu
Plenty, Bay of 150 E3 *bay* North Island, New Zealand
Plérin 90 A3 Côtes d'Armor, NW France
Plesetsk 110 C3 Arkhangel'skaya Oblast', NW Russian Federation
Pleshchenitsy *see* Plyeshchanitsy
Pleskau *see* Pskov
Pleskauer See *see* Pskov, Lake
Pleskava *see* Pskov
Pleszew 98 C4 Wielkopolskie, C Poland
Pleven 104 C2 *prev.* Plevna. Pleven, N Bulgaria
Plevlja/Plevlje *see* Pljevlja
Plevna *see* Pleven
Pljevlja 100 C4 *prev.* Plevlja, Plevlje. N Montenegro
Plocce *see* Ploče
Ploče 100 B4 *It.* Plocce; *prev.* Kardeljevo. Dubrovnik-Neretva, SE Croatia
Płock 98 D3 *Ger.* Plozk. Mazowieckie, C Poland
Plöcken Pass 95 C7 *Ger.* Plöckenpass, *It.* Passo di Monte Croce Carnico. *pass* SW Austria
Plöckenpass *see* Plöcken Pass
Ploești *see* Ploiești
Ploiești 108 C5 *prev.* Ploești. Prahova, SE Romania
Plomári 105 D5 *prev.* Plomárion. Lésvos, E Greece
Plomárion *see* Plomári
Płońsk 98 D3 Mazowieckie, C Poland
Plovdiv 104 C3 *prev.* Eumolpias; *anc.* Evmolpia, Philippopolis, *Lat.* Trimontium. Plovdiv, C Bulgaria
Plozk *see* Płock
Plungė 106 B3 Telšiai, W Lithuania
Plyeshchanitsy 107 D5 *Rus.* Pleshchenitsy. Minskaya Voblasts', N Belarus
Plymouth 55 G3 *dependent territory capital* (Montserrat) SW Montserrat
Plymouth 89 C7 SW England, United Kingdom
Plzeň 99 A5 *Ger.* Pilsen, *Pol.* Pilzno. Plzeňský Kraj, W Czech Republic
Po 80 D4 *river* N Italy
Pobedy, Pik 126 B3 *Chin.* Tomür Feng. *mountain* China/Kyrgyzstan
Po, Bocche del *see* Po, Foci del
Pocahontas 42 B1 Arkansas, C USA
Pocatello 46 E4 Idaho, NW USA
Pochinok 111 A5 Smolenskaya Oblast', W Russian Federation

Pocking 95 D6 Bayern, SE Germany
Poděbrady 99 B5 *Ger.* Podiebrad. Středočeský Kraj, C Czech Republic
Podgorica 101 C5 *prev.* Titograd. *country capital* (Montenegro) S Montenegro
Podiebrad *see* Poděbrady
Podil's'ka Vysochina 108 D3 *plateau* W Ukraine
Podium Anicensis *see* le Puy
Podol'sk 111 B5 Moskovskaya Oblast', W Russian Federation
Podravska Slatina *see* Slatina
Podujevě 101 D5 *Serb.* Podujevo. N Kosovo
Podujevo *see* Podujevě
Podunajská Rovina *see* Little Alföld
Poetovio *see* Ptuj
Pograded 101 D6 *var.* Pogradeci. Korçë, SE Albania
Pogradeci *see* Pograded
Pohjanlahti *see* Bothnia, Gulf of
Pohnpei 144 C2 *prev.* Ponape Ascension Island. *island* E Micronesia
Poiciters *see* Poitiers
Poinsett, Cape 154 D4 *headland* Antarctica
Point de Galle *see* Galle
Pointe-à-Pitre 55 G3 Grande Terre, C Guadeloupe
Pointe-Noire 77 B6 Kouilou, S Congo
Point Lay 36 C2 Alaska, USA
Poitiers 90 B4 *prev.* Poictiers; *anc.* Limonum. Vienne, W France
Poitou 90 B4 *cultural region* W France
Pokharā 135 E3 Western, C Nepal
Pokrovka *see* Kyzyl-Suu
Pokrovs'ke 109 G3 *Rus.* Pokrovskoye. Dnipropetrovs'ka Oblast', E Ukraine
Pokrovskoye *see* Pokrovs'ke
Pola *see* Pula
Pola de Lena 92 D1 Asturias, N Spain
Poland 98 B4 *off.* Republic of Poland, *var.* Polish Republic, *Pol.* Polska, Rzeczpospolita Polska; *prev.* Pol. Polska Rzeczpospolita Ludowa, The Polish People's Republic. *country* C Europe

POLAND
Northern Europe

Official name	Republic of Poland
Formation	1918 / 1945
Capital	Warsaw
Population	38.5 million / 328 people per sq mile (126 people per sq km) / 62%
Total area	120,728 sq. miles (312,685 sq. km)
Languages	Polish*
Religions	Roman Catholic 93%, Other and nonreligious 5%, Orthodox Christian 2%
Ethnic mix	Polish 97%, Other 3%
Government	Parliamentary system
Currency	Zloty = 100 groszy
Literacy rate	99%
Calorie consumption	3374 calories

Poland, Republic of *see* Poland
Polatlı 116 C3 Ankara, C Turkey
Polatsk 107 D5 *Rus.* Polotsk. Vitsyebskaya Voblasts', N Belarus
Pol-e Khomrī 123 E4 *var.* Pul-i-Khumri. Baghlān, NE Afghanistan
Poli *see* Pólis
Polikastro/Polikastron *see* Polýkastro
Polikrayshte 104 D2 Veliko Tŭrnovo, N Bulgaria
Pólis 102 C5 *var.* Poli. W Cyprus
Polish People's Republic, The *see* Poland
Polish Republic *see* Poland
Polkowice 98 B4 *Ger.* Heerwegen. Dolnośląskie, W Poland
Pollença 93 G3 Mallorca, Spain, W Mediterranean Sea
Pologi *see* Polohy
Polohy 109 G3 *Rus.* Pologi. Zaporiz'ka Oblast', SE Ukraine
Polokwane 78 D4 *prev.* Pietersburg. Limpopo, NE South Africa
Polonne 108 D2 *Rus.* Polonnoye. Khmel'nyts'ka Oblast', NW Ukraine
Polonnoye *see* Polonne
Polotsk *see* Polatsk
Polska/Polska, Rzeczpospolita/Polska Rzeczpospolita Ludowa *see* Poland
Polsko Kosovo 104 D2 Ruse, N Bulgaria

Poltava 109 F2 Poltavs'ka Oblast', NE Ukraine
Poltoratsk *see* Aşgabat
Põlva 106 E3 *Ger.* Pölwe. Põlvamaa, SE Estonia
Pölwe *see* Põlva
Polyarnyy 110 C2 Murmanskaya Oblast', NW Russian Federation
Polýkastro 104 B3 *var.* Polikastro; *prev.* Polikastron. Kentrikí Makedonía, N Greece
Polynesia 143 F4 *island group* C Pacific Ocean
Pomeranian Bay 94 D2 *Ger.* Pommersche Bucht, *Pol.* Zatoka Pomorska. *bay* Germany/Poland
Pomir, Dar''yoi *see* Pamir/Pāmir, Daryā-ye
Pommersche Bucht *see* Pomeranian Bay
Pomorska, Zatoka *see* Pomeranian Bay
Pomorskiy Proliv 110 D2 *strait* NW Russian Federation
Po, Mouth of the 96 C2 *var.* Bocche del Po. *river* NE Italy
Pompaelo *see* Pamplona
Pompano Beach 43 F5 Florida, SE USA
Ponape Ascension Island *see* Pohnpei
Ponca City 49 G1 Oklahoma, C USA
Ponce 55 F3 C Puerto Rico
Pondicherry 132 C2 *var.* Puduchcheri, *Fr.* Pondichéry. Pondicherry, SE India
Ponferrada 92 C1 Castilla-León, NW Spain
Poniatowa 98 E4 Lubelskie, E Poland
Pons Aelii *see* Newcastle upon Tyne
Pons Vetus *see* Pontevedra
Ponta Delgada 92 B5 São Miguel, Azores, Portugal, NE Atlantic Ocean
Ponta Grossa 63 E4 Paraná, S Brazil
Pontarlier 90 D4 Doubs, E France
Ponteareas 92 B2 Galicia, NW Spain
Ponte da Barca 92 B2 Viana do Castelo, N Portugal
Pontevedra 92 B1 *anc.* Pons Vetus. Galicia, NW Spain
Pontiac 40 D3 Michigan, N USA
Pontianak 138 C4 Borneo, C Indonesia
Pontisarae *see* Pontoise
Pontivy 90 A3 Morbihan, NW France
Pontoise 90 C3 *anc.* Briva Isarae, Cergy-Pontoise, Pontisarae. Val-d'Oise, N France
Ponziane Island 97 C5 *island* C Italy
Poole 89 D7 S England, United Kingdom
Poona *see* Pune
Poopó, Lago 61 F4 *var.* Lago Pampa Aullagas. *lake* W Bolivia
Popayán 58 B4 Cauca, SW Colombia
Poperinge 87 A6 West-Vlaanderen, W Belgium
Poplar Bluff 45 G5 Missouri, C USA
Popocatépetl 51 E4 *volcano* S Mexico
Popper *see* Poprad
Poprad 99 D5 *Ger.* Deutschendorf, *Hung.* Poprád. Prešovský Kraj, E Slovakia
Poprád 99 D5 *Ger.* Popper, *Hung.* Poprád. *river* Poland/Slovakia
Porbandar 134 B4 Gujarāt, W India
Porcupine Plain 80 B3 *undersea feature* E Atlantic Ocean
Pordenone 96 C2 *anc.* Portenau. Friuli-Venezia Giulia, NE Italy
Poreč 100 A2 *It.* Parenzo. Istra, NW Croatia
Porech'ye *see* Parechcha
Pori 85 D5 *Swe.* Björneborg. Länsi-Suomi, SW Finland
Porirua 151 D5 Wellington, North Island, New Zealand
Porkhov 110 A4 Pskovskaya Oblast', W Russian Federation
Porlamar 59 E1 Nueva Esparta, NE Venezuela
Póros 105 D6 Póros, S Greece
Póros 105 A5 Kefallinía, Iónia Nisiá, Greece, C Mediterranean Sea
Pors *see* Porsangenfjorden
Porsangenfjorden 84 D2 *Lapp.* Pors. *fjord* N Norway
Porsgrunn 85 B6 Telemark, S Norway
Portachuelo 61 G4 Santa Cruz, C Bolivia
Portadown 89 B5 *Ir.* Port an Dúnáin. S Northern Ireland, United Kingdom
Portalegre 92 C3 *anc.* Ammaia, Amoea. Portalegre, E Portugal

Port Alexander 36 D4 Baranof Island, Alaska, USA
Port Alfred 78 D5 Eastern Cape, S South Africa
Port Amelia see Pemba
Port An Dúnáin see Portadown
Port Angeles 46 B1 Washington, NW USA
Port Antonio 54 B5 NE Jamaica
Port Arthur 49 H4 Texas, SW USA
Port Augusta 149 B6 South Australia
Port-au-Prince 54 D3 country capital (Haiti) (Haiti) C Haiti
Port Blair 133 F2 Andaman and Nicobar Islands, SE India
Port Charlotte 43 E4 Florida, SE USA
Port Darwin see Darwin
Port d'Envalira 91 B8 E Andorra Europe
Port Douglas 148 D3 Queensland, NE Australia
Port Elizabeth 78 C5 Eastern Cape, S South Africa
Portenau see Pordenone
Porterville 47 C7 California, W USA
Port-Étienne see Nouâdhibou
Port Florence see Kisumu
Port-Francqui see Ilebo
Port-Gentil 77 A6 Ogooué-Maritime, W Gabon
Port Harcourt 75 G5 Rivers, S Nigeria
Port Hardy 36 D5 Vancouver Island, British Columbia, SW Canada
Port Harrison see Inukjuak
Port Hedland 146 B4 Western Australia
Port Huron 40 D3 Michigan, N USA
Portimão 92 B4 var. Vila Nova de Portimão. Faro, S Portugal
Port Jackson 148 E1 harbour New South Wales, E Australia
Portland 149 B7 Victoria, SE Australia
Portland 41 G2 Maine, NE USA
Portland 46 B3 Oregon, NW USA
Portland 49 G4 Texas, SW USA
Portland Bight 54 B5 bay S Jamaica
Portlaoighise see Port Laoise
Port Laoise 89 B6 var. Portlaoise, Ir. Portlaoighise; prev. Maryborough. C Ireland
Portlaoise see Port Laoise
Port Lavaca 49 G4 Texas, SW USA
Port Lincoln 149 A6 South Australia
Port Louis 79 H3 country capital (Mauritius) (Mauritius) NW Mauritius
Port-Lyautey see Kénitra
Port Macquarie 149 E6 New South Wales, SE Australia
Portmore 54 B5 C Jamaica
Port Moresby 144 B3 country capital (Papua New Guinea) (Papua New Guinea) Central/National Capital District, SW Papua New Guinea
Port Natal see Durban
Porto 92 B2 Eng. Oporto; anc. Portus Cale. Porto, NW Portugal
Porto Alegre 63 E5 var. Pôrto Alegre. state capital Rio Grande do Sul, S Brazil
Porto Alegre 76 E2 São Tomé, S Sao Tome and Principe, Africa
Porto Alegre 76 E2 São Tomé, S Sao Tome and Principe, Africa
Porto Alexandre see Tombua
Porto Amélia see Pemba
Porto Bello see Portobelo
Portobelo 53 G4 var. Porto Bello, Puerto Bello. Colón, N Panama
Port O'Connor 49 G4 Texas, SW USA
Porto Edda see Sarandë
Portoferraio 96 B4 Toscana, C Italy
Port-of-Spain 55 H5 country capital (Trinidad and Tobago) (Trinidad and Tobago) Trinidad, Trinidad and Tobago
Porto Grande see Mindelo
Portogruaro 96 C2 Veneto, NE Italy
Porto-Novo 75 F5 country capital (Benin) (Benin) S Benin
Porto Rico see Puerto Rico
Porto Santo 70 A2 var. Ilha do Porto Santo. island Madeira, Portugal, NE Atlantic Ocean
Porto Santo, Ilha do see Porto Santo
Porto Torres 97 A5 Sardegna, Italy, C Mediterranean Sea
Porto Velho 62 D2 var. Velho. state capital Rondônia, W Brazil

Portoviejo 60 A2 var. Puertoviejo. Manabí, W Ecuador
Port Pirie 149 B6 South Australia
Port Rex see East London
Port Said see Bûr Sa'îd
Portsmouth 89 D7 S England, United Kingdom
Portsmouth 41 G3 New Hampshire, NE USA
Portsmouth 40 D4 Ohio, N USA
Portsmouth 41 F5 Virginia, NE USA
Port Stanley see Stanley
Port Sudan 72 C3 Red Sea, NE Sudan
Port Swettenham see Klang/Pelabuhan Klang
Port Talbot 89 C7 S Wales, United Kingdom
Portugal 92 B3 off. Portuguese Republic. country SW Europe

PORTUGAL
Southwest Europe

Official name The Portuguese Republic
Formation 1139 / 1640
Capital Lisbon
Population 10.6 million / 299 people per sq mile (115 people per sq km) / 55%
Total area 35,672 sq. miles (92,391 sq. km)
Languages Portuguese*
Religions Roman Catholic 97%, Other 2%, Protestant 1%
Ethnic mix Portuguese 98%, African and other 2%
Government Parliamentary system
Currency Euro = 100 cents
Literacy rate 92%
Calorie consumption 3741 calories

Portuguese East Africa see Mozambique
Portuguese Guinea see Guinea-Bissau
Portuguese Republic see Portugal
Portuguese Timor see East Timor
Portuguese West Africa see Angola
Portus Cale see Porto
Portus Magnus see Almería
Portus Magonis see Mahón
Port-Vila 144 D4 var. Vila. country capital (Vanuatu) (Vanuatu) Éfaté, C Vanuatu
Porvenir 61 E3 Pando, NW Bolivia
Porvenir 65 B8 Magallanes, S Chile
Porvoo 85 E6 Swe. Borgå. Etelä-Suomi, S Finland
Porzecze see Parechcha
Posadas 64 D3 Misiones, NE Argentina
Poschega see Požega
Posen see Poznań
Posnania see Poznań
Postavy/Postawy see Pastavy
Posterholt 87 D5 Limburg, SE Netherlands
Postojna 95 D8 Ger. Adelsberg, It. Postumia. SW Slovenia
Postumia see Postojna
Pöstyén see Piešťany
Potamós 105 C7 Antikýthira, S Greece
Potentia see Potenza
Potenza 97 D5 anc. Potentia. Basilicata, S Italy
P'ot'i 117 F2 W Georgia
Potiskum 75 G4 Yobe, NE Nigeria
Potomac River 41 E5 river NE USA
Potosí 61 F4 Potosí, S Bolivia
Potsdam 94 D3 Brandenburg, NE Germany
Potwar Plateau 134 C2 plateau NE Pakistan
Poŭthĭsăt 137 D6 prev. Pursat. Poŭthĭsăt, W Cambodia
Po, Valle del see Po Valley
Po Valley 96 C2 It. Valle del Po. valley N Italy
Považská Bystrica 99 C5 Ger. Waagbistritz, Hung. Vágbeszterce. Trenčiansky Kraj, W Slovakia
Poverty Bay 150 E4 inlet North Island, New Zealand
Póvoa de Varzim 92 B2 Porto, NW Portugal
Powder River 44 D2 river Montana/ Wyoming, NW USA
Powell 44 C2 Wyoming, C USA
Powell, Lake 44 B5 lake Utah, W USA
Požarevac 100 D4 Ger. Passarowitz. Serbia, NE Serbia
Poza Rica 51 F4 var. Poza Rica de Hidalgo. Veracruz-Llave, E Mexico

Poza Rica de Hidalgo see Poza Rica
Požega 100 D4 prev. Slavonska Požega, Ger. Poschega, Hung. Pozsega. Požega-Slavonija, NE Croatia
Požega 100 D4 Serbia
Poznań 98 C3 Ger. Posen. Posnania. Wielkolpolskie, C Poland
Pozoblanco 92 D4 Andalucía, S Spain
Pozsega see Požega
Pozsony see Bratislava
Pozzallo 97 C8 Sicilia, Italy, C Mediterranean Sea
Prachatice 99 A5 Ger. Prachatitz. Jihočeský Kraj, S Czech Republic
Prachatitz see Prachatice
Prado del Ganso see Goose Green
Prae see Phrae
Prag/Praga/Prague see Praha
Praha 99 A5 Eng. Prague, Ger. Prag, Pol. Praga. country capital (Czech Republic) (Czech Republic) Středočeský, NW Czech Republic
Praia 74 A3 country capital (Cape Verde) (Cape Verde) Santiago, S Cape Verde
Prairie State see Illinois
Prathet Thai see Thailand
Prato 96 B3 Toscana, C Italy
Pratt 45 E5 Kansas, C USA
Prattville 42 D2 Alabama, S USA
Pravda 104 D1 prev. Dogrular. Silistra, NE Bulgaria
Pravia 92 C1 Asturias, N Spain
Preny see Prienai
Prenzlau 94 D3 Brandenburg, NE Germany
Prerau see Přerov
Přerov 99 C5 Ger. Prerau. Olomoucký Kraj, E Czech Republic
Preschau see Prešov
Prescott 48 B2 Arizona, SW USA
Preševo 101 D5 Serbia, SE Serbia
Presidente Epitácio 63 E4 São Paulo, S Brazil
Presidente Stroessner see Ciudad del Este
Prešov 99 D5 var. Preschau, Ger. Eperies, Hung. Eperjes. Prešovský Kraj, E Slovakia
Prespa, Lake 101 D6 Alb. Liqen i Prespës, Gk. Límni Megáli Préspa, Limni Prespa, Mac. Prespansko Ezero, Serb. Prespansko Jezero. lake SE Europe
Prespa, Limni/Prespansko Ezero/ Prespansko Jezero/Prespës, Liqen i see Prespa, Lake
Presque Isle 41 H1 Maine, NE USA
Pressburg see Bratislava
Preston 89 D5 NW England, United Kingdom
Prestwick 88 C4 W Scotland, United Kingdom
Preussisch Eylau see Bagrationovsk
Preußisch Holland see Pasłęk
Preussisch-Stargard see Starogard Gdański
Préveza 105 A5 Ípeiros, W Greece
Pribilof Islands 34 A3 island group Alaska, USA
Priboj 100 C4 Serbia, W Serbia
Price 44 B4 Utah, W USA
Prichard 42 C3 Alabama, S USA
Priekulė 106 B3 Ger. Prökuls. Klaipėda, W Lithuania
Prienai 107 B5 Pol. Preny. Kaunas, S Lithuania
Prieska 78 C4 Northern Cape, C South Africa
Prijedor 100 B3 Republika Srpska, NW Bosnia and Herzegovina
Prijepolje 100 D4 Serbia, W Serbia
Prikaspiyskaya Nizmennost' see Caspian Depression
Prilep 101 D6 Turk. Perlepe. S FYR Macedonia
Priluki see Pryluky
Primorsk 106 A4 Ger. Fischhausen. Kaliningradskaya Oblast', W Russian Federation
Primorsko 104 E2 prev. Keupriya. Burgas, E Bulgaria
Primorsk/Primorskoye see Prymors'k
Prince Albert 37 F5 Saskatchewan, S Canada
Prince Edward Island 39 F4 Fr. Île-du Prince-Édouard. province SE Canada

Prince Edward Islands 69 E8 island group S South Africa
Prince George 37 E5 British Columbia, SW Canada
Prince of Wales Island 148 B1 island Queensland, E Australia
Prince of Wales Island 37 F2 island Queen Elizabeth Islands, Nunavut, NW Canada
Prince of Wales Island see Pinang, Pulau
Prince Patrick Island 37 E2 island Parry Islands, Northwest Territories, NW Canada
Prince Rupert 36 D4 British Columbia, SW Canada
Prince's Island see Príncipe
Princess Charlotte Bay 148 C2 bay Queensland, NE Australia
Princess Elizabeth Land 154 C3 physical region Antarctica
Príncipe 77 A5 var. Príncipe Island, Eng. Prince's Island. island N Sao Tome and Principe
Príncipe Island see Príncipe
Prinzapolka 53 E3 Región Autónoma Atlántico Norte, E Nicaragua
Pripet 107 C7 Bel. Prypyats', Ukr. Pryp"yat'. river Belarus/Ukraine
Pripet Marshes 107 B7 wetland Belarus/ Ukraine
Prishtinë 101 D5 Eng. Pristina, Serb. Priština. C Kosovo
Priština see Prishtinë
Pristina see Prishtinë
Privas 91 D5 Ardèche, E France
Prizren 101 D5 S Kosovo
Probolinggo 138 D5 Jawa, C Indonesia
Probstberg see Wyszków
Progreso 51 H3 Yucatán, SE Mexico
Prokhladnyy 111 B8 Kabardino-Balkarskaya Respublika, SW Russian Federation
Prokletije see North Albanian Alps
Prökuls see Priekulė
Prokuplje 101 D5 Serbia, SE Serbia
Prome see Pyay
Promyshlennyy 110 E3 Respublika Komi, NW Russian Federation
Prościejów see Prostějov
Proskurov see Khmel 'nyts'kyy
Prossnitz see Prostějov
Prostějov 99 C5 Ger. Prossnitz, Pol. Prościejów. Olomoucký Kraj, E Czech Republic
Provence 91 D6 cultural region SE France
Providence 41 G3 state capital Rhode Island, NE USA
Providence see Fort Providence
Providencia, Isla de 53 F3 island NW Colombia, Caribbean Sea
Provideniya 155 B1 Chukotskiy Avtonomnyy Okrug, NE Russian Federation
Provo 44 B4 Utah, W USA
Prudhoe Bay 36 D2 Alaska, USA
Prusa see Bursa
Pruszków 98 D3 Ger. Kaltdorf. Mazowieckie, C Poland
Prut 108 D4 Ger. Pruth. river E Europe
Pruth see Prut
Pružana see Pruzhany
Pruzhany 107 B6 Pol. Pružana. Brestskaya Voblasts', SW Belarus
Prychornomor'ska Nyzovyna see Black Sea Lowland
Prydniprovs'ka Nyzovyna/ Prydnyprowskaya Nizina see Dnieper Lowland
Prydz Bay 154 D3 bay Antarctica
Pryluky 109 E2 Rus. Priluki. Chernihivs'ka Oblast', NE Ukraine
Prymors'k 109 G4 Rus. Primorsk; prev. Primorskoye. Zaporiz'ka Oblast', SE Ukraine
Pryp"yat'/Prypyats' see Pripet
Przemyśl 99 E5 Rus. Peremyshl. Podkarpackie, C Poland
Przheval'sk see Karakol
Psará 105 D5 island E Greece
Psel 109 F2 Rus. Psël. river Russian Federation/Ukraine
Psël see Psel
Pskov 114 B2 Ger. Pleskau, Latv. Pleskava. Pskovskaya Oblast', W Russian Federation
Pskov, Lake 106 E3 Est. Pihkva Järv, Ger. Pleskauer See, Rus. Pskovskoye Ozero. lake Estonia/Russian Federation

Pskovskoye Ozero *see* Pskov, Lake
Ptich' *see* Ptsich
Ptsich *107 C7 Rus.* Ptich'.
    Homyel'skaya
    Voblasts', SE Belarus
Ptsich *107 C7 Rus.* Ptich'. *river*
    SE Belarus
Ptuj *95 E7 Ger.* Pettau; *anc.* Poetovio.
    NE Slovenia
Pucallpa *60 C3* Ucayali, C Peru
Puck *98 C2* Pomorskie, N Poland
Pudasjärvi *84 D4* Oulu, C Finland
Puebla *51 F4 var.* Puebla de Zaragoza.
    Puebla, S Mexico
Puebla de Zaragoza *see* Puebla
Pueblo *44 D5* Colorado, C USA
Puerto Acosta *61 E4* La Paz, W Bolivia
Puerto Aisén *65 B6* Aisén, S Chile
Puerto Ángel *51 F5* Oaxaca, SE Mexico
Puerto Argentino *see* Stanley
Puerto Ayacucho *58 D3* Amazonas,
    SW Venezuela
Puerto Baquerizo Moreno *60 B5 var.*
    Baquerizo Moreno. Galapagos Islands,
    Ecuador, E Pacific Ocean
Puerto Barrios *52 C2* Izabal,
    E Guatemala
Puerto Bello *see* Portobelo
Puerto Berrío *58 B2* Antioquia,
    C Colombia
Puerto Cabello *58 D1* Carabobo,
    N Venezuela
Puerto Cabezas *53 E2 var.* Bilwi.
    Región Autónoma Atlántico Norte,
    NE Nicaragua
Puerto Carreño *58 D3* Vichada,
    E Colombia
Puerto Cortés *52 C2* Cortés,
    NW Honduras
Puerto Cumarebo *58 C1* Falcón,
    N Venezuela
Puerto Deseado *65 C7* Santa Cruz,
    SE Argentina
Puerto Escondido *51 F5* Oaxaca,
    SE Mexico
Puerto Gallegos *see* Río Gallegos
Puerto Inírida *58 D3 var.* Obando.
    Guainía, E Colombia
Puerto La Cruz *59 E1* Anzoátegui,
    NE Venezuela
Puerto Lempira *53 E2* Gracias a Dios,
    E Honduras
Puerto Limón *see* Limón
Puertollano *92 D4* Castilla-La Mancha,
    C Spain
Puerto López *58 C1* La Guajira,
    N Colombia
Puerto Maldonado *61 E3* Madre de
    Dios, E Peru
Puerto México *see* Coatzacoalcos
Puerto Montt *65 B5* Los Lagos, C Chile
Puerto Natales *65 B7* Magallanes, S Chile
Puerto Obaldía *53 H5* Kuna Yala,
    NE Panama
Puerto Plata *55 E3 var.* San Felipe de
    Puerto Plata. N Dominican Republic
Puerto Presidente Stroessner *see* Ciudad
    del Este
Puerto Princesa *132 E2 off.* Puerto
    Princesa City. Palawan, W Philippines
Puerto Princesa City *see* Puerto Princesa
Puerto Príncipe *see* Camagüey
Puerto Rico *135 F3 off.* Commonwealth
    of Puerto Rico; *prev.* Porto Rico. *US*
    commonwealth territory C West Indies
Puerto Rico *56 B1 island* C West Indies
Puerto Rico, Commonwealth of *see*
    Puerto Rico
Puerto Rico Trench *56 B1 trench*
    NE Caribbean Sea
Puerto San José *see* San José
Puerto San Julián *65 B7 var.* San Julián.
    Santa Cruz, SE Argentina
Puerto Suárez *61 H4* Santa Cruz,
    E Bolivia
Puerto Vallarta *50 D4* Jalisco,
    SW Mexico
Puerto Varas *65 B5* Los Lagos, C Chile
Puerto Viejo *53 E4* Heredia, NE Costa
    Rica
Puertoviejo *see* Portoviejo
Puget Sound *46 B1 sound* Washington,
    NW USA
Puglia *97 E5 var.* Le Puglie, *Eng.* Apulia.
    region SE Italy
Pukaki, Lake *151 B6 lake* South Island,
    New Zealand

Pukekohe *150 D3* Auckland, North
    Island, New Zealand
Puket *see* Phuket
Pukhavichy *107 C6 Rus.* Pukhovichi.
    Minskaya Voblasts', C Belarus
Pukhovichi *see* Pukhavichy
Pula *100 A3 It.* Pola; *prev.* Pulj. Istra,
    NW Croatia
Pulaski *40 D5* Virginia, NE USA
Puławy *98 D4 Ger.* Neu Amerika.
    Lubelskie, E Poland
Pul-i-Khumri *see* Pol-e Khomrī
Pulj *see* Pula
Pullman *46 C2* Washington, NW USA
Pułtusk *98 D3* Mazowieckie, C Poland
Puná, Isla *60 A2 island* SW Ecuador
Pune *134 C5 prev.* Poona. Mahārāshtra,
    W India
Punjab *134 C2 prev.* West Punjab,
    Western Punjab. *province* E Pakistan
Puno *61 E4* Puno, SE Peru
Punta Alta *65 C5* Buenos Aires,
    E Argentina
Punta Arenas *65 B8 prev.* Magallanes.
    Magallanes, S Chile
Punta Gorda *52 C2* Toledo, SE Belize
Punta Gorda *53 E4* Región Autónoma
    Atlántico Sur, SE Nicaragua
Puntarenas *52 D4* Puntarenas, W Costa
    Rica
Punto Fijo *58 C1* Falcón, N Venezuela
Pupuya, Nevado *61 E4 mountain*
    W Bolivia
Puri *135 F5 var.* Jagannath. Orissa,
    E India
Puriramya *see* Buriram
Purmerend *86 C3* Noord-Holland,
    C Netherlands
Pursat *see* Poŭthĭsăt, Poŭthĭsăt, W
    Cambodia
Purus, Rio *62 C2 var.* Río Purús. *river*
    Brazil/Peru
Pusan *129 E4 off.* Pusan-gwangyŏksi, *var.*
    Busan, *Jap.* Fusan. SE South Korea
Pusan-gwangyŏksi *see* Pusan
Pushkino *see* Biläsuvar
Püspökladány *99 D6* Hajdú-Bihar,
    E Hungary
Putorana, Gory/Putorana Mountains
    see Putorana, Plato
Putorana Mountains *115 E3 var.*
    Gory Putorana, *Eng.* Putorana
    Mountains. *mountain range* N Russian
    Federation
Putrajaya *138 B3 country capital*
    (Malaysia) (Malaysia) Kuala Lumpur,
    Peninsular Malaysia
Puttalam *132 C3* North Western
    Province, W Sri Lanka
Puttgarden *94 C2* Schleswig-Holstein,
    N Germany
Putumayo, Río *58 B5 var.* Içá, Rio. *river*
    NW South America
Putumayo, Río *see* Içá, Rio
Puurmani *106 D2 Ger.* Talkhof.
    Jõgevamaa, E Estonia
Pyatigorsk *111 B7* Stavropol'skiy Kray,
    SW Russian Federation
Pyatikhatki *see* P''yatykhatky
P''yatykhatky *109 F3 Rus.* Pyatikhatki.
    Dnipropetrovs'ka Oblast', E Ukraine
Pyay *136 B4 var.* Prome, Pye. Bago,
    C Burma (Myanmar)
Pye *see* Pyay
Pyetrykaw *107 C7 Rus.* Petrikov.
    Homyel'skaya Voblasts', SE Belarus
Pyinmana *136 B4 country capital*
    (Myanmar (Burma)) Mandalay,
    C Burma (Myanmar)
Pyin-Oo-Lwin *136 B3 var.* Maymyo.
    Mandalay, C Burma (Myanmar)
Pýlos *105 B6 var.* Pilos. Pelopónnisos,
    S Greece
Pyongyang *see* P'yŏngyang
P''yŏngyang *128 B4 var.* P'yŏngyang-si,
    Eng. Pyongyang. *country capital*
    (North Korea) (North Korea) SW North
    Korea
P'yŏngyang-si *see* P''yŏngyang
Pyramid Lake *47 C5 lake* Nevada,
    W USA
Pyrenaei Montes *see* Pyrenees
Pyrenees *102 B2 Fr.* Pyrénées, *Sp.*
    Pirineos; *anc.* Pyrenaei Montes.
    mountain range SW Europe
Pýrgos *105 B6 var.* Pirgos. Dytikí Ellás,
    S Greece
Pyritz *see* Pyrzyce

Pyryatyn *109 E2 Rus.* Piryatin.
    Poltavs'ka Oblast', NE Ukraine
Pyrzyce *98 B3 Ger.* Pyritz. Zachodnio-
    pomorskie, NW Poland
Pyu *see* Phyu
Pyuntaza *136 B4* Bago, SW Burma
    (Myanmar)

Q

Qā' al Jafr *119 C7 lake* S Jordan
Qaanaaq *82 D1 var.* Qânâq, *Dan.* Thule.
    Avannaarsua, N Greenland
Qabātiya *119 E6* N West Bank Asia
Qābis *see* Gabès
Qābis, Khalij *see* Gabès, Golfe de
Qacentina *see* Constantine
Qafṣah *see* Gafsa
Qagan Us *see* Dulan
Qahremānshahr *see* Kermānshāh
Qaidam Pendi *126 C4 basin* C China
Qal'aikhum *123 F3* Kuloba. Laikhum.
    S Tajikistan
Qalāt *123 E5* Per. Kalāt. Zābol,
    S Afghanistan
Qal'at Bishah *121 B5* 'Asīr, SW Saudi
    Arabia
Qalqīliya *see* Qalqilya
Qalqilya *119 D6 var.* Qalqiliya. Central,
    W West Bank Asia
Qamdo *126 D5* Xizang Zizhiqu, W China
Qamishly *see* Al Qāmishlī
Qânâq *see* Qaanaaq
Qaqortoq *82 C4 Dan.* Julianehåb.
    Kitaa, S Greenland
Qaraghandy/Qaraghandy Oblysy *see*
    Karaganda
Qara Qum *see* Garagum
Qarataū *see* Karatau, Zhambyl,
    Kazakhstan
Qarkilik *see* Ruoqiang
Qarokŭl *123 F3 Rus.* Karakul'.
    E Tajikistan
Qarqannah, Juzur *see* Kerkenah, Îles de
Qars *see* Kars
Qarshi *123 E3 Rus.* Karshi; *prev.*
    Bek-Budi. Qashqadaryo Viloyati,
    S Uzbekistan
Qasigianguit *see* Qasigiannguit
Qasigiannguit *82 C3 var.* Qasigianguit,
    Dan. Christianshåb. Kitaa,
    C Greenland
Qaṣr al Farāfirah *72 B2 var.* Qasr
    Farāfra. W Egypt
Qasr Farāfra *see* Qaṣr al Farāfirah
Qaṭana *119 B5 var.* Katana. Dimashq,
    S Syria
Qatar *120 C4 off.* State of Qatar, *Ar.*
    Dawlat Qaṭar. *country* SW Asia

| **QATAR** |
| *Southwest Asia* |

Official name State of Qatar
Formation 1971 / 1971
Capital Doha
Population 907,229 / 214 people
    per sq mile (82 people per sq km) / 92%
Total area 4416 sq miles (11,437 sq km)
Languages Arabic*
Religions Muslim (mainly Sunni) 95%,
    Other 5%
Ethnic mix Arab 40%, Indian 18%,
    Pakistani 18%, Other 14%, Iranian 10%
Government Monarchy
Currency Qatar riyal = 100 dirhams
Literacy rate 89%
Calorie consumption Not available

Qatar, State of *see* Qatar
Qattara Depression *72 A1 var.*
    Munkhafaḍ al Qaṭṭāra; *var.* Monkhafad
    el Qaṭṭâra, *Eng.* Qattara Depression.
    desert NW Egypt
**Qattara Depression/Qaṭṭārah,
    Munkhafaḍ al** *see* Qaṭṭārah,
    Munkhafaḍ al
Qaṭṭāra, Monkhafad el *see* Qaṭṭārah,
    Munkhafaḍ al
Qaṭṭārah, Munkhafaḍ al *see* Qaṭṭārah,
    Munkhafaḍ al
Qausuittuq *see* Resolute
Qazaqstan/Qazaqstan Respublikasy *see*
    Kazakhstan
Qazimämmäd *117 H3 Rus.* Kazi
    Magomed. SE Azerbaijan
Qazris *see* Cáceres

Qazvīn *120 C2 var.* Kazvin. Qazvīn,
    N Iran
Qena *see* Qinā
Qeqertarssuaq *see* Qeqertarsuaq
Qeqertarsuaq *82 C3 var.* Qeqertarssuaq,
    Dan. Godhavn. Kitaa, S Greenland
Qeqertarsuaq *82 C3 island* W Greenland
Qeqertarsuup Tunua *82 C3 Dan.* Disko
    Bugt. *inlet* W Greenland
Qerveh *see* Qorveh
Qeshm *120 D4 var.* Jazīreh-ye Qeshm,
    Qeshm Island. *island* S Iran
Qeshm Island/Qeshm, Jazīreh-ye
    see Qeshm
Qilian Shan *126 D3 var.* Kilien
    Mountains. *mountain range* N China
Qimusseriarsuaq *82 C2 Dan.*
    Melville Bugt, *Eng.* Melville Bay. *bay*
    NW Greenland
Qinā *72 B2 var.* Qena; *anc.* Caene,
    Caenepolis. E Egypt
Qing *see* Qinghai
Qingdao *128 D4 var.* Ching-Tao,
    Ch'ing-tao, Tsingtao, Tsintao, *Ger.*
    Tsingtau. Shandong, E China
Qinghai *126 C4 var.* Chinghai, Koko
    Nor, Qing, Qinghai Sheng, Tsinghai.
    province C China
Qinghai Hu *126 D4 var.* Ch'ing Hai,
    Tsing Hai, *Mong.* Koko Nor. *lake*
    C China
Qinghai Sheng *see* Qinghai
Qinhuangdao *128 D3* Hebei, E China
Qinzhou *128 B6* Guangxi Zhuangzu
    Zizhiqu, S China
Qiong *see* Hainan
Qiqihar *128 D2 var.* Ch'i-ch'i-ha-
    erh, Tsitsihar; *prev.* Lungkiang.
    Heilongjiang, NE China
Qira *126 B4* Xinjiang Uygur Zizhiqu,
    NW China
Qīta Ghazzah *see* Gaza Strip
Qitai *126 C3* Xinjiang Uygur Zizhiqu,
    NW China
Qīzān *see* Jīzān
Qizil Orda *see* Kzylorda
Qizil Qum/Qizilqum *see* Kyzyl Kum
Qizilrabot *123 G3 Rus.* Kyzylrabot.
    SE Tajikistan
Qogir Feng *see* K2
Qom *120 C3 var.* Kum, Qum, Qom,
    N Iran
Qomolangma Feng *see* Everest, Mount
Qomul *see* Hami
Qo'qon *123 F2 var.* Khokand,
    Rus. Kokand. Farg'ona Viloyati,
    E Uzbekistan
Qorveh *120 C3 var.* Qerveh, Qurveh.
    Kordestān, W Iran
Qostanay/Qostanay Oblysy *see*
    Kostanay
Qoubaīyāt *118 B4 var.* Al Qubayyāt.
    N Lebanon
Qoussantina *see* Constantine
Quang Ngai *137 E5 var.* Quangngai,
    Quang Nghia. Quang Ngai, C Vietnam
Quangngai *see* Quang Ngai
Quang Nghia *see* Quang Ngai
Quan Long *see* Ca Mau
Quanzhou *128 D6 var.* Ch'uan-chou,
    Tsinkiang; *prev.* Chin-chiang. Fujian,
    SE China
Quanzhou *128 C6* Guangxi Zhuangzu
    Zizhiqu, S China
Qu'Appelle *37 F5 river* Saskatchewan,
    S Canada
Quarles, Pegunungan *139 E4 mountain*
    range Sulawesi, C Indonesia
Quarnero *see* Kvarner
Quartu Sant' Elena *97 A6* Sardegna,
    Italy, C Mediterranean Sea
Quba *117 H2 Rus.* Kuba. N Azerbaijan
Qubba *see* Ba'qūbah
Québec *39 E4 var.* Quebec. *province*
    capital Québec, SE Canada
Québec *38 D3 var.* Quebec. *province*
    SE Canada
Queen Charlotte Islands *36 C5 Fr.* Îles
    de la Reine-Charlotte. *island group*
    British Columbia, SW Canada
Queen Charlotte Sound *36 C5 sea area*
    British Columbia, W Canada
Queen Elizabeth Islands *37 E1 Fr.* Îles
    de la Reine-Élisabeth. *island group*
    Nunavut, N Canada
Queensland *148 B4 state* N Australia

Queenstown 151 B7 Otago, South Island,
New Zealand
Queenstown 78 D5 Eastern Cape,
S South Africa
Quelimane 79 E3 var. Kilimane,
Kilmain, Quilimane. Zambézia,
NE Mozambique
Quelpart see Cheju-do
Quepos 53 E4 Puntarenas, S Costa Rica
Que Que see Kwekwe
Quera see Chur
Querétaro 51 E4 Querétaro de Arteaga,
C Mexico
Quesada 53 E4 var. Ciudad Quesada,
San Carlos. Alajuela, N Costa Rica
Quetta 134 B2 Baluchistān, SW Pakistan
Quetzalcoalco see Coatzacoalcos
Quezaltenango 52 A2 var.
Quetzaltenango. Quezaltenango,
W Guatemala
Quibdó 58 A3 Chocó, W Colombia
Quilimane see Quelimane
Quillabamba 60 D3 Cusco, C Peru
Quilon 132 C3 var. Kollam. Kerala,
SW India
Quimper 90 A3 anc. Quimper Corentin.
Finistère, NW France
Quimper Corentin see Quimper
Quimperlé 90 A3 Finistère, NW France
Quincy 40 A4 Illinois, N USA
Qui Nhon/Quinhon see Quy Nhon
Quissico 79 E4 Inhambane,
S Mozambique
Quito 60 B1 country capital (Ecuador)
(Ecuador) Pichincha, N Ecuador
Qulyndy Zhazyghy see Kulunda Steppe
Qum see Qom
Qurein see Al Kuwayt
Qŭrghonteppa 123 E3 Rus. Kurgan-
Tyube. SW Tajikistan
Qurlurtuuq see Kugluktuk
Qurveh see Qorveh
Quşayr see Al Quşayr
Quxar see Lhazê
Quy Nhon 137 E5 var. Quinhon, Qui
Nhon. Bình Định, C Vietnam
Qyteti Stalin see Kuçovë
Qyzylorda see Kzylorda

R

Raab 100 B1 Hung. Rába. river Austria/
Hungary
Raab see Rába
Raab see Győr
Raahe 84 D4 Swe. Brahestad. Oulu,
W Finland
Raalte 86 D3 Overijssel, E Netherlands
Raamsdonksveer 86 C4 Noord-Brabant,
S Netherlands
Raasiku 106 D2 Ger. Rasik. Harjumaa,
NW Estonia
Rába 99 B7 Ger. Raab. river Austria/
Hungary
Rába see Raab
Rabat 70 C2 var. al Dar al Baida.
country capital (Morocco) (Morocco)
NW Morocco
Rabat 102 B5 W Malta
Rabat see Victoria
Rabbah Ammon/Rabbath Ammon
see 'Ammān
Rabinal 52 B2 Baja Verapaz, C Guatemala
Rabka 99 D5 Małopolskie, S Poland
Râbnița see Rîbnița
Rabyanah Ramlat 71 G4 var. Rebiana
Sand Sea, Şaḩrā' Rabyānah. desert
SE Libya
Rabyānah, Şaḩrā' see Rabyānah, Ramlat
Răcari see Durankulak
Race , Cape 39 H3 headland
Newfoundland, Newfoundland and
Labrador, E Canada
Rach Gia 137 D6 Kiên Giang, S Vietnam
Rach Gia, Vinh 137 D6 bay S Vietnam
Racine 40 B3 Wisconsin, N USA
Rácz-Becse see Bečej
Rădăuți 108 C3 Ger. Radautz, Hung.
Rádóc. Suceava, N Romania
Radautz see Rădăuți
Rádeyilikóé see Fort Good Hope
Rádóc see Rădăuți
Radom 98 D4 Mazowieckie, C Poland
Radomsko 98 D4 Rus. Novoradomsk.
Łódzkie, C Poland

Radomyshl' 108 D2 Zhytomyrs'ka
Oblast', N Ukraine
Radoviš 101 E6 prev. Radovište.
E Macedonia
Radovište see Radoviš
Radviliškis 106 B4 Šiaulai, N Lithuania
Radzyń Podlaski 98 E4 Lubelskie,
E Poland
Rae-Edzo see Edzo
Raetihi 150 D4 Manawatu-Wanganui,
North Island, New Zealand
Rafa see Rafah
Rafaela 64 C3 Santa Fe, E Argentina
Rafah 119 A7 var. Rafa, Rafaḩ, Heb.
Rafiaḩ, Raphiah. SW Gaza Strip
Rafḩah 120 B4 Al Ḩudūd ash
Shamālīyah, N Saudi Arabia
Rafiaḩ see Rafah
Raga 73 A5 Western Bahr el Ghazal,
SW Sudan
Ragged Island Range 54 C2 island group
S Bahamas
Ragnit see Neman
Ragusa 97 C7 Sicilia, Italy,
C Mediterranean Sea
Ragusa see Dubrovnik
Rahachow 107 D7 Rus. Rogachëv.
Homyel'skaya Voblasts', SE Belarus
Rahaeng see Tak
Rahaṭ, Ḩarrat 121 B5 lava flow W Saudi
Arabia
Rahīmyār Khān 134 C3 Punjab,
SE Pakistan
Rahovec 101 D5 Serb. Orahovac.
W Kosovo
Raiatea 145 G4 island Îles Sous le Vent,
W French Polynesia
Räichür 132 C1 Karnātaka, C India
Raidestos see Tekirdağ
Rainier, Mount 34 A4 volcano
Washington, NW USA
Rainy Lake 38 A4 lake Canada/USA
Raipur 135 E4 Chhattisgarh, C India
Rājahmundry 135 E5 Andhra Pradesh,
E India
Rajang see Rajang, Batang
Rajang, Batang 138 D3 var. Rajang.
river East Malaysia
Rājapālaiyam 132 C3 Tamil Nādu,
SE India
Rājasthān 134 C3 cultural region
NW India
Rājkot 134 C4 Gujarāt, W India
Rāj Nāndgaon 135 E4 Chhattisgarh,
C India
Rajshahi 135 G3 prev. Rampur Boalia.
Rajshahi, W Bangladesh
Rakahanga 145 F3 atoll N Cook Islands
Rakaia 151 B6 river South Island, New
Zealand
Rakka see Ar Raqqah
Rakke 106 E2 Lääne-Virumaa,
NE Estonia
Rakvere 106 E2 Ger. Wesenberg. Lääne-
Virumaa, N Estonia
Raleigh 43 F1 state capital North
Carolina, SE USA
Ralik Chain 144 D1 island group Ralik
Chain, W Marshall Islands
Ramadi see Ar Ramādī
Râmnicul-Sărat see Râmnicu Sărat
Râmnicu Sărat 108 C4 prev. Râmnicul-
Sărat, Rîmnicu-Sărat. Buzău, E Romania
Râmnicu Vâlcea 108 B4 prev. Rîmnicu
Vîlcea. Vâlcea, C Romania
Rampur Boalia see Rajshahi
Ramree Island 136 A4 island W Burma
(Myanmar)
Ramtha see Ar Ramthā
Rancagua 64 B4 Libertador, C Chile
Rānchi 135 F4 Jhārkhand, N India
Randers 85 B7 Århus, C Denmark
Ráneš see Ringvassøya
Rangiora 151 C6 Canterbury, South
Island, New Zealand
Rangitikei 150 D4 river North Island,
New Zealand
Rangoon see Yangon
Rangpur 135 G3 Rajshahi, N Bangladesh
Rankin Inlet 37 G3 Nunavut, C Canada
Rankovićevo see Kraljevo
Ranong 137 B6 Ranong, SW Thailand
Rapa Nui see Pascua, Isla de
Raphiah see Rafah
Rapid City 44 D3 South Dakota, N USA
Räpina 106 E3 Ger. Rappin. Põlvamaa,
SE Estonia

Rapla 106 D2 Ger. Rappel. Raplamaa,
NW Estonia
Rappel see Rapla
Rappin see Räpina
Rarotonga 145 G5 island S Cook Islands,
C Pacific Ocean
Ras al'Ain see Ra's al 'Ayn
Ra's al 'Ayn 118 D1 var. Ras al'Ain. Al
Ḩasakah, N Syria
Ra's an Naqb 119 B7 Ma'ān, S Jordan
Raseiniai 106 B4 Kaunas, C Lithuania
Rasht 120 C2 var. Resht. Gīlān, NW Iran
Rasik see Raasiku
Râşnov 108 C4 prev. Rîşno, Rozsnyó,
Hung. Barcarozsnyó. Brașov,
C Romania
Rastenburg see Kętrzyn
Ratak Chain 144 D1 island group Ratak
Chain, E Marshall Islands
Ratān 85 C5 Jämtland, C Sweden
Rat Buri see Ratchaburi
Ratchaburi 137 C5 var. Rat Buri.
Ratchaburi, W Thailand
Ratisbon/Ratisbona/Ratisbonne see
Regensburg
Rat Islands 36 A2 island group Aleutian
Islands, Alaska, USA
Ratlām 134 D4 prev. Rutlam. Madhya
Pradesh, C India
Ratnapura 132 D4 Sabaragamuwa
Province, S Sri Lanka
Raton 48 D1 New Mexico, SW USA
Rättvik 85 C5 Dalarna, C Sweden
Raudhatain see Ar Rawdatayn
Raufarhöfn 83 E4 Norðhurland Eystra,
NE Iceland
Raukawa see Cook Strait
Raukumara Range 150 E3 mountain
range North Island, New Zealand
Räulakela 135 F4 var. Raurkela; prev.
Rourkela. Orissa, E India
Rauma 85 D5 Swe. Raumo. Länsi-
Suomi, SW Finland
Raumo see Rauma
Raurkela see Räulakela
Ravenna 96 C3 Emilia-Romagna, N Italy
Ravi 134 C2 river India/Pakistan
Rāwalpindi 134 C1 Punjab, NE Pakistan
Rawa Mazowiecka 98 D4 Łódzkie,
C Poland
Rawicz 98 C4 Ger. Rawitsch.
Wielkopolskie, C Poland
Rawitsch see Rawicz
Rawlins 44 C3 Wyoming, C USA
Rawson 65 C6 Chubut, SE Argentina
Rayak 118 B4 var. Rayaq, Riyāq.
E Lebanon
Rayaq see Rayak
Rayong 137 C5 Rayong, S Thailand
Razazah, Buhayrat ar 120 B3 var. Bahr
al Milḩ. lake C Iraq
Razdolnoye see Rozdol'ne
Razelm, Lacul see Razim, Lacul
Razgrad 104 D2 Razgrad, N Bulgaria
Razim, Lacul 108 D5 prev. Lacul Razelm.
lagoon NW Black Sea
Reading 89 D7 S England, United
Kingdom
Reading 41 F4 Pennsylvania, NE USA
Realicó 64 C4 La Pampa, C Argentina
Reăng Kesei 137 D5 Bătdâmbâng,
W Cambodia
Greater Antarctica see East Antarctica
Rebecca, Lake 147 C6 lake Western
Australia
Rebiana Sand Sea see Rabyānah, Ramlat
Rebun-to 130 C2 island NE Japan
Rechitsa see Rechytsa
Rechytsa 107 D7 Rus. Rechitsa.
Brestskaya Voblasts', SW Belarus
Recife 63 G2 prev. Pernambuco. state
capital Pernambuco, E Brazil
Recklinghausen 94 A4 Nordrhein-
Westfalen, W Germany
Recogne 87 C7 Luxembourg, SE Belgium
Reconquista 64 D3 Santa Fe,
C Argentina
Red Deer 37 E5 Alberta, SW Canada
Redding 47 B5 California, W USA
Redon 90 B4 Ille-et-Vilaine, NW France
Red River 67 E1 river Louisiana, S USA
Red River 35 C6 river S USA
Red River 42 B3 river Louisiana, S USA

Red Sea 72 C3 var. Sinus Arabicus. sea
Africa/Asia
Red Wing 45 G2 Minnesota, N USA
Reefton 151 C5 West Coast, South
Island, New Zealand
Reese River 47 C5 river Nevada, W USA
Refahiye 117 E3 Erzincan, C Turkey
Regensburg 95 C6 Eng. Ratisbon, Fr.
Ratisbonne, hist. Ratisbona; anc. Castra
Regina, Reginum. Bayern, SE Germany
Regenstauf 95 C6 Bayern, SE Germany
Reggane 70 D3 C Algeria
Reggio see Reggio nell'Emilia
Reggio Calabria see Reggio di Calabria
Reggio di Calabria 97 D7 var. Reggio
Calabria, Gk. Rhegion; anc. Regium,
Rhegium. Calabria, SW Italy
Reggio Emilia see Reggio nell'Emilia
Reggio nell'Emilia 96 B2 var. Reggio
Emilia, abbrev. Reggio; anc. Regium
Lepidum. Emilia-Romagna, N Italy
Reghin 108 C4 Ger. Sächsisch-Reen,
Hung. Szászrégen; prev. Reghinul
Săsesc, Ger. Sächsisch-Regen. Mureş,
C Romania
Reghinul Săsesc see Reghin
Regina 37 F5 province capital
Saskatchewan, S Canada
Reginum see Regensburg
Registan see Rīgestān
Regium see Reggio di Calabria
Regium Lepidum see Reggio nell'Emilia
Rehoboth 78 B3 Hardap, C Namibia
Rehovot 119 A6 ; prev. Reḩovot. Central,
C Israel
Reḩovot see Rehovot
Reichenbach see Dzierżoniów
Reichenau see Bogatynia, Poland
Reichenberg see Liberec
Reid 147 D6 Western Australia
Reikjavik see Reykjavík
Ré, Île de 90 A4 island W France
Reims 90 D3 Eng. Rheims; anc.
Durocortorum, Remi. Marne, N France
Reindeer Lake 37 F4 lake Manitoba/
Saskatchewan, C Canada
Reine-Charlotte, Îles de la see Queen
Charlotte Islands
Reine-Élisabeth, Îles de la see Queen
Elizabeth Islands
Reinga, Cape 150 C1 headland North
Island, New Zealand
Reinosa 92 D1 Cantabria, N Spain
Reka see Rijeka
Rekhovot see Rehovot
Reliance 37 F4 Northwest Territories,
C Canada
Remi see Reims
Rendina see Rentína
Rendsburg 94 B2 Schleswig-Holstein,
N Germany
Rengat 138 B4 Sumatera, W Indonesia
Reni 108 D4 Odes'ka Oblast',
SW Ukraine
Rennell 144 C4 var. Mu Nggava. island
S Solomon Islands
Rennes 90 B3 Bret. Roazon; anc.
Condate. Ille-et-Vilaine, NW France
Reno 47 C5 Nevada, W USA
Renqiu 128 C4 Hebei, E China
Rentína 105 B5 var. Rendina. Thessalía,
C Greece
Reps see Rupea
Repulse Bay 37 G3 Northwest
Terretories, N Canada
Reschitza see Reşiţa
Resht see Rasht
Resicabánya see Reşiţa
Resistencia 64 D3 Chaco, NE Argentina
Reşiţa 108 A4 Ger. Reschitza, Hung.
Resicabánya. Caraş-Severin,
W Romania
Resolute 37 F2 Inuit Qausuittuq.
Cornwallis Island, Parry Channel,
N Canada
Resolution Island 39 E1 island Nunavut,
NE Canada
Resolution Island 151 A7 island
SW New Zealand
Réunion 79 H4 off. La Réunion. French
overseas department W Indian Ocean
Réunion 69 E2 island W Indian Ocean
Reus 93 F2 Cataluña, E Spain
Reutlingen 95 B6 Baden-Württemberg,
S Germany
Reuver 87 D5 Limburg, SE Netherlands
Reval/Revel see Tallinn

Revillagigedo Island 50 B5 *island*
  Alexander Archipelago, Alaska, USA
Rexburg 46 E3 Idaho, NW USA
Reyes 61 F3 Beni, NW Bolivia
Rey, Isla del 53 G5 *island* Archipiélago
  de las Perlas, SE Panama
Reykjanes Basin 82 C5 *var.* Irminger
  Basin. *undersea basin* N Atlantic Ocean
Reykjanes Ridge 80 A1 *undersea ridge*
  N Atlantic Ocean
Reykjavík 83 E5 *var.* Reikjavik.
  country capital (Iceland) (Iceland)
  Höfudhborgarsvaedhi, W Iceland
Reynosa 51 E2 Tamaulipas, C Mexico
Rezā'īyeh, Daryācheh-ye *see* Orūmīyeh,
  Daryācheh-ye
Rezé 90 A4 Loire-Atlantique, NW France
Rēzekne 106 D4 *Ger.* Rositten; *prev. Rus.*
  Rezhitsa. Rēzekne, SE Latvia
Rezhitsa *see* Rēzekne
Rezovo 104 E3 *Turk.* Rezve. Burgas,
  E Bulgaria
Rezve *see* Rezovo
Rhaedestus *see* Tekirdağ
Rhegion/Rhegium *see* Reggio di Calabria
Rheims *see* Reims
Rhein *see* Rhine
Rheine 94 A3 *var.* Rheine in Westfalen.
  Nordrhein-Westfalen, NW Germany
Rheine in Westfalen *see* Rheine
Rheinisches Schiefergebirge 95 A5 *var.*
  Rhine State Uplands, *Eng.* Rhenish
  Slate Mountains. *mountain range*
  W Germany
Rhenish Slate Mountains *see* Rheinisches
  Schiefergebirge
Rhin *see* Rhine
Rhine 80 D4 *Dut.* Rijn, *Fr.* Rhin, *Ger.*
  Rhein. *river* W Europe
Rhinelander 40 B2 Wisconsin, N USA
Rhine State Uplands *see* Rheinisches
  Schiefergebirge
Rho 96 B2 Lombardia, N Italy
Rhode Island 41 G3 *off.* State of Rhode
  Island and Providence Plantations, *also
  known as* Little Rhody, Ocean State.
  state NE USA
Rhodes 105 E7 *var.* Ródhos, *Eng.*
  Rhodes, *It.* Rodi; *anc.* Rhodos. *island*
  Dodekánisa, Greece, Aegean Sea
Rhodes *see* Ródos
Rhodesia *see* Zimbabwe
Rhodope Mountains 104 C3 *var.*
  Rodhópi Óri, *Bul.* Rhodope Planina,
  Rodopi, *Gk.* Orosirá Rodhópis, *Turk.*
  Dospad Dagh. *mountain range*
  Bulgaria/Greece
Rhodope Planina *see* Rhodope Mountains
Rhône 80 C4 *river* France/Switzerland
Rhum 88 B3 *var.* Rum. *island*
  W Scotland, United Kingdom
Ribble 89 D5 *river* NW England, United
  Kingdom
Ribeira 92 B1 Galicia, NW Spain
Ribeirão Preto 63 F4 São Paulo, S Brazil
Riberalta 61 F2 Beni, N Bolivia
Rîbniţa 108 D3 *var.* Râbniţa, *Rus.*
  Rybnitsa. NE Moldova
Rice Lake 40 A2 Wisconsin, N USA
Richard Toll 74 B3 N Senegal
Richfield 44 B4 Utah, W USA
Richland 46 C2 Washington, NW USA
Richmond 151 C5 Tasman, South Island,
  New Zealand
Richmond 40 C5 Kentucky, S USA
Richmond 41 E5 *state capital* Virginia,
  NE USA
Richmond Range 151 C5 *mountain
  range* South Island, New Zealand
Ricobayo, Embalse de 92 C2 *reservoir*
  NW Spain
Ricomagus *see* Riom
Ridder 114 D4 *Kaz.* Leninogor.
  Vostochnyy Kazakhstan, E Kazakhstan
Ridgecrest 47 C7 California, W USA
Ried *see* Ried im Innkreis
Ried im Innkreis 95 D6 *var.* Ried.
  Oberösterreich, NW Austria
Riemst 87 D6 Limburg, NE Belgium
Riesa 94 D4 Sachsen, E Germany
Rift Valley *see* Great Rift Valley
Riga 106 C3 *Eng.* Riga. *country capital*
  (Latvia) (Latvia) Rīga, C Latvia
Rigaer Bucht *see* Riga, Gulf of
Riga, Gulf of 106 C3 *Est.* Liivi Laht, *Ger.*
  Rigaer Bucht, *Latv.* Rīgas Jūras Līcis,
  Rus. Rizhskiy Zaliv; *prev. Est.* Riia Laht.
  gulf Estonia/Latvia

Rīgas Jūras Līcis *see* Riga, Gulf of
Rigestan 122 D5 *var.* Registan. *desert
  region* S Afghanistan
Riia Laht *see* Riga, Gulf of
Riihimäki 85 D5 Etelä-Suomi, S Finland
Rijeka 100 A2 *Ger.* Sankt Veit am Flaum,
  It. Fiume, *Slvn.* Reka; *anc.* Tarsatica.
  Primorje-Gorski Kotar, NW Croatia
Rijn *see* Rhine
Rijssel *see* Lille
Rijssen 86 E3 Overijssel, E Netherlands
Rimah, Wadi ar 120 B4 *var.* Wādī ar
  Rummah. *dry watercourse* C Saudi
  Arabia
Rimini 96 C3 *anc.* Ariminum. Emilia-
  Romagna, N Italy
Rîmnicu-Sărat *see* Râmnicu Sărat
Rîmnicu Vîlcea *see* Râmnicu Vâlcea
Rimouski 39 E4 Québec, SE Canada
Ringebu 85 B5 Oppland, S Norway
Ringen *see* Rõngu
Ringkøbing Fjord 85 A7 *fjord*
  W Denmark
Ringvassøya 84 C2 Lapp. Ráneš. *island*
  N Norway
Rio *see* Rio de Janeiro
Riobamba 60 B1 Chimborazo,
  C Ecuador
Rio Branco 62 C4 *state capital* Acre,
  W Brazil
Rio Branco, Território de *see* Roraima
Rio Bravo 51 E2 Tamaulipas, C Mexico
Río Cuarto 64 C4 Córdoba, C Argentina
Rio de Janeiro 63 F4 *var.* Rio. *state
  capital* Rio de Janeiro, SE Brazil
Río Gallegos 65 B7 *var.* Gallegos, Puerto
  Gallegos. Santa Cruz, S Argentina
Rio Grande 51 E3 *var.* São Pedro do
  Rio Grande do Sul. Rio Grande do
  Sul, S Brazil
Rio Grande 50 D3 Zacatecas, C Mexico
Rio Grande do Norte 63 G2 *off.* Estado
  do Rio Grande do Norte. *region* E Brazil
Rio Grande do Norte 63 G2 *off.* Estado
  do Rio Grande do Norte. *state* E Brazil
Rio Grande do Norte, Estado do *see* Rio
  Grande do Norte
Rio Grande do Sul 63 E5 *off.* Estado do
  Rio Grande do Sul. *region* S Brazil
Rio Grande do Sul 63 E5 *off.* Estado do
  Rio Grande do Sul. *state* S Brazil
Rio Grande do Sul, Estado do *see* Rio
  Grande do Sul
Rio Grande Plateau *see* Rio Grande Rise
Rio Grande Rise 57 E6 *var.* Rio Grande
  Plateau. *undersea plateau* SW Atlantic
  Ocean
Riohacha 58 B1 La Guajira, N Colombia
Río Lagartos 51 H3 Yucatán, SE Mexico
Riom 91 C5 *anc.* Ricomagus. Puy-de-
  Dôme, C France
Río Verde 51 E4 *var.* Rioverde. San Luis
  Potosí, C Mexico
Rioverde *see* Río Verde
Ripoll 93 G2 Cataluña, NE Spain
Rishiri-tō 130 C2 *var.* Risiri Tō. *island*
  NE Japan
Risiri Tō *see* Rishiri-tō
Rišno *see* Râsnov
Risti 106 D2 *Ger.* Kreuz. Läänemaa,
  W Estonia
Rivas 52 D3 Rivas, SW Nicaragua
Rivera 64 D3 Rivera, NE Uruguay
River Falls 40 A2 Wisconsin, N USA
Riverside 47 C7 California, W USA
Riverton 151 A7 Southland, South
  Island, New Zealand
Riverton 44 C3 Wyoming, C USA
Rivière-du-Loup 39 E4 Québec,
  SE Canada
Rivne 108 C2 *Pol.* Równe, *Rus.* Rovno.
  Rivnens'ka Oblast', NW Ukraine
Rivoli 96 A2 Piemonte, NW Italy
Riyadh/Riyāḍ, Minṭaqat ar *see* Ar Riyāḍ
Riyāq *see* Rayak
Rize 117 E2 Rize, NE Turkey
Rizhao 128 D4 Shandong, E China
Rizhskiy Zaliv *see* Riga, Gulf of
Rkiz 74 C3 Trarza, W Mauritania
Road Town 55 F3 *dependent territory
  capital* (British Virgin Islands) Tortola,
  C British Virgin Islands
Roanne 91 C5 *anc.* Rodunma. Loire,
  E France
Roanoke 41 E5 Virginia, NE USA
Roanoke River 43 F1 *river* North
  Carolina/Virginia, SE USA

Roatán 52 C2 *var.* Coxen Hole, Coxin
  Hole. Islas de la Bahía, N Honduras
Roat Kampuchea *see* Cambodia
Roazon *see* Rennes
Robbie Ridge 143 E3 *undersea ridge*
  W Pacific Ocean
Robert Williams *see* Caála
Robinson Range 147 B5 *mountain range*
  Western Australia
Robson, Mount 37 E5 *mountain* British
  Columbia, SW Canada
Robstown 49 G4 Texas, SW USA
Roca Partida, Isla 50 B5 *island*
  W Mexico
Rocas, Atol das 63 G2 *island* E Brazil
Rochefort 87 C7 Namur, SE Belgium
Rochefort 90 B4 *var.* Rochefort sur Mer.
  Charente-Maritime, W France
Rochefort sur Mer *see* Rochefort
Rochester 45 G3 Minnesota, N USA
Rochester 41 G2 New Hampshire,
  NE USA
Rochester 41 G2 New York, NE USA
Rocheuses, Montagnes/Rockies *see*
  Rocky Mountains
Rockall Bank 80 B2 *undersea bank*
  N Atlantic Ocean
Rockall Trough 80 B2 *trough* N Atlantic
  Ocean
Rockdale 148 E2 Texas, SW USA
Rockford 40 B3 Illinois, N USA
Rockhampton 148 D4 Queensland,
  E Australia
Rock Hill 43 E1 South Carolina, SE USA
Rock Island 40 B3 Illinois, N USA
Rock Sound 54 C1 Eleuthera Island,
  C Bahamas
Rock Springs 44 C3 Wyoming, C USA
Rockstone 59 F3 C Guyana
Rocky Mount 43 F1 North Carolina,
  SE USA
Rocky Mountains 34 B4 *var.* Rockies,
  Fr. Montagnes Rocheuses. *mountain
  range* Canada/USA
Rodez 91 C5 *anc.* Segodunum. Aveyron,
  S France
Rodhópi Óri *see* Rhodope Mountains
Ródhos/Rodi *see* Ródos
Rodopi *see* Rhodope Mountains
Rodosto *see* Tekirdağ
Rodunma *see* Roanne
Roermond 87 D5 Limburg, SE
  Netherlands
Roeselare 87 A6 *Fr.* Roulers; *prev.*
  Rousselaere. West-Vlaanderen,
  W Belgium
Rogachev *see* Rahachow
Rogatica 100 C4 Republika Srpska,
  SE Bosnia and Herzegovina
Rogers 42 A1 Arkansas, C USA
Roger Simpson Island *see* Abemama
Roi Ed *see* Roi Et
Roi Et 137 D5 *var.* Muang Roi Et, Roi
  Ed. Roi Et, E Thailand
Roja 106 C2 Talsi, NW Latvia
Rokiškis 106 C4 Panevėžys,
  NE Lithuania
Rokycany 99 A5 *Ger.* Rokytzan.
  Plzeňský Kraj, W Czech Republic
Rokytzan *see* Rokycany
Rôlas, Ilha das 76 E2 *island* S Sao Tome
  and Principe, Africa, E Atlantic Ocean
Rolla 45 G5 Missouri, C USA
Rōm *see* Rømø
Roma 149 D5 Queensland, E Australia
Roma 104 C2 Vratsa, NW Bulgaria
Roman 104 C4 Hung. Románvásár.
  Neamţ, NE Romania
Romania 108 B4 Bul. Rumŭniya; *prev.*
  Rumänien, *Hung.* Románia, *Rom.*
  România, *Scr.* Rumunjska, *Ukr.*
  Rumuniya, *prev.* Republica Socialistă
  România, Rumania, Rumania,
  Socialist Republic of Romania, *prev.*
  Rom. România. *country* SE Europe

ROMANIA
Southeast Europe

Official name Romania
Formation 1878 / 1947
Capital Bucharest
Population 21.5 million / 242 people
  per sq mile (93 people per sq km) / 55%

ROMANIA
(continued)

Total area 91,699 sq. miles (237,500 sq. km)
Languages Romanian*, Hungarian
  (Magyar), Romani, German
Religions Romanian Orthodox 87%,
  Roman Catholic 5%, Protestant 4%,
  Other 2%, Greek Orthodox 1%,
  Greek Catholic (Uniate) 1%
Ethnic mix Romanian 89%, Magyar 7%,
  Roma 2%, Other 2%
Government Presidential system
Currency New Romanian leu = 100 bani
Literacy rate 97%
Calorie consumption 3455 calories

România, Republica Socialistă *see*
  Romania
Romania, Socialist Republic of *see*
  Romania
Romaniv 109 F3 *Rus.* Dneprodzerzhinsk,
  prev. Dniprodzerzhyns'k, *prev.*
  Kamenskoye. Dnipropetrovs'ka
  Oblast', E Ukraine
Románvásár *see* Roman
Rome 42 D2 Georgia, SE USA
Rome *see* Roma
Rominia *see* Romania
Romny 109 F2 Sums'ka Oblast',
  NE Ukraine
Rømø 85 A7 *Ger.* Röm. *island*
  SW Denmark
Roncador, Serra do 56 D4 *mountain
  range* C Brazil
Ronda 92 D5 Andalucía, S Spain
Rondônia 62 D3 *off.* Estado de
  Rondônia; *prev.* Território de
  Rondônia. *state* W Brazil
Rondônia 62 D3 *off.* Estado de
  Rondônia; *prev.* Território de
  Rondônia. *region* W Brazil
Rondônia, Estado de *see* Rondônia
Rondônia, Território de *see* Rondônia
Rondonópolis 63 E3 Mato Grosso,
  W Brazil
Rongelap Atoll 144 D1 *var.* Rönlap.
  atoll Ralik Chain, NW Marshall Islands
Róngu 106 D3 *Ger.* Ringen. Tartumaa,
  SE Estonia
Rönlap *see* Rongelap Atoll
Rønne 85 B8 Bornholm, E Denmark
Ronne Ice Shelf 154 A3 *ice shelf*
  Antarctica
Roosendaal 87 C5 Noord-Brabant,
  S Netherlands
Roosevelt Island 154 B4 *island*
  Antarctica
Roraima 62 D1 *off.* Estado de Roraima;
  prev. Território de Rio Branco,
  Território de Roraima. *state* N Brazil
Roraima 62 D1 *off.* Estado de Roraima;
  prev. Território de Rio Branco,
  Território de Roraima. *region* N Brazil
Roraima, Estado de *see* Roraima
Roraima, Mount 59 E3 *mountain*
  N South America
Roraima, Território de *see* Roraima
Røros 85 B5 Sør-Trøndelag, S Norway
Ross 151 B6 West Coast, South Island,
  New Zealand
Rosa, Lake 54 D2 *lake* Great Inagua,
  S Bahamas
Rosario 64 D3 Santa Fe, C Argentina
Rosario 64 D2 San Pedro, C Paraguay
Rosario *see* Rosarito
Rosarito 50 A1 *var.* Rosario. Baja
  California Norte, NW Mexico
Roscianum *see* Rossano
Roscommon 40 C2 Michigan, N USA
Roseau 55 G4 *prev.* Charlotte Town.
  country capital (Dominica) (Dominica)
  SW Dominica
Roseburg 46 B4 Oregon, NW USA
Rosenau *see* Rožňava
Rosenberg 49 G4 Texas, SW USA
Rosenberg *see* Ružomberok, Slovakia
Rosengarten 94 B3 Niedersachsen,
  N Germany
Rosenheim 95 C6 Bayern, S Germany
Rosia 93 H5 *var.* SW Gibraltar
Rosia Bay 93 H5 *bay* SW Gibraltar
  Europe W Mediterranean Sea Atlantic
  Ocean
Roşiori de Vede 108 B5 Teleorman,
  S Romania
Rositten *see* Rēzekne

Roslavl' *111 A5* Smolenskaya Oblast', W Russian Federation
Rosmalen *86 C4* Noord-Brabant, S Netherlands
Rossano *97 E6 anc.* Roscianum. Calabria, SW Italy
Ross Ice Shelf *154 B4 ice shelf* Antarctica
Rossiyskaya Federatsiya *see* Russian Federation
Rosso *74 B3* Trarza, SW Mauritania
Rossosh' *111 B6* Voronezhskaya Oblast', W Russian Federation
Ross Sea *154 B4 sea* Antarctica
Rostak *see* Ar Rustāq
Rostock *94 C2* Mecklenburg-Vorpommern, NE Germany
Rostov *see* Rostov-na-Donu
Rostov-na-Donu *111 B7 var.* Rostov, *Eng.* Rostov-on-Don. Rostovskaya Oblast', SW Russian Federation
Rostov-on-Don *see* Rostov-na-Donu
Roswell *48 D2* New Mexico, SW USA
Rota *144 B1 island* S Northern Mariana Islands
Rotcher Island *see* Tamana
Rothera *154 A2* UK research station Antarctica
Rotomagus *see* Rouen
Rotorua *150 D3* Bay of Plenty, North Island, New Zealand
Rotorua, Lake *150 D3 lake* North Island, New Zealand
Rotterdam *86 C4* Zuid-Holland, SW Netherlands
Rottweil *95 B6* Baden-Württemberg, S Germany
Rotuma *145 E4 island* NW Fiji Oceania S Pacific Ocean
Roubaix *90 C2* Nord, N France
Rouen *90 C3 anc.* Rotomagus. Seine-Maritime, N France
Roulers *see* Roeselare
Roumania *see* Romania
Round Rock *49 G3* Texas, SW USA
Rourkela *see* Rāulakela
Rousselaere *see* Roeselare
Roussillon *91 C6 cultural region* S France
Rouyn-Noranda *38 D4* Québec, SE Canada
Rovaniemi *84 D3* Lappi, N Finland
Rovigno *see* Rovinj
Rovigo *96 C2* Veneto, NE Italy
Rovinj *100 A3 It.* Rovigno. Istra, NW Croatia
Rovno *see* Rivne
Rovuma, Rio *79 F2 var.* Ruvuma. *river* Mozambique/Tanzania
Rovuma, Rio *see* Ruvuma
Równe *see* Rivne
Roxas City *139 E2* Panay Island, C Philippines
Royale, Isle *40 B1 island* Michigan, N USA
Royan *91 B5* Charente-Maritime, W France
Rozdol'ne *109 F4 Rus.* Razdolnoye. Respublika Krym, S Ukraine
Rožňava *99 D6 Ger.* Rosenau, *Hung.* Rozsnyó. Košický Kraj, E Slovakia
Rózsahegy *see* Ružomberok
Rozsnyó *see* Râşnov, Romania
Rozsnyó *see* Rožňava, Slovakia
Ruanda *see* Rwanda
Ruapehu, Mount *150 D4 volcano* North Island, New Zealand
Ruapuke Island *151 B8 island* SW New Zealand
Ruatoria *150 E3* Gisborne, North Island, New Zealand
Ruawai *150 D2* Northland, North Island, New Zealand
Rubeznhoye *see* Rubizhne
Rubizhne *109 H3 Rus.* Rubezhnoye. Luhans'ka Oblast', E Ukraine
Ruby Mountains *47 D5 mountain range* Nevada, W USA
Rucava *106 B3* Liepāja, SW Latvia
Rudensk *see* Rudzyensk
Rūdiškes *107 B5* Vilnius, S Lithuania
Rudnik *104 E2* Varna, E Bulgaria
Rudny *see* Rudnyy
Rudnyy *114 C4 var.* Rudny. Kostanay, N Kazakhstan
Rudolf, Lake *see* Turkana, Lake
Rudolfswert *see* Novo mesto
Rudzyensk *107 C6 Rus.* Rudensk. Minskaya Voblasts', C Belarus

Rufiji *73 C7 river* E Tanzania
Rufino *64 C4* Santa Fe, C Argentina
Rugāji *106 D4* Balvi, E Latvia
Rügen *94 D1 headland* NE Germany
Ruggell *94 E1* N Liechtenstein Europe
Ruhja *see* Rūjiena
Ruhnu *106 C2 var.* Ruhnu Saar, *Swe.* Runö. *island* SW Estonia
Ruhnu Saar *see* Ruhnu
Rujen *see* Rūjiena
Rūjiena *106 D3 Est.* Ruhja, *Ger.* Rujen. Valmiera, N Latvia
Rukwa, Lake *73 B7 lake* SE Tanzania
Rum *see* Rhum
Ruma *100 D3* Vojvodina, N Serbia
Rumadiya *see* Ar Ramādī
Rumania/Rumänien *see* Romania
Rumbek *73 B5* El Buhayrat, S Sudan
Rum Cay *54 D2 island* C Bahamas
Rumia *98 C2* Pomorskie, N Poland
Rummah, Wādi ar *see* Rimah, Wādi ar
Rummelsburg in Pommern *see* Miastko
Rumuniya/Rumŭniya/Rumunjska *see* Romania
Runanga *151 B5* West Coast, South Island, New Zealand
Rundu *78 C3 var.* Runtu. Okavango, NE Namibia
Runö *see* Ruhnu
Runtu *see* Rundu
Ruoqiang *126 C3 var.* Jo-ch'iang, *Uigh.* Charkhlik, Charkhliq, Qarkilik. Xinjiang Uygur Zizhiqu, NW China
Rupea *108 C4 Ger.* Reps, *Hung.* Kőhalom; *prev.* Cohalm. Braşov, C Romania
Rupel *87 B5 river* N Belgium
Rupella *see* la Rochelle
Rupert, Rivière de *38 D3 river* Québec, C Canada
Rusaddir *see* Melilla
Ruschuk/Ruşçuk *see* Ruse
Ruse *104 D1 var.* Ruschuk, Rustchuk, *Turk.* Rusçuk. Ruse, N Bulgaria
Russadir *see* Melilla
Russellville *42 A1* Arkansas, C USA
Russia *see* Russian Federation
Russian America *see* Alaska
Russian Federation *112 D2 off.* Russian Federation, *var.* Russia, *Latv.* Krievija, *Rus.* Rossiyskaya Federatsiya. *country* Asia/Europe

Rustaq *see* Ar Rustāq
Rust'avi *117 G2* SE Georgia
Rustchuk *see* Ruse
Ruston *42 B2* Louisiana, S USA
Rutanzige, Lake *see* Edward, Lake
Rutba *see* Ar Ruţbah
Rutlam *see* Ratlām
Rutland *41 F2* Vermont, NE USA
Rutog *126 A4 var.* Rutög, Rutok. Xizang Zizhiqu, W China
Rutok *see* Rutog
Ruvuma *69 E5 var.* Rio Rovuma. *river* Mozambique/Tanzania
Ruvuma, Rio *see* Rovuma, Rio
Ruwenzori *77 E5 mountain range* Dem. Rep. Congo/Uganda
Ruzhany *107 B6* Brestskaya Voblasts', SW Belarus

Ružomberok *99 C5 Ger.* Rosenberg, *Hung.* Rózsahegy. Žilinský Kraj, N Slovakia
Rwanda *73 B6 off.* Rwandese Republic; *prev.* Ruanda. *country* C Africa

RWANDA
Central Africa

Official name Republic of Rwanda
Formation 1962 / 1962
Capital Kigali
Population 9.4 million / 976 people per sq mile (377 people per sq km) / 20%
Total area 10,169 sq. miles (26,338 sq. km)
Languages Kinyarwanda*, French*, English*, Kiswahili
Religions Roman Catholic 56%, Traditional beliefs 25%, Muslim 10%, Protestant 9%
Ethnic mix Hutu 90%, Tutsi 9%, Other (including Twa) 1%
Government Presidential system
Currency Rwanda franc = 100 centimes
Literacy rate 65%
Calorie consumption 2084 calories

Rwandese Republic *see* Rwanda
Ryazan' *111 B5* Ryazanskaya Oblast', W Russian Federation
Rybach'ye *see* Balykchy
Rybinsk *110 B4 prev.* Andropov. Yaroslavskaya Oblast', W Russian Federation
Rybnik *99 C5* Śląskie, S Poland
Rybnitsa *see* Rîbniţa
Ryde *148 E1* United Kingdom
Ryki *98 D4* Lubelskie, E Poland
Rykovo *see* Yenakiyeve
Rypin *98 C3* Kujawsko-pomorskie, C Poland
Ryssel *see* Lille
Rysy *99 C5 mountain* S Poland
Ryukyu Islands *130 A2 Eng.* Ryukyu Islands. *island group* SW Japan
Ryukyu Islands *125 E3 Eng.* Ryukyu Islands. *island group* SW Japan
Ryukyu Islands *see* Nansei-shotō
Ryukyu Islands *see* Nansei-shotō
Ryukyu Trench *125 F3 var.* Nansei Syotō Trench. *trench* E East China Sea
Rzeszów *99 E5* Podkarpackie, SE Poland
Rzhev *110 B4* Tverskaya Oblast', W Russian Federation

S

Saale *94 C4 river* C Germany
Saalfeld *95 C5 var.* Saalfeld an der Saale. Thüringen, C Germany
Saalfeld an der Saale *see* Saalfeld
Saarbrücken *95 A6 Fr.* Sarrebruck. Saarland, SW Germany
Sääre *106 C2 var.* Sjar. Saaremaa, W Estonia
Saare *see* Saaremaa
Saaremaa *106 C2 Ger.* Oesel, Ösel; *prev.* Saare. *island* W Estonia
Saariselkä *84 D2 Lapp.* Suoločielgi. Lappi, N Finland
Sab' Ābār *118 C4 var.* Sab'a Biyar, Sa'b Bi'ār. Ḩimş, C Syria
Sab'a Biyar *see* Sab' Ābār
Šabac *100 D3* Serbia, W Serbia
Sabadell *93 G2* Cataluña, E Spain
Sabah *138 D3 prev.* British North Borneo, North Borneo. *state* East Malaysia
Sabanalarga *58 B1* Atlántico, N Colombia
Sabaneta *58 C1* Falcón, N Venezuela
Sab'atayn, Ramlat as *121 C6 desert* C Yemen
Sabaya *61 F4* Oruro, S Bolivia
Sa'b Bi'ār see Sab' Ābār
Saberi, Hamun-e *122 C5 var.* Daryācheh-ye Hāmun, Daryācheh-ye Sīstān. *lake* Afghanistan/Iran
Sabhā *71 F3* C Libya
Sabi *see* Save
Sabinas *51 E2* Coahuila, NE Mexico
Sabinas Hidalgo *51 E2* Nuevo León, NE Mexico
Sabine River *49 H3 river* Louisiana/Texas, SW USA

Sabkha *see* As Sabkhah
Sable, Cape *43 E5 headland* Florida, SE USA
Sable Island *39 G4 island* Nova Scotia, SE Canada
Şabyā *121 B6* Jīzān, SW Saudi Arabia
Sabzawar *see* Sabzevār
Sabzevār *120 D2 var.* Sabzawar. Khorāsān-Razavī, NE Iran
Sachsen *94 D4 Eng.* Saxony, *Fr.* Saxe. *state* E Germany
Sachs Harbour *37 E2 var.* Ikaahuk. Banks Island, Northwest Territories, N Canada
Sächsisch-Reen/Sächsisch-Regen *see* Reghin
Sacramento *47 B5 state capital* California, W USA
Sacramento Mountains *48 D2 mountain range* New Mexico, SW USA
Sacramento River *47 B5 river* California, W USA
Sacramento Valley *47 B5 valley* California, W USA
Sá da Bandeira *see* Lubango
Şa'dah *121 B6* NW Yemen
Sado *131 C5 var.* Sadoga-shima. *island* C Japan
Sadoga-shima *see* Sado
Saena Julia *see* Siena
Safad *see* Tsefat
Şāfāqis *see* Sfax
Şafāshahr *120 D3 var.* Deh Bīd. Fārs, C Iran
Safed *see* Tsefat
Säffle *85 B6* Värmland, C Sweden
Safford *48 C3* Arizona, SW USA
Safi *70 B2* W Morocco
Selseleh-ye Safid Kuh *122 D4 Eng.* Paropamisus Range. *mountain range* W Afghanistan
Sagaing *136 B3* Sagaing, C Burma (Myanmar)
Sagami-nada *131 D6 inlet* SW Japan
Sagan *see* Żagań
Sāgar *134 D4 prev.* Saugor. Madhya Pradesh, C India
Sagarmāthā *see* Everest, Mount
Sagebrush State *see* Nevada
Saghez *see* Saqqez
Saginaw *40 D3* Michigan, N USA
Saginaw Bay *40 D2 lake bay* Michigan, N USA
Sagua la Grande *54 B2* Villa Clara, C Cuba
Sagunto *93 F3 Cat.* Sagunt, *Ar.* Murviedro; *anc.* Saguntum. País Valenciano, E Spain
Sagunt/Saguntum *see* Sagunto
Sahara *68 B3 desert* Libya/Algeria
Sahara el Gharbiya *see* Şaḩrā' al Gharbīyah
Saharan Atlas *70 D2 var.* Saharan Atlas. *mountain range* Algeria/Morocco
Saharan Atlas *see* Atlas Saharien
Sahel *74 D3 physical region* C Africa
Şāḩiliyah, Jibāl as *118 B3 mountain range* NW Syria
Sāhīwāl *134 C2 prev.* Montgomery. Punjab, E Pakistan
Saïda *119 A5 var.* Şaydā, Sayida; *anc.* Sidon. W Lebanon
Sa'īdābād *see* Sīrjān
Saidpur *135 G3 var.* Syedpur. Rajshahi, NW Bangladesh
Saidu Sharif *134 C1 var.* Mingora, Mongora. North-West Frontier Province, N Pakistan
Saigon *see* Hồ Chí Minh
Saimaa *85 E5 lake* SE Finland
St Albans *89 E6 anc.* Verulamium. E England, United Kingdom
Saint Albans *40 D5* West Virginia, NE USA
St Andrews *88 C4* E Scotland, United Kingdom
Saint Anna Trough *see* Svyataya Anna Trough
St. Ann's Bay *54 B4* C Jamaica
St. Anthony *39 G3* Newfoundland and Labrador, SE Canada
Saint Augustine *43 E3* Florida, SE USA
St Austell *89 C7* SW England, United Kingdom
St.Botolph's Town *see* Boston
St-Brieuc *90 A3* Côtes d'Armor, NW France

RUSSIAN FEDERATION
Europe / Asia

Official name Russian Federation
Formation 1480 / 1991
Capital Moscow
Population 142 million / 22 people per sq mile (8 people per sq km) / 73%
Total area 6,592,735 sq. miles (17,075,200 sq. km)
Languages Russian*, Tatar, Ukrainian, Chavash, various other national languages
Religions Orthodox Christian 75%, Muslim 14%, Other 11%
Ethnic mix Russian 80%, Other 12%, Tatar 4%, Ukrainian 2%, Bashkir 1%, Chavash 1%
Government Mixed Presidential–Parliamentary system
Currency Russian rouble = 100 kopeks
Literacy rate 99%
Calorie consumption 3072 calories

St. Catharines 38 D5 Ontario, S Canada
St-Chamond 91 D5 Loire, E France
Saint Christopher and Nevis, Federation of see Saint Kitts and Nevis
Saint Christopher-Nevis see Saint Kitts and Nevis
Saint Clair, Lake 40 D3 var. Lac à L'Eau Claire. lake Canada/USA
St-Claude 91 D5 anc. Condate. Jura, E France
Saint Cloud 45 F2 Minnesota, N USA
Saint Croix 55 F3 island S Virgin Islands (US)
Saint Croix River 40 A2 river Minnesota/Wisconsin, N USA
St-Denis 79 G4 dependent territory capital (Réunion) NW Réunion
St-Dié 90 E4 Vosges, NE France
St-Egrève 91 D5 Isère, E France
Sainte Marie, Cap see Vohimena, Tanjona
Saintes 91 B5 anc. Mediolanum. Charente-Maritime, W France
St-Étienne 91 D5 Loire, E France
St-Flour 91 C5 Cantal, C France
St-Gall/Saint Gall/St. Gallen see Sankt Gallen
St-Gaudens 91 B6 Haute-Garonne, S France
Saint George 149 D5 Queensland, E Australia
St George 42 B4 N Bermuda
Saint George 44 A5 Utah, W USA
St. George's 55 G5 country capital (Grenada) (Grenada) SW Grenada
St-Georges 39 E4 Québec, SE Canada
St-Georges 59 H3 E French Guiana
Saint George's Channel 89 B6 channel Ireland/Wales, United Kingdom
St George's Island 42 B4 island E Bermuda
Saint Helena 69 B6 UK dependent territory C Atlantic Ocean
St Helier 89 D8 dependent territory capital (Jersey) S Jersey, Channel Islands
St.Iago de la Vega see Spanish Town
Saint Ignace 40 C2 Michigan, N USA
St-Jean, Lac 39 E4 lake Québec, SE Canada
Saint Joe River 46 D2 river Idaho, NW USA North America
St. John 39 F4 New Brunswick, SE Canada
Saint-John see Saint John
Saint John River 41 H1 Fr. Saint-John. river Canada/USA
St John's 55 G3 country capital (Antigua and Barbuda) (Antigua and Barbuda) Antigua, Antigua and Barbuda
St. John's 39 H3 province capital Newfoundland and Labrador, E Canada
Saint Joseph 45 F4 Missouri, C USA
St Julian's 102 B5 N Malta
St Kilda 88 A3 island NW Scotland, United Kingdom
Saint Kitts and Nevis 55 F3 off. Federation of Saint Christopher and Nevis, var. Saint Christopher-Nevis. country E West Indies

St-Laurent see St-Laurent-du-Maroni

St-Laurent-du-Maroni 59 H3 var. St-Laurent. NW French Guiana
St-Laurent, Fleuve see St. Lawrence
St. Lawrence 39 E4 Fr. Fleuve St-Laurent. river Canada/USA
St. Lawrence, Gulf of 39 F3 gulf NW Atlantic Ocean
Saint Lawrence Island 36 B2 island Alaska, USA
St-Lô 90 B3 anc. Briovera, Laudus. Manche, N France
St-Louis 90 E4 Haut-Rhin, NE France
Saint Louis 74 B3 NW Senegal
Saint Louis 45 G4 Missouri, C USA
Saint Lucia 55 E1 country SE West Indies

SAINT LUCIA
West Indies

Official name Saint Lucia
Formation 1979 / 1979
Capital Castries
Population 170,649 / 723 people per sq mile (280 people per sq km) / 31%
Total area 239 sq. miles (620 sq. km)
Languages English*, French Creole
Religions Roman Catholic 90%, Other 10%
Ethnic mix Black 83%, Mulatto (mixed race) 13%, Asian 3%, Other 1%
Government Parliamentary system
Currency Eastern Caribbean dollar = 100 cents
Literacy rate 95%
Calorie consumption 2988 calories

Saint Lucia Channel 55 H4 channel Martinique/Saint Lucia
St-Malo 90 B3 Ille-et-Vilaine, NW France
St-Malo, Golfe de 90 A3 gulf NW France
St.Matthew's Island see Zadetkyi Kyun
Saint Martin see Sint Maarten
St.Matthias Group 144 B3 island group NE Papua New Guinea
St. Moritz 95 B7 Ger. Sankt Moritz, Rmsch. San Murezzan. Graubünden, SE Switzerland
St-Nazaire 90 A4 Loire-Atlantique, NW France
Saint Nicholas see São Nicolau
Saint-Nicolas see Sint-Niklaas
St-Omer 90 C2 Pas-de-Calais, N France
Saint Paul 45 F2 state capital Minnesota, N USA
St-Paul, Île 141 C6 var. St.Paul Island. island Île St-Paul, NE French Southern and Antarctic Territories Antarctica Indian Ocea
St.Paul Island see St-Paul, Île
St Peter Port 89 D8 dependent territory capital (Guernsey) C Guernsey, Channel Islands
Saint Petersburg 43 E4 Florida, SE USA
Saint Petersburg see Sankt-Peterburg
St-Pierre and Miquelon 39 G4 Fr. Îles St-Pierre et Miquelon. French territorial collectivity NE North America
St-Quentin 90 C3 Aisne, N France
Saint Thomas see São Tomé, Sao Tome and Principe
Saint Thomas see Charlotte Amalie, Virgin Islands (US)
Saint Ubes see Setúbal
Saint Vincent 55 G4 island N Saint Vincent and the Grenadines
Saint Vincent see São Vicente
Saint Vincent and the Grenadines 55 H4 country SE West Indies

SAINT VINCENT & THE GRENADINES
West Indies

Official name Saint Vincent and the Grenadines
Formation 1979 / 1979
Capital Kingstown
Population 118,149 / 902 people per sq mile (347 people per sq km) / 59%
Total area 150 sq. miles (389 sq. km)
Languages English*, English Creole
Religions Anglican 47%, Methodist 28%, Roman Catholic 13%, Other 12%
Ethnic mix Black 77%, Mulatto (mixed race) 16%, Other 3%, Carib 3%, Asian 1%
Government Parliamentary system

SAINT VINCENT & THE GRENADINES
(continued)

Currency Eastern Caribbean dollar = 100 cents
Literacy rate 88%
Calorie consumption 2599 calories

Saint Vincent, Cape see São Vicente, Cabo de
Saint Vincent Passage 55 H4 passage Saint Lucia/Saint Vincent and the Grenadines
Saint Yves see Setúbal
Saipan 142 B1 island/country capital (Northern Mariana Islands) S Northern Mariana Islands
Saishū see Cheju-do
Sajama, Nevado 61 F4 mountain W Bolivia
Sajószentpéter 99 D6 Borsod-Abaúj-Zemplén, NE Hungary
Sakākah 120 B4 Al Jawf, NW Saudi Arabia
Sakakawea, Lake 44 D1 reservoir North Dakota, N USA
Sak'art'velo see Georgia
Sakata 130 D4 Yamagata, Honshū, C Japan
Sakhalin 115 G4 var. Sakhalin. island SE Russian Federation
Sakhalin see Sakhalin, Ostrov
Sakhon Nakhon see Sakon Nakhon
Şäki 117 G2 Rus. Sheki; prev. Nukha. NW Azerbaijan
Saki see Saky
Sakishima-shoto 130 A3 var. Sakisima Syotō. island group SW Japan
Sakisima Syotō see Sakishima-shotō
Sakiz see Saqqez
Sakiz-Adasi see Chíos
Sakon Nakhon 136 D4 var. Muang Sakon Nakhon, Sakhon Nakhon. Sakon Nakhon, E Thailand
Saky 109 F5 Rus. Saki. Respublika Krym, S Ukraine
Sal 74 A3 island Ilhas de Barlavento, NE Cape Verde
Sala 85 C6 Västmanland, C Sweden
Salacgriva 106 C3 Est. Salatsi. Limbāži, N Latvia
Sala Consilina 97 D5 Campania, S Italy
Salado, Río 62 D5 river E Argentina
Salado, Río 64 C3 river C Argentina
Şalālah 121 D6 SW Oman
Salamá 52 B2 Baja Verapaz, C Guatemala
Salamanca 64 B4 Coquimbo, C Chile
Salamanca 92 D2 anc. Helmantica, Salmantica. Castilla-León, NW Spain
Salamīyah 118 B3 var. As Salamīyah. Ḥamāh, W Syria
Salang see Phuket
Salantai 106 B3 Klaipėda, NW Lithuania
Salatsi see Salacgriva
Salavan 137 D5 var. Saravan, Saravane. Salavan, S Laos
Salavat 111 D6 Respublika Bashkortostan, W Russian Federation
Sala y Gómez 153 F4 island Chile, E Pacific Ocean
Sala y Gomez Fracture Zone see Sala y Gomez Ridge
Sala y Gomez Ridge 153 G4 var. Sala y Gomez Fracture Zone. fracture zone SE Pacific Ocean
Salazar see N'Dalatando
Šalčininkai 107 C5 Vilnius, SE Lithuania
Saldaba see Zaragoza
Saldus 106 B3 Ger. Frauenburg. Saldus, W Latvia
Sale 149 C7 Victoria, SE Australia
Salé 70 C2 NW Morocco
Salekhard 114 D3 prev. Obdorsk. Yamalo-Nenetskiy Avtonomnyy Okrug, N Russian Federation
Salem 132 C2 Tamil Nādu, SE India
Salem 46 B3 state capital Oregon, NW USA
Salerno 97 D5 anc. Salernum. Campania, S Italy
Salerno, Gulf of 97 C5 Eng. Gulf of Salerno. gulf S Italy
Salerno, Gulf of see Salerno, Golfo di
Salernum see Salerno

Salihorsk 107 C7 Rus. Soligorsk. Minskaya Voblasts', S Belarus
Salima 79 E2 Central, C Malawi
Salina 45 E5 Kansas, C USA
Salina Cruz 51 F5 Oaxaca, SE Mexico
Salinas 60 A2 Guayas, W Ecuador
Salinas 47 B6 California, W USA
Salisbury 89 D7 var. New Sarum. S England, United Kingdom
Salisbury see Harare
Sállan see Sørøya
Sallyana see Şalyān
Salmantica see Salamanca
Salmon River 46 D3 river Idaho, NW USA
Salmon River Mountains 46 D3 mountain range Idaho, NW USA
Salo 85 D6 Länsi-Suomi, SW Finland
Salon-de-Provence 91 D6 Bouches-du-Rhône, SE France
Salonica/Salonika see Thessaloníki
Salonta 108 A3 Hung. Nagyszalonta. Bihor, W Romania
Sal'sk 111 B7 Rostovskaya Oblast', SW Russian Federation
Salt see As Salt
Salta 64 C2 Salta, NW Argentina
Saltash 89 C7 SW England, United Kingdom
Saltillo 51 E3 Coahuila, NE Mexico
Salt Lake City 44 B4 state capital Utah, W USA
Salto 64 D4 Salto, N Uruguay
Salton Sea 47 D8 lake California, W USA
Salvador 63 G3 prev. São Salvador. state capital Bahia, E Brazil
Salween 124 C2 Bur. Thanlwin, Chin. Nu Chiang, Nu Jiang. river SE Asia
Şalyān 135 E3 var. Sallyana. Mid Western, W Nepal
Salzburg 95 D6 anc. Juvavum. Salzburg, N Austria
Salzgitter 94 C4 prev. Watenstedt-Salzgitter. Niedersachsen, C Germany
Salzwedel 94 C3 Sachsen-Anhalt, N Germany
Šamac see Bosanski Šamac
Samakhixai 137 E5 var. Attapu, Attopeu. Attapu, S Laos
Samalayuca 50 C1 Chihuahua, N Mexico
Samar 139 F2 island C Philippines
Samara 114 B3 prev. Kuybyshev. Samarskaya Oblast', W Russian Federation
Samarang see Semarang
Samarinda 138 D4 Borneo, C Indonesia
Samarkand see Samarqand
Samarkandski/Samarkandskoye see Temirtau
Samarobriva see Amiens
Samarqand 123 E2 Rus. Samarkand. Samarqand Viloyati, C Uzbekistan
Samawa see As Samāwah
Sambalpur 135 F4 Orissa, E India
Sambava 79 G2 Antsiranana, NE Madagascar
Sambir 108 B2 Rus. Sambor. L'vivs'ka Oblast', NW Ukraine
Sambor see Sambir
Sambre 90 D2 river Belgium/France
Samfya 78 D2 Luapula, N Zambia
Saminatal 94 E2 valley Austria/Liechtenstein Europe
Samnān see Semnān
Sam Neua see Xam Nua
Samoa 145 E4 off. Independent State of Western Samoa, var. Sāmoa; prev. Western Samoa. country W Polynesia

SAMOA
Australasia & Oceania

Official name Independent State of Samoa
Formation 1962 / 1962
Capital Apia
Population 214,265 / 196 people per sq mile (76 people per sq km) / 22%
Total area 1104 sq. miles (2860 sq. km)
Languages Samoan*, English*
Religions Christian 99%, Other 1%
Ethnic mix Polynesian 90%, Euronesian 9%, Other 1%
Government Parliamentary system
Currency Tala = 100 sene
Literacy rate 99%
Calorie consumption 2945 calories

Sāmoa see Samoa
Samoa Basin 143 E3 undersea basin
W Pacific Ocean
Samobor 100 A2 Zagreb, N Croatia
Sámos 105 E6 prev. Limín Vathéos.
Sámos, Dodekánisa, Greece, Aegean Sea
Sámos 105 D6 island Dodekánisa,
Greece, Aegean Sea
Samothrace see Samothráki
Samothráki 104 D4 Samothráki,
NE Greece
Samothráki 104 C4 anc. Samothrace.
island NE Greece
Sampít 138 C4 Borneo, C Indonesia
Samsun 116 D2 anc. Amisus. Samsun,
N Turkey
Samtredia 117 F2 W Georgia
Samui, Ko 137 C6 island SW Thailand
Samut Prakan 137 C5 var. Muang Samut
Prakan, Paknam. Samut Prakan,
C Thailand
San 74 D3 Ségou, C Mali
San 99 E5 river SE Poland
Şan'ā' 121 B6 Eng. Sana. country capital
(Yemen) (Yemen) W Yemen
Sana 100 B3 river NW Bosnia and
Herzegovina
Sanae 154 B2 South African research
station Antarctica
Sanaga 77 B5 river C Cameroon
San Ambrosio, Isla 57 A5 Eng. San
Ambrosio Island. island W Chile
San Ambrosio Island see San Ambrosio,
Isla
Sanandaj 120 C3 prev. Sinneh.
Kordestān, W Iran
San Andrés, Isla de 53 F3 island
N Colombia, Caribbean Sea
San Andrés Tuxtla 51 F4 var. Tuxtla.
Veracruz-Llave, E Mexico
San Angelo 49 F3 Texas, SW USA
San Antonio 52 B2 Toledo, S Belize
San Antonio 64 B4 Valparaíso, C Chile
San Antonio 49 F4 Texas, SW USA
San Antonio Oeste 65 C5 Río Negro,
E Argentina
San Antonio River 49 G4 river Texas,
SW USA
Sanāw 121 C6 var. Sanaw. NE Yemen
San Benedicto, Isla 50 B4 island
W Mexico
San Benito 52 B1 Petén, N Guatemala
San Benito 49 G5 Texas, SW USA
San Bernardino 47 C7 California,
W USA
San Blas 50 C3 Sinaloa, C Mexico
San Blas, Cape 42 D3 headland Florida,
SE USA
San Blas, Cordillera de 53 G4 mountain
range NE Panama
San Carlos 52 D4 Río San Juan,
S Nicaragua
San Carlos 48 B2 Arizona, SW USA
San Carlos see Quesada, Costa Rica
San Carlos de Ancud see Ancud
San Carlos de Bariloche 65 B5 Río
Negro, SW Argentina
San Carlos del Zulia 58 C2 Zulia,
W Venezuela
San Clemente Island 47 B8 island
Channel Islands, California, W USA
San Cristóbal 58 C2 Táchira,
W Venezuela
San Cristobal 144 C4 var. Makira. island
SE Solomon Islands
San Cristóbal see San Cristóbal de
Las Casas
San Cristóbal de Las Casas 51 G5 var.
San Cristóbal. Chiapas, SE Mexico
San Cristóbal, Isla 60 B5 var. Chatham
Island. island Galapagos Islands,
Ecuador, E Pacific Ocean
Sancti Spíritus 54 B2 Sancti Spíritus,
C Cuba
Sandakan 138 D3 Sabah, East Malaysia
Sandalwood Island see Sumba, Pulau
Sandanski 104 C3 prev. Sveti Vrach.
Blagoevgrad, SW Bulgaria
Sanday 88 D2 island NE Scotland, United
Kingdom
Sanders 48 C2 Arizona, SW USA
Sand Hills 44 D3 mountain range
Nebraska, C USA
San Diego 47 C8 California, W USA
Sandnes 85 A6 Rogaland, S Norway
Sandomierz 98 D4 Rus. Sandomir.
Świętokrzyskie, C Poland

Sandomir see Sandomierz
Sandoway see Thandwe
Sandpoint 46 C1 Idaho, NW USA
Sand Springs 49 G1 Oklahoma, C USA
Sandusky 40 D3 Ohio, N USA
Sandvika 85 A6 Akershus, S Norway
Sandviken 85 C6 Gävleborg, C Sweden
Sandwich Island see Efate
Sandwich Islands see Hawaiian Islands
Sandy Bay 93 H5 Saskatchewan,
C Canada
Sandy City 44 B4 Utah, W USA
Sandy Lake 38 B3 lake Ontario,
C Canada
San Esteban 52 D2 Olancho, C Honduras
San Eugenio/San Eugenio del Cuareim
see Artigas
San Felipe 58 D1 Yaracuy, NW Venezuela
San Felipe de Puerto Plata see Puerto
Plata
San Félix, Isla 57 A5 Eng. San Felix
Island. island W Chile
San Felix Island see San Félix, Isla
San Fernando 92 C5 prev. Isla de León.
Andalucía, S Spain
San Fernando 55 H5 Trinidad, Trinidad
and Tobago
San Fernando 46 D1 California, W USA
San Fernando 58 D2 var. San Fernando
de Apure. Apure, C Venezuela
San Fernando de Apure see San
Fernando
San Fernando del Valle de Catamarca
64 C3 var. Catamarca. Catamarca,
NW Argentina
San Fernando de Monte Cristi see
Monte Cristi
San Francisco 47 B6 California, W USA
San Francisco del Oro 50 C2
Chihuahua, N Mexico
San Francisco de Macorís 55 E3
C Dominican Republic
San Fructuoso see Tacuarembó
San Gabriel 60 B1 Carchi, N Ecuador
San Gabriel Mountains 46 E1 mountain
range California, USA
Sangihe, Kepulauan see Sangir,
Kepulauan
Sangir, Kepulauan 139 F3 var.
Kepulauan Sangihe. island group
N Indonesia
Sāngli 132 B1 Mahārāshtra, W India
Sangmélima 77 B5 Sud, S Cameroon
Sangre de Cristo Mountains 48 D1
mountain range Colorado/New Mexico,
C USA
San Ignacio 52 B1 prev. Cayo, El Cayo.
Cayo, W Belize
San Ignacio 61 F3 Beni, N Bolivia
San Ignacio 50 B2 Baja California Sur,
NW Mexico
San Joaquin Valley 47 B7 valley
California, W USA
San Jorge, Gulf of 65 C6 var. Gulf of San
Jorge. gulf S Argentina
San Jorge, Gulf of see San Jorge, Golfo
San José 53 E4 country capital (Costa
Rica) (Costa Rica) San José, C Costa
Rica
San José 61 G3 var. San José de
Chiquitos. Santa Cruz, E Bolivia
San José 52 A2 var. Puerto San José.
Escuintla, S Guatemala
San José 47 B6 California, W USA
San José see San José del Guaviare,
Colombia
San José de Chiquitos see San José
San José de Cúcuta see Cúcuta
San José del Guaviare 58 C4 var. San
José. Guaviare, S Colombia
San Juan 64 B4 San Juan, W Argentina
San Juan 55 F3 dependent territory
capital (Puerto Rico) NE Puerto Rico
San Juan see San Juan de los Morros
San Juan Bautista 64 D3 Misiones,
S Paraguay
San Juan Bautista see Villahermosa
San Juan Bautista Tuxtepec see Tuxtepec
San Juan de Alicante 93 F4 País
Valenciano, E Spain
San Juan del Norte 53 E4 var. Greytown.
Río San Juan, SE Nicaragua
San Juan de los Morros 58 D2 var. San
Juan. Guárico, N Venezuela
San Juanito, Isla 50 C4 island C Mexico
San Juan Mountains 48 D1 mountain
range Colorado, C USA

San Juan, Río 53 E4 river Costa Rica/
Nicaragua
San Juan River 48 C1 river Colorado/
Utah, W USA
San Julián see Puerto San Julián
Sankt-Bartholomäi see Palamuse
Sankt Gallen 95 B7 var. St. Gallen, Eng.
Saint Gall, Fr. St-Gall. Sankt Gallen,
NE Switzerland
Sankt-Georgen see Sfântu Gheorghe
Sankt-Jakobi see Pärnu-Jaagupi,
Pärnumaa, Estonia
Sankt Martin see Martin
Sankt Moritz see St. Moritz
Sankt-Peterburg 110 B4 prev.
Leningrad, Petrograd, Eng.
Saint Petersburg, Fin. Pietari.
Leningradskaya Oblast', NW Russian
Federation
Sankt Pölten 95 E6 Niederösterreich,
N Austria
Sankt Veit am Flaum see Rijeka
Sankuru 77 D6 river C Dem. Rep. Congo
Şanlıurfa 117 E4 prev. Sanli Urfa, Urfa;
anc. Edessa. şanlıurfa, S Turkey
Sanli Urfa see Şanlıurfa
San Lorenzo 61 G5 Tarija, S Bolivia
San Lorenzo 60 A1 Esmeraldas,
N Ecuador
San Lorenzo, Isla 60 C4 island W Peru
Sanlúcar de Barrameda 92 C5
Andalucía, S Spain
San Luis 64 C4 San Luis, C Argentina
San Luis 52 B2 Petén, NE Guatemala
San Luis 50 A1 var. San Luis Río
Colorado. Sonora, NW Mexico
San Luis Obispo 47 B7 California,
W USA
San Luis Potosí 51 E3 San Luis Potosí,
C Mexico
San Luis Río Colorado see San Luis
San Marcos 52 A2 San Marcos,
W Guatemala
San Marcos 49 G4 Texas, SW USA
San Marcos de Arica see Arica
San Marino 96 E1 country capital (San
Marino) (San Marino) C San Marino
San Marino 96 D1 ♦ Republic of San
Marino. country S Europe

SAN MARINO
Southern Europe

Official name Republic of San Marino
Formation 1631 / 1631
Capital San Marino
Population 29,615 / 1234 people
per sq mile (489 people per sq km) / 89%
Total area 23.6 sq. miles (61 sq. km)
Languages Italian*
Religions Roman Catholic 93%,
Other and nonreligious 7%
Ethnic mix Sammarinese 88%,
Italian 10%, Other 2%
Government Parliamentary system
Currency Euro = 100 cents
Literacy rate 99%
Calorie consumption Not available

San Marino, Republic of see San Marino
San Martín 154 A2 Argentinian research
station Antarctica
San Mateo 59 E2 Anzoátegui,
NE Venezuela
San Matías 61 H3 Santa Cruz, E Bolivia
San Matías, Gulf of 65 C5 var. Gulf of
San Matías. gulf E Argentina
San Matías, Gulf of see Matías, Golfo
Sanmenxia 128 C4 var. Shan Xian.
Henan, C China
San Miguel 52 C3 San Miguel,
SE El Salvador
San Miguel 50 D2 Coahuila, N Mexico
San Miguel de Ibarra see Ibarra
San Miguel de Tucumán 64 C3 var.
Tucumán. Tucumán, N Argentina
San Miguelito 53 G4 Panamá, C Panamá
San Miguel, Río 61 G3 river E Bolivia
San Murezzan see St. Moritz
Sannār see Sennar
Sânnicolaul-Mare see Sânnicolau Mare
Sânnicolau Mare 108 A4 var.
Sânnicolaul-Mare, Hung.
Nagyszentmiklós; prev. Sânmiclăuş
Mare, Sînnicolau Mare. Timiş,
W Romania

Sanok 99 E5 Podkarpackie, SE Poland
San Pablo 61 F5 Potosí, S Bolivia
San Pedro 52 C1 Corozal, NE Belize
San-Pédro 74 D5 S Côte d'Ivoire
San Pedro 50 D3 var. San Pedro de las
Colonias. Coahuila, N Mexico
San Pedro de la Cueva 50 C2 Sonora,
NW Mexico
San Pedro de las Colonias see San Pedro
San Pedro de Lloc 60 B3 La Libertad,
NW Peru
San Pedro Mártir, Sierra 50 A1
mountain range NW Mexico
San Pedro Sula 52 C2 Cortés,
NW Honduras
San Rafael 64 B4 Mendoza, W Argentina
San Rafael Mountains 47 C7 mountain
range California, W USA
San Ramón de la Nueva Orán 64 C2
Salta, N Argentina
San Remo 96 A3 Liguria, NW Italy
San Salvador 52 B3 country capital (El
Salvador) (El Salvador) San Salvador,
SW El Salvador
San Salvador 54 D2 prev. Watlings
Island. island E Bahamas
San Salvador de Jujuy 64 C2 var. Jujuy.
Jujuy, N Argentina
San Salvador, Isla 60 A4 island Ecuador
Sansanné-Mango 75 E4 var. Mango.
N Togo
Sansepolcro 96 C3 Toscana, C Italy
San Severo 97 D5 Puglia, SE Italy
Santa Ana 61 F3 Beni, N Bolivia
Santa Ana 52 B3 Santa Ana,
NW El Salvador
Santa Ana 46 D2 California, W USA
Santa Ana de Coro see Coro
Santa Ana Mountains 46 E2 mountain
range California, W USA
Santa Barbara 50 C2 Chihuahua,
N Mexico
Santa Barbara 47 C7 California, W USA
Santa Catalina Island 47 B8 island
Channel Islands, California, W USA
Santa Catarina 63 E5 off. Estado de
Santa Catarina. region S Brazil
Santa Catarina 63 E5 off. Estado de
Santa Catarina. state S Brazil
Santa Catarina, Estado de see Santa
Catarina
Santa Clara 54 B2 Villa Clara, C Cuba
Santa Clarita 46 D1 California, W USA
Santa Comba 92 B1 Galicia, NW Spain
Santa Cruz 76 E2 São Tomé, S Sao Tome
and Principe, Africa
Santa Cruz 47 B6 California, W USA
Santa Cruz 61 G4 department E Bolivia
Santa Cruz Barillas see Barillas
Santa Cruz del Quiché 52 B2 Quiché,
W Guatemala
Santa Cruz de Tenerife 70 A3 Tenerife,
Islas Canarias, Spain, NE Atlantic Ocean
Santa Cruz, Isla 60 B5 var. Indefatigable
Island, Isla Chávez. island Galapagos
Islands, Ecuador, E Pacific Ocean
Santa Cruz Islands 144 D3 island group
E Solomon Islands
Santa Cruz, Rio 65 B7 river
S Argentina
Santa Elena 52 B1 Cayo, W Belize
Santa Fe 64 C4 Santa Fe, C Argentina
Santa Fe 48 D1 state capital New Mexico,
SW USA
Santa Fe see Bogotá
Santa Fe de Bogotá see Bogotá
Santa Genoveva 50 B3 mountain
NW Mexico
Santa Isabel 144 C3 var. Bughotu. island
N Solomon Islands
Santa Isabel see Malabo
Santa Lucia Range 47 B7 mountain
range California, W USA
Santa Margarita, Isla 50 B3 island
NW Mexico
Santa Maria 63 E5 Rio Grande do Sul,
S Brazil
Santa Maria 47 B7 California, USA
Santa Maria 92 A5 island Azores,
Portugal, NE Atlantic Ocean
Santa María del Buen Aire see Buenos
Aires
Santa María, Isla 60 A5 var. Isla
Floreana, Charles Island. island
Galapagos Islands, Ecuador, E Pacific
Ocean

Santa Marta 58 B1 Magdalena, N Colombia
Santa Maura see Lefkáda
Santa Monica 46 D1 California, W USA
Santana 76 E2 São Tomé, C Sao Tome and Principe, Africa
Santander 92 D1 Cantabria, N Spain
Santarém 63 E2 Pará, N Brazil
Santarém 92 B3 anc. Scalabis. Santarém, W Portugal
Santa Rosa 64 C4 La Pampa, C Argentina
Santa Rosa see Santa Rosa de Copán
Santa Rosa de Copán 52 C2 var. Santa Rosa. Copán, W Honduras
Santa Rosa Island 47 B8 island California, W USA
Sant Carles de la Rápida see Sant Carles de la Ràpita
Sant Carles de la Ràpita 93 F3 var. Sant Carles de la Rápida. Cataluña, NE Spain
Santiago 64 B4 var. Gran Santiago. country capital (Chile) (Chile) Santiago, C Chile
Santiago 55 E3 var. Santiago de los Caballeros. N Dominican Republic
Santiago 53 F5 Veraguas, S Panama
Santiago 92 B1 var. Santiago de Compostela, Eng. Compostella; anc. Campus Stellae. Galicia, NW Spain
Santiago 74 A3 var. São Tiago. island Ilhas de Sotavento, S Cape Verde
Santiago see Santiago de Cuba, Cuba
Santiago de Compostela see Santiago
Santiago de Cuba 54 C3 var. Santiago. Santiago de Cuba, E Cuba
Santiago de Guayaquil see Guayaquil
Santiago del Estero 64 C3 Santiago del Estero, C Argentina
Santiago de los Caballeros see Santiago, Dominican Republic
Santiago de los Caballeros see Ciudad de Guatemala, Guatemala
Santiago Pinotepa Nacional see Pinotepa Nacional
Santiago, Río 60 B2 river N Peru
Santi Quaranta see Sarandë
Santissima Trinidad see Chilung
Sant Julià de Lòria 91 A8 Sant Julià de Lòria, SW Andorra Europe
Santo see Espiritu Santo
Santo Antão 74 A2 island Ilhas de Barlavento, N Cape Verde
Santo António 76 E1 Príncipe, N Sao Tome and Principe, Africa
Santo Domingo 55 D3 prev. Ciudad Trujillo. country capital (Dominican Republic) (Dominican Republic) SE Dominican Republic
Santo Domingo de los Colorados 60 B1 Pichincha, NW Ecuador
Santo Domingo Tehuantepec see Tehuantepec
San Tomé de Guayana see Ciudad Guayana
Santos 63 F4 São Paulo, S Brazil
Santos Plateau 57 D5 undersea plateau SW Atlantic Ocean
Santo Tomé 64 D3 Corrientes, NE Argentina
Santo Tomé de Guayana see Ciudad Guayana
San Valentín, Cerro 65 A6 mountain S Chile
San Vicente 52 C3 San Vicente, C El Salvador
São Francisco, Rio 63 F3 river E Brazil
Sao Hill 73 C7 Iringa, S Tanzania
São João da Madeira 92 B2 Aveiro, N Portugal
São Jorge 92 A5 island Azores, Portugal, NE Atlantic Ocean
São Luís 63 F2 state capital Maranhão, NE Brazil
São Mandol see São Manuel, Rio
São Manuel, Rio 63 E3 var. São Mandol, Teles Pirés. river C Brazil
São Marcos, Baía de 63 F1 bay N Brazil
São Miguel 92 A5 island Azores, Portugal, NE Atlantic Ocean
Saona, Isla 55 E3 island SE Dominican Republic
Saône 91 D5 river E France
São Nicolau 74 A3 Eng. Saint Nicholas. island Ilhas de Barlavento, N Cape Verde

São Paulo 63 E4 state capital São Paulo, S Brazil
São Paulo 63 E4 off. Estado de São Paulo. state S Brazil
São Paulo 63 E4 off. Estado de São Paulo. region S Brazil
São Paulo de Loanda see Luanda
São Paulo, Estado de see São Paulo
São Pedro do Rio Grande do Sul see Rio Grande
São Roque, Cabo de 63 G2 headland E Brazil
São Salvador see Salvador, Brazil
São Salvador/São Salvador do Congo see M'Banza Congo, Angola
São Tiago see Santiago
São Tomé 77 A5 country capital (Sao Tome and Principe) (Sao Tome and Principe) São Tomé, S São Tomé and Principe
São Tomé 76 E2 Eng. Saint Thomas. island S Sao Tome and Principe
Sao Tome and Principe 76 D1 off. Democratic Republic of Sao Tome and Principe. country E Atlantic Ocean

SÃO TOMÉ & PRÍNCIPE
West Africa

Official name The Democratic Republic of Sao Tome and Principe
Formation 1975 / 1975
Capital São Tomé
Population 199,579 / 538 people per sq mile (208 people per sq km) / 38%
Total area 386 sq. miles (1001 sq. km)
Languages Portuguese*, Portuguese Creole
Religions Roman Catholic 84%, Other 16%
Ethnic mix Black 90%, Portuguese and Creole 10%
Government Presidential system
Currency Dobra = 100 céntimos
Literacy rate 83%
Calorie consumption 2460 calories

Sao Tome and Principe, Democratic Republic of see Sao Tome and Principe
São Tomé, Pico de 76 D2 mountain São Tomé, C Sao Tome and Principe, Africa
São Vicente 74 A3 Eng. Saint Vincent. island Ilhas de Barlavento, N Cape Verde
São Vicente, Cabo de 92 B5 Eng. Cape Saint Vincent, Port. Cabode São Vicente. cape S Portugal
São Vicente, Cabo de see São Vicente, Cabo de
Sápai see Sápes
Sápes 104 D3 var. Sápai. Anatoliki Makedonía kai Thráki, NE Greece
Sapir 119 B7 prev. Sappir. Southern, S Israel
Sa Pobla 93 G3 Mallorca, Spain, W Mediterranean Sea
Sappir see Sapir
Sapporo 130 D2 Hokkaidō, NE Japan
Sapri 97 D6 Campania, S Italy
Sapulpa 49 G1 Oklahoma, C USA
Saqqez 120 C2 var. Saghez, Sakiz, Saqqiz. Kordestän, NW Iran
Saqqiz see Saqqez
Sara Buri 137 C5 var. Saraburi. Saraburi, C Thailand
Saraburi see Sara Buri
Saragossa see Zaragoza
Saragt see Sarahs
Saraguro 60 B2 Loja, S Ecuador
Sarahs 122 D3 var. Saragt, Rus. Serakhs. Ahal Welaýaty, S Turkmenistan
Sarajevo 100 C4 country capital (Bosnia and Herzegovina) (Bosnia and Herzegovina) Federacija Bosna I Hercegovina, SE Bosnia and Herzegovina
Sarakhs 120 E2 Khorāsān-Razavī, NE Iran
Saraktash 111 D6 Orenburgskaya Oblast', W Russian Federation
Saran' 114 C4 Kaz. Saran. Karaganda, C Kazakhstan
Saranda see Sarandë
Sarandë 101 C7 var. Saranda, It. Porto Edda; prev. Santi Quaranta. Vlorë, S Albania

Saransk 111 C5 Respublika Mordoviya, W Russian Federation
Sarasota 43 E4 Florida, SE USA
Saratov 114 B3 Saratovskaya Oblast', W Russian Federation
Saravan/Saravane see Salavan
Sarawak 138 D3 state East Malaysia
Sarawak see Kuching
Sarcelles 90 D1 Val-d'Oise, Ile-de-France, N France Europe
Sardinia 97 A5 Eng. Sardinia. island Italy, C Mediterranean Sea
Sardinia see Sardegna
Sarera, Teluk see Cenderawasih, Teluk
Sargasso Sea 66 B4 sea W Atlantic Ocean
Sargodha 134 C2 Punjab, NE Pakistan
Sarh 76 C4 prev. Fort-Archambault. Moyen-Chari, S Chad
Sāri 120 D2 var. Sari, Sāri. Māzandarān, N Iran
Saría 105 E7 island SE Greece
Sarıkamış 117 F3 Kars, NE Turkey
Sarikol Range 123 G3 Rus. Sarykol'skiy Khrebet. mountain range China/Tajikistan
Sark 89 D8 Fr. Sercq. island Channel Islands
Şarkışla 116 D3 Sivas, C Turkey
Sarmiento 65 B6 Chubut, S Argentina
Sarnia 38 C5 Ontario, S Canada
Sarny 108 C1 Rivnens'ka Oblast', NW Ukraine
Sarochyna 107 D5 Rus. Sorochino. Vitsyebskaya Voblasts', N Belarus
Sarov 111 C5 var. Sarova. Respublika Mordoviya, SW Russian Federation
Sarova see Sarov
Sarpsborg 85 B6 Østfold, S Norway
Sarrebruck see Saarbrücken
Sartène 91 E7 Corse, France, C Mediterranean Sea
Sarthe 90 B4 river N France
Sárti 104 C4 Kentriki Makedonía, N Greece
Saruhan see Manisa
Saryarqa see Kazakhskiy Melkosopochnik
Sarykol'skiy Khrebet see Sarikol Range
Sary-Tash 123 F2 Oshskaya Oblast', SW Kyrgyzstan
Saryyesik-Atyrau, Peski 123 G1 desert E Kazakhstan
Sasebo 131 A7 Nagasaki, Kyūshū, SW Japan
Saskatchewan 37 F5 province SW Canada
Saskatchewan 37 F5 river Manitoba/Saskatchewan, C Canada
Saskatoon 37 F5 Saskatchewan, S Canada
Sasovo 111 B5 Ryazanskaya Oblast', W Russian Federation
Sassandra 74 D5 S Côte d'Ivoire
Sassandra 74 D5 var. Ibo, Sassandra Fleuve. river S Côte d'Ivoire
Sassandra Fleuve see Sassandra
Sassari 97 A5 Sardegna, Italy, C Mediterranean Sea
Sassenheim 86 C3 Zuid-Holland, W Netherlands
Sassnitz 94 D2 Mecklenburg-Vorpommern, NE Germany
Sathmar see Satu Mare
Sátoraljaújhely 99 D6 Borsod-Abaúj-Zemplén, NE Hungary
Satpura Range 134 D4 mountain range C India
Satsuma-Sendai see Sendai
Satsunan-shoto 130 A3 island group Nansei-shotō, SW Japan Asia
Sattanen 84 D3 Lappi, NE Finland
Satu Mare 108 B3 var. Satmar, Hung. Szatmárrnémeti. Satu Mare, NW Romania
Sau see Sava
Saudi Arabia 121 B5 off. Kingdom of Saudi Arabia, Al 'Arabīyah as Su'ūdīyah, Ar. Al Mamlakah al 'Arabīyah as Su'ūdīyah. country SW Asia

SAUDI ARABIA
Southwest Asia

Official name Kingdom of Saudi Arabia
Formation 1932 / 1932
Capital Riyadh
Population 25.8 million / 32 people per sq mile (12 people per sq km) / 88%

SAUDI ARABIA
(continued)

Total area 756,981 sq. miles (1,960,582 sq. km)
Languages Arabic*
Religions Sunni Muslim 85%, Shi'a Muslim 15%
Ethnic mix Arab 90%, Afro-Asian 10%
Government Monarchy
Currency Saudi riyal = 100 halalat
Literacy rate 79%
Calorie consumption 2844 calories

Saudi Arabia, Kingdom of see Saudi Arabia
Sauer see Sûre
Saugor see Sāgar
Saulkrasti 106 C3 Rīga, C Latvia
Sault Sainte Marie 40 C1 Michigan, N USA
Sault Sainte Marie 38 C4 Michigan, N USA
Sault Ste. Marie 38 C4 Ontario, S Canada
Saumur 90 B4 Maine-et-Loire, NW France
Saurimo 78 C1 Port. Henrique de Carvalho, Vila Henrique de Carvalho. Lunda Sul, NE Angola
Sava 107 E6 Mahilyowskaya Voblasts', E Belarus
Savá 52 D2 Colón, N Honduras
Savai'i 145 E4 island NW Samoa
Savannah 43 E2 Georgia, SE USA
Savannah River 43 E2 river Georgia/South Carolina, SE USA
Savannakhét see Khanthabouli
Savanna-La-Mar 54 A5 W Jamaica
Savaria see Szombathely
Save 100 B3 Eng. Save, Ger. Sau, Hung. Száva. river SE Europe
Save see Sava
Save, Rio 79 E3 var. Sabi. river Mozambique/Zimbabwe
Saverne 90 E3 var. Zabern; anc. Tres Tabernae. Bas-Rhin, NE France
Savigliano 96 A2 Piemonte, NW Italy
Savigsivik see Savissivik
Savinski see Savinskiy
Savinskiy 110 C3 var. Savinski. Arkhangel'skaya Oblast', NW Russian Federation
Savissivik 82 D1 var. Savigsivik. Avannaarsua, N Greenland
Savoie 91 D5 cultural region E France
Savona 96 A2 Liguria, NW Italy
Savu Sea 139 E5 Ind. Laut Sawu. sea S Indonesia
Sawakin see Suakin
Sawdiri see Sodiri
Sawhāj 72 B2 var. Sohág var. Sawhāj, Suliag. C Egypt
Sawhāj see Sawhāj
Şawqirah 121 D6 var. Suqrah. S Oman
Sawu, Laut see Savu Sea
Saxe see Sachsen
Saxony see Sachsen
Sayaboury see Xaignabouli
Sayanskiy Khrebet 112 D3 mountain range S Russian Federation
Sayat 122 D3 Rus. Sayat. Lebap Welaýaty, E Turkmenistan
Sayaxché 52 B2 Petén, N Guatemala
Şaydā/Sayida see Saïda
Sayhūt 121 D6 E Yemen
Saynshand 127 E2 Dornogovi, SE Mongolia
Sayre 41 E3 Pennsylvania, NE USA
Say'ūn 121 C6 var. Saywūn. C Yemen
Saywūn see Say'ūn
Scalabis see Santarém
Scandinavia 66 D2 geophysical region NW Europe
Scarborough 89 D5 N England, United Kingdom
Scarpanto see Kárpathos
Scebeli see Shebeli
Schaan 94 E1 W Liechtenstein Europe
Schaerbeek 87 C6 Brussels, C Belgium
Schaffhausen 95 B7 Fr. Schaffhouse. Schaffhausen, N Switzerland
Schaffhouse see Schaffhausen
Schagen 86 C2 Noord-Holland, NW Netherlands
Schaulen see Šiauliai
Schebschi Mountains see Shebshi Mountains

Scheessel *94 B3* Niedersachsen, NW Germany
Schefferville *39 E2* Québec, E Canada
Schelde *see* Scheldt
Scheldt *87 B5 Dut.* Schelde, *Fr.* Escaut. *river* W Europe
Schell Creek Range *47 D5 mountain range* Nevada, W USA
Schenectady *41 F3* New York, NE USA
Schertz *49 G4* Texas, SW USA
Schiermonnikoog *86 D1 Fris.* Skiermûntseach. *island* Waddeneilanden, N Netherlands
Schijndel *86 D4* Noord-Brabant, S Netherlands
Schil *see* Jiu
Schiltigheim *90 E3* Bas-Rhin, NE France
Schivelbein *see* Świdwin
Schleswig *94 B2* Schleswig-Holstein, N Germany
Schleswig-Holstein *94 B2 state* N Germany
Schlettstadt *see* Sélestat
Schlochau *see* Człuchów
Schneekoppe *see* Sněžka
Schneidemühl *see* Piła
Schoden *see* Skuodas
Schönebeck *94 C4* Sachsen-Anhalt, C Germany
Schönlanke *see* Trzcianka
Schooten *see* Schoten
Schoten *87 C5 var.* Schooten. Antwerpen, N Belgium
Schouwen *86 B4 island* SW Netherlands
Schwabenalb *see* Schwäbische Alb
Schwäbische Alb *95 B6 var.* Schwabenalb, *Eng.* Swabian Jura. *mountain range* S Germany
Schwandorf *95 C5* Bayern, SE Germany
Schwaz *95 C7* Tirol, W Austria
Schweidnitz *see* Świdnica
Schweinfurt *95 B5* Bayern, SE Germany
Schweiz *see* Switzerland
Schwerin *94 C3* Mecklenburg-Vorpommern, N Germany
Schwertberg *see* Świecie
Schwiebus *see* Świebodzin
Schwyz *95 B7 var.* Schwiz. Schwyz, C Switzerland
Schyl *see* Jiu
Scio *see* Chíos
Scoresby Sound/Scoresbysund *see* Ittoqqortoormiit
Scoresby Sund *see* Kangertittivaq
Scotia Sea *57 C8 sea* SW Atlantic Ocean
Scotland *88 C3 cultural region* Scotland, UK
Scott Base *154 B4 NZ research station* Antarctica
Scott Island *154 B5 island* Antarctica
Scottsbluff *44 D3* Nebraska, C USA
Scottsboro *42 D1* Alabama, S USA
Scottsdale *48 B2* Arizona, SW USA
Scranton *41 F3* Pennsylvania, NE USA
Scrobesbyrig' *see* Shrewsbury
Scupi *see* Skopje
Scutari *see* Shkodër
Scutari, Lake *101 C5 Alb.* Liqeni i Shkodrës, *SCr.* Skadarsko Jezero. *lake* Albania/Montenegro
Scyros *see* Skýros
Searcy *42 B1* Arkansas, C USA
Seattle *46 B2* Washington, NW USA
Sébaco *52 D3* Matagalpa, W Nicaragua
Sebaste/Sebastia *see* Sivas
Sebastián Vizcaíno, Bahía *50 A2 bay* NW Mexico
Sebastopol *see* Sevastopol'
Sebenico *see* Šibenik
Sechura, Bahía de *60 A3 bay* NW Peru
Secunderābād *134 D5 var.* Sikandarabad. Andhra Pradesh, C India
Sedan *90 D3* Ardennes, N France
Seddon *151 D5* Marlborough, South Island, New Zealand
Seddonville *151 C5* West Coast, South Island, New Zealand
Sédhiou *74 B3* SW Senegal
Sedlez *see* Siedlce
Sedona *48 B2* Arizona, SW USA
Sedunum *see* Sion
Seeland *see* Sjælland
Seenu Atoll *see* Addu Atoll
Seesen *94 B4* Niedersachsen, C Germany
Segestica *see* Sisak

Segezha *110 B3* Respublika Kareliya, NW Russian Federation
Seghedin *see* Szeged
Segna *see* Senj
Segodunum *see* Rodez
Ségou *74 D3 var.* Segu. Ségou, C Mali
Segovia *92 D2* Castilla-León, C Spain
Segoviao Wangki *see* Coco, Río
Segu *see* Ségou
Séguédine *75 H2* Agadez, NE Niger
Seguin *49 G4* Texas, SW USA
Segura *93 E4 river* S Spain
Seinäjoki *85 D5 Swe.* Östermyra. Länsi-Suomi, W Finland
Seine *90 D1 river* N France
Seine, Baie de la *90 B3 bay* N France
Sekondi *see* Sekondi-Takoradi
Sekondi-Takoradi *75 E5 var.* Sekondi. S Ghana
Selânik *see* Thessaloníki
Selenga *127 E1 Mong.* Selenge Mörön. *river* Mongolia/Russian Federation
Selenge Mörön *see* Selenga
Sélestat *90 E4 Ger.* Schlettstadt. Bas-Rhin, NE France
Seleucia *see* Silifke
Selfoss *83 E5* Sudhurland, SW Iceland
Sélibabi *74 C3 var.* Sélibaby. Guidimaka, S Mauritania
Sélibaby *see* Sélibabi
Selma *47 C6* California, W USA
Selway River *46 D2 river* Idaho, NW USA North America
Selwyn Range *148 B3 mountain range* Queensland, C Australia
Selzaete *see* Zelzate
Semarang *138 C5 var.* Samarang. Jawa, C Indonesia
Sembé *77 B5* Sangha, NW Congo
Semendria *see* Smederevo
Semey *see* Semipalatinsk
Semezhevo *see* Syemyezhava
Seminole *49 E3* Texas, SW USA
Seminole, Lake *42 D3 reservoir* Florida/Georgia, SE USA
Semipalatinsk *114 D4 Kaz.* Semey. Vostochnyy Kazakhstan, E Kazakhstan
Semnān *120 D3 var.* Samnān. Semnān, N Iran
Semois *87 C8 river* SE Belgium
Sendai *131 A8 var.* Satsuma-Sendai. Kagoshima, Kyūshū, SW Japan
Sendai *130 D4* Miyagi, Honshū, C Japan
Sendai-wan *130 D4 bay* E Japan
Senec *99 C6 Ger.* Wartberg, *Hung.* Szenc; *prev.* Szempcz. Bratislavský Kraj, W Slovakia
Senegal *74 B3 off.* Republic of Senegal, *Fr.* Sénégal. *country* W Africa

SENEGAL
West Africa

Official name Republic of Senegal
Formation 1960 / 1960
Capital Dakar
Population 12.2 million / 164 people per sq mile (63 people per sq km) / 50%
Total area 75,749 sq. miles (196,190 sq. km)
Languages French*, Wolof, Pulaar, Serer, Diola, Mandinka, Malinke, Soninke
Religions Sunni Muslim 90%, Christian (mainly Roman Catholic) 5%, Traditional beliefs 5%
Ethnic mix Wolof 43%, Serer 15%, Other 14%, Peul 14%, Toucouleur 9%, Diola 5%
Government Presidential system
Currency CFA franc = 100 centimes
Literacy rate 39%
Calorie consumption 2279 calories

Senegal *74 C3 Fr.* Sénégal. *river* W Africa
Senegal, Republic of *see* Senegal
Senftenberg *94 D4* Brandenburg, E Germany
Senia *see* Senj
Senica *99 C6 Ger.* Senitz, *Hung.* Szenice. Trnavský Kraj, W Slovakia
Seniça *see* Sjenica
Senitz *see* Senica
Senj *100 A3 Ger.* Zengg, *It.* Segna; *anc.* Senia. Lika-Senj, NW Croatia
Senja *84 C2 prev.* Senjen. *island* N Norway
Senjen *see* Senja

Senkaku-shoto *130 A3 island group* SW Japan
Senlis *90 C3* Oise, N France
Sennar *72 C4 var.* Sannār. Sinnar, C Sudan
Senones *see* Sens
Sens *90 C3 anc.* Agendicum, Senones. Yonne, C France
Sensburg *see* Mragowo
Sên, Stœng *137 D5 river* C Cambodia
Senta *100 D3 Hung.* Zenta. Vojvodina, N Serbia
Seo de Urgel *see* La See d'Urgel
Seoul *see* Sŏul
Şepşi-Sângeorz/Sepsiszentgyörgy *see* Sfântu Gheorghe
Sept-Îles *39 E3* Québec, SE Canada
Seraing *87 D6* Liège, E Belgium
Serakhs *see* Sarahs
Seram, Laut *see* Ceram Sea
Pulau Seram *139 F4 var.* Serang, *Eng.* Ceram. *island* Maluku, E Indonesia
Serang *138 C5* Jawa, C Indonesia
Serang *see* Seram, Pulau
Serasan, Selat *138 C3 strait* Indonesia/Malaysia
Serbia *100 D4 off.* Federal Republic of Serbia; *prev.* Yugoslavia, SCr. Jugoslavija. *country* SE Europe

SERBIA
Southeast Europe

Official name Republic of Serbia
Formation 2006 / 2008
Capital Belgrade
Population 8.1 million / 271 people per sq mile (105 people per sq km) / 52%
Total area 29,905 sq miles (77,453 sq km)
Languages Serbian*, Hungarian (Magyar)
Religions Orthodox Christian 85%, Other 6%, Roman Catholic 6%, Muslim 3%
Ethnic mix Serb 83%, Other 10%, Magyar 4%, Bosniak 2%, Roma 1%
Government Parliamentary system
Currency Dinar = 100 para
Literacy rate 98%
Calorie consumption 2678 calories

Serbia, Federal Republic of *see* Serbia
Sercq *see* Sark
Serdar *122 C2 prev. Rus.* Gyzyrlabat, Kizyl-Arvat. Balkan Welaýaty, W Turkmenistan
Serdica *see* Sofiya
Serdobol' *see* Sortavala
Serenje *78 D2* Central, E Zambia
Seres *see* Sérres
Seret/Sereth *see* Siret
Serhetabat *122 D4 prev. Rus.* Gushgy, Kushka. Mary Welaýaty, S Turkmenistan
Sérifos *105 C6 anc.* Seriphos. *island* Kykládes, Greece, Aegean Sea
Seriphos *see* Sérifos
Serov *114 C3* Sverdlovskaya Oblast', C Russian Federation
Serowe *78 D3* Central, SE Botswana
Serpa Pinto *see* Menongue
Serpent's Mouth, The *59 F2 Sp.* Boca de la Serpiente. *strait* Trinidad and Tobago/Venezuela
Serpiente, Boca de la *see* Serpent's Mouth, The
Serpukhov *111 B5* Moskovskaya Oblast', W Russian Federation
Sérrai *see* Sérres
Serrana, Cayo de *53 F2 island group* NW Colombia South America
Serranilla, Cayo de *53 F2 island group* NW Colombia South America Caribbean Sea
Serravalle *96 E1* N San Marino
Sérres *104 C3 var.* Seres; *anc.* Sérrai. Kentrikí Makedonía, NE Greece
Sesdlets *see* Siedlce
Sesto San Giovanni *96 B2* Lombardia, N Italy
Sesvete *100 B2* Zagreb, N Croatia
Setabis *see* Xàtiva
Sète *91 C6 prev.* Cette. Hérault, S France
Setesdal *85 A6 valley* S Norway
Sétif *71 E2 var.* Stif. N Algeria
Setté Cama *77 A6* Ogooué-Maritime, SW Gabon

Setúbal *92 B4 Eng.* Saint Ubes, Saint Yves. Setúbal, W Portugal
Setúbal, Baía de *92 B4 bay* W Portugal
Seul, Lac *38 B3 lake* Ontario, S Canada
Sevan *117 G2* C Armenia
Sevan, Lake *117 G3 Eng.* Lake Sevan, *Rus.* Ozero Sevan. *lake* E Armenia
Sevan, Lake/Sevan, Ozero *see* Sevana Lich
Sevastopol' *109 F5 Eng.* Sebastopol. Respublika Krym, S Ukraine
Severn *38 B2 river* Ontario, S Canada
Severn *89 D6 Wel.* Hafren. *river* England/Wales, United Kingdom
Severnaya Zemlya *115 E2 var.* Nicholas II Land. *island group* N Russian Federation
Severnyy *110 E3* Respublika Komi, NW Russian Federation
Severodonetsk *see* Syeverodonets'k
Severodvinsk *110 C3 prev.* Molotov, Sudostroy. Arkhangel'skaya Oblast', NW Russian Federation
Severomorsk *110 C2* Murmanskaya Oblast', NW Russian Federation
Seversk *114 D4* Tomskaya Oblast', C Russian Federation
Sevier Lake *44 A4 lake* Utah, W USA
Sevilla *92 C4 Eng.* Seville; *anc.* Hispalis. Andalucía, SW Spain
Seville *see* Sevilla
Sevlievo *104 D2* Gabrovo, N Bulgaria
Sevluš/Sevlyush *see* Vynohradiv
Seward's Folly *see* Alaska
Seychelles *79 G1 off.* Republic of Seychelles. *country* W Indian Ocean

SEYCHELLES
Indian Ocean

Official name Republic of Seychelles
Formation 1976 / 1976
Capital Victoria
Population 81,895 / 787 people per sq mile (303 people per sq km) / 50%
Total area 176 sq. miles (455 sq. km)
Languages French Creole*, English*, French*
Religions Roman Catholic 90%, Anglican 8%, Other (including Muslim) 2%
Ethnic mix Creole 89%, Indian 5%, Other 4%, Chinese 2%
Government Presidential system
Currency Seychelles rupee = 100 cents
Literacy rate 92%
Calorie consumption 2465 calories

Seychelles, Republic of *see* Seychelles
Seydhisfjördhur *83 E5* Austurland, E Iceland
Seýdi *122 D2 Rus.* Seýdi; *prev.* Neftezavodsk. Lebap Welaýaty, E Turkmenistan
Seyhan *see* Adana
Sfákia *see* Chóra Sfakíon
Sfântu Gheorghe *108 C4 Ger.* Sankt-Georgen, *Hung.* Sepsiszentgyörgy; *prev.* Şepşi-Sângeorz, Sfîntu Gheorghe. Covasna, C Romania
Sfax *71 F2 Ar.* Şafāqis. E Tunisia
Sfîntu Gheorghe *see* Sfântu Gheorghe
's-Gravenhage *86 B4 var.* Den Haag, *Eng.* The Hague, *Fr.* La Haye. *country capital* (Netherlands-seat of government) (Netherlands-seat of government) Zuid-Holland, W Netherlands
's-Gravenzande *86 B4* Zuid-Holland, W Netherlands
Shaan/Shaanxi Sheng *see* Shaanxi
Shaanxi *128 B5 var.* Shaan, Shaanxi Sheng, Shan-hsi, Shenshi, Shensi. *province* C China
Shabani *see* Zvishavane
Shabeelle, Webi *see* Shebeli
Shache *126 A3 var.* Yarkant. Xinjiang Uygur Zizhiqu, NW China
Shacheng *see* Huailai
Shackleton Ice Shelf *154 D3 ice shelf* Antarctica
Shaddādi *see* Ash Shadādah
Shāhābād *see* Eslāmābād
Sha Hi *see* Orūmīyeh, Daryācheh-ye
Shahjahanabad *see* Delhi
Shahr-e Kord *120 C3 var.* Shahr Kord. Chahār Maḩall va Bakhtīārī, C Iran

Shahr Kord *see* Shahr-e Kord
Shāhrūd 120 D2 *prev.* Emāmrūd,
Emāmshahr. Semnān, N Iran
Shalkar 114 B4 *var.* Chelkar.
Aktyubinsk, W Kazakhstan
Shām, Bādiyat ash *see* Syrian Desert
Shana *see* Kuril'sk
Shandī *see* Shendi
Shandong 128 D4 *var.* Lu, Shandong
Sheng, Shantung. *province* E China
Shandong Sheng *see* Shandong
Shanghai 128 D5 *var.* Shang-hai.
Shanghai Shi, E China
Shangrao 128 D5 Jiangxi, S China
Shan-hsi *see* Shaanxi, China
Shan-hsi *see* Shanxi, China
Shannon 89 A6 *Ir.* An tSionainn. *river*
W Ireland
Shan Plateau 136 B3 *plateau* E Burma
(Myanmar)
Shansi *see* Shanxi
Shantar Islands *see* Shantarskiye Ostrova
Shantarskiye Ostrova 115 G3 *Eng.*
Shantar Islands. *island group* E Russian
Federation
Shantou 128 D6 *var.* Shan-t'ou, Swatow.
Guangdong, S China
Shan-t'ou *see* Shantou
Shantung *see* Shandong
Shanxi 128 C4 *var.* Jin, Shan-hsi,
Shansi, Shanxi Sheng. *province*
C China
Shan Xian *see* Sanmenxia
Shanxi Sheng *see* Shanxi
Shaoguan 128 C6 *var.* Shao-kuan,
Cant. Kukong; *prev.* Ch'u-chiang.
Guangdong, S China
Shao-kuan *see* Shaoguan
Shaqrā' 120 B4 Ar Riyāḍ, C Saudi Arabia
Shaqrā *see* Shuqrah
Shar 114 D5 *var.* Charsk. Vostochnyy
Kazakhstan, E Kazakhstan
Shari 130 D2 Hokkaidō, NE Japan
Shari *see* Chari
Sharjah *see* Ash Shāriqah
Shark Bay 147 A5 *bay* Western Australia
Sharqī, Al Jabal ash/Sharqi, Jebel esh
see Anti-Lebanon
Shashe 78 D3 *var.* Shashi. *river*
Botswana/Zimbabwe
Shashi *see* Shashe
Shatskiy Rise 125 G1 *undersea rise*
N Pacific Ocean
Shawnee 49 G1 Oklahoma, C USA
Shaykh, Jabal ash *see* Hermon, Mount
Shchadryn 107 D7 *Rus.* Shchedrin.
Homyel'skaya Voblasts', SE Belarus
Shchedrin *see* Shchadryn
Shcheglovsk *see* Kemerovo
Shchëkino 111 B5 Tul'skaya Oblast',
W Russian Federation
Shchors 109 E1 Chernihivs'ka Oblast',
N Ukraine
Shchuchin *see* Shchuchyn
Shchuchinsk 114 C4 *prev.* Shchuchye.
Akmola, N Kazakhstan
Shchuchye *see* Shchuchinsk
Shchuchyn 107 B5 *Pol.* Szczuczyn
Nowogródzki, *Rus.* Shchuchin.
Hrodzyenskaya Voblasts', W Belarus
Shebekino 111 A6 Belgorodskaya
Oblast', W Russian Federation
Shebelē Wenz, Wabē *see* Shebeli
Shebeli 73 D5 *Amh.* Wabē Shebelē Wenz,
It. Scebeli, *Som.* Webi Shabeelle. *river*
Ethiopia/Somalia
Sheberghān 123 E3 *var.* Shibarghān,
Shiberghan, Shibirghan. Jowzjān,
N Afghanistan
Sheboygan 40 B2 Wisconsin, N USA
Shebshi Mountains 76 A4 *var.*
Schebschi Mountains. *mountain range*
E Nigeria
Shechem *see* Nablus
Shedadi *see* Ash Shadādah
Sheffield 89 D5 N England, United
Kingdom
Shekhem *see* Nablus
Sheki *see* Şäki
Shelby 44 B1 Montana, NW USA
Sheldon 45 F3 Iowa, C USA
Shelekhov Gulf 115 G2 *Eng.* Shelekhov
Gulf. *gulf* E Russian Federation
Shelekhov Gulf *see* Shelikhova, Zaliv
Shendi 72 C4 *var.* Shandī. River Nile,
NE Sudan
Shengking *see* Liaoning

Shenking *see* Liaoning
Shenshi/Shensi *see* Shaanxi
Shenyang 128 D3 *Chin.* Shen-yang, *Eng.*
Moukden, Mukden; *prev.* Fengtien.
province capital Liaoning, NE China
Shen-yang *see* Shenyang
Shepetivka 108 D2 *Rus.* Shepetovka.
Khmel'nyts'ka Oblast', NW Ukraine
Shepetovka *see* Shepetivka
Shepparton 149 C7 Victoria,
SE Australia
Sherbrooke 39 E4 Québec, SE Canada
Shereik 72 C3 River Nile, N Sudan
Sheridan 44 C2 Wyoming, C USA
Sherman 49 G2 Texas, SW USA
's-Hertogenbosch 86 C4 *Fr.* Bois-le-
Duc, *Ger.* Herzogenbusch. Noord-
Brabant, S Netherlands
Shetland Islands 88 D1 *island group*
NE Scotland, United Kingdom
Shevchenko *see* Aktau
Shibarghān *see* Sheberghān
Shiberghan/Shibirghān *see* Sheberghān
Shibetsu 130 D2 *var.* Sibetu. Hokkaidō,
NE Japan
Shibh Jazīrat Sīnā' *see* Sinai
Shibushi-wan 131 B8 *bay* SW Japan
Shigatse *see* Xigazè
Shih-chia-chuang/Shihmen *see*
Shijiazhuang
Shihezi 126 C2 Xinjiang Uygur Zizhiqu,
NW China
Shiichi *see* Shyichy
Shijiazhuang 128 C4 *var.* Shih-chia-
chuang; *prev.* Shihmen. *province
capital* Hebei, E China
Shikārpur 134 B3 Sind, S Pakistan
Shikoku 131 C7 *var.* Sikoku. *island*
SW Japan
Shikoku Basin 125 F2 *var.* Sikoku Basin.
undersea basin N Philippine Sea
Shikotan, Ostrov 130 E2 *Jap.* Shikotan-
tō. *island* NE Russian Federation
Shikotan-tō *see* Shikotan, Ostrov
Shilabo 73 D5 Sumalē, E Ethiopia
Shiliguri 135 F3 *prev.* Siliguri. West
Bengal, NE India
Shilka 115 F4 *river* S Russian Federation
Shillong 135 G3 *state capital* Meghālaya,
NE India
Shimanto *see* Nakamura
Shimbir Berris *see* Shimbiris
Shimbiris 72 E4 *var.* Shimbir Berris.
mountain N Somalia
Shimoga 132 C2 Karnātaka, W India
Shimonoseki 131 A7 *var.* Simonoseki,
hist. Akamagaseki, Bakan. Yamaguchi,
Honshū, SW Japan
Shinano-gawa 131 C5 *var.* Sinano Gawa.
river Honshū, C Japan
Shindand 122 D4 Herāt, W Afghanistan
Shingū 131 C6 *var.* Singū. Wakayama,
Honshū, SW Japan
Shinjō 130 D4 *var.* Sinzyô. Yamagata,
Honshū, C Japan
Shinyanga 73 C7 Shinyanga,
NW Tanzania
Shiprock 48 C1 New Mexico, SW USA
Shirāz 120 D4 *var.* Shīrāz. Fārs, S Iran
Shishchitsy *see* Shyshchytsy
Shivpuri 134 D3 Madhya Pradesh,
C India
Shizugawa 130 D4 Miyagi, Honshū,
NE Japan
Shizuoka 131 D6 *var.* Sizuoka. Shizuoka,
Honshū, S Japan
Shklov *see* Shklow
Shklow 107 D6 *Rus.* Shklov.
Mahilyowskaya Voblasts', E Belarus
Shkodër 101 C5 *var.* Shkodra, *It.* Scutari,
SCr. Skadar. NW Albania
Shkodra *see* Shkodër
Shkodrës, Liqeni i *see* Scutari, Lake
Shkumbinit, Lumi i 101 C6 *var.*
Shkumbi, Shkumbin. *river* C Albania
Shkumbi/Shkumbin *see* Shkumbinit,
Lumi i
Sholāpur *see* Solāpur
Shostka 109 F1 Sums'ka Oblast',
NE Ukraine
Show Low 48 B2 Arizona, SW USA
Show Me State *see* Missouri
Shpola 109 E3 Cherkas'ka Oblast',
N Ukraine
Shqipëria/Shqipërisë, Republika e
see Albania

Shreveport 42 A2 Louisiana, S USA
Shrewsbury 89 D6 *hist.* Scrobesbyrig'.
W England, United Kingdom
Shu 114 C5 *Kaz.* Shū. Zhambyl,
SE Kazakhstan
Shuang-liao *see* Liaoyuan
Shū, Kazakhstan *see* Shu
Shumagin Islands 36 B3 *island group*
Alaska, USA
Shumen 104 D2 Shumen, NE Bulgaria
Shumilina 107 E5 *Rus.* Shumilino.
Vitsyebskaya Voblasts', NE Belarus
Shumilino *see* Shumilina
Shunsen *see* Ch'unch'ŏn
Shuqrah 121 B7 *var.* Shaqrā. SW Yemen
Shwebo 136 B3 Sagaing, C Burma
(Myanmar)
Shyichy 107 C7 *Rus.* Shiichi.
Homyel'skaya Voblasts', SE Belarus
Shymkent 114 B5 *prev.* Chimkent.
Yuzhnyy Kazakhstan, S Kazakhstan
Shyshchytsy 107 C6 *Rus.* Shishchitsy.
Minskaya Voblasts', C Belarus
Siam *see* Thailand
Siam, Gulf of *see* Thailand, Gulf of
Sian *see* Xi'an
Siang *see* Brahmaputra
Siangtan *see* Xiangtan
Šiauliai 106 B4 *Ger.* Schaulen. Šiauliai,
N Lithuania
Siazan' *see* Siyäzän
Sibay 111 D6 Respublika Bashkortostan,
W Russian Federation
Šibenik 100 B4 *It.* Sebenico. Šibenik-
Knin, S Croatia
Siberia 115 E3 *var.* Sibiria. *physical
region* NE Russian Federation
Siberia *see* Sibir'
Siberoet *see* Siberut, Pulau
Siberut, Pulau 138 A4 *prev.* Siberoet.
island Kepulauan Mentawai,
W Indonesia
Sibi 134 B2 Baluchistān, SW Pakistan
Sibiti 77 B6 Lékoumou, S Congo
Sibiu 108 B4 *Ger.* Hermannstadt, *Hung.*
Nagyszeben. Sibiu, C Romania
Sibolga 138 B3 Sumatera, W Indonesia
Sibu 138 D3 Sarawak, East Malaysia
Sibut 76 C4 *prev.* Fort-Sibut. Kémo,
S Central African Republic
Sibuyan Sea 139 E2 *sea* W Pacific Ocean
Sichon 137 C6 *var.* Ban Sichon, Si Chon.
Nakhon Si Thammarat, SW Thailand
Si Chon *see* Sichon
Sichuan 128 B5 *var.* Chuan, Sichuan
Sheng, Ssu-ch'uan, Szechuan,
Szechwan. *province* C China
Sichuan Pendi 128 B5 *basin* C China
Sichuan Sheng *see* Sichuan
Sicilian Channel *see* Sicily, Strait of
Sicily 97 C7 *Eng.* Sicily; *anc.* Trinacria.
island Italy, C Mediterranean Sea
Sicily, Strait of 97 B7 *var.* Sicilian
Channel. *strait* C Mediterranean Sea
Sicuani 61 E4 Cusco, S Peru
Sidári 104 A4 Kérkyra, Iónia Nisiá,
Greece, C Mediterranean Sea
Sidas 138 C4 Borneo, C Indonesia
Siderno 97 D7 Calabria, SW Italy
Sidhirókastron *see* Sidirókastro
Sīdī Barrānī 72 A1 NW Egypt
Sidi Bel Abbès 70 D2 *var.* Sidi bel Abbès,
Sidi-Bel-Abbès. NW Algeria
Sidirókastro 104 C3 *prev.*
Sidhirókastron. Kentrikí Makedonía,
NE Greece
Sidley, Mount 154 B4 *mountain*
Antarctica
Sidney 44 D1 Montana, NW USA
Sidney 44 D3 Nebraska, C USA
Sidney 40 C4 Ohio, N USA
Sidon *see* Saïda
Sidra *see* Surt
Sidra/Sidra, Gulf of *see* Surt, Khalīj,
N Libya
Siebenbürgen *see* Transylvania
Siedlce 98 E3 *Ger.* Sedlez, *Rus.* Sesdlets.
Mazowieckie, C Poland
Siegen 94 B4 Nordrhein-Westfalen,
W Germany
Siemiatycze 98 E3 Podlaskie, NE Poland
Siena 96 B3 *Fr.* Sienne; *anc.* Saena Julia.
Toscana, C Italy
Sienne *see* Siena
Sieradz 98 C4 Sieradz, C Poland
Sierpc 98 D3 Mazowieckie, C Poland
Sierra Leone 74 C4 *off.* Republic of Sierra
Leone. *country* W Africa

SIERRA LEONE
West Africa

Official name	Republic of Sierra Leone
Formation	1961 / 1961
Capital	Freetown
Population	5.8 million / 210 people per sq mile (81 people per sq km) / 40%
Total area	27,698 sq. miles (71,740 sq. km)
Languages	English*, Mende, Temne, Krio
Religions	Muslim 30%, Traditional beliefs 30%, Other 30%, Christian 10%
Ethnic mix	Mende 35%, Temne 32%, Other 21%, Limba 8%, Kuranko 4%
Government	Presidential system
Currency	Leone = 100 cents
Literacy rate	35%
Calorie consumption	1936 calories

Sierra Leone Basin 66 C4 *undersea basin*
E Atlantic Ocean
Sierra Leone, Republic of *see* Sierra Leone
Sierra Leone Ridge *see* Sierra Leone Rise
Sierra Leone Rise 66 C4 *var.* Sierra
Leone Ridge, Sierra Leone Schwelle.
undersea rise E Atlantic Ocean
Sierra Leone Schwelle *see* Sierra
Leone Rise
Sierra Vista 48 B3 Arizona, SW USA
Sífnos 105 C6 *anc.* Siphnos. *island*
Kykládes, Greece, Aegean Sea
Sigli 138 A3 Sumatera, W Indonesia
Siglufjördhur 83 E4 Nordhurland
Vestra, N Iceland
Signal Peak 48 A2 *mountain* Arizona,
SW USA
Signan *see* Xi'an
Signy 154 A2 UK research station South
Orkney Islands, Antarctica
Siguatepeque 52 C2 Comayagua,
W Honduras
Siguiri 74 D4 NE Guinea
Sihanoukville *see* Kâmpóng Saôm
Siilinjärvi 84 E4 Itä-Suomi, C Finland
Siirt 117 F4 *var.* Sert; *anc.* Tigranocerta.
Siirt, SE Turkey
Sikandarabad *see* Secunderābād
Sikasso 74 D4 Sikasso, S Mali
Sikeston 45 H5 Missouri, C USA
Sikhote-Alin', Khrebet 115 G4
mountain range SE Russian Federation
Siking *see* Xi'an
Siklós 99 C7 Baranya, SW Hungary
Sikoku *see* Shikoku
Sikoku Basin *see* Shikoku Basin
Šilalė 106 B4 Tauragé, W Lithuania
Silchar 135 G3 Assam, NE India
Silesia 98 B4 *physical region* SW Poland
Silifke 116 C4 *anc.* Seleucia. İçel,
S Turkey
Siliguri *see* Shiliguri
Siling Co 126 C5 *lake* W China
Silinhot *see* Xilinhot
Silistra 104 E1 *var.* Silistria; *anc.*
Durostorum. Silistra, NE Bulgaria
Silistria *see* Silistra
Sillamäe 106 E2 *Ger.* Sillamäggi. Ida-
Virumaa, NE Estonia
Sillamäggi *see* Sillamäe
Sillein *see* Žilina
Šilutė 106 B4 *Ger.* Heydekrug. Klaipéda,
W Lithuania
Silvan 117 E4 Diyarbakır, SE Turkey
Silva Porto *see* Kuito
Silver State *see* Colorado
Silver State *see* Nevada
Simanichi 107 C7 *Rus.* Simonichi.
Homyel'skaya Voblasts', SE Belarus
Simav 116 B3 Kütahya, W Turkey
Simav Çayı 116 A3 *river* NW Turkey
Simbirsk *see* Ul'yanovsk
Simeto 97 C7 *river* Sicily, Italy,
C Mediterranean Sea
Simeulue, Pulau 138 A3 *island*
NW Indonesia
Simferopol' 109 F5 Respublika Krym,
S Ukraine
Simitli 104 C3 Blagoevgrad, SW Bulgaria
Şimlăul Silvaniei/Şimleu Silvaniei
see Şimleu Silvaniei
Şimleu Silvaniei 108 B3 *Hung.*
Szilágysomlyó; *prev.* Şimlăul Silvaniei,
Şimleul Silvaniei. Sălaj, NW Romania
Simonichi *see* Simanichi
Simonoseki *see* Shimonoseki
Simpelveld 87 D6 Limburg,
SE Netherlands

Simplon Pass 95 B8 *pass* S Switzerland
Simpson *see* Fort Simpson
Simpson Desert 148 B4 *desert* Northern Territory/South Australia
Sinai 72 C2 *var.* Sinai Peninsula, *Ar.* Shibh Jazirat Sīnā', Sīnā. *physical region* NE Egypt
Sinaia 108 C4 Prahova, SE Romania
Sinano Gawa *see* Shinano-gawa
Sinā/Sinai Peninsula *see* Sinai
Sincelejo 58 B2 Sucre, NW Colombia
Sind 134 B3 *var.* Sindh. *province* SE Pakistan
Sindelfingen 95 B6 Baden-Württemberg, SW Germany
Sindh *see* Sind
Sindi 106 D2 Ger. Zintenhof. Pärnumaa, SW Estonia
Sines 92 B4 Setúbal, S Portugal
Singan *see* Xi'an
Singapore 138 B3 *country capital* (Singapore) (Singapore) S Singapore
Singapore 138 A1 *off.* Republic of Singapore. *country* SE Asia

SINGAPORE
Southeast Asia

Official name Republic of Singapore
Formation 1965 / 1965
Capital Singapore
Population 4.4 million / 18644 people per sq mile (7213 people per sq km) / 100%
Total area 250 sq. miles (648 sq. km)
Languages Mandarin*, Malay*, Tamil*, English*
Religions Buddhist 55%, Taoist 22%, Muslim 16%, Hindu, Christian, and Sikh 7%
Ethnic mix Chinese 77%, Malay 14%, Indian 8%, Other 1%
Government Parliamentary system
Currency Singapore dollar = 100 cents
Literacy rate 93%
Calorie consumption Not available

Singapore, Republic of *see* Singapore
Singen 95 B6 Baden-Württemberg, S Germany
Singida 73 C7 Singida, C Tanzania
Singkang 139 E4 Sulawesi, C Indonesia
Singkawang 138 C3 Borneo, C Indonesia
Singora *see* Songkhla
Singū *see* Shingū
Sining *see* Xining
Siniscola 97 A5 Sardegna, Italy, C Mediterranean Sea
Sinj 100 B4 Split-Dalmacija, SE Croatia
Sinkiang/Sinkiang Uighur Autonomous Region *see* Xinjiang Uygur Zizhiqu
Sinnamarie *see* Sinnamary
Sinnamary 59 H3 *var.* Sinnamarie. N French Guiana
Sinneh *see* Sanandaj
Sinnicolau Mare *see* Sânnicolau Mare
Sinoe, Lacul *see* Sinoie, Lacul
Sinoie, Lacul 108 D5 *prev.* Lacul Sinoe. *lagoon* SE Romania
Sinop 116 D2 *anc.* Sinope. Sinop, N Turkey
Sinope *see* Sinop
Sinsheim 95 B6 Baden-Württemberg, SW Germany
Sint Maarten 55 G3 *Eng.* Saint Martin. *Dutch autonomous region* S Caribbean Sea
Sint-Michielsgestel 86 C4 Noord-Brabant, S Netherlands
Sin-Miclǎuş *see* Gheorgheni
Sint-Niklaas 87 B5 *Fr.* Saint-Nicolas. Oost-Vlaanderen, N Belgium
Sint-Pieters-Leeuw 87 B6 Vlaams Brabant, C Belgium
Sintra 92 B3 *prev.* Cintra. Lisboa, W Portugal
Sinujiif 73 E5 Nugaal, NE Somalia
Sinus Aelaniticus *see* Aqaba, Gulf of
Sinus Gallicus *see* Lion, Golfe du
Sinyang *see* Xinyang
Sinzyô *see* Shinjô
Sion 95 A7 *Ger.* Sitten; *anc.* Sedunum. Valais, SW Switzerland
Sioux City 45 F3 Iowa, C USA
Sioux Falls 45 F3 South Dakota, N USA
Sioux State *see* North Dakota
Siphnos *see* Sífnos

Siping 128 D3 *var.* Ssu-p'ing, Szeping; *prev.* Ssu-p'ing-chieh. Jilin, NE China
Siple, Mount 154 A4 *mountain* Siple Island, Antarctica
Siquirres 53 E4 Limón, E Costa Rica
Siracusa 97 D7 *Eng.* Syracuse. Sicilia, Italy, C Mediterranean Sea
Sir Edward Pellew Group 148 B2 *island group* Northern Territory, NE Australia
Siret 108 C3 *var.* Siretul, *Ger.* Sereth, *Rus.* Seret. *river* Romania/Ukraine
Siretul *see* Siret
Siria *see* Syria
Sirikit Reservoir 136 C4 *lake* N Thailand
Sīrjān 120 D4 *prev.* Sa'īdābād. Kermān, S Iran
Sirna *see* Sýrna
Şırnak 117 F4 Şırnak, SE Turkey
Síros *see* Sýros
Sirte *see* Surt
Sirte, Gulf of 71 F2 *Eng.* Gulf of Sidra, Gulf of Sirti, Sidra. *gulf* N Libya
Sirti, Gulf of *see* Surt, Khalīj
Sisak 100 B3 *var.* Siscia, *Ger.* Sissek, *Hung.* Sziszek; *anc.* Segestica. Sisak-Moslavina, C Croatia
Siscia *see* Sisak
Sisimiut 82 C3 *var.* Holsteinborg, Holsteinsborg, Holstenborg, Holstensborg. Kitaa, S Greenland
Sissek *see* Sisak
Sīstān, Daryācheh-ye *see* Şāberī, Hāmūn-e
Sitaş Cristuru *see* Cristuru Secuiesc
Siteía 105 D8 *var.* Sitía. Kríti, Greece, E Mediterranean Sea
Sitges 93 G2 Cataluña, NE Spain
Sitía *see* Siteía
Sittang *see* Sittoung
Sittard 87 D5 Limburg, SE Netherlands
Sitten *see* Sion
Sittoung 136 B4 *var.* Sittang. *river* S Burma (Myanmar)
Sittwe 136 A3 *var.* Akyab. Rakhine State, W Burma (Myanmar)
Siuna 52 D3 Región Autónoma Atlántico Norte, NE Nicaragua
Siut *see* Asyūt
Sivas 116 D3 *anc.* Sebastia, Sebaste. Sivas, C Turkey
Siverek 117 E4 Şanlıurfa, S Turkey
Siwa *see* Siwah
Sīwah 72 A2 *var.* Siwa. NW Egypt
Six Counties, The *see* Northern Ireland
Six-Fours-les-Plages 91 D6 Var, SE France
Siyäzän 117 H2 *Rus.* Siazan'. NE Azerbaijan
Sjar *see* Sääre
Sjenica 101 D5 *Turk.* Seniça. Serbia, SW Serbia
Skadar *see* Shkodër
Skadarsko Jezero *see* Scutari, Lake
Skagerak *see* Skagerrak
Skagerrak 85 A6 *var.* Skagerak. *channel* N Europe
Skagit River 46 B1 *river* Washington, NW USA
Skalka 84 C3 *lake* N Sweden
Skarżysko-Kamienna 98 D4 Świętokrzyskie, C Poland
Skaudvilė 106 B4 Tauragė, SW Lithuania
Skegness 89 E6 E England, United Kingdom
Skíathos 105 C5 Skíathos, Vóreies Sporádes, Greece, Aegean Sea
Skídal' 107 B5 Rus. Skidel'.
Skidel' *see* Skidal'
Skiermûntseach *see* Schiermonnikoog
Skierniewice 98 D3 Łódzkie, C Poland
Skiftet 106 C1 *strait* Finland Atlantic Ocean Baltic Sea Gulf of Bothnia/Gulf of Finland
Skíros *see* Skýros
Skópelos 105 C5 Skópelos, Vóreies Sporádes, Greece, Aegean Sea
Skopje 101 D6 *var.* Üsküb, *Turk.* Üsküp, *prev.* Skoplje; *anc.* Scupi. *country capital* (Macedonia) (FYR Macedonia) N FYR Macedonia
Skoplje *see* Skopje
Skovorodino 115 F4 Amurskaya Oblast', SE Russian Federation

Skuodas 106 B3 *Ger.* Schoden, *Pol.* Szkudy. Klaipėda, NW Lithuania
Skye, Isle of 88 B3 *island* NW Scotland, United Kingdom
Skylge *see* Terschelling
Skýros 105 C5 *var.* Skíros. Skńyros, Vóreies Sporádes, Greece, Aegean Sea
Skýros 105 C5 *var.* Skíros; *anc.* Scyros. *island* Vóreies Sporádes, Greece, Aegean Sea
Slagelse 85 B7 Vestsjælland, E Denmark
Slatina 100 C3 *Hung.* Szlatina; *prev.* Podravska Slatina. Virovitica-Podravina, NE Croatia
Slatina 108 B5 Olt, S Romania
Slavgorod *see* Slawharad
Slavonski Brod 100 C3 *Ger.* Brod, *Hung.* Bród; *prev.* Brod, Brod na Savi. Brod-Posavina, NE Croatia
Slavuta 108 C2 Khmel'nyts'ka Oblast', NW Ukraine
Slavyansk *see* Slov"yans'k
Slawharad 107 E7 *Rus.* Slavgorod. Mahilyowskaya Voblasts', E Belarus
Slawno 98 C2 Zachodnio-pomorskie, NW Poland
Slēmānī *see* As Sulaymānīyah
Sliema 102 B5 N Malta
Sligo 89 A5 *Ir.* Sligeach. Sligo, NW Ireland
Sliven 104 D2 *var.* Slivno. Sliven, C Bulgaria
Slivnitsa 104 B2 Sofiya, W Bulgaria
Slivno *see* Sliven
Slobozia 108 C5 Ialomiţa, SE Romania
Slonim 107 B6 Pol. Słonim. Hrodzyenskaya Voblasts', W Belarus
Słonim *see* Slonim
Slovakia 99 C6 *off.* Slovenská Republika, *Ger.* Slowakei, *Hung.* Szlovákia, *Slvk.* Slovensko. *country* C Europe

SLOVAKIA
Central Europe

Official name Slovak Republic
Formation 1993 / 1993
Capital Bratislava
Population 5.4 million / 285 people per sq mile (110 people per sq km) / 58%
Total area 18,859 sq. miles (48,845 sq. km)
Languages Slovak*, Hungarian (Magyar), Czech
Religions Roman Catholic 60%, Other 18%, Atheist 10%, Protestant 8%, Orthodox Christian 4%
Ethnic mix Slovak 86%, Magyar 10%, Roma 2%, Other 1%, Czech 1%
Government Parliamentary system
Currency Euro = 100 cents
Literacy rate 99%
Calorie consumption 2889 calories

Slovak Ore Mountains *see* Slovenské rudohorie
Slovenia 95 D8 *off.* Republic of Slovenia, *Ger.* Slowenien, *Slvn.* Slovenija. *country* SE Europe

SLOVENIA
Central Europe

Official name Republic of Slovenia
Formation 1991 / 1991
Capital Ljubljana
Population 2 million / 256 people per sq mile (99 people per sq km) / 51%
Total area 7820 sq. miles (20,253 sq. km)
Languages Slovenian*
Religions Roman Catholic 96%, Other 3%, Muslim 1%
Ethnic mix Slovene 83%, Other 12%, Serb 2%, Croat 2%, Bosniak 1%
Government Parliamentary system
Currency Euro = 100 cents
Literacy rate 99%
Calorie consumption 3001 calories

Slovenia, Republic of *see* Slovenia
Slovenija *see* Slovenia
Slovenské rudohorie *see* Slovakia
Slovenské rudohorie 99 D6 *Eng.* Slovak Ore Mountains, *Ger.* Slowakisches Erzgebirge, Ungarisches Erzgebirge. *mountain range* C Slovakia
Slovensko *see* Slovakia

Slov"yans'k 109 G3 *Rus.* Slavyansk. Donets'ka Oblast', E Ukraine
Slowakei *see* Slovakia
Slowakisches Erzgebirge *see* Slovenské rudohorie
Slowenien *see* Slovenia
Słubice 98 B3 *Ger.* Frankfurt. Lubuskie, W Poland
Sluch 108 D1 *river* NW Ukraine
Słupsk 98 C2 *Ger.* Stolp. Pomorskie, N Poland
Slutsk 107 C6 Minskaya Voblasts', S Belarus
Smallwood Reservoir 39 F2 *lake* Newfoundland and Labrador, S Canada
Smara 70 B3 *var.* Es Semara. N Western Sahara
Smarhon' 107 C5 *Pol.* Smorgonie, *Rus.* Smorgon'. Hrodzyenskaya Voblasts', W Belarus
Smederevo 100 D4 *Ger.* Semendria. Serbia, N Serbia
Smederevska Palanka 100 D4 Serbia, C Serbia
Smela *see* Smila
Smila 109 E2 *Rus.* Smela. Cherkas'ka Oblast', C Ukraine
Smilten *see* Smiltene
Smiltene 106 D3 *Ger.* Smilten. Valka, N Latvia
Smola 84 A4 *island* W Norway
Smolensk 111 A5 Smolenskaya Oblast', W Russian Federation
Smorgon'/Smorgonie *see* Smarhon'
Smyrna *see* İzmir
Snake 34 B4 *river* Yukon Territory, NW Canada
Snake River 46 C3 *river* NW USA
Snake River Plain 46 D4 *plain* Idaho, NW USA
Sneek 86 D2 Friesland, N Netherlands
Sneeuw-gebergte *see* Maoke, Pegunungan
Snežka 98 B4 *Ger.* Schneekoppe, *Pol.* Śnieżki. *mountain* N Czech Republic/ Poland
Śniardwy, Jezioro 98 D2 *Ger.* Spirdingsee. *lake* NE Poland
Snieckus *see* Visaginas
Sniežka *see* Snežka
Snina 99 E5 *Hung.* Szinna. Prešovský Kraj, E Slovakia
Snowdonia 89 C6 *mountain range* NW Wales, United Kingdom
Snowdrift *see* Łutselk'e
Snow Mountains *see* Maoke, Pegunungan
Snyder 49 F3 Texas, SW USA
Sobradinho, Barragem de *see* Sobradinho, Represa de
Sobradinho, Represa de 63 F2 *var.* Barragem de Sobradinho. *reservoir* E Brazil
Sochi 111 A7 Krasnodarskiy Kray, SW Russian Federation
Société, Îles de la/Society Islands *see* Société, Archipel de la
Society Islands 145 G4 *var.* Archipel de Tahiti, Îles de la Société, Îles Tahiti. Society Islands. *island group* W French Polynesia
Soconusco, Sierra de *see* Madre, Sierra
Socorro 48 D2 New Mexico, SW USA
Socorro, Isla 50 B5 *island* W Mexico
Socotra 121 C7 *var.* Suḳuṭrā. Socotra. *island* SE Yemen
Socotra *see* Suquṭrā
Soc Trăng 137 D6 *var.* Khanh Hung. Soc Trăng, S Vietnam
Socuéllamos 93 E3 Castilla-La Mancha, C Spain
Sodankylä 84 D3 Lappi, N Finland
Sodari *see* Sodiri
Söderhamn 85 C5 Gävleborg, C Sweden
Södertälje 85 C6 Stockholm, C Sweden
Sodiri 72 B4 *var.* Sawdirī, Sodari. Northern Kordofan, C Sudan
Sodoe-kaboemi *see* Sukabumi
Soemba *see* Sumba, Pulau
Soembawa *see* Sumbawa
Soengaipenoeh *see* Sungaipenuh
Soerabaja *see* Surabaya
Soerakarta *see* Surakarta
Sofia *see* Sofiya
Sofia 104 B2 *var.* Sofia, *Eng.* Sofia, *Lat.* Serdica. *country capital* (Bulgaria) (Bulgaria) Sofiya-Grad, W Bulgaria
Sogamoso 58 B3 Boyacá, C Colombia
Sognefjorden 85 A5 *fjord* NE North Sea

Sohâg see Sawhāj
Sohar see Şuḩār
Sohm Plain 66 B3 abyssal plain
  NW Atlantic Ocean
Sohrau see Żory
Sokal' 108 C2 Rus. Sokal. L'vivs'ka
  Oblast', NW Ukraine
Söke 116 A4 Aydın, SW Turkey
Sokhumi 117 E1 Rus. Sukhumi.
  NW Georgia
Sokodé 75 F4 C Togo
Sokol 110 C4 Vologodskaya Oblast',
  NW Russian Federation
Sokółka 98 E3 Podlaskie, NE Poland
Sokolov 99 A5 Ger. Falkenau an der Eger;
  prev. Falknov nad Ohří. Karlovarský
  Kraj, W Czech Republic
Sokone 74 B3 W Senegal
Sokoto 75 F3 Sokoto, NW Nigeria
Sokoto 75 F4 river NW Nigeria
Sokotra see Suquţrá
Solāpur 124 B3 var. Sholāpur.
  Mahārāshtra, W India
Solca 108 C3 Ger. Solka. Suceava,
  N Romania
Sol, Costa del 92 D5 coastal region
  S Spain
Soldeu 91 B7 NE Andorra Europe
Solec Kujawski 98 C3 Kujawsko-
  pomorskie, C Poland
Soledad 58 B1 Atlántico, N Colombia
Isla Soledad see East Falkland
Soligorsk see Salihorsk
Solikamsk 114 C3 Permskaya Oblast',
  NW Russian Federation
Sol'-Iletsk 111 D6 Orenburgskaya
  Oblast', W Russian Federation
Solingen 94 A4 Nordrhein-Westfalen,
  W Germany
Solka see Solca
Sollentuna 85 C6 Stockholm, C Sweden
Solo see Surakarta
Solok 138 B4 Sumatera, W Indonesia
Solomon Islands 144 C3 prev. British
  Solomon Islands Protectorate. country
  W Solomon Islands N Melanesia
  W Pacific Ocean

SOLOMON ISLANDS
Australasia & Oceania

Official name Solomon Islands
Formation 1978 / 1978
Capital Honiara
Population 566,842 / 52 people
  per sq mile (20 people per sq km) / 17%
Total area 10,985 sq. miles (28,450 sq. km)
Languages English*, Pidgin English,
  Melanesian Pidgin
Religions Church of Melanesia
  (Anglican) 34%, Roman Catholic 19%,
  South Seas Evangelical Church 17%,
  Methodist 11%, Seventh-day
  Adventist 10%, Other 9%
Ethnic mix Melanesian 94%,
  Polynesian 4%, Other 2%
Government Parliamentary system
Currency Solomon Islands dollar
  = 100 cents
Literacy rate 77%
Calorie consumption 2265 calories

Solomon Islands 144 C3 island group
  Papua New Guinea/Solomon Islands
Solomon Sea 144 B3 sea W Pacific Ocean
Soltau 94 B3 Niedersachsen,
  NW Germany
Sol'tsy 110 A4 Novgorodskaya Oblast',
  W Russian Federation
Solun see Thessaloníki
Solwezi 78 D2 North Western,
  NW Zambia
Sōma 130 D4 Fukushima, Honshū,
  C Japan
Somalia 73 D5 off. Somali Democratic
  Republic, Som. Jamuuriyada
  Demuqraadiga Soomaaliyeed,
  Soomaaliya; prev. Italian Somaliland,
  Somaliland Protectorate. country
  E Africa

SOMALIA
East Africa

Official name The Somali
  Democratic Republic
Formation 1960 / 1960

SOMALIA
(continued)

Capital Mogadishu
Population 8.8 million / 36 people
  per sq mile (14 people per sq km) / 35%
Total area 246,199 sq. miles
  (637,657 sq. km)
Languages Somali*, Arabic*,
  English, Italian
Religions Sunni Muslim 98%, Christian 2%
Ethnic mix Somali 85%, Other 15%
Government Transitional regime
Currency Somali shilin = 100 senti
Literacy rate 24%
Calorie consumption 1628 calories

Somali Basin 69 E5 undersea basin
  W Indian Ocean
Somali Democratic Republic see
  Somalia
Somaliland 73 D5 disputed territory
  N Somalia
Somaliland Protectorate see Somalia
Sombor 100 C3 Hung. Zombor.
  Vojvodina, NW Serbia
Someren 87 D5 Noord-Brabant,
  SE Netherlands
Somerset 42 A5 var. Somerset Village.
  W Bermuda
Somerset 40 C5 Kentucky, S USA
Somerset Island 42 A5 island
  W Bermuda
Somerset Island 37 F2 island
  Queen Elizabeth Islands, Nunavut,
  NW Canada
Somerset Village see Somerset
Somers Islands see Bermuda
Somerton 48 A2 Arizona, SW USA
Someş 108 B3 river Hungary/Romania
  Europe
Somme 90 C2 river N France
Sommerfeld see Lubsko
Somotillo 52 C3 Chinandega,
  NW Nicaragua
Somoto 52 D3 Madriz, NW Nicaragua
Songea 73 C8 Ruvuma, S Tanzania
Söngjin see Kimch'aek
Songkhla 137 C7 var. Songkla, Mal.
  Singora. Songkhla, SW Thailand
Songkla see Songkhla
Sonoran Desert 48 A3 var. Desierto de
  Altar. desert Mexico/USA
Sonsonate 52 B3 Sonsonate,
  W El Salvador
Soochow see Suzhou
Soomaaliya/Soomaaliyeed,
  Jamuuriyada Demuqraadiga see
  Somalia
Soome Laht see Finland, Gulf of
Sop Hao 136 D3 Houaphan, N Laos
Sophia see Sofiya
Sopianae see Pécs
Sopot 98 C2 Ger. Zoppot. Pomorskie,
  N Poland
Sopron 99 B6 Ger. Ödenburg. Győr-
  Moson-Sopron, NW Hungary
Sorau/Sorau in der Niederlausitz
  see Żary
Sorgues 91 D6 Vaucluse, SE France
Sorgun 116 D3 Yozgat, C Turkey
Soria 93 E2 Castilla-León, N Spain
Soroca 108 D3 Rus. Soroki. N Moldova
Sorochinsk see Sarochyna
Sorong 139 F4 Papua, E Indonesia
Sørøy see Sørøya
Sørøya 84 C2 var. Sørøy, Lapp. Sállan.
  island N Norway
Sortavala 110 B3 prev. Serdobol'.
  Respublika Kareliya, NW Russian
  Federation
Sotavento, Ilhas de 74 A3 var. Leeward
  Islands. island group S Cape Verde
Sotkamo 84 E4 Oulu, C Finland
Souanké 77 B5 Sangha, NW Congo
Soueida see As Suwaydā'
Souflí 104 D3 prev. Soúflion. Anatolikí
  Makedonía kai Thráki, NE Greece
Soúflion see Souflí
Soufrière 55 F2 W Saint Lucia
Soukhné see As Sukhnah
Sŏul 129 E4 off. Sŏul-t'ŭkpyŏlsi, Eng.
  Seoul, Jap. Keijō; prev. Kyŏngsŏng.
  country capital (South Korea) (South
  Korea) NW South Korea
Sŏul-t'ŭkpyŏlsi see Sŏul

Soûr 119 A5 var. Şūr; anc. Tyre.
  SW Lebanon
Souris River 45 E1 var. Mouse River.
  river Canada/USA
Soúrpi 105 B5 Thessalía, C Greece
Sousse 71 F2 var. Süsah. NE Tunisia
South Africa 78 C4 off. Republic of
  South Africa, Afr. Suid-Afrika. country
  S Africa

SOUTH AFRICA
Southern Africa

Official name Republic of South Africa
Formation 1934 / 1994
Capital Tshwane / Pretoria; Cape Town;
  Bloemfontein
Population 47.7 million / 101 people
  per sq mile (39 people per sq km) / 57%
Total area 471,008 sq. miles
  (1,219,912 sq. km)
Languages English, isiZulu, isiXhosa,
  Afrikaans, Sepedi, Setswana, Sesotho,
  Xitsonga, siSwati, Tshivenda, isiNdebele
Religions Christian 68%, Traditional
  beliefs and animist 29%, Muslim 2%,
  Hindu 1%
Ethnic mix Black 79%, Colored 10%,
  White 9%, Asian 2%
Government Presidential system
Currency Rand = 100 cents
Literacy rate 82%
Calorie consumption 2956 calories

South Africa, Republic of see South Africa
South America 56 continent
Southampton 89 D7 hist. Hamwih,
  Lat. Clausentum. S England, United
  Kingdom
Southampton Island 37 G3 island
  Nunavut, NE Canada
South Andaman 133 F2 island Andaman
  Islands, India, NE Indian Ocean
South Australia 149 A5 state S Australia
South Australian Basin 142 B5 undersea
  basin SW Indian Ocean
South Bend 40 C3 Indiana, N USA
South Beveland see Zuid-Beveland
South Bruny Island 149 C8 island
  Tasmania, SE Australia
South Carolina 43 E2 off. State of South
  Carolina, also known as The Palmetto
  State. state SE USA
South Carpathians see Carpaţii
  Meridionalii
South China Basin 125 E4 undersea
  basin SE South China Sea
South China Sea 125 E4 Chin. Nan Hai,
  Ind. Laut Cina Selatan, Vtn. Biên Đông.
  sea SE Asia
South Dakota 44 D2 off. State of South
  Dakota, also known as The Coyote
  State, Sunshine State. state N USA
Southeast Indian Ridge 141 D7 undersea
  ridge Indian Ocean/Pacific Ocean
Southeast Pacific Basin 153 E5 var.
  Belling Hausen Mulde. undersea basin
  SE Pacific Ocean
South East Point 149 C7 headland
  Victoria, S Australia
Southend-on-Sea 89 E6 E England,
  United Kingdom
Southern Alps 151 B6 mountain range
  South Island, New Zealand
Southern Cook Islands 145 F4 island
  group S Cook Islands
Southern Cross 147 B6 Western
  Australia
Southern Indian Lake 37 F4 lake
  Manitoba, C Canada
Southern Ocean 67 B7 ocean Atlantic
  Ocean/Indian Ocean/Pacific Ocean
Southern Uplands 88 C4 mountain
  range S Scotland, United Kingdom
South Fiji Basin 142 D4 undersea basin
  S Pacific Ocean
South Geomagnetic Pole 154 B3 pole
  Antarctica
South Georgia 57 D8 island South
  Georgia and the South Sandwich
  Islands, SW Atlantic Ocean
South Goulburn Island 146 E2 island
  Northern Territory, N Australia
South Huvadhu Atoll 132 A5 atoll
  S Maldives
South Indian Basin 141 D7 undersea
  basin Indian Ocean/Pacific Ocean

South Island 151 C6 island S New
  Zealand
South Korea 129 E4 off. Republic of
  Korea, Kor. Taehan Min'guk. country
  E Asia

SOUTH KOREA
East Asia

Official name Republic of Korea
Formation 1948 / 1953
Capital Seoul
Population 48.1 million / 1262 people
  per sq mile (487 people per sq km) / 81%
Total area 38,023 sq. miles (98,480 sq. km)
Languages Korean*
Religions Mahayana Buddhist 47%,
  Protestant 38%, Roman Catholic 11%,
  Confucianist 3%, Other 1%
Ethnic mix Korean 100%
Government Presidential system
Currency South Korean won = 100 chon
Literacy rate 98%
Calorie consumption 3058 calories

South Lake Tahoe 47 C5 California,
  W USA
South Orkney Islands 154 A2 island
  group Antarctica
South Ossetia 117 F2 former autonomous
  region SW Georgia
South Pacific Basin 153 E4 var. Southwest
  Pacific Basin
South Platte River 44 D4 river
  Colorado/Nebraska, C USA
South Pole 154 B3 pole Antarctica
South Sandwich Islands 57 D8 island
  group SW Atlantic Ocean
South Sandwich Trench 57 E8 trench
  SW Atlantic Ocean
South Shetland Islands 154 A2 island
  group Antarctica
South Shields 88 D4 NE England, United
  Kingdom
Sioux City 45 F3 Nebraska, C USA
South Taranaki Bight 150 C4 bight
  SE Tasman Sea
South Tasmania Plateau see Tasman
  Plateau
South Uist 88 B3 island NW Scotland,
  United Kingdom
South-West Africa/South West Africa
  see Namibia
South West Cape 151 A8 headland
  Stewart Island, New Zealand
Southwest Indian Ocean Ridge see
  Southwest Indian Ridge
Southwest Indian Ridge 141 B6 var.
  Southwest Indian Ocean Ridge.
  undersea ridge SW Indian Ocean
Southwest Pacific Basin 153 E4 var.
  South Pacific Basin. undersea basin
  SE Pacific Ocean
Sovereign Base Area 102 C5 uk military
  installation S Cyprus
Soweto 78 D4 Gauteng, NE South Africa
Sōya-kaikyō see La Perouse Strait
Spain 92 D3 off. Kingdom of Spain, Sp.
  España; anc. Hispania, Iberia, Lat.
  Hispana. country SW Europe

SPAIN
Southwest Europe

Official name Kingdom of Spain
Formation 1492 / 1713
Capital Madrid
Population 43.6 million / 226 people
  per sq mile (87 people per sq km) / 77%
Total area 194,896 sq. miles
  (504,782 sq. km)
Languages Spanish*, Catalan*,
  Galician*, Basque*
Religions Roman Catholic 96%, Other 4%
Ethnic mix Castilian Spanish 72%,
  Catalan 17%, Galician 6%, Basque 2%,
  Other 2%, Roma 1%
Government Parliamentary system
Currency Euro = 100 cents
Literacy rate 98%
Calorie consumption 3371 calories

Spain, Kingdom of see Spain
Spalato see Split
Spanish Town 54 B5 hist. St.Iago de la
  Vega. C Jamaica
Sparks 47 C5 Nevada, W USA

Sparta *see* Spárti
Spartanburg *43 E1* South Carolina, SE USA
Spárti *105 B6 Eng.* Sparta. Pelopónnisos, S Greece
Spearfish *44 D2* South Dakota, N USA
Speightstown *55 G1* NW Barbados
Spencer *45 F3* Iowa, C USA
Spencer Gulf *149 B6 gulf* South Australia
Spey *88 C3 river* NE Scotland, United Kingdom
Spice Islands *see* Maluku
Spiess Seamount *67 C7 seamount* S Atlantic Ocean
Spijkenisse *86 B4* Zuid-Holland, SW Netherlands
Spíli *105 C8* Kríti, Greece, E Mediterranean Sea
Spīn Būldak *123 E5* Kandahār, S Afghanistan
Spirdingsee *see* Śniardwy, Jezioro
Spitsbergen *83 F2 island* NW Svalbard
Split *100 B4 It.* Spalato. Split-Dalmacija, S Croatia
Špoği *106 D4* Daugvapils, SE Latvia
Spokane *46 C2* Washington, NW USA
Spratly Islands *138 B2 Chin.* Nansha Qundao. *disputed territory* SE Asia
Spree *94 D4 river* E Germany
Springfield *40 B4 state capital* Illinois, N USA
Springfield *41 G3* Massachusetts, NE USA
Springfield *45 G5* Missouri, C USA
Springfield *40 C4* Ohio, N USA
Springfield *46 B3* Oregon, NW USA
Spring Garden *59 F2* NE Guyana
Spring Hill *43 E4* Florida, SE USA
Springs Junction *151 C5* West Coast, South Island, New Zealand
Springsure *148 D4* Queensland, E Australia
Sprottau *see* Szprotawa
Spruce Knob *41 E4 mountain* West Virginia, NE USA
Srbinje *see* Foča
Srbobran *100 D3 var.* Bácsszenttamás, *Hung.* Szenttamás. Vojvodina, N Serbia
Srebrenica *100 C4* Republika Srpska, E Bosnia and Herzegovina
Sredets *104 D2 prev.* Syulemeshlii. Stara Zagora, C Bulgaria
Sredets *104 E2 prev.* Grudovo. Burgas, E Bulgaria
Sremska Mitrovica *100 C3 prev.* Mitrovica, *Ger.* Mitrowitz. Vojvodina, NW Serbia
Srepok, Sông *see* Srêpôk, Tônle
Srêpôk, Tônle *137 E5 var.* Sông Srepok. *river* Cambodia/Vietnam
Sri Aman *138 C3* Sarawak, East Malaysia
Sri Jayawardanapura *see* Sri Jayewardanapura Kotte
Sri Jayewardanapura Kotte *132 D3 var.* Sri Jayawardanapura. Western Province, W Sri Lanka
Srikākulam *135 F5* Andhra Pradesh, E India
Sri Lanka *132 D3 off.* Democratic Socialist Republic of Sri Lanka; *prev.* Ceylon. *country* S Asia

SRI LANKA
South Asia

Official name Democratic Socialist Republic of Sri Lanka
Formation 1948 / 1948
Capital Colombo
Population 21.1 million / 844 people per sq mile (326 people per sq km) / 21%
Total area 25,332 sq. miles (65,610 sq. km)
Languages Sinhala*, Tamil*, Sinhala-Tamil, English
Religions Buddhist 69%, Hindu 15%, Muslim 8%, Christian 8%
Ethnic mix Sinhalese 82%, Tamil 9%, Moor 8%, Other 1%
Government Mixed presidential–parliamentary system
Currency Sri Lanka rupee = 100 cents
Literacy rate 91%
Calorie consumption 2385 calories

Sri Lanka, Democratic Socialist Republic of *see* Sri Lanka

Srinagarind Reservoir *137 C5 lake* W Thailand
Srpska, Republika *100 B3 republic* Bosnia and Herzegovina
Ssu-ch'uan *see* Sichuan
Ssu-p'ing/Ssu-p'ing-chieh *see* Siping
Stabroek *87 B5* Antwerpen, N Belgium
Stade *94 B3* Niedersachsen, NW Germany
Stadskanaal *86 E2* Groningen, NE Netherlands
Stafford *89 D6* C England, United Kingdom
Staicele *106 D3* Limbaži, N Latvia
Ştaierdorf-Anina *see* Anina
Stájerlakanina *see* Anina
Stakhanov *109 H3* Luhans'ka Oblast', E Ukraine
Stalin *see* Varna
Stalinabad *see* Dushanbe
Stalingrad *see* Volgograd
Stalino *see* Donets'k
Stalinobod *see* Dushanbe
Stalinsk *see* Novokuznetsk
Stalinski Zaliv *see* Varnenski Zaliv
Stalin, Yazovir *see* Iskŭr, Yazovir
Stalowa Wola *98 E4* Podkarpackie, SE Poland
Stamford *41 F3* Connecticut, NE USA
Stampalia *see* Astypálaia
Stanislau *see* Ivano-Frankivs'k
Stanislav *see* Ivano-Frankivs'k
Stanisławów *see* Ivano-Frankivs'k
Stanke Dimitrov *see* Dupnitsa
Stanley *57 D7 var.* Port Stanley, Puerto Argentino. *dependent territory capital* (Falkland Islands) East Falkland, Falkland Islands
Stanleyville *see* Kisangani
Stann Creek *see* Dangriga
Stanovoy Khrebet *113 E3 mountain range* SE Russian Federation
Stanthorpe *149 D5* Queensland, E Australia
Staphorst *86 D2* Overijssel, E Netherlands
Starachowice *98 D4* Świętokrzyskie, C Poland
Stara Kanjiža *see* Kanjiža
Stara Pazova *100 D3 Ger.* Altpasua, *Hung.* Ópazova. Vojvodina, N Serbia
Stara Planina *see* Balkan Mountains
Stara Zagora *104 D2 Lat.* Augusta Trajana. Stara Zagora, C Bulgaria
Starbuck Island *145 G5 prev.* Volunteer Island. *island* E Kiribati
Stargard in Pommern *see* Stargard Szczeciński
Stargard Szczeciński *98 B3 Ger.* Stargard in Pommern. Zachodnio-pomorskie, NW Poland
Stari Bečej *see* Bečej
Starobel'sk *see* Starobil's'k
Starobil's'k *109 H2 Rus.* Starobel'sk. Luhans'ka Oblast', E Ukraine
Starobin *107 C7 var.* Starobyn. Minskaya Voblasts', S Belarus
Starobyn *see* Starobin
Starogard Gdański *98 C2 Ger.* Preussisch-Stargard. Pomorskie, N Poland
Starokonstantinov *see* Starokostyantyniv
Starokostyantyniv *108 D2 Rus.* Starokonstantinov. Khmel'nyts'ka Oblast', NW Ukraine
Starominskaya *111 A7* Krasnodarskiy Kray, SW Russian Federation
Staryya Darohi *107 C6 Rus.* Staryye Dorogi. Minskaya Voblasts', S Belarus
Staryye Dorogi *see* Staryya Darohi
Staryy Oskol *111 B6* Belgorodskaya Oblast', W Russian Federation
State College *41 E4* Pennsylvania, NE USA
Staten Island *see* Estados, Isla de los
Statesboro *43 E2* Georgia, SE USA
States, The *see* United States of America
Staunton *41 E5* Virginia, NE USA
Stavanger *85 A6* Rogaland, S Norway
Stavers Island *see* Vostok Island
Stavropol' *111 B7 prev.* Voroshilovsk. Stavropol'skiy Kray, SW Russian Federation
Stavropol' *see* Tol'yatti
Steamboat Springs *44 C4* Colorado, C USA
Steenwijk *86 D2* Overijssel, N Netherlands

Steier *see* Steyr
Steierdorf/Steierdorf-Anina *see* Anina
Steinamanger *see* Szombathely
Steinkjer *84 B4* Nord-Trøndelag, C Norway
Stejarul *see* Karapelit
Stendal *94 C3* Sachsen-Anhalt, C Germany
Stepanakert *see* Xankändi
Stephenville *49 F3* Texas, SW USA
Sterling *44 D4* Colorado, C USA
Sterling *40 B3* Illinois, N USA
Sterlitamak *114 B3* Respublika Bashkortostan, W Russian Federation
Stettin *see* Szczecin
Stettiner Haff *see* Szczeciński, Zalew
Stevenage *89 E6* E England, United Kingdom
Stevens Point *40 B2* Wisconsin, N USA
Stewart Island *151 A8 island* S New Zealand
Steyerlak-Anina *see* Anina
Steyr *95 D6 var.* Steier. Oberösterreich, N Austria
St. Helena Bay *78 B5 bay* SW South Africa
Stif *see* Sétif
Stillwater *49 G1* Oklahoma, C USA
Štip *101 E6* E FYR Macedonia
Stirling *88 C4* C Scotland, United Kingdom
Stjørdalshalsen *84 B4* Nord-Trøndelag, C Norway
St-Maur-des-Fossés *90 E2* Val-de-Marne, Île-de-France, N France Europe
Stockach *95 B6* Baden-Württemberg, S Germany
Stockholm *85 C6 country capital* (Sweden) (Sweden) Stockholm, C Sweden
Stockmannshof *see* Pļaviņas
Stockton *47 B6* California, W USA
Stockton Plateau *49 E4 plain* Texas, SW USA
Stœng Trêng *137 D5 prev.* Stung Treng. Stœng Trêng, NE Cambodia
Stoke *see* Stoke-on-Trent
Stoke-on-Trent *89 D6 var.* Stoke. C England, United Kingdom
Stolbce *see* Stowbtsy
Stolbtsy *see* Stowbtsy
Stolp *see* Słupsk
Stolpmünde *see* Ustka
Stómio *104 B4* Thessalía, C Greece
Store Bælt *see* Storebælt
Storebelt *see* Storebælt
Støren *85 B5* Sør-Trøndelag, S Norway
Storfjorden *83 G2 fjord* S Norway
Storhammer *see* Hamar
Stornoway *88 B2* NW Scotland, United Kingdom
Storsjön *85 B5 lake* C Sweden
Storuman *84 C4* Västerbotten, N Sweden
Storuman *84 C4 lake* N Sweden
Stowbtsy *107 C6 Pol.* Stolbce, *Rus.* Stolbtsy. Minskaya Voblasts', C Belarus
Strabane *89 B5 Ir.* An Srath Bán. N Northern Ireland, United Kingdom
Strakonice *99 A5 Ger.* Strakonitz. Jihočeský Kraj, S Czech Republic
Strakonitz *see* Strakonice
Stralsund *94 D2* Mecklenburg-Vorpommern, NE Germany
Stranraer *89 C5* S Scotland, United Kingdom
Strasbourg *90 E3 Ger.* Strassburg; *anc.* Argentoratum. Bas-Rhin, NE France
Strășeni *108 D3 var.* Strasheny. C Moldova
Strasheny *see* Strășeni
Strassburg *see* Strasbourg, France
Strassburg *see* Aiud, Romania
Stratford *150 D4* Taranaki, North Island, New Zealand
Strathfield *148 E2* New South Wales, E Australia
Straubing *95 C6* Bayern, SE Germany
Strehaia *108 B5* Mehedinți, SW Romania
Strelka *114 D4* Krasnoyarskiy Kray, C Russian Federation
Strigonium *see* Esztergom
Strofília *see* Strofyliá
Strofyliá *105 C5 var.* Strofilia. Évvoia, C Greece
Stromboli *97 D6 island* Isole Eolie, S Italy

Stromeferry *88 C3* N Scotland, United Kingdom
Strömstad *85 B6* Västra Götaland, S Sweden
Strömsund *84 C4* Jämtland, C Sweden
Struga *101 D6* SW FYR Macedonia
Struma *see* Strymónas
Strumica *101 E6* E FYR Macedonia
Strumyani *104 C3* Blagoevgrad, SW Bulgaria
Strymónas *104 C3 Bul.* Struma. *river* Bulgaria/Greece
Stryy *108 B2* L'vivs'ka Oblast', NW Ukraine
Studholme *151 B6* Canterbury, South Island, New Zealand
Stuhlweissenberg *see* Székesfehérvár
Stung Treng *see* Stœng Trêng
Sturgis *44 D3* South Dakota, N USA
Stuttgart *95 B6* Baden-Württemberg, SW Germany
Stykkishólmur *83 E4* Vesturland, W Iceland
Styr *108 C1 Rus.* Styr'. *river* Belarus/Ukraine
Su *see* Jiangsu
Suakin *72 C4 var.* Sawakin. Red Sea, NE Sudan
Subačius *106 C4* Panevėžys, NE Lithuania
Subaykhān *118 E3* Dayr az Zawr, E Syria
Subotica *100 D2 Ger.* Maria-Theresiopel, *Hung.* Szabadka. Vojvodina, N Serbia
Suceava *108 C3 Ger.* Suczawa, *Hung.* Szucsava. Suceava, NE Romania
Su-chou *see* Suzhou
Suchow *see* Suzhou, Jiangsu, China
Suchow *see* Xuzhou, Jiangsu, China
Sucker State *see* Illinois
Sucre *61 F4 hist.* Chuquisaca, La Plata. *country capital* (Bolivia-legal capital) (Bolivia-legal capital) Chuquisaca, S Bolivia
Sucuma *see* Sawakin
Sudan *72 A4 off.* Republic of Sudan, *Ar.* Jumhuriyat as-Sudan; *prev.* Anglo-Egyptian Sudan. *country* N Africa

SUDAN
East Africa

Official name Republic of the Sudan
Formation 1956 / 1956
Capital Khartoum
Population 37.8 million / 39 people per sq mile (15 people per sq km) / 40%
Total area 967,493 sq. miles (2,505,810 sq. km)
Languages Arabic / Arabic, Dinka, Nuer, Nubian, Beja, Zande, Bari, Fur, Shilluk, Lotuko
Religions Muslim (mainly Sunni) 70%, Traditional beliefs 20%, Christian 5%, Other 1%
Ethnic mix Other Black 52%, Arab 40%, Dinka and Beja 7%, Other 1%
Government Presidential system
Currency new Sudanese pound or dinar = 100 piastres
Literacy rate 61%
Calorie consumption 2228 calories

Sudanese Republic *see* Mali
Sudan, Jumhuriyat as- *see* Sudan
Sudan, Republic of *see* Sudan
Sudbury *38 C4* Ontario, S Canada
Sudd *73 B5 swamp region* S Sudan
Sudeten *see var.* Sudetes, Sudetic Mountains, *Cz./Pol.* Sudety. *mountain range* Czech Republic/Poland
Sudetes/Sudetic Mountains/Sudety *see* Sudeten
Südkarpaten *see* Carpații Meridionali
Südliche Morava *see* Južna Morava
Sudong, Pulau *134 A2 island* SW Singapore Asia
Sudostroy *see* Severodvinsk
Sue *73 B5 river* S Sudan
Sueca *93 F3* País Valenciano, E Spain
Sue Wood Bay *42 B5 bay* W Bermuda North America W Atlantic Ocean
Suez *72 B1 Ar.* As Suways, El Suweis. NE Egypt
Suez Canal *72 B1 Ar.* Qanāt as Suways. *canal* NE Egypt
Suez, Gulf of *see* Khalīj as Suways

Suğla Gölü 116 C4 *lake* SW Turkey
Şuḥār 121 D5 *var.* Sohar.
Sühbaatar 127 E1 Selenge, N Mongolia
Suhl 95 C5 Thüringen, C Germany
Suicheng *see* Suixi
Suid-Afrika *see* South Africa
Suidwes-Afrika *see* Namibia
Suixi 128 C6 *var.* Suicheng. Guangdong,
  S China
Sujāwal 134 B3 Sind, SE Pakistan
Sukabumi 138 C5 *prev.* Soekaboemi.
  Jawa, C Indonesia
Sukagawa 131 D5 Fukushima, Honshū,
  C Japan
Sukarnapura *see* Jayapura
Sukarno, Puntjak *see* Jaya, Puncak
Sukhne *see* As Sukhnah
Sukhona 110 C4 *var.* Tot'ma. *river*
  NW Russian Federation
Sukhumi *see* Sokhumi
Sukkertoppen *see* Maniitsoq
Sukkur 134 B3 Sind, SE Pakistan
Sukumo 131 B7 Kōchi, Shikoku,
  SW Japan
Sulaimaniya *see* As Sulaymānīyah
Sulaiman Range 134 C2 *mountain range*
  C Pakistan
Sula, Kepulauan 139 E4 *island group*
  C Indonesia
Sulawesi, Laut *see* Celebes Sea
Sulechów 98 B3 *Ger.* Züllichau.
  Lubuskie, W Poland
Suliag *see* Sawhāj
Sullana 60 B2 Piura, NW Peru
Sullivan Island *see* Lanbi Kyun
Sulphur Springs 49 G2 Texas, SW USA
Sultānābād *see* Arāk
Sulu Archipelago 139 E3 *island group*
  SW Philippines
Sülüktü *see* Sulyukta
Sulu, Laut *see* Sulu Sea
Sulu Sea 139 E2 *var.* Laut Sulu. *sea*
  SW Philippines
Sulyukta 123 E2 *Kir.* Sülüktü.
  Batkenskaya Oblast', SW Kyrgyzstan
Sumatra 137 B8 *Eng.* Sumatra. *island*
  W Indonesia
Sumatra *see* Sumatera
Šumava *see* Bohemian Forest
Sumba, Pulau 139 E5 *Eng.* Sandalwood
  Island; *prev.* Soemba. *island* Nusa
  Tenggara, C Indonesia
Sumba, Selat 139 E5 *strait* Nusa
  Tenggara, S Indonesia
Sumbawanga 73 B7 Rukwa, W Tanzania
Sumbe 78 B2 *var.* N'Gunza, Port. Novo
  Redondo. Cuanza Sul, W Angola
Sumeih 73 B5 Southern Darfur, S Sudan
Sumgait *see* Sumqayıt, Azerbaijan
Summer Lake 46 B4 *lake* Oregon,
  NW USA
Summit 93 H5 Alaska, USA
Sumqayıt 117 H2 *Rus.* Sumgait.
  E Azerbaijan
Sumy 109 F2 Sums'ka Oblast',
  NE Ukraine
Sunbury 149 C7 Victoria, SE Australia
Sunda Islands *see* Greater Sunda Islands
Sunda, Selat 138 B5 *strait* Jawa/
  Sumatera, SW Indonesia
Sunda Trench *see* Java Trench
Sunderland 88 D4 *var.* Wearmouth.
  NE England, United Kingdom
Sundsvall 85 C5 Västernorrland,
  C Sweden
Sunflower State *see* Kansas
Sungaipenuh 138 B4 *prev.*
  Soengaipenoeh. Sumatera,
  W Indonesia
Sunnyvale 47 A6 California, W USA
Sunset State *see* Oregon
Sunshine State *see* Florida
Sunshine State *see* New Mexico
Sunshine State *see* South Dakota
Suntar 115 F3 Respublika Sakha
  (Yakutiya), NE Russian Federation
Sunyani 75 E5 W Ghana
Suoločielgi *see* Saariselkä
Suomenlahti *see* Finland, Gulf of
Suomen Tasavalta/Suomi *see* Finland
Suomussalmi 84 E4 Oulu, E Finland
Suŏng 137 D6 Kâmpóng Cham,
  C Cambodia
Suoyarvi 110 B3 Respublika Kareliya,
  NW Russian Federation
Supe 60 C3 Lima, W Peru
Supérieur, Lac *see* Superior, Lake

Superior 40 A1 Wisconsin, N USA
Superior, Lake 40 B1 *Fr.* Lac Supérieur.
  lake Canada/USA
Suqrah *see* Şawqirah
Şūr 121 E5 NE Oman
Şūr *see* Soûr
Surabaja *see* Surabaya
Surabaya 138 D5 *prev.* Surabaja,
  Soerabaja. Jawa, C Indonesia
Surakarta 138 C5 *Eng.* Solo; *prev.*
  Soerakarta. Jawa, S Indonesia
Šurany 99 C6 *Hung.* Nagysurány.
  Nitriansky Kraj, SW Slovakia
Sūrat 134 C4 Gujarāt, W India
Suratdhani *see* Surat Thani
Surat Thani 137 C6 *var.* Suratdhani.
  Surat Thani, SW Thailand
Surazh 107 E5 Vitsyebskaya Voblasts',
  NE Belarus
Surdulica 101 E5 Serbia, SE Serbia
Sûre 87 D7 *var.* Sauer. *river* W Europe
Surendranagar 134 C4 Gujarāt, W India
Surfers Paradise 149 E5 Queensland,
  E Australia
Surgut 114 D3 Khanty-Mansiyskiy
  Avtonomnyy Okrug-Yugra, C Russian
  Federation
Surin 137 D5 Surin, E Thailand
Surinam *see* Suriname
Suriname 59 G3 *off.* Republic of
  Suriname. *var.* Surinam; *prev.* Dutch
  Guiana, Netherlands Guiana. *country*
  N South America

SURINAME
South America

Official name Republic of Suriname
Formation 1975 / 1975
Capital Paramaribo
Population 470,784 / 8 people
per sq mile (3 people per sq km) / 77%
Total area 63,039 sq. miles (163,270 sq. km)
Languages Sranan (Creole), Dutch*,
Javanese, Sarnami Hindi, Saramaccan,
Chinese, Carib
Religions Hindu 27%, Protestant 25%,
Roman Catholic 23%, Muslim 20%,
Traditional beliefs 5%
Ethnic mix Creole 34%, South Asian 34%,
Javanese 18%, Black 9%, Other 5%
Government Parliamentary system
Currency Surinamese dollar = 100 cents
Literacy rate 90%
Calorie consumption 2652 calories

Suriname, Republic of *see* Suriname
**Sūriya/Sūriyah, Al-Jumhūrīyah al-
  'Arabīyah as-** *see* Syria
Surkhab, Darya-i- *see* Kahmard,
  Daryā-ye
Surkhob 123 F3 *river* C Tajikistan
Surt 71 G2 *var.* Sidra, Sirte. N Libya
Surtsey 83 E5 *island* S Iceland
Suruga-wan 131 D6 *bay* SE Japan
Susa 96 A2 Piemonte, NE Italy
Sūsah *see* Sousse
Susanville 47 B5 California, W USA
Susitna 36 C3 Alaska, USA
Susteren 87 D5 Limburg, SE Netherlands
Susuman 115 G3 Magadanskaya Oblast',
  E Russian Federation
Sutlej 134 C2 *river* India/Pakistan
Suur Munamägi 106 D3 *var.* Munamägi,
  Ger. Eier-Berg. *mountain* SE Estonia
Suur Väin 106 C2 *Ger.* Grosser Sund.
  strait W Estonia
Suva 145 E4 *country capital* (Fiji) (Fiji)
  Viti Levu, W Fiji
Suvalkai/Suvalki *see* Suwalki
Suwalki 98 E2 *Lith.* Suvalkai, *Rus.*
  Suvalki. Podlaskie, NE Poland
Suways, Qanāt as *see* Suez Canal
Suweida *see* As Suwayda'
Suzhou 128 D5 *var.* Soochow, Su-chou,
  Suchow; *prev.* Wuhsien. Jiangsu,
  E China
Svalbard 83 E1 *Norwegian dependency*
  Arctic Ocean
Svartisen 84 C3 *glacier* C Norway
Svay Riĕng 137 D6 Svay Riĕng,
  S Cambodia
Sveg 85 B5 Jämtland, C Sweden
Svenstavik 85 C5 Jämtland, C Sweden
Sverdlovsk *see* Yekaterinburg
Sverige *see* Sweden

Sveti Vrach *see* Sandanski
Svetlogorsk *see* Svyetlahorsk
Svetlogorsk *see* Svyetlahorsk
Svetlograd 111 B7 Stavropol'skiy Kray,
  SW Russian Federation
Svetlovodsk *see* Svitlovods'k
Svetozarevo *see* Jagodina
Svilengrad 104 D3 *prev.* Mustafa-Pasha.
  Khaskovo, S Bulgaria
Svitlovods'k 109 F3 *Rus.* Svetlovodsk.
  Kirovohrads'ka Oblast', C Ukraine
Svizzera *see* Switzerland
Svobodnyy 115 G4 Amurskaya Oblast',
  SE Russian Federation
Svyataya Anna Trough 155 C4 *var.*
  Saint Anna Trough. *trough* N Kara Sea
Svyetlahorsk 107 D7 *Rus.* Svetlogorsk.
  Homyel'skaya Voblasts', SE Belarus
Swabian Jura *see* Schwäbische Alb
Swakopmund 78 B3 Erongo, W Namibia
Swan Islands 53 E1 *island group*
  NE Honduras North America
Swansea 89 C7 *Wel.* Abertawe. S Wales,
  United Kingdom
Swarzędz 98 C3 Poznań, W Poland
Swatow *see* Shantou
Swaziland 78 D4 *off.* Kingdom of
  Swaziland. *country* S Africa

SWAZILAND
Southern Africa

Official name Kingdom of Swaziland
Formation 1968 / 1968
Capital Mbabane
Population 1 million / 151 people
per sq mile (58 people per sq km) / 24%
Total area 6704 sq. miles (17,363 sq. km)
Languages English*, siSwati*,
isiZulu, Xitsonga
Religions Christian 60%, Traditional
beliefs 40%
Ethnic mix Swazi 97%, Other 3%
Government Monarchy
Currency Lilangeni = 100 cents
Literacy rate 80%
Calorie consumption 2322 calories

Swaziland, Kingdom of *see* Swaziland
Sweden 84 B4 *off.* Kingdom of Sweden,
  Swe. Sverige. *country* N Europe

SWEDEN
Northern Europe

Official name Kingdom of Sweden
Formation 1523 / 1921
Capital Stockholm
Population 9.1 million / 57 people
per sq mile (22 people per sq km) / 83%
Total area 173,731 sq. miles
(449,964 sq. km)
Languages Swedish*, Finnish, Sámi
Religions Evangelical Lutheran 82%,
Other 13%, Roman Catholic 2%,
Muslim 2%, Orthodox Christian 1%
Ethnic mix Swedish 86%, Foreign-born
or first-generation immigrant 12%,
Finnish and Sámi 2%
Government Parliamentary system
Currency Swedish krona = 100 öre
Literacy rate 99%
Calorie consumption 3185 calories

Sweden, Kingdom of *see*
  Sweden
Sweetwater 49 F3 Texas, SW USA
Świdnica 98 B4 *Ger.* Schweidnitz.
  Wałbrzych, SW Poland
Świdwin 98 B2 *Ger.* Schivelbein.
  Zachodnio-pomorskie,
  NW Poland
Świebodzice 98 B4 *Ger.* Freiburg in
  Schlesien, Swiebodzice. Wałbrzych,
  SW Poland
Świebodzin 98 B3 *Ger.* Schwiebus.
  Lubuskie, W Poland
Świecie 98 C3 *Ger.* Schwertberg.
  Kujawsko-pomorskie, C Poland
Swindon 89 D7 S England, United
  Kingdom
Swinemünde *see*
  Świnoujście
Świnoujście 98 B2 *Ger.*
  Swinemünde. Zachodnio-pomorskie,
  NW Poland
Swiss Confederation *see* Switzerland

Switzerland 95 A7 *off.* Swiss
  Confederation, Fr. La Suisse, Ger.
  Schweiz, It. Svizzera; anc. Helvetia.
  country C Europe

SWITZERLAND
Central Europe

Official name Swiss Confederation
Formation 1291 / 1857
Capital Bern
Population 7.3 million / 475 people
per sq mile (184 people per sq km) / 68%
Total area 15,942 sq. miles (41,290 sq. km)
Languages German*, Swiss-German,
French*, Italian*, Romansch
Religions Roman Catholic 42%,
Protestant 35%, Other and
nonreligious 19%, Muslim 4%
Ethnic mix German 64%, French 20%,
Other 9%, Italian 6%, Romansch 1%
Government Parliamentary system
Currency Swiss franc = 100
rappen/centimes
Literacy rate 99%
Calorie consumption 3526 calories

Sycaminum *see* Hefa
Sydenham Island *see* Nonouti
Sydney 148 D1 *state capital* New South
  Wales, SE Australia
Sydney 39 G4 Cape Breton Island, Nova
  Scotia, SE Canada
Sydney Island *see* Manra
Syedpur *see* Saidpur
Syemyezhava 107 C6 *Rus.* Semezhevo.
  Minskaya Voblasts', C Belarus
Syene *see* Aswān
Syeverodonets'k 109 H3 *Rus.*
  Severodonetsk. Luhans'ka Oblast',
  E Ukraine
Syktyvkar 110 D4 *prev.* Ust'-Sysol'sk.
  Respublika Komi, NW Russian
  Federation
Sylhet 135 G3 Sylhet,
  NE Bangladesh
Synel'nykove 109 G3 Dnipropetrovs'ka
  Oblast', E Ukraine
Syowa 154 C2 *Japanese research station*
  Antarctica
Syracuse 41 E3 New York,
  NE USA
Syracuse *see* Siracusa
Syrdar'ya 114 B4 Sirdaryo Viloyati,
  E Uzbekistan
Syria 118 B3 *off.* Syrian Arab Republic,
  var. Siria, Syrie, Ar. Al-Jumhūrīyah
  al-'Arabiyah as-Sūriyah, Sūriya.
  country SW Asia

SYRIA
Southwest Asia

Official name Syrian Arab Republic
Formation 1941 / 1967
Capital Damascus
Population 20 million / 281 people
per sq mile (109 people per sq km) / 50%
Total area 71,498 sq. miles (184,180 sq. km)
Languages Arabic*, French, Kurdish,
Armenian, Circassian, Turkic languages,
Assyrian, Aramaic
Religions Sunni Muslim 74%, Other
Muslim 16%, Christian 10%
Ethnic mix Arab 89%, Kurdish 6%,
Other 3%, Armenian, Turkmen, and
Circassian 2%
Government One-party state
Currency Syrian pound = 100 piastres
Literacy rate 80%
Calorie consumption 3038 calories

Syrian Arab Republic *see* Syria
Syrian Desert 119 D5 *Ar.* Al Hamad,
  Bādiyat ash Shām. *desert* SW Asia
Syrie *see* Syria
Sýrna 105 E7 *var.* Sirna. *island* Kykládes,
  Greece, Aegean Sea
Sýros 105 C6 *var.* Síros. *island* Kykládes,
  Greece, Aegean Sea
Syulemeshlii *see* Sredets
Syvash, Zaliv *see* Syvash, Zatoka
Syvash, Zatoka 109 F4 *Rus.* Zaliv Syvash.
  inlet S Ukraine
Syzran' 111 C6 Samarskaya Oblast',
  W Russian Federation
Szabadka *see* Subotica

243

Szamotuły 98 B3 Poznań, W Poland
Szászrégen see Reghin
Szatmárrnémeti see Satu Mare
Száva see Sava
Szczecin 98 B3 Eng./Ger. Stettin.
Zachodnio-pomorskie, NW Poland
Szczecinek 98 B2 Ger. Neustettin.
Zachodnio-pomorskie, NW Poland
Szczeciński, Zalew 98 A2 var. Stettiner
Haff, Ger. Oderhaff. bay Germany/
Poland
Szczuczyn Nowogródzki see Shchuchyn
Szczytno 98 D3 Ger. Ortelsburg.
Warmińsko-Mazurskie, NE Poland
Szechuan/Szechwan see Sichuan
Szeged 99 D7 Ger. Szegedin, Rom.
Seghedin. Csongrád, SE Hungary
Szegedin see Szeged
Székelykeresztúr see Cristuru Secuiesc
Székesfehérvár 99 C6 Ger.
Stuhlweissenberg; anc. Alba Regia.
Fejér, W Hungary
Szeklerburg see Miercurea-Ciuc
Szekler Neumarkt see Târgu Secuiesc
Szekszárd 99 C7 Tolna, S Hungary
Szempcz/Szenc see Senec
Szenice see Senica
Szeping see Siping
Szilágysomlyó see Şimleu Silvaniei
Szinna see Snina
Sziszek see Sisak
Szitás-Keresztúr see Cristuru Secuiesc
Szkudy see Skuodas
Szlatina see Slatina
Szlovákia see Slovakia
Szolnok 99 D6 Jász-Nagykun-Szolnok,
C Hungary
Szombathely 99 B6 Ger. Steinamanger;
anc. Sabaria, Savaria. Vas, W Hungary
Szprotawa 98 B4 Ger. Sprottau.
Lubuskie, W Poland
Sztálinváros see Dunaújváros
Szucsava see Suceava

T

Tabariya, Bahrat see Tiberias, Lake
Table Rock Lake 49 G1 reservoir
Arkansas/Missouri, C USA
Tábor 99 B5 Jihočeský Kraj, S Czech
Republic
Tabora 73 B7 Tabora, W Tanzania
Tabriz 120 C2 var. Tebriz; anc. Tauris.
Āzarbāyjān-e Sharqī, NW Iran
Tabuaeran 145 G2 prev. Fanning Island.
atoll Line Islands, E Kiribati
Tabūk 120 A4 Tabūk, NW Saudi Arabia
Täby 85 C6 Stockholm, C Sweden
Tachau see Tachov
Tachov 99 A5 Ger. Tachau. Plveňský
Kraj, W Czech Republic
Tacloban 139 F2 off. Tacloban City.
Leyte, C Philippines
Tacloban City see Tacloban
Tacna 61 E4 Tacna, SE Peru
Tacoma 46 B2 Washington,
NW USA
Tacuarembó 64 D4 prev. San Fructuoso.
Tacuarembó, C Uruguay
Tademait, Plateau du 70 D3 plateau
C Algeria
Tadmor/Tadmur see Tudmur
Tādpatri 132 C2 Andhra Pradesh,
E India
Tadzhikistan see Tajikistan
Taegu 129 E4 off. Taegu-gwangyŏksi,
var. Daegu, Jap. Taikyū. SE South
Korea
Taegu-gwangyŏksi see Taegu
Taehan-haehyŏp see Korea Strait
Taehan Min'guk see South Korea
Taejŏn 129 E4 off. Taejŏn-gwangyŏksi,
Jap. Taiden. C South Korea
Taejŏn-gwangyŏksi see Taejŏn
Tafassâsset, Ténéré du 75 G2 desert
N Niger
Tafila/Ṭafīlah, Muḥāfaẓat aṭ see Aṭ
Ṭafīlah
Taganrog 111 A7 Rostovskaya Oblast',
SW Russian Federation
Taganrog, Gulf of 109 G4 Rus.
Taganrogskiy Zaliv, Ukr. Tahanroz'ka
Zatoka. gulf Russian Federation/
Ukraine

Taganrogskiy Zaliv see Taganrog,
Gulf of
Taguatinga 63 F3 Tocantins, C Brazil
Tagus 92 C3 Port. Rio Tejo, Sp. Río Tajo.
river Portugal/Spain
Tagus Plain 80 A4 abyssal plain
E Atlantic Ocean
Tahanroz'ka Zatoka see Taganrog,
Gulf of
Tahat 71 E4 mountain SE Algeria
Tahiti 145 H4 island Îles du Vent,
W French Polynesia
Tahiti, Archipel de see Société, Archipel
de la
Tahlequah 49 G1 Oklahoma, C USA
Tahoe, Lake 47 B5 lake California/
Nevada, W USA
Tahoua 75 F3 Tahoua, W Niger
Taichū see T'aichung
T'aichung 128 D6 Jap. Taichū; prev.
Taiwan. C Taiwan
Taiden see Taejŏn
Taieri 151 B7 river South Island, New
Zealand
Taihape 150 D4 Manawatu-Wanganui,
North Island, New Zealand
Taihoku see T'aipei
Taikyū see Taegu
Tailem Bend 149 B7 South Australia
T'ainan 128 D6 Jap. Tainan; prev.
Dainan. S Taiwan
T'aipei 128 D6 Jap. Taihoku; prev.
Daihoku. country capital (Taiwan)
(Taiwan) N Taiwan
Taiping 138 B3 Perak, Peninsular
Malaysia
Taiwan 128 D6 off. Republic of China,
var. Formosa, Formo'sa. country
E Asia

TAIWAN
East Asia

Official name Republic of China (ROC)
Formation 1949 / 1949
Capital Taipei
Population 22.9 million / 1835 people
per sq mile (709 people per sq km) / 80%
Total area 13,892 sq. miles (35,980 sq. km)
Languages Amoy Chinese, Mandarin
Chinese*, Hakka Chinese
Religions Buddhist, Confucianist, and
Taoist 93%, Christian 5%, Other 2%
Ethnic mix Han (20th-century
migration) 84%, Han (20th-century
migration) 14%, Aboriginal 2%
Government Presidential system
Currency Taiwan dollar = 100 cents
Literacy rate 97%
Calorie consumption Not available

Taiwan see T'aichung
T'aiwan Haihsia/Taiwan Haixia see
Taiwan Strait
Taiwan Strait 128 D6 var. Formosa
Strait, Chin. T'aiwan Haihsia, Taiwan
Haixia. strait China/Taiwan
Taiyuan 128 C4 var. T'ai-yuan, T'ai-
yüan; prev. Yangku. province capital
Shanxi, C China
T'ai-yuan/T'ai-yüan see Taiyuan
Ta'izz 121 B7 SW Yemen
Tajikistan 123 E3 off. Republic of
Tajikistan, Rus. Tadzhikistan, Taj.
Jumhurii Tojikiston; prev. Tajik S.S.R.
country C Asia

TAJIKISTAN
Central Asia

Official name Republic of Tajikistan
Formation 1991 / 1991
Capital Dushanbe
Population 6.4 million / 121 people
per sq mile (47 people per sq km) / 25%
Total area 55,251 sq. miles (143,100 sq. km)
Languages Tajik*, Uzbek, Russian
Religions Sunni Muslim 80%, Other 15%,
Shi'a Muslim 5%
Ethnic mix Tajik 80%, Uzbek 15%,
Other 3%, Russian 1%, Kyrgyz 1%
Government Presidential system
Currency Somoni = 100 diram
Literacy rate 99%
Calorie consumption 1828 calories

Tajikistan, Republic of see Tajikistan

Tajik S.S.R see Tajikistan
Tajo, Río see Tagus
Tak 136 C4 var. Rahaeng. Tak,
W Thailand
Takao see Kaohsiung
Takaoka 131 C5 Toyama, Honshū,
SW Japan
Takapuna 150 D2 Auckland, North
Island, New Zealand
Takhiatash see Taxiatosh
Takhtakupyr see Taxtako'pir
Takikawa 130 D2 Hokkaidō, NE Japan
Takla Makan Desert 126 B3 Eng. Takla
Makan Desert. desert NW China
Takla Makan Desert see Taklimakan
Shamo
Takow see Kaohsiung
Takutea 145 G4 island S Cook Islands
Talabriga see Aveiro, Portugal
Talabriga see Talavera de la Reina, Spain
Talachyn 107 D6 Rus. Tolochin.
Vitsyebskaya Voblasts', NE Belarus
Talamanca, Cordillera de 53 E5
mountain range S Costa Rica
Talara 60 B2 Piura, NW Peru
Talas 123 F2 Talasskaya Oblast',
NW Kyrgyzstan
Talaud, Kepulauan 139 F3 island group
E Indonesia
Talavera de la Reina 92 D3 anc.
Caesarobriga, Talabriga. Castilla-La
Mancha, C Spain
Talca 64 B4 Maule, C Chile
Talcahuano 65 B5 Bío Bío, C Chile
Taldykorgan 114 C5 Kaz. Taldyqorghan;
prev. Taldy-Kurgan. Taldykorgan,
SE Kazakhstan
Taldy-Kurgan/Taldyqorghan see
Taldykorgan
Ta-lien see Dalian
Taliq-an see Tāloqān
Tal'ka 107 C6 Minskaya Voblasts',
C Belarus
Talkhof see Puurmani
Tallahassee 42 D3 mvrc. Muskogean.
state capital Florida, SE USA
Tall al Abyaḍ see At Tall al Abyaḍ
Tallin see Tallinn
Tallinn 106 D2 Ger. Reval, Rus. Tallin;
prev. Revel. country capital (Estonia)
(Estonia) Harjumaa, NW Estonia
Tall Kalakh 118 B4 var. Tell Kalakh.
Ḥimş, C Syria
Tallulah 42 B2 Louisiana, S USA
Talnakh 114 D3 Taymyrskiy (Dolgano-
Nenetskiy) Avtonomnyy Okrug,
N Russian Federation
Tal'ne 109 E3 Rus. Tal'noye. Cherkas'ka
Oblast', C Ukraine
Tal'noye see Tal'ne
Taloga 49 F1 Oklahoma, C USA
Tāloqān 123 E3 var. Taliq-an. Takhār,
NE Afghanistan
Talsen see Talsi
Talsi 106 C3 Ger. Talsen. Talsi,
NW Latvia
Taltal 64 B2 Antofagasta, N Chile
Talvik 84 D2 Finnmark, N Norway
Tamabo, Banjaran 138 D3 mountain
range East Malaysia
Tamale 75 E4 C Ghana
Tamana 145 E3 prev. Rotcher Island.
atoll Tungaru, W Kiribati
Tamanrasset 71 E4 var. Tamenghest.
S Algeria
Tamar 89 C7 river SW England, United
Kingdom
Tamar see Tudmur
Tamatave see Toamasina
Tamazunchale 51 E4 San Luis Potosí,
C Mexico
Tambacounda 74 C3 SE Senegal
Tambov 111 B6 Tambovskaya Oblast',
W Russian Federation
Tambura 73 B5 Western Equatoria,
SW Sudan
Tamchaket see Tâmchekkeṭ
Tâmchekkeṭ 74 C3 var. Tamchaket.
Hodh el Gharbi, S Mauritania
Tamenghest see Tamanrasset
Tamil Nādu 132 C3 prev. Madras.
cultural region SE India
Tam Ky 137 E5 Quang Nam-fa Năng,
C Vietnam
Tammerfors see Tampere
Tampa 43 E4 Florida, SE USA
Tampa Bay 43 E4 bay Florida, SE USA

Tampere 85 D5 Swe. Tammerfors.
Länsi-Suomi, W Finland
Tampico 51 E3 Tamaulipas, C Mexico
Tamworth 149 D6 New South Wales,
SE Australia
Tanabe 131 C7 Wakayama, Honshū,
SW Japan
Tana Bru 84 D2 Finnmark, N Norway
Tanais see Don
Lake Tana 72 C4 var. Lake Tana. lake
NW Ethiopia
Tana, Lake see T'ana Hāyk'
Tanami Desert 146 D3 desert Northern
Territory, N Australia
Tananarive see Antananarivo
Ţāndārei 108 D5 Ialomiţa, SE Romania
Tandil 65 D5 Buenos Aires, E Argentina
Tandjoengkarang see Bandar Lampung
Tanega-shima 131 B8 island Nansei-
shotō, SW Japan
Tanen Taunggyi see Tane Range
Tane Range 136 B4 Bur. Tanen
Taunggyi. mountain range W Thailand
Tanezrouft 70 D4 desert Algeria/Mali
Ţanf, Jabal aṭ 118 D4 mountain SE Syria
Tanga 73 C7 Tanga, E Tanzania
Tanganyika and Zanzibar see Tanzania
Tanganyika, Lake 73 B7 lake E Africa
Tanger 70 C2 var. Tangiers, Tangier, Fr./
Ger. Tangerk, Sp. Tánger; anc. Tingis.
NW Morocco
Tangerk see Tanger
Tanggula Shan 126 C4 mountain W China
Tangier see Tanger
Tangiers see Tanger
Tangra Yumco 126 B5 var. Tangro Tso.
lake W China
Tangro Tso see Tangra Yumco
Tangshan 128 D3 var. T'ang-shan.
Hebei, E China
T'ang-shan see Tangshan
Tanimbar, Kepulauan 139 F5 island
group Maluku, E Indonesia
Tanjungkarang/Tanjungkarang-
Telukbetung see Bandar Lampung
Tanna 144 D4 island S Vanuatu
Tannenhof see Krynica
Tan-Tan 70 B3 SW Morocco
Tan-tung see Dandong
Tanzania 73 C7 off. United Republic of
Tanzania, Swa. Jamhuri ya Muungano
wa Tanzania; prev. German East Africa,
Tanganyika and Zanzibar. country
E Asia

TANZANIA
East Africa

Official name United Republic
of Tanzania
Formation 1964 / 1964
Capital Dodoma
Population 39.7 million / 116 people
per sq mile (45 people per sq km) / 36%
Total area 364,898 sq. miles
(945,087 sq. km)
Languages Kiswahili*, Sukuma, Chagga,
Nyamwezi, Hehe, Makonde, Yao,
Sandawe, English*
Religions Muslim 35%, Christian 30%,
Traditional beliefs 30%, Other 4%
Ethnic mix Native African (over 120
tribes) 99%, European, Asian, and Arab 1%
Government Presidential system
Currency Tanzanian shilling = 100 cents
Literacy rate 69%
Calorie consumption 1975 calories

Tanzania, Jamhuri ya Muungano wa
see Tanzania
Tanzania, United Republic of see
Tanzania
Taoudenni see Taoudenni
Taoudenni 75 E2 var. Taoudenit.
Tombouctou, N Mali
Tapa 106 E2 Ger. Taps. Lääne-Virumaa,
NE Estonia
Tapachula 51 G5 Chiapas, SE Mexico
Tapaiu see Gvardeysk
Tapajós, Rio 63 E2 var. Tapajóz. river
NW Brazil
Tapajóz see Tapajós, Rio
Taps see Tapa
Ṭarābulus 71 F2 var. Ṭarābulus al Gharb,
Eng. Tripoli. country capital (Libya)
(Libya) NW Libya
Ṭarābulus al Gharb see Ṭarābulus

Tarābulus/Ṭarābulus ash Shām *see*
Tripoli
Taraclia *108 D4 Rus.* Tarakilya.
S Moldova
Tarakilya *see* Taraclia
Mount Taranaki *150 C4 var.* Egmont.
volcano North Island, New Zealand
Tarancón *93 E3* Castilla-La Mancha,
C Spain
Taranto *97 E5 var.* Tarentum. Puglia,
SE Italy
Taranto, Gulf of *97 E6 Eng.* Gulf of
Taranto. *gulf* S Italy
Taranto, Gulf of *see* Taranto, Golfo di
Tarapoto *60 C2* San Martín, N Peru
Tarare *91 D5* Rhône, E France
Tarascon *91 D6* Bouches-du-Rhône,
SE France
Tarawa *144 D2 atoll* Tungaru, W Kiribati
Taraz *114 C5 prev.* Aulie Ata, Auliye-
Ata, Dzhambul, Zhambyl. Zhambyl,
S Kazakhstan
Tarazona *93 E2* Aragón, NE Spain
Tarbes *91 B6 anc.* Bigorra. Hautes-
Pyrénées, S France
Tarcoola *149 A6* South Australia
Taree *149 D6* New South Wales,
SE Australia
Tarentum *see* Taranto
Târgovişte *108 C5 prev.* Tîrgovişte.
Dâmboviţa, S Romania
Targu Jiu *108 B4 prev.* Tîrgu Jiu. Gorj,
W Romania
Târgul-Neamţ *see* Târgu-Neamţ
Târgul-Săcuiesc *see* Târgu Secuiesc
Târgu Mureş *108 B4 prev.* Oşorhei,
Tîrgu Mures, Ger. Neumarkt, *Hung.*
Marosvásárhely. Mureş, C Romania
Târgu-Neamţ *108 C3 var.* Târgul-
Neamţ; *prev.* Tîrgu-Neamţ. Neamţ,
NE Romania
Târgu Ocna *108 C4 Hung.* Aknavásár;
prev. Tîrgu Ocna. Bacău, E Romania
Târgu Secuiesc *108 C4 Ger.*
Neumarkt, Szekler Neumarkt, *Hung.*
Kezdivásárhely; *prev.* Chezdi-Oşorheiu,
Târgul-Săcuiesc, Tîrgu Secuiesc.
Covasna, E Romania
Tar Heel State *see* North Carolina
Tarija *61 G5* Tarija, S Bolivia
Tarīm *121 C6* C Yemen
Tarim Basin *124 C2 Eng.* Tarim Basin.
basin NW China
Tarim Basin *see* Tarim Pendi
Tarim He *126 B3 river* NW China
Tarma *60 C3* Junín, C Peru
Tarn *91 C6 cultural region* S France
Tarn *91 C6 river* S France
Tarnobrzeg *98 D4* Podkarpackie,
SE Poland
Tarnopol *see* Ternopil'
Tarnów *99 D5* Małopolskie, S Poland
Tarraco *see* Tarragona
Tarragona *93 G2 anc.* Tarraco.
Cataluña, E Spain
Tarrasa *see* Terrassa
Tàrrega *93 F2 var.* Tarrega. Cataluña,
NE Spain
Tarsatica *see* Rijeka
Tarsus *116 C4* İçel, S Turkey
Tartous/Tartouss *see* Ṭarṭūs
Tartu *106 D3 Ger.* Dorpat; *prev. Rus.*
Yurev, Yury'ev. Tartumaa, SE Estonia
Ṭarṭūs *118 A3 off.* Muḥāfaẓat Ṭarṭūs,
var. Tartous, Tartus. *governorate*
W Syria
Ṭarṭūs, Muḥāfaẓat *see* Ṭarṭūs
Ta Ru Tao, Ko *137 B7 island* S Thailand
Asia
Tarvisio *96 D2* Friuli-Venezia Giulia,
NE Italy
Tarvisium *see* Treviso
Tashauz *see* Daşoguz
Tashi Chho Dzong *see* Thimphu
Tashkent *see* Toshkent
Tash-Kömür *see* Tash-Kumyr
Tash-Kumyr *123 F2 Kir.* Tash-
Kömür. Dzhalal-Abadskaya Oblast',
W Kyrgyzstan
Tashqurghan *see* Kholm
Tasikmalaja *see* Tasikmalaya
Tasikmalaya *138 C5 prev.* Tasikmalaja.
Jawa, C Indonesia
Tasman Basin *142 C5 var.* East
Australian Basin. *undersea basin*
S Tasman Sea

Tasman Bay *151 C5 inlet* South Island,
New Zealand
Tasmania *149 B8 prev.* Van Diemen's
Land. *state* SE Australia
Tasmania *152 B4 island* SE Australia
Tasman Plateau *142 C5 var.* South
Tasmania Plateau. *undersea plateau*
SW Tasman Sea
Tasman Sea *142 C5 sea* SW Pacific
Ocean
Tassili-n-Ajjer *71 E4 plateau* E Algeria
Tatabánya *99 C6* Komárom-Esztergom,
NW Hungary
Tatar Pazardzhik *see* Pazardzhik
Tathlīth *121 B5* 'Asīr, S Saudi Arabia
Tatra Mountains *99 D5 Ger.* Tatra,
Hung. Tátra, *Pol./Slvk.* Tatry.
mountain range Poland/Slovakia
Tatra/Tátra *see* Tatra Mountains
Tatry *see* Tatra Mountains
Ta-t'ung/Tatung *see* Datong
Tatvan *117 F3* Bitlis, SE Turkey
Ta'ū *145 F4 var.* Tau. *island* Manua
Islands, E American Samoa
Taukum, Peski *123 G1 desert*
SE Kazakhstan
Taumarunui *150 D4* Manawatu-
Wanganui, North Island, New Zealand
Taungdwingyi *136 B3* Magway,
C Burma (Myanmar)
Taunggyi *136 B3* Shan State, C Burma
(Myanmar)
Taungoo *136 B4* Bago, C Burma
(Myanmar)
Taunton *89 C7* SW England, United
Kingdom
Taupo *150 D3* Waikato, North Island,
New Zealand
Taupo, Lake *150 D3 lake* North Island,
New Zealand
Tauragė *106 B4 Ger.* Tauroggen.
Tauragė, SW Lithuania
Tauranga *150 D3* Bay of Plenty, North
Island, New Zealand
Tauris *see* Tabriz
Tauroggen *see* Tauragė
Taurus Mountains *116 C4 Eng.* Taurus
Mountains. *mountain range* S Turkey
Taurus Mountains *see* Toros Dağları
Tavas *116 B4* Denizli, SW Turkey
Tavastehus *see* Hämeenlinna
Tavira *92 C5* Faro, S Portugal
Tavoy *see* Dawei
Tavoy Island *see* Mali Kyun
Ta Waewae Bay *151 A7 bay* South
Island, New Zealand
Tawakoni, Lake *49 G2 reservoir* Texas,
SW USA
Tawau *138 D3* Sabah, East Malaysia
Ṭawkar *see* Tokar
Tawzar *see* Tozeur
Taxco *51 E4 var.* Taxco de Alarcón.
Guerrero, S Mexico
Taxco de Alarcón *see* Taxco
Taxiatosh *122 C2 Rus.* Takhiatash.
Qoraqalpog'iston Respublikasi,
W Uzbekistan
Taxtako'pir *122 D1 Rus.* Takhtakupyr.
Qoraqalpog'iston Respublikasi,
NW Uzbekistan
Tay *88 C3 river* C Scotland, United
Kingdom
Taylor *49 G3* Texas, SW USA
Taymā' *120 A4* Tabūk, NW Saudi Arabia
Taymyr, Ozero *115 E2 lake* N Russian
Federation
Taymyr, Poluostrov *115 E2 peninsula*
N Russian Federation
Taz *114 D3 river* N Russian Federation
T'bilisi *117 G2 Eng.* Tiflis. *country
capital* (Georgia) (Georgia) SE Georgia
Tchad *see* Chad
Tchad, Lac *see* Chad, Lake
Tchien *see* Zwedru
Tchongking *see* Chongqing
Tczew *98 C2 Ger.* Dirschau. Pomorskie,
N Poland
Te Anau *151 A7* Southland, South Island,
New Zealand
Te Anau, Lake *151 A7 lake* South Island,
New Zealand
Teapa *51 G4* Tabasco, SE Mexico
Teate *see* Chieti
Tebingtinggi *138 B3* Sumatera,
N Indonesia
Tebriz *see* Tabriz

Techirghiol *108 D5* Constanţa,
SE Romania
Tecomán *50 D4* Colima, SW Mexico
Tecpan *51 E5 var.* Tecpan de Galeana.
Guerrero, S Mexico
Tecpan de Galeana *see* Tecpan
Tecuci *108 C4* Galaţi, E Romania
Tedzhen *see* Harīrūd/Tejen
Tedzhen *see* Tejen
Tees *89 D5 river* N England, United
Kingdom
Tefé *62 D2* Amazonas, N Brazil
Tegal *138 C4* Jawa, C Indonesia
Tegelen *87 D5* Limburg, SE Netherlands
Tegucigalpa *52 C3 country capital*
(Honduras) (Honduras) Francisco
Morazán, SW Honduras
Teheran *see* Tehrān
Tehrān *120 C3 var.* Teheran. *country
capital* (Iran) (Iran) Tehrān, N Iran
Tehuacán *51 F4* Puebla, S Mexico
Tehuantepec *51 F5 var.* Santo Domingo
Tehuantepec. Oaxaca, SE Mexico
Gulf of Tehuantepec *51 F5 var.* Gulf of
Tehuantepec. *gulf* S Mexico
Tehuantepec, Gulf of *see* Tehuantepec,
Golfo de
Isthmus of Tehuantepec *51 F5 var.*
Isthmus of Tehuantepec. *isthmus*
SE Mexico
Tehuantepec, Isthmus of *see*
Tehuantepec, Istmo de
Tejen *122 C3 Rus.* Tedzhen. Ahal
Welaýaty, S Turkmenistan
Tejen *see* Harīrūd
Tejo, Rio *see* Tagus
Te Kao *150 C1* Northland, North Island,
New Zealand
Tekax *51 H4 var.* Tekax de Álvaro
Obregón. Yucatán, SE Mexico
Tekax de Álvaro Obregón *see* Tekax
Tekeli *114 C5* Almaty, SE Kazakhstan
Tekirdağ *116 A2 It.* Rodosto; *anc.*
Bisanthe, Raidestos, Rhaedestus.
Tekirdağ, NW Turkey
Te Kuiti *150 D3* Waikato, North Island,
New Zealand
Tela *52 C2* Atlántida, NW Honduras
Telanaipura *see* Jambi
Tel Aviv-Jaffa *see* Tel Aviv-Yafo
Tel Aviv-Yafo *119 A6 var.* Tel Aviv-Jaffa.
Tel Aviv, C Israel
Teles Pirés *see* São Manuel, Rio
Telish *104 C2 prev.* Azizie. Pleven,
N Bulgaria
Tell Abiad/Tell Abyad *see* At Tall al
Abyaḍ
Tell Kalakh *see* Tall Kalakh
Tell Shedadi *see* Ash Shadādah
Tel'man/Tel'mansk *see* Gubadag
Teloekbetoeng *see* Bandar Lampung
Telo Martius *see* Toulon
Telschen *see* Telšiai
Telšiai *106 B3 Ger.* Telschen. Telšiai,
NW Lithuania
Telukbetung *see* Bandar Lampung
Temerin *100 D3* Vojvodina, N Serbia
Temeschburg/Temeschwar *see*
Timişoara
Temesvár/Temeswar *see* Timişoara
Temirtau *114 C4 prev.* Samarkandski,
Samarkandskoye. Karaganda,
C Kazakhstan
Tempio Pausania *97 A5* Sardegna, Italy,
C Mediterranean Sea
Temple *49 G3* Texas, SW USA
Temuco *65 B5* Araucanía, C Chile
Temuka *151 B6* Canterbury, South
Island, New Zealand
Tenasserim *137 B6* Tanintharyi,
S Burma (Myanmar)
Ténenkou *74 D3* Mopti, C Mali
Ténéré *75 G3 physical region* C Niger
Tenerife *70 A3 island* Islas Canarias,
Spain, NE Atlantic Ocean
Tengger Shamo *127 E3 desert* N China
Tengréla *74 D4 var.* Tingréla. N Côte
d'Ivoire
Tenkodogo *75 E4* S Burkina Faso
Tennant Creek *148 A3* Northern
Territory, C Australia
Tennessee *42 C1 off.* State of Tennessee,
also known as The Volunteer State.
state SE USA
Tennessee River *42 C1 river* S USA
Tenos *see* Tínos
Tepelena *see* Tepelenë

Tepelenë *101 C7 var.* Tepelena, *It.*
Tepeleni. Gjirokastër, S Albania
Tepeleni *see* Tepelenë
Tepic *50 D4* Nayarit, C Mexico
Teplice *98 A4 Ger.* Teplitz; *prev.* Teplice-
Šanov, Teplitz-Schönau. Ústecký Kraj,
NW Czech Republic
Teplice-Šanov/Teplitz/Teplitz-Schönau
see Teplice
Tequila *50 D4* Jalisco, SW Mexico
Teraina *145 G2 prev.* Washington Island.
atoll Line Islands, E Kiribati
Teramo *96 C4 anc.* Interamna. Abruzzi,
C Italy
Tercan *117 E3* Erzincan, NE Turkey
Terceira *92 A5 var.* Ilha Terceira. *island*
Azores, Portugal, NE Atlantic Ocean
Terceira, Ilha *see* Terceira
Terekhovka *see* Tsyerakhowka
Teresina *63 F2 var.* Therezina. *state
capital* Piauí, NE Brazil
Termez *see* Termiz
Termia *see* Kýthnos
Términos, Laguna de *51 G4 lagoon*
SE Mexico
Termiz *123 E3 Rus.* Termez.
Surkhondaryo Viloyati, S Uzbekistan
Termoli *96 D4* Molise, C Italy
Terneuzen *87 B5 var.* Neuzen. Zeeland,
SW Netherlands
Terni *96 C4 anc.* Interamna Nahars.
Umbria, C Italy
Ternopil' *108 C2 Pol.* Tarnopol, *Rus.*
Ternopol'. Ternopil's'ka Oblast',
W Ukraine
Ternopol' *see* Ternopil'
Terracina *97 C5* Lazio, C Italy
Terranova di Sicilia *see* Gela
Terranova Pausania *see* Olbia
Terrassa *93 G2 Cast.* Tarrasa. Cataluña,
E Spain
Terre Adélie *154 C4 physical region*
Antarctica
Terre Haute *40 B4* Indiana, N USA
Terre Neuve *see* Newfoundland and
Labrador
Terschelling *86 C1 Fris.* Skylge. *island*
Waddeneilanden, N Netherlands
Teruel *93 F3 anc.* Turba. Aragón,
E Spain
Tervel *104 E1 prev.* Kurtbunar, *Rom.*
Curtbunar. Dobrich, NE Bulgaria
Tervueren *see* Tervuren
Tervuren *87 C6 var.* Tervueren. Vlaams
Brabant, C Belgium
Teseney *72 C4 var.* Tessenei. W Eritrea
Tessalit *75 E2* Kidal, NE Mali
Tessaoua *75 G3* Maradi, S Niger
Tessenderlo *87 C5* Limburg, NE Belgium
Tessenei *see* Teseney
Testigos, Islas los *59 E1 island group*
N Venezuela
Tete *79 E2* Tete, NW Mozambique
Teterow *94 C3* Mecklenburg-
Vorpommern, NE Germany
Tétouan *70 C2 var.* Tetouan, Tetuán.
N Morocco
Tetovo *101 D5* Razgrad, N Bulgaria
Tetschen *see* Děčín
Tetuán *see* Tétouan
Teverya *see* Tverya
Te Waewae Bay *151 A7 bay* South
Island, New Zealand
Texarkana *42 A2* Arkansas, C USA
Texarkana *49 H2* Texas, SW USA
Texas *49 F3 off.* State of Texas, *also
known as* Lone Star State. *state* S USA
Texas City *49 H4* Texas, SW USA
Texel *86 C2 island* Waddeneilanden,
NW Netherlands
Texoma, Lake *49 G2 reservoir*
Oklahoma/Texas, C USA
Teziutlán *51 F4* Puebla, S Mexico
Thaa Atoll *see* Kolhumadulu
Thai, Ao *see* Thailand, Gulf of
Thai Binh *136 D3* Thai Binh, N Vietnam
Thailand *137 C5 off.* Kingdom of
Thailand, Th. Prathet Thai; *prev.* Siam.
country SE Asia

THAILAND
Southeast Asia

Official name Kingdom of Thailand
Formation 1238 / 1907
Capital Bangkok
Population 68.3 million / 346 people

THAILAND
(continued)

per sq mile (134 people per sq km) / 32%
Total area 198,455 sq. miles
(514,000 sq. km)
Languages Thai*, Chinese, Malay, Khmer,
Mon, Karen, Miao
Religions Buddhist 95%, Muslim 4%,
Other (including Christian) 1%
Ethnic mix Thai 83%, Chinese 12%,
Malay 3%, Khmer and Other 2%
Government Parliamentary system
Currency Baht = 100 satang
Literacy rate 93%
Calorie consumption 2467 calories

Thailand, Gulf of *137 C6 var.* Gulf of
Siam, *Th.* Ao Thai, *Vtn.* Vinh Thai Lan.
gulf SE Asia
Thailand, Kingdom of *see* Thailand
Thai Lan, Vinh *see* Thailand, Gulf of
Thai Nguyên *136 D3* Bắc Thai, N Vietnam
Thakhèk *136 D4 var.* Muang
Khammouan. Khammouan, C Laos
Thamarīd *see* Thamarīt
Thamarīt *121 D6 var.* Thamarid,
Thumrayt. SW Oman
Thames *150 D3* Waikato, North Island,
New Zealand
Thames *89 B8 river* S England, United
Kingdom
Thandwe *136 A4 var.* Sandoway.
Rakhine State, W Burma (Myanmar)
Thanh Hoa *136 D3* Thanh Hoa,
N Vietnam
Thanintari Taungdan *see* Bilauktaung
Range
Thanlwin *see* Salween
Thar Desert *134 C3 var.* Great Indian
Desert, Indian Desert. *desert* India/
Pakistan
Tharthar, Buhayrat ath *120 B3 lake*
C Iraq
Thásos *104 C4* Thásos, E Greece
Thásos *104 C4 island* E Greece
Thaton *136 B4* Mon State, S Burma
(Myanmar)
Thayetmyo *136 A4* Magway, C Burma
(Myanmar)
The Crane *55 H2 var.* Crane. S Barbados
The Dalles *46 B3* Oregon, NW USA
The Flatts Village *see* Flatts Village
The Hague *see* 's-Gravenhage
Theodosia *see* Feodosiya
The Pas *37 F5* Manitoba, C Canada
Therezina *see* Teresina
Thérma *105 D6* Ikaría, Dodekánisa,
Greece, Aegean Sea
Thermaic Gulf *104 B4 Eng.* Thermaic
Gulf; *anc.* Thermaicus Sinus. *gulf*
N Greece
Thermaic Gulf/Thermaicus Sinus *see*
Thermaïkós Kólpos
Thermiá *see* Kýthnos
Thérmo *105 B5* Dytikí Ellás, C Greece
The Rock *93 H4* New South Wales,
SE Australia
The Sooner State *see* Oklahoma
Thessaloníki *104 C3 Eng.* Salonica,
Salonika, *SCr.* Solun, *Turk.* Selânik.
Kentrikí Makedonía, N Greece
The Valley *55 G3 dependent territory
capital* (Anguilla) E Anguilla
The Village *49 G1* Oklahoma, C USA
The Volunteer State *see* Tennessee
Thiamis *see* Kalamás
Thian Shan *see* Tien Shan
Thibet *see* Xizang Zizhiqu
Thief River Falls *45 F1* Minnesota,
N USA
Thienen *see* Tienen
Thiers *91 C5* Puy-de-Dôme, C France
Thiès *74 B3* W Senegal
Thikombia *see* Cikobia
Thimbu *see* Thimphu
Thimphu *135 G3 var.* Thimbu; *prev.*
Tashi Chho Dzong. *country capital*
(Bhutan) W Bhutan
Thionville *90 D3 Ger.* Diedenhofen.
Moselle, NE France
Thíra *105 D7* Santoríni, Kykládes,
Greece, Aegean Sea
Thíra *105 D7* Santoríni, Kykládes,
Greece, Aegean Sea
Thíra *105 D7* Santoríni, Kykládes,
Greece, Aegean Sea

Thitu Island *128 C8 island* NW Spratly
Islands
Tholen *86 B4 island* SW Netherlands
Thomasville *42 D3* Georgia, SE USA
Thompson *37 F4* Manitoba, C Canada
Thonon-les-Bains *91 D5* Haute-Savoie,
E France
Thorenburg *see* Turda
Thorlákshöfn *83 E5* Sudhurland,
SW Iceland
Thorn *see* Toruń
Thornton Island *see* Millennium Island
Thorshavn *see* Tórshavn
Thospitis *see* Van Gölü
Thouars *90 B4* Deux-Sèvres, W France
Thoune *see* Thun
Thracian Sea *104 D4 Gk.* Thrakikó
Pélagos; *anc.* Thracium Mare. *sea*
Greece/Turkey
Thracium Mare/Thrakikó Pélagos *see*
Thracian Sea
Three Kings Islands *150 C1 island
group* N New Zealand
Thuin *87 B7* Hainaut, S Belgium
Thule *see* Qaanaaq
Thumrayt *see* Thamarīt
Thun *95 A7 Fr.* Thoune. Bern,
W Switzerland
Thunder Bay *38 B4* Ontario, S Canada
Thuner See *95 A7 lake* C Switzerland
Thung Song *137 C7 var.* Cha Mai.
Nakhon Si Thammarat, SW Thailand
Thurso *88 C2* N Scotland, United
Kingdom
Thýamis *see* Kalamás
Tianjin *128 D4 var.* Tientsin. Tianjin
Shi, E China
Tianjin Shi *128 D4 var.* Jin, Tianjin,
T'ien-ching, Tientsin. *municipality*
E China
Tian Shan *see* Tien Shan
Tianshui *128 B4* Gansu, C China
Tiba *see* Chiba
Tiber *96 C4 Eng.* Tiber. *river* C Italy
Tiber *see* Tevere, Italy
Tiber *see* Tivoli, Italy
Tiberias *see* Tverya
Tiberias, Lake *119 B5 var.* Chinnereth,
Sea of Bahr Tabariya, Sea of Galilee, *Ar.*
Bahrat Tabariya, *Heb.* Yam Kinneret.
lake N Israel
Tibesti *76 C2 var.* Tibesti Massif, *Ar.*
Tibistī. *mountain range* N Africa
Tibesti Massif *see* Tibesti
Tibet *see* Xizang Zizhiqu
Tibetan Autonomous Region *see* Xizang
Zizhiqu
Tibet, Plateau of *126 B4 var.* Xizang
Gaoyuan, *Eng.* Plateau of Tibet. *plateau*
W China
Tibet, Plateau of *see* Qingzang Gaoyuan
Tibistī *see* Tibesti
Tibni *see* At Tibnī
Tiburón, Isla *50 B2 var.* Isla del Tiburón.
island NW Mexico
Tiburón, Isla del *see* Tiburón, Isla
Tichau *see* Tychy
Tichît *74 D3 var.* Tichitt. Tagant,
C Mauritania
Tichitt *see* Tichît
Ticinum *see* Pavia
Ticul *51 H3* Yucatán, SE Mexico
Tidjikdja *see* Tidjikja
Tidjikja *74 C2 var.* Tidjikdja; *prev.* Fort-
Cappolani. Tagant, C Mauritania
T'ien-ching *see* Tianjin Shi
Tienen *87 C6 var.* Thienen, *Fr.*
Tirlemont. Vlaams Brabant, C Belgium
Tiên Giang, Sông *see* Mekong
Tien Shan *126 B3 Chin.* Thian Shan,
Tian Shan, T'ien Shan, *Rus.* Tyan'-
Shan'. *mountain range* C Asia
Tientsin *see* Tianjin
Tierp *85 C6* Uppsala, C Sweden
Tierra del Fuego *65 B8 island* Argentina/
Chile
Tiflis *see* T'bilisi
Tifton *42 D3* Georgia, SE USA
Tifu *139 F4* Pulau Buru, E Indonesia
Tighina *108 D4 Rus.* Bendery; *prev.*
Bender. E Moldova
Tigranocerta *see* Siirt
Tigris *120 B2 Ar.* Dijlah, *Turk.* Dicle.
river Iraq/Turkey
Tiguentourine *71 E3* E Algeria
Ti-hua/Tihwa *see* Ürümqi

Tijuana *50 A1* Baja California Norte,
NW Mexico
Tikhoretsk *111 A7* Krasnodarskiy Kray,
SW Russian Federation
Tikhvin *110 B4* Leningradskaya Oblast',
NW Russian Federation
Tiki Basin *143 G3 undersea basin*
S Pacific Ocean
Tiksi *115 F2* Respublika Sakha
(Yakutiya), NE Russian Federation
Tilburg *86 C4* Noord-Brabant,
S Netherlands
Tilimsen *see* Tlemcen
Tilio Martius *see* Toulon
Tillabéri *75 F3 var.* Tillabéry. Tillabéri,
W Niger
Tillabéry *see* Tillabéri
Tílos *105 E7 island* Dodekánisa, Greece,
Aegean Sea
Timan Ridge *110 D3 Eng.* Timan Ridge.
ridge NW Russian Federation
Timan Ridge *see* Timanskiy Kryazh
Timaru *151 B6* Canterbury, South Island,
New Zealand
Timbaki/Timbákion *see* Tympáki
Timbedgha *74 D3 var.* Timbédra. Hodh
ech Chargui, SE Mauritania
Timbédra *see* Timbedgha
Timbuktu *see* Tombouctou
Timiş *108 A4 county* SW Romania
Timişoara *108 A4 Ger.* Temeschwar,
Temeswar, *Hung.* Temesvár; *prev.*
Temeschburg. Timiş, W Romania
Timmins *38 C4* Ontario, S Canada
Timor *125 F5 island* Nusa Tenggara,
C Indonesia
Timor Sea *125 F5 sea* E Indian Ocean
Timor Timur *see* East Timor
Timor Trench *see* Timor Trough
Timor Trough *125 F5 var.* Timor
Trench. *trough* NE Timor Sea
Timrå *85 C5* Västernorrland,
C Sweden
Tindouf *70 C3* W Algeria
Tineo *92 C1* Asturias, N Spain
Tingis *see* Tanger
Tingo María *60 C3* Huánuco, C Peru
Tingréla *see* Tengréla
Tinhosa Grande *76 E2 island*
N Sao Tome and Principe, Africa,
E Atlantic Ocean
Tinhosa Pequena *76 E1 island*
N Sao Tome and Principe, Africa,
E Atlantic Ocean
Tinian *144 B1 island* S Northern Mariana
Islands
Tínos *105 D6* Tínos, Kykládes, Greece,
Aegean Sea
Tínos *105 D6 anc.* Tenos. *island*
Kykládes, Greece, Aegean Sea
Tip *101 E6* Papua, E Indonesia
Tipitapa *52 D3* Managua, W Nicaragua
Tip Top Mountain *38 C4 mountain*
Ontario, S Canada
Tirana *see* Tiranë
Tiranë *101 C6 var.* Tirana. *country
capital* (Albania) (Albania) Tiranë,
C Albania
Tiraspol *108 D4 Rus.* Tiraspol'.
E Moldova
Tiraspol' *see* Tiraspol
Tiree *88 B3 island* W Scotland, United
Kingdom
Tîrgoviște *see* Târgoviște
Tîrgu Jiu *see* Targu Jiu
Tîrgu Mureş *see* Târgu Mureş
Tîrgu-Neamţ *see* Târgu-Neamţ
Tîrgu Ocna *see* Târgu Ocna
Tîrgu Secuiesc *see* Târgu Secuiesc
Tirlemont *see* Tienen
Tîrnaveni *see* Veliko Târnovo
Tîrnavos *see* Týrnavos
Tirol *95 C7 off.* Land Tirol, *var.* Tyrol, *It.*
Tirolo. *state* W Austria
Tirol, Land *see* Tirol
Tirolo *see* Tirol
Tirreno, Mare *see* Tyrrhenian Sea
Tiruchchirāppalli *132 C3 prev.*
Trichinopoly. Tamil Nādu,
SE India
Tiruppattūr *132 C2* Tamil Nādu,
SE India
Tiruvannamalai Thiruvanathapuram/
Trivandrum
Tisa *101 F1 Ger.* Theiss, *Rom./Slvn./
SCr.* Tisa, *Rus.* Tissa, *Ukr.* Tysa. *river*
SE Europe

Tisa *see* Tisza
Tiszakécske *99 D7* Bács-Kiskun,
C Hungary
Titano, Monte *96 E1 mountain* C San
Marino
Titicaca, Lake *61 E4 lake* Bolivia/Peru
Titograd *see* Podgorica
Titose *see* Chitose
Titova Mitrovica *see* Mitrovicë
Títovo Užice *see* Užice
Titu *108 C5* Dâmbovița, S Romania
Titule *77 D5* Orientale, N Dem. Rep.
Congo
Tiverton *89 C7* SW England, United
Kingdom
Tivoli *96 C4 anc.* Tiber. Lazio, C Italy
Tizimín *51 H3* Yucatán, SE Mexico
Tizi Ouzou *71 E1 var.* Tizi-Ouzou.
N Algeria
Tizi-Ouzou *see* Tizi Ouzou
Tiznit *70 B3* SW Morocco
Tjilatjap *see* Cilacap
Tjirebon *see* Cirebon
Tlaquepaque *50 D4* Jalisco, C Mexico
Tlaxcala *see* Tlaxcala
Tlaxcala *51 F4 var.* Tlaxcala, Tlaxcala de
Xicohténcatl. Tlaxcala, C Mexico
Tlaxcala de Xicohténcatl *see* Tlaxcala
Tlemcen *70 D2 var.* Tilimsen, Tlemsen.
NW Algeria
Tlemsen *see* Tlemcen
Toamasina *79 G3 var.* Tamatave.
Toamasina, E Madagascar
Toba, Danau *138 B3 lake* Sumatera,
W Indonesia
Tobago *55 H5 island* NE Trinidad and
Tobago
Toba Kakar Range *134 B2 mountain
range* NW Pakistan
Tobol *114 C4 Kaz.* Tobyl. *river*
Kazakhstan/Russian Federation
Tobol'sk *114 C3* Tyumenskaya Oblast',
C Russian Federation
Tobruch/Tobruk *see* Ţubruq
Tobyl *see* Tobol
Tocantins *63 E3 off.* Estado do
Tocantins. *state* C Brazil
Tocantins *63 E3 off.* Estado do
Tocantins. *region* C Brazil
Tocantins, Estado do *see* Tocantins
Tocantins, Rio *63 F2 river* N Brazil
Tocoa *52 D2* Colón, N Honduras
Tocopilla *64 B2* Antofagasta, N Chile
Todi *96 C4* Umbria, C Italy
Todos os Santos, Baía de *63 G3 bay*
E Brazil
Toetoes Bay *151 B8 bay* South Island,
New Zealand
Tofua *145 E4 island* Ha'apai Group,
C Tonga
Togo *75 E4 off.* Togolese Republic; *prev.*
French Togoland. *country* W Africa

TOGO
West Africa

Official name The Togolese Republic
Formation 1960 / 1960
Capital Lomé
Population 6.5 million / 310 people
per sq mile (120 people per sq km) / 36%
Total area 21,924 sq. miles (56,785 sq. km)
Languages French*, Ewe, Kabye, Gurma
Religions Traditional beliefs 50%,
Christian 35%, Muslim 15%
Ethnic mix Ewe 46%, Other African 41%,
Kabye 12%, European 1%
Government Presidential system
Currency CFA franc = 100 centimes
Literacy rate 53%
Calorie consumption 2345 calories

Togolese Republic *see* Togo
Tojikiston, Jumhurii *see* Tajikistan
Tokanui *151 B7* Southland, South Island,
New Zealand
Tokar *72 C4 var.* Ţawkar. Red Sea,
NE Sudan
Tokat *116 D3* Tokat, N Turkey
Tokelau *145 E3 NZ overseas territory*
W Polynesia
Tőketerebes *see* Trebišov
Tokio *see* Tōkyō
Tokmak *123 G2 Kir.* Tokmok.
Chuyskaya Oblast', N Kyrgyzstan
Tokmak *109 G4 var.* Velykyy Tokmak.
Zaporiz'ka Oblast', SE Ukraine

Tokmok see Tokmak
Tokoroa 150 D3 Waikato, North Island, New Zealand
Tokounou 74 C4 C Guinea
Tokushima 131 C6 var. Tokusima. Tokushima, Shikoku, SW Japan
Tōkyō 130 A1 var. Tokio. country capital (Japan) (Japan) Tōkyō, Honshū, S Japan
Tōkyō-wan 130 A2 bay S Japan
Tolbukhin see Dobrich
Toledo 92 D3 anc. Toletum. Castilla-La Mancha, C Spain
Toledo 40 D3 Ohio, N USA
Toledo Bend Reservoir 49 G3 reservoir Louisiana/Texas, SW USA
Toletum see Toledo
Toliara 79 F4 var. Toliary; prev. Tuléar. Toliara, SW Madagascar
Toliary see Toliara
Tolmein see Tolmin
Tolmin 95 D7 Ger. Tolmein, It. Tolmino. W Slovenia
Tolmino see Tolmin
Tolna 99 C7 Ger. Tolnau. Tolna, S Hungary
Tolnau see Tolna
Tolochin see Talachyn
Tolosa 93 E1 País Vasco, N Spain
Tolosa see Toulouse
Toluca 51 F4 var. Toluca de Lerdo. México, S Mexico
Toluca de Lerdo see Toluca
Tol'yatti 111 C6 prev. Stavropol'. Samarskaya Oblast', W Russian Federation
Tomah 40 B2 Wisconsin, N USA
Tomakomai 130 D2 Hokkaidō, NE Japan
Tomar 92 B3 Santarém, W Portugal
Tomaschow see Tomaszów Mazowiecki
Tomaschow see Tomaszów Lubelski
Tomaszów see Tomaszów Mazowiecki
Tomaszów Lubelski 98 E4 Ger. Tomaschow. Lubelskie, E Poland
Tomaszów Mazowiecka see Tomaszów Mazowiecki
Tomaszów Mazowiecki 98 D4 var. Tomaszów Mazowiecka; prev. Tomaszów, Ger. Tomaschow. Łódzkie, C Poland
Tombigbee River 42 C3 river Alabama/Mississippi, S USA
Tombouctou 75 E3 Eng. Timbuktu. Tombouctou, N Mali
Tombua 78 A2 Port. Porto Alexandre. Namibe, SW Angola
Tomelloso 93 E3 Castilla-La Mancha, C Spain
Tomini, Gulf of 139 E4 var. Teluk Tomini; prev. Teluk Gorontalo. bay Sulawesi, C Indonesia
Tomini, Teluk see Tomini, Gulf of
Tomsk 114 D4 Tomskaya Oblast', C Russian Federation
Tomür Feng see Pobedy, Pik
Tonezh see Tonyezh
Tonga 145 E4 off. Kingdom of Tonga, var. Friendly Islands. country SW Pacific Ocean

TONGA
Australasia & Oceania

Official name Kingdom of Tonga
Formation 1970 / 1970
Capital Nuku'alofa
Population 116,921 / 421 people per sq mile (162 people per sq km) / 34%
Total area 289 sq. miles (748 sq. km)
Languages English*, Tongan*
Religions Free Wesleyan 41%, Other 17%, Roman Catholic 16%, Church of Jesus Christ of Latter-day Saints 14%, Free Church of Tonga 12%
Ethnic mix Tongan 98%, Other 2%
Government Monarchy
Currency Pa'anga (Tongan dollar) = 100 seniti
Literacy rate 99%
Calorie consumption Not available

Tonga, Kingdom of see Tonga
Tongatapu 145 E5 island Tongatapu Group, S Tonga
Tongatapu Group 145 E5 island group S Tonga

Tonga Trench 143 E3 trench S Pacific Ocean
Tongchuan 128 C4 Shaanxi, C China
Tongeren 87 D6 Fr. Tongres. Limburg, NE Belgium
Tongking, Gulf of 128 B7 Chin. Beibu Wan, Vtn. Vinh Băc Bô. gulf China/Vietnam
Tongliao 127 G2 Nei Mongol Zizhiqu, N China
Tongres see Tongeren
Tongshan see Xuzhou, Jiangsu, China
Tongtian He 126 C4 river C China
Tonj 73 B5 Warab, SW Sudan
Tônlé Sap 137 D5 Eng. Great Lake. lake W Cambodia
Tonopah 47 C6 Nevada, W USA
Tonyezh 107 C7 Rus. Tonezh. Homyel'skaya Voblasts', SE Belarus
Tooele 44 B4 Utah, W USA
Toowoomba 149 E5 Queensland, E Australia
Topeka 45 F4 state capital Kansas, C USA
Toplicza see Topliţa
Topliţa 108 C3 Ger. Töplitz, Hung. Maroshévíz; prev. Topliţa Română, Hung. Oláh-Toplicza, Toplicza. Harghita, C Romania
Topliţa Română/Töplitz see Topliţa
Topol'čany 99 C6 Hung. Nagytapolcsány. Nitriansky Kraj, W Slovakia
Topolovgrad 104 D3 prev. Kavakli. Khaskovo, S Bulgaria
Topolya see Bačka Topola
Top Springs Roadhouse 146 E3 Northern Territory, N Australia
Torda see Turda
Torez 109 H3 Donets'ka Oblast', SE Ukraine
Torgau 94 D4 Sachsen, E Germany
Torhout 87 A5 West-Vlaanderen, W Belgium
Torino 96 A2 Eng. Turin. Piemonte, NW Italy
Tornacum see Tournai
Torneå see Tornio
Torneträsk 84 C3 lake N Sweden
Tornio 84 D4 Swe. Torneå. Lappi, NW Finland
Tornionjoki 84 D3 river Finland/Sweden
Tornionjoki 84 D3 river Finland/Sweden
Toro 92 D2 Castilla-León, N Spain
Toronto 38 D5 province capital Ontario, S Canada
Torquay 89 C7 SW England, United Kingdom
Torrance 46 D2 California, W USA
Torre, Alto da 92 B3 mountain C Portugal
Torre del Greco 97 D5 Campania, S Italy
Torrejón de Ardoz 93 E3 Madrid, C Spain
Torrelavega 92 D1 Cantabria, N Spain
Torrens, Lake 149 A6 salt lake South Australia
Torrent 93 F3 Cas. Torrente, var. Torrent de l'Horta. País Valenciano, E Spain
Torrent de l'Horta/Torrente see Torrent
Torreón 50 D3 Coahuila, NE Mexico
Torres Strait 148 C1 strait Australia/Papua New Guinea
Torres Vedras 92 B3 Lisboa, C Portugal
Torrington 44 D3 Wyoming, C USA
Tórshavn 83 F5 Dan. Thorshavn. Dependent territory capital Faeroe Islands
To'rtko'l 122 D2 var. Türtkül, Rus. Turtkul'; prev. Petroaleksandrovsk. Qoraqalpog'iston Respublikasi, W Uzbekistan
Tortoise Islands see Colón, Archipiélago de
Tortosa 93 F2 anc. Dertosa. Cataluña, E Spain
Tortue, Montagne 59 H3 mountain range C French Guiana
Tortuga, Isla see La Tortuga, Isla
Toruń 98 C3 Ger. Thorn. Toruń, Kujawsko-pomorskie, C Poland
Tõrva 106 D3 Ger. Törwa. Valgamaa, S Estonia
Törwa see Tõrva
Torzhok 110 B4 Tverskaya Oblast', W Russian Federation
Tosa-wan 131 B7 bay SW Japan

Toscana 96 B3 Eng. Tuscany. region C Italy
Toscano, Archipelago 96 B4 Eng. Tuscan Archipelago. island group C Italy
Toshkent 123 E2 Eng./Rus. Tashkent. country capital (Uzbekistan) Toshkent Viloyati, E Uzbekistan
Totana 93 E4 Murcia, SE Spain
Tot'ma see Sukhona
Totness 59 G3 Coronie, N Suriname
Tottori 131 B6 Tottori, Honshū, SW Japan
Touâjîl 74 C2 Tiris Zemmour, N Mauritania
Touggourt 71 E2 NE Algeria
Toukoto 74 C3 Kayes, W Mali
Toul 90 D3 Meurthe-et-Moselle, NE France
Toulon 91 D6 anc. Telo Martius, Tilio Martius. Var, SE France
Toulouse 91 B6 anc. Tolosa. Haute-Garonne, S France
Toungoo see Taungoo
Touraine 90 B4 cultural region C France
Tourane see Đà Năng
Tourcoing 90 C2 Nord, N France
Tournai 87 A6 var. Tournay, Dut. Doornik; anc. Tornacum. Hainaut, SW Belgium
Tournay see Tournai
Tours 90 B4 anc. Caesarodunum, Turoni. Indre-et-Loire, C France
Tovarkovskiy 111 B5 Tul'skaya Oblast', W Russian Federation
Tower Island see Genovesa, Isla
Townsville 148 D3 Queensland, NE Australia
Towoeti Meer see Towuti, Danau
Towraghoudi 122 D4 Herāt, NW Afghanistan
Towson 41 F4 Maryland, NE USA
Towuti, Danau 139 E4 Dut. Towoeti Meer. lake Sulawesi, C Indonesia
Toyama 131 C5 Toyama, Honshū, SW Japan
Toyama-wan 131 B5 bay W Japan
Toyohara see Yuzhno-Sakhalinsk
Toyota 131 C6 Aichi, Honshū, SW Japan
Tozeur 71 E2 var. Tawzar. W Tunisia
Trâblous see Tripoli
Trabzon 117 E2 Eng. Trebizond; anc. Trapezus. Trabzon, NE Turkey
Traiectum ad Mosam/Traiectum Tungorum see Maastricht
Traiskirchen 95 E6 Niederösterreich, NE Austria
Trajani Portus see Civitavecchia
Trajectum ad Rhenum see Utrecht
Trakai 107 C5 Ger. Traken, Pol. Troki. Vilnius, SE Lithuania
Traken see Trakai
Tralee 89 A6 Ir. Trá Li. SW Ireland
Tralles Aydin see Aydin
Trang 137 C7 Trang, S Thailand
Transantarctic Mountains 154 B3 mountain range Antarctica
Transilvania see Transylvania
Transilvaniei, Alpi see Carpaţii Meridionali
Transjordan see Jordan
Transsylvanische Alpen/Transylvanian Alps see Carpaţii Meridionali
Transylvania 108 B4 Eng. Ardeal, Transilvania, Ger. Siebenbürgen, Hung. Erdély. cultural region NW Romania
Transylvanian Alps 108 B4 var. Alpi Transilvaniei, Carpaţii Sudici, Eng. South Carpathians, Transylvanian Alps, Ger. Südkarpaten, Transsylvanische Alpen, Hung. Déli-Kárpátok, Erdélyi-Havasok. mountain range C Romania
Trapani 97 B7 anc. Drepanum. Sicilia, Italy, C Mediterranean Sea
Trâpeăng Vêng 137 D5 Kâmpóng Thum, C Cambodia
Trapezus see Trabzon
Traralgon 149 C7 Victoria, SE Australia
Trasimenische See see Trasimeno, Lago
Trasimeno, Lago 96 C4 Eng. Lake of Perugia, Ger. Trasimenischersee. lake C Italy
Traù see Trogir
Traverse City 40 C2 Michigan, N USA
Tra Vinh 137 D6 var. Phu Vinh. Tra Vinh, S Vietnam

Travis, Lake 49 F3 reservoir Texas, SW USA
Travnik 100 C4 Federacija Bosna I Hercegovina, C Bosnia and Herzegovina
Trbovlje 95 E7 Ger. Trifail. C Slovenia
Treasure State see Montana
Třebíč 99 B5 Ger. Trebitsch. Vysočina, C Czech Republic
Trebinje 101 C5 Republika Srpska, S Bosnia and Herzegovina
Trebišov 99 D6 Hung. Tőketerebes. Košický Kraj, E Slovakia
Trebitsch see Třebíč
Trebnitz see Trzebnica
Tree Planters State see Nebraska
Trélazé 90 B4 Maine-et-Loire, NW France
Trelew 65 C6 Chubut, SE Argentina
Tremelo 87 C5 Vlaams Brabant, C Belgium
Trenčín 99 C5 Ger. Trentschin, Hung. Trencsén. Trenčiansky Kraj, W Slovakia
Trencsén see Trenčín
Trengganu, Kuala see Kuala Terengganu
Trenque Lauquen 64 C4 Buenos Aires, E Argentina
Trent see Trento
Trento 96 C2 Eng. Trent, Ger. Trient; anc. Tridentum. Trentino-Alto Adige, N Italy
Trenton 41 F4 state capital New Jersey, NE USA
Trentschin see Trenčín
Tres Arroyos 65 D5 Buenos Aires, E Argentina
Treskavica 100 C4 mountain range SE Bosnia and Herzegovina
Tres Tabernae see Saverne
Treves/Trèves see Trier
Treviso 96 C2 anc. Tarvisium. Veneto, NE Italy
Trichinopoly see Tiruchchirāppalli
Trichūr 132 C3 var. Thrissur. Kerala, SW India
Tridentum/Trient see Trento
Trier 95 A5 Eng. Treves, Fr. Trèves; anc. Augusta Treverorum. Rheinland-Pfalz, SW Germany
Triesen 94 E2 SW Liechtenstein
Triesenberg 94 E2 SW Liechtenstein Europe
Trieste 96 D2 Slvn. Trst. Friuli-Venezia Giulia, NE Italy
Trifail see Trbovlje
Tríkala 104 B4 prev. Trikkala. Thessalía, C Greece
Trikkala see Tríkala
Trimontium see Plovdiv
Trinacria see Sicilia
Trincomalee 132 D3 var. Trinkomali. Eastern Province, NE Sri Lanka
Trindade, Ilha da 67 C5 island Brazil, W Atlantic Ocean
Trinidad 61 F3 Beni, N Bolivia
Trinidad 64 D4 Flores, S Uruguay
Trinidad 44 D5 Colorado, C USA
Trinidad 55 H5 island C Trinidad and Tobago
Trinidad and Tobago 55 H5 off. Republic of Trinidad and Tobago. country SE West Indies

TRINIDAD & TOBAGO
West Indies

Official name Republic of Trinidad and Tobago
Formation 1962 / 1962
Capital Port-of-Spain
Population 1.3 million / 656 people per sq mile (253 people per sq km) / 76%
Total area 1980 sq. miles (5128 sq. km)
Languages English Creole, English*, Hindi, French, Spanish
Religions Roman Catholic 32%, Hindu 24%, Protestant 14%, Anglican 14%, Other and nonreligious 9%, Muslim 7%
Ethnic mix East Indian 40%, Black 40%, Mixed race 18%, Other 1%, White and Chinese 1%
Government Parliamentary system
Currency Trinidad and Tobago dollar = 100 cents
Literacy rate 99%
Calorie consumption 2732 calories

Trinidad and Tobago, Republic of *see* Trinidad and Tobago
Trinité, Montagnes de la *59 H3 mountain range* C French Guiana
Trinity River *49 G3 river* Texas, SW USA
Trinkomali *see* Trincomalee
Trípoli *105 B6 prev.* Trípolis. Pelo*ó*nnisos, S Greece
Tripoli *118 B4 var.* Tarābulus, Tarābulus ash Shām, Trāblous; *anc.* Tripolis. N Lebanon
Tripoli *see* Tarābulus
Trípolis *see* Trípoli, Greece
Tripolis *see* Tripoli, Lebanon
Tristan da Cunha *69 B7 dependency of Saint Helena* SE Atlantic Ocean
Triton Island *128 B7 island* S Paracel Islands
Trivandrum *132 C3 var.* Thiruvanathapuram, Tiruvantapuram. *state capital* Kerala, SW India
Trnava *99 C6 Ger.* Tyrnau, *Hung.* Nagyszombat. Trnavský Kraj, W Slovakia
Trnovo *see* Veliko Tŭrnovo
Trogir *100 B4 It.* Traù. Split-Dalmacija, S Croatia
Troglav *100 B4 mountain* Bosnia and Herzegovina/Croatia
Trois-Rivières *39 E4* Québec, SE Canada
Troki *see* Trakai
Trollhättan *85 B6* Västra Götaland, S Sweden
Tromsø *84 C2 Fin.* Tromssa. Troms, N Norway
Tromssa *see* Tromsø
Trondheim *84 B4 Ger.* Drontheim; *prev.* Nidaros, Trondhjem. Sør-Trøndelag, S Norway
Trondheimsfjorden *84 B4 fjord* S Norway
Trondhjem *see* Trondheim
Troódos *102 C5 var.* Troodos Mountains. *mountain range* C Cyprus
Troodos Mountains *see* Troódos
Troppau *see* Opava
Troy *42 D3* Alabama, S USA
Troy *41 F3* New York, NE USA
Troyan *104 C2* Lovech, N Bulgaria
Troyes *90 D3 anc.* Augustobona Tricassium. Aube, N France
Trst *see* Trieste
Trstenik *100 E4* Serbia, C Serbia
Trucial States *see* United Arab Emirates
Trujillo *52 D2* Colón, NW Honduras
Trujillo *60 D3* La Libertad, NW Peru
Trujillo *92 C3* Extremadura, W Spain
Truk Islands *see* Chuuk Islands
Trūn *104 B2* Pernik, W Bulgaria
Truro *39 F4* Nova Scotia, SE Canada
Truro *89 C7* SW England, United Kingdom
Trzcianka *98 B3 Ger.* Schönlanke. Pila, Wielkopolskie, C Poland
Trzebnica *98 C4 Ger.* Trebnitz. Dolnośląskie, SW Poland
Tsalka *117 F2* S Georgia Asia
Tsamkong *see* Zhanjiang
Tsangpo *see* Brahmaputra
Tsarevo *104 E2 prev.* Michurin. Burgas, E Bulgaria
Tsarigrad *see* Istanbul
Tsaritsyn *see* Volgograd
Tschakathurn *see* Čakovec
Tschaslau *see* Čáslav
Tschenstochau *see* Częstochowa
Tsefat *119 B5 var.* Safed, *Ar.* Safad; *prev.* Zefat. Northern, N Israel
Tselinograd *see* Astana
Tsetsen Khan *see* Öndörhaan
Tsetserleg *126 D2* Arhangay, C Mongolia
Tshela *77 B6* Bas-Congo, W Dem. Rep. Congo
Tshikapa *77 C7* Kasai-Occidental, SW Dem. Rep. Congo
Tshuapa *77 D6 river* C Dem. Rep. Congo
Tshwane *78 D4 var.* Epitoli; *prev.* Pretoria. *country capital* (South Africa-administrative capital) Gauteng, NE South Africa
Tsinan *see* Jinan
Tsing Hai *see* Qinghai Hu, China
Tsinghai *see* Qinghai, China
Tsingtao/Tsingtau *see* Qingdao
Tsinkiang *see* Quanzhou
Tsintao *see* Qingdao
Tsitsihar *see* Qiqihar

Tsu *131 C6 var.* Tu. Mie, Honshū, SW Japan
Tsugaru-kaikyo *130 C3 strait* N Japan
Tsumeb *78 B3* Otjikoto, N Namibia
Tsuruga *131 C6 var.* Turuga. Fukui, Honshū, SW Japan
Tsuruoka *130 D4 var.* Turuoka. Yamagata, Honshū, C Japan
Tsushima *131 A7 var.* Tsushima-tō, Tusima. *island group* SW Japan
Tsushima-tō *see* Tsushima
Tsyerakhowka *107 D8 Rus.* Terekhovka. Homyel'skaya Voblasts', SE Belarus
Tsyurupinsk *see* Tsyurupyns'k
Tsyurupyns'k *109 E4 Rus.* Tsyurupinsk. Khersons'ka Oblast', S Ukraine
Tu *see* Tsu
Tuamotu, Archipel des *see* Tuamotu, Îles
Tuamotu Fracture Zone *143 H3 fracture zone* E Pacific Ocean
Tuamotu Islands *145 H4 var.* Archipel des Tuamotu, Dangerous Archipelago, Tuamotu Islands. *island group* N French Polynesia
Tuamotu Islands *see* Tuamotu, Îles
Tuapi *53 E2* Región Autónoma Atlántico Norte, NE Nicaragua
Tuapse *111 A7* Krasnodarskiy Kray, SW Russian Federation
Tuba City *48 B1* Arizona, SW USA
Tubbergen *86 E3* Overijssel, E Netherlands
Tubeke *see* Tubize
Tubize *87 B6 Dut.* Tubeke. Walloon Brabant, C Belgium
Tubmanburg *74 C5* NW Liberia
Tubruq *71 H2 Eng.* Tobruk, *It.* Tobruch. NE Libya
Tubuai, Îles/Tubuai Islands *see* Australes, Îles
Tucker's Town *42 B5* E Bermuda
Tuckum *see* Tukums
Tucson *48 B3* Arizona, SW USA
Tucumán *see* San Miguel de Tucumán
Tucumcari *49 E2* New Mexico, SW USA
Tucupita *59 E2* Delta Amacuro, NE Venezuela
Tucuruí, Represa de *63 F2 reservoir* NE Brazil
Tudela *93 E2 Basq.* Tutera; *anc.* Tutela. Navarra, N Spain
Tudmur *118 C3 var.* Tadmur, Tamar, *Gk.* Palmyra, *Bibl.* Tadmor. Ḥimş, C Syria
Tuguegarao *139 E1* Luzon, N Philippines
Tuktoyaktuk *37 E3* Northwest Territories, NW Canada
Tukums *106 C3 Ger.* Tuckum. Tukums, W Latvia
Tula *111 B5* Tul'skaya Oblast', W Russian Federation
Tulancingo *51 E4* Hidalgo, C Mexico
Tulare Lake Bed *47 C7 salt flat* California, W USA
Tulcán *60 B1* Carchi, N Ecuador
Tulcea *108 D5* Tulcea, E Romania
Tul'chin *see* Tul'chyn
Tul'chyn *108 D3 Rus.* Tul'chin. Vinnyts'ka Oblast', C Ukraine
Tuléar *see* Toliara
Tulia *49 E2* Texas, SW USA
Tülkarm *119 D7* West Bank, Israel
Tulle *91 C5 anc.* Tutela. Corrèze, C France
Tulln *95 E6 var.* Oberhollabrunn. Niederösterreich, NE Austria
Tully *148 D3* Queensland, NE Australia
Tulsa *49 G1* Oklahoma, C USA
Tuluá *58 B3* Valle del Cauca, W Colombia
Tulun *115 E4* Irkutskaya Oblast', S Russian Federation
Tumaco *58 A4* Nariño, SW Colombia
Tumba, Lac *see* Ntomba, Lac
Tumbes *60 A2* Tumbes, NW Peru
Tumkür *132 C2* Karnātaka, W India
Tumuc-Humac Mountains *63 E1 var.* Serra Tumucumaque. *mountain range* N South America
Tumucumaque, Serra *see* Tumuc-Humac Mountains
Tunca Nehri *see* Tundzha
Tunduru *73 C8* Ruvuma, S Tanzania
Tundzha *104 D3 Turk.* Tunca Nehri. *river* Bulgaria/Turkey
Tungabhadra Reservoir *132 C2 lake* S India

Tungaru *145 E2 prev.* Gilbert Islands. *island group* W Kiribati
T'ung-shan *see* Xuzhou
Tungsten *36 D4* Northwest Territories, W Canada
Tung-t'ing Hu *see* Dongting Hu
Tunis *71 E1 var.* Tūnis. *country capital* (Tunisia) (Tunisia) NE Tunisia
Tunis, Golfe de *102 D3 Ar.* Khalīj Tūnis. *gulf* NE Tunisia
Tunisia *71 F2 off.* Tunisian Republic, *Ar.* Al Jumhūrīyah at Tūnisīyah, *Fr.* République Tunisienne. *country* N Africa

TUNISIA
North Africa

Official name The Tunisian Republic
Formation 1956 / 1956
Capital Tunis
Population 10.3 million / 172 people per sq mile (66 people per sq km) / 64%
Total area 63,169 sq. miles (163,610 sq. km)
Languages Arabic*, French
Religions Muslim (mainly Sunni) 98%, Christian 1%, Jewish 1%
Ethnic mix Arab and Berber 98%, Jewish 1%, European 1%
Government Presidential system
Currency Tunisian dinar = 1000 millimes
Literacy rate 74%
Calorie consumption 3238 calories

Tunisian Republic *see* Tunisia
Tunisienne, République *see* Tunisia
Tūnisīyah, Al Jumhūrīyah at *see* Tunisia
Tūnis, Khalīj *see* Tunis, Golfe de
Tunja *58 B3* Boyacá, C Colombia
Tuong Buong *see* Tương Đương
Tương Đương *136 D4 var.* Tuong Buong. Nghê An, N Vietnam
Tüp *see* Tyup
Tupelo *42 C2* Mississippi, S USA
Tupiza *61 G5* Potosí, S Bolivia
Turabah *121 B5* Makkah, W Saudi Arabia
Turangi *150 D4* Waikato, North Island, New Zealand
Turan Lowland *122 C2 var.* Turan Plain, *Kaz.* Turan Oypaty, *Rus.* Turanskaya Nizmennost', *Turk.* Turan Pesligi, *Uzb.* Turan Pasttekisligi. *plain* C Asia
Turan Oypaty/Turan Pesligi/Turan Plain/Turanskaya Nizmennost' *see* Turan Lowland
Turan Pasttekisligi *see* Turan Lowland
Ţurayf *120 A3* Al Ḩudūd ash Shamālīyah, NW Saudi Arabia
Turba *see* Teruel
Turbat *134 A3* Baluchistān, SW Pakistan
Turda *108 B4 Ger.* Thorenburg, *Hung.* Torda. Cluj, NW Romania
Turek *98 C3* Wielkopolskie, C Poland
Turfan *see* Turpan
Turin *see* Torino
Turkana, Lake *73 C6 var.* Lake Rudolf. *lake* N Kenya
Turkestan *114 B5 Kaz.* Türkistan. Yuzhnyy Kazakhstan, S Kazakhstan
Turkey *116 B3 off.* Republic of Turkey, *Turk.* Türkiye Cumhuriyeti. *country* SW Asia

TURKEY
Asia / Europe

Official name Republic of Turkey
Formation 1923 / 1939
Capital Ankara
Population 75.2 million / 253 people per sq mile (98 people per sq km) / 67%
Total area 301,382 sq. miles (780,580 sq. km)
Languages Turkish*, Kurdish, Arabic, Circassian, Armenian, Greek, Georgian, Ladino
Religions Muslim (mainly Sunni) 99%, Other 1%
Ethnic mix Turkish 70%, Kurdish 20%, Other 8%, Arab 2%
Government Parliamentary system
Currency new Turkish lira = 100 kurus
Literacy rate 98%
Calorie consumption 3357 calories

Turkey, Republic of *see* Turkey
Turkish Republic of Northern Cyprus *102 D5 disputed territory* Cyprus
Türkistan *see* Turkestan
Türkiye Cumhuriyeti *see* Turkey
Türkmenabat *122 D3 prev. Rus.* Chardzhev, Chardzhou, Chardzhui, Lenin-Turkmenski, *Turkm.* Chärjew. Lebap Welaýaty, E Turkmenistan
Türkmen Aylagy *122 B2 Rus.* Turkmenskiy Zaliv. *lake gulf* W Turkmenistan
Türkmenbashi *see* Türkmenbaşy
Türkmenbaşy *122 B2 Rus.* Turkmenbashi; *prev.* Krasnovodsk. Balkan Welaýaty, W Turkmenistan
Türkmenbaşy Aylagy *122 A2 prev. Rus.* Krasnovodskiy Zaliv, *Turkm.* Krasnowodsk Aylagy. *lake Gulf* W Turkmenistan
Turkmenistan *122 B2 ; prev.* Turkmenskaya Soviet Socialist Republic. *country* C Asia

TURKMENISTAN
Central Asia

Official name Turkmenistan
Formation 1991 / 1991
Capital Ashgabat
Population 5 million / 27 people per sq mile (10 people per sq km) / 46%
Total area 188,455 sq. miles (488,100 sq. km)
Languages Turkmen*, Uzbek, Russian, Kazakh, Tatar
Religions Sunni Muslim 87%, Orthodox Christian 11%, Other 2%
Ethnic mix Turkmen 77%, Uzbek 9%, Russian 7%, Other 4%, Kazakh 2%, Tatar 1%
Government One-party state
Currency Manat = 100 tenge
Literacy rate 99%
Calorie consumption 2742 calories

Turkmenskaya Soviet Socialist Republic *see* Turkmenistan
Turkmenskiy Zaliv *see* Türkmen Aylagy
Turks and Caicos Islands *55 E2 UK dependent territory* N West Indies
Turku *85 D6 Swe.* Åbo. Länsi-Suomi, SW Finland
Turlock *47 B6* California, W USA
Turnagain, Cape *150 D4 headland* North Island, New Zealand
Turnau *see* Turnov
Turnhout *87 C5* Antwerpen, N Belgium
Turnov *98 B4 Ger.* Turnau. Liberecký Kraj, N Czech Republic
Tŭrnovo *see* Veliko Tŭrnovo
Turnu Măgurele *108 B5 var.* Turnu-Măgurele. Teleorman, S Romania
Turnu Severin *see* Drobeta-Turnu Severin
Turócszentmárton *see* Martin
Turoni *see* Tours
Turpan *126 C3 var.* Turfan. Xinjiang Uygur Zizhiqu, NW China
Turpan Depression *see* Turpan Pendi
Turpan Pendi *126 C3 Eng.* Turpan Depression. *depression* NW China
Turpentine Isle *see* North'kola'l
Türtkül/Turtkul' *see* To'rtkol'
Turuga *see* Tsuruga
Turuoka *see* Tsuruoka
Tuscaloosa *42 C2* Alabama, S USA
Tuscan Archipelago *see* Toscano, Archipelago
Tuscany *see* Toscana
Tusima *see* Tsushima
Tutela *see* Tulle, France
Tutela *see* Tudela, Spain
Tutera *see* Tudela
Tuticorin *132 C3* Tamil Nādu, SE India
Tutrakan *104 D1* Silistra, NE Bulgaria
Tutuila *145 F4 island* W American Samoa
Tuvalu *145 E3 prev.* Ellice Islands. *country* SW Pacific Ocean

TUVALU
Australasia & Oceania

Official name Tuvalu
Formation 1978 / 1978
Capital Fongafale, on Funafuti Atoll
Population 11,992 / 1199 people

TUVALU
(continued)
per sq mile (461 people per sq km) / 57%
Total area 10 sq. miles (26 sq. km)
Languages English*, Tuvaluan, Kiribati
Religions Church of Tuvalu 97%,
Baha'i 1%, Seventh-day Adventist 1%,
Other 1%
Ethnic mix Polynesian 92%, Other 6%,
Kiribati 2%
Government Nonparty system
Currency Australian dollar and Tuvaluan
dollar = 100 cents
Literacy rate 98%
Calorie consumption Not available

Tuwayq, Jabal *121 C5 mountain range*
C Saudi Arabia
Tuxpan *50 D4* Jalisco, C Mexico
Tuxpan *50 D4* Nayarit, C Mexico
Tuxpán *51 F4 var.* Tuxpán de Rodríguez
Cano. Veracruz-Llave, E Mexico
Tuxpán de Rodríguez Cano *see* Tuxpán
Tuxtepec *51 F4 var.* San Juan Bautista
Tuxtepec. Oaxaca, S Mexico
Tuxtla *51 G5 var.* Tuxtla Gutiérrez.
Chiapas, SE Mexico
Tuxtla *see* San Andrés Tuxtla
Tuxtla Gutiérrez *see* Tuxtla
Tuy Hoa *137 E5* Phu Yên, S Vietnam
Tuz, Lake *116 C3 lake* C Turkey
Tver' *110 B4 prev.* Kalinin. Tverskaya
Oblast', W Russian Federation
Tverya *119 B5 var.* Tiberias; *prev.*
Teverya. Northern, N Israel
Twin Falls *46 D4* Idaho, NW USA
Tyan'-Shan' *see* Tien Shan
Tychy *99 D5 Ger.* Tichau. Śląskie,
S Poland
Tyler *49 G3* Texas, SW USA
Tylos *see* Bahrain
Tympáki *105 C8 var.* Timbaki;
prev. Timbákion. Kriti, Greece,
E Mediterranean Sea
Tynda *115 F4* Amurskaya Oblast',
SE Russian Federation
Tyne *88 D4 river* N England, United
Kingdom
Tyôsi *see* Chôshi
Tyras *see* Dniester
Tyre *see* Soûr
Tyrnau *see* Trnava
Týrnavos *104 B4 var.* Tírnavos.
Thessalía, C Greece
Tyrol *see* Tirol
Tyros *see* Bahrain
Tyrrhenian Sea *97 B6 It.* Mare Tirreno.
sea N Mediterranean Sea
Tyumen' *114 C3* Tyumenskaya Oblast',
C Russian Federation
Tyup *123 G2 Kir.* Tüp. Issyk-Kul'skaya
Oblast', NE Kyrgyzstan
Tywyn *89 C6* W Wales, United Kingdom
Tzekung *see* Zigong
Tziá *105 C6 prev.* Kéa, Kéos; *anc.* Ceos.
island Kykládes, Aegean Sea

U

UAE *see* United Arab Emirates
Uanle Uen *see* Wanlaweyn
Uaupés, Rio *see* Vaupés, Río
Ubangi-Shari *see* Central African
Republic
Ube *131 B7* Yamaguchi, Honshū,
SW Japan
Ubeda *93 E4* Andalucía, S Spain
Uberaba *63 F4* Minas Gerais, SE Brazil
Uberlândia *63 F4* Minas Gerais, SE Brazil
Ubol Rajadhani/Ubol Ratchathani *see*
Ubon Ratchathani
Ubon Ratchathani *137 D5 var.*
Muang Ubon, Ubol Rajadhani, Ubol
Ratchathani, Udon Ratchathani. Ubon
Ratchathani, E Thailand
Ubrique *92 D5* Andalucía, S Spain
Ubsu-Nur, Ozero *see* Uvs Nuur
Ucayali, Río *60 D3 river* C Peru
Uchiura-wan *130 D3 bay* NW Pacific
Ocean
Uchkuduk *see* Uchquduq
Uchquduq *122 D2 Rus.* Uchkuduk.
Navoiy Viloyati, N Uzbekistan
Uchtagan Gumy/Uchtagan, Peski *see*
Uçtagan Gumy

Uçtagan Gumy *122 C2 var.* Uchtagan
Gumy, *Rus.* Peski Uchtagan. *desert*
NW Turkmenistan
Udaipur *134 C3 prev.* Oodeypore.
Rājasthān, N India
Uddevalla *85 B6* Västra Götaland,
S Sweden
Udine *96 D2 anc.* Utina. Friuli-Venezia
Giulia, NE Italy
Udintsev Fracture Zone *154 A5 tectonic
feature* S Pacific Ocean
Udipi *see* Udupi
Udon Ratchathani *see* Ubon Ratchathani
Udon Thani *136 C4 var.* Ban Mak
Khaeng, Udorndhani. Udon Thani,
N Thailand
Udorndhani *see* Udon Thani
Udupi *132 B2 var.* Udipi. Karnātaka,
SW India
Uele *77 D5 var.* Welle. *river* NE Dem.
Rep. Congo
Uelzen *94 C3* Niedersachsen, N Germany
Ufa *111 D6* Respublika Bashkortostan,
W Russian Federation
Ugāle *106 C2* Ventspils, NW Latvia
Uganda *73 B6 off.* Republic of Uganda.
country E Africa

UGANDA
East Africa

Official name Republic of Uganda
Formation 1962 / 1962
Capital Kampala
Population 30.9 million / 401 people
per sq mile (155 people per sq km) / 12%
Total area 91,135 sq. miles (236,040 sq. km)
Languages English*, Luganda, Nkole,
Chiga, Lango, Acholi, Teso, Lugbara
Religions Roman Catholic 38%,
Protestant 33%, Traditional beliefs 13%,
Muslim (mainly Sunni) 8%, Other 8%
Ethnic mix Other 50%, Baganda 17%,
Banyakole 10%, Basoga 9%, Iteso 7%,
Bakiga 7%
Government Presidential system
Currency New Uganda shilling = 100 cents
Literacy rate 67%
Calorie consumption 2410 calories

Uganda, Republic of *see* Uganda
Uhorshchyna *see* Hungary
Uhuru Peak *see* Kilimanjaro
Uíge *78 B1 Port.* Carmona, Vila
Marechal Carmona. Uíge, NW Angola
Uinta Mountains *44 B4 mountain range*
Utah, W USA
Uitenhage *78 C5* Eastern Cape, S South
Africa
Uithoorn *86 C3* Noord-Holland,
C Netherlands
Ujda *see* Oujda
Ujelang Atoll *144 C1 var.* Wujlān. *atoll*
Ralik Chain, W Marshall Islands
Ujgradiska *see* Nova Gradiška
Újmoldova *see* Moldova Nouă
Ujungpandang *see* Makassar
Ujung Salang *see* Phuket
Újvidék *see* Novi Sad
UK *see* United Kingdom
Ukhta *114 C3* Respublika Komi,
NW Russian Federation
Ukiah *47 B5* California, W USA
Ukmergė *106 C4 Pol.* Wiłkomierz.
Vilnius, C Lithuania
Ukraina *see* Ukraine
Ukraine *108 C2 off.* Ukraine, *Rus.*
Ukraina, *Ukr.* Ukrayina; *prev.*
Ukrainian Soviet Socialist Republic,
Ukrainskay S.S.R. *country* SE Europe

UKRAINE
Eastern Europe

Official name Ukraine
Formation 1991 / 1991
Capital Kiev
Population 45.5 million / 195 people
per sq mile (75 people per sq km) / 67%
Total area 233,089 sq. miles
(603,700 sq. km)
Languages Ukrainian*, Russian, Tatar
Religions Christian (mainly
Orthodox) 95%, Other 5%
Ethnic mix Ukrainian 78%, Russian 17%,
Other 5%
Government Presidential system

UKRAINE
(continued)

Currency Hryvna = 100 kopiykas
Literacy rate 99%
Calorie consumption 3054 calories

Ukraine *see* Ukraine
Ukrainian Soviet Socialist Republic
see Ukraine
Ukrainskay S.S.R/Ukrayina *see* Ukraine
Ulaanbaatar *127 E2 Eng.* Ulan Bator;
prev. Urga. *country capital* (Mongolia)
(Mongolia) Töv, C Mongolia
Ulaangom *126 C2* Uvs, NW Mongolia
Ulan Bator *see* Ulaanbaatar
Ulanhad *see* Chifeng
Ulan-Ude *115 E4 prev.* Verkhneudinsk.
Respublika Buryatiya, S Russian
Federation
Uleåborg *see* Oulu
Uleälv *see* Oulujoki
Uleträsk *see* Oulujärvi
Ulft *86 E4* Gelderland, E Netherlands
Ullapool *88 C3* N Scotland, United
Kingdom
Ulm *95 B6* Baden-Württemberg,
S Germany
Ulsan *129 E4 Jap.* Urusan. SE South Korea
Ulster *89 B5 province* Northern Ireland,
United Kingdom/Ireland
Ulungur Hu *126 B2 lake* NW China
Uluru *147 D5 var.* Ayers Rock. *monolith*
Northern Territory, C Australia
Ulyanivka *109 E3 Rus.* Ul'yanovka.
Kirovohrads'ka Oblast', C Ukraine
Ul'yanovka *see* Ulyanivka
Ul'yanovsk *111 C5 prev.* Simbirsk.
Ul'yanovskaya Oblast', W Russian
Federation
Umán *51 H3* Yucatán, SE Mexico
Uman' *109 E3 Rus.* Uman. Cherkas'ka
Oblast', C Ukraine
Uman *see* Uman'
Umanak/Umanaq *see* Uummannaq
'Umān, Khalīj *see* Oman, Gulf of
'Umān, Salţanat *see* Oman
Umbrian-Machigian Mountains *see*
Umbro-Marchigiano, Appennino
Umbro-Marchigiano, Appennino
96 C3 Eng. Umbrian-Machigian
Mountains. *mountain range* C Italy
Umeå *84 C4* Västerbotten, N Sweden
Umeälven *84 C4 river* N Sweden
Umiat *36 D2* Alaska, USA
Umm Buru *72 A4* Western Darfur,
W Sudan
Umm Durmān *see* Omdurman
Umm Ruwaba *72 C4 var.* Umm
Ruwābah, Um Ruwāba. Northern
Kordofan, C Sudan
Umm Ruwābah *see* Umm Ruwaba
Umnak Island *36 A3 island* Aleutian
Islands, Alaska, USA
Um Ruwāba *see* Umm Ruwaba
Umtali *see* Mutare
Umtata *78 D5* Eastern Cape, SE South
Africa
Una *100 B3 river* Bosnia and
Herzegovina/Croatia
Unac *100 B3 river* W Bosnia and
Herzegovina
Unalaska Island *36 A3 island* Aleutian
Islands, Alaska, USA
'Unayzah *120 B4 var.* Anaiza. Al Qaşim,
C Saudi Arabia
Unci *see* Almería
Uncía *61 F4* Potosí, C Bolivia
Uncompahgre Peak *44 B5 mountain*
Colorado, C USA
Undur Khan *see* Öndörhaan
Ungaria *see* Hungary
Ungarisches Erzgebirge *see* Slovenské
rudohorie
Ungarn *see* Hungary
Ungava Bay *39 E1 bay* Québec, E Canada
Ungava Peninsula *38 D1 peninsula*
Québec, SE Canada
Ungeny *see* Ungheni
Ungheni *108 D3 Rus.* Ungeny.
W Moldova
Unguja *see* Zanzibar
Üngüz Angyrsyndaky Garagum *122 C2
Rus.* Zaunguzskiye Garagumy. *desert*
N Turkmenistan
Ungvár *see* Uzhhorod
Unimak Island *36 B3 island* Aleutian
Islands, Alaska, USA

Union *43 E1* South Carolina, SE USA
Union City *42 C1* Tennessee, S USA
Union of Myanmar *see* Burma
United Arab Emirates *121 C5 Ar.* Al
Imārāt al 'Arabīyah al Muttaḩidah,
abbrev. UAE; *prev.* Trucial States.
country SW Asia

UNITED ARAB EMIRATES
Southwest Asia

Official name United Arab Emirates
Formation 1971 / 1972
Capital Abu Dhabi
Population 4.8 million / 149 people
per sq mile (57 people per sq km) / 85%
Total area 32,000 sq. miles (82,880 sq. km)
Languages Arabic*, Farsi, Indian and
Pakistani languages, English
Religions Muslim (mainly Sunni) 96%,
Christian, Hindu, and other 4%
Ethnic mix Asian 60%, Emirian 25%,
Other Arab 12%, European 3%
Government Monarchy
Currency UAE dirham = 100 fils
Literacy rate 77%
Calorie consumption 3225 calories

United Arab Republic *see* Egypt
United Kingdom *89 B5 off.* United
Kingdom of Great Britain and
Northern Ireland, *abbrev.* UK. *country*
NW Europe

UNITED KINGDOM
Northwest Europe

Official name United Kingdom of Great
Britain and Northern Ireland
Formation 1707 / 1922
Capital London
Population 60 million / 643 people
per sq mile (248 people per sq km) / 89%
Total area 94,525 sq. miles
(244,820 sq. km)
Languages English*, Welsh* *(in Wales)*,
Scottish Gaelic, Irish Gaelic
Religions Anglican 45%, Roman
Catholic 9%, Presbyterian 4%, Other 42%
Ethnic mix English 80%, Scottish 9%,
West Indian, Asian, and other 5%,
Northern Irish 3%, Welsh 3%
Government Parliamentary system
Currency Pound sterling = 100 pence
Literacy rate 99%
Calorie consumption 3412 calories

United Kingdom of Great Britain and
Northern Ireland *see* United Kingdom
United Mexican States *see* Mexico
United Provinces *see* Uttar Pradesh
United States of America *35 B5 off.*
United States of America, *var.* America,
The States, *abbrev.* U.S., USA. *country*
North America

UNITED STATES
North America

Official name United States of America
Formation 1776 / 1959
Capital Washington D.C.
Population 304 million / 86 people
per sq mile (33 people per sq km) / 80%
Total area 3,717,792 sq. miles
(9,626,091 sq. km)
Languages English 82%, Spanish 11%,
other 7%
Religions Protestant 52%, Roman Catholic
25%, Muslim 2%, Jewish 2%, Other 19%
Ethnic mix White 62%, Hispanic 13%,
Black American/African 13%, Other 7%,
Asian 4%, Native American 1%
Government Presidential system
Currency US dollar = 100 cents
Literacy rate 99%
Calorie consumption 3774 calories

United States of America *see* United
States of America
Unst *88 D1 island* NE Scotland, United
Kingdom
Ünye *116 D2* Ordu, W Turkey
Upala *53 E4* Alajuela, NW Costa Rica
Upata *59 E2* Bolívar, E Venezuela
Upemba, Lac *77 D7 lake* SE Dem.
Rep. Congo

249

Upernavik *82 C2 var.* Upernivik. Kitaa,
C Greenland
Upernivik *see* Upernavik
Upington *78 C4* Northern Cape,
W South Africa
'Upolu *145 F4 island* SE Samoa
Upper Klamath Lake *46 A4 lake*
Oregon, NW USA
Upper Lough Erne *89 A5 lake*
SW Northern Ireland, United Kingdom
Upper Red Lake *45 F1 lake* Minnesota,
N USA
Upper Volta *see* Burkina Faso
Uppsala *85 C6* Uppsala, C Sweden
Uqsuqtuuq *see* Gjoa Haven
Ural *112 B3 Kaz.* Zayyq. *river*
Kazakhstan/Russian Federation
Ural Mountains *114 C3 var.* Ural'skiy
Khrebet, *Eng.* Ural Mountains.
mountain range Kazakhstan/Russian
Federation
Ural Mountains *see* Ural'skiye Gory
Ural'sk *114 B3 Kaz.* Oral. Zapadnyy
Kazakhstan, NW Kazakhstan
Ural'skiye Khrebet *see* Ural'skiye Gory
Uraricoera *62 D1* Roraima, N Brazil
Ura-Tyube *see* Ŭroteppa
Urbandale *45 F3* Iowa, C USA
Urdunn *see* Jordan
Uren' *111 C5* Nizhegorodskaya Oblast',
W Russian Federation
Urga *see* Ulaanbaatar
Urganch *122 D2 Rus.* Urgench; *prev.*
Novo-Urgench. Xorazm Viloyati,
W Uzbekistan
Urgench *see* Urganch
Urgut *123 E3* Samarqand Viloyati,
C Uzbekistan
Lake Urmia *121 C2 var.* Matianus, Sha
Hi, Urumi Yeh, *Eng.* Lake Urmia; *prev.*
Daryācheh-ye Reẓā'īyeh. *lake* NW Iran
Urmia, Lake *see* Orūmīyeh, Daryācheh-ye
Uroševac *see* Ferizaj
Ŭroteppa *123 E2 Rus.* Ura-Tyube.
NW Tajikistan
Uruapan *51 E4 var.* Uruapan del
Progreso. Michoacán, SW Mexico
Uruapan del Progreso *see* Uruapan
Uruguai, Rio *see* Uruguay
Uruguay *64 D4 off.* Oriental Republic
of Uruguay; *prev.* La Banda Oriental.
country E South America

URUGUAY
South America

Official name The Oriental Republic
of Uruguay
Formation 1828 / 1828
Capital Montevideo
Population 3.5 million / 52 people
per sq mile (20 people per sq km) / 93%
Total area 68,039 sq. miles (176,220 sq. km)
Languages Spanish*
Religions Roman Catholic 66%, Other
and nonreligious 30%,
Jewish 2%, Protestant 2%
Ethnic mix White 90%, Mestizo 6%,
Black 4%
Government Presidential system
Currency Uruguayan peso
= 100 centésimos
Literacy rate 98%
Calorie consumption 2828 calories

Uruguay *64 D3 var.* Rio Uruguai, Río
Uruguay. *river* E South America
Uruguay, Oriental Republic of *see*
Uruguay
Uruguay, Río *see* Uruguay
Urumchi *see* Ürümqi
Urumi Yeh *see* Orūmīyeh, Daryācheh-ye
Ürümqi *126 C3 var.* Tihwa, Urumchi,
Urumqi, Urumtsi, Wu-lu-k'o-mu-shi,
Wu-lu-mu-ch'i; *prev.* Ti-hua. Xinjiang
Uygur Zizhiqu, NW China
Urumtsi *see* Ürümqi
Urundi *see* Burundi
Urup, Ostrov *115 H4 island* Kuril'skiye
Ostrova, SE Russian Federation
Urusan *see* Ulsan
Urziceni *108 C5* Ialomiţa, SE Romania
Usa *110 E3 river* NW Russian Federation
Uşak *116 B3 prev.* Ushak. Uşak,
W Turkey
Ushak *see* Uşak
Ushant *see* Ouessant, Île d'

Ushuaia *65 B8* Tierra del Fuego,
S Argentina
Usinsk *110 E3* Respublika Komi,
NW Russian Federation
Üsküb/Üsküp *see* Skopje
Usmas Ezers *106 B3 lake* NW Latvia
Usol'ye-Sibirskoye *115 E4* Irkutskaya
Oblast', C Russian Federation
Ussel *91 C5* Corrèze, C France
Ussuriysk *115 G5 prev.* Nikol'sk,
Nikol'sk-Ussuriyskiy, Voroshilov.
Primorskiy Kray, SE Russian
Federation
Ustica *97 B6 island* S Italy
Ust'-Ilimsk *115 E4* Irkutskaya Oblast',
C Russian Federation
Ústí nad Labem *98 A4 Ger.* Aussig.
Ústecky Kraj, NW Czech Republic
Ustinov *see* Izhevsk
Ustka *98 C2 Ger.* Stolpmünde.
Pomorskie, N Poland
Ust'-Kamchatsk *115 H2* Kamchatskaya
Oblast', E Russian Federation
Ust'-Kamenogorsk *114 D5 Kaz.*
Öskemen. Vostochnyy Kazakhstan,
E Kazakhstan
Ust'-Kut *115 E4* Irkutskaya Oblast',
C Russian Federation
Ust'-Olenëk *115 E3* Respublika Sakha
(Yakutiya), NE Russian Federation
Ustrzyki Dolne *99 E5* Podkarpackie,
SE Poland
Ust'-Sysol'sk *see* Syktyvkar
Ust Urt *see* Ustyurt Plateau
Ustyurt Plateau *122 B1 var.* Ust
Urt, *Uzb.* Ustyurt Platosi. *plateau*
Kazakhstan/Uzbekistan
Ustyurt Platosi *see* Ustyurt Plateau
Usulután *52 C3* Usulután, SE El Salvador
Usumacinta, Río *52 B1 river* Guatemala/
Mexico
Usumbura *see* Bujumbura
U.S./USA *see* United States of America
Utah *44 B4 off.* State of Utah, *also known
as* Beehive State, Mormon State. *state*
W USA
Utah Lake *44 B4 lake* Utah, W USA
Utena *106 C4* Utena, E Lithuania
Utica *41 F3* New York, NE USA
Utina *see* Udine
Utrecht *86 C4 Lat.* Trajectum ad
Rhenum. Utrecht, C Netherlands
Utsunomiya *131 D5 var.* Utunomiya.
Tochigi, Honshū, S Japan
Uttarakhand *135 E2 cultural region*
N India
Uttar Pradesh *135 E3 prev.* United
Provinces, United Provinces of Agra
and Oudh. *cultural region* N India
Utunomiya *see* Utsunomiya
Uulu *106 D2* Pärnumaa, SW Estonia
Uummannaq *82 C3 var.* Umanak,
Umanaq. Kitaa, C Greenland
Uummannarsuaq *see* Nunap Isua
Uvalde *49 F4* Texas, SW USA
Uvarovichi *107 D7 Rus.* Uvarovichi.
Homyel'skaya Voblasts', SE Belarus
Uvarovichi *see* Uvarovichy
Uvea, Île *145 E4 island* N Wallis and
Futuna
Uvs Nuur *126 C1 var.* Ozero Ubsu-Nur.
lake Mongolia/Russian Federation
'Uwaynāt, Jabal al *88 A3 var.* Jebel
Uweinat. *mountain* Libya/Sudan
Uweinat, Jebel *see* 'Uwaynāt, Jabal al
Uyo *75 G5* Akwa Ibom, S Nigeria
Uyuni *61 F5* Potosí, W Bolivia
Uzbekistan *122 D2 off.* Republic of
Uzbekistan. *country* C Asia

UZBEKISTAN
Central Asia

Official name Republic of Uzbekistan
Formation 1991 / 1991
Capital Tashkent
Population 27.4 million / 159 people
per sq mile (61 people per sq km) / 37%
Total area 172,741 sq. miles
(447,400 sq. km)
Languages Uzbek*, Russian, Tajik, Kazakh
Religions Sunni Muslim 88%,
Orthodox Christian 9%, Other 3%
Ethnic mix Uzbek 80%, Other 6%,
Russian 6%, Tajik 5%, Kazakh 3%
Government Presidential system
Currency Som = 100 tiyin

UZBEKISTAN
(continued)

Literacy rate 99%
Calorie consumption 2241 calories

Uzbekistan, Republic of *see* Uzbekistan
Uzhgorod *see* Uzhhorod
Uzhhorod *108 B2 Rus.* Uzhgorod;
prev. Ungvár. Zakarpats'ka Oblast',
W Ukraine
Užice *100 D4 prev.* Titovo Užice. Serbia,
W Serbia

V

Vaal *78 D4 river* C South Africa
Vaals *87 D6* Limburg, SE Netherlands
Vaasa *85 D5 Swe.* Vasa; *prev.*
Nikolainkaupunki. Länsi-Suomi,
W Finland
Vaassen *86 D3* Gelderland,
E Netherlands
Vác *99 C6 Ger.* Waitzen. Pest,
N Hungary
Vadodara *134 C4 prev.* Baroda. Gujarāt,
W India
Vaduz *94 E2 country capital*
(Liechtenstein) (Liechtenstein)
W Liechtenstein
Vág *see* Váh
Vágbeszterce *see* Považská Bystrica
Váh *99 C5 Ger.* Waag, *Hung.* Vág. *river*
W Slovakia
Váhtjer *see* Gällivare
Väinameri *106 C2 prev.* Muhu Väin,
Ger. Moon-Sund. *sea* E Baltic Sea
Vajdahunyad *see* Hunedoara
Valachia *see* Wallachia
Valday *110 B4* Novgorodskaya Oblast',
W Russian Federation
Valdecañas, Embalse de *92 D3 reservoir*
W Spain
Valdepeñas *93 E4* Castilla-La Mancha,
C Spain
Valdés, Península *65 C6 peninsula*
SE Argentina
Valdez *36 C3* Alaska, USA
Valdia *see* Weldiya
Valdivia *65 B5* Los Lagos, C Chile
Val-d'Or *38 D4* Québec, SE Canada
Valdosta *43 E3* Georgia, SE USA
Valence *91 D5 anc.* Valentia, Valentia
Julia, Ventia. Drôme, E France
Valencia *93 F3* País Valenciano, E Spain
Valencia *46 D1* California, W USA
Valencia *58 D1* Carabobo, N Venezuela
Valencia, Gulf of *93 F3 var.* Gulf of
Valencia. *gulf* E Spain
Valencia, Gulf of *see* Valencia, Golfo de
Valencia/València *see* País Valenciano
Valenciennes *90 D2* Nord, N France
Valentia *see* Valence, France
Valentia *see* País Valenciano
Valentia Julia *see* Valence
Valentine State *see* Oregon
Valera *58 C2* Trujillo, NW Venezuela
Valetta *see* Valletta
Valga *106 D3 Ger.* Walk, *Latv.* Valka.
Valgamaa, S Estonia
Valira *91 A8 river* Andorra/Spain Europe
Valjevo *100 C4* Serbia, W Serbia
Valjok *see* Válljohka
Valka *106 D3 Ger.* Walk. Valka, N Latvia
Valka *see* Valga
Valkenswaard *87 D5* Noord-Brabant,
S Netherlands
Valladolid *51 H3* Yucatán, SE Mexico
Valladolid *92 D2* Castilla-León,
NW Spain
Vall D'Uxó *see* La Vall d'Uixó
Valle de La Pascua *58 D2* Guárico,
N Venezuela
Valledupar *58 B1* Cesar, N Colombia
Vallejo *47 B6* California, W USA
Vallenar *64 B3* Atacama, N Chile
Valletta *97 C8 prev.* Valetta. *country
capital* (Malta) (Malta) E Malta
Valley City *45 E2* North Dakota,
N USA
Válljohka *84 D2 var.* Valjok. Finnmark,
N Norway
Valls *93 G2* Cataluña, NE Spain
Valmiera *106 D3 Est.* Volmari, *Ger.*
Wolmar. Valmiera, N Latvia
Valona *see* Vlorë

Valozhyn *107 C5 Pol.* Wołożyn, *Rus.*
Volozhin. Minskaya Voblasts', C Belarus
Valparaíso *64 B4* Valparaíso, C Chile
Valparaiso *40 C3* Indiana, N USA
Valverde del Camino *92 C4* Andalucía,
S Spain
Van *117 F3* Van, E Turkey
Vanadzor *117 F2 prev.* Kirovakan.
N Armenia
Vancouver *36 D5* British Columbia,
SW Canada
Vancouver *46 B3* Washington, NW USA
Vancouver Island *36 D5 island* British
Columbia, SW Canada
Vanda *see* Vantaa
Van Diemen Gulf *146 D2 gulf* Northern
Territory, N Australia
Van Diemen's Land *see* Tasmania
Vaner, Lake *see* Vänern
Vänern *85 B6 Eng.* Lake Vaner; *prev.*
Lake Vener. *lake* S Sweden
Vangaindrano *79 G4* Fianarantsoa,
SE Madagascar
Van Horn *48 D3* Texas, SW USA
Lake Van *117 F3 Eng.* Lake Van; *anc.*
Thospitis. *salt lake* E Turkey
Lake Van *see* Van Gölü
Vannes *90 A3 anc.* Dariorigum.
Morbihan, NW France
Vantaa *85 D6 Swe.* Vanda. Etelä-Suomi,
S Finland
Vanua Levu *145 E4 island* N Fiji
Vanuatu *144 C4 off.* Republic of
Vanuatu; *prev.* New Hebrides. *country*
SW Pacific Ocean

VANUATU
Australasia & Oceania

Official name Republic of Vanuatu
Formation 1980 / 1980
Capital Port Vila
Population 211,971 / 45 people per sq mile
(17 people per sq km) / 23%
Total area 4710 sq. miles (12,200 sq. km)
Languages Bislama* (Melanesian
pidgin), English*, French*, other
indigenous languages
Religions Presbyterian 37%, Other 19%,
Anglican 15%, Roman Catholic 15%,
Traditional beliefs 8%, Seventh-day
Adventist 6%
Ethnic mix Melanesian 98%, Other 1%,
European 1%
Government Parliamentary system
Currency Vatu = 100 centimes
Literacy rate 74%
Calorie consumption 2587 calories

Vanuatu, Republic of *see* Vanuatu
Van Wert *40 C4* Ohio, N USA
Vapincum *see* Gap
Varakļāni *106 D4* Madona, C Latvia
Vārānasi *135 E3 prev.* Banaras, Benares,
hist. Kasi. Uttar Pradesh, N India
Varangerfjorden *84 E2 Lapp.*
Várjjatvuotna. *fjord* N Norway
Varangerhalvøya *84 D2 Lapp.*
Várnjárga. *peninsula* N Norway
Varannó *see* Vranov nad Topl'ou
Varasd *see* Varaždin
Varaždin *100 B2 Ger.* Warasdin, *Hung.*
Varasd. Varaždin, N Croatia
Varberg *85 B7* Halland, S Sweden
Vardar *101 E6 Gk.* Axiós. *river*
FYR Macedonia/Greece
Varde *85 A7* Ribe, W Denmark
Vareia *see* Logroño
Varéna *107 B5 Pol.* Orany. Alytus,
S Lithuania
Varese *96 B2* Lombardia, N Italy
Vârful Moldoveanu *108 B4 var.*
Moldoveanul; *prev.* Vîrful Moldoveanu.
mountain C Romania
Várjjatvuotna *see* Varangerfjorden
Varkaus *85 E5* Itä-Suomi, C Finland
Varna *104 E2 prev.* Stalin; *anc.* Odessus.
Varna, E Bulgaria
Varnenski Zaliv *104 E2 prev.* Stalinski
Zaliv. *bay* E Bulgaria
Várnjárga *see* Varangerhalvøya
Varshava *see* Warszawa
Vasa *see* Vaasa
Vasilikí *105 A5* Lefkáda, Iónia Nisiá,
Greece, C Mediterranean Sea
Vasilishki *107 B5 Pol.* Wasiliszki.
Hrodzyenskaya Voblasts', W Belarus

Vasil'kov *see* Vasyl'kiv
Vaslui *108 D4* Vaslui, C Romania
Västerås *85 C6* Västmanland, C Sweden
Vasyl'kiv *109 E2 var.* Vasil'kov.
  Kyyivs'ka Oblast', N Ukraine
Vaté *see* Efate
Vatican City *97 A7 off.* Vatican City.
  country S Europe

VATICAN CITY
Southern Europe

Official name The Vatican City
Formation 1929 / 1929
Capital Vatican City
Population 821 / 4829 people per sq mile
(1866 people per sq km) / 100%
Total area 0.17 sq. miles (0.44 sq. km)
Languages Italian*, Latin*
Religions Roman Catholic 100%
Government Papal state
Currency Euro = 100 cents
Literacy rate 99%
Calorie consumption Not available

Vatican City *see* Vatican City
Vatnajökull *83 E5 glacier* SE Iceland
Vatter, Lake *see* Vättern
Vättern *85 B6 Eng.* Lake Vatter; *prev.*
  Lake Vetter. *lake* S Sweden
Vaughn *48 D2* New Mexico, SW USA
Vaupés, Río *58 C4 var.* Rio Uaupés.
  river Brazil/Colombia
Vava'u Group *145 E4 island group*
  N Tonga
Vavuniya *132 D3* Northern Province,
  N Sri Lanka
Vawkavysk *107 B6 Pol.* Wołkowysk,
  Rus. Volkovysk. Hrodzyenskaya
  Voblasts', W Belarus
Växjö *85 C7 var.* Vexiö. Kronoberg,
  S Sweden
Vaygach, Ostrov *110 E2 island*
  NW Russian Federation
Veendam *86 E2* Groningen,
  NE Netherlands
Veenendaal *86 D4* Utrecht, C Netherlands
Vega *84 B4 island* C Norway
Veglia *see* Krk
Veisiejai *107 B5* Alytus, S Lithuania
Vejer de la Frontera *92 C5* Andalucía,
  S Spain
Veldhoven *87 D5* Noord-Brabant,
  S Netherlands
Velebit *100 A3 mountain range*
  C Croatia
Velenje *95 E7 Ger.* Wöllan. N Slovenia
Veles *101 E6 Turk.* Köprülü. C
  FYR Macedonia
Velho *see* Porto Velho
Velika Kikinda *see* Kikinda
Velika Morava *100 D4 var.* Glavn'a
  Morava, Morava, *Ger.* Grosse Morava.
  river C Serbia
Velikaya *113 G2 river* NE Russian
  Federation
Veliki Bečkerek *see* Zrenjanin
Velikiye Luki *110 A4* Pskovskaya
  Oblast', W Russian Federation
Velikiy Novgorod *110 B4 prev.*
  Novgorod. Novgorodskaya Oblast',
  W Russian Federation
Veliko Tŭrnovo *104 D2 prev.* Tirnovo,
  Trnovo, Tŭrnovo. Veliko Tŭrnovo,
  N Bulgaria
Velingrad *104 C3* Pazardzhik, C Bulgaria
Vel'ký Krtíš *99 D6* Banskobystrický
  Kraj, C Slovakia
Vellore *132 C2* Tamil Nādu, SE India
Velobriga *see* Viana do Castelo
Velsen *see* Velsen-Noord
Velsen-Noord *86 C3 var.* Velsen.
  Noord-Holland, W Netherlands
Vel'sk *110 C4 var.* Velsk.
  Arkhangel'skaya Oblast', NW Russian
  Federation
Velykyy Tokmak *see* Tokmak
Vendôme *90 C4* Loir-et-Cher,
  C France
Venedig *see* Venezia
Vener, Lake *see* Vänern
Venetia *see* Venezia
Venezia *96 C2 Eng.* Venice, *Fr.* Venise,
  Ger. Venedig; *anc.* Venetia. Veneto,
  NE Italy
Venezia, Golfo di *see* Venice,
  Gulf of

Venezuela *58 D2 off.* Republic of
  Venezuela; *prev.* Estados Unidos de
  Venezuela, United States of Venezuela.
  country N South America

VENEZUELA
South America

Official name Bolivarian Republic of
Venezuela
Formation 1830 / 1830
Capital Caracas
Population 27.7 million / 81 people
per sq mile (31 people per sq km) / 88%
Total area 352,143 sq. miles
(912,050 sq. km)
Languages Spanish*,
Amerindian languages
Religions Roman Catholic 89%,
Protestant and other 11%
Ethnic mix Mestizo 69%, White 20%,
Black 9%, Amerindian 2%
Government Presidential system
Currency Bolívar = 100 céntimos
Literacy rate 93%
Calorie consumption 2336 calories

Venezuela, Estados Unidos de *see*
  Venezuela
Venezuela, Gulf of *58 C1 Eng.* Gulf of
  Maracaibo, Gulf of Venezuela. *gulf*
  NW Venezuela
Venezuela, Gulf of *see* Venezuela,
  Golfo de
Venezuelan Basin *56 B1 undersea basin*
  E Caribbean Sea
Venezuela, Republic of *see* Venezuela
Venezuela, United States of *see*
  Venezuela
Venice *42 C4* Louisiana, S USA
Venice *see* Venezia
Venice, Gulf of *96 C2 It.* Golfo di
  Venezia, *Slvn.* Beneški Zaliv. *gulf*
  N Adriatic Sea
Venise *see* Venezia
Venlo *87 D5 prev.* Venloo. Limburg,
  SE Netherlands
Venloo *see* Venlo
Venta *106 B3 Ger.* Windau. *river* Latvia/
  Lithuania
Venta Belgarum *see* Winchester
Ventia *see* Valence
Ventimiglia *96 A3* Liguria, NW Italy
Ventspils *106 B2 Ger.* Windau.
  Ventspils, NW Latvia
Vera *64 D3* Santa Fe, C Argentina
Veracruz *51 F4 var.* Veracruz Llave.
  Veracruz-Llave, E Mexico
Veracruz Llave *see* Veracruz
Vercellae *see* Vercelli
Vercelli *96 A2 anc.* Vercellae. Piemonte,
  NW Italy
Verdal *see* Verdalsøra
Verdalsøra *84 B4 var.* Verdal. Nord-
  Trøndelag, C Norway
Verde, Cabo *see* Cape Verde
Verde, Costa *92 D1 coastal region*
  N Spain
Verden *94 B3* Niedersachsen,
  NW Germany
Veria *see* Véroia
Verkhnedvinsk *see* Vyerkhnyadzvinsk
Verkhneudinsk *see* Ulan-Ude
Verkhoyanskiy Khrebet *115 F3*
  mountain range NE Russian Federation
Vermillion *45 F3* South Dakota, N USA
Vermont *41 F2 off.* State of Vermont,
  also known as Green Mountain State.
  state NE USA
Vernal *44 B4* Utah, W USA
Vernon *49 F2* Texas, SW USA
Veröcze *see* Virovitica
Véroia *104 B4 var.* Veria, Vérroia,
  Turk. Karaferiye. Kentrikí Makedonía,
  N Greece
Verona *96 C2* Veneto, NE Italy
Vérroia *see* Véroia
Versailles *90 D1* Yvelines, N France
Versecz *see* Vršac
Verulamium *see* St Albans
Verviers *87 D6* Liège, E Belgium
Vesdre *87 D6 river* E Belgium
Veselinovo *104 D2* Shumen, NE Bulgaria
Vesontio *see* Besançon
Vesoul *90 D4 anc.* Vesulium, Vesulum.
  Haute-Saône, E France
Vesterålen *84 B2 island group* N Norway

Vestfjorden *84 C3 fjord* C Norway
Vestmannaeyjar *83 E5* Sudhurland,
  S Iceland
Vesulium/Vesulum *see* Vesoul
Vesuna *see* Périgueux
Vesuvius *97 D5 Eng.* Vesuvius. *volcano*
  S Italy
Vesuvius *see* Vesuvio
Veszprém *99 C7 Ger.* Veszprim.
  Veszprém, W Hungary
Veszprim *see* Veszprém
Vetrino *104 E2* Varna, E Bulgaria
Vetrino *see* Vyetryna
Vetter, Lake *see* Vättern
Veurne *87 A5 var.* Furnes. West-
  Vlaanderen, W Belgium
Vexiö *see* Växjö
Viacha *61 F4* La Paz, W Bolivia
Viana de Castelo *see* Viana do Castelo
Viana do Castelo *92 B2 var.* Viana de
  Castelo; *anc.* Velobriga. Viana do
  Castelo, NW Portugal
Vianen *86 C4* Utrecht, C Netherlands
Viangchan *136 C4 Eng./Fr.* Vientiane.
  country capital (Laos) (Laos) C Laos
Viangphoukha *136 C3 var.* Vieng Pou
  Kha. Louang Namtha, N Laos
Viareggio *96 B3* Toscana, C Italy
Viborg *85 A7* Viborg, NW Denmark
Vic *93 G2 var.* Vich; *anc.* Ausa, Vicus
  Ausonensis. Cataluña, NE Spain
Vicentia *see* Vicenza
Vicenza *96 C2 anc.* Vicentia. Veneto,
  NE Italy
Vich *see* Vic
Vichy *91 C5* Allier, C France
Vicksburg *42 B2* Mississippi, S USA
Victoria *79 H1 country capital*
  (Seychelles) (Seychelles) Mahé,
  SW Seychelles
Victoria *36 D5 province capital*
  Vancouver Island, British Columbia,
  SW Canada
Victoria *102 A5 var.* Rabat. Gozo,
  NW Malta
Victoria *49 G4* Texas,
  SW USA
Victoria *149 C7 state*
  SE Australia
Victoria *see* Masvingo, Zimbabwe
Victoria Bank *see* Vitória Seamount
Victoria de Durango *see* Durango
Victoria de las Tunas *see* Las Tunas
Victoria Falls *78 C3* Matabeleland
  North, W Zimbabwe
Victoria Falls *78 C2 waterfall* Zambia/
  Zimbabwe
Victoria Falls *see* Iguaçu, Salto do
Victoria Island *37 F3 island* Northwest
  Territories/Nunavut, NW Canada
Victoria, Lake *73 B6 var.* Victoria
  Nyanza. *lake* E Africa
Victoria Land *154 C4 physical region*
  Antarctica
Victoria Nyanza *see* Victoria, Lake
Victoria River *146 D3 river* Northern
  Territory, N Australia
Victorville *47 C7* California,
  W USA
Vicus Ausonensis *see* Vic
Vicus Elbii *see* Viterbo
Vidalia *43 E2* Georgia, SE USA
Videm-Krško *see* Krško
Videň *see* Wien
Vidin *104 B1 anc.* Bononia. Vidin,
  NW Bulgaria
Vidzy *107 C5* Vitsyebskaya Voblasts',
  NW Belarus
Viedma *65 C5* Río Negro,
  E Argentina
Vieja, Sierra *48 D3 mountain range*
  Texas, SW USA
Vieng Pou Kha *see* Viangphoukha
Vienna *see* Wien, Austria
Vienna *see* Vienne, France
Vienne *91 D5 anc.* Vienna. Isère,
  E France
Vienne *90 B4 river* W France
Vientiane *see* Viangchan
Vientos, Paso de los *see* Windward
  Passage
Vierzon *90 C4* Cher, C France
Viesīte *106 C4 Ger.* Eckengraf. Jēkabpils,
  S Latvia
Vietnam *136 D4 off.* Socialist Republic of
  Vietnam, *Vtn.* Cộng Hoa Xa Hôi Chu
  Nghia Việt Nam. *country* SE Asia

VIETNAM
Southeast Asia

Official name Socialist Republic
of Vietnam
Formation 1976 / 1976
Capital Hanoi
Population 86.4 million / 688 people
per sq mile (266 people per sq km) / 26%
Total area 127,243 sq. miles
(329,560 sq. km)
Languages Vietnamese*, Chinese, Thai,
Khmer, Muong, Nung, Miao, Yao, Jarai
Religions Nonreligious 81%, Buddhist 9%,
Christian 7%, Other 3%
Ethnic mix Vietnamese 86%, Other 10%,
Tay 2%, Thai 2%
Government One-party state
Currency Đông = 10 hao = 100 xu
Literacy rate 90%
Calorie consumption 2566 calories

Vietnam, Socialist Republic of *see*
  Vietnam
Vietri *see* Việt Tri
Việt Tri *136 D3 var.* Vietri. Vinh Phu,
  N Vietnam
Vieux Fort *55 F2* S Saint Lucia
Vigo *92 B2* Galicia, NW Spain
Viipuri *see* Vyborg
Vijayawāda *132 D1 prev.* Bezwada.
  Andhra Pradesh, SE India
Vila *see* Port-Vila
Vila Artur de Paiva *see* Cubango
Vila da Ponte *see* Cubango
Vila de João Belo *see* Xai-Xai
Vila de Mocímboa da Praia *see*
  Mocímboa da Praia
Vila do Conde *92 B2* Porto,
  NW Portugal
Vila do Zumbo *78 D2 prev.*
  Vila do Zumbu, Zumbo. Tete,
  NW Mozambique
Vila do Zumbu *see* Vila do Zumbo
Vilafranca del Penedès *93 G2 var.*
  Villafranca del Panadés. Cataluña,
  NE Spain
Vila General Machado *see* Camacupa
Vila Henrique de Carvalho *see* Saurimo
Viļaka *106 D4 Ger.* Marienhausen. Balvi,
  NE Latvia
Vilalba *92 C1* Galicia, NW Spain
Vila Marechal Carmona *see* Uíge
Vila Nova de Gaia *92 B2* Porto,
  NW Portugal
Vila Nova de Portimão *see* Portimão
Vila Pereira de Eça *see* N'Giva
Vila Real *92 C2 var.* Vila Rial. Vila Real,
  N Portugal
Vila Rial *see* Vila Real
Vila Robert Williams *see* Caála
Vila Salazar *see* N'Dalatando
Vila Serpa Pinto *see* Menongue
Vileyka *see* Vilyeyka
Vilhelmina *84 C4* Västerbotten, N Sweden
Vilhena *62 D3* Rondônia, W Brazil
Vília *105 C5* Attikí, C Greece
Viliya *107 C5 Lith.* Neris. *river*
  W Belarus
Viliya *see* Neris
Viljandi *106 D2 Ger.* Fellin.
  Viljandimaa, S Estonia
Vilkaviškis *106 B4 Pol.* Wyłkowyszki.
  Marijampolė, SW Lithuania
Villa Acuña *see* Ciudad Acuña.
  Coahuila, NE Mexico
Villa Bella *61 F2* Beni, N Bolivia
Villacarrillo *93 E4* Andalucía, S Spain
Villa Cecilia *see* Ciudad Madero
Villach *95 D7 Slvn.* Beljak. Kärnten,
  S Austria
Villacidro *97 A5* Sardegna, Italy,
  C Mediterranean Sea
Villa Concepción *see* Concepción
Villa del Pilar *see* Pilar
Villafranca de los Barros *92 C4*
  Extremadura, W Spain
Villafranca del Panadés *see* Vilafranca
  del Penedès
Villahermosa *51 G4 prev.* San Juan
  Bautista. Tabasco, SE Mexico
Villajoyosa *93 F4 Cat.* La Vila Joiosa.
  País Valenciano, E Spain
Villa María *64 C4* Córdoba, C Argentina
Villa Martín *61 F5* Potosí, SW Bolivia
Villa Mercedes *64 C4* San Juan,
  Argentina

Villanueva *50 D3* Zacatecas, C Mexico
Villanueva de la Serena *92 C3* Extremadura, W Spain
Villanueva de los Infantes *93 E4* Castilla-La Mancha, C Spain
Villarrica *64 D2* Guairá, SE Paraguay
Villavicencio *58 B3* Meta, C Colombia
Villaviciosa *92 D1* Asturias, N Spain
Villazón *61 G5* Potosí, S Bolivia
Villena *93 F4* País Valenciano, E Spain
Villeurbanne *91 D5* Rhône, E France
Villingen-Schwenningen *95 B6* Baden-Württemberg, S Germany
Villmanstrand *see* Lappeenranta
Vilna *see* Vilnius
Vilnius *107 C5* Pol. Wilno, Ger. Wilna; *prev.* Rus. Vilna. *country capital* (Lithuania) (Lithuania) Vilnius, SE Lithuania
Vil'shanka *109 E3* Rus. Olshanka. Kirovohrads'ka Oblast', C Ukraine
Vilvoorde *87 C6* Fr. Vilvorde. Vlaams Brabant, C Belgium
Vilvorde *see* Vilvoorde
Vilyeyka *107 C5* Pol. Wilejka, Rus. Vileyka. Minskaya Voblasts', NW Belarus
Vilyuy *115 F3* river NE Russian Federation
Viña del Mar *64 B4* Valparaíso, C Chile
Vinarós *93 F3* País Valenciano, E Spain
Vincennes *40 B4* Indiana, N USA
Vindhya Mountains *see* Vindhya Range
Vindhya Range *134 D4* var. Vindhya Mountains. *mountain range* N India
Vindobona *see* Wien
Vineland *41 F4* New Jersey, NE USA
Vinh *136 D4* Nghê An, N Vietnam
Vinh Loi *see* Bac Liêu
Vinishte *104 C2* Montana, NW Bulgaria
Vinita *49 G1* Oklahoma, C USA
Vinkovci *100 C3* Ger. Winkowitz, Hung. Vinkovcze. Vukovar-Srijem, E Croatia
Vinkovcze *see* Vinkovci
Vinnitsa *see* Vinnytsya
Vinnytsya *108 D2* Rus. Vinnitsa. Vinnyts'ka Oblast', C Ukraine
Vinogradov *see* Vynohradiv
Vinson Massif *154 A3* mountain Antarctica
Viranşehir *117 E4* Şanlıurfa, SE Turkey
Virful Moldoveanu *see* Vârful Moldoveanu
Virginia *45 G1* Minnesota, N USA
Virginia *41 E5* off. Commonwealth of Virginia, also known as Mother of Presidents, Mother of States, Old Dominion. state NE USA
Virginia Beach *41 F5* Virginia, NE USA
Virgin Islands *see* British Virgin Islands
Virgin Islands (US) *55 F3* var. Virgin Islands of the United States; prev. Danish West Indies. US unincorporated territory E West Indies
Virgin Islands of the United States *see* Virgin Islands (US)
Viróchey *137 E5* Rôtánôkiri, NE Cambodia
Virovitica *100 C2* Ger. Virovititz, Hung. Verőcze; prev. Ger. Werowitz. Virovitica-Podravina, NE Croatia
Virovititz *see* Virovitica
Virton *87 D8* Luxembourg, SE Belgium
Virtsu *106 D2* Ger. Werder. Läänemaa, W Estonia
Vis *100 B4* It. Lissa; anc. Issa. island S Croatia
Vis *see* Fish
Visaginas *106 C4* prev. Sniečkus. Utena, E Lithuania
Visākhapatnam *135 E5* var. Vishakhapatnam. Andhra Pradesh, SE India
Visalia *47 C6* California, W USA
Visby *85 C7* Ger. Wisby. Gotland, SE Sweden
Viscount Melville Sound *37 F2* prev. Melville Sound. sound Northwest Territories, N Canada
Visé *87 D6* Liège, E Belgium
Viseu *92 C2* prev. Vizeu. Viseu, N Portugal
Vishakhapatnam *see* Visākhapatnam
Vislinski Zaliv *see* Vistula Lagoon
Visoko *100 C4* Federacija Bosna I Hercegovina, C Bosnia and Herzegovina
Visttasjohka *84 D3* river N Sweden

Vistula *98 C2* Eng. Vistula, Ger. Weichsel. river C Poland
Vistula *see* Wisła
Vistula Lagoon *98 C2* Ger. Frisches Haff, Pol. Zalew Wislany, Rus. Vislinskiy Zaliv. lagoon Poland/Russian Federation
Vitebsk *see* Vitsyebsk
Viterbo *96 C4* anc. Vicus Elbii. Lazio, C Italy
Viti *see* Fiji
Viti Levu *145 E4* island W Fiji
Vitim *115 F4* river C Russian Federation
Vitória *63 F4* state capital Espírito Santo, SE Brazil
Vitoria *see* Vitoria-Gasteiz
Vitoria Bank *see* Vitória Seamount
Vitória da Conquista *63 F3* Bahia, E Brazil
Vitoria-Gasteiz *93 E1* var. Vitoria, Eng. Vittoria. País Vasco, N Spain
Vitória Seamount *67 B5* var. Victoria Bank, Vitoria Bank. seamount C Atlantic Ocean
Vitré *90 B3* Ille-et-Vilaine, NW France
Vitsyebsk *107 E5* Rus. Vitebsk. Vitsyebskaya Voblasts', NE Belarus
Vittoria *97 C7* Sicilia, Italy, C Mediterranean Sea
Vittoria *see* Vitoria-Gasteiz
Vizcaya, Golfo de *see* Biscay, Bay of
Vizianagram *135 E5* var. Vizianagram. Andhra Pradesh, E India
Vizianagram *see* Vizianagaram
Vjosës, Lumi i *101 C7* var. Vijosa, Vijosë, Gk. Aóos. river Albania/Greece
Vlaanderen *see* Flanders
Vlaardingen *86 B4* Zuid-Holland, SW Netherlands
Vladikavkaz *111 B8* prev. Dzaudzhikau, Ordzhonikidze. Respublika Severnaya Osetiya, SW Russian Federation
Vladimir *111 B5* Vladimirskaya Oblast', W Russian Federation
Vladimirovka *see* Yuzhno-Sakhalinsk
Vladimir-Volynskiy *see* Volodymyr-Volyns'kyy
Vladivostok *115 G5* Primorskiy Kray, SE Russian Federation
Vlagtwedde *86 E2* Groningen, NE Netherlands
Vlasotince *101 E5* Serbia, SE Serbia
Vlieland *86 C1* Fris. Flylân. island Waddeneilanden, N Netherlands
Vlijmen *86 C4* Noord-Brabant, S Netherlands
Vlissingen *87 B5* Eng. Flushing, Fr. Flessingue. Zeeland, SW Netherlands
Vlodava *see* Włodawa
Vlonë/Vlora *see* Vlorë
Vlorë *101 C7* prev. Vlonë, It. Valona, Vlora. Vlorë, SW Albania
Vlotslavsk *see* Włocławek
Vöcklabruck *95 D6* Oberösterreich, NW Austria
Vogelkop *see* Doberai, Jazirah
Vohimena, Tanjona *79 F4* Fr. Cap Sainte Marie. headland S Madagascar
Voiron *91 D5* Isère, E France
Vojvodina *100 D3* Ger. Wojwodina. Vojvodina, N Serbia
Volga *111 B7* river NW Russian Federation
Volga Uplands *81 G3* var. Volga Uplands. mountain range W Russian Federation
Volga Uplands *see* Privolzhskaya Vozvyshennost'
Volgodonsk *111 B7* Rostovskaya Oblast', SW Russian Federation
Volgograd *111 B7* prev. Stalingrad, Tsaritsyn. Volgogradskaya Oblast', SW Russian Federation
Volkhov *110 B4* Leningradskaya Oblast', NW Russian Federation
Volkovysk *see* Vawkavysk
Volmari *see* Valmiera
Volnovakha *109 G3* Donets'ka Oblast', SE Ukraine
Volodymyr-Volyns'kyy *108 C1* Pol. Włodzimierz, Rus. Vladimir-Volynskiy. Volyns'ka Oblast', NW Ukraine
Vologda *110 B4* Vologodskaya Oblast', W Russian Federation
Vólos *105 B5* Thessalía, C Greece
Volozhin *see* Valozhyn

Vol'sk *111 C6* Saratovskaya Oblast', W Russian Federation
Volta *75 E5* river SE Ghana
Volta Blanche *see* White Volta
Volta, Lake *75 E5* reservoir SE Ghana
Volta Noire *see* Black Volta
Volturno *97 D5* river S Italy
Volunteer Island *see* Starbuck Island
Volzhskiy *111 B6* Volgogradskaya Oblast', SW Russian Federation
Võnnu *106 E3* Ger. Wendau. Tartumaa, SE Estonia
Voorst *86 D3* Gelderland, E Netherlands
Voranava *107 C5* Pol. Werenów, Rus. Voronovo. Hrodzyenskaya Voblasts', W Belarus
Vorderrhein *95 B7* river SE Switzerland
Vóreioi Sporádes *see* Vóreies Sporádes
Vórioi Sporádhes *see* Vóreies Sporádes
Vorkuta *114 C2* Respublika Komi, NW Russian Federation
Vormsi *106 C2* var. Vormsi Saar, Ger. Worms, Swed. Ormsö. island W Estonia
Vormsi Saar *see* Vormsi
Voronezh *111 B6* Voronezhskaya Oblast', W Russian Federation
Voronovo *see* Voranava
Voroshilov *see* Ussuriysk
Voroshilovgrad *see* Luhans'k, Ukraine
Voroshilovsk *see* Stavropol', Russian Federation
Võru *106 D3* Ger. Werro. Võrumaa, SE Estonia
Vosges *90 E4* mountain range NE France
Vostochnyy Sayan *see* Eastern Sayans
Vostock Island *see* Vostok Island
Vostok *154 C3* Russian research station Antarctica
Vostok Island *145 G3* var. Vostock Island; prev. Stavers Island. island Line Islands, SE Kiribati
Voznesens'k *109 E3* Rus. Voznesensk. Mykolayivs'ka Oblast', S Ukraine
Vranje *101 E5* Serbia, SE Serbia
Vranov *see* Vranov nad Topl'ou
Vranov nad Topl'ou *99 D5* var. Vranov, Hung. Varannó. Prešovský Kraj, E Slovakia
Vratsa *104 C2* Vratsa, NW Bulgaria
Vrbas *100 C3* Vojvodina, NW Serbia
Vrbas *100 C3* river N Bosnia and Herzegovina
Vršac *100 D3* Ger. Werschetz, Hung. Versecz. Vojvodina, NE Serbia
Vsetín *99 C5* Ger. Wsetin. Zlínský Kraj, E Czech Republic
Vučitrn *see* Vushtrri
Vukovar *100 C3* Hung. Vukovár. Vukovar-Srijem, E Croatia
Vulcano, Isola *97 C7* island Isole Eolie, S Italy
Vung Tau *137 E6* prev. Fr. Cape Saint Jacques, Cap Saint-Jacques. Ba Ria-Vung Tau, S Vietnam
Vushtrri *101 D5* Serb. Vučitrn. N Kosovo
Vyatka *111 C5* river NW Russian Federation
Vyatka *see* Kirov
Vyborg *110 B3* Fin. Viipuri. Leningradskaya Oblast', NW Russian Federation
Vyerkhnyadzvinsk *107 D5* Rus. Verkhnedvinsk. Vitsyebskaya Voblasts', N Belarus
Vyetryna *107 D5* Rus. Vetrino. Vitsyebskaya Voblasts', N Belarus
Vynohradiv *108 B3* Cz. Sevluš, Hung. Nagyszöllős, Rus. Vinogradov; prev. Sevlyush. Zakarpats'ka Oblast', W Ukraine

W

Wa *75 E4* NW Ghana
Waag *see* Váh
Waagbistritz *see* Považská Bystrica
Waal *86 C4* river S Netherlands
Wabash *40 C4* river N USA
Wabash River *40 B5* river N USA
Waco *49 G3* Texas, SW USA
Wad Al-Hajarah *see* Guadalajara
Waddān *71 F3* NW Libya

Waddenzee *86 C1* var. Wadden Zee. sea SE North Sea
Wadden Zee *see* Waddenzee
Waddington, Mount *36 D5* mountain British Columbia, SW Canada
Wādī as Sīr *119 B6* var. Wadi es Sir. 'Ammān, NW Jordan
Wadi es Sir *see* Wādī as Sīr
Wadi Halfa *72 B3* var. Wādī Ḥalfā'. Northern, N Sudan
Wādī Mūsā *119 B7* var. Petra. Ma'ān, S Jordan
Wad Madani *see* Wad Medani
Wad Medani *72 C4* var. Wad Madanī. Gezira, C Sudan
Waflia *139 F4* Pulau Buru, E Indonesia
Wagadugu *see* Ouagadougou
Wagga Wagga *149 C7* New South Wales, SE Australia
Wagin *147 B7* Western Australia
Wāh *134 C1* Punjab, NE Pakistan
Wahai *139 F4* Pulau Seram, E Indonesia
Wahaybah, Ramlat Āl *see* Wahibah, Ramlat Āl
Wahiawā *47 A8* var. Wahiawa. O'ahu, Hawaii, USA, C Pacific Ocean
Wahibah, Ramlat Āl *see* Wahibah, Ramlat Āl
Wahibah Sands *121 E5* var. Ramlat Ahl Wahibah, Ramlat Al Wahaybah, Eng. Wahibah Sands. desert N Oman
Wahibah Sands *see* Wahibah, Ramlat Āl
Wahpeton *45 F2* North Dakota, N USA
Wahran *see* Oran
Waiau *151 A7* river South Island, New Zealand
Waigeo, Pulau *139 G4* island Maluku, E Indonesia
Waikaremoana, Lake *150 E4* lake North Island, New Zealand
Wailuku *47 B8* Maui, Hawaii, USA, C Pacific Ocean
Waimate *151 B6* Canterbury, South Island, New Zealand
Waiouru *150 D4* Manawatu-Wanganui, North Island, New Zealand
Waipara *151 C6* Canterbury, South Island, New Zealand
Waipawa *150 E4* Hawke's Bay, North Island, New Zealand
Waipukurau *150 D4* Hawke's Bay, North Island, New Zealand
Wairau *151 C5* river South Island, New Zealand
Wairoa *150 E4* Hawke's Bay, North Island, New Zealand
Wairoa *150 D2* river North Island, New Zealand
Waitaki *151 B6* river South Island, New Zealand
Waitara *150 D4* Taranaki, North Island, New Zealand
Waitzen *see* Vác
Waiuku *150 D3* Auckland, North Island, New Zealand
Wakasa-wan *131 C6* bay C Japan
Wakatipu, Lake *151 A7* lake South Island, New Zealand
Wakayama *131 C6* Wakayama, Honshū, SW Japan
Wake Island *152 C2* US unincorporated territory NW Pacific Ocean
Wake Island *142 D1* atoll NW Pacific Ocean
Wakkanai *130 C1* Hokkaidō, NE Japan
Wałbrzych *98 B4* Ger. Waldenburg, Waldenburg in Schlesien. Dolnośląskie, SW Poland
Walcourt *87 C7* Namur, S Belgium
Wałcz *98 B3* Ger. Deutsch Krone. Zachodnio-pomorskie, NW Poland
Waldenburg/Waldenburg in Schlesien *see* Wałbrzych
Waldia *see* Weldiya
Wales *36 C2* Alaska, USA
Wales *89 C6* Wel. Cymru. cultural region Wales, United Kingdom
Walgett *149 D5* New South Wales, SE Australia
Walk *see* Valga, Estonia
Walk *see* Valka, Latvia
Walker Lake *47 C5* lake Nevada, W USA
Wallachia *108 B5* var. Walachia, Ger. Walachei, Rom. Valachia. cultural region S Romania

Walla Walla *46 C2* Washington,
NW USA
Wallenthal *see* Hațeg
Wallis and Futuna *145 E4* Fr. Territoire
de Wallis et Futuna. *French overseas
territory* C Pacific Ocean
Wallis et Futuna, Territoire de *see*
Wallis and Futuna
Walnut Ridge *42 B1* Arkansas, C USA
Waltenberg *see* Zalău
Walthamstow *89 B7* Waltham Forest,
SE England, United Kingdom
Walvisbaai *see* Walvis Bay
Walvis Bay *78 A4* Afr. Walvisbaai.
Erongo, NW Namibia
Walvis Ridge *see* Walvis Ridge
Walvis Ridge *69 B7* var. Walvish Ridge.
undersea ridge E Atlantic Ocean
Wan *see* Wau
Wanaka *151 B6* Otago, South Island,
New Zealand
Wanaka, Lake *151 A6* lake South Island,
New Zealand
Wanchuan *see* Zhangjiakou
Wandel Sea *83 E1* sea Arctic Ocean
Wandsworth *89 A8* Wandsworth,
SE England, United Kingdom
Wanganui *150 D4* Manawatu-
Wanganui, North Island, New Zealand
Wangaratta *149 C7* Victoria,
SE Australia
Wankie *see* Hwange
Wanki, Río *see* Coco, Río
Wanlaweyn *73 D6* var. Wanle Weyn,
It. Uanle Uen. Shabeellaha Hoose,
SW Somalia
Wanle Weyn *see* Wanlaweyn
Wanxian *see* Wanzhou
Wanzhou *128 B5* var. Wanxian.
Chongqing Shi, C China
Warangal *135 E5* Andhra Pradesh,
C India
Warasdin *see* Varaždin
Warburg *94 B4* Nordrhein-Westfalen,
W Germany
Ware *37 E4* British Columbia, W Canada
Waremme *87 C6* Liège, E Belgium
Waren *94 C3* Mecklenburg-
Vorpommern, NE Germany
Wargla *see* Ouargla
Warkworth *150 D2* Auckland, North
Island, New Zealand
Warnemünde *94 C2* Mecklenburg-
Vorpommern, NE Germany
Warner *49 G1* Oklahoma, C USA
Warnes *61 G4* Santa Cruz, C Bolivia
Warrego River *149 C5* seasonal river
New South Wales/Queensland,
E Australia
Warren *40 D3* Michigan, N USA
Warren *41 D3* Ohio, N USA
Warren *41 E3* Pennsylvania, NE USA
Warri *75 F5* Delta, S Nigeria
Warrnambool *149 B7* Victoria,
SE Australia
Warsaw/Warschau *see* Warszawa
Warszawa *98 D3* Eng. Warsaw, Ger.
Warschau, Rus. Varshava. country
capital (Poland) (Poland) Mazowieckie,
C Poland
Warta *98 B3* Ger. Warthe. river W Poland
Wartberg *see* Senec
Warthe *see* Warta
Warwick *149 E5* Queensland, E Australia
Washington *44 A2* NE England, United
Kingdom
Washington DC *41 E4* country capital
(USA) (USA) District of Columbia,
NE USA
Washington Island *see* Teraina
Washington, Mount *41 G2* mountain
New Hampshire, NE USA
Wash, The *89 E6* inlet E England, United
Kingdom
Wasiliszki *see* Vasilishki
Waspam *53 E2* var. Waspán. Región
Autónoma Atlántico Norte,
NE Nicaragua
Waspán *see* Waspam
Watampone *139 E4* var. Bone. Sulawesi,
C Indonesia
Watenstedt-Salzgitter *see* Salzgitter
Waterbury *41 F3* Connecticut, NE USA
Waterford *89 B6* Ir. Port Láirge.
Waterford, S Ireland
Waterloo *45 G3* Iowa, C USA
Watertown *41 F2* New York, NE USA

Watertown *45 F2* South Dakota,
N USA
Waterville *41 G2* Maine, NE USA
Watford *89 A7* E England, United
Kingdom
Watlings Island *see* San Salvador
Watsa *77 E5* Orientale, NE Dem. Rep.
Congo
Watts Bar Lake *42 D1* reservoir
Tennessee, S USA
Wau *73 B5* var. Wāw. Western Bahr el
Ghazal, S Sudan
Waukegan *40 B3* Illinois, N USA
Waukesha *40 B3* Wisconsin, N USA
Wausau *40 B2* Wisconsin, N USA
Waverly *45 G3* Iowa, C USA
Wavre *87 C6* Walloon Brabant,
C Belgium
Wāw *see* Wau
Wawa *38 C4* Ontario, S Canada
Waycross *42 E3* Georgia, SE USA
Wearmouth *see* Sunderland
Webfoot State *see* Oregon
Webster City *45 F3* Iowa, C USA
Weddell Plain *154 A2* abyssal plain
SW Atlantic Ocean
Weddell Sea *154 A2* sea SW Atlantic
Ocean
Weener *94 A3* Niedersachsen,
NW Germany
Weert *87 D5* Limburg, SE Netherlands
Weesp *86 C3* Noord-Holland,
C Netherlands
Wegorzewo *98 D2* Ger. Angerburg.
Warmińsko-Mazurskie, NE Poland
Weichsel *see* Wisła
Weimar *94 C4* Thüringen, C Germany
Weissenburg *see* Alba Iulia, Romania
Weissenburg in Bayern *95 C6* Bayern,
SE Germany
Weissenstein *see* Paide
Weisskirchen *see* Bela Crkva
Weisswampach *87 D7* Diekirch,
N Luxembourg
Wejherowo *98 C2* Pomorskie,
NW Poland
Welchman Hall *55 G1* C Barbados
Weldiya *72 C4* var. Waldia, It. Valdia.
Āmara, N Ethiopia
Welkom *78 D4* Free State, C South Africa
Welle *see* Uele
Wellesley Islands *148 B2* island group
Queensland, N Australia
Wellington *151 D5* country capital (New
Zealand) Wellington, North Island,
New Zealand
Wellington *45 F5* Kansas, C USA
Wellington *see* Wellington, Isla
Wellington, Isla *65 A7* var. Wellington.
island S Chile
Wells *46 D3* Nevada, W USA
Wellsford *150 D2* Auckland, North
Island, New Zealand
Wells, Lake *147 C5* lake Western
Australia
Wels *95 D6* anc. Ovilava. Oberösterreich,
N Austria
Wembley *89 A8* Alberta, W Canada
Wemmel *87 B6* Vlaams Brabant,
C Belgium
Wenatchee *46 B2* Washington, NW USA
Wenchi *75 E4* W Ghana
Wen-chou/Wenchow *see* Wenzhou
Wendau *see* Võnnu
Wenden *see* Cēsis
Wenzhou *128 D5* var. Wen-chou,
Wenchow. Zhejiang, SE China
Werda *78 C4* Kgalagadi, S Botswana
Werder *see* Virtsu
Werenów *see* Voranava
Werkendam *86 C4* Noord-Brabant,
S Netherlands
Werowitz *see* Virovitica
Werro *see* Võru
Werschetz *see* Vršac
Wesenberg *see* Rakvere
Weser *94 B3* river NW Germany
Wessel Islands *148 B1* island group
Northern Territory, N Australia
West Antarctica *154 A3* var. Lesser
Antarctica. physical region Antarctica
West Australian Basin *see* Wharton Basin
West Bank *119 A6* disputed region
SW Asia
West Bend *40 B3* Wisconsin, N USA
West Bengal *135 F4* cultural region
NE India

West Cape *151 A7* headland South
Island, New Zealand
West Des Moines *45 F3* Iowa, C USA
Westerland *94 B2* Schleswig-Holstein,
N Germany
Western Australia *146 B4* state
W Australia
Western Bug *see* Bug
Western Carpathians *99 E7* mountain
range W Romania Europe
Western Desert *72 B2* var. Sahara el
Gharbîya, Eng. Western Desert. desert
C Egypt
Western Desert *see* Şaḥrā' al Gharbīyah
Western Dvina *85 E7* Bel. Dzvina, Ger.
Düna, Latv. Daugava, Rus. Zapadnaya
Dvina. river W Europe
Western Ghats *134 C5* mountain range
SW India
Western Isles *see* Outer Hebrides
Western Punjab *see* Punjab
Western Sahara *70 B3* disputed territory
N Africa
Western Samoa *see* Samoa
**Western Samoa, Independent State
of** *see* Samoa
Western Sayans *114 D4* Eng. Western
Sayans. mountain range S Russian
Federation
Western Sayans *see* Zapadnyy Sayan
Western Scheldt *87 B5* Eng. Western
Scheldt; prev. Honte. inlet S North Sea
Western Scheldt *see* Westerschelde
Western Sierra Madre *see* Madre
Occidental, Sierra
West Falkland *65 C7* var. Gran Malvina,
Isla Gran Malvina. island W Falkland
Islands
West Fargo *45 F2* North Dakota, N USA
West Frisian Islands *86 C1* Eng.
West Frisian Islands. island group
N Netherlands
West Frisian Islands *see*
Waddeneilanden
West Irian *see* Papua
Westliche Morava *see* Zapadna Morava
West Mariana Basin *142 B1* var. Perece
Vela Basin. undersea feature W Pacific
Ocean
West Memphis *42 B1* Arkansas, C USA
West New Guinea *see* Papua
Weston-super-Mare *89 D7* SW England,
United Kingdom
West Palm Beach *43 F4* Florida, SE USA
West Papua *see* Papua
Westport *151 C5* West Coast, South
Island, New Zealand
West Punjab *see* Punjab
West River *see* Xi Jiang
West Siberian Plain *114 C3* Eng.
West Siberian Plain. plain C Russian
Federation
West Siberian Plain *see* Zapadno-
Sibirskaya Ravnina
West Virginia *40 D4* off. State of West
Virginia, also known as Mountain State.
state NE USA
Wetar, Pulau *139 F5* island Kepulauan
Damar, E Indonesia
Wetzlar *95 B5* Hessen, W Germany
Wevok *36 C2* var. Wewuk. Alaska, USA
Wewuk *see* Wevok
Wexford *89 B6* Ir. Loch Garman.
SE Ireland
Weyburn *37 F5* Saskatchewan, S Canada
Weymouth *89 D7* S England, United
Kingdom
Wezep *86 D3* Gelderland, E Netherlands
Whakatane *150 E3* Bay of Plenty, North
Island, New Zealand
Whale Cove *37 G3* Nunavut, C Canada
Whangarei *150 D2* Northland, North
Island, New Zealand
Wharton Basin *141 D5* var. West
Australian Basin. undersea feature
E Indian Ocean
Whataroa *151 B6* West Coast, South
Island, New Zealand
Wheatland *44 D3* Wyoming, C USA
Wheeler Peak *48 D1* mountain New
Mexico, SW USA
Wheeling *40 D4* West Virginia, NE USA
Whitby *89 D5* N England, United
Kingdom
Whitefish *44 B1* Montana, NW USA
Whitehaven *89 C5* NW England, United
Kingdom

Whitehorse *36 D4* territory capital
Yukon Territory, W Canada
White Nile *72 B4* var. Bahr el Jebel.
river S Sudan
White Nile *72 B4* Ar. Al Baḥr al Abyaḍ,
An Nîl al Abyaḍ, Bahr el Jebel. river
SE Sudan
White River *44 D3* river South Dakota,
N USA
White Sea *110 C3* Eng. White Sea. sea
NW Russian Federation
White Sea *see* Beloye More
White Volta *75 E4* var. Nakambé, Fr.
Volta Blanche. river Burkina/Ghana
Whitianga *150 D2* Waikato, North
Island, New Zealand
Whitney, Mount *47 C6* mountain
California, USA
Whitsunday Group *148 D3* island group
Queensland, E Australia
Whyalla *149 B6* South Australia
Wichita *45 F5* Kansas, C USA
Wichita Falls *49 F2* Texas, SW USA
Wichita River *49 F2* river Texas,
SW USA
Wickenburg *48 B2* Arizona, SW USA
Wicklow *89 B6* Ir. Cill Mhantáin. county
E Ireland
Wicklow Mountains *89 B6* Ir. Sléibhte
Chill Mhantáin. mountain range
E Ireland
Wieliczka *99 D5* Małopolskie, S Poland
Wieluń *98 C4* Sieradz, C Poland
Wien *95 E6* Eng. Vienna, Hung.
Bécs, Slvk. Viedeň, Slvn. Dunaj; anc.
Vindobona. country capital (Austria)
(Austria) Wien, NE Austria
Wiener Neustadt *95 E6*
Niederösterreich, E Austria
Wierden *86 E3* Overijssel, E Netherlands
Wiesbaden *95 B5* Hessen, W Germany
**Wieselburg and Ungarisch-Altenburg/
Wieselburg-Ungarisch-Altenburg**
see Mosonmagyaróvár
Wiesenhof *see* Ostrołęka
Wight, Isle of *89 D7* island United
Kingdom
Wigorna Ceaster *see* Worcester
Wijchen *86 D4* Gelderland,
SE Netherlands
Wijk bij Duurstede *86 D4* Utrecht,
C Netherlands
Wilcannia *149 C6* New South Wales,
SE Australia
Wilejka *see* Vilyeyka
Wilhelm, Mount *144 B3* mountain
C Papua New Guinea
Wilhelm-Pieck-Stadt *see* Guben
Wilhelmshaven *94 B3* Niedersachsen,
NW Germany
Wilia/Wilja *see* Neris
Wilkes Barre *41 F3* Pennsylvania,
NE USA
Wilkes Land *154 C4* physical region
Antarctica
Wiłkomierz *see* Ukmergė
Willard *48 D2* New Mexico, SW USA
Willcox *48 C3* Arizona, SW USA
Willebroek *87 B5* Antwerpen, C Belgium
Willemstad *55 E5* dependent territory
capital (Netherlands Antilles) Curaçao,
Netherlands Antilles
Williston *44 D1* North Dakota, N USA
Wilmington *41 F4* Delaware, NE USA
Wilmington *43 F2* North Carolina,
SE USA
Wilmington *40 C4* Ohio, N USA
Wilna/Wilno *see* Vilnius
Wilrijk *87 C5* Antwerpen, N Belgium
Winchester *89 D7* hist. Wintanceaster,
Lat. Venta Belgarum. S England,
United Kingdom
Winchester *41 E4* Virginia, NE USA
Windau *see* Ventspils, Latvia
Windau *see* Venta, Latvia/Lithuania
Windhoek *78 B3* Ger. Windhuk. country
capital (Namibia) (Namibia) Khomas,
C Namibia
Windhuk *see* Windhoek
Windorah *148 C4* Queensland,
C Australia
Windsor *38 C5* Ontario, S Canada
Windsor *89 D7* S England, United
Kingdom
Windsor *41 G3* Connecticut, NE USA
Windward Islands *55 H4* island group
E West Indies

Windward Islands *see* Barlavento, Ilhas de, Cape Verde
Windward Passage 54 D3 *Sp.* Paso de los Vientos. *channel* Cuba/Haiti
Winisk 38 C2 *prev.* Winisk. Ontario, C Canada
Winisk *see* Winisk
Winkowitz *see* Vinkovci
Winnebago, Lake 40 B2 *lake* Wisconsin, N USA
Winnemucca 47 C5 Nevada, W USA
Winnipeg 37 G5 *province capital* Manitoba, S Canada
Winnipeg, Lake 37 G5 *lake* Manitoba, C Canada
Winnipegosis, Lake 38 A3 *lake* Manitoba, C Canada
Winona 45 G3 Minnesota, N USA
Winschoten 86 E2 Groningen, NE Netherlands
Winsen 94 B3 Niedersachsen, N Germany
Winston Salem 43 E1 North Carolina, SE USA
Winsum 86 D1 Groningen, NE Netherlands
Wintanceaster *see* Winchester
Winterswijk 86 E4 Gelderland, E Netherlands
Winterthur 95 B7 Zürich, NE Switzerland
Winton 148 C4 Queensland, E Australia
Winton 151 A7 Southland, South Island, New Zealand
Wisby *see* Visby
Wisconsin 40 A2 *off.* State of Wisconsin, *also known as* Badger State. *state* N USA
Wisconsin Rapids 40 B2 Wisconsin, N USA
Wisconsin River 40 B3 *river* Wisconsin, N USA
Wiślany, Zalew *see* Vistula Lagoon
Wismar 94 C2 Mecklenburg-Vorpommern, N Germany
Wittenberge 94 C3 Brandenburg, N Germany
Wittlich 95 A5 Rheinland-Pfalz, SW Germany
Wittstock 94 C3 Brandenburg, NE Germany
W. J. van Blommesteinmeer 59 G3 *reservoir* E Suriname
Władysławowo 98 C2 Pomorskie, N Poland
Włocławek 98 C3 *Ger./Rus.* Vlotslavsk. Kujawsko-pomorskie, C Poland
Włodawa 98 E4 *Rus.* Vlodava. Lubelskie, SE Poland
Włodzimierz *see* Volodymyr-Volyns'kyy
Wlotzkasbaken 78 B3 Erongo, W Namibia
Wodonga 149 C7 Victoria, SE Australia
Wodzisław Śląski 99 C5 *Ger.* Loslau. Śląskie, S Poland
Wojerecy *see* Hoyerswerda
Wójja *see* Wotje Atoll
Wojwodina *see* Vojvodina
Woking 89 D7 SE England, United Kingdom
Wolf, Isla 60 A4 *island* Galápagos, Galapagos Islands, W Ecuador South America
Wolfsberg 95 D7 Kärnten, SE Austria
Wolfsburg 94 C3 Niedersachsen, N Germany
Wolgast 94 D2 Mecklenburg-Vorpommern, NE Germany
Wołkowysk *see* Vawkavysk
Wöllan *see* Velenje
Wollaston Lake 37 F4 Saskatchewan, C Canada
Wollongong 149 D6 New South Wales, SE Australia
Wolmar *see* Valmiera
Wołożyn *see* Valozhyn
Wolvega 86 D2 *Fris.* Wolvegea. Friesland, N Netherlands
Wolvegea *see* Wolvega
Wolverhampton 89 D6 C England, United Kingdom
Wolverine State *see* Michigan
Wŏnsan 129 E3 SE North Korea
Woodburn 46 B3 Oregon, NW USA
Woodland 47 B5 California, W USA
Woodruff 40 B2 Wisconsin, N USA
Woods, Lake of the 38 A3 *Fr.* Lac des Bois. *lake* Canada/USA

Woodville 150 D4 Manawatu-Wanganui, North Island, New Zealand
Woodward 49 F1 Oklahoma, C USA
Worcester 78 C5 Western Cape, SW South Africa
Worcester 89 D6 *hist.* Wigorna Ceaster. W England, United Kingdom
Worcester 41 G3 Massachusetts, NE USA
Workington 89 C5 NW England, United Kingdom
Worland 44 C3 Wyoming, C USA
Wormatia *see* Worms
Worms 95 B5 *anc.* Augusta Vangionum, Borbetomagus, Wormatia. Rheinland-Pfalz, SW Germany
Worms *see* Vormsi
Worthington 45 F3 Minnesota, N USA
Wotje Atoll 144 D1 *var.* Wójjä. *atoll* Ratak Chain, E Marshall Islands
Woudrichem 86 C4 Noord-Brabant, S Netherlands
Wrangel Island 115 F1 *Eng.* Wrangel Island. *island* NE Russian Federation
Wrangel Island *see* Vrangelya, Ostrov
Wrangel Plain 155 B2 *undersea feature* Arctic Ocean
Wrocław 98 C4 *Eng./Ger.* Breslau. Dolnośląskie, SW Poland
Września 98 C3 Wielkopolskie, C Poland
Wsetin *see* Vsetín
Wuchang *see* Wuhan
Wuday'ah 121 C6 *spring/well* S Saudi Arabia
Wuhai 127 E3 *var.* Haibowan. Nei Mongol Zizhiqu, N China
Wuhan 128 C5 *var.* Han-kou, Han-k'ou, Hanyang, Wuchang, Wu-han; *prev.* Hankow. *province capital* Hubei, C China
Wu-han *see* Wuhan
Wuhsien *see* Suzhou
Wuhsi/Wu-his *see* Wuxi
Wuhu 128 D5 *var.* Wu-na-mu. Anhui, E China
Wujlân *see* Ujelang Atoll
Wukari 75 G4 Taraba, E Nigeria
Wuliang Shan 128 A6 *mountain range* SW China
Wu-lu-k'o-mu-shi/Wu-lu-mu-ch'i *see* Ürümqi
Wu-na-mu *see* Wuhu
Wuppertal 94 F4 *prev.* Barmen-Elberfeld. Nordrhein-Westfalen, W Germany
Würzburg 95 B5 Bayern, SW Germany
Wusih *see* Wuxi
Wuxi 128 D5 *var.* Wuhsi, Wu-his, Wusih. Jiangsu, E China
Wuyi Shan 125 E3 *mountain range* SE China
Wye 89 C6 *Wel.* Gwy. *river* England/Wales, United Kingdom
Wyłkowyszki *see* Vilkaviškis
Wyndham 146 D3 Western Australia
Wyoming 40 C3 Michigan, N USA
Wyoming 44 B3 *off.* State of Wyoming, *also known as* Equality State. *state* C USA
Wyszków 98 D3 *Ger.* Probstberg. Mazowieckie, NE Poland

X

Xaafuun, Raas 72 E4 *var.* Ras Hafun. *cape* NE Somalia
Xaçmaz 117 H2 *Rus.* Khachmas. N Azerbaijan
Xaignabouli 136 C4 *prev.* Muang Xaignabouri, *Fr.* Sayaboury. Xaignabouli, N Laos
Xai-Xai 79 E4 *prev.* João Belo, Vila de João Belo. Gaza, S Mozambique
Xalapa 51 F4 Veracruz-Llave, Mexico
Xam Nua 136 D3 *var.* Sam Neua. Houaphan, N Laos
Xankändi 117 G3 *Rus.* Khankendi; *prev.* Stepanakert. SW Azerbaijan
Xánthi 104 C3 Anatolikí Makedonía kai Thráki, NE Greece
Xàtiva 93 F3 *Cas.* Xátiva; *anc.* Setabis, *var.* Jativa. País Valenciano, E Spain
Xauen *see* Chefchaouen
Xäzär Dänizi *see* Caspian Sea
Xeres *see* Jeréz de la Frontera
Xiaguan *see* Dali
Xiamen 128 D6 *var.* Hsia-men; *prev.* Amoy. Fujian, SE China

Xi'an 128 C4 *var.* Changan, Sian, Signan, Siking, Singan, Xian. *province capital* Shaanxi, C China
Xiang *see* Hunan
Xianggang *see* Hong Kong
Xiangkhoang *see* Pèk
Xiangtan 128 C5 *var.* Hsiang-t'an, Siangtan. Hunan, S China
Xiao Hinggan Ling 128 D2 *Eng.* Lesser Khingan Range. *mountain range* NE China
Xichang 128 B5 Sichuan, C China
Xieng Khouang *see* Pèk
Xieng Ngeun *see* Muong Xiang Ngeun
Xigazê 126 C5 *var.* Jih-k'a-tse, Shigatse, Xigaze. Xizang Zizhiqu, W China
Xi Jiang 124 D3 *var.* Hsi Chiang, *Eng.* West River. *river* S China
Xilinhot 127 F2 *var.* Silinhot. Nei Mongol Zizhiqu, N China
Xilokastro *see* Xylókastro
Xin *see* Xinjiang Uygur Zizhiqu
Xingkai Hu *see* Khanka, Lake
Xingu, Rio 63 E2 *river* C Brazil
Xingxingxia 126 D3 Xinjiang Uygur Zizhiqu, NW China
Xining 127 E4 *var.* Hsining, Hsi-ning, Sining. *province capital* Qinghai, C China
Xinjiang *see* Xinjiang Uygur Zizhiqu
Xinjiang Uygur Zizhiqu 126 B3 *var.* Sinkiang, Sinkiang Uighur Autonomous Region, Xin, Xinjiang. *autonomous region* NW China
Xinpu *see* Lianyungang
Xinxiang 128 C4 Henan, C China
Xinyang 128 C5 *var.* Hsin-yang, Sinyang. Henan, C China
Xinzo de Limia 92 C2 Galicia, NW Spain
Xiqing Shan 124 D2 *mountain range* C China
Xiva 122 D2 *Rus.* Khiva, Khiwa. Xorazm Viloyati, W Uzbekistan
Xixón *see* Gijón
Xizang *see* Xizang Zizhiqu
Xizang Gaoyuan *see* Qingzang Gaoyuan
Xizang Zizhiqu 126 B4 *var.* Thibet, Tibetan Autonomous Region, Xizang, *Eng.* Tibet. *autonomous region* W China
Xolotlán *see* Managua, Lago de
Xucheng *see* Xuwen
Xuddur 73 D5 *var.* Hudur, *It.* Oddur. Bakool, SW Somalia
Xuwen 128 C7 *var.* Xucheng. Guangdong, S China
Xuzhou 128 D4 *var.* Hsu-chou, Suchow, Tongshan; *prev.* T'ung-shan. Jiangsu, E China
Xylókastro 105 B5 *var.* Xilokastro. Pelopónnisos, S Greece

Y

Ya'an 128 B5 *var.* Yaan. Sichuan, C China
Yabēlo 73 C5 Oromīya, C Ethiopia
Yablis 53 E2 Región Autónoma Atlántico Norte, NE Nicaragua
Yablonovyy Khrebet 115 F4 *mountain range* S Russian Federation
Yabrai Shan 127 E3 *mountain range* NE China
Yafran 71 F2 NW Libya
Yaghan Basin 67 B7 *undersea feature* SE Pacific Ocean
Yagotin *see* Yahotyn
Yahotyn 109 E2 *Rus.* Yagotin. Kyyivs'ka Oblast', N Ukraine
Yahualica 50 D4 Jalisco, SW Mexico
Yakima 46 B2 Washington, NW USA
Yakima River 46 B2 *river* Washington, NW USA
Yakoruda 104 C3 Blagoevgrad, SW Bulgaria
Yaku-shima 131 B8 *island* Nansei-shotō, SW Japan
Yakutat 36 D4 Alaska, USA
Yakutsk 115 F3 Respublika Sakha (Yakutiya), NE Russian Federation
Yala 137 C7 Yala, SW Thailand
Yalizava 107 D6 *Rus.* Yelizovo. Mahilyowskaya Voblasts', E Belarus
Yalong Jiang 128 A3 *river* C China
Yalova 116 B3 Yalova, NW Turkey
Yalpug, Ozero *see* Yalpuh, Ozero

Yalpuh, Ozero 108 D4 *Rus.* Ozero Yalpug. *lake* SW Ukraine
Yalta 109 F5 Respublika Krym, S Ukraine
Yalu 125 E2 *Chin.* Yalu Jiang, *Jap.* Oryokko, *Kor.* Amnok-kang. *river* China/North Korea
Yalu Jiang *see* Yalu
Yamaguchi 131 B7 *var.* Yamaguti. Yamaguchi, Honshū, SW Japan
Yamal, Poluostrov 114 D2 *peninsula* N Russian Federation
Yamaniyah, Al Jumhūrīyah al *see* Yemen
Yambio 73 B5 *var.* Yambiyo. Western Equatoria, S Sudan
Yambiyo *see* Yambio
Yambol 104 D2 *Turk.* Yanboli. Yambol, E Bulgaria
Yamdena, Pulau 139 G5 *prev.* Jamdena. *island* Kepulauan Tanimbar, E Indonesia
Yamoussoukro 74 D5 *country capital* (Côte d'Ivoire) C Côte d'Ivoire
Yamuna 134 D3 *prev.* Jumna. *river* N India
Yana 115 F2 *river* NE Russian Federation
Yanboli *see* Yambol
Yanbu 'al Baḥr 121 A5 Al Madinah, W Saudi Arabia
Yangambi 77 D5 Orientale, N Dem. Rep. Congo
Yangchow *see* Yangzhou
Yangiyo'l 123 E2 *Rus.* Yangiyul'. Toshkent Viloyati, E Uzbekistan
Yangiyul' *see* Yangiyo'l
Yangku *see* Taiyuan
Yangon 136 B4 *Eng.* Rangoon. Yangon, S Burma (Myanmar)
Yangtze 128 B5 *var.* Yangtze Kiang, *Eng.* Yangtze. *river* C China
Yangtze *see* Chang Jiang/Jinsha Jiang
Yangtze Kiang *see* Chang Jiang
Yangzhou 128 D5 *var.* Yangchow. Jiangsu, E China
Yankton 45 E3 South Dakota, N USA
Yannina *see* Ioánnina
Yanskiy Zaliv 113 F2 *bay* N Russian Federation
Yantai 128 D4 *var.* Yan-t'ai; *prev.* Chefoo, Chih-fu. Shandong, E China
Yaoundé 77 B5 *var.* Yaunde. *country capital* (Cameroon) Centre, S Cameroon
Yap 144 A1 *island* Caroline Islands, W Micronesia
Yapanskoye More East Sea/Japan, Sea of
Yapen, Pulau 139 G4 *prev.* Japen. *island* E Indonesia
Yap Trench 142 B2 *var.* Yap Trough. *undersea feature* W Pacific Ocean
Yap Trough *see* Yap Trench
Yapurá *see* Caquetá, Río, Brazil/Colombia
Yapurá *see* Japurá, Rio, Brazil/Colombia
Yaqui, Río 50 C2 *river* NW Mexico
Yaransk 111 C5 Kirovskaya Oblast', NW Russian Federation
Yarega 110 D4 Respublika Komi, NW Russian Federation
Yarkant *see* Shache
Yarlung Zangbo Jiang *see* Brahmaputra
Yarmouth 39 F5 Nova Scotia, SE Canada
Yarmouth *see* Great Yarmouth
Yaroslav *see* Jarosław
Yaroslavl' 110 B4 Yaroslavskaya Oblast', W Russian Federation
Yarumal 58 B2 Antioquia, NW Colombia
Yasyel'da 107 B7 *river* Brestskaya Voblasts', SW Belarus Europe
Yatsushiro 131 A7 *var.* Yatusiro. Kumamoto, Kyūshū, SW Japan
Yatusiro *see* Yatsushiro
Yaunde *see* Yaoundé
Yavarí *see* Javari, Rio
Río Yavari 62 C2 *var.* Yavarí. *river* Brazil/Peru
Yaviza 53 H5 Darién, SE Panama
Yavoriv 108 B2 *Pol.* Jaworów, *Rus.* Yavorov. L'vivs'ka Oblast', NW Ukraine
Yavorov *see* Yavoriv
Yazd 120 D3 *var.* Yezd. Yazd, C Iran
Yazoo City 42 B2 Mississippi, S USA
Yding Skovhøj 85 A7 *hill* C Denmark
Ýdra 105 C6 *var.* Ídhra. *island* Ýdra, S Greece

Ye *137 B5* Mon State, S Burma (Myanmar)
Yecheng *126 A3 var.* Kargilik. Xinjiang Uygur Zizhiqu, NW China
Yefremov *111 B5* Tul'skaya Oblast', W Russian Federation
Yekaterinburg *114 C3 prev.* Sverdlovsk. Sverdlovskaya Oblast', C Russian Federation
Yekaterinodar *see* Krasnodar
Yekaterinoslav *see* Dnipropetrovs'k
Yelets *111 B5* Lipetskaya Oblast', W Russian Federation
Yelisavetpol *see* Gäncä
Yelizavetgrad *see* Kirovohrad
Yelizovo *see* Yalizava
Yell *88 D1 island* NE Scotland, United Kingdom
Yellowhammer State *see* Alabama
Yellowknife *37 E4 territory capital* Northwest Territories, W Canada
Yellow River *128 C4 var.* Yellow River. *river* C China
Yellow River *see* Huang He
Yellow Sea *128 D4 Chin.* Huang Hai, *Kor.* Hwang-Hae. *sea* E Asia
Yellowstone River *44 C2 river* Montana/ Wyoming, NW USA
Yel'sk *107 C7* Homyel'skaya Voblasts', SE Belarus
Yelwa *75 F4* Kebbi, W Nigeria
Yemen *121 C7 off.* Republic of Yemen, *Ar.* Al Jumhuriyah al Yamaniyah, Al Yaman. *country* SW Asia

---

YEMEN
Southwest Asia

Official name Republic of Yemen
Formation 1990 / 1990
Capital Sana
Population 22.3 million / 103 people per sq mile (40 people per sq km) / 26%
Total area 203,849 sq. miles (527,970 sq. km)
Languages Arabic*
Religions Sunni Muslim 55%, Shi'a Muslim 42%, Christian, Hindu, and Jewish 3%
Ethnic mix Arab 99%, Other 1%
Government Presidential system
Currency Yemeni rial = 100 fils
Literacy rate 49%
Calorie consumption 2038 calories

Yemen, Republic of *see* Yemen
Yemva *110 D4 prev.* Zheleznodorozhnyy. Respublika Komi, NW Russian Federation
Yenakiyeve *109 G3 Rus.* Yenakiyevo; *prev.* Ordzhonikidze, Rykovo. Donets'ka Oblast', E Ukraine
Yenakiyevo *see* Yenakiyeve
Yenangyaung *136 A3* Magway, W Burma (Myanmar)
Yendi *76 E4* NE Ghana
Yengisar *126 A3* Xinjiang Uygur Zizhiqu, NW China
Yenierenköy *102 D4 var.* Yialousa, *Gk.* Agialoúsa. NE Cyprus
Yenipazar *see* Novi Pazar
Yenisei *114 D3 river* Mongolia/Russian Federation
Yenping *see* Nanping
Yeovil *89 D7* SW England, United Kingdom
Yeppoon *148 D4* Queensland, E Australia
Yerevan *117 F3 Eng.* Erivan. *country capital* (Armenia) (Armenia) C Armenia
Yeriho *see* Jericho
Yerushalayim *see* Jerusalem
Yeso *see* Hokkaidō
Yeu, Île d' *90 A4 island* NW France
Yevlakh *see* Yevlax
Yevlax *117 G2 Rus.* Yevlakh. C Azerbaijan
Yevpatoriya *109 F5* Respublika Krym, S Ukraine
Yeya *109 H4 river* SW Russian Federation
Yezerishche *see* Yezyaryshcha
Yezo *see* Hokkaidō
Yezyaryshcha *107 E5 Rus.* Yezerishche. Vitsyebskaya Voblasts', NE Belarus
Yialousa *see* Yenierenköy

Yiannitsá *see* Giannitsá
Yichang *128 C5* Hubei, C China
Yıldızeli *116 D3* Sivas, N Turkey
Yinchuan *128 B4 var.* Yinch'uan, Yin-ch'uan, Yinchwan. *province capital* Ningxia, N China
Yinchwan *see* Yinchuan
Yindu He *see* Indus
Yin-hsien *see* Ningbo
Yining *126 B2 var.* I-ning, *Uigh.* Gulja, Kuldja. Xinjiang Uygur Zizhiqu, NW China
Yin-tu Ho *see* Indus
Yisrael/Yisra'el *see* Israel
Yíthion *see* Gýtheio
Yogyakarta *138 C5 prev.* Djokjakarta, Jogjakarta, Jokyakarta. Jawa, C Indonesia
Yokohama *131 D5* Aomori, Honshū, C Japan
Yokohama *130 A2* Kanagawa, Honshū, S Japan
Yokote *130 D4* Akita, Honshū, C Japan
Yola *75 H4* Adamawa, E Nigeria
Yonago *131 B6* Tottori, Honshū, SW Japan
Yong'an *128 D6 var.* Yongan. Fujian, SE China
Yongzhou *129 C6 var.* Lengshuitan. Hunan, S China
Yonkers *41 F3* New York, NE USA
Yonne *90 C4 river* C France
Yopal *58 C3 var.* El Yopal. Casanare, C Colombia
York *89 D5 anc.* Eboracum, Eburacum. N England, United Kingdom
York *105 E4* Nebraska, C USA
York, Cape *148 C1 headland* Queensland, NE Australia
York, Kap *see* Innaanganeq
Yorkton *37 F5* Saskatchewan, S Canada
Yoro *52 C2* Yoro, C Honduras
Yoshkar-Ola *111 C5* Respublika Mariy El, W Russian Federation
Yösönbulag *see* Altay
Youngstown *40 D4* Ohio, N USA
Youth, Isle of *54 A2 var.* Isla de Pinos, *Eng.* Isle of Youth; *prev.* The Isle of the Pines. *island* W Cuba
Youth, Isle of *see* Juventud, Isla de la
Ypres *see* Ieper
Yreka *46 B4* California, W USA
Yrendagüe *see* General Eugenio A. Garay
Yssel *see* IJssel
Ysyk-Köl *see* Balykchy
Ysyk-Köl *see* Issyk-Kul', Ozero
Yu *see* Henan
Yuan *see* Red River
Yuan Jiang *see* Red River
Yuba City *47 B5* California, W USA
Yucatán, Canal de *see* Yucatan Channel
Yucatan Channel *51 H3 Sp.* Canal de Yucatán. *channel* Cuba/Mexico
Yucatán Peninsula *35 C7 Eng.* Yucatan Peninsula. *peninsula* Guatemala/ Mexico
Yucatan Peninsula *see* Yucatán, Península de
Yuci *see* Jinzhong
Yue *see* Guangdong
Yue Shan, Tai *see* Lantau Island
Yueyang *128 C5* Hunan, S China
Yugoslavia *see* Serbia
Yukhavichy *107 D5 Rus.* Yukhovichi. Vitsyebskaya Voblasts', N Belarus
Yukhovichi *see* Yukhavichy
Yukon *see* Yukon Territory
Yukon River *36 C2 river* Canada/USA
Yukon, Territoire du *see* Yukon Territory
Yukon Territory *36 D3 var.* Yukon, *Fr.* Territoire du Yukon. *territory* NW Canada
Yulin *128 C6* Guangxi Zhuangzu Zizhiqu, S China
Yuma *48 A2* Arizona, SW USA
Yun *see* Yunnan
Yungki *see* Jilin
Yung-ning *see* Nanning
Yunjinghong *see* Jinghong
Yunki *see* Jilin
Yunnan *see* Yunnan
Yunnan Sheng *see* Yunnan
Yünnan/Yun-nan *see* Yunnan

ZAMBIA
Southern Africa

Official name Republic of Zambia
Formation 1964 / 1964
Capital Lusaka
Population 12.1 million / 42 people per sq mile (16 people per sq km) / 36%
Total area 290,584 sq. miles

Yurev *see* Tartu
Yurihonjō *see* Honjō
Yuruá, Río *see* Juruá, Rio
Yury'ev *see* Tartu
Yushu *126 D4 var.* Gyêgu. Qinghai, C China
Yuty *64 D3* Caazapá, S Paraguay
Yuzhno-Sakhalinsk *115 H4 Jap.* Toyohara; *prev.* Vladimirovka. Ostrov Sakhalin, Sakhalinskaya Oblast', SE Russian Federation
Yuzhnyy Bug *see* Pivdennyy Buh
Yuzhou *see* Chongqing
Ýylanly *see* Gurbansoltan Eje

Z

Zaandam *see* Zaanstad
Zaanstad *86 C3 prev.* Zaandam. Noord-Holland, C Netherlands
Zabaykal'sk *115 F5* Chitinskaya Oblast', S Russian Federation
Zabern *see* Saverne
Zabid *121 B7* W Yemen
Zabinka *see* Zhabinka
Ząbkowice *see* Ząbkowice Śląskie
Ząbkowice Śląskie *98 B4 var.* Ząbkowice, *Ger.* Frankenstein, Frankenstein in Schlesien. Dolnośląskie, SW Poland
Zábřeh *99 C5 Ger.* Hohenstadt. Olomoucký Kraj, E Czech Republic
Zacapa *52 B2* Zacapa, E Guatemala
Zacatecas *50 D3* Zacatecas, C Mexico
Zacatepec *51 E4* Morelos, S Mexico
Záchary *see* Zacháro
Zadar *100 A3 It.* Zara; *anc.* Iader. Zadar, SW Croatia
Zadetkyi Kyun *137 B6 var.* St.Matthew's Island. *island* Mergui Archipelago, S Burma (Myanmar)
Zafra *92 C4* Extremadura, W Spain
Żagań *98 B4 var.* Zagań, Żegań, *Ger.* Sagan. Lubuskie, W Poland
Zagazig *see* Az Zaqāzīq
Zágráb *see* Zagreb
Zagreb *100 B2 Ger.* Agram, *Hung.* Zágráb. *country capital* (Croatia) (Croatia) Zagreb, N Croatia
Zagros Mountains *120 C3 Eng.* Zagros Mountains. *mountain range* W Iran
Zagros Mountains *see* Zāgros, Kūhhā-ye
Záharo *see* Zacháro
Zähedän *120 E4 var.* Zahidan; *prev.* Duzdab. Sīstān va Balūchestān, SE Iran
Zahidan *see* Zähedän
Zahlah *see* Zahlé
Zahlé *118 B4 var.* Zahlah. C Lebanon
Záhony *99 E6* Szabolcs-Szatmár-Bereg, NE Hungary
Zaire *see* Congo (river)
Zaire *see* Congo (Democratic Republic of)
Zaječar *100 E4* Serbia, E Serbia
Zakataly *see* Zaqatala
Zakháro *see* Zacháro
Zakhidnyy Buh/Zakhodni Buh *see* Bug
Zākhō *120 B2 var.* Zākhū. Dahūk, N Iraq
Zākhū *see* Zākhō
Zakopane *99 D5* Małopolskie, S Poland
Zákynthos *105 A6 var.* Zákinthos, *It.* Zante. *island* Iónia Nísoi, Greece, C Mediterranean Sea
Zalaegerszeg *99 B7* Zala, W Hungary
Zaläu *108 B3 Ger.* Waltenberg, *Hung.* Zilah; *prev.* Ger. Zillenmarkt. Sălaj, NW Romania
Zalim *121 B5* Makkah, W Saudi Arabia
Zambesi/Zambeze *see* Zambezi
Zambezi *78 C2* North Western, W Zambia
Zambezi *78 D2 var.* Zambesi, *Port.* Zambeze. *river* S Africa
Zambia *78 C2 off.* Republic of Zambia; *prev.* Northern Rhodesia. *country* S Africa

---

ZAMBIA
(continued)

(752,614 sq. km)
Languages English*, Bemba, Tonga, Nyanja, Lozi, Lala-Bisa, Nsenga
Religions Christian 63%, Traditional beliefs 36%, Muslim and Hindu 1%
Ethnic mix Bemba 34%, Other African 26%, Tonga 16%, Nyanja 14%, Lozi 9%, European 1%
Government Presidential system
Currency Zambian kwacha = 100 ngwee
Literacy rate 68%
Calorie consumption 1927 calories

Zambia, Republic of *see* Zambia
Zamboanga *139 E3 off.* Zamboanga City. Mindanao, S Philippines
Zamboanga City *see* Zamboanga
Zambrów *98 E3* Łomża, E Poland
Zamora *92 D2* Castilla-León, NW Spain
Zamora de Hidalgo *50 D4* Michoacán, SW Mexico
Zamość *98 E4 Rus.* Zamoste. Lubelskie, E Poland
Zamoste *see* Zamość
Zancle *see* Messina
Zanda *126 A4* Xizang Zizhiqu, W China
Zanesville *40 D4* Ohio, N USA
Zanjān *120 C2 var.* Zenjan, Zinjan. Zanjān, NW Iran
Zante *see* Zákynthos
Zanthus *147 C6* Western Australia, S Australia Oceania
Zanzibar *73 D7* Zanzibar, E Tanzania
Zanzibar *73 C7 Swa.* Unguja. *island* E Tanzania
Zaozhuang *128 D4* Shandong, E China
Zapadna Morava *100 D4 Ger.* Westliche Morava. *river* C Serbia
Zapadnaya Dvina *110 A4* Tverskaya Oblast', W Russian Federation
Zapadnaya Dvina *see* Western Dvina
Zapadnyy Bug *see* Bug
Zapala *65 B5* Neuquén, W Argentina
Zapiola Ridge *67 B6 undersea feature* SW Atlantic Ocean
Zapolyarnyy *110 C2* Murmanskaya Oblast', NW Russian Federation
Zaporizhzhya *109 F3 Rus.* Zaporozh'ye; *prev.* Aleksandrovsk. Zaporiz'ka Oblast', SE Ukraine
Zaporozh'ye *see* Zaporizhzhya
Zapotiltic *50 D4* Jalisco, SW Mexico
Zaqatala *117 G2 Rus.* Zakataly. NW Azerbaijan
Zara *116 D3* Sivas, C Turkey
Zara *see* Zadar
Zarafshan *see* Zarafshon
Zarafshon *122 D2 Rus.* Zarafshan. Navoiy Viloyati, N Uzbekistan
Zarafshon *see* Zeravshan
Zaragoza *93 F2 Eng.* Saragossa; *anc.* Caesaraugusta, Salduba. Aragón, NE Spain
Zarand *120 D3* Kermän, C Iran
Zaranj *122 D5* Nīmrūz, SW Afghanistan
Zarasai *106 C4* Utena, E Lithuania
Zárate *64 D4 prev.* General José F.Uriburu. Buenos Aires, E Argentina
Zarautz *93 E1 var.* Zarauz. País Vasco, N Spain
Zarauz *see* Zarautz
Zaraza *59 E2* Guárico, N Venezuela
Zarghün Shahr *123 E4 var.* Katawaz. Paktīkā, SE Afghanistan
Zaria *75 G4* Kaduna, C Nigeria
Zarós *105 D8* Kríti, Greece, E Mediterranean Sea
Zarqa *see* Az Zarqā'
Żary *98 B4 Ger.* Sorau, Sorau in der Niederlausitz. Lubuskie, W Poland
Zaunguzskiye Garagumy *see* Üngüz Angyrsyndaky Garagum
Zavertse *see* Zawiercie
Zavet *104 D1* Razgrad, NE Bulgaria
Zavidović *100 C3* Federacija Bosna I Hercegovina, N Bosnia and Herzegovina
Zawia *see* Az Zāwiyah
Zawiercie *98 D4 Rus.* Zavertse. Śląskie, S Poland
Zawilah *71 F3 var.* Zuwaylah, *It.* Zueila. C Libya
Zaysan Köl *see* Zaysan, Ozero

Zaysan, Ozero 114 D5 *Kaz.* Zaysan Köl.
lake E Kazakhstan
Zayyq *see* Ural
Zbarazh 108 C2 Ternopil's'ka Oblast',
W Ukraine
Zduńska Wola 98 C4 Sieradz, C Poland
Zealand 85 B8 *Eng.* Zealand, *Ger.*
Seeland. *island* E Denmark
Zealand *see* Sjælland
Zeebrugge 87 A5 West-Vlaanderen,
NW Belgium
Zeewolde 86 D3 Flevoland,
C Netherlands
Zefat *see* Tsefat
Żegań *see* Żagań
Zeiden *see* Codlea
Zeist 86 C4 Utrecht, C Netherlands
Zele 87 B5 Oost-Vlaanderen,
NW Belgium
Zelle *see* Celle
Zel'va 107 B6 *Pol.* Zelwa. Hrodzyenskaya
Voblasts', W Belarus
Zelwa *see* Zel'va
Zelzate 87 B5 *var.* Selzaete. Oost-
Vlaanderen, NW Belgium
Žemaičių Aukštumas 106 B4 *physical
region* W Lithuania
Zemst 87 C5 Vlaams Brabant, C Belgium
Zemun 100 D3 Serbia, N Serbia
Zengg *see* Senj
Zenica 100 C4 Federacija Bosna
I Hercegovina, C Bosnia and
Herzegovina
Zenta *see* Senta
Zeravshan 123 E3 *Taj./Uzb.* Zarafshon.
river Tajikistan/Uzbekistan
Zevenaar 86 D4 Gelderland,
SE Netherlands
Zevenbergen 86 C4 Noord-Brabant,
S Netherlands
Zeya 113 E3 *river* SE Russian Federation
Zgerzh *see* Zgierz
Zgierz 98 C4 *Ger.* Neuhof, *Rus.* Zgerzh.
Łódź, C Poland
Zgorzelec 98 B4 *Ger.* Görlitz.
Dolnośląskie, SW Poland
Zhabinka 107 A6 *Pol.* Żabinka.
Brestskaya Voblasts', SW Belarus
Zhambyl *see* Taraz
Zhanaozen 114 A4 *Kaz.* Zhangaözen;
prev. Novyy Uzen'. Mangistau,
W Kazakhstan
Zhangaözen *see* Zhanaozen
Zhangaqazaly *see* Ayteke Bi
Zhang-chia-k'ou *see* Zhangjiakou
Zhangdian *see* Zibo
Zhangjiakou 128 C3 *var.* Changkiakow,
Zhang-chia-k'ou, *Eng.* Kalgan; *prev.*
Wanchuan. Hebei, E China
Zhangzhou 128 D6 Fujian, SE China
Zhanjiang 128 C7 *var.* Chanchiang,
Chan-chiang, *Cant.* Tsamkong, *Fr.*
Fort-Bayard. Guangdong, S China

Zhaoqing 128 C6 Guangdong, S China
Zhdanov *see* Mariupol'
Zhe *see* Zhejiang
Zhejiang 128 D5 *var.* Che-chiang,
Chekiang, Zhe, Zhejiang Sheng.
province SE China
Zhejiang Sheng *see* Zhejiang
Zheleznodorozhnyy 106 A4 Irkutskaya
Oblast', C Russian Federation
Zheleznodorozhnyy *see* Yemva
Zheleznogorsk 111 A5 Kurskaya Oblast',
W Russian Federation
Zhëltyye Vody *see* Zhovti Vody
Zhengzhou 128 C4 *var.* Ch'eng-chou,
Chengchow; *prev.* Chenghsien.
province capital Henan, C China
Zhezkazgan 114 C4 *Kaz.* Zhezqazghan;
prev. Dzhezkazgan. Karaganda,
C Kazakhstan
Zhezqazghan *see* Zhezkazgan
Zhidachov *see* Zhydachiv
Zhitkovichi *see* Zhytkavichy
Zhitomir *see* Zhytomyr
Zhlobin 107 D7 Homyel'skaya Voblasts',
SE Belarus
Zhmerinka *see* Zhmerynka
Zhmerynka 108 D2 *Rus.* Zhmerinka.
Vinnyts'ka Oblast', C Ukraine
Zhodino *see* Zhodzina
Zhodzina 107 D6 *Rus.* Zhodino.
Minskaya Voblasts', C Belarus
Zholkev/Zholkva *see* Zhovkva
Zhonghua Renmin Gongheguo *see*
China
Zhosaly *see* Dzhusaly
Zhovkva 108 B2 *Pol.* Żółkiew, *Rus.*
Zholkev, Zholkva; *prev.* Nesterov.
L'vivs'ka Oblast', NW Ukraine
Zhovti Vody 109 F3 *Rus.* Zhëltyye Vody.
Dnipropetrovs'ka Oblast', E Ukraine
Zhovtneve 109 E4 *Rus.* Zhovtnevoye.
Mykolayivs'ka Oblast', S Ukraine
Zhovtnevoye *see* Zhovtneve
Zhydachiv 108 B2 *Pol.* Żydaczów,
Rus. Zhidachov. L'vivs'ka Oblast',
NW Ukraine
Zhytkavichy 107 C7 *Rus.* Zhitkovichi.
Homyel'skaya Voblasts', SE Belarus
Zhytomyr 108 D2 *Rus.* Zhitomir.
Zhytomyrs'ka Oblast', NW Ukraine
Zibo 128 D4 *var.* Zhangdian. Shandong,
E China
Zichenau *see* Ciechanów
Zielona Góra 98 B4 *Ger.* Grünberg,
Grünberg in Schlesien, Grüneberg.
Lubuskie, W Poland
Zierikzee 86 B4 Zeeland,
SW Netherlands
Zigong 128 B5 *var.* Tzekung. Sichuan,
C China
Ziguinchor 74 B3 SW Senegal
Zilah *see* Zalău
Žilina 99 C5 *Ger.* Sillein, *Hung.* Zsolna.
Zlínský Kraj, N Slovakia
Zillenmarkt *see* Zalău
Zimbabwe 78 D3 *off.* Republic of
Zimbabwe; *prev.* Rhodesia. *country*
S Africa

ZIMBABWE
Southern Africa

Official name Republic of Zimbabwe
Formation 1980 / 1980
Capital Harare
Population 13.2 million / 88 people
per sq mile (34 people per sq km) / 35%
Total area 150,803 sq. miles
(390,580 sq. km)
Languages English*, Shona, isiNdebele
Religions Syncretic (Christian/traditional
beliefs) 50%, Christian 25%, Traditional
beliefs 24%, Other (including Muslim) 1%
Ethnic mix Shona 71%, Ndebele 16%,
Other African 11%, White 1%Asian 1%
Government Presidential system
Currency Zimbabwe dollar = 100 cents
Literacy rate 90%
Calorie consumption 1943 calories

Zimbabwe, Republic of *see* Zimbabwe
Zimnicea 108 C5 Teleorman, S Romania
Zimovniki 111 B7 Rostovskaya Oblast',
SW Russian Federation
Zinder 75 G3 Zinder, S Niger
Zinov'yevsk *see* Kirovohrad
Zintenhof *see* Sindi
Zipaquirá 58 B3 Cundinamarca,
C Colombia
Zittau 94 D4 Sachsen, E Germany
Zlatni Pyasŭtsi 104 E2 Dobrich,
NE Bulgaria
Zlin 99 C5 *prev.* Gottwaldov. Zlínský
Kraj, E Czech Republic
Złoczów *see* Zolochev
Złotów 98 C3 Wielkopolskie,
C Poland
Znamenka *see* Znam"yanka
Znam"yanka 109 F3 *Rus.* Znamenka.
Kirovohrads'ka Oblast', C Ukraine
Žnin 98 C3 Kujawsko-pomorskie,
C Poland
Zoetermeer 86 C4 Zuid-Holland,
W Netherlands
Żółkiew *see* Zhovkva
Zolochev 108 C2 *Pol.* Złoczów, *Rus.*
Zolochiv. L'vivs'ka Oblast', W Ukraine
Zolochiv 109 G2 *Rus.* Zolochev.
Kharkivs'ka Oblast', E Ukraine
Zolochiv *see* Zolochev
Zolote 109 H3 *Rus.* Zolotoye. Luhans'ka
Oblast', E Ukraine
Zolotonosha 109 E2 Cherkas'ka Oblast',
C Ukraine
Zolotoye *see* Zolote
Zólyom *see* Zvolen
Zomba 79 E2 Southern, S Malawi
Zombor *see* Sombor
Zongo 77 C5 Equateur, N Dem. Rep.
Congo
Zonguldak 116 C2 Zonguldak,
NW Turkey
Zonhoven 87 D6 Limburg,
NE Belgium
Zoppot *see* Sopot
Żory 99 C5 *var.* Zory, *Ger.* Sohrau.
Śląskie, S Poland

Zouar 76 C2 Borkou-Ennedi-Tibesti,
N Chad
Zouérat 74 C2 *var.* Zouérate, Zouîrât.
Tiris Zemmour, N Mauritania
Zouérate *see* Zouérat
Zouîrât *see* Zouérat
Zrenjanin 100 D3 *prev.* Petrovgrad,
Veliki Bečkerek, *Ger.* Grossbetschkerek,
Hung. Nagybecskerek. Vojvodina,
N Serbia
Zsil/Zsily *see* Jiu
Zsolna *see* Žilina
Zsombolya *see* Jimbolia
Zsupanya *see* Županja
Zubov Seamount 67 D5 *undersea
feature* E Atlantic Ocean
Zueila *see* Zawilah
Zug 95 B7 *Fr.* Zoug. Zug, C Switzerland
Zugspitze 95 C7 *mountain* S Germany
Zuid-Beveland 87 B5 *var.* South
Beveland. *island* SW Netherlands
Zuider Zee *see* IJsselmeer
Zuidhorn 86 E1 Groningen,
NE Netherlands
Zuidlaren 86 E2 Drenthe, NE Netherlands
Zula 72 C4 E Eritrea
Züllichau *see* Sulechów
Zumbo *see* Vila do Zumbo
Zundert 87 C5 Noord-Brabant,
S Netherlands
Zunyi 128 B5 Guizhou, S China
Županja 100 C3 *Hung.* Zsupanya.
Vukovar-Srijem, E Croatia
Zürich 95 B7 *Eng./Fr.* Zurich, *It.* Zurigo.
Zürich, N Switzerland
Zurich, Lake 95 B7 *Eng.* Lake Zurich.
lake NE Switzerland
Zürich, Lake *see* Zürichsee
Zurigo *see* Zürich
Zutphen 86 D3 Gelderland,
E Netherlands
Zuwärah 71 F2 NW Libya
Zuwaylah *see* Zawilah
Zuyevka 111 D5 Kirovskaya Oblast',
NW Russian Federation
Zvenigorodka *see* Zvenyhorodka
Zvenyhorodka 109 E2 *Rus.*
Zvenigorodka. Cherkas'ka Oblast',
C Ukraine
Zvishavane 78 D3 *prev.* Shabani.
Matabeleland South, S Zimbabwe
Zvolen 99 C6 *Ger.* Altsohl, *Hung.*
Zólyom. Banskobystrický Kraj,
C Slovakia
Zvornik 100 C4 E Bosnia and
Herzegovina
Zwedru 74 D5 *var.* Tchien. E Liberia
Zwettl 95 E6 Wien, NE Austria
Zwevegem 87 A6 West-Vlaanderen,
W Belgium
Zwickau 95 C5 Sachsen, E Germany
Zwolle 86 D3 Overijssel, E Netherlands
Żydaczów *see* Zhydachiv
Zyóetu *see* Jõetsu
Żyrardów 98 D3 Mazowieckie, C Poland
Zyryanovsk 114 D5 Vostochnyy
Kazakhstan, E Kazakhstan